BENCHMARK Series

MICROSOFT®

OFFICE 2000

CORE CERTIFICATION

NITA RUTKOSKY

Pierce College at Puyallup
Puyallup, Washington

MICROSOFT OFFICE
Microsoft®
OFFICE
USER SPECIALIST

APPROVED COURSEWARE

EMCParadigm

Senior Editor	Sonja M. Brown
Developmental Editor	Tom Modl
Copy Editor	Kathryn A. Savoie
Art Director	Joan D'Onofrio
Cover and Icons Designer	Chris Vern Johnson
Text Designer	Jennifer Wreisner
Desktop Production Specialists	Leslie Anderson, Julie Hansen
Tester	Nancy Sauro
Proofreader	Kathryn A. Savoie
Indexer	Nancy Fulton

Publishing Team—George Provol, Publisher; Wesley Lawton, Executive Editor; Janice Johnson, Director of Product Development; Lori Landwer, Marketing Manager; Shelley Clubb, Electronic Design and Production Manager.

Registered Trademarks—Microsoft, Windows, PowerPoint, Outlook, and the MOUS icon are registered trademarks of Microsoft Corporation in the United States and other countries. IBM is a registered trademark of IBM Corporation.

Permissions—Material for selected documents has been excerpted from *Telecommunications: Systems and Applications*, by William Mitchell, Robert Hendricks, and Leonard Sterry, published by Paradigm Publishing Inc., 1993; *Advanced WordPerfect: Desktop Publishing 6.1 for Windows*, by Nita Hewitt Rutkosky, Judy Dwyer Burnside, and Joanne Marschke Arford, published by Paradigm Publishing Inc., 1996.

Acknowledgments—The author and publisher wish to thank the following reviewers for their technical and academic assistance: Tony D. Gabriel, Computer Learning Center, Glendale, California; Denise Seguin, Fanshawe College, London, Ontario; and Janet Sheppard, Collin County Community College, Plano, Texas.

Library of Congress Cataloging-in-Publication Data
       Rutkosky, Nita Hewitt.
           Microsoft Office 2000 / Nita Rutkosky.
               p.   cm.
           ISBN 0-7638-0255-7
              1. Microsoft Office. 2. Business—Computer programs. I. Title.
     HF5548.4.M525R868 2000   99-10805
     005.369—dc21   CIP

Text + CD: ISBN 0-7638-0255-7
Order number: 04336

© 2000 by Paradigm Publishing Inc.
        Published by **EMC**Paradigm
        875 Montreal Way
        St. Paul, MN 55102
        (800) 535-6865
        E-mail: educate@emcp.com
        Web Site: www.emcp.com

Printed in the United States of America
10 9 8 7 6 5 4 3

Contents

Introduction

Most personal computers purchased today come preloaded with the Microsoft® Windows 95 or Windows 98 operating system and some are preloaded with Windows-based applications. Windows-based applications control a large portion of the application industry. One of the most popular Windows-based suites of programs is Microsoft Office 2000. This suite contains a word processing program (Word), a spreadsheet program (Excel), a slide presentation program (PowerPoint), a database program (Access), and a desktop information management program (Outlook). Virtually all business tasks can be performed with the programs in this suite. For example, an employee can prepare correspondence in Word, prepare financial worksheets in Excel, prepare presentations in PowerPoint, organize and save data in Access, and schedule appointments and maintain contact lists in Outlook.

In this textbook, students will learn basic and intermediate features of the five programs in the Microsoft Office suite as well as the basics of the operating systems Microsoft Windows 95 and 98. Students do not need any previous computer experience to use this textbook and only basic high school freshman mathematics is required.

Focus on Integration

Microsoft Office is an integrated suite of programs that lets the user import and export data from one program to the other. Microsoft Office also contains several tools that can be used in any program in the suite. The chapters in this textbook were designed to take advantage of the integration of Microsoft Office. Wherever feasible, students work with more than one application to complete an exercise. In addition, each unit ends with an *Integrated Topic* chapter that emphasizes related skills or a related application that can be incorporated with the unit content.

► **Unit 1** focuses on creating, saving, printing, editing, formatting, and enhancing Word documents; managing documents on disk; exploring the Internet; and creating and formatting Web pages.

► **Unit 2** deals with the concept of presenting, manipulating, and calculating numerical data in columns and rows using Excel. Students also learn to present Excel data more visually by charting the data. Integrated topics presented in this unit include inserting clip art images in Word documents and Excel worksheets and creating maps with Excel data.

► **Unit 3** provides information on creating, saving, printing, editing, formatting, and enhancing PowerPoint presentations as well as inserting hyperlinks in a presentation. The Microsoft tools introduced in this unit include WordArt and organizational charts. Students also learn to link and embed objects between Word, Excel, and PowerPoint.

► **Unit 4** is developed around the concept of organizing, sorting, and managing data. In this unit, students learn to create, organize, edit, and extract data in Access files and to link Access data to an Excel worksheet and a Word document. Students also learn to schedule appointments and create a task list, contact list, and e-mail message using Outlook.

> **Chapter structure:** Each chapter contains the following sections:
> - performance objectives that identify what will specifically be learned in the chapter
> - material introducing and explaining new concepts and features
> - step-by-step exercises at the computer
> - a chapter summary
> - a knowledge self-check (called "Thinking Offline")
> - skill assessment exercises (called "Working Hands-On")
> - a skill assessment exercise requiring the use of the Help feature

The step-by-step exercises integrated within the chapters provide students with the opportunity to practice using the feature(s) presented in the chapter. Skill assessments at the end of each chapter require students to complete exercises without step-by-step instructions. Additional simulation exercises in each unit require students to make decisions about document preparation and formatting. These practical exercises provide ample opportunity to practice new features as well as previously learned features. Composing activities in each unit provide students with the opportunity to compose and format business documents. In recognition of the importance of lifelong learning skills, each unit also includes an Internet exercise designed to encourage students to search for specific information and data using specific URLs, keyword searches, online directories, and search engine indexes.

After they have learned the features of the various programs in the Microsoft Office suite, students are presented with a final Integrated Project. In this project, students are presented with various business situations and are required to use problem-solving, critical-thinking, and creative-thinking skills to design documents for each situation.

Approved Courseware for the Microsoft Office User Specialist (MOUS) Program

The logo on the cover of this text means the book has been approved as courseware that teaches all the skills you need to pass the Core-level certification exams in Word, Excel, PowerPoint, and Access. The MOUS program is used to test and validate your skills in using Office. It supplies objective proof to an employer that you know how to use the programs efficiently and productively. For more information on the MOUS program and where to take the test, visit Microsoft's Web site at www.microsoft.com.

SCANS Standards

This textbook covers important SCANS (Secretary's Commission on Achieving Necessary Skills) goals. The SCANS report was the result of a joint commission from the Departments of Education and Labor. The goal of the commission was to establish the interdisciplinary standards that should be required for all students. SCANS skill standards emphasize the integration of competencies from the areas of information gathering and research, technology, basic skills, and thinking skills.

Educators agree that all curricula can be strengthened by emphasizing classroom work that is more authentic and relevant to learners, i.e., connecting context to content. Teaching in context helps students move away from the subject-specific orientation to integrative learning that includes decision making, problem solving, and critical thinking. The concepts and applications material in each unit of this book has been designed to reflect this important interdisciplinary emphasis as well as implement the SCANS standards. For example, the chapter skill assessments reinforce acquired technical skills while providing practice in decision making and problem solving. The unit performance assessments offer simulations that require students to demonstrate their understanding of the major skills and technical features taught in the unit within the framework of critical and creative thinking. The composing activities toward the end of each unit make it clear that students are not just producers, but editors and writers as well. SCANS places heavy emphasis on communication skills as well as on the planning and follow-through activities.

Emphasis on Visual Learning

Microsoft Office is a suite of programs that operates within the Windows environment, a graphical user interface (GUI) providing a visually oriented environment that uses icons to represent program features. This textbook also emphasizes a graphical environment with icons that represent specific learning components. For example, a computer icon 🖱️ appears next to unit performance assessments. This visually represents that the exercise is done at the computer. A hands-at-keyboard icon ⌨️ identifies the writing activities in each unit. A globe icon 🌐 displays next to the Internet activity at the end of each unit. Also, the integrated exercises are marked with icons representing the applications used.

Upon completion of the course, students will have mastered the basic and intermediate features of Office. They also will have acquired basic skills in using Windows 95 and 98 and a solid foundation in the problem-solving and communication competencies so important in the contemporary workplace.

Getting Started in Office 2000

In this textbook, you will learn to operate several microcomputer application programs that combine to make an application "suite." This suite of programs is called Microsoft Office Professional 2000. The programs you will learn to operate are the *software*, which include instructions telling the computer what to do. The software programs in the suite include a word processing program called *Word*, a spreadsheet program called *Excel*, a presentation program called *PowerPoint*, a database program called *Access*, and a desktop information management program called *Outlook*. Before you learn how to use the Office suite, you need to have a basic understanding of how computers and the related devices work.

Identifying Computer Hardware

The computer equipment you will use to operate the suite of programs is referred to as *hardware*. You will need access to an IBM PC or an IBM-compatible computer. This computer system should consist of the CPU, monitor, keyboard, printer, disk drive, and mouse. If you are not sure what equipment you will be operating, check with your instructor. The computer system displayed in figure G.1 consists of six components. Each component is discussed separately in the material that follows.

figure
G.1   *IBM Personal Computer System*

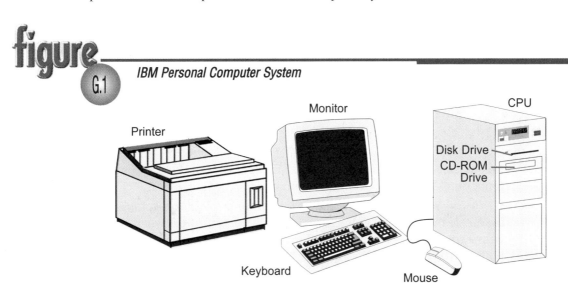

Printer Monitor CPU Disk Drive CD-ROM Drive Keyboard Mouse

CPU

CPU stands for Central Processing Unit and is the intelligence of the computer. All the processing occurs in the CPU. Silicon chips, which contain miniaturized circuitry, are placed on boards that are plugged into slots within the CPU. Whenever an instruction is given to the computer, that instruction is processed through circuitry in the CPU.

Monitor

The monitor is a piece of equipment that looks like a television screen. It displays the information of a program and the text being input at the keyboard. The quality of display for monitors varies depending on the type of monitor and the type of resolution. Monitors can also vary in size—generally from 14-inch size up to 21-inch size.

Keyboard

The keyboard is used to input information into the computer. Keyboards for microcomputers vary in the number and location of the keys. Microcomputers have the alphabetic and numeric keys in the same location as the keys on a typewriter. The symbol keys, however, may be placed in a variety of locations, depending on the manufacturer. In addition to letters, numbers, and symbols, most microcomputer keyboards contain function keys, arrow keys, and a numeric keypad. Figure G.2 shows an enhanced keyboard.

Microcomputer Enhanced Keyboard

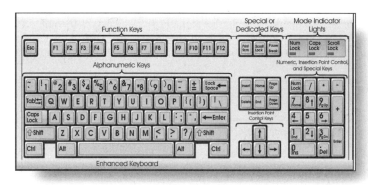

The 12 keys at the top of the enhanced keyboard, labeled with the letter F followed by a number, are called *function keys*. These keys can be used to perform functions within each of the suite programs.

To the right of the regular keys is a group of *special* or *dedicated keys*. These keys are labeled with specific functions that will be performed when you press the key. Below the special keys are arrow keys. These keys are used to move the insertion point in the document screen.

In the upper right corner of the keyboard are three mode indicator lights. When certain modes have been selected, a light appears on the keyboard. For example, if you press the Caps Lock key, which disables the lowercase alphabet, a light appears next to Caps Lock. Similarly, pressing the Num Lock key will disable the special functions on the numeric keypad, which is located at the right side of the keyboard.

Disk Drive

Depending on the computer system you are using, Microsoft Office Professional is installed on a hard drive or as part of a network system. Whether you are using the suite on a hard drive or network system, you will need to have a disk drive available for inserting a 3.5-inch disk, on which you will save and open documents.

The memory capacity for disks varies depending on the density of the disk. Disk memory is measured in kilobytes (thousands) and megabytes (millions). The memory capacity for a 3.5-inch double density (DD) disk is 720,000 bytes (720 kilobytes, which is written as 720Kb). The memory capacity for a 3.5-inch high density disk (HD) is 1,440,000 bytes (1.44 megabytes, which is written as 1.44Mb).

Printer

When you create a document in one of the suite programs, it is considered *soft copy*. If you want a *hard copy* of a document, you need to print it. To print documents you will need to access a printer. Printers are either *impact* or *nonimpact*. Impact printers have a mechanism that strikes the paper to create text. Nonimpact printers use a variety of methods—heat, ink jet, laser—to print characters. These printers are much quieter and faster than impact printers.

Mouse

Many functions in the suite programs are designed to operate more efficiently with a *mouse*. A mouse is an input device that sits on a flat surface next to the computer. A mouse can be operated with the left or the right hand. Moving the mouse on the flat surface causes a corresponding mouse pointer to move on the screen. Figure G.1 shows an illustration of a mouse. For specific instructions on how to use a mouse, please refer to the "Using the Mouse" text later in this section.

Maintaining Disks

You will be copying chapter folders onto a 3.5-inch disk and then saving and opening files from this disk. To ensure that you will be able to retrieve information from the disk, you need to follow certain rules of disk maintenance. To properly maintain a 3.5-inch disk, follow these rules:

- Do not expose the disk to extreme heat or cold.
- Keep the disk away from magnets and magnetic fields. They can erase the information saved on the disk.
- Do not wipe or clean the magnetic surface of the disk.
- Keep the disk away from food, liquids, and smoke.
- Never remove the disk from the disk drive when the drive light is on.
- Carry the disk in a plastic case to prevent damage to the metal shutter.

The 3.5-inch disk on which you will open and save files must be formatted. Most likely, any disk you purchase will already be formatted. Formatting is a process that establishes tracks and sectors on which information is stored and prepares the disk to accept data from the disk operating system (and erases anything previously saved on the disk). If you are using a disk that is not formatted, check with your instructor on the steps needed to format. (You can also look up the steps to format using the Windows Help feature. The Windows Help feature is presented later in this section.)

Using the Mouse

The programs in the Microsoft Office Professional suite can be operated using a keyboard or they can be operated with the keyboard and a mouse. The mouse may have two or three buttons on top, which are tapped to execute specific functions and commands. To use the mouse, rest it on a flat surface or a mouse pad. Put your hand over it with your palm resting on top of the mouse and your wrist resting on the table surface. As you move the mouse on the flat surface, a corresponding pointer moves on the screen.

When using the mouse, there are four terms you should understand—point, click, double-click, and drag. When operating the mouse, you may need to *point* to a specific command, button, or icon. Point means to position the mouse pointer on the desired item. With the mouse pointer positioned on the desired item, you may need to *click* a button on the mouse. Click means quickly tapping a button on the mouse once. To complete two steps at one time, such as choosing and then executing a function, *double-click* a mouse button. Double-click means to tap the left mouse button twice in quick succession. The term *drag* means to press and hold the left mouse button, move the mouse pointer to a specific location, and then release the button.

Using the Mouse Pointer

The mouse pointer will change appearance depending on the function being performed or where the pointer is positioned. The mouse pointer may appear as one of the following images:

I

The mouse pointer appears as an I-beam (called the *I-beam pointer*) in the document screen and can be used to move the insertion point or select text.

The mouse pointer appears as an arrow pointing up and to the left (called the *arrow pointer*) when it is moved to the Title bar, Menu bar, or one of the toolbars at the top of the screen or when a dialog box is displayed. For example, to open a new document with the mouse, you would move the I-beam pointer to the File option on the Menu bar. When the I-beam pointer is moved to the Menu bar, it turns into an arrow pointer. To make a selection, position the tip of the arrow pointer on the File option, and then click the left mouse button. At the drop-down menu that displays, make selections by positioning the arrow pointer on the desired option, and then clicking the left mouse button.

The mouse pointer becomes a double-headed arrow (either pointing left and right, pointing up and down, or pointing diagonally) when performing certain functions such as changing the size of a picture.

In certain situations, such as moving a picture or frame, the mouse pointer becomes a four-headed arrow. The four-headed arrow means that you can move the object left, right, up, or down.

When a request is being processed or when a program is being loaded, the mouse pointer may appear with an hourglass beside it. The hourglass image means "please wait." When the process is completed, the hourglass image is removed.

The mouse pointer displays as a hand with a pointing index finger in certain functions such as Help and indicates that there is more information available about the item.

Choosing Commands

Once a program is open, several methods can be used in the program to choose commands. A command is an instruction that tells the program to do something. You can choose a command with one of the following methods:

- Click a toolbar button with the mouse.
- Choose a command from a menu.
- Use shortcut keys.
- Use a shortcut menu.

Choosing Commands on Toolbars

When a program such as Word or PowerPoint is open, several toolbars containing buttons for common tasks are available. In many of the suite programs, two toolbars are visible on the screen (unless your system has been customized). One toolbar is called the Standard toolbar; the other is referred to as the Formatting toolbar. To choose a command from a toolbar, position the tip of the arrow pointer on a button, and then click the left mouse button. For example, to print the document currently displayed in the document screen, position the tip of the arrow pointer on the Print button on the Standard toolbar, and then click the left mouse button.

Choosing Commands on the Menu Bar

Each of the suite applications contains a Menu bar that displays toward the top of the screen. This Menu bar contains a variety of options you can use to perform functions and commands on data. Functions are grouped logically into options, which display on the Menu bar. For example, features to work with files (documents) are grouped in the File option. Either the mouse or the keyboard can be used to make choices from the Menu bar or make a choice at a dialog box.

To use the mouse to make a choice from the Menu bar, move the I-beam pointer to the Menu bar. This causes the I-beam pointer to display as an arrow pointer. Position the tip of the arrow pointer on the desired option, and then click the left mouse button.

To use the keyboard, press the Alt key to make the Menu bar active. Options on the Menu bar display with an underline below one of the letters. To choose an option from the Menu bar, key the underlined letter of the desired option, or move the insertion point with the left or right arrow keys to the option desired, and then press Enter. This causes a drop-down menu to display.

For example, to display the File drop-down menu in Word as shown in figure G.3 using the mouse, position the arrow pointer on File on the Menu bar, and then click the left mouse button. To display the File drop-down menu with the keyboard, press the Alt key, and then key the letter F for File.

Word File Drop-Down Menu

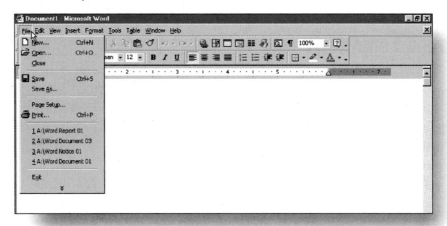

Choosing Commands from Drop-Down Menus

To choose a command from a drop-down menu with the mouse, position the arrow pointer on the desired option, and then click the left mouse button. At the drop-down menu that displays, drag the arrow pointer down the menu to the desired option, and then click the left mouse button.

To make a selection from the drop-down menu with the keyboard, key the underlined letter of the desired option. Once the drop-down menu displays, you do not need to hold down the Alt key with the underlined letter. If you want to close a drop-down menu without making a choice, click in the document screen outside the drop-down menu; or, press the Esc key twice.

If an option can be accessed by clicking a button on a toolbar, the button is displayed preceding the option in the drop-down menu. For example, buttons display before the New, Open, Save, and Print options at the File drop-down menu (see figure G.3).

Some menu options may be gray shaded (dimmed). When an option is dimmed, that option is currently not available. For example, if you choose the Table option on the Menu bar, the Table drop-down menu displays with dimmed options including Merge Cells and Table AutoFormat.

Some menu options are preceded by a check mark. The check mark indicates that the option is currently active. To make an option inactive (turn it off) using the mouse, position the arrow pointer on the option, and then click the left mouse button. To make an option inactive (turn it off) with the keyboard, key the underlined letter of the option.

If an option from a drop-down menu displays followed by an ellipsis (...), a dialog box will display when that option is chosen. A dialog box provides a variety of options to let you specify how a command is to be carried out. For example, if you choose File and then Print from the PowerPoint Menu bar, the Print dialog box shown in figure G.4 displays.

figure
G.4

PowerPoint Print Dialog Box

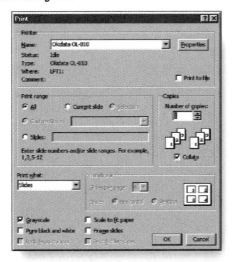

Or, if you choose Format and then Font from the Word Menu bar, the Font dialog box shown in figure G.5 displays.

figure
G.5

Word Font Dialog Box

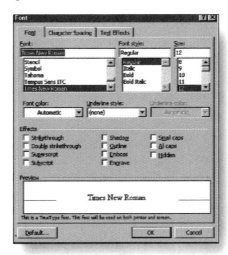

Some dialog boxes provide a set of options. These options are contained on separate tabs. For example, the Font dialog box shown in figure G.5 contains a tab at the top of the dialog box with the word Font on it. Two other tabs display to the right of the Font tab. The tab that displays in the front is the active tab. To make a tab active using the mouse, position the arrow pointer on the desired tab, and then click the left mouse button. If you are using the keyboard, press Ctrl + Tab or press Alt + the underlined letter on the desired tab. For example, to change the tab to Character Spacing in the Font dialog box, click Character Spacing, or press Ctrl + Tab, or press Alt + R.

To choose options from a dialog box with the mouse, position the arrow pointer on the desired option, and then click the left mouse button. If you are using the keyboard, press the Tab key to move the insertion point forward from option to option. Press Shift + Tab to move the insertion point backward from option to option. You can also hold down the Alt key then press the underlined letter of the desired option. When an option is selected, it displays either in reverse video (white letters on a blue background) or surrounded by a dashed box called a *marquee*.

A dialog box contains one or more of the following elements: text boxes, list boxes, check boxes, option buttons, spin boxes, and command buttons.

Text Boxes

Some options in a dialog box require text to be entered. For example, the boxes below the Find what and Replace with options at the Excel Replace dialog box shown in figure G.6 are text boxes. In a text box, you key text or edit existing text. Edit text in a text box in the same manner as normal text. Use the left and right arrow keys on the keyboard to move the insertion point without deleting text and use the Delete key or Backspace key to delete text.

Excel Replace Dialog Box

G.6

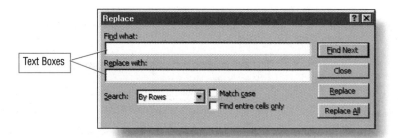

List Boxes

Some dialog boxes such as the Access Open dialog box shown in figure G.7 may contain a list box. The list of files below the Look in: option is contained in a list box. To make a selection from a list box with the mouse, move the arrow pointer to the desired option, and then click the left mouse button.

figure

G.7   *Access Open Dialog Box*

Some list boxes may contain a scroll bar. This scroll bar will display at the right side of the list box (a vertical scroll bar) or at the bottom of the list box (a horizontal scroll bar). Either a vertical scroll bar or a horizontal scroll bar can be used to move through the list if the list is longer than the box. To move down through a list on a vertical scroll bar, position the arrow pointer on the down scroll triangle and hold down the left mouse button. To scroll up through the list in a vertical scroll bar, position the arrow pointer on the up scroll triangle and hold down the left mouse button. You can also move the arrow pointer above the scroll box and click the left mouse button to scroll up the list or move the arrow pointer below the scroll box and click the left mouse button to move down the list. To move through a list with a horizontal scroll bar, click the left scroll triangle to scroll to the left of the list or click the right scroll triangle to scroll to the right of the list.

To make a selection from a list using the keyboard, move the insertion point into the box by holding down the Alt key and pressing the underlined letter of the desired option. Press the up and/or down arrow keys on the keyboard to move through the list.

In some dialog boxes where there is not enough room for a list box, lists of options are inserted in a drop-down list box. Options that contain a drop-down list box display with a down-pointing triangle. For example, the Underline style option at the Word Font dialog box (refer to figure G.5) contains a drop-down list. To display the list, click the down-pointing triangle to the right of the Underline style text box. If you are using the keyboard, press Alt + U.

Check Boxes

Some dialog boxes contain options preceded by a box. A check mark may or may not appear in the box. The Word Font dialog box (refer to figure G.5) displays a variety of check boxes within the Effects section. If a check mark appears in the box, the option is active (turned on). If there is no check mark in the check box, the option is inactive (turned off).

Any number of check boxes can be active. For example, in the Word Font dialog box, you can insert a check mark in any or all of the boxes in the Effects section and these options will be active.

To make a check box active or inactive with the mouse, position the tip of the arrow pointer in the check box, and then click the left mouse button. If you are using the keyboard, press Alt + the underlined letter of the desired option.

Option Buttons

In the PowerPoint Print dialog box (refer to figure G.4), the options in the Print range section are preceded by option buttons. Only one option button can be selected at any time. When an option button is selected, a dark circle displays in the button.

To select an option button with the mouse, position the tip of the arrow pointer inside the option button, and then click the left mouse button. To make a selection with the keyboard, hold down the Alt key, and then press the underlined letter of the desired option.

Spin Boxes

Some options in a dialog box contain measurements or numbers that can be increased or decreased. These options are generally located in a spin box. For example, the Word Paragraph dialog box shown in figure G.8 contains a variety of spin boxes located after the Left, Right, Before, and After options. To increase a number in a spin box, position the tip of the arrow pointer on the up-pointing triangle to the right of the desired option, and then click the left mouse button. To decrease the number, click the down-pointing triangle. If you are using the keyboard, press Alt + the underlined letter of the desired option, and then press the up arrow key to increase the number or the down arrow key to decrease the number.

Word Paragraph Dialog Box

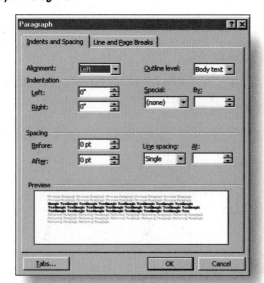

Getting Started

Command Buttons

In the Excel Replace dialog box (refer to figure G.6), the boxes at the right side of the dialog box are called *command buttons*. A command button is used to execute or cancel a command. Some command buttons display with an ellipsis (...). A command button that displays with an ellipsis will open another dialog box. To choose a command button with the mouse, position the arrow pointer on the desired button, and then click the left mouse button. To choose a command button with the keyboard, press the Tab key until the desired command button contains the marquee, and then press the Enter key.

Choosing Commands with Shortcut Keys

At the left side of a drop-down menu is a list of options. At the right side, shortcut keys for specific options may display. For example, the shortcut keys to save a document are Ctrl + S and are displayed to the right of the Save option at the File drop-down menu (refer to figure G.3). To use shortcut keys to choose a command, hold down the Ctrl key, key the letter for the command, and then release the Ctrl key.

Choosing Commands with Shortcut Menus

The software applications in the suite include menus that contain commands related to the item with which you are working. A shortcut menu appears right where you are working in the document. To display a shortcut menu, click the *right* mouse button or press Shift + F10.

For example, if the insertion point is positioned in a paragraph of text in a Word document, clicking the *right* mouse button or pressing Shift + F10 will cause the shortcut menu shown in figure G.9 to display in the document screen.

To select an option from a shortcut menu with the mouse, click the desired option. If you are using the keyboard, press the up or down arrow key until the desired option is selected, and then press the Enter key. To close a shortcut menu without choosing an option, click anywhere outside the shortcut menu or press the Esc key.

G.9   *Word Shortcut Menu*

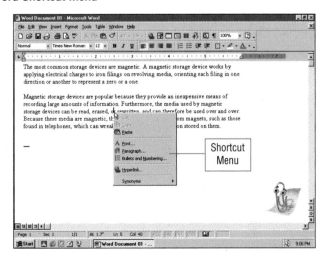

Using the Microsoft Office Assistant

Microsoft Office Professional 2000 includes an *Office Assistant*. This Assistant is a link to the on-screen Help feature that anticipates the type of help you need and suggests Help topics related to the work you are doing. The Assistant will also point out ways to perform tasks more easily and provide visual examples and step-by-step instructions for specific tasks. When you open a program, the Assistant displays, by default, in the lower right corner of the screen as shown in figure G.10. The default Assistant is named "Clippit," and is an image of a paper clip. (This image can be changed.)

figure
G.10

Office Assistant

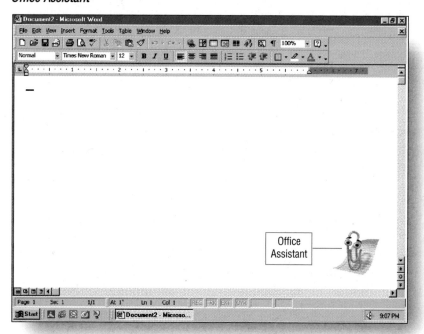

The Assistant will perform a variety of functions. For example, if you try to close a document without saving it, the Assistant will make a sound to get your attention and display a question box like the one shown in figure G.11. At this question, click the desired response.

figure
G.11

Assistant Question Box

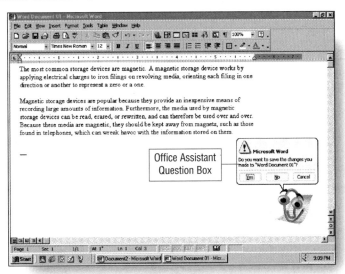

Office Assistant
Question Box

If you are completing a task that one of the Office programs will automatically format, the Assistant will specify what the particular program is doing. For example, if you key a numbered paragraph in Word, Word will automatically format this numbered paragraph. As you are keying the numbered paragraph, the Assistant will tell you that Word is automatically formatting the text and ask if you want to learn more about the feature.

If you are working on a task and want help, just click the Assistant. The Assistant will guess what kind of help you want and display a list of Help topics like the list shown in figure G.12. If the desired topic does not display, key a question in the text box that displays below the list of topics, and then click the Search button.

figure
G.12

Office Assistant Help Topics List

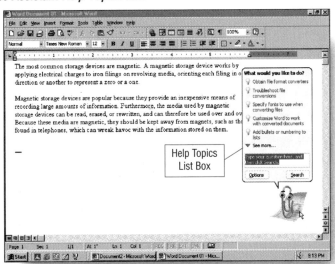

Help Topics
List Box

Occasionally, a light bulb will display above the Assistant. Click this light bulb and the Assistant will display a tip about the type of work you are doing.

Hiding/Turning Off the Office Assistant

To hide the Office Assistant, click <u>H</u>elp and then Hide the <u>O</u>ffice Assistant. Redisplay the Office Assistant by clicking <u>H</u>elp and then Show the <u>O</u>ffice Assistant. The Office Assistant can also be turned off for the entire Word session. To do this, click the Office Assistant and then click the <u>O</u>ptions button that displays in the yellow box. At the Office Assistant dialog box that displays, click the <u>U</u>se the Office Assistant option to remove the check mark, and then click OK.

Changing the Assistant

Microsoft Office Professional offers a variety of other Office Assistants. To display and choose another Assistant, position the arrow pointer on the Assistant, and then click the *right* mouse button. At the shortcut menu that displays, click <u>C</u>hoose Assistant. This displays the Office Assistant dialog box shown in figure G.13. At this dialog box, the current Assistant displays. To display other Assistants, click the <u>N</u>ext button. You can choose from The Dot, F1, The Genius, Office Logo, Mother Nature, Links, and Rocky.

Office Assistant Dialog Box

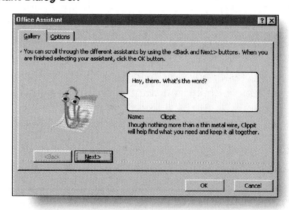

You can customize the Office Assistant by clicking the <u>O</u>ptions tab at the Office Assistant dialog box. This displays a dialog box with a variety of Help options. Insert a check mark before the features you want active and remove the check mark for those features you want inactive.

Working with Multiple Programs

As you learn the various applications in the Microsoft Office Professional suite, you will notice how executing commands in each is very similar. For example, the steps to save, close, and print are virtually the same whether you are working in Word, Excel, PowerPoint, or Access. This consistency among programs greatly enhances a user's ability to easily transfer knowledge learned in one program to another within the suite.

Another appeal of Microsoft Office Professional is the ability to have more than one program open at the same time. For example, you can open Word, create a document, and then open Excel, create a spreadsheet, and copy the spreadsheet into Word.

When a program is open, the name of the program followed by a document name displays in a button on the Taskbar. When another program is opened, the name of the program displays in a button that is positioned to the right of the first program button. Figure G.14 shows the Taskbar with Word, Excel, and PowerPoint open. To move from one program to another, all you need to do is click the button on the Taskbar representing the desired program.

Taskbar with Word, Excel, and PowerPoint Open

As you learn the applications in the Microsoft Office Professional suite, you will learn more about the features presented in this section.

Installing Additional Features

During a standard installation of Microsoft Office Professional, all features and applications may not be installed. To install additional features or applications, you would complete the following basic steps (you may want to refer to the Microsoft Office documentation for specific information):

1. At the Windows desktop, double-click the *My Computer* icon.
2. At the My Computer window, double-click the Control Panel icon.
3. At the Control Panel window, double-click the Add/Remove Program icon.
4. At the Add/Remove Programs Properties dialog box, click Install.
5. At the next screen, insert the Microsoft Office setup CD in the appropriate drive. Follow the steps provided by the Install Wizard to install additional features or applications.

Completing Computer Exercises

Some computer exercises in this textbook require that you open an existing file. Exercise files are saved on the CD that accompanies this textbook. The files you need for each chapter are saved in individual folders. Before beginning a chapter, copy the necessary folder from the CD to a preformatted data disk. After completing the exercises in a chapter, delete the chapter folder before copying the next chapter folder. (Check with your instructor before deleting a folder.)

Copying a Folder

The CD that accompanies this textbook contains numerous files you use to complete some exercises and assessments in chapters. As you begin working in a chapter, copy the chapter folder from the CD to your disk. (Not every chapter contains a folder on the CD. For example, when completing exercises in the Access chapters, you will copy database files from the CD rather than individual chapter folders. This is to ensure that there is adequate space on your disk for saving files.) Copy the chapter folder from the CD to your disk using Windows Explorer by completing the following steps:

1. Insert the CD that accompanies this textbook in the CD-ROM drive.
2. Insert a formatted 3½-inch disk in the disk drive.
3. At the Windows desktop, click the Start button on the Taskbar, point to <u>P</u>rograms, and then click Windows Explorer.
4. In Windows Explorer, click the down-pointing triangle at the right side of the A<u>d</u>dress list box.
5. At the drop-down list that displays, click the drive where the CD is located.
6. In the list box, click the chapter folder you want to copy.
7. Click the Copy button on the Windows Explorer toolbar.
8. Click the down-pointing triangle at the right side of the A<u>d</u>dress list box and then click the drive where your disk is located.
9. Click the Paste button on the Windows Explorer toolbar.
10. After the folder is copied to your disk, close Windows Explorer by clicking the Close button located in the upper right corner of Windows Explorer.

Deleting a Folder

Before copying a chapter folder onto your disk, delete any previous chapter folders. Do this in Windows Explorer by completing the following steps:

1. Insert your disk in the disk drive.
2. At the Windows desktop, click the Start button on the Taskbar, point to <u>P</u>rograms, and then click Windows Explorer.
3. In Windows Explorer, click the down-pointing triangle at the right side of the A<u>d</u>dress list box.
4. At the drop-down list that displays, click the drive where your disk is located.
5. Click the chapter folder in the list box.
6. Click the Delete button on the Windows Explorer toolbar.
7. At the message asking if you want to remove the folder and all its contents, click the <u>Y</u>es button.
8. At the message asking if you want to delete a read-only file, click the yes to <u>A</u>ll button.
9. Close Windows Explorer by clicking the Close button located in the upper right corner of Windows Explorer.

Using Windows 95 and Windows 98

A computer requires an operating system to provide instructions on a multitude of processes, including loading programs, managing data, directing the flow of information to peripheral equipment, and displaying information. Windows 95 and Windows 98 are operating systems that provide functions of this type (along with much more) in a graphical environment. Both Windows operating systems are referred to as a *graphical user interface* (GUI—pronounced *gooey*) that provides a visual display of information with features such as icons (pictures) and buttons. Windows 95 and Windows 98 perform their basic functions in an almost identical manner. New features of Windows 98 will be noted in paragraphs such as the one below.

NEW in Windows 98

The major difference between Windows 95 and Windows 98 is that Windows 98 combines general computer operations with easy access to the Internet. The Internet Explorer browser, which is installed with the operating system, is integrated with the desktop. The Active Desktop permits you to display Web pages as part of your desktop. Windows Update connects directly with Microsoft's Web site, and the Help system provides direct contact with Microsoft's technical support pages. Even for those without Internet connections, the desktop, Taskbar, Start menu, Window views, and folder options can be more easily personalized and adjusted to suit the user's demands.

In this introduction you will learn basic features of Windows 95 and Windows 98. For a more in-depth look at either of the systems, consider reading *Microsoft Windows 95* or *Microsoft Windows 98,* written by Edward J. Coburn and published by EMC/Paradigm Publishing.

Before using one of the software programs in the Microsoft Office Professional suite, you will need to start the operating system. To do this, turn on the computer. Depending on your computer equipment configuration, you may also need to turn on the monitor and printer. When the computer is turned on, the Windows 95 or Windows 98 operating system is automatically started and, after a few moments, the desktop will display, as shown in figure W.1 (Windows 95) and figure W.2 (Windows 98).

figure W.1

Windows 95 Desktop

Start Button

Taskbar

figure W.2

Windows 98 Desktop

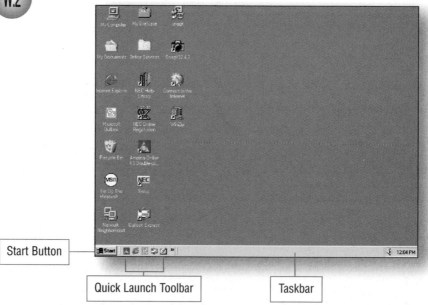

Start Button

Quick Launch Toolbar

Taskbar

Exploring the Desktop

The main portion of the screen that displays when Windows 95 or Windows 98 is loaded is called the *desktop*. Think of the desktop in Windows as the top of a desk in an office. A business person places necessary tools—such as pencils, pens, paper, files, calculator—on his or her desktop to perform functions. Like the tools that are located on a desk, the desktop contains tools for operating the computer. These tools are logically grouped and placed in dialog boxes or panels that can be displayed using one of the icons at the left side of the desktop.

NEW in Windows 98

The Channel Bar is part of the Windows 98 desktop. Channels are regularly updated links to Web pages. Initially the Channel Bar includes advertisements for channels to which you can subscribe; you can also select your own channels from the World Wide Web. Use of the Channel Bar requires an active Internet connection.

The desktop contains a variety of icons and features for using your computer and software programs installed on the computer. The features available on the desktop are described in the following text.

Using Icons

Icons are visual symbols that represent programs, files, or folders. In figure W.3, the figure on the left shows an icon for the Microsoft program Internet Explorer in Windows 95; the figure in the middle shows the icon for that same program in Windows 98. Icons in Windows 95 and Windows 98 are very similar to those in earlier versions of Windows. The biggest difference is the folder icon. The figure on the right shows the Windows folder icon. Windows 95 and Windows 98 folders are just like directories from Windows 3.1 or DOS. To open a folder or start a program, you double-click the icon.

Windows Icons: Windows 95 Internet Explorer; Windows 98 Internet Explorer; Windows Folder

Using the Taskbar

The bar that displays at the bottom of the desktop, shown in figures W.1 and W.2, is called the Taskbar. The Taskbar in Windows 95 contains three areas: the Start button, the program button area, and the System tray. The Windows 98 Taskbar is divided into four areas: the Start button, the Quick Launch toolbar, the program button area, and the System tray.

The Start button is located at the left side of the Taskbar. Use this button to start a program, use the Help feature, change settings, and open files. To display the options available with the Start button, position the arrow pointer on the Start button, and then click the left mouse button. This causes a pop-up menu to display, as shown in figure W.4.

Start Button Pop-up Menu

| America Online 4.0 |
| Network Neighborhood |
| New Office Document |
| Open Office Document |
| Windows Update |
| WinZip |
| Programs ▶ |
| Favorites ▶ |
| Documents ▶ |
| Settings ▶ |
| Find ▶ |
| Help |
| Run... |
| Log Off |
| Shut Down... |

To choose an option from this pop-up menu, drag the arrow pointer to the desired option (referred to as *pointing*), and then click the left mouse button. Pointing to options at the Start pop-up menu followed by a right-pointing triangle will cause a side menu to display with additional options.

NEW in Windows 98

The Start menu includes two new options, both of which require an Internet connection: *Windows Update* takes you to the Microsoft product support and update pages, from which you can select any updates that might not be available in your copy of Windows 98; Favorites provides shortcuts to frequently used files and Web sites.

When a program is open, a program button appears in the middle of the Taskbar. In the Taskbar shown below, taken from Windows 95, the Word 2000 program is open. An icon representing Word displays in the program button area of the Taskbar.

Windows 95 Taskbar with Word 2000 Open

Switching Between Open Programs

To switch between open programs, click the program's button on the Taskbar. In the Taskbar shown below, the Word button is depressed, indicating that it is the active program. Clicking either the Excel or PowerPoint button will activate that program.

Taskbar with Word 2000 Program Active

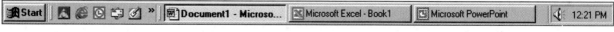

When Excel is the active program, the Word button is now raised and the Excel button is depressed, as shown below:

Taskbar with Excel 2000 Program Active

Almost every program you open will appear on the Taskbar. (A few specialized tools may not.) On the Taskbar shown below there are 11 programs running at the same time. Each button on the Taskbar gets a little smaller each time you open a program.

Taskbar with 11 Programs Running

exercise

Opening Programs and Switching Between Programs

1. Open Windows 95 or Windows 98. (To do this, turn on the computer and, if necessary, turn on the printer.)
2. When the desktop displays, open Word 2000 by completing the following steps:
   a. Position the arrow pointer on the Start button on the Taskbar and then click the left mouse button.
   b. At the Start pop-up menu, point to Programs. (This causes a side menu to display.)
   c. Drag the arrow pointer to *Microsoft Word* and then click the left mouse button.
   d. When the Word 2000 program is opened, notice that an icon representing Word displays in the program button area of the Taskbar.
3. Open Excel 2000 by completing the following steps:
   a. Position the arrow pointer on the Start button on the Taskbar and then click the left mouse button.
   b. At the Start pop-up menu, point to Programs.
   c. Drag the arrow pointer to *Microsoft Excel* and then click the left mouse button.
   d. When the Excel 2000 program is opened, notice that an icon representing Excel displays in the program button area of the Taskbar to the right of the button representing Word.
4. Switch to the Word program by clicking the button on the Taskbar representing Word.
5. Switch to the Excel program by clicking the button on the Taskbar representing Excel.
6. Exit Excel by clicking File on the Excel Menu bar and then clicking Exit at the drop-down menu.
7. Click the button on the Taskbar representing Word.
8. Exit Word by clicking File on the Word Menu bar and then clicking Exit at the drop-down menu.

The System tray is the recessed area on the far right side of the Taskbar. The System tray contains a digital clock and specialized programs that run in the background. Position the arrow pointer over the current time on the Taskbar and today's date displays in a small yellow box:

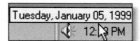

Double-click the current time displayed on the Taskbar and the Date/Time Properties dialog box displays, as shown:

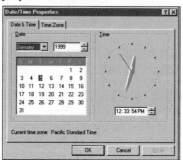

Change the date with options in the Date section of the dialog box. For example, to change the month, click the down-pointing triangle at the right side of the text box containing the current month, and then click the desired month at the drop-down list. Change the year by clicking the up- or down-pointing triangle at the right side of the text box containing the current year until the desired year displays. To change the day, click the desired day in the monthly calendar that displays in the dialog box. To change the time, double-click either the hour, minute, or seconds and use the up and down arrows to adjust the time.

NEW in Windows 98

The Quick Launch toolbar is positioned between the Start button and the program button area on the Taskbar. It contains icons for programs that can be launched with a single click, such as the Internet Explorer Browser. The appearance of the Quick Launch toolbar can vary considerably, depending on your installation of Windows 98. A typical installation is shown in figure W.5.

figure W.5

Windows 98 Taskbar with Quick Launch Toolbar

Quick Launch Toolbar

Setting Taskbar Properties

The default setting for the Taskbar displays it at the bottom of the desktop with the time displayed. These default settings can be changed with options at the

Taskbar Properties dialog box, shown in figure W.6. To display this dialog box, position the arrow pointer on any empty spot on the Taskbar, and then click the *right* mouse button. At the pop-up menu that displays, click P<u>r</u>operties.

Taskbar Properties Dialog Box

Each property is controlled by a check box. Property options containing a check mark are active. Click the option to remove the check mark and make the option inactive. If an option is inactive, clicking the option will insert a check mark in the check box and turn on the option (make it active). The Taskbar Properties dialog box contains these options:

Always on <u>t</u>op: Keeps the Taskbar visible at all times. Check this if you want to see the Taskbar even when you are running programs.

A<u>u</u>to hide: Collapses the Taskbar into a thin line at the bottom of the screen. When you move the insertion point to the bottom of the screen, the Taskbar will display.

Show <u>s</u>mall icons in Start menu: Displays small icons in the Start menu. If unchecked, large icons are used (see figure W.7).

Show <u>C</u>lock: Shows or hides the clock.

Start Menu for Windows 98, Showing Large and Small Icons

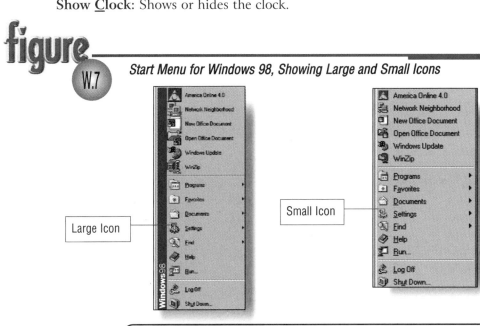

Large Icon

Small Icon

exercise 2

Changing Taskbar Properties

1. Make sure Windows 95 or Windows 98 is open and the desktop is displayed.
2. Change the size of the icons in the Start pop-up menu and remove the display of the clock by completing the following steps:
   a. Position the arrow pointer on any empty area on the Taskbar and then click the *right* mouse button.
   b. At the pop-up menu that displays, click Properties.
   c. At the Taskbar Properties dialog box, click Show small icons in Start menu. (This inserts a check mark in the check box.)
   d. Click Show Clock. (This removes the check mark from the check box.)
   e. Click the Apply button.
   f. Click OK to close the dialog box.
3. Notice that the time no longer displays at the right side of the Taskbar. Click the Start button at the left side of the Taskbar and notice that the icons in the pop-up menu are smaller. Click on any empty spot on the Taskbar to remove the pop-up menu.
4. Return to the default settings for the Taskbar by completing the following steps:
   a. Position the arrow pointer on any empty area on the Taskbar and then click the *right* mouse button.
   b. At the pop-up menu that displays, click Properties.
   c. At the Taskbar Properties dialog box, click Show small icons in Start menu. (This removes the check mark from the check box.)
   d. Click Show Clock. (This inserts a check mark in the check box.)
   e. Click the Apply button.
   f. Click OK to close the dialog box.

Using Windows Explorer

Windows Explorer is the file management program for Windows 95 and Windows 98. You can use Windows Explorer to see the contents of every drive and folder attached to your computer. You can even look into drives and folders on a network.

Looking at the Explorer Window

To open Windows Explorer, click the Start button on the Taskbar, point to Programs, and then click *Windows Explorer*. This displays the Windows Explorer window similar to the one of those shown in figure W.8. The Windows Explorer displays with two panes—the All Folders pane (called the Folders pane in Windows 98) and the Contents pane (called the Files pane in Windows 98). The names of the two panes in Windows Explorer vary between Windows 95 and Windows 98. In this section, they will be referred to as All Folders/Folders (representing the Windows 95 name and the Windows 98 name) and Contents/Files pane.

Windows Explorer Window for Windows 95 (left) and Windows 98 (right)

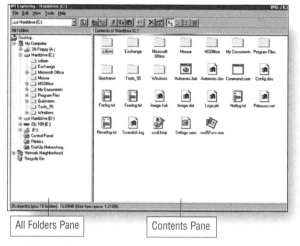 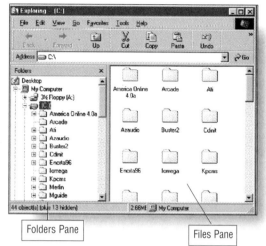

| All Folders Pane | Contents Pane | Folders Pane | Files Pane |

The All Folders/Folders pane shows all the drives connected to your computer (including network drives if you are attached to a network), every printer you can use, and special system folders such as Control Panel or Dial-Up Networking. This pane gives you the large view of your computer system. The computer using Windows 95 in figure W.8 has two hard drives (C: and D:), a floppy drive (A:), an Iomega Zip drive (E:), a CD-ROM drive (F:), and Network access (Network Neighborhood). Your system will vary from this one.

The All Folders/Folders pane is based on a *hierarchy*. At the top is the Desktop. As you can see from figure W.8, all the other icons are shown below the Desktop icon. A plus sign next to an icon means you can double-click the icon and open up folders that are hidden inside. In figure W.9, if the Windows icon is clicked in the All Folders pane in the Windows 95 computer, a number of folders appear.

Contents of "Windows" in Windows Explorer (Windows 95)

Notice that the contents in the Contents/Files pane has changed. After double-clicking on the Windows folder in the All Folders/Folders pane, the Contents/Files pane shows the contents of the Windows folder.

The Contents/Files pane gives you the local view of your computer. In this pane you will see all the folders, files, or programs that are a part of the current disk or folder. In Windows 95, you can tell what drive or folder you are viewing by looking at the top of the Contents pane. In figure W.9 it reads *Contents of 'Windows.'* This means that you are looking at the contents of the Windows folder.

NEW in Windows 98

In Windows 98, you can tell what drive or folder you are viewing by finding the open folder in the Folders pane.

Double-clicking a drive or folder icon within the Contents/Files pane opens that drive or folder within the All Folders/Folders pane and shows the contents of that drive or folder in the Contents/Files pane. Double-clicking a program or file icon starts the application.

Clicking the Up One Level button (Windows 95) or the Up button (Windows 98) on the toolbar moves Windows Explorer up the hierarchy. Clicking the Up One Level button opens the C drive in the All Folders/Folders pane, and displays the contents of the C drive in the Contents pane.

Copying, Moving, and Deleting Files in Windows Explorer

File management activities can be performed in Windows Explorer. These activities include copying and moving files from a folder or drive to another or deleting files. To copy a file to another folder, position the arrow pointer on the file to be moved and then hold down the *right* mouse button. Drag the file to the desired folder and then release the right mouse button. At the pop-up menu that displays, click Copy Here. This inserts a copy of the file in the position of the arrow pointer. In figure W.10, the file named *Faclog.txt* is being copied from the C drive to the A drive.

figure
W.10

Copying a File in Windows Explorer

The document Faclog.txt is being copied from C drive to A drive.

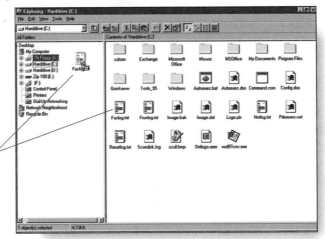

You can move a file by completing similar steps. The only difference is that you click <u>M</u>ove Here at the pop-up menu rather than <u>C</u>opy Here. When a file is moved to a new location it leaves its original location.

A file or selected files can be easily removed from Windows Explorer. To delete a file, position the arrow pointer on the file in the Contents/Files pane to be deleted and then click the *right* mouse button. At the pop-up menu that displays, click <u>D</u>elete. At the Confirm File Delete dialog box, click the <u>Y</u>es button. Complete similar steps to delete selected files.

Deleted files are sent to the Recycle Bin. You will learn more about the Recycle Bin in the next section.

Copying and File and Folder and Deleting a File

1. Open Windows 95 or Windows 98.
2. Open Windows Explorer by completing the following steps:
   a. Click the Start button located at the left side of the Taskbar.
   b. At the pop-up menu that displays, point to <u>P</u>rograms, and then click *Windows Explorer*.
3. Copy a file from the CD that accompanies this textbook to a disk in drive A by completing the following steps:
   a. Insert the CD that accompanies this textbook into the CD drive.
   b. Insert a formatted 3.5-inch disk in drive A
   .
   c. Click the down-pointing triangle at the right side of the All Folders/Folders pane until the drive containing the CD displays (depending on your system—this is probably drive D or drive F).
   d. Click once on the CD drive. (This displays the folders on the CD in the Contents/Files pane.)
   e. Double-click the *Window* folder (located in the Contents/Files pane).
   f. Click the up-pointing triangle at the right side of the All Folders/Folders pane until drive A: is visible.
   g. Position the arrow pointer on *Word Document 01* in the Content/Files pane and then hold down the *right* mouse button.
   h. Drag the arrow pointer (an outline of the file will move with the arrow pointer) to the All Folders/Folders pane to the *A* drive (make sure *A:* is selected [displays with a blue background]) and then release the mouse button.
   i. At the pop-up menu that displays, click <u>C</u>opy Here. (This copies the file to the A: drive.)
4. Click *3½ Floppy (A:)* in the All Folders/Folders pane.
5. Delete Word Document 01 from drive A by completing the following steps:
   a. Position the arrow pointer on *Word Document 01* and then click the *right* mouse button.
   b. At the drop-down menu that displays, click <u>D</u>elete.
   c. At the message asking you to confirm the deletion, click the <u>Y</u>es button.
6. Copy the *Window* folder from the CD drive to the disk in drive A by completing the following steps:
   a. Click the down-pointing triangle at the right side of the All Folders/Folders pane until the drive containing the CD displays.

b. Click once on the CD drive. (This displays the folders on the CD in the Contents/Files pane.)

c. Click once on the *Window* folder.

d. Click the up-pointing triangle at the right side of the All Folders/Folders pane until drive A is visible.

e. Position the arrow pointer on *Window* folder and then hold down the *right* mouse button.

f. Drag the arrow pointer to the All Folders/Folders pane to the drive A (make sure *A:* is selected [displays with a blue background]) and then release the mouse button.

g. At the pop-up menu that displays, click Copy Here. (This copies the folder to the A drive.)

7. Close Windows Explorer by clicking File and then Close, or clicking the Close button (contains an X) located in the upper right corner of Windows Explorer.

Selecting Files

More than one file can be moved, copied, or deleted at one time. Before moving, copying, or deleting files, select the desired files. Selecting files in Windows Explorer is easier when the display of the Contents/Files pane is changed to Details. To change the display, display Windows Explorer and then click View. At the drop-down menu, click Details. This displays the contents of the Windows Explorer in a manner similar to that shown in figure W.11.

Windows Explorer with Details View Selected

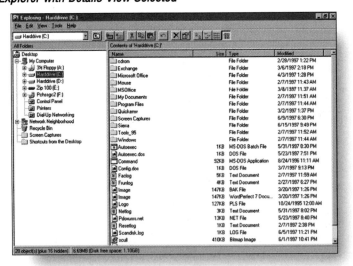

To move adjacent files, click the first file, hold down the Shift key, and then click the last file. This selects and highlights all files from the first file clicked to the last file clicked. With the adjacent files selected, position the arrow pointer on any selected file, and then hold down the *right* mouse button. Drag the files to the desired destination and then release the mouse button.

To select nonadjacent files, click the first file to select it, hold down the Ctrl key and then click any other files to be moved. With the desired files selected, position the arrow pointer on one of the selected files and then hold down the *right* mouse button. Drag the files to the desired destination and then release the mouse button.

Copying and Deleting Files

1. Open Windows 95 or Windows 98.
2. Open Windows Explorer by completing the following steps:
   a. Click the Start button located at the left side of the Taskbar.
   b. At the pop-up menu that displays, point to Programs, and then click *Windows Explorer*.
3. Change the display to Details by clicking View and then Details.
4. Copy files from the CD that accompanies this textbook to a disk in drive A: by completing the following steps:
   a. Insert the CD that accompanies this textbook into the CD drive.
   b. Insert your disk in drive A.
   c. Click the down-pointing triangle at the right side of the All Folders/Folders pane until the drive containing the CD displays (depending on your system—this is probably drive D or drive F).
   d. Click once on the CD drive. (This displays the folders on the CD in the Contents/Files pane.)
   e. Double-click the *Window* folder.
   f. Click the up-pointing triangle at the right side of the All Folders/Folders pane until drive A: is visible.
   g. Position the arrow pointer on *Word Document 01* in the Contents/Files pane and then click the left mouse button.
   h. Hold down the Shift key, click *Word Document 05*, and then release the Shift key. (This selects *Word Document 01, Word Document 02, Word Document 03, Word Document 04,* and *Word Document 05*.)
   i. Position the arrow pointer on one of the selected files and then hold down the *right* mouse button.
   j. Drag the arrow pointer (an outline of the files will move with the arrow pointer) to the All Folders/Folders pane to the *A:* drive (make sure *A:* is selected [displays with a blue background]) and then release the mouse button.
   k. At the pop-up menu that displays, click Copy Here. (This copies the files to the A drive.)
5. Click *3½ Floppy (A:)* in the All Folders/Folders pane to display the files located in the A drive.
6. Delete the files from drive A: that you just copied by completing the following steps:
   a. Position the arrow pointer on *Word Document 01* in the Contents/Files pane and then click the left mouse button.
   b. Hold down the Shift key, click *Word Document 05*, and then release the Shift key. (This selects *Word Document 01, Word Document 02, Word Document 03, Word Document 04,* and *Word Document 05*.)
   c. Position the arrow pointer on one of the selected files and then click the *right* mouse button.

d. At the drop-down menu that displays, click Delete.

e. At the message asking you to confirm the deletion, click the Yes button.

7. Close Windows Explorer by clicking File and then Close, or clicking the Close button (contains an X) located in the upper right corner of Windows Explorer.

Manipulating and Creating Folders in Windows Explorer

In Windows 95 and Windows 98, files are grouped logically and placed in folders. A folder can be created within a folder. The main folder on a disk or drive is called the root folder. Additional folders can be created as a branch of this root folder. To create a folder while in Windows Explorer, display the Contents/Files pane of the folder or drive in which you want your new folder to be. Position the arrow pointer in the Contents/Files pane and then click the *right* mouse button. (Do not right-click on an icon.) This displays a pop-up menu like that shown in figure W.12.

NEW in Windows 98

The pop-up menu adds Customize this Folder and Refresh to the options available in Windows 95.

Pop-up Menu in Windows Explorer

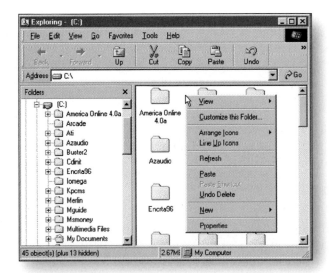

At the pop-up menu, point to New and then click Folder. This places a New Folder icon in the Contents/Files pane, as shown in figure W.13.

figure

New Folder Icon in Windows Explorer

With *New Folder* selected below the icon, as shown in figure W.13, key the desired name for the folder, and then press Enter. The new folder is automatically placed in the All Folders/Folders pane.

To delete a folder in Windows Explorer, position the arrow pointer on the folder, and then click the *right* mouse button. At the pop-up menu that displays, click <u>D</u>elete. At the Confirm Folder Delete dialog box, click the <u>Y</u>es button.

Creating a New Folder

1. Open Windows 95 or Windows 98.
2. Open Windows Explorer by completing the following steps:
   a. Click the Start button located at the left side of the Taskbar.
   b. At the pop-up menu that displays, point to <u>P</u>rograms, and then click *Windows Explorer*.
3. Change the display to List by clicking <u>V</u>iew and then <u>L</u>ist.
4. Create a new folder by completing the following steps:
   a. Insert your disk in drive A (this disk contains the *Window* folder you copied in exercise 3).
   b. Click the up-pointing triangle at the right side of the All Folders/Folders pane until *3½ Floppy (A:)* displays.
   c. Click once on *3½ Floppy (A:)*.
   d. Double-click the *Window* folder. (This opens the folder.)
   e. Position the arrow pointer in a blank area in the Contents/Files pane and then click the *right* mouse button. (Do not right-click on an icon.)
   f. At the pop-up menu that displays, point to Ne<u>w</u>, and then click <u>F</u>older. (This places a New Folder icon in the Contents/Files pane.)
   g. With *New Folder* selected, key **Spell Check Files**, and then press Enter.
5. Copy *Word Spell Check 01, Word Spell Check 02, Word Spell Check 03,* and *Word Spell Check 04* into the Spell Check Files folder you just created by completing the following steps:
   a. Click once on the file named *Word Spell Check 01* located in the Contents/Files pane.

b. Hold down the Shift key, click once on the file named *Word Spell Check 04*, and then release the Shift key. (This selects *Word Spell Check 01*, *Word Spell Check 02*, *Word Spell Check 03*, and *Word Spell Check 04*.)

c. Position the arrow pointer on one of the selected files and then hold down the *right* mouse button.

d. Drag the arrow pointer (an outline of the selected files will move with the arrow pointer) to the *Spell Check Files* folder located in the Contents/Files pane (make sure the *Spell Check Files* folder displays with a blue background) and then release the mouse button.

e. At the pop-up menu that displays, click <u>C</u>opy Here. (This copies the selected files to the *Spell Check Files* folder.)

6. Display the files you just copied by double-clicking the *Spell Check Files* folder in the Contents/Files pane.

7. Click *3½ Floppy (A:)* in the All Folders/Folders pane. (This displays the contents of the your disk in the Contents/Files pane.)

8. Delete the *Spell Check Files* folder and its contents by completing the following steps:

a. Double-click the *Window* folder in the Contents/Files pane.

b. Position the arrow pointer on the *Spell Check Files* folder in the Contents/Files pane and then click the *right* mouse button.

c. At the drop-down menu that displays, click <u>D</u>elete.

d. At the message asking you to confirm the deletion, click <u>Y</u>es.

9. Close Windows Explorer by clicking <u>F</u>ile and then <u>C</u>lose, or clicking the Close button (contains an X) located in the upper right corner of Windows Explorer.

Formatting Floppy Disks in Windows Explorer

Before a disk can be used to save files, it must be formatted. Formatting is a process that prepares the surface of a disk for receiving data from the particular disk operating system that you are using.

A disk can be formatted while in Windows Explorer. To do this, insert the disk you want formatted in drive A. Click the up-pointing triangle at the right side of the All Folders/Folders pane until *3½ Floppy (A:)* displays. Position the arrow pointer on *3½ Floppy (A:)* and then click the *right* mouse button.

At the pop-up menu that displays (figure W.14), click For<u>m</u>at. At the Format dialog box shown in figure W.15, set the capacity to meet the inserted disk (most disks are 1.44 Mb floppies), choose a format type, and add a label, if necessary, to identify the disk. Click the <u>S</u>tart button and the formatting begins. The progress of the formatting is shown in the program bar located toward the bottom of the dialog box.

figure

W.14

Menu Options for Drive A: Windows 95 (left), Windows 98 (right)

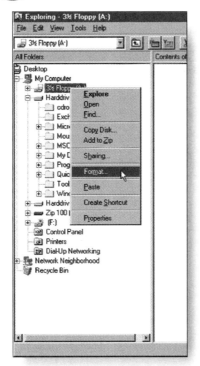

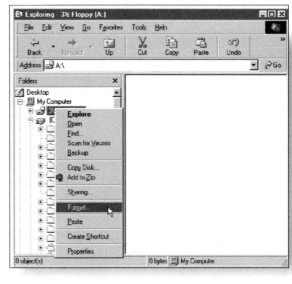

figure

W.15

Format Dialog Box

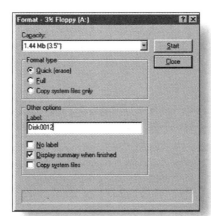

Using the Recycle Bin

Deleting the wrong file can be a disaster. Windows 95 and Windows 98 help protect you and your work with the Recycle Bin (see figure W.16). The Recycle Bin acts just like an office wastepaper basket; you can throw away unwanted files, but you can reach in and take paper out if you threw it away by accident.

Recycle Bin Icon

Deleting Files to the Recycle Bin

In the *Using Windows Explorer* section, you learned how to delete files from the hard drive. A file or selected files deleted from the hard drive are automatically sent to the Recycle Bin. Files deleted from a disk are deleted permanently. (There are recovery programs, however, that will help you recover deleted text. If you accidentally delete a file(s) from a disk, do not do anything more with the disk until you can run a recovery program.)

Another method for deleting a file is to drag the file to the Recycle Bin icon on the desktop. Drag a file icon to the Recycle Bin until the *Recycle Bin* icon is selected (displays with a blue background) and then release the mouse button. This drops the file you are dragging into the Recycle Bin. When a file is dropped into the Recycle Bin, the Recycle Bin displays with paper spilling out the top.

As you learned in the *Using Windows Explorer* section, a file can also be deleted and sent to the Recycle Bin by right-clicking the file, and then clicking <u>D</u>elete at the pop-up menu that displays. At the Confirm File Delete dialog box, click <u>Y</u>es.

Recovering Files from the Recycle Bin

If you accidentally delete a file to the Recycle Bin, it can be easily restored. To restore a file, double-click the Recycle Bin icon on the desktop. This opens the Recycle Bin window shown in figure W17. (The contents of the Recycle Bin will vary.)

Recycle Bin Window with Details View Selected

To restore a file, click the file you want restored. With the file selected, click File on the Recycle Bin Menu bar and then click Restore at the drop-down menu. The file is removed from the Recycle Bin and returned to its original location. You can also restore a file by positioning the arrow pointer on the file, clicking the *right* mouse button, and then clicking Restore at the pop-up menu.

Deleting Files to and Recovering Files from the Recycle Bin

1. Open Windows 95 or Windows 98.
2. Open Windows Explorer by completing the following steps:
   a. Click the Start button located at the left side of the Taskbar.
   b. At the pop-up menu that displays, point to Programs, and then click *Windows Explorer*.
3. Copy files from your disk in drive A to drive C by completing the following steps:
   a. Insert your disk in drive A (this disk contains the *Window* folder).
   b. Click the up-pointing triangle at the right side of the All Folders/Folders pane until *3½ Floppy (A:)* displays.
   c. Click once on *3½ Floppy (A:)*.
   d. Double-click the *Window* folder in the Contents/Files pane.
   e. Position the arrow pointer on *Word Spell Check 01* and then click the left mouse button.
   f. Hold down the Shift key, click *Word Spell Check 04,* and then release the Shift key.
   g. Position the arrow pointer on one of the selected files and then hold down the *right* mouse button.
   h. Drag the arrow pointer (an outline of the files will move with the arrow pointer) to the All Folders/Folders pane to the *C:* drive (make sure *C:* is selected [displays with a blue background]) and then release the mouse button.
   i. At the pop-up menu that displays, click Copy Here. (This copies the files to the C drive.)
4. Click *C:* in the All Folders/Folders pane to display the files located in the C drive. (The files you copied, *Word Spell Check 01* through *Word Spell Check 04*, will display in the Contents/Files pane in alphabetical order.)
5. Delete *Word Spell Check 01* through *Word Spell Check 04* from the C drive and send them to the Recycle Bin by completing the following steps:
   a. Select *Word Spell Check 01* through *Word Spell Check 04* in the Contents/Files pane. (If these files are not visible, you will need to scroll down the list of files.)
   b. Position the arrow pointer on one of the selected files and then click the *right* mouse button.
   c. At the pop-up menu that displays, click Delete.
   d. At the message asking you to confirm the deletion, click Yes.
6. Close Windows Explorer by clicking File and then Close, or clicking the Close button (contains an X) located in the upper right corner of the Windows Explorer Title bar.
7. At the desktop, display the contents of the Recycle Bin by double-clicking the *Recycle Bin* icon.
8. At the Recycle Bin window, restore Word Spell Check 01 through Word Spell Check 04 to the C drive by completing the following steps:
   a. Scroll to the end of the list of files.
   b. When *Word Spell Check 01* through *Word Spell Check 04* display in the list box, select all four files.

  c. With the files selected, position the arrow pointer on one of the selected files, and then click the *right* mouse button.

  d. At the pop-up menu that displays, click <u>R</u>estore.

 9. Close the Recycle Bin window by clicking <u>F</u>ile on the Recycle Bin Menu bar and then clicking <u>C</u>lose at the drop-down menu.

10. Open Windows Explorer.

11. With the contents of drive C displayed in the Contents/Files pane, complete the following steps:

  a. Select *Word Spell Check 01* through *Word Spell Check 04* in the Contents/Files pane. (If these files are not visible, you will need to scroll down the list of files. These are the files you recovered from the Recycle Bin.)

  b. Delete the four files.

12. Close Windows Explorer.

Emptying the Recycle Bin

Just like a wastepaper basket, the Recycle Bin can get too full. To empty the Recycle Bin, position the arrow pointer on the *Recycle Bin* icon on the desktop and then click the *right* mouse button. At the pop-up menu that displays, click Empty Recycle <u>B</u>in. At the Confirm Multiple File Delete dialog box, click <u>Y</u>es. You can also empty the Recycle Bin by double-clicking the *Recycle Bin* icon. At the Recycle Bin window that displays, click <u>F</u>ile on the Menu bar and then click Empty Recycle <u>B</u>in at the drop-down menu. At the Confirm Multiple File Delete dialog box, click <u>Y</u>es.

  Emptying the Recycle Bin deletes all files. You can delete a specific file or files from the Recycle Bin (rather than all files). To do this, double-click the *Recycle Bin* icon on the desktop. At the Recycle Bin window, select the file or files to be deleted, position the arrow pointer on one of the selected files, and then click the *right* mouse button. At the pop-up menu that displays, click <u>D</u>elete. At the dialog box asking you to confirm the deletion, click <u>Y</u>es.

 *exercise* 7

Emptying the Recycle Bin

(Note: Check with your instructor before completing this exercise.)

1. At the desktop, double-click the *Recycle Bin* icon.

2. At the Recycle Bin window, empty the contents of the Recycle Bin by completing the following steps:

  a. Click <u>F</u>ile on the Recycle Bin Menu bar and then click Empty Recycle <u>B</u>in at the drop-down menu.

  b. At the message asking you to confirm the deletion, click <u>Y</u>es.

3. Close the Recycle Bin window by clicking <u>F</u>ile and then <u>C</u>lose.

When the Recycle Bin is emptied the files cannot be recovered by the Recycle Bin or by Windows 95 or Windows 98. If you have to recover a file, you will need to use a file recovery program such as Norton Utilities. These utilities are separate programs, but might be worth their cost if you ever need them.

Customizing the Recycle Bin

The Recycle Bin settings can be customized at the Recycle Bin Properties dialog box shown in figure W.18. To display this dialog box, position the arrow pointer on the *Recycle Bin* icon on the desktop and then click the *right* mouse button. At the pop-up menu that displays, click Properties.

W.18 *Recycle Bin Properties Dialog Box*

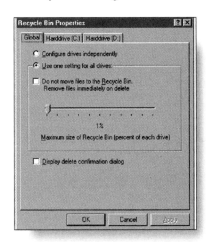

The Recycle Bin can operate differently on each drive contained by your computer, or you can have one setting for all components of the computer. In figure W.19, the settings are the same for all drives.

Until you remove files from the Recycle Bin, they take up space on your hard drive. You can limit the maximum size of the Recycle Bin by moving the slide bar in the Recycle Bin Properties dialog box. You can pick any percentage between 1 and 100. The larger the Recycle Bin, the less room there is for all your other work. Once the Recycle Bin is filled, it begins to delete old files to make room for new ones.

After making any desired changes to the Recycle Bin Properties dialog box, click OK to close the dialog box.

Using My Computer

My Computer is a special icon that Windows 95 or Windows 98 creates and places on your desktop. *My Computer* provides instant access into components of your computer including drives attached to the computer (floppies, hard drives, and CD-ROM drives), printers, dial-up connections (modems used to attach to another computer), and the Control Panel. To display the My Computer window shown in figure W.19, double-click the *My Computer* icon on the desktop.

figure W.19

My Computer Window: Windows 95 (left) and Windows 98 (right)

Double-click the *Harddrive (C:)* icon and another window is opened (see figure W.20). The desktop now has two open windows: My Computer and Harddrive (C:).

figure W.20

Harddrive (C:) Window in Windows 95

Double-click the *3½ Floppy (A:)* icon and three windows open: My Computer, Harddrive (C:), and 3½ Floppy (A:). With the C: and A: windows open, you can easily drag files from one drive to the other. Dragging files from the C drive to a disk in the floppy drive is an easy way to save files to a disk.

If you continue clicking on folders, you will open up window after window onto your desktop. To stop this from happening, hold down the Ctrl key while double-clicking any folder in My Computer. This forces the new window to replace the one already open.

You can start any application from My Computer. Double-click any document icon and the correct application is started with the document opened. In figure W.21, Word was started and the file Document.doc was opened by double-clicking the *Document.doc* icon in the My Computer window named Document Folder.

W.21 *Starting an Application from My Computer in Windows 95*

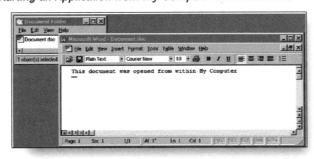

Changing the My Computer Window Display

By default, the My Computer window displays objects in the window as large icons. This default setting can be seen by clicking the <u>V</u>iew option on the My Computer Menu bar. Notice in the drop-down menu in figure W.22 that the Large Icons option is selected.

NEW in Windows 98

The default <u>V</u>iew setting in Windows 98 also includes the as <u>W</u>eb Page option.

W.22 *Drop-Down View Menu in Windows 98 with Large Icons Option Selected*

Click the Small Icons option at the View drop-down menu and the icons in the My Computer window are reduced in size. Clicking the List option will display objects in the My Computer window in a list beginning at the left side of the window. Click the Details option at the View drop-down menu and a detailed view of each object displays in the My Computer window as shown in figure W.23.

Details View of My Computer Window in Windows 98

Changing the Window Display and Moving and Deleting a File in My Computer

If you are using Windows 95:

1. At the desktop, double-click the My Computer icon.
2. At the My Computer window, display folders and files in a list (rather than large icons) by clicking View and then List.
3. Insert your disk in drive A.
4. Open the drive A: window and the drive C: window by completing the following steps:
   a. Double-click *3½ Floppy (A:)* in the My Computer list box.
   b. Change the display of the files in drive A to a list by clicking View on the drive A: Menu bar and then clicking List.
   c. Click the Title bar of the My Computer window. (This displays the My Computer window on top of the window for drive A.)
   d. Double-click *C:* in the My Computer list box.
   e. Change the display of folders and files in drive C to a list by clicking View on the drive C: Menu bar and then clicking List.
5. Make a copy of *Word Document 01* located in the *Window* folder on your disk in drive A: by completing the following steps:

    a.   Click the drive A: Taskbar button.

    b.   Double-click the *Window* folder.

    c.   Position the arrow pointer on *Word Document 01*, click the *right* mouse button, and then click <u>C</u>opy at the pop-up menu.

    d.   Click the Up One Level button (this changes to drive A).

    e.   Position the arrow pointer in a blank portion of the drive A: window (not on a file), and then click the *right* mouse button.

    f.   At the pop-up menu that displays, click <u>P</u>aste.

6.   Move *Word Document 01* to drive C by completing the following steps:

    a.   Reduce the size of the drive A: window by clicking on the Restore button located on the right side of the drive A: Title bar. Scroll as necessary to place *Word Document 01* in the window.

    b.   Position the arrow pointer on *Word Document 01* and then hold down the *right* mouse button.

    c.   Drag the arrow pointer (an outline of the file will move with the arrow pointer) to the drive C window and then release the mouse button.

    d.   At the pop-up menu that displays, click <u>M</u>ove Here.

7.   Delete *Word Document 01* from the drive C: window by completing the following steps:

    a.   Position the arrow pointer on *Word Document 01* and then click the *right* mouse button.

    b.   At the pop-up menu that displays, click <u>D</u>elete.

    c.   At the Confirm File Delete dialog box, click <u>Y</u>es.

8.   Close the drive C: window by clicking the Close button located at the right side of the drive C: Title bar. (The Close button displays with an X.)

9.   Close the drive A: window.

10.   Close the My Computer window.

If you are using Windows 98:

1.   At the desktop, double-click the *My Computer* icon.

2.   At the My Computer window, display folders and files in a list (rather than large icons) by clicking <u>V</u>iew and then <u>L</u>ist.

3.   Insert your disk in drive A.

4.   Copy a document from the *Window* folder on the disk in drive A to drive C by completing the following steps:

    a.   Double-click *3½ Floppy (A:)* in the My Computer list box.

    b.   Double-click the *Window* folder (this displays the documents in the folder).

    c.   Change the display of the files in the *Window* folder to a list by clicking <u>V</u>iew on the Menu bar and then clicking <u>L</u>ist.

    d.   Click once on the document named *Word Document 01*.

    e.   Click the Copy button on the toolbar.

    f.   Click twice on the Back button on the toolbar.

    g.   At the My Computer window, double-click *C:* in the list box.

    h.   Click the Paste button on the toolbar.

5.   Delete *Word Document 01* from the drive C: window by completing the following steps:

    a.   Position the arrow pointer on *Word Document 01* and then click the *right* mouse button.

    b.   At the pop-up menu that displays, click <u>D</u>elete.

    c.   At the message asking you to confirm the deletion, click <u>Y</u>es.

6.   Close the My Computer window by clicking the Close button located at the right side of the My Computer Title bar. (The Close button displays with an X.)

Creating a Shortcut

Shortcuts are specialized icons. They are very small files that point the operating system to the actual item, whether it is a file, a folder, or an application. For example, in figure W.24, the *Shortcut to Dynamic.doc* icon represents a path to a specific file in the Word 2000 program. The icon is not the actual file but a path to the file. Double-click the shortcut icon and Windows 95 or Windows 98 will open the Word 2000 program and also open the file named Dynamic.doc.

Shortcut Icons

Shortcuts provide quick and easy access to files or programs used every day without having to remember where the file is stored. You will learn one method for creating a shortcut in exercise 9. A shortcut icon can be easily deleted from the desktop by dragging the shortcut icon to the Recycle Bin icon. This deletes the shortcut icon but does not delete the file to which the shortcut pointed.

Creating a Shortcut

1. At the desktop, double-click the *My Computer* icon. If necessary, reduce the size of the My Computer window by clicking the Restore button located at the right side of the My Computer window Title bar.
2. Insert your disk in drive A.
3. At the My Computer window, double-click *3½ Floppy (A:)*.
4. Double-click the *Window* folder.
5. Change the display of files to a list by clicking <u>V</u>iew on the Menu bar and then clicking <u>L</u>ist at the drop-down menu.
6. Create a shortcut to the file named *Word Letter 01* by completing the following steps:
   a. Position the arrow pointer on *Word Letter 01* located in the *Window* folder window.
   b. Hold down the *right* mouse button, drag the outline of the file to the desktop window, and then release the mouse button.
   c. At the pop-up menu that displays, click Create <u>S</u>hortcut(s) Here.
7. Close the *Windows* window by clicking the Close button located at the right side of the Title bar. (If you are using Windows 95 you may need to close the My Computer window by clicking the Close button located at the right side of the My Computer window Title bar.)
8. Open Word 2000 and the file named *Word Letter 01* by double-clicking the *Word Letter 01* shortcut icon on the desktop.
9. After viewing the file in Word, exit Word by clicking <u>F</u>ile on the Menu bar and then clicking E<u>x</u>it at the drop-down menu.
10. Delete the Word Letter 01 shortcut icon by completing the following steps:

a. At the desktop, position the arrow pointer on the *Word Letter 01* shortcut icon.
b. Hold down the left mouse button, drag the icon on top of the Recycle Bin icon, and then release the mouse button.
c. At the message asking you to confirm the deletion, click Yes.

Customizing the Desktop

The Windows 95 or Windows 98 operating environment is very customizable. You can change background patterns and colors and set screen savers directly from the desktop. To change display properties, position the arrow pointer anywhere on any empty location on the desktop and then click the *right* mouse button. At the pop-up menu that displays, click Properties. This displays the Display Properties dialog box shown in figure W.25.

W.25 *Display Properties Dialog Box with Background Tab Selected*

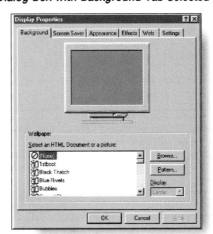

Changing the Desktop Background

The desktop background is customized at the Display Properties dialog box with the Background tab selected. In Windows 95, add a pattern to the desktop with options from the Pattern list box. Patterns are simple backgrounds that fill the desktop surface with a repeated geometric pattern. Click any pattern in the Pattern list box and preview the results in the preview screen at the top of the dialog box.

Add a wallpaper background to the Windows 95 desktop with options in the Wallpaper list box. Click any wallpaper option in the Wallpaper list box and preview the results in the preview screen. Wallpaper can be displayed as tiled or centered. Tiled wallpaper covers the entire screen with a repeated series of images. Centered wallpaper is one image set in the middle of the screen.

If you want, you can choose (None) for both the pattern and wallpaper. This leaves the desktop one solid color. When you are satisfied with the pattern and wallpaper choices, click OK to set the changes and close the Display Properties dialog box.

Display the Display Properties dialog box as described above. Choose a desktop background from the Wallpaper list box. You can use the Browse button to select an HTML document from the network for your desktop background. By default, the Wallpaper image will be placed in the center of the desktop. You can use the Display drop-down menu to *Tile* the image, or repeat it across the desktop, or *Stretch* it to cover the desktop. The Pattern button opens the Pattern dialog box, where you can choose a pattern to fill any space left around the Wallpaper image. You can choose (None) for both Wallpaper and Pattern.

Adding a Screen Saver

If your computer sits idle for periods of time, consider adding a screen saver. If a screen sits idle for a long period of time, you run the risk of burning any images onto the screen. (Fortunately, monitor technology has improved and burning images on the screen is becoming less of a problem.) A screen saver is a pattern that changes constantly, thus eliminating the problem of an image staying on the screen too long.

To add a screen saver, display the Display Properties dialog box and then click the Screen Saver tab. This displays the dialog box as shown in figure W.26.

figure

W.26   *Display Properties Dialog Box with Screen Saver Tab Selected*

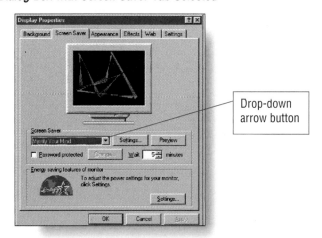

Drop-down arrow button

Click the down-pointing arrow at the right side of the Screen Saver text box to display a list of installed screen savers. Click a screen saver and a preview displays in the monitor located toward the top of the dialog box. Click the Preview button and the dialog box is hidden and the screen saver displays on your monitor. Move the mouse or click a button on the mouse and the dialog box will reappear.

Click the Settings button to display additional options for customizing a screen saver. Protect the screen saver with a password by clicking the Password protected check box. If a check mark appears in this check box, you must enter the correct password to clear the screen saver and return to the desktop.

If your computer's hardware is Energy Star compatible, the Energy saving features of monitor section is enabled. In Windows 95, this places the monitor or CPU into a sleep mode to save energy. Many new computers have this feature.

NEW in Windows 98

> The Energy saving features of monitor Settings dialog box permits you to choose a power scheme appropriate to the way you use your computer, and to decide how long the computer can be left unused before the monitor and the hard disk are turned off.

Changing Colors

Click the Appearance tab at the Display Properties dialog box and the dialog box displays as shown in figure W.27. At this dialog box, you can change the desktop scheme.

figure

W.27 *Display Properties Dialog Box with Appearance Tab Selected*

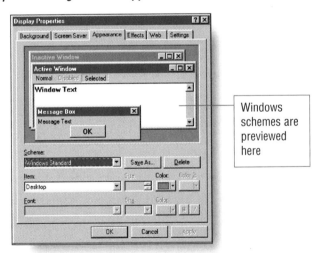

Windows schemes are previewed here

Schemes are predefined collections of colors that are used in windows, menus, title bars, and system fonts. Windows 95 and Windows 98 load with the Windows Standard scheme. Click the down-pointing triangle at the right side of the Scheme text box to display a list of available schemes. When you choose a scheme, the results are previewed in the dialog boxes as shown in figure W.28.

figure

W.28

Examples of Appearance Schemes: Windows 95 (left) and Windows 98 (right)

Schemes set the appearance of the entire operating system. If you want to set the desktop to a unique color, but leave the rest of the scheme intact, specify options at the Item drop-down box. Click the down-pointing triangle at the right side of the Item text box and then click the specific object to which you want the scheme applied.

NEW in Windows 98

The Effects tab in the Display Properties dialog box, as shown in figure W.29, allows you to change desktop icons from the default icons used by Windows 98. Select the icon you want to change, click the Change Icon button, and select a new icon from the Current icon box in the Change Icon dialog box, or use the Browse... button to select an icon of your own design.

figure

W.29

Display Properties Dialog Box (left) and Change Icon Dialog Box (right)

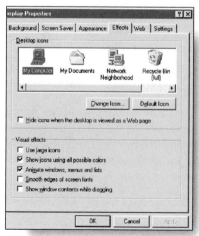 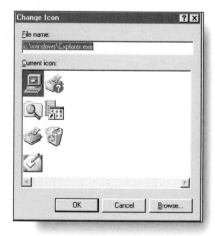

NEW in Windows 98

The Web tab in the Display Properties dialog box, shown in figure W.30, uses your Internet browser to display Web pages and other Internet files on your desktop. Using the tab requires a working Internet connection.

With check marks selecting both View my Active Desktop as a web page and Internet Explorer Channel Bar, clicking the New... button will enable you to select material from the Internet to add to your Active Desktop.

figure

W.30 *Display Properties Dialog Box with Web Tab Selected*

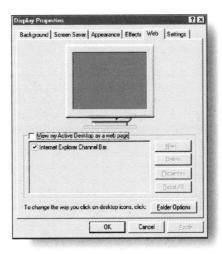

Changing Settings

Click the Settings tab at the Display Properties dialog box and the dialog box displays as shown in figure W.31. At this dialog box, you can set color and screen resolution.

figure

W.31 *Display Properties Dialog Box with Settings Tab Selected: Windows 95 (left) and 98 (right)*

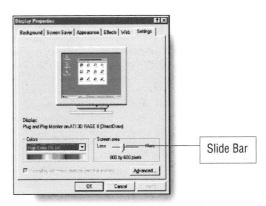

Slide Bar

The <u>C</u>olor palette option in Windows 95, or the Colors option in Windows 98, determines how many colors are displayed on your monitor. In general, you can choose 16 colors, 256 colors, 65,535 colors (High Color), or 16.7 million colors (True Color) to be shown on your monitor. The more colors that are shown, the more realistic the images will appear. However, a lot of computer memory is required to show thousands of colors. Your exact choice is determined by the specific hardware you are using.

The <u>D</u>esktop area slide bar in Windows 95, or Screen area slide bar in Windows 98, sets the screen's resolution. Generally, resolutions are 640 x 480, 800 x 600, or 1024 x 1280. The higher the number, the more you can fit onto your screen. Again, your actual values depend on your particular hardware.

In Windows 95, the <u>F</u>ont size option sets the text size used throughout the operating system. This includes icon names, menu text, dialog box text, and the Start button, among other items. If reading text on the monitor is difficult, consider increasing the system font size.

NEW in Windows 98

Clicking the A<u>d</u>vanced button on the Settings tab of the Display Properties dialog box will display a new dialog box with access to advanced display settings, as shown in figure W.32. The Display box lets you change font size for menus, icons, and window text.

Dialog Box for Advanced Display Settings with General Tab Selected

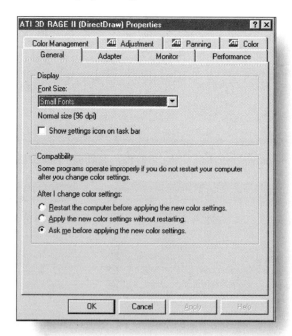

exercise 10

Customizing the Desktop

(Note: Check with your instructor before completing this exercise.)

If you are using Windows 95:

1. At the desktop, display the Display Properties dialog box by positioning the arrow pointer on an empty location on the desktop, clicking the *right* mouse button, and then clicking Properties at the pop-up menu.

2. At the Display Properties dialog box, add a pattern to the desktop by completing the following steps:
   a. At the Display Properties dialog box, make sure the Background tab is selected. (If it is not, click the Background tab.)
   b. Click *Buttons* in the Pattern list box.
   c. Click OK to close the dialog box.

3. After viewing the desktop with the Buttons pattern applied, remove the pattern and add a wallpaper design to the desktop by completing the following steps:
   a. Display the Display Properties dialog box.
   b. At the Display Properties dialog box with the Background tab selected, click *(None)* located at the top of the Pattern list box. (This removes the Buttons pattern.)
   c. Click the down-pointing triangle in the Wallpaper list box until *Clouds* is visible, and then click *Clouds*.
   d. Click OK to close the dialog box.

4. After viewing the desktop with the Clouds wallpaper applied, add a screen saver by completing the following steps:
   a. Display the Display Properties dialog box.
   b. At the Display Properties dialog box, click the Screen Saver tab. (If a screen saver is already selected in the Screen Saver text box, make a note of this screen saver name.)
   b. Click the down-pointing triangle at the right side of the Screen Saver text box.
   d. At the drop-down list that displays, click a screen saver that interests you. (A preview of the screen saver displays in the screen located toward the top of the dialog box.)
   e. Click a few other screen savers to see how they will display on the monitor.
   f. With a screen saver selected, click OK. (This closes the dialog box.)

5. At the desktop the screen saver will display, by default, after the monitor has sat idle for 15 minutes.

6. Return all settings back to the default by completing the following steps:
   a. Display the Display Properties dialog box.
   b. Click the Background tab.
   c. At the Display Properties dialog box with the Background tab selected, click *(None)* in the Wallpaper list box. (You will need to scroll up the list to display this option.)
   d. Click the Screen Saver tab.
   e. At the Display Properties dialog box with the Screen Saver tab selected, click the down-pointing triangle at the right side of the Screen Saver text box, and then click *(None)* in the Screen Saver list box. (If a screen saver was selected before completing this exercise, return to that screen saver.)
   f. Click OK to close the Display Properties dialog box.

If you are using Windows 98:

1. At the desktop, display the Display Properties dialog box by positioning the arrow pointer on an empty location on the desktop, clicking the *right* mouse button, and then clicking Properties at the pop-up menu.
2. At the Display Properties dialog box, add wallpaper to the desktop by completing the following steps:
   a. At the Display Properties dialog box, make sure the Background tab is selected. (If it is not, click the Background tab.)
   b. Click *Bubbles* in the Wallpaper list box. Be sure Center is selected in the Display list box.
   c. Click OK to close the dialog box.
3. After viewing the desktop with the Bubbles wallpaper pattern displayed, add a pattern to fill in the space around the wallpaper by completing the following steps:
   a. Display the Display Properties dialog box.
   b. At the Display Properties dialog box with the Background tab selected, click the Pattern... button. (This displays the Pattern dialog box.)
   c. Click the down-pointing triangle in the Pattern list box until *Daisies* is visible, and then click *Daisies*.
   d. Click OK to close the Pattern dialog box, and then click OK to close the Display Properties dialog box.
4. After viewing the desktop with the Bubbles wallpaper and the Daisies pattern applied, add a screen saver by completing the following steps:
   a. Display the Display Properties dialog box.
   b. At the Display Properties dialog box, click the Screen Saver tab. (If a screen saver is already selected in the Screen Saver text box, make a note of this screen saver name.)
   c. Click the down-pointing triangle at the right side of the Screen Saver text box.
   d. At the drop-down list that displays, click a screen saver that interests you. (A preview of the screen saver displays in the screen located toward the top of the dialog box.)
   e. Click a few other screen savers to see how they will display on the monitor.
   f. With a screen saver selected, click OK. (This closes the dialog box.)
5. At the desktop the screen saver will display, by default, after the monitor has sat idle for 15 minutes.
6. Return all settings back to the default by completing the following steps:
   a. Display the Display Properties dialog box.
   b. Click the Background tab.
   c. At the Display Properties dialog box with the Background tab selected, click *(None)* in the Wallpaper list box.
   d. Click the Pattern... button.
   e. At the Pattern dialog box, click *(None)* in the Pattern list box. (You will need to scroll up the list to display this option.)
   f. Click OK to close the Pattern dialog box.
   g. Click the Screen Saver tab.
   h. At the Display Properties dialog box with the Screen Saver tab selected, click the down-pointing triangle at the right side of the Screen Saver text box, and then click *(None)* in the Screen Saver list box. (If a screen saver was selected before completing this exercise, return to that screen saver.)
   i. Click OK to close the Display Properties dialog box.

Exploring Windows 95 and Windows 98 Help Files

Windows 95 and Windows 98 include an on-screen reference guide providing information, explanations, and interactive help on learning Windows features. The on-screen reference guide, referred to as "Help," contains complex files with hypertext used to access additional information by clicking a word or phrase. The Help feature can interact with open programs to help guide you through difficult tasks.

NEW in Windows 98

You can get direct help from the Microsoft Web site by clicking the Web Help button in the Windows Help window. There will be a link in the window that appears labeled *Support Online*. Click the underlined text to connect with the Web, provided, of course, you have an Internet connection.

Using Windows Help Files

To display the Help Topics dialog box (Windows 95) or Windows Help dialog box (Windows 98) shown in figure W.33, click the Start button on the Taskbar and then click <u>H</u>elp at the pop-up menu.

W.33 Windows 95 Help Topics Dialog Box and Windows 98 Windows Help Dialog Box

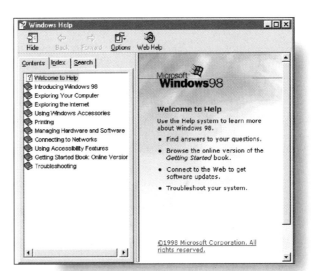

The dialog boxes shown in figure W.33 each contain three tabs: Contents, Index, and Find in Windows 95; <u>C</u>ontents, <u>I</u>ndex, and <u>S</u>earch in Windows 98. Book icons display before options in the list box. Click a book icon that displays before a topic, such as *Introducing Windows* or *Introducing Windows 98*, and a list of subtopics will appear. Select the subtopic you want to read about, and a help box displays with information on the particular topic.

Using the Help Topics or Windows Help Dialog Box with the Contents Tab Selected

(Note: Depending on the type of installation completed on Windows, some of the Help categories may not be available. If some of the Help categories in exercise 11 do not display, experiment with other categories that interest you.)

If you are using Windows 95:

1. Make sure Windows 95 is open and the desktop displayed.
2. Use the Help feature to learn about basic Windows 95 features by completing the following steps:
   a. Click the Start button located at the left side of the Taskbar.
   b. At the pop-up menu that displays, click Help.
   c. At the Help Topics dialog box, make sure the Contents tab is selected. (If not, click the Contents tab.)
   d. Position the arrow pointer on *Introducing Windows* and then double-click the left mouse button. (This causes the book icon preceding *Introducing Windows* to display as an open book and a list of topics to display below *Introducing Windows*.)
   e. Double-click *Getting Your Work Done*.
   f. Double-click *The basics*. (This option displays preceded by a page containing a question mark.)
   g. At the Windows Help dialog box, click the gray button immediately in front of *Moving windows*.
   h. To view a demonstration on how to move a window, click the button containing a right-pointing black triangle located at the left side of the desktop window.
   i. After the demonstration is completed, click the gray button immediately in front of *Sizing windows*.
   j. View a demonstration on how to size a window by clicking the button containing a right-pointing black triangle located at the left side of the desktop window.
   k. Complete similar steps to those in 2i and 2j to view demonstrations on *Scrolling, Closing windows, Switching between windows*, and *Using dialog boxes*.
3. After viewing the *Using dialog boxes* demonstration, close the Windows Help dialog box by clicking the Close button (displays with an X) that displays in the upper right corner of the dialog box.

If you are using Windows 98:

1. Make sure Windows 98 is open and the desktop displayed.
2. Use the Help feature to learn about basic Windows 98 features by completing the following steps:
   a. Click the Start button located at the left side of the Taskbar.
   b. At the pop-up menu that displays, click Help.
   c. At the Windows Help dialog box, make sure the Contents tab is selected. (If not, click the Contents tab.)
   d. Position the arrow pointer on *Introducing Windows 98* and then click the left mouse button. (This causes the *book* icon preceding *Introducing Windows 98* to display as an open book and a list of topics to display below *Introducing Windows 98*.)
   e. Position the arrow pointer on *What's New in Windows 98* and click the left mouse button. (This causes the *book* icon preceding *What's New in Windows 98* to display as an open book and a list of topics to display below *What's New in Windows 98*, with each item preceded by a *question mark* icon.)

f.   Position the arrow pointer on *Innovative, easy-to-use features* and click the left mouse button. This causes a list of topics to appear in the help box at the right of the Windows Help window.

g.   Position the arrow pointer on *Web integration* and click the left mouse button.

h.   Read the information displayed in the help box.

i.   Click the other topics in the help box and read the information supplied. If you wish to pursue one of the topics further, click <u>click here</u> at the end of the text.

j.   Close the open *book* icons by clicking on the icons. This will remove the list of subtopics and restore the list to its original form.

3.   After reading the information and closing the open *book* icons, close the Windows Help dialog box by clicking the Close button (displays with an X) that displays in the upper right corner of the dialog box.

Click the Index tab and the Help Topics or Windows Help dialog box displays as shown in figure W.34. The Index tab is just like a book's written index.

Windows 95 Help Topics Dialog Box with Index Tab Selected (left)
Windows 98 Windows Help Dialog Box with Index Tab Selected (right)

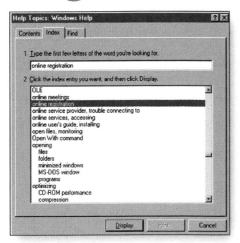 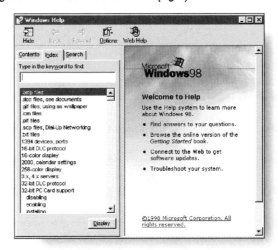

Key **online** in the text box at the top of the Index tab. (In Windows 95 the text box is labeled *Type the first few letters of the word you're looking for*; in Windows 98 it is labeled *Type in the keyword to find*.) This displays index entries as shown in figure W.34. Double-click *online registration* in the list box and the help information box containing information on on-line registration displays.

Using the Help Topics or Windows Help dialog box with the Index tab selected is often easier than looking through the dialog box with the Contents tab selected, since you can enter specific phrases into the text box.

In Windows 95, use the Help Topics dialog box with the Find tab selected to search for an individual word or words. The first time you display the Help Topics dialog box with the Find tab selected, the message shown in figure W.35 displays. Make sure <u>M</u>inimize database size (recommended) is selected and then click the <u>N</u>ext> button. At the next step click the <u>F</u>inish button and Windows 95 builds an index of every word used in the help file.

figure
W.35

Help Topics Contents and Help Box in Windows 95

At the Help Topics dialog box with the Find tab selected as shown, key **online** in the first text box. In the second text box Windows 95 suggests some words that might narrow your search, and in the bottom box is a list of every topic that includes the word "online."

NEW in Windows 98

In Windows 98, use the Windows Help dialog box with the Search tab selected to search for an individual word or words. At the Windows Help dialog box with the Search tab selected, as shown in figure W.36, key **online** in the first text box. Then click the List Topics button to display a list in the bottom box of every topic that includes the word "online." For further information on your chosen topic, either click the Display button or double-click the topic itself; your information will display in the help window at the right.

figure
W.36

Windows 98 Windows Help Dialog Box with Search Tab Selected

exercise 12

Using the Help Topics or Windows Help Dialog Box with the Index Tab Selected

If you are using Windows 95:

1. Make sure Windows 95 is opened and the desktop displays.
2. Use the Help feature to learn about deleting files and folders by completing the following steps:
   a. Click the Start button located at the left side of the Taskbar.
   b. At the pop-up menu that displays, click <u>H</u>elp.
   c. At the Help Topics dialog box, click the I<u>n</u>dex tab.
   d. With the insertion point positioned in the top text box, key **deleting**.
   e. At the list of topics that displays in the list box, double-click *files or folders* that displays below *deleting*.
   f. At the Topics Found dialog box with the *Deleting a file or folder* option selected, click the <u>D</u>isplay button.
   g. Read the information that displays in the yellow help box.
   h. Click the gray button that displays immediately in front of *Related Topics* (located at the bottom of the yellow box).
   i. At the Topics Found dialog box, double-click *Retrieving deleted files or shortcuts*.
   j. Read the information that displays in the yellow help box.
   k. Click the Close button (contains an X) that displays in the upper right corner of the yellow help box.
3. Use the Help feature to learn more about the look of Windows 95 by completing the following steps:
   a. Click the Start button located at the left side of the Taskbar.
   b. At the pop-up menu that displays, click <u>H</u>elp.
   c. At the Help Topics dialog box, click the I<u>n</u>dex tab.
   d. With the insertion point positioned in the top text box, key **buttons**.
   e. With *buttons* selected in the list box, click the <u>D</u>isplay button.
   f. At the Topics Found dialog box, double-click *The new look and feel of Windows* located in the list box.
   g. At the yellow help box, click the gray button immediately in front of *Start button and taskbar.*
   h. Read the information displayed on the Start button and taskbar and then click the gray button immediately in front of *My Computer*.
   i. Read the information that displays on the My Computer feature and then click the gray button immediately in front of the next option. Continue in this manner until you have clicked each gray button in the yellow help box.
   j. After reading the information on the last option, click the Close button (contains an X) located in the upper right corner of the yellow help box.
   k. Click the Close button in the yellow help box that displays with the title *A new look and feel.*

If you are using Windows 98:

1. Make sure Windows 98 is opened and the desktop displays.
2. Use the Help feature to learn about deleting files and folders by completing the following steps:

a. Click the Start button located at the left side of the Taskbar.
b. At the pop-up menu that displays, click Help.
c. At the Windows Help dialog box, click the Index tab.
d. With the insertion point positioned in the top text box, key **deleting**.
e. At the list of topics that displays in the list box, double-click *deleting files, folders*.
f. At the Topics Found dialog box with the *To delete a file or folder* option selected, click the Display button.
g. Read the information that displays in the help box.
h. Click *Related Topics* at the bottom of the help box.
i. At the list that displays, click *To retrieve deleted files or shortcuts*.
j. Read the information that displays in the help box.
k. Click the Close button (contains an X) that displays in the upper right corner of the Windows Help dialog box.

3. Use the Help feature to learn more about the look of Windows 98 by completing the following steps:
a. Click the Start button located at the left side of the taskbar.
b. At the pop-up menu that displays, click Help.
c. At the Windows Help dialog box, click the Index tab.
d. With the insertion point positioned in the top text box, key **buttons**.
e. With *buttons* selected in the list box, click the Display button.
f. At the Topics Found dialog box, double-click *Manipulating windows in Windows*.
g. Read the information displayed in the help box and then, with *buttons* still selected in the left list box, click the Display button again.
h. At the Topics Found dialog box, double-click *To cancel your last action within a program or in My Computer or Windows Explorer*.
i. Read the information displayed in the help box and then continue in this manner until you have read about each option involving *buttons* in the Topics Found dialog box.
j. After you have read the information on the last option, click the Close button (contains an X) located in the upper right corner of the Windows Help dialog box.

Word

UNIT ONE

MICROSOFT® WORD 2000

CORE LEVEL MOUS SKILLS

Coding No.	SKILL	Pages
W2000.1	**Working with text**	
W2000.1.1	Use the Undo, Redo, and Repeat command	25-27, 76-77
W2000.1.2	Apply font formats (Bold, Italic and Underline)	38-39
W2000.1.3	Use the SPELLING feature	128-133
W2000.1.4	Use the THESAURUS feature	139-141
W2000.1.5	Use the GRAMMAR feature	133-136
W2000.1.6	Insert page breaks	113-114
W2000.1.7	Highlight text in document	121-122
W2000.1.8	Insert and move text	161-163
W2000.1.9	Cut, Copy, Paste, and Paste Special using the Office Clipboard	161-166
W2000.1.10	Copy formats using the Format Painter	57-58
W2000.1.11	Select and change font and font size	40-45
W2000.1.12	Find and replace text	205-210
W2000.1.13	Apply character effects (superscript, subscript, strikethrough, small caps and outline)	46-47
W2000.1.14	Insert date and time	119-120
W2000.1.15	Insert symbols	71-74
W2000.1.16	Create and apply frequently used text with AutoCorrect	136-139
W2000.2	**Working with paragraphs**	
W2000.2.1	Align text in paragraphs (Center, Left, Right and Justified)	51-56
W2000.2.2	Add bullets and numbering	63-70
W2000.2.3	Set character, line, and paragraph spacing options	48-50, 56-57, 74-76
W2000.2.4	Apply borders and shading to paragraphs	77-82
W2000.2.5	Use indentation options (Left, Right, First Line and Hanging Indent)	58-63
W2000.2.6	Use TABS command (Center, Decimal, Left and Right)	101-110
W2000.2.7	Create an outline style numbered list	220-221
W2000.2.8	Set tabs with leaders	109-110
W2000.3	**Working with documents**	
W2000.3.1	Print a document	7, 10, 172-174
W2000.3.2	Use print preview	114-116
W2000.3.3	Use Web Page Preview	304-305
W2000.3.4	Navigate through a document	15-20
W2000.3.5	Insert page numbers	202-205
W2000.3.6	Set page orientation	180-182
W2000.3.7	Set margins	111-113
W2000.3.8	Use GoTo to locate specific elements in a document	210-211
W2000.3.9	Create and modify page numbers	202-205
W2000.3.10	Create and modify headers and footers	193-202
W2000.3.11	Align text vertically	116-117
W2000.3.12	Create and use newspaper columns	122-128
W2000.3.13	Revise column structure	127-128
W2000.3.14	Prepare and print envelopes and labels	175-180
W2000.3.15	Apply styles	215-220
W2000.3.16	Create sections with formatting that differs from other sections	123-127, 201-202
W2000.3.17	Use click & type	118-119
W2000.4	**Managing files**	
W2000.4.1	Use save	6-7, 11
W2000.4.2	Locate and open an existing document	12, 17, 159-160
W2000.4.3	Use Save As (different name, location or format)	21-22
W2000.4.4	Create a folder	150-151
W2000.4.5	Create a new document using a Wizard	213-215, 311-314
W2000.4.6	Save as Web Page	303-305
W2000.4.7	Use templates to create a new document	211-213
W2000.4.8	Create Hyperlinks	309-310
W2000.4.9	Use the Office Assistant	82-87
W2000.4.10	Send a Word document via e-mail	182-183
W2000.5	**Using tables**	
W2000.5.1	Create and format tables	235-275
W2000.5.2	Add borders and shading to tables	244-249
W2000.5.3	Revise tables (insert & delete rows and columns, change cell formats)	255-256, 258-261
W2000.5.4	Modify table structure (merge cells, change height and width)	249-254, 261-262
W2000.5.5	Rotate text in a table	265, 269-270
W2000.6	**Working with pictures and charts**	
W2000.6.1	Use the drawing toolbar	722-731
W2000.6.2	Insert graphics into a document (WordArt, ClipArt, Images)	533-541, 713-722

Chapter 01

Creating, Printing, and Editing Word Documents

PERFORMANCE OBJECTIVES

Upon successful completion of chapter 1, you will be able to:

- Open Microsoft Word.
- Create, save, name, print, open, and close a Word document.
- Exit Word and Windows.
- Edit a document.
- Move the insertion point within a document.
- Scroll within a document.
- Select text in a document.

In this chapter, you will learn to create, save, print, open, close, and edit a Word document. Before continuing in this chapter, make sure you have read the *Getting Started* section presented at the beginning of this book. This section contains information about computer hardware and software, using the mouse, executing commands, and the Microsoft Office Assistant.

Opening Microsoft Word

Microsoft Office Professional 2000 contains a word processing program, named Word, that you can use to create, save, edit, and print documents. The steps to open Word may vary depending on your system setup. Generally, to open Word, you would complete the following steps:

1. Turn on the monitor and the CPU. (Depending on your system, you may also need to turn on the printer.)
2. After a few moments, the Windows 98 (or Windows 95) screen displays (your screen may vary). At the Windows 98 (or Windows 95) screen, position the arrow pointer on the Start button on the Taskbar (located at the bottom left side of the screen), and then click the left mouse button. This causes a pop-up menu to display.

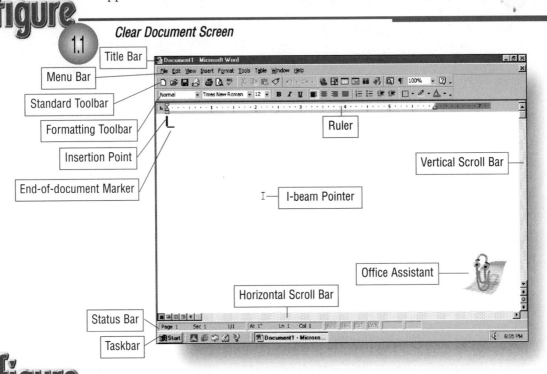

Loading a program that is already open can cause unnecessary use of memory. Use the Taskbar to see what programs are open before loading another.

3. Point to Programs. (To do this, move the mouse pointer up until Programs is selected—do not click the mouse button). This causes another menu to display to the right of the first pop-up menu.
4. Move the arrow pointer to *Microsoft Word* and then click the left mouse button.

Creating a Word Document

When Microsoft Word is open, a clear document screen displays as shown in figure 1.1. The features of the document screen are described in figure 1.2. (The Standard and Formatting toolbars at your clear document screen may appear on the same line. The two toolbars have been separated for figure 1.1.)

figure 1.1

Clear Document Screen

Title Bar
Menu Bar
Standard Toolbar
Formatting Toolbar
Insertion Point
End-of-document Marker
Ruler
Vertical Scroll Bar
I-beam Pointer
Office Assistant
Horizontal Scroll Bar
Status Bar
Taskbar

figure 1.2

Microsoft Word Screen

Feature	Description
Title Bar	The document name displays at the left side of the Title bar followed by the program name (such as *Microsoft Word*).
Menu Bar	The Menu bar contains a list of options to manage and customize documents. Word functions and features are grouped into menu options. For example, functions to save, close, or open a new document are contained in the File option on the Menu bar. (Shortcut commands to some common features display at the right side of menus.)
Standard Toolbar	The Standard toolbar contains buttons that are shortcuts for the most popular commands. For example, buttons are available for opening and saving a document. Position the arrow pointer on a button on the Standard toolbar and, after one second, a ScreenTip displays with the name of the button.

Formatting Toolbar	The Formatting toolbar contains buttons that can quickly apply formatting to text in a document such as bold, italics, and underlining. Position the arrow pointer on a button on the Formatting toolbar and, after one second, a ScreenTip displays with the name of the button.
Ruler	Set margins, indents, and tabs with the Ruler.
Insertion Point	The insertion point indicates the location where the next character entered at the keyboard will appear.
End-of-document Marker	The end-of-document marker indicates the end of the document.
Scroll Bars	Use the scroll bars to view various parts of the document.
Status Bar	The Status bar displays information about the text in the document and whether certain working modes are active. The Status bar also displays the current location of the insertion point by page number, section number, line measurement, line count, and column position. At the right side of the Status bar, working modes are displayed. When a working mode is dimmed, it is inactive. When a working mode is active, it displays in black.
Taskbar	The bottom line on the screen is the Taskbar. Information on the Taskbar was presented in the *Getting Started* section.
Office Assistant	The Office Assistant is a link to the on-screen Help feature that anticipates the type of help you need and suggests Help topics related to the work you are doing. The Assistant will also point out ways to perform tasks more easily and will provide visual examples and step-by-step instructions for specific tasks.

At a clear document screen, key (type) the information to create a document. A document is any information you choose; for instance, a letter, memo, report, term paper, table, and so on. Some things to consider when keying text are:

* **Word Wrap:** As you key (type) text to create a document, you do not need to press the Enter key at the end of each line because Word wraps text to the next line. A word is wrapped to the next line if it begins before the right margin and continues past the right margin. The only times you need to press Enter are to end a paragraph, create a blank line, or end a short line.

* **AutoCorrect:** Word contains a feature that automatically corrects certain words as they are being keyed (typed). For example, if you key the word *adn* instead of *and*, Word automatically corrects it when you press the space bar after the word.

* **Spell It:** A feature in Word called Spell It automatically inserts a wavy red line below words that are not contained in the Spelling dictionary or are not automatically corrected by AutoCorrect. This group may include misspelled words, proper names, some terminology, and some foreign words. If you key a word not recognized by the Spelling dictionary, Word inserts a red wavy line below the word. If the word is correct, you can leave it as written. If, however, the word is incorrect, you have two choices—you can backspace over the word using the Backspace key and then key it correctly, or you can position the I-beam pointer on the word, click the *right* mouse button, and then click the correct spelling in the pop-up menu.

A book icon diplays in the Status bar. A checkmark on the book indicates no spelling errors detected in the document by Spell It, while an X in the book indicates errors. Double-click the book icon to move to the next error.

- **Automatic Grammar Checker:** Word includes an automatic grammar checker. If the grammar checker detects a sentence containing a grammatical error, a green wavy line is inserted below the sentence. At this point, leave the green wavy line. You will learn more about the grammar checker in chapter 3.
- **Spacing Punctuation:** Typically, Word uses Times New Roman as the default typeface. Times New Roman is a proportional typeface. (You will learn more about typefaces in chapter 2.) When keying text in a proportional typeface, space once (rather than twice) after end-of-sentence punctuation such as a period, question mark, or exclamation point, and after a colon. Proportional typefaces are set closer together, and extra white space at the end of a sentence or after a colon is not needed.

Saving a Document

Save any open documents before exiting Word.

Save

Save a document approximately every 15 minutes or when interrupted by a telephone call or visitors.

When you have created a document, the information will need to be saved on your disk. A variety of methods can be used to save a document. You can save by clicking the Save button on the Standard toolbar; by clicking File and then Save; or with the shortcut command, Ctrl + S. For many features in this textbook, instructions for using the mouse will be emphasized. (For information on using the keyboard, refer to the *Choosing Commands* section in *Getting Started*.) To save a document with the Save button on the Standard toolbar, you would complete the following steps:

1. Position the arrow pointer on the Save button (the third button from the left) on the Standard toolbar and then click the left mouse button.
2. At the Save As dialog box shown in figure 1.3, key the name of the document.
3. Click the Save button located in the lower right corner of the dialog box.

figure
1.3

Save As Dialog Box

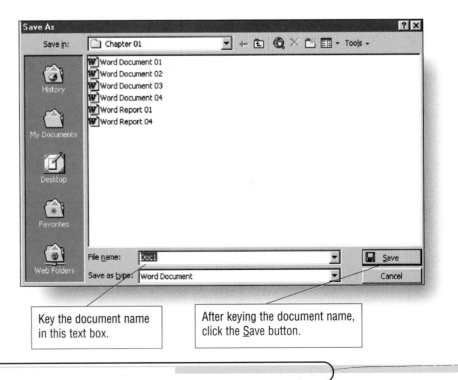

Key the document name in this text box.

After keying the document name, click the Save button.

You can also display the Save As dialog box by clicking <u>F</u>ile on the Menu bar and then clicking Save <u>A</u>s at the drop-down menu.

Naming a Document

Document names created in Word and other suite applications can be up to 255 characters in length, including the drive letter and any folder names, and may include spaces. File names cannot include any of the following characters:

<table>
<tr><td>forward slash (/)</td><td>question mark (?)</td></tr>
<tr><td>backslash (\)</td><td>quotation mark (")</td></tr>
<tr><td>greater than sign (>)</td><td>colon (:)</td></tr>
<tr><td>less than sign (<)</td><td>semicolon (;)</td></tr>
<tr><td>asterisk (*)</td><td>pipe symbol (|)</td></tr>
</table>

You cannot give a document the same name in first uppercase and then lowercase letters.

Canceling a Command

If a drop-down menu is displayed in the document screen, it can be removed with the mouse by positioning the I-beam pointer in the document screen (outside the drop-down menu), and then clicking the left mouse button. If you are using the keyboard, press the Alt key. You can also press the Esc key twice. The first time you press Esc, the drop-down menu is removed but the menu option on the Menu bar is still selected. The second time you press Esc, the option on the Menu bar is no longer selected.

Several methods can be used to remove a dialog box from the document screen. To remove a dialog box with the mouse, click the Cancel button or Close button. You can also click the Close button located in the upper right corner of the dialog box containing the "X." A dialog box can be removed from the document screen with the keyboard by pressing the Esc key.

Closing a Document

When a document is saved with the <u>S</u>ave or Save <u>A</u>s options, the document is saved on the disk and remains in the document screen. To remove the document from the screen, click the Close button located at the far right side of the Menu bar (contains the X) or click <u>F</u>ile and then <u>C</u>lose. (If you close a document with the Close button, be sure to use the Close button on the Menu bar, not the Close button on the Title bar. The Close button on the Title bar will close the Word program.) When you close a document, the document is removed and a blank screen is displayed. At this screen, you can open a previously saved document, create a new document, or exit the Word program.

Printing a Document

Many of the computer exercises you will be creating will need to be printed. A printing of a document is referred to as hard copy. (Soft copy is a document displayed in the document screen and hard copy is a document printed on paper.) A document can be sent immediately to the printer by clicking the Print button on the Standard toolbar or through the Print dialog box. Display the Print dialog box by clicking <u>F</u>ile and then <u>P</u>rint. At the Print dialog box, click the OK button.

Print

Exiting Word and Windows

When you are finished working with Word and have saved all necessary information, exit Word by clicking File and then Exit. You can also exit the Word program by clicking the Close button located at the right side of the Title bar. (The Close button contains an X.) After exiting Word, you may also need to exit the Windows 98 (or Windows 95) program. To exit Windows, you would complete the following steps:

1. Click the Start button located at the left side of the Taskbar.
2. At the pop-up menu, click Shut Down.
3. At the Shut Down Windows dialog box, make sure *Shut down* is selected, and then click Yes.

Completing Computer Exercises

At the end of sections within chapters and at the end of chapters, you will be completing hands-on exercises at the computer. These exercises will provide you with the opportunity to practice the presented functions and commands. The skill assessment exercises at the end of each chapter include general directions. If you do not remember how to perform a particular function, refer to the text in the chapter.

Copying Data Documents

In several exercises in each chapter, you will be opening documents provided with this textbook. Before beginning each chapter, copy the chapter folder from the CD that accompanies this textbook to a floppy disk (or other folder). Detailed steps on how to copy a folder from the CD to your floppy disk are presented in the Getting Started section. Abbreviated steps are printed on the inside back cover of this textbook.

Changing the Default Folder

At the end of this and the remaining chapters in the textbook, you will be saving documents. More than likely, you will want to save documents onto your disk. You will also be opening documents that have been saved on your disk.

To save documents on and open documents from your data disk, you will need to specify the drive where your disk is located as the default folder. Once you specify the drive where your data disk is located, Word uses this as the default folder until you exit the Word program. The next time you open Word, you will again need to specify the drive where your data disk is located. You only need to change the default folder once each time you enter the Word program.

You can change the default folder at the Open dialog box or the Save As dialog box. To change the folder to the *Chapter 01* folder on the disk in drive A at the Open dialog box, you would complete the following steps (see figure 1.4):

1. Click the Open button on the Standard toolbar (the second button from the left); or click File and then Open.
2. At the Open dialog box, click the down-pointing triangle at the right side of the Look in text box.
3. From the drop-down list that displays, click *3½ Floppy (A:)*.

4. Double-click *Chapter 01* that displays in the list box.
5. Click the Cancel button in the lower right corner of the dialog box.

If you want to change the default folder permanently, make the change at the Options dialog box with the File Locations tab selected. To permanently change the default folder to drive A, you would complete these steps:

1. Click Tools and then Options.
2. At the Options dialog box, click the File Locations tab.
3. At the Options dialog box with the File Locations tab selected, make sure *Documents* is selected in the File types list box and then click the Modify button.
4. At the Modify Location dialog box, click the down-pointing triangle at the right side of the Look in list box, and then click *3½ Floppy (A:)*.
5. Click the OK button.

Changing the Default Folder

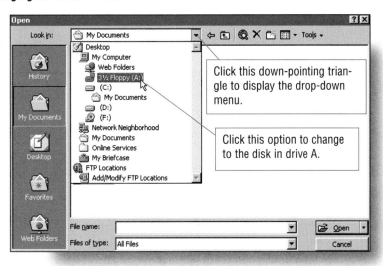

Click this down-pointing triangle to display the drop-down menu.

Click this option to change to the disk in drive A.

Changing the Default Type Size

Typically, Word uses 10-point Times New Roman as the default font. (You will learn more about fonts in chapter 2.) Exercises in this and other chapters will generally display text in 12-point size. If the system you are operating uses a point size other than 12, you can change the default type size to 12 by completing the following steps (see figure 1.5):

figure
1.5

Changing the Default Font

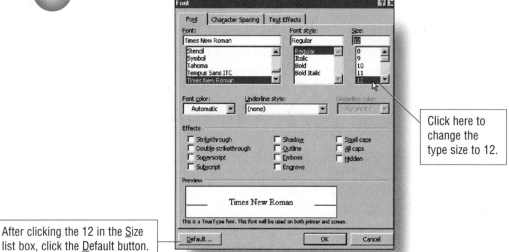

Click here to change the type size to 12.

After clicking the 12 in the <u>S</u>ize list box, click the <u>D</u>efault button.

1. Click F<u>o</u>rmat and then <u>F</u>ont.
2. At the Font dialog box, click *12* in the <u>S</u>ize list box.
3. Click the <u>D</u>efault command button located in the lower left corner of the dialog box.
4. At the message box asking if you want to change the default font, click <u>Y</u>es.

Once the default type size has been changed in this manner, the new type size will be in effect each time you open the Word program. You need to change the default only once.

exercise

Creating and Printing a Document

1. Follow the instructions in this chapter to open Windows and then Word.
2. At the clear document screen, change to the default folder where your disk is located by completing the following steps: (If the default folder has been changed permanently, these steps are not necessary. Check with your instructor before changing the default folder.)
   a. Click the Open button on the Standard toolbar.

b. At the Open dialog box, click the down-pointing triangle to the right of the Look in option.

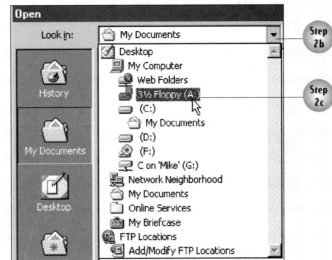
Step 2b

Step 2c

c. From the drop-down list that displays, click *3½ Floppy (A:)* (this may vary depending on your system).
d. Double-click the *Chapter 01* folder.
e. Click the Cancel command button located in the lower right corner of the dialog box.

3. At the document screen, make sure that 12-point Times New Roman is the default font. (If not, change the default type size to 12 following the directions listed in the *Changing the Default Type Size* section of this chapter; or, check with your instructor.)

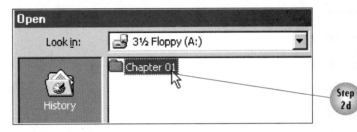
Step 2d

4. Key (type) the text in figure 1.6. If you make a mistake while keying and Spell It inserts a wavy red line, backspace over the incorrect word using the Backspace key, and then rekey the correct word. Ignore any green wavy lines inserted by Word. (Do not worry about doing a lot of correcting—you will learn more about editing a document later in this chapter.) Remember to space only once after end-of-sentence punctuation when keying the text.

5. When you are done keying the text, save the document and name it Word Ch 01, Ex 01 (for Chapter 1, Exercise 1) by completing the following steps:

a. Click the Save button on the Standard toolbar.
b. At the Save As dialog box, key **Word Ch 01, Ex 01**. (Key a zero when naming documents, not the letter O. In this textbook, the zero, 0, displays thinner than the letter O. As you key **Word Ch 01, Ex 01**, the selected text in the File name text box is automatically deleted and replaced with the text you key.)
c. Press the Enter key or click the Save button located in the lower right corner of the dialog box.

Step 5b

6. Print the document by clicking the Print button on the Standard toolbar.
7. Close Word Ch 01, Ex 01 by clicking File and then Close or by clicking the Close button located at the far right side of the Menu bar. (This displays a blank screen, rather than a clear screen.)

figure 1.6

Exercise 1

A mainframe is a very large computer used, typically, in a large organization to handle high-volume processing. A typical use of a mainframe computer would be to process the financial transactions and maintain the accounts of a large bank.

A keyboard or a keyboard and a display connected to a mainframe or other computer is referred to as a dumb terminal. A dumb terminal is generally used to input raw information and takes its name from the fact that it has no processor of its own. In the early days of computers, the mainframe/dumb terminal configuration was the only one available for computing.

Opening a Document

Open

When a document has been saved and closed, it can be opened at the Open dialog box shown in figure 1.7. To display this dialog box, click the Open button on the Standard toolbar or click File and then Open. At the Open dialog box, double-click the document name.

The names of the most recently opened documents display toward the bottom of the expanded File drop-down menu. To open a document from this drop-down menu, click File, expand the drop-down menu, and then click the desired document.

figure 1.7

Open Dialog Box

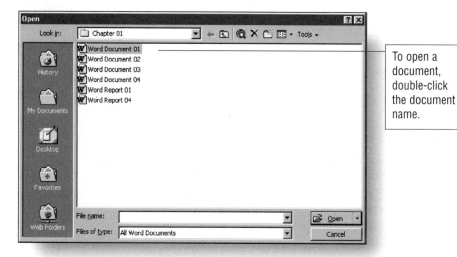

To open a document, double-click the document name.

Creating a New Document

When you close a document, a blank screen is displayed. If you want to create a new document, display a clear document screen. To do this, click the New Blank Document button on the Standard toolbar (the first button).

New Blank
Document

Creating and Printing a New Document

1. At a blank screen, create a new document by clicking the New Blank Document button on the Standard toolbar (the first button from the left).
2. At the clear document screen, key the information shown in figure 1.8. (Correct any errors highlighted by Spell It as they occur and remember to space once after end-of-sentence punctuation. Ignore any wavy green lines inserted by Word.)
3. Save the document and name it Word Ch 01, Ex 02 by completing the following steps:
   a. Click the Save button on the Standard toolbar.
   b. At the Save As dialog box, key **Word Ch 01, Ex 02**.
   c. Click the Save button (or press Enter).
4. Print the document by completing the following steps:
   a. Click File and then Print.
   b. At the Print dialog box, click OK (located in the lower right corner of the dialog box.)
5. Close the document by clicking File and then Close or clicking the Close button located at the right side of the Menu bar.

Make sure correct printer name displays here.

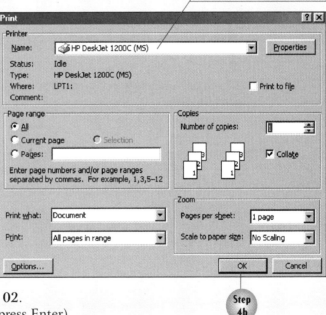

Step 4b

figure

1.8 *Exercise 2*

A workstation is a desktop computer powerful enough to rival the performance of a minicomputer or, in some cases, of a small mainframe. Workstations are used widely for scientific, engineering, and research applications.

A personal computer, or PC, is a desktop computer that is less powerful than a workstation. As personal computers have become more powerful, the distinction between them and workstations has blurred. During the 1980s and early 1990s, networked personal computers took over many of the functions previously performed by mainframes and minis.

Displaying and Moving Toolbars

The Standard and Formatting toolbars display below the Menu bar at the top of the screen. These toolbars may display side by side with only a portion of the buttons visible. To display the hidden buttons, click the More Buttons button (displays with two right-pointing arrows). Clicking the More Buttons button displays a palette of buttons.

The Formatting toolbar in the figures in this textbook displays immediately below the Standard toolbar. At this display, all buttons on the toolbars are visible. To move the Formatting toolbar below the Standard toolbar, complete the following steps:

1. Click Tools and then Customize.
2. At the Customize dialog box, click the Options tab. (Skip this step if the Options tab is already selected.)
3. Click the *Standard and Formatting toolbars share one row* option. (This removes the check mark.)
4. Click the Close button to close the dialog box.

The display of the Standard and Formatting toolbars (as well as other toolbars) can be turned on or off. To do this, position the mouse pointer anywhere on a toolbar, and then click the *right* mouse button. At the drop-down menu that displays, click the toolbar name you want turned on or off. You can also turn on or off the display of a toolbar by clicking View on the Menu bar, pointing to Toolbars, and then clicking the toolbar name.

Expanding Drop-Down Menus

Microsoft Word personalizes menus and toolbars as you work. When you click an option on the Menu bar, only the most popular options display (considered first-rank options). This is referred to as an *adaptive menu*. To expand the drop-down menu and display the full set of options (first-rank options as well as second-rank options), click the down-pointing arrows that display at the bottom of the drop-down menu. A drop-down menu will also expand if you click an option on the Menu bar and then pause on the menu for a few seconds. Second-rank options on the expanded drop-down menu display with a lighter gray background. If you choose a second-rank option, it is promoted and becomes a first-rank option the next time the drop-down menu is displayed.

If you want all menu options displayed when you click an option on the Menu bar, turn off the adaptive menu feature. To do this, you would complete the following steps:

1. Click Tools, expand the drop-down menu by clicking the down-pointing arrows that display at the bottom of the menu, and then click Customize.
2. At the Customize dialog box, click the Options tab.
3. At the Customize dialog box with the Options tab selected, click in the *Menus show recently used commands first* check box to remove the check mark.
4. Click the Close button to close the dialog box.

Editing a Document

Many documents that are created need to have changes made to them. These changes may include adding text, called *inserting*, or removing text, called *deleting*. To insert or delete text, you need to be able to move the insertion point to specific locations in a document without erasing the text through which it passes. To move the insertion point without interfering with text, you can use the mouse, the keyboard, or the mouse combined with the keyboard.

Moving the Insertion Point with the Mouse

The mouse can be used to move the insertion point quickly to specific locations in the document. To do this, position the I-beam pointer at the location where you want the insertion point, and then click the left mouse button.

Scrolling with the Mouse

In addition to moving the insertion point to a specific location, the mouse can be used to move the display of text in the document screen. Scrolling in a document changes the text displayed but does not move the insertion point. If you want to move the insertion point to a new location in a document, scroll to the location, position the I-beam pointer in the desired location, and then click the left mouse button.

You can use the mouse with the *horizontal scroll bar* and/or the *vertical scroll bar* to scroll through text in a document. The horizontal scroll bar displays toward the bottom of the Word screen and the vertical scroll bar displays at the right side. Figure 1.9 displays the Word screen with the scroll bars and scroll boxes identified.

figure

1.9

Scroll Bars

Click a scroll triangle to scroll the text in the document in the direction indicated on the triangle. The vertical and horizontal scrollbars each contain a scroll box. A scroll box indicates the location of the text in the document screen in relation to the remainder of the document. To scroll up one screen at a time, position the arrow pointer above the scroll box (but below the up scroll triangle) on the vertical scroll bar, and then click the left mouse button. Position the arrow pointer below the scroll box and click the left button to scroll down a screen. If you hold the left button down, the action becomes continuous. You can also position the arrow pointer on the scroll box, hold down the left mouse button, and then drag the scroll box along the scroll bar to reposition text in the document screen.

As you drag the scroll box along the vertical scroll bar in a longer document, page numbers display at the right side of the document screen in a yellow box. (You will notice this when completing exercise 3.)

Moving the Insertion Point to a Specific Page

Along with scrolling options, Word also contains navigation buttons for moving the insertion point to a specific location. Navigation buttons are shown in figure 1.9 and include the Previous button, the Select Browse Object button, and the Next button. The full names of and the task completed by the Previous and Next buttons varies depending on the last navigation completed. Click the Select Browse Object button and a palette of browsing choices displays. You will learn more about the Select Browse Object button in the next section.

Word includes a Go To option that you can use to move the insertion point to a specific page within a document. To move the insertion point to a specific page, you would complete the following steps:

1. Click <u>E</u>dit, expand the drop-down menu by clicking the down-pointing arrows that display at the bottom of the menu, and then click <u>G</u>o To; or, double-click the page number at the left side of the Status bar.
2. At the Find and Replace dialog box with the <u>G</u>o To tab selected, key the page number. (If you are using the 10-key pad at the right side of the keyboard, make sure the Num Lock key is on.)
3. Click the Go <u>T</u>o button or press Enter. (The Go <u>T</u>o button displays as the Nex<u>t</u> button until a page number is entered.)
4. Click the Close button to close the Find and Replace dialog box.

Browsing in a Document

The Select Browse Object button located at the bottom of the vertical scroll bar contains options for browsing through a document. Click this button and a palette of browsing choices displays as shown in figure 1.10. Use the options on the palette to move the insertion point to various features in a Word document. Position the arrow pointer on an option in the palette and the option name displays below the options. For example, position the arrow pointer on the last option in the top row and *Browse by Page* displays below the options. When you click the Browse by Page option, the insertion point moves to the next page in the document. Use the other options in the palette to move to the next specified object in the document.

Select Browse
Object

Select Browse Object Palette

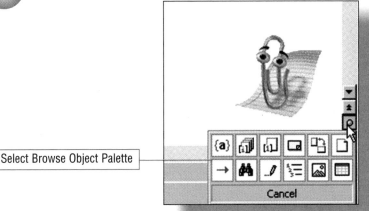

Select Browse Object Palette

Scrolling, Browsing, and Moving the Insertion Point in a Document
1. At a clear document screen, open Word Report 04.
2. Practice moving the insertion point and scrolling and browsing through the document using the mouse by completing the following steps:
   a. Position the I-beam pointer at the beginning of the first paragraph and then click the left mouse button. (This moves the insertion point to the location of the I-beam pointer.)

b. Position the mouse pointer on the down scroll triangle on the vertical scroll bar and then click the left mouse button several times. (This scrolls down lines of text in the document.) With the mouse pointer on the down scroll triangle, hold down the left mouse button and keep it down until the end of the document displays.

c. Position the mouse pointer on the up scroll triangle and hold down the left mouse button until the beginning of the document displays.

d. Position the mouse pointer below the scroll box and then click the left mouse button. Continue clicking the mouse button (with the mouse pointer positioned below the scroll box) until the end of the document displays.

e. Position the mouse pointer on the scroll box in the vertical scroll bar. Hold down the left mouse button, drag the scroll box to the top of the vertical scroll bar, and then release the mouse button. (Notice that the document page numbers display in a yellow box at the right side of the document screen.)

f. Click on the title at the beginning of the document. (This moves the insertion point to the location of the mouse pointer.)

g. Move the insertion point to page 4 by completing the following steps:

 1) Click Edit, expand the drop-down menu by clicking the down-pointing arrows that display at the bottom of the menu, and then click Go To; or, double-click the page number at the left side of the Status bar.

 2) At the Find and Replace dialog box with the Go To tab selected, make sure *Page* is selected in the Go to what list box, and then key 4 in the Enter page number text box.

 3) Click the Go To button or press Enter.

 4) Click the Close button to close the Find and Replace dialog box.

h. Click the Previous Page button located immediately above the Select Browse Object button on the vertical scroll bar. (This moves the insertion point to page 3.)

i. Click the Previous Page button again. (This moves the insertion point to page 2.)

j. Click twice on the Next Page button located immediately below the Select Browse Object button on the vertical scroll bar. (This moves the insertion point to the beginning of page 4.)

k. Move the insertion point to page 1 by completing the following steps:

 1) Click the Select Browse Object button located toward the bottom of the vertical scroll bar.

 2) At the palette of browsing choices, click the first choice in the bottom row (Go To).

 3) At the Find and Replace dialog box with the Go To tab selected, press the Delete key to delete the *4* in the Enter page number text box, and then key **1**.

 4) Click the Go To button or press Enter.

 5) Click the Close button to close the Find and Replace dialog box.

l. Move to the beginning of page 2 by completing the following steps:

 1) Click the Select Browse Object button.

2) At the palette of browsing choices, click the last choice in the top row (Browse by Page). (This moves the insertion point to page 2.)
3) Click the Select Browse Object button again and then click the last choice in the top row (Browse by Page). (This moves the insertion point to page 3.)

3. Close Word Report 04.

Step 212

Step 213

Browse by Page

Moving the Insertion Point with the Keyboard

To move the insertion point with the keyboard, use the arrow keys located to the right of the regular keyboard. (You can also use the arrow keys on the numeric keypad. If you use these keys, make sure Num Lock is off.) Use the arrow keys together with other keys to move the insertion point to various locations in the document as shown in figure 1.11.

figure 1.11

Insertion Point Movement Commands

To move insertion point	*Press*
One character left	left arrow
One character right	right arrow
One line up	up arrow
One line down	down arrow
One word to the left	Ctrl + left arrow
One word to the right	Ctrl + right arrow
To end of a line	End
To beginning of a line	Home
To beginning of current paragraph	Ctrl + up arrow
To beginning of previous paragraph	Ctrl + up arrow twice
To beginning of next paragraph	Ctrl + down arrow
Up one screen	Page Up
Down one screen	Page Down
To top of previous page	Ctrl + Page Up
To top of next page	Ctrl + Page Down
To beginning of document	Ctrl + Home
To end of document	Ctrl + End

When moving the insertion point, Word considers a word to be any series of characters between spaces. A paragraph is any text that is followed by a stroke of the Enter key. A page is text that is separated by a soft or hard page break.

If you open a previously saved document, you can move the insertion point to where the insertion point was last located when the document was closed by pressing Shift + F5.

exercise 4

Moving the Insertion Point Using the Keyboard

1. Open Word Report 01.
2. Practice moving the insertion point using the keyboard by completing the following steps:
   a. Press the right arrow key to move the insertion point to the next character to the right. Continue pressing the right arrow key until the insertion point is positioned at the end of the first paragraph.
   b. Press Ctrl + right arrow key to move the insertion point to the next word to the right. Continue pressing Ctrl + right arrow until the insertion point is positioned on the last word of the second paragraph.
   c. Press Ctrl + left arrow key until the insertion point is positioned at the beginning of the document.
   d. Press the End key to move the insertion point to the end of the title.
   e. Press the Home key to move the insertion point to the beginning of the title.
   f. Press Ctrl + Page Down to position the insertion point at the beginning of page 2.
   g. Press Ctrl + Page Up to position the insertion point at the beginning of page 1 (the beginning of the document).
   h. Press Ctrl + End to move the insertion point to the end of the document.
   i. Press Ctrl + Home to move the insertion point to the beginning of the document.
3. Close Word Report 01.

Inserting Text

Once you have created a document, you may want to insert information you forgot or have since decided to include. At the default document screen, Word moves existing characters to the right as you key additional text.

If you want to key over something, switch to the Overtype mode. You can do this by pressing the Insert key or by double-clicking the OVR mode button on the Status bar. When Overtype is on, the OVR mode button displays in black. To turn off Overtype, press the Insert key or double-click the OVR mode button.

> If you key a character that takes the place of an existing character, deactivate the Overtype mode by pressing the Insert key or double-clicking the OVR button on the Status bar. *Hint*

Deleting Text

When you edit a document, you may want to delete (remove) text. Commands for deleting text are presented in figure 1.12.

figure

To delete	Press
Character right of insertion point	Delete key
Character left of insertion point	Backspace key
Text from insertion point to beginning of word	Ctrl + Backspace
Text from insertion point to end of word	Ctrl + Delete

Saving a Document with Save As

Earlier in this chapter, you learned to save a document with the Save button on the Standard toolbar or the Save option from the File drop-down menu. The File drop-down menu also contains a Save As option. The Save As option is used to save a previously created document with a new name.

For example, suppose you create and save a document named Market Funds, and then open it later. If you save the document again with the Save button on the Standard toolbar or the Save option from the File drop-down menu, Word will save the document with the same name. You will not be prompted to key a name for the document. This is because Word assumes that when you use the Save option on a previously saved document, you want to save it with the same name. If you open the document named Market Funds, make some changes to it, and then want to save it with a new name, you must use the Save As option. When you use the Save As option, Word displays the Save As dialog box where you can key a new name for the document.

exercise

5

Editing and Saving a Document

1. Open Word Document 01.
2. Save the document with the name Word Ch 01, Ex 05 using Save As by completing the following steps:
   a. Click File and then Save As.
   b. At the Save As dialog box, key **Word Ch 01, Ex 05**.
   c. Click the Save button or press Enter.
3. Make the following changes to the document:
   a. Change the word *works* in the second sentence of the first paragraph to *operates*.
   b. Delete the words *means of* in the first sentence of the second paragraph and insert the words *method for*.

c. Delete the word *Furthermore* and the comma and space following it that begins the second sentence of the second paragraph. Capitalize the *t* in *the* that now begins the second sentence.

d. Delete the word *therefore* in the second sentence of the second paragraph.

e. Delete the words *over and over* in the second sentence of the second paragraph and insert the words *again and again*.

f. Delete the words *which can wreak havoc with the information stored on them* located at the end of the last sentence of the document.

g. Delete the comma located immediately following the word *telephones* and, if necessary, insert a period.

4. Save the document again with the same name (Word Ch 01, Ex 05) by clicking the Save button on the Standard toolbar or by clicking <u>F</u>ile and then <u>S</u>ave.

5. Print and then close Word Ch 01, Ex 05.

Selecting Text

The mouse and/or keyboard can be used to select a specific amount of text. Once you select the text, you can delete or perform other Word functions involving the selected text. When text is selected, it displays as white text on a black background as shown in figure 1.13.

figure

1.13

Selected Text

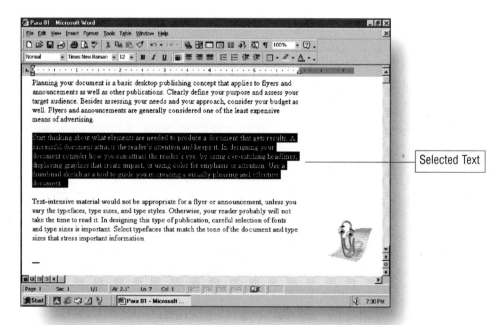

Selected Text

Selecting Text with the Mouse

You can use the mouse to select a word, line, sentence, paragraph, or the entire document. Figure 1.14 indicates the steps to follow to select various amounts of text. To select specific amounts of text such as a line, the instructions in the figure tell you to click in the selection bar. The selection bar is the space at the left side of the document screen between the left edge of the screen and the text. When the mouse pointer is positioned in the selection bar, the pointer turns into an arrow pointing up and to the right (instead of to the left).

figure

1.14 *Selecting with the Mouse*

To select	Complete these steps using the mouse
A word	Double-click the word.
A line of text	Click in the selection bar to the left of the line.
Multiple lines of text	Drag in the selection bar to the left of the lines.
A sentence	Hold down the Ctrl key, then click anywhere in the sentence.
A paragraph	Double-click in the selection bar next to the paragraph or triple-click anywhere in the paragraph.
Multiple paragraphs	Drag in the selection bar.
An entire document	Triple-click in the selection bar.

To select an amount of text other than a word, sentence, or paragraph, position the I-beam pointer on the first character of the text to be selected, hold down the left mouse button, drag the I-beam pointer to the last character of the text to be selected, and then release the mouse button. You can also select all text between the current insertion point and the I-beam pointer. To do this, position the insertion point where you want the selection to begin, hold down the Shift key, click the I-beam pointer at the end of the selection, and then release the Shift key.

To cancel a selection using the mouse, click anywhere in the document screen outside the selected text.

> To select text vertically, hold down the Alt key while dragging with the mouse.

Hint

Selecting Text with the Keyboard

To select a specific amount of text using the keyboard, use the Extend Selection key, F8, along with the arrow keys. When you press F8, the extend selection mode is turned on and the EXT mode button on the Status bar displays in black letters. (You can also turn on the extend selection mode by double-clicking the EXT mode button on the Status bar.) As you move the insertion point through text, the text is selected. If you want to cancel the selection, press the Esc key, and then press any arrow key (or double-click the EXT mode button on the Status bar and then press any arrow key). You can also select text with the commands shown in figure 1.15.

> If text is selected, any character you key replaces the selected text.

Hint

figure
1.15 *Selecting with the Keyboard*

To select	Press
One character to right	Shift + right arrow
One character to left	Shift + left arrow
To end of word	Ctrl + Shift + right arrow
To beginning of word	Ctrl + Shift + left arrow
To end of line	Shift + End
To beginning of line	Shift + Home
One line up	Shift + up arrow
One line down	Shift + down arrow
To beginning of paragraph	Ctrl + Shift + up arrow
To end of paragraph	Ctrl + Shift + down arrow
One screen up	Shift + Page Up
One screen down	Shift + Page Down
To end of document	Ctrl + Shift + End
To beginning of document	Ctrl + Shift + Home
Entire document	Ctrl + A or click Edit, Select All

exercise 6

Selecting and Deleting Text

1. Open Word Document 02.
2. Save the document with Save As and name it Word Ch 01, Ex 06.
3. Make the following changes to the document:
   a. Select the words *and use no cabling at all* and the period that follows located at the end of the last sentence in the first paragraph and then press the Delete key.
   b. Insert a period immediately following the word *signal*.
   c. Delete the heading line containing the text *QWERTY Keyboard* and the blank line below it using the Extend key, F8, by completing the following steps:
      1) Position the insertion point immediately before the *Q* in *QWERTY*.
      2) Press F8 to turn on select.
      3) Press the down arrow key twice. (This selects the heading and the blank line below it.)
      4) Press the Delete key.

d. Complete steps similar to those in c1) through c4) to delete the heading line containing the text *DVORAK Keyboard* and the blank line below it.

e. Begin a new paragraph with the sentence that reads *Keyboards have different physical appearances.* by completing the following steps:
1) Position the insertion point immediately left of the *K* in *Keyboards* (the first word of the fifth sentence in the last paragraph).
2) Press the Enter key twice.

f. Delete the last sentence in the last paragraph using the mouse by completing the following steps:
1) Position the I-beam pointer anywhere in the sentence that begins *All keyboards have modifier keys....*
2) Hold down the Ctrl key and then click the left mouse button.
3) Press the Delete key.

g. Delete the last paragraph by completing the following steps:
1) Position the I-beam pointer anywhere in the last paragraph (the paragraph that reads *Keyboards have different physical appearances.*).
2) Triple-click the left mouse button.
3) Press the Delete key.

4. Save the document with the same name (Word Ch 01, Ex 06) by clicking the Save button on the Standard toolbar or clicking <u>F</u>ile and then <u>S</u>ave.

5. Print and then close Word Ch 01, Ex 06.

Using the Undo and Redo Buttons

If you make a mistake and delete text that you did not intend to, or if you change your mind after deleting text and want to retrieve it, you can use the Undo or Redo buttons on the Standard toolbar. For example, if you key text and then click the Undo button, the text will be removed. Word removes text to the beginning of the document or up to the point where text had been previously deleted. You can undo text or commands. For example, if you add formatting such as bolding to text and then click the Undo button, the bolding is removed.

Undo

Redo

If you use the Undo button and then decide you do not want to reverse the original action, click the Redo button. For example, if you select and underline text, and then decide to remove underlining, click the Undo button. If you then decide you want the underlining back on, click the Redo button. Many Word actions can be undone or redone. Some actions, however, such as printing and saving cannot be undone or redone.

You cannot undo a save.

In addition to the Undo and Redo buttons on the Standard toolbar, you can use options from the <u>E</u>dit drop-down menu to undo and redo actions. The first option at the <u>E</u>dit drop-down menu will vary depending on the last action completed. For example, if you click the Numbering button on the Formatting toolbar, and then click <u>E</u>dit on the Menu bar, the first option displays as <u>U</u>ndo Number Default. If you decide you do not want the numbering option on, click the <u>U</u>ndo Number Default option at the <u>E</u>dit drop-down menu. You can also just click the Undo button on the Standard toolbar.

Word maintains actions in temporary memory. If you want to undo an action performed earlier, click the down-pointing triangle to the right of the Undo button. This causes a drop-down menu to display as shown in figure 1.16.

figure

Undo Drop-Down List

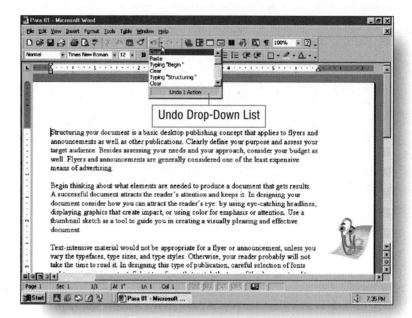

To make a selection from this drop-down menu, click the desired action. Any actions preceding a chosen action are also undone. You can do the same with the actions in the Redo drop-down list. To display the Redo drop-down list, click the down-pointing triangle to the right of the Redo button. To redo an action, click the desired action. Any actions preceding the chosen action are also redone. Multiple actions must be undone or redone in sequence.

exercise

Deleting and Restoring Text with the Undo Button

1. Open Word Document 01.
2. Save the document with Save As and name it Word Ch 01, Ex 07.
3. Make the following changes to the document:
   a. Move the insertion point to the end of the document. Press the Backspace key until the last three words of the document (*stored on them.*) are deleted. Be sure to delete the space before *stored*.
   b. Undo the deletion by clicking the Undo button on the Standard toolbar.
   c. Redo the deletion by clicking the Redo button on the Standard toolbar.
   d. Key a period after the word *information* to end the sentence.
   e. Select the first sentence in the first paragraph (the sentence that begins *The most common storage...*) and then delete it.
   f. Select the second paragraph in the document and then delete it.
   g. Undo the two deletions by completing the following steps:
      1) Click the down-pointing triangle to the right of the Undo button.

2) Click the *second* Clear listed in the drop-down menu. (This will redisplay the first sentence in the first paragraph and the second paragraph. The sentence will be selected.)

    h. With the first sentence of the first paragraph selected, press the Delete key.

4. Save the document with the same name (Word Ch 01, Ex 07) by clicking the Save button on the Standard toolbar or clicking <u>F</u>ile and then <u>S</u>ave.

5. Print and then close Word Ch 01, Ex 07.

chapter summary

► Open Microsoft Word by clicking the Start button on the Taskbar, pointing to <u>P</u>rograms, and then clicking *Microsoft Word*.

► The Title bar is the top line of the Word screen and displays the name of the current document. The Menu bar is the second line on the screen and contains a list of options that are used to customize a Word document.

► The Standard and Formatting toolbars display below the Menu bar and contain shortcuts for the most popular Word commands. Position the arrow pointer on a button on a toolbar and after one second a Screentip displays with the name of the button.

► The blinking vertical line is called the insertion point and indicates the position of the next character to be entered at the document screen. The underline symbol is the end-of-document marker and indicates the end of the document.

► The mouse pointer displays on the screen as an I-beam called the I-beam pointer or as an arrow pointing up and to the left called the mouse pointer.

► The scroll bars appear as gray shaded bars along the right and toward the bottom of the document screen and are used to view various sections of a document.

► The Status bar appears as a gray bar below the horizontal scroll bar toward the bottom of the Word screen. It displays such information as the current location of the insertion point and whether certain modes are active.

► The Office Assistant is an on-screen Help feature that anticipates the type of help you need, as well as suggesting Help topics related to the work you are doing. The Assistant will also point out ways to perform tasks more easily and provide visual examples and step-by-step instructions for specific tasks.

► Word automatically wraps text to the next line as you key information. Press the Enter key only to end a paragraph, create a blank line, or end a short line.

► Word contains a feature named AutoCorrect that automatically corrects certain words as they are keyed.

► When keying text, the Spell It feature automatically inserts a wavy red line below words not contained in the Spelling dictionary, and the automatic grammar checker inserts a green wavy line below a sentence containing a grammatical error.

- Document names can contain a maximum of 255 characters, including the drive letter and folder names, and may include spaces. The following characters cannot be used when naming a document: / \ < > * ? " \ : ; and |.

- Drop-down menus and dialog boxes can be removed from the editing window with the mouse or keyboard.

- When a document is saved on the disk using the <u>S</u>ave or Save <u>A</u>s options, the document remains in the document screen. To remove the document from the screen, click <u>F</u>ile and then <u>C</u>lose or click the Close button located at the right side of the Menu bar.

- To print a document, open the document and then click the Print button on the Standard toolbar or click <u>F</u>ile, <u>P</u>rint, and then OK.

- Be sure to save all needed documents before exiting Word and Windows.

- In order to save on or open documents from your data disk, the default folder should be changed. Change the default folder at the Open dialog box or the Save As dialog box or change it permanently at the Options dialog box with the File Locations tab selected.

- Open a document by displaying the Open dialog box and then double-clicking the desired document name.

- Click the New Blank Document button on the Standard toolbar to display a clear document screen.

- The display of toolbars can be turned on or off and toolbars can be moved to different locations on the screen.

- Word uses *adaptive* menus containing first-rank and second-rank options. Only the first-rank options are visible when the drop-down menu first displays. To display second-rank options, either click the down-pointing arrows at the bottom of the menu or pause on the menu for a few seconds. If you choose a second-rank option, it is promoted and becomes a first-rank option the next time the drop-down menu is displayed.

- The insertion point can be moved throughout the document without interfering with text by using the mouse, the keyboard, or the mouse combined with the keyboard.

- The insertion point can be moved by character, word, screen, or page, and from the first to the last character in a document.

- The horizontal/vertical scroll bars and the mouse can be used to scroll through a document. The scroll box indicates the location of the text in the document screen in relation to the remainder of the document.

- Click the Select Browse Object button located at the bottom of the vertical scroll bar to display options for browsing through a document.

- Switch to the Overtype mode if you want to key over something. When Overtype is on, the OVR mode button in the Status bar displays in black.

- Text can be deleted by character, word, line, several lines, or partial page using specific keys or by selecting text using the mouse or the keyboard.

- A specific amount of text can be selected using the mouse or the keyboard. That text can then be deleted or manipulated in other ways using Word functions.

- The selection bar can be used to select specific units of text such as a line. The selection bar is the space at the left side of the document screen between the left edge of the screen and the text.

- Use the Undo button on the Standard toolbar if you change your mind after keying, deleting, or formatting text and want to undo the deleting or formatting. Use the Redo button to redo something that had been undone with the Undo button.

commands review

Opening Word

1. Turn on the computer.
2. At the Windows 98 (or Windows 95) screen, position the arrow pointer on the Start button on the Taskbar (located at the bottom left side of the screen), and then click the left mouse button.
3. At the pop-up menu, point to Programs (you do not need to click the mouse button). This causes another menu to display to the right of the first pop-up menu.
4. Move the arrow pointer to *Microsoft Word* and then click the left mouse button.

Saving a Document

1. Click the Save button on the Standard toolbar or click File and then Save.
2. At the Save As dialog box, key the name of the document.
3. Click the Save button or press Enter.

Changing the Default Folder

1. Click the Open button on the Standard toolbar or click File and then Open.
2. At the Open dialog box, click the down-pointing triangle at the right side of the Look in text box.
3. From the drop-down list that displays, click *3½ Floppy (A:)*.
4. Click the Cancel button that displays in the lower right corner of the dialog box.

Changing the Default Folder Permanently

1. Click Tools and then Options.
2. At the Options dialog box, click the File Locations tab.
3. Make sure *Documents* is selected in the File types list box and then click the Modify button.
4. At the Modify Location dialog box, change to the desired folder.
5. Click the OK button.

Closing a Document Using the Mouse

1. Click the Close button on the Menu bar or click File and then Close.

Opening a Document

1. Click the Open button on the Standard toolbar or click File and then Open.
2. At the Open dialog box, double-click the document name.

Printing a Document

1. Open the document.
2. Click the Print button on the Standard toolbar.
        or
1. Open the document.
2. Click File and then Print.
3. At the Print dialog box, click OK.

Exiting Word

1. Be sure all needed documents have been saved.
2. Click the Close button on the Title bar or click File and then Exit.

Exiting Windows

1. Click the Start button at the left side of the Taskbar.
2. At the pop-up menu, click Shut Down.
3. At the Shut Down Windows dialog box, make sure *Shut down* is selected, and then click OK.

Scrolling Review

Changing the Display Using the Mouse and the Vertical Scroll Bar

Up one line	Click the up scroll triangle on the vertical scroll bar
Up several lines	Position the arrow pointer as above and then hold down left mouse button
Down one line	Click the down scroll triangle on the vertical scroll bar
Down several lines	Position the arrow pointer as above and then hold down left mouse button
Up one screen	Click with arrow pointer above the scroll box on the scroll bar
Down one screen	Click with arrow pointer below the scroll box on the scroll bar
To beginning of document	Position the arrow pointer on the scroll box, hold down left mouse button, drag the scroll box to the beginning of the scroll bar, and then release the mouse button
To end of document	Position the arrow pointer on the scroll box, hold down left mouse button, drag the scroll box to the end of the scroll bar, and then release the mouse button

Insertion Point Movement Review

Moving the Insertion Point Using the Mouse

To move to a specific location	Move arrow pointer to desired location and then click left mouse button
To move to the next page	Click the Next Page button
To move to the previous page	Click the Previous Page button
To move to a specific page	1. Click Edit and then Go To or double-click the page number at the left side of the Status bar. 2. Key the page number. 3. Click the Go To button or press Enter. 4. Click the Close button.

Moving the Insertion Point Using the Keyboard

To move insertion point	Press
One character left	left arrow
One character right	right arrow
One line up	up arrow
One line down	down arrow
One word to the left	Ctrl + left arrow
One word to the right	Ctrl + right arrow
To end of line	End

To beginning of a line	Home
To beginning of current paragraph	Ctrl + up arrow
To beginning of previous paragraph	Ctrl + up arrow twice
To beginning of next paragraph	Ctrl + down arrow
Up one screen	Page Up
Down one screen	Page Down
To top of previous page	Ctrl + Page Up
To top of next page	Ctrl + Page Down
To beginning of document	Ctrl + Home
To end of document	Ctrl + End
To last location when document was closed	Shift + F5

Deletion Commands Review

To delete	Press
Character right of insertion point	Delete key
Character left of insertion point	Backspace key
Word before insertion point	Ctrl + Backspace
Word after insertion point	Ctrl + Delete

Selecting Text Review

Selecting Text Using the Mouse

To select text	Position I-beam pointer at the beginning of text to be selected, hold down left mouse button, drag the I-beam pointer to the end of text to be selected, and then release the mouse button
To select	Complete these steps
A word	Double-click the word
A line of text	Click in the selection bar to the left of line
Multiple lines of text	Drag in the selection bar to left of lines
A sentence	Hold down Ctrl key and then click anywhere in the sentence
A paragraph	Double-click in the selection bar next to paragraph or triple-click anywhere in the paragraph
Multiple paragraphs	Drag in the selection bar
An entire document	Triple-click in the selection bar
To cancel a selection	Click anywhere outside the selected text in the document screen

Selecting Text Using the Keyboard

To select	Press
One character to right	Shift + right arrow
One character to left	Shift + left arrow
To end of word	Ctrl + Shift + right arrow
To beginning of word	Ctrl + Shift + left arrow

To end of line	Shift + End
To beginning of line	Shift + Home
One line up	Shift + up arrow
One line down	Shift + down arrow
To beginning of paragraph	Ctrl + Shift + up arrow
To end of paragraph	Ctrl + Shift + down arrow
One screen up	Shift + Page Up
One screen down	Shift + Page Down
To end of document	Ctrl + Shift + End
To beginning of document	Ctrl + Shift + Home
Entire document	Ctrl + A or click Edit, Select All
To cancel a selection	Press any arrow key

Other Commands Review

Turn on Overtype	Double-click the OVR mode button on the Status bar, or press the Insert key
Undo	Click Undo button on the Standard toolbar
Redo	Click Redo button on the Standard toolbar
Save As	1. Click File and then Save As.
	2. At the Save As dialog box, key the document name.
	3. Click the Save button or press Enter.

thinking offline

Matching: In the space provided at the left, indicate the correct letter or letters that match each description.

Ⓐ ButtonTip
Ⓑ Fix It
Ⓒ Formatting toolbar
Ⓓ Horizontal scroll bar
Ⓔ Menu bar

Ⓕ Office Assistant
Ⓖ Save As
Ⓗ Scrolling
Ⓘ Spell It
Ⓙ Standard toolbar

Ⓚ Status bar
Ⓛ Title bar
Ⓜ ScreenTip
Ⓝ Vertical scroll bar

_____ 1. This toolbar contains buttons for working with documents such as the Open button and the Save button.

_____ 2. This toolbar contains buttons for formatting a document such as bold, italics, and underline.

_____ 3. This displays below the horizontal scroll bar and displays the current location of the insertion point.

_____ 4. This displays along the right side of the screen and is used to view various sections of a document.

_____ 5. This displays in the document screen and is an on-screen Help feature that anticipates the type of help you need as well as suggesting Help topics related to the work you are doing.

_____ 6. Doing this in a document changes the text displayed but does not move the insertion point.

_____ 7. This displays at the top of the Word screen and displays the name of the currently open document.

_____ 8. This appears after approximately one second when the mouse pointer is positioned on a button on a toolbar.

_____ 9. Use this option to save a previously created document with a new name.

_____ 10. This feature inserts a wavy red line below words not contained in the Spelling dictionary.

Completion: In the space provided at the right, indicate the correct term, command, or number.

1. This feature automatically corrects certain words as they are being keyed. _____

2. This displays in the document screen as a blinking vertical line. _____

3. This is the second line of the Word screen and contains a list of options that are used to customize a Word document. _____

4. At a blank screen, click this button on the Standard toolbar to open a new blank document. _____

5. Use this keyboard command to move the insertion point to the beginning of the previous page. _____

6. When Overtype is on, this mode button displays in black on the Status bar. _____

7. Press this key on the keyboard to delete the character left of the insertion point. _____

8. Complete these steps using the mouse to select one word. _____

9. Use this keyboard command to select text to the end of the line. _____

10. If you click this button on the Standard toolbar, text you just keyed will be removed. _____

11. Use this keyboard command to move the insertion point to the end of the document. _____

12. Use this keyboard command to select text to the end of the paragraph. _____

13. To select various amounts of text using the mouse, you can click in this bar. _____

working hands-on

Assessment 1

1. Open Windows and then Word.
2. At the clear document screen, change the default folder to the drive where your disk is located. (Check with your instructor to determine if this step is necessary.)
3. At the clear document screen, key the text in figure 1.17. (Correct any errors highlighted by Spell It as they occur and remember to space once after end-of-sentence punctuation.)
4. Save the document and name it Word Ch 01, SA 01.
5. Print and then close Word Ch 01, SA 01.

Assessment 1

The primary storage medium used with most personal computers today is the hard drive. Typically, a person uses a hard drive to store the computer's operating system, application programs, fonts, and data files created with the application programs.

Hard drives have large storage capacities, up to several gigabytes. However large or small a hard drive is, at least 10 to 15 percent of its total capacity should be left free. If the hard drive becomes too full, the computer user is likely to experience various difficulties, such as printing problems caused by an inability to spool, or write temporarily to the drive, files that are to be printed.

Assessment 2

1. Open Word Document 03.
2. Save the document with Save As and name it Word Ch 01, SA 02.
3. Make the following changes to the document:
   a. Delete the word *rare* in the first sentence of the first paragraph.
   b. Delete % in the second sentence of the second paragraph and then key *percent*.
   c. Delete the word *actually* in the last sentence of the second paragraph.
   d. Delete the word *general* in the last sentence of the second paragraph.
   e. Change the word *primary* in the first sentence of the third paragraph to *main*.

     f.   Delete the words *in this phase of the expansion* in the second sentence of the third paragraph.

     g.   Join the first and second paragraphs.

4. Save the document again with the same name (Word Ch 01, SA 02).

5. Print and then close Word Ch 01, SA 02.

Assessment 3

1. Open Word Document 04.

2. Save the document with Save As and name it Word Ch 01, SA 03.

3. Make the following changes to the document:

     a.   Delete the words *the ongoing* in the first sentence of the first paragraph.

     b.   Delete the last sentence in the first paragraph.

     c.   Delete the words *(last year's market catalyst)* in the second sentence of the second paragraph.

     d.   Change the word *Moreover* in the first sentence of the third paragraph to *Additionally*.

     e.   Insert the word *rapid* after *earlier* in the first sentence of the third paragraph.

     f.   Change the word *a* in the second sentence of the third paragraph to *an important*.

     g.   Change the word *Plus* in the last sentence of the third paragraph to *Second*.

4. Save the document again with the same name (Word Ch 01, SA 03).

5. Print and then close Word Ch 01, SA 03.

Assessment 4

1. At a clear document screen (click the New Blank Document button), compose a paragraph explaining when you would use the Save As command when saving a document rather than the Save command, and the advantages to Save As.

2. Save the document and name it Word Ch 01, SA 04.

3. Print and then close Word Ch 01, SA 04.

Chapter 02

Formatting Text and Using Help

Upon successful completion of chapter 2, you will be able to:
- Apply bold, italic, and underlining formatting.
- Change the font.
- Adjust character spacing.
- Animate text.
- Turn on/off the display of nonprinting characters.
- Change the alignment of text in paragraphs.
- Change spacing before and after paragraphs.
- Automate formatting with Format Painter.
- Indent text in paragraphs.
- Create numbered and bulleted paragraphs.
- Insert special symbols in a document.
- Change line spacing in a document.
- Apply borders and shading to text.
- Repeat the last action.
- Use the Help feature.

As you work with Word, you will learn a number of commands and procedures that affect how the document appears when printed. The appearance of a document in the document screen and how it looks when printed is called the *format*. Formatting can include such elements as bolding, italicizing, and underlining characters, and inserting special symbols. Text in paragraphs can also be formatted, by changing text alignment, indenting text, applying formatting with Format Painter, inserting numbers and bullets, changing line spacing, and applying borders and shading.

Microsoft Word contains an on-screen reference manual containing information on features and commands for each program within the suite. In this chapter, you will learn to use the Help feature to display information about Word.

Formatting Characters

Formatting a document can include adding enhancements to characters such as bolding, underlining, and italicizing. A variety of formatting options is displayed in figure 2.1.

Character Formatting

Formatting	Method
Uppercase letters	Press the Caps Lock key
Bold	Press Ctrl + B or click the Bold button on the Formatting toolbar
Underline	Press Ctrl + U or click the Underline button on the Formatting toolbar
Italics	Press Ctrl + I or click the Italic button on the Formatting toolbar

Bold

Underline

Italic

More than one type of character formatting can be applied to the same text. For example, you can both bold and underline a section of text as has been done to the title in figure 2.2. If formatting is applied to text, it can be removed by selecting the text and then clicking the appropriate button on the Formatting toolbar or pressing the shortcut command. For example, to remove underlining from text, you would select the text to which you want the underlining removed, and then click the Underline button on the Formatting toolbar or press Ctrl + U.

All character formatting can be removed from selected text with the shortcut command, Ctrl + spacebar. This removes *all* character formatting. For example, if bold and italics are applied to text, selecting the text and then pressing Ctrl + spacebar will remove both bold and italics.

(Before completing computer exercises, delete the Chapter 01 *folder on your disk. Next, copy the* Chapter 02 *folder from the CD that accompanies this textbook to your disk and then make* Chapter 02 *the active folder.)*

exercise

Applying Character Formatting to Text as It Is Keyed

1. At a clear document screen, key the document shown in figure 2.2 with the following specifications:
   a. While keying the document, bold the text shown bolded in the figure by completing the following steps:
      1) Click the Bold button on the Formatting toolbar or press Ctrl + B. (This turns on bold.)
      2) Key the text.
      3) Click the Bold button on the Formatting toolbar or press Ctrl + B. (This turns off bold.)
   b. While keying the document, underline the text shown underlined in the figure by completing the following steps:

      1) Click the Underline button on the Formatting toolbar or press Ctrl + U.
      2) Key the text.
      3) Click the Underline button on the Formatting toolbar or press Ctrl + U.
  c. While keying the document, italicize the text shown in italics in the figure by completing the followings steps:
      1) Click the Italic button on the Formatting toolbar or press Ctrl + I.
      2) Key the text.
      3) Click the Italic button on the Formatting toolbar or press Ctrl + I.
2. Save the document and name it Word Ch 02, Ex 01a.
3. Print Word Ch 02, Ex 01a.
4. With the document still open, make the following changes:
  a. Remove underlining from the title by completing the following steps:
      1) Select the title *COMPUTER MOTHERBOARD*.
      2) Click the Underline button on the Formatting toolbar.
  b. Add underlining to the bolded word *Buses* by completing the following steps:
      1) Select the word *Buses* (do not include the colon).
      2) Click the Underline button on the Formatting toolbar.
  c. Select and then underline each of the other bolded words that begin the remaining paragraphs (*System Clock, Microprocessor, Read-only Memory, Expansion Slots*).
5. Save the document with Save As and name it Word Ch 02, Ex 01b.
6. Print and then close Word Ch 02, Ex 01b.

figure

2.2   *Exercise 1*

COMPUTER MOTHERBOARD

The main circuit board in a computer is called the *motherboard*. The motherboard is a thin sheet of fiberglass or other material with electrical pathways, called *traces*, etched onto it. These traces connect components that are soldered to the motherboard or attached to it by various connectors. Many components are found on the motherboard, including the following:

Buses: The electronic connections that allow communication between components in the computer are referred to as buses.

System Clock: A system clock synchronizes the computer's activities.

Microprocessor: The microprocessor, also called the *processor*, processes data and controls the functions of the computer.

Read-only Memory: The read-only memory (ROM) chip contains the computer's permanent memory in which various instructions are stored.

Expansion Slots: The expansion slots are used to add various capabilities to a computer such as the ability to access files over a network or digitize sound or video.

Changing Fonts

The default font used by Word is 10-point Times New Roman (or 12-point Times New Roman, if you followed the steps presented in chapter 1 on changing the default font). You may want to change this default to some other font for such reasons as changing the mood of a document, enhancing the visual appeal, and increasing the readability of the text. A font consists of three elements—typeface, type size, and type style.

Choosing a Typeface

A *typeface* is a set of characters with a common design and shape. (Word refers to typeface as *font*.) Typefaces may be decorative or plain and are either *monospaced* or *proportional*. A monospaced typeface allots the same amount of horizontal space for each character. Courier is an example of a monospaced typeface. Proportional typefaces allot a varying amount of space for each character. The space allotted is based on the width of the character. For example, the lowercase *i* will take up less space than the uppercase *M*.

Use a serif typeface for text-intensive documents

Proportional typefaces are divided into two main categories: *serif* and *sans serif*. A serif is a small line at the end of a character stroke. Traditionally, a serif typeface is used with documents that are text intensive (documents that are mainly text) because the serifs help move the reader's eyes across the page. A sans serif typeface does not have serifs (*sans* is French for *without*). Sans serif typefaces are often used for headlines and advertisements that are not text intensive. Figure 2.3 shows examples of serif and sans serif typefaces.

As mentioned earlier in chapter 1, space once after end-of-sentence punctuation and after a colon when text is set in a proportional typeface. Proportional typefaces are set closer together and extra white space at the end of a sentence or after a colon is not needed.

figure
2.3
Serif and Sans Serif Typefaces

Serif Typefaces	Sans Serif Typefaces
Bookman Old Style	Arial
Garamond	Eurostile
Goudy Old Style	**Haettenschweiler**
Modern No. 20	**Impact**
Rockwell	Lucinda Sans
Times New Roman	Tahoma

Choosing a Type Size

Type size is divided into two categories: *pitch* and *point size*. Pitch is a measurement used for monospaced typefaces; it reflects the number of characters that can be printed in 1 horizontal inch. (For some printers, the pitch is referred to as *cpi*, or *characters per inch*. For example, the font Courier 10 cpi is the same as 10-pitch Courier.)

Proportional typefaces can be set in different sizes. The size of proportional type is measured vertically in units called *points*. A point is approximately 1/72 of an inch. The higher the point size, the larger the characters. Examples of different point sizes in the Arial typeface are shown in figure 2.4.

2.4 *Different Point Sizes in Arial*

8-point Arial
12-point Arial
18-point Arial
24-point Arial

Choosing a Type Style

Within a typeface, characters may have a varying style. There are four main categories of type styles: normal (for some typefaces, this may be referred to as *light*, *black*, *regular*, or *roman*), bold, italic, and bold italic. Figure 2.5 illustrates the four main type styles in 12 points.

2.5 *Four Main Type Styles*

Tahoma regular	Times New Roman regular
Tahoma bold	**Times New Roman Bold**
Tahoma italic	*Times New Roman Italic*
Tahoma bold italic	***Times New Roman bold italic***

The term *font* describes a particular typeface in a specific style and size. Some examples of fonts include 10-pitch Courier, 10-point Arial, 12-point Tahoma bold, and 12-point Times New Roman bold italic.

Using the Font Dialog Box

The fonts available display in the <u>F</u>ont list box at the Font dialog box. To display the Font dialog box, shown in figure 2.6, click F<u>o</u>rmat and then <u>F</u>ont. You can also display the Font dialog box with a shortcut menu. To do this, position the I-beam pointer anywhere within the document screen, click the *right* mouse button, and then click the left mouse button on <u>F</u>ont.

Font Dialog Box

Choose a typeface in this list box. Use the scroll bar at the right side of the box to view various typefaces available.

Choose a type style in this list box. The options in the box may vary depending on the typeface selected.

Choose a type size in this list box; or, select the current measurement in the top box and then key the desired measurement.

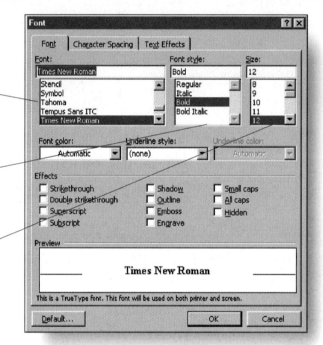

The <u>F</u>ont list box at the Font dialog box displays the typefaces (fonts) available with your printer. Figure 2.6 shows the typefaces available with a laser printer (the fonts displayed with your printer may vary from those shown). To select a typeface, select the desired typeface (font), and then click OK or press Enter. The Preview box at the bottom of the dialog box displays the appearance of the selected font.

The <u>S</u>ize list box at the Font dialog box displays a variety of common type sizes. Decrease point size to make text smaller or increase point size to make text larger. To select a point size with the mouse, click the desired point size. To view more point sizes, click the down-pointing triangle in the <u>S</u>ize scroll bar. You can also key a specific point size. To do this, select the number in the <u>S</u>ize text box, and then key the desired point size.

The Font st<u>y</u>le list box displays the styles available with the selected typeface. As you select different typefaces at the Font dialog box, the list of styles changes in the Font st<u>y</u>le list box. Choose from a variety of type styles such as regular, bold, italic, or bold and italic.

Make adjustments to character spacing such as expanding or condensing the space between characters with options at the Font dialog box with the Cha<u>r</u>acter Spacing tab selected.

exercise 2

Changing the Font at the Font Dialog Box

1. Open Word Document 01.
2. Save the document with Save As and name it Word Ch 02, Ex 02.
3. Change the typeface to 13-point Bookman Old Style italic by completing the following steps:
   a. Select the entire document. (*Hint: To select the entire document press Ctrl + A or click Edit and then Select All.*)
   b. Display the Font dialog box by clicking Format and then Font.
   c. At the Font dialog box, click the up-pointing triangle at the right side of the Font list box until *Bookman Old Style* displays, and then click *Bookman Old Style*. (If Bookman Old Style is not available, choose another serif typeface such as Galliard BT or Garamond.)

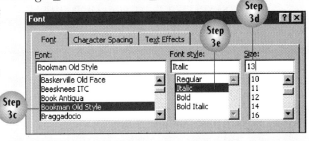

   d. Change the Size option to 13 by selecting the *12* displayed in the Size list box and then keying **13**.
   e. Click *Italic* in the Font style list box.
   f. Click OK or press Enter.
4. At the document screen, deselect the text by clicking anywhere in the document screen outside the selected text.
5. Save the document again with the same name (Word Ch 02, Ex 02).
6. Print and then close Word Ch 02, Ex 02.

In addition to using the Font dialog box to select a typeface, you can use the Font button on the Formatting toolbar. The Font button displays a font name followed by a down-pointing triangle. For example, if your default typeface is Times New Roman, that name displays in the Font button. If you click the down-pointing triangle at the right side of the Font button, a drop-down list displays. Click the desired typeface at this drop-down list.

Font

Font size can be changed with options from the Font Size button on the Formatting toolbar. The Font Size button contains the current point size followed by a down-pointing triangle. To change the type size with the Font Size button, click the down-pointing triangle at the right side of the Font Size button, and then click the desired size at the drop-down list.

Font Size

The Formatting toolbar also contains a Font Color button to change the color of selected text. Click the Font Color button and the selected text changes to the color that displays on the button (below the A). To choose a different color, click the down-pointing triangle at the right side of the button and then click the desired color at the palette of color choices.

Font Color

Changing the Font, Size, and Color Using Buttons on the Formatting Toolbar

1. Open Word Document 02.
2. Save the document with Save As and name it Word Ch 02, Ex 03.
3. Change the typeface to 14-point Arial and the color to Indigo using buttons on the Formatting toolbar by completing the following steps:
   a. Select the entire document. (*Hint: To select the entire document press Ctrl + A or click Edit and then Select All.*)
   b. Click the down-pointing triangle at the right side of the Font button on the Formatting toolbar and then click *Arial* at the drop-down list. (You may need to scroll up the list to display *Arial*.)
   c. Click the down-pointing triangle at the right side of the Font Size button on the Formatting toolbar and then click *14* at the drop-down list.
   d. Change the font color to Indigo by completing the following steps:
      1) Click the down-pointing triangle at the right side of the Font Color button (the last button on the Formatting toolbar).
      2) At the palette of color choices that displays, click *Indigo* (second color choice from the *right* in the top row).
4. Deselect the text to see what it looks like set in 14-point Arial and in Indigo.
5. Save the document again with the same name (Word Ch 02, Ex 03).
6. Print and then close Word Ch 02, Ex 03.

The Font dialog box contains a variety of underlining options. Click the down-pointing triangle at the right side of the Underline style option box and a drop-down palette of underlining styles displays containing options such as a double line, thick line, dashed line, and so on.

Click the down-pointing triangle at the right side of the Font color text box and a palette of choices displays. Position the arrow pointer on a color and after one second a yellow box displays with the color name. Use this option to change the color of selected text.

Changing the Font and Text Color and Underlining Text

1. Open Word Notice 01.
2. Save the document with Save As and name it Word Ch 02, Ex 04.

3. Change the font and text color by completing the following steps:
   a. Select the entire document.
   b. Display the Font dialog box.
   c. Change the font to 14-point Goudy Old Style bold. (If Goudy Old Style is not available, consider using another serif typeface such as Bookman Old Style or Century Schoolbook.)
   d. With the Font dialog box still displayed, change the text color to Blue by clicking the down-pointing triangle at the right side of the Font color text box, and then clicking *Blue* (sixth color option from the left in the second row).
   e. Click OK or press Enter.
   f. Deselect the text.

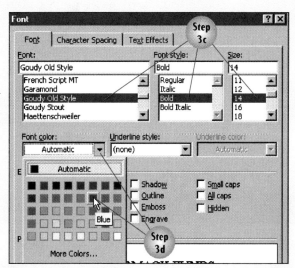

4. Double underline the text *Annual Stockholders' Meeting* by completing the following steps:
   a. Select *Annual Stockholders' Meeting*.
   b. Display the Font dialog box.
   c. Click the down-pointing triangle at the right side of the Underline style option box and then click the double-line option (see figure) at the drop-down list.
   d. Click OK to close the dialog box.

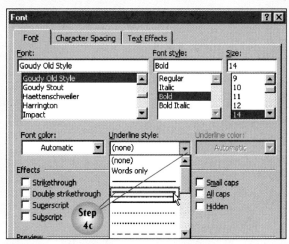

5. Apply a thick underline to the text *6:30 p.m.* by completing the following steps:
   a. Select *6:30 p.m.*
   b. Display the Font dialog box.
   c. Click the down-pointing triangle at the right side of the Underline style option box and then click the thick line option (see figure) that displays below the double-line option.
   d. Click OK to close the dialog box.
   e. Deselect the text
6. Save the document again with the same name (Word Ch 02, Ex 04).
7. Print and then close Word Ch 02, Ex 04.

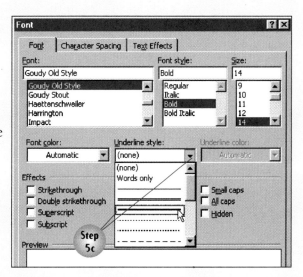

The Effects section of the Font dialog box contains a variety of options that can be used to create different character styles. For example, you can strikethrough text (which has a practical application for some legal documents in which deleted text must be retained in the document), or create superscript and subscript text. With the Hidden option from the Font dialog box, you can include such items as comments, personal messages, or questions in a document. These items can be displayed, printed, or hidden. The Small caps option lets you print small capital letters. This works for some printers, but not all. Additional effects include Double strikethrough, Shadow, Outline, Emboss, Engrave, and All caps.

Changing Text to Small Caps

1. Open Word Notice 01.
2. Save the document with Save As and name it Word Ch 02, Ex 05.
3. Select the entire document and then make the following changes:
   a. Display the Font dialog box and change the font to 14-point Modern No. 20 bold. (Do not close the dialog box.) (If Modern No. 20 is not available, consider using another decorative serif typeface such as Dauphin or BernhardMod BT.)
   b. With the Font dialog box still displayed, change the font color to violet (see the figure).
   c. With the Font dialog box still displayed, click Small caps in the Effects section.
   d. Click OK or press Enter to close the Font dialog box.
   e. Deselect the text.
4. Save the document again with the same name (Word Ch 02, Ex 05).
5. Print and then close Word Ch 02, Ex 05.

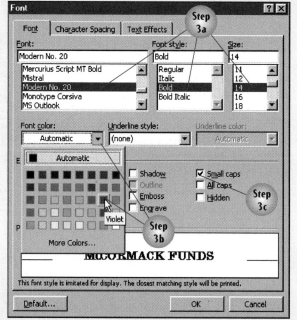

Superscript text is raised slightly above the text line and subscripted text is lowered slightly below the text line. Use the superscript effect for some mathematical equations such as four to the third power (written as 4^3) and use the subscript effect to create some chemical formulas such as H_2O. Create superscript text with the Superscript effect and subscript with the Subscript effect at the Font dialog box. Superscript text can also be created with the shortcut command Ctrl + Shift + =, and subscript text can be created with the shortcut command Ctrl + =.

exercise 6

Applying Superscript Effect to Text and Changing the Font

1. At a clear document screen, key the text shown in figure 2.7 with the following specifications:
   a. Create the first superscript numbers in the document by completing the following steps:
      1) Key text to the point where the superscript number is to appear.
      2) Display the Font dialog box.
      3) At the Font dialog box, click the Superscript check box located in the Effects section.
      4) Click OK to close the Font dialog box.
      5) Key the superscript number.
      6) Turn off Superscript by displaying the Font dialog box, clicking the Superscript check box (this removes the check mark), and then clicking OK to close the dialog box.
   b. Create the second superscript number in the document by completing the following steps:
      1) Key text to the point where the superscript number is to appear.
      2) Press Ctrl + Shift + =.
      3) Key the superscript number.
      4) Press Ctrl + Shift + =.
   c. Finish keying the remainder of the document using either the method described in step a or the one in step b to create the remaining superscript text.
   d. Select the entire document and then change the font to 12-point Bookman Old Style (or a similar serif typeface such as Century Schoolbook or Garamond).
2. Save the document and name it Word Ch 02, Ex 06.
3. Print and then close Word Ch 02, Ex 06.

figure 2.7

Exercise 6

The Chinese abacus consisted of pebbles strung on rods inside a frame. The columns represented decimal places (ones place, tens place, hundreds place, and so on). Pebbles in the upper part of an abacus correspond to 5×10^0, or 5, for the first column; 5×10^1, or 50, for the second column; 5×10^2, or 500, for the third column; and so on. Pebbles in the lower part correspond to 1×10^0, or 1, for the first column; 1×10^1, or 10, for the second column; 1×10^2, or 100, for the third column; and so on.

Adjusting Character Spacing

Each typeface is designed with a specific amount of space between characters. This character spacing can be changed with options at the Font dialog box with the Character Spacing tab selected as shown in figure 2.8. To display this dialog box, click Format and then Font. At the Font dialog box, click the Character Spacing tab.

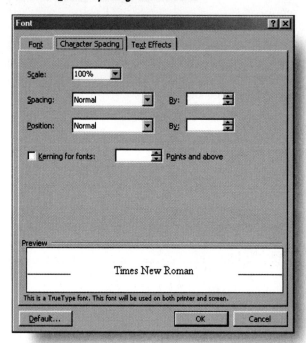

Font Dialog Box with Character Spacing Tab Selected

Choose the Scale option to stretch or compress text horizontally as a percentage of the current size. You can choose a percentage from 1 to 600. Expand or condense the spacing between characters with the Spacing option. Choose either the *Expanded* or *Condensed* option and then enter the desired percentage amount in the By text box. Raise or lower selected text in relation to the baseline with the Spacing option. Choose either the *Raised* or *Lowered* option and then enter the percentage amount in the By text box.

Kerning is a term that refers to the adjustment of spacing between certain character combinations. Kerning provides text with a more evenly spaced look and works only with TrueType or Adobe Type manager fonts. Turn on automatic kerning by inserting a check mark in the Kerning for fonts check box. Specify the beginning point size that you want kerned in the Points and above text box.

Animating Text

Animation effects can be added to text at the Font dialog box with the Text Effects tab selected. To display this dialog box, shown in figure 2.9, click Format and then Font. At the Font dialog box click the Text Effects tab.

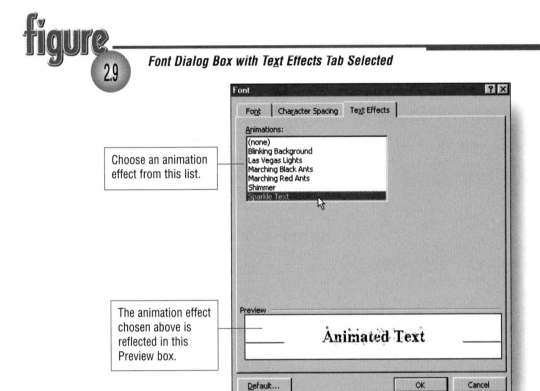

figure
2.9

Font Dialog Box with Text Effects Tab Selected

Choose an animation effect from this list.

The animation effect chosen above is reflected in this Preview box.

Animation effects can be added to text, such as a blinking background, a shimmer or sparkle. To add an animation effect, select the text, display the Font dialog box with the Text Effects tab selected, click the desired effect, and then close the Font dialog box. Animation effects added to text display in the screen but do not print.

exercise 7

Adjusting Character Spacing and Scaling, Turning on Kerning, and Animating Text

1. Open Word Document 02.
2. Save the document with Save As and name it Word Ch 02, Ex 07.
3. Adjust character spacing and turn on kerning by completing the following steps:
   a. Select the entire document.
   b. Click Format and then Font.

c. At the Font dialog box, click the Character Spacing tab.
d. At the Font dialog box with the Character Spacing tab selected, click the down-pointing triangle at the right side of the Spacing option, and then click *Expanded* at the drop-down list. (This inserts *1 pt* in the By text box.)

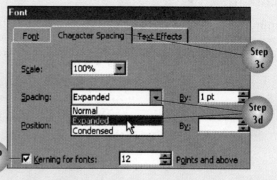

e. Click in the Kerning for fonts check box. (This inserts a check mark in the check box and also inserts *12* in the Points and above text box.)
f. Click OK to close the dialog box.
g. Deselect the text.
4. Save the document again with the same name (Word Ch 02, Ex 07).
5. Print Word Ch 02, Ex 07.
6. With Word Ch 02, Ex 07 still open, compress text horizontally by completing the following steps:

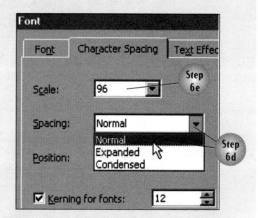

a. Select the entire document.
b. Click Format and then Font.
c. At the Font dialog box, click the Character Spacing tab.
d. At the Font dialog box with the Character Spacing tab selected, click the down-pointing triangle at the right side of the Spacing option, and then click *Normal* at the drop-down list.
e. Select *100%* in the Scale option text box and then key **96**. (This compresses text to 96 percent of the original horizontal spacing.)
f. Click OK to close the dialog box.
g. Deselect the text.
7. Add a blinking background to the title of the document by completing the following steps:

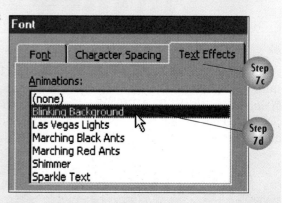

a. Select the title *COMPUTER KEYBOARDS*.
b. Click Format and then Font.
c. At the Font dialog box, click the Text Effects tab.
d. Click the *Blinking Background* option in the list box.
e. Click OK to close the dialog box.
8. Save the document again with the same name (Word Ch 02, Ex 07).
9. Print and then close Word Ch 02, Ex 07.

Formatting Paragraphs

Formatting such as changing alignment, indenting text, inserting bullets and numbers, and changing line spacing can be applied to paragraphs. In Word, a paragraph is any amount of text followed by a paragraph mark. A paragraph mark is inserted in a document each time the Enter key is pressed. By default, this paragraph mark is not visible. When changes are made to a paragraph, the formatting changes are inserted in the paragraph mark. If the paragraph mark is deleted, the formatting in the mark is eliminated and the text returns to the default.

Nonprinting characters do not print whether they are displayed or not.

Displaying Nonprinting Characters

When you begin formatting text by paragraph, displaying nonprinting characters can be useful. If you want to remove paragraph formatting from text, delete the paragraph mark. To display the paragraph mark and other nonprinting characters, click the Show/Hide ¶ button on the Standard toolbar. This causes nonprinting characters to display as shown in the document in figure 2.10. Click the Show/Hide ¶ button on the Standard toolbar to turn off the display of nonprinting characters.

¶

Show/Hide ¶

figure

2.10

Document with Nonprinting Symbols Displayed

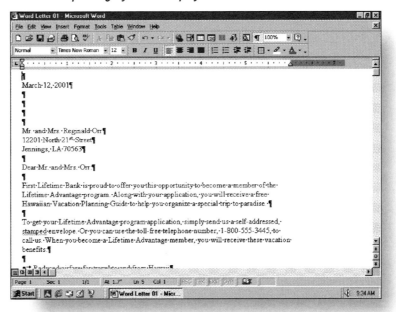

Changing the Alignment of Text in Paragraphs

By default, paragraphs in a Word document are aligned at the left margin and ragged at the right margin. This default alignment can be changed with buttons on the Formatting toolbar or with shortcut commands. Text in a paragraph can be aligned at the left margin, between margins, at the right margin, or at the left and right margins. Figure 2.11 illustrates the different paragraph alignments.

figure
2.11 *Paragraph Alignments*

Left Aligned Text

Center Aligned Text

Right Aligned Text

Fully Aligned Text

Use the buttons on the Formatting toolbar or the shortcut commands shown in figure 2.12 to change the alignment of text in paragraphs.

figure
2.12 *Paragraph Alignment Buttons and Commands*

To align text	Button	Shortcut command
at the left margin	☰	Ctrl + L
between margins	☰	Ctrl + E
at the right margin	☰	Ctrl + R
at the left and right margins	☰	Ctrl + J

You can change the alignment of text in paragraphs before you key the text or you can change the alignment of existing text. If you change the alignment before keying text, the alignment formatting is inserted in the paragraph mark. As you key text and press Enter, the paragraph formatting is continued. For example, if you press Ctrl + E to turn on center aligning, key text for the first paragraph, and then press Enter, the center alignment formatting is still active and the insertion point displays in the middle of the left and right margins.

Align Left

To return paragraph alignment to the default (left aligned), click the Align Left button on the Formatting toolbar or press Ctrl + L. You can also return all paragraph formatting to the default by pressing Ctrl + Q. This shortcut command returns all paragraph formatting (not just alignment) to the default settings.

To change the alignment of existing text in a paragraph, position the insertion point anywhere within the paragraph. The entire paragraph does not have to be selected. To change the alignment of several adjacent paragraphs in a document, select a portion of the first paragraph through a portion of the last paragraph. Only a portion of the first and last paragraphs needs to be selected.

Using AutoComplete

Microsoft Word and other Office applications include an AutoComplete feature that inserts an entire item when you key a few identifying characters. For example, key the letters *Mond* and *Monday* displays in a ScreenTip above the letters. Press the Enter key or press F3 and Monday is inserted in the document. When entering Thursday in exercise 8, key the first four characters (Thur) and then press the Enter key.

Changing Paragraph Alignment to Center

1. At a clear document screen, turn on the display of nonprinting characters by clicking the Show/Hide ¶ button on the Standard toolbar.
2. Key the text shown in figure 2.13.
3. Make the following changes to the document:
   a. Select the entire document.
   b. With the entire document still selected, change the font to 16-point Arial bold and the font color to Blue.
   c. With the entire document still selected, change the alignment of paragraphs to center by clicking the Center button on the Formatting toolbar.
   d. Deselect the text by clicking in the document screen outside the selected text.
4. Click the Show/Hide ¶ button on the Standard toolbar to turn off the display of nonprinting characters.
5. Save the document and name it Word Ch 02, Ex 08.
6. Print and then close Word Ch 02, Ex 08.

Exercise 8

McCORMACK FUNDS

McCormack LifeLine Trust Annuities Seminar

Thursday, March 15

8:30 a.m. to 11:30 a.m.

Conference Room C

Changing Paragraph Alignment to Justified

1. Open Word Document 02.
2. Save the document with Save As and name it Word Ch 02, Ex 09.
3. Change the alignment of the text in paragraphs to justified by selecting the entire document and then clicking the Justify button on the Formatting toolbar.
4. Save the document again with the same name (Word Ch 02, Ex 09).
5. Print and then close Word Ch 02, Ex 09.

Changing Alignment at the Paragraph Dialog Box

Paragraph alignment can also be changed at the Paragraph dialog box with the Indents and Spacing tab selected as shown in figure 2.14. To change the alignment of text in a paragraph, display the Paragraph dialog box by clicking Format and then Paragraph. At the Paragraph dialog box with the Indents and Spacing tab selected, click the down-pointing triangle in the Alignment option box. From the drop-down menu that displays, click an alignment option, and then click OK or press Enter.

figure

2.14

Paragraph Dialog Box with Indents and Spacing Tab Selected

Change paragraph alignment by clicking this down-pointing triangle and then clicking the desired alignment at the drop-down list.

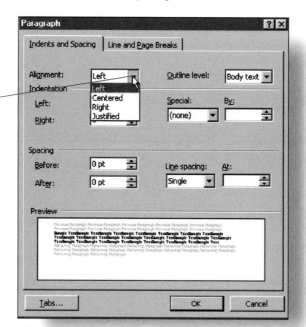

exercise 10

Changing Paragraph Alignment to Justified Using the Paragraph Dialog Box

1. Open Word Document 01.
2. Save the document with Save As and name it Word Ch 02, Ex 10.
3. Change the alignment of text in paragraphs to justified using the Paragraph dialog box by completing the following steps:
   a. Select the entire document.
   b. Click Format and then Paragraph.
   c. At the Paragraph dialog box, click the down-pointing triangle at the right of the Alignment option box, and then click *Justified*.
   d. Click OK or press Enter.
   e. Deselect the text.
4. Save the document again with the same name (Word Ch 02, Ex 10).
5. Print and then close Word Ch 02, Ex 10.

Using Shortcut Menus

Word provides shortcut menus that display commands related to the text or item of selected text or the positioning of the insertion point. Another method for displaying the Paragraph dialog box is to use a shortcut menu. To do this, position the insertion point in the text that you want formatted and then click the *right* button on the mouse. At the shortcut menu that displays, click Paragraph. This displays the Paragraph dialog box.

Some keyboards include a Shortcut Menu key (an image of a menu) located in the bottom row of the keyboard to the right of the space bar. When pressed, this key will display a shortcut menu with the Paragraph option.

exercise 11

Changing Paragraph Alignment to Right Using a Shortcut Menu

1. At a clear document screen, turn on the display of nonprinting characters.
2. Change the alignment of text to Right by completing the following steps:
   a. Position the I-beam pointer anywhere in the document screen and then click the *right* mouse button.
   b. At the shortcut menu that displays, click Paragraph.
   c. At the Paragraph dialog box, change the setting in the Alignment option box to *Right*.
   d. Click OK or press Enter.
3. Key the first line of text shown in figure 2.15 and then press Enter. Key the remaining

lines of text. (Each time you press Enter, the formatting from the previous paragraph is carried to the next paragraph.)

4. Select the entire document and then change the font to 14-point Arial bold.
5. Save the document and name it Word Ch 02, Ex 11.
6. Turn off the display of nonprinting characters.
7. Print and then close Word Ch 02, Ex 11.

Exercise 11

McCORMACK FUNDS
5499 Fourth Street
New York, NY 10223
(212) 555-2277

Spacing before and after Paragraphs

Spacing before and after paragraphs in a document can be increased or decreased with options at the Paragraph dialog box. To increase or decrease spacing before a paragraph, display the Paragraph dialog box, select the current measurement in the Before text box (in the Spacing section), and then key a new measurement. Complete similar steps to increase or decrease spacing after paragraphs except choose the After option. You can also click the up- or down-pointing triangles to the right of the Before or After options to increase or decrease the measurement. Word uses a point measurement for spacing before and after paragraphs. Enter or display a higher point measurement to increase the spacing or enter or display a lower point measurement to decrease the spacing.

Spacing before Paragraphs

1. Open Word List.
2. Save the document with Save As and name it Word Ch 02, Ex 12.
3. Make the following changes to the document:
   a. Select the entire document and then change the font to 12-point Bookman Old Style (or a similar serif typeface).
   b. With the document still selected, change the alignment of the paragraphs to Center.
   c. Select the title *LIFETIME REAL ESTATE ACCOUNT* and then change the font to 14-point Arial bold.

d. Add 6 points of spacing before certain paragraphs by completing the following steps:

1) Select from *Investment Practices of the Account* through *Expense Deductions*.

2) With the text selected, display the Paragraph dialog box.

3) At the Paragraph dialog box, click once on the up-pointing triangle at the right side of the <u>B</u>efore option (in the Spacing section). (This changes the measurement in the text box to *6 pt*.)

4) Click OK to close the dialog box.

4. Save the document again with the same name (Word Ch 02, Ex 12).

5. Print and then close Word Ch 02, Ex 12.

Formatting with Format Painter

Format
Painter

The Standard toolbar contains a button that can be used to copy character formatting to different locations in the document. This button is called the Format Painter and displays on the Standard toolbar as a paintbrush. To use the Format Painter button, position the insertion point on a character containing the desired character formatting, click the Format Painter button, and then select text to which you want the character formatting applied. When you click the Format Painter button, the mouse I-beam pointer displays with a paintbrush attached. If you want to apply character formatting a single time, click the Format Painter button once. If, however, you want to apply the character formatting in more than one location in the document, double-click the Format Painter button. If you have double-clicked the Format Painter button, turn off the feature by clicking the Format Painter button once.

Formatting Headings with the Format Painter

1. Open Word Report 01.

2. Save the document with Save As and name it Word Ch 02, Ex 13.

3. Make the following changes to the document:

a. Select the entire document and then change the font to 12-point Garamond (or a similar serif typeface such as Bookman Old Style or New Century Schoolbook).

b. Select the title, *GRAPHICS SOFTWARE*, and then change the font to 14-point Arial bold.

c. Use the Format Painter button to center the three headings in the report and change the font for the headings to 14-point Arial bold by completing the following steps:

1) Position the insertion point next to any character in the title *GRAPHICS SOFTWARE*.
2) Double-click the Format Painter button on the Standard toolbar.
3) Select the heading *Early Painting and Drawing Programs*.
4) Select the heading *Developments in Painting and Drawing Programs*.
5) Select the heading *Painting and Drawing Programs Today*.
6) Click once on the Format Painter button on the Standard toolbar. (This turns the feature off.)
7) Deselect the heading.

4. Save the document again with the same name (Word Ch 02, Ex 13). (The formatting you apply to this document may create a page break in an undesirable location. You will learn how to control page breaks in chapter 3.)

5. Print and then close Word Ch 02, Ex 13.

Indenting Text in Paragraphs

By now you are familiar with the word wrap feature of Word, which ends lines and wraps the insertion point to the next line. To indent text from the left margin, or the left and right margins, or to create numbered items, use indent buttons on the Formatting toolbar, shortcut commands, options from the Paragraph dialog box, markers on the Ruler, or the Alignment button on the Ruler. Indent markers on the Ruler are identified in figure 2.16. Refer to figure 2.17 for methods for indenting text in a document.

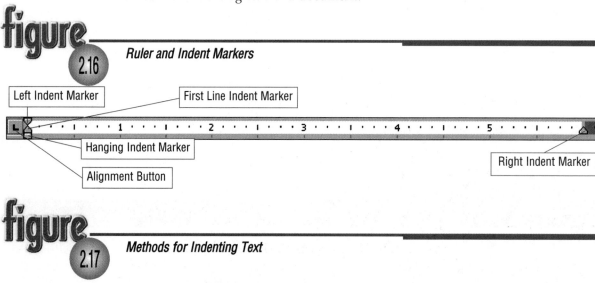

figure 2.16

Ruler and Indent Markers

Left Indent Marker
First Line Indent Marker
Hanging Indent Marker
Alignment Button
Right Indent Marker

figure 2.17

Methods for Indenting Text

Indent	Methods for Indenting
First line of paragraph	• Press the Tab key. • Display Paragraph dialog box, click down-pointing triangle to the right of the <u>S</u>pecial text box, click *First line*, and then click OK.

	• Drag the first line indent marker on the Ruler.
	• Click the Alignment button located at the left side of the Ruler until the First Line Indent button displays and then click on the Ruler at the desired location.
Text from left margin	• Click the Increase Indent button on the Formatting toolbar to increase indent or click the Decrease Indent button to decrease the indent.
	• Press Ctrl + M to increase indent or press Ctrl + Shift + M to decrease indent.
	• Display the Paragraph dialog box, key the desired indent measurement in the Left text box, and then click OK.
	• Drag the left indent marker on the Ruler.
Text from left and right margins	• Display the Paragraph dialog box, key the desired indent measurement in the Left text box and the Right text box, and then click OK.
	• Drag the left indent marker and the right indent marker on the Ruler.
All lines of text except the first (called a hanging indent)	• Press Ctrl + T. (Press Ctrl + Shift + T to remove hanging indent.)
	• Display the Paragraph dialog box, click the down-pointing triangle to the right of the Special text box, click *Hanging*, and then click OK.
	• Click the Alignment button located at the left side of the Ruler until the Hanging Indent button displays and then click on the Ruler at the desired location.

Indents can be set on the Ruler using the left indent marker, the right indent marker, first line indent marker, and hanging indent marker. A first-line indent and a hanging indent can also be set on the Ruler using the Alignment button. The Alignment button displays at the left side of the Ruler. Click this button to display the desired alignment (such as First Line Indent and Hanging Indent) and then click on the Ruler at the location where you want to set the indent.

exercise 14

Indenting the First Line of Paragraphs Using the First Line Indent Button
1. Open Word Document 03.
2. Save the document with Save As and name it Word Ch 02, Ex 14.
3. Indent the first line of each paragraph 0.25 inches by completing the following steps:
   a. Select the entire document.
   b. Click the Alignment button located at the left side of the Ruler until the First Line Indent button displays.

c. Click on the 0.25-inch mark on the Ruler.
d. Deselect the text
4. Save the document again with the same name (Word Ch 02, Ex 14).
5. Print and then close Word Ch 02, Ex 14.

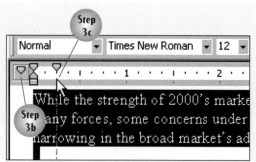

exercise 15

Indenting Text from the Left Margin

1. Open Word Ch 02, Ex 01a. (You created this document in exercise 1.)
2. Save the document with Save As and name it Word Ch 02, Ex 15.
3. Indent the second paragraph in the document to the first tab setting by completing the following steps:
   a. Position the insertion point anywhere in the second paragraph (begins with *Buses:*).
   b. Click the Increase Indent button on the Formatting toolbar.
4. Indent the third paragraph by completing the following steps:
   a. Position the insertion point anywhere in the third paragraph (begins with *System Clock:*).
   b. Click Format and then Paragraph.
   c. At the Paragraph dialog box with the Indents and Spacing tab selected, select *0"* in the Left text box, and then key **0.5**.
   d. Click OK or press Enter.

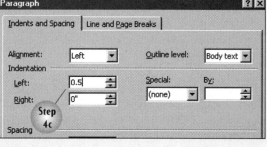

5. Indent the remaining three paragraphs in the document by completing the following steps:
   a. Make sure the Ruler is displayed. (If not, click View, expand the drop-down menu [if necessary], and then click Ruler.)
   b. Select from the fourth paragraph (begins with *Microprocessor:*) to the end of the document.
   c. Position the arrow pointer on the left indent marker on the Ruler, hold down the left mouse button, drag the marker to the 0.5-inch mark on the Ruler, and then release the mouse button.
   d. Deselect the text. (To do this with the mouse, click anywhere in the text outside the selected text.)
6. Save the document again with the same name (Word Ch 02, Ex 15).
7. Print and then close Word Ch 02, Ex 15.

Indenting Text from the Left and Right Margins

1. At a clear document screen, key the document shown in figure 2.18. Bold and center align the title as shown.
2. After keying the document, indent the second paragraph of the document from the left and right margins by completing the following steps:
   a. Make sure the Ruler is displayed.
   b. Position the insertion point anywhere in the second paragraph (begins with *I deeply care about...*).
   c. Position the arrow pointer on the left indent marker on the Ruler, hold down the left mouse button, drag the marker to the 0.5-inch mark on the Ruler, and then release the mouse button.
   d. Position the arrow pointer on the right indent marker on the Ruler, hold down the left mouse button, drag the marker to the 5.5-inch mark on the Ruler, and then release the mouse button.
3. Indent the fourth paragraph in the document from the left and right margins by completing the following steps:

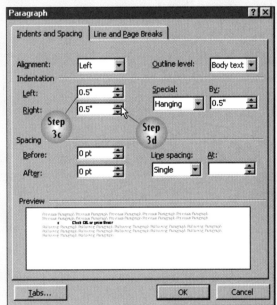

   a. Position the insertion point anywhere within the fourth paragraph (begins with *I plan to increase...*).
   b. Click Format and then Paragraph.
   c. At the Paragraph dialog box with the Indents and Spacing tab selected, select the *0"* in the Left text box, and then key **0.5**.
   d. Click the up-pointing triangle at the right of the Right text box until *0.5"* displays in the text box.
   e. Click OK or press Enter.
4. Select all the paragraphs in the document (excluding the title) and then change the paragraph alignment to justified.
5. Save the document and name it Word Ch 02, Ex 16.
6. Print and then close Word Ch 02, Ex 16.

figure
2.18   *Exercise 16*

McCORMACK FUNDS APPOINTS NEW CEO

On September 3, 2001, Kelly Millerton became Chief Executive Officer of McCormack Funds. Ms. Millerton has been with McCormack Funds for twelve years. She began her career as the Director of Marketing and has held the position of Chief Operating Officer for the past three years. When asked about her appointment, Ms. Millerton stated:

I deeply care about McCormack Funds and our shareholders and am committed to keeping the company strong and providing a wide range of high-quality investments.

Ms. Millerton's commitment to the strength of the company is apparent in the ambitious nature of her goals. When asked what specific goals she has for McCormack Funds, she stated:

I plan to increase the assets under management by the company and its subsidiaries from their present level of $41 billion to an amount over $100 billion by the year 2002. To do this, McCormack Funds has to continue to provide both topnotch investment products and superior service, but also must expand our expertise to a broader level.

exercise 17

Creating Hanging Paragraphs

1. Open Word Bibliography.
2. Save the document with Save As and name it Word Ch 02, Ex 17.
3. Create a hanging indent for the first two paragraphs by completing the following steps:
    a. Select at least a portion of the first and second paragraphs.
    b. Position the arrow pointer on the hanging indent marker on the Ruler.
    c. Hold down the left mouse button, drag the marker to the 0.5-inch mark on the Ruler, and then release the mouse button.
4. Create a hanging indent for the third paragraph by completing the following steps:
    a. Position the insertion point anywhere in the third paragraph.
    b. Click the Alignment button located at the left

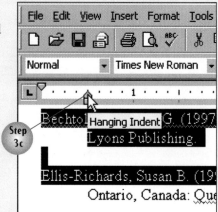

side of the Ruler until the Hanging Indent button displays.

c. Click on the 0.5-inch mark on the Ruler.

5. Create a hanging indent for the fourth paragraph by completing the following steps:
    a. Position the insertion point anywhere in the fourth paragraph.
    b. Press Ctrl + T.

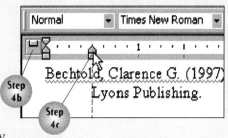

6. Create a hanging indent for the fifth paragraph by completing the following steps:
    a. Position the insertion point somewhere in the fifth paragraph.
    b. Click Format and then Paragraph.
    c. At the Paragraph dialog box with the Indents and Spacing tab selected, click the down-pointing triangle to the right of the Special text box, and then click *Hanging* at the drop-down menu.
    d. Click OK or press Enter.

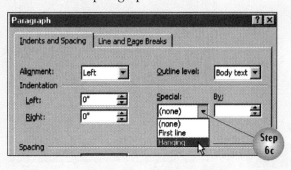

7. Select the entire document and then change to a serif typeface (other than Times New Roman) in 12-point size.
8. Save the document again with the same name (Word Ch 02, Ex 17).
9. Print and then close Word Ch 02, Ex 17.

Creating Numbered and Bulleted Paragraphs

If you key **1.**, press the space bar, key a paragraph of text, and then press Enter, Word will indent the number approximately 0.25 inches and then hang indent the text in the paragraph approximately 0.5 inches from the left margin. Additionally, *2.* will be inserted 0.25 inches from the left margin at the beginning of the next paragraph. This is part of Word's AutoFormat feature. (If this feature is not activated, you can turn it on by clicking Tools and then AutoCorrect. At the AutoCorrect dialog box, click the AutoFormat As You Type tab. Click in the Automatic numbered lists check box to insert a check mark and then click OK.) Continue keying numbered items and Word will insert the next number in the list. To turn off numbering, press the Enter key twice or click the Numbering button on the Formatting toolbar. (You can also remove all paragraph formatting from a paragraph, including automatic numbering, by pressing Ctrl + Q.)

If you press Enter twice between numbered paragraphs, the automatic number is removed. To turn it back on, key the next number in the list (and the period) followed by a space, key the paragraph of text, and then press Enter. Word will automatically indent the number and hang indent the text.

If the automatic bullet or numbering feature is on, Press Shift + Enter to insert a line break without inserting a bullet or number.

Hint

exercise 18

Creating Numbered Paragraphs

1. At a clear document screen, key the text shown in figure 2.19. When keying the numbered paragraph, complete the following steps:
   a. Key **1.** and then press the space bar.
   b. Key the paragraph of text and then press Enter. (This moves the insertion point down to the next line, inserts *2.* indented 0.25 inches from the left margin, and also indents the first paragraph of text approximately 0.5 inches from the left margin.)
   c. Continue keying the remaining text. (Remember, you do not need to key the paragraph number and period—these are automatically inserted.)
2. Save the document and name it Word Ch 02, Ex 18.
3. Print and then close Word Ch 02, Ex 18.

figure
2.19
Exercise 18

FREQUENTLY ASKED QUESTIONS

1. What influence did the Jacquard loom have on the subsequent development of computers?
2. Why is Charles Babbage known as the "father of the computer"?
3. What is a transistor, and what effect did its invention have on electronics in general and on computers in particular?
4. What are the main components of a computer, and what do they do?
5. How do computers encode information?
6. What is the motherboard of a computer, and what does it contain?
7. What are the main types of memory in a computer, and how do they differ from one another?
8. What are the major types of printers, and how do they differ from one another?

If you do not want automatic numbering in a document, turn the feature off at the AutoCorrect dialog box with the AutoFormat As You Type tab selected as shown in figure 2.20. To display this dialog box, click Tools and then AutoCorrect. At the AutoCorrect dialog box, click the AutoFormat As You Type tab. To turn off automatic numbering, remove the check mark from the *Automatic numbered lists* option.

figure
2.20

AutoCorrect Dialog Box with AutoFormat As You Type Tab Selected

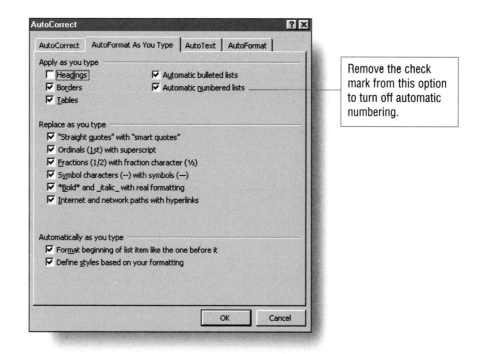

Remove the check mark from this option to turn off automatic numbering.

You can also automate the creation of numbered paragraphs with the Numbering button on the Formatting toolbar. To use this button, key the text (do not key the number) for each paragraph to be numbered, select the paragraphs to be numbered, and then click the Numbering button on the Formatting toolbar.

Numbering

In addition to automatically numbering paragraphs, Word's AutoFormat feature will create bulleted paragraphs. (If this feature is not activated, you can turn it on by clicking Tools and then AutoCorrect. At the AutoCorrect dialog box, click the AutoFormat As You Type tab. Click in the Automatic bulleted lists check box to insert a check mark, and then click OK.)

Figure 2.21 shows an example of bulleted paragraphs. Bulleted lists with hanging indents are automatically created when a paragraph begins with the symbol *, >, or -. Key one of the symbols, press the space bar, key text, and then press Enter. The AutoFormat feature inserts a bullet indented 0.25 inches from the left margin and indents the text following the bullet 0.5 inches. The type of bullet inserted depends on the type of character entered. For example, if you use the asterisk (*) symbol, a round bullet is inserted. An arrow bullet is inserted if the greater than symbol (>) is used.

figure
2.21

Bulleted Paragraphs

- This is a paragraph preceded by a bullet. A bullet is used to indicate a list of items or topics.
- This is another paragraph preceded by a bullet. Bulleted paragraphs can be easily created by keying certain symbols before the text or with the Bullets button on the Formatting toolbar.

exercise 19

Creating Bullets

1. At a clear document screen, key the text shown in figure 2.22 with the following specifications:
   a. Bold and center the title in uppercase letters as shown in figure 2.22.
   b. Key the first paragraph in the figure and then create the bulleted paragraphs by completing the following steps:
      1) With the insertion point positioned at the left margin of the first paragraph to contain a bullet, key the greater than symbol (>).
      2) Press the space bar once.
      3) Key the text of the first bulleted paragraph (the text that begins *Loads during start-up....*).
      4) Press the Enter key once and then continue keying the text after the bullets.
   c. After keying the last bulleted paragraph, press the Enter key twice (this turns off bullets), and then key the last paragraph shown in the figure.
2. Save the document and name it Word Ch 02, Ex 19.
3. Print and then close Word Ch 02, Ex 19.

figure
2.22

Exercise 19

COMPUTER OPERATING SYSTEM

The most important piece of software used on a personal computer system is its *operating system*, or OS. The OS performs a number of interdependent functions such as the following:

➢ Loads during start-up, recognizes the CPU and devices connected to it, such as keyboards, monitors, hard drives, and floppy disk drives

➢ Manages the operations of the CPU and of devices connected to it

➢ Creates a *user interface*, an environment displayed on the computer screen with which the user interacts when working at the computer

➢ Creates and updates a file system, or *directory*, for each storage device that is attached to the computer; this directory shows the location of each file on each storage device and thus enables the user to access programs and documents

➢ Supports operations performed from within other programs, such as opening and closing programs, calling resources such as fonts and sounds, and saving and printing documents

Without an OS, a computer is just a paperweight. The OS brings the system to life and gives the system its character. When a person starts a computer, instructions built into the machine's ROM look for an OS, first on any disk inserted into a floppy disk drive at start-up and then on the system's primary hard drive. When found, the OS is loaded, in part, into the computer's RAM, where it remains until the computer is turned off.

Bullets can be applied to existing text by selecting the text and then clicking the Bullets button on the Formatting toolbar. Insert bullets to selected text by clicking the Bullets button on the Formatting toolbar.

Bullets

Using the Bullets and Numbering Buttons

1. Open Word List.
2. Save the document with Save As and name it Word Ch 02, Ex 20.
3. Add bullets to text by completing the following steps:
   a. Select text from *The Real Estate Account* through *Expense Deductions*.
   b. Click the Bullets button on the Formatting toolbar.
   c. Deselect the text.
4. Save the document with the same name (Word Ch 02, Ex 20).
5. Print Word Ch 02, Ex 20.
6. With the document still open, change the bullets to numbers by completing the following steps:
   a. Select text from *The Real Estate Account* through *Expense Deductions*.
   b. Click the Numbering button on the Formatting toolbar.
   c. Deselect the text.
7. Save the document again with the same name (Word Ch 02, Ex 20).
8. Print and then close Word Ch 02, Ex 20.

In addition to the Bullets and Numbering buttons on the Formatting toolbar, you can also use options from the Bullets and Numbering dialog box to number paragraphs or insert bullets. To display this dialog box, click Format and then Bullets and Numbering. The Bullets and Numbering dialog box contains three tabs: Bulleted, Numbered, and Outline Numbered. Figure 2.23 shows the Bullets and Numbering dialog box with each tab selected. Select the Bulleted tab if you want to insert bullets before selected paragraphs and select the Numbered tab to insert numbers.

At the Bullets and Numbering dialog box with the Outline Numbered tab displayed, you can specify the type of numbering for paragraphs at the left margin, first tab setting, second tab setting, and so on. (The options that display with *Heading 1*, *Heading 2*, or *Heading 3* are not available unless the text to be numbered has been formatted with a Heading style. You will learn more about styles in chapter 5.)

figure
2.23

Bullets and Numbering Dialog Box with Each Tab Selected

Click a bulleting option to select it and then click OK or double-click the desired option.

Click a numbering option to select it and then click OK or double-click the desired option.

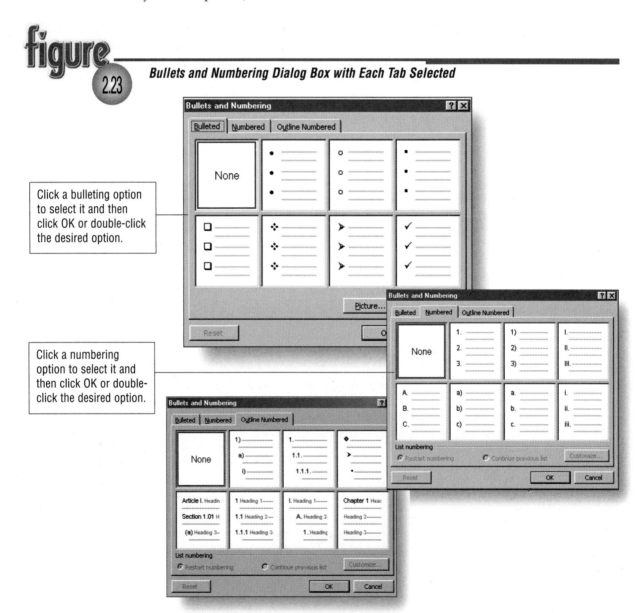

Chapter Two

exercise 21

Numbering Paragraphs Using the Bullets and Numbering Dialog Box

1. Open Word List.
2. Save the document with Save As and name it Word Ch 02, Ex 21.
3. Number the paragraphs in the document using the Bullets and Numbering dialog box by completing the following steps:
   a. Select the paragraphs in the document *excluding* the title and the blank lines below the title.
   b. Click Format and then Bullets and Numbering.
   c. At the Bullets and Numbering dialog box, click the Numbered tab.
   d. Click the third numbering option box in the top row.
   e. Click OK or press Enter.

Bullets and Numbering — Step 3c			Step 3d / ? X
Bulleted Numbered Outline Numbered			
None	1. —— 2. —— 3. ——	1) —— 2) —— 3) ——	I. —— II. —— III. ——
A. —— B. —— C. ——	a) —— b) —— c) ——	a. —— b. —— c. ——	i. —— ii. —— iii. ——

List numbering
○ Restart numbering   ○ Continue previous list   [Customize...]
[Reset]   [OK]   [Cancel]

4. Add *Annuity Contracts* between paragraphs 4 and 5 by completing the following steps:
   a. Position the insertion point immediately to the right of the last letter in *Role of Account*.
   b. Press Enter. (This moves the insertion point a double space below the previous paragraph.)
   c. Key **Annuity Contracts**.
5. Select and then delete *Investment Practices of the Account* (paragraph 2).
6. Select the entire document and then change to a sans serif typeface in 12-point size (you determine the typeface).
7. Save the document again with the same name (Word Ch 02, Ex 21).
8. Print and then close Word Ch 02, Ex 21.

exercise 22

Creating an Outline Numbered List

1. Open Word Agenda.
2. Save the document with Save As and name it Word Ch 02, Ex 22.
3. Apply outline numbering to the document by completing the following steps:
   a. Select the paragraphs in the document *excluding* the title, subtitle, and blank lines below the subtitle.
   b. Click Format and then Bullets and Numbering.

c. At the Bullets and Numbering dialog box, click the Outline Numbered tab.
d. Click the second option from the left in the top row.
e. Click OK or press Enter to close the dialog box.

4. Save the document again with the same name (Word Ch 02, Ex 22).
5. Print Word Ch 02, Ex 22.
6. With the document still open, make the following changes:
   a. Delete *Sponsors* in the Education section.
   b. Move the insertion point immediately right of the last letter in *Personal Lines* (in the Sales and Marketing section), press the Enter key, and then key **Production Report**.
7. Select the entire document and then change to a serif typeface of your choosing (other than Times New Roman).
8. Save the document again with the same name (Word Ch 02, Ex 22).
9. Print and then close Word Ch 02, Ex 22.

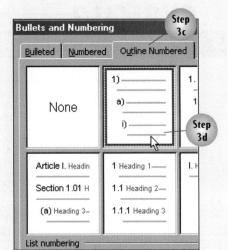

Creating Ordinals

Word's AutoFormat feature automatically formats ordinal numbers. For example, if you key **1st** and then press the space bar, Word will correct it to 1st. Word automatically changes the font size of the *st* and formats the letters as superscript text. This automatic feature will change other ordinal numbers such as 2nd, 3rd, 4th, and so on.

Creating Ordinals

1. At a clear document screen, key the text shown in figure 2.24. Let Word's AutoFormat feature insert the bullets (key an asterisk and then press the space bar before the first bulleted paragraph) and automatically change the formatting of the ordinal numbers.
2. Save the document and name it Word Ch 02, Ex 23.
3. Print and then close Word Ch 02, Ex 23.

figure 2.24   *Exercise 23*

NOTES ON CHANGING CONTRACT

After reading the contract prepared by Neimi and Gleason, I recommend the following changes:

- Delete the 1ˢᵗ paragraph in the 2ⁿᵈ section.
- Add a paragraph between the 2ⁿᵈ and 3ʳᵈ paragraphs in the 4ᵗʰ section that fully describes the responsibilities of the contract holder.
- Remove the words *and others* in the 4ᵗʰ paragraph of the 6ᵗʰ section.

Inserting Symbols

Many of the typefaces (fonts) include special symbols such as bullets, publishing symbols, and letters with special punctuation (such as É, ö, and ñ). To insert a symbol, display the Symbol dialog box with the <u>S</u>ymbols tab selected as shown in figure 2.25 by clicking <u>I</u>nsert and then <u>S</u>ymbol. At the Symbol dialog box, double-click the desired symbol, and then click Close; or click the desired symbol, click <u>I</u>nsert, and then click Close.

figure 2.25   *Symbol Dialog Box with <u>S</u>ymbols Tab Selected*

Click this down-pointing triangle to display a list of fonts. Choose the font that contains the desired symbol.

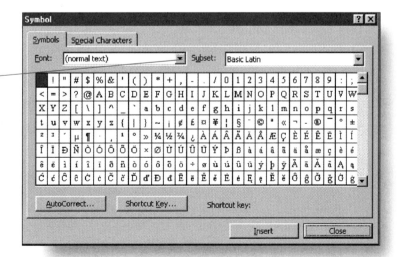

Changing the Font for Symbols

At the Symbol dialog box with the Symbols tab selected, you can change the font with the Font option. When you change the font, different symbols display in the dialog box. To change the font, display the Symbol dialog box with the Symbols tab selected, click the down-pointing triangle to the right of the Font text box, and then click the desired font at the drop-down list.

exercise 24

Creating Special Symbols

1. At a clear document screen, create the document shown in figure 2.26 by completing the following steps:
   a. Key the text in the document to the point where the ® symbol is to be inserted and then complete the following steps:
      1) Click Insert and then Symbol.
      2) At the Symbol dialog box with the Symbols tab selected, click the down-pointing triangle at the right side of the Font text box, and then click *(normal text)* at the drop-down list. (You may need to scroll up to see this option. Skip this step if *(normal text)* is already selected.)
      3) Double-click the ® symbol (approximately the third symbol from the *right* in the fourth row).
      4) Click the Close button.
   b. Key the text in the memo to the point where the ó is to be inserted and then complete the following steps:
      1) Click Insert and then Symbol.
      2) At the Symbol dialog box with the Symbols tab selected, make sure Font displays as *(normal text)*.
      3) Double-click the ó symbol (approximately the eleventh symbol from the left in the seventh row).
      4) Click the Close button.
   c. Key the text in the memo to the point where the ñ is to be inserted and then complete the following steps:
      1) Click Insert and then Symbol.
      2) At the Symbol dialog box, make sure the Font is *(normal text)*, and then double-click the ñ symbol (approximately the ninth symbol from the left in the seventh row).
      3) Click the Close button.

4) Repeat these steps when you key the other occurrences of Viña.

d. Key the text in the memo to the point where the first bullet (☎) is to be inserted and then complete the following steps:

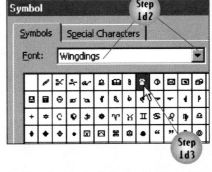

1) Click Insert and then Symbol.
2) At the Symbol dialog box, change the font to *Wingdings*. To do this, click the down-pointing triangle at the right side of the Font text box, click the down scroll triangle until *Wingdings* displays, and then click it.
3) Double-click the ☎ symbol (approximately the ninth symbol from the left in the top row).
4) Click the Close button.

e. Press the Tab key, key the text following the first bullet, and then press Enter. (If the automatic bulleting feature is on, Word inserts another bullet.)

f. Key the remaining text following the bullets. (The bullets will be automatically inserted.)

g. After keying the text following the last bullet, press Enter twice. (This turns off the automatic bullets.)

h. Key the remainder of the text in the document.

2. Save the document and name it Word Ch 02, Ex 24.
3. Print and then close Word Ch 02, Ex 24.

figure 2.26 *Exercise 24*

ENHANCED SERVICES

New Options in Retirement

"You can now change the source of your annuity income from any MIRA® account to any other MIRA account," states Concepción Viña, Fund Manager for retirement accounts. In addition, Viña states that retirees receiving annuity income through the graduated payment method can now switch to the standard payment method.

Automated Telephone Service Improvements

Access to your accumulation is now available 24 hours a day, 7 days a week through the Automated Telephone Service. You can use this service to:

☎   Find out your last premium paid

☎ Set up future accumulation transfers
☎ Make multiple transfers in the same call
☎ Get a confirmation statement automatically

Faster Cash Withdrawals

You can get cash from a supplemental retirement annuity or a preferred personal annuity. "Often, this cash can be available the next business day," states Viña.

Changing Line Spacing

By default, the word wrap feature single spaces text. There may be occasions when you want to change to another spacing, such as line and a half or double. Line spacing can be changed with shortcut commands or options from the Paragraph dialog box. Figure 2.27 illustrates the shortcut commands to change line spacing.

2.27 *Line Spacing Shortcut Commands*

Press	To change line spacing to
Ctrl + 1*	single spacing
Ctrl + 2	double spacing
Ctrl + 5	1.5 line spacing

(*Use the numbers on the keyboard, not the numeric keypad.)

Changing Line Spacing

1. Open Word Document 02.
2. Save the document with Save As and name it Word Ch 02, Ex 25.
3. Change the line spacing for all paragraphs to 1.5 line spacing by completing the following steps:
   a. Select the entire document.

    b.   Press Ctrl + 5.
4. Change the alignment of all paragraphs to justified.
5. Save the document again with the same name (Word Ch 02, Ex 25).
6. Print and then close Word Ch 02, Ex 25.

Line spacing can also be changed at the Paragraph dialog box. At the Paragraph dialog box, you can change line spacing with the Line spacing option or the At option. If you click the down-pointing triangle to the right of the Line spacing text box at the Paragraph dialog box, a drop-down list displays with a variety of spacing options. For example, to change the line spacing to double you would click *Double* at the drop-down list. You can key a specific line spacing measurement in the At text box at the Paragraph dialog box. For example, to change the line spacing to double, key **2** in the At text box.

Increase the ease with which a person can read text in a document by slightly increasing the line spacing.

Changing Line Spacing at the Paragraph Dialog Box

1. Open Word Document 03.
2. Save the document with Save As and name it Word Ch 02, Ex 26.
3. Change the line spacing to double using the Paragraph dialog box by completing the following steps:

    a.   Select the entire document.
    b.   Click Format and then Paragraph.
    c.   At the Paragraph dialog box, make sure the Indents and Spacing tab is selected, and then click the down-pointing triangle to the right of the Line spacing text box (this box contains the word *Single*).
    d.   From the drop-down list that displays, click *Double*.
    e.   Click OK or press Enter to close the dialog box.
    f.   Click outside the selected text to deselect it.

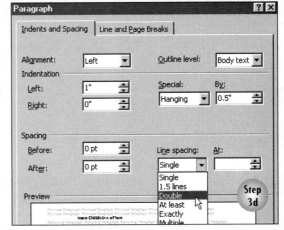

4. Save the document again with the same name (Word Ch 02, Ex 26).
5. Print Word Ch 02, Ex 26.
6. With Word Ch 02, Ex 26 still open, change the line spacing to 1.3 by completing the following steps:

    a.   Select the entire document.
    b.   Click Format and then Paragraph.
    c.   At the Paragraph dialog box, make sure the Indents and Spacing tab is selected.

d. Click in the <u>A</u>t text box and then key **1.3**.
e. Click OK or press Enter to close the dialog box.
f. Click outside the text to deselect it.
7. Save the document again with the same name (Word Ch 02, Ex 26).
8. Print and then close Word Ch 02, Ex 26.

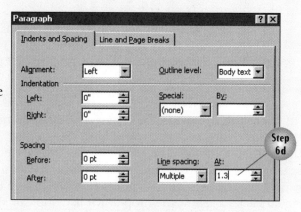

Step 6d

Repeating the Last Action

Another method for repeating the last action is pressing F4.

Hint

Use the Format Painter feature to copy character formatting to different locations in a document. If you want to apply other types of formatting, such as paragraph formatting, to a document, consider using the Repeat command. To use the Repeat command, apply the desired formatting, move the insertion point to the next location where you want the formatting applied, click <u>E</u>dit, expand the drop-down menu, and then click <u>R</u>epeat; or press Ctrl + Y.

exercise 27

Formatting Using the Repeat Command

1. Open Word Report 01.
2. Save the document with Save As and name it Word Ch 02, Ex 27.
3. Make the following changes to the document:
    a. Select the entire document.
    b. Change the line spacing to single.
    c. Deselect the text.
    d. Bold the headings *Early Painting and Drawing Programs, Developments in Painting and Drawing Programs,* and *Painting and Drawing Programs Today.*
4. Apply paragraph formatting and repeat the formatting by completing the following steps:
    a. Position the insertion point anywhere in the heading *Early Painting and Drawing Programs.*
    b. Click F<u>o</u>rmat and then <u>P</u>aragraph.
    c. At the Paragraph dialog box, click twice on the up-pointing triangle at the right side of the <u>B</u>efore option (in the Spacing section). (This changes the measurement in the text box to *12 pt.*)
    d. Click once on the up-pointing triangle at the right side of the Af<u>t</u>er option. (This changes the measurement in the text box to *6 pt.*)

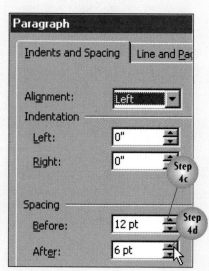

Step 4c

Step 4d

e. Click OK to close the Paragraph dialog box.

f. Repeat the paragraph formatting for the second heading by completing the following steps:

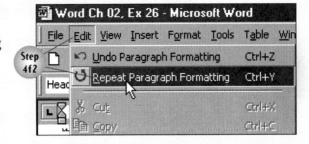

1) Position the insertion point anywhere in the heading *Developments in Painting and Drawing Programs*.

2) Click Edit, expand the drop-down menu, and then click Repeat Paragraph Formatting.

g. Repeat the paragraph formatting for the third heading by positioning the insertion point anywhere in the heading *Painting and Drawing Programs Today* and then pressing Ctrl + Y.

5. Move the insertion point to any character in the title *GRAPHICS SOFTWARE* and then insert 12 points of space after the paragraph.

6. Save the document again with the same name (Word Ch 02, Ex 27).

7. Print and then close Word Ch 02, Ex 27.

Applying Borders and Shading

Every paragraph you create in Word contains an invisible frame. A border that appears around this frame can be applied to a paragraph. A border can be added to specific sides of the paragraph or to all sides. The type of border line and thickness of the line can be customized. In addition, you can add shading and fill within the border.

When a border is added to a paragraph of text, the border expands and contracts as text is inserted or deleted from the paragraph. You can create a border around a single paragraph or a border around selected paragraphs.

Creating a Border with the Border Button

One method for creating a border is to use options from the Border button on the Formatting toolbar. The name of the button changes depending on the border choice that was previously selected at the button drop-down palette. When Word is first opened, the button name displays as Outside Border. Click the down-pointing triangle at the right side of the button and a palette of border choices displays as shown in figure 2.28.

figure

2.28 *Border Palette*

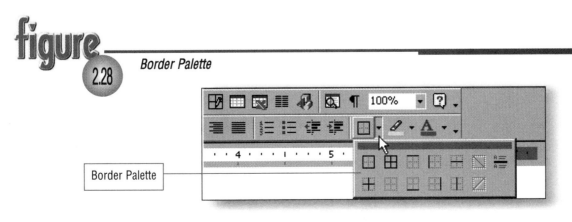

Border Palette

Click the option that will insert the desired border. For example, to insert a border at the bottom of the paragraph, click the Bottom Border option (third option from the left in the bottom row). Clicking an option will add the border to the paragraph where the insertion point is located. To add a border to more than one paragraph, select the paragraphs first and then click the desired option.

Adding Borders to Paragraphs of Text

1. Open Word Document 03.
2. Save the document with Save As and name it Word Ch 02, Ex 28.
3. Create a border around the first paragraph by completing the following steps:
   a. Position the insertion point anywhere in the first paragraph.
   b. Position the mouse pointer on the Border button on the Formatting toolbar and wait for the ScreenTip to display. Make sure the ScreenTip displays as Outside Border and then click the button. (If this is not the name for the button, click the down-pointing triangle at the right side of the button and then click the Outside Border option [first option in the first row].)

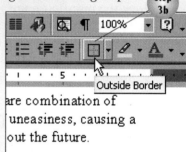

4. Complete steps similar to those in 3 to add a border to the second paragraph.
5. Complete steps similar to those in 3 to add a border to the third paragraph.
6. Save the document again with the same name (Word Ch 02, Ex 28).
7. Print Word Ch 02, Ex 28.
8. With the document still open, remove the borders by completing the following steps:
   a. Select the three paragraphs in the document. (You do not have to select all the text in the first and last paragraphs, just a portion.)
   b. Click the down-pointing triangle at the right side of the Border button on the Formatting toolbar and then click the No Border option (second option from the left in the bottom row). (This removes the borders from the three paragraphs.)
   c. Deselect the text.

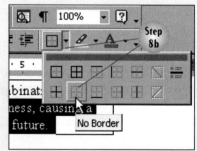

9. Add a border around and between the paragraphs by completing the following steps:
   a. Select from the middle of the first paragraph to somewhere in the middle of the third paragraph.
   b. Click the down-pointing triangle at the right side of the Border button and then click the All Borders option (second option from the left in the top row).
   c. Deselect the text.

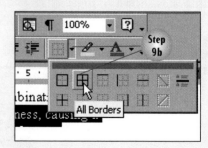

10. Save the document again with the same name (Word Ch 02, Ex 28).
11. Print and then close Word Ch 02, Ex 28.

Adding Borders and Shading

As you learned in the previous section, borders can be added to a paragraph or selected paragraphs with options from the Border button on the Formatting toolbar. If you want to customize the line creating the border or add shading, use options from the Borders and Shading dialog box. To display this dialog box, shown in figure 2.29, click Format and then Borders and Shading.

figure
2.29

Borders and Shading Dialog Box with the Borders Tab Selected

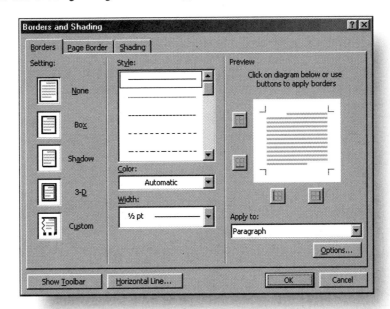

The buttons in the Setting section of the dialog box contain a visual display of line options. For example, click the Box button to insert a border around the paragraph (or selected paragraphs). Click the 3-D button to insert a border with a shadow, creating a three-dimensional look.

With the options in the Style list box, you can change the line style by clicking the desired style in the list box. The default line color is black. This can be changed to a different color by clicking the down-pointing triangle at the right side of the Color text box and then clicking the desired color at the drop-down list. If the desired color is not visible, scroll down the list. The default line width is ½ point. The line width can be changed by clicking the down-pointing triangle at the right side of the Width text box and then clicking the desired width at the pop-up list.

The diagram in the Preview section offers another method for inserting border lines. Specify where you want a border line to appear by clicking the desired location on the diagram. For example, if you want to insert a border at the bottom of the paragraph (or selected paragraphs), click the bottom portion of the diagram in the Preview section. This adds a border line to the diagram. You can also click a button in the Preview section that displays the desired border. For example, to add a border at the right side of the paragraph (or selected paragraphs), click the button that displays at the bottom of the diagram at the right side.

The Apply to option has a setting of *Paragraph*. This specifies to what the border and shading will apply. Click the Options button and options display for setting the desired distance between the edge of the border and the text.

Adding a Customized Border to a Document

1. Open Word Notice 01.
2. Save the document with Save As and name it Word Ch 02, Ex 29.
3. Make the following changes to the document:
   a. With the insertion point at the beginning of the document, press the Enter key twice.
   b. Select the entire document and then change the font to 18-point Mistral bold and the text color to Dark Red. (If Mistral is not available, choose a fancy, decorative typeface.)
   c. With the entire document still selected, add a dark blue shadow border by completing the following steps:
      1) Click Format and then Borders and Shading.
      2) At the Borders and Shading dialog box with the Borders tab selected, click the Shadow button.
      3) Click the down-pointing triangle at the right side of the Width text box and then click the *6 pt* line at the pop-up list.
      4) Click the down-pointing triangle at the right side of the Color text box and then click *Dark Blue* at the drop-down list.
      5) Click OK or press Enter.
4. Deselect the text.
5. Save the document again with the same name (Word Ch 02, Ex 29).
6. Print and then close Word Ch 02, Ex 29.

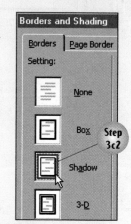

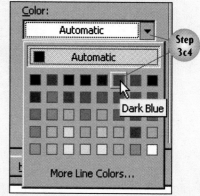

Adding Shading

With choices from the Borders and Shading dialog box with the Shading tab selected, shown in figure 2.30, you can add shading to the border around text. Fill color choices display in the upper left corner of the dialog box. To add a fill, click the desired color in this section. If you want to add a pattern, click the down-pointing triangle at the right side of the Style text box and then click the desired pattern at the drop-down list. If a pattern is added inside a border, the color of the pattern can be changed with the Color option. Click the down-pointing triangle at the right side of the Color text box and then click the desired color at the drop-down list.

The Preview area of the Borders and Shading dialog box with the Shading tab selected displays how the border shading and/or pattern will display.

figure
2.30

Borders and Shading Dialog Box with Shading Tab Selected

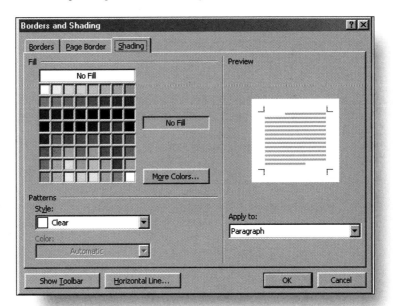

exercise 30

Adding Borders and Shading to Paragraphs of Text

1. Open Word Document 03.
2. Save the document with Save As and name it Word Ch 02, Ex 30.
3. Create a border around all the paragraphs in the document that is 3 points thick and contains 25% shading by completing the following steps:

   a. Select all paragraphs in the document.
   b. Click Format and then Borders and Shading.
   c. At the Borders and Shading dialog box with the Borders tab selected, click the Box button located at the left side of the dialog box.
   d. Click the down-pointing triangle at the right side of the Width text box and then click *3 pt* at the pop-up list.
   e. Make sure that *Automatic* is selected in the Color text box. If not, click the down-pointing triangle at the right side of the Color text box and then click *Automatic* at the drop-down list. (This option is located at the beginning of the list.)
   f. Click the Shading tab.
   g. Click the light turquoise color in the Fill section of the dialog box.
   h. Click the down-pointing triangle at the right side of the Style list box and then click *5%* at the drop-down list.
   i. Click OK to close the dialog box.

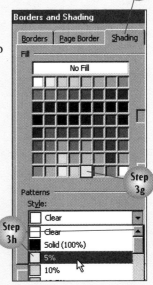

Step 3f

Step 3g

Step 3h

4. Deselect the text.
5. Save the document again with the same name (Word Ch 02, Ex 30).
6. Print and then close Word Ch 02, Ex 30.

Using Help

Word's Help feature is an on-screen reference manual containing information about all Word features and commands. Word's Help feature is similar to the Windows Help and the Help features in Excel, PowerPoint, and Access. Get help using the Office Assistant or turn off the Assistant and get help from the Microsoft Word Help dialog box.

Getting Help from the Office Assistant

Press F1 to display the yellow box above the Office Assistant.

The Office Assistant will provide information about specific topics. To get help using the Office Assistant, click the Office Assistant or click Help and then Microsoft Word Help. This causes a box to display above the Office Assistant as shown in figure 2.31. (If the Office Assistant is not visible, click the Microsoft Word Help button on the Standard toolbar.)

figure
2.31

Office Assistant Help Box

Microsoft
Word Help

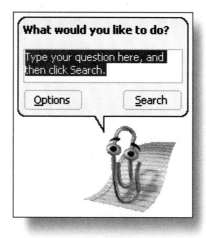

When the help box displays above the Office Assistant, the text *Type your question here, and then click Search* displays in the text box below the question *What would you like to do?* This text is already selected, so key a question about a specific Word feature, and then click the Search button. The Office Assistant will display a list of related topics. At this list, click the desired topic and information will display in a Microsoft Word Help dialog box. After reading the information, click the Close button located in the upper right corner of the dialog box (contains an X).

Show

Forward

The Microsoft Word Help dialog box contains a toolbar with the buttons shown in figure 2.32. Click the Show button to expand the dialog box and display three tabs—Contents, Answer Wizard, and Index. If you move to various help items, click the

Back button to return to the previous window. The Forward button is dimmed until the Back button has been clicked. When the Forward button is active, click the button to move forward to a help item. Send the Help information to the printer by clicking the Print button. Click the Options button and a drop-down menu displays with many of the same features as the buttons. For example, there is a Show <u>T</u>abs option that will expand the dialog box, and <u>B</u>ack and <u>F</u>orward options that do the same thing as the Back and Forward buttons. Additional options include <u>H</u>ome, <u>S</u>top, <u>R</u>efresh, <u>I</u>nternet Options, and <u>P</u>rint.

Back

Print

Options

Microsoft Word Help Dialog Box Toolbar

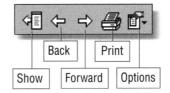

exercise 31

Using the Office Assistant to Learn How to Automatically Insert Arrows

1. At a clear document screen, use the Office Assistant to read information about automatically inserting arrows by completing the following steps:

   a. Make sure the Office Assistant is visible. If it is not, click <u>H</u>elp and then Show the <u>O</u>ffice Assistant.
   b. Click the Office Assistant.
   c. At the yellow box that displays above the Office Assistant, key **How do I automatically insert an arrow in a document?**
   d. Click the <u>S</u>earch button.
   e. At the list that displays in the yellow box, click *Insert symbols and special characters*. (When you position the arrow pointer on the topic, the pointer turns into a hand.)
   f. At the Microsoft Word Help dialog box, click *Automatically insert an arrow, face, or other symbol* in the *What do you want to do?* section.
   g. Read the information about automatically inserting arrows and faces and then print the information by clicking the Print button on the dialog box toolbar, and then clicking OK at the Print dialog box.
   h. Click on *turn on AutoCorrect* that displays in blue and underlined in the Microsoft Word Help dialog box. (This displays information about turning on AutoCorrect.)

    i. After reading the information on AutoCorrect, click the Back button on the dialog box toolbar.
    j. Click the Close button located in the upper right corner of the dialog box (contains an X).
2. If necessary, remove the Office Assistant yellow box by clicking in the document screen outside the yellow box.

Using the Expanded Microsoft Word Help Dialog Box

The Microsoft Word Help dialog box toolbar contains a Show button. Click the Show button and the dialog box expands as shown in figure 2.33. Three tabs display in the expanded dialog box—Contents, Answer Wizard, and Index.

figure

2.33

Expanded Microsoft Word Help Dialog Box

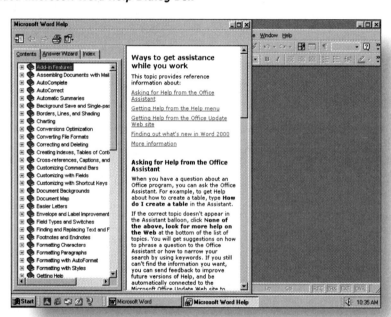

Select the Contents tab at the expanded Microsoft Word Help dialog box and a variety of categories display preceded by an icon of a closed book. Most of these categories contain additional categories. To display these additional categories, double-click a category. This causes the *closed book* icon to change to an *open book* icon and the additional categories to display below the selected category.

Click the Answer Wizard tab and a text box displays preceded by the question "What would you like to do?" Key your question in the text box and then click the Search button. This displays a list of categories in the Select topic to display list box. Click a topic in the list box, and information about the topic displays at the right side of the dialog box.

With the Index tab selected, enter a keyword in the Type keywords list box, and then click the Search button. Topics related to the keyword display in the

Choose a topic list box. Click a topic in this list box and information about that topic displays at the right side of the dialog box. You can also scroll through the Or choose keywords list box to display the desired topic. The topics in this list box are alphabetized.

Hiding/Turning Off the Office Assistant

To hide the Office Assistant, click Help and then Hide the Office Assistant. Redisplay the Office Assistant by clicking the Microsoft Word Help button on the Standard toolbar or by clicking Help and then Show the Office Assistant.

The Office Assistant can also be turned off. To do this, click the Office Assistant and then click the Options button that displays in the yellow box. At the Office Assistant dialog box that displays as shown in figure 2.34, click the Use the Office Assistant option to remove the check mark, and then click OK.

figure

2.34   *Office Assistant Dialog Box*

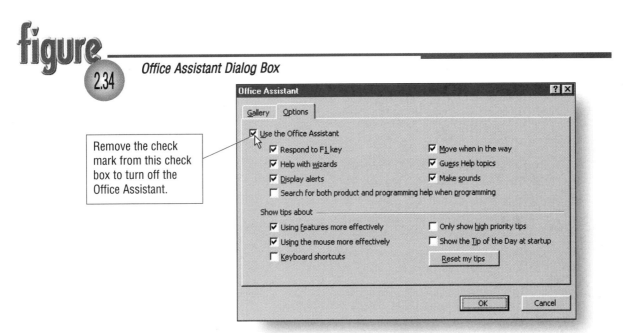

Remove the check mark from this check box to turn off the Office Assistant.

Turning Off the Office Assistant and Using Help

1. At a clear document screen, turn off the Office Assistant by completing the following steps:
   a. Make sure the Office Assistant is visible.
   b. Click the Office Assistant.
   c. Click the Options button in the yellow box.
   d. At the Office Assistant dialog box, click the Use the Office Assistant option (this removes the check mark).
   e. Click OK to close the dialog box.

2. Use the Help feature with the <u>C</u>ontents tab selected to find information on formatting characters by completing the following steps:
   a. Click <u>H</u>elp on the Menu bar and then click Microsoft Word <u>H</u>elp.
   b. At the Microsoft Word Help dialog box, click the <u>C</u>ontents tab. (Skip this step if the <u>C</u>ontents tab is already selected.)
   c. Double-click *Formatting* in the <u>C</u>ontents list box. (This displays subcategories below *Formatting*.)
   d. Double-click *Formatting Characters* in the <u>C</u>ontents list box. (This displays subcategories below *Formatting Characters*.)
   e. Click a subcategory topic that interests you and then read the information about the subcategory that displays at the right side of the dialog box.
   f. Click several other subcategories that interest you and read the information about each subcategory.

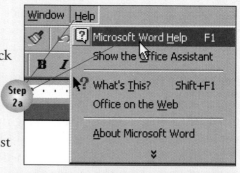

3. Use the Help feature with the <u>A</u>nswer Wizard tab selected to search for information on indenting paragraphs by completing the following steps:
   a. Click the <u>A</u>nswer Wizard tab.
   b. Key **How do I indent text in paragraphs?** in the <u>W</u>hat would you like to do? text box and then click the <u>S</u>earch button.
   c. At the list of topics that displays in the Select <u>t</u>opic to display list box, click *Indent paragraphs*.
   d. Look at the topics that display at the right side of the dialog box and then click a topic that interests you.
   e. After reading information about the topic, click the Back button on the dialog box toolbar.
   f. Click the topic *About paragraph alignment* in the Select <u>t</u>opic to display list box.
   g. Read the information that displays at the right side of the dialog box.

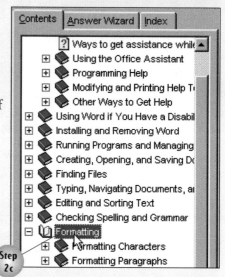

4. Use the Help feature with the <u>I</u>ndex tab selected to search for information on line spacing by completing the following steps:
   a. Click the <u>I</u>ndex tab.

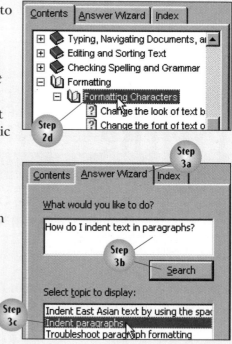

b. Key **line space** in the Type keywords text box and then click the Search button.

c. Click the topic *About line spacing* that displays in the Choose a topic list box.

d. Read the information that displays at the right side of the dialog box.

5. Click the Close button that displays in the upper right corner of the dialog box (contains an X) to close the Microsoft Word Help dialog box.

6. Turn on the display of the Office Assistant by clicking Help and then Show the Office Assistant.

7. Click in the document screen to remove the yellow box above the Office Assistant.

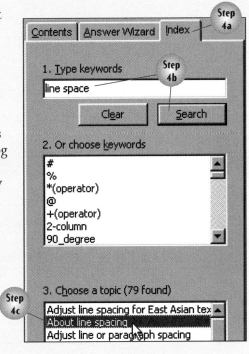

Using Additional Help Features

Click the Help option on the Menu bar, expand the drop-down menu, and a variety of help features are available. You have already learned about the Microsoft Word Help option and the Hide the Office Assistant (or Show the Office Assistant) option. The drop-down menu contains a number of other options.

Choose the What's This option to point to a specific item and display information about that item. For example, to display information about a button on a toolbar, click Help and then What's This. This causes the mouse pointer to display with a question mark attached. Click a button on a toolbar and the name of the button along with information about the button displays in a yellow box. You can also use this option to display information on what formatting has been applied to specific text. To do this, click Help and then What's This. Click specific text in the document and a gray box displays containing information on paragraph formatting and font formatting.

Click Office on the Web from the Help drop-down menu and you are connected to the Microsoft Office Update web site. From this site, you can get answers to the most frequently asked questions about Word. You can also get up-to-date tips, templates, clip art, and Help files.

If you have been a WordPerfect user and would like information on how to carry out a command in Word, click Help, expand the drop-down menu, and then click WordPerfect Help.

Word contains a self-repairing feature that will find and fix errors in Word. To run this feature, click Help, expand the drop-down menu, and then click Detect and Repair. This displays the Detect and Repair dialog box with a message telling you that during the process you may be asked to provide the installation source

Click Help, About Microsoft Word, and then click the System Info button to display information about your computer such as your processor type, operating system, memory, and hard disk space.

and to exit or open applications. Click the Start button to begin the detect and repair process.

The last option at the Help drop-down menu, About Microsoft Word, displays information such as the release date, license number, and system information. You can also display information about Microsoft's technical support such as a listing of support telephone numbers.

exercise 33

Using What's This and Displaying System Information

1. At a clear document screen, use the What's This feature by completing the following steps:
   a. Click Help and then What's This. (This causes the mouse pointer to display with a question mark attached.)
   b. Click the Bold button on the Formatting toolbar. (This causes a yellow box to display with information on the Bold button.)
   c. Click in the document screen outside the yellow box. (This removes the box.)
   d. Click Help and then What's This.
   e. Click the Select Browse Object button (displays towards the bottom of the vertical scroll bar). (This causes a yellow box to display with information on the Select Browse Object.)
   f. Click in the document screen outside the yellow box. (This removes the box.)
2. Read information about Word by completing the following steps:
   a. Click Help and then About Microsoft Word.
   b. At the About Microsoft Word dialog box, click the System Info button that displays in the lower right corner of the dialog box.
   c. At the Microsoft System Information dialog box, read the information, then exit the dialog box by clicking File (on the dialog box menu bar) and then Exit.
   d. At the About Microsoft Word dialog box, click the Tech Support button that displays in the lower right corner of the dialog box.
   e. Read the information that displays in the Microsoft Word Help dialog box and then click the Close button that displays in the upper right corner of the dialog box (contains an X).
   f. At the About Microsoft Word dialog box, click OK.

Using ScreenTips

ScreenTips

Word includes a ScreenTips feature that is available in every dialog box and displays as a button containing a question mark. This button displays in the upper right corner of dialog boxes. To use the ScreenTips feature, click the ScreenTips button, and then click an item in the dialog box. Word will display an explanation about the particular item.

exercise 34

Using ScreenTips

1. At a clear document screen, display information about specific items in the Paragraph dialog box by completing the following steps:
   a. Display the Paragraph dialog box.
   b. Click the ScreenTips button. (This button is located in the upper right corner of the dialog box and contains a question mark.)
   c. Move the arrow pointer (displays with a question mark attached) to the Alignment option and then click the left mouse button. (This displays a yellow box containing information on alignment.)
   d. Click the ScreenTips button and then click the Line spacing option.
   e. Close the Paragraph dialog box.
2. Display information about specific options (you choose the options) in the Font dialog box by completing steps similar to those in step 1.
3. Close the Font dialog box.

chapter summary

▶ The appearance of a document in the document screen and how it looks when printed is called the format.

▶ Text can be bolded, italicized, and underlined with buttons on the Formatting toolbar or with shortcut commands. Do this as text is keyed or apply the features later by selecting the text then choosing the desired feature.

▶ You can remove all character formatting from selected text by pressing Ctrl + spacebar.

▶ A font consists of three parts: typeface, type style, and type size.

▶ A typeface is a set of characters with a common design and shape. Typefaces are either monospaced, allotting the same amount of horizontal space to each character, or proportional, allotting a varying amount of space for each character.

▶ A type style is a variation of style within a certain typeface. There are four main kinds of type styles: normal, bold, italic, and bold italic.

▶ Type size is measured in pitch or point size. Pitch is the number of characters per inch—the higher the pitch, the smaller the characters. Point size is a vertical measurement—the higher the point size, the larger the characters.

▶ Change the font at the Font dialog box or use the Font button on the Formatting toolbar. Click the Font Size button on the Formatting toolbar to change the font size or click the Font Color button to change the text color.

▶ The Effects section of the Font dialog box contains a variety of options that can be used to create different character styles such as Strikethrough, Double strikethrough, Superscript, Subscript, Shadow, Outline, Emboss, Engrave, Small caps, All caps, and Hidden.

- Adjust character spacing and turn on kerning with options at the Font dialog box with the Character Spacing tab selected.
- Animate text in the screen with options at the Font dialog box with the Text Effects tab selected.
- To turn on or off the display of nonprinting characters such as paragraph marks, click the Show/Hide ¶ button on the Standard toolbar.
- In Word, a paragraph is any amount of text followed by a paragraph mark (a stroke of the Enter key). Word inserts into the paragraph mark any paragraph formatting that is turned on before the text is keyed.
- To remove paragraph formatting from text, delete the paragraph mark or remove all paragraph formatting by pressing Ctrl + Q.
- By default, paragraphs in a Word document are aligned at the left margin and ragged at the right margin. This default alignment can be changed with buttons on the Formatting toolbar, at the Paragraph dialog box, or with shortcut commands for left, center, right, or fully aligned.
- Increase or decrease space before or after a paragraph or selected paragraphs with the Before and After options at the Paragraph dialog box.
- Use the Format Painter button (displays on the Standard toolbar as a paintbrush) to copy character formatting already applied to text to different locations in the document.
- The first line of text in a paragraph can be indented by pressing the Tab key, with an option from the Paragraph dialog box, or with the first-line indent marker on the Ruler.
- All lines of text in a paragraph can be indented to a tab setting or to a specific measurement from the left margin with an option from the Paragraph dialog box or with the left indent marker on the Ruler.
- Text in paragraphs can be indented from the left and the right margins with options at the Paragraph dialog box or with the left and right indent markers on the Ruler.
- In a hanging paragraph, the first line of the paragraph remains at the left margin, while the remaining lines are indented to the first tab setting. Hanging paragraphs can be created with a shortcut command, with options from the Paragraph dialog box, with the hanging indent marker on the Ruler, or with the Hanging Indent button.
- Word's AutoFormat feature will automatically format numbered and bulleted lists as well as create ordinal numbers.
- Bulleted lists with hanging indents are automatically created when a paragraph begins with *, >, or -. The type of bullet inserted depends on the type of character entered.
- Paragraphs can also be numbered with the Numbering button on the Formatting toolbar and bullets can be inserted before paragraphs with the Bullets button. Numbers or bullets can also be inserted with options at the Bullets and Numbering dialog box.
- Many of the typefaces (fonts) include special symbols such as bullets and publishing symbols. Insert a symbol in a document at the Symbols dialog box.
- Line spacing can be changed with shortcut commands or options from the Paragraph dialog box.
- Repeat the last action by clicking Edit, expanding the drop-down menu, and then clicking Repeat; or by pressing Ctrl + Y.
- Every paragraph created in Word contains an invisible frame. A border that appears around this frame can be added to a paragraph.
- Use options from the Border button on the Formatting toolbar to insert borders around a paragraph or selected paragraphs.

- Use options at the Borders and Shading dialog box with the Borders tab selected to add a customized border to a paragraph or selected paragraphs.
- Use options at the Borders and Shading dialog box with the Shading tab selected to add shading or a pattern to a paragraph of text or selected paragraphs.
- Word's Help feature is an on-screen reference manual containing information about all Word features and commands.
- To get help from the Office Assistant, click the Assistant, key a question, and then click the Search button.
- Some Help information displays in the Microsoft Word Help dialog box. This dialog box contains a toolbar with the following buttons—Show, Forward, Back, Print, and Options.
- The expanded Microsoft Word Help dialog box displays with three tabs—Contents, Answer Wizard, and Index.
- Hide the Office Assistant by clicking Help and then Hide the Office Assistant. Redisplay the Office Assistant by clicking the Microsoft Word Help button on the Standard toolbar or by clicking Help and then Show the Office Assistant.
- Turn off the Office Assistant for the entire Word session by clicking the Office Assistant and then clicking the Options button. At the Office Assistant dialog box, click the Use the Office Assistant option to remove the check mark, and then click OK.
- Additional options from the Help drop-down menu include: What's This, Office on the Web, WordPerfect Help, Detect and Repair, and About Microsoft Word.
- Use the ScreenTips button in any dialog box to read information about specific items in the dialog box.

commands review

	Mouse	Keyboard
Uppercase function		Caps Lock Key
Bold	Click Bold button on Formatting toolbar	Ctrl + B
Italics	Click Italic button on Formatting toolbar	Ctrl + I
Underline	Click Underline button on Formatting toolbar	Ctrl + U
Remove all character formatting from selected text		Ctrl + space bar
Display Font dialog box	Format, Font	Format, Font
Turn on/off display of nonprinting characters	Click Show/Hide ¶ button on Standard toolbar	
Align text at the left margin	Click Align Left button on Formatting toolbar	Ctrl + L
Align text between margins	Click Center button on Formatting toolbar	Ctrl + E
Align text at the right margin	Click Align Right button on Formatting toolbar	Ctrl + R
Align text at the left and right margins	Click Justify button on Formatting toolbar	Ctrl + J
Return all paragraph formatting to normal		Ctrl + Q

Paragraph dialog box	F<u>o</u>rmat, <u>P</u>aragraph	
Format Painter	Click Format Painter button on Standard toolbar	
Indent first line of a paragraph	At the Paragraph dialog box, click <u>S</u>pecial, then *First line*; or drag first-line indent marker on Ruler to desired measurement; or change to the First Line Indent button and then click on Ruler at desired measurement	Tab key
Indent left margin of all lines of text in a paragraph or selected paragraphs	At the Paragraph dialog box, key indent measurement in the <u>L</u>eft text box; or drag left indent marker on Ruler to desired measurement; or click Increase Indent button on Formatting toolbar	Ctrl + M
Decrease indent of text in a paragraph	Decrease number in the <u>L</u>eft text box at the Paragraph dialog box; or drag left indent marker on Ruler to desired measurement; or click Decrease Indent button on Formatting toolbar	Ctrl + Shift + M
Indent left and right margins of paragraph	At the Paragraph dialog box, key indent measurement in the <u>L</u>eft and <u>R</u>ight text boxes; or drag left indent marker on Ruler to desired measurement, and then drag right indent marker to desired measurement	
Create a hanging paragraph	At the Paragraph dialog box, key the desired indent measurement in the <u>L</u>eft text box, click <u>S</u>pecial, then *Hanging*; or drag hanging indent marker on Ruler to desired measurement; or change to the Hanging Indent button and then click on Ruler at desired measurement	Ctrl + T
Create numbered/bulleted paragraphs	Select paragraphs, click Numbering or Bullets button on Formatting toolbar; or display the Bullets and Numbering dialog box	
Bullets and Numbering dialog box	F<u>o</u>rmat, <u>B</u>ullets and <u>N</u>umbering	F<u>o</u>rmat, <u>B</u>ullets and <u>N</u>umbering
Display Symbol dialog box	<u>I</u>nsert, <u>S</u>ymbol	<u>I</u>nsert, <u>S</u>ymbol
Change to single spacing		Ctrl + 1
Change to double spacing		Ctrl + 2
Change to 1.5 line spacing		Ctrl + 5
Change line spacing at Paragraph dialog box	Click the up/down pointing triangle to the right of <u>A</u>t box; key measurement in <u>A</u>t box; or click Li<u>n</u>e Spacing	
Repeat the last action	<u>E</u>dit, expand drop-down menu, <u>R</u>epeat	Ctrl + Y
Display Borders and Shading dialog box	Format, <u>B</u>orders and Shading	F<u>o</u>rmat, <u>B</u>orders and Shading
Microsoft Word Help dialog box	Click Office Assistant, key question, click <u>S</u>earch button, and then click desired topic; or turn off Office Assistant and then click <u>H</u>elp and then Microsoft Word <u>H</u>elp	
Office Assistant dialog box	Click Office Assistant and then click <u>O</u>ptions button	

thinking offline

Matching: In the space provided at the left, indicate the correct letter or letters that match each description.

- Ⓐ Arial
- Ⓑ Century Schoolbook
- Ⓒ Garamond
- Ⓓ italic
- Ⓔ font
- Ⓕ pitch
- Ⓖ point
- Ⓗ proportional
- Ⓘ sans serif
- Ⓙ serif
- Ⓚ subscript
- Ⓛ super script
- Ⓜ Times New Roman
- Ⓝ type size
- Ⓞ type style
- Ⓟ typeface

_____ 1. This kind of typeface does not have a small line at the end of each character stroke.

_____ 2. This term refers to a particular typeface in a specific style and size.

_____ 3. This is a set of characters with a common design and shape.

_____ 4. This term refers to text that is lowered slightly below the regular line of text.

_____ 5. With this type of measurement, the higher the number, the larger the characters.

_____ 6. These are examples of different typefaces.

_____ 7. This term refers to text that is raised slightly above the regular line of text.

Completion: In the space provided at the right, indicate the correct term, symbol, or command.

1. To use the Format Painter to apply formatting to several locations in a document, do this to the Format Painter button. _____

2. Change the font of selected text with this button on the Formatting toolbar. _____

3. This is the shortcut command to bold text. _____

4. This is the shortcut command to underline text. _____

5. This keyboard command removes all character formatting from selected text. _____

6. Word inserts paragraph formatting into this mark. _____

7. To turn on or off the display of nonprinting characters, click this button on the Standard toolbar. _____

8. This is the Word default paragraph alignment. _____

9. You can return all paragraph formatting to normal with this keyboard command. _____

10. In this kind of paragraph, the first line remains at the left margin and the remaining lines are indented to the first tab setting. _____

11. Insert spacing before or after paragraphs with options at this dialog box. _____

12. The number 2nd is referred to as this.

13. Automate the creation of bulleted paragraphs with the Bullets button on this toolbar.

14. At the Paragraph dialog box, change line spacing with the Line spacing option or this.

15. This is the shortcut command to change line spacing to 2.

16. This is the shortcut command to repeat the last action.

17. The Border button is located on this toolbar.

18. Click this option on the Menu bar and then click Borders and Shading to display the Borders and Shading dialog box.

19. Click this button, located in the Setting section of the Borders and Shading dialog box, to add a border that has a three-dimensional look to paragraphs.

20. Display the Office Assistant dialog box by clicking the Office Assistant and then clicking this button.

21. Click this button on the Microsoft Word Help dialog box toolbar to expand the dialog box.

22. Click this tab at the expanded Microsoft Word Help dialog box to display a variety of categories preceded by an icon of a closed book.

23. In the space provided below, list the steps you would complete to insert the symbol ✂ into a document. (*Hint: The* ✂ *symbol is located in the* Wingdings *font.*)

_____

_____

24. In the space provided below, list the steps you would complete to change the line spacing to 1.25.

_____

_____

working hands-on

Assessment 1

1. At a clear document screen, key the document shown in figure 2.35. Bold, italicize, and underline the text as shown.
2. After keying the document, make the following changes:
   a. Change the line spacing to 1.5 for the two paragraphs in the body of the document.
   b. Change the paragraph alignment to justified for the two paragraphs in the body of the document.

3. Save the document and name it Word Ch 02, SA 01.
4. Print and then close Word Ch 02, SA 01.

Assessment 1

RATES REDUCED

As a result of anticipated lower claims costs and other expected cost savings, premiums for LongLife insurance policies have been reduced, **effective February 1, 2001**. The new, lower premiums will apply to both existing and new policies. Policy benefits will remain the same.

The actual rate of reduction will vary depending on the policyholder's age and plan option. If you are between the ages of 45 and 64 and have a policy with a *periodic* inflation option, your premium reduction will be between <u>13 and 32 percent</u>! Premiums of a colleague in the same age bracket with an *automatic* inflation option will be reduced by between <u>5 and 29 percent</u>! Reductions may be higher or lower at other ages.

Assessment 2

1. Open Word Document 03.
2. Save the document with Save As and name it Word Ch 02, SA 02.
3. Make the following changes:
   a. Add a title to the document by completing the following steps:
      1) With the insertion point positioned on the first character in the document, press the Enter key twice.
      2) Press the up arrow key twice. (This moves the insertion point to the beginning blank line.)
      3) Click the Center button on the Formatting toolbar and then click the Bold button.
      4) Key **ECONOMIC GAINS**.
   b. Select and then bold the following text in the document:
      1) *25%* (located in the second paragraph)
      2) *5000* (located in the second paragraph)
      3) *economic slowdown* (located in the third paragraph)
   c. Select and then italicize the following text in the document:
      1) *strength* (located in the first paragraph)
      2) *second half of 2000* (located in the second paragraph)
      3) *third-quarter 2000 earnings* (located in the third paragraph)
   d. Select the entire document and then compress text horizontally by 97 percent of the original horizontal spacing.
4. Save the document again with the same name (Word Ch 02, SA 02).
5. Print and then close Word Ch 02, SA 02.

Assessment 3

1. Open Word Report 03.
2. Save the document with Save As and name it Word Ch 02, SA 03.
3. Make the following changes to the document:
   a. Select the entire document and then change the font to 12-point Garamond (or a similar serif typeface).
   b. Select the title *NETWORK TOPOLOGIES* and then change the font to 18-point Tahoma bold (or a similar sans serif typeface).
   c. Use Format Painter to center and change the formatting to 18-point Tahoma bold for the three headings *Linear Bus Networks*, *Star Networks*, and *Ring Networks*.
4. Save the document again with the same name (Word Ch 02, SA 03).
5. Print and then close Word Ch 02, SA 03.

Assessment 4

1. Open Word Document 05.
2. Save the document with Save As and name it Word Ch 02, SA 04.
3. Make the following changes to the document:
   a. Select the entire document and then change the font to 12-point Century Schoolbook (or a similar serif typeface).
   b. Select the title *ARE YOU PREPARING FOR RETIREMENT?* and then change the font to 14-point Century Schoolbook bold (or the serif typeface you chose in step 3a).
   c. Select from the second paragraph (that begins *Living longer than ever,...*) to the end of the document and then add the following:
      1) Add paragraph numbering.
      2) Add 3 points of spacing before paragraphs. (To do this, select the current measurement in the Before text box at the Paragraph dialog box, and then key **3**.)
   d. Move the insertion point to the end of the document, and then add the following text:

      The Growth Account® is a registered trademark of McCormack Funds.

      Edited by Anya Volochëk

4. Save the document again with the same name (Word Ch 02, SA 04).
5. Print and then close Word Ch 02, SA 04.

Assessment 5

1. At a clear document screen, key the document shown in figure 2.36.
2. After keying the text in the document, make the following changes the document:
   a. Select the entire document and then change the font to 13-point Bookman Old Style.
   b. Select the title and then change the font to 18-point Bookman Old Style bold.
   c. Select the heading *Choices and Changes* and then change the font to 16-point Bookman Old Style bold.
3. Save the document and name it Word Ch 02, SA 05.
4. Print and then close Word Ch 02, SA 05.

GENERAL MATTERS

Choices and Changes

As long as your annuity fund certificate permits, you can choose or change any of the following:

► an annuity starting date;
► an income option;
► a transfer;
► a method of payment for death benefits;
► a date when the commuted value of an annuity becomes payable;
► an annuity partner, beneficiary, or other person named to receive payments;
► a cash withdrawal or other distribution; and
► a repurchase.

You have to make your choices or changes via a written notice satisfactory to us and received at our home offices. Transfers between accounts can currently be made by telephone. You can change the terms of a transfer, cash withdrawal, repurchase, or other cash distribution only before they are scheduled to take place.

Assessment 6

1. At a clear document screen, key the document shown in figure 2.37.
2. After keying the text in the document, make the following changes to the document:
   a. Select the paragraphs of text in the body of the document (all paragraphs except the title and the blank line below the title).
   b. With the paragraphs of text selected, change the paragraph alignment to justified.
   c. Select the paragraphs that begin with bolded words and then indent the text 0.5 inches from the left margin.
3. Save the document and name it Word Ch 02, SA 06.
4. Print Word Ch 02, SA 06.
5. With the document still open, select the paragraphs that begin with the bolded words, and then indent 0.5 inches from the right margin (the left margin should already be indented 0.5 inches).
6. Save the document again with the same name (Word Ch 02, SA 06).
7. Print and then close Word Ch 02, SA 06.

figure

2.37

Assessment 6

TOTAL RETURN CHARTS

The total return charts for the annuity accounts represent past performance. The value of your accumulation may rise or fall. The units you own may be worth more or less than their original price upon redemption. The following terms are used in the total return charts:

Average annual total return: The average rate that an investment grew each year over a specified period of time.

Annual total return: The rate at which an investment grew during a given twelve-month period ending December 31. In some cases, only part-year results are available if, for example, an account began operations during a year, or if a current year is not yet completed.

Accumulation units: The value of a single unit as it stood on March 31. The total return charts show how the value of accumulation units has fluctuated over time.

Accumulative rates: The compounded total growth of an investment over an extended period of time (not just a year).

As you read the total return charts, remember that past performance is no guarantee of future results. Historical information can, however, help you decide which accounts may meet your risk-tolerance and growth expectations.

Assessment 7

1. At a clear document screen, create the document shown in figure 2.38 with the following specifications:
   a. Change the line spacing to double.
   b. Center, bold, and italicize text as indicated.
   c. Create hanging paragraphs as indicated.
   d. Change the paragraph alignment for all paragraphs to justified.
2. Save the document and name it Word Ch 02, SA 07.
3. Print and then close Word Ch 02, SA 07.

figure
2.38   *Assessment 7*

BIBLIOGRAPHY

Amaral, Howard G. (1998). *Economic Growth in America*, 2nd edition (pp. 103-112).

Denver, CO: Goodwin Publishing Group.

Cuevas, Roxanne A. (1999). *Establishing a Stock Portfolio* (pp. 18-35). Los Angeles, CA:

North Ridge, Inc.

Forsyth, Stuart M. (1999). *International Investing* (pp. 23-31). San Francisco, CA:

Roosevelt & Carson Publishing.

Gudroe, Andrea G. (2000). *Global Economics*, 3rd edition (pp. 67-72). Phoenix, AZ:

Desert Palm Press.

Assessment 8

1. At a clear document screen, create the document shown in figure 2.39.
2. After keying the document, insert numbering before each paragraph in the document (except the title and the blank line below the title).
3. Save the document and name it Word Ch 02, SA 08.
4. Print Word Ch 02, SA 08.
5. Make the following changes to the document:
   a. Delete *External fund raising*.
   b. Change *Internal fund raising* so it reads *Fund raising*.
   c. Add *Corporate* between the fourth and fifth paragraphs.
6. Save the document again with the same name (Word Ch 02, SA 08).
7. Print and then close Word Ch 02, SA 08.

figure
2.39 *Assessment 8*

COMMUNITY CONNECTIONS PROJECT

Mission statement
Project planning
Education
Government
Private business
External fund raising
Internal fund raising
Environmental issues
Recommendations
Evaluation

Assessment 9

1. Open Word Document 02.
2. Save the document with Save As and name it Word Ch 02, SA 09.
3. Make the following changes to the document:
   a. Select the entire document, change to a serif typeface other than Times New Roman, and then deselect the text.
   b. Select the heading *QWERTY KEYBOARD* and the paragraph that follows it, and then add a double line border of your choosing and light green shading.
   c. Select the heading *DVORAK KEYBOARD* and the paragraph that follows it, and apply the same border and shading as in step 3b. *(Hint: Use the Repeat command.)*
4. Save the document again with the same name (Word Ch 02, SA 09).
5. Print and then close Word Ch 02, SA 09.

Assessment 10

1. Use the Office Assistant to help you find information about AutoFormat. (Key the question **What changes will AutoFormat make?** in the text box below the question *What would you like to do?* At the list that displays in the yellow box, click *Format a document automatically*.) Make sure you learn about what AutoFormat automatically formats in a document and also learn about the dialog box where you can make changes to AutoFormat. Print this information.
2. After reading about and experimenting with the AutoFormat feature, write a description of the feature that includes the following:
   a. Create a title for the description that is keyed in all capital letters and is centered and bolded.
   b. List the steps to display the dialog box where you can make changes to AutoFormat.
   c. List three changes that Word can make automatically.
   d. Consider adding enhancements to the document such as bold and/or italics, and bullets and/or numbering.
3. Save the completed description and name it Word Ch 02, SA 10.
4. Print and then close Word Ch 02, SA 10.

Chapter 03

Enhancing the Visual Display and Clarity of Documents

3

PERFORMANCE OBJECTIVES

Upon successful completion of chapter 3, you will be able to:

- Set, clear, and move tabs on the Ruler and at the Tabs dialog box.
- Change the document view.
- Change the top, bottom, left, and right margins in a document.
- Insert a hard page break in a document.
- Preview a document.
- Vertically align text in a document.
- Insert optional and nonbreaking hyphens in text.
- Format text into newspaper columns.
- Complete a spelling check on text in a document.
- Complete a grammar check on text in a document.
- Add words to and delete words from the AutoCorrect dialog box.
- Display synonyms and antonyms for specific words using the Thesaurus.

Formatting can be applied to a document such as setting tabs, changing the document margins, and inserting page breaks. In this chapter, you will learn to apply these types of formatting along with formatting text into newspaper columns, completing a spelling check on text in a document, improving the grammar of text in a document by completing a grammar check, and using the Thesaurus to find synonyms and related words for a specific word.

Manipulating Tabs

When you work with a document, Word offers a variety of default settings such as margins and line spacing. One of these defaults is a left tab set every 0.5 inches. In some situations, these default tabs are appropriate; in others, you may want to create your own. Two methods exist for setting tabs. Tabs can be set on the Ruler or at the Tabs dialog box.

Manipulating Tabs on the Ruler

Use the Ruler to set, move, and delete tabs. By default, the Ruler displays below the Formatting Toolbar as shown in figure 3.1. If the Ruler is not displayed, turn on the display by clicking <u>V</u>iew, expanding the drop-down menu, and then clicking <u>R</u>uler.

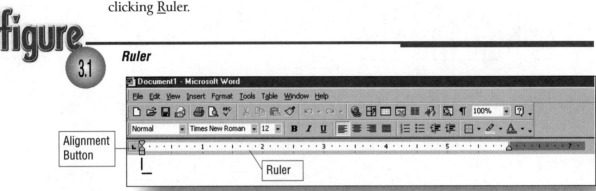

figure

3.1

Ruler

The Ruler displays left tabs set every 0.5 inches. These default tabs are indicated by tiny vertical lines along the bottom of the Ruler. With a left tab, text aligns at the left edge of the tab. The other types of tabs that can be set on the Ruler are center, right, decimal, and bar.

Alignment

The small button at the left side of the Ruler is called the Alignment button. (You used this button in chapter 2 to indent the first line of text in a paragraph and to create a hanging indent.) Each time you click the Alignment button, a different tab or paragraph alignment symbol displays. Figure 3.2 shows the tab alignment symbols and what type of tab each will set.

figure

3.2

Tab Alignment Symbols

L	=	left tab
⊥	=	center tab
⅃	=	right tab
⅂·	=	decimal tab
❘	=	bar tab

The columns displayed in figure 3.3 show text aligned at different tabs. The text in the first column in figure 3.3 was keyed at a left tab. The second column of text was keyed at a center tab, the third column at a right tab, and the fourth column at a decimal tab. (Refer to figure 3.7 for an example of a bar tab.)

figure 3.3 — Examples of Left, Center, Right, and Decimal Tabs

Valencia	Washington	Olympia	22.908
Yang	Oregon	Salem	1,655.05555
Nicholson	California	Sacramento	623.5

Setting Tabs

To set a left tab on the Ruler, make sure the left alignment symbol **L** displays in the Alignment button. Position the arrow pointer just below the tick mark (the marks on the Ruler) where you want the tab symbol to appear and then click the left mouse button. When you set a tab on the Ruler, any default tabs to the left are automatically deleted by Word. Set a center, right, decimal, or bar tab on the Ruler in a similar manner.

Before setting a tab on the Ruler, click the Alignment button at the left side of the Ruler until the appropriate tab symbol is displayed, and then set the tab. If you change the tab symbol in the Alignment button, the symbol remains until you change it again or you exit Word. If you exit then reenter Word, the tab symbol returns to the default of left tab.

When setting tabs on the Ruler, a dotted guideline displays to help align tabs.

(Before completing computer exercises, delete the Chapter 02 *folder on your disk. Next, copy the* Chapter 03 *folder from th CD that accompanies this textbook to your disk and then make* Chapter 03 *the active folder.)*

Setting Left Tabs on the Ruler

1. At a clear document screen, key the document shown in figure 3.4 by completing the following steps:
   a. Key the heading **TORRES ENTERPRISES**, centered and bolded.
   b. Press Enter twice. (Be sure to return the paragraph alignment back to left and turn off bold.)
   c. Set left tabs at the 1.25-inch mark and the 3.5-inch mark on the Ruler by completing the following steps:
      1) Click the Show/Hide ¶ button on the Standard toolbar to turn on the display of nonprinting characters.
      2) Make sure the Ruler is displayed.
      3) Make sure the left tab symbol displays in the Alignment button at the left side of the Ruler.
      4) Position the arrow pointer below the 1.25-inch mark on the Ruler and then click the left mouse button.

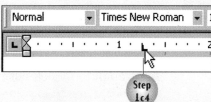

Step 1c4

5) Position the arrow pointer below the 3.5-inch tick mark on the Ruler and then click the left mouse button.

d. Key the text in columns as shown in figure 3.4. Press the Tab key before keying each column entry. (Make sure you press Tab before keying the text in the first column as well as the second column.)

e. Click the Show/Hide ¶ button on the Standard toolbar to turn off the display of nonprinting characters.

2. Save the document and name it Word Ch 03, Ex 01.

3. Print and then close Word Ch 03, Ex 01.

figure

3.4   *Exercise 1*

TORRES ENTERPRISES

Michele Yabe	Manager
Jason Edmondson	Assistant Manager
Kimberly Pascual	Supervisor
Eduardo Ross	Training Specialist
Troy Zimmerman	Administrative Assistant

When you press the Enter key, the insertion point is moved down to the next line and a paragraph mark is inserted in the document. Paragraph formatting is stored in this paragraph mark. For example, if you make changes to tab settings, these changes are inserted in the paragraph mark. In some situations, you may want to start a new line but not a new paragraph. To do this, press Shift + Enter. Word inserts a line break symbol (visible when nonprinting characters have been turned on) and moves the insertion point to the next line.

If you change tab settings and then create columns of text using the New Line command, Shift + Enter, the tab formatting is stored in the paragraph mark at the end of the columns. If you want to make changes to the tab settings for text in the columns, position the insertion point anywhere within the columns (all the text in the columns does not have to be selected), and then make the changes.

If you want to set a tab at a specific measurement on the Ruler, hold down the Alt key, position the arrow pointer at the desired position, and then hold down the left mouse button. This displays two measurements on the Ruler. The first measurement displays the location of the arrow pointer on the Ruler in relation to the left edge of the page. The second measurement is the distance from the location of the arrow pointer on the Ruler to the right margin. With the left mouse button held down, position the tab symbol at the desired location, and then release the mouse button and the Alt key.

Position the insertion point in any paragraph of text and tabs for the paragraph appear on the Ruler.

exercise 2

Setting Left, Center, and Right Tabs on the Ruler

1. At a clear document screen, key the document shown in figure 3.5 by completing the following steps:
   a. Key the heading **WORKSHOPS** centered and bolded.
   b. Press Enter three times. (Be sure to return the paragraph alignment back to left and turn off bold.)
   c. Set a left tab at the 0.5-inch mark, a center tab at the 3.5-inch mark, and a right tab at the 5.5-inch mark by completing the following steps:
      1) Click the Show/Hide ¶ button on the Standard toolbar to turn on the display of nonprinting characters.
      2) Make sure the Ruler is displayed.
      3) Make sure the left tab symbol displays in the Alignment button at the left side of the Ruler.
      4) Position the arrow pointer below the 0.5-inch tick mark on the Ruler. Hold down the Alt key and then the left mouse button. Make sure the first measurement on the Ruler

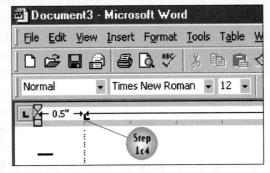

      displays as 0.5" and then release the mouse button and the Alt key.
      5) Position the arrow pointer on the Alignment button at the left side of the Ruler and then click the left mouse button until the center tab symbol ⊥ displays.
      6) Position the arrow pointer below the 3.5-inch tick mark on the Ruler. Hold down the Alt key and then the left mouse button. Make sure the first measurement on the

      Ruler displays as 3.5" and then release the mouse button and the Alt key.
      7) Position the arrow pointer on the Alignment button at the left side of the Ruler and then click the left mouse button until the right tab symbol ⌐ displays.
      8) Position the arrow pointer below the 5.5-inch tick mark on the Ruler. Hold down the Alt key and then the left mouse button. Make

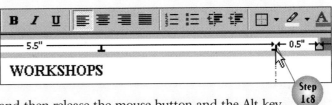

      sure the first measurement on the Ruler displays as 5.5" and then release the mouse button and the Alt key.
   d. Key the text in columns as shown in figure 3.5. Press the Tab key before keying each column entry and press Shift + Enter twice after keying the text in the third column. (This moves the insertion point a double space below the text and inserts the New Line command.)
2. Save the document and name it Word Ch 03, Ex 02.
3. Print and then close Word Ch 03, Ex 02.

figure
3.5
Exercise 2

WORKSHOPS

Quality Management	February 5	$150
Staff Development	February 12	130
Streamlining Production	March 1	115
Managing Records	March 27	90

Moving Tabs

After a tab has been set on the Ruler, it can be moved to a new location. To move a single tab, position the arrow pointer on the tab symbol on the Ruler, hold down the left mouse button, drag the symbol to the new location on the Ruler, and then release the mouse button.

Deleting Tabs

To delete a tab from the Ruler, position the arrow pointer on the tab symbol you want deleted, hold down the left mouse button, drag the symbol down into the document screen, and then release the mouse button.

exercise 3

Moving and Deleting Tabs on the Ruler

1. Open Word Tab 01.
2. Save the document with Save As and name it Word Ch 03, Ex 03.
3. Move the tab settings so the columns are more balanced by completing the following steps:
   a. Select only the text in columns (do not include any blank lines above the columns of text).
   b. Position the arrow pointer on the left tab symbol at the 0.5-inch mark, hold down the left mouse button, drag the left tab symbol to the 1.25-inch mark on the Ruler, and then release the mouse button. (*Hint: Use the Alt key to help you precisely position the tab symbol.*)
   c. Position the arrow pointer on the decimal tab symbol at the 3.5-inch mark, hold down the left mouse button, drag the decimal tab symbol into the document screen, and then release the mouse button. (This deletes the tab and merges the second column of text with the first column.)

   d. Click the Alignment button at the left side of the Ruler until the right tab symbol displays.

   e. Position the arrow pointer on the 4.75-inch mark on the Ruler and then click the left mouse button. (*Hint: Use the Alt key to help you precisely position the tab symbol.*)

   f. Deselect the text.

4. Save the document again with the same name (Word Ch 03, Ex 03).

5. Print and then close Word Ch 03, Ex 03.

Manipulating Tabs at the Tabs Dialog Box

Use the Tabs dialog box shown in figure 3.6 to set tabs at a specific measurement. You can also use the Tabs dialog box to set tabs with preceding leaders and clear one tab or all tabs. To display the Tabs dialog box, click Format, expand the drop-down menu, and then click Tabs.

figure

3.6   *Tabs Dialog Box*

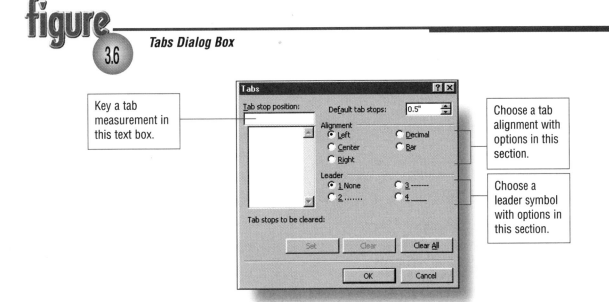

Key a tab measurement in this text box.

Choose a tab alignment with options in this section.

Choose a leader symbol with options in this section.

Clearing Tabs

At the Tabs dialog box, you can clear an individual tab or all tabs. To clear all tabs, click the Clear All button. To clear an individual tab, specify the tab position, and then click the Clear button.

Setting Tabs

At the Tabs dialog box, you can set a left, right, center, or decimal tab as well as a bar. (For an example of a bar tab, refer to figure 3.7.) You can also set a left, right, center, or decimal tab with preceding leaders. To change the type of tab at the

Tabs dialog box, display the dialog box, and then click the desired tab in the Alignment section. Key the desired measurement for the tab in the Tab stop position text box.

Setting Left Tabs and a Bar Tab at the Tabs Dialog Box

1. At a clear document screen, key the document shown in figure 3.7 by completing the following steps:
   a. Key the title **TRAINING DATES** bolded and centered, press the Enter key twice, and then change the paragraph alignment back to Left.
   b. Display the Tabs dialog box and then set left tabs and a bar tab by completing the following steps:
      1) Click Format, expand the drop-down menu, and then click Tabs.
      2) Make sure Left is selected in the Alignment section of the dialog box. (If not, click Left.)
      3) Key **1.75** in the Tab stop position text box. (The insertion point should automatically be positioned in the Tab stop position text box. If not, click in the text box.)
      4) Click the Set button.
      5) Key **3.5** in the Tab stop position text box and then click the Set button.
      6) Key **3** in the Tab stop position text box, click Bar in the Alignment section, and then click the Set button.
      7) Click OK to close the Tabs dialog box.
   c. Key the text in columns as shown in figure 3.7. Press the Tab key before keying each column entry. (The vertical line between columns will appear automatically. You need only key the dates. Do not press Enter after keying the date *February 27*.)
2. Save the document and name it Word Ch 03, Ex 04.
3. Print and then close Word Ch 03, Ex 04.

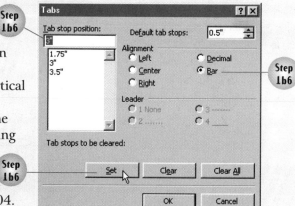

Exercise 4

TRAINING DATES

January 9	February 6
January 17	February 12
January 22	February 15
January 30	February 27

Setting Leader Tabs

The four types of tabs can also be set with leaders. Leaders are useful in a table of contents or other material where you want to direct the reader's eyes across the page. Figure 3.8 shows an example of leaders. Leaders can be periods (.), hyphens (-), or underlines (_). To add leaders to a tab, click the type of leader desired in the Leader section of the Tabs dialog box.

Set a tab with leaders at the Tabs dialog box.

Setting a Left Tab and a Right Tab with Dot Leaders

1. At a clear document screen, create the document shown in figure 3.8 by completing the following steps:
   a. Change the font to 12-point Tahoma. (If your printer does not support Tahoma, choose a similar sans serif typeface such as Univers.)
   b. Center and bold the title *TABLE OF CONTENTS*.
   c. Press Enter three times. (Be sure to return the alignment of the paragraph back to left and turn off bold.)
   d. Change the line spacing to 2.
   e. Set a left tab and a right tab with dot leaders by completing the following steps:
      1) Click Format and then Tabs.
      2) At the Tabs dialog box, make sure Left is selected in the Alignment section of the dialog box. (If not, click Left.)
      3) Make sure the insertion point is positioned in the Tab stop position text box, key **1**, and then click the Set button.
      4) Key **5** in the Tab stop position text box.
      5) Click Right in the Alignment section of the dialog box.
      6) Click 2....... in the Leader section of the dialog box and then click the Set button.
      7) Click OK or press Enter.
   f. Key the text in columns as shown in figure 3.8. Press the Tab key before keying each column entry.

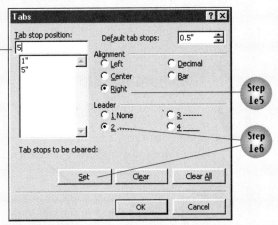

2. Save the document and name it Word Ch 03, Ex 05.
3. Print and then close Word Ch 03, Ex 05.

figure

3.8

Exercise 5

TABLE OF CONTENTS

> View the positioning of elements on a page in Print Preview.

> The insertion point remains where it was in the preceding view when you change to a different view

Preparing Multiple-Paged Documents

Word assumes that you are using standard-sized paper, which is 8.5 inches wide and 11 inches long. By default, a Word document contains 1-inch top and bottom margins and 1.25-inch left and right margins. With the default top and bottom margins of 1 inch, a total of 9 inches of text will print on a page (1 inch for the top margin, 9 inches of printed text, and then 1 inch for the bottom margin). As you create long documents, you will notice that when the insertion point nears 9.8 inches (or approximately Line 45 [this number may vary]) a page break is inserted in the document. The page break is inserted at the next line (at the 10-inch measurement). The line below the page break is the beginning of the next page.

Changing the View

The display of a page break will change depending on the view. At the Normal view, a page break displays as a row of dots. Change to the Print Layout view and a page break displays as an actual break in the page. Figure 3.9 shows an example of a page break in a document in the Normal view and another in the Print Layout view.

figure

3.9

Page Break in Normal View

> The pixelization problem in painting programs was resolved in two ways. First, as the
>
> RAM and storage capacities of personal computers grew, raster image-processing programs were
>
> created that could handle images with a greater number of dots per inch. Today's high-end raster
>
> image programs can handle full-screen images at 2400 dpi or higher in 16.7 million different
>
> colors. Another solution to the pixelization problem was the development of antialiasing,
>
> whereby pixels along the edge of an image are progressively lightened or darkened to produce

Page break
Normal vie

Page Break in Print Layout View

The pixelization problem in painting programs was resolved in two ways. First, as the RAM and storage capacities of personal computers grew, raster image-processing programs were created that could handle images with a greater number of dots per inch. Today's high-end raster

image programs can handle full-screen images at 2400 dpi or higher in 16.7 million different colors. Another solution to the pixelization problem was the development of antialiasing, whereby pixels along the edge of an image are progressively lightened or darkened to produce

Page break in Print Layout view

To change to the Print Layout view, click <u>V</u>iew and then <u>P</u>rint Layout or click the Print Layout View button at the left side of the horizontal scroll bar. (The Print Layout View button is the third button from the left side of the screen before the horizontal scroll bar.) To change back to the Normal view, click <u>V</u>iew and then <u>N</u>ormal or click the Normal View button at the left side of the horizontal scroll bar. (The Normal View button is the first button from the left.)

Print Layout
View

Normal View

When you are working in a document containing more than one page of text, the Status bar displays the page where the insertion point is positioned and will also display the current page followed by the total number of pages in a document. For example, if the insertion point is positioned somewhere on page 3 of a 12-page document (with one section), the left side of the Status bar will display *Page 3 Sec 1 3/12*. The *3/12* indicates that the insertion point is positioned on page 3 in a document containing 12 pages.

Changing Margins

The default margin settings are displayed in the Page Setup dialog box shown in figure 3.10. To display the Page Setup dialog box, click <u>F</u>ile and then Page Set<u>u</u>p or double-click a gray area at the top of the Ruler. At the Page Setup dialog box, make sure the <u>M</u>argins tab is selected.

To change margins in a document, display the Page Setup dialog box, select the current measurement in the <u>T</u>op, <u>B</u>ottom, Le<u>f</u>t, or Ri<u>g</u>ht text boxes, key the new measurement for the margin, and then click OK or press Enter. As you make changes to the margin measurements at the Page Setup dialog box, the sample page in the Preview box illustrates the adjustments to the margins. You can also click the up- and down-pointing triangles after each margin option to increase or decrease the margin measurement.

figure
3.10

Page Setup Dialog Box with Margins Tab Selected

> Notice the default settings for the top, bottom, left, and right margins.

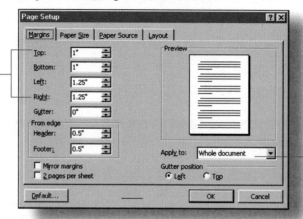

> If you want margin changes to affect the entire document, leave the Apply to option set at *Whole document*. If you want margin changes to affect the document from the insertion point to the end of the document, change the Apply to option to *This point forward*.

> Margin changes are applied to the entire document until the document is divided into sections.

Hint

If you want the new margins to affect the entire document, position the insertion point anywhere within the document, and then make margin changes at the Page Setup dialog box. You can also specify that margin changes affect the text in a document from the position of the insertion point to the end of the document. To do this, click the down-pointing triangle at the right of the Apply to option box in the Page Setup dialog box, and then click *This point forward* at the drop-down list.

> Most printers contain a required margin (between one-quarter and three-eighths of an inch) because printers cannot print to the edge of the page.

Hint

Inserting a Section Break

By default, changes made to margins in a document are applied to all text in the document. If you want margin changes to apply to specific text in a document, select the text first. Text in a document can also be divided into sections. When a document is divided into sections, each section can be formatted separately. For example, different margin settings can be applied to each section in a document, Insert a section break at the Break dialog box. Display this dialog box by clicking Insert and then Break.

exercise 6

Changing Margins and View

1. Open Word Report 01.
2. Save the report with Save As and name it Word Ch 03, Ex 06.
3. Change the top margin to 1.5 inches and the left and right margins to 1 inch by completing the following steps:
   a. Click File and then Page Setup or double-click a gray area at the top of the Ruler.
   b. At the Page Setup dialog box, click the Margins tab.
   c. Click the up-pointing triangle after the Top option until *1.5"* displays in the Top text box.
   d. Click the down-pointing triangle after the Left option until *1"* displays in the Left text box.
   e. Click the down-pointing triangle after the Right option until *1"* displays in the Right text box.
   f. Click OK or press Enter.

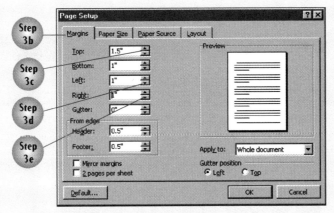

Step 3b
Step 3c
Step 3d
Step 3e

4. Make the following changes to the document:
    a. Select the title *GRAPHICS SOFTWARE* and then change the font to 18-point Arial bold.
    b. Select the heading *Early Painting and Drawing Programs* and then change the font to 14-point Arial bold.
    c. Use Format Painter to change the formatting to 14-point Arial bold for the remaining two headings, *Developments in Painting and Drawing Programs* and *Painting and Drawing Programs Today*.
5. Change to the document view by completing the following steps:
    a. Change to Print Layout view by clicking the Print Layout View button located at the left side of the horizontal scroll bar (third button from the left).
    b. Scroll through the document and notice how page breaks appear in the document.
    c. Change back to Normal view by clicking View and then Normal.
6. Save the document again with the same name (Word Ch 03, Ex 06).
7. Print and then close Word Ch 03, Ex 06.

Inserting Hard Page Breaks

Word's default settings break each page after Line 45 (approximately 9.8 inches). Word automatically inserts page breaks in a document as you edit it. Since Word does this automatically, you may find that page breaks sometimes occur in undesirable locations. To remedy this, you can insert your own page break. A page break inserted automatically by Word is called a *soft page break* and a break inserted by you is called a *hard page break*.

To insert a hard page break, position the insertion point where you want the break to occur, click Insert and then Break. At the Break dialog box, make sure Page break is selected, and then click OK or press Enter. You can also insert a hard page break by positioning the insertion point in the document where you want the break to occur and then pressing Ctrl + Enter.

A hard page break displays in the Normal view as a line of dots with the words *Page Break* in the middle of the line. A hard page break displays in the same manner as a soft page break in the Print Layout view.

Soft page breaks automatically adjust if text is added to or deleted from a document. A hard page break does not adjust and is therefore less flexible than a soft page break. If you add or delete text from a document with a hard page break, check the break to determine whether it is still in a desirable location.

A hard page break can be deleted from a document. To delete a hard page break, position the insertion point on the page break and then press the Delete key.

exercise 7

Inserting Hard Page Breaks

1. Open Word Report 01.
2. Save the document with Save As and name it Word Ch 03, Ex 07.
3. Make the following changes to the document:
   a. Change the left and right margins to 1 inch.
   b. Insert a hard page break at the beginning of the heading *Developments in Painting and Drawing Programs* by completing the following steps:
      1) Position the insertion point at the beginning of the heading *Developments in Painting and Drawing Programs*.
      2) Press Ctrl + Enter.
   c. Insert a hard page break at the beginning of the remaining heading *Painting and Drawing Programs Today*.
4. Save the document again with the same name (Word Ch 03, Ex 07).
5. Print and then close Word Ch 03, Ex 07.

Previewing a Document

Press Ctrl + F2 to display Print Preview

Print Preview

Before printing a document, viewing the document may be useful. Word's Print Preview feature displays the document on the screen as it will appear when printed. With this feature, you can view a partial page, single page, multiple pages, or zoom in on a particular area of a page.

To view a document, click File and then Print Preview or click the Print Preview button on the Standard toolbar. (The Print Preview button is the sixth button from the left on the Standard toolbar.) In Print Preview, the page where the insertion point is located displays on the screen. Figure 3.11 shows a document in Print Preview and figure 3.12 identifies the buttons on the Print Preview toolbar.

figure 3.11

Document in Print Preview

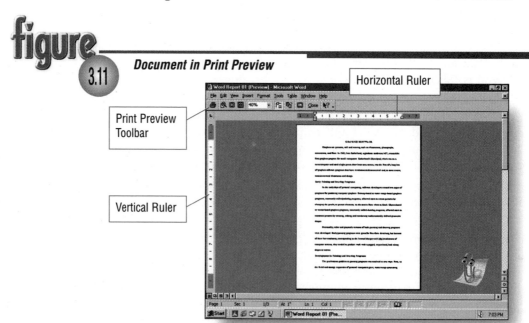

figure
3.12

Print Preview Toolbar Buttons

Click this button	Named	To do this
🖨	Print	Send the current document to the printer.
🔍	Magnifier	Toggle the mouse pointer between a magnifying glass, which is used to view the document, and the normal mouse pointer, which is used to edit the document.
▯	One Page	Display individual pages in the document.
▦	Multiple Pages	Display multiple pages in the document (up to 18 pages).
42% ▾	Zoom	Change viewing by percentage option or to Page Width, Text Width, Whole Page, or Two Pages.
📝	View Ruler	Turn the display of the Ruler on or off.
📑	Shrink to Fit	Try to "shrink" the contents of the last page in the document onto the previous page if there is only a small amount of text on the last page.
🔲	Full Screen	Toggle the screen display between the normal display and full screen display, which removes everything from the Print Preview screen except the document and the Print Preview toolbar.
Close	Close Preview	Close Print Preview and return to document screen.
▸? ▾	Context Sensitive Help	Display context-sensitive help.

While in Print Preview, you can move through a document using the insertion point movement keys, the horizontal and vertical scroll bars, and/or the Page Up and Page Down keys.

Viewing a Document with Print Preview

1. Open Word Report 01.
2. View the document by completing the following steps:

   a. Click File and then Print Preview or click the Print
      Preview button on the Standard toolbar.
   b. Click the Multiple Pages button on the Print Preview
      Toolbar. (This causes a grid to appear immediately below
      the button.)
   c. Position the arrow pointer in the upper left portion of the grid, move the
      arrow pointer down and to the right until the message at the bottom of the
      grid displays as *2 x 2 Pages,* and then click the mouse
      button.

   d. Click the Full Screen button on the Print Preview
      toolbar. This displays only the pages in the document
      and the Print Preview toolbar.
   e. Click the Full Screen button again to restore the screen display.
   f. Click the One Page button on the Print Preview toolbar.
   g. Click the down-pointing triangle at the right of the Zoom
      button and then click *50%* at the drop-down list.
   h. Click the down-pointing triangle at the right of the Zoom
      button and then click *75%* at the drop-down list.
   i. Click the One Page button on the Print Preview toolbar.
   j. Click the Close button on the Print Preview toolbar.
3. Close Word Report 01.

Vertically Aligning Text

Text in a Word document is aligned at the top of the page by default. This
alignment can be changed using the Vertical alignment option at the Page Setup
dialog box with the Layout tab selected as shown in figure 3.13. Display this
dialog box by clicking File and then Page Setup. At the Page Setup dialog box,
click the Layout tab.

Page Setup Dialog Box with Layout Tab Selected

Click this down-pointing triangle to display a list of vertical alignment options.

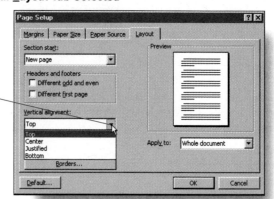

The Vertical alignment option from the Page Setup dialog box contains four choices—*Top*, *Center*, *Justified*, and *Bottom*. The default setting is *Top*, which aligns text at the top of the page. Choose *Center* if you want text centered vertically on the page. The *Justified* option will align text between the top and the bottom margins. The *Center* option positions text in the middle of the page vertically, while the *Justified* option adds space between paragraphs of text (not within) to fill the page from the top to bottom margins. If you center or justify text, the text does not display centered or justified on the screen in the Normal view but it does display centered or justified in the Print Layout view. Choose the *Bottom* option to align text in the document vertically along the bottom of the page.

Vertically Aligning Text in a Document

1. Open Word Ch 03, Ex 02.
2. Save the document with Save As and name it Word Ch 03, Ex 09.
3. Change to the Print Layout view by clicking View and then Print Layout or clicking the Print Layout View button located at the left side of the screen before the horizontal scroll bar.
4. Vertically center the text in the document by completing the following steps:
   a. Click File and then Page Setup.
   b. At the Page Setup dialog box, click the Layout tab. (Skip this step if the Layout tab is already selected.)
   c. Click the down-pointing triangle at the right side of the Vertical alignment option box and then click *Center* at the drop-down list.
   d. Click OK to close the dialog box.

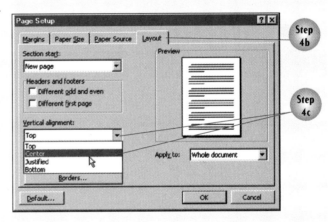

5. Display the document in Print Preview by clicking the Print Preview button on the Standard toolbar.
6. After viewing the document, click the Close button on the Print Preview toolbar.
7. Save the document again with the same name (Word Ch 03, Ex 09).
8. Print and then close Word Ch 03, Ex 09.

Using the Click and Type Feature

In chapter 2, you learned to change paragraph alignment with buttons on the Formatting toolbar, shortcut commands, or options at the Paragraph dialog box. Another method for changing paragraph alignment is to use the *click and type* feature. Before using this feature, you must change to the Print Layout view.

In Print Layout view, hover the mouse pointer between the left and right margins (at approximately the three-inch mark on the Ruler). After a few seconds, four short horizontal lines display below the I-beam pointer. These horizontal lines represent center alignment. Double-click the mouse button and the insertion point is moved to the center of the margins and the Center button on the Formatting toolbar is activated.

You can change to right alignment in a similar manner. Hover the mouse pointer near the right margin and after a few seconds horizontal lines display at the left side of the I-beam pointer. These horizontal lines represent right alignment and are similar in appearance to the lines on the Align Right button on the Formatting toolbar. With the right alignment lines displayed at the left side of the I-beam pointer, double-click the left mouse button.

If the alignment lines are not displayed near the I-beam pointer and you double-click the left mouse button, a left tab is set at the position of the insertion point. If you want to change the alignment and not set a tab, be sure the alignment lines display near the I-beam pointer before double-clicking the mouse button. To change to left alignment, hover the mouse pointer near the left margin. When horizontal lines display representing left alignment, double-click the left mouse button.

Using Click and Type to Align Text

1. At a clear document screen, create the document shown in figure 3.14 by completing the following steps:
   a. Change to the Print Layout view by clicking <u>V</u>iew and then <u>P</u>rint Layout.
   b. Position the I-beam pointer between the left and right margins at about the 3-inch mark on the horizontal ruler and the 2½-inch mark on the vertical ruler.
   c. When the center alignment lines display below the I-beam pointer, double-click the left mouse button.
   d. Key the centered text shown in figure 3.14.
   e. After keying the centered text, change to right alignment by completing the following steps:
      1) Position the I-beam pointer near the right margin at approximately the 4-inch mark on the vertical ruler until the right alignment lines display at the left side of the I-beam pointer. (You may need to scroll down the document to display the 4-inch mark on the vertical ruler.)
      2) Double-click the left mouse button.
   f. Key the right aligned text shown in figure 3.14.
2. Make the following changes to the document:
   a. Select the centered text and then change the font to 14-point Arial bold and the line spacing to double.

b. Select the right aligned text and then change the font to 8-point Arial bold.
   c. Deselect the text.
3. Save the document and name it Word Ch 03, Ex 10.
4. Print and then close Word Ch 03, Ex 10.

Exercise 10

MICROSOFT EXCEL TRAINING
Developing Financial Spreadsheets
Tuesday, October 16, 2001
Training Center
9:00 a.m. - 3:30 p.m.

Sponsored by
Cell Systems

Inserting the Date and Time

The current date and/or time can be inserted in a document with options from the Date and Time dialog box shown in figure 3.15. To display this dialog box, click Insert and then Date and Time.

Date and Time Dialog Box

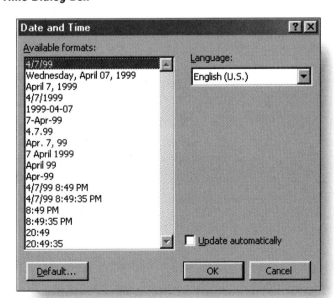

The Date and Time dialog box contains a list of date and time options in the Available formats list box. Click the desired date or time format, then click OK or press Enter.

The date can also be inserted in a document with the shortcut command, Alt + Shift + D. When you press Alt + Shift + D, the date is inserted in figures (such as 10/1/01). Press Alt + Shift + T to insert the current time in the document. The time is inserted in figures followed by AM or PM (such as 2:33 PM).

The date and/or time is inserted in the document as regular text. The date and/or time can also be inserted in a document as a field. If a date is inserted in a document as a field, the date is automatically updated if the document is opened on a different day. If the time is inserted as a field, the time is automatically updated when the document is opened again. To insert the date and/or time as a field, click the Update automatically check box that displays towards the bottom of the Date and Time dialog box.

Inserting the Date and Time

1. Open Word Document 05.
2. Save the document with Save As and name it Word Ch 03, Ex 11.
3. Make the following changes to the document:
   a. Bold the title *ARE YOU PREPARING FOR RETIREMENT?*.
   b. Select from the paragraph that begins *Living longer than ever...* through the last paragraph in the document (do not include the blank lines at the end of the document) and then click the Bullets button on the Formatting toolbar.
   c. Move the insertion point to the end of the document (at the beginning of a blank line) and then complete the following steps:
      1) Key **Date:** and then press the space bar once.
      2) Press Alt + Shift + D. (This inserts the current date.)
      3) Press the Enter key.
      4) Key **Time:** and then press the space bar once.
      5) Press Alt + Shift + T. (This inserts the current time.)
4. Print Word Ch 03, Ex 11.
5. Change the current date format by completing the following steps:
   a. Delete the current date.
   b. Click Insert and then Date and Time.
   c. At the Date and Time dialog box, click the fourth option in the Available formats list box.
   d. Click OK or press Enter.
6. Save the document again with the same name (Word Ch 03, Ex 11).
7. Print and then close Word Ch 03, Ex 11.

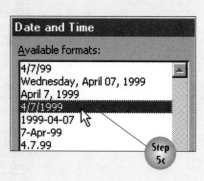

Highlighting Text

As people read information in books, magazines, periodicals, papers, and so on, they may highlight important information with a highlighting pen. A highlighting pen creates a colored background through which the text can be read. This colored background draws the reader's eyes to the specific text.

Word provides a button on the Formatting toolbar that lets you highlight text in a document using the mouse. With this highlighting feature, you can select and highlight specific text in a document with a variety of colors. To use this feature, click the Highlight button on the Formatting toolbar, and then select the desired text using the mouse. When the Highlight button is activated, the I-beam pointer displays with a pen attached. Continue selecting text you want highlighted and when completed, click once on the Highlight button to deactivate it.

The default highlighting color is yellow. You can change this color by clicking the down-pointing triangle to the right of the Highlight button. From the drop-down list of colors that displays, click the desired color. This changes the color of the small rectangle below the pen on the Highlight button. If you are using a noncolor printer, highlighted text will print with a gray background. To remove highlighting from text, change the highlighting color to *None*, activate the Highlight button, and then select the highlighted text.

exercise 12

Highlighting Text in a Document

1. Open Word Document 04.
2. Save the document with Save As and name it Word Ch 03, Ex 12.
3. Highlight text in the document by completing the following steps:
   a. Click the Highlight button on the Formatting toolbar.
   b. Select the sentence *While an agreement would be positive for the financial markets, the uncertainty surrounding the budget discussion is a lingering concern.* that displays in the first paragraph.
   c. Click the Highlight button to deactivate it.
4. Change the highlighting color and then highlight text in the document by completing the following steps:
   a. Click the down-pointing triangle to the right of the Highlight button on the Formatting toolbar.
   b. From the drop-down list of colors, click the Turquoise color.
   c. Select the sentence *While the sign of healthy cyclical rotation to other sections such as financial services and consumer non-durables has been noticed, no group has yet emerged as a clear leader.* that displays at the end of the second paragraph.
   d. Click the Highlight button to deactivate it.
5. Save the document again with the same name (Word Ch 03, Ex 12).

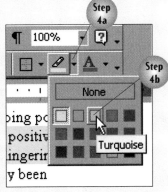

Step 4a

Step 4b

None

Turquoise

6. Print Word Ch 03, Ex 12.
7. Deselect text in the document by completing the following steps:
   a. Click the down-pointing triangle to the right of the Highlight button on the Formatting toolbar.
   b. From the drop-down list that displays, click the *None* option (ScreenTip displays with *No Highlight*).
   c. Select the sentence *While an agreement would be positive for the financial markets, the uncertainty surrounding the budget discussion is a lingering concern.* that displays in the first paragraph.
   d. Select the sentence *While the sign of healthy cyclical rotation to other sections such as financial services and consumer non-durables has been noticed, no group has yet emerged as a clear leader.* that displays at the end of the second paragraph.
   e. Return the highlight color to yellow.
   f. Click the Highlight button to deactivate it.
8. Save the document again with the same name (Word Ch 03, Ex 12).
9. Print and then close Word Ch 03, Ex 12.

Creating Newspaper Columns

When preparing a document containing text, an important point to consider is the readability of the document. Readability refers to the ease with which a person can read and understand groups of words. The line length of text in a document can enhance or detract from the readability of text. If the line length is too long, the reader may lose his or her place on the line and have a difficult time moving to the next line below. To improve the readability of some documents such as newsletters or reports, you may want to set the text in columns.

Text can be set in two different types of columns in Word. One type, called newspaper columns, is commonly used for text in newspapers, newsletters, and magazines. The other type, called side-by-side columns, is used for text that you want to keep aligned horizontally. Side-by-side columns are created using the Tables feature (covered in chapter 6).

Newspaper columns contain text that flows up and down in the document, as shown in figure 3.16. When the first column on the page is filled with text, the insertion point moves to the top of the next column on the same page. When the last column on the page is filled with text, the insertion point moves to the beginning of the first column on the next page.

Create newspaper columns using the Columns button on the Standard toolbar or options from the Columns dialog box. The formatting for newspaper columns can be established before the text is keyed or it can be applied to existing text. A document can include as many columns as there is room for on the page. Word determines how many columns can be included on the page based on the page width, the margin widths, and the size and spacing of the columns.

figure

3.16   *Newspaper Columns*

Text flows from top to bottom in the first column...

...then to the top of the next column and so on.

Formatting Sections

Changes in column affect the entire document or the section of the document in which the insert point is positioned. If you want to create different numbers or styles of columns in a document, divide the document into sections. There are three methods for inserting a section break in a document.

Columns

One method is to use the Break dialog box. Display this dialog box by clicking Insert and then Break. In the Section break types section of the Break dialog box, choose to insert a section break that begins a new page or choose to insert a continuous section break. A continuous section break displays in the Normal view as a double line of dots across the screen with the words *Section Break (Continuous)* inserted in the middle. In the Print Layout view, a section break does not display on the screen. However, the section number where the insertion point is located displays in the Status bar as *Sec* followed by the number. A section break that begins a new page displays as a double row of dots across the screen with the words *Section Break (Next Page)* inserted in the middle. In the Print Layout view, a section break that begins a new page displays as a new page.

Another method for inserting a section break in a document is to use the Columns dialog box and specify that text is to be formatted into columns from the location of the insertion point forward in the document. The third method is to select the text first and then apply column formatting.

Creating Newspaper Columns with the Columns Button

To create newspaper columns using the Columns button on the Standard toolbar, click the Columns button. This causes a grid to display as shown in figure 3.17. Move the mouse down and to the right until the desired number of columns displays with a blue background on the Columns grid and then click the mouse button.

figure 3.17

Columns Grid

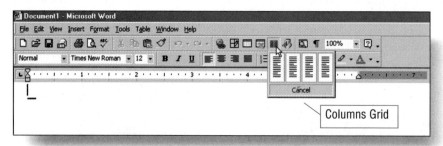

Columns Grid

If a document contains a title and you want that title to span both columns, position the insertion point at the left margin at the first line of text that will begin the columns and then click Insert and then Break. At the Break dialog box shown in figure 3.18, click Continuous, and then click OK or press Enter.

figure 3.18

Break Dialog Box

Click Continuous to insert a continuous section break

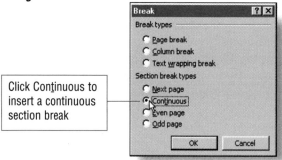

In addition to using the method just described, you could also format the text in a document into columns and not the title by selecting the text in the document (excluding the title), and then using the Columns button on the Standard toolbar to create the columns. A third method is explained in the next section on creating columns with options from the Columns dialog box.

In Normal view, text displays in a single column at the left side of the document screen. If you want to view columns as they will appear when printed, change to the Print Layout view.

Formatting Text into Newspaper Columns Using the Columns Button

1. Open Word Report 01.
2. Save the document with Save As and name it Word Ch 03, Ex 13.
3. Make the following changes to the document:
   a. Change to the Print Layout view.
   b. Select the title and then change the font to 18-point Times New Roman bold.
   c. Select the text in the document from the beginning of the first paragraph (begins with *Graphics are pictures...*) to the end of the document. With the text selected, make the following changes:
      1) Change the font to 11-point Times New Roman.
      2) Change the line spacing to single.
      3) Set a left tab on the Ruler at the 0.25-inch mark.
      4) Format the text into two newspaper columns by clicking the Columns button on the Standard toolbar, moving the arrow pointer down and to the right until two columns display with a blue background on the Columns grid (and *2 Columns* displays below the grid), and then clicking the mouse button again.
      5) Deselect the text.
      6) Insert six points of space before and after each of the three headings in the document (*Early Painting and Drawing Programs*, *Developments in Painting and Drawing Programs* and *Painting and Drawing Programs Today*). (*Hint: Do this with the Before and After options at the Paragraph dialog box.*)

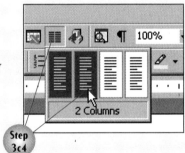

Step 3c4

4. Save the document again with the same name (Word Ch 03, Ex 13).
5. Print and then close Word Ch 03, Ex 13.

Creating Newspaper Columns with the Columns Dialog Box

The Columns dialog box can be used to create newspaper columns that are equal or unequal in width. To display the Columns dialog box shown in figure 3.19, click Format, expand the drop-down menu, and then click Columns.

figure

3.19

Columns Dialog Box

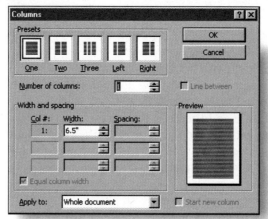

At the Columns dialog box, you can choose from a number of preset columns, choose your own number of columns, specify the width and spacing of specific columns, insert a line between columns, and specify where column formatting is to apply.

exercise

14

Formatting Text into Uneven Newspaper Columns with a Line Between

1. Open Word Report 02.
2. Save the document with Save As and name it Word Ch 03, Ex 14.
3. Delete the section 2 portion of the document by completing the following steps:
   a. Select the text in the document from the beginning of the title *SECTION 2: COMPUTERS IN ENTERTAINMENT* (located on page 2) to the end of the document.
   b. Press the Delete key.
4. Make the following changes to the document:
   a. Select the entire document and then change the font to 12-point Bookman Old Style (or a similar serif typeface).
   b. Select the title *SECTION 1: COMPUTERS IN COMMUNICATION* and then change the font to 14-point Arial bold.
   c. Select the heading *Telecommunications* and then change the font to 12-point Arial bold.
   d. Use Format Painter to apply 12-point Arial bold to the two remaining headings (*Publishing* and *News Services*).
   e. Select the text from the beginning of the first paragraph to the end of the document and then make the following changes:
      1) Change the line spacing to single.
      2) Set a left tab on the Ruler at the 0.25-inch mark.
   f. Insert 6 points of space above and below each of the three headings (*Telecommunications*, *Publishing*, and *News Services*).

5. Format the text of the report into uneven columns with a line between by completing the following steps:
   a. Change to the Print Layout view.
   b. Position the insertion point at the left margin of the first paragraph.
   c. Click Format, expand the drop-down menu, and then click Columns.
   d. At the Columns dialog box, click the down-pointing triangle at the right side of the Apply to text box, and then click *This point forward* at the drop-down list.
   e. Click the Right option in the Presets section of the Columns dialog box.
   f. Click the Line between check box.
   g. Click OK or press Enter.
   h. If the heading *News Services* displays at the top of the second column, remove the six points of space before the heading. (If the heading moves to the bottom of the first column, position the insertion point at the beginning of the heading, and then press the Enter key. This should move the heading to the top of the second column.)
6. Save the document again with the same name (Word Ch 03, Ex 14).
7. Print and then close Word Ch 03, Ex 14.

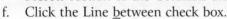

Inserting a Column and/or Page Break

When formatting text into columns, Word automatically breaks the columns to fit the page. At times, column breaks may appear in an undesirable location. For example, a heading may appear at the bottom of the column, while the text after the heading begins at the top of the next column. You can insert a column break by positioning the insertion point where you want the column to end and begin a new page by pressing Ctrl + Shift + Enter. You can also insert a column break by positioning the insertion point at the location where the new column is to begin, and then clicking Insert and then Break. At the Break dialog box, click Column break, and then click OK or press Enter.

Editing Text in Columns

To move the insertion point in a document using the mouse, position the arrow pointer where desired, and then click the left button. On the keyboard, the left and right arrow keys move the insertion point in the direction indicated within the column. When the insertion point gets to the end of the line within the column, it moves down to the beginning of the next line within the same column.

You can use the mouse or the keyboard to move the insertion point between columns. If you are using the mouse, position the I-beam pointer where desired, and then click the left button. If you are using the keyboard, press Alt + up arrow to move the insertion point to the top of the previous column, or press Alt + down arrow to move the insertion point to the top of the next column.

Editing Text in Newspaper Columns

1. Open Word Ch 03, Ex 13.
2. Save the document with Save As and name it Word Ch 03, Ex 15.
3. Make the following changes to the report:
   a. Change the left and right margins to 1 inch.
   b. Select the entire document and then change the font to 11-point Bookman Old Style (or a similar serif typeface).
   c. Change the spacing between the two columns by completing the following steps:
      1) Position the insertion point somewhere in the first paragraph.
      2) Click Format and then Columns.
      3) At the Columns dialog box, click the down-pointing triangle at the right side of the Spacing text box (located in the Width and spacing section) until *0.3"* displays.
      4) Click OK or press Enter to close the dialog box.
   d. Select the title and then change the font to 16-point Tahoma bold.
   e. Select the heading *Early Painting and Drawing Programs* and then change the font to 11-point Tahoma bold.

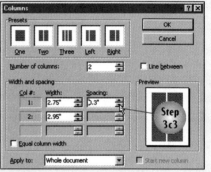

   f. Use Format Painter to apply 11-point Tahoma bold to the two remaining headings.
   g. If the heading *Developments in Painting and Drawing Programs* displays at the top of the second column, remove the six points of space before the heading. (If the heading moves to the bottom of the first column, position the insertion point at the beginning of the heading, and then press the Enter key. This should move the heading to the top of the second column.)
4. Save the document again with the same name (Word Ch 03, Ex 15).
5. Print and then close Word Ch 03, Ex 15.

Removing Column Formatting

To remove column formatting using the Columns button, position the insertion point in the section containing columns, or select the text in columns. Click the Columns button on the Standard toolbar and then click the first column in the Columns grid. To remove column formatting using the Columns dialog box, position the insertion point in the section containing columns, or select the text in columns, and then click Format and then Columns. At the Columns dialog box, click One in the Presets section, and then click OK or press Enter.

Checking the Spelling and Grammar of a Document

Word includes writing tools to help create a thoughtful and well-written document. Two of these tools are a spelling checker and a grammar checker. The spelling checker finds misspelled words and offers replacement words. It also finds duplicate words and irregular capitalizations. When you spell check a document, the spelling checker compares the words in your document with the words in its dictionary. If a match is found, the word is passed over. If there is no match for the word, the spelling checker will stop, select the word, and offer replacements.

The grammar checker will search a document for errors in grammar, style, punctuation, and word usage. The spelling checker and the grammar checker can help you create a well-written document but do not replace the need for proofreading. You would complete the following steps to complete a spelling and grammar check:

1. Click the Spelling and Grammar button on the Standard toolbar or click <u>T</u>ools and then <u>S</u>pelling and Grammar.
2. If a spelling error is detected, the misspelled word is selected and a Spelling and Grammar dialog box similar to the one shown in figure 3.20 displays. The sentence containing the misspelled word is displayed in the Not in Dictionary: text box. If a grammatical error is detected, the sentence containing the error is selected and the Spelling and Grammar dialog box similar to the one shown in figure 3.21 displays.
3. If a misspelled word is selected, replace the word with the correct spelling, tell Word to ignore it and continue checking the document, or add the word to a custom dictionary. If a sentence containing a grammatical error is selected, the grammar checker displays the sentence in the top text box in the Spelling and Grammar dialog box. Choose to ignore or change errors found by the grammar checker.
4. When the spelling and grammar check is completed, the Office Assistant displays the message *The spelling and grammar check is complete*. Click anywhere in the document screen outside the message box to remove the box.

Complete a spelling and grammar check on a portion of a document by selecting the text first and then clicking the Spelling and Grammar button.

Spelling and Grammar

figure
3.20

Spelling and Grammar Dialog Box with Spelling Error Selected

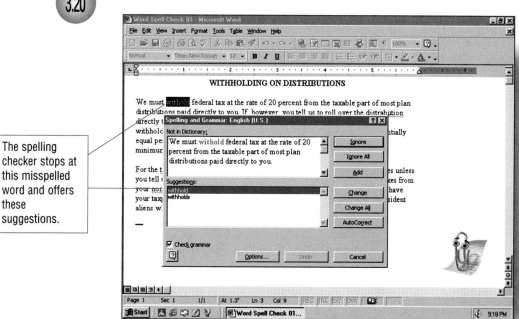

The spelling checker stops at this misspelled word and offers these suggestions.

figure
3.21

Spelling and Grammar Dialog Box with Grammar Error Selected

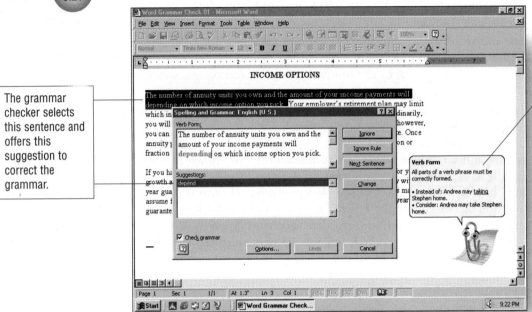

The grammar checker selects this sentence and offers this suggestion to correct the grammar.

The Office Assistant provides information on the grammar rule.

When a word is selected during a spelling and grammar check, you need to determine if the word should be corrected or if it should be ignored. Word provides buttons at the right side and bottom of the Spelling and Grammar dialog box to make decisions. The buttons will change depending on whether a misspelled word is selected or a sentence containing a grammatical error. Figure 3.22 describes the buttons and the functions performed by the buttons.

figure
3.22

Spelling and Grammar Checking Buttons

Button	Function
Ignore	During spell checking, skips that occurrence of the word; in grammar checking, leaves the currently selected text as written.
Ignore All	During spell checking, skips that occurrence of the word and all other occurrences of the word in the document.
Ignore Rule	During grammar checking, leaves the currently selected text as written and also ignores the current rule for the remainder of the grammar check in the document.

<u>A</u>dd	Adds the selected word to the main spelling checker dictionary.
<u>C</u>hange	Replaces the selected word in the sentence with the selected word in the Suggestio<u>n</u>s list box.
Change A<u>l</u>l	Replaces the selected word in the sentence with the selected word in the Suggestio<u>n</u>s list box and all other occurrences of the word in the document.
AutoCo<u>r</u>rect	Inserts the selected word and the correct spelling of the word in the AutoCorrect dialog box.
<u>U</u>ndo Edit	Reverses the most recent spelling and grammar action.
Ne<u>x</u>t Sentence	Accepts manual changes made to a sentence and then continues grammar checking.
<u>O</u>ptions	Displays a dialog box with options for customizing a spelling and grammar check.

By default, the spelling and grammar in a document is checked. You can turn off the grammar checker and perform only a spelling check. To do this, click the Chec<u>k</u> grammar option at the Spelling and Grammar dialog box (located in the lower left corner) to remove the check mark.

The buttons in the Spelling and Grammar dialog box change depending on the type of error selected.

Spell Checking a Document

1. Open Word Spell Check 01.
2. Save the document with Save As and name it Word Ch 03, Ex 16.
3. Perform a spelling check by completing the following steps:
   a. Click the Spelling and Grammar button on the Standard toolbar (the seventh button from the left).
   b. The spelling checker selects the word *withold*. The proper spelling is selected in the Suggestio<u>n</u>s list box so click the Change A<u>l</u>l button. (Because this word is misspelled in other locations in the document, clicking the Change A<u>l</u>l button will change the other misspellings.)
   c. The spelling checker selects the word *distrabution*. The proper spelling is selected in the Suggestio<u>n</u>s list box so click the <u>C</u>hange button. (Click the <u>C</u>hange button because the word is only misspelled once.)
   d. The spelling checker selects the word *imployer*. The proper spelling is selected in the Suggestio<u>n</u>s list box so click the <u>C</u>hange button.
   e. The spelling checker selects the word *fedaral*. The proper spelling is selected in the Suggestio<u>n</u>s list box so click the Change A<u>l</u>l button.
   f. The spelling checker selects *yaers*. The proper spelling is selected in the Suggestio<u>n</u>s list box so click the <u>C</u>hange button.
   g. The spelling checker selects *taxible*. The proper spelling is selected in the Suggestio<u>n</u>s list box so click the <u>C</u>hange button.

h. If the spelling checker selects *noneligible*, click Ignore All to skip the word (it is spelled properly).

i. The spelling checker selects the word *identificatoin*. The proper spelling is selected in the Suggestions list box so click the Change button.

j. The Office Assistant displays the message, *The spelling and grammar check is complete*. Click in the document screen outside this message to remove the message.

4. Save the document again with the same name (Word Ch 03, Ex 16).

5. Print and then close Word Ch 03, Ex 16.

Editing while Spell Checking

When spell checking a document, you can temporarily leave the Spelling and Grammar dialog box, make corrections in the document, and then resume spell checking. For example, suppose while spell checking you notice a sentence that you want to change. To correct the sentence, move the I-beam pointer to the location in the sentence where the change is to occur, click the left mouse button, and then make changes to the sentence. To resume spell checking, click the Resume button, which was formerly the Ignore button.

Spell Checking a Document with Words in Uppercase and with Numbers

1. Open Word Spell Check 02.

2. Save the document with Save As and name it Word Ch 03, Ex 17.

3. Check spell checking options by completing the following steps:

   a. Click Tools and then Options.

   b. At the Options dialog box, click the Spelling & Grammar tab.

   c. Make sure there is a check mark in the Ignore words in UPPERCASE check box. (If there is no check mark, click in the check box before Ignore words in UPPERCASE to insert one.)

   d. Make sure there is a check mark in the Ignore words with numbers check box. (If there is no check mark, click in the check box before Ignore words with numbers to insert one.)

   e. Click OK or press Enter to close the dialog box.

4. Perform a spelling check by completing the following steps:

   a. Click the Spelling and Grammar button on the Standard toolbar.

   b. The spelling checker selects the word *beigin*. The proper spelling is selected in the Suggestions list box so click the Change button (or Change All button).

   c. The spelling checker selects the word *aney*. The proper spelling of the word is selected in the Suggestions list box so click the Change button (or Change All button).

   d. The grammar checker selects *the distribution is because you are disabled* and displays information on capitalization. Click the Ignore Rule button to tell the grammar checker to ignore the rule.

   e. The spelling checker selects *seperated*. The proper spelling is selected in the Suggestions list box so click the Change button (or Change All button).

f.   The spelling checker selects *annuty*. The proper spelling is selected in the Suggestions list box so click the Change button (or Change All button).

g.   The spelling checker selects *searies*. The proper spelling is selected in the Suggestions list box so click the Change button (or Change All button).

h.   The spelling checker selects *gros*. The proper spelling is selected in the Suggestions list box so click the Change button (or Change All button).

i.   The spelling checker selects *laess*. The proper spelling *less* is not selected in the Suggestions list box but it is one of the words suggested. Click *less* in the Suggestions list box, and then click the Change button.

j.   The grammar checker selects *you are required to make a payment to someone besides yourself under a MIRA plan.* and displays information on commonly confused words. Click the Ignore Rule button to tell the grammar checker to ignore the rule.

k.   When the spelling and grammar check is completed, click outside the Office Assistant message box to remove the message box.

5.   Save the document again with the same name (Word Ch 03, Ex 17).

6.   Print and then close Word Ch 03, Ex 17.

Checking the Grammar and Style of a Document

Word includes a grammar checking feature that you can use to search a document for grammar, style, punctuation, and word usage. Like the spelling checker, the grammar checker does not find every error in a document and may stop at correct phrases. The grammar checker can help you create a well-written document but does not replace the need for proofreading.

To complete a grammar check (as well as a spelling check) on a document, click the Spelling and Grammar button on the Standard toolbar or click Tools, and then Spelling and Grammar. (At the Spelling and Grammar dialog box, make sure there is a check mark in the Check grammar check box.) The grammar checker selects the first sentence with a grammatical error and displays the sentence in the top text box in the dialog box. The grammar rule that is violated is displayed above the text box and the Office Assistant displays information about the grammar rule. Choose to ignore or change errors found by the grammar checker. When the grammar checker is done, the open document is displayed on the screen. The changes made during the check are inserted in the document. By default, a spelling check is completed on a document during a grammar check.

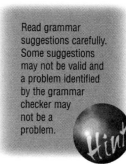

Read grammar suggestions carefully. Some suggestions may not be valid and a problem identified by the grammar checker may not be a problem.

Checking Grammar in a Document

1.   Open Word Grammar Check 01.

2.   Save the document with Save As and name it Word Ch 03, Ex 18.

3.   Perform a grammar check by completing the following steps:

a.   Click the Spelling and Grammar button on the Standard toolbar.

b.   The grammar checker selects the sentence *The number of annuity units you own and the amount of your income payments will depending on which income option you pick.* and displays *depend* in the Suggestions list box. The Office Assistant displays information on verb form. Read this information and then click the Change button.

c. The grammar checker selects the sentence *Once annuity payments start, you cannot change the income option for the accumulation or fraction of accumulation on which their based.* and displays *they're* in the Suggestions list box. The Office Assistant displays information on commonly confused words. Read this information and then click the Change button.

d. The grammar checker selects the sentence *If your married, McCormack Funds may assume for you a survivor annuity with half-benefit to annuity partner and a 10-year guaranteed period, with your spouse as your annuity partner.* and displays *you're* in the Suggestions list box. The Office Assistant displays information on commonly confused words. (This is the same information displayed in the previous step.) Click the Change button to change *your* to *you're*.

e. The Office Assistant displays a message box telling you that the spelling and grammar check is completed. Click in the document screen outside this box to remove the box.

4. Save the document again with the same name (Word Ch 03, Ex 18).

5. Print and then close Word Ch 03, Ex 18.

Changing Grammar Checking Options

If you click the Options button in the Spelling and Grammar dialog box, the Spelling and Grammar dialog box displays with options for customizing the grammar checking. One of the options is Show readability statistics. Insert a check mark in this option and readability statistics about the document will display when grammar checking is completed. Most of the readability information is self-explanatory. The last two statistics included, however, are described in figure 3.23.

figure

3.23   *Readability Statistics*

Flesch Reading Ease	The Flesch reading ease is based on the average number of syllables per word and the average number of words per sentence. The higher the score, the greater the number of people who will be able to understand the text in the document. Standard writing generally scores in the 60-70 range.
Flesch-Kincaid Grade Level	This is based on the average number of syllables per word and the average number of words per sentence. The score indicates a grade level. Standard writing is generally written at the seventh- or eighth-grade level.

Changing Writing Style

At the Spelling and Grammar dialog box (as well as the Options dialog box with the Spelling & Grammar tab selected), you can specify a writing style. The default writing style is *Standard*. This can be changed to *Casual, Formal, Technical*, or *Custom*. Choose the writing style that matches the document you are checking. For example, if you are checking a scientific document, change the writing style to *Technical*. If you are checking a short story, consider changing the writing style to *Casual*. To change the writing style, click the down-pointing triangle at the right of the Writing style text box, and then click the desired style at the drop-down list.

Changing Grammar Checking Options, Then Grammar Checking a Document

1. Open Word Document 05.
2. Save the document with Save As and name it Word Ch 03, Ex 19.
3. Change grammar checking options by completing the following steps:
   a. Click Tools and then Options.
   b. At the Options dialog box, click the Spelling & Grammar tab.
   c. At the Options dialog box with the Spelling & Grammar tab selected, click the Show readability statistics. (This inserts a check mark in the option.)
   d. Click the down-pointing triangle at the right of the Writing style text box and then click *Formal* at the drop-down list.
   e. Click OK to close the dialog box.
4. Complete a grammar check on the document by completing the following steps:
   a. Click the Spelling and Grammar button on the Standard toolbar.
   b. The grammar checker selects the sentence *That is all changing—here's why.*, displays *here is* in the Suggestions list box, and the Office Assistant displays information about contraction use. Read this information and then click the Change button to change *here's* to *here is*.

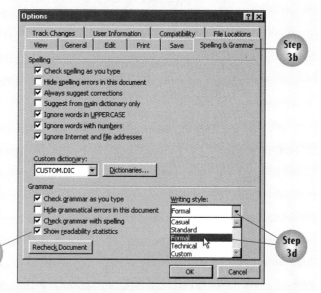

c. The grammar checker selects the sentence *Your house is not expected to skyrocket in value as in past years.* and displays *Passive Voice (no suggestions)* in the Suggestions list box. Read the information on passive voice displayed by the Office Assistant. Leave the sentence as written and continue grammar checking by clicking the Next Sentence button.

d. The grammar checker selects the sentence *By the time you are ready to retire, your nest egg may seem substantial—but it isn't going to buy what it would buy today.*, displays *time,* in the Suggestions list box, and the Office Assistant displays information about comma use. This sentence is correct as written so click the Ignore button

e. The grammar checker again selects the sentence *By the time you are ready to retire, your nest egg may seem substantial—but it isn't going to buy what it would buy today.* and displays *is not* in the Suggestions list box; the Office Assistant displays information about contraction use. Click the Change button to change *isn't* to *is not.*

f. If the grammar checker selects the same sentence again and displays information about comma use, click the Ignore button.

g. The grammar checker displays the Readability Statistics for the document. Read these statistics and then click OK to close the dialog box.

5. Change the checking options back to the default by completing the following steps:
   a. Click Tools and then Options.
   b. At the Options dialog box, click the Spelling & Grammar tab.
   c. At the Options dialog box with the Spelling & Grammar tab selected, click the Show readability statistics. (This removes the check mark from the check box.)
   d. Click the down-pointing triangle at the right of the Writing style text box and then click *Standard* at the drop-down list.
   e. Click OK to close the dialog box.

6. Make the following changes to the document:
   a. Select the entire document and then change to a serif typeface (other than Times New Roman) in 12-point size.
   b. Select the title *ARE YOU PREPARING FOR RETIREMENT?* and then change the font to 14-point Arial bold.
   c. Select from the second paragraph (that begins *Living longer than ever...*) to the end of the document and then click the Bullets button on the Formatting toolbar.

7. Save the document again with the same name (Word Ch 03, Ex 19).

8. Print and then close Word Ch 03, Ex 19.

Customizing AutoCorrect

Earlier in this chapter, you learned that during a spelling check a selected word can be added to AutoCorrect. You can add, delete, or change words at the AutoCorrect dialog box. To display the AutoCorrect dialog box with the AutoCorrect tab selected as shown in figure 3.24, click Tools and then AutoCorrect. Several options display at the beginning of the AutoCorrect dialog box. If a check appears in the check box before the option, the option is active.

figure

3.24

AutoCorrect Dialog Box

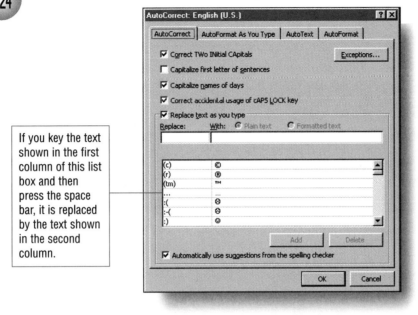

If you key the text shown in the first column of this list box and then press the space bar, it is replaced by the text shown in the second column.

Adding a Word to AutoCorrect

Commonly misspelled words or typographical errors can be added to AutoCorrect. For example, if you consistently key *oopen* instead of *open*, you can add *oopen* to AutoCorrect and tell it to correct it as *open*. To do this, you would display the AutoCorrect dialog box, key *oopen* in the Replace text box, key *open* in the With text box, and then click the Add button. The next time you key *oopen* and then press the space bar, AutoCorrect changes it to *open*.

Deleting a Word from AutoCorrect

A word that is contained in AutoCorrect can be deleted. To delete a word, display the AutoCorrect dialog box, click the desired word in the list box (you may need to click the down-pointing triangle to display the desired word), and then click the Delete button.

Adding Text to and Deleting Text from AutoCorrect

1. At a clear document screen, add words to AutoCorrect by completing the following steps:
   a. Click Tools and then AutoCorrect.
   b. At the AutoCorrect dialog box with the AutoCorrect tab selected, make sure the insertion point is positioned in the Replace text box. If not, click in the Replace text box.

c. Key **dtp**.

d. Press the Tab key (this moves the insertion point to the <u>W</u>ith text box) and then key **desktop publishing**.

e. Click the <u>A</u>dd button. (This adds *dtp* and *desktop publishing* to the AutoCorrect and also selects *dtp* in the <u>R</u>eplace text box.)

f. Key **particuler** in the Replace text box. (When you begin keying *particuler*, *dtp* is automatically deleted.)

g. Press the Tab key and then key **particular**.

h. Click the <u>A</u>dd button.

i. With the insertion point positioned in the <u>R</u>eplace text box, key **populer**.

j. Press the Tab key and then key **popular**.

k. Click the <u>A</u>dd button.

l. With the insertion point positioned in the <u>R</u>eplace text box, key **tf**.

m. Press the Tab key and then key **typeface**.

n. Click the <u>A</u>dd button.

o. Click OK or press Enter.

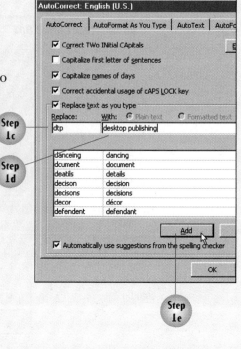

Step 1c

Step 1d

Step 1e

2. Key the text shown in figure 3.25. (Key the text exactly as shown. AutoCorrect will correct words as you key.)

3. Save the document and name it Word Ch 03, Ex 20.

4. Print Word Ch 03, Ex 20.

5. Delete the words you added to AutoCorrect by completing the following steps:

a. Click <u>T</u>ools and then <u>A</u>utoCorrect.

b. At the AutoCorrect dialog box, click *dtp* in the list box. (Click the down-pointing triangle in the list box scroll bar until *dtp* is visible and then click *dtp*.)

c. Click the <u>D</u>elete button.

d. Click the *particuler* option in the list box.

e. Click the <u>D</u>elete button.

f. Click the *populer* option in the list box.

Step 5b

g. Click the <u>D</u>elete button.

h. Click the *tf* option in the list box.

Step 5c

i. Click the <u>D</u>elete button.

j. Click OK or press Enter.

6. Close Word Ch 03, Ex 20.

figure 3.25

Exercise 20

CHOOSING A TYPEFACE

Λ tf is a sct of characters with a common general design and shape. One of teh most important considerations in establishing a particuler mood or feeling in a document is the tf. For example, a decorative tf may be chosen for invitations or menus, while a simple block-style tf may be chosen for headlines or reports. Choose a tf that reflects the contents, your audience expectations, and the image you want to project.

There are many typefaces, adn new designs are created on a regular basis. The most populer tf for typewriters is Courier. There are a variety of typefaces populer with dtp programs including Arial, Bookman, Century Schoolbook, Garamond, Helvetica, and Times New Roman.

Using the Thesaurus

Word offers a Thesaurus program that can be used to find synonyms, antonyms, and related words for a particular word. Synonyms are words that have the same or nearly the same meaning. When using the Thesaurus, Word may display antonyms for some words. Antonyms are words with opposite meanings. With the Thesaurus, you can improve the clarity of business documents.

To use the Thesaurus, position the insertion point next to any character in the word for which you want to find a synonym or antonym, click Tools, expand the drop-down menu, point to Language, and then click Thesaurus. At the Thesaurus dialog box shown in figure 3.26, select the desired synonym (or antonym) in the Replace with Synonym list box, and then click the Replace button.

figure 3.26

Thesaurus Dialog Box

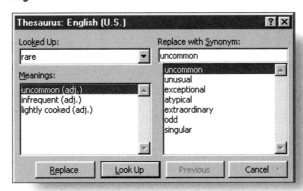

At the Thesaurus dialog box, a list of words displays in the Meanings list box. Depending on the word you are looking up, the words in the Meanings list box may display followed by *(n.)* or *(adj)*. You might also see the words *Antonym*, and *Related Words*. The first word in the Meanings list box is selected by default and synonyms for that word are displayed in the Replace with Synonym list box. You can view synonyms in the Replace with Synonym list box for the words shown in the Meanings list box by clicking the desired word.

Displaying Synonyms Using a Shortcut Menu

Another method for displaying synonyms for a word is to use a shortcut menu. To do this, position the mouse pointer on the word and then click the *right* mouse button. At the shortcut menu that displays, point to Synonyms, and then click the desired synonym at the side menu. Figure 3.27 shows synonyms in the shortcut menu side menu for the word *expectation*. Click the Thesaurus option at the bottom of the side menu to display the Thesaurus dialog box.

figure

3.27

Shortcut Menu Synonym Side Menu

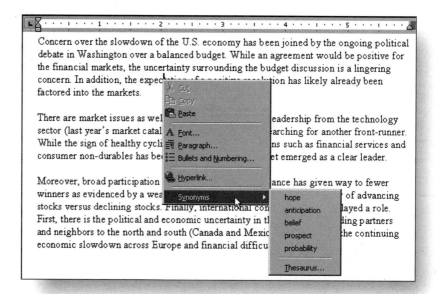

Changing Words Using the Thesaurus

1. Open Word Document 03.
2. Save the document with Save As and name it Word Ch 03, Ex 21.
3. Change the word *rare* in the first paragraph to *unusual* using the Thesaurus by completing the following steps:

a. Position the insertion point anywhere in the word *rare* (located in the first paragraph).
b. Click <u>T</u>ools, expand the drop-down menu, point to <u>L</u>anguage, and then click <u>T</u>hesaurus.
c. At the Thesaurus dialog box, click *unusual* in the Replace with Synonym list box, and then click the <u>R</u>eplace button.

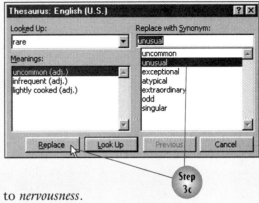

Step 3c

4. Follow similar steps to make the following changes using the Thesaurus:
   a. Change *uneasiness* in the first paragraph to *nervousness*.
   b. Change *relatively* in the second paragraph to *comparatively*.
5. Change *phase* in the third paragraph to *stage* using a shortcut menu by completing the following steps:
   a. Position the mouse pointer on the word *phrase* located in the second sentence of the third paragraph.
   b. Click the *right* mouse button.
   c. At the shortcut menu that displays, point to S<u>y</u>nonyms and then click *stage* at the side menu.
6. Save the document again with the same name (Word Ch 03, Ex 21).
7. Print and then close Word Ch 03, Ex 21.

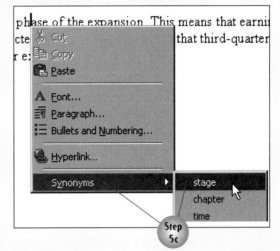

Step 5c

chapter summary

▶ By default, tabs are set every 0.5 inches. These settings can be changed on the Ruler or at the Tabs dialog box.

▶ Use the Alignment button at the left side of the Ruler to select a left, right, center, or decimal tab. When you set a tab on the Ruler, any tabs to the left are automatically deleted.

▶ Turning on the display of nonprinting characters, such as those for paragraphs and tabs, is useful when creating tabbed text.

▶ After a tab has been set on the Ruler, it can be moved or deleted using the mouse pointer.

▶ At the Tabs dialog box, you can set any of the four types of tabs as well as a bar tab at a specific measurement. You can also set tabs with preceding leaders and clear one tab or all tabs. Preceding leaders can be periods, hyphens, or underlines.

▶ Change to the Print Layout view by clicking <u>V</u>iew and then <u>P</u>rint Layout or by clicking the Print Layout View button at the left side of the horizontal scroll bar. Change back to the Normal view by clicking <u>V</u>iew and then <u>N</u>ormal or clicking the Normal View button at the left side of the horizontal scroll bar.

- By default, a Word document contains 1.25-inch left and right margins and 1-inch top and bottom margins.

- Word inserts a page break at approximately 10 inches from the top of each page. With the default 1-inch top and bottom margins, this allows a total of 9 inches to be printed on a standard page. The page break displays as a row of dots in the Normal view and as an actual break in the page in Print Layout view.

- The page break that Word inserts automatically is a soft page break. A page break that you insert is a hard page break.

- With Word's Print Preview feature, you can view a partial page, single page, multiple pages, or zoom in on a particular area of a page. With buttons from the Print Preview toolbar at the top of the Print Preview screen, you can change the display of the document, send a document to the printer, and turn the display of the rulers on or off.

- Vertically align text in a document with the Vertical alignment option at the Page Setup dialog box with the Layout tab selected.

- Use the click and type feature to center, right align, and left align text.

- Insert the current date and/or time with options at the Date and Time dialog box or with shortcut commands.

- Highlight text in a document by clicking the Highlight button on the Formatting toolbar and then selecting the text. A variety of highlighting colors is available.

- Newspaper columns can be created with the Columns button on the Standard toolbar or with options at the Columns dialog box.

- In the Normal view, text will display in a single column at the left side of the document screen. Change to the Print Layout view to view columns as they will appear when printed.

- Options at the Columns dialog box let you change the spacing between columns, apply columns formatting from the point of the insertion point forward, insert a line between columns, or start a new column.

- To move the insertion point in a document with columns using the mouse, position the mouse pointer where desired, and then click the left button. To move the insertion point with the keyboard, use the arrow keys.

- Column formatting can be removed with the Columns button on the Standard toolbar or at the Columns dialog box.

- Word includes a spelling and grammar checker.

- The spelling checker matches the words in your document with the words in its dictionary. If a match is not found, the word is selected and possible corrections are suggested.

- When checking the spelling and/or grammar in a document, you can temporarily leave the Spelling and Grammar dialog box, make corrections in the document, and then resume checking.

- With the grammar checker, you can search a document for correct grammar, style, punctuation, and word usage.

- When a grammar error is detected, the Office Assistant displays information about the specific error.

- Commonly misspelled words, typographical errors, or abbreviations can be added to or deleted from the AutoCorrect dialog box.

- The Thesaurus finds synonyms, antonyms, and related words for a particular word.

commands review

	Mouse	Keyboard
Display the Ruler	View, Ruler	View, Ruler
New Line command		Shift + Enter
Tabs dialog box	Format, Tabs	Format, Tabs
Print Layout view	Click Print Layout View button at left side of horizontal scroll bar	View, Print Layout
Normal view	Click Normal View button at left side of horizontal scroll bar	View, Normal
Insert a hard page break	Insert, Break, Page Break	Ctrl + Enter
Print Preview	Click Print Preview button on Standard toolbar or click File, Print Preview	File, Print Preview
Page Setup dialog box	File, Page Setup or double-click a gray area at top of the Ruler	File, Page Setup
Display Columns dialog box	Format, Columns	Format, Columns
Insert a column break	Insert, Break, Column break	Ctrl + Shift + Enter
Spelling and Grammar dialog box	Click Spelling and Grammar button on Standard toolbar	Tools, Spelling and Grammar
AutoCorrect dialog box	Tools, AutoCorrect	Tools, AutoCorrect
Thesaurus dialog box	Tools, Language, Thesaurus	Tools, Language, Thesaurus
Insert date/time	Insert, Date and Time, click desired selection, click OK	Alt + Shift + D (date)
Highlight text	Click Highlight button on Formatting toolbar, select text	Alt + Shift + T (time)

thinking offline

Completion: In the space provided at the right, indicate the correct term, symbol, or command.

1. By default, each tab is set apart from the other by this measurement. _____

2. These are the four types of tabs that can be set on the Ruler. _____
   _____
   _____
   _____

3. This is the default tab type. _____

4. When setting tabs on the Ruler, choose the tab type with this button.

5. Press these keys on the keyboard to insert a New Line command. _____

6. Tabs can be set on the Ruler or here. _____

7. To remove all previous tabs, click this button at the Tabs dialog box. _____

8. This is the default left and right margin measurement. _____

9. Press these keys on the keyboard to insert a hard page break. _____

10. This view displays the document on the screen as it will appear when printed. _____

11. Vertically align text with the Vertical alignment option at the Page Setup dialog box with this tab selected. _____

12. This is the shortcut command to insert the current date. _____

13. The Columns button is located on this toolbar. _____

14. Change to this view to display columns as they will appear when printed. _____

15. To complete a spelling and grammar check, click this button on the Standard toolbar. _____

16. When spell checking a document, click this button at the Spelling and Grammar dialog box to skip all occurrences of the selected word. _____

17. This is the default writing style that the grammar checker uses when checking grammar in a document. _____

18. This feature finds synonyms, antonyms, and related words for a particular word. _____

19. In the space provided below, list the steps you would complete to add the letters *hs* and the replacement words *holographic system* at the AutoCorrect dialog box.

_____

_____

_____

working hands-on

Assessment 1

1. At a clear document screen, complete the following steps:
   a. Change the font to 12-point Arial.
   b. Key the document shown in figure 3.28. For the text in columns, set a left tab at the 1-inch mark, the 2.5-inch mark, and the 4-inch mark on the Ruler.
   c. Change the vertical alignment for text to *Center*.
2. Save the document and name it Word Ch 03, SA 01.
3. Print Word Ch 03, SA 01.
4. With the document still open, select the text in columns and then move the tab at the 1-inch mark on the Ruler to the 0.75-inch mark, the tab at the 2.5-inch mark to the 2.75-inch mark, and the tab on the 4-inch mark on the Ruler to the 4.5-inch mark.
5. Save the document again with the same name (Word Ch 03, SA 01).
6. Print and then close Word Ch 03, SA 01.

figure

3.28 **Assessment 1**

SOFTWARE TRAINING SCHEDULE

Word	April 9	8:30 - 11:30 a.m.
PowerPoint	April 11	1:00 - 3:30 p.m.
Excel	May 8	8:30 - 11:30 a.m.
Access	May 10	1:00 - 3:30 p.m.

Assessment 2

1. At a clear editing window, key the document shown in figure 3.29 with the following specifications:
   a. Change the font to 12-point Century Schoolbook (or a similar serif typeface such as Bookman Old Style or Garamond).
   b. Bold and center the title as shown.
   c. Before keying the text in columns, display the Tabs dialog box, and then set left tabs at the 0.5-inch mark and the 1-inch mark, and a right tab with dot leaders at the 5.5-inch mark.
2. Save the document and name it Word Ch 03, SA 02.
3. Print and then close Word Ch 03, SA 02.

figure
3.29 *Assessment 2*

> ### TABLE OF CONTENTS
>

Assessment 3

1. Open Word Ch 03, SA 02.
2. Save the document with Save As and name it Word Ch 03, SA 03.
3. Select the text in columns and then move the tab symbols on the Ruler as follows:
   a. Move the left tab symbol at the 1-inch mark to the 1.5-inch mark.
   b. Move the left tab symbol at the 0.5-inch mark to the 1-inch mark.
   c. Move the right tab symbol at the 5.5-inch mark to the 5-inch mark.
4. Save the document again with the same name (Word Ch 03, SA 03).
5. Print and then close Word Ch 03, SA 03.

Assessment 4

1. Open Word Report 03.
2. Save the document with Save As and name it Word Ch 03, SA 04.
3. Make the following changes to the report:
   a. Change the left and right margins to 1 inch.
   b. Set the title *NETWORK TOPOLOGIES* in 16-point Times New Roman bold.
   c. Set the three headings in the document (*Linear Bus Networks*, *Star Networks*, and *Ring Networks*) in 14-point Times New Roman bold.
   d. Select the text from the beginning of the first paragraph (begins with *A network's layout...*) to the end of the document and then make the following changes:

        1) Change the line spacing to single.

        2) Set a left tab at the 0.25-inch mark on the Ruler.

        3) Format the selected text into two columns.

    e. Insert six points of space before and after each of the three headings in the document (*Linear Bus Networks*, *Star Networks*, and *Ring Networks*).

4. Save the document again with the same name (Word Ch 03, SA 04).
5. Print and then close Word Ch 03, SA 04.

Assessment 5

1. Open Word Ch 03, SA 04.
2. Save the document with Save As and name it Word Ch 03, SA 05.
3. Make the following changes to the document:
    a. Change the left and right margins to 1.25 inches.
    b. Change the width between the columns to 0.3 inches and insert a line between the columns.
4. Save the document again with the same name (Word Ch 03, SA 05).
5. Print and then close Word Ch 03, SA 05.

Assessment 6

1. Open Word Spell Check 03.
2. Save the document with Save As and name it Word Ch 03, SA 06.
3. Complete a spelling check on the document.
4. After completing the spell check, make the following changes to the document:
    a. Set the entire document in a serif typeface of your choosing (other than Times New Roman).
    b. Set the title and two headings in a sans serif typeface.
    c. Move the insertion point to the end of the document. Insert the current date, press the Enter key, and then insert the current time.
5. Save the document again with the same name (Word Ch 03, SA 06).
6. Print and then close Word Ch 03, SA 06.

Assessment 7

1. Open Word Grammar Check 02.
2. Save the document with Save As and name it Word Ch 03, SA 07.
3. Display the Options dialog box with the Spelling & Grammar tab selected, change the writing style to *Formal*, and then close the dialog box.
4. Complete a grammar check on the document. You determine what to change and what to leave as written. Not all sentences selected by the grammar checker contain errors. After the grammar checking is completed, proofread the document and make any necessary changes not selected by the grammar checker.
5. Make the following changes to the document:
    a. Set the entire document in a serif typeface of your choosing (other than Times New Roman).
    b. Set the title in a larger sans serif font.
    c. Double-space the paragraph in the document and change the alignment of the paragraph to justified.
6. Save the document again with the same name (Word Ch 03, SA 07).
7. Display the Options dialog box with the Spelling & Grammar tab selected, change the writing style to *Standard*, and then close the dialog box.
8. Print and then close Word Ch 03, SA 07.

Assessment 8

1. In some Word documents, especially documents with left and right margins wider than 1 inch, the right margin may appear quite ragged. If the paragraph alignment is changed to justified, the right margin will appear even, but there will be extra space added throughout the line. In these situations, hyphenating long words that fall at the end of the text line provides the document with a more balanced look. Use Word's Help feature to learn how to automatically hyphenate words in a document.
2. Open Word Report 01.
3. Save the document with Save As and name it Word Ch 03, SA 08.
4. Automatically hyphenate words in the document, limiting the consecutive hyphens to 2. *(Hint: Specify the number of consecutive hyphens at the Hyphenation dialog box.)*
5. Save the document again with the same name (Word Ch 03, SA 08).
6. Print and then close Word Ch 03, SA 08.

 Chapter 04

Working with Multiple Documents

PERFORMANCE OBJECTIVES

Upon successful completion of chapter 4, you will be able to:

- Create a folder.
- Copy, move, rename, delete, and print documents.
- Move and copy blocks of text within a document.
- Move and copy blocks of text between documents.
- Print specific pages in a document.
- Print multiple copies of a document.
- Print envelopes and labels.
- Change paper size and orientation.
- Send a Word document by e-mail.

Almost every company that conducts business maintains a filing system. The system may consist of documents, folders, and cabinets; or it may be a computerized filing system where information is stored on tapes and disks. Whatever type of filing system a business uses, daily maintenance of files is important to a company's operation. In this chapter, you will learn to maintain files (documents) in Word, including such activities as copying, moving, renaming, and printing documents, and creating additional file folders.

Some documents may need to be heavily revised, and these revisions may include deleting, moving, or copying blocks of text. This kind of editing is generally referred to as *cut and paste*. Cutting and pasting can be done within the same document, or, text can be selected and then moved or copied to another document.

In chapter 1, you learned to print a document with the Print button on the Standard toolbar or through the Print dialog box. By default, one copy of all pages of the currently open document is printed. In this chapter, you will learn to customize a print job with selections from the Print dialog box and to change the paper size and orientation.

Maintaining Documents

Many file (document) management tasks can be completed at the Open and Save As dialog boxes. These tasks can include copying, moving, printing, and renaming documents; opening multiple documents; opening a document as read only; and creating a new folder. To display the Open dialog box, shown in figure 4.1, click the Open button on the Standard toolbar or click File and then Open. To display the Save As dialog box, click File and then Save As.

Open Dialog Box

- Current folder
- Folder icon
- Document icon

Some document maintenance tasks such as creating a folder and deleting documents are performed by using buttons on the Open dialog box or Save As dialog box toolbar. Figure 4.2 displays the Open dialog box toolbar buttons.

Open Dialog Box Toolbar Buttons

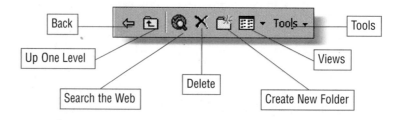

Back — Up One Level — Search the Web — Delete — Create New Folder — Views — Tools

If possible, do all your work in Microsoft Office on the hard drive or network drive. Use a floppy disk primarily for transporting and archiving documents.

Creating a Folder

In Word, documents are grouped logically and placed in *folders*. A folder can be created within a folder. The main folder on a disk or drive is called the *root* folder. Additional folders can be created as a branch of this root folder.

At the Open or Save As dialog boxes, a document displays in the list box preceded by a *document* icon , and a folder is preceded by a *folder* icon.

Create a new folder by clicking the Create New Folder button located on the dialog box toolbar at the Open dialog box or Save as dialog box. At the New Folder dialog box shown in figure 4.3, key a name for the folder, and then click OK or press Enter. The new folder becomes the active folder.

Create New Folder

If you want to make the previous folder the active folder, click the Up One Level button on the dialog box toolbar. Clicking this button changes to the folder that was up one level from the current folder. After clicking the Up One Level button, the Back button becomes active. Click this button and the previously active folder becomes active again.

Up One Level

A folder name can contain a maximum of 255 characters. Numbers, spaces, and symbols can be used in the folder name, except those symbols explained in chapter 1 in the *Naming a Document* section.

Back

(Before completing computer exercises, delete the Chapter 03 *folder on your disk. Next, copy the* Chapter 04 *folder from the CD that accompanies this textbook to your disk and then make* Chapter 04 *the active folder.)*

New Folder Dialog Box

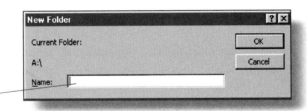

Key a folder name in this text box and then press Enter or click OK.

exercise

Creating a Folder

1. Create a folder named *Documents* on your disk by completing the following steps:
   a. Display the Open dialog box and open the *Chapter 04* folder on your disk.
   b. Click the Create New Folder button (located on the dialog box toolbar).
   c. At the New Folder dialog box, key **Documents**.
   d. Click OK or press Enter. (The *Documents* folder is now the active folder.)
   e. Change back to the *Chapter 04* folder by clicking the Up One Level button on the dialog box toolbar.

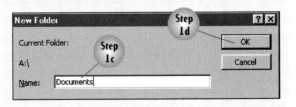

2. Click the Cancel button to close the Open dialog box.

Selecting Documents

Document management tasks can be completed on one document or selected documents. For example, you can move one document to a different folder, or you can select several documents and move them at one time. Selected documents can be deleted, copied, moved, or printed.

To select one document, display the Open dialog box, and then click the desired document. To select several adjacent documents (documents displayed next to each other) using the mouse, you would complete the following steps:

1. Display the Open dialog box.
2. Click the first document to make it active.
3. Position the arrow pointer on the last document to be selected, hold down the Shift key, and then click the left mouse button.

You can also select documents that are not adjacent in the Open dialog box. To do this with the mouse, you would complete the following steps:

1. Display the Open dialog box.
2. Click the first document you want selected.
3. Hold down the Ctrl key.
4. Click each document you want selected.
5. When all desired documents are selected, release the Ctrl key.

When the Open dialog box is displayed, the first document in the Look in list box is automatically selected. Before selecting documents, deselect the first document (unless this first document is to be included with the other selected documents). To deselect the first document, position the arrow pointer anywhere in a clear portion of the Look in list box (not on a document name), and then click the left mouse button.

If your disk is full, use Save As to save the document to a different drive or folder.

Deleting Documents and Folders

At some point, you may want to delete certain documents from your data disk or any other disk or folder in which you may be working. If you use Word on a regular basis, you should establish a system for deleting documents. The system you choose depends on the work you are doing and the amount of folder or disk space available. To delete a document, display the Open or Save As dialog box, select the document, and then click the Delete button on the dialog box toolbar. At the dialog box asking you to confirm the deletion, click Yes.

Delete

You can also delete a document by displaying the Open dialog box, selecting the document to be deleted, clicking the Tools button on the dialog box toolbar, and then clicking Delete at the drop-down menu. Another method for deleting a document is to display the Open dialog box, right-click the document to be deleted, and then click Delete at the shortcut menu.

Tools

Deleting a Document

1. Delete a document by completing the following steps:
   a. Display the Open dialog box with *Chapter 04* the active folder.
   b. Click Word Document 06 to select it.
   c. Click the Delete button on the dialog box toolbar.
   d. At the question asking if you want to delete the items, click <u>Y</u>es.
2. Close the Open dialog box.

Deleting Selected Documents

1. Delete selected documents by completing the following steps:
   a. Display the Open dialog box with *Chapter 04* the active folder.
   b. Click Word Report 02.
   c. Hold down the Shift key and then click Word Report 04.
   d. Click the Tools button on the dialog box toolbar.
   e. At the drop-down menu that displays, click <u>D</u>elete.
   f. At the question asking if you are sure you want to delete the items, click <u>Y</u>es.
   g. At the message telling you that Word Report 02 is a read-only file and asking if you are sure you want to delete it, click the Yes to <u>A</u>ll button.
2. Close the Open dialog box.

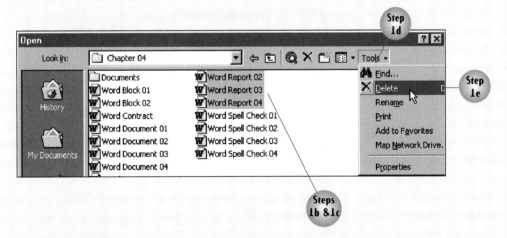

A folder and all its contents can be deleted at the Open or Save As dialog box. Delete a folder and its contents in the same manner as deleting a document or selected documents.

Deleting to the Recycle Bin

Documents deleted from your data disk are deleted permanently. (There are recovery programs, however, that will help you recover deleted text. If you accidentally delete a document or documents from a disk, do not do anything more with the disk until you can run a recovery program.) Documents deleted from the hard drive are automatically sent to the Windows Recycle Bin. If you accidentally delete a document to the Recycle Bin, it can be easily restored. To free space on the drive, empty the Recycle Bin on a periodic basis. Restoring a document from or emptying the contents of the Recycle Bin is done at the Windows desktop (not in Word). To empty the Recycle Bin, you would complete the following steps:

Remember to empty the Recycle Bin on a regular basis.

1. Display the Windows desktop. (If you are just beginning, turn on the computer, and Windows will open. If you are currently working in Word, click the Minimize button at the right side of the Title bar. (The Minimize button contains the single underline symbol (_). Be sure to click the Minimize button on the Title bar and not the one just below it on the Menu bar.)

Minimize

2. At the Windows desktop, double-click the *Recycle Bin* icon (located at the left side of the desktop).
3. At the Recycle Bin dialog box, shown in figure 4.4, click File and then Empty Recycle Bin.
4. At the question asking if you are sure you want to delete these items, click Yes.

4.4

Recycle Bin Dialog Box

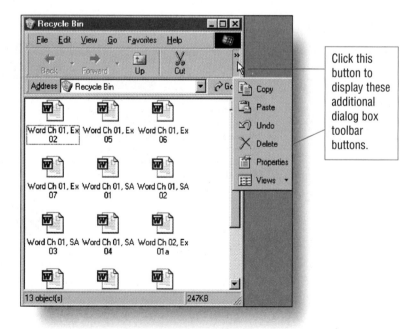

Click this button to display these additional dialog box toolbar buttons.

If you want to empty only specific documents from the Recycle Bin, hold down the Ctrl key while clicking the documents to be emptied. Position the arrow pointer on one of the selected documents, click the *right* mouse button, and then click the left mouse button on Delete. At the question asking if you want to delete the selected documents, click Yes. You can also delete selected documents by expanding the Recycle Bin dialog box toolbar (click the right-pointing arrows that display at the right side of the toolbar—see figure 4.4) and then clicking the Delete button.

A document or selected documents can also be restored from the Recycle Bin. To do this, you would complete the following steps:

1. At the Windows desktop, double-click the Recycle Bin icon.
2. At the Recycle Bin dialog box, click the document to be restored. (If you are restoring more than one document, hold down the Ctrl key while clicking the desired documents.)
3. Click File and then Restore.

At the Recycle Bin dialog box, you can also restore a document by positioning the arrow pointer on the document to be restored, clicking the *right* mouse button, and then clicking the left mouse button on Restore.

If you minimized the Word program by clicking the Minimize button, you can maximize (display the Word screen) the Word program at the desktop by clicking the Microsoft Word button located on the Taskbar (at the bottom of the screen).

Copying Files

In previous chapters, you opened a document from the data disk and saved it with a new name on the same disk. This process makes an exact copy of the document, leaving the original on the disk. You copied documents and saved the new document in the same folder as the original document. You can also copy a document into another folder and use the document's original name or give it a different name, or select documents at the Open dialog box and copy them to the same folder or into a different folder. To copy a document into another folder, you would complete the following steps:

1. Open the document you want to copy.
2. Display the Save As dialog box.
3. At the Save As dialog box, change to the desired folder. To do this, click the down-pointing triangle to the right of the Save in text box, and then click the desired folder at the drop-down menu.
4. Click the Save button in the lower right corner of the dialog box.

The Open and Save As dialog boxes contain an Up One Level button (located on the dialog box toolbar). Use this button if you want to change to the folder that is up one level from the current folder.

Saving a Copy of an Open Document

1. Open Word Document 02.
2. Save the document with Save As and name it Keyboards. (Make sure *Chapter 04* is the active folder.)
3. Save a copy of the Keyboards document in the *Documents* folder created in exercise 1 by completing the following steps: (If your system does not contain this folder, check with your instructor to determine if there is another folder you can use.)
   a. With Keyboards still open, display the Save As dialog box.
   b. At the Save As dialog box, change to the *Documents* folder. To do this, double-click *Documents* at the beginning of the list box (folders are listed before documents).
   c. Click the Save button located in the lower right corner of the dialog box.
4. Close Keyboards.
5. Change back to the *Chapter 04* folder by completing the following steps:
   a. Display the Open dialog box.
   b. Click the Up One Level button located on the dialog box toolbar.
   c. Click Cancel to close the Open dialog box.

A document can be copied to another folder without opening the document first. To do this, use the Copy and Paste options from a shortcut menu at the Open (or Save As) dialog box.

Copying a Document at the Open Dialog Box

1. Copy Word Document 01 to the *Documents* folder by completing the following steps:
   a. Display the Open dialog box with *Chapter 04* the active folder.
   b. Position the arrow pointer on Word Document 01, click the *right* mouse button, and then click Copy at the shortcut menu.
   c. Change to the *Documents* folder by double-clicking *Documents* at the beginning of the list box.
   d. Position the arrow pointer in any white area (not on a document name) in the list box, click the *right* mouse button, and then click Paste at the shortcut menu.
2. Change back to the *Chapter 04* folder by clicking the Up One Level button located on the dialog box toolbar.
3. Close the Open dialog box.

A document or selected documents can be copied into the same folder. When you do this, Word names the document(s) "Copy of xxx" (where xxx is the current document name). You can copy one document or selected documents into the same folder.

exercise

Copying Selected Documents into the Same Folder

1. Copy documents into the same folder by completing the following steps:
    a. Display the Open dialog box with *Chapter 04* the active folder.
    b. Select Word Document 03, Word Document 04, and Word Document 05. (To do this, click Word Document 03, hold down the Shift key, and then click Word Document 05.)
    c. Position the arrow pointer on one of the selected documents, click the *right* mouse button, and then click Copy at the shortcut menu.
    d. Position the arrow pointer in any white area in the list box, click the *right* mouse button, and then click Paste at the shortcut menu. (In a few seconds, Word will redisplay the Open dialog box with the following documents added: Copy of Word Document 03, Copy of Word Document 04, and Copy of Word Document 05.)
2. Close the Open dialog box.

exercise

Copying Selected Documents into a Different Folder

1. Copy several documents to the *Documents* folder by completing the following steps:
    a. Display the Open dialog box with *Chapter 04* the active folder.
    b. Select Word Document 02, Word Document 04, and Word Document 05 by completing the following steps:
        1) Click once on Word Document 02. (This selects the document.)
        2) Hold down the Ctrl key, click Word Document 04, click Word Document 05, and then release the Ctrl key.
    c. Position the arrow pointer on one of the selected documents, click the *right* mouse button, and then click Copy at the shortcut menu.
    d. Double-click the folder named *Documents*. (This folder is located at the beginning of the list box.)
    e. When the *Documents* folder displays, position the arrow pointer in any white area in the list box, click the *right* mouse button, and then click Paste at the shortcut menu.
    f. Click the Up One Level button to change back to the *Chapter 04* folder.
2. Close the Open dialog box by clicking the Cancel button.

Sending Documents to a Different Drive or Folder

With the Copy and Paste options from the shortcut menu at the Open or Save As dialog box, you can copy documents to another folder or drive. With the Send To option, you can quickly send a copy of a document to another drive or folder. To use this option, position the arrow pointer on the document you want copied, click the *right* mouse button, position the arrow pointer on Send To (this causes a side menu to display), and then click the desired drive or folder.

Cutting and Pasting a Document

A document can be removed from one folder or disk and inserted in another folder or on a disk using the Cut and Paste options from the shortcut menu at the Open dialog box. To do this you would display the Open dialog box, position the arrow pointer on the document to be removed (cut), click the *right* mouse button, and then click Cut at the shortcut menu. Change to the desired folder, position the arrow pointer in a white area in the list box, click the *right* mouse button, and then click Paste at the shortcut menu.

Cutting and Pasting a Document

1. Save and move a document into a different folder by completing the following steps:
    a. Open Word Document 04.
    b. Save the document with Save As and name it Economic Outlook.
    c. Close Economic Outlook.
    d. Move Economic Outlook to the *Documents* folder by completing the following steps:
        1) Display the Open dialog box with *Chapter 04* the active folder.
        2) Position the arrow pointer on Economic Outlook, click the *right* mouse button, and then click Cut at the shortcut menu.
        3) Double-click *Documents* to make it the active folder.
        4) Position the arrow pointer in the white area in the list box, click the *right* mouse button, and then click Paste at the shortcut menu.
    e. Click the Up One Level button to make the *Chapter 04* folder the active folder.
2. Close the Open dialog box.

Renaming Documents

At the Open dialog box, use the Rename option from the Tools drop-down menu to give a document a different name. The Rename option changes the name of the document and keeps it in the same folder. To use Rename, display the Open dialog box, click once on the document to be renamed, click the Tools button on the dialog box toolbar and then click the Rename Option. This causes a black border to surround the document name and the name to be selected. Key the desired name and then press Enter.

You can also rename a document by right-clicking the document name at the Open dialog box and then clicking Rename at the shortcut menu. Key the desired name for the document and then press the Enter key.

Renaming a Document

1. Rename a document located in the *Documents* folder by completing the following steps:
   a. Display the Open dialog box with *Chapter 04* the active folder.
   b. Double-click *Documents* to make it the active folder.
   c. Click once on Word Document 05 to select it.
   d. Click the Tools button on the dialog box toolbar.
   e. At the drop-down menu that displays, click Rename.
   f. Key **Retirement** and then press the Enter key. (Depending on your system setup, you may need to key **Retirement.doc**.)
   g. At the message asking if you are sure you want to change the name of the read-only file, click Yes.
   h. Complete steps similar to those in 1c through 1g to rename Word Document 04 to Stock Market (or Stock Market.doc).
   i. Click the Up One Level button.
2. Close the Open dialog box.

Deleting a Folder and Its Contents

As you learned earlier in this chapter, a document or selected documents can be deleted. In addition to documents, a folder (and all its contents) can be deleted. Delete a folder in the same manner as a document is deleted.

Deleting a Folder and Its Contents

1. Delete the *Documents* folder and its contents by completing the following steps:
   a. Display the Open dialog box with *Chapter 04* the active folder.
   b. Click once on the *Documents* folder to select it.
   c. Click the Delete button on the dialog box toolbar.
   d. At the question asking if you want to remove the folder and its contents, click Yes.
   e. At the message telling you that Word Document 01 is a read-only file and asking if you are sure you want to delete it, click the Yes to All button.
2. Close the Open dialog box.

Opening Documents

A document or selected documents can be opened at the Open dialog box. To open one document, display the Open dialog box, position the arrow pointer on the desired document, click the *right* mouse button, and then click Open at the shortcut menu. To open more than one document, select the documents in the Open dialog box, position the arrow pointer on one of the selected documents, click the *right* mouse button, and then click Open at the shortcut menu.

Closing Documents

If more than one document is open, all open documents can be closed at the same time. To do this, hold down the Shift key, click File and then Close All. Holding down the Shift key before clicking File causes the Close option to change to Close All.

Opening and Closing Several Documents

1. Open several documents by completing the following steps:
   a. Display the Open dialog box with *Chapter 04* the active folder.
   b. Select Word Document 01, Word Document 02, Word Document 03, and Word Document 04.
   c. Position the arrow pointer on one of the selected documents, click the *right* mouse button, and then click the left mouse button on Open.
2. Close the open documents by completing the following steps:
   a. Hold down the Shift key.
   b. Click File and then Close All.

Printing Documents

Up to this point, you have opened a document and then printed it. With the Print option from the Tools drop-down menu or the Print option from the shortcut menu at the Open dialog box, you can print a document or several documents without opening them.

Printing Documents

1. Display the Open dialog box with *Chapter 04* the active folder.
2. Select Word Document 03, Word Document 04, and Word Document 05.
3. Click the Tools button on the dialog box toolbar.
4. At the drop-down menu that displays, click Print.

Working with Blocks of Text

When cutting and pasting, you work with blocks of text. A block of text is a portion of text that you have selected. (Chapter 1 explained the various methods for selecting text.) A block of text can be as small as one character or as large as an entire page or document. Once a block of text has been selected, it can be deleted, moved to a new location, or copied and pasted within a document or to other open documents.

Deleting a Block of Text

Word offers different methods for deleting text from a document. To delete a single character, you can use either the Delete key or the Backspace key. To delete more than a single character, select the portion of text to be deleted, and then choose one of the following options:

- Press Delete.
- Click the Cut button on the Standard toolbar.
- Click Edit and then click Cut.

If you press Delete, the text is deleted permanently. (You can, however, restore deleted text with the Undo Typing option from the Edit menu or with the Undo or Redo buttons on the Standard toolbar.) The Cut button on the Standard toolbar and the Cut option from the Edit drop-down menu will delete the selected text and insert it in the *Clipboard*. Word's Clipboard is a temporary area of memory. The Clipboard holds text while it is being moved or copied to a new location in the document or to a different document. Text inserted in the Clipboard stays there until other text is inserted. Delete selected text with the Delete key if you do not need it again. Use the other methods if you might want to insert deleted text in the current document or a different document.

Moving a Block of Text

Word offers a variety of methods for moving text. After you have selected a block of text, move the text with buttons on the Standard toolbar or options from the Edit drop-down menu. To move a block of selected text from one location to another using buttons on the Standard toolbar, you would complete the following steps:

1. Select the text.
2. Click the Cut button on the Standard toolbar.
3. Position the insertion point at the location where the selected text is to be inserted.
4. Click the Paste button on the Standard toolbar.

To move a block of selected text from one location to another using options from the Edit menu, you would complete the following steps:

1. Select the text.
2. Click Edit and then click Cut.
3. Position the insertion point at the location where the selected text is to be inserted.
4. Click Edit and then Paste.

In addition to the methods just described, a block of selected text can also be moved with the mouse. There are two methods for moving text with the mouse. You can use the mouse to drag selected text to a new location or use a shortcut menu.

To drag selected text to a new location, you would complete the following steps:

1. Select the text to be moved with the mouse.
2. Move the I-beam pointer inside the selected text until it becomes an arrow pointer.
3. Hold down the left mouse button, drag the arrow pointer (displays with a gray box attached) to the location where you want the selected text inserted, and then release the button.
4. Deselect the text.

Cut

Undo

Redo

Consider using the Cut button rather than the Delete key to delete text. If you want to bring back the deleted text, position the insertion point and then click the Paste button.

Paste

If you drag and then drop selected text in the wrong location, immediately click the Undo button.

When you hold down the left mouse button and drag the mouse, the arrow pointer displays with a small gray box attached. In addition, the insertion point displays as a grayed vertical bar. When the insertion point (grayed vertical bar) is located in the desired position, release the mouse button. The selected text is removed from its original position and inserted in the new location.

To move selected text with a shortcut menu, you would complete the following steps:

1. Select the text to be moved with the mouse.
2. Move the I-beam pointer inside the selected text until it becomes an arrow pointer.
3. Click the *right* mouse button.
4. At the shortcut menu that displays, click Cut.
5. Position the insertion point where the text is to be inserted.
6. Click the *right* mouse button to display the shortcut menu and then click <u>P</u>aste.

The Clipboard contents are deleted when the computer is turned off. Save text you want permanently as a separate document.

When selected text is cut from a document and inserted in the Clipboard, it stays in the Clipboard until other text is inserted in the Clipboard. For this reason, you can paste text from the Clipboard more than just once. For example, if you cut text to the Clipboard, you can paste this text in different locations within the document or other documents as many times as desired.

exercise 13

Moving Selected Text

1. Open Word Document 03.
2. Save the document with Save As and name it Word Ch 04, Ex 13.
3. Move the following text in the document:
   a. Move the second paragraph above the first paragraph by completing the following steps:
      1) Select the second paragraph including the blank line below the paragraph.
      2) Click the Cut button on the Standard toolbar.
      3) Position the insertion point at the beginning of the first paragraph.
      4) Click the Paste button on the Standard toolbar.
   b. Move the third paragraph above the second paragraph by completing the following steps:
      1) Select the third paragraph including the blank line below the paragraph.
      2) Click <u>E</u>dit and then click Cu<u>t</u>. (This may display the Clipboard toolbar. You will learn about this toolbar later in this chapter.)
      3) Position the insertion point at the beginning of the second paragraph.
      4) Click <u>E</u>dit and then <u>P</u>aste.
   c. Move the first paragraph to the end of the document using the mouse by completing the following steps:

1) Using the mouse, select the first paragraph including the blank line below the paragraph.
2) Move the I-beam pointer inside the selected text until it becomes an arrow pointer.
3) Hold down the left mouse button, drag the arrow pointer (displays with a small gray box attached) a double space below the last paragraph (make sure the insertion point, which displays as a grayed vertical bar, is positioned a double space below the last paragraph), and then release the mouse button.

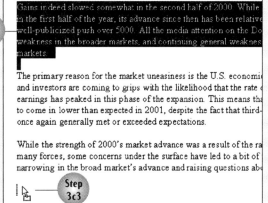

Step 3c1

Step 3c3

4) Deselect the text.
5) If necessary, press Enter to create space between paragraphs. (Skip this step if the paragraphs are already separated by a double space.)

d. If the Clipboard toolbar is displayed, close it.
4. Save the document again with the same name (Word Ch 04, Ex 13).
5. Print and then close Word Ch 04, Ex 13.

Copying a Block of Text

Copying selected text can be useful in documents that contain repetitive portions of text. You can use this function to insert duplicate portions of text in a document instead of rekeying the text. After you have selected a block of text, copy the text to a different location with buttons on the Standard toolbar or options from the Edit drop-down menu. To copy text with the buttons on the Standard toolbar, you would complete the following steps:

1. Select the text to be copied.
2. Click the Copy button on the Standard toolbar.
3. Move the insertion point to the location where the copied text is to be inserted.
4. Click the Paste button on the Standard toolbar.

Copy

To copy text with options from the Edit drop-down menu, you would complete the following steps:

1. Select the text to be copied.
2. Click Edit and then click Copy.
3. Move the insertion point to the location where the copied text is to be inserted.
4. Click Edit and then Paste.

Copying Selected Text with Buttons on the Standard Toolbar

1. Open Word Block 01.
2. Save the document with Save As and name it Word Ch 04, Ex 14.
3. Select the entire document and then change the font to 14-point Goudy Old Style bold (or a similar serif typeface).
4. Copy the text in the document to the end of the document by completing the following steps:
   a. Select all the text in the document including two blank lines below the text.
   b. Click the Copy button on the Standard toolbar.
   c. Move the insertion point to the end of the document.
   d. Click the Paste button on the Standard toolbar.
5. Copy the text again at the end of the document. To do this, position the insertion point at the end of the document, and then click the Paste button on the Standard toolbar. (This inserts a copy of the text from the Clipboard.)
6. Save the document with the same name (Word Ch 04, Ex 14).
7. Print and then close Word Ch 04, Ex 14.

The mouse can also be used to copy a block of text in a document to a new location. To do this, you would complete the following steps:

1. Select the text with the mouse.
2. Move the I-beam pointer inside the selected text until it becomes an arrow pointer.
3. Hold down the left mouse button and hold down the Ctrl key. Drag the arrow pointer (displays with a small gray box and a box containing a plus symbol) to the location where you want the copied text inserted (make sure the insertion point, which displays as a grayed vertical bar, is positioned in the desired location), and then release the mouse button and then the Ctrl key.
4. Deselect the text.

If you select a block of text and then decide you selected the wrong text or you do not want to do anything with the block, you can deselect it. If you are using the mouse, click the left mouse button outside the selected text. If you are using the keyboard, press an arrow key to deselect text. If you selected with the Extend mode (F8), press Esc and then press an arrow key to deselect text.

Copying Selected Text Using the Mouse

1. Open Word Block 02.
2. Save the document with Save As and name it Word Ch 04, Ex 15.

3. Copy the text in the document using the mouse by completing the following steps:
   a. Select all the text with the mouse and include two blank lines below the text. (Consider turning on the display of nonprinting characters.)
   b. Move the I-beam pointer inside the selected text until it becomes an arrow pointer.
   c. Hold down the Ctrl key and then the left mouse button. Drag the arrow pointer (displays with a small gray box and a box with a plus symbol inside) to the end of the document immediately above the end-of-document marker (make sure the insertion point, which displays as a grayed vertical bar, is positioned immediately above the end-of-document marker), then release the mouse button and then the Ctrl key.

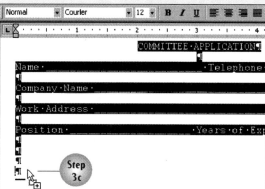

   d. Deselect the text.
4. Select both forms using the mouse (including two blank lines below the second form) and then copy the selected forms to the end of the document.
5. Make sure all forms fit on one page. If the forms do not fit on one page, consider deleting any extra blank lines between forms.
6. Save the document again with the same name (Word Ch 04, Ex 15).
7. Print and then close Word Ch 04, Ex 15.

Collecting and Pasting Multiple Items

Office 2000 includes a new feature called *collecting and pasting* that you can use to collect up to 12 different items and then paste them in various locations. Display the Clipboard toolbar shown below when you want to collect and paste items. Display this toolbar by right-clicking an existing toolbar and then clicking Clipboard.

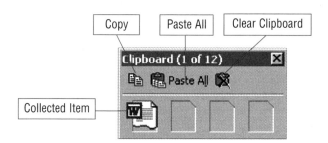

Select text or an object you want to copy and then click the Copy button on the Clipboard toolbar. Continue selecting text or items and clicking the Copy button. To insert an item, position the insertion point in the desired location and then click the button on the Clipboard representing the item. Position the insertion point on a button and a ScreenTip displays with information on the item. If the item is text, the first 50 characters display. When all desired items are inserted, click the Clear Clipboard button to remove any remaining items.

Usually, if you cut or copy any two items consecutively, the Clipboard toolbar automatically displays. If you close the Clipboard toolbar three times in a row without clicking a button on the toolbar, the Clipboard toolbar will no longer appear automatically. To display the Clipboard toolbar, right-click any currently displayed toolbar, and then click Clipboard. You can also click <u>V</u>iew, point to <u>T</u>oolbars, and then click Clipboard. When you display the Clipboard toolbar and then click a button on the toolbar, the count is reset, and from that point on the Clipboard toolbar appears automatically again.

Collecting and Pasting Paragraphs of Text

1. Open Word Contract.
2. Display the Clipboard toolbar by right-clicking an existing toolbar and then clicking Clipboard at the drop-down list. (If there are any items in the Clipboard, click the Clear Clipbard button.)
3. Select paragraph 2 in the *TRANSFERS AND MOVING EXPENSES* section and then click the Copy button on the Clipboard toolbar.
4. Select and then copy each of the following paragraphs:
   a. Paragraph 4 in the *TRANSFERS AND MOVING EXPENSES* section.
   b. Paragraph 1 in the *SICK LEAVE* section.
   c. Paragraph 3 in the *SICK LEAVE* section.
   d. Paragraph 5 in the *SICK LEAVE* section.
5. Paste the paragraphs by completing the following steps:
   a. Click the New Blank Document button on the Standard toolbar.
   b. Key **CONTRACT NEGOTIATION ITEMS** centered and bolded.
   c. Press Enter twice, turn off bold, and return the paragraph alignment back to Left.
   d. Click the button on the Clipboard representing paragraph 2. (When the paragraph is inserted in the document, the paragraph number changes.)
   e. Click the button on the Clipboard representing paragraph 4.
   f. Click the button on the Clipboard representing paragraph 3.
   g. Click the button on the Clipboard representing paragraph 5.
6. Click the Clear Clipboard button on the Clipboard toolbar.
7. Select the numbered paragraphs and then click the Numbering button on the Formatting toolbar. (This properly renumbers the paragraphs.)
8. Deselect the text and then close the Clipboard toolbar.
9. Save the document and name it Word Ch 04, Ex 16.
10. Print and then close Word Ch 04, Ex 16.
11. Close Word Contract without saving the changes.

Inserting One Document into Another

Some documents may contain standard information—information that remains the same. For example, a legal document, such as a will, may contain text that is standard and appears in all wills. Repetitive text can be saved as a separate document and then inserted into an existing document whenever needed. Insert a separate document into an existing document by displaying the Insert File dialog box and double-clicking the desired document. To display the Insert File dialog box shown in figure 4.5, click Insert, expand the drop-down menu, and then click File.

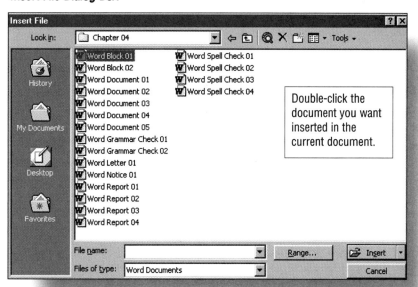

figure

4.5

Insert File Dialog Box

Double-click the document you want inserted in the current document.

exercise

17

Saving Selected Text and Inserting One Document into Another

1. Open Word Document 04.
2. Select the first paragraph and then save it as a separate document named Budget by completing the following steps:
   a. Select the first paragraph in the document.
   b. Click the Copy button on the Standard toolbar.
   c. Click the New Blank Document button on the Standard toolbar (first button on the left).
   d. At the clear document screen, click the Paste button on the Standard toolbar.
   e. Save the document and name it Budget.
   f. Close the Budget document.
3. Close Word Document 04 without saving any changes.
4. At a clear document screen, key the title and the first paragraph of text shown in figure 4.6. After keying the first paragraph of text, press Enter twice and then insert the Budget document by completing the following steps:

a. Click Insert, expand the drop-down menu, and then click File.
b. At the Insert File dialog box, double-click Budget.
5. Move the insertion point a double space below the last paragraph and then key the last paragraph shown in figure 4.6.
6. Save the document and name it Word Ch 04, Ex 17.
7. Print and then close Word Ch 04, Ex 17.

Exercise 17

LOOKING FORWARD

The basic, underlying conditions that have driven the markets thus far, such as moderate growth with low inflation and falling interest rates, remain firmly in place. Importantly, continued low inflation and lackluster economic growth have set the stage for further interest rate cuts, and rates do indeed have room to move even lower, particularly if the current administration and Congress can reach a compromise on a balanced budget.

[Insert *Budget* document here.]

Even beyond the core fundamentals in the U.S. economy, there are clear reasons to be optimistic over the longer term, including reasonable stock valuations, stable labor costs, rising savings rates from baby boomers, increasing demand for U.S. exports in light of expanding economies overseas, and U.S. superiority in the technologies of the future.

Working with Windows

Word operates within the Windows environment created by the Windows 98 program. However, when working in Word, a *window* refers to the document screen. The Windows 98 program creates an environment in which various software programs are used with menu bars, scroll bars, and icons to represent programs and files. With the Windows 98 program, you can open several different software programs and move between them quickly. Similarly, using windows in Word, you can open several different documents and move between them quickly.

Opening Multiple Windows

With multiple documents open, you can move the insertion point between them. You can move or copy information between documents or compare the contents of several documents. The maximum number of documents (windows) that you can have open at one time depends on the memory of your computer system and the amount of text in each document. When you open a new window, it is placed on top of the original window. Once multiple windows are opened, you can resize the windows to see all or a portion of them on the screen.

When a document is open, a button displays on the taskbar. This button represents the open document and contains a document icon, and the document name. (Depending on the length of the document name and the size of the button, not all of the name may be visible.) Another method for determining what documents are open is to click the Window option on the Menu bar. This displays a drop-down menu similar to the one shown in figure 4.7. (The number of documents and document names displayed at the bottom of the menu will vary.)

Window Drop-Down Menu

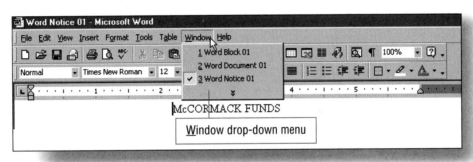

Window drop-down menu

The open document names display at the bottom of the menu. The document name with the check mark in front of it is the *active* document. The active document is the document containing the insertion point. To make one of the other documents active, click the desired document name. When you change the active document, the Window menu is removed and the new active document displays.

Closing Multiple Windows

All open documents can be closed at the same time. To do this, hold down the Shift key, and then click File on the Menu bar. This causes the File drop-down menu to display with the Close option changed to Close All. Click the Close All option and all open documents will be closed.

Opening and Closing Multiple Windows

(Note: If you are using Word on a network system that contains a virus checker, you may not be able to open multiple documents at once. Continue by opening each document individually.)

1. Open several documents at the same time by completing the following steps:
   a. Display the Open dialog box.
   b. Click the document named Word Block 01.
   c. Hold down the Ctrl key, click Word Document 01, and then click Word Notice 01.
   d. Release the Ctrl key.
   e. Position the arrow pointer on one of the selected documents, click the *right* mouse button, and then click the left mouse button on Open.

2. Make Word Document 01 the active document by clicking the button on the Taskbar containing the name Word Document 01.
3. Make Word Block 01 the active document by clicking <u>W</u>indow and then clicking <u>1</u>.
4. Close all open documents by holding down the Shift key, clicking <u>F</u>ile, and then clicking <u>C</u>lose All.

Arranging Windows

If you have more than one document open, you can use the <u>A</u>rrange All option from the <u>W</u>indow drop-down menu to view a portion of all open documents. To do this, click <u>W</u>indow, expand the menu, and then click <u>A</u>rrange All. Figure 4.8 shows a document screen with four documents open that have been arranged.

Arranged Documents

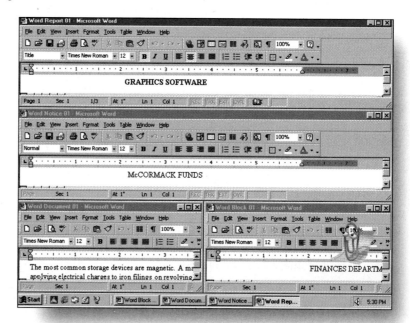

Arranging Windows

1. Open the following documents: Word Block 01, Word Document 01, Word Notice 01, and Word Report 01.
2. Arrange the windows by clicking <u>W</u>indow, expanding the drop-down menu, and then clicking <u>A</u>rrange All.

3. Make Word Block 01 the active document by positioning the arrow pointer on the title bar for Word Block 01 and then clicking the left mouse button.
4. Close Word Block 01.
5. Make Word Notice 01 active and then close it.
6. Close the remaining documents.

Maximizing, Restoring, and Minimizing Documents

Use the Maximize and Minimize buttons in the upper right corner of the active document window to change the size of the window. The Maximize button is the button in the upper right corner of the active document immediately to the left of the Close button. (The Close button is the button containing the X.) The Minimize button is located immediately to the left of the Maximize button.

If you arrange all open documents and then click the Maximize button in the active document, the active document expands to fill the document screen. In addition, the Maximize button changes to the Restore button. To return the active document back to its size before it was maximized, click the Restore button. If you click the Minimize button in the active document, the document is reduced and a button displays on the Taskbar representing the document. To maximize a document that has been minimized, click the button on the Taskbar representing the document.

Maximize

Minimize

Restore

You can minimize all open programs by right-clicking an empty spot on the Taskbar and then clicking Minimize All Windows.

Minimizing, Maximizing, and Restoring Documents

1. Open Word Block 02.
2. Maximize Word Block 02 by clicking the Maximize button at the right side of the Title bar. (The Maximize button is the button at the right side of the Title bar, immediately left of the Close button.)
3. Open Word Document 03.
4. Open Word Report 01.
5. Arrange the windows.
6. Make Word Block 02 the active window.
7. Minimize Word Block 02 by clicking the Minimize button in the upper right corner of the active window.
8. Make Word Document 03 the active document and then minimize Word Document 03.
9. Restore Word Document 03 by clicking the button on the Taskbar representing the document.
10. Restore Word Block 02.
11. Make Word Report 01 the active document and then close it.
12. Close Word Document 03.
13. Maximize Word Block 02 by clicking the Maximize button at the right side of the Title bar.
14. Close Word Block 02.

Cutting and Pasting Text Between Windows

With several documents open, you can easily move, copy, and/or paste text from one document to another. To move, copy, and/or paste text between documents, use the cutting and pasting options you learned earlier in this chapter together with the information about windows.

Copying Selected Text from One Open Document to Another

1. Open Word Document 03.
2. Save the document with Save As and name it Word Ch 04, Ex 21.
3. With Word Ch 04, Ex 21 still open, open Word Document 04.
4. With Word Document 04 the active document, copy the first two paragraphs in the document and paste them into Word Ch 04, Ex 21 by completing the following steps:
   a. Select the first two paragraphs in Word Document 04.
   b. Click the Copy button on the Standard toolbar.
   c. Deselect the text.
   d. Make Word Ch 04, Ex 21 the active document.
   e. Position the insertion point a double space below the last paragraph and then click the Paste button on the Standard toolbar.
5. Make Word Document 04 the active document and then close it. (This displays Word Ch 04, Ex 21.)
6. With Word Ch 04, Ex 21 displayed, make the following changes to the document:
   a. Key the title **ECONOMIC OUTLOOK** at the beginning of the document, centered and in bold.
   b. Select the entire document and then change the font to 12-point Garamond (or a similar serif typeface).
7. Save the document again with the same name (Word Ch 04, Ex 21).
8. Print and then close Word Ch 04, Ex 21.

Printing Documents

Save a document before printing it.

In chapter 1, you learned to print the document displayed in the document screen at the Print dialog box. By default, one copy of all pages of the currently open document prints. With options at the Print dialog box, you can specify the number of copies to print and also specific pages for printing. To display the Print dialog box shown in figure 4.9, click File and then Print.

figure
4.9

Print Dialog Box

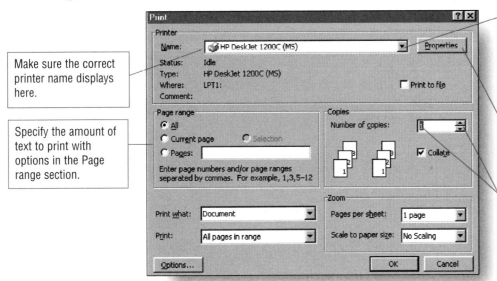

Make sure the correct printer name displays here.

Specify the amount of text to print with options in the Page range section.

Click this down-pointing triangle to display a list of installed printers.

Click this button to set options for the selected printer such as paper size, layout, orientation, paper source, and paper quality.

Print multiple copies of a document by increasing this number.

If you want to cancel the current print job, double-click the *Print Status* icon on the Status bar (located at the far right side). Depending on how much of the document has been sent to the printer, this may or may not stop the printing of the entire document.

Printing Specific Text or Pages

The Page range section of the Print dialog box contains settings you can use to specify the amount of text you want printed. At the default setting of <u>A</u>ll, all pages of the current document are printed. Choose the Curr<u>e</u>nt page option to print the page where the insertion point is located. If you want to select and then print a portion of the document, choose the <u>S</u>election option at the Print dialog box. This prints only the text that has been selected in the current document. (This option is dimmed unless text is selected in the document.)

With the Pages option, you can identify a specific page, multiple pages, and/or a range of pages. If you want specific multiple pages printed, use a comma (,) to indicate *and* and use a hyphen (-) to indicate *through*. For example, to print pages 2 and 5, you would key **2,5** in the Pages text box. To print pages 6 through 10, you would key **6-10**.

Click the Properties button at the Print dialog box to display a dialog box with options for specifying the paper size, orientation, and paper source.

Hint

Printing Specific Pages

1. Open Word Report 01.
2. Save the document with Save As and name it Word Ch 04, Ex 22.
3. Make the following changes to the document:
   a. Change the top, left, and right margins to 1.5 inches.
   b. Set the entire document in 13-point Bookman Old Style (or a similar serif typeface).
   c. Set the title *GRAPHICS SOFTWARE* in 14-point Arial bold.
   d. Set the first heading *Early Painting and Drawing Programs* in 13-point Arial bold.
   e. Use Format Painter to set the two remaining headings in the report in 13-point Arial bold.
   f. Check the page breaks in the document and, if necessary, adjust the page breaks. (Consider inserting your own hard page break with Ctrl + Enter if Word breaks a page in an undesirable location.)
4. Save the document again with the same name (Word Ch 04, Ex 22).
5. Print pages 1 and 3 of the report by completing the following steps:
   a. Display the Print dialog box by clicking File and then Print.
   b. At the Print dialog box, click Pages.
   c. Key **1,3** in the Pages text box.
   d. Click OK or press Enter.
6. Close Word Ch 04, Ex 22.

Printing Multiple Copies

If you want to print more than one copy of a document, use the Number of copies option from the Print dialog box. If you print several copies of a document containing multiple pages, Word prints the pages in the document collated. For example, if you print two copies of a three-page document, pages 1, 2, and 3 are printed, and then the pages are printed a second time. Printing pages collated is helpful but takes more printing time. To speed up the printing time, you can tell Word not to print the pages collated. To do this, remove the check mark from the Collate option at the Print dialog box. With the check mark removed, Word will print all copies of the first page, and then all copies of the second page, and so on.

Printing Multiple Copies of a Document

1. Open Word Document 02.
2. Print three copies of the document by completing the following steps:
   a. Display the Print dialog box.
   b. Key **3**. (The insertion point is automatically positioned in the Number of copies text box when the Print dialog box displays.)
   c. Click OK or press Enter.
3. Close Word Document 02.

Printing Envelopes

Word automates the creation of envelopes with options at the Envelopes and Labels dialog box with the Envelopes tab selected as shown in figure 4.10. Key the delivery address in the Delivery address text box and the return address in the Return address text box. If you open the Envelopes and Labels dialog box in a document containing a name and address, the name and address are automatically inserted in the Delivery address text box in the dialog box.

At the Envelopes and Labels dialog box, you can send the envelope directly to the printer by clicking the Print button, or you can insert the envelope in the current document by clicking the Add to Document button.

figure
4.10

Envelopes and Labels Dialog Box with Envelopes Tab Selected

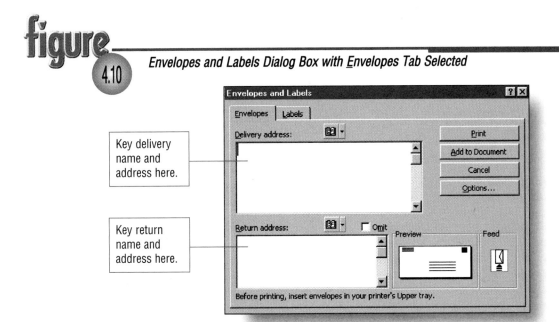

Key delivery name and address here.

Key return name and address here.

If you enter a return address before printing the envelope, Word will display the question *"Do you want to save the new return address as the default return address?"* At this question, click Yes if you want the current return address available for future envelopes. Click No if you do not want the current return address used as the default. If a default return address displays in the Return address section of the dialog box, you can tell Word to omit the return address when printing the envelope by clicking the Omit check box to remove the check mark.

The Envelopes and Labels dialog box contains a Preview sample box and a Feed sample box. The Preview sample box shows how the envelope will appear when printed and the Feed sample box shows how the envelope should be inserted into the printer. (This will vary for different printers.)

exercise 24

Printing an Envelope

1. At a clear document screen, create an envelope that prints the delivery address and return address shown in figure 4.11 by completing the following steps:
   a. Click Tools and then Envelopes and Labels.
   b. At the Envelopes and Labels dialog box with the Envelopes tab selected, key the delivery address shown in figure 4.11 (the one containing the name *Mr. Gregory Watanabe*). (Press the Enter key to end the line containing the name and the line containing the street address. Do not press Enter after keying the city, state, and zip code because that will cause an extra page to print.)
   c. Click in the Return address text box. (If there is any text in the Return Address text box, select and then delete it.)
   d. Key the return address shown in figure 4.11 (the one containing the name *Mrs. Wendy Steinberg*).
   e. Click the Add to Document button.
   f. At the message *"Do you want to save the new return address as the default return address?"*, click No.
2. Save the document and name it Word Ch 04, Ex 24.
3. Print and then close Word Ch 04, Ex 24. *(Note: Manual feed of the envelope may be required. Please check with your instructor.)*

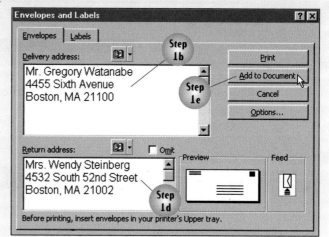

figure 4.11

Exercise 24

Mrs. Wendy Steinberg
4532 South 52nd Street
Boston, MA 21002

Mr. Gregory Watanabe
4455 Sixth Avenue
Boston, MA 21100

Creating an Envelope in an Existing Document

1. Open Word Letter 01.
2. Create and print an envelope for the document by completing the following steps:
   a. Click Tools and then Envelopes and Labels.
   b. At the Envelopes and Labels dialog box (with the Envelopes tab selected), make sure the delivery address displays properly in the Delivery address section.
   c. If any text displays in the Return address section, insert a check mark in the Omit check box (located to the right of the Return address option. (This tells Word not to print the return address on the envelope.)
   d. Click the Print button.
3. Close Word Letter 01.

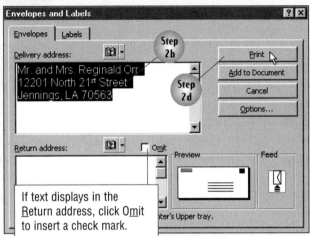

Printing Labels

Use Word's labels feature to print text on mailing labels, file labels, disk labels, or other types of labels. Word includes a variety of predefined labels that can be purchased at an office supply store. To create a sheet of mailing labels with the same name and address using the default options, display the Envelopes and Labels dialog box with the Labels tab selected as shown in figure 4.12. Key the desired address in the Address text box and then click the New Document button to insert the mailing label in a new document or click the Print button to send the mailing label directly to the printer.

Envelopes and Labels Dialog Box with Labels Tab Selected

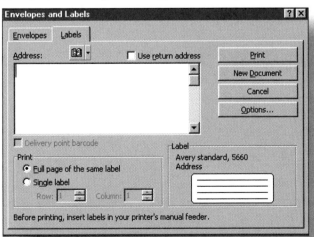

Creating Mailing Labels

1. Open Word Letter 01.
2. Create mailing labels with the delivery address by completing the following steps:

    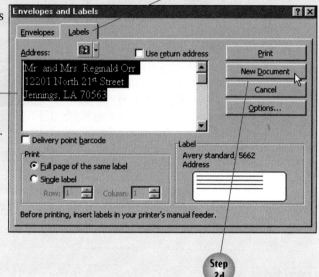

    Step 2b

    Step 2c

    Step 2d

    a. Click Tools and then Envelopes and Labels.
    b. At the Envelopes and Labels dialog box, click the Labels tab.
    c. Make sure the delivery address displays properly in the Address section.
    d. Click the New Document button.
3. Save the mailing label document and name it Word Ch 04, Ex 26.
4. Print and then close Word Ch 04, Ex 26.
5. Close Word Letter 01.

If you open the Envelopes and Labels dialog box (with the Labels tab selected) in a document containing a name and address, the name and address are automatically inserted in the Address section of the dialog box. To enter different names in each of the mailing labels, start at a clear document screen, display the Envelopes and Labels dialog box with the Labels tab selected, and then click the New Document button. The Envelopes and Labels dialog box is removed from the screen and the document screen displays with label forms. The insertion point is positioned in the first label form. Key the name and address in this label and then press the Tab key to move the insertion point to the next label. Pressing Shift + Tab will move the insertion point to the preceding label.

Changing Label Options

Click the Options button at the Envelopes and Labels dialog box with the Labels tab selected and the Label Options dialog box displays as shown in figure 4.13.

figure
4.13

Label Options Dialog Box

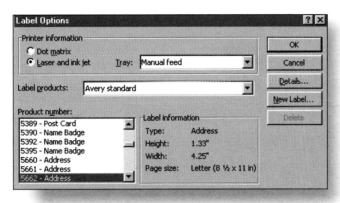

At the Label Options dialog box, choose the type of printer, the desired label product, and the product number. This dialog box also displays information about the selected label such as type, height, width, and paper size. When you select a label, Word automatically determines label margins. If, however, you want to customize these default settings, click the Details button at the Label Options dialog box.

exercise 27

Creating Customized Mailing Labels

1. At a clear document screen, create mailing labels by completing the following steps:
   a. Click Tools and then Envelopes and Labels.
   b. Make sure the Labels tab is selected. (If not, click Labels.)
   c. Click the Options button.
   d. At the Label Options dialog box, make sure *Avery standard* displays in the Label products text box.
   e. Click the down-pointing triangle at the right side of the Product number list box until *5662 - Address* is visible and then click *5662 - Address*.
   f. Click OK or press Enter.
   g. At the Envelopes and Labels dialog box, click the New Document button.

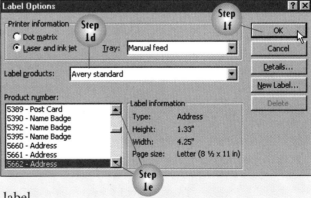

   h. At the document screen, key the first name and address shown in figure 4.14 in the first label.
   i. Press Tab to move the insertion point to the next label and then key the second name and address shown in figure 4.14. Continue in this manner until all names and addresses have been keyed.
2. Save the document and name it Word Ch 04, Ex 27.
3. Print and then close Word Ch 04, Ex 27.
4. At the clear document screen, close the document screen without saving changes.

figure
4.14

Exercise 27

Mr. David Lowry
12033 South 152nd Street
Houston, TX 77340

Ms. Marcella Santos
394 Apple Blossom
Friendswood, TX 77533

Mr. and Mrs. Al Sasaki
1392 Pioneer Drive
Baytown, TX 77903

Mrs. Jackie Rhyner
29039 107th Avenue East
Houston, TX 77302

Changing Paper Size and Orientation

Word assumes that you are printing on standard stationery—8.5 inches wide by 11 inches long. If you need to print text on different size stationery, change the paper size at the Page Setup dialog box with the Paper Size tab selected as shown in figure 4.15.

figure
4.15

Page Setup Dialog Box with Paper Size Tab Selected

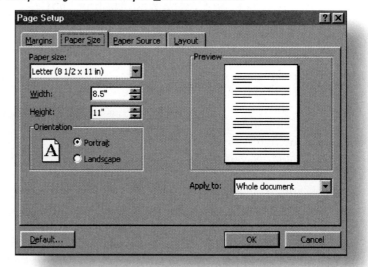

Word provides several predefined paper sizes. The number and type of paper sizes will vary depending on the selected printer. Use the predefined paper sizes if they are the necessary sizes. If the predefined sizes do not include what you need, create your own paper size with the Custom size option. If you choose the Custom size option at the Page Setup dialog box, you can enter the desired measurements for the width and height of the paper size.

Word provides two orientations for paper sizes—portrait and landscape. Figure 4.16 illustrates how text appears on the page in portrait and landscape orientations.

figure 4.16 **Portrait and Landscape Orientations**

By default, the change in paper size will affect the entire document. At the Page Setup dialog box, the Apply to option has a default setting of *Whole document*. This can be changed to *This point forward*. At this setting, the paper size change will affect text from the current position of the insertion point to the end of the document.

Changing to a Predesigned Paper Size

(Note: Check with your instructor before completing this exercise. Your printer may not be capable of printing on legal-sized stationery.)

1. Open Word Report 01.
2. Save the document with Save As and name it Word Ch 04, Ex 28.
3. Change the paper size to Legal by completing the following steps:
   a. Click File and then Page Setup.
   b. At the Page Setup dialog box click the Paper Size tab. (Skip this step if the Paper Size tab is already selected.)
   c. Click the down-pointing triangle at the right of the Paper size option and then click *Legal (8 1/2 x 14 in)* at the drop-down list. (This paper size may be listed as *Legal 8.5 x 14 in* or *US Legal.*)
   d. Click OK or press Enter.

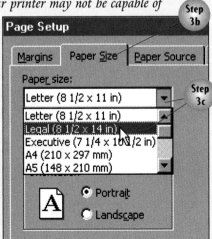

Step 3b

Step 3c

4. Save the document again with the same name (Word Ch 04, Ex 28).
5. Print and then close Word Ch 04, Ex 28. (Check with your instructor before printing to see if your printer is capable of printing legal-sized documents.)

exercise 29

Changing to Landscape Orientation

1. Open Word Document 02.
2. Save the document with Save As and name it Word Ch 04, Ex 29.
3. Change margins and page orientation by completing the following steps:
   a. Display the Page Setup dialog box with the Margins tab selected.
   b. Change the left and right margins to 1.5 inches.
   c. Click the Paper Size tab.
   d. At the Page Setup dialog box with the Paper Size tab selected, click Landscape in the Orientation section.
   e. Click OK to close the dialog box.
4. Save the document again with the same name (Word Ch 04, Ex 29).
5. Print and then close Word Ch 04, Ex 29.

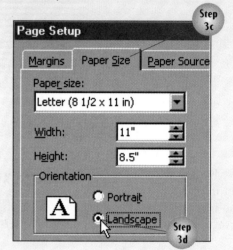

Sending a Word Document by E-Mail

Computers within a company can be connected by a private network referred to as an "intranet." With an intranet, employees within a company can send a Word document by e-mail. To send a Word document by e-mail, you will need to have Outlook available on your system. System configurations can be quite varied and you may find that your screen does not exactly match what you see in the figure in this section. Steps in exercise 30 may need to be modified to accommodate your system.

To send a document by e-mail, open the document in Word, and then click the E-mail button on the Standard toolbar. (You can also click File, point to Send To, and then click Mail Recipient.) This displays the e-mail header below the Formatting toolbar as shown in figure 4.17. When the e-mail header displays, Outlook is automatically opened.

At the e-mail header, fill in the recipient information and then click the Send a Copy button. Word sends a copy of the document to the recipient and closes the e-mail header. The original document remains open for editing. When the document is saved, the e-mail information is saved with the document.

The e-mail header contains buttons you can use to customize the e-mail message. Buttons are available for sending a copy of a document, selecting a name from an address book, establishing a priority level, and specifying delivery options.

figure 4.17

E-mail Header

E-mail Header

> Word Contract - Microsoft Word
>
> File Edit View Insert Format Tools Table Window Help
>
> Normal ▾ Times New Roman ▾ 12 ▾ B I U
>
> Send a Copy
>
> To:
>
> Cc:
>
> Subject: Word Contract
>
> AGREEMENT BETWEEN
>
> REINBERG MANUFACTURING AND LABOR WORKER'S UNION

In the exercise in this chapter, you will send the e-mail to your instructor. If your system is networked and your computer is not part of an intranet system, skip step 3d (clicking the Send a Copy button).

exercise 30

Creating and Printing an Outlook E-mail Message

(Note: Before completing this exercise, check to see if you can send e-mail messages. If you cannot, consider completing all the steps in the exercise except step 3d.)

1. Open Word Contract.
2. Save the document with Save As and name it Word Ch 04, Ex 30.
3. Send Word Ch 04, Ex 30 by e-mail by completing the following steps:
   a. Click the E-mail button on the Standard toolbar.
   b. At the e-mail header, key your instructor's name in the To... text box. (Depending on how the system is configured, you may need to key your instructor's e-mail address.)
   c. Click the down-pointing triangle at the right side of the Set Priority button and then click High Priority at the drop-down list.
   d. Click the Send a Copy button.
   e. Click the E-mail button on the Standard toolbar to turn off the display of the e-mail header.
4. Save the document again with the same name (Word Ch 04, Ex 30).
5. Close the Word Ch 04, Ex 30 document.

chapter summary

▶ A new folder can be created at the Open dialog box or the Save As dialog box.

▶ One document or several documents can be selected at the Open dialog box. A document or selected documents can be copied, moved, renamed, deleted, printed, or opened.

▶ A copy of a document can be made by opening the document and then saving it with a different name. A document can also be copied with the Copy option from the Open dialog box shortcut menu. A document or selected documents can be copied to the same folder or to a different folder. If a document is copied to the same folder, Word adds *Copy of* before the document name.

▶ Use the Cut and Paste options from the Open dialog box shortcut menu to move a document from one folder to another.

▶ Use the Rename option from the Open dialog box Tools drop-down menu or the shortcut menu to give a document a different name.

▶ Documents and/or folders can be deleted with the Delete button on the Open or Save As dialog box toolbar or the Delete option from the shortcut menu. Documents deleted from the hard drive are sent to the Windows Recycle Bin. Documents can be emptied or recovered from the Recycle Bin at the Windows desktop.

▶ Several documents can be opened at one time at the Open dialog box. All open documents can be closed at the same time by holding down the Shift key, then clicking File and then Close All.

▶ A document or selected documents can be printed at the Open dialog box.

▶ Deleting, moving, or copying blocks of text within a document is generally referred to as *cutting and pasting*. A block of text can be as small as one character or as large as an entire page or document.

▶ When deleting a block of text, use the Delete key if you do not need that text again; use the Cut button on the Standard toolbar or the Cut option from the Edit drop-down menu if you might want to insert the deleted text in the current or a different document.

▶ Selected text can be copied in a document or a different document using the Copy and Paste buttons on the Standard toolbar or the Copy and Paste options from the Edit drop-down menu.

▶ With the collect and paste feature, you can collect up to 12 items and then paste them in various locations.

▶ Insert one document into another by displaying the Insert File dialog box and then double-clicking the desired document.

▶ When working in Word for Windows, a window refers to the document screen.

▶ You can open multiple documents and copy or move text between documents.

▶ Each open document fills the entire editing window. Move among the open documents by clicking the button on the Taskbar representing the desired document or by clicking Window and then clicking the desired document name. The active document is the document containing the insertion point.

▶ Use the Arrange All option from the Window drop-down menu to view a portion of all open documents.

- Use the Minimize, Maximize, and Restore buttons in the upper right corner of the window to reduce or increase the size of the active window.
- With several documents open, you can easily move, copy, and/or paste text from one document to another.
- The options available at the Print dialog box can help to customize a print job.
- To cancel a print job, double-click the Print Status icon on the Status bar (located at the right side).
- The Page range section of the Print dialog box contains settings you can use to specify the amount of text you want printed. With the Pages option, you can identify a specific page, multiple pages, and/or a range of pages for printing.
- If you want to print more than one copy of a document, use the Number of copies option from the Print dialog box.
- Create and print an envelope with options at the Envelopes and Labels dialog box.
- Use Word's labels feature to print text on mailing labels, file labels, disk labels, or other types of labels. These additional options are available at the Label Options dialog box: Printer information, Label products (to choose the type of label), and Details (to change label margins).
- The default paper size is 8.5 inches wide by 11 inches long. Paper size can be changed at the Page Setup dialog box with the Paper Size tab selected.
- Word provides two page orientations—portrait and landscape. Change the page orientation at the Page Setup dialog box with the Paper Size tab selected.
- When computers are connected by an intranet, a Word document can be sent by e-mail. Click the E-mail button on the Standard toolbar to display the e-mail header.

commands review

	Mouse/Keyboard
Open dialog box	File, Open; or click Open button on Standard toolbar
Save As dialog box	File, Save As
Minimize Word	Click Minimize button at right side of Title bar
Close all open documents	Hold Shift key, click File, Close All
Delete selected text permanently	Press Delete
Delete selected text and insert it in the Clipboard	Edit, Cut; or click Cut button on Standard toolbar
Insert text from Clipboard to new location	Edit, Paste; or click Paste button on Standard toolbar
Copy selected text	Edit, Copy, move insertion point to new location, then Edit, Paste; or click Copy button on Standard toolbar, move insertion point to new location, and then click Paste button
Deselect text	Click left mouse button outside selected text; or press any arrow key

Save selected text as separate document	Edit, Copy or click Copy button on Standard toolbar; click New Blank Document button on Standard toolbar; click Edit, Paste or click Paste button on Standard toolbar; then save in the normal manner
Display Clipboard toolbar	Right-click any displayed toolbar and then click Clipboard
Insert document into another	With insertion point at the desired location for the standard text, click Insert, then File, then double-click the desired document
Arrange all open documents	Window, Arrange All
Minimize a document	Click Minimize button
Maximize a document	Click Maximize button
Display Print dialog box	File, Print
Display Envelopes and Labels dialog box	Tools, Envelopes and Labels
Display the Page Setup dialog box	File, Page Setup
Display e-mail header	Click E-mail button on Standard toolbar; or click File, point to Send To, then click Mail Recipient

thinking offline

Completion: In the space provided at the right, indicate the correct term, command, or number.

1. A new folder can be created with this button at the Open or Save As dialog box.

2. Click this button at the Open or Save As dialog box to change to the folder that is up one level from the current folder.

3. To display the Open dialog box shortcut menu, display the Open dialog box, position the arrow pointer on a document, and then click this mouse button.

4. To select documents at the Open dialog box that are not adjacent using the mouse, hold down this key while clicking the desired documents.

5. A document can be copied to another folder without opening the document using the Copy option and this option from the Open dialog box shortcut menu.

6. To close all open documents at once, hold down this key, click File and then click Close All.

7. When a document or selected documents are deleted from the hard drive, the documents are sent to this bin.

8. This choice from the Window drop-down menu causes each open document to appear in a separate window with no windows overlapping.

9. If more than one document is open, this word describes the document where the insertion point is located.

_____

10. Do this if you want a document to fill the editing window.

_____

11. To print pages 1 through 4 in a document, key this in the Pages text box at the Print dialog box.

_____

12. Word provides two page orientations—portrait and this.

_____

13. Click the E-mail button on this toolbar to display the e-mail header.

_____

14. In the space provided below, list the steps you would complete to open several consecutive documents at one time.

_____

_____

15. In the space provided below, list the steps you would complete to print pages 2 through 8 and page 12 of the open document.

_____

_____

16. In the space provided below, list the steps you would complete to save the second paragraph of a document named Loan Agreement as a separate document named Disclosure.

_____

_____

working hands-on

Assessment 1

1. Display the Open dialog box with *Chapter 04* the active folder and then create a new folder named *Checking Tools*.
2. Copy (be sure to use the <u>C</u>opy option and not the Cu<u>t</u> option) all documents that begin with *Word Spell Check* and *Word Grammar Check* into the *Checking Tools* folder.
3. With the *Checking Tools* folder as the active folder, rename the following documents:
   a. Rename Word Spell Check 01 to Plans. (Depending on your system setup, you make need to rename it to Plans.doc.)
   b. Rename Word Spell Check 02 to Total Return. (Depending on your system setup, you may need to rename it to Total Return.doc.)
4. Make *Chapter 04* the active folder and then close the Open dialog box.

Assessment 2

1. Display the Open dialog box and then delete the *Checking Tools* folder and all documents contained within it.

2. Delete the following documents:
   Copy of Word Document 03
   Copy of Word Document 04
   Copy of Word Document 05
3. Close the Open dialog box.

Assessment 3

1. Open Word Report 01.
2. Save the document with Save As and name it Word Ch 04, SA 03.
3. Make the following changes to the report:
   a. Select the entire document and then change to a serif typeface other than Times New Roman (you determine the typeface) and change the line spacing to single.
   b. Select and then delete the last sentence in the document.
   c. Move the section titled *Painting and Drawing Programs Today* above the section titled *Developments in Painting and Drawing Programs*.
   d. Set the title and three headings in a larger, bold, sans serif typeface.
   e. Change the top, left, and right margins to 1.5 inches.
4. Save the document again with the same name (Word Ch 04, SA 03).
5. Print and then close Word Ch 04, SA 03.

Assessment 4

1. At a clear document screen, create the document shown in figure 4.15. Double-space between lines and triple-space after the last line in the document.
2. Make the following changes to the document:
   a. Change the font for the entire document to 14-point Copperplate Gothic Bold. (If this font is not available, choose Bookman Old Style.)
   b. Select and then copy the text a triple space below the original text.
   c. Paste the text two more times. (There should be a total of four forms when you are done, and they should fit on one page.)
3. Save the document and name it Word Ch 04, SA 04.
4. Print and then close Word Ch 04, SA 04.

Assessment 4

NEWS FLASH!!

LIFETIME ANNUITY FUNDS WORKSHOP TODAY!

Friday, October 20, 2000

North Bay Conference Hall

Assessment 5

1. Open Word Block 01, Word Document 01, Word Notice 01, and Word Spell Check 01.
2. Make Word Notice 01 the active document.
3. Make Word Block 01 the active document.
4. Arrange all the windows.
5. Make Word Spell Check 01 the active document and then minimize it.
6. Minimize the remaining documents.
7. Restore Word Block 01 by clicking the button on the Taskbar representing the document.
8. Restore Word Document 01.
9. Restore Word Notice 01.
10. Restore Word Spell Check 01.
11. Close Word Spell Check 01.
12. Close Word Notice 01.
13. Close Word Document 01.
14. Maximize Word Block 01.
15. Close Word Block 01.

Assessment 6

1. Open Word Document 03 and Word Document 04.
2. Make Word Document 03 the active document and then save it with Save As and name it Word Ch 04, SA 06.
3. Make the following changes to the open documents:
   a. Select and then delete the last paragraph of text in Word Ch 04, SA 06.
   b. Copy the first two paragraphs in Word Document 04 and then paste them at the end of Word Ch 04, SA 06.
   c. Check the spacing of paragraphs in Word Ch 04, SA 06 and make sure there is a blank line between each paragraph.
4. Make sure Word Ch 04, SA 06 is the active document and then make the following changes:
   a. Add the title *ECONOMIC GROWTH IN THE 90s* at the beginning of the document, making it bold and centered.
   b. Set the entire document in a serif typeface (other than Times New Roman).
5. Save the document again with the same name (Word Ch 04, SA 06).
6. Print and then close Word Ch 04, SA 06.
7. Close Word Document 04.

Assessment 7

1. Open Word Document 01.
2. Print two copies of the document, displaying the Print dialog box only once.
3. Close Word Document 01.

Assessment 8

1. Open Word Report 01.
2. Save the document with Save As and name it Word Ch 04, SA 08.
3. Make the following changes to the document:
   a. Select the entire document and then change the font to 13-point Century Schoolbook.
   b. Set the title in 16-point Century Schoolbook bold.
   c. Set the three headings in 14-point Century Schoolbook bold. (*Hint: Use Format Painter.*)
   d. Change the top, bottom, left, and right margins to 1.5 inches.
   e. Change the page orientation to landscape.
4. Save the document again with the same name (Word Ch 04, SA 08).
5. Print page 2 of the report.
6. Close Word Ch 04, SA 08.

Assessment 9

1. At a clear document screen, create an envelope with the text shown in figure 4.16.
2. Save the envelope document and name it Word Ch 04, SA 09.
3. Print and then close Word Ch 04, SA 09.

figure

4.16

Assessment 9

Dr. Roseanne Holt
21330 Cedar View Drive
Logan, UT 84598

Mr. Gene Mietzner
4559 Corrin Avenue
Smithfield, UT 84521

Assessment 10

1. Create mailing labels with the names and addresses shown in figure 4.17. Use the Avery standard, 5660 – Address label.
2. Save the document and name it Word Ch 04, SA 10.
3. Print and then close Word Ch 04, SA 10.
4. At the clear document screen, close the document screen without saving changes.

figure

4.17 *Assessment 10*

Ms. Susan Lutovsky	Mr. Leonard Krueger	Mr. and Mrs. Jim Kiel
1402 Mellinger Drive	13290 North 120th	413 Jackson Street
Fairhope, OH 43209	Canton, OH 43291	Avondale, OH 43887
Mr. Vince Kiley	Mrs. Irene Hagen	Ms. Helga Gundstrom
14005 288th South	12930 147th Avenue East	P.O. Box 3112
Canton, OH 43287	Canton, OH 43296	Avondale, OH 43887

Assessment 11

1. Use Word's Help feature to learn how to create a postnet bar code and a FIM-A code for an envelope. Print the information.
2. After reading about and experimenting with creating a postnet bar code and a FIM-A code, write a description of the features that includes the following:
   a. Create a title for the description that is keyed in all capital letters and is centered and bolded.
   b. Describe the purpose of the postnet bar code and the FIM-A code.
   c. Set the document in a serif typeface (other than Times New Roman).
   d. Set the document title in a sans serif typeface.
3. Save the completed description and name it Word Ch 04, SA 11.
4. Print and then close Word Ch 04, SA 11.
5. At a clear document screen, create an envelope that contains the addresses shown in figure 4.18. Add a postnet bar code and a FIM-A code to the envelope.
6. Save the envelope document and name it Word Ch 04, Envelope.
7. Print and then close Word Ch 04, Envelope.

figure

4.18 *Assessment 11*

Ms. Candace Bryner
2604 Linden Boulevard
Montgomery, AL 36334

Mr. Chad Frazier
610 Valley Avenue
Montgomery, AL 36336

Chapter 05

Formatting Documents

In a Word document, text can be created that prints at the top of every page and/or the bottom of every page and page numbering can be added to documents. Word contains a variety of features to automate the formatting of documents such as find and replace, styles, templates, and outlining.

Working with Headers and Footers

Text that appears at the top of every page is called a *header* and text that appears at the bottom of every page is referred to as a *footer*. Headers and footers are common in manuscripts, textbooks, reports, and other publications.

Creating a Header or Footer

With the <u>H</u>eader and Footer option from <u>V</u>iew, you can create a header or a footer. When you click <u>V</u>iew and then <u>H</u>eader and Footer, Word automatically changes to the Print Layout view, dims the text in the document, inserts a pane where the header or footer is entered, and also inserts the Header and Footer toolbar. Figure 5.1 shows a document with a header pane and the Header and Footer toolbar displayed. Figure 5.2 identifies the buttons on the Header and Footer toolbars.

5.1

Header Pane and Header and Footer Toolbar

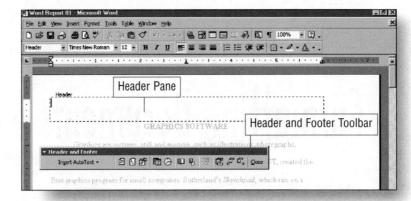

5.2

Header and Footer Toolbar Buttons

Click this button	Named	To do this
Insert AutoText ▾	Insert AutoText	Insert AutoText into header/footer.
▣	Insert Page Number	Insert page number in header/footer.
▣	Insert Number of Pages	Prints the total number of pages in the active document.
▣	Format Page Number	Format the page numbers in the current section.
▣	Insert Date	Insert date in header/footer.
◷	Insert Time	Insert time in header/footer.
▣	Page Setup	Display Page Setup dialog box.
▣	Show/Hide Document Text	Turn on/off the display of document text.
▣	Same as Previous	Link/Unlink header/footer to or from previous section.
▣	Switch Between Header and Footer	Switch between the header pane and the footer pane.
▣	Show Previous	Show previous section's header/footer.
▣	Show Next	Show next section's header/footer.
Close	Close Header and Footer	Close header/footer pane.

By default, the insertion point is positioned in the header pane. Key the header text in the header pane. If you are creating a footer, click the Switch Between Header and Footer button on the Header and Footer toolbar. This displays a footer pane where footer text is keyed.

Switch Between
Header and Footer

Header and footer text can be formatted in the same manner as text in the document. For example, the font of header or footer text can be changed, character formatting such as bolding, italicizing, and underlining can be added, margins can be changed, and much more.

After keying the header or footer text, click the Close button on the Header and Footer toolbar. Clicking Close returns you to the previous view. If the Normal view was selected before a header was created, you are returned to the Normal view. If the Print Layout view was selected before a header was created, you are returned to that view. In the Normal view, a header or footer does not display on the screen. A header or footer will display dimmed in the Print Layout view. If you want to view how a header and/or footer will print, click the Print Preview button on the Standard toolbar. By default, a header and/or footer prints on every page in the document. Later in this chapter you will learn how to create headers/footers for specific sections of a document.

For reference purposes in a document, consider inserting a footer that contains the document name and path.

When creating a header or footer, the main document text displays but is dimmed. This dimmed text can be hidden while creating a header or footer by clicking the Show/Hide Document Text button on the Header and Footer toolbar. To redisplay the dimmed document text, click the button again.

Show/Hide
Document Text

exercise

Creating a Header and a Footer

1. Open Word Report 01.
2. Save the document with Save As and name it Word Ch 05, Ex 01.
3. Create the header *Graphics Software* and a footer that inserts the filename and path by completing the following steps:
   a. Click View and then Header and Footer.
   b. At the header pane, turn on bold, and then key **Graphics Software**.
   c. Click the Switch Between Header and Footer button on the Header and Footer toolbar. (This displays the footer pane.)
   d. At the footer pane, click the Insert AutoText button on the Header and Footer toolbar and then click *Filename and path* at the drop-down list.
   e. Click the Close button on the Header and Footer toolbar.

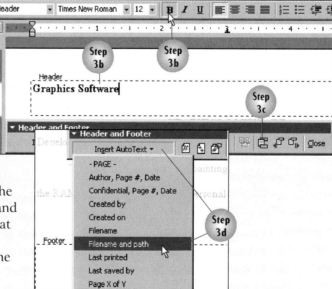

4. Display Print Preview to see how the header and footer will appear on each page when printed. (Press the Page Down key to view the second and then third page of the report.) After previewing the document, close Print Preview.
5. Check page breaks in the document and, if necessary, adjust the page breaks.
6. Save the document again with the same name (Word Ch 05, Ex 01).
7. Print and then close Word Ch 05, Ex 01.

(Note: Most printers cannot print to the edge of the page. If your footer does not print in exercise 1, you may need to increase the distance from the footer to the edge of the page. To increase this measurement, display the Page Setup dialog box by clicking File and then Page Setup. At the Page Setup dialog box, make sure the Margins tab is selected, and then increase the number for the Footer: option in the From edge section of the dialog box. The amount of increase depends on your printer.)

Formatting a Header or Footer

Header or footer text does not take on the character formatting of the document. For example, if you change the font for the document text, header or footer text remains at the default font. However, margin changes made to the document text do affect header or footer text. If you want header or footer text character formatting to be the same as the document text, you must format header or footer text in the header or footer pane in the normal manner.

A header or footer contains three tab settings. (These settings are designed to work with the default left and right margins of 1.25 inches. If changes are made to the margins, these settings may not operate as described.) If you want text aligned at the left margin, make sure the insertion point is positioned at the left side of the header or footer pane, and then key the text. To center text in the header or footer pane, press the Tab key. This moves the insertion point to a preset tab. From the left margin, pressing the Tab key twice will move the insertion point to the right margin of the header or footer pane. Text keyed at this tab will be right aligned.

Creating and Formatting a Footer

1. Open Word Report 01.
2. Save the document with Save As and name it Word Ch 05, Ex 02.
3. Make the following changes to the document:
   a. Change the top margin to 1.5 inches.
   b. Select the entire document and then change the font to 12-point Century Schoolbook. (If Century Schoolbook is not available, choose another serif typeface such as Bookman Old Style or Garamond.)
4. Create the footer *Painting and Drawing Programs* in 12-point Century Schoolbook bold (or the serif typeface you chose in step 3b) that prints at the left margin of every page and *Page #* (where # represents the page number) in 12-point Century Schoolbook bold that prints at the right margin of every page by completing the following steps:
   a. Click View and then Header and Footer.
   b. Click the Switch Between Header and Footer button on the Header and Footer toolbar. (This displays the footer pane.)

c. Change the font to 12-point Century Schoolbook bold (or the serif typeface you chose in step 3b).

d. Key **Painting and Drawing Programs**.

e. Press the Tab key twice.

f. Key **Page** and then press the spacc bar once.

g. Click the Insert Page Number button on the Header and Footer toolbar.

h. Select the page number and then change the font to 12-point Century Schoolbook bold (or the serif typeface you chose in step 3b).

i. Click the Close button on the Header and Footer toolbar.

5. View the document in Print Preview.

6. Check page breaks in the document and, if necessary, adjust the page breaks.

7. Save the document again with the same name (Word Ch 05, Ex 02).

8. Print and then close Word Ch 05, Ex 02.

Editing a Header or Footer

Edit a header or footer by changing to the Print Layout view and then double-clicking the dimmed header or footer you want to edit. Edit the header or footer and then double-click the dimmed document text to make the document active.

Another method for editing a header or footer is to click View and then Header and Footer. Edit the header and then click the Close button on the Header and Footer toolbar. If you want to edit a footer, click the Switch Between Header and Footer button to display the footer. If there is more than one header or footer in a document, click the Show Next button or Show Previous button to display the desired header/footer.

1. Open Word Ch 05, Ex 02.

2. Save the document with Save As and name it Word Ch 05, Ex 03.

3. Change the left and right margins to 1 inch.

4. Edit the footer by completing the following steps:

a. Click <u>V</u>iew and then <u>H</u>eader and Footer.

b. Click the Switch Between Header and Footer button on the Header and Footer toolbar. (This displays the footer pane containing the footer created in exercise 2.)

c. Delete *Painting and Drawing Programs* from the footer pane. (Leave *Page #*, which is located toward the right margin.)

d. Key **GRAPHICS SOFTWARE** at the left margin in the footer pane.

e. Click the <u>C</u>lose button on the Header and Footer toolbar.

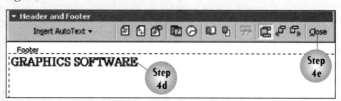

> Double-click a header or footer in Print Layout view to open the header or footer pane for editing.

Show Next

Show Previous

Editing a Footer

5. View the document in Print Preview.
6. Check page breaks in the document and, if necessary, adjust the page breaks.
7. Save the document again with the same name (Word Ch 05, Ex 03).
8. Print and then close Word Ch 05, Ex 03.

Deleting a Header or Footer

Delete a header or footer from a document by deleting it from the header or footer pane. Display the pane containing the header or footer to be deleted, select the header or footer text, and then press the Delete key.

Creating Different Headers/Footers in a Document

By default, Word will insert a header or footer on every page in the document. You can create different headers or footers within one document. For example, you can do the following:

Page Setup

- create a unique header or footer on the first page;
- omit a header or footer on the first page;
- create different headers or footers for odd and even pages; or
- create different headers or footers for sections in a document.

Creating a First Page Header/Footer

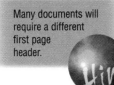

Many documents will require a different first page header.

A different header or footer can be created on the first page of a document. To do this, display the header or footer pane and then click the Page Setup button on the Header and Footer toolbar. At the Page Setup dialog box with the Layout tab selected as shown in figure 5.3, click the Different first page option to insert a check mark, and then click OK to close the dialog box. At the document, open another header or footer pane by clicking the Show Next button on the Header and Footer toolbar. Key the text for the other header or footer that will print on all but the first page and then click the Close button on the Header and Footer toolbar.

figure
5.3

Page Setup Dialog Box with Layout Tab Selected

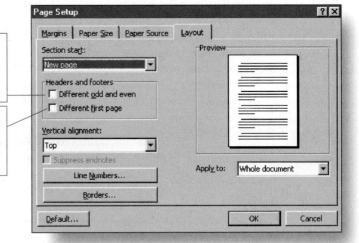

Click this option if you want to create different headers or footers on odd and even pages.

Click this option if you want to create a unique header or footer on the first page.

After creating the headers or footers, preview the document to see how the headers or footers will display when printed. You can follow similar steps to omit a header or footer on the first page. For example, to omit a header or footer on the first page, complete the same steps as described above except do not key text when the first header or footer pane is opened.

Creating a Header that Prints on all Pages Except the First Page

1. Open Word Report 02.
2. Save the document with Save As and name it Word Ch 05, Ex 04.
3. Create the header *Computer Technology* that is bolded and prints at the right margin on all pages except the first page by completing the following steps:
   a. Position the insertion point anywhere in the first page.
   b. Click View and then Header and Footer.
   c. Click the Page Setup button on the Header and Footer toolbar.
   d. At the Page Setup dialog box, make sure the Layout tab is selected, and then click Different first page. (This inserts a check mark in the check box.)
   e. Click OK or press Enter.
   f. With the header pane displayed, click the Show Next button on the Header and Footer toolbar. (This opens another header pane.)
   g. Press the Tab key twice, turn on bold, and then key **Computer Technology**.
   h. Click the Close button on the Header and Footer toolbar.

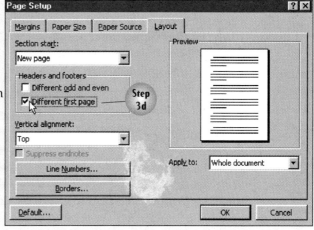

4. Check page breaks in the document and, if necessary, adjust the page breaks.
5. Save the document again with the same name (Word Ch 05, Ex 04).
6. Print and then close Word Ch 05, Ex 04. (You may want to preview the document before printing.)

Creating a Header/Footer for Odd/Even Pages

Printing one header or footer on even pages and another header or footer on odd pages may be useful. You may want to do this in a document that will be bound after printing. To create a header or footer that prints on odd pages and another that prints on even pages, you would complete the following steps:

1. Click View and then Header and Footer. (If you are creating a footer, click the Switch Between Header and Footer button.)
2. Click the Page Setup button. At the Page Setup dialog box, make sure the Layout tab is selected, click Different odd and even, and then click OK or press Enter. (Make sure there is no check mark in the Different first page option.)

3. At the odd page header or footer pane, key the desired text.
4. Click the Show Next button on the Header and Footer toolbar.
5. At the even header or footer pane, key the desired text, and then click the Close button on the Header and Footer toolbar.

Creating a Footer for Odd Pages and Another for Even Pages

1. Open Word Report 02.
2. Save the document with Save As and name it Word Ch 05, Ex 05.
3. Make the following changes to the document:
   a. Change the top margin to 1.5 inches.
   b. Change the font for the entire document to 12-point Century Schoolbook (or a similar typeface).
   c. Insert a page break at the line containing the title *SECTION 2: COMPUTERS IN ENTERTAINMENT* (located on page 2).
4. Create a footer that prints on all odd pages and another that prints on all even pages by completing the following steps:
   a. Move the insertion point to the beginning of the document and then click View and then Header and Footer.
   b. Click the Switch Between Header and Footer button.
   c. Click the Page Setup button.
   d. At the Page Setup dialog box, make sure the Layout tab is selected, and then click Different odd and even. (Make sure there is no check mark in the Different first page option.)
   e. Click OK or press Enter.
   f. At the odd page footer pane press the Tab key twice and then key **Communication and Entertainment**.

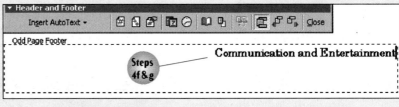

   g. Select the footer text *Communication and Entertainment* and then change the font to 12-point Century Schoolbook bold (or the serif typeface you chose in step 3b).
   h. Click the Show Next button on the Header and Footer toolbar.
   i. At the even page footer pane, key **Computers**.
   j. Select the footer text *Computers* and then change

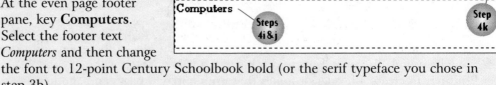

   the font to 12-point Century Schoolbook bold (or the serif typeface you chose in step 3b).
   k. Click the Close button on the Header and Footer toolbar.
5. Check page breaks in the document and, if necessary, adjust the page breaks.
6. Save the document again with the same name (Word Ch 05, Ex 05).
7. Print and then close Word Ch 05, Ex 05. (You may want to preview the document before printing.)

Creating a Header/Footer for Different Sections

A section can be created that begins a new page or a continuous section can be created. If you want different headers and/or footers for pages in a document, divide the document into sections.

For example, if a document contains several chapters, you can create a section for each chapter, and then create a different header or footer for each section. When dividing a document into sections by chapter, insert a section break that also begins a new page.

When a header or footer is created for a specific section in a document, the header or footer can be created for all previous and next sections or just for next sections. If you want a header or footer to print on only those pages in a section and not the previous or next sections, you must deactivate the Same as Previous button. This tells Word not to print the header or footer on previous sections. Word will, however, print the header or footer on following sections. If you do not want the header or footer to print on following sections, create a blank header or footer at the next section. When creating a header or footer for a specific section in a document, preview the document to determine if the header or footer appears on the correct pages.

Same as
Previous

exercise
6

Creating Footers for Different Sections

1. Open Word Report 02.
2. Save the document with Save As and name it Word Ch 05, Ex 06.
3. Insert a section break by completing the following steps:
   a. Position the insertion point at the beginning of the title *SECTION 2: COMPUTERS IN ENTERTAINMENT* (located on page 2).
   b. Click Insert and then Break.
   c. At the Break dialog box, click Next page.
   d. Click OK to close the dialog box.
4. Create section and page numbering footers for the two sections by completing the following steps:
   a. Position the insertion point at the beginning of the document.
   b. Click View and then Header and Footer.
   c. Click the Switch Between Header and Footer button.
   d. At the footer pane, turn on bold, key **Section 1**, and then press the Tab key twice. (This moves the insertion point to the right margin.) Key **Page**, press the space bar, key a hyphen (-), press the space bar again, and then click the Insert Page Number button on the Header and Footer toolbar.

> ▼ Header and Footer
>
> Insert AutoText ▾   Close
>
> Footer -Section 1-
> Section 1   Page - 1
>
> Step 4d
> Step 4d
> Step 4d
> Step 4f

e. Select and then bold the page number.
f. Click the Show Next button.
g. Click the Same as Previous button to deactivate it.
h. Change *Section 1* to *Section 2* in the footer.
i. Click the Close button on the Header and Footer toolbar.

5. Check page breaks in the document and, if necessary, adjust the page breaks.

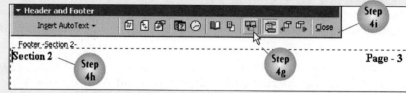

6. Save the document again with the same name (Word Ch 05, Ex 06).

7. Print and then close Word Ch 05, Ex 06. (You may want to preview the document before printing.)

Inserting Page Numbering in a Document

Word, by default, does not print page numbers on a page. For documents such as memos and letters, this is appropriate. For longer documents, however, page numbers may be needed. Page numbers can be added to documents with options from the Page Numbers dialog box or in a header or footer. Earlier in this chapter, you learned about the Insert Page Number button on the Header and Footer toolbar. Clicking this button inserts page numbering in a header or footer.

In addition to a header or footer, page numbering can be added to a document with options from the Page Numbers dialog box shown in figure 5.4. To display this dialog box, click Insert and then Page Numbers.

Page Numbers Dialog Box

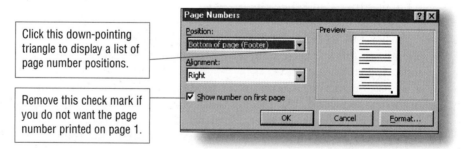

Click this down-pointing triangle to display a list of page number positions.

Remove this check mark if you do not want the page number printed on page 1.

The Position option at the Page Numbers dialog box contains two choices—Top of page (Header) and Bottom of page (Footer). With choices from the Alignment option, you can insert page numbering at the left margin, center of the page, right margin, at the inside margin (the margin closest to the binding in bound material), and at the outside margin (the margin furthest from the binding in bound material).

If you turn on page numbering in a document, the page number will appear on all pages in the document including the first page. If you do not want page numbering to appear on the first page, remove the check mark from the <u>S</u>how number on first page option at the Page Numbers dialog box.

Numbering Pages at the Bottom Right Margin

1. Open Word Report 01.
2. Save the document with Save As and name it Word Ch 05, Ex 07.
3. Change the top margin to 1.5 inches.
4. Number pages, except the first page, at the top of the page at the right margin by completing the following steps:
   a. Click <u>I</u>nsert and then Page N<u>u</u>mbers.
   b. At the Page Numbers dialog box, click the down-pointing triangle at the right of the <u>P</u>osition text box, and then click *Top of page (Header)*.
   c. Make sure the <u>A</u>lignment option displays as *Right*. (If not, click the down-pointing triangle at the right of the <u>A</u>lignment text box, and then click *Right* at the drop-down list.)
   d. Click the <u>S</u>how number on first page option to remove the check mark.
   e. Click OK or press Enter.
5. Check page breaks in the document and, if necessary, adjust the page breaks.
6. Save the document again with the same name (Word Ch 05, Ex 07).
7. Print and then close Word Ch 05, Ex 07. (You may want to preview the document before printing.)

Deleting Page Numbering

Page numbering in a document can be deleted in the same manner as deleting a header or footer. To delete page numbering in a document, click <u>V</u>iew and then <u>H</u>eader and Footer. Display the header or footer pane containing the page numbering, select the page numbering, and then press the Delete key. Click the <u>C</u>lose button on the Header and Footer toolbar.

Modifying Page Numbering Format

At the Page Number Format dialog box shown in figure 5.5, you can change the numbering format, add chapter numbering, and specify where you want page numbering to begin and in what sections you want page numbering to appear. To display the Page Number Format dialog box, click the <u>F</u>ormat button at the Page Numbers dialog box.

figure

5.5

Page Number Format Dialog Box

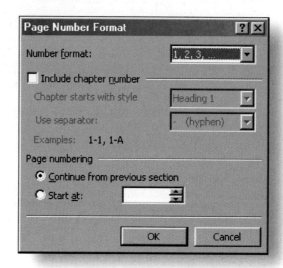

Click the Number format option from the Page Number Format dialog box to change the numbering from Arabic numbers (1, 2, 3, etc.), to lowercase letters (a, b, c, etc.), uppercase letters (A, B, C, etc.), lowercase Roman numerals (i, ii, iii, etc.), or uppercase Roman numerals (I, II, III, etc.).

Chapter numbering can be included in a document. Word will number chapters in a document if the chapter heading is formatted with a heading style. You will learn about heading styles in a later chapter.

By default, page numbering begins with 1 and continues sequentially from 1 through all pages and sections in a document. You can change the beginning page number with the Start at option at the Page Number Format dialog box. You can change the beginning page number at the beginning of the document or change the page number at the beginning of a section.

exercise

Numbering Pages with Roman Numerals at the Outside Margins

1. Open Word Report 02.
2. Save the document with Save As and name it Word Ch 05, Ex 08.
3. Turn on page numbering, change the page numbering to outside margins, use lowercase Roman numerals, and change the beginning number to 3 by completing the following steps:
   a. Click Insert and then Page Numbers.
   b. At the Page Numbers dialog box, change the Alignment to *Outside*.
   c. Click the Format button.

d. At the Page Number Format dialog box, click the down-pointing triangle at the right of the Number format text box and then click *i, ii, iii, ...* at the drop-down list.

e. Click Start at and then key **3**.

f. Click OK or press Enter to close the Page Number Format dialog box.

g. Click OK or press Enter to close the Page Numbers dialog box.

4. Check page breaks in the document and, if necessary, adjust the page breaks.

5. Save the document again with the same name (Word Ch 05, Ex 08).

6. Print and then close Word Ch 05, Ex 08. (You may want to preview the document before printing.)

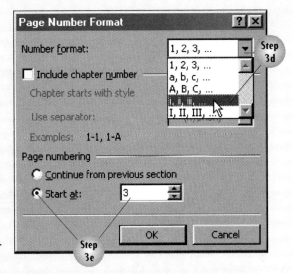

Finding and Replacing Text

With Word's find feature you can search for specific characters or formatting. With the find and replace feature, you can search for specific characters or formatting and replace with other characters or formatting. Using the find feature, or the find and replace feature, you can:

- Search for overly used words or phrases in a document.
- Use abbreviations for common phrases when entering text and then replace the abbreviations with the actual text later.
- Set up standard documents with generic names and replace them with other names to make personalized documents.
- Find and replace formatting.

The keyboard shortcut for Find is Ctrl + F.

Finding Text

To find specific text or formatting in a document, click Edit and then Find. This displays the Find and Replace dialog box with the Find tab selected as shown in figure 5.6. Enter the characters for which you are searching in the Find what text box. You can enter up to 256 characters in this text box. Click the Find Next button and Word searches for and selects the first occurrence of the text in the document. Make corrections to the text if needed and then search for the next occurrence by clicking the Find Next button again. Click the Cancel button to close the Find and Replace dialog box.

figure

5.6

Find and Replace Dialog Box with Find Tab Selected

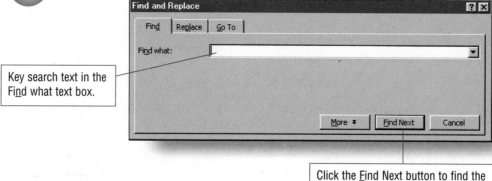

Key search text in the Find what text box.

Click the Find Next button to find the next occurrence of the search text.

exercise 9

Finding Words

1. Open Word Report 01.
2. Find every occurrence of *painting programs* in the document by completing the following steps:
   a. With the insertion point positioned at the beginning of the document, click Edit and then Find.
   b. At the Find and Replace dialog box with the Find tab selected, key **painting programs** in the Find what text box.
   c. Click the Find Next button.
   d. Word searches for and selects the first occurrence of *painting programs*.
   e. Search for the next occurrence of *painting programs* by clicking the Find Next button again.
   f. Continue clicking the Find Next button until the message *Word has finished searching the document* displays.
   g. Click the Cancel button to close the Find and Replace dialog box (and remove the message).
3. Close Word Report 01.

The next time you open the Find and Replace dialog box, you can display a list of text for which you have searched by clicking the down-pointing triangle after the Find what text box. For example, if you searched for *type size* and then performed another search for *type style*, the third time you open the Find and Replace dialog box, clicking the down-pointing triangle after the Find what text

The keyboard shortcut for Replace is Ctrl + H.

box will display a drop-down list with *type style* and *type size*. Click text from this drop-down list if you want to perform a search on that text.

Finding and Replacing Text

To use Find and Replace, click Edit, expand the drop-down menu, and then click Replace. This displays the Find and Replace dialog box with the Replace tab selected as shown in figure 5.7.

Find and Replace Dialog Box with the Replace Tab Selected

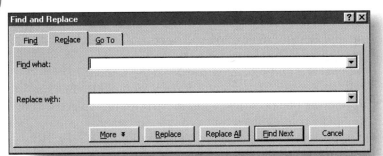

Enter the characters and/or formatting for which you are searching in the Find what text box. Press the Tab key to move the insertion point to the Replace with text box and then key the replacement text or insert the replacement formatting. You can also move the insertion point to the Replace with text box by clicking inside the text box.

The Find and Replace dialog box contains several command buttons. Click the Find Next button to tell Word to find the next occurrence of the characters and/or formatting. Click the Replace button to replace the characters or formatting and find the next occurrence. If you know that you want all occurrences of the characters or formatting in the Find what text box replaced with the characters or formatting in the Replace with text box, click the Replace All button. This replaces every occurrence from the location of the insertion point to the beginning or end of the document (depending on the search direction). Click the Cancel button to close the Find and Replace dialog box.

Finding and Replacing Text

1. Open Word Legal 01.
2. Save the document with Save As and name it Word Ch 05, Ex 10.
3. Find all occurrences of NAME1 and replace with SUSAN R. LOWE by completing the following steps:
    a. With the insertion point positioned at the beginning of the document, click Edit, expand the drop-down menu, and then click Replace.

b. At the Find and Replace dialog box with the Replace tab selected, key **NAME1** in the Fi_n_d what text box.

c. Press the Tab key to move the insertion point to the Replace with text box.

d. Key **SUSAN R. LOWE**.

e. Click the Replace A_l_l button.

f. When all replacements are made, the message *Word has completed its search of the document and has made 5 replacements* displays. (Do not close the Find and Replace dialog box.)

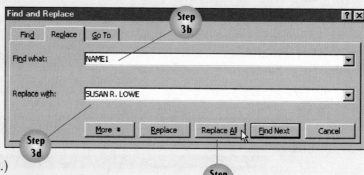

4. With the Find and Replace dialog box still open, complete steps similar to those in 3b through 3f to find all occurrences of NAME2 and replace with MARY A. LANGE.

5. With the Find and Replace dialog box still open, complete steps similar to those in 3b through 3f to find the one occurrence of NUMBER and replace with C-3546.

6. Close the Find and Replace dialog box.

7. Save the document again with the same name (Word Ch 05, Ex 10).

8. Print and then close Word Ch 05, Ex 10.

Choosing Find Check Box Options

The Find and Replace dialog box contains a variety of check boxes with options you can choose for completing a search. To display these options, click the M_o_re button located at the bottom of the dialog box. This causes the Find and Replace dialog box to expand as shown in figure 5.8. Each option and what will occur if it is selected is described in figure 5.9.

Expanded Find and Replace Dialog Box

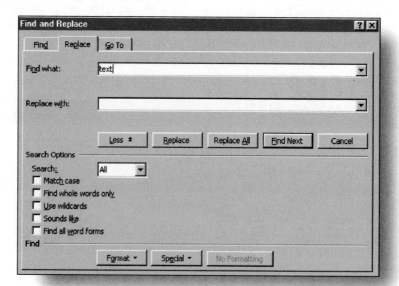

figure
5.9

Options at the Find and Replace Dialog Box

Choose this option	To
Match case	Exactly match the case of the search text. For example, if you search for *Book* and select the Match case option, Word will stop at *Book* but not *book* or *BOOK*.
Find whole words only	Find a whole word, not a part of a word. For example, if you search for *her* and did not select Find whole words only, Word would stop at *there*, *here*, *hers*, and so on.
Use wildcards	Search for wildcards, special characters, or special search operators.
Sounds like	Match words that sound alike but are spelled differently such as *know* and *no*.
Find all word forms	Find all forms of the word entered in the Find what text box. For example, if you enter *hold*, Word will stop at *held* and *holding*.

To remove the display of options toward the bottom of the Find and Replace dialog box, click the Less button. (The Less button was previously the More button.)

exercise
11

Finding and Replacing Word Forms

1. Open Word Document 06.
2. Save the document with Save As and name it Word Ch 05, Ex 11.
3. Find all forms of the word *produce* and replace it with forms of *create* by completing the following steps:
   a. Make sure the insertion point is positioned at the beginning of the document.
   b. Click Edit and then Replace.
   c. At the Find and Replace dialog box with the Replace tab selected, key **produce** in the Find what text box.
   d. Press the Tab key and then key **create** in the Replace with text box.
   e. Click the More button.
   f. Click the Find all word forms option. (This inserts a check mark in the check box.)
   g. Click the Replace All button.
   h. At the message, *Replace All is*

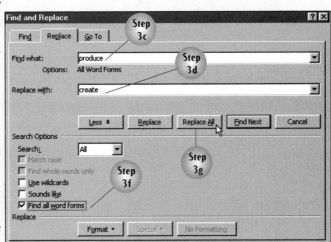

not recommended with Find All Word Forms. Continue with Replace All?, click OK.
   i. When the find and replace is completed, click the Find all word forms option to
       remove the check mark.
   j. Click the Less button.
   k. Click the Close button to close the Find and Replace dialog box.
4. Save the document again with the same name (Word Ch 05, Ex 11).
5. Print and then close Word Ch 05, Ex 11.

Navigating in a Document Using Go To

As you learned, you can use the Find and Replace dialog box to find specific text
or formatting in a document, and to find and replace specific text or formatting.
You can also use the Find and Replace dialog box with the Go To tab selected, as
shown in figure 5.10, to find or go to a specific location or item. To display this
dialog box, display the Find and Replace dialog box and then click the Go To tab
or click Edit, expand the drop-down menu, and then click Go To.

Find and Replace Dialog Box with Go To Tab Selected

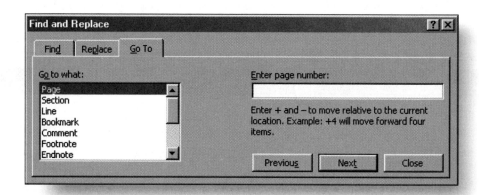

   To find a specific item in a document such as a page or line, click the desired
item in the Go to what list box, and then click the Go To button.

Navigating in a Document Using Go To

1. Open Word Report 02.
2. Save the document with Save As and name it Word Ch 05, Ex 12.
3. Make the following changes to the document:
   a. Change the top, left, and right margins to 1.5 inches.

b. Insert page numbering that prints at the bottom, center, of each page.
c. Insert a section break that begins a new page at the title *SECTION 2: COMPUTERS IN ENTERTAINMENT.*

4. Position the insertion point at the beginning of the document and then move the insertion point to specific locations in the document by completing the following steps:

a. Click <u>E</u>dit, expand the drop-down menu, and then click <u>G</u>o To.

b. At the Find and Replace dialog box with the <u>G</u>o To tab selected, click *Line* in the <u>G</u>o to what list box.

c. Click in the <u>E</u>nter line number text box and then key **10**.

d. Click the Go <u>T</u>o button. (This moves the insertion point to line 10 on the first page of the document—check the Status bar.)

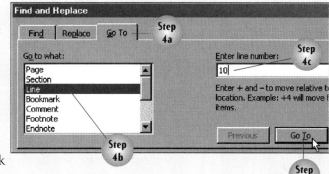

e. At the Find and Replace dialog box with the <u>G</u>o To tab selected, click *Page* in the <u>G</u>o to what list box.

f. Click in the <u>E</u>nter page number text box and then key **2**.

g. Click the Go <u>T</u>o button. (This moves the insertion point to the beginning of page 2.

h. At the Find and Replace dialog box with the <u>G</u>o To tab selected, click *Section* in the <u>G</u>o to what list box.

i. Click in the <u>E</u>nter section number list box and then key **2**.

j. Click the Go <u>T</u>o button. (This moves the insertion point to the beginning of the second section.)

k. Click the Close button to close the Find and Replace dialog box.

5. Save the document again with the same name (Word Ch 05, Ex 12).

6. Print and then close Word Ch 05, Ex 12.

Using Templates

Word has included a number of *template* documents that are formatted for specific uses. Each Word document is based on a template document with the *Normal* template the default. With Word templates, you can easily create a variety of documents, such as letters, memos, and awards, with specialized formatting. Along with templates, Word also includes *Wizards*. Wizards are templates that do most of the work for you. *(Note: During a typical installation, not all templates may be installed. Before completing the template exercises, check to see if the templates are available.)*

Templates and Wizards are available at the New dialog box. To display this dialog box, shown in figure 5.11, click <u>F</u>ile and then <u>N</u>ew. The New dialog box contains several tabs for displaying a variety of templates and wizards. If the default tab, General, is selected as shown in figure 5.11, the *Blank Document* template displays. To view other templates and wizards, click a different tab at the top of the New dialog box.

Use Word wizards and templates to create a variety of professionally designed documents

The template wizard is a template that asks questions and uses your responses to format a document auto-matically.

figure

5.11

New Dialog Box with General Tab Selected

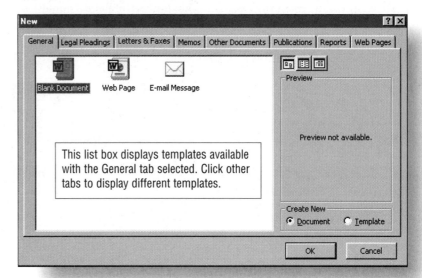

To create a document based on a different template, click the desired template, and then click OK, or double-click the desired template. If you click once on the desired template, a sample template displays in the Preview box at the right side of the dialog box. When you double-click a template, a template document is opened with certain formatting already applied. Specific information is then entered in the template document. After all information has been entered, the template document is saved in the normal manner.

exercise 13

Creating a Memo with a Memo Template

1. Use the Contemporary Memo template to create a memo by completing the following steps:
   a. Click File and then New.
   b. At the New dialog box, click the Memos tab.
   c. At the New dialog box with the Memos tab selected, double-click *Contemporary Memo*.

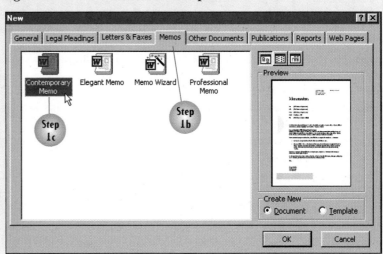

    d. At the contemporary memo template document, complete the following steps to key the text in the memo:

        1) Position the I-beam pointer on the word *here* in the bracketed text *[Click **here** and type name]* after *To:*, click the left mouse button, and then key **Sylvia Monroe, Vice President**.

        2) Position the I-beam pointer on the word *here* in the bracketed text *[Click **here** and type name]* after *CC:*, click the left mouse button, and then key **Jacob Sharify, President**.

        3) Position the I-beam pointer on the word *here* in the bracketed text *[Click **here** and type name]* after *From:*, click the left mouse button, and then key **Jamie Rodriquez, Design Department Manager**.

        4) Position the I-beam pointer on the word *here* in the bracketed text *[Click **here** and type subject]* after *Re:*, click the left mouse button, and then key **Color Scanners**.

        5) Select and then delete the text in the memo from ***How To Use This Memo Template*** to the end of the document.

        6) Key the text shown in figure 5.12.

  2. Save the memo and name it Word Ch 05, Ex 13.

  3. Print and then close Word Ch 05, Ex 13. (This memo template will print with several graphics including horizontal and vertical lines as well as lightened images.)

Exercise 13

The amount of company material produced by the Graphics Department has increased 200 percent in the past six months. To meet the demands of the increased volume, I am requesting two new color scanners. These scanners are needed to scan photographs, pictures, and other images. The total price of the two scanners is approximately $425. I will complete a product request form and forward it to you immediately.

Using Wizards

Wizards are template documents that do most of the work for you. When you select a Wizard template document, Word asks you questions and gives you choices about what type of formatting you want applied to the document. Follow the steps provided by the Wizard to complete the document.

Creating a Letter Using a Wizard

1. Create a letter using the Letter Wizard by completing the following steps:
   a. Click File and then New.
   b. At the New dialog box, click the Letters & Faxes tab.
   c. At the New dialog box with the Letters & Faxes tab selected, double-click the *Letter Wizard* icon.
   d. At the message displayed by the Office Assistant, click the *Send one letter* option.
   e. At the Letter Wizard—Step 1 of 4 dialog box, complete the following steps:
      1) Click the down-pointing triangle at the right side of the *Choose a page design* option, and then click *Contemporary Letter* at the drop-down list.
      2) Click the Next> button.

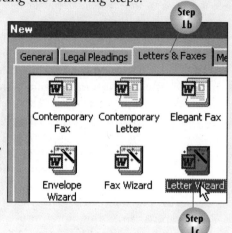

   f. At the Letter Wizard—Step 2 of 4 dialog box, complete the following steps:
      1) Key **Mr. Gregory Todd** in the Recipient's name text box.
      2) Press the Tab key. (This moves the insertion point to the Delivery address text box.)
      3) Key **12001 North 32nd Avenue**.
      4) Press Enter.
      5) Key **New York, NY 10225**.
      6) Click the Business option located in the lower right corner of the dialog box.
      7) Click the Next> button.
   g. At the Letter Wizard—Step 3 of 4 dialog box, click the Next> button.
   h. At the Letter Wizard—Step 4 of 4 dialog box, complete the following steps:
      1) Select the text that currently displays in the Sender's name text box, and then key **Louis Hamilton**.

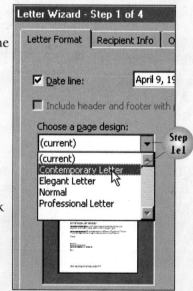

      2) Click in the Job title text box and then key **Investment Manager**.
      3) Click in the Writer/typist's initials text box and then key your initials.
      4) Click the Finish button.
   i. At the Office Assistant message, click Cancel.
   j. At the letter, insert a file for the body of the letter by completing the following steps:
      1) Select the text *Type your letter here. To add, remove, or change letter elements, choose Letter Wizard from the Tools menu.* and then press the Delete key.
      2) Click Insert and then File.

3) At the Insert File dialog box, make sure *Chapter 05* is the active folder, and then double-click *Word Letter 06*.
    k. Move down the name and inside address by positioning the insertion point at the beginning of the name *Mr. Gregory Todd* and then pressing the Enter key twice.
2. Save the letter and name it Word Ch 05, Ex 14.
3. Print and then close Word Ch 05, Ex 14.

Formatting with Predesigned Styles

A Word document, by default, is based on the Normal template document. Within a normal template document, a Normal style is applied to text by default. This Normal style sets text in the default font (this may vary depending on what you have selected or what printer you are using) and uses left alignment and single spacing. In addition to this Normal style, other predesigned styles are available in a document based on the Normal template document. Display these styles by clicking the down-pointing triangle to the right of the Style button on the Formatting toolbar.

Other template documents also contain predesigned styles. If you choose a different template document from the New dialog box, click the down-pointing triangle to the right of the Style button on the Formatting toolbar to display the names of styles available for that particular template document.

To apply a style with the Style button on the Formatting toolbar, position the insertion point in the paragraph to which you want the style applied, or select the text, and then click the down-pointing triangle to the right of the Style button (the first button on the left). This causes a drop-down list to display as shown in figure 5.13. Click the desired style in the list to apply the style to the text in the document.

Style

Applying a ready-to-use style ensures a consistent visual appearance of document elements.

figure

5.13

Style Drop-Down List

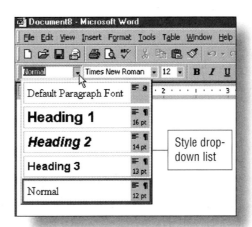

Style drop-down list

When you click a style in the drop-down list, the list is removed from the screen and the style is applied to the text. This formatting applied by the style will vary. For example, the Heading 1 style applies the font 16-point Arial bold and the Heading 2 style applies the font 14-point Arial bold italic.

When a style is applied to text, the style name displays in the Style button on the Formatting toolbar. In addition, the font for the style displays in the Font button and the size for the style displays in the Font Size button.

exercise 15

Formatting a Document with Styles

1. Open Word Report 01.
2. Save the document with Save As and name it Word Ch 05, Ex 15.
3. Make the following changes to the report:
   a. Select the entire document.
   b. Press Ctrl + 1 to change to single spacing.
4. Format the title with a style on the Formatting toolbar by completing the following steps:
   a. Position the insertion point anywhere within the title *GRAPHICS SOFTWARE*.
   b. Click the down-pointing triangle at the right side of the Style button on the Formatting toolbar.
   c. At the drop-down list that displays, click *Heading 1*.
5. Format the first heading with a style on the Formatting toolbar by completing the following steps:
   a. Position the insertion point anywhere within the first heading, *Early Painting and Drawing Programs*.
   b. Click the down-pointing triangle at the right side of the Style button on the Formatting toolbar and then click *Heading 2* at the drop-down list.
6. Format the two remaining headings (*Developments in Painting and Drawing Programs* and *Painting and Drawing Programs Today*) with the Heading 2 style.
7. Save the document again with the same name (Word Ch 05, Ex 15).
8. Print and then close Word Ch 05, Ex 15.

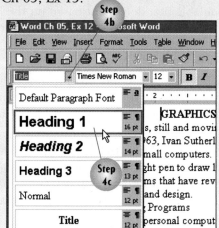

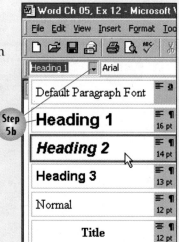

Formatting with Styles at the Style Dialog Box

The Style drop-down list only displays a few styles. Word provides many more predesigned styles than this that you can use to format text in a document. You can display the list of styles available with Word at the Style dialog box, shown in figure 5.14. To display the Style dialog box, click Format and then Style.

figure
5.14

Style Dialog Box

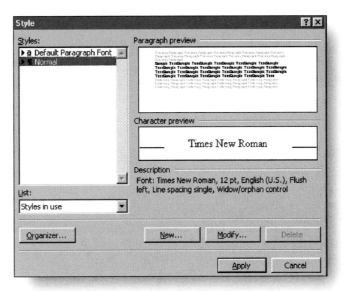

To display the entire list of styles provided by Word, click the down-pointing triangle at the right side of the List text box, and then click *All styles* at the drop-down list. When you click *All styles*, the list of styles in the Styles list box displays as shown in figure 5.15. The list is longer than the list box. In the Styles list box, paragraph styles are preceded by a paragraph mark (¶) and character styles are preceded by the symbol (a).

figure
5.15

Style Dialog Box with All Styles Displayed

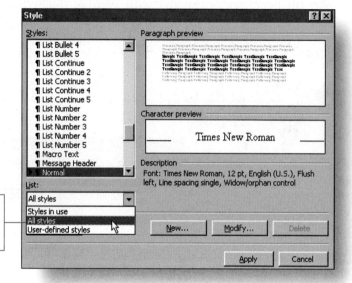

Click *All styles* to display all available styles in the Styles list box.

View attributes of a style in the Description area of the Style dialog box.

At the right side of the Style dialog box, the Paragraph preview box displays an example of how the selected style will format text. The Character preview box displays the font used to format text. A description of the style is displayed in the Description section of the dialog box.

To apply a style at the Style dialog box, position the insertion point within the paragraph of text to be formatted; or, if applying a character style, select the text, click Format and then Style. At the Style dialog box, click the down-pointing triangle at the right side of the List text box, and then click *All styles*. Click the desired style in the list and then click the Apply button.

exercise 16

Formatting with a Style at the Style Dialog Box

1. Open Word Document 05.
2. Save the document with Save As and name it Word Ch 05, Ex 16.
3. Make the following changes to the document:
   a. Bold the heading *ARE YOU PREPARING FOR RETIREMENT?*.
   b. Apply the List Bullet 2 style to text in the document by completing the following steps:
      1) Select from the paragraph that begins *"Living longer than ever,…"* through the last paragraph of text in the document.
      2) Click Format and then click Style.

3) At the Style dialog box, click the down-pointing triangle at the right side of the List text box, and then click *All styles* at the drop-down list.
4) Click the *List Bullet 2* style in the Styles list box. (You will need to scroll up to see this style.)
5) Click the Apply button.
   c. Deselect the text.
4. Save the document again with the same name (Word Ch 05, Ex 16).
5. Print and then close Word Ch 05, Ex 16.

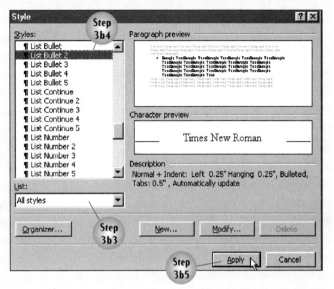

Formatting with Styles at the Style Gallery

Each template document contains predesigned styles. Use the Style Gallery dialog box to apply styles from other templates to the current document. This provides you with a large number of predesigned styles for formatting text. To display the Style Gallery dialog box shown in figure 5.16, click Format and then Theme. At the Theme dialog box, click the Style Gallery button (located at the bottom of the dialog box).

figure

5.16   *Style Gallery Dialog Box*

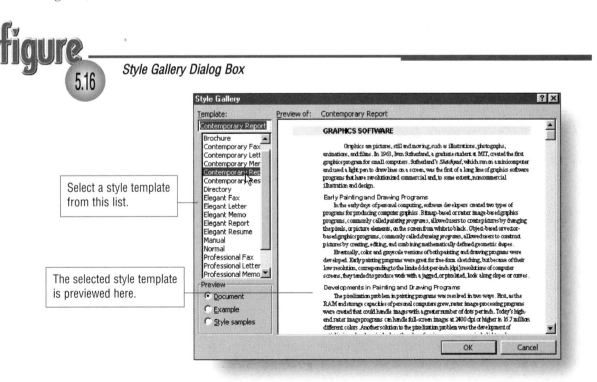

At the Style Gallery dialog box, the template documents are displayed in the Template list box. The open document is displayed in the Preview of section of the dialog box. With this section, you can choose templates from the Template list box and see how the formatting is applied to the open document.

At the bottom of the Style Gallery dialog box, the Document option is selected in the Preview section. If you click Example, Word will insert a sample document in the Preview of section that displays the formatting applied to the document. Click Style samples and styles will display in the Preview of section of the dialog box rather than the document or sample document.

exercise 17

Formatting a Report with Styles from a Report Template

1. Open Word Ch 05, Ex 15.
2. Save the document with Save As and name it Word Ch 05, Ex 17.
3. Format the document at the Style Gallery by completing the following steps:
   a. Click Format and then click Theme.
   b. At the Theme dialog box, click the Style Gallery button (located at the bottom of the dialog box).
   c. At the Style Gallery dialog box, click *Contemporary Report* in the Template list box.
   d. Click OK or press Enter.
4. Save the document again with the same name (Word Ch 05, Ex 17).
5. Print and then close Word Ch 05, Ex 17.

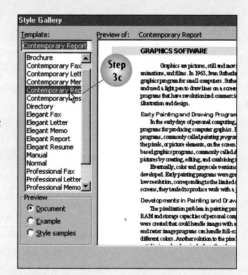

Creating Outline Style Numbered List

In chapter 2, you learned how to apply numbering to selected text with options at the Bullets and Numbering dialog box. Certain options at the Bullets and Numbering dialog box with the Outline Numbered tab selected are available only when heading styles have been applied to text. In exercise 18, you will apply heading styles to text and then apply outline style numbering to the text.

Creating an Outline Style Numbered List

1. Open Word Agenda.
2. Save the document with Save As and name it Word Ch 05, Ex 18.
3. Make the following changes to the document:
    a. Delete the following text:
        First Quarter (below *Income Report*)
        Second Quarter (below *Income Report*)
        First Quarter (below *Expense Report*)
        Second Quarter (below *Expense Report*)
    b. Apply the Heading 1 style to the following text:
        Sales and Marketing
        Financial
        Services and Procedures
        Education
    c. Apply the Heading 2 style to the following text:
        Commercial Lines
        Personal Lines
        Year-end Production Report
        Income Report
        Expense Report
        Accounts Receivable
        Accounts Payable
        Collections
        Update
        Sponsors
        Seminars
        Training
    d. Apply outline style numbering by completing the following steps:
        1) Select the text from the beginning of *Sales and Marketing* to the end of the document.
        2) Click Format and then Bullets and Numbering.
        3) At the Bullets and Numbering dialog box, click the Outline Numbered tab.
        4) Click the third option from the left in the bottom row.
        5) Click OK to close the dialog box.
    e. Select the title *COMMERCIAL LINES DEPARTMENT* and the subtitle *MEETING AGENDA* and then change the font to 16-point Arial bold.
4. Save the document again with the same name (Word Ch 05, Ex 18).
5. Print and then close Word Ch 05, Ex 18.

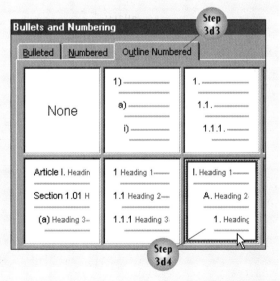

Creating an Outline

Create an outline in Word and then use the outline as a basis for preparing a PowerPoint presentation.

Word's outlining feature will format headings within a document as well as let you view formatted headings and body text in a document. With the outlining feature you can quickly see an overview of a document by collapsing parts of a document so that only the headings show. With headings collapsed, you can perform such editing functions as moving or deleting sections of a document.

To create an outline, you identify particular headings and subheadings within a document as certain heading levels. The Outline view is used to assign particular heading levels to text. You can also enter text and edit text while working in Outline view. To change to Outline view, click the Outline View button at the left side of the horizontal scroll bar, expand the drop-down menu, then click Outline. Figure 5.17 shows the Word Report 01 document as it will appear in exercise 19 with heading formatting applied in Outline view.

Outline View

Document in Outline View

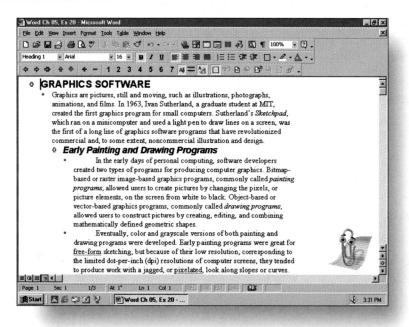

In figure 5.17, the title *GRAPHICS SOFTWARE* is identified as a first-level heading, the heading *Early Painting and Drawing Programs* is identified as a second-level heading, and the paragraphs following are normal text.

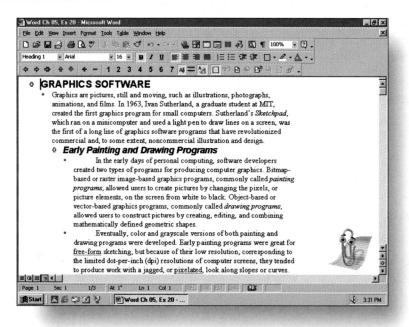
Outline an existing document or create a new document in Outline view.

When a document contains headings and text that have been formatted in the Outline view, each paragraph is identified as a particular heading level or as normal text. Paragraphs are identified by *outline selection symbols* that appear in the selection bar at the left side of the screen. Figure 5.18 describes the three outline selection symbols and what they indicate.

figure
5.18

Outline Selection Symbols

⊕   Indicates that subtext appears below the heading. Subtext may be body text or other subordinate headings.

▭   Indicates that no subtext appears below the heading.

☐   Indicates the paragraph is normal text.

The outline selection symbols can be used to select text in the document. To do this, position the arrow pointer on the outline selection symbol next to text you want to select until it turns into a four-headed arrow, and then click the left mouse button.

Assigning Headings

When a document is displayed in Outline view, the Outlining toolbar displays below the Formatting toolbar. The buttons on the Outlining toolbar are shown in figure 5.19.

figure
5.19

Outlining Toolbar Buttons

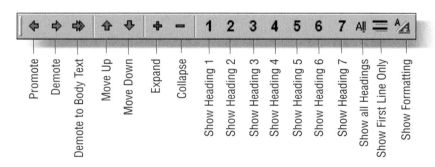

To change a paragraph that is identified as normal text to a first-level heading, position the insertion point on any character in the text (or select the text), and then click the Promote button on the Outlining toolbar. This applies the Heading 1 style to the paragraph. The Heading 1 style is a style that has been predefined by Word. This style displays in the Style button on the Formatting toolbar. (First button at left side.) The Heading 1 style sets the text in 16-point Arial bold.

To change a paragraph to a second-level heading, position the insertion point anywhere within the text, and then click the Demote button. This applies the Heading 2 style to the text. The Heading 2 style sets text in 14-point Arial bold italic and indents the text one-half inch.

Promote

Demote

Formatting a Document with Buttons on the Outlining Toolbar

1. Open Word Report 01.
2. Save the document with Save As and name it Word Ch 05, Ex 19.
3. Change to the Outline viewing mode by clicking the Outline View button at the left side of the horizontal scroll bar.
4. Promote and demote heading levels by completing the following steps:
   a. Position the insertion point anywhere in the title *GRAPHICS SOFTWARE* and then click the Promote button on the Outlining toolbar. (*Heading 1* will display in the Style button on the Formatting toolbar.)
   b. Position the insertion point anywhere in the heading *Early Painting and Drawing Programs* and then click the Demote button on the Outlining toolbar. (*Heading 2* will display in the Style button on the Formatting toolbar.)
   c. Position the insertion point anywhere in the heading *Developments in Painting and Drawing Programs* and then click the Promote button on the Outlining toolbar. (*Heading 2* will display in the Style button on the Formatting toolbar.)
   d. Position the insertion point anywhere in the heading *Painting and Drawing Programs Today* and then click the Promote button on the Outlining toolbar. (*Heading 2* will display in the Style button on the Formatting toolbar.)
5. Save the document again with the same name (Word Ch 05, Ex 19).
6. Print and then close Word Ch 05, Ex 19.

Collapsing and Expanding Outline Headings

One of the major benefits of working in the Outline view is the ability to see a condensed outline of your document without all of the text in between headings or subheadings. Word lets you collapse a heading level in an outline. This causes any text or subsequent lower heading levels to disappear temporarily. When heading levels are collapsed, viewing the outline of a document is much easier. For example, when an outline is collapsed, you can see an overview of the entire document and move easily to different locations in the document. You can also move headings and their subordinate headings to new locations in the outline.

Show Heading 2

To collapse the entire outline, click the Show Heading button containing the number of heading levels desired. For example, if a document contains three heading levels, clicking the Show Heading 2 button on the Outlining toolbar will collapse the outline so only Heading 1 and Heading 2 text is displayed.

Click the Show All Headings button to deactivate the button and the document collapses displaying only heading text, not body text. Click the Show All Headings button again to activate it and the document expands to show all heading levels and body text. If you click the Show All Headings button to deactivate it, the document would display as shown in figure 5.20. (The document in figure 5.20 is the document from figure 5.17.) When a heading is collapsed, a gray horizontal line displays beneath it.

Show All Headings

Collapsed Outline

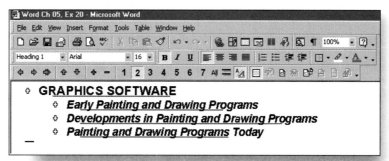

exercise 20

Collapsing an Outline

1. Open Word Ch 05, Ex 19.
2. Save the document with Save As and name it Word Ch 05, Ex 20.
3. Make the following changes to the document:
   a. Make sure the document is displayed in the Outline viewing mode.
   b. Click the Show All Headings button on the Outlining toolbar to deactivate it.
   c. With the outline collapsed, select the heading *Painting and Drawing Programs Today*, and then delete it. (This deletes the heading and all text below the heading.)
4. Save the document again with the same name (Word Ch 05, Ex 20).
5. Print and then close Word Ch 05, Ex 20. (This will print the collapsed outline, not the entire document.)

To collapse all of the text beneath a particular heading (including the text following any subsequent headings), position the insertion point within the heading, and then click the Collapse button on the Outlining toolbar. To make the text appear again, click the Expand button on the Outlining toolbar. For example, if you collapsed the first second-level heading shown in the document in figure 5.17, the document would display as shown in figure 5.21.

Collapse

Expand

figure

5.21

Collapsed Second-Level Heading

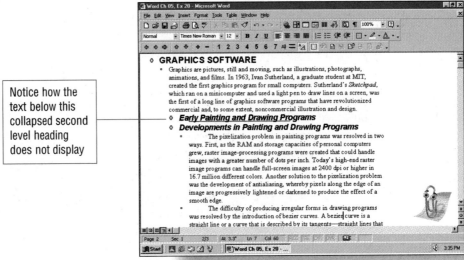

Notice how the text below this collapsed second level heading does not display

Organizing an Outline

Collapsing and expanding headings within an outline is only part of the versatility offered by Word's outline feature. It also offers you the ability to rearrange an entire document by reorganizing an outline. Whole sections of a document can quickly be rearranged by moving the headings at the beginning of those sections. The text that is collapsed beneath the headings is moved at the same time.

Collapse an outline before moving text.

For example, to move a second-level heading below other second-level headings, you would collapse the outline, select the second-level heading to be moved, and then click the Move Down button on the Outlining toolbar until the second-level heading is in the desired position.

If headings are collapsed, you only need to select the heading and move it to the desired location. Any subsequent text that is hidden is moved automatically. You can also move headings in a document by positioning the arrow pointer on the plus symbol before the desired heading until it turns into a four-headed arrow, holding down the mouse button, dragging the heading to the desired location, and then releasing the mouse button. As you drag the mouse, a gray horizontal line displays in the document with an arrow attached. Use this horizontal line to help you move the heading to the desired location.

Move Down

exercise

Moving Headings in a Document

1. Open Word Ch 05, Ex 20.
2. Save the document with Save As and name it Word Ch 05, Ex 21.
3. Make the following changes to the document:

a. With the Outline viewing mode turned on, click the Show Heading 2 button on the Outlining toolbar.

b. Move *Painting and Drawing Programs Today* above *Developments in Painting and Drawing Programs* by completing the following steps:
   1) Position the insertion point anywhere in the heading *Painting and Drawing Programs Today*.
   2) Click once on the Move Up button on the Outlining toolbar.

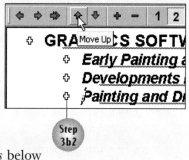

Step 3b2

c. Move the heading *Early Painting and Drawing Programs* below *Developments in Painting and Drawing Programs* by completing the following steps:
   1) Position the arrow pointer on the plus symbol immediately left of the heading *Early Painting and Drawing Programs* until it turns into a four-headed arrow.
   2) Hold down the left mouse button, drag the mouse down until the gray horizontal line with the arrow attached is positioned below *Developments in Painting and Drawing Programs*, and then release the mouse button.

Step 3c2

   3) Deselect the text.

4. Save the document again with the same name (Word Ch 05, Ex 21).

5. Print Word Ch 05, Ex 21. (Only the title and headings will print.)

6. Click the Show All Headings button on the Outlining toolbar to display the document text and then close the document.

chapter summary

▶ Text that appears at the top of every page is called a header; text that appears at the bottom of every page is called a footer.

▶ Click View and then Header and Footer to display the Header and Footer toolbar and a header pane.

▶ Click the Switch Between Header and Footer button on the Header and Footer toolbar to display a footer pane.

▶ A header or footer does not display in the Normal view but will display dimmed in the Print Layout view. To see how the header or footer will print, display Print Preview.

▶ Header or footer text does not take on any character formatting applied to the document. If you want header or footer text character formatting to be the same as the document text, format that text in the header or footer pane in the normal manner.

▶ A header or footer contains three tab alignment settings: left, center, and right. Press the Tab key to move the insertion point to the center alignment setting and then press the Tab key again to move the insertion point to the right alignment setting.

▶ Edit a header or footer in Print Layout view or in the header or footer pane.

▶ Delete a header or footer at the header or footer pane.

▶ More than one header or footer can be created in a document.

- Insert page numbering in a document with options from the Page Numbers dialog box or in a header or footer.
- Modify page numbers at the Page Number Format dialog box.
- Use the find feature to search for specific characters or formatting. Use the find and replace feature to search for specific characters or formatting and replace with other characters or formatting.
- Click Edit and then Find to display the Find and Replace dialog box with the Find tab selected.
- Click Edit and then Replace to display the Find and Replace dialog box with the Replace tab selected.
- At the Find and Replace dialog box, click the Find Next button to find the next occurrence of the characters and/or formatting. Click the Replace button to replace the characters or formatting and find the next occurrence; or, click the Replace All button to replace all occurrences of the characters or formatting.
- Click the More button at the Find and Replace dialog box to display additional options for completing a search.
- Navigate through a document with options at the Find and Replace dialog box with the Go To tab selected.
- Create a variety of documents such as letters, memos, and awards, using Word templates and Wizards.
- Wizards are templates that do most of the work for you.
- Templates and Wizards provided by Word are available at the New dialog box.
- A style is a set of formatting instructions saved with a specific name in order to use the formatting over and over.
- All styles provided by Word can be displayed in the Style dialog box with *All styles* selected.
- Apply a style using the Style button on the Formatting toolbar or at the Style dialog box.
- Use the Outline view to format headings in a document and assign particular heading levels to text.
- Headings and text formatted in the Outline view are identified by outline selection symbols that display at the left side of the screen. These symbols can be used to select text in the document.
- The Outlining toolbar displays below the Formatting toolbar in Outline view. Use buttons on this toolbar to assign various level headings to text.

commands review

	Mouse/Keyboard
Create a header or footer	View, Header and Footer
Print Preview	File, Print Preview; or click Print Preview button on Standard toolbar
Find and Replace dialog box with Find tab selected	Edit, Find
Find and Replace dialog box with Replace tab selected	Edit, Replace

Find and Replace dialog box with <u>G</u>o To tab selected	<u>E</u>dit, <u>G</u>o To
Page Numbers dialog box	<u>I</u>nsert, Page N<u>u</u>mbers
New dialog box	<u>F</u>ile, <u>N</u>ew
Style dialog box	Fo<u>r</u>mat, <u>S</u>tyle
Style Gallery dialog box	Fo<u>r</u>mat, T<u>h</u>eme, Style <u>G</u>allery
Outline view	<u>V</u>iew, <u>O</u>utline; or click Outline View button at left side of horizontal scroll bar

thinking offline ·····················

Completion: In the space provided at the right margin, indicate the correct term, command, or number.

1. Clicking <u>V</u>iew and then <u>H</u>eader and Footer automatically positions the insertion point here.

2. To create a footer, click this button on the Header and Footer toolbar.

3. Create footers on odd and/or even pages at this dialog box.

4. Page numbers can be inserted in a header or footer or with options at this dialog box.

5. Change the beginning page number with this option at the Page Number Format dialog box.

6. If you want to replace every occurrence of what you are searching for in a document, click this button at the Find and Replace dialog box.

7. Click this button at the Find and Replace dialog box if you do not want to replace an occurrence with the replace text.

8. Click this option at the Find and Replace dialog box if you are searching for a word and all its forms.

9. Choose a template at this dialog box.

10. Display the styles available in a document by clicking the down-pointing triangle at the right side of this button on the Formatting toolbar.

11. Use this view to format headings in a document and assign particular heading levels to text.

12. Click this button on the Outlining toolbar to display only first level headings.

13. Click this button on the Outlining toolbar to move the selected heading up one level.

14. In the space provided below, list the steps you would complete to create the footer *Computers and Technology* that prints bolded and centered on each page of the document.

_____

_____

_____

_____

15. In the space provided below, list the steps you would complete to insert page numbering in a document that prints at the bottom right side on each page and begins with page number 5.

_____

_____

_____

_____

working hands-on

Assessment 1

1. Open Word Report 03.
2. Save the document with Save As and name it Word Ch 05, SA 01.
3. Make the following changes to the document:
   a. Change the top margin to 1.5 inches.
   b. Select the entire document and then change the font to 12-point Bookman Old Style (or a similar serif typeface).
   c. Select the title *NETWORK TOPOLOGIES* and then change the font to 18-point Tahoma bold.
   d. Select the heading *Linear Bus Networks* and then change the font to 14-point Tahoma bold.
   e. Use the Format Painter to change the font to 14-point Tahoma bold for the remaining two headings *Star Networks* and *Ring Networks*.
   f. Create the footer *Network Topologies* that is set in 12-point Tahoma bold and prints at the center of the footer pane.
4. Check page breaks in the document and, if necessary, adjust the page breaks.
5. Save the document again with the same name (Word Ch 05, SA 01).
6. Print and then close Word Ch 05, SA 01.

Assessment 2

1. Open Word Ch 05, SA 01.
2. Save the document with Save As and name it Word Ch 05, SA 02.

3. Make the following changes to the document:
   a. Delete the footer in the document.
   b. Create the footer *Page #* (where the correct page number is inserted at the #) that is set in 12-point Tahoma bold and prints at the right margin on all odd pages.
   c. Create the footer *Types of Networks* that is set in 12-point Tahoma bold and prints at the left margin on all even pages.
4. Save the document again with the same name (Word Ch 05, SA 02).
5. Print and then close Word Ch 05, SA 02.

Assessment 3

1. Open Word Report 04.
2. Save the document with Save As and name it Word Ch 05, SA 03.
3. Make the following changes to the document:
   a. Select the entire document and then change the font to 12-point Century Schoolbook (or a similar serif typeface).
   b. Select the title *CHAPTER 1: COMPUTER INPUT DEVICES* and then change the font to 14-point Arial bold.
   c. Change the font to 14-point Arial bold for the following title and headings:
      Keyboard
      Mouse
      Trackball
      Touch Pad and Touch Screen
      CHAPTER 2: COMPUTER OUTPUT DEVICES
      Monitor
      Printer
   d. Insert a section break that begins a new page at the beginning of the line containing the title *CHAPTER 2: COMPUTER OUTPUT DEVICES*. (Be sure to insert a section break and not a page break.)
   e. Create the footer *Chapter 1: Computer Input Devices* that is set in 12-point Arial bold, is centered, and prints in the first section.
   f. Create the footer *Chapter 2: Computer Output Devices* that is set in 12-point Arial bold, is centered, and prints in the second section.
4. Check page breaks in the document and, if necessary, adjust the page breaks.
5. Save the document again with the same name (Word Ch 05, SA 03).
6. Print and then close Word Ch 05, SA 03.

Assessment 4

1. Open Word Contract.
2. Save the document with Save As and name it Word Ch 05, SA 04.
3. Make the following changes to the document:
   a. Find all occurrences of REINBERG MANUFACTURING and replace with QUALITY SYSTEMS.
   b. Find all occurrences of RM and replace with QS.
   c. Find all occurrences of LABOR WORKERS' UNION and replace with INDUSTRIAL WORKERS' UNION.
   d. Find all occurrences of LWU and replace with IWU.
4. Save the document again with the same name (Word Ch 05, SA 04).
5. Print and then close Word Ch 05, SA 04.

Assessment 5

1. Use the Contemporary Fax template (displays when the Letter & Faxes tab is selected at the New dialog box) to create a fax cover sheet. Select the text in brackets, delete it, and then key the information as shown below:

   Click anywhere in the text *[Click here and type address]* located in the upper right corner of the fax page and then key the following:

   4509 Jackson Avenue
   St. Paul, MN 55230

   Key the following text in the specified location:

To:	**Rene LeJeune**
Fax:	**(412) 555-8122**
From:	**Claire Monroe**
Re:	**Order Number 3420**
Pages:	**1**
CC:	(leave this blank)

   Select the text in the body of the fax, delete it, and then key the following:

   This fax is to confirm your order number 3420. All items on that order are in stock and will be shipped within three business days. This order will be shipped by two-day express delivery. If you need overnight delivery, please call (304) 555-9855.

2. Save the completed fax and name it Word Ch 05, SA 05.
3. Print and then close Word Ch 05, SA 05.

Assessment 6

1. Open Word Report 03.
2. Save the document with Save As and name it Word Ch 05, SA 06.
3. Make the following changes to the document:
   a. Apply the following heading styles:

NETWORK TOPOLOGIES	=	Heading 1
Linear Bus Networks	=	Heading 2
Star Networks	=	Heading 2
Ring Networks	=	Heading 2

   b. Format the document at the Style Gallery with the *Professional Report* template.
4. Save the document again with the same name (Word Ch 05, SA 06).
5. Print and then close Word Ch 05, SA 06.

Assessment 7

1. Open Word Report 04.
2. Save the document with Save As and name it Word Ch 05, SA 07.
3. Make the following changes to the document:
   a. Change to the Outline view and then promote or demote the following titles and headings:

CHAPTER 1: COMPUTER INPUT DEVICES	=	Heading 1
Keyboard	=	Heading 2
Mouse	=	Heading 2
Trackball	=	Heading 2

Touch Pad and Touch Screen	=	Heading 2
CHAPTER 2: COMPUTER OUTPUT DEVICES	=	Heading 1
Monitor	=	Heading 2
Printer	=	Heading 2

    b. Collapse the outline so only the two heading levels display.

    c. Move the chapter 1 title and the headings below it after the chapter 2 title and the headings below it.

    d. Renumber the chapters (chapter 1 becomes 2 and chapter 2 becomes 1).

    e. Move the heading *Trackball* below the heading *Touch Pad and Touch Screen*.

4. Save the document again with the same name (Word Ch 05, SA 07).

5. Print and then close Word Ch 05, SA 07.

Assessment 8

1. In this chapter, you learned to find specific text and replace with other text. You can also find formatting and replace with other formatting. Use Word's Help feature to learn how to find formatting and replace with other formatting and then complete the following steps:

    a. At a clear document screen, write the steps you would follow to find 14-point Times New Roman bold formatting and replace with 16-point Arial bold formatting.

    b. Save the completed document and name it Word Ch 05 Steps.

    c. Print and then close Word Ch 05 Steps.

2. Search and replace character formatting by completing the following steps:

    a. Open Word Ch 05, SA 01.

    b. Save the document with Save As and name it Word Ch 05, SA 08.

    c. Search for 18-point Tahoma bold formatting and replace with 16-point Bookman Old Style bold. (If Bookman Old Style is not available, choose a similar serif typeface.)

    d. Search for 14-point Tahoma bold formatting and replace with 13-point Bookman Old Style bold (or the font you chose in steps 2c).

    e. Save the document again with the same name (Word Ch 05, SA 08).

    f. Print and then close Word Ch 05, SA 08.

Chapter 06

Creating and Formatting Tables

PERFORMANCE OBJECTIVES

Upon successful completion of chapter 6, you will be able to:

- Create a table.
- Enter and edit text within cells in a table.
- Delete a table.
- Format a table by adding borders and shading, changing column width, aligning text within cells, inserting and deleting columns and rows, and merging and splitting cells.
- Apply formatting to a table with one of Word's predesigned AutoFormats.
- Create and format a table using buttons on the Tables and Borders toolbar.
- Perform calculations on values in a table.

Word provides a variety of features that help you organize data. With Word's Tables feature, you can create data in columns and rows. This data can consist of text, values, and formulas. The Tables feature can create columns of data in a manner similar to a spreadsheet. Many basic spreadsheet functions, such as inserting values, totaling numbers, and inserting formulas, can be performed in a Word table.

With a Word table, a form can be created that contains boxes of information called *cells*. A cell is the intersection between a row and a column. A cell can contain text, characters, numbers, data, graphics, or formulas. Data within a cell can be formatted to display left, right, center, or fully aligned, and can include character formatting such as bold, italics, and underlining. The formatting choices available with the Tables feature are quite extensive and allow flexibility in creating a variety of tables.

Creating a Table

A table can be created with the Insert Table button on the Standard toolbar or the Table option from the Menu bar. To create a table with the Insert Table button, click the Insert Table button on the Standard toolbar. This causes a grid to

Insert Table

appear as shown in figure 6.1. Move the mouse pointer down and to the right until the correct number of rows and columns displays below the grid and then click the left mouse button. As you move the mouse pointer in the grid, note that selected columns and rows are highlighted, and the number of rows and columns displays below the grid.

6.1

Table Grid

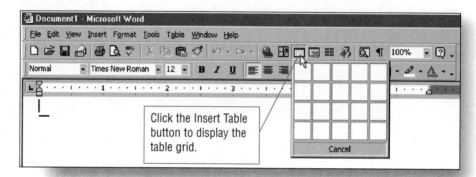

Click the Insert Table button to display the table grid.

Before creating a table, try to determine the number of columns needed since Word automatically determines column width.

A table can also be created with options at the Insert Table dialog box shown in figure 6.2. Display the Insert Table dialog box by clicking Table, pointing to Insert, and then clicking Table. At the Insert Table dialog box, key the desired number of columns in the Number of columns text box. Press the Tab key or click in the Number of rows text box, key the desired number of rows, and then click OK or press Enter. A table is inserted in the document at the location of the insertion point.

6.2

Insert Table Dialog Box

If you think you will be adding text above a table, press Enter at least once at a new document screen, and then create the table.

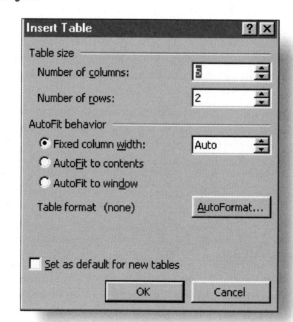

Figure 6.3 shows an example of a table with four columns and three rows. Various parts of the table are identified in figure 6.3 such as the gridlines, move table column marker, end-of-cell marker, and end-of-row marker. In a table, nonprinting characters identify the end of a cell and the end of a row. To view these characters, click the Show/Hide ¶ button on the Standard toolbar. The end-of-cell marker displays inside each cell and the end-of-row marker displays at the end of a row of cells. These markers are identified in figure 6.3.

figure
6.3

Table

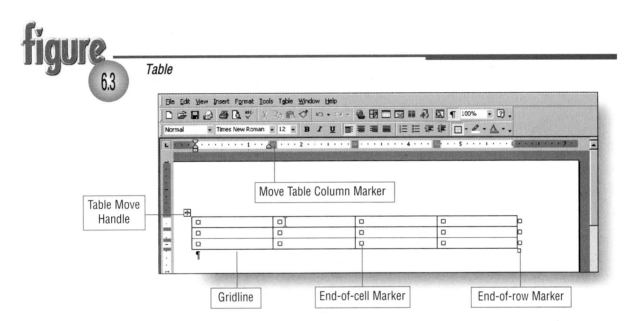

Table Move Handle

Move Table Column Marker

Gridline

End-of-cell Marker

End-of-row Marker

When a table is created, the insertion point is located in the cell in the upper left corner of the table. Cells in a table contain a cell designation. Columns in a table are lettered from left to right, beginning with A. Rows in a table are numbered from top to bottom beginning with 1. The cell in the upper left corner of the table is cell A1. The cell to the right of A1 is B1, the cell to the right of B1 is C1, and so on. The cells below A1 are A2, A3, A4, and so on. Some cell designations are shown in figure 6.4.

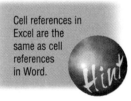

Cell references in Excel are the same as cell references in Word.

figure
6.4

Cell Designations

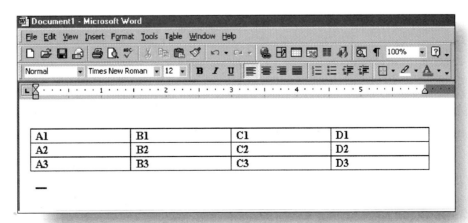

A1	B1	C1	D1
A2	B2	C2	D2
A3	B3	C3	D3

If the Ruler is displayed at the top of the document screen, move table column markers display on the Ruler. These markers represent the end of a column and are useful in changing the width of columns. Figure 6.3 identifies a move table column marker.

Entering Text in Cells

With the insertion point positioned in a cell, key or edit text. Move the insertion point to other cells with the mouse by clicking in the desired cell. If you are using the keyboard, press the Tab key to move the insertion point to the next cell or press Shift + Tab to move the insertion point to the previous cell.

If the text you key does not fit on one line, it wraps to the next line within the same cell. Or, if you press Enter within a cell, the insertion point is moved to the next line within the same cell. The cell vertically lengthens to accommodate the text, and all cells in that row also lengthen. Pressing the Tab key in a table causes the insertion point to move to the next cell in the table. If you want to move the insertion point to a tab stop within a cell, press Ctrl + Tab.

If the insertion point is located in the last cell of the table and you press the Tab key, Word adds another row to the table. To avoid this situation, make sure you do not press the Tab key after entering text in the last cell, or, immediately click the Undo button on the Standard toolbar. You can insert a page break within a table by pressing Ctrl + Enter. The page break is inserted between rows, not within.

When all information has been entered in the cells, move the insertion point below the table and, if necessary, continue keying the document, or save the document in the normal manner.

Moving the Insertion Point within a Table

To move the insertion point to a different cell within the table using the mouse, click in the desired cell. To move the insertion point to different cells within the table using the keyboard, refer to the information shown in figure 6.5.

Pressing the Tab key in a table moves the insertion point to the next cell. Pressing Ctrl + Tab moves the insertion point to the next tab within a cell. *Hint*

figure
6.5 *Insertion Point Movement within a Table Using the Keyboard*

To move the insertion point	Press these keys
to next cell	Tab
to preceding cell	Shift + Tab
forward one character	right arrow key
backward one character	left arrow key
to previous row	up arrow key
to next row	down arrow key
to first cell in the row	Alt + Home (or Alt + 7 on numeric keypad*)
to last cell in the row	Alt + End (or Alt + 1 on numeric keypad*)
to top cell in the column	Alt + Page Up (or Alt + 9 on numeric keypad*)
to bottom cell in the column	Alt + Page Down (or Alt + 3 on numeric keypad*)
	Num Lock must be off.

238

Creating a Table with the Insert Table Button

1. At a clear editing window, create the table shown in figure 6.6 by completing the following steps:

    a. Click the Insert Table button on the Standard toolbar.

    b. Move the mouse pointer down and to the right until the number below the grid displays as 5 x 3 and then click the mouse button.

    c. Key the text in the cells as indicated in figure 6.6. Press the Tab key to move to the next cell or press Shift + Tab to move to the preceding cell. (If you accidentally press the Enter key within a cell, immediately press the Backspace key. Do not press Tab after keying the text in the last cell. If you do, another row is inserted in the table. If this happens, immediately click the Undo button on the Standard toolbar.)

2. Save the table and name it Word Ch 06, Ex 01.

3. Print and then close Word Ch 06, Ex 01.

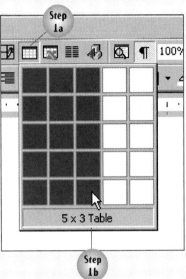

Exercise 1

Maggie Rivera	First Trust Bank	(203) 555-3440
Regina Stahl	United Fidelity	(301) 555-1221
Stanley White Cloud	Key One Savings	(360) 555-8966
Les Cromwell	Madison Trust	(602) 555-4900
Cecilia Nordyke	American Financial Trust	(509) 555-3995

exercise 2

Creating a Table at the Insert Table Dialog Box

1. At a clear document screen, create the table shown in figure 6.7 by completing the following steps:
   a. Change the paragraph alignment to center and turn on bold.
   b. Key **OPTIONAL PLAN PREMIUM RATES**.
   c. Press Enter three times.
   d. Turn off bold and change the paragraph alignment to left.
   e. Create the table by completing the following steps:
      1) Click Table, point to Insert, and then click Table.
      2) At the Insert Table dialog box, key **3** in the Number of columns text box. (The insertion point is automatically positioned in this text box.)
      3) Press the Tab key (this moves the insertion point to the Number of rows option) and then key **8**.
      4) Click OK or press Enter.

   f. Key the text in the cells as indicated in figure 6.7. Press the Tab key to move to the next cell or press Shift + Tab to move to the preceding cell. To indent the text in cells B2 through B8 and cells C2 through C8, press Ctrl + Tab to move the insertion to a tab within cells, and then key the text.
2. Save the table and name it Word Ch 06, Ex 02.
3. Print and then close Word Ch 06, Ex 02.

Exercise 2

6.7

OPTIONAL PLAN PREMIUM RATES

Waiting Period	Plan 2002 Employees	Basic Plan Employees
60 days	0.79%	0.67%
90 days	0.59%	0.49%
120 days	0.35%	0.30%
180 days	0.26%	0.23%
240 days	0.25%	0.22%
300 days	0.23%	0.21%
360 days	0.22%	0.20%

Selecting Cells

A table can be formatted in special ways. For example, the alignment of text in cells or rows can be changed or character formatting can be added. To identify the cells that are to be affected by the formatting, the specific cells need to be selected.

Selecting in a Table with the Mouse

The mouse pointer can be used to select a cell, row, column, or an entire table. Figure 6.8 describes methods for selecting in a table with the mouse. The left edge of each cell, between the left column border and the end-of-cell marker or first character in the cell, is called the *cell selection bar*. When the mouse pointer is positioned in the cell selection bar, it turns into an arrow pointing up and to the right (instead of the left). Each row in a table contains a *row selection bar*, which is the space just to the left of the left edge of the table. When the mouse pointer is positioned in the row selection bar, the mouse pointer turns into an arrow pointing up and to the right.

figure
6.8

Selecting in a Table with the Mouse

To select this	Do this
a cell	Position the mouse pointer in the cell selection bar at the left edge of the cell until it turns into an arrow pointing up and to the right and then click the left mouse button.
a row	Position the mouse pointer in the row selection bar at the left edge of the table until it turns into an arrow pointing up and to the right and then click the left mouse button.
a column	Position the mouse pointer on the uppermost horizontal gridline of the table in the appropriate column until it turns into a short, downward-pointing arrow and then click the left mouse button.
adjacent cells	Position the mouse pointer in the first cell to be selected, hold down the left mouse button, drag the mouse pointer to the last cell to be selected, and then release the mouse button.
all cells in a table	Click the table move handle; or position the mouse pointer in any cell in the table, hold down the Alt key, and then double-click the left mouse button. You can also position the mouse pointer in the row selection bar in the first row at the left edge of the table until it turns into an arrow pointing up and to the right, hold down the left mouse button, drag down to select all rows in the table, and then release the left mouse button.
text within a cell	Position the mouse pointer at the beginning of the text and then hold down the left mouse button as you drag the mouse across the text. (When a cell is selected, the entire cell is changed to black. When text within cells is selected, only those lines containing text are selected.)

Selecting and Formatting Cells in a Table

1. Open Word Ch 06, Ex 01.
2. Save the document with Save As and name it Word Ch 06, Ex 03.
3. Select and then bold the text in the cells in the first column using the mouse by completing the following steps:
   a. Position the mouse pointer on the uppermost horizontal gridline of the first column in the table until it turns into a short, downward-pointing arrow.
   b. Click the left mouse button.
   c. Click the Bold button on the Standard toolbar.
   d. Deselect the column.
4. Select and then italicize the text in the cells in the third column by completing steps similar to those in step 3.
5. Save the document again with the same name (Word Ch 06, Ex 03).
6. Print and then close Word Ch 06, Ex 03.

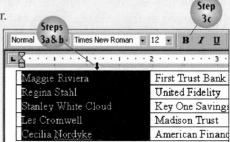

Selecting in a Table with the Keyboard

The keyboard can be used to select specific cells within a table. Figure 6.9 displays the commands for selecting specific amounts of a table.

6.9 *Selecting in a Table with the Keyboard*

To select	Press
the next cell's contents	Tab
the preceding cell's contents	Shift + Tab
the entire table	Alt + 5 (on numeric keypad with Num Lock off)
adjacent cells	Hold Shift key, then press an arrow key repeatedly
a column	Position insertion point in top cell of column, hold down the Shift key, then press down arrow key until column is selected

If you want to select only text within cells, rather than the entire cell, press F8 to turn on the Extend mode, and then move the insertion point with an arrow key. When a cell is selected, the entire cell is changed to black. When text within a cell is selected, only those lines containing text are selected.

Selecting Cells with the Table Drop-Down Menu

A row or column of cells or all cells in a table can be selected with options from the Table drop-down menu. For example, to select a row of cells in a table, position the insertion point in any cell in the row, click T<u>a</u>ble, point to Sele<u>c</u>t, and then click <u>R</u>ow.

To select cells in a column, position the insertion point in any cell in the column, click T<u>a</u>ble, point to Sele<u>c</u>t, and then click <u>C</u>olumn. To select all cells in the table, position the insertion point in any cell in the table, click T<u>a</u>ble, point to Sele<u>c</u>t, and then click <u>T</u>able.

Selecting and Formatting Cells Using the Table Drop-Down Menu

1. Open Word Ch 06, Ex 02.
2. Save the document with Save As and name it Word Ch 06, Ex 04.
3. Select and then bold the text in the cells in the first column using the keyboard to complete the following steps:
   a. Position the insertion point in the first cell of the first column (cell A1).
   b. Hold down the Shift key and then press the down arrow key seven times. (This should select all cells in the first column.)
   c. Press Ctrl + B.
4. Select and then bold the text in the cells in the second column using the T<u>a</u>ble drop-down menu by completing the following steps:
   a. Position the insertion point in any cell in the second column.
   b. Click T<u>a</u>ble, point to Sele<u>c</u>t, and then click <u>C</u>olumn.
   c. Click the Bold button on the Standard toolbar.
5. Select and then italicize the text in the cells in the third column by completing steps similar to those in steps 3 or 4.
6. Save the document again with the same name (Word Ch 06, Ex 04).
7. Print and then close Word Ch 06, Ex 04.

Deleting a Table

All text in cells within a table can be deleted, leaving the table gridlines, or all text and the gridlines can be deleted. To delete the text, leaving the gridlines, select the table, and then press the Delete key. To delete the text in cells and the gridlines, click T<u>a</u>ble, point to <u>D</u>elete, and then click <u>T</u>able.

Copying and Deleting a Table

1. Open Word Ch 06, Ex 02.
2. Save the document with Save As and name it Word Ch 06, Ex 05.
3. Make the following changes to the document:
   a. Select and then delete the title *OPTIONAL PLAN PREMIUM RATES*.
   b. Move the insertion point below the table and then press the Enter key three times.

c. Select the table by completing the following steps:
   1) Position the insertion point in any cell in the table.
   2) Click Table, point to Select, and then click Table.
d. With the table selected, click the Copy button on the Standard toolbar.
e. Move the insertion point to the end of the document and then click the Paste button on the Standard toolbar. (This inserts a copy of the table at the end of the document.)
f. Select and then delete the first table in the document by completing the following steps:
   1) Position the insertion point in any cell in the table.
   2) Change to the Print Layout view.
   3) Click the table move handle located in the upper left corner of the table.
   4) Click Table, point to Delete, and then click Table.
g. Delete any extra blank lines at the beginning of the document.

4. Save the document again with the same name (Word Ch 06, Ex 05).
5. Print and then close Word Ch 06, Ex 05.

Formatting a Table

A table that has been created with Word's Tables feature can be formatted in a variety of ways. For example, borders and shading can be added to cells; rows and columns can be inserted or deleted; cells can be split or merged; and the alignment of the table can be changed.

Adding Borders

If you make a mistake while formatting a table, immediately click the Undo button on the Standard toolbar.

The gridlines creating a table can be customized with border options. Borders can be added to a selected cell(s) or an entire table with options at the Borders and Shading dialog box shown in figure 6.10. To display this dialog box, click Format and then Borders and Shading.

figure

6.10

Borders and Shading Dialog Box with Borders Tab Selected

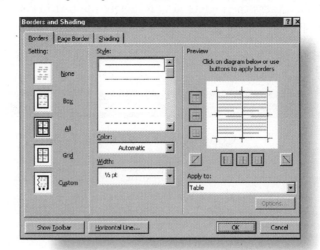

If you want a border option to apply to a specific cell, select the cell first and then display the Borders and Shading dialog box. The Borders and Shading Apply to option will display with *Cell* in the text box. If the insertion point is positioned in a table (with no cell selected) or if the entire table is selected, changes made at the Borders and Shading dialog box will affect the entire table and the Apply to option will display with *Table*. Figure 6.11 describes the options available at the Borders and Shading dialog box.

figure

6.11   *Options at the Borders and Shading Dialog Box with the Borders Tab Selected*

Choose this option	To do this
None	Remove all borders from selected cell(s) or table
Box	Insert a box border around the selected cell(s) or table
All	Insert a box border around and between selected cell(s) or table and apply preset shadow formatting to border
Grid	Insert a box border around selected cell(s) or table and apply preset 3-D border formatting, making the border look like a "window"
Custom	Create a custom border using options in the Preview diagram
Style	Choose a border style
Color	Choose a border color
Width	Specify the width of the border
Preview diagram	Click the sides of the Preview diagram to add or remove the currently selected settings
Apply to	Specify to what the border and shading should be applied
Options	Set additional margin and position settings (only available when Apply to is set at *Paragraph* or when Page Border tab is selected)

exercise

6

Creating a Table with Border Lines Around and Between Cells

1. At a clear document screen, create the document shown in figure 6.12 by completing the following steps:
   a. Change the paragraph alignment to center and turn on bold.
   b. Key **DIVERSIFICATION OF ASSETS**.
   c. Press Enter, turn off bold, and then change the paragraph alignment to left.
   d. Press Enter twice and then create a table with 2 columns and 8 rows (8 x 2).
   e. Key the text in the first cell (cell A1) by completing the following steps:
      1) Click the Center button on the Formatting toolbar.

2) Click the Bold button on the Formatting toolbar.
3) Key **Asset**.

f.   Press the Tab key to move the insertion point to the next cell (cell B1). Complete steps similar to those in step 1e to center and bold the column heading *Percentage*.

g.   Key the text in the remaining cells as indicated in figure 6.12. Press the Tab key to move to the next cell or press Shift + Tab to move to the preceding cell. Press Ctrl + Tab before keying each entry in cells A2 through A8. Press Ctrl + Tab *twice* before keying each entry in cells B2 through B8.

h.   Add blue thick/thin lines around the table by completing the following steps:
   1) Position the insertion point in any cell in the table. (Make sure no text or cell is selected.)
   2) Click Format and then Borders and Shading.
   3) At the Borders and Shading dialog box with the Borders tab selected, click the None option. (This removes all borders from the Preview diagram.)
   4) Click the Custom option.
   5) Scroll to the end of the line styles in the Style list box until the third line option from the end displays and then click it.
   6) Change the line color to blue by clicking the down-pointing triangle at the right side of the Color option and then clicking *Blue* at the drop-down list.
   7) Apply the border to the outside of the table by completing the following steps:
      a) Click the top button at the left side of the Preview diagram. (This inserts a blue shadow border to the top of the Preview diagram.)
      b) Click the third button from the top at the left side of the Preview diagram. (This inserts a blue shadow border at the bottom of the table.)
      c) Click the second button from the left at the bottom of the Preview diagram. (This inserts a blue shadow border at the left side of the table.)
      d) Click the fourth button from the left at the bottom of the Preview diagram. (This inserts a blue shadow border at the right side of the table.)
   8) Click OK to close the Borders and Shading dialog box.

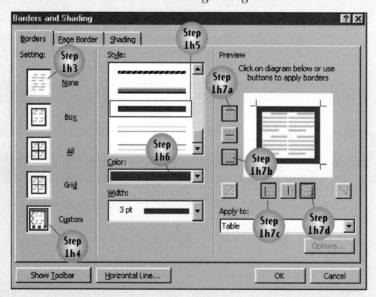

i.   Add a single blue line between columns by completing the following steps:
   1) Click Format and then Borders and Shading.
   2) At the Borders and Shading dialog box, scroll to the beginning of the line

styles in the Style list box and then click the first line style (a single line).

3) Change the line color to blue. (To do this, click the down-pointing triangle at the right of the Color option, and then click *Blue* at the drop-down list.)

4) Click the third button from the left at the bottom of the Preview diagram. (This inserts a single blue line between columns.)

5) Click OK to close the Borders and Shading dialog box.

2. Save the document and name it Word Ch 06, Ex 06.

3. Print and then close Word Ch 06, Ex 06.

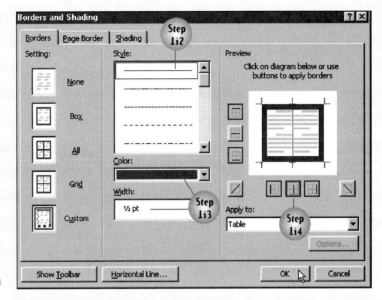

 *Exercise 6*

DIVERSIFICATION OF ASSETS

Asset	Percentage
Office buildings	20%
Shopping centers	18%
Utilities	15%
Other mortgage and real estate	14%
Manufacturing	12%
Government	11%
Communications	10%

Adding Shading

Shaded cells add visual appeal to a table. Shading can be added to cells or selected cells with options at the Borders and Shading dialog box with the Shading tab selected as shown in figure 6.13. Figure 6.14 describes the options available at the Borders and Shading dialog box with the Shading tab selected.

figure
6.13

Borders and Shading Dialog Box with Shading Tab Selected

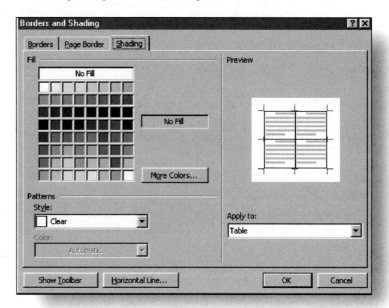

figure
6.14

Options at the Borders and Shading Dialog Box with Shading Tab Selected

Choose this option	To do this
Fill	Choose a fill color for selected cell(s) or entire table
Style	Choose a shading style to apply "over" fill color
Color	Choose a color for the lines and dots in the selected shading pattern
Preview diagram	Click the sides of the Preview diagram to add or remove the currently selected fill, style, and color
Apply to	Specify to what the border and shading should be applied

Adding a Border and Shading to a Table

1. Open Word Ch 06, Ex 02.
2. Save the document with Save As and name it Word Ch 06, Ex 07.
3. Add a border and shading to the table by completing the following steps:
   a. Move the insertion point to a cell within the table.
   b. Click Format and then Borders and Shading.
   c. At the Borders and Shading dialog box, make sure the Borders tab is selected.

d. Choose a double line style in the St**y**le list box.
e. Click the Gri**d** option located at the left side of the dialog box.
f. Click the **S**hading tab.
g. At the Borders and Shading dialog box with the **S**hading tab selected, click the light turquoise color in the Fill section. (The light turquoise color is the fifth color from the left in the bottom row.)
h. Click OK to close the dialog box.
4. Add a fill to the first row of cells by completing thc following steps:
a. Select cells A1, B1, and C1.
b. Click F**o**rmat and then **B**orders and Shading.
c. At the Borders and Shading dialog box, make sure the **S**hading tab is selected.
d. At the Borders and Shading dialog box with the **S**hading tab selected, click the down-pointing triangle at the right side of the St**y**le option, and then click *20%* at the drop-down list.
e. Click OK to close the Borders and Shading dialog box.
f. Deselect the cells.
5. Save the document again with the same name (Word Ch 06, Ex 07).
6. Print and then close Word Ch 06, Ex 07.

Changing Column Width

When a table is created, the columns are the same width. The width of the columns depends on the number of columns as well as the document margins. In some tables, you may want to change the width of certain columns to accommodate more or less text. You can change the width of columns using the mouse on the Ruler, in a table, or with options from the Table Properties dialog box.

Changing Column Width with the Ruler

When the insertion point is positioned in a table, move the table column markers display on the Ruler (see figure 6.3). To change the column width with move table column markers, position the mouse pointer on the move table column marker until it turns into a left- and right-pointing arrow, hold down the left mouse button, drag the marker to make the column wider or narrower, and then release the mouse button. As you drag a marker, any move table column markers to the right are also moved.

If you want to see the column measurements as you move a move table column marker, hold down the Alt key while dragging the marker. You can also view the column measurements by positioning the mouse pointer on a move table column marker, holding down the Alt key, and then holding down the left mouse button.

If you only want to move the move table column marker where the mouse pointer is positioned, hold down the Shift key, and then drag the marker on the Ruler. This does not change the overall size of the table. To change the column width of the column where the insertion point is positioned and all columns to the right, hold down the Ctrl key and the Shift key while you drag the move table column marker.

The first-line indent marker, the left indent marker, the right indent marker, and the hanging indent marker display on the Ruler for the column where the insertion point is positioned. These markers can be used to adjust the left or right

Change column width by dragging column markers on the Ruler.

column margins, indent the first line in a cell, or create a hanging indent. Changes made to the column margins affect only the column where the insertion point is positioned.

Creating a Table and Then Changing Column Width with the Ruler

1. At a clear document screen, create the document shown in figure 6.15 by completing the following steps:
   a. Create a table with 3 columns and 7 rows (7 x 3).
   b. Change the width of the second column using the mouse by completing the following steps:
      1) Make sure the Ruler is displayed.
      2) Position the mouse pointer on the move table column marker on the 4-inch mark on the Ruler until it turns into an arrow pointing left and right.

      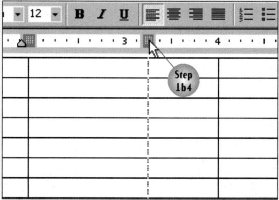

      3) Hold down the Shift key and then the left mouse button.
      4) Drag the marker to the 3¼-inch mark, release the Shift key, and then release the mouse button.
   c. Change the width of the third column using the mouse by completing the following steps:
      1) Position the mouse pointer on the move table column marker on the 6-inch mark on the Ruler until it turns into an arrow pointing left and right.

      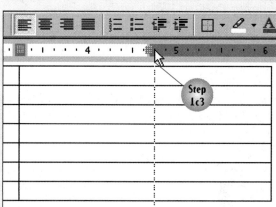

      2) Hold down the Shift key and then the left mouse button.
      3) Drag the marker to the 4¾-inch mark, release the Shift key and then release the mouse button.
   d. Key the text in the cells, bolding and centering the text as shown.
   e. Add a thick/thin double-line border around the table by completing the following steps:
      1) With the insertion point positioned in any cell in the table, click Format and then Borders and Shading.
      2) At the Borders and Shading dialog box, make sure the Borders tab is selected.
      3) Scroll down the Style list box until the first thick/thin double-line option displays and then click the double line option.
      4) Click Grid option that displays at the left side of the dialog box.
      5) Click OK to close the dialog box.

f.   Add 10% fill to cells A1, B1, and C1 by completing the following steps:
1)   Select cells A1, B1, and C1.
2)   Click Format and then Borders and Shading.
3)   At the Borders and Shading dialog box, click the Shading tab.
4)   At the Borders and Shading dialog box with the Shading tab selected, click the down-pointing triangle at the right side of the Style option, and then click *10%* at the drop-down list.
5)   Click OK to close the Borders and Shading dialog box.
6)   Deselect the cells.
2.   Save the document and name it Word Ch 06, Ex 08.
3.   Print and then close Word Ch 06, Ex 08.

Exercise 8

Name	Employee #	Department
Kevin Gerome	222-104-6608	Human Resources
Louella Arellano	433-196-9817	Human Resources
Gale Meschke	533-119-6780	Financial Planning
Paul Tjerne	114-457-3221	Sales
William Whitlock	652-671-9910	Sales
Madeline Zevenbergen	552-900-6221	Support Services

Changing Column Width with the Mouse

You can use the gridlines to change column widths within the table. To change column widths using the gridlines, position the mouse pointer on the gridline separating columns until the insertion point turns into a left- and right-pointing arrow with a vertical double line between. Hold down the left mouse button, drag the gridline to the desired location, and then release the mouse button. Only the gridline where the insertion point is positioned is moved. If you want to change column widths for all columns to the right, hold down the Shift key while dragging the gridline. Hold down the Shift key and Ctrl key while dragging the gridline if you want to change the width of all columns to the right without changing the size of the table.

Changing Column Width at the Table Properties Dialog Box

If you know the exact measurement for columns in a table, you can change column widths at the Table Properties dialog box with the Column tab selected as shown in figure 6.16. To display this dialog box, click Table and then Table Properties. At the Table Properties dialog box, click the Column tab. To change the column width, select the current measurement in the Preferred width text box, and then key the desired measurement. You can also click the up- or down-pointing triangle to increase or decrease the current measurement.

figure
6.16

Table Properties Dialog Box with Column Tab Selected

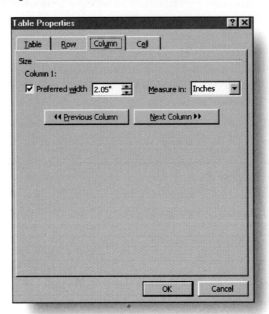

In a table containing text or other features, you can adjust the width of one column to accommodate the longest line of text in the column. To do this, position the mouse pointer on the right column gridline until it turns into a left- and right-pointing arrow with a vertical double line, and then double-click the left mouse button. To automatically size more than one column, select the columns first, and then double-click on a gridline.

Changing Column Width in a Table

1. Open Word Ch 06, Ex 02.
2. Save the document with Save As and name it Word Ch 06, Ex 09.
3. Select and then delete the title *OPTIONAL PLAN PREMIUM RATES*.
4. Change the width of the first column by completing the following steps:
   a. Click in the top cell in the first column.
   b. Position the mouse pointer on the gridline separating the first and second columns until it turns into a left- and right-pointing arrow with a vertical double line between.

c. Hold down the Alt key and then the left mouse button, drag the gridline to the left until the first measurement on the horizontal ruler displays as *1.25"*, then release the mouse button and then the Alt key.

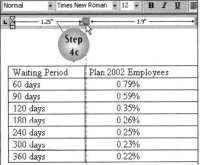

5. Change the width of the second column by completing the following steps:
   a. Click in the top cell in the middle column.
   b. Click Table and then Table Properties.
   c. At the Table Properties dialog box, click the Column tab.
   d. At the Table Properties dialog box with the Column tab selected, click the down-pointing triangle at the right side of the Preferred width text box until *1.7"* displays.
   e. Click OK or press Enter.

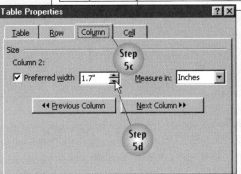

Waiting Period	Plan 2002 Employees
60 days	0.79%
90 days	0.59%
120 days	0.35%
180 days	0.26%
240 days	0.25%
300 days	0.23%
360 days	0.22%

6. Change the width of the third column to 1.7" by completing steps similar to those in step 5.
7. Add the following to the table
   a. Add a thick/thin double line border around the table.
   b. Add a single line between the columns.
   c. Add a light color fill to all cells in the table. (You determine the color.)
8. Save the document again with the same name (Word Ch 06, Ex 09).
9. Print and then close Word Ch 06, Ex 09. (The table will not be centered between the margins.)

Changing Column Width with AutoFit

Use the AutoFit option from the Table drop-down menu to make the column widths in a table automatically fit the contents. To do this, position the insertion point in any cell in the table, click Table, point to AutoFit, and then click AutoFit to Contents at the side menu.

Changing Column Widths Using AutoFit

1. Open Word Ch 06, Ex 01.
2. Save the document with Save As and name it Word Ch 06, Ex 10.
3. Change the width of the columns to fit the contents by completing the following steps:
   a. Make sure the insertion point is positioned in a cell within the table.
   b. Click Table, point to AutoFit, and then click AutoFit to Contents at the side menu.
4. Make the following changes to the table:

a. Change the border line around the table from a single line to a line of your choosing (other than single).
b. Add shading of your choosing to the table.
5. Save the document again with the same name (Word Ch 06, Ex 10).
6. Print and then close Word Ch 06, Ex 10.

Changing Row Height

Change row height in a table in much the same manner as changing column width. You can change row height with an adjust table row marker on the vertical ruler, using a gridline, or with options at the Table Properties dialog box.

To change row height using the vertical ruler, position the mouse pointer on the desired adjust table row marker, hold down the left mouse button, drag the marker to the desired position, and then release the mouse button. Hold down the Alt key while dragging an adjust table row marker and measurements display on the vertical ruler.

To change row height using a gridline, position the mouse pointer on the desired gridline until the pointer turns into an up- and down-pointing arrow with a vertical double line between. Hold down the left mouse button, drag the gridline to the desired position, and then release the mouse button. Hold down the Alt key while dragging a gridline and measurements display on the vertical ruler.

Another method for adjusting row height is to display the Table Properties dialog box with the Row tab selected as shown in figure 6.17. At this dialog box, click the Specify height option, key the desired row measurement in the Specify height text box, and then close the dialog box.

Table Properties Dialog Box with Row Tab Selected

6.17

To change row height, click the Specify height option, and then enter the desired measurement in the Specify height text box.

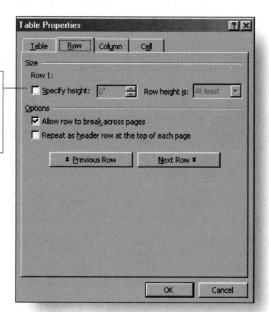

Changing Cell Alignment

By default, text in cells aligns at the left side of the cell. Like normal text, this alignment can be changed to center, right, or justified. To change the alignment of text in cells, select the cells, then click the desired alignment button on the Formatting toolbar. You can also change the alignment of text in selected cells with the Alignment option at the Paragraph dialog box with the Indents and Spacing tab selected or with a shortcut command. For example, to change the alignment of text to center in all cells in the second column of a table, you would select all cells in the second column, and then click the Center button on the Formatting toolbar.

The methods just described change the horizontal alignment of text in cells. You can also change the vertical alignment of text in cells at the Table Properties dialog box with the Cell tab selected as shown in figure 6.18. The default vertical alignment of text in a cell is Top. This can be changed to Center or Bottom.

Table Properties Dialog Box with Cell Tab Selected

Choose a vertical alignment for text in cells with options in this section of the dialog box.

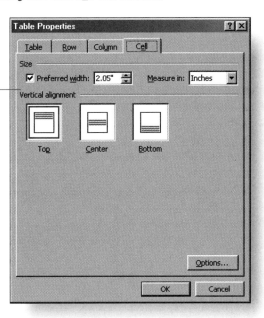

Changing Row Height and Cell Alignment

1. Open Word Table 04.
2. Save the document with Save As and name it Word Ch 06, Ex 11.
3. Change row heights in the table by completing the following steps:
   a. Increase the height of the first row in the table by completing the following steps:
      1) Change to the Print Layout view.

2) Position the mouse pointer on the first adjust table row marker on the vertical ruler.
3) Hold down the left mouse button and hold down the Alt key.
4) Drag the adjust table row marker down until the first row measurement on the vertical ruler displays as *1*", then release the mouse button and then the Alt key.

b. Increase the height of second row by completing the following steps:

1) Position the arrow pointer on the gridline that displays at the bottom of the second row until the arrow pointer turns into an up- and down-pointing arrow with a horizontal double line between.
2) Hold down the left mouse button and then hold down the Alt key.
3) Drag the gridline down until the second row measurement on the vertical ruler displays as *0.58*", then release the mouse button and then the Alt key.

c. Increase the height of rows 3 through 11 (the remaining rows) by completing the following steps:

1) Select rows 3 through 11.
2) Click Table and then Table Properties.
3) At the Table Properties dialog box, click the Row tab.
4) At the Table Properties dialog box with the Row tab selected, click the Specify height option.
5) Click the up-pointing triangle at the right side of the Specify height option until *0.5*" displays in the Specify height text box.
6) Click OK to close the dialog box.

4. Make the following changes to the table:

a. Change the vertical and horizontal alignment of text in rows 1 and 2 by completing the following steps:

1) Select rows 1 and 2.
2) Click Table and then Table Properties.
3) At the Table Properties dialog box, click the Cell tab.
4) At the Table Properties dialog box with the Cell tab selected, click the Center option in the Vertical alignment section of the dialog box.
5) Click OK to close the dialog box.
6) With rows 1 and 2 still selected, click the Center button on the Formatting toolbar.

b. Select only row 1 and then change the font to 24-point Arial bold.
c. Select only row 2 and then change the font to 14-point Arial bold.

5. Save the document again with the same name (Word Ch 06, Ex 11).
6. Print and then close Word Ch 06, Ex 11.

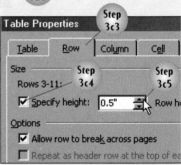

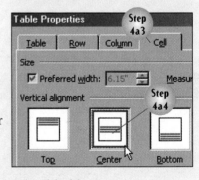

Aligning the Table

By default, a table aligns at the left margin. This alignment can be changed with options at the Table Properties dialog box with the Table tab selected as shown in figure 6.19. To change the alignment, click the desired alignment option in the Alignment section of the dialog box.

Table Properties Dialog Box with Table Tab Selected

6.19

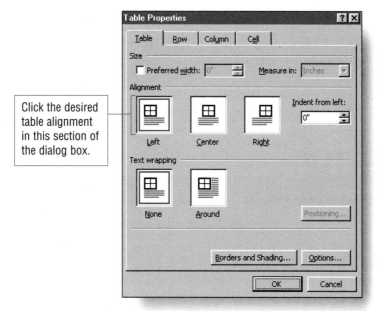

Click the desired table alignment in this section of the dialog box.

Horizontally Aligning a Table

1. Open Word Ch 06, Ex 09.
2. Save the document with Save As and name it Word Ch 06, Ex 12.
3. Center the table horizontally by completing the following steps:
   a. Position the insertion point in any cell in the table.
   b. Click Table and then Table Properties.
   c. At the Table Properties dialog box, click the Table tab.
   d. At the Table Properties dialog box with the Table tab selected, click the Center option in the Alignment section.
   e. Click OK or press Enter.
4. Save the document again with the same name (Word Ch 06, Ex 12).
5. Print and then close Word Ch 06, Ex 12.

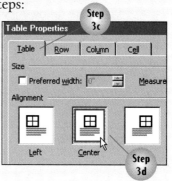

Inserting Rows

After a table has been created, rows can be added (inserted) to the table. There are several methods you can use to insert rows. You can use options from the Insert side menu to insert rows above or below the current row. To do this, position the insertion point in a row below next to the row is to be inserted, click Table, point to Insert, and then click either Rows Above or Rows Below (depending on where you want the row inserted). If you want more than one row inserted, select the desired number of rows and then click Table, point to Insert, and choose Rows Above or Rows Below.

You can also insert rows by selecting a row or several rows and then clicking the Insert Rows button on the Standard toolbar. The Insert Table button becomes the Insert Rows button on the Standard toolbar when a row or several rows are selected in a table.

Another method for inserting a row or several rows is to select a row (or rows) in a table, position the mouse pointer inside the table, click the *right* mouse button, and then click Insert Rows. Also, a row can be inserted at the end of the table by positioning the insertion point in the last cell in the table and then pressing the Tab key.

Add a row to the bottom of a table by positioning the insertion point in the last cell and then pressing the Tab key.

Insert Rows

Inserting Rows in a Table

1. Open Word Ch 06, Ex 08.
2. Save the document with Save As and name it Word Ch 06, Ex 13.
3. Add two rows to the table by completing the following steps:
   a. Select the fourth and fifth rows in the table.
   b. Click Table, point to Insert, and then click Rows Above.
   c. Deselect the rows.
   d. Position the insertion point in cell A4 (below *Louella Arellano*), and then key **Steven Haarberg**.
   e. Key the following text in the specified cell:

B4	=	**627-220-9880**
C4	=	**Human Resources**
A5	=	**Howard Kline**
B5	=	**149-395-4009**
C5	=	**Financial Planning**

4. Make the following changes to the table:
   a. Use the AutoFit feature to make the columns in the table automatically fit the contents.
   b. Center the table horizontally.
5. Save the document again with the same name (Word Ch 06, Ex 13).
6. Print and then close Word Ch 06, Ex 13.

Inserting Columns

Columns can be inserted in a table in much the same way as rows. To insert a column, position the insertion point in a cell within the table, click T<u>a</u>ble, point to <u>I</u>nsert, and then click Columns to the <u>L</u>eft or Columns to the <u>R</u>ight. If you want to insert more than one column, select the desired number of columns first.

Another method for inserting a column (or columns) is to select the column and then click the Insert Columns button on the Standard toolbar. The Insert Table button on the Standard toolbar becomes the Insert Columns button when a column or columns are selected.

Insert Columns

A column or group of columns can also be inserted by selecting the column(s), clicking the *right* mouse button, and then clicking <u>I</u>nsert Columns at the drop-down menu. Word inserts a column or columns to the left of the selected column or columns. If you want to add a column to the right side of the table, select all the end-of-row markers, and then click the Insert Columns button on the Standard toolbar.

Inserting a Column in a Table

1. Open Word Ch 06, Ex 01.
2. Save the document with Save As and name it Word Ch 06, Ex 14.
3. Make the following changes to the table:
   a. Add a row to the table, apply bold, and change the alignment to center by completing the following steps:
      1) Position the insertion point in any cell in the first row.
      2) Click T<u>a</u>ble, point to <u>I</u>nsert, and then click Rows <u>A</u>bove.
      3) With the new row selected, click the Bold button on the Formatting toolbar and then click the Center button.
   b. Key the following text in the specified cell:

A1	=	**Name**
B1	=	**Company**
C1	=	**Phone Number**

   c. Add a column to the right side of the table and change the alignment to center by completing the following steps:
      1) Click the Show/Hide ¶ button on the Standard toolbar to turn on the display of nonprinting characters.
      2) Position the mouse pointer above the first end-of-row marker at the top of the row at the far right side of the table until it turns into a small downward-pointing arrow.
      3) Click the left mouse button. (This will select all of the end-of-row markers at the right side of the table.)
      4) Click T<u>a</u>ble, point to <u>I</u>nsert, and then click Columns to the <u>R</u>ight.
      5) With the column selected, click the Center button on the Formatting toolbar.

      6) Deselect the column.
  d. Key the following text in the specified cells:

D1	=	**Ext.**
D2	=	**2331**
D3	=	**1035**
D4	=	**2098**
D5	=	**1564**
D6	=	**2109**

  e. Click the Show/Hide ¶ button to turn off the display of nonprinting characters.
  f. Make the following changes to the table:
      1) Use the AutoFit feature to make the columns in the table automatically fit the contents.
      2) Center the table horizontally.
4. Save the document again with the same name (Word Ch 06, Ex 14).
5. Print and then close Word Ch 06, Ex 14.

Deleting Cells, Rows, or Columns

Delete a column, row, or cell with options from the Delete side menu. For example, to delete a column, position the insertion point in any cell within the column, click Table, point to Delete, and then click Columns. To delete a row, click Table, point to Delete, and then click Rows. To delete a specific cell, position the insertion point in the cell, click Table, point to Delete, and then click Cells. This displays the Delete Cells dialog box shown in figure 6.20.

figure

6.20

Delete Cells Dialog Box

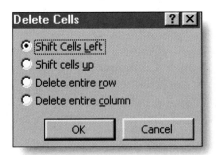

    At the Delete Cells dialog box, the Shift Cells Left option is selected by default. At this option, cells will shift left after the cell (or selection of cells) is deleted. Click the Shift cells up option if you want cells moved up after the cell (or selected cells) is deleted. Click Delete entire row to delete the row where the insertion point is positioned or click Delete entire column to delete the column where the insertion point is positioned.

    The Delete Cells dialog box can also be displayed by positioning the mouse pointer in the table, clicking the *right* mouse button, and then clicking Delete Cells at the drop-down menu.

Deleting Rows and Columns in a Table

1. Open Word Ch 06, Ex 13.
2. Save the document with Save As and name it Word Ch 06, Ex 15.
3. Make the following changes to the table:
   a. Delete the bottom row in the table by completing the following steps:
      1) Position the insertion point in any cell in the bottom row.
      2) Click Table, point to Delete, and then click Rows.
   b. Delete the middle column by completing the following steps:
      1) Position the insertion point in any cell in the middle column.
      2) Click Table, point to Delete, and then click Columns.
4. Save the document again with the same name (Word Ch 06, Ex 15).
5. Print and then close Word Ch 06, Ex 15.

Merging Cells

Cells can be merged with the Merge Cells option from the Table drop-down menu. To do this, select the cells to be merged, click Table and then click Merge Cells.

Splitting Cells

Split a cell or a row or column of cells with options at the Split Cells dialog box shown in figure 6.21. To display this dialog box, position the insertion point in the cell to be split, click Table, expand the drop-down menu, and then click Split Cells. At the Split Cells dialog box, make sure the desired number of columns displays in the Number of columns text box, and then click OK or press Enter. To split an entire column or row of cells, select the column or row first, click Table and then click Split Cells.

Split Cells Dialog Box

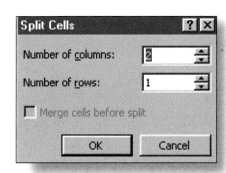

Creating a Table with Merged Cells

1. At a clear document screen, create the table shown in figure 6.22 by completing the following steps:
   a. Create a table with 3 columns and 10 rows (10 x 3).
   b. Change the width of the first column to 3 inches and the width of the second and third columns to 1.5 inches.
   c. Merge the cells in the first row by completing the following steps:
      1) Select the first row.
      2) Click Table and then Merge Cells.
   d. Merge the cells in the second row by completing steps similar to those in step 1c.
   e. Select the entire table and then change the font to 12-point Arial bold.
   f. Key the text in the cells as shown in figure 6.22, center aligning the text as indicated.
   g. Add a double line border around the outside of the table and a single line border on the inside of the table.
   h. Select the third row and then add 20% fill.
2. Save the document and name it Word Ch 06, Ex 16.
3. Print and then close Word Ch 06, Ex 16.

figure
6.22
Exercise 16

McCORMACK FUNDS CORPORATION		
Common Stocks		
Stock	Shares	Market Value

Save a document containing a table before applying an auto-format.

Formatting with AutoFormat

Formatting a table by adding borders or shading, aligning text in cells, changing fonts, and so on, can take some time. Word has provided predesigned table formats that can quickly format your table for you. Table formats are contained in the Table AutoFormat dialog box shown in figure 6.23. To display this dialog box, position the insertion point in any cell in a table, click Table and then Table AutoFormat.

figure
6.23

Table AutoFormat Dialog Box

Click a format in this list box and preview it in the Preview section.

Remove the check mark from those formats you do not want applied to the autoformat.

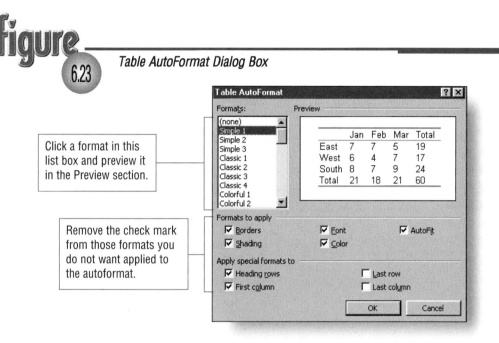

Table formats are displayed in the Formats list box. Select a table format in the Formats list box and preview the appearance of the table in the Preview section. When previewing table formats, you can make some changes to the format by removing check marks from the options in the Formats to apply section of the dialog box. For example, if you like a format created by Word except for the shading, select the format in the Formats list box in the dialog box, and then click the Shading check box. This removes the check mark from the Shading check box and also removes the shading from the table shown in the Preview section.

If you want to apply the special formatting only to specific parts of the table, select the parts of the table you want the formatting applied to in the Apply special formats to section of the dialog box. For example, if you want the table formatting applied only to the first column in the table, insert a check mark in the First column option and remove the check marks from the other options.

exercise 17

Formatting a Table Using the Table AutoFormat Dialog Box

1. Open Word Ch 06, Ex 01.
2. Save the document with Save As and name it Word Ch 06, Ex 17.
3. Make the following changes to the table:
   a. Make sure the insertion point is positioned in cell A1.

    b. Insert a row above the current row.

    c. With the new row selected, click the Bold button on the Formatting toolbar and then the Center button.

    d. Key the following text in the specified cells (the text will be bold and centered):

A1	=	**Name**
B1	=	**Company**
C1	=	**Telephone Number**

    e. Automatically format the table by completing the following steps:

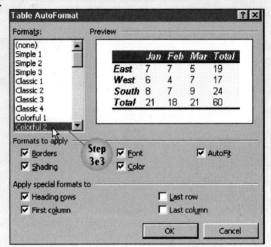

       1) Position the insertion point in any cell in the table.

       2) Click Table and then Table AutoFormat.

       3) At the Table AutoFormat dialog box, click *Colorful 2* in the Formats list box.

       4) Click OK or press Enter.

    f. Center the table horizontally.

4. Save the document again with the same name (Word Ch 06, Ex 17).

5. Print and then close Word Ch 06, Ex 17.

Use buttons on the Tables and Borders toolbar to create a more free-form table.

Tables and Borders

Creating a Table Using the Tables and Borders Toolbar

Word includes a Tables and Borders toolbar with options you can use to create a more free-form table. With buttons on the Tables and Borders toolbar shown in figure 6.24, you can draw a table with specific borders as well as add shading and fill. To display this toolbar, click the Tables and Borders button on the Standard toolbar. Figure 6.25 identifies the buttons on the toolbar and the purpose of each.

figure
6.24

Tables and Borders Toolbar

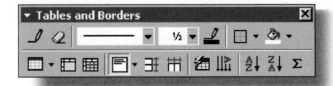

figure
6.25

Buttons on the Tables and Borders Toolbar

Click this button	Named	To do this
	Draw Table	Insert a table where you drag in the document.
	Eraser	Erase border and/or cell lines.
	Line Style	Specify the border line style.
	Line Weight	Specify the thickness of the border line.
	Border Color	Specify the border line color.
	Outside Border	Add or remove border around selected text, paragraph, cells, or other object.
	Shading Color	Add, modify, or remove fill color from selected object.
	Insert Table	Display a pop-up menu with options to insert a table; insert a column, row, or cells; and specify the fit of cell contents.
	Merge Cells	Combine contents of selected adjacent cells into one cell.
	Split Cells	Split selected cells in number of rows and columns specified.
	Align Top Left	Display a palette of alignment options such as top center, top right, center, center left, center right, bottom left, bottom center, and bottom right.
	Distribute Rows Evenly	Change selected rows or cells to equal row height.
	Distribute Columns Evenly	Change selected columns or cells to equal column width.
	Table AutoFormat	Apply predesigned formats to table or selected cells.
	Change Text Direction	Orient selected text in a cell horizontally left to right.
	Sort Ascending	Sort selected items alphabetically or numerically in ascending order.
	Sort Descending	Sort selected items alphabetically or numerically in descending order.
	AutoSum	Insert total of a column or row in cell.

To create a table using buttons on the Tables and Borders toolbar, you would complete the following steps:

1. Turn on the display of the Tables and Borders toolbar by clicking the Tables and Borders button on the Standard toolbar. (The viewing mode is automatically changed to Print Layout.)
2. Position the mouse pointer (displays as a pencil) in the area of the editing window where you want the upper left corner of the table to display.
3. Hold down the left mouse button, drag the pencil pointer down and to the right until the outline displays the desired size of the table, and then release the mouse button. (This creates the border of the table.)
4. Use the pencil pointer to draw the row and column lines.
5. Click inside the cell where you want to key text.
6. Key the desired text. (When you key text, the pencil pointer turns into the normal mouse pointer.)

Many of the buttons on the Tables and Borders toolbar can be used to customize the table. For example, you can change the line style with Line Style options and then draw the desired portion of the table. Or, you can change the line style and then redraw lines in an existing table. Use options from the Shading Color button to add color to a cell or selected cells in a table.

exercise 18

Drawing a Table Using the Tables and Borders Toolbar

1. At a clear editing window, draw the table shown in figure 6.26 by completing the following steps:
   a. Key the title centered and bolded as shown in figure 6.26. (Press the Enter key once, turn off bold and return paragraph alignment to left, and then press the Enter key two more times.)
   b. Turn on the display of the Tables and Borders toolbar by clicking the Tables and Borders button on the Standard toolbar.
   c. Change the line style to single by clicking the down-pointing triangle at the right side of the Line Style button and then clicking the single line option.

Step 1c

   d. Position the mouse pointer (displays as a pencil) in the editing window and draw the table, row, and column lines as shown in figure 6.26. (To draw the lines, position the pencil in the desired location, hold down the left mouse button, draw the line, and then release the button. If you want to erase a line, click the Eraser button on the Tables and Borders toolbar and then drag across the line. To continue drawing the table, click the Draw Table button.)
   e. When the table is drawn, click the Draw Table button on the Tables and Borders toolbar button to deactivate it.
   f. Change the vertical alignment of text in cells by completing the following steps:

Step 1f2

      1) Select all cells in the table.
      2) Click the down-pointing triangle at the right side of the Align Top Left button located on the Tables and Borders toolbar.

Step 1f3

3) At the palette of alignment choices, click the Align Center Left option (first option from the left in the second row).

g. With all cells in the table still selected, click the Distribute Rows Evenly button on the Tables and Borders toolbar.

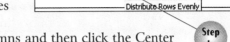

Step 1g

h. Select all cells in the second and third columns and then click the Center button on the Formatting toolbar (not the Tables and Borders toolbar).

i. Click in the first cell.

j. Key the text in the cells as shown in figure 6.26. (If text wraps in a cell, widen the column.)

2. Turn off the display of the Tables and Borders toolbar by clicking the Tables and Borders button on the Standard toolbar.

3. Save the document and name it Word Ch 06, Ex 18.

4. Print and then close Word Ch 06, Ex 18.

figure
6.26

Exercise 18

CURRENT JOBS AND FUTURE PROJECTIONS

Occupation	1998	2010
Agriculture, Forestry, Fishery	18,342	15,423
Executive, Managerial, Administrative	26,459	28,109
Marketing, Sales	32,188	33,009
Operators, Fabricators, Laborers	35,429	32,677
Professional, Technical	51,239	55,438

exercise 19

Customizing a Table with the Tables and Borders Toolbar

1. Open Word Ch 06, Ex 18.
2. Save the document with Save As and name it Word Ch 06, Ex 19.
3. Customize the table by completing the following steps:
   a. Turn on the display of the Tables and Borders toolbar by clicking the Tables and Borders button on the Standard toolbar.
   b. Change the outside table border lines to double lines by completing the following steps:

1) Click the down-pointing triangle at the right side of the Line Style button.
2) At the drop-down list that displays, click the first double-line style.
3) Position the pencil pointer in the upper left corner of the table, hold down the left mouse button, drag the pencil down the left side of the table until it reaches the bottom, and then release the mouse button. (This changes the single line to a double line.)
4) Change the bottom border of the table to a double line by dragging the pencil across the bottom border. (Be sure to hold the left mouse button down as you drag.)
5) Change the right border of the table to a double line by dragging the pencil along the right border.
6) Change the top border of the table to a double line by dragging the pencil along the top border.

c. Click the Draw Table button to deselect it.
d. Add gray shading to cells by completing the following steps:
1) Select cells A2 through C6.
2) Click the down-pointing triangle at the right side of the Shading Color button on the Tables and Borders toolbar.
3) At the palette of color choices that displays, click the Gray-25% color (this is the second option from the *right* in the top row).

e. Add light turquoise shading to cells by completing the following steps:
1) Select cells A1, B1, and C1.
2) Click the down-pointing arrow at the right side of the Shading Color button on the Tables and Borders toolbar.
3) At the palette of color choices, click the light turquoise color (fifth color from the left in the bottom row).

f. Turn off the display of the Tables and Borders toolbar.

4. Save the document again with the same name (Word Ch 06, Ex 19).
5. Print and then close Word Ch 06, Ex 19.

Moving a Table

Position the mouse pointer in a table and a table move handle displays in the upper left corner. Use this handle to move the table in the document. Position the mouse pointer on the table move handle until the pointer turns into a four-headed arrow, hold down the left mouse button, drag the table to the desired position, and then release the mouse button.

To move a table, changing the document view can be helpful. With options from the Zoom button on the Standard toolbar, you can change the display percentage and also select options such as Page Width, Text Width, Whole Page, and Two Pages. The options available from the Zoom button depend on the view selected. To move a table, consider changing to the Print Layout view and then changing the Zoom to *Whole Page*. To change the zoom, click the down-pointing triangle at the right side of the Zoom button and then click *Whole Page* at the drop-down list.

Zoom

Inserting a Column, Changing Text Direction, and Moving the Table

1. Open Word Ch 06, Ex 18.
2. Save the document with Save As and name it Word Ch 06, Ex 20.
3. Customize the table so it appears as shown in figure 6.27 by completing the following steps:
   a. Delete the title *CURRENT JOBS AND FUTURE PROJECTIONS*.
   b. Click in the first cell.
   c. Click Table, point to Insert, expand the side menu, and then click Columns to the Left. (This inserts a column at the left side of the table.)
   d. Deselect the column.
   e. Change the width of the first and second columns by completing the following steps:
      1) Position the insertion point in the first cell (cell A1).
      2) Position the mouse pointer on the gridline that separates the first and second column until the pointer turns into a left- and right-pointing arrow with a vertical double line between.
      3) Hold down the left mouse button, drag to the left to approximately the ¾-inch mark on the horizontal ruler and then release the mouse button.
   f. Merge the cells in the first column by completing the following steps:
      1) Display the Tables and Borders toolbar.
      2) Click the Draw Table button to deactivate it.
      3) Select the first column.
      4) Click the Merge Cells button on the Tables and Borders toolbar.
   g. Key the text in the first cell as shown in figure 6.27 by completing the following steps:
      1) Make sure the insertion point is positioned in the first cell.
      2) Change the text direction by clicking twice on the Change Text Direction button on the Tables and Borders toolbar.
      3) Click the Center button on the Formatting toolbar.
      4) Change the font to 24-point Times New Roman bold.
      5) Key **Future Jobs**.
   h. Turn off the display of the Tables and Borders toolbar.
4. Move the table to the middle of the page by completing the following steps:
   a. Click the down-pointing triangle at the right side of the Zoom button on the Standard toolbar and then click *Whole Page* at the drop-down list.
   b. Position the mouse pointer in the table until the table move handle displays in the upper left corner of the table.
   c. Position the mouse pointer on the table move handle until the pointer turns into a four-headed arrow.
   d. Hold down the left mouse button, drag the outline of the table to the middle of the page, and then release the mouse button.

e. Click the down-pointing triangle at the right side of the Zoom button on the Standard toolbar and then click *100%* at the drop-down list.
5. Save the document again with the same name (Word Ch 06, Ex 20).
6. Print and then close Word Ch 06, Ex 20.

Exercise 20

	Occupation	1998	2010
Future Jobs	Agriculture, Forestry, Fishery	18,342	15,423
	Executive, Managerial, Administrative	26,459	28,109
	Marketing, Sales	32,188	33,009
	Operators, Fabricators, Laborers	35,429	32,677
	Professional, Technical	51,239	55,438

Performing Calculations

Click the insert Microsoft Excel Worksheet button to use Excel functions and tables in Word.

Hint

Numbers in a table can be calculated. Numbers can be added, subtracted, multiplied, and divided. In addition, you can calculate averages, percentages, and minimum and maximum values. Calculations can be performed in a Word table; however, for complex calculations, use a Microsoft Excel worksheet.

To perform a calculation in a table, position the insertion point in the cell where you want the result of the calculation to display. This cell should be empty. By default, Word assumes that you want to calculate the sum of cells immediately above or to the left of the cell where the insertion point is positioned. This default calculation can be changed.

As an example of how to calculate sums, you would complete the following steps to calculate the sum of cells in C2 through C5 and insert the result of the calculation in cell C6:

1. Position the insertion point in cell C6.
2. Click Table, expand the drop-down menu, and then click Formula.
3. At the Formula dialog box shown in figure 6.28, the calculation =SUM(ABOVE) displays in the Formula text box. This is the desired formula to calculate the sum.
4. Click OK or press Enter.

Formula Dialog Box

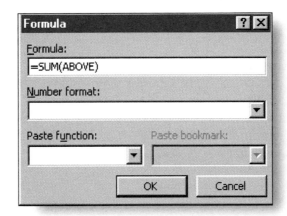

Word adds the numbers in cells C2 through C5 and then inserts the result of this calculation in cell C6. To perform other types of calculations such as subtraction, multiplication, and division, the formula displayed in the Formula text box at the Formula dialog box must be changed. You can use an arithmetic sign to write a formula. For example, the formula =A2-A3 (A2 minus A3) can be inserted in cell A4, which tells Word to insert the difference of A2 and A3 in cell A4. If changes are made to the numbers in cells A2 and A3, the value in A4 can be recalculated.

Begin a formula with the equal symbol (=). This identifies the data that follows as a formula.

Four basic operators can be used when writing formulas: the plus sign (+) for addition, the minus sign (hyphen) for subtraction, the asterisk (*) for multiplication, and the forward slash (/) for division. If there are two or more operators in a calculation, Word calculates from left to right. If you want to change the order of calculation, use parentheses around the part of the calculation to be performed first.

In the default formula, the SUM part of the formula is called a function. Word provides other functions you can use to write a formula. These functions are available with the Paste function option at the Formula dialog box. For example, you can use the AVERAGE function to average numbers in cells. Examples of how formulas can be written are shown in figure 6.29.

The numbering format can be specified at the Formula dialog box. For example, if you are calculating money amounts, you can specify that the calculated numbers display with two numbers following the decimal point. To specify the numbering format, display the Formula dialog box, and then click the down-pointing triangle to the right of the Number format option. Click the desired formatting at the drop-down list.

figure
6.29

Example Formulas

Cell E4 is the total price of items.
Cell B4 contains the quantity of items, and cell D4 contains the unit price. The formula for cell E4 is **=B4*D4**. (This formula multiplies the quantity of items in cell B4 by the unit price in cell D4.)

Cell D3 is the percentage of increase in sales from the previous year.
Cell B3 contains the amount of sales for the previous year, and cell C3 contains the amount of sales for the current year. The formula for cell D3 is **=C3-B3/C3*100**. (This formula subtracts the amount of sales last year from the amount of sales this year. The remaining amount is divided by the amount of sales this year and then multiplied by 100 to display the product as a percentage.)

Cell E1 is the average of test scores.
Cells A1 through D1 contain test scores. The formula to calculate the average score is **=(A1+B1+C1+D1)/4**. (This formula adds the scores from cells A1 through D1 and then divides that sum by 4.) You can also enter the formula as **AVERAGE(LEFT)**. The AVERAGE function tells Word to average all entries left of cell E1.

exercise 21

Calculating Net Profit

1. At a clear document screen, create the document shown in figure 6.30 by completing the following steps:
   a. Press the Enter key once.
   b. Create a table with 4 columns and 6 rows (6 x 4).
   c. Select the first row and then merge the cells.
   d. Position the insertion point in the first row, press the Enter key once, change the alignment to center, turn on bold, key **McCORMACK FUNDS CORPORATION**, and then press Enter once.
   e. Select the second row in the table and then click the Bold and the Center buttons on the Formatting toolbar.

f. Select cells A3 through A6 and then change the alignment to center.
g. Select cells B3 through D6 and then change the alignment to right.
h. Key the text in the cells as shown in figure 6.30.
i. Add border lines and 20% shading to the table as shown in figure 6.30.
j. Insert a formula in cell D3 by completing the following steps:
   1) Position the insertion point in cell D3 (the cell below *Net Profit*).
   2) Click Table, expand the drop-down menu, and then click Formula.
   3) At the Formula dialog box, delete the formula in the Formula text box.
   4) Key **=B3-C3** in the Formula text box.
   5) Click the down-pointing triangle at the right side of the Number format text box and then click the third option from the top of the drop-down list.
   6) Click OK or press Enter.

Formula	? X
Formula: **Step 1j4**	
=B3-C3	
Number format:	
Step 1j5	▼
#,##0	
#,##0.00	
$#,##0.00;($#,##0.00)	
0	
0%	
0.00	
0.00%	▼

k. Insert the formula =B4-C4 in cell D4 by completing the following steps:
   1) Position the insertion point in cell D4.
   2) Click Table and then click Formula.
   3) At the Formula dialog box, delete the formula in the Formula text box.
   4) Key **=B4-C4** in the Formula text box.
   5) Click the down-pointing triangle at the right side of the Number format text box and then click the second option from the top of the drop-down list.
   6) Click OK or press Enter.
l. Insert the formula =B5-C5 in cell D5 by completing steps similar to those in step 1k.
m. Insert the formula =B6-C6 in cell D6 by completing steps similar to those in step 1k.
2. Save the document and name it Word Ch 06, Ex 21.
3. Print and then close Word Ch 06, Ex 21.

figure
6.30

Exercise 21

McCORMACK FUNDS CORPORATION			
Year	Income	Expenses	Net Profit
1997	$6,890,309.10	$4,224,980.00	
1998	7,822,899.80	3,199,554.30	
1999	7,904,899.20	4,328,167.90	
2000	8,218,287.75	5,325,211.65	

exercise 22

Averaging Test Scores

1. Open Word Table 01.
2. Save the document with Save As and name it Word Ch 06, Ex 22.
3. Insert a formula in cell F3 to average test scores by completing the following steps:
   a. Position the insertion point in cell F3 (the cell below *Ave.*).
   b. Click Table and then Formula.
   c. Delete the formula in the Formula text box *except* the equals sign.
   d. With the insertion point positioned immediately after the equals sign, click the down-pointing triangle to the right of the Paste function text box.
   e. At the drop-down list that displays, click AVERAGE.
   f. With the insertion point positioned between the left and right parentheses, key **left**.
   g. Click the down-pointing triangle to the right of the Number format text box and then click the fifth option from the top (*0%*) at the drop-down list.
   h. Click OK or press Enter.
4. Position the insertion point in cell F4 and then complete steps similar to those in step 3 to insert a formula to average test scores.
5. Position the insertion point in cell F5 and then complete steps similar to those in step 3 to insert a formula to average test scores.
6. Position the insertion point in cell F6 and then complete steps similar to those in step 3 to insert a formula to average test scores.
7. Position the insertion point in cell F7 and then complete steps similar to those in step 3 to insert a formula to average test scores.
8. Position the insertion point in cell F8 and then complete steps similar to those in step 3 to insert a formula to average test scores.
9. Save the document again with the same name (Word Ch 06, Ex 22).
10. Print and then close Word Ch 06, Ex 22.

Formula dialog box (? X)

Step 3f

Formula:
=AVERAGE(left)

Number format:

```
#,##0
#,##0.00
$#,##0.00;($#,##0.00)        Step
0                             3g
0%
0.00
0.00%
```

If changes are made to numbers in cells that are part of a formula, select the result of the calculation, and then press the F9 function key. This recalculates the formula and inserts the new result of the calculation in the cell. You can also recalculate by completing the following steps:

1. Select the number in the cell containing the formula.
2. Click Table, expand the drop-down menu, and then click Formula.
3. At the Formula dialog box, click OK or press Enter.

Recalculating Test Scores

1. Open Word Ch 06, Ex 22.
2. Save the document with Save As and name it Word Ch 06, Ex 23.
3. Make the following changes to the table:
   a. Change the number in cell C3 from *79* to *85*.
   b. Change the number in cell D5 from *74* to *86*.
   c. Change the number in cell D8 from *78* to *92*.
   d. Position the mouse pointer in cell F3, click the left mouse button (this inserts a gray background around the numbers in the cell), and then press F9. (Pressing F9 recalculates the average.)
   e. Click the number in cell F5 and then press F9.
   f. Click the number in cell F8 and then press F9.
4. Save the document again with the same name (Word Ch 06, Ex 23).
5. Print and then close Word Ch 06, Ex 23.

chapter summary

- Word's Tables feature can be used to create columns and rows of information. A cell is the intersection between a row and a column.
- A table can contain text, characters, numbers, data, graphics, or formulas. It can be extensively formatted and can include calculations.
- A table can be created with the Insert Table button on the Standard toolbar or at the Insert Table dialog box.
- Columns in a table are lettered from left to right beginning with A. Rows are numbered from top to bottom beginning with 1.
- The lines that form the cells of the table are called gridlines.
- With the insertion point positioned in a cell, key or edit text as you would normal text.
- To move the insertion point to different cells within the table using the mouse, position the mouse pointer in the desired cell, and then click the left button.
- To move the insertion point to different cells within the table using the keyboard, refer to the information shown in figure 6.5 in this chapter.
- To use the mouse to select specific cells within a table, refer to the information shown in figure 6.8 in this chapter.
- To use the keyboard to select specific cells within a table, refer to the information shown in figure 6.9 in this chapter.
- A row or column of cells or all cells in a table can be selected with options from the Table drop-down menu.
- All text in cells within a table can be deleted, leaving the table gridlines, or all text and gridlines can be deleted.

- Borders and shading can be added to cells; rows and columns can be inserted or deleted; cells can be split or merged; and the alignment of the table can be changed.
- Column width and row height can be changed using the mouse on the Ruler, within a table, or at the Table Properties dialog box.
- After a table has been created, various methods can be used to add rows and/or columns.
- Specific cells in a table or rows or columns in a table can be deleted.
- Word has provided predesigned table formats in the Table AutoFormat dialog box that can quickly format a table.
- Use buttons on the Tables and Borders toolbar to create and customize a table. Click the Tables and Borders button on the Standard toolbar to turn on the display of the Tables and Borders toolbar.
- Numbers in a table can be calculated by inserting a formula in a cell at the Formula dialog box.

commands review

	Mouse/Keyboard
Create table with Standard toolbar	With mouse pointer on Insert Table button on Standard toolbar, hold down left mouse button, move mouse pointer down and right until desired table size displays, release button
Display Insert Table dialog box	Click Table, point to Insert, then click Table
Move insertion point to next cell	Tab
Move insertion point to previous cell	Shift + Tab
Insert tab within a cell	Ctrl + Tab
Insert page break within a table	Ctrl + Enter
Select a row, column, or all cells with Table drop-down menu	Position insertion point, click Table, point to Select, and then click Table, Column, Row or Cell
Delete text only from table	Select table, press Delete
Delete table	Click Table, point to Delete, then click Table
Display Table Properties dialog box	Click Table, then Table Properties
Delete cells, rows, or columns	Click Table, point to Delete, then click Columns, Rows, or Cells
Display Table AutoFormat dialog box	With insertion point in a cell, click Table, then Table AutoFormat
Turn on/off display of Tables and Borders toolbar	Click Tables and Borders button on Standard toolbar
Display Formula dialog box	Click Table, expand the drop-down menu, then click Formula

thinking offline

Completion: In the space provided at the right, indicate the correct term, command, or number.

1. Use this button on the Standard toolbar to create a table.
2. This is another name for the lines that form the cells of the table.
3. The end-of-row marker shows only when this button is active on the Standard toolbar.
4. The move table column markers display here.
5. Use this keyboard command to move the insertion point to the previous cell.
6. Use this keyboard command to insert a tab within a cell.
7. This is the name given to the space just to the left of the left edge of a table.
8. To add shading to a cell or selected cells, display this dialog box.
9. Change the width of columns at this dialog box with the Column tab selected.
10. Text in cells aligns at this side of the cell by default.
11. Choose this option at the Delete Cells dialog box if you want cells moved up after selected cells are deleted.
12. To merge cells A1 and B1, select A1 and B1, and then click this at the Table drop-down menu.
13. To divide one cell into two columns, click this at the Table drop-down menu.
14. Choose predesigned table formats at this dialog box.
15. Click this button on the Tables and Borders toolbar to add, modify, or remove fill color from selected objects.
16. Click this button on the Tables and Borders toolbar to change the border line style.
17. This is the operator for multiplication that is used when writing formulas in a table.
18. This is the formula to add cells D2, D3, and D4, and then divide the total by 5.
19. This is the formula to multiply A1 by B1.
20. This calculation will display in the Formula text box in the Formula dialog box by default.

working hands-on

Assessment 1

1. At a clear document screen, create the table shown in figure 6.31. Bold and center the text as shown.
2. Save the document and name it Word Ch 06, SA 01.
3. Print and then close Word Ch 06, SA 01.

figure
6.31   *Assessment 1*

Name and Title	Department
Charles (Kit) G. Bloomquist, Manager	Facilities Maintenance
Penny M. Fitzpatrick, Director	Marketing, Continental United States
Jeffrey J. Hartnett, Assistant Manager	Computer Technical Support
Raymond D. Johnson, Manager	Communications Operations, International
Sandra L. Kvasnikoff, Vice President	Customer Service
Kenneth R. Morrison, Assistant Manager	System Support Services

Assessment 2

1. At a clear document screen, create the table shown in figure 6.32 with the following specifications:
   a. Press the Enter key once and then create a table with 2 columns and 9 rows (9 x 2).
   b. Change the width of the first column to 4.5 inches and the width of the second column to 1.5 inches.
   c. Change the alignment of cells in the second column to right.
   d. Select the entire table and then change the font to 12-point Arial.
   e. Merge cells in the first row (cells A1 and B1).
   f. Key the text in the cells as indicated. Bold and center the text in the first cell. Before keying the text in the first cell, press the Enter key once. After keying the text in the cell centered and bolded, press the Enter key once.
2. Save the document and name it Word Ch 06, SA 02.
3. Print and then close Word Ch 06, SA 02.

figure

6.32

Assessment 2

PROPERTY Replacement Cost	
Business Personal Property Including Stock & Equipment	$1,367,400
Blanket Earnings & Expenses	4,883,432
Total Valuable Papers	73,000
Transit Domestic & Foreign	41,000
Excess Legal Liability	550,000
Accounts Receivable	40,000
Computer Coverage	35,000
Fire Department Service Charge	15,000

Assessment 3

1. At a clear document screen, create the table shown in figure 6.33 with the following specifications:
   a. Press the Enter key once.
   b. Create a table with 3 columns and 8 rows (8 x 3).
   c. Merge the cells in the first row (cells A1, B1, and C1).
   d. Select the first and second rows and then click the Bold button and the Center button on the Formatting toolbar.
   e. Select cells B3 through C8 and then change the alignment to Right.
   f. Key the text in the cells shown in figure 6.33. (Before keying the text in the first cell, press the Enter key once. After keying the text in the cell centered and bolded, press the Enter key once.)
   g. Add border lines and shading to the table as shown in figure 6.33.
   h. Use the AutoFit feature to make the columns in the table automatically fit the contents.
   i. Center the table horizontally.
2. Save the document and name it Word Ch 06, SA 03.
3. Print and then close Word Ch 06, SA 03.

figure

6.33   *Assessment 3*

STOCK OPTION LEDGER REPORT		
Type of Transaction	**# of Shares**	**Future**
Beginning Inventory	93,000	1,000
Portion Exercised	2,000	3,000
One Hundred Percent Split	3,000	4,400
Exercised	(1,000)	4,400
Exercised	2,000	4,400
Portion Exercised	1,000	5,400

Assessment 4

1. Open Word Table 05.
2. Save the document with Save As and name it Word Ch 06, SA 04.
3. Make the following changes to the table:
   a. Select cells B1 through C7 and then change the alignment to right.
   b. With the insertion point positioned in any cell in the table, apply the *Columns 5* formatting at the Table AutoFormat dialog box.
   c. Center the table horizontally.
   d. Position the insertion point in cell B7 and then display the Formula dialog box. At this dialog box, leave the formula in the Formula text box as written. Click the down-pointing triangle at the right of the Number format option and then click the first numbering format in the drop-down menu. Click OK to close the Formula dialog box.
   e. Position the insertion point in cell C7 and then display the Formula dialog box. At this dialog box, leave the formula in the Formula text box as written. Click the down-pointing triangle to the right of the Number format option and then click the first numbering format in the drop-down menu. Click OK to close the Formula dialog box. (Key a dollar sign before each total.)
4. Save the document again with the same name (Word Ch 06, SA 04).
5. Print and then close Word Ch 06, SA 04.

Assessment 5

1. Open Word Table 06.
2. Save the document with Save As and name it Word Ch 06, SA 05.
3. Customize the table in the document so it displays as shown in figure 6.34.
4. Save the document again with the same name (Word Ch 06, SA 05).
5. Print and then close Word Ch 06, SA 05.

Assessment 5

JOBS IN GREATEST DEMAND

BA or Graduate Degree Required

Position	Weekly Income	Yearly Openings
Accountants/Auditors	$675	821
Financial Managers	$645	357
Loan Officers	$695	278
Registered Nurses	$752	1,450
Teachers, Elementary	$680	1,008
Teachers, Secondary	$750	1,326

Assessment 6

1. At a clear document screen, create a table using the information shown in figure 6.35. Format the table following steps similar to those in Assessment 4.
2. Save the document and name it Word Ch 06, SA 06.
3. Print and then close Word Ch 06, SA 06.

figure
6.35   *Assessment 6*

Expenses	Budgeted	Actual
Basic education	$17,349,233	$17,213,455
Support services	13,239,441	12,987,345
Special education	5,123,325	5,236,415
Vocational education	1,945,674	1,895,350
Learning assistance	1,134,095	1,056,394
Other education programs	754,342	698,560
Community services	693,548	701,359
Total		

Assessment 7

1. Open Word Table 07.
2. Save the document with Save As and name it Word Ch 06, SA 07.
3. Format the table so it appears as shown in figure 6.36 by making the following changes:
    a. Position the insertion point in any cell in the table.
    b. Position the mouse pointer on the move table column marker that displays on the Ruler between the 1-inch mark and the 2-inch mark, hold down the Ctrl key and the Shift key, and then drag the marker to the 2¼-inch mark on the Ruler.
    c. Select the first two rows and then change the alignment to center and change the font to 14-point Tahoma bold.
    d. Select cells B3 through D8 and then change the alignment to right.
    e. Select cells A3 through D8 and then change the font to 11-point Tahoma.
    f. Insert the formula **=C3-B3** in cell D3 and change the <u>N</u>umber format option to the third option from the top at the drop-down menu.
    g. Insert the appropriate formula in cells D4, D5, D6, D7, and D8 to subtract This Year numbers from Last Year numbers. (Change the <u>N</u>umber format option to the second option from the top at the drop-down menu.)
    h. Insert border lines and shading as shown in figure 6.36. (To create the double-line border, you will need to select the double-line border option and then increase the width to 1 ½ pts.)
4. Save the document again with the same name (Word Ch 06, SA 07).
5. Print and then close Word Ch 06, SA 07.

figure
6.36
Assessment 7

McCORMACK FUNDS CORPORATION Computer Operations Expenses			
Expense	**Last Year**	**This Year**	**Difference**
Payroll	$1,102,003.90	$1,320,229.20	
New Equipment	690,340.24	750,345.98	
Equipment Maintenance	20,435.33	22,820.45	
Personnel Training	19,485.45	20,460.00	
Consultation Fees	14,309.00	12,683.50	
Supplies and Printing	1,783.48	2,009.42	

Assessment 8

1. Using Word's Help feature, learn how to convert a table to text. Print the information.
2. After reading the information on converting a table to text, complete the following steps:
   a. Create a Word document that describes the steps.
   b. Save the document and name it Word Ch 06, Steps.
   c. Print and then close Word Ch 06, Steps.
3. Open Word Ch 06, SA 02 and then complete the following steps:
   a. Convert the table in Word Ch 06, SA 02 to text. (You determine with what to separate the text.)
   b. Save the converted table and name it Word Ch 06, SA 08.
   c. Print and then close Word Ch 06, SA 08.
4. Using Word's Help feature, learn how to convert text to a table.
5. After reading the information, key the text shown in figure 6.37 exactly as written and then convert the text to a table.
6. Save the table and name it Word Ch 06, Table.
7. Print and then close Word Ch 06, Table.

figure
6.37 *Assessment 8*

Title,Name
President,Martin Sherwood
Vice President,Gina Lopez
Vice President,Sydney Fox
Manager,Stephen Powell
Manager,Linda Wang

Chapter 07

Exploring the Internet

Increasingly, businesses are accessing the Internet to conduct research, publish product or catalog information, communicate, and market products globally. In many Microsoft Office applications, you can jump to the Internet and browse the World Wide Web. You can also create a document in an office application and then save it as a Web document with HyperText Markup Language (HTML) codes. HTML "tags" attached to information in a Web document enable the links and jumps between documents and data resources to operate. Information provided by the tags also instructs the browser software how to display text, images, animations, or sounds.

Understanding the Internet

The *Internet* is a network of computers connected around the world. In 1969, the U.S. Defense Department created a network to allow researchers at different sites to exchange information. The first network consisted of only four computers. Since then, the number of networks that have connected has grown exponentially, and the Internet is no longer just a vehicle of information for researchers, but can be used by anyone whose computer has a *modem*, a device that allows data to be sent over telephone lines.

Users access the Internet for several purposes: to communicate using e-mail, to subscribe to news groups, to transfer files, to socialize with other users around the globe in "chat" rooms, and largely to access virtually any kind of information imaginable.

INTEGRATED TOPIC

To use the Internet, you generally need three things—an Internet Service Provider (ISP), a program to browse the Web (called a *Web browser*), and a *search engine* (software used to locate specific data on the Internet).

A variety of Internet Service Providers are available. Local ISPs are available as well as commercial ISPs such as Microsoft Network®, America Online®, AT&T Worldnet Service®, and CompuServe®. To complete the exercises in this chapter, you will need access to the Internet through an ISP. Check with your instructor to determine the ISP used by your school to connect to the Internet.

Once you are connected to the Internet, you can access the *World Wide Web*. The World Wide Web is the most commonly used application on the Internet. The Web is a set of standards and protocols used to access information available on the Internet. The Internet is the physical network utilized to carry the data. To access the Web and maneuver within the Web, you need a Web browser. A Web browser allows you to move around the Internet by pointing and clicking with the mouse. A popular Web browser designed by Microsoft is the Microsoft Internet Explorer. The exercises in this chapter are created with the assumption that you will have Microsoft Internet Explorer available. If you will be using a different Web browser, some of the steps in the exercises may vary.

A phenomenal amount of information is available on the Internet. Searching through all that information to find the specific information you need can be an overwhelming task. Software programs, called *search engines*, have been created to help you search more quickly and easily for the desired information. There are many search engines available on the Internet, each offering the opportunity to search for specific information. As you use different search engines, you may find you prefer one over the others.

Browsing the World Wide Web

In this chapter, you will be completing several exercises and assessments that require you to search for locations and information on the World Wide Web. To do this, you will need the following:

1. A modem or network connection to a server with Internet access.
2. Browser software installed and configured. (This chapter will explore the World Wide Web using Microsoft Internet Explorer.)
3. An Internet Service Provider account.

A modem is a hardware device that converts digital data into a form that can be transmitted over telephone lines. The word "modem" is derived from MOdulator/DEModulator. The modem attached to your computer converts digital data into an analog signal that can be transferred over telephone lines. At the other end of the connection is another modem that converts the analog signal back to digital data for the receiving computer. There are internal and external modems available in a variety of speeds. Modem speed is measured in terms of the number of bits per second data is transferred. If you are using a computer connected to a network, the network server will route the data through its modem, or to another server with a modem.

An Internet Service Provider (ISP) sells access to the Internet. In order to provide this access, the ISP must have in place the hardware and software necessary to support access to the Internet, phone lines to accept the modem

The Web is used to locate information, distribute sales and marketing data, advertise products and services, and deliver software.

Hint

A company may set up a network infrastructure called an "intranet" to allow employees access to company information.

Hint

connections, and support staff to assist their customers. Each ISP is responsible for configuring its computers, routers, and software to enable connectivity to every other individual and computer that make up the Internet.

Locating URLs on the Internet

We all know that we can dial a telephone number of a friend or relative in any country around the world and establish a connection within seconds. The global telephone system is an amazing network that functions because of a common set of protocols and standards that are agreed upon by each country. The Internet operates on the same principle. Computer protocols known as TCP/IP (Transmission Control Protocol/Internet Protocol) form the base of the Internet. Protocols are simply agreements on how various hardware and software should communicate with each other. The Internet Service Provider becomes the Domain Name Service (DNS), *the route to the Internet*. The DNS and IP determine how to route your computer to another location/computer on the Internet. Every computer directly linked to the Internet has a unique IP address.

This explanation has been overly simplified. The technical details on how computer A can "talk" to computer B do not directly involve a computer user any more than does picking up a phone in Vancouver, British Columbia, and dialing a number in San Diego, California.

Uniform Resource Locators, referred to as URLs, are the method used to identify locations on the Internet. The format of a URL is *http://server-name.path*. The first part of the URL, *http://*, identifies the protocol. The letters *http* stand for HyperText Transfer Protocol, which is the protocol or language used to transfer data within the World Wide Web. The colon and slashes separate the protocol from the server name. The server name is the second component of the URL. For example, in the URL http://home.netscape.com, the server name is identified as *home.netscape*. The last part of the URL specifies the domain to which the server belongs. For example, *.com* refers to "commercial" and establishes that the URL is a commercial company. Other examples of domains include *.edu* for "educational," *.gov* for "government," and *.mil* for "military." Some examples of URLs are displayed in figure 7.1.

7.1 *Sample URLs*

URL	Connects to
http://www.microsoft.com	Microsoft Corporation home page
http://www.emcp.com	EMC/Paradigm Publishing home page
http://lcweb.loc.gov	Library of Congress home page
http://www.washington.edu	University of Washington home page
http://www.xerox.com	Xerox home page
http://www.kodak.com	Eastman Kodak home page
http://www.alaska-air.com	Alaska Airlines home page

If you know the URL for a specific Web site and would like to visit that site, key the URL in the Address section of the Web toolbar. To display the Web toolbar shown in figure 7.2, click <u>V</u>iew, point to <u>T</u>oolbars, and then click Web at the drop-down list. You can also display the Web toolbar by positioning the mouse pointer on a toolbar, clicking the *right* mouse button, and then clicking Web at the drop-down list.

Before keying a URL in the Address text box on the Web toolbar, make sure you are connected to the Internet through your Internet Service Provider. When keying a URL, you must key the address exactly as written, including any colons (:) or slashes (/).

When you key a URL in the Address section of the Web toolbar and then press Enter, your default Web browser is automatically activated. The home page for the specific URL displays on the screen in the Web browser. Figure 7.3 shows the Microsoft home page in the Internet Explorer Web browser. You will learn more about Internet Explorer later in this chapter.

When you are connected to a URL, the home page for the specific URL (Web site) displays. The home page is the starting point for viewing the Web site. At the home page, you can choose to "branch off" the home page to other pages within the Web site or jump to other Web sites. You do this with hyperlinks that are embedded in the home page. You will learn more about hyperlinks in the next section of this chapter. In exercise 1, you will be visiting some Web site home pages using URLs.

Another method for displaying a URL is to display the Open dialog box, key the URL address in the File name text box, and then click OK.

figure
7.2

Web Toolbar

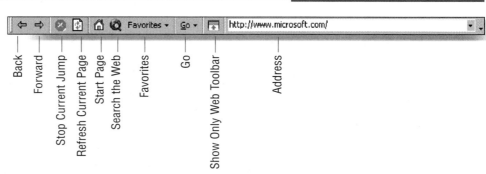

Back | Forward | Stop Current Jump | Refresh Current Page | Start Page | Search the Web | Favorites | Go | Show Only Web Toolbar | Address

exercise 1

Visiting Web Site Home Pages

1. Make sure you are connected to the Internet through an Internet Service Provider.
2. Explore several sites on the World Wide Web from within Word by completing the following steps:
   a. At a clear document screen, display the Web toolbar by clicking <u>V</u>iew, pointing to <u>T</u>oolbars, and then clicking Web.
   b. Click in the Address text box located on the Web toolbar. (This will select the current document name in the text box.)
   c. Display the Web site home page for Microsoft Corporation by keying **http://www.microsoft.com** and then pressing Enter.
   d. In a few moments, the Microsoft home page

Step 2c

http://www.microsoft.com

displays. The home page will display in your default Web browser similar to what is shown in figure 7.3. Home pages are updated frequently so the Microsoft home page you are viewing will vary slightly from what you see in figure 7.3. Scroll down the home page, reading the information about Microsoft.

   e. After reading about Microsoft, view the home page for NASA. To do this, click the current address located in the A̲ddress text box, key **http://www.nasa.gov** and then press Enter. Scroll down the home page reading the information displayed about NASA.

3. After reading the information displayed on the NASA home page, close your Web browser by clicking F̲ile and then C̲lose.

In exercise 1, step 2c, you keyed the Microsoft Web site URL as http://www.microsoft.com. When keying a URL, you can leave off the http://. Office adds this automatically to the URL.

Microsoft Home Page

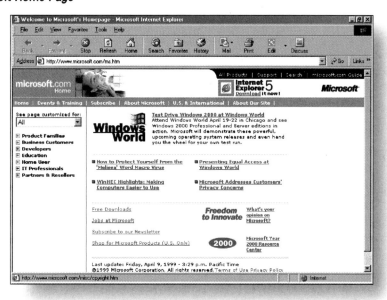

Using Hyperlinks

As you were viewing the Web site home pages for Microsoft and NASA, did you notice text that displayed in a different color and was also underlined? Text displayed in a different color and underlined indicates text that has been identified as a *hyperlink*. A hyperlink allows you to link or connect to another item. A hyperlink can display in a variety of ways. It can display as text in a different color and underlined or as a heading or button. Move the mouse pointer to a hyperlink and the mouse pointer turns into a hand. This is one method for determining if an item is a hyperlink.

To use a hyperlink, position the mouse pointer on the desired hyperlink until the pointer turns into a hand, and then click the left mouse button. For example, when you displayed the Microsoft home page, you could have clicked the hyperlink button About Microsoft located towards the top of the page to display information about

Back

Forward

Microsoft Corporation. Most pages contain a variety of hyperlinks. Using these links, you can zero in on the exact information for which you are searching.

The Web toolbar as well as the Internet Explorer Web browser contain a Back button you can click to display the previous Web page. If you click the Back button and then would like to go back to the hyperlink, click the Forward button. By clicking the Back button, you can back your way out of any hyperlinks and return to the default Web home page. In exercise 2, you will be exploring two sites on the World Wide Web and using hyperlinks to display specific information.

exercise 2

Visiting Web Sites and Using Hyperlinks

1. Make sure you are connected to the Internet through an Internet Service Provider.
2. Explore several sites on the World Wide Web by completing the following steps:
   a. At a clear document screen, make sure the Web toolbar displays.
   b. Click in the Address text box located on the Web toolbar.
   c. Key **http://www.time.com** and then press Enter.
   d. When the Time home page displays, click the hyperlink to the cover story by positioning the mouse pointer over an image or text that represents the cover story until the pointer turns into a hand and then clicking the left mouse button.
   e. When the cover story page displays, click the Print button on the Internet Explorer toolbar to print the page.
   f. Click the Back button to return to the Time home page.
   g. Click the current address located in the Address text box.
   h. Key **http://www. amazon.com** and then press Enter.
   i. When the Amazon.com home page displays, click the BESTSELLERS hyperlink button. (This hyperlink is probably located towards the top of the Amazon.com page. If this hyperlink is not available, choose any other hyperlink that interests you.)
   j. When the bestseller page displays, print the page.
3. After printing the bestseller page, close your Web browser by clicking File and then Close.

Searching the Internet Using Internet Explorer

In the previous exercises, you jumped around the Web by keying URLs, which is a fast way to move from site to site. Often, however, you will access the Web to search for information and you will not know the URL that you want to visit.

Search engines are valuable tools to assist a user in locating information on a particular topic by simply keying a few words or a short phrase. There are many search engines available on the Internet such as Excite, Infoseek, Lycos, Yahoo, AltaVista, and HotBot. Each offers the opportunity to search for specific information. As you use different search engines, you may find you prefer one over the others.

Search the Web

To search for information on the Web, click the Search the Web button on the Web toolbar. This displays the Internet Explorer Search Setup page as shown in figure 7.4. As mentioned earlier in this chapter, Internet Explorer is a Web browser, which creates an environment in which you can search and display Web sites. Figure 7.4 identifies the features of the Internet Explorer program window and figure 7.5 describes the features.

figure 7.4

Internet Explorer Window

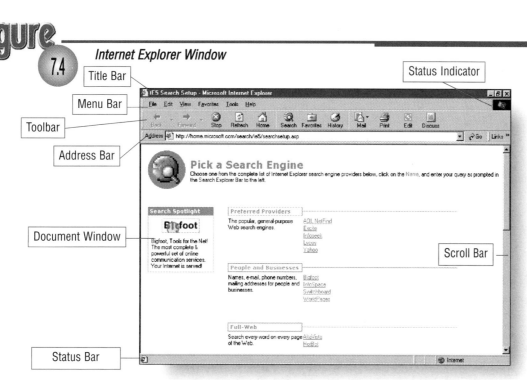

figure 7.5

Internet Explorer Program Window Features

Internet Explorer Feature	Description
Title bar	Displays the name of the Web page followed by the name of the program—Microsoft Internet Explorer
Menu bar	Contains a list of options for using and customizing Internet Explorer
Toolbar	Contains buttons for commonly used features such as navigating, searching, printing, and formatting

Address bar	Displays the address of the current Web site page
Status indicator	Status indicator is the Microsoft logo; animates (moves) when a Web site is being loaded
Document window	Displays the contents of the current Web site
Scroll bar	Use the scroll bar to display information in the current Web page
Status bar	Displays information about connection progress and the percentage of information that has been transferred

The Internet Explorer toolbar contains buttons for accessing a variety of commands. Figure 7.6 shows the buttons and describes each button.

figure

7.6

Internet Explorer Toolbar Buttons

Click this button	*To do this*
Back	Display previous Web page
Forward	Display next Web page
Stop	Stop loading a page
Refresh	Refresh (update) contents of current page
Home	Display the default home page
Search	Display the Search side bar
Favorites	Display the Favorites side bar
History	Display the History side bar containing a list of sites visited on specific days or during specific weeks
Mail	Display mail and news options
Print	Print the current Web page
Edit	Display the current Web page in a Word document screen for editing
Discuss	Chat with others connected to the same server. (You must specify the discussion server.)

Searching for Specific Information on the Web

Click the Search the Web button on the Web toolbar and the Internet Explorer Search Setup page displays as shown in figure 7.4. This page lists a variety of search engines in different categories. (Web pages and search engines are constantly changing so you may discover that your Internet Explorer Search Setup page may vary from what you see in figure 7.4. If that is the case, you may need to modify some steps in the exercises in this chapter.) Click the desired search engine name and a side bar displays. For example, click the Excite search engine name and a side bar displays as shown in figure 7.7. Key specific text in the white text box that displays towards the top of the Excite side bar and then click the Search button. A list of sites displays in the Excite side bar containing the specific text you entered in the white text box. Click a site listing to jump to that site on the Web.

figure
7.7

Excite Side Bar

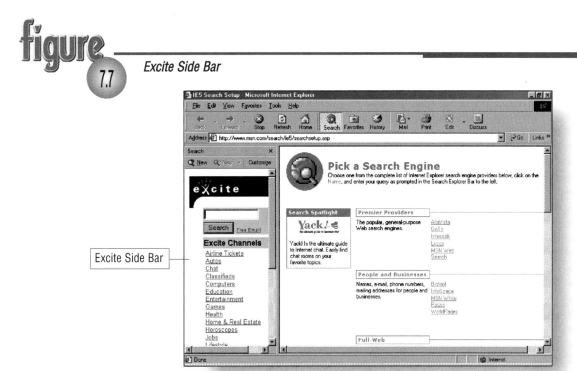

Excite Side Bar

As you gain experience searching the Web, you will develop methods to refine your search techniques and tools to limit the time spent browsing. Before you begin a research project, jot down your key words or phrases and think about ways to limit the sites that will be selected by being as specific as possible without restricting the search. As you will see in the next exercise, you can become overwhelmed with the number of sites that will be selected.

If the downloading process is taking too long and you want to quit, click the Stop button on the Internet Explorer toolbar.

Hint

Using Search Engines to Locate Information on the Web

(Note: Web pages and search engines are changing constantly. If the instructions in this exercise do not match what you are viewing, you may need to substitute different steps than the ones instructed here.)

1. Jump to the World Wide Web from within Word and search for information on lahars (dense, viscous flows of volcanic debris) using the Excite search engine by completing these steps:

   a. At a clear document screen, make sure the Web toolbar displays, and then click the Search the Web button on the Web toolbar.

   b. At the Internet Explorer Search Setup page (like the one shown in figure 7.4), complete the following steps:

      1) Click the hyperlink *Excite* that displays in the *Full-Web* column.
      2) Click in the white text box (above the Search button) that displays towards the top of the Excite side bar (see figure 7.7).
      3) Key **lahars** in the text box.
      4) Click the Search button.

   c. In a few moments, the Excite search engine will return with the first ten sites in the side bar that meet your search criteria. Click a site that interests you.

   d. Click the Print button on the Internet Explorer toolbar to print the Web page displayed.

   e. After printing the information, click the Back button on the Internet Explorer toolbar. (This displays the Search Setup page at the right side of the screen.)

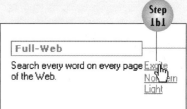

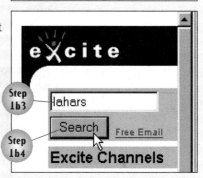

2. Search for information on the Australian platypus using the Infoseek search engine by completing the following steps:

   a. Click *Infoseek*, which displays in the *Premier Providers* column.

   b. Click in the white text box that displays towards the top of the Infoseek side bar.

   c. Key **Australian platypus** in the text box and then press Enter.

   d. In a few moments, the Infoseek search engine will return with information that meets the search criteria. Scroll through the side bar and read the information presented by Infoseek.

   e. Click a site about the Australian platypus that interests you.

   f. After viewing the site in the side bar, click the Search button on the Internet Explorer toolbar to remove the Search side bar.

3. Close Internet Explorer by clicking <u>F</u>ile on the Internet Explorer Menu bar and then clicking <u>C</u>lose at the drop-down menu.

Narrowing a Search

The Internet contains a phenomenal amount of information. For example, if you search for *physician-assisted suicide* using the Infoseek search engine, more than 500,000 sites may be found. Some searches can result in millions of "hits" (sites). Wading through all these sites can be very time consuming and counterproductive. Narrowing a search to very specific criteria can greatly reduce the number of hits for a search.

To reduce the number of documents found and to find only those documents containing very specific information, use *search operators*. Search operators may vary between search engines. Some operators may work within many engines, while others are specific to certain search engines. Some common search operators include symbols such as a quotation mark ("), a plus symbol (+), and a minus symbol (-). Figure 7.8 lists the operators and an explanation of each.

figure 7.8

Search Operators

Operator	Explanation
Plus (+)	Key a plus symbol directly in front of a word and only those documents containing the word will be found. Do not space after the symbol. If you are including more than one word, space between the first word and the next symbol or word.
	Example: Key **+baseball +rules** and only those documents containing both *baseball* and *rules* will be found
Minus (-)	Key a minus symbol directly in front of a word that you do not want included in the search. This symbol is helpful in situations where you want to find a specific topic but want to narrow it by excluding certain parts of the topic.
	Example: Key **+whales -blue -killer** and the search engine will find those documents containing *whales* but <u>not</u> *blue* or *killer*.
Quotation Marks (")	If you enter terms for a search such as *University of Arizona*, a search engine will find documents containing any or all of the three words in any order. If you want only those documents found containing *University of Arizona* in this specific order, enclose the words in quotation marks.
	Example: Key **"University of Arizona"** and the search engine will find those documents containing the three words in the order specified between the quotation marks.

In addition to search operators, some search engines recognize Boolean operators when conducting a search. (Boolean operators are based on Boolean algebra [named after George Boole, an English mathematician], which is a mathematical system originally devised for the analysis of symbolic logic.)

Boolean operators include AND, AND NOT, OR, and parentheses. Boolean operators must be keyed in all capital letters with a space on either side. Boolean operators are explained in figure 7.9.

figure
7.9

Boolean Operators

Operator	Function
AND	Find documents with words joined by AND.
	Example: Key **Disneyland AND California** and the search engine will find those documents containing both *Disneyland* and *California*.
OR	Find documents that contain at least one of the words joined by OR.
	Example: Key **volcanoes OR lahars** and the search engine will find those documents containing either *volcanoes* or *lahars*.
AND NOT	Find documents that contain the word before AND NOT but not the word after.
	Example: Key **bicycling AND NOT racing** and the search engine will find those documents containing the word *bicycling* but not the word *racing*.

Each search engine uses its own set of search guidelines. Research the guidelines for your favorite search engine.

Not all search engines use Boolean operators to limit searches. Each search engine should contain a Web page that explains how to conduct what is considered an advanced search. In exercise 4, you will be using two different search engines to find information and also print information on how to perform an advanced search with each of the two search engines.

exercise 4

Using Search Operators to Search for Specific Information on the Web

1. Jump to the World Wide Web from within Word and search for information on the University of Michigan using the Northern Light search engine by completing these steps:
   a. At a clear document screen, click the Search the Web button on the Web toolbar.
   b. At the Internet Explorer Search Setup page (like the one shown in figure 7.4), complete the following steps:
      1) Click *Northern Light*, which displays in the *Full-Web* column.
      2) Click in the white text box that displays towards the top of the Northern Light side bar, key **University of Michigan**, and then press Enter.
   c. In a few moments, the Northern Light search engine will return with a list of sites that meets your search criteria. Write down the total number of sites found by Northern Light.
   d. Scroll down the side bar to see some of the sites that have been selected.
   e. Learn more about searching with Northern Light by completing the following steps:

1) Click the HELP hyperlink button that displays towards the top of the Northern Light side bar.

2) Click the *Optimize Your Search* hyperlink that displays in the window at the far right side of the screen. (You will need to scroll to the right to see this hyperlink.)

3) When the Optimize Your Search page displays, print the information by clicking the Print button on the Internet Explorer toolbar.

f. Narrow the search by completing the following steps:

1) Select the text *University of Michigan* that displays in the white text box located towards the top of the Northern Light side bar, key **"University of Michigan"**, and then press Enter.

2) When Northern Light returns with a list of sites, write down the total number of sites. Compare this number to the previous number. The number found with the search containing the quotation marks should be considerably lower than the search without the quotation marks.

g. Click the Back button on the Internet Explorer toolbar until the Internet Explorer Search Setup page displays at the right side of the screen.

2. Find information on Ralph Nader using the Excite search engine and then find information on Ralph Nader but not the Green Party by completing the following steps:

a. At the Internet Explorer Search Setup page, click *Excite* in the *Full-Web* column.

b. Click in the white text box that displays towards the top of the Excite side bar and then key **Ralph Nader**.

c. Click the Search button.

d. When Excite returns with a list of sites, view the full screen by clicking the hyperlink *View Full Screen* that displays in the Excite side bar. (This displays additional information on Excite at the right side of the screen.)

e. At the Excite full screen that displays at the right, look for the total number of hits for *Ralph Nader* and then write down the number. (This number will probably display below *Web Results*.)

f. Display information on advanced searches in Excite by completing the following steps:

1) Click the *Help* hyperlink that displays at the right side of the white text box in the side bar.

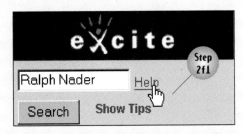

2) At the Excite help page that displays at the right side of the screen, click the *Advanced Search Tips* hyperlink.
3) When the Advanced Search Tips page displays, click the Print button on the Internet Explorer toolbar.
4) Read the information on advanced searches.

g. Narrow the search to documents containing Ralph Nader but <u>not</u> the Green Party by completing the following steps:
   1) Select *Ralph Nader* in the white text box that displays towards the top of the Excite side bar and then key **+Ralph +Nader -Green -Party**.
   2) Click the Search button.
   3) When Excite returns with a list of sites, click the *View Full Screen* hyperlink. (This updates the information at the right side of the screen.)
   4) Look at the information that displays at the right side of the screen and then write down the total number of sites found. Compare this number to the previous number. The number found with the search containing the plus and minus symbols should be considerably lower than the search without the symbols.

h. Click the Search button on the Internet Explorer toolbar to turn off the display of the Search side bar.

3. Click <u>F</u>ile and then <u>C</u>lose to close the Internet Explorer.

Search Help

Search Description
General Search Tips
Advanced Search Tips
Search Results
Relevance Rating
List by Web Site
Show Summaries
Search Wizard
Browser Error Messages

Step 2f2

Each search engine Web site should contain information on how to narrow a search or conduct an advanced search. You may want to experiment with some of the other search engines to see if you can find information on how to conduct advanced searches within each.

Favorites

Adding Favorite Sites to the Favorites List

If you find a site that you would like to visit on a regular basis, that site can be added to a Favorites list. To do this, display the site, and then click the Favorites button on the Internet Explorer toolbar. This causes a side bar to display similar to the one shown in figure 7.10 (your folder names may vary).

figure
7.10

Favorites Side Bar

Favorites Side Bar

To add a favorite site, click the Add button located at the top of the Favorites side bar. This displays the Add Favorite dialog box shown in figure 7.11. At this dialog box, make sure the information in the Name text box is correct (if not, select the text and then key your own information), and then click OK. The new site displays at the bottom of the list in the Favorites side bar. After a site has been added to the Favorites list, you can jump quickly to that site by clicking the Favorites button on the Internet Explorer toolbar and then clicking the site name at the Favorites side bar.

Keep your Favorites list a reasonable length by adding only those pages that you expect to visit several times.

Hint

figure
7.11

Add Favorite Dialog Box

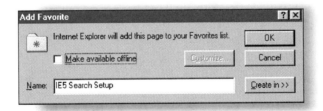

If you want to insert a favorites site into a folder, display the site, and then click the Add button. At the Add Favorite dialog box, click the Create in button located at the right side of the dialog box. This expands the dialog box and displays a list of folders. Click the folder into which you want the site listed and then click the OK button. To display the list of sites within a folder, click the folder name at the Favorite side bar. To turn off the display of sites within a folder, click the folder name again.

To delete a site from the Favorites side bar, position the mouse pointer on the site, click the *right* mouse button, and then click <u>D</u>elete at the pop-up menu that displays. At the Confirm File Delete dialog box, click the <u>Y</u>es button.

If you want to organize the list of favorite sites, click the Organize button located at the top of the Favorites side bar. This displays the Organize Favorites dialog box shown in figure 7.12. Use this dialog box to create a new folder, delete or rename a folder, or move a folder name up or down the Favorites list.

figure
7.12

Organize Favorites Dialog Box

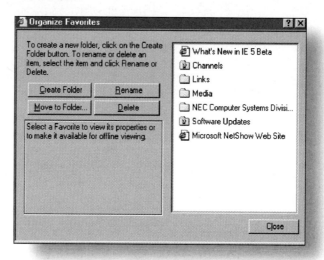

Displaying a List of Sites Visited

History

As you visit different Web sites, Internet Explorer keeps track of the sites. Click the History button on the Internet Explorer toolbar and a History side bar displays as shown in figure 7.13. You can display sites visited today or the past three weeks. To display the sites, click the desired day or week. This information can be useful for remembering Internet addresses previously visited and for monitoring Internet use. Close the History side bar by clicking the History button again or by clicking the Close button (contains an X) located in the upper right corner of the History side bar.

figure

7.13

Internet Explorer History Side Bar

History Side Bar

exercise 5

Exploring the Web, Adding Favorite Sites, and Displaying Sites Visited

1. Explore several locations on the World Wide Web from within Word using Internet Explorer and hyperlinks by completing the following steps:

   a. Click the Search the Web button on the Web toolbar.

   b. At the Internet Explorer Search Setup page, click in the Address text box. (This selects the current address.)

   c. Display the home page for *USA Today* by keying **http://www.usatoday.com** and then pressing Enter.

   d. Add the *USA Today* Web site to the Favorites list by completing the following steps:

      1) Click the Favorites button located on the Internet Explorer toolbar.

      2) At the Favorites side bar, click the Add button (displays towards the top of the side bar).

      3) At the Add Favorite dialog box, make sure *USA TODAY* displays in the Name text box, and then click OK.

      4) Click the Favorites button on the Internet Explorer toolbar to remove the Favorites side bar.

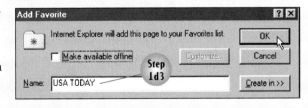

   e. Display the Alaska Airlines Web page, add it to the Favorites list, and then search for flight departure times from Los Angeles, California, to Anchorage, Alaska, by completing the following steps:

1) Click in the Address text box to select the current URL, key **http://www.alaska-air.com**, and then press Enter.
2) When the Alaska Airlines home page displays, add it to the Favorites list by completing steps similar to those in step 1d.
3) At the Alaska Airlines home page, click the *Schedules* hyperlink.
4) At the schedule Web page, click the down-pointing triangle at the right side of the From text box, and then click *Los Angeles, California* at the drop-down list. (You will need to scroll down the list.)
5) Make sure the To text box displays *Anchorage, Alaska*.

6) Change the departing date from one week from today. (You will need to change the day and perhaps the month.)
7) Click the CONTINUE button.
8) When the flight schedule page displays, click the Print button on the Internet Explorer toolbar.

f. Jump to the home page for *USA Today* by completing the following steps:
1) Click the Favorites button on the Internet Explorer toolbar to display the Favorites side bar.
2) At the Favorites side bar, click *USA TODAY*.
3) Click the Favorites button to turn off the display of the Favorites side bar.

g. Display a list of sites visited by completing the following steps:
1) Click the History button on the Internet Explorer toolbar. (Sites visited today display in the side bar.)
2) Display sites visited last week by clicking *Last Week*.
3) Click the History button on the Internet Explorer toolbar to turn off the display of the History side bar.

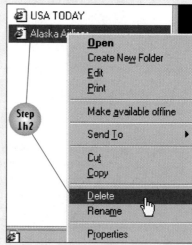

h. Remove *Alaska Airlines* and *USA TODAY* from the Favorites side bar by completing the following steps:
1) Click the Favorites button on the Internet Explorer toolbar.
2) Right-click *Alaska Airlines* in the Favorites side bar and then click Delete at the drop-down menu.
3) At the Confirm File Delete dialog box, click Yes.
4) Right-click on *USA TODAY* in the Favorites side bar and then click Delete at the drop-down menu.
5) At the Confirm File Delete dialog box, click Yes.

6) Click the Favorites button on the Internet Explorer toolbar to turn off the display of the Favorites side bar.
2. Close Internet Explorer by clicking File and then Close.
3. If the Windows desktop displays, click the Microsoft Word button that displays on the taskbar. (This will display the Word document screen.)

Creating a Web Page

Now that you have been "surfing the net," you have visited several Web site home pages and have an idea how a home page displays. Home pages are Web documents that describe a company, school, government, or individual and are created using a language called HyperText Markup Language (HTML). This is a language that Web browsers use to read hypertext documents. In the past, a person needed knowledge of HTML to design a Web page. Now a Web page can be created in Word and saved as a Web page or created with a Web Page Wizard.

Before creating a Web page, consider the information you want contained in the Web page. Carefully plan the layout of the information and where to position hyperlinks. Good Web page design is a key element to a successful Web page. Often a company will hire a professional Web page designer to create their home page. Before designing a Web page, you may want to visit a variety of Web pages and consider some of the following questions: What elements are included on the Web page? How are the elements distributed on the page? Is the information organized logically and is it easy to read? Is the Web page visually appealing? Evaluating Web pages on the Web will help you when designing your own.

To save a Word document as a Web page, click File, expand the drop-down menu, and then click Save as Web Page. At the Save As dialog box, key a name for the Web page document, and then press Enter or click the Save button. (Word automatically changes the Save as type option to Web Page.)

Changing to the Web Layout View

When you save a document as a Web page, Word automatically changes to the Web Layout view. The Web Layout view displays a page as it will appear when published to the Web or an intranet. You can also change to the Web Layout view by clicking the Web Layout View button located at the left side of the horizontal scroll bar or by clicking View and then Web Layout.

Web Layout View

Formatting a Web Page

Word provides a variety of predesigned styles and formatting that can be applied to a document. You learned about the styles in the Style Gallery in chapter 5. Themes and backgrounds can also be applied to documents. Themes and backgrounds are designed for viewing in a Word document, in an e-mail message, or on the Web. Backgrounds and some theme formatting do not print.

Applying a Theme to a Web Page

Some interesting and colorful formatting can be applied to a document with options at the Theme dialog box shown in figure 7.14. To display this dialog box, click Format expand the drop-down menu, and then click Theme. Click a theme in the Choose a Theme list box and a preview displays at the right side. Click OK to close the dialog box and apply the theme to the document. (You can also double-click a theme at the Theme dialog box.)

When a theme is applied to a document, Word automatically changes to the Web Layout view. Theme formatting is designed for documents that will be published on the Web, on an intranet, or sent as an e-mail. Not all of the formatting applied by a theme will print.

figure

7.14   *Theme Dialog Box*

Click a theme in this list box and preview it at the right.

Previewing a Document in Web Page Preview

When creating a Web page, you may want to preview it in your default Web browser. To do this, click File, expand the drop-down menu, and then click Web Page Preview. This displays the currently open document in the default Web browser and displays formatting supported by the browser.

exercise 6

Creating and Formatting a Web Page

1. Open Beltway Home Page.
2. Save the document as a Web page by completing the following steps:
   a. Click File, expand the drop-down menu, and then click Save as Web Page.
   b. Key **Beltway Web Page** and then press Enter.
3. Make the following formatting changes to the document:
   a. Apply the Heading 1 style to the company name *BELTWAY TRANSPORTATION*.
   b. Center the company name *BELTWAY TRANSPORTATION*.
   c. Select the company address, telephone number, and Web address and then apply the Heading 2 style.
   d. With the text still selected, display the Paragraph dialog box, change the spacing before paragraphs to 3 points (leave the spacing after at 3 points), and then close the dialog box.
   e. With the text still selected, click the Center button on the Formatting toolbar, and then deselect the text.
   f. Apply the Travel theme by completing the following steps:
      1) Click Format, expand the drop-down menu, and then click Theme.
      2) Scroll through the list of themes in the Choose a Theme list box until *Travel* is visible and then click *Travel*.
      3) Click OK to close the dialog box.
   g. Select the text from the paragraph that begins *Let Beltway Transportation take care of all...* to the end of the document, change the font color to lime green, and then deselect the text.
4. Preview the document in Web Page Preview by completing the following steps:
   a. Click File, expand the drop-down menu, and then click Web Page Preview.
   b. After viewing the document in the Web browser, click File and then Close.
5. Save the document again with the same name (Beltway Web Page).
6. Print and then close Beltway Web Page. (Not all of the theme formatting will print.)

Applying a Background to a Document

Apply a colorful background to a document by clicking Format, expanding the drop-down menu, and then clicking Background. This causes a palette of color choices to display at the right side of the drop-down menu as shown in figure 7.15. Click the desired color or click the More Colors option to display the Colors dialog box.

Apply a background and the view is automatically changed to Web Layout. A background color does not display in the Normal or Print Layout views and will not print. Like a theme, background color is designed for formatting documents such as Web pages or e-mail messages that are viewed on the screen.

figure
7.15

Background Side Menu

Click the Fill Effects option from the Background side menu and the Fill Effects dialog box displays as shown in figure 7.16. Use options from this dialog box to apply formatting such as a gradient, texture, and pattern.

figure
7.16

Fill Effects Dialog Box

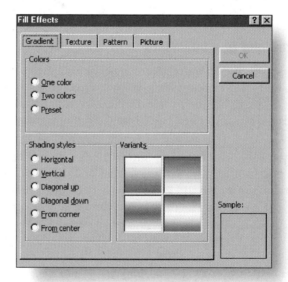

exercise 7

Applying a Background to a Web Page

1. Open Beltway Web Page. (If this document is not visible, change the Files of type option at the Open dialog box to All Files.)
2. Save the document with Save As and name it Beltway Background. (Make sure the Save as type option is *Web Page*.)
3. Change the background color of the Web page and add a gradient and texture by completing the following steps:
   a. Click Format, expand the drop-down menu, point to Background, and then click the Sea Green color (fourth color from the left in the third row).
   b. Click Format, point to Background, and then click Fill Effects.
   c. At the Fill Effects dialog box with the Gradient tab selected, click From center in the Shading styles section.
   d. Click OK to close the dialog box.
   e. Notice how the Web page displays.
4. Add a texture to the Web page by completing the following steps:
   a. Click Format, point to Background, and then click Fill Effects.
   b. At the Fill Effects dialog box, click the Texture tab.
   c. At the Fill Effects dialog box with the Texture tab selected, click the third texture option from the left in the bottom row (*Purple mesh*).
   d. Click OK to close the dialog box.
   e. Notice how the Web page displays.
5. Preview the Web page in Web Page Preview. (You may need to maximize the Internet Explorer window.) After viewing the document, close the Web browser.
6. Save the document again with the same name (Beltway Background).
7. Close Beltway Background. (Printing is optional—the texture does not print.)

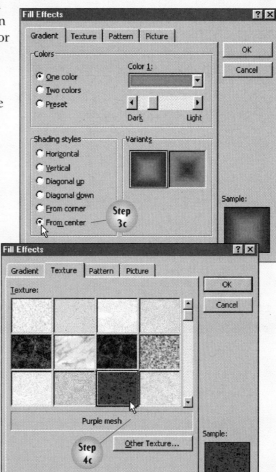

Formatting with Buttons on the Web Tools Toolbar

A Web page designer uses a variety of tools to prepare an appealing and successful Web page. Tools are available for formatting a Web page with buttons on the Web Tools toolbar shown in figure 7.17. Display the Web Tools toolbar by clicking View, pointing to Toolbars, and then clicking Web Tools. You can also display the Web Tools toolbar by right-clicking a currently displayed toolbar and then clicking Web Tools at the drop-down list. The shape of the toolbar shown in figure

7.17 has been changed to show the button names. The shape of your Web Tools toolbar will vary.

An interactive Web page, a page in which the viewer will provide input or answer questions, might include check boxes and option buttons. A Web page with a variety of options and choices might include drop-down boxes and list boxes. In exercise 8 you will be using two of the buttons on the Web Tools toolbar. As you continue to create and design Web pages, consider experimenting with other buttons on the Web Tools toolbar.

figure 7.17

Web Tools Toolbar Buttons

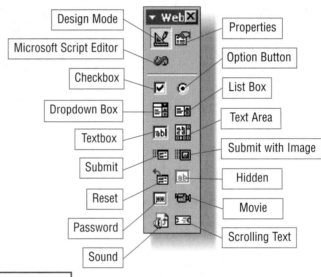

- Design Mode
- Microsoft Script Editor
- Checkbox
- Dropdown Box
- Textbox
- Submit
- Reset
- Password
- Sound
- Properties
- Option Button
- List Box
- Text Area
- Submit with Image
- Hidden
- Movie
- Scrolling Text

exercise 8

Inserting a Sound Clip and Scrolling Text to a Web Page

1. Open Beltway Web Page.
2. Save the document with Save As and name it Beltway Formatted.
3. Insert scrolling text in the Web page by completing the following steps:
   a. Display the Web Tools toolbar by clicking View, pointing to Toolbars, and then clicking Web Tools.
   b. Position the insertion point at the left margin on the blank line below the company Web address and then click the Center button on the Formatting toolbar.
   c. Click the Scrolling Text button on the Web Tools toolbar.
   d. At the Scrolling Text dialog box, select *Scrolling Text* that displays in

the Type the scrolling text here text box and then key **Let Beltway Transportation take care of all your moving needs!**

    e. Click the down-pointing triangle at the right side of the Background color text box and then click *Dark Yellow* at the drop-down list.

    f. Click OK to close the Scrolling Text dialog box.

4. Add a sound clip to the Web page by completing the following steps:

    a. Click the Sound button on the Web Tools toolbar.

    b. At the Background Sound dialog box, click the Browse button.

    c. At the File Open dialog box (with the Media folder displayed), double-click *Canyon* in the list box.

    d. At the Background Sound dialog box, click the down-pointing triangle at the right side of the Loop text box, and then click *Infinite* at the drop-down list.

    e. Click OK to close the Background Sound dialog box.

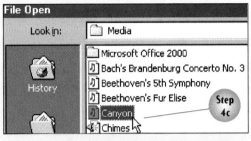

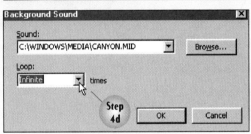

5. Save the document again with the same name (Beltway Formatted).

6. Close the Web Tools toolbar.

7. Print and then close Beltway Formatted.

Creating Hyperlinks

The business Web sites you have visited, such as Microsoft and *USA Today*, have included hyperlinks to connect you to other pages or Web sites. You can create your own hyperlink in your Web page. To do this, select the text you want specified as the hyperlink, and then click the Insert Hyperlink button on the Standard toolbar. At the Insert Hyperlink dialog box shown in figure 7.18, key the Web site URL in the Type the file or Web page name text box, and then click OK.

Insert
Hyperlink

Insert Hyperlink Dialog Box

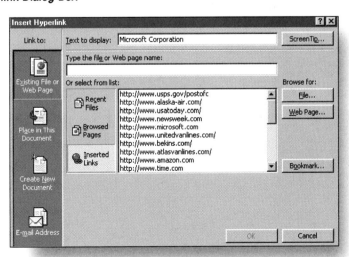

Position the arrow pointer (turns into a hand) on a hyperlink and, after a few moments, the URL associated with the hyperlink displays in a yellow box.

Another method for creating a hyperlink is to key the URL in a Word document. When you key the complete URL, Word automatically converts the URL to a hyperlink and changes the color of the URL. In exercise 9, you will be establishing hyperlinks from the Beltway Transportation Web page to moving company sites.

exercise 9

Creating Hyperlinks

1. Open Beltway Web Page.
2. Create a hyperlink so that clicking Atlas Van Lines displays the Atlas Van Lines Web page by completing the following steps:
   a. Select the text *Atlas Van Lines* that displays towards the end of the document (after a bullet).
   b. Click the Insert Hyperlink button on the Standard toolbar.
   c. At the Insert Hyperlink dialog box, key **http://www.atlasvanlines.com** in the Type the file or Web page name text box.
   d. Click OK. (This changes the color of the *Atlas Van Lines* text and also adds underlining to the text.)
3. Complete steps similar to those in step 2 to create a hyperlink from *Bekins* to the URL *http://www.bekins.com*.
4. Complete steps similar to those in step 2 to create a hyperlink from *United Van Lines* to the URL *http://www.unitedvanlines.com*.
5. Click the Save button on the Standard toolbar to save the Web page with the hyperlinks added.

Insert Hyperlink dialog box

Link to:	Text to display:	Atlas Van Lines		ScreenTip...

Step 2c

Type the file or Web page name:
http://www.atlasvanlines.com|

Or select from list:
- http://www.usps.gov/postofc
- http://www.alaska-air.com/
- http://www.usatoday.com/
- http://www.newsweek.com
- http://www.microsoft.com
- http://www.unitedvanlines.com/
- http://www.bekins.com/
- http://www.atlasvanlines.com/
- http://www.amazon.com
- http://www.time.com

Existing File or Web Page
Place in This Document
Create New Document
E-mail Address

Recent Files
Browsed Pages
Inserted Links

Browse for:
File...
Web Page...
Bookmark...

OK   Cancel

6. Jump to the hyperlink sites by completing the following steps:
   a. Click the hyperlink *Atlas Van Lines* that displays towards the end of the document.
   b. When the Atlas Van Lines Web page displays, scroll through the page, and then click on a hyperlink that interests you.
   c. After looking at this next page, click File and then Close.
   d. At the Beltway Web page document, click the hyperlink *Bekins*.
   e. After viewing the Bekins home page, click File and then Close.
   f. At the Beltway Web page document, click the hyperlink *United Van Lines*.
   g. After viewing the United Van Lines home page, click File and then Close.
7. Close the Beltway Web Page document.

Creating a Web Page Using the Web Page Wizard

Word provides a wizard that will help you prepare a Web page. To use the Web Page Wizard, click File and then New. At the New dialog box, click the Web Pages tab. At the New dialog box with the Web Pages tab selected, as shown in figure 7.19, double-click the *Web Page Wizard* icon. This displays the Web Page Wizard Start dialog box shown in figure 7.20. With the Web Page Wizard, you will choose a title and location for the page, specify and organize pages, and choose a visual theme for the page.

figure

7.19

New Dialog Box with Web Pages Tab Selected

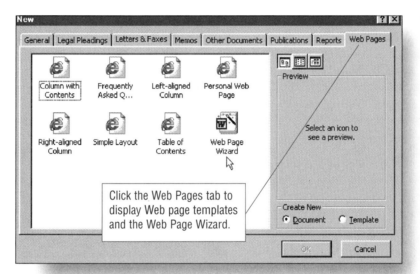

Click the Web Pages tab to display Web page templates and the Web Page Wizard.

figure

7.20

Web Page Wizard Short Dialog Box

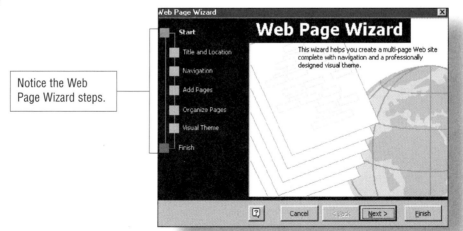

Notice the Web Page Wizard steps.

When using the Web Page Wizard, you will need to specify the location of the Web page document and related documents. In exercise 10, you will create a subfolder on the your data disk and then specify that subfolder as the location for the Web page documents.

Creating a Web Page Using the Web Page Wizard

1. Create a subfolder on your disk by completing the following steps:
   a. Display the Open dialog box.
   b. Make sure *Chapter 07* is the active folder on your disk.
   c. Click the Create New Folder button on the dialog box toolbar.
   d. At the New Folder dialog box, key **Web Pages** in the Name text box, and then click OK.
   e. Click the Cancel button to close the Open dialog box.
2. Create a Web page using the Web Page Wizard by completing the following steps:
   a. At a blank Word screen, click File and then New.
   b. At the New dialog box, click the Web Pages tab.
   c. At the New dialog box with the Web Pages tab selected, double-click the *Web Page Wizard* icon.
   d. At the Web Page Wizard Start dialog box, click the Next> button.

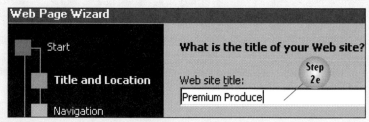

   e. At the Web Page Wizard Title and Location dialog box, key **Premium Produce** in the Web site title text box.
   f. Click the Next> button.
   g. At the Web Page Wizard Navigation dialog box, make sure Vertical frame is selected, and then click the Next> button.
   h. At the Web Page Wizard Add Pages dialog box, make the following changes:
      1) Click *Personal Web Page* in the Current pages in Web site list box and then click the Remove Page button.
      2) Click *Blank Page 2* in the Current pages in Web site list box and then click the Remove Page button.
      3) Click the Add Template Page button.
      4) At the Web Page Templates dialog box, double-click *Left-aligned Column* in the list box.
      5) At the Web Page Wizard Add Pages dialog box, click the Next> button.
   i. At the Web Page Wizard Organize Pages dialog box, click the Move Up button (to move *Left-aligned Column* above *Blank Page 1*), and then click the Next> button.

j. At the Web Page Wizard Visual Theme dialog box, choose a theme by completing the following steps:

   1) Click the Browse Themes button.

   2) At the Theme dialog box, scroll down the list of themes in the Choose a Theme list box until *Nature* is visible and then click *Nature*.

   3) Click OK to close the dialog box.

   4) At the Web Page Wizard Visual Theme dialog box, click the Next> button.

   k. At the Web Page Wizard Finish dialog box, click the Finish button. (If you are saving onto a disk, this may take some time.)

3. Format the Web page document by completing the following steps:

   a. Turn off the display of the Frames toolbar by clicking the Close button (contains an X) that displays in the upper right corner of the toolbar.

   b. Select the text *Main Heading Goes Here* and then key **Premium Produce**.

   c. Select the text (below the picture) *Captions goes here.* and then key **Premium Produce—Premium Flavor**. (To create the dash between Produce and Premium, key two hyphens. AutoCorrect will change the two hyphens to a dash when you press the space bar after keying Premium.)

   d. Insert a file from your data disk by completing the following steps:

      1) Select from the beginning of the text *Section Heading Goes Here* (the first occurrence of this text) to the end of the text in the document. (Make sure you do not select the picture or anything other than the text.)

      2) With the text selected, press the Delete key.

      3) Click Insert and then File.

      4) At the Insert File dialog box, click the Up One Level button to make *Chapter 07* the active folder, and then double-click the document named *Prem Pro Insert*.

   e. Insert a pricing table in the blank page by completing the following steps:

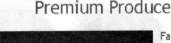

Premium Produce

Step 3b

Step 3d

Farm-fresh and Organic Produce

Premium Produce is your source for local, farm-fresh produce. All of our produce is organically grown without pesticides, herbicides or other sprays. We ship our produce daily to a

Step 3c

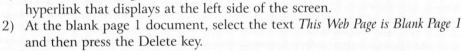

Premium Produce—Premium Flavor

      1) Click the *Blank Page 1* hyperlink that displays at the left side of the screen.

      2) At the blank page 1 document, select the text *This Web Page is Blank Page 1* and then press the Delete key.

      3) Click Insert and then File.

      4) At the Insert File dialog box, make sure *Chapter 07* is the active folder.

      5) Double-click *Prem Pro Pricing* in the list box. (This inserts the table into the blank page 1 document.)

      6) With the table inserted in the document, click the Save button on the Standard toolbar. (If you are saving onto a disk, this may take some time.)

   f. Return to the Premium Produce page by clicking the *Left-aligned Column* hyperlink that displays at the left side of the screen.

   g. Change the hyperlink text by completing the following steps:

      1) Select the *Left-aligned Column* hyperlink text and then key **Home**. (Make sure *Home* is underlined. If not, click the Undo button and try again.)

      2) Select the *Blank Page 1* hyperlink text and then key **Pricing**. (Make sure *Pricing* is underlined. If not, click the Undo button and try again.)

h. Display the pricing table by clicking the *Pricing* hyperlink.
  i. Return to the Premium Produce home page by clicking the *Home* hyperlink.
4. Save the Web document by clicking the Save button on the Standard toolbar. (This saves the document and names it *default*.)
5. Print and then close the document.

The Web Page Wizard specifies a folder and subfolders for Web page files. This is because a Web page generally consists of a variety of items that are inserted in individual files. For example, each bullet image and clip art image or picture in a Web page is saved in a separate image file. Inserting all of these files into folders makes it easier for you to take this information to another location. For example, you can copy the contents of a Web page folder and all its subfolders to another computer or onto a disk.

During the Web Page Wizard steps, a vertical frame was chosen. A frame in a Web page helps you organize information and make it easily accessible. When a single Web page is divided into sections that can display separate Web pages, each section is referred to as a frame. In exercise 10, your Web page contained two frames—the section at the left containing the hyperlinks and the section at the right containing the company home page information.

exercise 11

Viewing the Web Pages Folder

1. Display the Open dialog box.
2. If neccesary, change the Files of type option to All Files.
3. Display the contents of the *Web Pages* folder by completing the following steps:
    a. Make sure *Chapter 07* on your disk is the active folder.
    b. Double-click the *Web Pages* folder.
    c. At the *Web Pages* folder, double-click the *Premium Produce* folder.
    d. At the *Premium Produce* folder, notice the documents saved in this folder by the Web Page Wizard.
    e. Double-click the folder *Blank Page 1_files*.
    f. Notice the documents saved in this folder by the Web Page Wizard and then click the Up One Level button.
    g. At the *Premium Produce* folder, double-click the *Left-aligned Column_files* folder.
    h. Notice the documents saved in this folder by the Web Page Wizard and then click the Up One Level button.
    i. Click the Up One Level two more times. (This returns you to the *Chapter 07* folder.)
4. Close the Open dialog box.

chapter summary

- The Internet is a network of computers connected around the world allowing exchange of information.
- Word provides the ability to jump to the Internet from the Word document screen.
- The World Wide Web is the most commonly used application on the Internet and is a set of standards and protocols used to access information available on the Internet.
- A software program used to access the Web is referred to as a Web browser.
- To locate information on the World Wide Web you need a modem, browser software, and an Internet Service Provider account. An Internet Service Provider sells access to the Internet.
- A modem is a hardware device that carries data over telephone lines.
- Uniform Resource Locators (URLs) are the method used to identify locations on the Web.
- A Web page can contain hyperlinks. Click a link to connect to another site, location, or page.
- Use a search engine such as Yahoo, InfoSeek, or Excite to locate information on the Internet on a specific topic by keying a few words or a short phrase.
- Narrow a search by using search operators such as the plus symbol, minus symbol, quotation mark; or use Boolean operators such as AND, OR, and AND NOT.
- Add a site that you visit regularly to the Favorites list at the Internet Explorer Favorites side bar. You can also delete and organize favorite sites at the Favorites side bar.
- Click the History button on the Internet Explorer toolbar to display the History side bar. This side bar displays sites visited for the current day as well as two previous days and three previous weeks.
- Home pages are Web documents that describe a company, school, government, or individual and are created using a language called HyperText Markup Language (HTML).
- A home page can be created in Word and saved as a Web page, or you can create a Web page using the Web Page Wizard.
- When a document is saved as a Web page, Word automatically changes to the Web Layout view.
- Apply a theme to a Web page with options at the Theme dialog box.
- Preview a document in the default Web browser by clicking File, expanding the drop-down menu, and then clicking Web Page Preview.
- Apply a background color with options from the Background side menu.
- Apply a gradient, texture, or pattern to a Web page with options at the Fill Effects dialog box.
- Some theme formatting and background color, gradient, texture, and pattern do not print.
- The Web Tools toolbar contains buttons for customizing and designing a Web page.
- One method for creating a hyperlink is to select the text and then click the Insert Hyperlink button on the Standard toolbar. At the Insert Hyperlink dialog box, key the URL and then click OK.
- Start the Web Page Wizard by displaying the New dialog box, clicking the Web Pages tab, and then double-clicking the *Web Page Wizard* icon.

commands review

	Mouse
Display the Web toolbar	Click View, point to Toolbars, then click Web; or right-click any toolbar, then click Web at the drop-down menu
Display Internet Explorer Search Setup page	Click Search the Web button on the Web toolbar
Display the Favorites side bar	Click Favorites button on the Internet Explorer toolbar
Display the History side bar	Click History button on the Internet Explorer toolbar
Change to the Web Layout view	Click Web Layout View button at the left side of the horizontal scroll bar or click View and then Web Layout
Display the Theme dialog box	Click Format, expand the drop-down menu, and then click Theme
Web Page Preview	Click File, expand the drop-down menu, and then click Web Page Preview
Display the Background side menu	Click Format and then point to Background
Display Fill Effects dialog box	Click Format, point to Background, then click Fill Effects
Display Web Tools toolbar	Click View, point to Toolbars, then click Web Tools; or, right-click a toolbar and then click Web Tools at the drop-down list
Display the Insert Hyperlink dialog box	Click Insert Hyperlink button on the Standard toolbar
Display the New dialog box	Click File and then New

thinking offline

Completion: In the space provided at the right, indicate the correct term or command.

1. List three reasons why users access the Internet.

2. The word "modem" is derived from this.

3. The letters ISP stand for this.

4. This is the method used to identify locations on the Internet.

5. To search for information on the Web using a search engine, click this button on the Web toolbar.

6. Click this in a home page to link to another page or location.

7. Click this button on the Internet Explorer toolbar to display the previous Web page or location.

8. List at least three search engines that can be used to search for specific information on the Internet.

          _____

          _____

          _____

9. Click this button on the Internet Explorer toolbar to display a side bar containing a list of sites visited in the last few days, hours, or minutes.

          _____

10. A home page on the Web is created using this language.

          _____

11. When a document is saved as a Web page, the Web page displays in this view.

          _____

12. Use buttons on this toolbar to design and format a Web page.

          _____

13. Click File, expand the drop-down menu, and then click this option to display the currently open document in the default Web browser.

          _____

14. Click this button on the Standard toolbar to add a hypertext link to selected text.

          _____

In the space provided, list the text and operators you would use to complete the following searches using the Excite search engine.

1. Search for documents containing the words *better business bureau* in that sequence.

          _____

2. Search for documents containing *travel* but not *international*.

          _____

3. Search for documents containing *dolphins* or *porpoises*.

          _____

working hands-on

Assessment 1

1. Make sure you are connected to the Internet and then display the following sites:
   a. At a clear document screen, display the *USA Today* home page at http://www.usatoday.com.
   b. At the *USA Today* home page, find a section of the newspaper that interests you, find an article within that section, and then print the article.
   c. Display the Alaska Airlines home page at http://www.alaska-air.com.
   d. Search for flight departure times from Juneau, Alaska, to Orange County, California.
   e. Print the flight schedule.
   f. Display the United States Postal Service Web site at http://www.usps.gov/postofc.
   g. At the site, use hyperlinks to search for information on domestic postage rates, and then print the information.
2. Close Internet Explorer.

Assessment 2

1. Make sure you are connected to the Internet.
2. At a clear document screen, click the Search the Web button on the Toolbar.
3. At the Internet Explorer Search Setup page, complete the following searches:
   a. Use a search engine of your choosing to find information on bicycle racing.
   b. When the search engine displays a list of sites, scroll through the list, find a bicycle club that interests you, and then display the home page for the club.
   c. With the bicycle club home page displayed, print the page.
   d. Click the Back button until the Internet Explorer Search Setup page displays at the right side of the screen.
   e. Use a search engine of your choosing to find information on the White House.
   f. When the search engine displays a list of sites, scroll through the list, find a site that interests you, and then display the home page.
   g. With the home page displayed, print the page.
   h. Click the Back button until the Internet Explorer Search Setup page displays at the right side of the screen.
   i. Use a search engine of your choosing to find sites on kayaking in national parks.
   j. When the search engine displays a list of sites, find a national park site that interests you, display the site, and then print the page.
   k. Click the Back button until the Internet Explorer Search Setup page displays.
4. Close Internet Explorer.

Assessment 3

1. Open Apex Home Page.
2. Make the following changes to the document:
   a. Save the document as a Web page with the name Apex Web Page.
   b. Make the following formatting changes to the document:
      1) Apply a theme of your choosing to the document.
      2) Increase the font size of the company name, Web address, address, and telephone number.
      3) Select *Apple Computer* and then create a hyperlink to http://www.apple.com.
      4) Select *Blizzard Entertainment* and then create a hyperlink to http://www.blizzard.com.
      5) Select *id Software* and then create a hyperlink to http://www.idsoftware.com.
      6) Select *Microsoft Corporation* and then create a hyperlink to http://www.microsoft.com.
      7) Make sure the text for the home page fits on one page. (If it does not, delete some blank lines.)
3. Save the document again with the same name (Apex Web Page).
4. Print and then close Apex Web Page.

Assessment 4

1. Open Apex Web Page.
2. Save the document with Save As and name it Apex Background.
3. Make the following formatting changes to the document:
   a. Apply a background color and gradient of your choosing.
   b. Add the scrolling text *Apex Cyberware offers computer software at incredibly low prices!* somewhere in the document.
   c. Add a sound clip to the document.
   d. Preview the document in the default Web browser. (You may need to maximize the browser window.) After viewing the document, close the Web browser.
4. Save the document again with the same name (Apex Background).
5. Print and then close Apex Background.

Assessment 5

1. Some Web sites contain interactive pages where the viewer fills in information in various types of boxes and then submits the information to the Web site company. The Web Tools toolbar contains buttons for creating an interactive Web page with forms controls such as text boxes, check boxes, and option boxes. Use the Help feature to learn about Web form controls. (*Hint: Click the Office Assistant, key the question* What are Web form controls?, *and then click the Search button. At the list of items that displays, click* Form controls you can use on a Web page.) Continue using the Help to display information on the eleven standard form controls. Read specifically about the Checkbox control, Option Button control, and the Textbox control.
2. After reading the Help information on controls, complete the following steps:
   a. Create the document shown in figure 7.21. (Use Web Tools toolbar buttons to create the check boxes, option boxes, and text boxes.)
   b. Apply the same theme you applied to the Apex Web Page in assessment 4.
   c. After applying the theme, make sure spacing is correct.
3. Save the document and name it Apex Form.
4. Print and then close Apex Form. (Some of the theme formatting will not print.)

figure

7.21

Assessment 5

Top of Form

APEX CYBERWARE
http://www.apexcyber.com
540 Minor Avenue
Seattle, WA 98045
(206) 555-2233

Customer Name: [   ]

Address: [   ]

Company: [   ]

Have you ordered from Apex Cyberware in the past six months?   ◯ Yes   ◯ No

Please insert a check in the box next to software you are currently using on your computer:

☐ Education   ☐ Games

☐ Word processing   ☐ Spreadsheet

☐ Database   ☐ Presentation

☐ Scheduling   ☐ Money management

Bottom of Form

Performance Assessments

Unit 1 PA

WORD

ASSESSING CORE PROFICIENCIES

In this unit, you have learned to create, edit, format, save, print, and enhance Word documents; manage documents on disk; explore the Internet; and create and format Web pages.

(Before completing unit assessments, delete the Chapter 07 *folder on your disk. Next, copy the* Unit 1 PA *folder from the CD that accompanies this textbook to your disk and then make* Unit 1 PA *the active folder.)*

Assessment 1

1. At a clear document screen, key the text shown in figure U1.1.
2. Save the document and name it Unit 1, PA 01.
3. Print and then close Unit 1, PA 01.

GLOSSARY

Acoustical energy: A form of energy related to signals generated by some form of sound such as a voice.

Amplitude modulation (AM): A method of modifying the high to low ranges of a radio carrier wave according to the strength of the signal.

Analog signal: A continuously varying *electromagnetic wave* whose signal pattern changes based on the information being transmitted.

Asynchronous transmission: The transmission of data one character at a time through a method that denotes the beginning and end of each character; the devices used in sending and receiving the data are not synchronized for the transmission.

Attenuation: Decrease in the strength of a signal as it moves away from its source; the strength of the signal is generally measured in *decibels*, the method developed to measure the loudness of sound.

Figure U1.1 • Assessment 1

Assessment 2

1. Open Unit 1, PA 01.
2. Save the document with Save As and name it Unit 1, PA 02.
3. Make the following changes to the document:
   a. Change the top, left, and right margins to 1.5 inches.
   b. Select the paragraphs that begin with bolded words, change the paragraph alignment to justified, and then insert numbering.
   c. Select the entire document and then change the font to 12-point Century Schoolbook (or a similar serif typeface).
4. Save the document again with the same name (Unit 1, PA 02).
5. Print and then close Unit 1, PA 02.

Assessment 3

1. At a clear document screen, key the text shown in figure U1.2 with the following specifications:
   a. Change the font to 16-point Braggadocio and the color to dark blue. (If Braggadocio is not available, choose another font.)
   b. Animate the title *Telecommunications Seminar* with an animation effect of your choosing. (The animation effect will not print.)
   c. Change the line spacing to 1.5.
   d. Center the text vertically on the page.
2. Save the document and name it Unit 1, PA 03.
3. Print and then close Unit 1, PA 03.

Telecommunications Seminar

Thursday, March 15, 2001

Carson Convention Center

Room 108

8:30 a.m. - 4:30 p.m.

Figure U1.2 • Assessment 3

Assessment 4

1. At a clear document screen, key the text shown in figure U1.3 with the following specifications:
   a. Bold and center the title as shown.
   b. Determine the tab settings for the text in columns.

   c. Select the entire document and then change the font to 12-point Arial.
   d. Vertically center the text on the page.
2. Save the document and name it Unit 1, PA 04.
3. Print and then close Unit 1, PA 04.

INCOME BY DIVISION

	1997	1998	1999
Public Relations	$14,375	$16,340	$16,200
Database Services	9,205	15,055	13,725
Graphic Design	18,400	21,790	19,600
Technical Support	5,780	7,325	9,600

Figure U1.3 • Assessment 4

Assessment 5

1. At a clear document screen, key the text shown in figure U1.4 with the following specifications:
   a. Bold and center the title as shown.
   b. You determine the tab settings for the text in columns.
   c. Select the entire document and then change the font to 12-point Bookman Old Style (or a similar serif typeface).
   d. Vertically center the text on the page.
2. Save the document and name it Unit 1, PA 05.
3. Print and then close Unit 1, PA 05.

TABLE OF CONTENTS

Telecommunications Services 1

Telecommunications Facts and Figures 3

Technology in the Future 7

Electronic Mail and Messaging Systems 9

Cellular Mobile Telephone Technology 12

Local Area Networks 17

Figure U1.4 • Assessment 5

Assessment 6

1. Open Word Spell Check 04.
2. Save the document with Save As and name it Unit 1, PA 06.
3. Make the following changes to the document:
   a. Complete a spelling check and a grammar check on the document. (You determine what to edit and what to leave as written.)
   b. Select the document and then change the font to 12-point Century Schoolbook (or a similar serif typeface).
   c. Set the title in 14-point Century Schoolbook bold.
   d. Select the paragraphs in the body of the document (excluding the title), and then indent the first line of each paragraph 0.5 inches and change the paragraph alignment to justified.
   e. Proofread the document. (There are errors that are not selected by the spelling or grammar checker.)
4. Save the document again with the same name (Unit 1, PA 06).
5. Print and then close Unit 1, PA 06.

Assessment 7

1. At a clear document screen, create an envelope with the text shown in figure U1.5.
2. Save the envelope document and name it Unit 1, PA 07.
3. Print and then close Unit 1, PA 07.

Mrs. Eileen Hebert
15205 East 42nd Street
Lake Charles, LA 71098

Mr. Earl Robicheaux
1436 North Sheldon Street
Jennings, LA 70542

Figure U1.5 • Assessment 7

Assessment 8

1. Create mailing labels with the name and address for Mrs. Eileen Hebert shown in figure U1.5 using the Avery standard, 5660 – Address label.
2. Save the document and name it Unit 1, PA 08.
3. Print and then close Unit 1, PA 08.

1. Create a document by copying text from another document by completing the following steps:
   a. Key the title **KEY LIFE HEALTH PLAN** bolded and centered.
   b. Press Enter twice and then key the subtitle **Plan Information** bolded and centered.
   c. Press Enter three times, turn off bold, and return the paragraph alignment to left.
   d. Save the document and name it Unit 1, PA 09.
   e. With Unit 1, PA 09 still open, open the document named Key Life Health Plan.
   f. With Key Life Health Plan the active document, select the second heading *HOW THE PLAN WORKS* and the three paragraphs of text below this heading, and then copy and paste it at the end of the Unit 1, PA 09 document.
   g. Make Key Life Health Plan the active document. Select the first heading *PLAN HIGHLIGHTS* and the six paragraphs of text below this heading and then copy and paste the selected text at the end of the Unit 1, PA 09 document.
   h. Make Key Life Health Plan the active document. Select the fourth heading *PROVIDER NETWORK* and the two paragraphs of text below this heading and then copy and paste it to the end of the Unit 1, PA 09 document.
   i. Make Key Life Health Plan the active document. Select the third heading *QUALITY ASSESSMENT* and the six paragraphs of text below this heading (two paragraphs and four bulleted paragraphs) and then copy and paste it at the end of the Unit 1, PA 09 document.
2. Close Key Life Health Plan. (If you are asked if you want to save the changes, click No.)
3. Make the following changes to Unit 1, PA 09:
   a. Change the top margin to 1.5 inches and the left and right margins to 1 inch.
   b. Set the entire document in 12-point Century Schoolbook (or a similar serif typeface).
   c. Set the title and subtitle in 16-point Arial bold.
   d. Set the following headings in 14-point Arial bold: *(Hint: Use Format Painter.)*
      HOW THE PLAN WORKS
      PLAN HIGHLIGHTS
      PROVIDER NETWORK
      QUALITY ASSESSMENT
   e. Check the spacing in the document. There should only be a double space above and below headings (except between the subtitle and the first heading—that should be a triple space) and between paragraphs. If there are extra blank lines, delete them.

f. Insert a footer in the document that prints Key Life Health Plan set in 12-point Century Schoolbook bold at the left margin and prints the page number in bold at the right margin.
4. Save the document again with the same name (Unit 1, PA 09).
5. Print and then close Unit 1, PA 09.

Assessment 10

1. Open Unit 1, PA 09.
2. Save the document with Save As and name it Unit 1, PA 10.
3. Make the following changes to the document:
   a. Delete the footer.
   b. Select the entire document and then change line spacing to 1.2. (To do this, display the Paragraph dialog box, key **1.2** in the At text box, and then close the dialog box. This should increase the size of the document to three pages. If your document is not three pages in length, consider increasing the line spacing to *1.3*.)
   c. Create the header Key Life Health Plan that is set in 12-point Century Schoolbook bold and prints at the right margin on every page except the first page.
   d. Move the insertion point to the end of the document, a double-space below the text in the document and then insert the following:
      Key Life Health Plan®
      Prepared by Daria Caráquez
4. Save the document again with the same name (Unit 1, PA 10).
5. Print and then close Unit 1, PA 10.

Assessment 11

1. Open Unit 1, PA 09.
2. Save the document with Save As and name it Unit 1, PA 11.
3. Make the following changes to the document:
   a. Change the top margin to 1 inch.
   b. Delete the footer.
   c. Search for all occurrences of *Key Life Health Plan* and replace with Premium Health Care Plan.
   d. Insert a continuous section break at the beginning of the heading *HOW THE PLAN WORKS*.
   e. Format the text (below the section break) into two evenly spaced newspaper columns with a line between.
4. Save the document again with the same name (Unit 1, PA 11).
5. Print only the first page of the document.
6. Close Unit 1, PA 11.

Assessment 12

1. Open Word Report 04.
2. Save the document with Save As and name it Unit 1, PA 12.
3. Make the following changes to the document:
   a. Change to the Outline view.
   b. Promote or demote text to the headings specified below:

CHAPTER 1: COMPUTER INPUT DEVICES	= Heading 1
Keyboard	= Heading 2
Mouse	= Heading 2
Trackball	= Heading 2
Touch Pad and Touch Screen	= Heading 2
CHAPTER 2: COMPUTER OUTPUT DEVICES	= Heading 1
Monitor	= Heading 2
Printer	= Heading 2

   c. Change to the Print Layout view.
   d. Change the top margin to 1.5 inches.
   e. Insert a page break at the beginning of *CHAPTER 2: COMPUTER OUTPUT DEVICES*.
   f. Create the footer Computer Input and Output Devices that is bolded and prints at the right margin on all odd pages.
   g. Create a footer that inserts the filename and path at the left margin on all even pages.
4. Save the document again with the same name (Unit 1, PA 12).
5. Print pages 2 through 4 of the document.
6. Close Unit 1, PA 12.

Assessment 13

1. At a clear document screen, create the table shown in figure U1.6 with the following specifications:
   a. The width of the first column is 1.8 and the width of the second and third columns is 1.4.
   b. Insert the bold, center, and alignment formatting as shown in the figure.
   c. Include the border lines and shading as shown in the figure.
   d. Center the table horizontally.
   e. After creating the table, insert the formula =SUM(ABOVE) to calculate the amounts in the *First Half* column and the *Second Half* column.
2. Save the document and name it Unit 1, PA 13.
3. Print and then close Unit 1, PA 13.

McCORMACK FUNDS		
BALANCE SHEET		
Asset	**First Half**	**Second Half**
Bonds	$41,300,225.50	$45,100,670.00
Stocks	8,924,600.25	9,340,155.80
Mortgages	75,302,210.55	67,210,550.00
Real Estate	13,450,305.45	20,193,553.75
Long-term Investments	1,340,690.90	945,392.00
Short-term Investments	631,405.55	803,288.35
Other Assets	341,395.25	442,890.20
Total		

Figure U1.6 • Assessment 13

Assessment 14

1. At a clear document screen, create a table using the information shown in figure U1.7 with the following specifications:
   a. Insert formulas in the Difference column that calculate the difference between Class B and Class A funds.
   b. Apply an autoformat of your choosing to the table.
2. Save the document and name it Unit 1, PA 14.
3. Print and then close Unit 1, PA 14.

STRATEGIC INCOME FUND

	Class A	**Class B**	**Difference**
Expenses after 1 year	$ 56.25	$ 68.30	
Expenses after 3 years	85.10	93.00	
Expenses after 5 years	102.75	110.50	
Expenses after 10 years	178.00	220.15	

Figure U1.7 • Assessment 14

Assessment 15

1. Make sure you are connected to the Internet.
2. At a clear document screen in Word, click the Search the Web button on the toolbar.

3. At the Internet Explorer Search Setup page, complete the following searches.
   a. Search for information on endangered species but not fish or birds. (You determine the search engine.)
   b. Scroll through the list of sites and display a site that interests you. Read the information on the home page and then print the home page.
   c. Search for sailing clubs in the San Diego area. (You determine the search engine.)
   d. Display a home page for a sailing club in San Diego and then print the home page.
   e. Display one other home page for a sailing club in San Diego and then print that home page.
4. Close Internet Explorer.

Assessment 16

1. Open Goldburg Home Page.
2. Save the document as a Web page and name it Goldburg Web Page.
3. Make the following changes to the document:
   a. Apply the Heading 1 style to the name *DEVIN M. GOLDBURG*.
   b. Select the street address; city, state, and Zip code; and telephone number and then complete the following steps:
      1) Apply the Heading 2 style.
      2) Change the spacing before paragraphs to 3 points (leave the spacing after at 3 points).
   c. Apply the Heading 3 style to the following headings:
      Career Objective
      Education
      Work Experience
      Hobbies and Interests
      Relocation
   d. Apply a theme of your choosing to the document.
   e. Add scrolling text to the document. (You determine the text as well as the location.)
   f. Insert a sound clip of your choosing in the document.
   g. Create the following hyperlinks:
      1) Select the text *Albuquerque Technical Vocational Institute* in the *Work Experience* section of the document and link it to the URL http://www.tvi.cc.nm.us.
      2) Select the text *Presbyterian Healthcare Services* in the *Work Experience* section of the document and link it to the URL http://www.phs.org.
4. Save the document again with the same name (Goldburg Web Page).
5. Print and then close Goldburg Web Page.

WRITING ACTIVITIES

The following activities give you the opportunity to practice your writing skills along with demonstrating an understanding of some of the important Word features you have mastered in this unit. Follow the steps explained below to improve your writing skills.

The Writing Process

Plan Gather ideas, select which information to include, and choose the order in which to present the information.

   Checkpoints
- What is the purpose?
- What information do the readers need to reach your intended conclusion?

Write Following the information plan and keeping the reader in mind, draft the document using clear, direct sentences that say what you mean.

   Checkpoints
- What are the subpoints for each main thought?
- How can you connect paragraphs so the reader moves smoothly from one idea to the next?

Revise Improve what is written by changing, deleting, rearranging, or adding words, sentences, and paragraphs.

   Checkpoints
- Is the meaning clear?
- Do the ideas follow a logical order?
- Have you included any unnecessary information?
- Have you built your sentences around strong nouns and verbs?

Edit Check spelling, sentence construction, word use, punctuation, and capitalization.

   Checkpoints
- Can you spot any redundancies or cliches?
- Can you reduce any phrases to an effective word (for example, change *the fact that* to *because*)?
- Have you used commas only where there is a strong reason for doing so?
- Did you proofread the document for errors that your spell checker cannot identify?

Publish Prepare a final copy that could be reproduced and shared with others.

   Checkpoints
- Which design elements—for example, bolding and different fonts— would help highlight important ideas or sections?
- Would charts or other graphics help clarify meaning?

Use correct grammar, appropriate word choices, and clear sentence constructions.

Activity 1

Use Word's Help feature to learn about grammar and writing style options. Learn what options are available and the steps to display the options. Once you have determined this information, compose a memo to your instructor using the Contemporary Memo template. In the memo, explain grammar and writing style options and specifically describe at least two options. Also include in this memo, the steps required to change grammar and writing style options. Save the completed memo and name it Unit 1, Act 01. Print and then close Unit 1, Act 01.

Activity 2

Prepare a Web page résumé for yourself using the Web page résumé you formatted in Assessment 16 as a guide. Try to include as much information about yourself as possible. If there are any hyperlinks you can create, include those in your résumé. When completed, save the résumé Web page and name it Unit 1, Act 02. Print and then close Unit 1, Act 02.

INTERNET ACTIVITY

The Internet is made up of thousands of connecting networks, millions of computers, people from over 150 countries, and unlimited information and resources. Connect to the Internet and use this information resource to search for information on a specific hobby that interests you. Suggestions include collecting, antiques, sports, music, drama, gardening, travel, sailing, flying, etc. Find out as much information as you can about the hobby you choose. When you are done researching the hobby, create a Word document that describes the search process. Include the following information:

- The steps you completed to find Web sites containing information on your specific hobby.
- The types of resources available for your hobby (e.g., magazines, clubs, companies, retailers).
- Your favorite Web site for the hobby including the URL and a description of the site.

Include any other additional information to describe your search. Apply formatting to enhance the Word document. When the document is completed, save it and name it Unit 1, Internet Act. Print and then close Unit 1, Internet Act.

Excel

UNIT TWO

MICROSOFT® EXCEL 2000

CORE LEVEL MOUS SKILLS

Coding No.	SKILL	Pages
XL2000.1	**Working with cells**	
XL2000.1.1	Use Undo and Redo	401-402
XL2000.1.2	Clear cell content	386-387
XL2000.1.3	Enter text, dates, and numbers	338-341, 344-345
XL2000.1.4	Edit cell content	342, 349, 351
XL2000.1.5	Go to a specific cell	338-339
XL2000.1.6	Insert and delete selected cells	345-347, 384-387
XL2000.1.7	Cut, copy, paste, paste special and move selected cells, use the Office Clipboard	416-418, 488-490
XL2000.1.8	Use Find and Replace	402-404
XL2000.1.9	Clear cell formats	386-387
XL2000.1.10	Work with series (AutoFill)	339, 341, 352, 354
XL2000.1.11	Create hyperlinks	439-441
XL2000.2	**Working with files**	
XL2000.2.1	Use Save	342, 345
XL2000.2.2	Use Save As (different name, location, format)	342, 343, 438, 440, 448-450
XL2000.2.3	Locate and open an existing workbook	343
XL2000.2.4	Create a folder	439-440
XL2000.2.5	Use templates to create a new workbook	442-451
XL2000.2.6	Save a worksheet/workbook as a Web Page	343, 438, 440
XL2000.2.7	Send a workbook via email	441-442
XL2000.2.8	Use the Office Assistant	374-375
XL2000.3	**Formatting worksheets**	
XL2000.3.1	Apply font styles (typeface, size, color and styles)	365-366
XL2000.3.2	Apply number formats (currency, percent, dates, comma)	357-362
XL2000.3.3	Modify size of rows and columns	351-357
XL2000.3.4	Modify alignment of cell content	362-364
XL2000.3.5	Adjust the decimal place	358-362
XL2000.3.6	Use the Format Painter	431-432
XL2000.3.7	Apply autoformat	372-374
XL2000.3.8	Apply cell borders and shading	366-372
XL2000.3.9	Merging cells	362-364
XL2000.3.10	Rotate text and change indents	362-364
XL2000.3.11	Define, apply, and remove a style	432-438
XL2000.4	**Page setup and printing**	
XL2000.4.1	Preview and print worksheets & workbooks	343-344, 347-350, 418-420
XL2000.4.2	Use Web Page Preview	438, 440
XL2000.4.3	Print a selection	344, 351
XL2000.4.4	Change page orientation and scaling	388-391
XL2000.4.5	Set page margins and centering	392-394
XL2000.4.6	Insert and remove a page break	394-396
XL2000.4.7	Set print, and clear a print area	399-400
XL2000.4.8	Set up headers and footers	389-392
XL2000.4.9	Set print titles and options (gridlines, print quality, row & column headings)	396-400
XL2000.5	**Working with worksheets & workbooks**	
XL2000.5.1	Insert and delete rows and columns	383-387
XL2000.5.2	Hide and unhide rows and columns	399-400
XL2000.5.3	Freeze and unfreeze rows and columns	421-424
XL2000.5.4	Change the zoom setting	348, 350
XL2000.5.5	Move between worksheets in a workbook	419-420
XL2000.5.6	Check spelling	401-402
XL2000.5.7	Rename a worksheet	420-421
XL2000.5.8	Insert and Delete worksheets	418-421
XL2000.5.9	Move and copy worksheets	420-421
XL2000.5.10	Link worksheets & consolidate data using 3D References	488-491
XL2000.6	**Working with formulas & functions**	
XL2000.6.1	Enter a range within a formula by dragging	466-467, 491
XL2000.6.2	Enter formulas in a cell and using the formula bar	462-463
XL2000.6.3	Revise formulas	482
XL2000.6.4	Use references (absolute and relative)	464, 485-487
XL2000.6.5	Use AutoSum	462-463
XL2000.6.6	Use Paste Function to insert a function	468-481
XL2000.6.7	Use basic functions (AVERAGE, SUM, COUNT, MIN, MAX)	469-474
XL2000.6.8	Enter functions using the formula palette	469
XL2000.6.9	Use date functions (NOW and DATE)	480-481
XL2000.6.10	Use financial functions (FV and PMT)	474-480
XL2000.6.11	Use logical functions (IF)	481-483
XL2000.7	**Using charts and objects**	
XL2000.7.1	Preview and print charts	509-510
XL2000.7.2	Use chart wizard to create a chart	505-509, 518
XL2000.7.3	Modify charts	511-528
XL2000.7.4	Insert, move, and delete an object (picture)	533-538, 546-547
XL2000.7.5	Create and modify lines and objects	538, 542-543, 547-560 (Maps)

Chapter 08

Preparing and Formatting an Excel Worksheet

8

PERFORMANCE OBJECTIVES

Upon successful completion of chapter 8, you will be able to:
- Identify the various elements of an Excel worksheet.
- Create, save, and print a worksheet.
- Enter data in a worksheet.
- Edit data in a worksheet.
- Select cells in a worksheet.
- Apply formatting to data in cells.
- Change column widths and row heights.
- Format numbers in a worksheet.
- Add borders, shading, and patterns to cells in a worksheet.
- Apply an autoformat to selected cells in a worksheet.

In chapter 6, you learned about Word's Table feature. Many features in a table are similar to an Excel spreadsheet. Just as you learned to enter and edit data in cells, format cells, and calculate formulas in cells, in this chapter you will learn to perform the same functions in an Excel spreadsheet.

Many companies use a spreadsheet for numerical and financial data and to analyze and evaluate information. An Excel spreadsheet can be used for such activities as creating financial statements, preparing budgets, managing inventory, and analyzing cash flow. In addition, numbers and values can be easily manipulated to create "what if" situations. For example, using a spreadsheet, a person in a company can ask questions such as "What if the value in this category is decreased?" "How would that change affect the department budget?" Questions like these can be easily answered in an Excel spreadsheet. Change the value in a category and Excel will recalculate formulas for the other values. In this way, a spreadsheet can be used not only for creating financial statements or budgets but also as a planning tool.

Creating a Worksheet

Open Excel by clicking the Start button at the left side of the Taskbar, pointing to *Programs*, and then clicking *Microsoft Excel*. When Excel is opened, you are presented with a blank worksheet in a screen like the one shown in figure 8.1. The elements of a blank Excel worksheet are described in figure 8.2.

On your screen, the Standard and Formatting toolbars may display side by side with only a portion of the buttons visible. If this is the case, move the Formatting toolbar below the Standard toolbar by completing the following steps:

1. Click Tools and then Customize.
2. At the Customize dialog box, click the Options tab. (Skip this step if the Options tab is already selected.)
3. Click the Standard and Formatting toolbars share one row option. (This removes the check mark.)
4. Click the Close button to close the dialog box.

The display of the Standard and Formatting toolbars (as well as other toolbars) can be turned on or off. To do this, position the mouse pointer anywhere on a toolbar, and then click the *right* mouse button. At the drop-down menu that displays, click the toolbar name you want turned on or off. You can also turn on or off the display of a toolbar by clicking View on the Menu bar, pointing to Toolbars, and then clicking the toolbar name.

figure 8.1

Blank Excel Worksheet

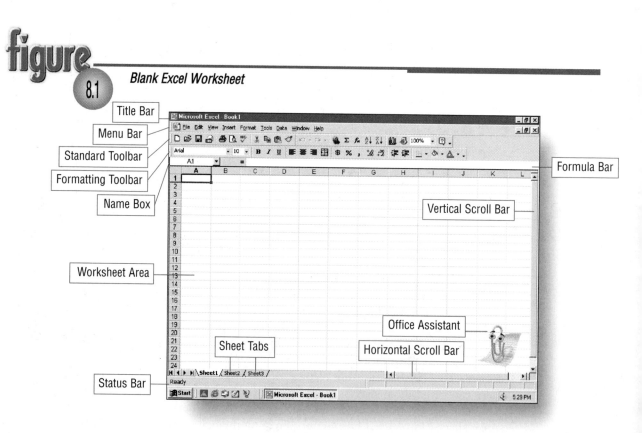

figure
8.2

Elements of an Excel Worksheet

Title bar:	The Title bar displays the name of the program along with the name of a workbook. The buttons at the far right side of the Title bar can be used to minimize, restore, or close Excel.
Menu bar:	Excel commands are grouped into related functions and placed on the Menu bar. For example, options for formatting cells, rows, or columns are grouped in the F<u>o</u>rmat option on the Menu bar.
Standard toolbar:	Icons for the most common commands in Excel are placed on the Standard toolbar.
Formatting toolbar:	Functions that are used to format elements of a worksheet are placed on buttons on the Formatting toolbar.
Name box:	The cell address, also called the cell reference, displays in the Name box and includes the column letter and row number.
Formula bar:	The Formula bar provides information about the active cell. Formulas can be entered and edited in the Formula bar.
Sheet tabs:	The sheet tabs identify the current worksheet. The tab for the active worksheet displays with a white background while the inactive worksheets display with a gray background (the background color may vary depending on the Windows color scheme).
Scroll bars:	A vertical scroll bar displays at the right side of the worksheet, and a horizontal scroll bar displays at the bottom of the Worksheet. These scroll bars are used to navigate within a worksheet.
Status bar:	The Status bar is located below the horizontal scroll bar and displays information about the worksheet and the currently active cell.
Worksheet area:	The worksheet area is a collection of cells where information such as labels, values, or formulas is entered. A cell is an intersection between a row and a column.

A document created in Excel is referred to as a *workbook*. An Excel workbook consists of individual worksheets (or *sheets*) like the sheets of paper in a notebook. Notice the tabs located toward the bottom of the Excel window that are named *Sheet1*, *Sheet2*, and so on. The area containing the gridlines in the Excel window is called the *worksheet area*. Figure 8.3 identifies the elements of the worksheet area. Create a worksheet in the worksheet area that will be saved as part of a workbook. Columns in a worksheet are labeled with letters of the alphabet, and rows are numbered.

figure
8.3

Elements of a Worksheet Area

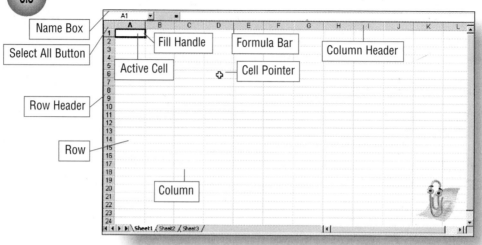

Name Box

Select All Button

Fill Handle

Formula Bar

Column Header

Active Cell

Cell Pointer

Row Header

Row

Column

The gray vertical and horizontal lines that define the cells in the worksheet area are called *gridlines*. When the insertion point (which displays as a thick white plus sign) is positioned in a cell, the *cell address*, also called the *cell reference*, displays at the left side of the Formula bar in what is called the *Name box*. The cell reference includes the column letter and row number. For example, if the insertion point is positioned in the first cell of the worksheet, the cell reference *A1* displays in the Name box located at the left side of the Formula bar. In a worksheet, the cell containing the insertion point is considered the *active cell*. The active cell is surrounded by a thick black border.

To make a cell active, position the cell pointer in the cell, and then click the left mouse button.

Hint

Entering Data in a Cell

Enter data such as a heading, number, or value, in a cell. To enter data in a cell, make the desired cell active, and then key the data. To move the insertion point to the next cell in the worksheet, press the Tab key. Other commands for moving the insertion point within a worksheet are displayed in figure 8.4.

figure
8.4

Commands for Moving Insertion Point in a Worksheet

To move the insertion point here	Press
Down to the next cell	Enter
Up to the next cell	Shift + Enter
Next cell	Tab
Previous cell	Shift + Tab
Cell at beginning of row	Home
Next cell in the direction of the arrow	Up, down, left, or right arrow keys
Last cell in worksheet	Ctrl + End

First cell in worksheet	Ctrl + Home
Cell in next window (approximately 16-24 rows)	Page Down
Cell in previous window (approximately 16-24 rows)	Page Up
Cell in window to right (approximately 8-11 columns)	Alt + Page Down
Cell in window to left (approximately 8-11 columns)	Alt + Page Up

Another method for moving the insertion point to a specific cell is to use the Go To feature. To use this feature, click Edit and then Go To. At the Go To dialog box, key the cell reference in the Reference text box, and then click OK.

When you are ready to key data into the active cell, check the Status bar. The word *Ready* should display at the left side. As data is being keyed in the cell, the word *Ready* changes to *Enter*. Data being keyed in a cell displays in the cell as well as in the Formula bar. If the data being keyed is longer than the cell can accommodate, the data overlaps the next cell to the right (it does not become a part of the next cell—it simply overlaps it). You will learn how to change column widths to accommodate data later in this chapter.

If the data you enter in a cell consists of text and the text does not fit into the cell, it overlaps the next cell. If, however, you enter a number in a cell, specify it as a number (rather than text) and the number is too long to fit in the cell, Excel changes the display of the number to number symbols *(###)*. This is because Excel does not want you to be misled by a number when you see only a portion of it in the cell.

In addition to moving the insertion point with the keyboard, you can also move it using the mouse. To make a specific cell active with the mouse, position the mouse pointer, which displays as a white plus sign (called the *cell pointer*), on the desired cell, and then click the left mouse button. The cell pointer displays as a white plus sign when positioned in a cell in the worksheet and displays as an arrow pointer when positioned on other elements of the Excel window such as toolbars or scroll bars.

Scroll through a worksheet using the vertical and/or horizontal scroll bars. Use the mouse on these scroll bars as you learned to do in a Word document. Scrolling shifts the display of cells in the worksheet area but does not change the active cell. Scroll through a worksheet until the desired cell is visible and then click the desired cell.

Using Automatic Entering Features

Excel contains several features that help you enter data into cells quickly and efficiently. These features include *AutoComplete*, which automatically inserts data in a cell that begins the same as a previous entry; *AutoCorrect*, which automatically corrects many common typographical errors; and *AutoFill*, which will automatically insert words, numbers, or formulas in a series.

Use the Go To dialog box to move to a specific cell.

If a cell entry displays as ##### or as a scientific notation (such as 2.35E+08), the column width is too narrow to display the entire entry.

Drag the vertical scroll box in a worksheet and row numbers display in a yellow box. Drag the horizontal scroll box and letters display.

The AutoComplete feature will automatically insert data in a cell that begins the same as a previous entry. For example, in exercise 1, you will key the name *Roger Bellamy* in a cell. Later you will key the name *Robert Jorgenson* in a cell. As you key the *R* in *Robert*, the AutoComplete feature will automatically insert *Roger Bellamy*. Since this is not the data you want in the cell, simply continue keying the correct name and it will take the place of the data inserted by AutoComplete. This feature can be very useful in a worksheet that contains repetitive data entries. For example, consider a worksheet that repeats the word *Payroll*. The second and subsequent times this word is to be inserted in a cell, simply keying the letter *P* will cause AutoComplete to insert the entire word.

While working in Word, you learned about the AutoCorrect feature. This feature automatically corrects many common typing (keying) errors. Excel contains the same AutoCorrect feature. To see what symbols and words are in the AutoCorrect feature, click Tools and then AutoCorrect. This displays the AutoCorrect dialog box shown in figure 8.5 with a list box containing the replacement data.

figure
8.5
AutoCorrect Dialog Box

Key the text displayed in the first column and then press the space bar. The text is replaced by text displayed in the second column.

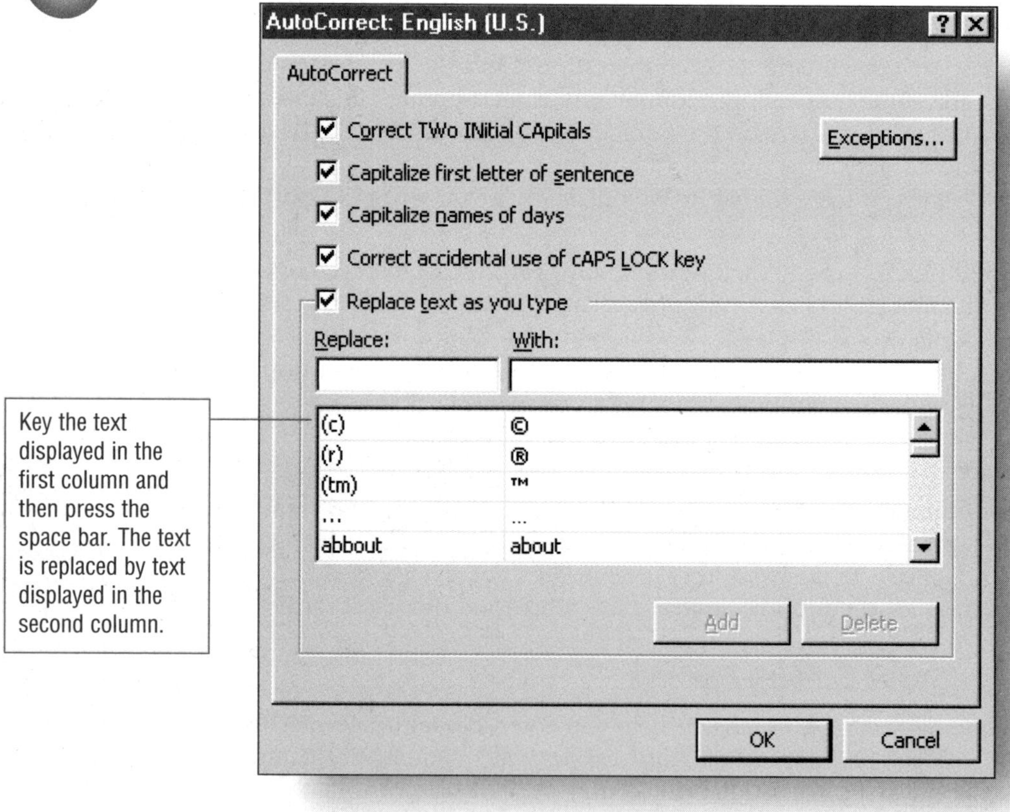

At the AutoCorrect dialog box, key the text shown in the first column in the list box, and the text in the second column is inserted in the cell. Along with symbols, the AutoCorrect dialog box contains commonly misspelled words and common typographical errors. The AutoCorrect feature is a helpful tool when entering text in cells.

When a cell is active, it is surrounded by a thick, black border. A small, black square is located at the bottom right side of this border. This black square is called the AutoFill *fill handle* (see figure 8.3). With the fill handle, you can quickly fill a range of cells with the same data or with consecutive data. For example, suppose you need to insert the year 2000 in consecutive cells. To do this quickly, key 2000 in the first cell, position the mouse pointer on the fill handle, hold down the left mouse button, drag across the cells where you want the year inserted, and then release the mouse button.

You can also use the AutoFill fill handle to insert a series in consecutive cells. For example, suppose you are creating a worksheet with data for all the months in the year. Key **January** in the first cell, position the mouse pointer on the fill handle, hold down the left mouse button, drag down or across to 11 more cells, and then release the mouse button. Excel automatically inserts the other eleven months in the year in the proper order. When using the fill handle, the cells must be adjacent. Figure 8.6 identifies the sequence inserted in cells by Excel when specific data is entered.

figure

8.6 *AutoFill Fill Handle Series*

Enter this data *(Commas represent data in separate cells.)*	And the AutoFill fill handle will insert this sequence in adjacent cells
January	February, March, April, etc…
Jan	Feb, Mar, Apr, etc…
Jan 98, Jan 99	Jan-98, Jan-99, Jan-00, Jan-01, etc…
Monday	Tuesday, Wednesday, Thursday, etc…
Product 1	Product 2, Product 3, Product 4, etc…
Qtr 1	Qtr 2, Qtr 3, Qtr 4
2, 4	6, 8, 10, etc…

Certain sequences, such as *2, 4* and *Jan 98, Jan 99* require that both cells be selected before using the fill handle. If only the cell containing *2* is active, the fill handle will insert *2*s in the selected cells. The list in figure 8.6 is only a sampling of what the AutoFill fill handle can do. You may find a variety of other sequences that can be inserted in a worksheet using the AutoFill fill handle.

If you do not want a series to increment, hold down the Ctrl key while dragging the fill handle.

Hint

Editing Data in a Cell

Edit data being keyed in a cell by pressing the Backspace key to delete the character left of the insertion point or pressing the Delete key to delete the character to the right of the insertion point. To change the data in a cell, click the cell once to make it active, and then key the new data. When a cell containing data is active, anything keyed will take the place of the existing data. If you want to edit only a portion of the data in a cell, double-click the cell. This makes the cell active, moves the insertion point inside the cell, and displays the word *Edit* at the left side of the Status bar. Move the insertion point using the arrow keys or the mouse and then make the needed corrections. If you are using the keyboard, you can press the Home key to move the insertion point to the first character in the cell or Formula bar, or press the End key to move the insertion point to the last character.

When you are done editing the data in the cell, be sure to change out of the *Edit* mode. To do this, make another cell active. You can do this by pressing Enter, Tab, or Shift + Tab. You can also change out of the *Edit* mode and return to the *Ready* mode by clicking another cell or the Enter button on the Formula bar.

Enter

If the active cell does not contain data, the Formula bar displays only the cell reference (by column letter and row number). As data is being keyed in a cell, the two buttons shown in figure 8.7 display on the Formula bar to the right of the name box. Click the Cancel button to delete the current cell entry. You can also delete the cell entry by pressing the Esc key. Click the Enter button to indicate that you are done keying or editing the cell entry. When you click the Enter button on the Formula bar, the word *Enter* (or *Edit*) located at the left side of the Status bar changes to *Ready*.

Cancel

8.7

Buttons on the Formula Bar

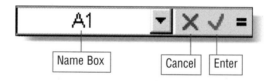

Name Box

Cancel   Enter

Save

Saving a Workbook

Save an Excel workbook, which may consist of a worksheet or several worksheets, by clicking the Save button on the Standard toolbar or clicking File and then Save. At the Save As dialog box, key a name for the workbook in the File name list box, and then press Enter or click Save. A workbook file name, like a Word file name, can contain up to 255 characters, including drive letter and any folder names, and can include spaces. Some symbols cannot be used in a file name. Refer to chapter 1 for a listing of these symbols.

Ctrl + S is the keyboard command to display the Save As dialog box.

To save an Excel workbook onto a disk, change to drive A (or the drive where the disk is located) before saving the workbook. You can do this at the Save As dialog box by clicking the down-pointing triangle at the right side of the Save in text box and then clicking *3½ Floppy (A:)* at the drop-down menu.

Saving an Excel Workbook as a Web Page

An Excel workbook can be saved in HTML format and made available for publishing on the Internet or on an intranet. The advantage to saving an Excel workbook as a Web page is that users can have access to the workbook data without having Excel installed. All a user needs to view the Excel Web page is a Web browser and access to the Internet or an intranet.

To save an Excel workbook as a Web page, open the desired workbook, then click File, and then Save as Web Page. At the Save As dialog box, key a name for the Excel Web page and then press Enter or click Save

Opening a Workbook

Open an Excel workbook by displaying the Open dialog box and then double-clicking the desired workbook name. Display the Open dialog box by clicking the Open button on the Standard toolbar or by clicking File and then Open.

Printing a Workbook

To print an Excel workbook, open the workbook you want printed, and then click the Print button on the Standard toolbar. This prints the active worksheet in the workbook. If you want more control over printing, click File and then Print to display the Print dialog box shown in figure 8.8.

Open

Ctrl + O is the keyboard command to display the Open dialog box.

Print

Ctrl + P is the keyboard command to display the Print dialog box.

figure
8.8

Print Dialog Box

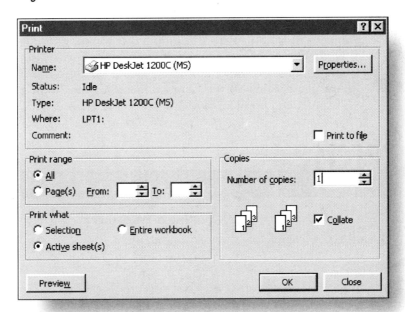

At the Print dialog box, the currently selected printer name displays in the Name text box. If other printers are installed, click the down-pointing triangle at the right side of the Name text box to display a list of printers.

The Active sheet(s) option in the Print what section is selected by default. At this setting, the currently active worksheet will print. If you want to print an entire workbook that contains several worksheets, click Entire workbook in the Print what section. Click the Selection option in the Print what section to print the currently selected cells.

If you want more than one copy of a worksheet or workbook printed, change to the desired number of copies with the Number of copies option in the Copies section. If you want the copies printed collated, make sure there is a check mark in the Collate check box in the Copies section.

A worksheet within a workbook can contain more than one page. If you want to print specific pages of a worksheet within a workbook, click Pages) in the Print range section, and then specify the desired page numbers in the From and To text boxes.

If you want to preview the worksheet before printing, click the Preview button that displays at the bottom left corner of the dialog box. This displays the worksheet as it will appear on the printed page. After viewing the worksheet, click the Close button that displays toward the top of the Preview screen.

Closing a Workbook and Exiting Excel

Close

To close an Excel workbook, click the Close button that displays at the right side of the Menu bar (the second Close button from the top) or click File and then Close. To exit Excel, click the Close button that displays at the right side of the Title bar (the first Close button from the top) or click File and then Exit. You can also exit Excel by double-clicking the Excel icon that displays at the left side of the Menu bar.

Using Drop-Down Menus

As you learned in unit 1, applications in the Office 2000 suite contain adaptive menus. In chapters in unit 1, instructions were included for expanding drop-down menus. Beginning with this unit and continuing through the remainder of this textbook, the "expand the drop-down menu" instruction will not be included. If you cannot find a menu option, expand the drop-down menu. You might also consider turning off the adaptive menu feature. To do this, refer to the "Expanding Drop-Down Menu" section in chapter 1.

exercise

Creating a Worksheet

1. Open Excel by completing the following steps:
   a. At the Windows desktop, click the Start button that displays at the left side of the Taskbar.
   b. At the pop-up menu that displays, point to Programs.
   c. At the next pop-up menu that displays, click *Microsoft Excel*.
2. At the Excel worksheet that displays, create the worksheet shown in figure 8.9 by completing the following steps:
   a. With cell A1 the active cell (displays with a thick black border), key **Name**.
   b. Press the Tab key. (This makes cell B1 the active cell.)
   c. Key **Hours** and then press the Tab key. (This makes cell C1 the active cell.)

   d. Key **Rate** and then press Enter to move the insertion point to cell A2.

   e. With A2 the active cell, key the name **Avery**.

   f. Continue keying the data shown in figure 8.9. Key the dollar signs as shown in the figure. Use the Tab key to move to the next cell in the row, press Shift + Tab to move to the previous cell in the row, or press the Enter key to move down a row to the cell at the left margin. (For other commands for moving the insertion point, refer to figure 8.4.)

3. After keying the data shown in the cells in figure 8.9, save the worksheet by completing the following steps:

   a. Click the Save button on the Standard toolbar.

   b. At the Save As dialog box, make the drive where your disk is located the active drive, and then key **Excel Ch 08, Ex 01** in the File name text box.

   c. Press Enter or click the Save button.

4. Print Excel Ch 08, Ex 01 by clicking the Print button on the Standard toolbar. (The gridlines will not print.)

5. Close Excel Ch 08, Ex 01.

Exercise 1

	A	B	C	D
1	Name	Hours	Rate	
2	Avery	45	$19.50	
3	Connors	35	$18.75	
4	Estrada	24	$15.00	
5	Juergens	24	$17.50	
6	Mikulich	20	$15.25	
7	Talbot	15	$10.00	
8				

Selecting Cells

Cells within a worksheet can be formatted in a variety of ways. For example, the alignment of data in cells or rows can be changed or character formatting can be added. To identify the cells that are to be affected by the formatting, the specific cells need to be selected.

Selecting Cells Using the Mouse

Select specific cells in a worksheet using the mouse or select columns or rows. Methods for selecting cells using the mouse display in figure 8.10.

Selecting with the Mouse

To select this	Do this
Column	Position the cell pointer on the column header (a letter) and then click the left mouse button.
Row	Position the cell pointer on the row header (a number) and then click the left mouse button.
Adjacent cells	Drag with mouse to select specific cells.
Nonadjacent cells	Hold down the Ctrl key while clicking column header, row header, or specific cells.
All cells in worksheet	Click the Select All button (refer to figure 8.3).

Selected cells, except the active cell, display with a light blue background (this may vary) rather than a white background. The active cell is the first cell in the selection block and displays in the normal manner (white background with black data). Selected cells remain selected until you click a cell with the mouse or press an arrow key on the keyboard.

Selecting Cells Using the Keyboard

The keyboard can be used to select specific cells within a worksheet. Figure 8.11 displays the commands for selecting specific cells.

Selecting Cells Using the Keyboard

To select	Press
Cells in direction of arrow key	Shift + arrow key
To beginning of row	Shift + Home
To beginning of worksheet	Shift + Ctrl + Home
To last cell in worksheet containing data	Shift + Ctrl + End
An entire column	Ctrl + spacebar
An entire row	Shift + spacebar
Entire worksheet	Ctrl + A or Ctrl + Shift + spacebar

Chapter Eight

Selecting Data within Cells

The selection commands presented select the entire cell. You can also select specific characters within a cell. To do this with the mouse, position the cell pointer in the desired cell, and then double-click the left mouse button. Drag with the I-beam pointer through the data you want selected. If you are using the keyboard, hold down the Shift key, and then press the arrow key that moves the insertion point in the desired direction. Data the insertion point passes through will be selected. You can also press F8 to turn on the Extend mode, move the insertion point in the desired direction to select the data, and then press F8 to turn off the Extend mode.

Applying Formatting with Buttons on the Formatting Toolbar

A variety of formatting can be applied to cells in a worksheet using buttons on the Formatting toolbar. With buttons on the Formatting toolbar shown in figure 8.12, you can change the font and font size and bold, italicize, and underline data in cells. To apply bold to a cell or selected cells, click the Bold button on the Formatting toolbar; click the Italic button to apply italics; and click the Underline button to apply underlining formatting.

With other buttons on the Formatting toolbar, you can change the alignment of text within cells, increase or decrease the number of digits after a decimal point, increase or decrease indents, change the cell border, add fill color to a cell, and change text color.

B
Bold

I
Italic

U
Underline

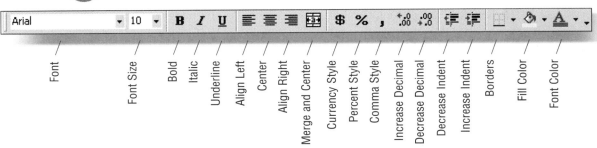

Formatting Toolbar

Previewing a Worksheet

Before printing a worksheet, consider previewing it to see how it will appear when printed. To preview a worksheet, click the Preview button in the Print dialog box; click the Print Preview button on the Standard toolbar; or click File and then Print Preview. This causes the document to display on the screen as it will appear when printed. Figure 8.13 displays the worksheet named Excel Worksheet 01 in Print Preview. Notice that the gridlines in the worksheet will not print.

Print Preview

figure

8.13

Worksheet in Print Preview

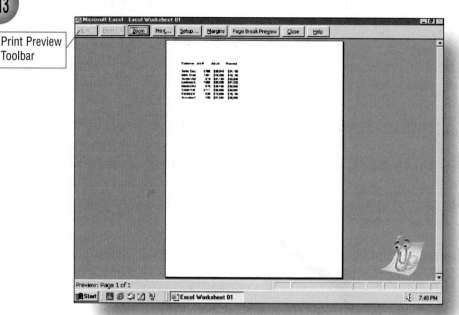

Print Preview Toolbar

Hint

In Print Preview with the Margins button active, change worksheet margins by dragging margin borders.

To zoom in on the worksheet and make the display bigger, click the Zoom button on the Print Preview toolbar. This toolbar displays at the top of the screen immediately below the Title bar. Click the Print button on the Print Preview toolbar to send the worksheet to the printer. Click the Setup button and the Page Setup dialog box displays where you can specify the orientation of the page and the paper size. Clicking the Margins button causes margin boundary lines to display on the worksheet. Clicking this button again removes the margin boundary lines. (You will learn more about these options in chapter 9.) After viewing the worksheet, click the Close button to remove Print Preview and return to the worksheet.

Changing the Zoom Setting

In Print Preview, you can zoom in on the worksheet and make the display bigger. You can also change the size of the display at the worksheet (not in Print Preview) with the options on the Zoom button. To change the percentage of display, click the down-pointing triangle at the right side of the Zoom button on the Standard toolbar and then click the desired percentage at the drop-down list. You can also click in the Zoom button to select the current percentage measurement, key a new percentage, and then press Enter.

exercise 2

Selecting and Applying Character Formatting to Cells

1. Open Excel Worksheet 01.
2. Save the worksheet with Save As and name it Excel Ch 08, Ex 02.
3. Apply character formatting to data within cells by completing the following steps:
   a. Select and then bold and italicize the first row by completing the following steps:
      1) Position the cell pointer on the row 1 header and then click the left mouse button. (This is the number 1 that displays at the left side of the screen, immediately left of *Customer*.)
      2) Click the Bold button and then click the Italic button on the Formatting toolbar.
   b. Select and then bold the data in cells A3 through A10 by completing the following steps:
      1) Position the cell pointer in cell A3, hold down the left mouse button, drag the cell pointer to cell A10, and then release the mouse button.
      2) Click the Bold button on the Formatting toolbar.
   c. Select and then italicize the data in cells B3 through D10 by completing the following steps:
      1) Position the cell pointer in cell B3, hold down the left mouse button, drag the cell pointer to cell D10, and then release the mouse button.
      2) Click the Italic button on the Formatting toolbar.
4. Make the following changes to data within cells in the worksheet:
   a. Double-click cell A5 (contains *Sunset Automotive*).
   b. Delete the word *Automotive* and then key **Transport**. (When completed, the company name should be *Sunset Transport*.)
   c. Click once in cell A9 (contains *Detailed Designs*) and then key **Mustang Supply**. (Clicking only once allows you to key over the existing data.)
   d. Click once in cell B6 (contains *1009*) and then key **885**.
   e. Edit cell D10 by completing the following steps:
      1) Click Edit and then Go To.
      2) At the Go To dialog box, key **D10** in the Reference text box, and then click OK.
      3) Key **75225** (over *$86,905*).
   f. Click once in any other cell.

5. Preview the worksheet by completing the following steps:
   a. Click the Print Preview button on the Standard toolbar.
   b. At the print preview screen, click the Zoom button. (This increases the display of the worksheet cells.)
6. Change the zoom display by completing the following steps:
   a. Click the down-pointing triangle at the right side of the Zoom button on the Standard toolbar and then click *200%* at the drop-down list.
   b. After viewing the document at 200% display, click in the Zoom button (this selects *200%*), key **150**, and then press Enter. (This changes the zoom percentage to 150%.)
   c. Change the zoom back to 100% by clicking the down-pointing triangle at the right side of the Zoom button and then clicking *100%* at the drop-down list.
   d. After viewing the worksheet, click the Close button.
7. Save the document again with the same name (Excel Ch 08, Ex 02).
8. Print and then close Excel Ch 08, Ex 02. (The gridlines will not print.)

exercise 3

Changing the Font and Font Color for Data in a Worksheet

1. Open Excel Worksheet 01.
2. Save the worksheet with Save As and name it Excel Ch 08, Ex 03.
3. Make the following changes to the worksheet:
   a. Select the entire worksheet and then change the font and font color by completing the following steps:
      1) Click the Select All button. (This is the gray button that displays immediately left of column header A and immediately above row header 1.)
      2) Click the down-pointing triangle at the right side of the Font button on the Formatting toolbar.
      3) At the drop-down menu that displays, scroll down the list and then click *Garamond*. (If Garamond is not available, choose another serif typeface such as Century Schoolbook.)
      4) Click the down-pointing triangle at the right side of the Font Size button on the Formatting toolbar and then click *11* at the drop-down menu.
      5) Click the down-pointing triangle at the right side of the Font Color button (this is the last button on the Formatting toolbar). At the palette of color choices, click the blue color that is the sixth color from the left in the second row.

b. Click once in cell A6 and then change *Linstrom Enterprises* to *Jefferson, Inc.*
c. Double-click in cell A7 and then change *Morcos Media* to *Morcos Corp.*
d. Click once in cell C6 and then change *$63,293* to *$59,578*.
e. Double-click in cell C10 and then change the second number from a *7* to an *8*.
f. Click once in any other cell.
4. Preview the worksheet by completing the following steps:
a. Click the Print Preview button on the Standard toolbar.
b. At the print preview screen, increase the size of the display by clicking the Zoom button. (Skip this step if the size is already increased.)
c. After viewing the worksheet, click the Close button.
5. Save the document again with the same name (Excel Ch 08, Ex 03).
6. Print Excel Ch 08, Ex 03. (The gridlines will not print. If you are not printing on a color printer, the data will print in black rather than blue.)
7. Print selected cells by completing the following steps:
a. Select cells A1 through C10.
b. Click File and then Print.
c. At the Print dialog box, click Selection in the Print what section.
d. Click OK.
8. Click outside the selected area to deselect the cells and then close Excel Ch 08, Ex 03.

Changing Column Width and Row Height

Columns in a worksheet are the same width by default, and rows are the same height. In some worksheets you may want to change column widths or row heights to accommodate more or less data. Changes to column widths or row heights can be made using the mouse on column or row boundaries or at a dialog box.

Changing Column Width

The width of one column or selected columns can be changed using the mouse on column boundaries or at the Column Width dialog box.

Changing Column Width with Column Boundaries

The mouse can be used to change the width of a column or selected columns. For example, to increase the size of column B, you would position the mouse pointer on the black boundary line between columns B and C in the column header until the mouse pointer turns into a double-headed arrow pointing left and right. With the double-headed arrow displayed, you would hold down the left mouse button, drag the boundary to the right to increase the size of column B, and then release the mouse button when the column is the desired width.

The width of selected columns that are adjacent can be changed at the same time. To do this, select the columns and then drag one of the column boundaries within the selected columns. As the boundary is being dragged, the column width changes for all selected columns.

As a column boundary is being dragged, the column width displays in a yellow box above the mouse pointer. The column width number that displays represents the average number of characters in the standard font that can fit in a cell.

exercise 4

Changing Column Width Using a Column Boundary

1. At a blank Excel worksheet, create the worksheet shown in figure 8.14 by completing the following steps:

   a. Change the width of column A by completing the following steps:

   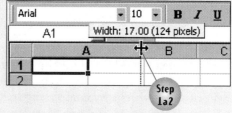

   1) Position the mouse pointer on the column boundary in the column header between columns A and B until it turns into a double-headed arrow pointing left and right.

   2) Hold down the left mouse button, drag the column boundary to the right until *Width: 17.00 (124 pixels)* displays in the yellow box, and then release the mouse button.

   b. Change the width of columns B, C, and D by completing the following steps:

   1) Select columns B, C, and D. To do this, position the cell pointer on the letter B in the column header, hold down the left mouse button, drag the cell pointer to the letter D in the column header, and then release the mouse button.

   2) Position the cell pointer on the column boundary between columns B and C until it turns into a double-headed arrow pointing left and right.

   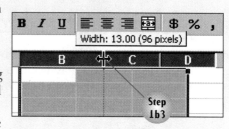

   3) Hold down the left mouse button, drag the column boundary to the right until *Width: 13.00 (96 pixels)* displays in the yellow box, and then release the mouse button.

   c. Key the data in the cells as shown in figure 8.14. Key the dollar signs and decimal points as shown. Use the Tab key to move to the next cell and then press Shift + Tab to move to the previous cell. For other commands for moving the insertion point, refer to figure 8.4. (Consider using the AutoFill fill handle for the months. To do this, key **October** in cell B1, position the mouse pointer on the fill handle, hold down the left mouse button, drag to cell D1, and then release the mouse button.)

   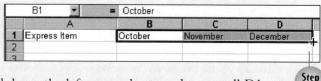

   d. After keying the data in the cells, make the following formatting changes:

   1) Select the entire worksheet and then change the font to 12-point Tahoma (or a similar sans serif typeface).

   2) Select row 1 and then apply bold and italic formatting.

2. Save the worksheet and name it Excel Ch 08, Ex 04.
3. Preview the worksheet.
4. Print and then close Excel Ch 08, Ex 04.

Exercise 4

	A	B	C	D	E
1	Expense Item	October	November	December	
2	Salaries	$25,450.50	$26,090.65	$26,445.00	
3	Lease	$5,650.00	$5,650.00	$5,560.00	
4	Insurance	$5,209.65	$5,335.55	$5,621.45	
5	Utilities	$2,100.50	$2,249.75	$2,441.35	
6	Maintenance	$1,430.00	$1,119.67	$1,450.50	
7					

A column width in an existing worksheet can be adjusted to fit the longest entry in the column. To automatically adjust a column width to the longest entry, position the cell pointer on the column boundary at the right side of the column, and then double-click the left mouse button.

Changing Column Width Automatically in an Existing Worksheet

1. Open Excel Worksheet 01.
2. Save the worksheet with Save As and name it Excel Ch 08, Ex 05.
3. Select the entire worksheet and then change the font to 14-point Times New Roman.
4. Adjust the width of the first column to accommodate the longest entry in the column by completing the following steps:
   a. Position the cell pointer on the column boundary between columns A and B until it turns into a double-headed arrow pointing left and right.
   b. Double-click the left mouse button.
5. Select row 1 and then click the Bold button on the Formatting toolbar.
6. Save the document again with the same name (Excel Ch 08, Ex 05).
7. Preview the worksheet.
8. Print and then close Excel Ch 08, Ex 05.

	A	B	C	D
	A1	= Customer		
1	Customer	Job #	Actual	Planned
2				
3	Sellar Corporation	2130	$30,349	$34,109
4	Main Street Photos	1201	$48,290	$48,100

Step 4a

Changing Column Width at the Column Width Dialog Box

At the Column Width dialog box shown in figure 8.15, you can specify a column width number. The column width number represents the average number of characters in the standard font that will fit in a cell. Increase the column width number to make the column wider or decrease the column width number to make the column narrower.

To display the Column Width dialog box, click Format, point to Column, and then click Width. At the Column Width dialog box, key the number representing the average number of characters in the standard font that you want to fit in the column, and then press Enter or click OK.

figure 8.15

Column Width Dialog Box

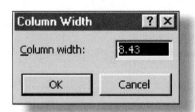

exercise 6

Changing Column Width at the Column Width Dialog Box

1. At a blank Excel worksheet, create the worksheet shown in figure 8.16 by completing the following steps:
   a. Change the width of column A by completing the following steps:
      1) Make sure any cell in column A is active.
      2) Click Format, point to Column, and then click Width.
      3) At the Column Width dialog box, key **10** in the Column width text box.
      4) Press Enter or click OK to close the dialog box.

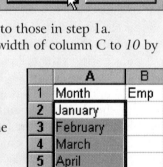

   b. Make any cell in column B active and then change the width of column B to *5* by completing steps similar to those in step 1a.
   c. Make any cell in column C active and then change the width of column C to *10* by completing steps similar to those in step 1a.
   d. Make any cell in column D active and then change the width of column D to *10* by completing steps similar to those in step 1a.
   e. Key the data in the cells as shown in figure 8.16. Use the fill handle to insert the months.
   f. After keying the data in the cells, make the following formatting changes:
      1) Select the entire worksheet and then change the font to 12-point Garamond (or a similar serif typeface).
      2) Select row 1 and then apply bold formatting.
2. Save the worksheet and name it Excel Ch 08, Ex 06.
3. Preview the worksheet.
4. Print and then close Excel Ch 08, Ex 06.

Exercise 6

	A	B	C	D	E
1	Month	Emp	Actual	Budget	
2	January	320	$3,121.50	$3,005.60	
3	February	197	$3,450.78	$3,500.20	
4	March	763	$2,109.45	$2,229.67	
5	April	804	$4,312.50	$4,110.30	
6	May	334	$5,110.40	$4,995.00	
7	June	105	$1,894.35	$1,995.15	
8					

Changing Row Height

Row height can be changed in much the same manner as column width. For example, you can change the row height using the mouse on a row boundary, or at the Row Height dialog box.

Changing Row Height with Row Boundaries

Change row height using a row boundary in the same manner as you learned to change column width. To do this, position the cell pointer on the boundary between rows in the row header until it turns into a double-headed arrow pointing up and down, hold down the left mouse button, drag up or down until the row is the desired height, and then release the mouse button.

The height of selected rows that are adjacent can be changed at the same time. (The height of nonadjacent rows will not all change at the same time.) To do this, select the rows, and then drag one of the row boundaries within the selected rows. As the boundary is being dragged, the row height changes for all selected rows.

As a row boundary is being dragged, the row height displays in a yellow box above the mouse pointer. The row height number that displays represents a point measurement. There are approximately 72 points in a vertical inch. Increase the point size to increase the row height; decrease the point size to decrease the row height.

Changing Row Height Using a Row Boundary

1. Open Excel Worksheet 05.
2. Save the worksheet with Save As and name it Excel Ch 08, Ex 07.
3. Make the following changes to the worksheet:
   a. Change the font size of January to 14 by completing the following steps:
      1) Make cell A1 the active cell.
      2) Click the down-pointing triangle at the right of the Font Size button on the Formatting toolbar.
      3) From the drop-down menu that displays, click *14*.

b. Change the height of row 1 by completing the following steps:
   1) Position the cell pointer in the row header on the row boundary between rows 1 and 2 until it turns into a double-headed arrow pointing up and down.
   2) Hold down the left mouse button, drag the row boundary down until *Height: 27.00 (36 pixels)* displays in the yellow box, and then release the mouse button

c. Change the height of rows 2 through 8 by completing the following steps:
   1) Select rows 2 through 8. To do this, position the cell pointer on the number 2 in the row header, hold down the left mouse button, drag the cell pointer to the number 8 in the row header, and then release the mouse button.
   2) Position the cell pointer on the row boundary between rows 2 and 3 until it turns into a double-headed arrow pointing up and down.
   3) Hold down the left mouse button, drag the row boundary down until *Height: 21.00 (28 pixels)* displays in the yellow box, and then release the mouse button.

4. Save the worksheet again with the same name (Excel Ch 08, Ex 07).
5. Preview the worksheet.
6. Print and then close Excel Ch 08, Ex 07.

Changing Row Height at the Row Height Dialog Box

At the Row Height dialog box shown in figure 8.17, you can specify a row height number. To display the Row Height dialog box, click Format, point to Row, and then click Height.

figure

8.17

Row Height Dialog Box

exercise 8

Changing Row Height at the Row Height Dialog Box

1. Open Excel Worksheet 07.
2. Save the worksheet with Save As and name it Excel Ch 08, Ex 08.
3. Make the following changes to the worksheet:
   a. Change the font size of *REAL PHOTOGRAPHY* to 14 and turn on bold.
   b. Change the height of row 1 by completing the following steps:
      1) Make any cell in row 1 active.
      2) Click Format, point to Row, and then click Height.
      3) At the Row Height dialog box, key **30** in the Row height text box, and then press Enter or click OK.
   c. Change the height of rows 2 through 10 by completing the following steps:
      1) Select rows 2 through 10.
      2) Click Format, point to Row, and then click Height.
      3) At the Row Height dialog box, key **20** in the Row height text box, and then press Enter or click OK.
4. Save the worksheet again with the same name (Excel Ch 08, Ex 08).
5. Preview the worksheet.
6. Print and then close Excel Ch 08, Ex 08.

Formatting Data in Cells

An Excel worksheet, like a Word document, contains default formatting. For example, by default, letters and words are aligned at the left of a cell, numbers are aligned at the right, and data is set in a 10-point sans serif typeface such as Arial. Depending on the data you are entering in cells, you may want to change some of these default settings.

> Use the Format Painter button on the Standard toolbar to copy formatting from one range of cells to another.
>
> *Hint*

Formatting Numbers

Numbers in a cell, by default, are aligned at the right and decimals and commas are not displayed unless they are keyed in the cell. Also, numbers display in a 10-point sans serif typeface such as Arial. Depending on the type of numbers used in a worksheet, you may want to change these default settings. You can format numbers using a *format symbol*, or change number formatting with buttons on the Formatting toolbar or with options at the Format Cells dialog box.

Format symbols you can use to format numbers include a percent sign (%), a comma (,), and a dollar sign ($). For example, if you key the number *$45.50* in a cell, Excel automatically applies Currency formatting to the number. If you key *45%*, Excel automatically applies the Percent formatting to the number.

Five buttons on the Formatting toolbar can be used to format numbers in cells. The five buttons are shown and described in figure 8.18.

Number Formatting Buttons on Formatting Toolbar

Click this button	Named	To do this
$	Currency Style	Add a dollar sign, any necessary commas, and a decimal point followed by two decimal digits, if none are keyed; right align number in cell
%	Percent Style	Multiply cell value by 100 and display result with a percent symbol; right align number in cell
,	Comma Style	Add any necessary commas and a decimal point followed by two decimal digits, if none are keyed; right align number in cell
.0 .00	Increase Decimal	Increase number of decimal places displayed after decimal point in selected cells
.00 .0	Decrease Decimal	Decrease number of decimal places displayed after decimal point in selected cells

(*Note: Before entering percent numbers in a cell, check to make sure automatic percent entry is enabled. To do this, click* Tools *and then* Options. *At the Options dialog box, click the Edit tab. Make sure there is a check mark in the* Enable automatic percent entry *option and then click OK.*)

Increase Decimal

Decrease Decimal

Specify the formatting for numbers in cells in a worksheet before keying the numbers, or format existing numbers in a worksheet. The Increase Decimal and Decrease Decimal buttons on the Formatting toolbar will change decimal places for existing numbers only.

Formatting Numbers with Buttons on the Formatting Toolbar

1. At a blank Excel worksheet, create the worksheet shown in figure 8.19 by completing the following steps:
   a. Change the width of column A to 13.00.
   b. Select columns B, C, and D, and then change the column width to 10.00.
   c. Change the width of column E to 8.00.
   d. Key the data in the cells as shown in figure 8.19.
   e. After keying the data in the cells, make the following number formatting changes:

1) Select cells B3 through D12.
2) Click the Currency Style button on the Formatting toolbar.
3) Click twice the Decrease Decimal button on the Formatting toolbar. (There should now be no decimal places in the numbers in the selected cells.)
4) Select cells E3 through E12.
5) Click the Percent Style button on the Formatting toolbar.
6) Click twice the Increase Decimal button on the Formatting toolbar. (There should now be two decimal places in the percent numbers in the selected cells.)

f. Select and then bold column A.
g. Select and then bold row 1.

2. Save the worksheet and name it Excel Ch 08, Ex 09.
3. Preview the worksheet.
4. Print and then close Excel Ch 08, Ex 09.

	10	B I U	三 三 三	$ % ,	.00 .00

= 624000

	B	C	D	E	F
	Sales	Break Even	Safety	Safety %	
	$ 624,000	$ 587,230	$ 36,770	0.0627	
	$ 725,400	$ 634,350	$ 91,050	0.144	
	$ 358,650	$ 315,350	$ 43,300	0.137	
	$ 402,805	$ 399,850	$ 2,955	0.0074	
	$ 768,293	$ 721,420	$ 46,873	0.065	
	$ 734,210	$ 706,780	$ 27,430	0.0389	

Step 1e2 Step 1e3
Step 1e1

$ % , .00 .00
Step 1e5 E Step 1e6
Safety %

70	6.27%
50	14.40%
00	13.70%
55	0.74%
73	6.50%
30	3.89%

Step 1e4

figure
8.19

Exercise 9

	A	B	C	D	E	F
1		Sales	Break Even	Safety	Safety %	
2	Product A					
3	Budget	624000	587230	36770	0.0627	
4	Actual	725400	634350	91050	0.144	
5						
6	Product B					
7	Budget	358650	315350	43300	0.137	
8	Actual	402805	399850	2955	0.0074	
9						
10	Product C					
11	Budget	768293	721420	46873	0.065	
12	Actual	734210	706780	27430	0.0389	
13						

Numbers in cells can also be formatted with options at the Format Cells dialog box with the Number tab selected as shown in figure 8.20. Display this dialog box by clicking Format and then Cells.

figure
8.20

Format Cells Dialog Box with Number Tab Selected

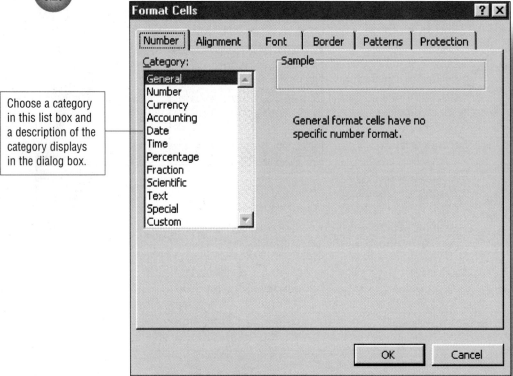

Choose a category in this list box and a description of the category displays in the dialog box.

Format Cells `? X`

| Number | Alignment | Font | Border | Patterns | Protection |

Category:

General
Number
Currency
Accounting
Date
Time
Percentage
Fraction
Scientific
Text
Special
Custom

Sample

General format cells have no specific number format.

`OK` `Cancel`

The left side of the dialog box displays number categories. The default category is *General*. At this setting no specific formatting is applied to numbers except right aligning numbers in cells. The other number categories are described in figure 8.21.

figure
8.21

Number Categories at the Format Cells Dialog Box

Click this category	To apply this number formatting
Number	Specify number of decimal places and whether or not a thousand separator should be used; choose the display of negative numbers; right align numbers in cell
Currency	Apply general monetary values; dollar sign is added as well as commas and decimal points, if needed; right align numbers in cell
Accounting	Line up the currency symbol and decimal points in a column; add dollar sign and two digits after a decimal point; right align numbers in cell
Date	Display date as date value; specify the type of formatting desired by clicking an option in the Type list box; right align date in cell

Time	Display time as time value; specify the type of formatting desired by clicking an option in the <u>T</u>ype list box; right align time in cell
Percentage	Multiply cell value by 100 and display result with a percent symbol; add decimal point followed by two digits by default; number of digits can be changed with the <u>D</u>ecimal places option; right align number in cell
Fraction	Specify how fraction displays in cell by clicking an option in the <u>T</u>ype list box; right align fraction in cell
Scientific	Use for very large or very small numbers. Use the letter E to tell Excel to move a decimal point a specified number of positions
Text	Treat number in cell as text; number is displayed in cell exactly as keyed
Special	Choose a number type, such as Zip Code, Phone Number, or Social Security Number in the <u>T</u>ype option list box; useful for tracking list and database values
Custom	Specify a numbering type by choosing an option in the <u>T</u>ype list box

Formatting Numbers at the Format Cells Dialog Box

1. Open Excel Worksheet 02.
2. Save the worksheet with Save As and name it Excel Ch 08, Ex 10.
3. Make the following changes to the worksheet:
   a. Change the number formatting by completing the following steps:
      1) Select cells B2 through D8.
      2) Click Format and then Cells.
      3) At the Format Cells dialog box with the Number tab selected, click *Currency* in the <u>C</u>ategory section.
      4) Click the down-pointing triangle at the right of the <u>D</u>ecimal places option until *0* displays in the <u>D</u>ecimal places text box.
      5) Click OK to close the dialog box.
   b. Select and then bold and italicize row 1.
4. Save the worksheet again with the same name (Excel Ch 08, Ex 10).
5. Print Excel Ch 08, Ex 10.
6. With Excel Ch 08, Ex 10 still open, change the display of negative numbers by completing the following steps:
   a. Select cells D2 through D8.
   b. Click Format and then Cells.

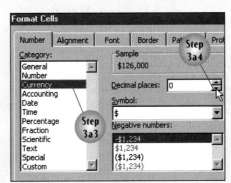

c. At the Format Cells dialog box, click the fourth option displayed in the <u>N</u>egative numbers list box (displays as *($1,234)*).

d. Click OK to close the dialog box.

7. Save the worksheet again with the same name (Excel Ch 08, Ex 10).

8. Preview the worksheet.

9. Print and then close Excel Ch 08, Ex 10.

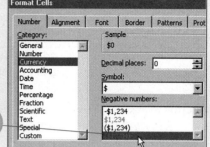

Step 6c

Alignment, Indenting and Rotating Data in Cells

Align Left

Center

Align Right

Merge and Center

The alignment of data in cells depends on the type of data entered. For example, words or text combined with numbers entered in a cell are aligned at the left edge of the cell while numbers are aligned at the right. Alignment of data can be controlled with buttons on the Formatting toolbar or options at the Format Cells dialog box with the Alignment tab selected.

Four buttons on the Formatting toolbar, shown in figure 8.22, can be used to control the alignment of data in a cell or selected cells. Click the Align Left button to align data at the left side of a cell, click the Center button to align data between the left and right side of a cell, and click Align Right to align data at the right side of a cell. Click the Merge and Center button to merge selected cells and center data within the merged cells.

Indent text within a cell or selected cells by clicking the Increase Indent button or the Decrease Indent button on the Formatting toolbar. These buttons are identified in figure 8.22. The Increase Indent button will move text within the cell or selected cells to the right while the Decrease Indent button will move text to the left.

8.22 Alignment and Indent Buttons on the Formatting Toolbar

Data aligning and indenting can also be controlled at the Format Cells dialog box with the Alignment tab selected as shown in figure 8.23.

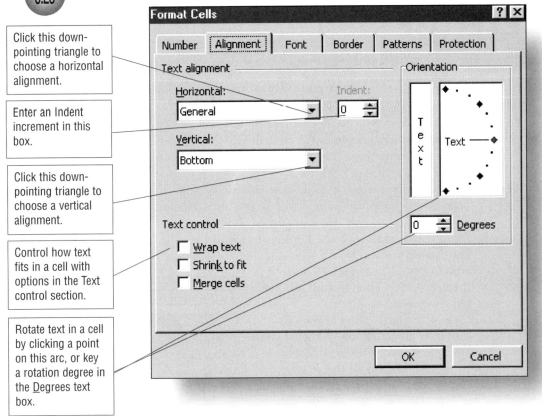

figure
8.23

Format Cells Dialog Box with Alignment Tab Selected

Click this down-pointing triangle to choose a horizontal alignment.

Enter an Indent increment in this box.

Click this down-pointing triangle to choose a vertical alignment.

Control how text fits in a cell with options in the Text control section.

Rotate text in a cell by clicking a point on this arc, or key a rotation degree in the Degrees text box.

Format Cells

Number | Alignment | Font | Border | Patterns | Protection

Text alignment

Horizontal:
General

Indent:
0

Vertical:
Bottom

Text control

☐ Wrap text
☐ Shrink to fit
☐ Merge cells

Orientation

T e x t   Text ——◆

0   Degrees

OK   Cancel

Click the down-pointing triangle at the right of the Horizontal option box and a list of alignment options displays. This list includes Left (Indent), Center, Right, Fill, Justify, and Center Across Selection. Choose the desired horizontal alignment from this list.

By default, data in a cell is aligned at the bottom of the cell. This alignment can be changed to top, center, or justify with choices from the Vertical drop-down list. To display this list, click the down-pointing triangle at the right side of the Vertical option.

Use the Indent box to indent cell contents from the left side of the cell. Each increment entered in the Indent box is equivalent to the width of one character.

In the Orientation section of the Format Cells dialog box with the Alignment tab selected, you can choose to rotate data. A portion of the Orientation section shows points on an arc. Click a point on the arc to rotate the text along that point. You can also key a rotation degree in the Degrees text box. Key a positive number to rotate selected text from the lower left to the upper right of the cell. Key a negative number to rotate selected text from the upper left to the lower right of the cell.

As you learned earlier, if data keyed in a cell is longer than the cell, it overlaps the next cell to the right. If you want data to remain in a cell and wrap to the next line within the same cell, click the Wrap text option in the Text control section of the dialog box. Click the Shrink to fit option to reduce the size of the text font so all selected data fits within the column. Use the Merge cells option to combine two or more selected cells into a single cell.

If you want to enter data on more than one line within a cell, enter the data on the first line and then press Alt + Enter. Pressing Alt + Enter moves the insertion point to the next line within the same cell.

Aligning and Rotating Data in Cells

1. Open Excel Worksheet 01.
2. Save the worksheet with Save As and name it Excel Ch 08, Ex 11.
3. Make the following changes to the worksheet:
    a. Select the entire worksheet and then change the font to 12-point Tahoma (or a similar sans serif typeface).
    b. Automatically increase the width of column A by positioning the cell pointer on the boundary between columns A and B and then double-clicking the left mouse button.
    c. Select row 1, then click the Bold button, and then the Center button on the Formatting toolbar.
    d. Select cells B3 through B10 and then click the Center button on the Formatting toolbar.
    e. Change the orientation of data in cells by completing the following steps:
        1) Select cells B1 through D1.
        2) Click Format and then Cells.
        3) At the Format Cells dialog box, click the Alignment tab.
        4) Select the 0 in the Degrees text box and then key **45**.
        5) Click OK to close the dialog box.

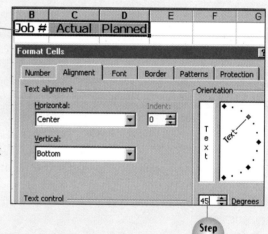

4. Merge and center data in a cell by completing the following steps:
    a. Select cells A12 through D12.
    b. Click the Merge and Center button on the Formatting toolbar.
    c. Double-click in the newly merged cell.
    d. Turn on bold, key **YEARLY JOB REPORT**, and then press Enter.
5. Enter text on a separate line in cell C1 by completing the following steps:
    a. Double-click cell C1
    b. Move the insertion point to the end of *Actual*.
    c. Press Alt + Enter.
    d. Key **Amount**.

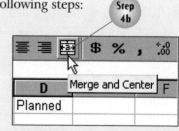

6. Follow steps similar to those in 5 to enter the word *Amount* below *Planned* in cell D1.
7. Save the worksheet again with the same name (Excel Ch 08, Ex 11).
8. Preview the worksheet.
9. Print and then close Excel Ch 08, Ex 11.

Changing the Font at the Format Cells Dialog Box

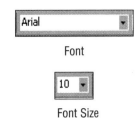

Font

10

Font Size

As you learned earlier in this chapter, the font for data can be changed with the Font button on the Formatting toolbar and the font size can be changed with the Font Size button. The font for data in selected cells can also be changed at the Format Cells dialog box with the Font tab selected as shown in figure 8.24.

figure
8.24

Format Cells Dialog Box with Font Tab Selected

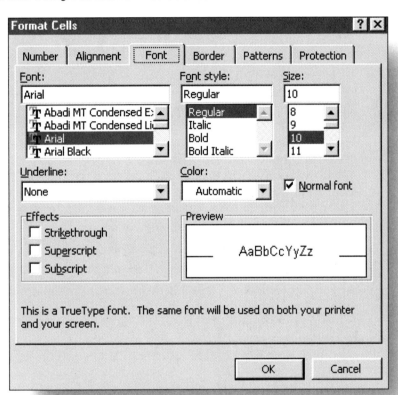

At the Format Cells dialog box with the Font tab selected, you can change the font, font style, font size, and font color. You can also change the underlining method and add effects such as superscript and subscript.

Changing the Font and Font Color of Data in Cells

1. Open Excel Worksheet 02.
2. Save the worksheet with Save As and name it Excel Ch 08, Ex 12.
3. Make the following changes to the worksheet:
   a. Change the font and font color by completing the following steps:
      1) Select the entire worksheet.
      2) Click Format and then Cells.
      3) At the Format Cells dialog box, click the Font tab.

4) At the Format Cells dialog box with the Font tab selected, click *Garamond* in the Font list box (you will need to scroll down the list to make this font visible).

5) Click *12* in the Size list box (you will need to scroll down the list to make this size visible).

6) Click the down-pointing triangle at the right of the Color text box (contains the word *Automatic*).

7) At the palette of color choices that displays, click the Blue color.

8) Click OK to close the dialog box.

b. Change the font color for the cells in row 1 by completing the following steps:

1) Select row 1.

2) Click Format and then Cells.

3) At the Format Cells dialog box, make sure the Font tab is selected.

4) Click the down-pointing triangle at the right side of the Color text box.

5) At the palette of color choices, click a red color (you choose the red).

6) Click OK to close the dialog box.

c. Select cells B2 through D8 and then change the number formatting to *Currency* with zero decimal places.

d. Select cells A2 through A8 and then click twice on the Increase Indent button on the Formatting toolbar. (This indents the text from the left side of the cells.)

e. Automatically adjust the width of columns A, B, C, and D.

4. Save the worksheet again with the same name (Excel Ch 08, Ex 12).

5. Preview the worksheet.

6. Print and then close Excel Ch 08, Ex 12.

Borders

Formatting Cells

Formatting can be applied to cells in a worksheet. For example, borders can be added to cells as well as patterns and shading. Excel also offers a feature called *AutoFormat* that applies predesigned formatting to a worksheet.

Adding Borders to Cells

One method for applying borders is to select the cell or range of cells, click the down-pointing triangle at the right of the Borders button, and then click a border.

The gridlines that display in a worksheet do not print. Borders that will print can, however, be added to cells. Borders can be added by clicking the Borders button on the Formatting toolbar or with options from the Format Cells dialog box with the Border tab selected.

To add a border to a cell or selected cells, make the desired cell active or select the desired cells, and then click the Borders button on the Formatting toolbar. By default, a single line border is added to the bottom of the active cell or the selected cells. To change the style of border, click the down-pointing triangle at the right of the Borders button. This causes a palette of border style choices to display. Click the choice that represents the type of border desired for the cell or selected cells. Clicking the desired border style removes the palette and also applies that border style to the active cell or the selected cells.

Adding Borders to Cells Using the Borders Button

1. Open Excel Worksheet 01.
2. Save the worksheet with Save As and name it Excel Ch 08, Ex 13.
3. Make the following changes to the worksheet:
   a. Select the entire worksheet and then change the font size to 11 points.
   b. Automatically adjust the width of column A.
   c. Select row 1 and then turn on bold and change the alignment to center.
   d. Select cells B3 through B10 and then change the alignment to center.
   e. Add a border to all cells in the worksheet (that contain data) by completing the following steps:

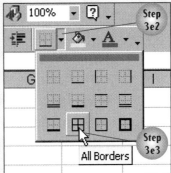

   1) Select cells A1 through D10 (this includes all the cells containing data in the worksheet).
   2) Click the down-pointing triangle at the right of the Borders button on the Formatting toolbar.
   3) At the palette of border style choices that displays, click the All Borders option (second option from the left in the bottom row).

   f. Add a double-line border to the bottom of selected cells by completing the following steps:
   1) Select cells A1 through D1.
   2) Click the down-pointing triangle at the right of the Borders button on the Formatting toolbar.
   3) At the palette of border style choices that displays, click the Bottom Double Border option (first option from the left in the middle row).

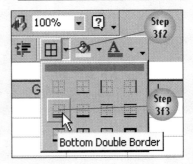

4. Preview the worksheet.
5. Save the worksheet again with the same name (Excel Ch 08, Ex 13).
6. Print and then close Excel Ch 08, Ex 13.

Borders can also be added to the active cell or selected cells with options at the Format Cells dialog box with the Border tab selected as shown in figure 8.25.

figure

8.25

Format Cells Dialog Box with Border Tab Selected

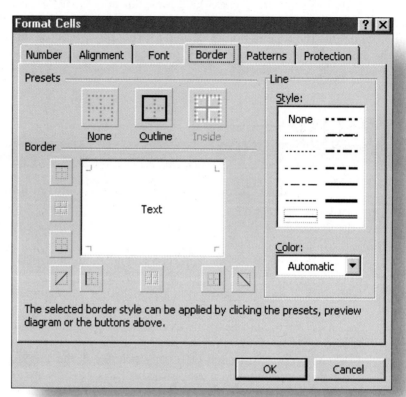

With options in the Presets section, you can remove borders with the <u>N</u>one option, add only outside borders with the <u>O</u>utline option, or click the <u>I</u>nside option to add borders to the inside of selected cells. In the Border section of the dialog box, specify the side of the cell or selected cells to which you want to apply a border. Choose the style of line desired for the border with the options that display in the <u>S</u>tyle list box. Add color to border lines with choices from the color palette that displays when you click the down-pointing triangle located at the right side of the <u>C</u>olor text box (contains the word *Automatic*).

exercise 14

Adding Borders to Cells at the Format Cells Dialog Box

1. Open Excel Worksheet 02.
2. Save the worksheet with Save As and name it Excel Ch 08, Ex 14.
3. Make the following changes to the worksheet:
   a. Select the entire worksheet, display the Format Cells dialog box with the Font tab selected, change the font to 12-point Century Schoolbook (or a similar serif typeface), change the color to green (you determine the green), and then close the dialog box.

b. Select row 1 and then turn on bold and change the alignment to center.
c. Select cells B2 through D8, display the Format Cells dialog box with the Number tab selected, change the Category option to *Currency* with zero decimal places, and then close the dialog box.
d. Automatically adjust the width of columns A, B, C, and D.
e. Add a green outline border to the worksheet by completing the following steps:

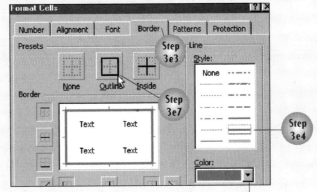

1) Select cells A1 through D8 (all cells containing data).
2) Click Format and then Cells.
3) At the Format Cells dialog box, click the Border tab.
4) Click the sixth option from the top in the second column in the Style list box.
5) Click the down-pointing triangle located at the right side of the Color text box (contains the word *Automatic*).
6) At the palette of color choices, click the same green color that you chose for the font.
7) Click the Outline option in the Presets section of the dialog box.
8) Click OK to close the dialog box.

4. Save the worksheet again with the same name (Excel Ch 08, Ex 14).
5. Preview the worksheet.
6. Print and then close Excel Ch 08, Ex 14.

Adding Shading and a Pattern to Cells

To enhance the visual display of cells and data within cells, consider adding shading and/or a pattern to cells. Color shading can be added to cells in a worksheet by clicking the Fill Color button on the Formatting toolbar. Color shading and/or a pattern can be added to cells in a worksheet with options at the Format Cells dialog box with the Patterns tab selected.

To add color shading using the Fill Color button on the Formatting toolbar, make the desired cell active or select the desired cells, and then click the Fill Color button. By default, the color yellow is added to the cell or selected cells. To add a shading of a different color, click the down-pointing triangle at the right of the Fill Color button, and then click the desired color at the palette that displays.

Fill Color

Apply shading and patterns to cells at the Format Cells dialog box with the Patterns tab selected.

Hint

exercise 15

Adding Borders and Shading to Cells

1. Open Excel Worksheet 02.
2. Save the worksheet with Save As and name it Excel Ch 08, Ex 15.
3. Make the following changes to the worksheet:
   a. Select the entire worksheet, display the Format Cells dialog box with the Font tab selected, change the font to 12-point Arial and the color to blue (sixth color from the left in the second row), and then close the dialog box.
   b. Select row 1 and then turn on bold and change the alignment to center.
   c. Select cells B2 through D8, display the Format Cells dialog box with the Number tab selected, change the Category option to *Currency* with zero decimal places, and then click OK to close the dialog box.
   d. Automatically adjust the width of columns A through D.
   e. Add a border to all cells in the worksheet that contain data by completing the following steps:
      1) Select cells A1 through D8 (this includes all the cells containing data in the worksheet).
      2) Click the down-pointing triangle at the right of the Borders button on the Formatting toolbar.
      3) At the palette of border style choices that displays, click the All Borders option (second option from the left in the bottom row).
   f. Add light turquoise shading to the cells in the worksheet containing data by completing the following steps:
      1) Select cells A1 through D8. (Skip this step if the cells are already selected.)
      2) Click the down-pointing triangle at the right of the Fill Color button on the Formatting toolbar.
      3) At the palette of shading color choices that displays, click the light turquoise color that is the fifth option from the left in the bottom row.
4. Save the worksheet again with the same name (Excel Ch 08, Ex 15).
5. Preview the worksheet.
6. Print and then close Excel Ch 08, Ex 15.

Color shading as well as a pattern can be added to the active cell or selected cells with options at the Format Cells dialog box with the Patterns tab selected as shown in figure 8.26.

figure
8.26

Format Cells Dialog Box with Patterns Tab Selected

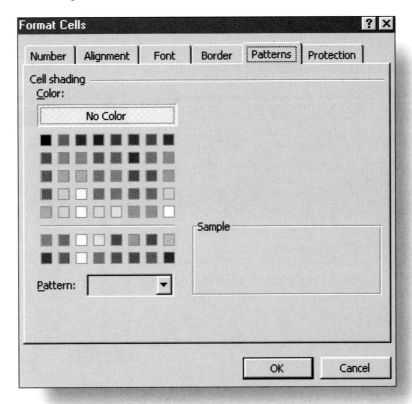

Choose a color shading for a cell or selected cells by clicking a color choice in the Color palette. To add a pattern to a cell or selected cells, click the down-pointing triangle at the right of the Pattern text box, and then click the desired pattern. When you click a pattern, that pattern displays in the Sample box in the dialog box. The Sample box also displays any color shading that has been chosen.

exercise 16

Adding Shading and a Pattern to Cells

1. Open Excel Worksheet 01.
2. Save the worksheet with Save As and name it Excel Ch 08, Ex 16.
3. Make the following changes to the worksheet:
   a. Select the entire worksheet and then change the font to 12-point Garamond (or a similar serif typeface).
   b. Automatically adjust the width of columns A through D.
   c. Select row 1 and then turn on bold and change the alignment to center.
   d. Select cells B3 through B10 and then change the alignment to center.
   e. Add a border to cells A1 through D10 in the worksheet by completing the following steps:

1) Select cells A1 through D10.
2) Click Format and then Cells.
3) At the Format Cells dialog box, click the Border tab.
4) Click the fifth option from the top in the second column in the Style list box.
5) Click the Outline button in the Presets section of the dialog box.
6) Click the Inside button in the Presets section of the dialog box.
7) Click OK to close the dialog box.

4. Add a color shading to cells in the worksheet by completing the following steps:
   a. With cells A1 through D10 still selected, click Format and then Cells.
   b. At the Format Cells dialog box, click the Patterns tab.
   c. At the Format Cells dialog box with the Patterns tab selected, click the light blue color in the Color palette.
   d. Click OK to close the dialog box.

5. Add a pattern to the cells in the first row by completing the following steps:
   a. Select cells A1 through D1.
   b. Click Format and then Cells.
   c. At the Format Cells dialog box, make sure the Patterns tab is selected.
   d. Click the down-pointing triangle at the right side of the Pattern text box.
   e. From the palette of pattern choices that displays, click the fourth pattern choice in the top row.
   f. Click OK to close the dialog box.

6. Save the worksheet again with the same name (Excel Ch 08, Ex 16).
7. Preview the worksheet.
8. Print and then close Excel Ch 08, Ex 16.

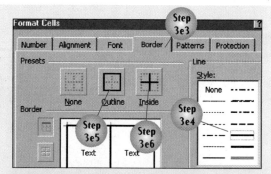

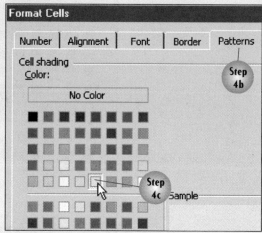

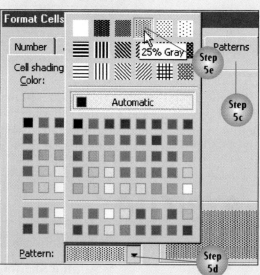

Formatting with AutoFormat

In chapter 6, you learned about Word's AutoFormat feature that automatically applies formatting to a table. Excel also contains an AutoFormat feature. To display the AutoFormat dialog box in Excel, click Format and then AutoFormat. At the AutoFormat dialog box, shown in figure 8.27, predesigned autoformats display along with the name for the format.

AutoFormat Dialog Box

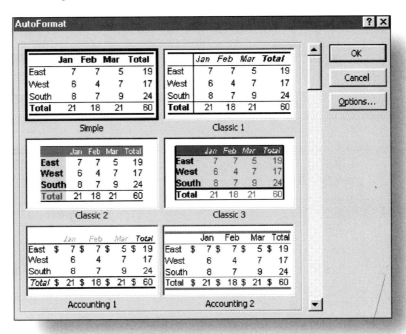

To automatically format a worksheet, select the cells that make up the worksheet, and then click Format and then AutoFormat. (Do not click the Select All button—this selects the entire worksheet, even the empty cells. If you apply an autoformat to all cells, it may lock up your computer.) At the AutoFormat dialog box, click the desired worksheet format, and then click OK; or, double-click the desired worksheet format. Not all formats display at one time. Use the vertical scroll bar at the right side of the list box to view additional formats.

You can make some changes to the predesigned autoformat. To do this, click the Options button that displays at the right side of the AutoFormat dialog box. This causes a number of check box options to display at the bottom of the dialog box. Remove the check mark from options that you do not want applied to the worksheet. For example, suppose you like a predesigned format except the font. To change back to the default font, select the format in the list box, click the Options button, and then click Font. This removes the check mark from the Font check box and also changes the font in the sample worksheet.

If you want to apply the special formatting only to specific portions of the worksheet, select the portions of the worksheet to which you want the formatting applied, and then display the AutoFormat dialog box.

Formatting a Worksheet with AutoFormat

1. Open Excel Worksheet 01.
2. Save the worksheet with Save As and name it Excel Ch 08, Ex 17.
3. Apply autoformatting to the worksheet by completing the following steps:
   a. Select cells A1 through D10.
   b. Click Format and then AutoFormat.
   c. At the AutoFormat dialog box, click the down scroll arrow on the vertical scroll bar until the *Colorful 1* sample worksheet displays.
   d. Double-click *Colorful 1*.
4. Save the document again with the same name (Excel Ch 08, Ex 17).
5. Print and then close Excel Ch 08, Ex 17.

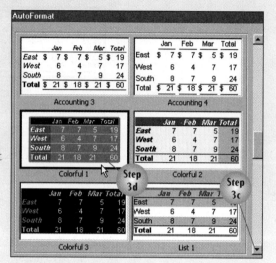

Using Help

Excel's Help feature is an on-screen reference manual containing information about Excel features and commands. Excel's Help feature is similar to the Windows Help and the Help features in Word, PowerPoint, and Access. Get help using the Office Assistant or turn off the Assistant and get help from the Help Topics dialog box.

Getting Help from the Office Assistant

The Office Assistant will provide information about specific topics. To get help using the Office Assistant, click the Office Assistant or click Help and then Microsoft Excel Help. This causes a box to display above the Office Assistant. Key a question in the box about a specific Excel feature and then click the Search button. The Office Assistant displays a list of topics related to the question. At this list, click the desired topic, and information will display in a Microsoft Excel Help dialog box. After reading the information, click the Close button located in the upper right corner of the dialog box (contains an X).

Hiding/Turning Off the Office Assistant

To hide the Office Assistant, click Help and then Hide the Office Assistant. Redisplay the Office Assistant by clicking the Microsoft Word Help button on the Standard toolbar or by clicking Help and then Show the Office Assistant.

The Office Assistant can also be turned off for the entire session. To do this, click the Office Assistant and then click the Options button that displays in the yellow box. At the Office Assistant dialog box that displays, click the Use the Office Assistant option to remove the check mark, and then click OK.

exercise 18

Getting Help from the Office Assistant

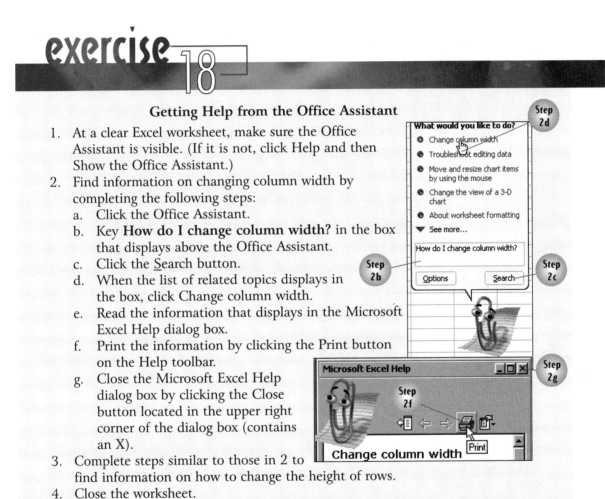

1. At a clear Excel worksheet, make sure the Office Assistant is visible. (If it is not, click Help and then Show the Office Assistant.)
2. Find information on changing column width by completing the following steps:
   a. Click the Office Assistant.
   b. Key **How do I change column width?** in the box that displays above the Office Assistant.
   c. Click the Search button.
   d. When the list of related topics displays in the box, click Change column width.
   e. Read the information that displays in the Microsoft Excel Help dialog box.
   f. Print the information by clicking the Print button on the Help toolbar.
   g. Close the Microsoft Excel Help dialog box by clicking the Close button located in the upper right corner of the dialog box (contains an X).
3. Complete steps similar to those in 2 to find information on how to change the height of rows.
4. Close the worksheet.

chapter summary

► Use an Excel spreadsheet to create financial statements, prepare budgets, manage inventory, and analyze cash flow. Numbers and values can be easily manipulated in an Excel spreadsheet to answer "what if" questions.

► A document created in Excel is called a workbook. A workbook consists of individual worksheets. The intersection of columns and rows in a worksheet are referred to as cells.

► An Excel window contains the following elements: Title bar, Menu bar, Standard toolbar, Formatting toolbar, Formula bar, worksheet area, sheet tabs, scroll bars, and Status bar.

► The gray vertical and horizontal lines that define cells in the worksheet area are called gridlines.

► When the insertion point is positioned in a cell, the cell reference displays in the Name box located at the left side of the Formula bar. The cell reference includes the column letter and row number.

► To enter data in a cell, make the cell active, and then key the data. To move the insertion point to the next cell, press the Tab key. To move the insertion point to the previous cell, press Shift + Tab. For other insertion point movement commands, refer to figure 8.4.

► Data being entered in a cell displays in the cell as well as in the Formula bar.

► The AutoComplete feature will automatically insert a previous entry if the character or characters being keyed in a cell match a previous entry.

► Use the AutoFill fill handle to fill a range of cells with the same or consecutive data.

► If data entered in a cell consists of text (letters) and the text does not fit into the cell, it overlaps the cell to the right. However, if the data being entered are numbers and do not fit in the cell, the numbers are changed to number symbols (###).

► To replace data in a cell, click the cell once, and then key the new data. To edit data within a cell, double-click the cell, and then make necessary changes.

► Save, open, print, and close an Excel workbook in the same manner as a Word document.

► Select all cells in a column by clicking the column header. Select all cells in a row by clicking the row header. Select all cells in a worksheet by clicking the Select All button located immediately to the left of the column headers.

► To select cells with the keyboard, refer to figure 8.11.

► Preview a worksheet by clicking the Preview button in the Print dialog box; clicking the Print Preview button on the Standard toolbar; or clicking File and then Print Preview.

► Change the size of the worksheet display with options on the Zoom button on the Standard toolbar.

► Apply character formatting to selected cells with buttons on the Formatting toolbar such as Font, Font Size, Bold, Italic, Underline, and Font Color.

► Change column width by dragging the column header boundary with the mouse. As a column header boundary is being dragged, the column width displays in a yellow box above the mouse pointer. This number represents the average number of characters in the standard font that will fit in a cell.

► To automatically adjust a column to accommodate the longest entry in the column, double-click the column header boundary on the right.

► Column width can be changed at the Column Width dialog box.

- Format numbers in cells with the Currency Style, Percent Style, Comma Style, Increase Decimal, and Decrease Decimal buttons on the Formatting toolbar.
- Numbers in cells can also be formatted at the Format Cells dialog box with the Number tab selected.
- Change alignment of data within cells with these buttons on the Formatting toolbar: Align Left, Center, Align Right, and Merge and Center.
- Alignment of data within cells can also be changed at the Format Cells dialog box with the Alignment tab selected.
- Indent text in a cell or selected cells by clicking the Increase Indent button on the Formatting toolbar. Decrease the indent of text in a cell or selected cells by clicking the Decrease Indent button.
- The font type, font size, font style, and font color for data in a cell or selected cells can be changed with options at the Format Cells dialog box with the Font tab selected.
- Add borders to a cell or selected cells with the Borders button on the Formatting toolbar or options at the Format Cells dialog box with the Border tab selected.
- Color shading can be added to a cell or selected cells with the Color button on the Formatting toolbar. Shading as well as a pattern can be added to a cell or selected cells with options at the Format Cells dialog box with the Patterns tab selected.
- Apply automatic formatting to selected cells in a worksheet with autoformats available at the AutoFormat dialog box.
- Excel's Help feature is an on-screen reference manual containing information about Excel features and commands.
- To get help from the Office Assistant, click the Assistant, key a question, and then click the Search button.

commands review

	Mouse/Keyboard
Display Save As dialog box	Click File and then Save As
Display Open dialog box	Click Open button on Standard toolbar; or click File and then Open
Display Print dialog box	Click File and then Print
Close a worksheet	Click File and then Close
Display worksheet in Print Preview	Click Preview button in Print dialog box; click Print Preview button on Standard toolbar; or click File and then Print Preview
Change Zoom display	Click down-pointing triangle at right side of Zoom button on Standard toolbar.
Display Column Width dialog box	Click Format, point to Column, and then click Width
Display Row Height dialog box	Click Format, point to Row, and then click Height
Display Format Cells dialog box	Click Format and then Cells
Display AutoFormat dialog box	Click Format and then AutoFormat

thinking offline

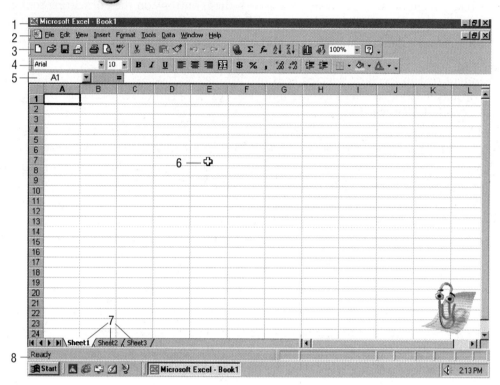

Identifying: Look at the Excel screen shown above. This screen contains numbers with lines pointing to specific items. Write the name of the item after the number below that corresponds with the number in the Excel screen.

1. _____   5. _____

2. _____   6. _____

3. _____   7. _____

4. _____   8. _____

Completion: In the space provided at the right, indicate the correct term or command.

1. Press this key on the keyboard to move the insertion point to the next cell. _____

2. Press these keys on the keyboard to move the insertion point to the previous cell. _____

3. Columns in a worksheet are labeled with this. _____

4. Rows in a worksheet are labeled with this. _____

5. Click this button in the worksheet area to select all cells in the table. _____

6. The gray vertical and horizontal lines that define the cells in a worksheet area are referred to as this. _____

7. If a number entered in a cell is too long to fit inside the cell, the number is changed to this. _____

8. Data being keyed in a cell displays in the cell as well as here. _____

9. This is the name of the small, black square that displays in the bottom right corner of the active cell. _____

10. To select nonadjacent columns using the mouse, hold down this key on the keyboard while clicking the column headers. _____

11. This toolbar contains buttons for applying character formatting to data within selected cells. _____

12. To automatically adjust a column width to accommodate the longest entry in the cell, do this with the mouse on the column header boundary. _____

13. As a column boundary is being dragged, the column width displays in this. _____

14. Click this button on the Formatting toolbar to multiply the value of numbers in selected cells by 100 and display the result followed by a percent symbol. _____

15. Click this button on the Formatting toolbar to add a dollar sign, any necessary commas, and a decimal point followed by two decimal digits to numbers in selected cells. _____

16. Click this button on the Formatting toolbar to merge selected cells and center any data within the cells. _____

17. Add color shading to selected cells in a document with options at the Format Cells dialog box with this tab selected. _____

18. Automatically apply formatting to selected cells in a worksheet with formats available at this dialog box. _____

working hands-on

Assessment 1

1. Create the worksheet shown in figure 8.28 by completing the following steps:
   a. Select the entire worksheet and then change the font to 12-point Garamond (or a similar serif typeface).
   b. Select column headers A, B, and C and then change the column width to 14.00.
   c. . Select row 1 and then turn on bold and change the alignment to center.
   d. Key the data shown in figure 8.28.
   e. After keying the data, select cells B2 through C6, and then change the number formatting to *Currency* with zero decimal places.
2. Save the worksheet and name it Excel Ch 08, SA 01.
3. Print and then close Excel Ch 08, SA 01.

Assessment 1

	A	B	C	D
1	**Expense**	**Original**	**Current**	
2	Labor	97000	98500	
3	Material	129000	153000	
4	Subcontracts	20450	21600	
5	Permits	1200	1350	
6	Tax	1950	2145	
7				

Assessment 2

1. Open Excel Worksheet 03.
2. Save the worksheet with Save As and name it Excel Ch 08, SA 02.
3. Make the following changes to the worksheet:
   a. Select the entire worksheet and then change the font to 11-point Tahoma (or a similar sans serif typeface).
   b. Select row 1 and then turn on bold.
   c. Select row 2 and then turn on bold and italics and change the alignment to center.
   d. Select cells A1 through D1 and then click the Merge and Center button on the Formatting toolbar.
   e. Select cells B3 through D8 and then click the Percent Style button on the Formatting toolbar.
   f. Select rows 1 through 8 and then change the row height to 18.00.
   g. Automatically adjust the widths of columns A through D.
4. Save the worksheet again with the same name (Excel Ch 08, SA 02).
5. Print and then close Excel Ch 08, SA 02.

Assessment 3

1. Open Excel Ch 08, SA 01.
2. Save the worksheet with Save As and name it Excel Ch 08, SA 03.
3. Make the following changes to the worksheet:
   a. Change the font for the entire worksheet to 14-point Arial and change the font color to violet.
   b. Change the font color to dark blue for the cells in row 1.
   c. Automatically adjust the widths of columns A, B, and C.
   d. Add a single-line outside border to cells A1 through C6.
4. Save the worksheet again with the same name (Excel Ch 08, SA 03).
5. Print and then close Excel Ch 08, SA 03.

Assessment 4

1. Open Excel Ch 08, SA 02.
2. Save the worksheet with Save As and name it Excel Ch 08, SA 04.
3. Make the following changes to the worksheet:
   a. Change the font for the entire worksheet to 12-point Garamond (or a similar serif typeface) and the font color to violet.
   b. Select row 2, turn off bold and italics, and then change the font color to dark blue.
   c. Select row 1 and then change the font color to dark blue.
   d. Select cells A1 through D8 and then add an outside border with a line style of your choosing.
4. Save the worksheet again with the same name (Excel Ch 08, SA 04).
5. Print and then close Excel Ch 08, SA 04.

Assessment 5

1. Open Excel Ch 08, SA 01.
2. Save the worksheet with Save As and name it Excel Ch 08, SA 05.
3. Add the following formatting to the worksheet:
   a. Select the cells that create the worksheet and then add a border around all cells (you choose the border line style).
   b. With the worksheet cells still selected, add light yellow shading to all cells.
   c. Select cells A1 through C1 and then add a pattern of your choosing to the cells.
4. Save the worksheet again with the same name (Excel Ch 08, SA 05).
5. Print and then close Excel Ch 08, SA 05.

Assessment 6

1. Create an Excel worksheet with the information shown in figure 8.29. You determine the following:
   a. Font
   b. Width of columns
   c. Number formatting
2. Add the following enhancements to the worksheet:
   a. Add a border to all cells in the worksheet containing data.
   b. Add a color shading to all cells in the worksheet containing data.

    c.   Add a pattern to column headings (the cells containing *Project, Projected,* and *Actual*).

3.   Save the completed worksheet and name it Excel Ch 08, SA 06.

4.   Print and then save Excel Ch 08, SA 06.

Assessment 6

CAPITAL PROJECT SUMMARY

Project	Projected	Actual
Rail siding installation	$43,300	$41,200
Cement slabs	$12,000	$13,980
Silos	$28,420	$29,600
Conveying system	$56,700	$58,200
Modulators	$8,210	$8,100
Winder	$6,400	$7,100

Assessment 7

1.   Open Excel Worksheet 02.

2.   Save the worksheet with Save As and name it Excel Ch 08, SA 07.

3.   Select cells A1 through D8 and then apply an autoformat. (Choose an autoformat that properly displays the numbers in the worksheet.)

4.   Save the worksheet again with the same name (Excel Ch 08, SA 07).

5.   Print and then close Excel Ch 08, SA 07.

Assessment 8

1.   Use the Office Assistant to learn more about how to move and scroll within an Excel worksheet.

2.   After reading and printing the information, create a worksheet containing the information. Set this up as a worksheet with two columns (cells will contain only text—not numbers). Create the worksheet with the following features:

    a.   Create a title for the worksheet.

    b.   Set the text in cells in a serif typeface and change the text color.

    c.   Add borders to the cells (you determine the border style).

    d.   Add a color shading to cells (you determine the color—make it complementary to the text color).

3.   Save the completed worksheet and name it Excel Ch 08, SA 08.

4.   Print and then close Excel Ch 08, SA 08.

 Chapter 09

Maintaining and Enhancing a Worksheet

PERFORMANCE OBJECTIVES

Upon successful completion of chapter 9, you will be able to:
- Insert rows and columns in a worksheet.
- Delete rows and columns in a worksheet.
- Clear data in cells.
- Change worksheet margins.
- Center a worksheet horizontally and vertically on the page.
- Insert a page break in a worksheet.
- Print gridlines and row and column headings.
- Hide and unhide a worksheet, column, or row.
- Set and clear a print area.
- Specify more than one print area in Page Break Preview.
- Change the print quality.
- Complete a spelling check on a worksheet.
- Find and replace data in a worksheet.
- Sort data in cells in ascending and descending order.

Some worksheets, once created, may require maintenance. This maintenance might include adding or deleting data and changing existing data. In this chapter, you will learn to add and delete rows and columns in a worksheet. You will also learn to control the formatting of a worksheet page. For example, you will learn to change worksheet margins, create headers and footers, print column and row titles, print gridlines, and center a worksheet horizontally and vertically on the page.

Inserting/Deleting Rows and Columns

New data may need to be included in an existing worksheet. For example, a row or several rows of new data may need to be inserted into a worksheet; or, data may need to be removed from a worksheet.

Inserting Rows

After a worksheet has been created, rows can be added to (inserted into) the worksheet. Insert a row with options from the Insert drop-down menu or with options at the Insert dialog box. By default, a row is inserted above the row containing the active cell. To insert a row in a worksheet, make a cell active in the row below where the row is to be inserted, then click Insert and then Rows. If you want to insert more than one row, select the number of rows in the worksheet that you want inserted, then click Insert and then Rows.

A row can also be inserted by making a cell active in the row below where the row is to be inserted, then clicking Insert, expanding the drop-down menu, and then clicking Cells. This causes the Insert dialog box to display as shown in figure 9.1. At the Insert dialog box, click Entire row. This inserts an entire row above the active cell.

figure
9.1

Insert Dialog Box

exercise 1

Inserting Rows in a Worksheet

1. Open Excel Worksheet 01.
2. Save the worksheet with Save As and name it Excel Ch 09, Ex 01.
3. Make the following changes to the worksheet:
   a. Add two rows and enter data in the new cells by completing the following steps:
      1) Select rows 7 and 8 in the worksheet.
      2) Click Insert and then Rows.
      3) Key the following data in the specified cells (you do not need to key the dollar sign or the comma in cells containing money amounts):

A7	=	**Summit Clinic**
B7	=	**570**
C7	=	**$33,056**
D7	=	**$32,500**
A8	=	**Franklin Center**
B8	=	**690**
C8	=	**$19,745**
D8	=	**$19,250**

    b. Select cells A1 through D12 and then apply an autoformat of your choosing. (Make sure the numbers display properly.)

4. Save the document again with the same name (Excel Ch 09, Ex 01).

5. Print and then close Excel Ch 09, Ex 01.

Inserting Columns

Columns can be inserted in a worksheet in much the same way as rows. Insert a column with options from the Insert drop-down menu or with options at the Insert dialog box. By default, a column is inserted immediately to the left of the column containing the active cell. To insert a column in a worksheet, make a cell active in the column immediately to the right of where the new column is to be inserted, then click Insert and then Columns. If you want to insert more than one column, select the number of columns in the worksheet that you want inserted, then click Insert and then Columns.

    A column can also be inserted by making a cell active in the column immediately to the right of where the new column is to be inserted, then clicking Insert and then Cells. This causes the Insert dialog box to display. At the Insert dialog box, click Entire column. This inserts an entire column immediately to the left of the active cell.

exercise 2

Inserting a Column in a Worksheet

1. Open Excel Worksheet 03.

2. Save the document with Save As and name it Excel Ch 09, Ex 02.

3. Make the following changes to the worksheet:

    a. Add a column to the worksheet and enter data in the new cells by completing the following steps:

      1) Click in any cell in column D.

      2) Click Insert and then Columns.

      3) Key the following data in the specified cell:

D2	=	**2001**
D3	=	**0.55**
D4	=	**0.4**
D5	=	**1.12**
D6	=	**1.85**
D7	=	**0.22**
D8	=	**0.055**

b. Change the contents of cell E2 from *Prior Year* to *2000*.
c. Select cells B3 through E8 and then click the Percent Style button on the Formatting toolbar.
d. Select cells A1 through E8 and then apply an autoformat of your choosing.
4. Save the worksheet again with the same name (Excel Ch 09, Ex 02).
5. Print and then close Excel Ch 09, Ex 02.

Deleting Cells, Rows, or Columns

Specific cells in a worksheet or rows or columns in a worksheet can be deleted. To delete a specific cell, make the cell active, and then press the Delete key. You can also select the cells to be deleted and then press the Delete key. If you use the Delete key to delete cell(s), only the cell text is deleted. The empty cell(s) remain(s) in the worksheet.

If you want to delete the cell(s) as well as the cell text, make the specific cell active or select cells, then click Edit and then Delete. At the Delete dialog box shown in figure 9.2, choose what you wanted deleted, and then click OK.

Delete Dialog Box

At the Delete dialog box, the Shift cells left option is selected by default. At this setting, cells will shift left after the selected cell (or cells) is deleted. Click Shift cells up and cells will shift up after the selected cell (or cells) is deleted. Click Entire row to delete the row containing the active cell or click Entire column to delete the column containing the active cell.

The Delete dialog box can also be displayed by positioning the cell pointer in the worksheet, clicking the *right* mouse button, and then clicking Delete on the shortcut menu. To delete several rows of cells, select the rows, then click Edit and then Delete. To delete several columns of cells, select the columns, then click Edit and then Delete.

Clearing Data in Cells

With the Clear option from the Edit drop-down menu, the contents of selected cells can be cleared. This is useful in a situation where the cells are to remain but the contents need to be changed. To clear cell contents, select the cells, click Edit, point to Clear, and then click All. This deletes the cell contents and the cell formatting. Click Formats to remove formatting from selected cells while leaving the data. Click Contents to remove the contents of the cell, leaving any formatting. You can also press the Delete key to clear the contents of the selected cells.

One method for clearing the contents of a cell is to right-click the cell and then click Clear Contents at the shortcut menu.

Deleting Columns and Deleting and Clearing Rows in a Worksheet

1. Open Excel Worksheet 02.
2. Save the worksheet with Save As and name it Excel Ch 09, Ex 03.
3. Make the following changes to the worksheet:
   a. Delete column D in the worksheet by completing the following steps:
      1) Click in any cell in column D.
      2) Click Edit and then Delete.
      3) At the Delete dialog box, click Entire column.
      4) Click OK or press Enter.

   b. Delete row 5 by completing the following steps:
      1) Select row 5.
      2) Click Edit and then Delete.
   c. Clear row contents by completing the following steps:
      1) Select rows 5 and 6.
      2) Click Edit, point to Clear, and then click Contents.

   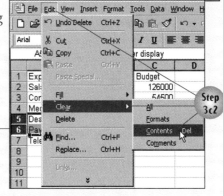

   d. Key the following data in the specified cell:
      A5 = **Lodging**
      B5 = **4535**
      C5 = **5100**
      A6 = **Entertainment**
      B6 = **3210**
      C6 = **3000**
   e. Select cells A1 through C7 and then apply the *Accounting 1* autoformat.
   f. Clear cell formatting and then apply different formatting by completing the following steps:
      1) Select cells A1 through C1.
      2) Click Edit, point to Clear, and then click Formats.
      3) With cells A1 through C1 still selected, click the Bold button on the Formatting toolbar and then click the Center button.
4. Save the worksheet again with the same name (Excel Ch 09, Ex 03).
5. Print and then close Excel Ch 09, Ex 03.

Formatting a Worksheet Page

The worksheets you have been creating and printing have fit on one sheet of paper. The worksheet has been printed in what is referred to as *portrait* orientation with default top and bottom margins of 1 inch and left and right margins of 0.75 inches. These settings can be changed with options at the Page Setup dialog box. The Page Setup dialog box contains several tabs for controlling the appearance of the worksheet page.

Controlling the Page Layout

Print Preview

The Page Setup dialog box with the Page tab selected as shown in figure 9.3 provides options for controlling the layout of the worksheet on the page. To display this dialog box, click File and then Page Setup. You can also display the Page Setup dialog box while in Print Preview. To do this, click the Print Preview button on the Standard toolbar. At the Print Preview screen, click the Setup button. At the Page Setup dialog box, make sure the Page tab is selected.

Page Setup Dialog Box with Page Tab Selected

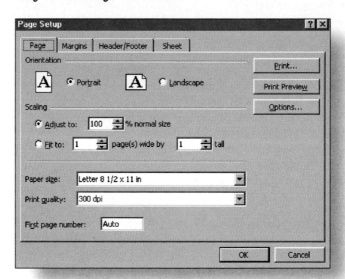

Control how information is printed on the page with choices in the Orientation section of the Page Setup dialog box. The two choices in the Orientation section are represented by sample pages. A sample page that is taller than it is wide shows how the default orientation (Portrait) prints data on the page. The other choice, Landscape, will rotate the data and print it on a page that is wider than it is tall. The Landscape orientation might be useful in a worksheet that contains more columns than rows.

With options in the Scaling section of the Page Setup dialog box, you can adjust the size of the data in the worksheet by percentage. You can also specify on how many pages you want the data to fit. For example, if a worksheet contains too many columns to print on one page, choosing Fit to and leaving *1* as the number of pages will cause the display percentage to be decreased until the columns all fit on one page.

By default, an Excel worksheet is printed on standard paper, which is 8.5 inches wide and 11 inches long. This paper size can be changed with options from the Paper size drop-down menu. Some paper size options include *Legal 8 1/2 x 14 in* and *Executive 7 1/4 x 10 1/2.* (Your paper size names may vary.) Paper size choices will vary depending on the selected printer. To view the list of paper sizes, click the down-pointing triangle at the right of the Paper size text box.

Depending on the printer you are using, you may or may not have choices for setting the print quality. The numbers that display in the Print quality text box will vary depending on the selected printer. To view a list of print quality choices, click the down-pointing triangle at the right side of the Print quality text box. Choose a higher *dpi* (dots per inch) number to improve the quality of the print.

The worksheets you have printed so far have not been numbered. If you turn page numbering on (discussed in the next section), the first worksheet page is numbered 1 and any additional pages are incrementally numbered. With the First page number option, you can specify a different beginning page number. To do this, select *Auto* in the First page number text box, and then key the new starting number.

Turning On Page Numbering

By default, worksheet pages are not numbered. Page numbering can be applied to a workbook with options at the Page Setup dialog box with the Header/Footer tab selected as shown in figure 9.4. To display this dialog box, click File and then Page Setup. At the Page Setup dialog box, click the Header/Footer tab.

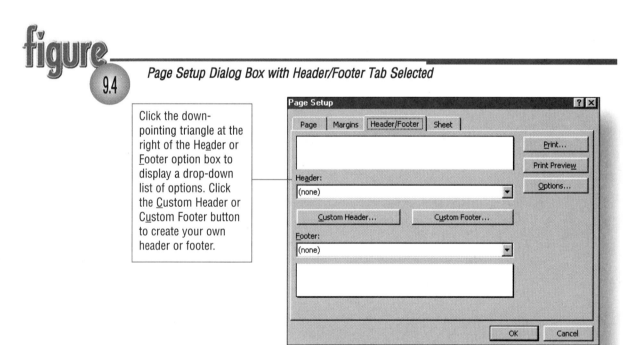

figure
9.4   *Page Setup Dialog Box with Header/Footer Tab Selected*

Click the down-pointing triangle at the right of the Header or Footer option box to display a drop-down list of options. Click the Custom Header or Custom Footer button to create your own header or footer.

To insert page numbering at the top of every page, click the Custom Header button on the Page Setup dialog box. Click the Custom Footer button to insert page numbering at the bottom of every page. If you click the Custom Footer button, the Footer dialog box shown in figure 9.5 displays. (The Header dialog box will display in a similar manner.) At the Footer dialog box, page numbering can be inserted at the Left section, Center section, or Right section of the page. Click in the text box below the desired location. Insert page numbering by clicking the Page Number button. (The buttons are identified in figure 9.5). Click OK to close the Footer dialog box and then click OK to close the Page Setup dialog box.

Page Number

figure

9.5 *Footer Dialog Box*

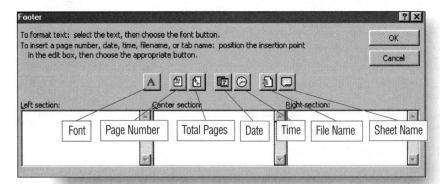

exercise 4

Changing Page Orientation and Inserting Page Numbering

1. Open Excel Worksheet 06.
2. Save the worksheet with Save As and name it Excel Ch 09, Ex 04.
3. Change the orientation of the worksheet and insert page numbering by completing the following steps:

   a. Click File and then Page Setup.
   b. At the Page Setup dialog box, click the Page tab.
   c. Click the Landscape option.
   d. Click twice on the up-pointing triangle at the right side of the Adjust to text box. (This inserts *110%* in the text box.)
   e. Click the Header/Footer tab.
   f. At the Page Setup dialog box with the Header/Footer tab selected, click the Custom Footer button.
   g. At the Footer dialog box, click in the text box below Center section.

   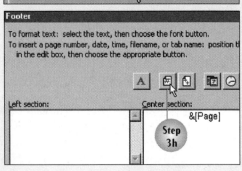

   h. Click the Page Number button (second button from the left).
   i. Click OK to close the Footer dialog box.
   j. Click OK to close the Page Setup dialog box.
4. Save the worksheet again with the same name (Excel Ch 09, Ex 04).
5. Preview the worksheet by clicking the Print Preview button on the Standard toolbar. After viewing the worksheet in Print Preview, click the Close button.
6. Print Excel Ch 09, Ex 04. (Before printing this worksheet, check with your instructor to determine if your printer can print in landscape orientation.)

7. With Excel Ch 09, Ex 04 still open, change the page orientation, scale the size of the worksheet so it fits on one page, and change the beginning page number to 3 by completing the following steps:
   a. Click File and then Page Setup.
   b. At the Page Setup dialog box, click the Page tab.
   c. Click the Portrait option.
   d. Click the Fit to option.
   e. Select *Auto* that displays in the First page number text box and then key **3**.
   f. Click OK to close the dialog box.
8. Save the worksheet again with the same name (Excel Ch 09, Ex 04).
9. Preview the worksheet and then print and close Excel Ch 09, Ex 04.

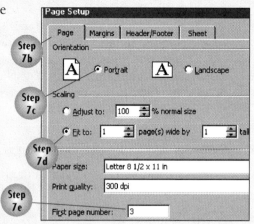

Inserting Headers/Footers

In the previous section, you learned how to insert page numbers in a header or footer. You can also create a header or footer containing text you want to print on every page. If you want specific text to print at the top of each page of the worksheet, create a header. Create a footer for text you want to print at the bottom of each page.

At the Page Setup dialog box with the Header/Footer tab selected (see figure 9.4), Excel offers a variety of header and footer text options. Click the down-pointing triangle after the Header text box and a drop-down list displays with options for inserting the user's name, document name, current date, and page number. The same list will display if you click the down-pointing triangle at the right of the Footer text box.

Creating a Header and Footer

1. Open Excel Worksheet 06.
2. Save the worksheet with Save As and name it Excel Ch 09, Ex 05.
3. Insert a header and footer in the worksheet by completing the following steps:
   a. Click File and then Page Setup.
   b. At the Page Setup dialog box, click the Header/Footer tab.
   c. At the Page Setup dialog box with the Header/Footer tab selected, click the Custom Header button.
   d. At the Header dialog box, click in the text box below Center section.
   e. Key **Microcomputer Applications**.
   f. Click OK to close the Header dialog box.

g. At the Page Setup dialog box with the Header/Footer tab selected, click the down-pointing triangle at the right side of the Footer text box.

h. At the drop-down list that displays, click *Page 1 of ?*.

i. Click OK to close the Page Setup dialog box.

4. Save the worksheet again with the same name (Excel Ch 09, Ex 05).

5. Preview the worksheet by clicking the Print Preview button on the Standard toolbar. After viewing the worksheet in Print Preview, click the Close button.

6. Print and then close Excel Ch 09, Ex 05.

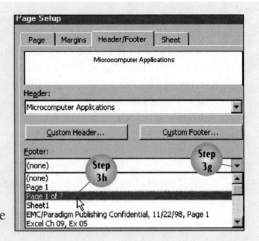

Changing Worksheet Margins

Excel uses 1-inch top and bottom margins for a worksheet and 0.75-inch left and right margins. These default margins can be changed at the Page Setup dialog box with the Margins tab selected as shown in figure 9.6.

Page Setup Dialog Box with Margins Tab Selected

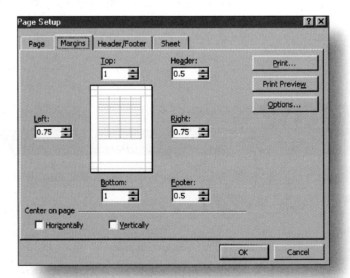

The Preview section of the dialog box displays the worksheet page showing the cells and margins. As you increase or decrease the Top, Bottom, Left, or Right margin measurements, the sample worksheet page reflects the change. You can also increase or decrease the measurement from the top of the page to the header with the Header option or the measurement from the footer to the bottom of the page with the Footer option.

Changing Worksheet Margins

1. Open Excel Worksheet 02.
2. Save the worksheet with Save As and name it Excel Ch 09, Ex 06.
3. Select cells A1 through D8 and then apply the *Accounting 2* autoformat.
4. Change the orientation of the worksheet and change the worksheet margins by completing the following steps:
   a. Click File and then Page Setup.
   b. At the Page Setup dialog box, click the Page tab.
   c. Click the Landscape option.
   d. Click the Margins tab.
   e. At the Page Setup dialog box with the Margins tab selected, click the up-pointing triangle at the right of the Top text box until *3.5* displays.
   f. Click the up-pointing triangle at the right of the Left text box until *3.5* displays.
   g. Click OK to close the dialog box.
5. Save the worksheet again with the same name (Excel Ch 09, Ex 06).
6. Preview the worksheet by clicking the Print Preview button on the Standard toolbar. After viewing the worksheet in Print Preview, click the Close button.
7. Print and then close Excel Ch 09, Ex 06.

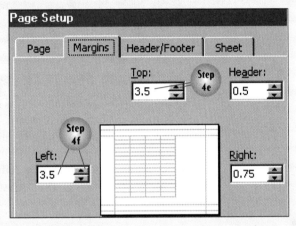

Centering a Worksheet Horizontally and/or Vertically

Many of the worksheets you have printed have been short and printed in the upper left corner of the page. A worksheet can be better centered on a page by changing the margins. But an easier method for centering a worksheet is to use the Horizontally and/or Vertically options that display at the bottom of the Page Setup dialog box with the Margins tab selected. If you choose one or both of these options, the worksheet page in the Preview section displays how the worksheet will print on the page.

Horizontally and Vertically Centering a Worksheet

1. Open Excel Worksheet 03.
2. Save the worksheet with Save As and name it Excel Ch 09, Ex 07.
3. Select cells B3 through D8 and then click the Percent Style button on the Formatting toolbar.

4. Select cells A1 through D8 and then apply the *Colorful 2* autoformat.
5. Horizontally and vertically center the worksheet by completing the following steps:
   a. Click File and then Page Setup.
   b. At the Page Setup dialog box, click the Margins tab.
   c. Click the Horizontally option.
   d. Click the Vertically option.
   e. Click OK to close the dialog box.
6. Save the worksheet again with the same name (Excel Ch 09, Ex 07).
7. Preview the worksheet by clicking the Print Preview button on the Standard toolbar. After viewing the worksheet in Print Preview, click the Close button.
8. Print and then close Excel Ch 09, Ex 07.

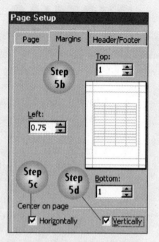

Inserting and Removing Page Breaks

The default left and right margins of 0.75 inches allow a total of 7 inches of cells across the page (8.5 inches minus 1.5 inches equals 7 inches). If a worksheet contains more than 7 inches of cells across the page, a page break is inserted in the worksheet and the remaining columns are moved to the next page. A page break displays as a broken line along cell borders. Figure 9.7 shows the page break in Excel Worksheet 06. (The location of your page break may vary.)

Page Break

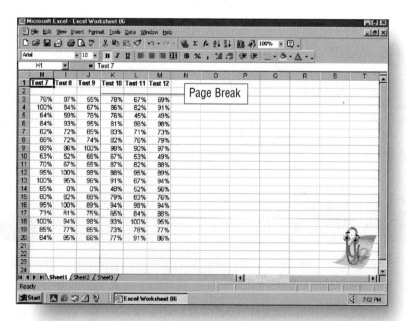

A page break also displays horizontally in a worksheet. By default, a worksheet can contain approximately 9 inches of cells vertically down the page. This is because the paper size is set by default at 11 inches. With the default top and bottom margins of 1 inch, this allows 9 inches of cells to print on one page.

Excel automatically inserts a page break in a worksheet. You can, however, insert your own if you would like more control over what cells print on a page. To insert your own page break, select the column or row, click Insert and then Page Break. A page break is inserted immediately left of the selected column or immediately above the selected row. If you want to insert both a vertical and horizontal page break at the same time, make a cell active, click Insert and then Page Break. This causes a vertical page break to be inserted at the left side of the active column and a horizontal page break to be inserted immediately above the active cell. To remove a page break, select the column or row or make the desired cell active, click Insert and then Remove Page Break.

The page break automatically inserted by Excel may not be visible initially in a worksheet. One way to display the page break is to preview the worksheet. When you close the Print Preview screen, the page break will display in the worksheet. In Print Preview, click the Next button on the Preview bar to display the next page in the worksheet. Click the Previous button to display the previous page in the worksheet.

Excel provides a page break view that will display worksheet pages and page breaks. To display this view, click View and then Page Break Preview. This causes the worksheet to display similar to the worksheet shown in figure 9.8. The word *Page* along with the page number is displayed in gray behind the cells in the worksheet. A blue line displays indicating the page break. You can move the page break by positioning the arrow pointer on the blue line, holding down the left mouse button, dragging the line to the desired location, and then releasing the mouse button. (If the Office Assistant is displaying a yellow box welcoming you to the page break preview, you must click OK before you can move the blue line.) To return to the normal view, click View and then Normal.

To display a page break in a worksheet, you may need to display the worksheet in Print Preview and then close Print Preview.

figure

9.8

Worksheet in Page Break Preview

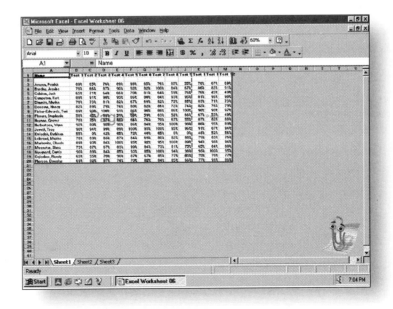

**exercise** 8

Inserting a Page Break in a Worksheet

1. Open Excel Worksheet 06.
2. Save the worksheet with Save As and name it Excel Ch 09, Ex 08.
3. View the default page break inserted automatically by Excel by completing the following steps:
   a. Click the Print Preview button on the Standard toolbar.
   b. After previewing the worksheet, click the Close button.
   c. At the worksheet, click the right scroll triangle at the right side of the horizontal scroll bar until columns J and K are visible. The default page break should display between columns J and K. (The default page break displays as a dashed line. The location of the page break may vary slightly.)
4. Make the following formatting changes:
   a. Select the entire table and then change the font to 12-point Century Schoolbook (or a similar serif typeface such as Garamond).
   b. If necessary, automatically adjust the width of column A.
   c. Select columns B through M and then drag one of the selected column boundaries to the right until the column width displays as *9.00* in the yellow box.
   d. Insert a page break between columns F and G by completing the following steps:
      1) Select column G.
      2) Click Insert and then Page Break.
      3) Click once in any cell in column F.
5. View the worksheet in Page Break Preview by completing the following steps:
   a. Click View and then Page Break Preview. (If a "Welcome to Page Break Preview" message box displays, click OK.)
   b. View the pages and page breaks in the worksheet.
   c. Click View and then Normal to return to the normal view.
6. Horizontally and vertically center the worksheet by completing the following steps:
   a. Click File and then Page Setup.
   b. At the Page Setup dialog box, click the Margins tab.
   c. Click the Horizontally option.
   d. Click the Vertically option.
   e. Click OK to close the dialog box.
7. Save the worksheet again with the same name (Excel Ch 09, Ex 08).
8. Preview the worksheet by clicking the Print Preview button on the Standard toolbar. After viewing the worksheet in Print Preview, click the Close button.
9. Print and then close Excel Ch 09, Ex 08.

Printing Column and Row Titles on Multiple Pages

Columns and rows in a worksheet are usually titled. For example, in Excel Worksheet 06, column titles include *Name, Test 1, Test 2, Test 3,* etc. Row titles include the names of the people who have taken the tests. If a worksheet prints on more than one page, having column and/or row titles printing on each page can be useful. For example, when you printed Excel Ch 09, Ex 08, the names of the people did not print on the second page. This makes matching test scores with names difficult.

Column and/or row titles can be printed on each page of a worksheet. To do this, click File and then Page Setup. At the Page Setup dialog box, click the Sheet tab. This displays the dialog box as shown in figure 9.9.

figure 9.9

Page Setup Dialog Box with Sheet Tab Selected

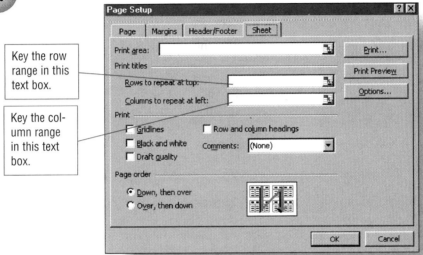

Key the row range in this text box.

Key the column range in this text box.

At the Page Setup dialog box with the Sheet tab selected, specify the range of row cells you want to print on every page in the Rows to repeat at top text box. Key a cell range using a colon. For example, if you want cells A1 through J1 to print on every page, you would key **A1:J1** in the Rows to repeat at top text box. Key the range of column cells you want to print on every page in the Columns to repeat at left text box.

Printing Column Titles on Each Page of a Worksheet

1. Open Excel Worksheet 06.
2. Save the worksheet with Save As and name it Excel Ch 09, Ex 09.
3. Make the following formatting changes to the worksheet:
   a. Select the entire table and then change the font to 12-point Garamond (or a similar serif typeface).
   b. If necessary, automatically adjust the width of column A.
   c. Select columns B through M and then drag one of the selected column boundaries to the right until the column width displays as *8.00* in the yellow box above the mouse pointer. (This will change the width of columns B through M to 8.00.)
   d. Select row 1 and then change the alignment to center.

4. Specify that you want column titles to print on each page by completing the following steps:
   a. Click File and then Page Setup.
   b. At the Page Setup dialog box, click the Sheet tab.
   c. At the Page Setup dialog box with the Sheet tab selected, click in the Columns to repeat at left text box.
   d. Key **A1:A20**.
   e. Click OK to close the dialog box.

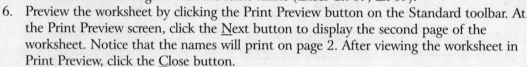

5. Save the worksheet again with the same name (Excel Ch 09, Ex 09).
6. Preview the worksheet by clicking the Print Preview button on the Standard toolbar. At the Print Preview screen, click the Next button to display the second page of the worksheet. Notice that the names will print on page 2. After viewing the worksheet in Print Preview, click the Close button.
7. Print and then close Excel Ch 09, Ex 09.

Printing Gridlines and Row and Column Headings

By default, gridlines do not print. Print gridlines by inserting a check mark in the Gridlines option at the Page Setup dialog box with the Sheet tab selected.

The gridlines that create the cells in a worksheet, by default, do not print. If you would like these gridlines to print, display the Page Setup dialog box with the Sheet tab selected, and then click Gridlines in the Print section. This inserts a check mark in the check box. At the Page Setup dialog box with the Sheet tab selected, you can also click Row and column headings and the row numbers and column letters will print with the worksheet.

If you are printing with a color printer, you can print the worksheet in black and white. To do this, display the Page Setup dialog box with the Sheet tab selected, and then click Black and white. This option is located in the *Print* section of the dialog box.

Printing Gridlines and Row and Column Headings

1. Open Excel Worksheet 05.
2. Save the worksheet with Save As and name it Excel Ch 09, Ex 10.
3. Make the following changes to the worksheet:
   a. Specify that the gridlines and row and column headings are to print by completing the following steps:
      1) Click File and then Page Setup.
      2) At the Page Setup dialog box, click the Sheet tab.
      3) Click the Gridlines check box in the Print section to insert a check mark.
      4) Click the Row and column headings check box in the Print section to insert a check mark.

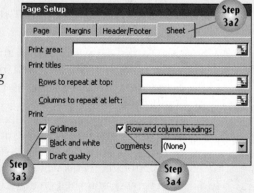

    b. With the Page Setup dialog box still displayed, click the Margins tab.

    c. At the Page Setup dialog box with the Margins tab selected, click the Horizontally option and then click the Vertically option.

    d. Click OK to close the dialog box.

4. Save the worksheet again with the same name (Excel Ch 09, Ex 10).

5. Preview the worksheet by clicking the Print Preview button on the Standard toolbar. After viewing the worksheet in Print Preview, click the Close button.

6. Print and then close Excel Ch 09, Ex 10.

Customizing Print Jobs

A variety of options are available for customizing print jobs. You can hide columns and/or rows before printing a worksheet, specify a printing area in a worksheet, and specify a print quality.

Hiding and Unhiding Workbook Elements

Various elements in a workbook, such as worksheets, columns, and rows, can be hidden. You may want to hide a worksheet that contains sensitive information, hide rows and/or columns that you are not using or do not want others to view, or hide elements in a workbook in order to use as much of the screen as possible to display specific worksheet data.

To hide a worksheet, display the worksheet, then click Format, point to Sheet, and then click Hide. To hide columns in a worksheet, select the columns to be hidden, click Format, point to Column, and then click Hide. To hide selected rows, click Format, point to Row, and then click Hide.

To make a hidden worksheet visible, click Format, point to Sheet, and then click Unhide. At the Unhide dialog box that displays, double-click the name of the hidden worksheet you want to display. To make a hidden column visible, select the column to the left and the column to the right of the hidden column, and then click Format, point to Columns, and then click Unhide. To make a hidden row visible, select the row above and the row below the hidden row, then click Format, point to Rows, and then click Unhide.

If the first row or column is hidden, use the Go To feature to make the row or column visible. To do this, click Edit and then Go To. At the Go To dialog box, key **A1** in the Reference text box, and then click OK. At the worksheet, click Format, point to Column or point to Row, and then click Unhide.

Printing a Specific Area of a Worksheet

Use the Print Area feature to select and print specific areas in a worksheet. To use this feature, select the cells you want to print, then click File, point to Print Area, and then click Set Print Area. This inserts a border around the selected cells. Click the Print button on the Standard toolbar and the cells within the border are printed.

You can specify more than one print area in a worksheet in Page Break Preview. To do this, display the worksheet in Page Break Preview. Select the first group of cells, then click File, point to Print Area, and then click Set Print Area. Select the next group of cells, right-click in the selected cells, and then click Add to Print Area at the shortcut menu. Clear a print area by selecting the area, clicking File, pointing to Print Area, and then clicking Clear Print Area.

Each area specified as a print area will print on a separate page. If you want nonadjacent print areas to print on the same page, consider hiding columns and/or rows in the worksheet to bring the areas together.

Changing Print Quality

Most printers have more than one level of print quality. The print quality choices vary with printers and may include options such as *High, Medium, Low,* and *Draft.* Print quality choices are available at the Page Setup dialog box with the Page tab selected. At this dialog box, click the down-pointing triangle at the right side of the Print quality option, and then click the desired print quality at the drop-down list.

Customizing a Printing Job

1. Open Excel Worksheet 06.
2. Specify a print area by completing the following steps:
   a. Select cells A1 through B20.
   b. Click File, point to Print Area, and then click Set Print Area.
   c. With the border surrounding the cells A1 through B20, click the Print button on the Standard toolbar.
   d. Clear the print area by making sure cells A1 through B20 are selected and then clicking File, pointing to Print Area, and then clicking Clear Print Area.
3. Suppose you want to print all the student names and just the percentages for Test 6 and you want the information to print on one page. To do this, hide columns B through F and select the print area by completing the following steps:
   a. Select columns B through F.
   b. Click Format, point to Column, and then click Hide.
   c. Select cells A1 through G20. (Columns A and G are now adjacent.)
   d. Click File, point to Print Area, and then click Set Print Area.
   e. Change the print quality and print the specified print area by completing the following steps:
      1) Click File and then Page Setup.
      2) At the Page Setup dialog box, click the Page tab.
      3) At the Page Setup dialog box with the Page tab selected, click the down-pointing triangle at the right side of the Print quality option, and then click *Draft* (or a similar quality) at the drop-down list.
      4) Click the Print... button.
      5) At the Print dialog box, click OK.
   f. Clear the print area by making sure cells A1 through G20 are selected and then clicking File, pointing to Print Area, and then clicking Clear Print Area.
   g. Make the hidden columns visible by selecting columns A and G and then clicking Format, pointing to Columns, and then clicking Unhide.
4. Close Excel Worksheet 06 without saving the changes.

Completing a Spelling Check

In chapter 3, you learned about Word's spell checking feature. Excel also includes a spell checker that operates the same as Word's. To spell check text in a worksheet, make the first cell in the worksheet active, then click the Spelling button on the Standard toolbar or click Tools and then Spelling. Figure 9.10 displays the Spelling dialog box. At this dialog box, you can click a button to tell Excel to ignore a word or you can replace a misspelled word with a word from the Suggestions list box.

Spelling

9.10 *Excel Spelling Dialog Box*

The word in the worksheet not found in the spell check dictionary displays here.

Suggested spellings display in the Suggestions list box.

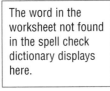

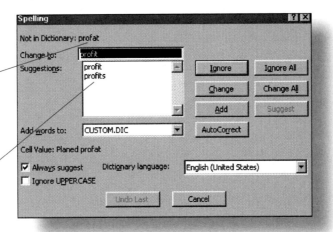

Using Undo and Redo

Undo

Excel includes an Undo button on the Standard toolbar that will reverse certain commands or delete the last data keyed in a cell. For example, if you apply an autoformat to selected cells in a worksheet and then decide you want the autoformatting removed, click the Undo button on the Standard toolbar. If you decide you want the autoformatting back again, click the Redo button on the Standard toolbar.

Redo

In addition to using the Undo and Redo buttons on the Standard toolbar, you can select options from the Edit drop-down menu to undo or repeat actions. The first two options at the Edit drop-down menu will vary depending on the last action completed. For example, if you just clicked the Currency Style button on the Formatting toolbar, and then displayed the Edit drop-down menu, the first option displays as Undo Style and the second option displays as Repeat Style. If you decide you do not want the currency style applied, click Edit and then Undo Style. You can also just click the Undo button on the Standard toolbar.

exercise 12

Spell Checking and Formatting a Worksheet

1. Open Excel Worksheet 04.
2. Save the worksheet with Save As and name it Excel Ch 09, Ex 12.
3. Complete a spelling check on the worksheet by completing the following steps:
   a. Make sure cell A1 is the active cell.
   b. Click the Spelling button on the Standard toolbar.
   c. Click Change as needed to correct misspelled words in the worksheet.
   d. At the message telling you the spelling check is completed, click OK.
4. Make the following formatting changes to the document:
   a. Select the entire worksheet and then change the font to 11-point Univers (or a similar sans serif typeface such as Tahoma).
   b. Select cells A1 through B12 and then apply the *Accounting 4* autoformat.
   c. Select cells B3 through B12 and then click the Currency Style button on the Formatting toolbar.
   d. With cells B3 through B12 still selected, click twice on the Decrease Decimal button on the Formatting toolbar.
   e. Make cell B4 active and then add a single-line border at the bottom of the cell. (To do this, click the down-pointing triangle at the right side of the Borders button on the Formatting toolbar and then click the Bottom Border option.)
   f. Make cell B5 active and then add a double-line border at the bottom of the cell. (To do this, click the down-pointing triangle at the right side of the Borders button on the Formatting toolbar and then click the Bottom Double Border option.)
   g. Make cell B10 active and then add a single-line border at the bottom of the cell.
   h. Make cell B12 active and then add a double-line border at the bottom of the cell.
   i. Select row 1 and then turn on bold.
   j. Select cells A1 through B12 and then add a pale blue color shading.
   k. After looking at the worksheet with the light blue color shading, you decide you want to remove it. To do this, click the Undo button on the Standard toolbar.
5. Save the worksheet again with the same name (Excel Ch 09, Ex 12).
6. Print and then close Excel Ch 09, Ex 12.

Finding and Replacing Data in a Worksheet

Excel provides a find feature you can use to look for specific data and either replace it with nothing or replace it with other data. This feature is particularly helpful in a large worksheet with data you want to find quickly. Excel also includes a find and replace feature. Use this to look for specific data in a worksheet and replace it with other data.

To find specific data in a worksheet, click Edit and then Find. This displays the Find dialog box shown in figure 9.11. Key the data you want to find in the Find what text box and then click the Find Next button. Continue clicking the Find Next button to move to the next occurrence of the data.

Ctrl + F is the keyboard command to display the Find dialog box.

Hint

figure
9.11

Find Dialog Box

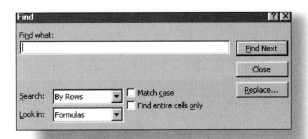

To find specific data in a worksheet and replace it with other data, click Edit and then Replace. This displays the Replace dialog box shown in figure 9.12. Enter the data for which you are looking in the Find what text box. Press the Tab key or click in the Replace with text box and then enter the data that is to replace the data in the Find what text box.

Ctrl + H is the keyboard command to display the Replace dialog box.

figure
9.12

Replace Dialog Box

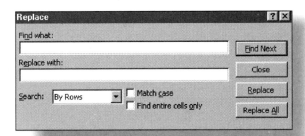

The Replace dialog box contains four command buttons at the right side. Click the Find Next button to tell Excel to find the next occurrence of the data. Click the Replace button to replace the data and find the next occurrence. If you know that you want all occurrences of the data in the Find what text box replaced with the data in the Replace with text box, click the Replace All button. Click the Close button to close the Replace dialog box.

By default, Excel will look for any data that contains the same characters as the data in the Find what text box, without concern for the characters before or after the entered data. For example, in exercise 12, you will be looking for test scores of 0%. If you do not specify to Excel that you want to find cells that contain just 0%, Excel will stop at any cell containing a 0%. In this example, Excel would stop at a cell containing 90% or a cell containing 100%. To specify that the only data that should be contained in the cell is what is entered in the Find what text box, insert a check mark in the Find entire cells only check box.

If the Find dialog box or the Replace dialog box obstructs your view of the worksheet, move the box by clicking and dragging the title bar.

If the Match case option at the Replace dialog box is active (contains a check mark) Excel will look for only that data that exactly matches the case of the data entered in the Find what text box. Remove the check mark from this check box if you do not want Excel to find exact case matches. Excel, by default, searches by rows in a worksheet. This can be changed to *By Columns* with the Search option.

Finding and Replacing Data

1. Open Excel Worksheet 06.
2. Save the worksheet with Save As and name it Excel Ch 09, Ex 13.
3. Find all occurrences of 0% in the worksheet and replace with 70% by completing the following steps:
   a. Click Edit and then Replace.
   b. At the Replace dialog box, key **0%** in the Find what text box.
   c. Press the Tab key (this moves the insertion point to the Replace with text box).
   d. Key **70%**.
   e. Click Find entire cells only.
   f. Click the Replace All button.
4. Select the entire worksheet and then change the font to 10-point Century Schoolbook (or a similar serif typeface).
5. Automatically adjust the width of columns A through M.
6. Save the worksheet again with the same name (Excel Ch 09, Ex 13).

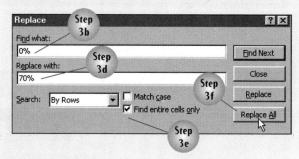

7. Display the Page Setup dialog box with the Page tab selected, click the Landscape option, and then close the dialog box.
8. Print and then close Excel Ch 09, Ex 13.

Excel's Find feature is very similar to the Find and Replace feature. The difference is that Find will only find data and will not replace it. To use Find, click Edit and then Find. This causes the Find dialog box to display. This dialog box contains many of the same options as the Find and Replace dialog box. Use Find if you are looking for specific data in a worksheet.

Sorting Data

Sort Ascending

Sort Descending

Excel is primarily a spreadsheet program, but it also includes some basic database functions. With a database program, you can alphabetize information or arrange numbers numerically. Data can be sorted by columns in a worksheet. By default, Excel will sort special symbols such as *, @, and # first, numbers second, and letters third. Sort data in a worksheet using the Sort Ascending or Sort Descending buttons on the Standard toolbar or at the Sort dialog box.

Sorting Data Using Buttons on the Standard Toolbar

To sort data in a worksheet using the buttons on the Standard toolbar, open the worksheet, select the cells containing data you want to sort, and then click the Sort Ascending button (sorts text A through Z; sorts numbers lowest to highest) or Sort Descending button (sorts text Z through A; sorts numbers highest to lowest). If you select more than one column in a worksheet, Excel will sort the data in the first selected column.

exercise 14

Sorting Data Using the Sort Ascending and Sort Descending Buttons

1. Open Excel Worksheet 03.
2. Save the worksheet with Save As and name it Excel Ch 09, Ex 14.
3. Make the following formatting changes to the worksheet:
   a. Merge and center the data in cell A1 across cells A1 through D1.
   b. Bold the data in cell A1.
   c. Bold the data in cells B2 through D2.
   d. Automatically adjust the width of columns A through D.
   e. Select cells B3 through D8 and then click the Percent Style button on the Formatting toolbar.
4. Sort the data in the first column alphabetically in ascending order by completing the following steps:
   a. Select cells A3 through D8.
   b. Click the Sort Ascending button on the Standard toolbar.

Step 4b

Step 4a

	A	B	C	D	E
1	ANALYSIS OF FINANCIAL CONDITION				
2		Actual	Planned	Prior Year	
3	Stockholder's equity ratio	62%	60%	57%	
4	Bond holder's equity ratio	45%	39%	41%	
5	Liability liquidity ratio	122%	115%	120%	
6	Fixed obligation security ratio	196%	190%	187%	
7	Fixed interest ratio	23%	20%	28%	
8	Earnings ratio	7%	6%	6%	

5. Save the worksheet again with the same name (Excel Ch 09, Ex 14).
6. Print Excel Ch 09, Ex 14. (Do not close the worksheet.)
7. Sort the data in the first column alphabetically in descending order by completing steps similar to those in step 4 except click the Sort Descending button on the Standard toolbar.
8. Save the worksheet again with the same name (Excel Ch 09, Ex 14).
9. Print and then close Excel Ch 09, Ex 14.

Sorting Data at the Sort Dialog Box

If you want to sort data in a column other than the first selected column, use the Sort dialog box. If you select just one column in a worksheet and then click the Sort Ascending or Sort Descending button on the Standard toolbar, only the data in that column is sorted. If this data was related to data to the left or right of the data in the column, that relationship is broken. For example, if you sort cells B3 through B8 in Excel Ch 09, Ex 13, the percentages for *Bondholder's equity ratio* are now *23%, 39% and 41%*, when they should be *45%, 39%, and 41%*.

Use the Sort dialog box to sort data and maintain the relationship of all cells. To sort using the Sort dialog box, select the cells you want sorted, then click <u>D</u>ata and then <u>S</u>ort. This displays the Sort dialog box shown in figure 9.13.

figure

9.13

Sort Dialog Box

The data displayed in the <u>S</u>ort by text box will vary depending on what you have selected. Generally, the data that displays is the title of the first column of selected cells. If the selected cells do not have a title, the data may display as *Column A*. Use this option to specify what column you want sorted. Using the Sort dialog box to sort data in a column maintains the relationship of the data.

exercise 15

Sorting Data Using the Sort Dialog Box

1. Open Excel Ch 09, Ex 14.
2. Save the worksheet with Save As and name it Excel Ch 09, Ex 15.
3. Sort the percentages in cells B3 through B8 in ascending order and maintain the relationship to the other data by completing the following steps:
   a. Select cells A3 through D8.
   b. Click <u>D</u>ata and then <u>S</u>ort.
   c. At the Sort dialog box, click the down-pointing triangle at the right of the Sort by text box, and then click *Actual* from the drop-down list.
   d. Make sure <u>A</u>scending is selected in the Sort by section of the dialog box. If not, click <u>A</u>scending.
   e. Click OK to close the dialog box.

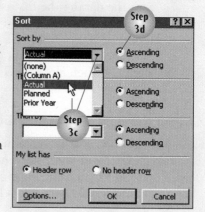

4. Save the worksheet again with the same name (Excel Ch 09, Ex 15).
5. Print Excel Ch 09, Ex 15.
6. Sort the percentages in cells B3 through B8 in *descending* order and maintain the relationship of the data by completing steps similar to those in step 3.
7. Save the worksheet again with the same name (Excel Ch 09, Ex 15).
8. Print and then close Excel Ch 09, Ex 15.

Sorting More than One Column

When sorting data in cells, you can sort on more than one column. For example, in exercise 15, you will be sorting the average test scores in ascending order and then sorting the names of the students alphabetically. In this sort, the test averages are sorted first and then students with the same average are sorted alphabetically within that average. For example, there are several average scores of 76%. Students within that average—not all students—are sorted alphabetically.

If you are not satisfied with the results of a sort, immediately click the Undo button on the Standard toolbar.

To sort on more than one column, select all columns in the worksheet that need to remain relative, and then display the Sort dialog box. At the Sort dialog box, specify the first column you want sorted in the Sort by text box, and then specify the second column in the first Then by text box. In Excel, you can sort on up to three columns. If you want to sort the data in a third column, you would specify that in the second Then by text box.

exercise 16

Sorting Data in Two Columns

1. Open Excel Worksheet 06.
2. Save the worksheet with Save As and name it Excel Ch 09, Ex 16.
3. Select and then delete row 2.
4. Sort the Test 1 percentages in cells B2 through B19 in ascending order and then sort alphabetically by the names in the first column by completing the following steps:
   a. Select cells A2 through M19.
   b. Click Data and then Sort.
   c. At the Sort dialog box, click the down-pointing triangle at the right side of the Sort by text box, and then click *Test 1* from the drop-down list.
   d. Make sure Ascending is selected in the Sort by section of the dialog box. If not, click Ascending.
   e. Click the down-pointing triangle at the right of the first Then by text box and then click *Name* in the drop-down list.
   f. Make sure Ascending is selected in the first Then by section.
   g. Click OK to close the dialog box.

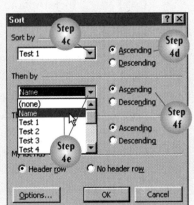

5. Save the worksheet again with the same name (Excel Ch 09, Ex 16).

6. Display the Page Setup dialog box with the Page tab selected, click the Landscape option, and then close the dialog box.
7. Print the worksheet. (Notice how the names of the students with the same Test 1 percentages are alphabetized.)
8. Close Excel Ch 09, Ex 16.

chapter summary

- ▶ Insert a row in a worksheet by clicking Insert and then Rows. To insert more than one row, select the number of rows you want inserted, and then click Insert and then Rows. A row can also be inserted at the Insert dialog box.

- ▶ Insert a column in a worksheet by clicking Insert and then Columns. To insert more than one column, select the number of columns you want inserted, and then click Insert and then Columns. A column can also be inserted at the Insert dialog box.

- ▶ Delete a specific cell by clicking Edit and then Delete. This displays the Delete dialog box where you can specify if you want to delete just the cell or an entire row or column.

- ▶ Contents of a cell can be removed with the Clear option from the Edit drop-down menu or by pressing the Delete key.

- ▶ By default, a worksheet prints on the page in portrait orientation. This can be changed to landscape orientation at the Page Setup dialog box with the Page tab selected.

- ▶ The percentage size of data in a worksheet can be adjusted with options in the Scaling section of the Page Setup dialog box with the Page tab selected.

- ▶ The paper size can be changed with the Paper size option at the Page Setup dialog box with the Page tab selected.

- ▶ Create a header and/or footer for worksheet pages with options at the Page Setup dialog box with the Header/Footer tab selected.

- ▶ The beginning page number in a worksheet can be changed with the First page number option at the Page Setup dialog box with the Page tab selected.

- ▶ Excel uses 1-inch top and bottom margins and 0.75-inch left and right margins for a worksheet. These default margins can be changed at the Page Setup dialog box with the Margins tab selected.

- ▶ Center a worksheet horizontally and/or vertically on a page with options at the Page Setup dialog box with the Margins tab selected.

- ▶ Insert a page break in a worksheet with Insert and then Page Break.

- ▶ Print column and row titles on every page of a multiple-paged worksheet with options at the Page Setup dialog box with the Sheet tab selected.

- ▶ Gridlines, column letters, and row numbers can be printed with options at the Page Setup dialog box with the Sheet tab selected.

- ▶ You can hide and unhide a worksheet in a workbook or columns or rows in a worksheet.

- ▶ Use the Print Area feature to select and print specific areas in a worksheet. Specify more than one print area in Page Break Preview.

- The print quality for most printers can be changed with the Print quality option at the Page Setup dialog box with the Page tab selected.
- Complete a spelling check on a worksheet by clicking the Spelling button on the Standard toolbar or clicking Tools and then Spelling.
- Click the Undo button to reverse certain commands or delete the last data keyed in a cell. Click the Redo button to repeat the last command or action, if possible.
- Find data with options at the Find dialog box and find and replace data in a worksheet with options at the Replace dialog box.
- Sort the first column of selected cells with the Sort Ascending or Sort Descending buttons on the Standard toolbar.
- Use the Sort dialog box to sort on a column other than the first column, to maintain the relationship of the data, or to sort on more than one column.

commands review

	Mouse/Keyboard
Insert a row	Click Insert, Rows
Insert a column	Click Insert, Columns
Display Insert dialog box	Click Insert, Cells
Display Delete dialog box	Click Edit, Delete
Clear cell	Click Edit, Clear or press the Delete key
Display Page Setup dialog box	Click File and then Page Setup
Insert a page break	Click Insert, Page Break
Hide columns	Select columns, click Format, point to Column, then click Hide
Hide rows	Select rows, click Format, point to Row, then click Hide
Unhide columns	Select column to left and right, then click Format, point to Column, click Unhide
Unhide rows	Select row above and below, then click Format, point to Row, click Unhide
Set a print area	Select cells, then click File, point to Print Area, then click Set Print Area
Clear a print area	Select cells, then click File, point to Print Area, then click Clear Print Area
Display Spelling dialog box	Click Spelling button on Standard toolbar or click Tools, Spelling
Display Find dialog box	Click Edit, Find
Display Replace dialog box	Click Edit, Replace

Sort first selected column in ascending order	Click Sort Ascending button on Standard toolbar
Sort first selected column in descending order	Click Sort Descending button on Standard toolbar
Display Sort dialog box	Click Data, Sort

thinking offline

Completion: In the space provided at the right, indicate the correct term, command, or number.

1. By default, a row is inserted in this direction from the row containing the active cell. _____

2. By default, a column is inserted in this direction from the column containing the active cell. _____

3. By default, a worksheet prints in this orientation on a page. _____

4. Change the page orientation at the Page Setup dialog box with this tab selected. _____

5. This is the default paper size. _____

6. This is the worksheet default top and bottom margin measurement. _____

7. This is the worksheet default left and right margin measurement. _____

8. A worksheet can be horizontally and/or vertically centered with options at the Page Setup dialog box with this tab selected. _____

9. Click this to insert a page break in a worksheet. _____

10. Print gridlines with an option at the Page Setup dialog box with this tab selected. _____

11. To make a hidden column visible, select these columns and then click Format, point to Column, and then click Unhide. _____

12. Use this feature to print specific areas in a worksheet. _____

13. To complete a spelling check on a worksheet, click this button on the Standard toolbar. _____

14. To display the Sort dialog box, click Sort from this drop-down menu. _____

15. List the steps you would complete to print column titles in a multiple-paged worksheet.

_____

_____

16. List the steps you would complete to find all occurrences of *January* in a worksheet and replace with *July*.

_____

_____

17. List the steps you would complete to sort the second column of data in ascending order in the worksheet displayed below.

	A	B	C	D
1	SALES BY GEOGRAPHIC TERRITORY			
2	Territory	Actual	Budget	
3	Northwest	$ 459,309	$ 465,000	
4	Northeast	$ 794,209	$ 820,000	
5	Southwest	$ 351,309	$ 350,000	
6	Southeast	$ 408,123	$ 400,000	
7				

working hands-on

Assessment 1

1. Open Excel Worksheet 07.
2. Save the worksheet with Save As and name it Excel Ch 09, SA 01.
3. Make the following changes to the worksheet:
   a. Delete column E.
   b. Bold the data in cell A1.
   c. Bold the data in row 2.
   d. Select columns B through D and then change the width of the columns to 13.00.
   e. Create a column between columns C and D (when the column is inserted, the data in column D moves over to column E).
   f. Select cells D3 through D10 and then change the number formatting to *General*. (Do this at the Format Cells dialog box with the Number tab selected.)
   g. Key the following data in the specified cells:
D2	=	**Periods**
D3	=	2 (*Hint: Use the fill handle to copy the 2s.*)
D4	=	2
D5	=	2
D6	=	2
D7	=	2
D8	=	2
D9	=	2
D10	=	2
   h. Select and then center the data in cells D3 through D10.
   i. Add a row above row 6 and then key the following data in the specified cells:

$$A6 = \text{Facsimile}$$
$$B6 = 670.00$$
$$C6 = 150.00$$
$$D6 = 2$$
$$E6 = 4$$

    j.   Select cells A1 through E11 and then apply the *Colorful 1* autoformat.

    k.   Select cells D3 through E11 and then change the alignment to center.

4. Save the worksheet again with the same name (Excel Ch 09, SA 01).

5. Print and then close Excel Ch 09, SA 01.

Assessment 2

1. Open Excel Worksheet 01.

2. Save the worksheet with Save As and name it Excel Ch 09, SA 02.

3. Make the following changes to the worksheet:

    a.   Select the worksheet and then change the font to 10-point Century Schoolbook (or a similar serif typeface).

    b.   Automatically adjust the width of column A.

    c.   Bold and center the data in row 1.

    d.   Delete row 2.

    e.   Select cells B2 through B9 and then change the alignment to center.

4. Change the worksheet top margin to 2 inches and the left margin to 2.25 inches and then print the worksheet.

5. Save the worksheet again with the same name (Excel Ch 09, SA 02).

6. Close Excel Ch 09, SA 02.

Assessment 3

1. Open Excel Worksheet 06.

2. Save the worksheet with Save As and name it Excel Ch 09, SA 03.

3. Make the following changes to the worksheet:

    a.   Select the worksheet and then change the font to 11-point Garamond (or a similar serif typeface).

    b.   If necessary, automatically adjust the width of column A.

    c.   If necessary, adjust slightly columns K, L, and M so the title (such as *Test 10, Test 11*, and so on) fits in the cell.

    d.   Delete row 2 and then delete rows 8 and 9.

    e.   Create the header *Excel Test Scores* that prints at the right margin on both pages.

    f.   Create a footer that prints *Page x* (where *x* represents the correct page number) at the bottom center of the page.

4. Save the worksheet again with the same name (Excel Ch 09, SA 03).

5. Print the worksheet so the column titles (names) print on both pages.

6. Print the worksheet again in landscape orientation.

7. Close Excel Ch 09, SA 03.

Assessment 4

1. Open Excel Worksheet 02.

2. Save the worksheet with Save As and name it Excel Ch 09, SA 04.

3. Make the following changes to the worksheet:

    a.   Select the entire worksheet and then change the font to 12-point Tahoma (or a similar sans serif typeface).

    b. Select row 1 and then bold and center the data.

    c. Select cells B2 through D8 and then click the Currency Style button on the Formatting toolbar.

    d. With cells B2 through D8 still selected, click twice the Decrease Decimal button on the Formatting toolbar.

    e. Select columns A through D and then automatically adjust the size of the columns to accommodate the amounts.

4. Save the worksheet again with the same name (Excel Ch 09, SA 04).

5. Print the worksheet, including gridlines and the row and column headings.

6. Close Excel Ch 09, SA 04.

Assessment 5

1. Open Excel Ch 09, SA 01.

2. Save the worksheet with Save As and name it Excel Ch 09, SA 05.

3. Make the following changes to the worksheet:

    a. Find all occurrences of cells containing only the number *2* and then replace it with the number *1*.

    b. Find all occurrences of cells containing only the number *6* and then replace it with the number *5*.

    c. Delete row 10.

4. Save the worksheet again with the same name (Excel Ch 09, SA 05).

5. Print the worksheet horizontally and vertically centered on the page.

6. Close Excel Ch 09, SA 05.

Assessment 6

1. Open Excel Ch 09, SA 01.

2. Save the worksheet with Save As and name it Excel Ch 09, SA 06.

3. Select cells A3 through E11 and then click the Sort Ascending button on the Standard toolbar.

4. Print the worksheet horizontally and vertically centered on the page.

5. With the worksheet still open, select cells A3 through E11, and then sort the numbers in column B in ascending order (do this at the Sort dialog box).

6. Print the worksheet horizontally and vertically centered on the page.

7. With the worksheet still open, select cells A3 through E11, and then sort by the numbers in the *Life of Asset* column in ascending order and then by *Equipment* in ascending order. (This is one sort.)

8. Save the worksheet again with the same name (Excel Ch 09, SA 06).

9. Print the worksheet horizontally and vertically centered on the page.

10. Close Excel Ch 09, SA 06.

Assessment 7

1. Open Excel Worksheet 06.

2. Save the worksheet with Save As and name it Excel Ch 09, SA 07.

3. Make the following changes to the worksheet:

    a. Delete columns J through M.

    b. Delete row 2 and then delete row 13.

    c. Select cells A2 through I18 and then sort by names in descending order.

      d. Select cells A1 through I18 and then apply an autoformat of your choosing.
4. Save the worksheet again with the same name (Excel Ch 09, SA 07).
5. Print the worksheet horizontally and vertically centered on the page and insert page numbering at the bottom center of the page.
6. Close Excel Ch 09, SA 07.

Assessment 8

1. Open Excel Worksheet 06.
2. Print student names and scores for Test 12 on one page by completing the following steps:
      a. Hide columns B through L.
      b. Specify A1 through M20 as a print area.
      c. Print the print area. (Make sure the cells print on one page.)
      d. Clear the print area.
      e. Make columns B through L visible.
3. Close Excel Worksheet 06 without saving the changes.

Assessment 9

1. Use Excel's Office Assistant and ask the question "What is Excel's default sorting order?"
2. Display information on default sort orders. After reading and printing the information presented by the Office Assistant, create a worksheet containing a summary of the information. Create the worksheet with the following features:

      a. Create a title for the worksheet.
      b. Set the data in cells in a serif typeface and change the data color.
      c. Add borders to the cells (you determine the border style).
      d. Add a color shading to cells (you determine the color—make it complementary to the data color).
3. Save the completed worksheet and name it Excel Ch 09, SA 09.
4. Print and then close Excel Ch 09, SA 09.

Chapter 10

Moving Data within and between Workbooks

PERFORMANCE OBJECTIVES

Upon successful completion of chapter 10, you will be able to:
- Move, copy, and paste cells within a worksheet.
- Create a workbook with multiple worksheets.
- Split a worksheet into windows and freeze panes.
- Open and close workbooks.
- Size, move, and arrange workbooks.
- Copy and paste data between windows.
- Automate formatting with Format Painter.
- Define, apply, remove, and delete styles.
- Copy styles from one workbook to another.
- Save an Excel workbook as a Web page.
- Preview a Web page using Web Page Preview.
- Create a hyperlink.
- Create a folder.
- Send a workbook by e-mail.
- Create financial forms using templates.
- Create customized templates.

Moving and pasting or copying and pasting selected cells in different locations in a worksheet can be useful for rearranging data in a worksheet or for saving time. Up to this point, the workbooks you have been working in have consisted of only one worksheet. In this chapter, you will learn to create a workbook with several worksheets and complete tasks such as copying and pasting data within and between worksheets. You will also work with multiple workbooks and complete tasks such as sizing, moving, and arranging workbooks, and opening and closing multiple workbooks.

Formatting in a large workbook containing multiple worksheets can be automated with styles. A style is a predefined set of formatting attributes. In this chapter, you will learn to define, apply, modify, remove, delete, and copy styles. You will also learn how to save an Excel workbook as a Web page, create a hyperlink in a workbook, and send a workbook as e-mail.

Moving, Copying, and Pasting Cells

Situations may arise where you need to move cells to a different location within a worksheet; or, you may need to copy repetitive data in a worksheet. You can perform these actions by selecting cells and then using the Move, Copy, and/or Paste buttons on the Standard toolbar. You can also perform these actions with the mouse or with options from the Edit drop-down menu.

Cut

Paste

Ctrl + X is the keyboard command to cut selected data.

Ctrl + V is the keyboard command to paste data.

Moving Selected Cells

Selected cells and cell contents can be moved in a worksheet and between worksheets. Selected cells can be moved with the Cut and Paste buttons on the Standard toolbar, by dragging with the mouse, or with options on the Edit drop-down menu.

To move selected cells with buttons on the Standard toolbar, select the cells, and then click the Cut button. This causes a moving dashed line to display around the selected cells. Click the cell where you want the first selected cell to be inserted and then click the Paste button on the Standard toolbar. If you change your mind and do not want to move the selected cells, press the Esc key to remove the moving dashed line or double-click in any cell.

To move selected cells with the mouse, select the cells, and then position the mouse pointer on any border of the selected cells until it turns into an arrow pointer. Hold down the left mouse button, drag the outline of the selected cells to the desired location, and then release the mouse button.

Selected cells can also be moved by selecting the cells and then clicking Edit and then Cut. This causes a moving dashed line to display around the selected cells. Click the cell where you want the first selected cell to be inserted and then click Edit and then Paste.

exercise

Moving Selected Cells in a Worksheet

1. Open Excel Worksheet 02.
2. Save the worksheet with Save As and name it Excel Ch 10, Ex 01.
3. Make the following changes to the worksheet:
   a. Move cells in column D to column E by completing the following steps:
      1) Select cells D1 through D8.
      2) Click the Cut button on the Standard toolbar.
      3) Click cell E1 to make it active.
      4) Click the Paste button on the Standard toolbar.
   b. Move cells in column B to column D by completing the following steps:
      1) Select cells B1 through B8.
      2) Position the mouse pointer on any boundary of the selected cells until it turns into an arrow pointer.
      3) Hold down the left mouse button, drag the outline of the selected cells to column D, and then release the mouse button.

	A	B	C	D	E
1	Expense	Actual	Budget		Variance
2	Salaries	126000	126000		0
3	Commissions	58000	54500	D1:D8	3500
4	Media space	8250	10100		1850
5	Travel expenses	6350	6000		-350
6	Dealer display	4140	4500		360
7	Payroll taxes	2430	2200		-230
8	Telephone	1450	1500		50

Step 3b1

Step 3b3

(After the cells are moved, they should occupy cells D1 through D8.)
   c.   Delete column B.
   d.   Select cells A1 through D8 and then apply the Accounting 2 autoformat.
   e.   Select row 1 and then turn on Bold and change the alignment to center.
4.   Save the worksheet again with the same name (Excel Ch 10, Ex 01).
5.   Print and then close Excel Ch 10, Ex 01.

Copying Selected Cells

Copying selected cells can be useful in worksheets that contain repetitive data. To copy cells, select the cells, and then click the Copy button on the Standard toolbar. Click the cell where you want the first selected cell to be copied and then click the Paste button on the Standard toolbar.

Copy

Selected cells can also be copied using the mouse and the Ctrl key. To do this, select the cells to be copied, and then position the mouse pointer on any border around the selected cells until it turns into an arrow pointer. Hold down the Ctrl key and the left mouse button, drag the outline of the selected cells to the desired location, and then release the left mouse button and then the Ctrl key.

Ctrl + C is the keyboard command to copy selected data.

The Copy and Paste options from the Edit drop-down menu can also be used to copy selected cells in a worksheet. To do this, select the cells, and then click Edit and then Copy. Click the cell where you want the first selected cell to be copied and then click Edit and then Paste.

Collecting and Pasting Multiple Items

In chapter 4, you learned about a new Office 2000 feature called *collecting and pasting*. With this feature, you can collect up to 12 different items and then paste them in various locations. Display the Clipboard toolbar when you want to collect and paste items. Display this toolbar by right-clicking an existing toolbar and then clicking Clipboard. Select text or an object you want to copy and then click the Copy button on the Clipboard toolbar. Continue selecting text or items and clicking the Copy button. To insert an item, position the insertion point in the desired location and then click the Clipboard button representing the item. Position the insertion point on a button and a ScreenTip displays with information on the item. If the item is text, the first 50 characters display. When all desired items are inserted, click the Clear Clipboard button to remove any remaining items.

When you click the Copy button on the Standard toolbar, selected cells display surrounded by a moving border.

exercise 2

Collecting and Pasting Cells
1.   Open Excel Worksheet 06.
2.   Save the worksheet with Save As and name it Excel Ch 10, Ex 02.
3.   Make cell A22 the active cell, turn on bold, and then key **Top Performers**.
4.   Display the Clipboard toolbar by right-clicking an existing toolbar and then clicking Clipboard at the drop-down list.
5.   Collect several rows of cells and then paste them by completing the following steps:
   a.   Click the row header for row 9 (this selects the entire row).

b. Click the Copy button on the Clipboard toolbar.
c. Click the row header for row 13 and then click the Copy button on the Clipboard toolbar.
d. Click the row header for row 16 and then click the Copy button on the Clipboard toolbar.

6. Paste the copied cells by completing the following steps:
a. Make cell A23 active.
b. Click the button on the Clipboard toolbar representing row 13. (To find this button, position the arrow pointer on a button on the Clipboard toolbar until the ScreenTip displays. Look for the ScreenTip that begins *Jewett, Troy 98% 94%...*).
c. Make cell A24 active.
d. Click the button on the Clipboard toolbar representing row 16 (look for the ScreenTip that begins *Markovits, Claude 89% 93%...*)
e. Make cell A25 active.
f. Click the button on the Clipboard toolbar representing row 9 (look for the ScreenTip that begins *Fisher-Edwards, Teri 89% 93%...*).

7. Click the Clear Clipboard button on the Clipboard toolbar.
8. Close the Clipboard toolbar.
9. Save the worksheet again with the same name (Excel Ch 10, Ex 02).
10. Print and then close Excel Ch 10, Ex 02.

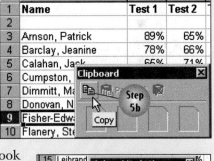

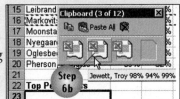

Creating a Workbook with Multiple Worksheets

Up to this point, each workbook you have been creating has contained one worksheet. As you learned in chapter 8, a workbook can contain several worksheets. You can create a variety of worksheets within a workbook for related data. For example, a workbook may contain a worksheet for the expenses for each salesperson in a company and another worksheet for the monthly payroll for each department within the company. Another example is recording sales statistics for each quarter in individual worksheets within a workbook.

The copy and paste features can be useful in creating more than one worksheet within a workbook. These features are helpful if there is some consistency in data within each worksheet. For example, you can create a worksheet containing information on a product and then this information can be copied to another worksheet where you would change data in specific cells. By default, a workbook contains three worksheets. To insert an additional worksheet in a workbook, click Insert and then Worksheet.

To copy selected cells to a new worksheet, select the cells, click the Copy button on the Standard toolbar, click the worksheet tab (displayed immediately above the Status bar) representing the desired worksheet, and then click the Paste button.

Printing a Workbook Containing Multiple Worksheets

You can print specific worksheets in a workbook by selecting the tabs of the desired worksheets.

In exercise 3, you will create a workbook that contains four worksheets. When printing this workbook, by default, Excel will print the worksheet currently displayed. If you want to print all worksheets in a workbook, display the Print dialog box by clicking File and then Print. At the Print dialog box, click Entire workbook in the Print what section, and then click OK.

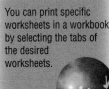

Another method for printing specific worksheets within a workbook is to select the tabs of the worksheets you want to print. To do this, open the desired workbook, hold down the Ctrl key, and then click the desired tabs. (If the tabs are adjacent, you can use the Shift key.)

Copying Cells to Different Worksheets

1. Open Excel Worksheet 02.
2. Save the worksheet with Save As and name it Excel Ch 10, Ex 03.
3. Add a fourth worksheet by clicking <u>I</u>nsert and then <u>W</u>orksheet. (This adds a *Sheet4* tab before the *Sheet1* tab.)
4. Click the *Sheet1* tab to make worksheet 1 active and then make the following changes to the worksheet:
   a. With any cell in row 1 active, add a row. (This adds a row at the beginning of the worksheet.)
   b. Key **First Quarter** in cell A1.
   c. Select cells A1 through D9 and then apply the Accounting 1 autoformat.
   d. Select cells A1 through D1 and then click the Merge and Center button on the Formatting toolbar.
   e. Select cells B3 through D9 and then decrease the decimal places to none.
   f. Copy cells and paste them into worksheets 2, 3, and 4 by completing the following steps:
      1) Click the Select All button that displays immediately to the left of the column A header and immediately above the row 1 header.
      2) Click the Copy button on the Standard toolbar.
      3) Click the *Sheet2* tab that displays immediately above the Status bar.
      4) At worksheet 2, make sure cell A1 is the active cell, and then click the Paste button.
      5) Click the *Sheet3* tab that displays immediately above the Status bar.
      6) At worksheet 3, make sure cell A1 is the active cell, and then click the Paste button.
      7) Click the *Sheet4* tab.
      8) At worksheet 4, make sure cell A1 is the active cell, and then click the Paste button.
   g. Click the *Sheet2* tab and then make the following changes to cell entries in worksheet 2:
      A1: From *First Quarter* to *Second Quarter*
      B4: From *58,000* to *60500*
      C4: From *54,500* to *58500*
      D4: From *(3,500)* to *-2000*
      B8: From *2,430* to *2510*
      C8: From *2,200* to *2350*
      D8: From *(230)* to *-160*
   h. Click the *Sheet3* tab and then make the following changes to cell entries in worksheet 3:
      A1: From *First Quarter* to *Third Quarter*
      B4: From *58,000* to *60200*
      C4: From *54,500* to *60500*
      D4: From *(3,500)* to *300*
      B8: From *2,430* to *2500*
      C8: From *2,200* to *2550*
      D8: From *(230)* to *50*

i.   Click the *Sheet4* tab and then make the following changes to cell entries in worksheet 4:
       A1: From *First Quarter* to *Fourth Quarter*
       B4: From *58,000* to *61000*
       C4: From *54,500* to *60500*
       D4: From *(3,500)* to *-500*
       B8: From *2,430* to *2550*
       C8: From *2,200* to *2500*
       D8: From *(230)* to *-50*
5.   Save the workbook again with the same name (Excel Ch 10, Ex 03).
6.   Print all the worksheets in the workbook by completing the following steps:
     a.   Make sure there are no selected cells (just an active cell).
     b.   Click File and then Print.
     c.   At the Print dialog box, click Entire workbook in the Print what section.
     d.   Click OK. (Each worksheet will print on a separate piece of paper.)
7.   Close Excel Ch 10, Ex 03.

Managing Worksheets

Right-click a sheet tab and a shortcut menu displays with the options Insert, Delete, Rename, Move or Copy, and Select All Sheets. Use these options to manage worksheets in a workbook. For example, remove a worksheet by clicking the Delete option. Move or copy a worksheet by clicking the Move or Copy option. Clicking this option causes a Move or Copy dialog box to display where you specify before what sheet you want to move or copy the selected sheet. By default, Excel names worksheets in a workbook *Sheet1, Sheet2, Sheet3,* and so on. To rename a worksheet, click the Rename option (this selects the default sheet name), and then key the desired name.

You can manage more than one worksheet at a time by selecting the worksheets first. If the tabs are adjacent, click the first tab, hold down the Shift key, and then click the last tab. If the tabs are nonadjacent, click the first tab, hold down the Ctrl key, and then click any other tabs you want selected.

Deleting Selected Worksheets

1.   Open Excel Ch 10, Ex 03.
2.   Save the workbook with Save As and name it Excel Ch 10, Ex 04.
3.   Delete worksheets 3 and 4 by completing the following steps:
     a.   Click the left mouse button on *Sheet3* that displays at the bottom of the workbook window.
     b.   Hold down the Ctrl key, click *Sheet4*, and then release the Ctrl key.
     c.   Position the arrow pointer on the *Sheet4* tab and then click the *right* mouse button.
     d.   At the pop-up menu that displays, click the left mouse button on Delete.
     e.   At the message telling you that the selected sheets will be permanently deleted, click OK.

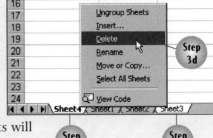

4. Rename worksheets 1 and 2 by completing the following steps:
   a. Right-click the *Sheet1* tab, click <u>R</u>ename at the shortcut menu, and then key **First Quarter**.
   b. Right-click the *Sheet2* tab, click <u>R</u>ename at the shortcut menu, and then key **Second Quarter**.
5. Move the Second Quarter sheet tab by completing the following steps:
   a. Right-click the Second Quarter sheet tab and then click <u>M</u>ove or Copy at the shortcut menu.
   b. At the Move or Copy dialog box, make sure *First Quarter* is selected in the <u>B</u>efore sheet list box, and then click OK.
6. Save the workbook again with the same name (Excel Ch 10, Ex 04).
7. Print the entire workbook (two worksheets).
8. Close Excel Ch 10, Ex 04.

Splitting a Worksheet into Windows and Freezing and Unfreezing Panes

In some worksheets, not all cells display at one time in the worksheet area (such as Excel Worksheet 06). When working in worksheets with more cells than can display at one time, you may find splitting the worksheet window into panes helpful. Split the worksheet window into panes with the <u>S</u>plit option from the <u>W</u>indow drop-down menu or using the split bars that display at the top of the vertical scroll bar and at the right side of the horizontal scroll bar. These split bars are identified in figure 10.1.

Split Bars

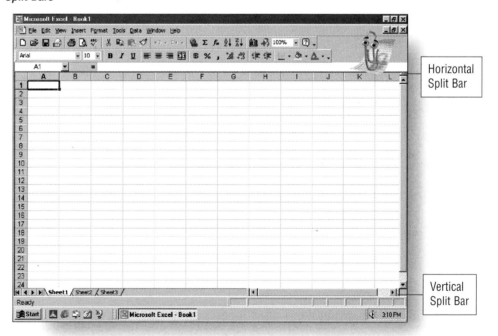

Horizontal Split Bar

Vertical Split Bar

To split a window with the split bar located at the top of the vertical scroll bar, position the mouse pointer on the split bar until it turns into a double-headed arrow with a short double line in the middle. Hold down the left mouse button, drag down the thick gray line that displays until the pane is the desired size, and then release the mouse button. Split the window vertically with the split bar at the right side of the horizontal scroll bar.

To split a worksheet window with the Window drop-down menu, click Window and then Split. This causes the worksheet to be split into four window panes as shown in figure 10.2. The windows are split by thick gray lines (with a three-dimensional look).

figure 10.2 *Split Window*

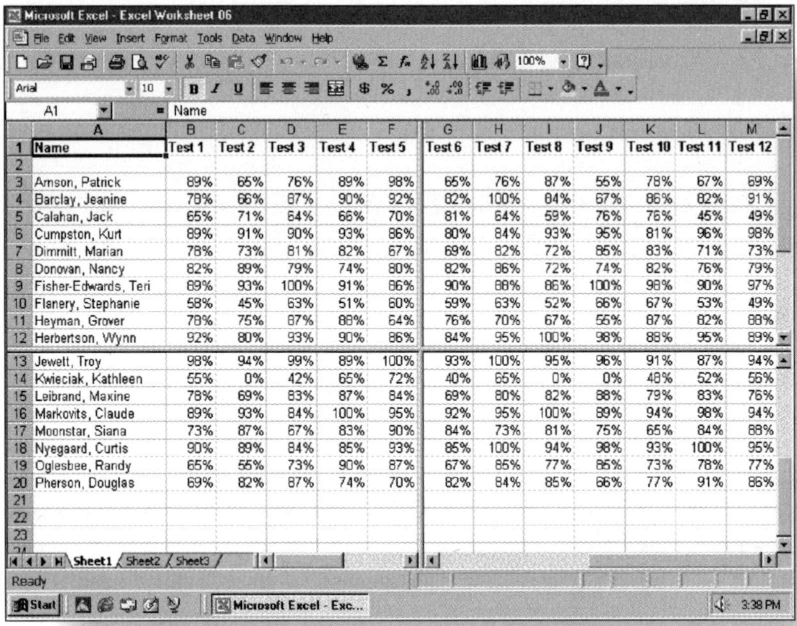

	A	B	C	D	E	F	G	H	I	J	K	L	M
1	Name	Test 1	Test 2	Test 3	Test 4	Test 5	Test 6	Test 7	Test 8	Test 9	Test 10	Test 11	Test 12
2													
3	Arnson, Patrick	89%	65%	76%	89%	98%	65%	76%	87%	55%	78%	67%	69%
4	Barclay, Jeanine	78%	66%	87%	90%	92%	82%	100%	84%	67%	86%	82%	91%
5	Calahan, Jack	65%	71%	64%	66%	70%	81%	64%	59%	76%	76%	45%	49%
6	Cumpston, Kurt	89%	91%	90%	93%	86%	80%	84%	93%	95%	81%	96%	98%
7	Dimmitt, Marian	78%	73%	81%	82%	67%	69%	82%	72%	85%	83%	71%	73%
8	Donovan, Nancy	82%	89%	79%	74%	80%	82%	86%	72%	74%	82%	76%	79%
9	Fisher-Edwards, Teri	89%	93%	100%	91%	86%	90%	88%	86%	100%	98%	90%	97%
10	Flanery, Stephanie	58%	45%	63%	51%	60%	59%	63%	52%	66%	67%	53%	49%
11	Heyman, Grover	78%	75%	87%	88%	64%	76%	70%	67%	55%	87%	82%	88%
12	Herbertson, Wynn	92%	80%	93%	90%	86%	84%	95%	100%	98%	88%	95%	89%
13	Jewett, Troy	98%	94%	99%	89%	100%	93%	100%	95%	96%	91%	87%	94%
14	Kwieciak, Kathleen	55%	0%	42%	65%	72%	40%	65%	0%	0%	48%	52%	56%
15	Leibrand, Maxine	78%	69%	83%	87%	84%	69%	80%	82%	88%	79%	83%	76%
16	Markovits, Claude	89%	93%	84%	100%	95%	92%	95%	100%	89%	94%	98%	94%
17	Moonstar, Siana	73%	87%	67%	83%	90%	84%	73%	81%	75%	65%	84%	88%
18	Nyegaard, Curtis	90%	89%	84%	85%	93%	85%	100%	94%	98%	93%	100%	95%
19	Oglesbee, Randy	65%	55%	73%	90%	87%	67%	85%	77%	85%	73%	78%	77%
20	Pherson, Douglas	69%	82%	87%	74%	70%	82%	84%	85%	66%	77%	91%	86%
21													
22													
23													

A window pane will display the active cell. As the insertion point is moved through the pane, another active cell with a blue background may display. This additional active cell displays when the insertion point passes over one of the gray lines that creates the pane. As you move through a worksheet, you may see both active cells—one with a normal background and one with a blue background. If you make a change to the active cell, the change is made in both. If you want only one active cell to display, freeze the window panes by clicking Window and then Freeze Panes. With panes frozen, only the display of the pane with the active cell will change. To unfreeze panes, click Window and the Unfreeze Panes.

The thick gray lines that divide the window into panes can be moved using the mouse. To do this, position the mouse pointer on the line until it turns into a double-headed arrow with a double line in the middle. Hold down the left mouse button, drag the outline of the gray line until it is positioned in the desired location, and then release the mouse button. If you want to move both the horizontal and vertical lines at the same time, position the mouse pointer on the intersection of the thick gray lines until it turns into a four-headed arrow. Hold down the left mouse button, drag the thick gray lines in the desired direction, and then release the mouse button.

By splitting a worksheet into windows, you can maintain the display of column headings while editing or keying text in cells. You can do the same for row headings. You will be doing this with a worksheet in exercise 5.

Splitting Windows and Editing Cells

1. Open Excel Worksheet 06.
2. Save the worksheet with Save As and name it Excel Ch 10, Ex 05.
3. Split the window by completing the following steps:
   a. Click <u>W</u>indow and then <u>S</u>plit. (This causes the window to be split into four panes.)
   b. Drag both the horizontal and vertical gray lines by completing the following steps:
      1) Position the mouse pointer on the intersection between the horizontal and vertical lines until it turns into a four-headed black arrow.
      2) Hold down the left mouse button, drag up and to the left until the horizontal gray line is immediately below the first row and the vertical gray line is immediately to the right of the first column, and then release the mouse button.
   c. Freeze the window panes by clicking <u>W</u>indow and then <u>F</u>reeze Panes.
   d. Add two rows by completing the following steps:
      1) Select rows 18 and 19.
      2) Click <u>I</u>nsert and then <u>R</u>ows.
   e. Key the following text in the specified cells:

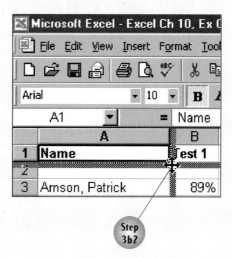

Step 3b2

A18	=	**Nauer, Sheryl**
B18	=	75
C18	=	83
D18	=	85
E18	=	78
F18	=	82
G18	=	80
H18	=	79
I18	=	82
J18	=	92
K18	=	90
L18	=	86
M18	=	84
A19	=	**Nunez, James**
B19	=	98
C19	=	96
D19	=	100
E19	=	90
F19	=	95
G19	=	93
H19	=	88
I19	=	91
J19	=	89
K19	=	100
L19	=	96
M19	=	98

f. Edit the text in the following cells:
D3: Change *76%* to *92%*
K6: Change *81%* to *74%*
E8: Change *74%* to *90%*
M12: Change *89%* to *95%*
C14: Change *0%* to *70%* (Hint: *Be sure to press Enter to change from the Edit mode to the Ready mode.*)
g. Unfreeze the window panes by clicking Window and then Unfreeze Panes.
h. Remove the panes by clicking Window and then Remove Split.
4. Save the worksheet again with the same name (Excel Ch 10, Ex 05).
5. Print the worksheet in landscape orientation and then close Excel Ch 10, Ex 05.

Working with Windows

In chapter 4, you learned about working with multiple documents in Word. You learned to open multiple documents and then arrange the open documents in the window. You also learned to cut and paste text between open documents. Many of the same functions can be performed in Excel. For example, you can open multiple workbooks, arrange the workbooks in the window, and also print and close multiple workbooks.

Opening Multiple Workbooks

With multiple workbooks open, you can move or copy information between workbooks or compare the contents of several workbooks. The maximum number of workbooks that you can have open at one time depends on the memory of your computer system and the amount of information in each workbook. When you open a new workbook, it is placed on top of the original workbook. Once multiple workbooks are opened, you can resize the workbooks to see all or a portion of them on the screen.

Multiple workbooks can be opened at one time at the Open dialog box. If workbooks are adjacent, display the Open dialog box, click the first workbook to be opened, hold down the Shift key, and then click the last workbook to be opened. If the workbooks are nonadjacent, click the first workbook to be opened, and then hold down the Ctrl key while clicking the remaining desired workbook names. Release the Shift key or the Ctrl key and then click the Open button.

To see what workbooks are currently open, click Window on the Menu bar. The names of the open workbooks display at the bottom of the drop-down menu. The workbook name with the check mark in front of it is the *active* workbook. The active workbook is the workbook containing the active cell. To make one of the other workbooks active, click the desired workbook.

Closing Multiple Workbooks

All open workbooks can be closed at the same time. To do this, hold down the Shift key, click File on the Menu bar, and then click Close All. Holding down the Shift key while clicking the File option causes the Close option to change to the Close All option.

exercise 6

Opening and Closing Multiple Workbooks

(Note: If you are using Microsoft Office on a network system that contains a virus checker, you may not be able to open multiple workbooks at one time.)

1. Open several workbooks at the same time by completing the following steps:
   a. Display the Open dialog box.
   b. Click the document named Excel Worksheet 02.
   c. Hold down the Ctrl key, click Excel Worksheet 04, and then click Excel Worksheet 06.
   d. Release the Ctrl key and then click the Open button in the dialog box.
2. Make Excel Worksheet 02 the active document by clicking Window and then 3.
3. Make Excel Worksheet 04 the active document by clicking Window and then 2.
4. Close all open documents by completing the following steps:
   a. Hold down the Shift key.
   b. Click File on the Menu bar.
   c. Click Close All.

Arranging Workbooks

If you have more than one workbook open, you can arrange the workbooks at the Arrange Windows dialog box shown in figure 10.3. To display this dialog box, open several workbooks, then click Window and then Arrange.

Arrange Windows Dialog Box

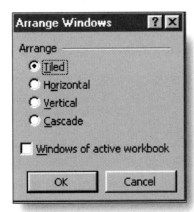

At the Arrange Windows dialog box, click Tiled to display a portion of each open workbook. Figure 10.4 shows four open workbooks that have been tiled.

figure

10.4

Tiled Workbooks

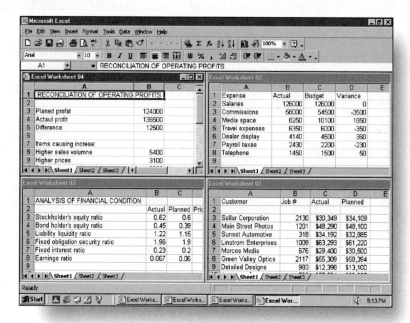

Choose the Horizontal option at the Arrange Windows dialog box and the open workbooks will be displayed across the screen. The Vertical option will display the open workbooks up and down the window. The last option, Cascade, will display the Title bar of each open workbook. Figure 10.5 shows four open workbooks that have been cascaded.

figure

10.5

Cascaded Workbooks

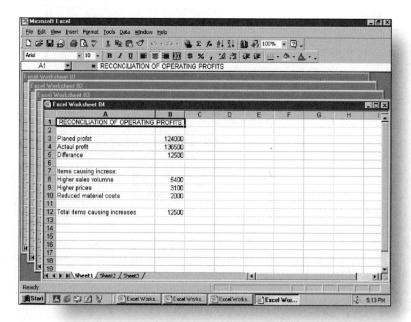

Arranging Workbooks

1. Open the following workbooks: Excel Worksheet 01, Excel Worksheet 02, Excel Worksheet 03, and Excel Worksheet 04.
2. Tile the workbooks by completing the following steps:
    a. Click <u>W</u>indow and then <u>A</u>rrange.
    b. At the Arrange Windows dialog box, make sure <u>T</u>iled is selected, and then click OK.
3. Tile the workbooks horizontally by completing the following steps:
    a. Click <u>W</u>indow and then <u>A</u>rrange.
    b. At the Arrange Windows dialog box, click H<u>o</u>rizontal.
    c. Click OK.
4. Cascade the workbooks by completing the following steps:
    a. Click <u>W</u>indow and then <u>A</u>rrange.
    b. At the Arrange Windows dialog box, click <u>C</u>ascade.
    c. Click OK.
5. Close all the open workbooks by holding down the Shift key and then clicking <u>F</u>ile and then <u>C</u>lose All.

Sizing and Moving Workbooks

The Maximize and Minimize buttons in the upper right corner of the active workbook window can be used to change the size of the window. The Maximize button is the button in the upper right corner of the active document immediately to the left of the Close button. (The Close button is the button containing the X.) The Minimize button is located immediately to the left of the Maximize button.

Maximize

Minimize

Close

If you arrange all open workbooks and then click the Maximize button in the active workbook, the active workbook expands to fill the screen. In addition, the Maximize button changes to the Restore button. To return the active workbook back to its size before it was maximized, click the Restore button.

Clicking the Minimize button causes the active workbook to be reduced and positioned as a button on the Taskbar. In addition, the Minimize button changes to the Restore button. To maximize a workbook that has been reduced, click the button on the Taskbar representing the workbook.

Restore

Minimizing, Maximizing, and Restoring Workbooks

1. Open Excel Worksheet 01.
2. Maximize Excel Worksheet 01 by clicking the Maximize button at the right side of the workbook Title bar. (The Maximize button is the button at the right side of the Title bar, immediately to the left of the Close button.)
3. Open Excel Worksheet 03 and Excel Worksheet 05.

4. Make the following changes to the open workbooks:
   a. Tile the workbooks.
   b. Make Excel Worksheet 01 the active workbook (Title bar displays with a blue background [the background color may vary depending on how Windows is customized]).
   c. Minimize Excel Worksheet 01 by clicking the Minimize button that displays at the right side of the Title bar.
   d. Make Excel Worksheet 03 the active workbook and then minimize it.
   e. Minimize Excel Worksheet 05.
5. Close all workbooks by holding down the Shift key, then clicking File and then Close All.

Cut/copy and paste a worksheet between programs in the Microsoft Office suite in the same manner as you cut/copy and paste between worksheets in Excel.

Moving, Copying, and Pasting Data between Workbooks

With more than one workbook open, you can move, copy, and/or paste data from one workbook to another. To move, copy, and/or paste data between workbooks, use the cutting and pasting options you learned earlier in this chapter, together with the information about windows in this chapter.

exercise 9

Copying Selected Cells from One Open Worksheet to Another

1. At a blank worksheet, create the worksheet shown in figure 10.6 by completing the following steps (if a blank worksheet is not displayed, click the New button on the Standard toolbar):
   a. If you just completed exercise 8, click the Maximize button so the worksheet fills the entire worksheet window.
   b. Change the width of column A to 21.00.
   c. Select cells A1 through D1 click the Merge and Center button on the Formatting toolbar, and then click the Bold button.
   d. Select row 2, click the Bold button on the Formatting toolbar, and then click the Center button.
   e. Select cells B3 through B6 and then click the Center button on the Formatting toolbar.
   f. Key the text in the cells as shown in figure 10.6.
   g. Select cells C3 through D6, click the Currency Style button on the Formatting toolbar, and then click twice on the Decrease Decimal button.
2. Save the worksheet and name it Excel Ch 10, Ex 09.
3. With Excel Ch 10, Ex 09 still open, open Excel Worksheet 01.
4. With Excel Worksheet 01 the active worksheet, change the width of column A to 21.00.

5. Select and then copy text from Excel Worksheet 01 to Excel Ch 10, Ex 09 by completing the following steps:
   a. With Excel Worksheet 01 the active workbook, select cells A5 through D10.
   b. Click the Copy button on the Standard toolbar.
   c. Click <u>W</u>indow and then click <u>2</u> Excel Ch 10, Ex 09.
   d. Make cell A7 the active cell and then click the Paste button on the Standard toolbar.

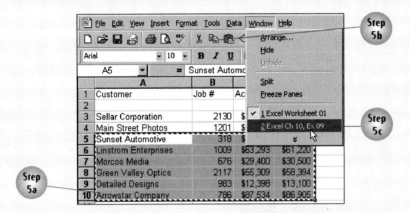

   e. Deselect the cells.
6. Select cells A1 through D12 in Excel Ch 10, Ex 09 and then apply the Colorful 1 autoformat.
7. Save the workbook again with the same name (Excel Ch 10, Ex 09).
8. Print and then close Excel Ch 10, Ex 09.
9. Close Excel Worksheet 01 without saving the changes.

figure
10.6

Exercise 9

	A	B	C	D
1		FEBRUARY		
2	Customer	Job #	Actual	Planned
3	Real Photography	129	$ 42,350	$ 41,000
4	Jenkins Corporation	3310	$ 88,450	$ 90,000
5	Bridgway Electronics	1023	$ 19,340	$ 17,500
6	Moss Bay Productions	894	$ 68,340	$ 65,000
7				

Copying and Pasting a Worksheet between Programs

Microsoft Office is a suite that allows integration, which is the combining of data from two or more programs into one document. Integration can occur by copying and pasting data between programs. The program containing the data to be copied is called the *source* program and the program where the data is pasted is called the *destination* program. For example, you can create a worksheet in Excel and then copy it to a Word document.

The steps to copy and paste between programs are basically the same as copying and pasting between documents within the same program. The only difference is that you need to open both programs and use the Taskbar to move between programs.

To copy a worksheet into a Word document, you would follow these basic steps:

1. Open Word and then create the document or open an existing document.
2. Open Excel and then create the worksheet or open an existing worksheet.
3. Select the worksheet and then click the Copy button on the Standard toolbar.
4. Click the button on the Taskbar representing Microsoft Word. (This makes Word the active program.)
5. Position the insertion point in the Word document where you want the worksheet inserted and then click the Paste button on the Standard toolbar.

When a worksheet is pasted into a Word document, it becomes a Word table. If you need to edit the worksheet (now a table), you are limited to the editing capabilities in Word. In a later chapter, you will learn about linking or embedding objects, which allows editing of the object with the tools available from the source program.

Copying and Pasting a Worksheet into a Word Document

1. Open the Word program and then open Word Letter 02.
2. Save the document and name it Word Ch 10, Ex 10.
3. With Word Ch 10, Ex 10 still open, make Excel the active program.
4. Open Excel Worksheet 03.
5. Save the worksheet with Save As and name it Excel Ch 10, Ex 10.
6. Make the following changes to the worksheet:
   a. Select cells B3 through D8 and then click the Percent Style button on the Formatting toolbar.
   b. Select cells A1 through D8 and then apply the Colorful 1 autoformat.

7. Save the worksheet again with the same name (Excel Ch 10, Ex 10).
8. Copy the worksheet to the letter in Word Ch 10, Ex 10 by completing the following steps:
   a. Select cells A1 through D8.
   b. Click the Copy button on the Standard toolbar.
   c. Click the button on the Taskbar representing the Word program.
   d. With Word Ch 10, Ex 10 displayed, position the insertion point a double space below the first paragraph of text in the body of the letter, and then click the Paste button on the Standard toolbar.
9. Make the following changes to the worksheet (which is now a Word table):
   a. Make the following changes to the specified cells (since there are no cell references in Word, you will need to count the columns and rows to find the correct cell):
      B6: Change *196%* to *110%*
      C6: Change *190%* to *104%*
      D6: Change *187%* to *101%*
   b. Horizontally center the worksheet (which is now a Word table) by completing the following steps:
      1) Position the insertion point in any cell in the table.
      2) Click Table and then Table Properties.
      3) At the Table Properties dialog box, click the Table tab.
      4) At the Table Properties dialog box with the Table tab selected, click the Center option in the Alignment section.
      5) Click OK or press Enter.
10. Save the Word document again with the same name (Word Ch 10, Ex 10).
11. Print and then close Word Ch 10, Ex 10.
12. Exit Word.
13. With Excel the active program, close Excel Ch 10, Ex 10.

You would follow the same basic steps to copy a worksheet and paste it into a PowerPoint presentation.

Formatting with Format Painter

The Standard toolbar contains a button that can be used to copy formatting to different locations in the worksheet. This button is called the Format Painter and displays on the Standard toolbar as a paintbrush. To use the Format Painter button, make a cell active that contains the desired formatting, click the Format Painter button, and then click the cell or select cells to which you want the formatting applied.

When you click the Format Painter button, the mouse pointer displays with a paintbrush attached. If you want to apply formatting a single time, click the Format Painter button once. If, however, you want to apply the character formatting in more than one location in the worksheet, double-click the Format Painter button. If you have double-clicked the Format Painter button, turn off the feature by clicking the Format Painter button once.

Format
Painter

Formatting with Format Painter

1. Open Excel Worksheet 06.
2. Save the worksheet with Save As and name it Excel Ch 10, Ex 11.
3. Use Format Painter to "paint" formatting to cells by completing these steps:
    a. Select cells B1 through B20 and then apply pale blue shading to the cells.
    b. Make a cell containing a percentage number in column B active.
    c. Double-click the Format painter button on the Standard toolbar.
    d. Select each of the following columns:
        Column D
        Column F
        Column H
        Column J
        Column L
    e. Select each of the following rows:
        Row 3
        Row 5
        Row 7
        Row 9
        Row 11
        Row 13
        Row 15
        Row 17
        Row 19
    f. Turn off Format Painter by clicking the Format Painter button on the Standard toolbar.
    g. Select row 1 and then click twice on the Bold button on the Formatting toolbar. (The Format Painter removed the bold formatting from the cells you formatted with pale blue shading. Selecting the row and then clicking the Bold button the first time removes bold from all headings. Clicking the Bold button the second time inserts bold formatting for the headings.)
4. Save the formatted worksheet with the same name (Excel Ch 10, Ex 11).
5. Print Excel Ch 10, Ex 11 in landscape orientation.
6. Close Excel Ch 10, Ex 11.

Formatting with Styles

To automate the formatting of cells in a workbook, consider defining and applying a style. A style, which is a predefined set of formatting attributes such as font, font size, alignment, borders, shading, and so on, is particularly useful in large workbooks with data requiring a considerable amount of formatting.

There are several advantages to using a style to apply formatting. A style helps to ensure consistent formatting from one worksheet to another. All attributes for a particular style are defined only once and you do not have to redefine attributes over and over. If you need to change the formatting, you need only change the style, and all cells formatted with that style automatically reflect the change.

Defining a Style

Excel contains some common number styles that can be applied with buttons on the Formatting toolbar. For example, clicking the Currency Style button on the Formatting toolbar applies currency formatting to the cell or selected cells. The Percent Style and Comma Style buttons also apply styles to cells.

Two basic methods are available for defining your own style. You can define a style with formats already applied to a cell or you can display the Style dialog box, click the Modify button, and then choose formatting options at the Format Cells dialog box. Styles you create are only available in the workbook in which they are created.

To define a style with existing formatting, you would complete these steps:

1. Select the cell or cells containing the desired formatting.
2. Click Format and then Style.
3. At the Style dialog box, shown in figure 10.7, key a name for the new style in the Style name text box.
4. Click OK to close the dialog box.

Style Dialog Box

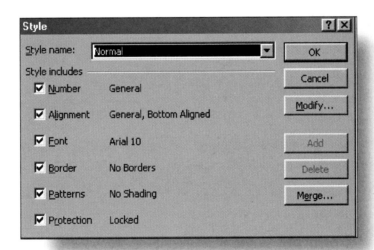

To define a new style without first applying the formatting, you would complete the following steps:

1. Click Format and then Style.
2. At the Style dialog box, key a name for the new style in the Style name text box.
3. Click the Modify button.
4. At the Format Cells dialog box, select the formats you want included in the style.
5. Click OK to close the Format Cells dialog box.
6. At the Style dialog box, remove the check mark from any formats that you do not want included in the style.
7. Click OK to define and apply the style to the selected cell. To define the style without applying it to the selected cell, click the Add button, and then click the Close button.

Applying a Style

To apply a style, select the cells you want to format, and then display the Style dialog box. At the Style dialog box, click the down-pointing triangle at the right side of the Style name text box, and then click the desired style name. Click OK to close the dialog box and apply the style.

Defining and Applying Styles

1. Open Excel Worksheet 02.
2. Save the worksheet with Save As and name it Excel Ch 10, Ex 12.
3. Format a cell and then define a style with the formatting by completing the following steps:
   a. Make sure cell A1 is active.
   b. Change the font and apply a bottom border by completing the following steps:
      1) Click Format and then Cells.
      2) At the Format Cells dialog box, click the Font tab.
      3) At the Font tab, change the font to Tahoma, the font style to Bold, the size to 12 points, and the color to Indigo. (Indigo is the second color from the right in the top row.)
      4) Click the Border tab.
      5) At the Format Cells dialog box with the Border tab selected, click the sixth Line Style option from the top in the second column.
      6) Click the down-pointing triangle at the right side of the Color option and then click the Violet color at the color palette (seventh color from the left in the third row from the top).
      7) Click the bottom border of the preview cell in the dialog box.
      8) Click OK to close the Formal Cells dialog box.
   c. With cell A1 still the active cell, define a style named Title with the formatting you just applied by completing the following steps:
      1) Click Format and then Style.
      2) At the Style dialog box, key Title in the Style name text box.
      3) Click the Add button.
      4) Click the Close button.
4. Apply the Title style to cells A1 through D1 by completing the following steps:

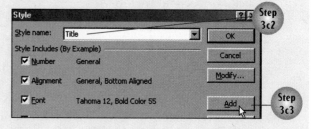

a. Select cells A1 through D1. (Even though cell A1 is already formatted, the style has not been applied to it. Later, you will modify the style and the style must be applied to the cell for the change to affect it.)

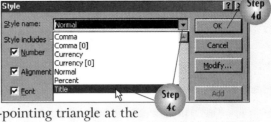

Step 4d
Step 4c

b. Click Format and then Style.
c. At the Style dialog box, click the down-pointing triangle at the right side of the Style name text box, and then click *Title* at the drop-down list.
d. Click OK to close the Style dialog box.

5. Define a new style named Font without first applying the formatting by completing the following steps:
   a. Click in any empty cell.
   b. Click Format and then Style.
   c. At the Style dialog box, key **Font** in the Style name text box.
   d. Click the Modify button.
   e. At the Format Cells dialog box, click the Font tab.

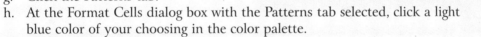

Step 5c
Step 5k
Step 5d
Step 5j

   f. At the Format Cells dialog box with the Font tab selected, change the font to Tahoma, the style to **12**, and the color to Indigo.
   g. Click the Patterns tab.
   h. At the Format Cells dialog box with the Patterns tab selected, click a light blue color of your choosing in the color palette.
   i. Click OK to close the Format Cells dialog box.
   j. At the Style dialog box, click the Add button.
   k. Click the Close button.

6. Apply the Font style by completing the following steps:
   a. Select cells A2 through D8.
   b. Click Format and then Style.
   c. At the Style dialog box, click the down-pointing triangle at the right side of the Style name text box, and then click *Font* at the drop-down list.
   d. Click OK to close the Style dialog box.

7. Make the following changes to the worksheet:
   a. Select cells B2 through D8.
   b. Click the Currency Style button on the Formatting toolbar.
   c. Click twice on the Decrease Decimal button on the Formatting toolbar.
   d. Automatically adjust columns A through D.

8. Save the worksheet again with the same name (Excel Ch 10, Ex 12).
9. Print Excel Ch 10, Ex 12.
10. With Excel Ch 10, Ex 12 still open, modify the Title style by completing the following steps:
    a. Click in any empty cell.
    b. Display the Style dialog box.
    c. Click the down-pointing triangle at the right side of the Style name text box and then click *Title* at the drop-down list.
    d. Click the Modify button.

  e. At the Format Cells dialog box, click the Alignment tab.
  f. At the Format Cells dialog box with the Alignment tab selected, click the down pointing triangle to the right of <u>H</u>orizontal option box, and then click *Center* at the drop-down list.
  g. Click OK to close the Format Cells dialog box.
  h. At the Style dialog box, click the <u>A</u>dd button.
  i. Click the Close button to close the Style dialog box.
 11. Save the document again with the same name (Excel Ch 10, Ex 12).
 12. Print and then close Excel Ch 10, Ex 12.

Copying Styles to Another Workbook

Styles you define are saved with the workbook in which they are created. You can, however, copy styles from one workbook to another. To do this, you would complete the following steps:

 1. Open the workbook containing the styles you want to copy.
 2. Open the workbook into which you want to copy the styles.
 3. Display the Style dialog box.
 4. At the Style dialog box, click the M<u>e</u>rge button.
 5. At the Merge Styles dialog box shown in figure 10.8, double-click the name of the workbook that contains the styles you want to copy.
 6. Click OK to close the Style dialog box.

10.8 *Merge Styles Dialog Box*

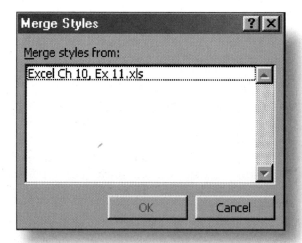

Removing a Style

If you apply a style to text and then decide you do not want the formatting applied, remove the style. To do this, select the cells formatted with the style you want to remove and then display the Style dialog box. At the Style dialog box, click the down-pointing arrow at the right side of the <u>S</u>tyle name text box, and then click *Normal* at the drop-down list.

Deleting a Style

Delete a style at the Style dialog box. To do this, display the Style dialog box, click the down-pointing triangle at the right side of the Style name text box. At the drop-down list that displays, click the style you want deleted, and then click the Delete button.

Copying and Removing Styles

1. Open Excel Ch 10, Ex 12.
2. Open Excel Worksheet 13.
3. Save the document with Save As and name it Excel Ch 10, Ex 13.
4. Delete column H.
5. Copy the styles in Excel Ch 10, Ex 12 into Excel Ch 10, Ex 13 by completing the following steps:
   a. Display the Style dialog box.
   b. At the Style dialog box, click the Merge button.
   c. At the Merge Styles dialog box, double-click *Excel Ch 10, Ex 12.xls* in the Merge styles from list box.
   d. Click OK to close the Style dialog box.
6. Modify the Font dialog box by completing the following steps:
   a. Click in any empty cell.
   b. Display the Style dialog box.
   c. At the Style dialog box, click the down-pointing triangle at the right side of the Style name text box, and then click *Font*.
   d. Click the Modify button.
   e. At the Format Cells dialog box, click the Font tab.
   f. Change the font to Arial and the size to *10* point.
   g. Click OK to close the Format Cells dialog box.
   h. At the Style dialog box, click the Add button.
   i. Click the Close button to close the Style dialog box.
7. Apply the following styles:
   a. Select cells A1 through G2 and then apply the Title style.
   b. Select cells A3 through G8 and then apply the Font style.
8. Remove the Font style from cells B3 through B8 by completing the following steps:
   a. Select cells B3 through B8.
   b. Display the Style dialog box.
   c. At the Style dialog box, click the down-pointing triangle at the right side of the Style name text box, and then click *Normal*.
   d. Click OK to close the dialog box.

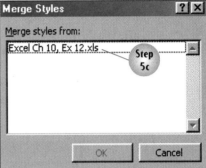

9. Complete steps similar to those in 8 to remove the style from cells D3 through D8 and cells F3 through F8.
10. Make the following changes to the document:

a. Change the width of columns B through G to 11.00.
b. Select cells B3 through G8, then click the Currency button on the Formatting toolbar, and then click twice on the Decrease Decimal button.
11. Save the worksheet again with the same name (Excel Ch 10, Ex 13).
12. Print and then close Excel Ch 10, Ex 13.
13. Close Excel Ch 10, Ex 12.

Creating a Web Page

In chapter 7, you visited a variety of Web sites on the Internet. You also saved a Word document as a Web page and created a Web page using a Web Page Wizard. An Excel workbook can also be saved as a Web page. The Web page can be viewed with the default Web browser, and hyperlinks can be inserted in the Web page.

Saving a Workbook as a Web Page

Save a workbook as a Web page by opening the workbook, then clicking File and then Save as Web Page. At the Save As dialog box shown in figure 10.9, key a name for the Web page in the File name text box, and then click the Save button.

10.9 *Save As Dialog Box*

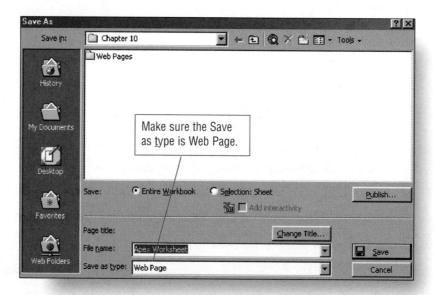

Previewing a Workbook in Web Page Preview

When creating a Web page, you may want to preview it in your default Web browser. Depending on the browser you are using, some of the formatting in a workbook may not display in the browser. To preview a workbook in your default Web browser, click File and then click Web Page Preview. This displays the currently open worksheet in the default Web browser and displays formatting supported by the browser.

Creating Hyperlinks

The business Web sites, such as Microsoft and USA Today, that you visited while completing some exercises in chapter 7 included hyperlinks to connect you to other pages or Web sites. You can create your own hyperlink in your Web page. To do this, select the text you want specified as the hyperlink, and then click the Insert Hyperlink button on the Standard toolbar. At the Insert Hyperlink dialog box shown in figure 10.10, key the Web site URL in the Type the file or Web page name text box, and then click OK.

Insert Hyperlink

figure

10.10   *Insert Hyperlink Dialog Box*

Key the URL in this text box.

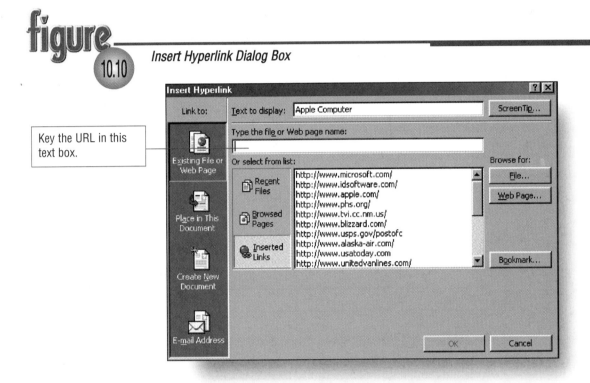

Another method for creating a hyperlink is to key the URL in an Excel worksheet. When you key the complete URL, Excel automatically converts the URL to a hyperlink and changes the color of the URL.

Maintaining Workbooks and Folders

In chapter 4, you learned document maintenance tasks such as creating a folder and copying, renaming, and deleting documents. These same tasks can be performed in Excel. The steps to create a folder or copy, rename, and delete a document are the same as the steps in Word. For example, to create a folder in Excel, display the Open dialog box or Save As dialog box and then click the Create New Folder button on the dialog box toolbar. At the Create New Folder dialog box, key a name for the folder, and then press Enter or click OK.

**Creating a Folder, Saving a Workbook as a Web Page,
Previewing the Web Page, and Creating Hyperlinks**

1. Create a folder named *Web Pages* by completing the following steps:
   a. Display the Open dialog box.
   b. Make sure *Chapter 10* is the active folder.
   c. Click the Create New Folder button on the dialog box toolbar.
   d. At the Create New Folder dialog box, key **Web Pages** and then press Enter.
   e. Click the Up One Level button to return to the *Chapter 10* folder.
   f. Close the Open dialog box.

Create New Folder

> **New Folder**
>
> Current Folder:
>
> A:\Chapter 10 [Step 1d]
>
> Name: | Web Pages

2. Open Apex Worksheet 01.
3. Save the worksheet as a Web page in the *Web Pages* folder by completing the following steps:
   a. Click File and then Save as Web Page.
   b. At the Save As dialog box, double-click *Web Pages* in the list box.
   c. Select the text in the File name text box and then key **Apex Web Page**.
   d. Click the Save button.

> File name: | Apex Web Page [Step 3c]
>
> Save as type: | Web Page   [Step 3d]   Save   Cancel

4. Preview the document in Web Page Preview by completing the following steps:
   a. Click File and then click Web Page Preview.
   b. If the viewing area in the browser is limited, click the Maximize button located in the upper right corner of the browser window.
   c. After viewing the worksheet in the Web browser, click File and then Close.
5. Create a hyperlink so that clicking *Apple Computer* displays the Apple Computer Web page by completing the following steps:
   a. Click cell A12 (this is the cell containing *Apple Computer*).
   b. Click the Insert Hyperlink button on the Standard toolbar.
   c. At the Insert Hyperlink dialog box, key **http://www.apple.com** in the Type the file or Web page name text box.
   d. Click OK. (This changes the color of the Apple Computer text and also adds underlining to the text.)

> **Insert Hyperlink**
>
> Link to: | Text to display: | Apple Computer
>
> | Type the file or Web page name:
>
> | http://www.apple.com

6. Complete steps similar to those in step 5 to create a hyperlink from *Microsoft Corporation* to the URL http://www.microsoft.com.
7. Click the Save button on the Standard toolbar to save the Web page with the hyperlinks added. [Step 5c]
8. Jump to the hyperlink sites by completing the following steps:

a. Make sure you are connected to the Internet.
b. Click the hyperlink *Apple Computer* that displays towards the bottom of the worksheet.
c. When the Apple Computer Web page displays, scroll through the page and then click on a hyperlink that interests you.
d. After looking at this next page, click <u>F</u>ile and then <u>C</u>lose.
e. At the Apex Web Page document, click the hyperlink *Microsoft Corporation*.
f. After viewing the Microsoft Web page, click <u>F</u>ile and then <u>C</u>lose.

9. Print and then close Apex Web Page.

Sending a Workbook by E-mail

Computers within a company can be connected by a private network referred to as an "intranet." With an intranet, employees within a company can send documents by e-mail. To send an Excel workbook by e-mail, you will need to have Outlook available on your system. System configurations can be quite varied and you may find that your screen does not exactly match what you see in the figure in this section. Steps in exercise 14 may need to be modified to accommodate your system.

To send a workbook by e-mail, open the workbook, and then click the E-mail button on the Standard toolbar. This displays the e-mail header below the Formatting toolbar as shown in figure 10.11. When the e-mail header displays, Outlook is automatically opened.

E-mail

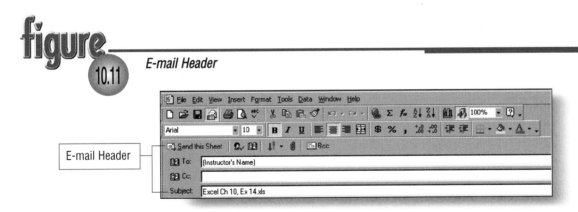

figure
10.11

E-mail Header

E-mail Header

At the e-mail header, fill in the recipient information and then click the <u>S</u>end this Sheet button. Excel sends a copy of the workbook to the recipient and closes the e-mail header. The original workbook remains open for editing. When the workbook is saved, the e-mail information is saved with the document.

The e-mail header contains buttons you can use to customize the e-mail message. Buttons are available for sending a copy of a document, selecting a name from an address book, establishing a priority level, and specifying delivery options.

In the exercise in this chapter, you will send the e-mail to your instructor. If your system is not networked or your computer is not part of an intranet system, skip step 3d (clicking the <u>S</u>end this Sheet button).

exercise 15

Sending a Workbook by E-mail

(Note: Before completing this exercise, check to see if you can send e-mail messages. If you cannot, consider completing all the steps in the exercise except step 3d.)

1. Open Excel Worksheet 05.
2. Save the workbook with Save As and name it Excel Ch 10, Ex 15.
3. Send Excel Ch 10, Ex 15 by e-mail by completing the following steps:

   a. Click the E-mail button on the Standard toolbar.

   b. At the e-mail header, key your instructor's name in the To: text box. (Depending on how the system is configured, you may need to key your instructor's e-mail address.)

   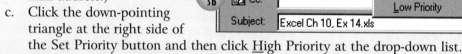

   c. Click the down-pointing triangle at the right side of the Set Priority button and then click <u>H</u>igh Priority at the drop-down list.

   d. Click the <u>S</u>end this Sheet button.

   e. Click the E-mail button on the Standard toolbar to turn off the display of the e-mail header.

4. Save the workbook again with the same name (Excel Ch 10, Ex 15).
5. Close Excel Ch 10, Ex 15.

If it fits your needs, consider using an Excel template worksheet form.

Using Excel Templates

Excel has included a number of *template* worksheet forms that are formatted for specific uses. For example, Excel has provided template forms for an expense statement, invoice, and purchase order. To view the templates available with Excel, click <u>F</u>ile and then <u>N</u>ew. This displays the New dialog box. At this dialog box, click the Spreadsheet Solutions tab and the template forms display as shown in figure 10.12.

figure
10.12

New Dialog Box with Spreadsheet Solutions Tab Selected

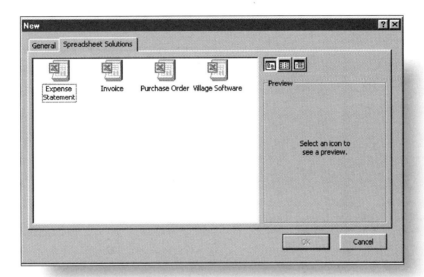

The templates in the New dialog box with the Spreadsheet Solutions tab selected are licensed to Microsoft by Village Software®. You can learn more about Village Software by double-clicking the Village Software template in the New dialog box.

Use the Expense template to itemize business expenses. The invoice is designed to help you prepare an invoice, which is an itemized list of goods shipped, specifying the price and terms of sale. Use the Purchase Order template to prepare a purchase order, which lists a description of products purchased, including quantity, number of units, and unit price.

Entering Data in a Template

Templates contain unique areas where information is entered at the keyboard. For example, in the Invoice template shown in figure 10.13, you enter information such as the customer name, address, and telephone number, and also the quantity, description, and unit price of products. To enter information in the appropriate location, position the mouse pointer (white plus sign) in the location where you want to key data, and then click the left mouse button. After keying the data, click the next location. You can also move the insertion point to another cell using the commands learned in chapter 8. For example, press the Tab key to make the next cell active, press Shift + Tab to make the previous cell active.

figure
10.13

Invoice Template

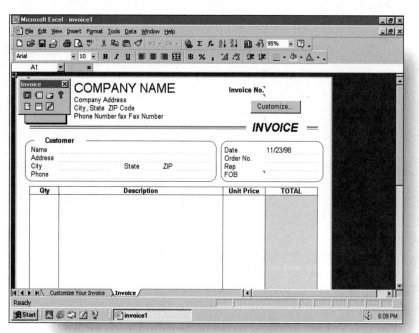

exercise
16

Preparing an Invoice Using a Template

(Note: The Invoice form created in this exercise will occupy a considerable amount of space on your disk. Consider creating the form in this exercise, printing it, and then closing it without saving it.)

1. Click File and then New.
2. At the New dialog box, click the Spreadsheet Solutions tab.
3. At the New dialog box with the Spreadsheet Solutions tab selected, double-click *Invoice*.
4. Depending on your system, Microsoft may display a message box telling you that the workbook you are opening contains macros. The message goes on to say, "Some macros may contain viruses that could be harmful to your computer. If you are sure this workbook is from a trusted source, click 'Enable Macros'." Check with your instructor to make sure your system is secure and, if it is, click Enable Macros.
5. If the Invoice form does not display at 100%, consider clicking the down-pointing triangle at the right side of the Zoom button on the Standard toolbar and then clicking *100%* at the drop-down list.

6. Key data in the invoice by completing the following steps:
   a. Position the mouse pointer to the right of the Name option (on the light gray dotted line) in the Customer section of the invoice until it turns into a white plus sign.
   b. Click the left mouse button. (This should make the cell immediately to the right of Name active.)
   c. Key **IN-FLOW SYSTEMS** and then press Enter. (This makes the cell immediately to the right of the Address option active.)
   d. Key **320 Milander Way** and then press Enter. (This makes the cell immediately to the right of the City option active.)
   e. Key **Boston** and then press the Tab key twice. (This makes the cell immediately to the right of State active.)
   f. Key **MA** and then press the Tab key twice. (This makes the cell immediately to the right of ZIP active.)
   g. Key **02188**.
   h. Position the mouse pointer (white plus sign) to the right of the Phone option (on the light gray dotted line) and then click the left mouse button.
   i. Key **(617) 555-3900**.
   j. Position the mouse pointer (white plus sign) to the right of the Order No. option until it turns into a white plus sign and then click the left mouse button. (This should make the cell immediately to the right of Order No. active.)
   k. Key **2388-348** and then press Enter. (This makes the cell immediately to the right of Rep active.)
   l. Key **Jenkins** and then press Enter. (This makes the cell immediately to the right of FOB active.)
   m. Key **Boston**.
   n. Key the following data immediately below the specified heading (use the mouse, the Tab key, and/or the Enter key to make the desired cell active):

Qty.	=	**40**
Description	=	**Oscillator**
Unit Price	=	**340**
Qty.	=	**25**
Description	=	**Discriminator**
Unit Price	=	**570**
Qty.	=	**300**
Description	=	**Clamps**
Unit Price	=	**3.49**

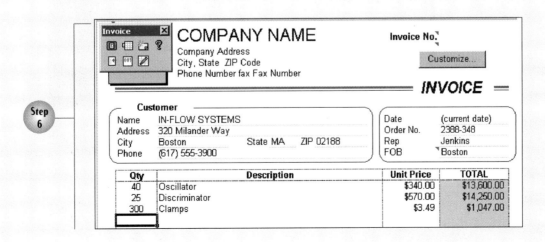

7. Save the completed invoice by completing the following steps (this step is optional; if you do not think you have enough room on your disk, print the form, and then close it without saving):
   a. Click File and then Save As.
   b. At the Save As dialog box, key **Excel Ch 10, Ex 16** in the File name text box, and then press Enter or click Save.
8. Print and then close Excel Ch 10, Ex 16.

When the Invoice template was displayed on the screen, did you notice small red triangles that displayed in various locations in the template? These small red triangles are comments that provide information about specific cells. To use a comment, position the mouse pointer on a small red triangle and a yellow box displays with information. For example, if you position the mouse pointer on the small red triangle above Invoice No., a yellow box displays as shown in figure 10.14.

Invoice Comment

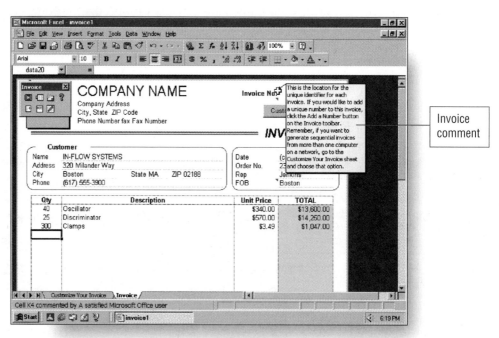

The Invoice toolbar that displays toward the upper left corner of the invoice contains buttons for performing functions in the template. There is a button that lets you hide the display of the red triangles. The buttons on the Invoice template are described in figure 10.15. The buttons that display in a template toolbar may vary slightly from those described in figure 10.15.

figure
10.15   *Invoice Toolbar Buttons*

Button	Name	Description
	Size to Screen/Return to Size	Reduces or expands the display of the invoice
	Hide Comments/ Display Comments	Hides or displays comments
	New Comment	Create your own note for a cell
	Template Help	Displays information about the template
	Display Example/ Remove Example	Turns on or off the display of example data in the template
001	Assign a Number	Assigns a permanent unique number to the invoice
	Capture Data in a Database	Updates the existing Template Wizard Database with values from the template

Customizing a Template

At the top of the invoice you prepared and printed in exercise 11, the text *COMPANY NAME* displayed at the top followed by *Company Address*, and so on. Information in a template can be customized and then the template can be saved with a new name. This allows you to create a customized template to use for subsequent invoices. You can also lock the customized template to prevent accidental changes to the customized information.

To customize a template, click the gray Customize button that generally displays in the upper right corner of a template. This causes a customize form to display. For example, if you click the Customize button at the Invoice template, the customize form displays as shown in figure 10.16.

Create customized templates for specific uses.

Hint

figure
10.16

Invoice Customize Form

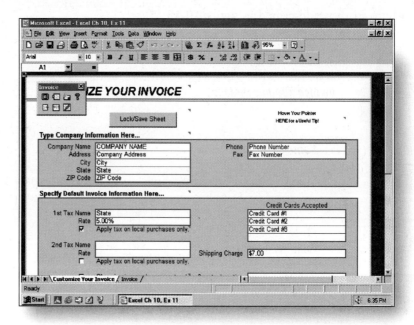

At the customize form shown in figure 10.16, key the information that you want to remain in the Invoice template for each use, and then click the gray Lock/Save Sheet button that displays toward the top of the invoice. When you click this button, the Lock/Save Sheet dialog box shown in figure 10.17 displays.

figure
10.17

Lock/Save Sheet Dialog Box

At the Lock/Save Sheet dialog box, specify whether you want to lock the invoice but not save it or lock it and save it as a template. If you want to use the template in the future, click Lock and save Template and then click OK. This displays the Save Template dialog box where you key a new name for the template. The default folder at the Save Template dialog box is the *Templates* folder. The new template you save will be saved in the *Templates* folder (rather than your disk in drive A). Key a new name for the template at the Save Template dialog box and then press Enter or click <u>S</u>ave. This displays a box containing information telling you that the new customized template has been saved to C:\WINDOWS\Application Data\Microsoft\Templates. *(Note: Depending on your system configuration, this folder may vary.)* The message also tells you that to begin using the new template, close the current invoice, and then open the new Invoice template from the New dialog box. A customized template that you create is displayed in the New dialog box with the General tab selected.

In exercise 17, you will create a customized Invoice template with the name XXX Invoice (where your initials are inserted instead of the XXX). Check with your instructor before completing this exercise to make sure your system will allow you to create a new template.

Creating a Customized Invoice Template

1. Click <u>F</u>ile and then <u>N</u>ew.
2. At the New dialog box, click the Spreadsheet Solutions tab.
3. At the New dialog box with the Spreadsheet Solutions tab selected, double-click *Invoice*.
4. If Microsoft displays the message box telling you that the workbook you are opening contains macros, click the <u>E</u>nable Macros button. *(Note: Be sure to check with your instructor before clicking this button.)*
5. At the Invoice template, click the gray Customize button that displays in the upper right corner of the Invoice template.
6. At the *CUSTOMIZE YOUR INVOICE* form that displays, key the following data in the specified cells. (To do this, position the mouse pointer [white plus sign] in the white area on top of the generic information [such as *COMPANY NAME*], click the left mouse button, and then key the text. Use the Enter key, the Tab key, Shift + Tab, and/or the mouse to move to the correct cell.)

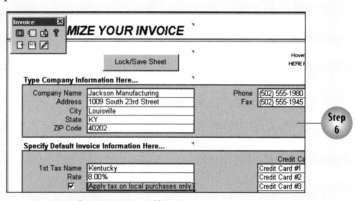

Company Name	=	**Jackson Manufacturing**
Address	=	**1009 South 23rd Street**
City	=	**Louisville**
State	=	**KY**
ZIP Code	=	**40202**
Phone Number	=	**(502) 555-1980**
Fax Number	=	**(502) 555-1945**
1st Tax Name	=	**Kentucky**
Rate	=	**8** *(Be sure to press Enter after keying 8.)*

7. Save the Invoice template with a new name by completing the following steps:
   a. Click the gray Lock/Save Sheet button that displays toward the top of the *CUSTOMIZE YOUR INVOICE* form.
   b. At the Lock/Save Sheet dialog box, click *Lock and save Template*, and then click OK.
   c. At the Save Template dialog box, key **XXX Invoice** (where your initials are inserted instead of the XXX), and then press Enter or click <u>S</u>ave.
   d. At the message telling you that the customized template has been saved to the directory, click OK.
8. Close the Invoice template.

When the *CUSTOMIZE YOUR INVOICE* form is displayed, tabs appear below the invoice at the left side of the horizontal scroll bar. The two tabs that display when customizing the Invoice template are Customize Your Invoice and Invoice. With these tabs you can move back and forth between the invoice and the customize form. You will notice similar types of tabs when customizing other templates.

Filling in a Customized Invoice Template

(Note: The Invoice form created in this exercise will occupy a considerable amount of space on your disk. Consider printing and then closing the Invoice form without saving it.)

1. Open the XXX Invoice template (where your initials display instead of the XXX) by completing the following steps:
   a. Click <u>F</u>ile and then <u>N</u>ew.
   b. At the New dialog box, click the General tab.
   c. At the New dialog box with the General tab selected, double-click the *XXX Invoice* icon (where your initials display instead of the *XXX*).
2. If Microsoft displays the message box telling you that the workbook you are opening contains macros, click the <u>E</u>nable Macros button. *(Note: Be sure to check with your instructor before clicking this button.)*
3. With the XXX Invoice template open, key the following data in the specified cells:

Name	=	**Seaside Marine Supplies**
Address	=	**1200 Camino Drive**
City	=	**San Diego**
State	=	**CA**
ZIP Code	=	**92031**
Phone	=	**(619) 555-9500**

Order No.	=	231-202
Rep	=	Thornton
FOB	=	Kentucky
Qty.	=	3
Description	=	Propeller
Unit Price	=	725
Qty.	=	10
Description	=	Fuel Rover
Unit Price	=	210
Qty.	=	7
Description	=	Balancing Fan
Unit Price	=	95

Step 3

Jackson Manufacturing
1009 South 23rd Street
Louisville, KY 40202
(502) 555-1980 fax (505) 555-1945

Invoice No.

Customize...

INVOICE

Customer

Name	Seaside Marine Supplies		Date	11/24/98
Address	1200 Camino Drive		Order No.	231-202
City	San Diego	State CA ZIP 92031	Rep	Thornton
Phone	(619) 555-9500		FOB	Kentucky

Qty	Description	Unit Price	TOTAL
3	Propeller	$725.00	$2,175.00
10	Fuel Rover	$210.00	$2,100.00
7	Balancing Fan	$95.00	$665.00

4. Delete information toward the bottom of the invoice by completing the following steps:
   a. Scroll down toward the bottom of the invoice until the text *Insert Fine Print Here* displays.
   b. Click anywhere in the text *Insert Fine Print Here* and then press the Delete key.
   c. Scroll down to the bottom of the invoice until the text *Insert Farewell Statement Here* displays.
   d. Click anywhere in the text *Insert Farewell Statement Here* and then press the Delete key.
5. Save the completed Invoice template in the normal manner to the *Chapter 10* folder on your disk in drive A with the name Excel Ch 10, Ex 18. *(You will need to change the drive location at the Save As dialog box.)* (This step is optional. If you do not think you have room on your disk for this exercise, print the form and then close it without saving it.)
6. Print and then close Excel Ch 10, Ex 18.

The Invoice template automatically calculates the total price of each product ordered, and inserts a subtotal amount for all items, shipping and handling costs, sales tax, and a final total. This template includes formulas that calculate these amounts. In the next chapter, you will learn how to insert your own formula in a worksheet.

chapter summary

► Selected cells and cell contents can be moved in and between worksheets using the Cut, Copy, and Paste buttons on the Standard toolbar; dragging with the mouse; or with options from the Edit drop-down menu.

► Selected cells can be moved with the mouse by dragging the outline of the selected cells to the desired position.

► Selected cells can be copied with the mouse by holding down the Ctrl key and the left mouse button, dragging the outline of the selected cells to the desired location, and then releasing the left mouse button and then the Ctrl key.

► A variety of worksheets with related data can be created within a workbook.

► To print all worksheets in a workbook, click Entire workbook in the Print what section of the Print dialog box. You can also print specific worksheets by holding down the Ctrl key and then clicking the tabs of the worksheets you want printed.

► Perform maintenance activities, such as deleting and renaming, on worksheets within a workbook by clicking the *right* mouse button on a sheet tab, and then clicking the desired option at the pop-up menu.

► The worksheet window can be split into panes with the Split option from the Window drop-down menu or with the split bars on the horizontal and vertical scroll bars.

► Remove the split window by clicking Window and then Remove Split; or drag the split bars.

► Freeze window panes by clicking Window and then Freeze Panes. When panes are frozen, only the display of the pane with the active cell changes. Unfreeze Window panes by clicking Window and then Unfreeze Panes.

► Open multiple workbooks that are adjacent by displaying the Open dialog box, clicking the first workbook to be opened, holding down the Shift key, and then clicking the last workbook. If workbooks are nonadjacent, click the first workbook, hold down the Ctrl key, and then click the desired workbook names.

► If multiple workbooks are opened, click Window on the Menu bar to see a list of the open workbooks.

► Close all open workbooks at one time by holding down the Shift key and then clicking File and then Close All.

► Multiple workbooks can be arranged in a window with options from the Arrange Windows dialog box.

► Click the Maximize button located at the right side of the Title bar of the active workbook to make the workbook fill the entire window area. Click the Minimize button to shrink the active workbook to a button on the Taskbar. Click the Restore button to return the workbook back to its previous size.

► Data can be moved, copied, and/or pasted between workbooks.

► Objects can be copied from a document in one program (called the source program) and then pasted into a document in another program (called the destination program). When an object is pasted in the destination program, it becomes a part of that program and the object can be edited with only those tools available in the destination program.

- Automate formatting of cells with Format Painter.
- Automate the formatting of cells in a workbook by defining and then applying styles. A style is a predefined set of formatting attributes.
- A style helps to ensure consistent formatting from one worksheet to another. All formatting attributes for a particular style are defined only once. Modify a style and all cells to which the style is applied automatically reflect the change.
- To define a style with formats already applied to a cell or display the Style dialog box, click the Modify button, and then choose formatting options at the Format Cells dialog box.
- Define, apply, modify, remove, and delete styles at the Style dialog box.
- Styles are saved in the workbook in which they are created. Styles can be copied, however, to another workbook. Do this with the Merge button at the Style dialog box.
- Save an Excel workbook as a Web page by clicking File and then Save as Web Page.
- Preview a Web page in your default browser by clicking File and then Web Page Preview.
- Create a hyperlink at the Insert Hyperlink dialog box. Display this dialog box by clicking the Insert Hyperlink button on the Standard toolbar.
- Create a new folder by clicking the Create New Folder button on the Open dialog box or Save As dialog box toolbar.
- To send a workbook as e-mail, open the workbook, and then click the E-mail button on the Standard toolbar. This displays the e-mail header where you specify who is to receive the e-mail, establish a priority level, and specify delivery options.
- Excel provides preformatted templates for creating forms such as an expense statement, invoice, or purchase order.
- Excel templates can be customized and the customized form can be locked and saved in the *Templates* folder.
- Templates contain unique areas where information is entered at the keyboard. These areas vary depending on the template.
- Each template contains comments that display as small red triangles and provide information about cells.
- A template contains a toolbar with buttons you can use to perform such actions as changing the size of the template, hiding or displaying comments, creating a note for a cell, displaying or removing an example, and assigning a number to the template. The buttons vary depending on the template displayed.
- To customize a template for personal use, click the gray Customize button that displays in the upper right corner of the template.
- A customized template that has been saved displays in the New dialog box with the General tab selected.
- When the customize form is displayed, tabs display below the template form. Use these tabs to switch between the customize form and the template.

commands review

	Mouse/Keyboard
Split window into panes	Click Window, Split; or drag split bar
Freeze window panes	Click Window, Freeze Panes
Unfreeze window panes	Click Window, Unfreeze Panes
Remove window panes	Click Window, Remove Split
Display Arrange Windows dialog box	Click Window, Arrange
Turn on Format Painter	Click Format Painter button on Standard toolbar
Display Style dialog box	Click Format, Style
Display Merge Styles dialog box	At Style dialog box, click Merge button
Save workbook as a Web page	Click File, Save as Web Page
Display Web page in Web Page Preview	Click File, Web Page Preview
Display Insert Hyperlink dialog box	Click Insert Hyperlink button on Standard toolbar
Display Create New Folder dialog box	At Open or Save As dialog box, click Create New Folder button on dialog box toolbar
Display e-mail header	Click E-mail button on Standard toolbar
Display New dialog box	Click File, New

thinking offline

Completion: In the space provided at the right, indicate the correct term, number, or symbol.

1. To copy selected cells with the mouse, hold down this key while dragging the outline of the selected cells to the desired location. _____

2. To split a window using a split bar, position the mouse pointer on the split bar until the mouse pointer turns into this. _____

3. Clicking Window and then Split causes the active worksheet to be split into this number of windows. _____

4. To see what workbooks are currently open, click this on the Menu bar. _____

5. To close all open workbooks at the same time, hold down this key while clicking File and then Close All. _____

6. Arrange all open workbooks with options from this dialog box. _____

7. Click this button to shrink the active workbook to a button on the Taskbar. _____

8. Click this button to return the workbook back to its original size. _____

9. Click this button to make the active workbook fill the entire window area. _____

10. When copying and pasting data between programs, the program containing the original data to be copied is called this. _____

11. Click this button at the Style dialog box to display the Format Cells dialog box. _____

12. Save an Excel workbook as a Web page by clicking File on the Menu bar and then clicking this option. _____

13. Click this button on the Standard toolbar to add a hyperlink to text in the active cell. _____

14. Click this tab at the New dialog box to display a list of Excel templates. _____

15. List the steps you would complete to open all of the following documents at one time: Excel Worksheet 02, Excel Worksheet 03, and Excel Worksheet 05.

_____

_____

_____

_____

16. List the steps you would complete to copy a range of cells from one workbook to another.

_____

_____

_____

_____

17. List the steps you would complete to display the *CUSTOMIZE YOUR PURCHASE ORDER* form.

_____

_____

_____

_____

working hands-on

Assessment 1

1. Open Excel Worksheet 03.
2. Save the worksheet with Save As and name it Excel Ch 10, SA 01.
3. Make the following changes to the worksheet:
   a. Insert a column between columns C and D. (The new column will be column D.)
   b. Move the cells in column B to the blank column D.
   c. Delete the blank column B.
   d. Select cells B3 through D8 and then click the Percent Style button.
   e. Select cells A1 through D8 and then apply an autoformat of your choosing.
4. Save the worksheet again with the same name (Excel Ch 10, SA 01).
5. Print and then close Excel Ch 10, SA 01.

Assessment 2

1. Open Excel Worksheet 05.
2. Save the worksheet with Save As and name it Excel Ch 10, SA 02.
3. Make the following changes:
   a. Copy cells A1 through C8 to *Sheet2*.
   b. With *Sheet2* active, make the following changes:
      A1: Change *January* to *February*
      B3: Change *35* to *40*
      B6: Change *24* to *20*
      B7: Change *15* to *20*
      C4: Change *$19.00* to *20.15*
      C6: Change *$16.45* to *17.45*
   c. Automatically adjust the width of column A.
   d. Copy cells A1 through C8 to *Sheet3*.
   e. With *Sheet3* active, make the following changes:
      A1: Change *February* to *March*
      B4: Change *20* to *35*
      B8: Change *15* to *20*
   f. Automatically adjust the width of column A.
4. Save the worksheets again with the same name (Excel Ch 10, SA 02).
5. Print all worksheets in the Excel Ch 10, SA 02 workbook.
6. Close Excel Ch 10, SA 02.

Assessment 3

1. Open Excel Worksheet 09.
2. Save the worksheet with Save As and name it Excel Ch 10, SA 03.
3. Make the following changes to the worksheet:
   a. Split the window.
   b. Drag the intersection of the horizontal and vertical gray lines so that the horizontal gray line is immediately below row 9 and the vertical gray line is immediately to the right of column A.

c.   Freeze the window panes.
d.   Add a new row 8 and then key the following in the specified cells:

A8	=	**Loaned Out**
B8	=	**10**
C8	=	**0**
D8	=	**5**
E8	=	**0**
F8	=	**11**
G8	=	**3**
H8	=	**16**
I8	=	**0**
J8	=	**0**
K8	=	**5**
L8	=	**0**
M8	=	**0**

e.   Remove the split.
f.   Select rows 1 through 10 and then change the row height to 18.00.
4.   Save the worksheet again with the same name (Excel Ch 10, SA 03).
5.   Print the worksheet in landscape orientation (it will take two pages) so the row titles print on each page.
6.   Close Excel Ch 10, SA 03.

Assessment 4

1.   Create the worksheet shown in figure 10.18 (change the width of column A to 21.00).
2.   Save the worksheet and name it Excel Ch 10, SA 04.
3.   With Excel Ch 10, SA 04 still open, open Excel Worksheet 09.
4.   Select and copy the following cells from Excel Worksheet 09 to Excel Ch 10, SA 04:
   a.   Copy cells A3 through G3 in Excel Worksheet 09 and paste them into Excel Ch 10, SA 04 beginning with cell A12.
   b.   Copy cells A9 through G9 in Excel Worksheet 09 and paste them into Excel Ch 10, SA 04 beginning with cell A13.
5.   With Excel Ch 10, SA 04 the active worksheet, apply an autoformat of your choosing to cells A1 through G13.
6.   Save the worksheet again with the same name (Excel Ch 10, SA 04).
7.   Print Excel Ch 10, SA 04 in landscape orientation and centered horizontally and vertically on the page.
8.   Close Excel Ch 10, SA 04.
9.   Close Excel Worksheet 09 without saving the changes.

figure

10.18

Assessment 4

	A	B	C	D	E	F	G	H
1		EQUIPMENT USAGE REPORT						
2		January	February	March	April	May	June	
3	Machine #12							
4	Total Hours Available	2,300	2,430	2,530	2,400	2,440	2,240	
5	In Use	2,040	2,105	2,320	2,180	2,050	1,995	
6								
7	Machine #25							
8	Total Hours Available	2,100	2,240	2,450	2,105	2,390	1,950	
9	In Use	1,800	1,935	2,110	1,750	2,215	1,645	
10								
11	Machine #30							
12								

Assessment 5

1. Open Apex Worksheet 02.
2. Save the worksheet as a Web page named Apex Web Page, SA 05 in the *Web Pages* folder.
3. Preview the document in Web Page Preview.
4. Create a hyperlink so that clicking *id Software* displays the id Software Web page.
5. Create a hyperlink so that clicking *Blizzard Entertainment* displays the Blizzard Entertainment Web page.
6. Make sure you are connected to the Internet and then jump to the id Software site. After viewing the site, close the Web browser.
7. Jump to the Blizzard Entertainment site. After viewing the site, close the Web browser.
8. Save the Web page again with the same name (Apex Web Page, SA 05).
9. Print and then close Apex Web Page, SA 05.

Assessment 6

1. At a clear worksheet, define the following styles:
   a. Define a style named Heading that contains the following formatting:
      1) 14-point Times New Roman bold in Blue-Gray color
      2) Horizontal alignment of Center
      3) Double-line top and bottom border in Dark Red color
      4) Light purple shading
   b. Define a style named Column 01 that contains the following formatting:
      1) 12-point Times New Roman in Blue-Gray color
      2) Light purple shading
   c. Define a style named Column 02 that contains 12-point Times New Roman in Blue-Gray color
2. Save the worksheet and name it Excel Ch 10, Style 01.
3. With Excel Ch 10, Style 01 open, open Excel Worksheet 09.
4. Save the worksheet with Save As and name it Excel Ch 10, SA 06.
5. Copy the styles from Excel Ch 10, Style 01 into Excel Ch 10, SA 06. *(Hint: Do this through the Style dialog box.)*
6. Select cells A1 through M1 and then click the Merge and Center button on the Formatting toolbar.
7. Apply the following styles:
   a. Select cells A1 through M2 and then apply the Heading style.

  b. Select cells A3 through A9 and then apply the Column 01 style.

  c. Select cells B3 through G9 and then apply the Column 02 style.

  d. Select cells H3 through M9 and then apply the Column 01 style.

 8. Automatically adjust the widths of columns A through M.

 9. Save the worksheet again with the same name (Excel Ch 10, SA 06).

10. Print Excel Ch 10, SA 06 on one page in Landscape orientation. *(Hint: Change the orientation and scaling at the Page Setup dialog box with the Page tab selected.)*

11. With Excel Ch 10, SA 06 still open, modify the following styles:

  a. Modify Heading so it changes the font color to Indigo (instead of Blue-Gray) and inserts a solid, thick top and bottom border in Violet (instead of a double-line top and bottom border in Dark Red).

  b. Modify Column 02 so it adds a font style of Bold Italic (leave all the other formatting attributes).

12. Save the worksheet again with the same name (Excel Ch 10, SA 06).

13. Print Excel Ch 10, SA 06 on one page and in Landscape orientation.

14. Close Excel Ch 10, SA 06.

15. Close Excel Ch 10, Style 01.

Assessment 7

 1. Create a customized template with the Purchase Order template. At the *CUSTOMIZE YOUR PURCHASE ORDER* form, key the following data in the specified cells:

COMPANY NAME	=	**K & N Corporation**
Company Address	=	**897 North 112th Street**
City	=	**White Plains**
State	=	**NY**
ZIP Code	=	**10609**
Phone Number	=	**(201) 555-4321**
Fax Number	=	**(201) 555-4330**
1st Tax Name	=	**New York**
Rate	=	**8.2** *(Be sure to press Enter after keying **8.2**.)*

 2. Click the Lock/Save Sheet button and save the customized Purchase Order template with the name XXX Purchase Order (where your initials are inserted instead of the XXX).

 3. Close the Purchase Order template.

 4. Display the New dialog box with the General tab selected, and then double-click XXX Purchase Order (where your initials display instead of the XXX) and then key the following data in the specified cells:

  In the Vendor section:

Name	=	**Evergreen Services**
Address	=	**1209 Princeville Drive**
City	=	**Pickerington**
State	=	**OH**
ZIP Code	=	**43145**
Phone	=	**(614) 555-9766**

  In the Ship To section:

Name	=	**K & N Corporation**
Address	=	**897 North 112th Street**
City	=	**White Plains**
State	=	**NY**
ZIP Code	=	**10609**

Phone	=	(201) 555-4321
Qty.	=	120
Units	=	dozen
Description	=	Heater ring
Unit Price	=	24.95
Qty.	=	10
Units	=	boxes
Description	=	Wheel bands
Unit Price	=	79.50
Qty.	=	7
Units	=	dozen
Description	=	Repair kit, 21B
Unit Price	=	19.50

5. Save the completed Purchase Order in the normal manner to the chapter 10 folder on your disk in drive A with the name Excel Ch 10, SA 07.
6. Print and then close Excel Ch 10, SA 07.

Assessment 8

1. Delete the XXX Invoice template you created in this chapter by completing the following steps:
   a. Click File and then New.
   b. At the New dialog box with the General tab selected, position the arrow pointer on *XXX Invoice* (where your initials display instead of the *XXX*), and then click the *right* mouse button.
   c. At the pop-up menu that displays, click Delete.
   d. At the dialog box asking if you are sure you want to send the *XXX Invoice* to the Recycle Bin, click Yes.
2. Complete steps similar to those in steps 1a through 1d to delete *XXX Purchase Order*.

Assessment 9

1. In this chapter, you learned about features that automate the formatting of cells in a worksheet such as Format Painter and Styles. Another formatting feature is Conditional Formatting. Use Excel's Help feature to learn about Conditional Formatting.
2. Open Excel Worksheet 06.
3. Save the worksheet with Save As and name it Excel Ch 10, SA 09.
4. Select cells B3 through M20 and then use Conditional Formatting to display all percentages between 95% and 100% in red and with a red border.
5. Save the worksheet again with the same name (Excel Ch 10, SA 09).
6. Print and then close Excel Ch 10, SA 09.

Chapter 11

Inserting Formulas in a Worksheet

PERFORMANCE OBJECTIVES

Upon successful completion of chapter 11, you will be able to:

- Insert a formula in a cell using the AutoSum button.
- Key a formula in the Formula bar.
- Use the Paste Function feature to insert a formula in a cell.
- Write formulas with the AVERAGE, MAX, MIN, COUNT, SLN, DDB, FV, PMT, DATE, NOW, and IF functions.
- Name a range of cells and use a range in a formula.
- Create an absolute and mixed cell reference.
- Automatically outline a worksheet.
- Link cells between worksheets.
- Link worksheets using 3-D references.
- Plan and create a worksheet.

Excel is a powerful decision-making tool containing data that can be manipulated to answer "what if" situations. Insert a formula in a worksheet and then manipulate the data to make projections, answer specific questions, and use as a planning tool. For example, the manager of a department might use an Excel worksheet to prepare a department budget and then determine the impact on the budget of hiring a new employee or increasing the volume of production.

Insert a formula in a worksheet to perform calculations on values. A formula contains a mathematical operator, value, cell reference, cell range, and a function. Formulas can be written that add, subtract, multiply, and/or divide values. Formulas can also be written that calculate averages, percentages, minimum and maximum values, and much more. Excel includes an AutoSum button on the Standard toolbar that inserts a formula to calculate the total of a range of cells. Paste Function is an Excel feature that offers a variety of functions to create a formula.

Using the AutoSum Button

In chapter 6, you learned to key basic formulas in a Word table. The process for keying a formula in an Excel worksheet is similar. To perform a calculation in a worksheet, make active the cell in which you want to insert the formula (this cell should be empty). Key the formula in the cell and the formula displays in the cell as well as the Formula bar. When the formula is completed, and you exit the cell, the result of the formula displays in the active cell while the actual formula displays in the Formula bar.

You can also enter a formula in the Formula bar located below the Formatting toolbar. To do this, click in the Formula bar text box, key the desired formula and then press Enter or click the Enter button (contains a green check mark) on the Formula toolbar.

One of the advantages of using formulas in a worksheet is that cell entries can be changed and the formula will automatically recalculate the values and insert the result in the cell containing the formula. This is what makes an Excel worksheet a decision-making tool.

In addition to keying a formula in a cell, you can also use the AutoSum button on the Standard toolbar. The AutoSum button adds numbers automatically with the SUM function. When you click the AutoSum button, Excel looks for a range of cells containing numbers above the active cell if there are none there, then it looks to the left of the active cell. Excel suggests the range of cells to be added. If the suggested range is not correct, drag through the desired range with the mouse, and then press Enter. You can also just double-click the AutoSum button and this will insert the SUM function with the range Excel chooses.

Enter

AutoSum

Use the AutoSum button to automatically add numbers in a range of cells.

exercise

Adding Values with the AutoSum Button

1. Open Excel Worksheet 02.
2. Save the worksheet with Save As and name it Excel Ch 11, Ex 01.
3. Calculate the sum of cells by completing the following steps:
   a. Make B9 the active cell.
   b. Click the AutoSum button on the Standard toolbar.
   c. Excel inserts the formula =SUM(B2:B8) in cell B9. This is the correct range of cells, so press Enter.

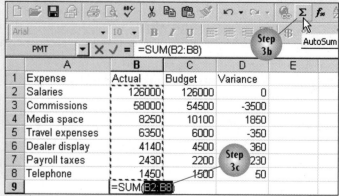

d. Make C9 the active cell.
e. Click the AutoSum button on the Standard toolbar.
f. Excel inserts the formula =SUM(C2:C8) in cell C9. This is the correct range of cells, so press Enter.
g. Make D9 the active cell.
h. Double-click the AutoSum button on the Standard toolbar. (This inserts the formula =SUM(D2:D8) in cell D9 and inserts the sum -1820.)

4. Select cells A1 through D9 and then apply the Accounting 1 autoformat.
5. Save the worksheet again with the same name (Excel Ch 11, Ex 01).
6. Print Excel Ch 11, Ex 01.
7. Make the following changes to cell entries:
   B4: Change 8,250.00 to 9550
   D4: Change 1,850.00 to 550
   B7: Change 2,430.00 to 2050
   D7: Change (230.00) to 150
8. Save the worksheet again with the same name (Excel Ch 11, Ex 01).
9. Print and then close Excel Ch 11, Ex 01.

Writing Formulas with Mathematical Operators

The AutoSum button on the Standard toolbar essentially creates the formula for you. You can also write your own formulas using mathematical operators. Commonly used mathematical formulas and their functions are described in figure 11.1.

When writing your own formula, begin the formula with the equals (=) sign. For example, to divide cell B2 by cell C2 and insert the result in cell D2, you would make D2 the active cell, and then key =B2/C2.

After keying a formula in a cell, press the Enter key, the Tab key, Shift + Tab, or click the Enter button on the Formula bar.

figure

11.1   *Mathematical Operators*

To perform this function	Key this operator
Addition	+
Subtraction	-
Multiplication	*
Division	/
Percent	%
Exponentiation	^

If there are two or more operators in a formula, Excel uses the same order of operations used in algebra. From left to right in a formula, this order, called the *order of operations*, is: negations (negative number—a number preceded by -) first, then percents (%), then exponentiations (^), followed by multiplications (*), divisions (/), additions (+), and finally subtractions (-). If you want to change the order of operations, use parentheses around the part of the formula you want calculated first.

Copying a Formula with Relative Cell References

In many worksheets, the same basic formula is used repetitively. In a situation where a formula is copied to other locations in a worksheet, use a *relative cell reference*. Copy a formula containing relative cell references and the cell references change. For example, if you enter the formula =SUM(A2:C2) in cell D2 and then copy it relatively to cell D3, the formula in cell D3 displays as =SUM(A3:C3). (Additional information on cell references is discussed later in this chapter in the "Using an Absolute Cell Reference in a Formula" section.)

You can display formulas in a worksheet rather than the calculated values by pressing Ctrl + ` (accent grave).

To copy a formula relatively in a worksheet, use the Fill option from the Edit drop-down menu. To do this, select the cell containing the formula as well as the cells to which you want the formula copied, and then click Edit. At the Edit drop-down menu, point to Fill. This causes another drop-down menu to display. The choices active in this drop-down menu will vary depending on the selected cells. For example, if you select cells down a column, options such as Down and Up will be active. If cells in a row are selected, options such as Right and Left will be active. Click the desired direction and the formula is copied relatively to the selected cells.

Finding Variances by Inserting and Copying a Formula

1. Open Excel Worksheet 01.
2. Save the worksheet with Save As and name it Excel Ch 11, Ex 02.
3. Make the following changes to the worksheet:
   a. Change the width of column A to 19.00.
   b. Make cell E1 active and then key **Variance**.
4. Insert a formula and then copy it to other cells by completing the following steps:
   a. Make E3 the active cell.
   b. Key the formula **=D3-C3**.
   c. Press Enter.
   d. Copy the formula to cells E4 through E10 by completing the following steps:
      1) Select cells E3 through E10.
      2) Click Edit, point to Fill, and then click Down.

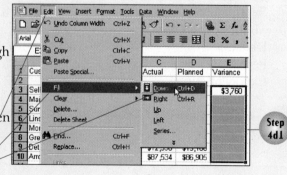

Step 4d2

Step 4d1

5. Select cells A1 through E10 and then apply the Colorful 1 autoformat.
6. Select cells B3 through B10 and then change the alignment to right.
7. Save the worksheet again with the same name (Excel Ch 11, Ex 02).
8. Print Excel Ch 11, Ex 02.
9. Make the following changes to cell contents:
    C4: Change *$48,290* to *46425*
    D6: Change *$61,220* to *60000*
    C8: Change *$55,309* to *57415*
    C9: Change *$12,398* to *14115*
10. Save the worksheet again with the same name (Excel Ch 11, Ex 02).
11. Print and then close Excel Ch 11, Ex 02.

Copying Formulas with the Fill Handle

Use the Autofill fill handle to copy a formula up, down, left, or right within a worksheet. To use the fill handle, insert the desired data in the cell (text, value, formula, etc.). With the cell active, position the mouse pointer (white plus sign) on the fill handle until the mouse pointer turns into a thin black cross. Hold down the left mouse button, drag and select the desired cells, and then release the mouse button. If you are dragging a cell containing a formula, a relative version of the formula is copied to the selected cells. You will use the fill handle in exercise 3 to copy a formula to adjacent cells.

Use the AutoFill fill handle to copy a relative version of a formula.

exercise 3

Calculating Salary by Inserting and Copying a Formula with the Fill Handle

1. Open Excel Worksheet 05.
2. Save the worksheet with Save As and name it Excel Ch 11, Ex 03.
3. Make cell D2 active, turn on bold, change the alignment to center, and then key **Salary**.
4. Insert a formula and then copy it to other cells using the fill handle by completing the following steps:
   a. Make D3 the active cell.
   b. Click the Formula bar text box and then key **=C3*B3**.
   c. Click the Enter button on the formula bar.
   d. Copy the formula to cells D4 through D8 by completing the following steps:
      1) Make cell D3 active.
      2) Position the mouse pointer (white plus sign) on the fill handle that displays at the lower right corner of cell D3 until the pointer turns into a thin black cross.
      3) Hold down the left mouse button, drag down to cell D8, and then release the mouse button.

	A	B	C	D
1		January		
2	Name	Hours	Rate	Salary
3	Carolyn Bentley	35	$23.15	$810.25
4	Lindon Cassini	20	$19.00	$380.00
5	Michelle DeFord	40	$18.75	$750.00
6	Javier Farias	24	$16.45	$394.80
7	Deborah Gould	15	$11.50	$172.50
8	William Jarman	15	$11.50	$172.50

Step 4d3

5. Save the worksheet again with the same name (Excel Ch 11, Ex 03).
6. Print Excel Ch 11, Ex 03.
7. Make the following changes to cell contents:
    B4: Change *20* to *28*
    C5: Change *$18.75* to *19.10*
    B7: Change *15* to *24*
8. Save the worksheet again with the same name (Excel Ch 11, Ex 03).
9. Print and then close Excel Ch 11, Ex 03.

Writing a Formula by Pointing

In exercises 2 and 3, you wrote formulas using cell references such as =C3-B3. Another method for writing a formula is to "point" to the specific cells that are to be part of the formula. Creating a formula by pointing is more accurate than keying the cell reference since a mistake can happen when entering the cell reference.

To write a formula by pointing, click the cell that will contain the formula, key the equals sign to begin the formula, and then click the cell you want to reference in the formula. This inserts a moving border around the cell and also changes the mode from *Enter* to *Point*. (The word *Point* displays at the left side of the Status bar.) Key the desired mathematical operator and then click the next cell reference. Continue in this manner until all cell references are specified and then press the Enter key. This ends the formula and inserts the result of the calculation of the formula in the active cell. When writing a formula by pointing, you can also select a range of cells you want included in a formula.

exercise 4

Writing a Formula by Pointing that Calculates Percentage of Down Time

1. Open Excel Worksheet 09.
2. Save the worksheet with Save As and name it Excel Ch 11, Ex 04.
3. Make the following changes to the worksheet:
   a. Make cell A11 active and then key **Percentage of Down Time**.
   b. Enter a formula by pointing that computes the percentage of equipment down time by completing the following steps:
      1) Make cell B11 active.
      2) Key the equals sign followed by the left parenthesis (=().
      3) Click cell B3. (This inserts a moving border around the cell and the mode changes from *Enter* to *Point*.)
      4) Key the minus symbol (-).
      5) Click cell B9.
      6) Key the right parenthesis followed by the forward slash ()/).
      7) Click cell B3.
      8) Make sure the formula looks like this: =(B3-B9)/B3 and then press Enter.

	A	B	
1			
2	**Hours**	**January**	
3	Total Hours Available	2,300	Step 3b7
4	Avoidable Delays	19	
5	Unavoidable Delays	9	
6	Repairs	5	
7	Servicing	6	
8	Unassigned	128	
9	In Use	2,040	
10			
11	Percentage of Down Time	=(B3-B9)/B3	Step 3b8
12			

c. Make cell B11 active and then click the Percent Style button on the Formatting toolbar.

d. With cell B11 still active, position the mouse pointer on the fill handle, drag across to cell M11, and then release the mouse button.

e. Enter a formula by dragging through a range of cells by completing the following steps:
1) Click in cell A13 and then key **Hours Available Jan – June.**
2) Click in cell B13 and then click the AutoSum button on the Standard toolbar.
3) Select cells B3 through G3.
4) Click the Enter key on the Formula bar.

f. Click in cell A14 and then key **Hours Available July – Dec.**

g. Click in cell B14 and then complete steps similar to those in steps 3e2 through 3e4 to create a formula that totals hours available from July through December.

4. Save the worksheet again with the same name (Excel Ch 11, Ex 04).

5. Print the worksheet in landscape orientation horizontally and vertically centered on the page and with column A titles repeated at the left side of the worksheet on the second page.

6. Close Excel Ch 11, Ex 04.

exercise 5

Writing a Formula by Pointing that Calculates Percentage of Actual Budget

1. Open Excel Worksheet 02.

2. Save the worksheet with Save As and name it Excel Ch 11, Ex 05.

3. Make the following changes to the worksheet:
   a. Delete column D.
   b. Make cell D1 active and then key **% of Actual**.
   c. Enter a formula by pointing that calculates the percentage of actual budget by completing the following steps:
      1) Make cell D2 active.
      2) Key the equals sign (=).
      3) Click cell C2. (This inserts a moving border around the cell and the mode changes from *Enter* to *Point*.)
      4) Key the forward slash symbol (/).
      5) Click cell B2.
      6) Make sure the formula looks like this: =C2/B2 and then press Enter.

	A	B	C	D
1	Expense	Actual	Budget	% of Actual
2	Salaries	126000	126000	=C2/B2
3	Commissions	58000	54500	
4	Media space	8250	10100	
5	Travel expenses	6350	6000	Step
6	Dealer display	4140	4500	3c
7	Payroll taxes	2430	2200	
8	Telephone	1450	1500	

   d. Make cell D2 active and then click the Percent Style button on the Formatting toolbar.
   e. With cell D2 still active, position the mouse pointer on the fill handle, drag down to cell D8, and then release the mouse button.
   f. Select cells B2 through C8 and then click the Currency Style button on the Formatting toolbar.
   g. Automatically increase the width of column D to accommodate the column heading.
   h. Select cells A1 through D8 and then apply the Classic 2 autoformat.

4. Save the worksheet again with the same name (Excel Ch 11, Ex 05).

5. Print the worksheet horizontally and vertically centered on the page.

6. Close Excel Ch 11, Ex 05.

Inserting a Formula with the Paste Function Button

In exercise 1, the AutoSum button inserted a formula that began with =SUM. This part of the formula is called a *function*. A function is a built-in formula. Using a function takes less keystrokes when creating a formula. For example, the =SUM function saved you from having to key each cell to be included in the formula with the plus (+) symbol between cell entries.

Excel provides other functions that can be used to write formulas. A function operates on what is referred to as an *argument*. An argument may consist of a constant, a cell reference, or another function (referred to as a nested function). In exercise 1, when you made cell B10 active and then clicked the AutoSum button, the formula *=SUM(B3:B9)* was inserted in the cell. The cell range (B3:B9) is an example of a cell reference argument. An argument may also contain a *constant*. A constant is a value entered directly into the formula. For example, if you enter the formula *=SUM(B3:B9,100)*, the cell range B3:B9 is a cell reference argument and 100 is a constant. In this formula, 100 is always added to the sum of the cells. If a function is included in an argument within a function, it is called a *nested function*. (You will learn about nested functions later in this chapter.)

Paste Function

When a value calculated by the formula is inserted in a cell, this process is referred to as *returning the result*. The term *returning* refers to the process of calculating the formula and the term *result* refers to the value inserted in the cell.

You can key a function in a cell in a worksheet or you can use the Paste Function button on the Standard toolbar to help you write the formula. When you click the Paste Function button, or click Insert and then Function, the Paste Function dialog box displays as shown in figure 11.2.

If you need to display a specific cell or cells behind the formula palette, move the palette by clicking and dragging it. *Hint*

Depending on your system, the Office Assistant may ask if you would like help with the feature. If you know the formula you want to write and do not need help from the Office Assistant, either leave the yellow message box displayed or close it by clicking the blue circle that precedes the option "No, don't provide help now." If you would like assistance on how to write a formula and what function to use, click the blue circle preceding "Yes, please provide help," located in the yellow message box.

figure 11.2

First Paste Function Dialog Box

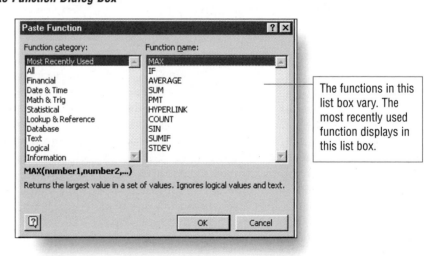

The functions in this list box vary. The most recently used function displays in this list box.

At the Paste Function dialog box, function categories display in a list box at the left and function names display in a list box at the right. The list of function names will change depending on what is selected in the function categories list box. For example, if you click *All* in the Function category list box, a much longer list of functions displays in the Function name list box.

Choose a function in the Function name list box and then click OK. This displays a formula palette, like the one shown in figure 11.3. At this palette, enter in the Number 1 text box the range of cells you want included in the formula, enter any constants that are to be included as part of the formula, or enter another function. After entering a range of cells, a constant, or another function, click the OK button. More than one argument can be included in a function. If the function you are creating contains more than one argument, press the Tab key to move the insertion point to the Number 2 text box, and then enter the second argument.

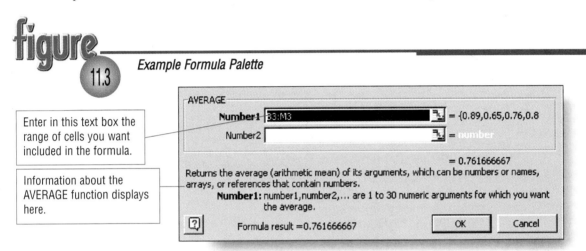

figure
11.3

Example Formula Palette

Enter in this text box the range of cells you want included in the formula.

Information about the AVERAGE function displays here.

Writing Formulas with Functions

Excel includes over 200 functions that are divided into nine different categories including Financial, Date & Time, Math & Trig, Statistical, Lookup & Reference, Database, Text, Logical, and Information. Clicking the AutoSum button on the Standard toolbar automatically adds numbers with the SUM function. The SUM function is included in the Math & Trig category. In some sections in this chapter, you will write formulas with functions in other categories including Statistical, Financial, Date & Time, and Logical.

Writing Formulas with Statistical Functions

In this section, you will learn to write formulas with the statistical functions AVERAGE, MAX, MIN, and COUNT. The AVERAGE function returns the average (arithmetic mean) of the arguments. The MAX function returns the largest value in a set of values and the MIN function returns the smallest number in a set of values. Use the COUNT function to count the number of cells that contain numbers within the list of arguments.

Finding Averages

A common function in a formula is the AVERAGE function. With this function, a range of cells is added together and then divided by the number of cell entries. In exercise 6 you will use the AVERAGE function, which will add all test scores for a student and then divide that number by the total number of tests. You will use the Paste Function feature to simplify the creation of the formula containing an AVERAGE function.

One of the advantages to using formulas in a worksheet is the ability to easily manipulate data to answer certain questions. In exercise 6 you will learn the impact of retaking certain tests on the final average score.

exercise 6

Extra Credit

Averaging Test Scores in a Worksheet

1. Open Excel Worksheet 06.
2. Save the worksheet with Save As and name it Excel Ch 11, Ex 06.
3. Make cell N1 the active cell, turn on bold, and then key **Average**.
4. Use the Paste Function feature to find the average of test scores and copy the formula down by completing the following steps:
   a. Make N3 the active cell.
   b. Click the Paste Function button on the Standard toolbar.
   c. At the Paste Function dialog box, click *Statistical* in the Function category list box.
   d. Click *AVERAGE* in the Function name list box.
   e. Click OK.
   f. At the formula palette, make sure *B3:M3* displays in the Number 1 text box. (If not, key **B3:M3** in the Number 1 text box.)
   g. Click OK.
   h. Copy the formula by completing the following steps:
      1) Make cell N3 active.
      2) Position the mouse pointer on the fill handle until the pointer turns into a thin black cross.
      3) Hold down the left mouse button, drag down to cell N20, and then release the mouse button.
5. Save the worksheet again with the same name (Excel Ch 11, Ex 06).
6. Specify that you want the names printed on each page of the worksheet and then print the worksheet by completing the following steps:
   a. Click File and then Page Setup.
   b. At the Page Setup dialog box, click the Sheet tab.
   c. Click inside the Columns to repeat at left text box.
   d. Key **A1:A20**.
   e. Click the Print button at the right side of the dialog box.

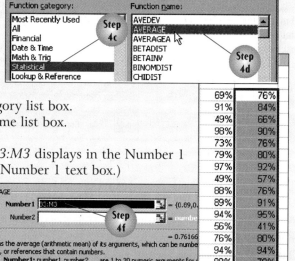

f. At the Print dialog box, click OK.

7. After viewing the averages of test scores, you notice that a couple of people have a low average. You decide to see what happens to the average score if students make up tests where they scored the lowest. You decide that a student can make up to 70% on a retake of the test. Make the following changes to test scores to see how the changes will affect the test average.

        L5: Change *45* to *70*
        M5: Change *49* to *70*
        C10: Change *45* to *70*
        M10: Change *49* to *70*
        C14: Change *0* to *70*
        I14: Change *0* to *70*
        J14: Change *0* to *70*

8. Save the worksheet again with the same name (Excel Ch 11, Ex 06).

9. Print and then close Excel Ch 11, Ex 06. (Compare the test averages for Jack Calahan, Stephanie Flanery, and Kathleen Kwieciak to see what the effect of retaking the tests has on their final test averages.)

When a formula such as the AVERAGE formula you inserted in a cell in exercise 6 calculates cell entries, it ignores certain cell entries. The AVERAGE function will ignore text in cells and blank cells (not zeros). For example, in the worksheet containing test scores, a couple of cells contained a 0% entry. This entry was included in the averaging of the test scores. If you did not want that particular test to be included in the average, enter text in the cell such as *N/A* (for not applicable) or leave the cell blank.

Finding Maximum and Minimum Values

The MAX function is used in a formula to return the maximum value in a cell range and the MIN function returns the minimum value in a cell range. As an example, you could use the MAX and MIN functions in a worksheet containing employee hours to determine which employee worked the most number of hours and which worked the least. In a worksheet containing sales commissions, you could use the MAX and MIN functions to determine the salesperson who earned the most commission dollars and the one who earned the least.

Insert a MAX and MIN function into a formula in the same manner as an AVERAGE function. In exercise 7, you will use the Paste Function feature to insert MAX and MIN functions in cells to determine the highest test score average and the lowest test score average.

Finding Maximum and Minimum Values in a Worksheet

1. Open Excel Ch 11, Ex 06.
2. Save the worksheet with Save As and name it Excel Ch 11, Ex 07.
3. Key the following in the specified cells:

   A22: Turn on bold and then key **Highest Test Average**.
   A23: Turn on bold and then key **Lowest Test Average**.
   A24: Turn on bold and then key **Average of All Tests**.
4. Insert the following formulas in the worksheet:
   a. Insert a formula to identify the highest test score average by completing the following steps:
      1) Make cell B22 active.
      2) Click the Paste Function button on the Standard toolbar.
      3) At the Paste Function dialog box, click *Statistical* in the Function category list box.
      4) Click *MAX* in the Function name list box. (You will need to scroll down the list to display *MAX*.)
      5) Click OK.
      6) At the formula palette, key **N3:N20** in the Number 1 text box, and then click OK.

   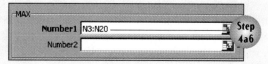

   b. Insert a formula to identify the lowest test score average by completing the following steps:
      1) Make cell B23 active.
      2) Click the Paste Function button on the Standard toolbar.
      3) At the Paste Function dialog box, make sure *Statistical* is selected in the Function category list box, and then click *MIN* in the Function name list box.
      4) Click OK.
      5) At the formula palette, key **N3:N20** in the Number 1 text box, and then click OK.
   c. Insert a formula to determine the average of all test scores by completing the following steps:
      1) Make cell B24 active.
      2) Click the Paste Function button on the Standard toolbar.
      3) At the Paste Function dialog box, make sure *Statistical* is selected in the Paste category list box, and then click *AVERAGE* in the Function name list box.
      4) Click OK.
      5) At the formula palette, key **N3:N20** in the Number 1 text box, and then click OK.
5. Save the worksheet again with the same name (Excel Ch 11, Ex 07).
6. Print Excel Ch 11, Ex 07 in landscape orientation. (Check with your instructor first to determine if your printer is capable of landscape printing.)

7. Change the 70% values (which were previously 0%) in cells C14, I14, and J14 to *N/A*. (This will cause the average of test scores for Kathy Kwieciak to increase and also will change the minimum number and average of all test scores.)
8. Save the worksheet again with the same name (Excel Ch 11, Ex 07).
9. Print Excel Ch 11, Ex 07 in landscape orientation.
10. Close Excel Ch 11, Ex 07.

Counting Numbers in a Range

Use the COUNT function to count the numeric values in a range. For example, in a range of cells containing cells with text and cells with numbers, you can count how many cells in the range contain numbers. In exercise 8, you will use the COUNT function to specify the number of students taking the midterm test and the number taking the final test. In this worksheet, a cell is left blank if a student did not take a test. If a value such as 0% was entered into the cell, the COUNT function would count this as a cell with a number.

Counting the Number of Students Taking Tests

1. Open Excel Worksheet 30.
2. Save the worksheet and name it Excel Ch 11, Ex 08.
3. Count the number of students who have taken the midterm test by completing the following steps:
   a. Make cell A22 active.
   b. Key **Number of students** and then press Alt + Enter (this moves the insertion point down to the next line within the cell).
   c. Key **completing the midterm**.
   d. Make cell B22 active.
   e. Insert a formula counting the number of students who have taken the midterm test by completing the following steps:
      1) Click the Paste Function button on the Standard toolbar.
      2) At the Paste Function dialog box, click *Statistical* in the Function c̲ategory list box.
      3) Scroll down the list of functions in the Function n̲ame list box until *COUNT* is visible and then double-click *COUNT*.
      4) At the formula palette, key **B3:B20** in the Value 1 text box, and then click OK.
4. Count the number of students who have taken the final test by completing the following steps:
   a. Make cell A23 active.
   b. Key **Number of students** and then press Alt + Enter (this moves the insertion point down to the next line within the cell).
   c. Key **completing the final**.
   d. Make cell B23 active.

COUNT		Step 3e4	
Value1	B3:B20		= {0.91;0.76;0.67;0;0
Value2			= number
			= 16

Counts the number of cells that contain numbers and numbers within the list of arguments.

e. Insert a formula counting the number of students who have taken the final test by completing the following steps:
1) Click the Paste Function button on the Standard toolbar.
2) At the Paste Function dialog box, click *Statistical* in the Function category list box.
3) Scroll down the list of functions in the Function name list box until *COUNT* is visible and then double-click *COUNT*.
4) At the formula palette, key **C3:C20** in the Value 1 text box, and then click OK.
5. Save the worksheet again with the same name (Excel Ch 11, Ex 08).
6. Print Excel Ch 11, Ex 08.
7. Add test scores by completing the following steps:
a. Make cell B14 active and then key **68**.
b. Make cell C14 active and then key **70**.
c. Make cell C19 active and then key **55**.
d. Press Enter.
8. Save the worksheet again with the same name (Excel Ch 11, Ex 08).
9. Print and then close Excel Ch 11, Ex 08.

Writing Formulas with Financial Functions

In this section, you will learn to write formulas with the financial functions SLN, DDB, FV, and PMT. The SLN function returns the straight-line depreciation of an asset for one period, while the DDB function returns the depreciation of an asset for a specified period of time using the double-declining balance method. Use the FV function to return the future value of an investment based on periodic, constant payments and a constant interest rate. The PMT function will calculate the payment for a loan based on constant payments and a constant interest rate.

Finding Depreciation Values

Assets within a company, such as equipment, can be depreciated over time. There are several methods for determining the amount of depreciation, such as the straight-line depreciation method, fixed-declining balance method, and the double-declining balance method. In determining depreciation, you need to create cell entries for some or all of the following categories: cost, salvage, life, period, and/or month. Figure 11.4 describes what each category should contain.

figure

11.4 *Depreciation Categories*

cost	=	initial cost of the asset
salvage	=	value of asset at the end of the depreciation
life	=	number of periods over which the asset is being depreciated
period	=	period for which you want to calculate the depreciation (must use the same units as life category)
month	=	number of months in the first year (if omitted, 12 is used)

The straight-line method uses the categories cost, salvage, and life. The fixed-declining balance method uses all the categories shown in figure 11.4, and the double-declining balance method uses cost, salvage, life, and period. An optional category named factor can be included in the double-declining balance method. This category is the rate at which the balance declines. If no cell entry is included, the number 2 is assumed (which is why it is referred to as the double-declining balance method).

Determining Depreciation Using the Straight-Line Method

1. Open Excel Worksheet 07.
2. Save the worksheet with Save As and name it Excel Ch 11, Ex 09.
3. Insert the function to determine straight-line depreciation by completing the following steps:
   a. Make cell E3 active.
   b. Click the Paste Function button on the Standard toolbar.
   c. At the Paste Function dialog box, click *Financial* in the Function category list box.
   d. Scroll down the Function name list until the function *SLN* is visible and then click *SLN*.
   e. Click OK.
   f. At the formula palette, key **B3** in the Cost category, and then press the Tab key.
   g. Key **C3** in the Salvage category and then press the Tab key.
   h. Key **D3** in the Life category.
   i. Click OK.
4. Copy the formula down to other cells by completing the following steps:
   a. Make cell E3 active.
   b. Using the fill handle, drag down to cell E10, and then release the mouse button.
5. Make the following formatting changes to the worksheet:
   a. Select cells A1 through E10 and then apply the Classic 3 autoformat.
   b. Select cells D3 through D10 and then click the Center button on the Formatting toolbar.
   c. Select cells E3 through E10 and then click the Currency Style button on the Formatting toolbar.

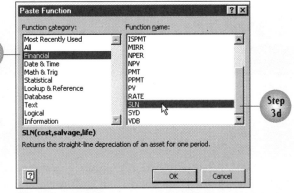

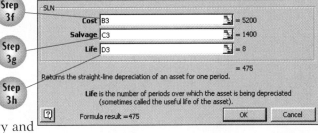

E
sset Depreciation
$475.00
$686.25
$900.00
$337.50
$150.00
$90.83
$55.00
$493.33

Step 4

6. Save the worksheet again with the same name (Excel Ch 11, Ex 09).
7. Print Excel Ch 11, Ex 09 horizontally and vertically centered on the page.
8. Close Excel Ch 11, Ex 09.

When you clicked the Financial option in the Function category in step 3c of exercise 9, Excel displayed information below the list box that showed the order of categories in the formula. At the formula palette, as a cell designation was entered in each category, such as Cost, Salvage, Life, and so on, Excel displayed information about the category toward the bottom of the palette. This information can be very helpful in understanding the categories of a formula and what functions Excel uses when creating a formula with the Paste Function feature. Try experimenting with other function names to see what Excel uses to build the formula.

exercise 10

Determining Depreciation Using the Fixed-Declining Method

1. Open Excel Worksheet 07.
2. Save the worksheet with Save As and name it Excel Ch 11, Ex 10.
3. Add a column by completing the following steps:
   a. Make any cell in column E active.
   b. Click Insert and then Columns.
   c. Key the following text in the specified cells:

E2	=	**Period of Dep.**
E3	=	1 *(Hint: Use the fill handle to copy the 1s.)*
E4	=	1
E5	=	1
E6	=	1
E7	=	1
E8	=	1
E9	=	1
E10	=	1

4. Add another column by completing the following steps:
   a. Make any cell in column F active.
   b. Click Insert and then Columns.
   c. Key the following text in the specified cells:

F2	=	**Months in Period**
F3	=	12 *(Hint: Use the fill handle to copy the 12s.)*
F4	=	12
F5	=	12
F6	=	12
F7	=	12
F8	=	12
F9	=	12
F10	=	12

   d. Automatically adjust the width of columns E and F.

5. Insert the function to determine fixed-declining depreciation by completing the following steps:
   a. Make cell G3 active.
   b. Click the Paste Function button on the Standard toolbar.
   c. At the Paste Function dialog box, make sure *Financial* is selected in the Function category list box.
   d. Click *DB* in the Function name list box and then click OK.
   e. At the formula palette, key **B3** in the Cost category, and then press the Tab key.
   f. Key **C3** in the Salvage category and then press the Tab key.
   g. Key **D3** in the Life category and then press the Tab key.
   h. Key **E3** in the Period category and then press the Tab key.
   i. Key **F3** in the Month category.
   j. Click OK.
6. Copy the formula down to cells G4 through G10.
7. Make the following formatting changes to the worksheet:
   a. Select cells A1 through G10 and then apply the Classic 3 autoformat.
   b. Select cells D3 through F10 and then click the Center button on the Formatting toolbar.
   c. Select cells G3 through G10 and then click the Currency Style button on the Formatting toolbar.
8. Save the worksheet again with the same name (Excel Ch 11, Ex 10).
9. Print Excel Ch 11, Ex 10 in landscape orientation.
10. Close Excel Ch 11, Ex 10.

E	F	G
PHY		
Period of Dep.	Months in Period	Depreciation
1	12	$785.20
1	12	$1,210.39
1	12	$1,489.50
1	12	$516.15
1	12	$234.40
1	12	$134.36
1	12	$92.88
1	12	$770.43

Step 6

exercise 11

Determining Depreciation Using the Double-Declining Method

1. Open Excel Worksheet 07.
2. Save the worksheet with Save As and name it Excel Ch 11, Ex 11.
3. Add a column between columns D and E and then key the following text in the specified cells:

E2	=	**Period of Dep.**
E3	=	1 *(Hint: Use the fill handle to copy the 1s.)*
E4	=	1
E5	=	1
E6	=	1
E7	=	1
E8	=	1
E9	=	1
E10	=	1

4. Insert the function to determine double-declining depreciation by completing the following steps:
   a. Make cell F3 active.
   b. Click the Paste Function button on the Standard toolbar.
   c. At the Paste Function dialog box, make sure *Financial* is selected in the Function category list box.
   d. Click *DDB* in the Function name list box and then click OK.
   e. At the formula palette, key **B3** in the Cost category, and then press the Tab key.
   f. Key **C3** in the Salvage category and then press the Tab key.
   g. Key **D3** in the Life category and then press the Tab key.
   h. Key **E3** in the Period category.
   i. Click OK.
5. Copy the formula down to cells F4 through F10.
6. Make the following formatting changes to the worksheet:
   a. Select cells A1 through F10 and then apply the Classic 3 autoformat.
   b. Select cells D3 through E10 and then click the Center button on the Formatting toolbar.
   c. Select cells F3 through F10 and then click the Currency Style button on the Formatting toolbar.
7. Save the worksheet again with the same name (Excel Ch 11, Ex 11).
8. Print Excel Ch 11, Ex 11 in landscape orientation.
9. Close Excel Ch 11, Ex 11.

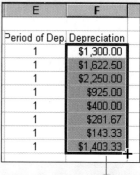

E	F
Period of Dep.	Depreciation
1	$1,300.00
1	$1,622.50
1	$2,250.00
1	$925.00
1	$400.00
1	$281.67
1	$143.33
1	$1,403.33

Step 5

Finding the Periodic Payments for a Loan

The PMT function finds the periodic payment for a loan based on constant payments and a constant interest rate. The PMT function contains the arguments nper, pv, fv, and type. The nper argument is the number of payments that will be made to an investment or loan, pv is the current value of amounts to be received or paid in the future, fv is the value of a loan or investment at the end of all periods, and type determines whether calculation will be based on payments made in arrears (at the end of each period) or in advance (at the beginning of each period).

exercise 12

Calculating Payments

1. Open Excel Worksheet 31.
2. Save the worksheet with Save As and name it Excel Ch 11, Ex 12.
3. The owner of Real Photography is interested in purchasing a new developer and needs to determine monthly payments on three different models. Insert a formula that calculates monthly payments and then copy that formula by completing the following steps:
   a. Position the insertion point in cell E7.
   b. Click the Paste Function button on the Standard toolbar.
   c. At the Paste Function dialog box, click *Financial* in the Function category list box.

d. Click *PMT* in the Function name list box.
e. Click OK.
f. At the formula palette, key **C7/12** in the Rate text box. (This tells Excel to divide the interest rate by 12 months.)
g. Press the Tab key. (This moves the insertion point to the Nper text box).

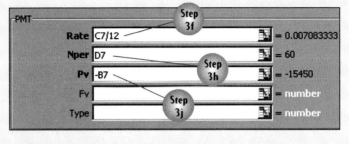

h. Key **D7**. (This is the total number of months in the payment period).
i. Press the Tab key. (This moves the insertion point to the Pv text box.)
j. Key **-B7**. (Excel displays the result of the PMT function as a negative number since the loan represents a negative cash flow to the borrower. Insert a minus sign before B7 to show the monthly payment as a positive number rather than a negative number.)
k. Click OK. (This closes the dialog box and also inserts the monthly payment of *$316.98* in cell E7.)
l. Copy the formula in cell E7 down to cells E8 and E9.
4. Insert a formula in cell F7 that calculates the total amount of the payments by completing the following steps:
   a. Make cell F7 active.
   b. Key **=E7*D7** and then press Enter.
   c. Make cell F7 active and then copy the formula down to cells F8 and F9.
5. Insert a formula in cell G7 that calculates to the total amount of interest paid by completing the following steps:
   a. Make cell G7 active.
   b. Key **=F7-B7** and then press Enter.
   c. Make cell G7 active and then copy the formula down to cells G8 and G9.
6. Save the worksheet again with the same name (Excel Ch 11, Ex 12).
7. Print and then close Excel Ch 11, Ex 12.

Finding the Future Value of a Series of Payments

The FV function calculates the future value of a series of equal payments or an annuity. Use this function to determine information such as how much money can be earned in an investment account with a specific interest rate and over a specific period of time.

Finding the Future Value on an Investment

1. Open Excel Worksheet 32.
2. Save the worksheet with Save As and name it Excel Ch 11, Ex 13.
3. The owner of Real Photography has decided to save money to purchase a new developer and wants to compute how much money can be earned by investing the

money in an investment account that returns a 9% annual interest. The owner determines that $1,200 per month can be invested in the account for three years. Complete the following steps to determine the future value of the investment account by completing the following steps:

a. Make cell C6 active.
b. Click the Paste Function button on the Standard toolbar.
c. At the Paste Function dialog box, click *Financial* in the Function category list box.
d. Click *FV* in the Function name list box.
e. Click OK.
f. At the formula palette, key **C3/12** in the Rate text box.
g. Press the Tab key.
h. Key **C4** in the Nper text box.
i. Press the Tab key.
j. Key **C5** in the Pmt text box.
k. Click OK. (This closes the dialog box and also inserts the future value of *$49,383.26* in cell C6.)

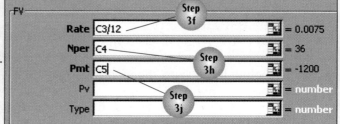

4. Save the worksheet again with the same name (Excel Ch 11, Ex 13).
5. Print Excel Ch 11, Ex 13.
6. The owner decides to determine the future return after two years. To do this, change the amount in cell C4 from *36* to *24* and then press Enter. (This recalculates the future investment amount in cell C6.)
7. Save the worksheet again with the same name (Excel Ch 11, Ex 13).
8. Print and then close Ch 11, Ex 13.

Writing Formulas with Date & Time Functions

In this section, you will learn to write formulas with the date and time functions NOW and DATE. The NOW function returns the serial number of the current date and time. The DATE function returns the serial number that represents a particular date. Excel can make calculations using dates because the dates are represented as serial numbers. To calculate a date's serial number, Excel counts the days since the beginning of the twentieth century. The date serial number for January 1, 1900 is 1. The date serial number for January 1, 2000, is 36,526.

Using the DATE and NOW Functions

1. Open Excel Worksheet 33.
2. Save the worksheet with Save As and name it Excel Ch 11, Ex 14.
3. This worksheet establishes overdue dates for accounts. Enter a formula in cell D5 that returns the serial number for the date March 21, 2001 by completing the following steps:
   a. Make cell D5 active.
   b. Click the Paste Function button on the Standard toolbar.

c. At the Paste Function dialog box, click Date & Time in the Function category.
d. Click *DATE* in the Function name list box.
e. Click OK.
f. At the formula palette, key **2001** in the Year text box.
g. Press the Tab key and then key **03** in the Month text box.
h. Press the Tab key and then key **21** in the Day text box.
i. Click OK.

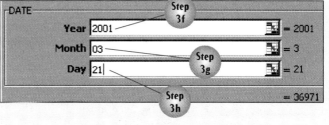

4. Complete steps similar to those in 3 to enter the following dates as serial numbers in the specified cells:

D6	=	**March 27, 2001**
D7	=	**April 2, 2001**
D8	=	**April 10, 2001**

5. Enter a formula in cell F5 that inserts the due date (the purchase date plus the number of days in the Terms column) by completing the following steps:
   a. Make cell F5 active.
   b. Key **=D5+E5** and then press Enter.
   c. Make cell F5 active and then copy the formula down to cells F6, F7, and F8.
6. Make cell A10 active and then key your name.
7. Insert the current date as a serial number by completing the following steps:
   a. Make cell A11 active.
   b. Click the Paste Function button on the Standard toolbar.
   c. At the Paste Function dialog box, make sure *Date & Time* is selected in the Function category list box, and then click *NOW* in the Function name list box.
   d. Click OK.
   e. At the formula palette telling you that the function takes no argument, click OK.
   f. With cell A11 still active, click the Align Left button on the Formatting toolbar.
8. Save the worksheet again with the same name (Excel Ch 10, Ex 14).
9. Print and then close Excel Ch 10, Ex 14.

Writing a Formula with the IF Logical Function

The IF function is considered a *conditional function*. With the IF function you can perform conditional tests on values and formulas. A question that can be answered with true or false is considered a *logical test*. The IF function makes a logical test and then performs a particular action if the answer is true and another action if the answer is false.

For example, an IF function can be used to write a formula that calculates a salesperson's bonus as 10 percent if the quota of $100,000 is met or exceeded and zero if the quota is less than $100,000. That formula would look like this: =IF(quota=>100000,quota*0.1,0). There are three parts to the formula—the condition or logical test IF(quota=>100000), action taken if the condition or logical test is true (quota*0.1), and the action taken if the condition or logical test is false (0). Commas separate the condition and the actions. In the bonus formula, if the quota is equal to or greater than $100,000, then the quota is multiplied by 10%. If the quota is less than $100,000, then the bonus is zero.

In exercise 15, you will write a formula with cell references rather than cell data. The formula in exercise 15 is =IF(C2>B2,C2*0.15,0). In this formula the condition or logical test is whether or not the number in cell C2 is greater than the number in cell B2. If the condition is true and the number is greater, then the number in cell C2 is multiplied by 0.15 (providing a 15% bonus). If the condition is false and the number in cell C2 is less than the number in cell B2, then nothing happens (no bonus). Notice how commas are used to separate the logical test from the actions.

Revising a Formula

Revise a formula by making active the cell containing the formula and then editing the formula in the cell or in the Formula bar text box. After revising the formula, press Enter or click the Enter button on the Formula bar and Excel will recalculate the result of the formula.

Writing a Formula with an IF Function

1. Open Excel Worksheet 10.
2. Save the worksheet with Save As and name it Excel Ch 11, Ex 15.
3. Write a formula with the IF function by completing the following steps: (The formula will determine if the quota has been met and, if it has, will insert the bonus [15% of the actual sales]. If the quota has not been met, the formula will insert a zero.)
   a. Make cell D2 active.
   b. Key **=IF(C2>B2,C2*0.15,0)** and then press Enter.
   c. Make cell D2 active and then use the fill handle to copy the formula to cells D3 through D7.
   d. Select cells D2 through D7 and then click the Currency Style button on the Formatting toolbar.
4. Print the worksheet.
5. Revise the formula so it will insert a 25% bonus if the quota has been met by completing the following steps:
   a. Make cell D2 active.
   b. Click in the Formula bar and then edit the formula so it displays as *IF(C2>B2,C2*0.25,0)* and then click the Enter button on the Formula bar.
   c. Copy the formula down to cells D3 through D7.
6. Save the worksheet again with the same name (Excel Ch 11, Ex 15).
7. Print and then close Excel Ch 11, Ex 15.

C	D
Actual Sales	**Bonus**
$ 103,295.00	15494.25
$ 129,890.00	0
$ 133,255.00	19988.25
$ 94,350.00	14152.5
$ 167,410.00	25111.5
$ 109,980.00	0

Step 3c

D
Bonus
$ 15,494.25
$ -
$ 19,988.25
$ 14,152.50
$ 25,111.50
$ -

Step 3d

Writing a Nested IF Condition

In exercise 15, the IF function had only two possible actions—the actual sales times 15 percent or a zero. In a formula where more than two actions are required, use nested IF functions. For example, in exercise 16, you will write a formula with IF conditions that has four possible actions—a letter grade of A, B, C, or D. When writing nested IF conditions, insert symbols such as commas, quotation marks, and parentheses in the proper locations. If you want an IF condition to insert text, insert quotation marks before and after the text. The formula you will be writing in exercise 16 is shown below.

=IF(E2>89,"A",IF(E2>79,"B",IF(E2>69,"C",IF(E2>59,"D"))))

This formula begins with the condition =IF(E2>89,"A",. If the number in cell E2 is greater than 89 then the condition is met and the grade of A is returned. The formula continues with a nested condition, IF(E2>79,"B",. If the number in cell E2 does not meet the first condition (greater than 89) then Excel looks to the next condition—is the number in cell E2 greater than 79. If it is, then the grade of B is inserted in cell E2. The formula continues with another nested condition, IF(E2>69,"C",. If the number in cell E2 does not match the first condition, Excel looks to the second condition, and if that condition is not met, then Excel looks to the third condition. If the number in cell E2 is greater than 69, then the grade of C is inserted in cell E2. The final nested condition is IF(E2>59,"D". If the first three conditions are not met but this one is, then the grade of D is inserted in cell E2. The four parentheses at the end of the formula end each condition in the formula.

exercise 16

Writing a Formula with Nested IF Conditions

1. Open Excel Worksheet 11.
2. Save the worksheet with Save As and name it Excel Ch 11, Ex 16.
3. Insert a formula to average the scores by completing the following steps:
    a. Make cell E2 active.
    b. Key **=AVERAGE(B2:D2)** and then press Enter.
    c. Make cell E2 active and then copy the formula down to cells E3 through E6.
    d. With cells E2 through E6 still selected, click the Decrease Decimal button on the Formatting toolbar five times.
4. Insert a formula with nested IF conditions by completing the following steps:
    a. Make cell F2 active.
    b. Key **=IF(E2>89,"A",IF(E2>79,"B",IF(E2>69,"C",IF(E2>59,"D"))))** and then press Enter.
    c. Make cell F2 active and then use the fill handle to copy the formula down to cells F3 through F6.
    d. With cells F2 through F6 still selected, click the Center button on the Formatting toolbar.
5. Save the worksheet again with the same name (Excel Ch 11, Ex 16).
6. Print and then close Excel Ch 11, Ex 16.

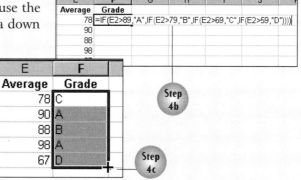

As you keyed the formula with nested IF conditions in step 4b of exercise 16, did you notice that the parentheses were different colors? Each color represents a condition. The four right parentheses at the end of the formula ended each of the conditions and each matched in color a left parenthesis. If an average in column E in Excel Ch 11, Ex 16 is less than 59, the nested formula inserts "FALSE" in the cell. If you want the formula to insert a letter grade, such as "F," instead of FALSE, include another nested IF condition in the formula.

If you enter a complicated formula in a worksheet, consider protecting the worksheet. To do this, click Tools, point to Protection, and then click Protect Sheet. At the Protect Sheet dialog box, enter a password, and then click OK.

Hint

Working with Ranges

A selected group of cells is referred to as a *range*. As you learned in an earlier chapter, a range of cells can be formatted, moved, copied, or deleted. A range of cells can also be named. Name a range of cells to quickly move the insertion point to the range or use a named range as part of a formula.

To name a range, select the cells, and then click in the Name Box button on the Formula bar (first button from the left on the Formula Bar). Key a name for the range (do not use a space) and then press Enter. To move the insertion point to a specific range and select the range, click the down-pointing triangle at the right side of the Name Box button and then click the range name.

A range name can be used in a formula. For example, if a range is named Profit and you wanted to insert the average of all cells in the Profit range, you would make the desired cell active and then key **=AVERAGE(Profit)**. A named range can be used in the current worksheet or in another worksheet within the workbook.

exercise 17

Naming a Range and Using a Range in a Formula

1. Open Excel Worksheet 09.
2. Save the worksheet with Save As and name it Excel Ch 11, Ex 17.
3. Click the *Sheet2* tab and then key the following text in the specified cell:

A1	=	**EQUIPMENT USAGE REPORT**
A2	=	**Yearly Hours**
A3	=	**Avoidable Delays**
A4	=	**Unavoidable Delays**
A5	=	**Total Delay Hours**
A6	=	**(leave blank)**
A7	=	**Repairs**
A8	=	**Servicing**
A9	=	**Total Repair/Servicing Hours**

	A
1	**EQUIPMENT USAGE REPORT**
2	**Yearly Hours**
3	Avoidable Delays
4	Unavoidable Delays
5	Total Delay Hours
6	
7	Repairs
8	Servicing
9	Total Repair/Servicing Hours
10	

4. Make the following formatting changes to the worksheet:
   a. Automatically adjust the width of column A.
   b. Center and bold the text in cells A1 and A2.

   Step 5d   Steps 3&4

5. Select a range of cells in worksheet 1, name the range, and use it in a formula in worksheet 2 by completing the following steps:

   adhours   = 19

	A	B	C
1			
2	**Hours**	**January**	**February**
3	Total Hours Available	2,300	2,430
4	Avoidable Delays	19	12
5	Unavoidable Delays	9	8
6	Repairs	5	7
7	Servicing	6	13
8	Unassigned	128	95
9	In Use	2,040	2,105

   a. Make worksheet 1 active by clicking the *Sheet1* tab.
   b. Select cells B4 through M4.
   c. Click in the Name Box button on the Formula bar.
   d. Key **adhours** (for Avoidable Delays Hours) and then press Enter.
   e. Click the *Sheet2* tab to make worksheet 2 active.

f. Make cell B3 active.

g. Key the equation **=SUM(adhours)** and then press Enter.

6. Make worksheet 1 active and then complete the following steps:

a. Select cells B5 through M5 and then name the range udhours.

b. Make worksheet 2 active, make cell B4 active, and then insert the equation *=SUM(udhours)*.

c. Make worksheet 1 active.

d. Select cells B6 through M6 and then name the range rhours.

e. Make worksheet 2 active, make cell B7 active, and then insert the equation *=SUM(rhours)*.

f. Make worksheet 1 active.

g. Select cells B7 through M7 and then name the range shours.

h. Make worksheet 2 active, make cell B8 active, and then insert the equation *=SUM(shours)*.

7. With worksheet 2 still active, make the following changes:

a. Make cell B5 active.

b. Click the AutoSum button on the Standard toolbar and then press Enter.

c. Make cell B9 active.

d. Double-click the AutoSum button on the Standard toolbar.

8. Save the workbook again with the same name (Excel Ch 11, Ex 17).

9. Print worksheet 2.

10. Make worksheet 1 active and then move to the range adhours by clicking the down-pointing triangle at the right side of the Name Box button and then clicking *adhours* at the drop-down list.

11. Close Excel Ch 11, Ex 17.

	A	B	
1	EQUIPMENT USAGE REPORT		
2	Yearly Hours		
3	Avoidable Delays	=SUM(adhours)	
4	Unavoidable Delays		
5	Total Delay Hours		
6			
7	Repairs		
8	Servicing		
9	Total Repair/Servicing Hours		

Step 5g

Using Absolute and Mixed Cell References in Formulas

A reference identifies a cell or a range of cells in a worksheet and can be relative, absolute, or mixed. Relative cell references refer to cells relative to a position in a formula. Absolute references refer to cells in a specific location. A relative cell reference adjusts when a formula is copied while an absolute cell reference remains constant when a formula is copied. A mixed cell reference does both— either the column remains absolute and the row is relative or the column is relative and the row is absolute. Distinguish between relative, absolute, and mixed cell references using the dollar sign ($). Key a dollar sign before the column and/or row cell reference in a formula to specify that the column or row is an absolute cell reference.

Using an Absolute Cell Reference in a Formula

In this chapter you have learned to copy a relative formula. For example, if the formula =SUM(A2:C2) in cell D2 is copied relatively to cell D3, the formula changes to =SUM(A3:C3). In some situations, you may want a formula to contain an absolute cell reference, which always refers to a cell in a specific location. In exercise 18, you will add a column for projected job earnings and then perform "what if" situations using a formula with an absolute cell reference.

To identify an absolute cell reference, insert a $ symbol before the row and also the column. For example, the absolute cell reference C12 would be keyed as *$C$12* in a formula.

Inserting and Copying a Formula with an Absolute Cell Reference

1. Open Excel Worksheet 01.
2. Save the worksheet with Save As and name it Excel Ch 11, Ex 18.
3. Make the following changes to the worksheet:
   a. Delete columns B and D by completing the following steps:
      1) Click the column B header (the letter B at the top of the column).
      2) Hold down the Ctrl key and then click the column D header. (This selects column B and column D.)
      3) Click Edit and then Delete.
   b. Key **Projected** in C1.
   c. Center and bold the text in cells A1 through C1.
4. Determine the effect on actual job earnings with a 20% increase by completing the following steps:
   a. Key **% Increase/Decrease** in cell A12.
   b. Key **1.2** in cell B12 and then press Enter. (This number will be used in a formula to determine a 20% increase.)
   c. Make cell B12 the active cell and make sure the number formatting is General. (If it is not, click Format and then Cells. At the Format Cells dialog box, click the Number tab, click *General* in the Category list box, and then click OK.)
   d. Make cell C3 active, key the formula **=B3*$B$12**, and then press Enter.
   e. Automatically adjust the width of column C.
   f. Make cell C3 active and then use the fill handle to copy the formula to cells C4 through C10.
   g. Select cells B3 through C10 and then click the Currency Style button on the Formatting toolbar.
   h. With cells B3 through C10 still selected, click twice on the Decrease Decimal button on the Formatting toolbar.
5. Save and then print the worksheet.

Step 3a1

Step 3a2

	B	C	D
1	Cus	#	Actual	Planned
2				
3	Sell	2130	$30,349	$34,109
4	Mai	1201	$48,290	$48,100
5	Sur	318	$34,192	$32,885
6	Lins	1009	$63,293	$61,220

Step 3a3

Step 4d

	A	B	C
1	Customer	Actual	Projected
2			
3	Sellar Corporation	$30,349	=B3*$B$12
4	Main Street Photos	$48,290	
5	Sunset Automotive	$34,192	
6	Linstrom Enterprises	$63,293	
7	Morcos Media	$29,400	
8	Green Valley Optics	$55,309	
9	Detailed Designs	$12,398	
10	Arrowstar Company	$87,534	
11			
12	% Increase/Decrease	1.2	

Step 4a

Step 4b

B	C
Actual	**Projected**
$30,349	36418.8
$48,290	57948
$34,192	41030.4
$63,293	75951.6
$29,400	35280
$55,309	66370.8
$12,398	14877.6
$87,534	105040.8
1.2	

Step 4f

6. With the worksheet still open, determine the effect on actual job earnings with a 10% decrease by completing the following steps:
   a. Make B12 active.
   b. Key **0.9** and then press Enter.
7. Save and then print the worksheet.
8. Determine the effects on actual job earnings with a 10% increase. (To do this, key **1.1** in cell B12.)
9. Save, print, and then close Excel Ch 11, Ex 18.

	A	B	C
1	Customer	Actual	Projected
2			
3	Sellar Corporation	$ 30,349	$ 27,314
4	Main Street Photos	$ 48,290	$ 43,461
5	Sunset Automotive	$ 34,192	$ 30,773
6	Linstrom Enterprises	$ 63,293	$ 56,964
7	Morcos Media	$ 29,400	$ 26,460
8	Green Valley Optics	$ 55,309	$ 49,778
9	Detailed Designs	$ 12,398	$ 11,158
10	Arrowstar Company	$ 87,534	$ 78,781
11			
12	% Increase/Decrease	0.9	
13			

Step 6b

Using a Mixed Cell Reference in a Formula

The formula you created in step 4d in exercise 18 contained a relative cell reference (B3) and an absolute cell reference ($B$12). A formula can also contain a mixed cell reference. In a mixed cell reference either the column remains absolute and the row is relative or the column is relative and the row is absolute. In exercise 19, you will create the formula =$A3*B$2. In the first cell reference in the formula, $A3, the column is absolute and the row is relative. In the second cell reference, B$2, the column is relative and the row is absolute. The formula containing the mixed cell references allows you to fill in the column and row data using only one formula.

exercise 19

Determining Simple Interest Using a Formula with Mixed Cell References

1. Open Excel Worksheet 12.
2. Save the worksheet with Save As and name it Excel Ch 11, Ex 19.
3. Insert a formula containing mixed cell references by completing the following steps:
   a. Make cell B3 the active cell.
   b. Key the formula =**$A3*B$2** and then press Enter.

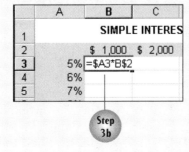

	A	B	C
1		SIMPLE INTERES	
2		$ 1,000	$ 2,000
3		5%	=$A3*B$2
4		6%	
5		7%	

Step 3b

4. Copy the formula down and to the right by completing the following steps:
   a. Make cell B3 active and then use the fill handle to copy the formula down to cell B13.
   b. Make cell B3 active and then use the fill handle to copy the formula across to cell F3.
   c. Make cell C3 active and then use the fill handle to copy the formula down to cell C13.
   d. Make cell D3 active and then use the fill handle to copy the formula down to cell D13.
   e. Make cell E3 active and then use the fill handle to copy the formula down to cell E13.
   f. Make cell F3 active and then use the fill handle to copy the formula down to cell F13.

	A	B
1		SIMPLE I
2		$ 1,000	$
3	5%	$ 50
4	6%	$ 60
5	7%	$ 70
6	8%	$ 80
7	9%	$ 90
8	10%	$ 100
9	11%	$ 110
10	12%	$ 120
11	13%	$ 130
12	14%	$ 140
13	15%	$ 150
14		

Step 4a

	A	B	C	D	E	F
1		SIMPLE INTEREST LOAN TABLE				
2		$ 1,000	$ 2,000	$ 3,000	$ 4,000	$ 5,000
3	5%	$ 50	$ 100	$ 150	$ 200	$ 250
4	6%	$ 60				

Step 4b

5. Save the worksheet again with the same name (Excel Ch 11, Ex 19).
6. Print the worksheet centered horizontally and vertically on the page.
7. Close Excel Ch 11, Ex 19.

	A	B	C
1		SIMPLE INTERES	
2		$ 1,000	$ 2,000
3	5%	$ 50	$ 100
4	6%	$ 60	$ 120
5	7%	$ 70	$ 140
6	8%	$ 80	$ 160
7	9%	$ 90	$ 180
8	10%	$ 100	$ 200
9	11%	$ 110	$ 220
10	12%	$ 120	$ 240
11	13%	$ 130	$ 260
12	14%	$ 140	$ 280
13	15%	$ 150	$ 300

Step 4c

You had to key only one formula in exercise 19 to create the data in the simple interest table. The mixed cell references allowed you to copy the formula down columns and across rows.

Linking Cells between Worksheets

In workbooks containing multiple worksheets or between related workbooks there may be data in cells that create a link between worksheets or workbooks. When data is linked, a change made in a linked cell is automatically made to the other cells in the link. Links can be made with individual cells or with a range of cells.

Linking cells between worksheets creates what is called a *dynamic link*. Dynamic links are useful in worksheets or workbooks that need to maintain consistency and control over critical data. The worksheet that contains the original data is called the *source* worksheet and the worksheet relying on the source worksheet for the data in the link is called the *dependent* worksheet.

To create a link, make active the cell containing the data to be linked (or select the cells), and then click the Copy button on the toolbar. Make active the worksheet where you want to paste the cell or cells and then click Edit and then Paste Special. This causes the Paste Special dialog box to display as shown in figure 11.5.

To maintain consistency and control over data shared between worksheets, consider creating a dynamic link with the data.

figure

11.5 *Paste Special Dialog Box*

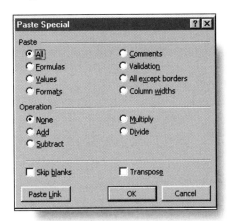

At the Paste Special dialog box, specify what in the cell you want to copy and what operators you want to include, and then click the Paste Link button at the bottom left side of the dialog box. When a change is made to the cell or cells in the source worksheet, the change is automatically made to the linked cell or cells in the dependent worksheet.

exercise 20

Linking Cells between Worksheets

1. Open Excel Worksheet 02.
2. Save the worksheet with Save As and name it Excel Ch 11, Ex 20.
3. Make the following changes to the worksheet:
   a. Insert a new row at the beginning of the worksheet.
   b. Make A1 the active cell.
   c. Click the Bold button and then key **FIRST HALF, 2000**.
   d. Align the text in cell A1 between columns A, B, C, and D (use the Merge and Center button).
   e. Delete the data in cells D3 through D9. (You are deleting the amounts in these cells because you are going to insert a formula instead.)

f.   Select cells B3 through D9, click the Currency Style button on the Standard toolbar, and then click twice the Decrease Decimal button on the Standard toolbar.

g.   Make cell D3 active, key the formula **=C3-B3**, and then press Enter.

h.   Copy the formula in cell D3 down to cells D4 through D9.

i.   Automatically adjust the width of columns A, B, C, and D.

	A	B	C	D
1	FIRST HALF, 2000			
2	Expense	Actual	Budget	Variance
3	Salaries	$126,000	$126,000	$ -
4	Commissions	$ 58,000	$ 54,500	$ (3,500)
5	Media space	$ 8,250	$ 10,100	$ 1,850
6	Travel expenses	$ 6,350	$ 6,000	$ (350)
7	Dealer display	$ 4,140	$ 4,500	$ 360
8	Payroll taxes	$ 2,430	$ 2,200	$ (230)
9	Telephone	$ 1,450	$ 1,500	$ 50
10				

Step 3h

4.   Save the worksheet again with the same name (Excel Ch 11, Ex 20).

5.   Copy the data in the worksheet to *Sheet2* by completing the following steps:
   a.   Select cells A1 through D9.
   b.   Click the Copy button on the Standard toolbar.
   c.   Click the *Sheet2* tab that displays to the left of the horizontal scroll bar.
   d.   With cell A1 the active cell, click the Paste button on the Standard toolbar.
   e.   Automatically adjust the width of columns A, B, C, and D.
   f.   Select cells C3 through C9 and then delete the cell data.

6.   Link cells C3 through C9 from *Sheet1* to *Sheet2* by completing the following steps:
   a.   Click the *Sheet1* tab.
   b.   With *Sheet1* displayed, select cells C3 through C9.
   c.   Click the Copy button on the Standard toolbar.
   d.   Click the *Sheet2* tab.
   e.   Make cell C3 active.
   f.   Click Edit and then Paste Special.
   g.   At the Paste Special dialog box, make sure All is selected in the Paste section of the dialog box, and then click the Paste Link button.

Step 6f

	File Edit View Insert Format Tools Data Window He

Undo Clear   Ctrl+Z

Arial   Cut   Ctrl+X   *I* U
C   Copy   Ctrl+C
    Paste   Ctrl+V

			C	D
1			2000	
2	Exp		Budget	Variance
3	Sal;	Fill		######
4	Cor	Clear		######
5	Mec	Delete...		$ (8,250)
6	Trav	Delete Sheet		$ (6,350)
7	Dea			$ (4,140)
8	Pay	Find... Ctrl+F		$ (2,430)
9	Tele	Replace... Ctrl+H		$ (1,450)

Paste Special...

Step 6e

7.   With *Sheet2* still the active worksheet, make the following changes to the specified cells:
   A1: Change *FIRST HALF, 2000* to *SECOND HALF, 2000*
   B3: Change *$126,000* to *123,500*
   B4: Change *$58,000* to *53,000*
   B6: Change *$6,350* to *6,125*

8.   Make *Sheet1* the active worksheet and then make the following changes to some of the linked cells:
   C3: Change *$126,000* to *128,000*
   C4: Change *$54,500* to *56,000*
   C8: Change *$2,200* to *2,400*

9.   Click the *Sheet2* tab and notice that the values in cells C3, C4, and C8 automatically changed. (This is because they are linked to *Sheet1*.)

10.   Save the workbook again with the same name (Excel Ch 11, Ex 20).

11.   Print both worksheets in the workbook.

12.   Close Excel Ch 11, Ex 20.

Linking Worksheets Using 3-D References

In a multiple worksheet workbook, you can use a 3-D reference to analyze data in the same cell or range of cells. A 3-D reference includes the cell or range of cells, preceded by a range of worksheet names. For example, you can add all the values contained in cells in B2 through B5 in worksheets 1 and 2 in a workbook using a 3-D reference. To do this, you would complete these basic steps:

1. Make active the cell where you want to enter the function.
2. Key =SUM(and then click the *Sheet1* tab.
3. Hold down the Shift key and then click the *Sheet2* tab.
4. Select cells B2 through B5 in thc worksheet.
5. Key) and then press Enter.

Linking Worksheets with a 3-D Reference

1. Open Excel Worksheet 34.
2. Save the workbook with Save As and name it Excel Ch 11, Ex 21.
3. Link worksheets 1, 2, and 3 with a 3-D reference by completing the following steps:
   a. Make cell B10 active.
   b. Click the Center button and then the Bold button on the Formatting toolbar.
   c. Key **January Sales** and then press Alt + Enter.
   d. Key **1998-2001** and then press Enter.
   e. With cell B11 active, insert a formula with a 3-D reference by completing the following steps:
      1) Key =SUM(.
      2) Hold down the Shift key and then click the *Sheet3* tab.
      3) Select cells B3 through B8.
      4) Key) (this is the closing parenthesis that ends the formula) and then press Enter.
      5) Make cell B11 active.
      6) Click the Currency Style button on the Formatting toolbar and then click twice on the Decrease Decimal button.

FIRST-QUARTER SALES - 1998		
Customer	January	February
Lakeside Trucking	$ 84,231	$ 73,455
Gresham Machines	$ 33,199	$ 40,390
Real Photography	$ 30,891	$ 35,489
Genesis Productions	$ 72,190	$ 75,390
Landower Company	$ 22,188	$ 14,228
Jewell Enterprises	$ 19,764	$ 50,801
	January Sales 1998-2001	
	=SUM('Sheet1:Sheet3'!B3:B8)	

Step
3e1-3e4

4. Complete steps similar to those in 3 to add February sales for 1998-2001. (Insert the heading *February Sales 1998-2001* [on two lines] in cell C10 and insert the formula with the 3-D reference in cell C11.)
5. Complete steps similar to those in 3 to add March sales for 1998-2001. (Insert the heading *March Sales 1998-2001* [on two lines] in cell D10 and insert the formula with the 3-D reference in cell D11.)
6. Save the workbook again with the same name (Excel Ch 11, Ex 21).
7. Print worksheet 1 of the workbook.
8. Close Excel Ch 11, Ex 21.

Automatically Outlining a Worksheet

Apply outlining to a worksheet to display specific rows and columns such as subtotals and totals. Apply an automatic outline to a worksheet by clicking Data, pointing to Group and Outline, and then clicking Auto Outline. Figure 11.6 shows a worksheet with outlining applied and identifies outlining buttons.

figure

11.6

Worksheet with Outlining Applied

Column Level Buttons

Hide Details Button

This line specifies a group of cells that are included in a subtotal.

Hours	January	February	March	April	May	June	1st Half	July
							EQUIPMENT USAGE REPORT	
Total Hours Available	2,300	2,430	2,530	2,400	2,440	2,240	14,340	2,5
Avoidable Delays	19	12	16	20	14	15	96	
Unavoidable Delays	9	8	6	12	9	10	54	
Repairs	5	7	12	9	10	6	49	
Servicing	6	13	7	6	4	5	41	
Unassigned	128	95	85	135	95	75	613	1
In Use	2,040	2,105	2,320	2,180	2,050	1,995	12,690	2,3

Hide Details

Show Details

Apply outlining to a document containing rows or columns that summarize data. For example, if you apply outlining to a document with subtotals and totals, you can then display the entire worksheet, only subtotals and totals in the worksheet, or only totals.

In the document in figure 11.6, notice the lines that display above the column headers. These lines identify a group of cells that are part of a subtotal or total. The button with the hyphen on it is called the Hide Details button. Click this button and all cells in the group are hidden except the subtotal or total cell. The Hide Details button changes to the Show Details button (a button with a plus symbol on it). Click the Show Details button to show all cells in the group.

You can also specify what cells to display by clicking a Column Level button (see figure 11.6). For example, in the worksheet shown in figure 11.6, click the Column Level 1 button to display the total column, and click the Column Level 2 button to display subtotal and total columns. Clicking the Column Level 3 button displays all cells in the worksheet.

exercise 22

Applying Automatic Outlining

1. Open Excel Worksheet 09.
2. Save the worksheet with Save As and name it Excel Ch 11, Ex 22.
3. Make the following changes to the worksheet:
   a. Insert a new column by completing the following steps:

G	H
IT USAGE REPORT	
June	1st Half
2,240	14,340
15	96
10	54
6	49
5	41
75	613
1,995	12,690

   1) Make any cell in column H active.
   2) Click Insert and then Columns.
   3) Key **1st Half** in cell H2 (in the new column).
   4) Make cell H3 active, key **=SUM(B3:G3)**, and then press Enter.
   5) Make cell H3 active again and then copy the formula down to cells H4 through H9.
   b. Create another subtotal column by completing the following steps:

Step 3a5

N	O
December	2nd Half
2,210	14,490
5	53
7	52
8	55
12	52
120	716
1,830	12,540

Step 3b1

   1) Key **2nd Half** centered and bolded in cell O2.
   2) Make cell O3 active, key **=SUM(I3:N3)**, and then press Enter.
   3) Make cell O3 active again and then copy the formula down to cells O4 through O9.
   c. Create a total column by completing the following steps:

Step 3b3

O	P
2nd Half	Total
14,490	28,830
53	149
52	106
55	104
52	93
716	1,329
12,540	25,230

Step 3c1

   1) Key **Total** centered and bolded in cell P2.
   2) Make cell P3 active, key **=H3+O3**, and then press Enter.
   3) Make cell P3 active again and then copy the formula down to cells P4 through P9.
   d. Apply automatic outlining to the worksheet by completing the following steps:
   1) Make cell A1 active.
   2) Click Data, point to Group and Outline, and then click Auto Outline.
   e. Display only subtotals and totals by clicking the Column Level 2 button.
   f. Print the worksheet.

Step 3c3

   g. Display only the total by clicking the Column Level 1 button.

Step 3e

   h. Print the worksheet.
4. Save and then close Excel Ch 11, Ex 22.

	A	H	O	P
1	EQUIPMENT USAGE REPORT			
2	Hours	1st Half	2nd Half	Total
3	Total Hours Available	14,340	14,490	28,830
4	Avoidable Delays	96	53	149
5	Unavoidable Delays	54	52	106
6	Repairs	49	55	104
7	Servicing	41	52	93
8	Unassigned	613	716	1,329
9	In Use	12,690	12,540	25,230

Planning a Worksheet

The worksheets you have worked with so far have already been basically planned. If you need to plan a worksheet yourself, there are some steps you can follow. These are basic steps—you may think of additional steps or additional information to help you plan a worksheet.

Before entering data in a worksheet, plan the worksheet.

- **Step 1: Identify the purpose of the worksheet.** The more definite you are about your purpose, the easier organizing your data into an effective worksheet will be. Consider things such as the purpose of the worksheet, the intended audience, the desired output or results, and the data required.
- **Step 2: Design the worksheet.** To do this, you need to determine how the data is to be organized, the titles of columns and rows, and how to emphasize important information. Designing the worksheet also includes determining any calculations that need to be performed.
- **Step 3: Create a sketch of the worksheet.** A diagram or sketch can help create a logical and well-ordered worksheet. With a sketch, you can experiment with alternative column and row configurations and titles and headings. When creating a sketch, start with the heading or title of the worksheet, which should provide a quick overview of what the data represents in the worksheet. Determine appropriate column and row titles that clearly identify the data.
- **Step 4: Enter the data in the worksheet.** Key the data in the worksheet, including the worksheet title, column titles, row titles, and data within cells. Enter any required formulas into the worksheet and then format the worksheet to make it appealing and easy to read.
- **Step 5: Test the worksheet data.** After preparing the worksheet and inserting any necessary formulas, check the data to be sure that the calculations are performed correctly. Consider verifying the formula results by completing the formula on a calculator.

exercise 23

Planning and Creating a Worksheet

1. Look at the data shown in figure 11.7. (The first paragraph is simply a description of the data—do not include this in the worksheet.) After reviewing the data, complete the following steps:
   a. Create a sketch of how you think the worksheet should be organized.
   b. Create a worksheet from the sketch. (Be sure to include the necessary formula to calculate the total costs.)
   c. Apply formatting to enhance the appearance of the worksheet.
2. Save the worksheet and name it Excel Ch 11, Ex 23.
3. Print and then close Excel Ch 11, Ex 23.

figure

11.7   *Exercise 23*

The following data itemizes budgeted direct labor hours and dollars by department for planning purposes. This data is prepared quarterly and sent to the plant manager and production manager.

DIRECT LABOR BUDGET

	Labor Rate	Total Hours	Total Costs
April			
Assembly	12.75	723	
Electronics	16.32	580	
Machining	27.34	442	
May			
Assembly	12.75	702	
Electronics	16.32	615	
Machining	27.34	428	
June			
Assembly	12.75	694	
Electronics	16.32	643	
Machining	27.34	389	

chapter summary

- ► Key a formula in a cell and the formula displays in the cell as well as in the Formula bar. If cell entries are changed, a formula will automatically recalculate the values and insert the result in the cell.
- ► Use the AutoSum button on the Standard toolbar to automatically add numbers in rows or columns.
- ► Create your own formula with commonly used operators such as addition (+), subtraction (-), multiplication (*), division (/), percent (%), and exponentiation (^). When writing a formula, begin with the equals (=) sign.

- Copy a formula to other cells in a row or column with the Fill option from the Edit drop-down menu or with the fill handle that displays in the bottom right corner of the active cell.

- Excel includes over 200 functions that are divided into nine categories. Use the Paste Function feature to create formulas using built-in functions.

- A function operates on an argument, which may consist of a cell reference, a constant, or another function. When a value calculated by a formula is inserted in a cell, this is referred to as returning the result.

- Use the IF function, considered a conditional function, to perform conditional tests on values and formulas.

- Use nested IF functions in a formula where more than two actions are required.

- A selected group of cells is referred to as a range. A range can be named and used in a formula. Name a range by keying the name in the Name Box button on the Formula bar.

- A reference identifies a cell or a range of cells in a worksheet and can be relative or absolute. Identify an absolute cell reference by inserting a $ symbol before the column and row.

- Cells can be linked between worksheets and workbooks. The worksheet containing the original cell is called the source worksheet and the worksheet relying on the source worksheet for the data in the link is called the dependent worksheet. To create a link, copy data in a cell, and then paste it with Edit and then Paste Special. At the Paste Special dialog box, click Paste Link.

- In a multiple worksheet workbook, use a 3-D reference to analyze data in the same cell or range of cells.

- Apply outlining to a worksheet to display specific rows and columns such as subtotals and totals.

- Plan a worksheet by completing these basic steps: identify the purpose of the worksheet, design the worksheet, create a sketch of the worksheet, enter the data in the worksheet, and test the worksheet data.

commands review

	Mouse/Keyboard
Automatically insert sum	Click AutoSum button on Standard toolbar
Display Paste Function dialog box	Click Paste Function button on Standard toolbar; or click Insert, Function
Display Paste Special dialog box	Click Edit, Paste Special
Apply automatic outlining	Click Data, point to Group and Outline, click Auto Outline

thinking offline

Completion: In the space provided at the right, indicate the correct term, symbol, or value.

1. Begin a formula with this sign. _____

2. Click this button on the Standard toolbar to automatically add numbers in cells. _____

3. This is the operator for division that is used when writing a formula. _____

4. This is the operator for multiplication that is used when writing a formula. _____

5. This is the name of the small black box located at the bottom right corner of a cell that can be used to copy a formula to adjacent cells. _____

6. A function operates on this, which may consist of a constant, a cell reference, or another function. _____

7. This function is considered a conditional function. _____

8. To identify an absolute cell reference, key this symbol before the column and row. _____

9. In worksheets that are linked, the worksheet containing the cell with the original data is called this. _____

10. When linking data in a cell, click this button at the Paste Special dialog box. _____

11. In a multiple worksheet workbook, use this reference to analyze data in the same cell or range of cells. _____

12. Apply automatic outlining to a worksheet by clicking this option on the Menu bar, pointing to Group and Outline, and then clicking Auto Outline. _____

13. Suppose that cell B2 contains the budgeted amount and cell C2 contains the actual amount. Write the formula below (including the IF conditions) that would insert the word "under" if the actual amount was less than the budgeted amount and insert the word "over" if the actual amount was greater than the budgeted amount.

_____

_____

14. List the steps you would complete to link the data in cell B2 in *Sheet1* with cell B2 in *Sheet2*.

_____

_____

_____

working hands-on

Assessment 1

1. Create a worksheet with the information shown in figure 11.8 with the following specifications:
   a. Key the data shown in figure 11.8 with the appropriate formatting.
   b. Insert the formula to calculate the difference (actual amount minus the budget amount) and then copy the formula down to the other cells.
   c. Use AutoSum to insert the total amounts.
   d. Format the numbers in cells as currency with zero decimal places.
2. Save the worksheet and name it Excel Ch 11, SA 01.
3. Print Excel Ch 11, SA 01 centered horizontally and vertically on the page.
4. Close Excel Ch 11, SA 01.

11.8 *Assessment 1*

SUMMARY OF PERFORMANCE

	Actual	Budget	Difference
Northeast division	2,505,250	2,250,000	
Southeast division	1,895,200	1,550,000	
Northwest division	2,330,540	2,200,000	
Southwest division	1,850,340	1,950,500	
Total			

Assessment 2

1. Open Excel Worksheet 13.
2. Save the worksheet with Save As and name it Excel Ch 11, SA 02.
3. Make the following changes to the worksheet:
   a. Determine the average monthly sales using the AVERAGE function.
   b. Format the numbers in cell B3 through H8 as currency with zero decimal places.
   c. Automatically adjust columns B through H.
4. Save the worksheet again with the same name (Excel Ch 11, SA 02).
5. Change the top margin to 2 inches and then print Excel Ch 11, SA 02.
6. Close Excel Ch 11, SA 02.

Assessment 3

1. Open Excel Ch 11, SA 02.
2. Save the worksheet with Save As and name it Excel Ch 11, SA 03.
3. Make the following changes to the worksheet:
   a. Total each monthly column. (Create an appropriate title for the row.)
   b. Use the MAX function to determine the highest monthly total (for cells B3 through G8). (You determine where you want this maximum monthly total to appear in the worksheet. Be sure to include a cell title.)
   c. Use the MIN function to determine the lowest monthly total (for cells B3 through G8). (You determine where you want this minimum monthly total to appear in the worksheet. Be sure to include a cell title.)
4. Save the worksheet again with the same name (Excel Ch 11, SA 03).
5. Print the worksheet in Landscape orientation and then close Excel Ch 11, SA 03.

Assessment 4

1. Open Excel Worksheet 08.
2. Save the worksheet with Save As and name it Excel Ch 11, SA 04.
3. Insert a formula in cell E3 that calculates depreciation using the straight-line method.
4. Copy the formula down to cells E4 through E9.
5. Make the following formatting changes to the worksheet:
   a. Select cells E3 through E9 and then click the Currency Style button on the Formatting toolbar.
   b. Select cells A1 through E9 and then apply an autoformat of your choosing. (Make sure values and numbers are displayed properly.)
6. Save the worksheet again with the same name (Excel Ch 11, SA 04).
7. Print Excel Ch 11, SA 04 centered horizontally and vertically on the page.
8. Close Excel Ch 11, SA 04.

Assessment 5

1. Open Excel Worksheet 35.
2. Save the worksheet with Save As and name it Excel Ch 11, SA 05.
3. The manager of Clearline Manufacturing is interested in refinancing a loan for either $125,000 or $300,000 and wants to determine the monthly payments, total payments, and total interest paid. Insert a formula with the following specifications:
   a. Make cell E5 active.
   b. Use the Paste Function button on the Standard toolbar to insert a formula using the PMT function. At the formula palette, enter the following:

Rate	=	C5/12
Nper	=	D5
Pv	=	-B5

   c. Copy the formula in cell E5 down to cells E6 and E8.
4. Insert a formula in cell F5 that multiplies the amount in E5 by the amount in D5.
5. Insert a formula in cell G5 that subtracts the amount in F5 from the amount in B5.
6. Save the worksheet again with the same name (Excel Ch 11, SA 05).
7. Print and then close Excel Ch 11, SA 05.

Inserting Formulas in a Worksheet

Assessment 6

1. Open Excel Worksheet 32.
2. Save the worksheet with Save As and name it Excel Ch 11, SA 06.
3. Make the following changes to the worksheet:
   a. Change the percentage in cell C3 from *9%* to *10%*.
   b. Change the number in cell C4 from *36* to *60*.
   c. Change the amount in cell C5 from *($1,200)* to *-500*.
   d. Use the FV function to insert a formula that calculates the future value of the investment. *(Hint: For help with the formula, refer to exercise 13.)*
4. Save the worksheet again with the same name (Excel Ch 11, SA 06).
5. Print Excel Ch 11, SA 06.

Assessment 7

1. Create the worksheet shown in figure 11.9 with the following specifications:
   a. Format the cells as shown in figure 11.9. (Before keying the percentages in cells B6 through B12, select the cells and then click the Percent Style button and then the Center button.)
   b. Key the data shown in the cells in figure 11.9.
   c. Make cell C6 active and then insert the formula =*$B$3*B6*. (In this formula, B3 is identified as an absolute cell reference because the budget amount remains in cell B3.)
   d. Copy the formula in cell C6 down to cell C12.
   e. Format the numbers in cells C6 through C12 as currency with zero decimal places. (If necessary, automatically adjust the column width.)
2. Save the workbook and name it Excel Ch 11, SA 07.
3. With Excel Ch 11, SA 07 open, copy the cells in the worksheet to *Sheet2* and *Sheet3* by completing the following steps:
   a. Select cells A1 through C12 and then copy the selected cells to *Sheet2*.
   b. Copy the selected cells to *Sheet3*.
4. With *Sheet3* displayed, make the following changes:
   a. Automatically adjust the widths of columns A, B, and C.
   b. Make the following changes to the specified cells:
      A5: Change *Production Department* to *Finance Department*
      B6: Change *15%* to *14*
      B7: Change *3%* to *2*
      B9: Change *9%* to *8*
      B10: Change *5%* to *4*
   c. Delete *$1,200,000* in cell B3.
5. Make *Sheet2* active and then make the following changes:
   a. Automatically adjust the widths of columns A, B, and C.
   b. Make the following changes to the specified cells:
      A5: Change *Production Department* to *Personnel Department*
      B6: Change *15%* to *13*
      B7: Change *3%* to *2*
      B9: Change *9%* to *6*
      B10: Change *5%* to *4*
   c. Delete *$1,200,000* in cell B3.
6. Make *Sheet1* active and then link the annual budget amount ($1,200,000) in cell B3 to cell B3 in *Sheet2* and B3 in *Sheet3*. *(Hint: Do this by copying and then pasting with Paste Link at the Paste Special dialog box.)*

7. Make *Sheet1* the active worksheet and then save the workbook again with the same name (Excel Ch 11, SA 07).
8. Rename *Sheet1 Production,* rename *Sheet2 Personnel,* and rename *Sheet3 Finance.*
9. Print the entire workbook.
10. With Excel Ch 11, SA 07 still open, determine the impact on the budget of a 10% increase in the annual budget. To do this, change the amount in cell B3 in *Sheet1* to *1,320,000.* (This will change the amounts in *Sheet2* and *Sheet3* because the cell was linked.)
11. Print the entire workbook.
12. With Excel Ch 11, SA 07 still open, determine the impact on the budget of a 10% decrease in the annual budget. To do this, change the amount in cell B3 to *1,080,000.*
13. Save, print (the entire workbook), and then close Excel Ch 11, SA 07.

figure
11.9
Assessment 7

	A	B	C
1	SELLAR CORPORATION		
2			
3	Annual Budget	$1,200,000	
4			
5	Prodution Department	% of Budget	Total
6	Salaries	15%	
7	Benefits	3%	
8	Payroll taxes	2%	
9	Operating costs	9%	
10	Training	5%	
11	Supplies	2%	
12	Miscellaneous	1%	
13			

Assessment 8

1. Open Excel Worksheet 01.
2. Save the worksheet with Save As and name it Excel Ch 11, SA 08.
3. Make the following changes to the worksheet:
   a. Key **Difference** in cell E1.
   b. Insert the formula *=D3-C3* in cell E3 and then copy it down to E4 through E10.
   c. Select cells E3 through E10 and then name the range Difference.
   d. Key **Max Difference** in cell A13.
   e. Insert the formula *=MAX(Difference)* in cell B13.
   f. Key **Min Difference** in cell A14.
   g. Insert the formula *=MIN(Difference)* in cell B14.
   h. Key **Ave Difference** in cell A15.
   i. Insert the formula *=AVERAGE(Difference)* in cell B15.
   j. Select cells C3 through E10 and then click the Currency Style button on the Formatting toolbar.
   k. Select cells B13 through B15 and then click the Currency Style button on the Formatting toolbar.

     l.   Bold and center the text in cells A1 through E1.

     m. Center the text in cells B3 through B10.

4. Save the worksheet again with the same name (Excel Ch 11, SA 08).

5. Print Excel Ch 11, SA 08.

6. Make the following changes to the worksheet:

     a. Change *63,293.00* in cell C6 to *55,500.00*.

     b. Change *12,398.00* in cell C9 to *13,450.00*.

     c. Create the header *Customer Jobs* that prints centered at the top of the page. (Create this header at the Page Setup dialog box with the Header/Footer tab selected.)

7. Save, print, and then close Excel Ch 11, SA 08.

Assessment 9

1. Open Excel Ch 11, SA 08.

2. Save the worksheet with Save As and name it Excel Ch 11, SA 09.

3. Make the following changes to the worksheet:

     a. Make cell F1 active and then key **Bonus**.

     b. Make cell F3 active and then insert the following formula to provide a 10% bonus for those jobs that were under the planned amount: *=IF(E3>0,C3*0.1,0)*.

     c. Copy the formula in cell F3 down to cells F4 through F10.

     d. Select cells F3 through F10 and then click the Currency Style button on the Formatting toolbar.

4. Save the worksheet again with the same name (Excel Ch 11, SA 09).

5. Print and then close Excel Ch 11, SA 09.

Assessment 10

1. Open Excel Worksheet 14.

2. Save the worksheet with Save As and name it Excel Ch 11, SA 10.

3. Make the following changes to the worksheet:

     a. Insert a formula using an absolute reference to determine the projected quotas at ten percent of the current quotas.

     b. Save the worksheet and name it Excel Ch 11, SA 10.

     c. Print Excel Ch 11, SA 10.

     d. Determine the projected quotas at fifteen percent of the current quota by changing cell A14 to *15% Increase* and cell B14 to *1.15*.

     e. Save and then print Excel Ch 11, SA 10.

     f. Determine the projected quotas at twenty percent of the current quota.

4. Save, print, and then close Excel Ch 11, SA 10.

Assessment 11

1. Open Excel Worksheet 34.

2. Save the workbook with Save As and name it Excel Ch 11, SA 11.

3. Make the following changes to the workbook:

     a. Insert the heading *Average January Sales 1998-2001* (on multiple lines) in cell B10.

     b. Insert a formula in cell B11 with a 3-D reference that averages the total in cells B3 through B8 in *Sheet1*, *Sheet2*, and *Sheet3*.

c. Make cell B11 active and then change to the Currency Style with zero decimal places.
d. Insert the heading *Average February Sales 1998-2001* (on multiple lines) in cell C10.
e. Insert a formula in cell C11 with a 3-D reference that averages the total in cells C3 through C8 in *Sheet1*, *Sheet2*, and *Sheet3*.
f. Make cell C11 active and then change to the Currency Style with zero decimal places.
g. Insert the heading *Average March Sales 1998-2001* (on multiple lines) in cell D10.
h. Insert a formula in cell D11 with a 3-D reference that averages the total in cells D3 through D8 in *Sheet1*, *Sheet2*, and *Sheet3*.
i. Make cell D11 active and then change to the Currency Style with zero decimal places.
4. Save the workbook again with the same name (Excel Ch 11, SA 11).
5. Print worksheet 1 of the workbook.
6. Close Excel Ch 11, SA 11.

Assessment 12

1. Learn about specific options in the Options dialog box by completing the following steps:
   a. Display the Options dialog box by clicking Tools and then Options.
   b. At the Options dialog box, click the View tab.
   c. Read information about each of the options in the Window options section of the dialog box. (To do this, click the Help button [displays with a question mark] that displays in the upper right corner of the dialog box, and then click the desired option.)
2. After reading information about the options in the Window options section, complete the following steps:
   a. Open Excel Ch 11, SA 04.
   b. Save the worksheet with Save As and name it Excel Ch 11, SA 12.
   c. Display the formulas in column E (rather than the results) using information you learned from the Options dialog box.
3. Save the worksheet again with the same name (Excel Ch 11, SA 12).
4. Print and then close Excel Ch 11, SA 12.

Chapter 12

Creating a Chart in Excel

PERFORMANCE OBJECTIVES

Upon successful completion of chapter 12, you will be able to:
- Create a chart with data in an Excel worksheet.
- Create a chart in a separate worksheet.
- Print a selected chart and print a worksheet containing a chart.
- Size, move, and delete a chart.
- Change the type of chart.
- Choose a custom chart type.
- Change data in a chart.
- Add, delete, and customize elements in a chart.

In the previous Excel chapters, you learned to create data in worksheets. While a worksheet does an adequate job of representing data, you can present some data more visually by charting the data. A chart is sometimes referred to as a *graph* and is a picture of numeric data. In this chapter, you will learn to create and customize charts in Excel.

Creating a Chart

In Excel, create a chart by selecting cells containing the data you want to chart, and then clicking the Chart Wizard button on the Standard toolbar. There are four steps involved in creating a chart with the Chart Wizard. Suppose you wanted to create a chart with the worksheet shown in figure 12.1. To create the chart with the Chart Wizard, you would complete the following steps:

> The Chart Wizard automates the process of creating charts.

Chart
Wizard

1. Select the cells containing data (in the worksheet in figure 12.1, this would be cells A1 through C4).
2. Click the Chart Wizard button on the Standard toolbar.
3. At the Chart Wizard - Step 1 of 4 - Chart Type dialog box shown in figure 12.2, choose the desired chart type and chart sub-type, and then click the Next > button.

Press F11 to create a chart using the Chart Wizard with all default settings.

4. At the Chart Wizard - Step 2 of 4 - Chart Source Data dialog box shown in figure 12.3, make sure the data range displays correctly (for the chart in figure 12.1, the range will display as =*Sheet1!$A$1:$C$4*), and then click the Next > button.

5. At the Chart Wizard - Step 3 of 4 - Chart Options dialog box shown in figure 12.4, make any changes to the chart, and then click the Next > button.

6. At the Chart Wizard - Step 4 of 4 - Chart Location dialog box shown in figure 12.5, specify where you want the chart inserted, and then click the Finish button.

If the chart was created with all the default settings at the Chart Wizard dialog boxes, the chart would display below the cells containing data as shown in figure 12.6.

figure
12.1

Excel Worksheet

	A	B	C	D
1	**Salesperson**	**June**	**July**	
2	Chaney	$34,239	$39,224	
3	Ferraro	$23,240	$28,985	
4	Jimenez	$56,892	$58,450	
5				
6				

figure
12.2

Chart Wizard - Step 1 of 4 - Chart Type Dialog Box

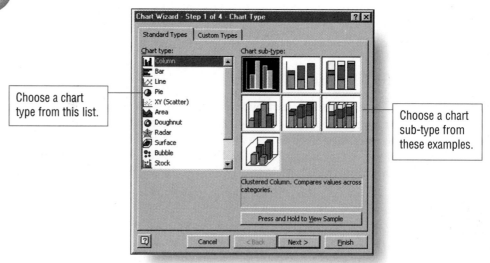

Choose a chart type from this list.

Choose a chart sub-type from these examples.

figure
12.3
Chart Wizard - Step 2 of 4 - Chart Source Data Dialog Box

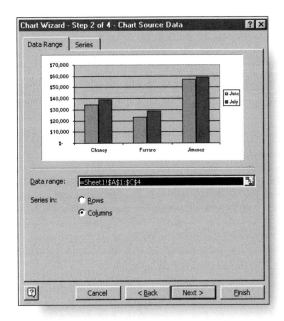

figure
12.4
Chart Wizard - Step 3 of 4 - Chart Options Dialog Box

Add and/or format chart elements with options from this dialog box with various tabs selected.

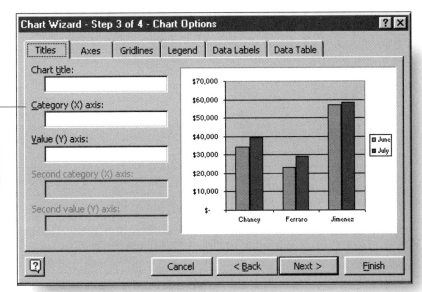

figure

Chart Wizard - Step 4 of 4 - Chart Location Dialog Box

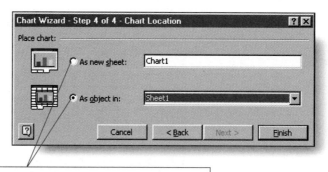

> Chart Wizard - Step 4 of 4 - Chart Location [?][X]
> Place chart:
> ○ As new sheet: `Chart1`
> ● As object in: `Sheet1` ▼
> [?]   [Cancel] [< Back] [Next >] [Finish]

To insert the chart in the active worksheet, leave this at the default setting of As object in. Choose As new sheet option to create the chart in a separate sheet.

figure

Chart Based on Excel Worksheet

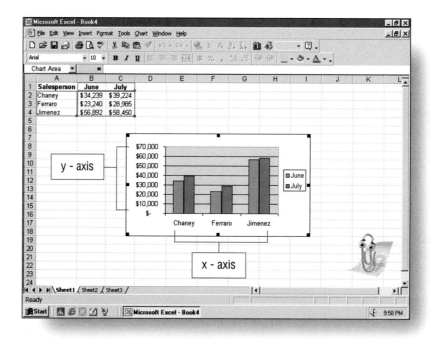

Preview the chart at step 1 of the Chart Wizard by positioning the arrow pointer on the Press and Hold to View Sample button and then holding down the left mouse button.

Hint

In the chart created in Excel, shown in figure 12.6, the left vertical side of the chart is referred to as the y-axis. The y-axis contains tick marks with amounts displaying the value at that particular point on the axis. The values in the chart in figure 12.6 are broken into tick marks by ten thousands beginning with zero and continuing to 70,000. The values for the y-axis will vary depending on the data in the table. The names in the first column are used for the x-axis, which runs along the bottom of the chart.

Creating a Chart in Excel with Data in a Worksheet

1. Open Excel and then open Excel Worksheet 15.
2. Save the worksheet with Save As and name it Excel Ch 12, Ex 01.
3. Create a chart using the Chart Wizard by completing the following steps:
    a. Select cells A1 through E5.
    b. Click the Chart Wizard button on the Standard toolbar.

Step 3b

Chart Wizard

	A	B	C	D	E	F	G	H	I
1	Region	1st Qtr.	2nd Qtr.	3rd Qtr.	4th Qtr.				
2	Northwest	300,560	320,250	287,460	360,745				
3	Southwest	579,290	620,485	490,125	635,340				
4	Northeast	890,355	845,380	795,460	890,425				
5	Southeast	290,450	320,765	270,450	300,455				

A1 = Region

Step 3a

    c. At the Chart Wizard - Step 1 of 4 - Chart Type dialog box, click the Next > button.
    d. At the Chart Wizard - Step 2 of 4 - Chart Source Data dialog box, make sure the data range displays as =Sheet1!$A$1:$E$5 and then click the Next > button.
    e. At the Chart Wizard - Step 3 of 4 - Chart Options dialog box, click the Next > button.
    f. At the Chart Wizard - Step 4 of 4 - Chart Location dialog box, make sure the As object in option is selected and that Sheet1 displays in the text box, and then click the Finish button.
    g. Click outside the chart to deselect the chart.
4. Save the worksheet again with the same name (Excel Ch 12, Ex 01).
5. Print and then close Excel Ch 12, Ex 01.

Printing Only the Chart

In a worksheet containing data in cells as well as a chart, you can print only the chart. To do this, click the chart to select it and then display the Print dialog box. At the Print dialog box, *Selected Chart* will automatically be selected in the Print what section. Click OK to print only the selected chart.

Previewing a Chart

Preview a chart by clicking the Print Preview button on the Standard toolbar or by clicking File and then Print Preview. This displays the worksheet containing the chart in Print Preview (refer to figure 8.13, page 348). After previewing the chart, click the Close button, or print the worksheet by clicking the Print button on the Print Preview toolbar and then clicking OK at the Print dialog box.

exercise

Previewing and Printing Only the Chart in Excel

1. Open Excel Ch 12, Ex 01.
2. Preview the chart by completing the following steps:
    a. Click the Print Preview button on the Standard toolbar.
    b. In Print Preview, click the Zoom button to make the display of the worksheet bigger.
    c. Click the Zoom button again to return to the full-page view.
    d. Click the Close button to close Print Preview.
3. Print only the chart by completing the following steps:
    a. Click the chart to select it.
    b. Click File and then Print.
    c. At the Print dialog box, make sure *Selected Chart* is selected in the Print what section of the dialog box and then click OK.
4. Close Excel Ch 12, Ex 01.

Creating a Chart in a Separate Worksheet

The chart you created in Excel in exercise 1 was inserted in the same worksheet as the cells containing data. You cannot delete the data (displaying only the chart) because the data in the chart will also be deleted. If you want to create a chart in a worksheet by itself, click the As new sheet option at the Chart Wizard - Step 4 of 4 - Chart Location dialog box. When the chart is completed, it displays in a separate sheet and fills most of the page. The sheet containing the chart is labeled *Chart1*. This sheet label displays on a tab located toward the bottom of the screen. The worksheet containing the data is located in Sheet 1. You can move between the chart and the worksheet by clicking the desired tab.

exercise

Creating a Chart in a Separate Excel Worksheet

1. Open Excel Worksheet 15.
2. Save the worksheet with Save As and name it Excel Ch 12, Ex 03.
3. Create a chart as a separate sheet using the Chart Wizard by completing the following steps:
    a. Select cells A1 through E5.
    b. Click the Chart Wizard button on the Standard toolbar.
    c. At the Chart Wizard - Step 1 of 4 - Chart Type dialog box, click the Next > button.
    d. At the Chart Wizard - Step 2 of 4 - Chart Source Data dialog box, make sure the data range displays as =*Sheet1!$A$1:$E$5*, and then click the Next > button.
    e. At the Chart Wizard - Step 3 of 4 - Chart Options dialog box, click the Next > button.
    f. At the Chart Wizard - Step 4 of 4 - Chart Location dialog box, click As new sheet, and then click the Finish button.

Step 3f

4. Save the workbook (two sheets) again with the same name (Excel Ch 12, Ex 03).
5. Print only the sheet containing the chart. (To do this, make sure the sheet containing the chart displays, and then click the Print button on the Standard toolbar.)
6. Close Excel Ch 12, Ex 03.

Deleting a Chart

A chart created in Excel can be deleted by clicking once in the chart to select it and then pressing the Delete key. If a chart created in a new worksheet is deleted, the chart is deleted but the worksheet is not. To delete the chart as well as the worksheet, position the mouse pointer on the *Chart1* tab, and then click the *right* mouse button. At the pop-up menu that displays, click the left mouse button on Delete. At the message box telling you that selected sheets will be permanently deleted, click OK.

Sizing and Moving a Chart

The size of a chart created in Excel in the same worksheet as the data containing cells can be changed. To do this, click the chart once to select it (this inserts black square sizing handles around the chart), and then drag the sizing handles in the desired direction.

A chart created with data in a worksheet can be moved by selecting the chart and then dragging it with the mouse. To move a chart, click once inside the chart to select it. Position the arrow pointer inside the chart, hold down the left mouse button, drag the outline of the chart to the desired location, and then release the button.

Sizing a Chart

1. Open Excel Ch 12, Ex 01.
2. Save the worksheet with Save As and name it Excel Ch 12, Ex 04.
3. Size the chart by completing the following steps:
   a. Select the chart by positioning the arrow pointer in the white portion of the chart just inside the chart border until a yellow box with the words *Chart Area* displays (takes approximately one second) next to the arrow pointer and then clicking the left mouse button. (Do not click on a chart element. This selects the element, not the entire chart.)

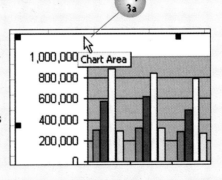

Step 3a

b. Position the arrow pointer on the black square sizing handle located in the middle of the bottom border until the arrow pointer turns into a double-headed arrow pointing up and down.

c. Hold down the left mouse button, drag the outline of the bottom border of the chart down approximately five rows, and then release the mouse button.

d. Position the arrow pointer on the black square sizing handle located in the middle of the right border until the arrow pointer turns into a double-headed arrow pointing left and right.

Step 3c

e. Hold down the left mouse button, drag the outline of the border to the right approximately two columns, and then release the mouse button.

f. Deselect the chart. (To do this, click in an empty cell somewhere in the worksheet.)

4. Save the worksheet again with the same name (Excel Ch 12, Ex 04).
5. Change the page orientation to landscape and then print Excel Ch 12, Ex 04.
6. Close Excel Ch 12, Ex 04.

Changing the Chart Type

In exercises 1 and 3, you created a column chart, which is the default. The Chart Wizard offers 14 basic chart types along with built-in autoformats that can be applied to save time to get the desired look for the chart. Figure 12.7 shows an illustration and explanation of the 14 chart types.

figure

12.7   Chart Types

	Area	An Area chart emphasizes the magnitude of change, rather than time and the rate of change. It also shows the relationship of parts to a whole by displaying the sum of the plotted values.
	Bar	A Bar chart shows individual figures at a specific time or shows variations between components but not in relationship to the whole.
	Bubble	A Bubble chart compares sets of three values in a manner similar to a scatter chart with the third value displayed as the size of the bubble marker.
	Column	A Column chart compares separate (noncontinuous) items as they vary over time.

	**Cone**	A Cone chart displays columns with a conical shape.
	**Cylinder**	A Cylinder chart displays columns with a cylindrical shape.
	**Doughnut**	A Doughnut chart shows the relationship of parts to the whole.
	**Line**	A Line chart shows trends and change over time at even intervals. It emphasizes the rate of change over time rather than the magnitude of change.
	**Pie**	A Pie chart shows proportions and relationships of parts to the whole.
	**Pyramid**	A Pyramid chart displays columns with a pyramid shape.
	**Radar**	A Radar chart emphasizes differences and amounts of change over time and variations and trends. Each category has its own value axis radiating from the center point. Lines connect all values in the same series.
	**Stock**	A Stock chart shows four values for a stock—open, high, low, and close.
	**Surface**	A Surface chart shows trends in values across two dimensions in a continuous curve.
	**XY (Scatter)**	A Scatter chart shows either the relationships among numeric values in several data series or plots the interception points between x and y values. It shows uneven intervals of data and is commonly used in scientific data.

You can choose a chart type in step 1 of the Chart Wizard steps or change the chart type for an existing chart. When creating a chart with the Chart Wizard, choose the desired chart type and sub-type at the first Chart Wizard dialog box. To change the chart type for an existing chart, make sure the chart is active and then click Chart and then Chart Type. This displays the Chart Type dialog box. Choose the desired chart type and chart sub-type at this dialog box and then click the OK button.

You can also change the chart type in an existing chart with a shortcut menu. To do this, position the arrow pointer in a white portion of the chart (inside the chart but outside any chart element), and then click the *right* mouse button. At the shortcut menu that displays, click Chart Type. This displays the Chart Type dialog box that contains the same options at the Chart Wizard - Step 1 of 4 - Chart Type dialog box.

Changing Chart Type in Excel

1. Open Excel Ch 12, Ex 03.
2. Save the workbook with Save As and name it Excel Ch 12, Ex 05.
3. Make sure the chart is displayed. If not, click the *Chart1* tab located at the bottom of the worksheet window.
4. Change the chart type to a Line chart by completing the following steps:
   a. Click Chart and then Chart Type.
   b. At the Chart Type dialog box, click *Line* in the Chart type list box.
   c. Change the chart sub-type by clicking the first chart in the second row in the Chart sub-type list box.

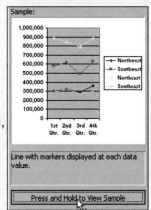

   d. View a sample of how this sub-type chart will display by positioning the arrow pointer on the Press and Hold to View Sample button and then holding down the left mouse button. After viewing a sample of the selected Line chart, release the mouse button.
   e. Click OK to close the dialog box.
5. Save the workbook again with the same name (Excel Ch 12, Ex 05).
6. Print only the sheet containing the chart. (To do this, make sure the sheet containing the chart is displayed, and then click the Print button on the Standard toolbar.)
7. With Excel Ch 12, Ex 05 still open, change the chart type to Bar by completing the following steps:
   a. Click Chart and then Chart Type.
   b. At the Chart Wizard dialog box, click *Bar* in the Chart type list box.
   c. Change the chart sub-type by clicking the first chart in the second row in the Chart sub-type list box.

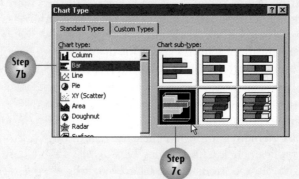

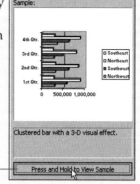

d. View a sample of how this sub-type chart will display by positioning the arrow pointer on the Press and Hold to View Sample button and then holding down the left mouse button. After viewing a sample of the selected Bar chart, release the mouse button.

e. Click OK to close the dialog box.

8. Save the workbook again with the same name (Excel Ch 12, Ex 05).

9. Print only the sheet containing the chart and then close Excel Ch 12, Ex 05.

Step 7d

Choosing a Custom Chart Type

The chart feature offers a variety of preformatted custom charts. A custom chart can be chosen in step 1 of the Chart Wizard steps or a custom chart type can be chosen for an existing chart. To choose a custom chart type while creating a chart, click the Custom Types tab at the Chart Wizard - Step 1 of 4 - Chart Type dialog box.

You can also choose a custom chart for an existing chart. To do this, click Chart and then Chart Type. At the Chart Type dialog box, click the Custom Types tab. This displays the Chart Type dialog box as shown in figure 12.8. You can also display the Chart Type dialog box by positioning the arrow pointer in the chart, clicking the *right* mouse button, and then clicking Chart Type at the shortcut menu. At the Chart Type dialog box with the Custom Types tab selected, click the desired custom chart type in the Chart type list box.

A variety of preformatted custom charts are available. Use one of these custom charts if the formatting is appropriate.

figure

12.8

Chart Type Dialog Box with Custom Types Tab Selected

Choose a custom chart type from this list box and preview it at the right in the Sample box.

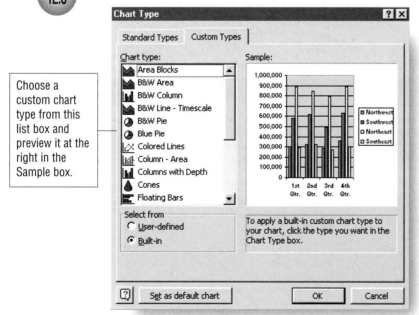

Choosing a Custom Chart Type

1. Open Excel Ch 12, Ex 03.
2. Save the workbook with Save As and name it Excel Ch 12, Ex 06.
3. Choose a custom chart type by completing the following steps:
    a. Click Chart and then Chart Type.
    b. At the Chart Type dialog box, click the Custom Types tab.
    c. At the Chart Type dialog box with the Custom Types tab selected, click *Columns with Depth* in the Chart type list box.
    d. Click OK to close the Chart Type dialog box.
4. Save the workbook again with the same name (Excel Ch 12, Ex 06).
5. Print only the sheet containing the chart. (To do this, make sure the sheet containing the chart displays, and then click the Print button on the Standard toolbar.)
6. Close Excel Ch 12, Ex 06.

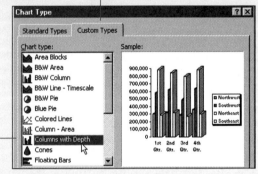

Changing Data in Cells

> The chart is linked to the selected cells. If data is changed in a selected cell, the chart is automatically updated.

The Excel chart feature uses data in cells to create a chart. This data can be changed and the chart will reflect the changes. When a change is made to data in a worksheet, the change is also made to any chart created with the cells in the worksheet. The change is reflected in a chart whether it is located in the same worksheet as the changed cells or in a new sheet.

Changing Numbers in an Excel Worksheet

1. Open Excel Ch 12, Ex 03.
2. Save the workbook with Save As and name it Excel Ch 12, Ex 07.
3. Make the following changes to the data in cells in *Sheet1*:
    a. Make sure the worksheet containing the cells (not the chart) is active. If not, click the *Sheet1* tab located at the bottom of the worksheet window.
    b. Make the following changes to the specified cells:
        C2: Change *320,250* to *295,785*
        D3: Change *490,125* to *550,350*
        C5: Change *320,765* to *298,460*
        E5: Change *300,455* to *275,490*

4. Display the worksheet containing the chart (Chart1).
5. Save the workbook again with the same name (Excel Ch 12, Ex 07).
6. Print only the sheet containing the chart.
7. Close Excel Ch 12, Ex 07.

Changing the Data Series

When a chart is created, the Chart Wizard uses the data in the first column (except the first cell) to create the x-axis (the information along the bottom of the chart) and uses the data in the first row (except the first cell) to create the legend. For example, in the chart in figure 12.6, the names (Chaney, Ferraro, and Jimenez) were used for the x-axis (along the bottom of the chart) and the months (June and July) were used for the legend.

A data series is information represented on the chart by bars, lines, columns, pie slices, etc.

When a chart is created, the option Rows is selected by default at the Chart Wizard - Step 2 of 4 - Chart Source Data dialog box. This can be changed to Columns and the data in the first column (except the first cell) will be used to create the x-axis and the data in the first row will be used to create the legend.

Change the data series in an existing chart by making the chart active and then clicking Chart and then Source Data. This displays the Source Data dialog box shown in figure 12.9. Another method for displaying the Source Data dialog box is to position the arrow pointer in a white portion of the chart (inside the chart but outside any chart element) and then click the *right* mouse button. At the shortcut menu that displays, click Source Data. The Source Data dialog box contains the same options as the Chart Wizard - Step 2 of 4 - Chart Source Data dialog box.

figure
12.9

Source Data Dialog Box

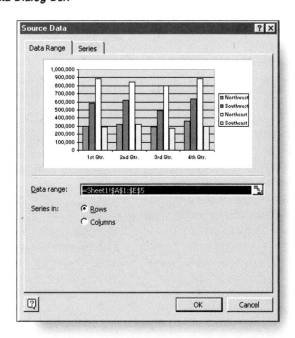

Changing Data Series in an Excel Chart

1. Open Excel Ch 12, Ex 01.
2. Save the workbook with Save As and name it Excel Ch 12, Ex 08.
3. Change the data series by completing the following steps:
   a. Position the arrow pointer in a white portion of the chart (inside the chart but outside any chart element) and then click the *right* mouse button.
   b. At the shortcut menu that displays, click Source Data.
   c. At the Source Data dialog box, click the Columns option.
   d. Click OK to close the Source Data dialog box.
   e. Click outside the chart to deselect it.
4. Save the workbook again with the same name (Excel Ch 12, Ex 08).
5. Print and then close Excel Ch 12, Ex 08.

Creating a Pie Chart in Excel Using Chart Wizard

1. Open Excel Worksheet 16.
2. Save the worksheet with Save As and name it Excel Ch 12, Ex 09.
3. Create a pie chart by completing the following steps:
   a. Select cells A4 through B10.
   b. Click the Chart Wizard button on the Standard toolbar.
   c. At the Chart Wizard - Step 1 of 4 - Chart Type dialog box, click *Pie* in the Chart type list box, and then click the Next > button.
   d. At the Chart Wizard - Step 2 of 4 - Chart Source Data dialog box, make sure the data range displays as =*Sheet1!$A$4:$B$10*. Click the Rows option to see what happens to the pie when the data series is changed, click Columns to return the data series back, and then click the Next > button.
   e. At the Chart Wizard - Step 3 of 4 - Chart Options dialog box, click the Data Labels tab.
   f. At the dialog box with the Data Labels tab selected, click Show percent.
   g. Click the Next > button.
   h. At the Chart Wizard - Step 4 of 4 - Chart Location dialog box, click As new sheet and then click the Finish button.
4. Save the workbook (two sheets) again with the same name (Excel Ch 12, Ex 09).
5. Print only the sheet containing the chart.
6. Close Excel Ch 12, Ex 09.

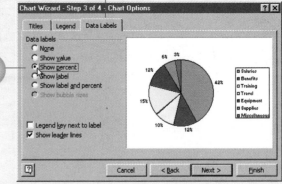

Adding Chart Elements

Certain chart elements are automatically inserted in a chart created by the Chart Wizard including a chart legend and labels for the x-axis and y-axis. Add other chart elements such as a chart title and data labels at the Chart Wizard - Step 3 of 4 - Chart Options dialog box. Add chart elements to an existing chart by making the chart active and then clicking Chart and then Chart Options. This displays the Chart Options dialog box shown in figure 12.10. Another method for displaying this dialog box is to position the arrow pointer in a white portion of the chart (inside the chart but outside any chart element), click the *right* mouse button, and then click Chart Options. The Chart Options dialog box contains the same options as the Chart Wizard - Step 3 of 4 - Chart Options dialog box.

The legend identifies which data series is represented by which data marker.

figure 12.10

Chart Options Dialog Box

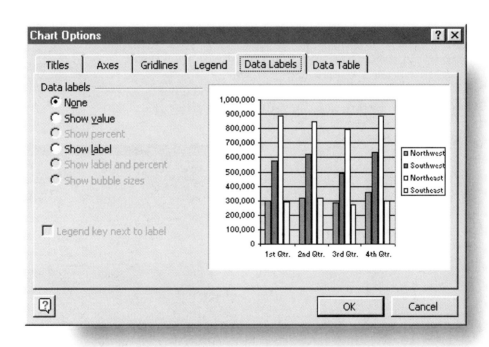

exercise 10

Adding a Title to a Chart and Changing the Legend Location

1. Open Excel Ch 12, Ex 09.
2. Save the workbook with Save As and name it Excel Ch 12, Ex 10.
3. Add a title and data labels to the chart and change the location of the chart legend by completing the following steps:
   a. Make sure the sheet (*Chart1*) containing the pie chart displays.
   b. Click Chart and then Chart Options.
   c. At the Chart Options dialog box, click the Titles tab. (Skip this step if the Titles tab is already selected.)
   d. Click inside the Chart title text box and then key **DEPARTMENT EXPENSES BY PERCENTAGE**.
   e. Click the Data Labels tab.
   f. Click the Legend key next to label check box.
   g. Click the Legend tab.
   h. At the Chart Options dialog box with the Legend tab selected, click Left.
   i. Click the OK button to close the dialog box.
4. Save the workbook again with the same name (Excel Ch 12, Ex 10).
5. Print only the sheet containing the pie chart.
6. Close Excel Ch 12, Ex 10.

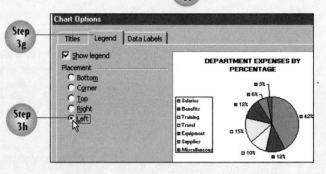

Moving/Sizing Chart Elements

Chart elements can be repositioned for easier viewing.

When additional elements are added to a chart, the chart can become quite full and elements may overlap. If elements in a chart overlap, an element can be selected and then moved. To select an element, position the arrow pointer on a portion of the element, and then click the left mouse button. This causes sizing handles to display around the element. Position the mouse pointer toward the edge of the selected element until it turns into an arrow pointer, hold down the left mouse button, drag the element to the desired location, and then release the mouse button. To change the size of an element, drag the sizing handles in the desired direction.

Deleting/Removing Chart Elements

Chart elements can be selected by clicking the desired element. Once an element is selected, it can be moved and it can also be deleted. To delete a selected element, press the Delete key. If you delete a chart element in a chart and then decide you want it redisplayed in the chart, immediately click the Undo button on the Standard toolbar.

Moving/Sizing/Adding Chart Elements

1. Open Excel Ch 12, Ex 10.
2. Save the workbook with Save As and name it Excel Ch 12, Ex 11.
3. Move and size chart elements by completing the following steps:
   a. Move the legend to the right side of the chart by completing the following steps:
      1) Click the legend to select it.
      2) With the arrow pointer positioned in the legend, hold down the left mouse button, drag the outline of the legend to the right side of the chart, and then release the mouse button.
   b. Move the pie to the left by completing the following steps:
      1) Select the pie. To do this, position the arrow pointer in a white portion of the chart immediately outside the pie (a yellow box displays with *Plot Area* inside) and then click the left mouse button. (This should insert a square border around the pie. If not, try selecting the pie again.)
      2) With the pie selected (square border around the pie), position the arrow pointer inside the square border that displays around the pie (not inside the pie), hold down the left mouse button, drag the outline of the pie to the left until it looks balanced with the legend, and then release the mouse button.

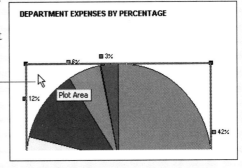

   c. Increase the size of the legend by completing the following steps:
      1) Click the legend to select it.
      2) Use the sizing handles that display around the legend to increase the size. (You determine the direction to drag the sizing handles and the final size of the legend. Make sure the pie and legend are balanced.)

4. Save the workbook again with the same name (Excel Ch 12, Ex 11).
5. Print only the sheet containing the pie chart.
6. With Excel Ch 12, Ex 11 still open, remove the legend, change the data labels, and move the pie by completing the following steps:
   a. Delete the legend by completing the following steps:
      1) Click the legend to select it.
      2) Press the Delete key.
   b. Change the data labels by completing the following steps:
      1) Position the arrow pointer in a white portion of the chart (outside any chart element) and then click the *right* mouse button.
      2) At the shortcut menu that displays, click Chart Options.
      3) At the Chart Options dialog box, click the Data Labels tab.
      4) At the Chart Options dialog box with the Data Labels tab selected, click the Show label and percent option.
      5) Click OK to close the Chart Options dialog box.
   c. Move the pie by completing the following steps:
      1) Make sure the pie is selected. (If the pie is not selected, select it by positioning the arrow pointer in a white portion of the chart immediately outside the pie [a yellow box displays with *Plot Area* inside] and then clicking the left mouse button).
      2) With the pie selected (square border around the pie), position the arrow pointer inside the square border that displays around the pie (not inside the pie), hold down the left mouse button, drag the outline of the pie until it looks centered between the left and right sides of the chart, and then release the mouse button.

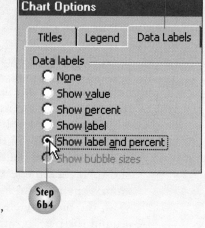

Step 6b3

Step 6b4

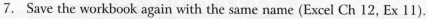

7. Save the workbook again with the same name (Excel Ch 12, Ex 11).
8. Print only the sheet containing the pie chart.
9. Close Excel Ch 12, Ex 11.

Adding Gridlines

Gridlines can be added to a chart for the category, series, and value. Depending on the chart, some but not all of these options may be available. To add gridlines, display the Chart Options dialog box and then click the Gridlines tab. This displays the Chart Options dialog box with the Gridlines tab selected as shown in figure 12.11. At this dialog box, insert a check mark in those options for which you want gridlines.

figure

12.11

Chart Options Dialog Box with Gridlines Tab Selected

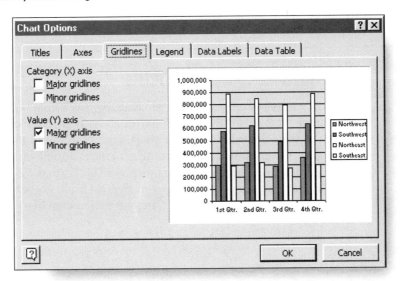

exercise 12

Adding Gridlines to a Chart

1. Open Excel Ch 12, Ex 03.
2. Save the workbook with Save As and name it Excel Ch 12, Ex 12.
3. Add gridlines to the chart by completing the following steps:
   a. Make sure the sheet containing the chart is displayed. (If not, click the *Chart1* tab located toward the bottom of the screen.)
   b. Click Chart and then Chart Options.
   c. At the Chart Options dialog box, click the Gridlines tab.
   d. At the Chart Options dialog box with the Gridlines tab selected, insert a check mark in the two options in the Category (X) axis section and also the two options in the Value (Y) axis section.
   e. Click OK to close the Chart Options dialog box.

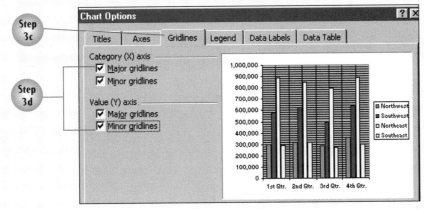

4. Save the workbook again with the same name (Excel Ch 12, Ex 12).
5. Print only the sheet containing the chart.
6. Close Excel Ch 12, Ex 12.

Formatting Chart Elements

A variety of formatting options are available for a chart or chart elements. Formatting can include adding a pattern, changing background and foreground colors of the selected element or chart, changing the font, and changing the alignment or placement. To customize a chart, double-click in the chart area (outside any chart element). This displays the Format Chart Area dialog box with the Patterns tab selected as shown in figure 12.12. You can also display this dialog box by clicking once in the chart area and then clicking Format and then Selected Chart Area.

12.12 *Format Chart Area Dialog Box with Patterns Tab Selected*

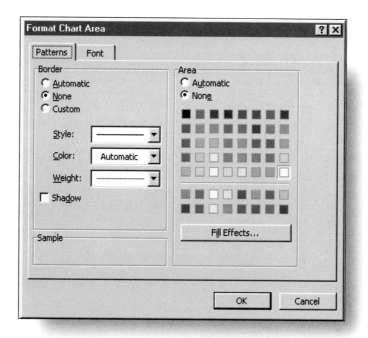

Customize the chart area by adding a pattern and/or fill color and background at the Format Chart Area dialog box with the Patterns tab selected. Click the Font tab and options for changing the typeface, type style, and type size display.

The font and pattern of chart elements can also be customized along with additional formatting for specific elements. For example, if you double-click a chart title, the Format Chart Title dialog box displays. (You can also display this dialog box by clicking once on the title and then clicking Format and then Selected Chart Title.) This dialog box contains three tabs—Patterns, Font, and Alignment. Clicking the Patterns or the Font tab displays the same options as those available at the Format Chart Area dialog box. Click the Alignment tab and options for changing the text alignment (horizontal or vertical) display along with options for the title orientation.

Double-click a chart legend and the Format Legend dialog box displays with three tabs—Patterns, Font, and Placement. (You can also display this dialog box by clicking once on the legend and then clicking Format and then Selected Legend.) Clicking the Patterns or the Font tab displays the same options as those available at the Format Chart Area dialog box. Click the Placement tab to display options for specifying the location of the legend in relation to the chart.

Each chart element contains a formatting dialog box. To display this dialog box, double-click the desired chart element. For example, double-click text in either the x-axis or the y-axis and the Format Axis dialog box displays.

Customizing Elements in an Excel Chart

1. Open Excel Worksheet 19.
2. Save the worksheet with Save As and name it Excel Ch 12, Ex 13.
3. Create a Column chart with the data in the worksheet by completing the following steps:
   a. Select cells A4 through C7.
   b. Click the Chart Wizard button on the Standard toolbar.
   c. At the Chart Wizard - Step 1 of 4 - Chart Type dialog box, click the Next > button.
   d. At the Chart Wizard - Step 2 of 4 - Chart Source Data dialog box, make sure the data range displays as =Sheet1!$A$4:$C$7 and then click the Next > button.
   e. At the Chart Wizard - Step 3 of 4 - Chart Options dialog box, make the following changes:
      1) Click the Titles tab.
      2) Click inside the Chart title text box and then key **NORTHWEST REGION**.
      3) Click the Next > button.
   f. At the Chart Wizard - Step 4 of 4 - Chart Location dialog box, click the As new sheet option, and then click the Finish button.
4. Change the font for the title and legend and add a border and shading by completing the following steps:
   a. Double-click the title NORTHWEST REGION.
   b. At the Format Chart Title dialog box, click the Font tab, and then change the font to 24-point Century Schoolbook bold (or a similar serif typeface).
   c. Click the Patterns tab.
   d. Click the white circle before Custom in the Border section of the dialog box.

e. Click the down-pointing triangle to the right of the <u>W</u>eight text box. From the drop-down menu that displays, click the third option.

f. Click the check box before the Sha<u>d</u>ow option.

g. Add light green color by clicking the fourth color from the left in the fifth row.

h. Click OK to close the Format Chart Title dialog box.

5. Format the legend with the same options as the title (complete steps similar to those in step 4, except change the font to 10-point Century Schoolbook bold [instead of 24-point].)

6. With the legend still selected, increase the width by dragging the left, middle sizing handle to the left so the legend slightly overlaps the chart. (Make sure *# of computers* is completely visible in the legend.)

7. Save the workbook again with the same name (Excel Ch 12, Ex 13).

8. Print only the sheet containing the chart.

9. Close Excel Ch 12, Ex 13.

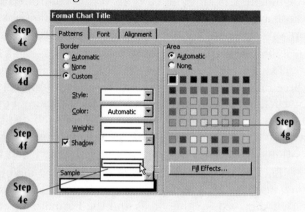

Changing Element Colors

Fill Color

A fill color can be added to a chart or a chart element with the Fill Color button on the Formatting toolbar. To add a fill color, select the chart or the chart element, and then click the down-pointing triangle at the right side of the Fill Color button on the Formatting toolbar. This displays a palette of color choices as shown in figure 12.13. Click the desired color on the palette.

figure

12.13

Fill Color Button Palette

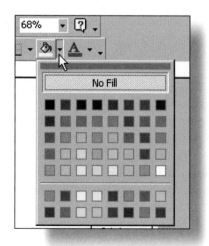

Changing Element Colors in a Chart

1. Open Excel Ch 12, Ex 09.
2. Save the workbook with Save As and name it Excel Ch 12, Ex 14.
3. Change the colors of the pieces of the pie by completing the following steps:
    a. Change the color of the piece of pie representing Salaries to red by completing the following steps:
        1) Position the arrow pointer on the Salaries piece of pie and then click the left mouse button. (Make sure the sizing handles surround only the Salaries piece of pie. You may need to experiment a few times to select the piece correctly.)
        2) Click the down-pointing triangle at the right of the Fill Color button on the Formatting toolbar.
        3) At the color palette, click the red color (first color in the third row).

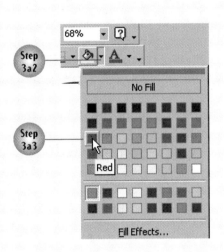

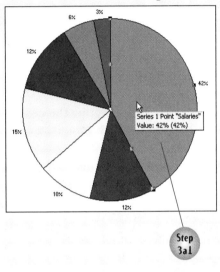

    b. Change the color of the Miscellaneous piece of pie to green by completing steps similar to those in step 3a. (You determine the shade of green.)
    c. Change the color of the Supplies piece of pie to yellow by completing steps similar to those in step 3a. (You determine the shade of yellow.)
    d. Change the color of the Equipment piece of pie to blue by completing steps similar to those in step 3a. (You determine the shade of blue.)
    e. Change the color of the Travel piece of pie to violet by completing steps similar to those in step 3a.
    f. Change the color of the Training piece of pie to light turquoise by completing steps similar to those in step 3a.
    g. Change the color of the Benefits piece of pie to a color you have not used on the other pieces of pie by completing steps similar to those in step 3a.

4. Add a background color to the chart by completing the following steps:
   a. Select the entire chart. (To do this, position the arrow pointer inside the chart window but outside the chart, and then click the left mouse button.)
   b. Click the down-pointing triangle at the right of the Fill Color button on the Formatting toolbar.
   c. From the color palette that displays, click a light blue color of your choosing.
5. Save the workbook again with the same name (Excel Ch 12, Ex 14).
6. Print only the sheet containing the Pie chart.
7. Close Excel Ch 12, Ex 14.

chapter summary

➤ Create a chart with data in an Excel worksheet. A chart is a visual presentation of data.

➤ Create a chart by selecting the cells containing the data to be charted and then clicking the Chart Wizard button on the Standard toolbar. Complete the four steps in the Chart Wizard.

➤ Insert a chart in the same worksheet as the cells containing data or in a separate sheet. If a chart is created in a separate sheet, the sheet is named *Chart1*.

➤ The left vertical side of a chart is referred to as the y-axis, and the bottom of the chart is referred to as the x-axis.

➤ In a worksheet containing cells of data as well as a chart, the chart can be printed (rather than all data in the worksheet) by selecting the chart first and then displaying the Print dialog box.

➤ To delete a chart in a worksheet, click the chart to select it, and then press the Delete key. To delete a chart created in a separate sheet, position the mouse pointer on the chart tab, click the right mouse button, and then click Delete.

➤ Change the size of a chart in an Excel worksheet by clicking the chart and then dragging the sizing handles in the desired direction. To move a chart, select the chart, position the arrow pointer inside the chart, hold down the left mouse button, drag the outline of the chart to the desired location, and then release the mouse button.

➤ Fourteen basic chart types are available and include Area, Bar, Bubble, Column, Cone, Cylinder, Doughnut, Line, Pie, Pyramid, Radar, Stock, Surface, and XY (scatter).

➤ The default chart type is a Column chart. This can be changed at the first Chart Wizard dialog box or at the Chart Type dialog box.

➤ A variety of custom charts are available at the Chart Type dialog box with the Custom Types tab selected.

➤ Change data in a cell used to create a chart and the data in the chart reflects the change.

➤ Chart elements can be added to a chart at the step 3 Chart Wizard dialog box or at the Chart Options dialog box.

➤ Move a chart element by selecting the element and then dragging the element to the desired location.

- Size a chart element by selecting the chart element and then dragging a sizing handle to the desired size.
- Delete a chart element by selecting the element and then pressing the Delete key.
- Customize the formatting of a chart element by double-clicking the element. This causes a formatting dialog box to display. The options at the dialog box will vary depending on the chart element.
- Add fill color to a chart or a chart element by selecting the chart or element and then clicking the Fill Color button on the Formatting toolbar. Click the desired color at the palette of color choices that displays.

commands review

	Mouse
Create a chart	Select the cells and then click the Chart Wizard button on the Standard toolbar. Complete steps 1 through 4 of the Chart Wizard.
Chart Type dialog box	Make chart active; click Chart, then Chart Type
Source Data dialog box	Make chart active; click Chart, then Source Data
Chart Options dialog box	Make chart active; click Chart, then Chart Options
Format Chart Area dialog box	Double-click in chart area outside any chart element
Format Chart Title dialog box	Double-click chart title
Format Legend dialog box	Double-click chart legend

thinking offline

Completion: In the space provided at the right, indicate the correct term or command.

1. Create a chart by selecting the cells containing data and then clicking this button on the Standard toolbar. _____

2. To create a chart as a separate worksheet, click this option at the Chart Wizard - Step 4 of 4 - Chart Location dialog box. _____

3. Change the size of a selected chart by dragging these. _____

4. This axis is located at the bottom of the chart. _____

5. Double-click a legend in a chart and this dialog box displays. _____

6. Choose a custom chart type at the Chart Type dialog box with this tab selected.

           _____

7. Double-click in a chart area and this dialog box displays.

           _____

8. Add fill color to a chart element by selecting the element and then clicking this button on the Formatting toolbar.

           _____

9. List the steps you would complete to create a default chart in Excel with cells A1 through D8 and insert the chart in a separate worksheet.

_____

_____

_____

working hands-on

Assessment 1

1. With Excel the active program, open Excel Worksheet 01.
2. Save the worksheet with Save As and name it Excel Ch 12, SA 01.
3. Make the following changes to the worksheet:
   a. Delete column B.
   b. Delete row 2.
4. Select cells A1 through C9 and then create a chart in a separate sheet with the following specifications:
   a. At step 1 of the Chart Wizard do not make any changes.
   b. At step 2, make sure the proper cell range displays.
   c. At step 3, add the title *COMPANY SALES*.
   d. At step 4, specify that the chart is to be created as a new sheet.
   e. After the chart is created, change the font size of the title to 24 points.
5. Save the workbook again with the same name (Excel Ch 12, SA 01).
6. Print only the sheet containing the chart.
7. Close Excel Ch 12, SA 01.

Assessment 2

1. Open Excel Worksheet 22.
2. Save the worksheet with Save As and name it Excel Ch 12, SA 02.
3. Select cells A1 through E3 and then create a chart in a new worksheet with the following specifications:
   a. At step 1 of the Chart Wizard, choose the Line chart type.
   b. At step 2, make sure the proper cell range displays.
   c. At step 3, add the title *COMPANY SALES*.
   d. At step 4, specify that the chart is to be created as a new sheet.

4. After the chart is created, make the following customizations:
   a. Add a light background color to the entire chart.
   b. Add a complementary light background color to the legend.
   c. Change the legend font to a serif typeface (you determine the typeface).
   d. Change the font for the title *COMPANY SALES* to the same serif typeface you chose for the legend and increase the font size.
   e. If some of the text in the legend is not visible, select the legend and then increase the size of the legend.
5. Save the workbook again with the same name (Excel Ch 12, SA 02).
6. Print only the sheet containing the chart.
7. Close Excel Ch 12, SA 02.

Assessment 3

1. Open Excel Worksheet 03.
2. Save the worksheet with Save As and name it Excel Ch 12, SA 03.
3. Make the following changes to the worksheet:
   a. Delete column D.
   b. Select cells B3 through C8 and then click the Percent Style button on the Standard toolbar.
4. Select cells A2 through C8 and then create a chart in a new sheet with the default settings in Chart Wizard, except add the chart title *ANALYSIS OF FINANCIAL CONDITION*.
5. Make the following changes to the chart:
   a. Change the color of the bars in the chart (you determine the colors).
   b. Change the font of the title and add a border (you determine the font and border style).
   c. Change the background shading of the chart to light turquoise.
   d. Add the following gridlines: <u>M</u>ajor gridlines in *Category (X) Axis* and Minor gridlines in *Value (Y) Axis*.
6. Save the workbook again with the same name (Excel Ch 12, SA 03).
7. Print only the sheet containing the chart.
8. Close Excel Ch 12, SA 03.

Assessment 4

1. At a clear worksheet window, create a worksheet with the following data:

Fund Allocations

Fund	Percentage
Annuities	23%
Stocks	42%
Bonds	15%
Money Market	20%

2. Create a pie chart as a separate worksheet with the data with the following specifications:
   a. Create a title for the pie chart.
   b. Add data labels to the chart.
   c. Add any other enhancements that will improve the visual presentation of the data.
3. Save the workbook and name it Excel Ch 12, SA 04.
4. Print only the sheet containing the chart.
5. Close Excel Ch 12, SA 04.

Assessment 5

1. Open Excel Ch 12, SA 04.
2. Save the workbook with Save As and name it Excel Ch 12, SA 05.
3. Choose a custom chart type at the Chart Type dialog box with the Custom Types tab selected. (Choose a custom pie chart.)
4. Save the workbook again with the same name (Excel Ch 12, SA 05).
5. Print only the sheet containing the chart.
6. Close Excel Ch 12, SA 05.

Assessment 6

1. Open Excel Worksheet 18.
2. Save the workbook with Save As and name it Excel Ch 12, SA 06.
3. Look at the data in the worksheet and then create a chart to represent the data. Add a title to the chart and add any other enhancements to improve the visual display of the chart.
4. Save the workbook again with the same name (Excel Ch 12, SA 06).
5. Print the chart and then close Excel Ch 12, SA 06.

Assessment 7

1. Use Excel's Help feature to learn more about an XY (scatter) chart.
2. After reading the information presented by Help, create a worksheet with the data shown in figure 12.14. Create a scatter chart from the data in a separate sheet and create an appropriate title for the chart. (Excel will change the date *July 1* to *1-Jul* and change the other dates in the same manner. The XY scatter chart will display time in five-day intervals.)
3. Save the completed workbook and name it Excel Ch 12, SA 07.
4. Print both sheets of the workbook (the sheet containing the data in cells and the sheet containing the chart).
5. Close Excel Ch 12, SA 07.

figure

12.14   *Assessment 7*

HIGHLAND PARK ATTENDANCE

Week	Projected	Actual
July 1	35,000	42,678
July 8	33,000	41,065
July 15	30,000	34,742
July 22	28,000	29,781
July 29	28,000	26,208

Chapter 13

Inserting Clip Art Images and Creating Maps

PERFORMANCE OBJECTIVES

Upon successful completion of chapter 13, you will be able to:

- Insert, size, and move a clip art image in a Word document and an Excel worksheet.
- Use the Map feature to create a map from data in an Excel worksheet.
- Customize a map created in an Excel worksheet.
- Copy and paste a map from an Excel worksheet to a Word document.

Microsoft Office contains several tools you can use in Word and Excel to create special objects. In this chapter, you will learn to use two of these tools—Clip Gallery and Map. With Clip Gallery, you can insert images into a document to add visual appeal. With Map you can use data in an Excel worksheet to create a map.

Adding Clip Art to Documents

Microsoft Office includes a gallery of clip art images that can be inserted in an Office application such as Word, Excel, or PowerPoint. The steps to insert a clip art image into any of the Office applications are basically the same. To insert a clip art image, click Insert, point to Picture, and then click Clip Art. This displays the Insert ClipArt dialog box with the Pictures tab selected as shown in figure 13.1.

INTEGRATED TOPIC

figure
13.1

Insert ClipArt Dialog Box with Pictures Tab Selected

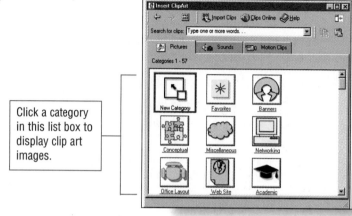

Click a category in this list box to display clip art images.

**Insert
Clip Art**

Alt + Home is the keyboard command to display all categories in the Insert ClipArt dialog box.

Increase the size of the Insert ClipArt dialog box by dragging a border.

Back

All Categories

Another method for displaying the Insert ClipArt dialog box is to click the Insert Clip Art button on the Drawing toolbar. To display the Drawing toolbar, position the mouse pointer on the Standard or Formatting toolbar, click the *right* mouse button, and then click Drawing at the drop-down list. You can also display clip art categories and images by clicking Insert and then Object. At the Object dialog box with the Create New tab selected, double-click *Microsoft Clip Gallery* in the list box. This displays the Microsoft Clip Gallery that contains the same options as the Insert ClipArt dialog box.

At the Insert ClipArt dialog box with the Pictures tab selected, click a category in the category list box. This displays a list of clip art available for the category. To insert a clip art image in the document, click the desired clip art, and then click the Insert clip button at the top of the callout side menu that displays. Remove the Insert ClipArt dialog box from the screen by clicking the Close button (contains an X) located in the upper right corner of the dialog box.

Maneuver through categories and clip art at the Insert ClipArt dialog box using buttons on the toolbar that displays at the top of the dialog box. For example, click the Back button to display clip art for the previously selected category. To redisplay all categories, click the All Categories button. (See figure 13.2.)

figure
13.2

Insert ClipArt Dialog Box Buttons

Forward

Back   All Categories

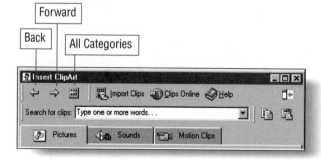

When you click a clip art image, a callout side menu displays containing several buttons as shown in figure 13.3. Click the Insert clip button to insert the image in the document. Click the Preview clip to view how the clip art image will display in the document. If you want to add a clip art image to the Favorites category or to any other category, click the Add clip to Favorites or other category button. This expands the side menu and displays an option for entering the desired category. The side menu will continue to display expanded until you click the button again. Clicking the Find similar clips button on the callout side menu causes the side menu to expand and display with keyboard for searching. The side menu will remain expanded until you click the button again.

Insert clip

Preview clip

Add clip to Favorites or other category

Clip Art Callout Side Menu Buttons

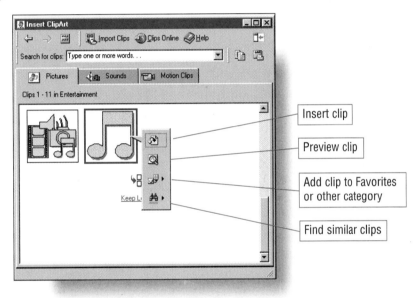

Insert clip

Preview clip

Add clip to Favorites or other category

Find similar clips

Sizing a Clip Art Image

Once a clip art image is inserted in a document, it can be sized using the white sizing handles that display around a selected clip art image. To change the size of a clip art image, click in the image to select it, and then position the mouse pointer on a sizing handle until the pointer turns into a double-headed arrow. Hold down the left mouse button, drag the sizing handle in or out to decrease or increase the size of the image, and then release the mouse button.

Use the middle sizing handle at the left or right side of the image to make the image wider or thinner. Use the middle sizing handle at the top or bottom of the image to make the image taller or shorter. Use the sizing handle at a corner of the image to change both the width and height at the same time. When sizing a clip art image in Word, consider using the horizontal and vertical rulers that display in the Print Layout view.

Use sizing handles to change the size of an image.

Hint

Moving and Deleting a Clip Art Image

Move a clip art image by dragging the image. To do this, click once on the image to select it. Position the arrow pointer on the image, hold down the left mouse button, drag the outline of the image to the desired position, and then release the mouse button. To deselect an image, click anywhere in the document outside the frame. Delete a clip art image from a document by clicking the image to select it and then pressing the Delete key.

exercise 1

Inserting and Sizing a Clip Art Image in a Word Document

1. Open Word and then create a title by completing the following steps:
   a. Change the font size to 28 points.
   b. Turn on bold and change the paragraph alignment to Center.
   c. Key **McCORMACK FUNDS**.
   d. Press the Enter key.
   e. Turn off bold and return the paragraph alignment to Left.

2. Insert a clip art image in the document by completing the following steps:
   a. Change to the Print Layout view.
   b. Click <u>I</u>nsert, point to <u>P</u>icture, and then click <u>C</u>lip Art.
   c. At the Insert ClipArt dialog box (see figure 13.1), scroll through the list of categories until *Business* is visible and then click *Business*.
   d. Click once on the image shown at the right. (The location of the image may vary.)
   e. At the callout side menu, click the Insert clip button (top button).
   f. Click the Close button (contains an X) that displays in the upper right corner of the dialog box.
   g. Decrease the size of the clip art image by completing the following steps:

   > Clips 1 - 34 in Business

   > Step 2e

   > Step 2d

   1) Click the image to select it. (White sizing handles should display around the image. If black sizing handles display around the image, click the Text Wrapping button on the Picture toolbar and then click T<u>h</u>rough at the drop-down list.)
   2) If necessary, click the down scroll triangle on the vertical scroll bar until the bottom sizing handles display.
   3) Position the mouse pointer on the bottom right sizing handle until the pointer turns into a diagonally pointing two-headed arrow.

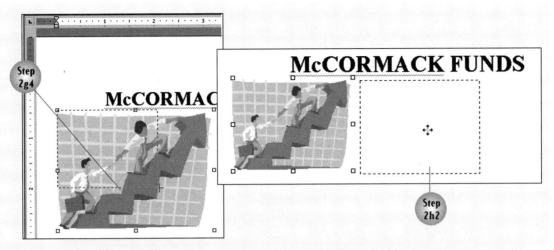

Step
2g4

Step
2h2

McCORMAC

McCORMACK FUNDS

4) Hold down the left mouse button, drag up and to the left until the size of the image is approximately 2 inches by 2 inches (use the horizontal and vertical rulers as visual aids), and then release the left mouse button.

h. Move the clip art image by completing the following steps:
1) With the clip art image still selected, position the arrow pointer inside the image. (The arrow pointer displays with a four-headed arrow attached.)
2) Hold down the left mouse button, drag the image until it is centered below the name *McCORMACK FUNDS*, and then release the left mouse button.

i. Click outside the image to deselect it.

3. Save the document and name it Word Ch 13, Ex 01.
4. Print and then close Word Ch 13, Ex 01.
5. Exit Word.

Inserting and Sizing a Clip Art Image in an Excel Worksheet

1. Open Excel and then open Excel Worksheet 03.
2. Save the document with Save As and name it Excel Ch 13, Ex 02.
3. Make the following changes to the worksheet:
   a. Select the first four rows of the worksheet and then click Insert and then Rows. (This inserts four new rows at the beginning of the worksheet.)
   b. Double-click in cell A2, key **MYLAN COMPUTERS**, and then press Enter.
   c. Select cells A1 through D12 and then apply the Accounting 1 autoformat.
   d. Select cells B7 through D12 and then click the Percent Style button on the Formatting toolbar.
4. Insert an image in the worksheet by completing the following steps:
   a. Make cell B1 the active cell.
   b. Click Insert, point to Picture, and then click Clip Art.
   c. At the Insert ClipArt dialog box, click the *Science & Technology* category in the category list box.
   d. Click once on the image shown on the right
   e. At the callout side menu, click the Insert clip button (top button).

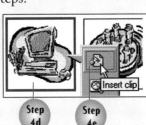

Insert clip

Step
4d

Step
4e

f. Click the Close button (contains an X) that displays in the upper right corner of the dialog box.

g. Decrease the size of the clip art image by completing the following steps:

    1) Click the image to select it (white sizing handles display around the image).

    2) Position the mouse pointer on the bottom right sizing handle until the pointer turns into a diagonally pointing two-headed arrow.

    3) Hold down the left mouse button, drag up and to the left until the outline of the image fits within cells B1 through D5 and then release the mouse button.

h. If necessary, move the image so it is centered within cells B1 through D4.

i. Click outside the image to deselect it.

5. Save the worksheet again with the same name (Excel Ch 13, Ex 02).

6. Print the worksheet horizontally and vertically centered on the page.

7. Close Excel Ch 13, Ex 02 and then exit Excel.

Searching for Clip Art Images

You can search for specific types of clip art images or for a specific image at the Insert ClipArt dialog box. To do this, display the Insert ClipArt dialog box, click in the Search for clips text box, and then key the type of clip art image desired or key the specific name. Press the Enter key and clip art images display that match what you entered.

Formatting Clip Art Images

Use buttons on the Picture toolbar to format a clip art image in Word, PowerPoint, or Excel.

Format clip art images using a variety of methods. The formatting available depends on the program in which the clip art is inserted. Moving and sizing clip art images is considered formatting. Other formatting available includes adding fill color and border lines, increasing or decreasing the brightness or contrast, choosing a wrapping style, and cropping the image. A variety of methods are available for changing the formatting of a clip art image. In this section, formatting will focus on using the buttons on the Picture toolbar.

Formatting Clip Art Images in Word

Format an image in a Word document with buttons on the Picture toolbar shown in figure 13.4. To display this toolbar, click a clip art image. (If the toolbar does not display, position the mouse pointer on the image, click the *right* mouse button, and then click Show Picture Toolbar at the shortcut menu.) The buttons on the Picture toolbar are described in figure 13.5.

figure
13.4

Word Picture Toolbar

figure
13.5

Word Picture Toolbar Buttons

Click this button	Named	To do this
	Insert Picture	Display the Insert Picture dialog box with a list of subfolders containing additional images.
	Image Control	Display a drop-down list with options for controlling how the image displays. Options include Automatic, Grayscale, Black & White, and Watermark.
	More Contrast	Increase contrast of the image.
	Less Contrast	Decrease contrast of the image.
	More Brightness	Increase brightness of the image.
	Less Brightness	Decrease brightness of the image.
	Crop	Crop image so only a specific portion of the image is visible.
	Line Style	Insert a border around the image and specify the border line style.
	Text Wrapping	Specify how text will wrap around or through the image. Choices include Square, Tight, Behind Text, In Front of Text, Top and Bottom, Through, and Edit Wrap Points.
	Format Picture	Display Format Picture dialog box with options for formatting the image. Tabs in the dialog box include Colors and Lines, Size, Layout, Picture, and Web.

Set Transparent
Color

This button is available only for drawing objects.

Reset Picture

Reset picture to its original size, position, and color.

exercise 3

Formatting a Clip Art Image in Word

1. With Word the active program, create the letterhead shown in figure 13.6 at a clear document screen by completing the following steps:

   a. Insert the image, change the wrapping style of the image and add a fill and border by completing the following steps:

      1) Change to the Print Layout view.
      2) Click Insert, point to Picture, and then click Clip Art.
      3) At the Insert ClipArt dialog box, click in the Search for clips text box, key **trees**, and then press Enter.
      4) Click once on the last image in the first row. The location of the image may vary.
      5) At the callout side menu, click the Insert clip button.
      6) Click the Close button (contains an X) that displays in the upper right corner of the dialog box.
      7) Change the wrapping style of the image by completing the following steps:
         a) Click the image to select it. (If the Picture toolbar is not visible, right-click the image and then click Show Picture Toolbar.)
         b) Click the Text Wrapping button on the Picture toolbar and then click Square at the drop-down list.
      8) Decrease the size of the clip art image by completing the followings steps:
         a) Click the Format Picture button on the Picture toolbar.
         b) At the Format Picture dialog box, click the Size tab.
         c) At the Format Picture dialog box with the Size tab selected, select the current measurement in the Height text box, and then key **1.5**.

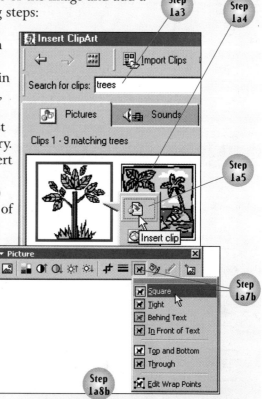

d) Click OK to close the dialog box.
9) Insert a single border line around the image by clicking the Line Style button on the Picture toolbar and then clicking the *2¼ pt* line style at the drop-down list.
10) Add a light green fill color by completing the following steps:
   a) Click the Format Picture button on the Picture toolbar.
   b) At the Format Picture dialog box, click the Colors and Lines tab.
   c) At the Format Picture dialog box with the Colors and Lines tab selected, click the down-pointing triangle at the right of the Color text box (displays with the words *No Fill*).
   d) At the palette of color choices that displays, click the light green color that is fourth from the left in the last row.
   e) Click OK to close the Format Picture dialog box.
11) Click outside the image to deselect it.
b. Key the text in the document in figure 13.6 by completing the following steps:
   1) Change the paragraph alignment to Right.
   2) Key the company name, address, telephone number, and Web address as shown in figure 13.6. (If Word converts the Web address to a hyperlink, immediately click the Undo button.)
   3) Select the company name *Alpine Nursery* and then change the font to 24-point Copperplate Gothic Bold. (If this typeface is not available, choose a similar decorative typeface.)
   4) Select the street address; city, state, and Zip code; and the telephone number and then change the font to 16-point Copperplate Gothic Bold.
   5) Select the Web address and then change the font to 10-point Copperplate Gothic Bold.
2. Save the document and name it Word Ch 13, Ex 03.
3. Print and then close Word Ch 13, Ex 03.

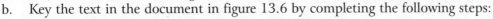

figure
13.6

Exercise 3

ALPINE NURSERY
5677 ROSEHILL DRIVE
SUMMERVILLE, OR 99031
(503) 555-3550
HTTP://WWW.ALPINE.COM

Formatting Clip Art Images in Excel

Formatting clip art images in Excel is basically the same as formatting images in Word. The Picture toolbar automatically displays in Excel when a clip art image is inserted in a worksheet and is similar to the Word Picture toolbar except there is no Text Wrapping button.

Formatting a Clip Art Image in Excel

1. Make Excel the active program and then open Excel Worksheet 13.
2. Save the worksheet with Save As and name it Excel Ch 13, Ex 04.
3. Make the following changes to the worksheet:
   a. Delete column H.
   b. Insert a row at the beginning of the worksheet.
   c. Change the height of the new row to 99.0.
   d. Select cells A1 through G1 and then click the Merge and Center button on the Formatting toolbar.
   e. With cell A1 the active cell, make the following changes:
      1) Display the Format Cells dialog box. (To do this, click Format and then Cells.)
      2) At the Format Cells dialog box, click the Alignment tab.
      3) At the Format Cells dialog box with the Alignment tab selected, change the Horizontal option to *Right* and the Vertical option to *Center* (in the Text alignment section).
      4) Click the Font tab.
      5) At the Format Cells dialog box with the Font tab selected, change the font to 34-point Arial bold.
      6) Click OK to close the dialog box.
   f. Key **Global Transport**.
4. Insert and format a clip art image by completing the following steps:
   a. Click outside cell A1 and then click cell A1 again.
   b. Display the Insert ClipArt dialog box.
   c. At the Insert ClipArt dialog box, click the *Maps* category.
   d. Click the image shown above and then click the Insert clip button. (The location of the image may vary.)
   e. Close the Insert ClipArt dialog box.
   f. Change the size of the image by completing the following steps:

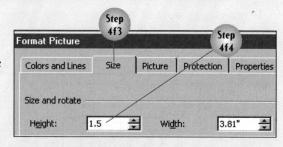

      1) Click the image to select it.
      2) Click the Format Picture button on the Picture toolbar. (If the Picture toolbar is not visible, click View, point to Toolbars, and then click Picture.)
      3) At the Format Picture dialog box, click the Size tab.
      4) Select the current measurement in the Height text box (in the Size and rotate section) and then key **1.5**.

5) Click OK to close the dialog box.
g. Click twice on the More Brightness button on the Picture toolbar.
5. Save the workbook again with the same name (Excel Ch 13, Ex 04).
6. Print the worksheet centered horizontally and vertically on the page.
7. Close Excel Ch 13, Ex 04.

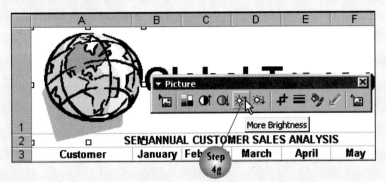

Creating a Watermark

An interesting effect can be created in a document with a watermark. A *watermark* is a lightened image that displays in a document. Text can be inserted in front of the watermark creating a document with a foreground and a background. The foreground is the text and the background is the watermark image. Figure 13.7 shows an example of a watermark you will create in exercise 5. The image of the business people is the watermark and creates the background; the text of the announcement displays in front of the watermark and creates the foreground.

Use a watermark to add visual appeal to a document.

 13.7

Watermark Example

A Word document contains three levels: the text layer, a layer above the text, and a layer behind. The text layer is the one in which you generally work in a document. A clip art image is inserted above the text layer, covering the text. If you do not want the clip art image to cover text, move the object behind the text. Do this by clicking the Text Wrapping button on the Picture toolbar and then clicking Behind Text at the drop-down list. Creating a watermark involves using the Image Control button on the Picture toolbar along with the Text Wrapping button

exercise 5

Creating a Watermark in a Word Document

1. With Word the active program, open Word Block 01.
2. Save the document with Save As and name it Word Ch 13, Ex 05.
3. Make the following changes to the document:
   a. Select the entire document and then change the font to 24-point Rockwell bold.
   b. Deselect the text.
   c. Move the insertion point to the beginning of the document.
   d. Display the Insert ClipArt dialog box.
   e. At the Insert ClipArt dialog box, click in the Search for clips text box, key **meetings**, and then press Enter.
   f. Click the image shown at the right and then click the Insert clip button.
   g. Close the Insert ClipArt dialog box.
   h. Click once on the image to select it. (Make sure the Picture toolbar displays. If it does not, right-click the image and then click Show Picture Toolbar.)
   i. Click the Image Control button on the Picture toolbar and then click Watermark at the drop-down list that displays.
   j. Click twice on the Less Brightness button on the Picture toolbar.
   k. Click the Text Wrapping button on the Picture toolbar and then click Behind Text. (If the clip art displays in front of the text, repeat this step.)
   l. With the watermark image still selected, drag it so it is centered horizontally and vertically behind the text (see figure 13.7).
   m. Click outside the image to deselect it.
4. Save the document again with the same name (Word Ch 13, Ex 05).
5. Print and then close Word Ch 13, Ex 05.

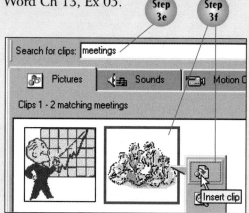

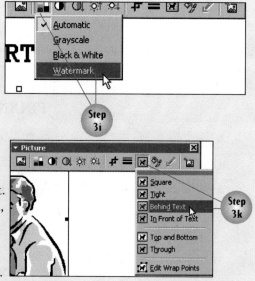

Downloading Clip Art

The Microsoft Web site offers a clip gallery with hundreds of clip art images you can download. To display the Microsoft Clip Gallery, you must have access to the Internet. To download a clip art image, you would complete these basic steps:

1. Make sure you are connected to the Internet and then display the Insert ClipArt dialog box.
2. At the Insert ClipArt dialog box, click the Clips Online button that displays towards the top of the dialog box.
3. At the message telling you to click OK to browse additional clips from a special Web page, click the OK button.
4. At the End-User License Agreement page, read the agreement, and then click the Accept button if you accept the terms of the agreement.
5. At the Microsoft Clip Gallery shown in figure 13.8 (your screen may vary), search for the desired image.
6. Download the desired image by clicking the download button that displays below the image.
7. Close the Insert ClipArt dialog box.
8. Close Microsoft Internet Explorer.

Microsoft Clip Gallery

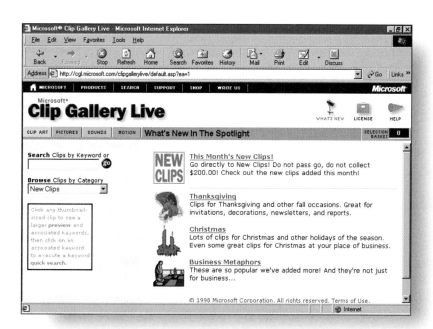

A downloaded clip is usually inserted in the Downloaded Clips category. To insert a downloaded clip art, display the Insert ClipArt dialog box, display the Downloaded Clips category, click the desired image, and then click the Insert clip button.

Deleting Downloaded Clip Art

Delete a clip art image from the Insert ClipArt dialog box by right-clicking the image and then clicking the <u>D</u>elete option from the shortcut menu. At the message telling you to click OK to delete the clip from all Clip Gallery categories, click the OK button.

Downloading a Clip Art Image from the Microsoft Clip Gallery

(Note: Check with your instructor before completing this exercise to determine if you can download clip art with your system configuration.)

1. Make Excel the active program and then open Excel Worksheet 07.
2. Save the worksheet with Save As and name it Excel Ch 13, Ex 06.
3. Make the following changes to the worksheet:
   a. Delete column E.
   b. Change the height of the first row to 100.
   c. With cell A1 the active cell, make the following changes
      1) Display the Format Cells dialog box with the Alignment tab selected.
      2) Change the <u>H</u>orizontal alignment to *Right* and the <u>V</u>ertical alignment to *Center*.
      3) Click the Font tab and then change the font style to Bold and the size to 14.
      4) Close the Format Cells dialog box.
4. Download a clip from the Microsoft Clip Gallery by completing the following steps:
   a. Make sure you are connected to the Internet.
   b. Display the Insert ClipArt dialog box.
   c. At the Insert ClipArt dialog box, click the <u>C</u>lips Online button.
   d. At the message telling you to click OK to browse additional clips from a special Web page, click the OK button.
   e. At the End-User License Agreement page, read the agreement, and then click the Accept button if you accept the terms of the agreement.
   f. At the Microsoft Clip Gallery (see figure 13.8), click in the Search text box and then key **Photography**.
   g. Click the go button that displays at the right side of the Search text box.
   h. When the photography clip images display, click the image of the camera. (This displays the image as a miniature in the box below the Browse text box.)
   i. Click the download button that displays immediately below the image (contains a small down-pointing red arrow).

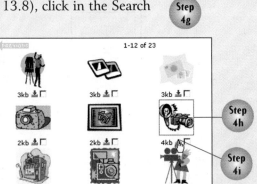

j.   At the Insert ClipArt dialog box with the camera image displayed, click the Close button.

k.   Click File and then Close to close the Microsoft Internet Explorer.

5.   Insert and size the camera image by completing the following steps:

a.   With cell A1 the active cell, display the Insert ClipArt dialog box.

b.   At the Insert ClipArt dialog box, click the *Downloaded Clips* category.

c.   Click the camera image and then click the Insert clip button.

d.   Close the Insert ClipArt dialog box.

e.   Decrease the size of the image so it fits inside cell A1.

Step 5e

6.   Save the worksheet again with the same name (Excel Ch 13, Ex 06).

7.   Print the worksheet centered horizontally and vertically on the page.

8.   Delete the downloaded clip by completing the following steps:

a.   Display the Insert ClipArt dialog box.

b.   At the ClipArt dialog box, click the *Downloaded Clips* category.

c.   Right-click the camera image you downloaded and then click Delete at the shortcut menu.

d.   At the message telling you to click OK to delete the clip from all Clip Gallery categories, click the OK button.

e.   Close the Insert ClipArt dialog box.

9.   Close Excel Ch 13, Ex 06.

Displaying Data in a Map

Data in a worksheet can be difficult to analyze and may not have the intended impact. Inserting data in a chart, as you learned in chapter 12, presents data in a form that is more easily analyzed. Visual impact for some data can be achieved by using the Map feature to display data that is geographic in nature. The Map feature displays geographic areas and information for data that is established in an Excel worksheet. Once the map is created, it can be inserted into a Word document or another Office application.

The Map feature will create a map and display data for the following areas: Australia, Canada, Europe, Mexico, North America, UK Standard Regions, US with AK & HI Inset, United States in North America, and World Countries.

Creating a Map

You must use geographic regions that the Map feature recognizes.

A map can be created using worksheet data such as product sales for specific states or provinces, population data, or international sales figures. Data that you want to insert in a map must be created in columns in an Excel worksheet. Figure 13.9 shows columns of data in an Excel worksheet that have been used to create a map.

figure
13.9

Map Created with Data in a Worksheet

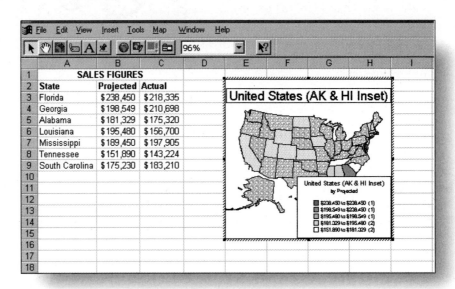

The map shown in figure 13.9 was created with all default settings. This map can be customized in a variety of ways. For example, you can display specific states, add color to the states, and change the column used to obtain data. In exercise 7, you will create the map shown in figure 13.9, and then learn how to customize the map.

Create a map by selecting specific cells in a worksheet and then clicking the Map button on the Standard toolbar. If the Map button does not display on the Standard toolbar, you can add it to the toolbar by completing the following steps:

Map

1. Click Tools and then Customize.
2. At the Customize dialog box, click the Commands tab.
3. At the Customize dialog box with the Commands tab selected, click *Insert* in the Categories list box (see figure 13.10).
4. Scroll down the Commands list box until *Map* displays (see figure 13.10).
5. Position the arrow pointer on *Map*, hold down the left mouse button, drag to the location on the Standard toolbar where you want the Map button inserted, and then release the mouse button.
6. Click the Close button to close the Customize dialog box.

figure
13.10

Customize Dialog Box

Click Insert in the Categories list box.

Scroll down the Commands list box until Map displays. Position arrow pointer on Map and then drag to desired position on toolbar.

If you do not add the Map button on the Standard toolbar, display the Map feature by clicking Insert and then Object. At the Object dialog box, scroll down the Object type list box until *Microsoft Map* is visible and then double-click *Microsoft Map*. These steps insert the map over the selected cells in the worksheet. If this is the method you use to complete exercises, you may need to modify some of the steps.

Creating a Map with an Excel Worksheet

(Note: If you are using a disk for saving exercise documents, you may want to delete the documents created earlier in this chapter. Check with your instructor before deleting any documents.)

1. Open Excel and then open Excel Worksheet 18.
2. Save the worksheet and name it Excel Ch 13, Ex 07.
3. Create a map with the data in the worksheet by completing the following steps:
   a. Select cells A2 through C9.
   b. Click the Map button on the Standard toolbar. (This causes the arrow pointer to turn into crosshairs.)
   c. Position the crosshairs in the upper left corner of cell E2, hold down the left mouse button, drag the crosshairs to the bottom right corner of cell H15, and then release the mouse button.
   d. At the Multiple Maps Available dialog box, shown in figure 13.11, make sure *United States (AK & HI Inset)* is selected in the list box, and then click OK.

e. At the Microsoft Map Control dialog box, shown in figure 13.12, click the Close button that displays in the upper right corner of the dialog box. (You can also close the dialog box by clicking the Show/Hide Microsoft Map Control button on the Map toolbar.)

f. Deselect the map by clicking in the worksheet area, outside the map.

4. Save the worksheet again with the same name (Excel Ch 13, Ex 07).

5. Print the worksheet (and map) centered horizontally and vertically on the page.

6. Close Excel Ch 13, Ex 07.

Multiple Maps Available Dialog Box

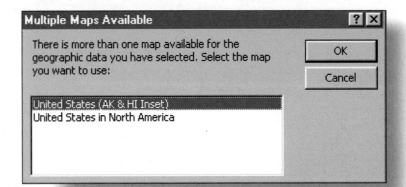

Microsoft Map Control Dialog Box

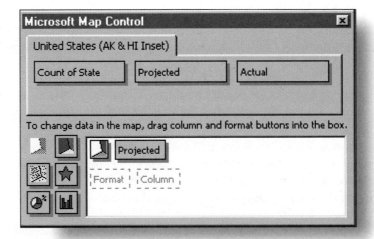

If changes are made to data in the worksheet used to create a map, click the Map Refresh button.

Customizing a Map

A data map can be customized in a variety of ways. Specific states or provinces can be displayed (rather than the entire North American continent), color can be added to specified states or provinces, dots can be used to indicate data, and different columns of data can be reflected in the map.

Changes can be made to the map with options and buttons at the Microsoft Map Control dialog box shown in figure 13.12 or with buttons on the Map toolbar. Figure 13.13 identifies each button on the Map toolbar and the function performed by the button.

Map Toolbar Buttons

Click this button	Named	To do this
 ▶	Select Objects	select objects in a data map and then move, size, or delete
 🖐	Grabber	move map within frame
 ▦	Center Map	specify the center of the map
 ▦	Map Labels	display Map Labels dialog box where labels can be added to features
 A	Add Text	add text to map
 📌	Custom Pin Map	display Custom Pin Map dialog box where special "push-pins" can be added to mark specific locations
 ●	Display Entire	zoom out and display map and all map features centered in the frame
 ▦	Redraw Map	redraw map that has been stretched
 ▦	Map Refresh	update map when changes have been made to data in the worksheet
 ▦	Show/Hide Microsoft Map Control	display or hide Microsoft Map Control dialog box
 96% ▾	Zoom Percentage of Map	zoom in on or zoom out of a specific area in a map

Zoom
Percentage of
Map

Grabber

Map Labels

Zooming In on Specific States

Zoom in on a specific area in a map using the Zoom Percentage of Map button on the Map toolbar along with the Grabber button. To do this, click the down-pointing triangle at the right side of the Zoom Percentage of Map button. At the drop-down menu that displays, click a higher percentage number to zoom in on the map. Finding the right percentage may take some time. You can also change the percentage of zoom by selecting the current percentage in the Zoom Percentage of Map button and then keying the desired percentage. After changing the zoom percentage, click the Grabber button on the Map toolbar. Position the arrow pointer (displays as a hand) in the map, hold down the left mouse button, drag the map until the desired location displays, and then release the mouse button.

Adding Labels

Labels can help the reader better understand the data displayed on the map. Click the Map Labels button on the Map toolbar and the Map Labels dialog box displays like the one shown in figure 13.14. At this dialog box, you can choose to label features based on the map displayed. For example, if the United States map displays, position the mouse pointer on a location on the map and a label displays. If you position the mouse pointer on a state, the state name displays. If you want the label to remain, click the left mouse button. You can also label values in the map by choosing the Values from option at the bottom of the dialog box. In exercise 8, you will add value labels to states showing the projected sales.

Add labels to a map to help the reader better understand the data.

figure

13.14

Map Labels Dialog Box

exercise 8

Zooming In on Specific States in a Map and Adding Value Labels

1. Open Excel Ch 13, Ex 07.
2. Save the worksheet and name it Excel Ch 13, Ex 08.
3. Zoom in on the specific states in the worksheet by completing the following steps:
    a. Double-click the map. (This displays the Map toolbar.)
    b. Click the Map Refresh button on the Map toolbar.
    c. Click the down-pointing triangle at the right side of the Zoom Percentage of Map button and then click *250%* at the drop-down menu. (This changes the size of the map to 250% of the original size.)
    d. Click the Grabber button on the Map toolbar.
    e. Position the mouse pointer (hand) on the map, hold down the left mouse button, drag the map to display the states in white and shades of gray as shown in figure 13.15, and then release the mouse button.
4. Add value labels to the states by completing the following steps:
    a. Click the Map Labels button on the Map toolbar.
    b. At the Map Labels dialog box, click in the white circle preceding Values from (located toward the bottom of the dialog box).
    c. Click OK to close the dialog box.
    d. Click once on each state. (This will add the value.)
    e. Click the Select Objects button on the Map toolbar. (This returns the mouse pointer to an arrow pointer.)
    f. If you are not satisfied with the location of a value, click once on the value to select it, and then drag the value to the desired location.
5. Click outside the map to deselect it.
6. Save the worksheet again with the same name (Excel Ch 13, Ex 08).
7. Print the worksheet (and map) centered horizontally and vertically on the page.
8. Close Excel Ch 13, Ex 08.

figure 13.15

Exercise 8, Map of Specific States with Values Added

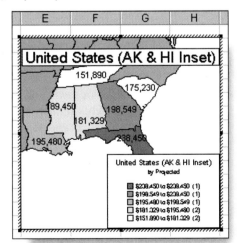

Remove a value label from a map by right-clicking the value and then clicking Clear at the pop-up menu that displays. If you want to format the value, right-click the value and then click Format Font. This displays the Font dialog box where you can change the font for the label.

Customizing a Legend and Title

By default, a legend is included in a data map. In figure 13.9, this default legend contains shaded boxes followed by the amounts of projected sales. A legend can be compacted displaying less information. To do this, right-click the legend, and then click Compact at the pop-up menu. This displays only two shaded boxes followed by *Projected*. You can also compact a legend at the Format Properties dialog box with the Legend Options tab selected as shown in figure 13.16. To display this dialog box, double-click the legend. To display the legend in compact form, insert a check mark in the Use Compact Format check box.

Format Properties Dialog Box with Legend Options Tab Selected

If a legend has been compacted and you would like to return it to its expanded form, display the Format Properties dialog box with the Legend Options tab selected and then remove the check mark from the Use Compact Format option. Removing the check mark makes the Title and Subtitle options available. Accept the title and subtitle provided or key your own. You can also right-click the legend and then click Compact. This removes the check mark preceding Compact and returns the legend to its expanded format.

If you do not want the legend to display in the map, right-click the legend, and then click Hide. You can also display the Format Properties dialog box with the Legend Options tab selected and then remove the check mark from the Show Legend option that displays at the bottom left corner of the dialog box.

The map shown in figure 13.9 displays with the title *United States (AK & HI Inset)*. This title may not accurately reflect the data in the table. You can change text in the title by double-clicking the title, deleting the existing text, and then keying the desired text. Format the text in the title by right-clicking the title and then clicking Format Font at the pop-up menu. This displays the Font dialog box where a different font can be chosen. If you do not want a title in the map, right-click the title, and then click Hide at the pop-up menu.

The legend and/or title can be moved within the map. To do this, click once in the title or legend and then use the mouse to drag the title or legend to the desired location.

exercise 9

Customizing the Legend and Changing the Title in a Map

1. Open Excel Ch 13, Ex 08.
2. Save the worksheet and name it Excel Ch 13, Ex 09.
3. Customize the legend so it appears as shown in figure 13.17 by completing the following steps:
   a. Double-click the map. (This displays the Map toolbar.)
   b. Click the Map Refresh button on the Map toolbar.
   c. Double-click the legend. (This displays the Format Properties dialog box with the Legend Options tab selected.)
   d. Make sure the text *United States (AK & HI Inset)* is selected in the Title text box and then press the Delete key. (This deletes the title.)
   e. Key **Projected Sales** in the Title text box.
   f. Select and then delete *by Projected* that displays in the Subtitle text box. (Do not key a subtitle.)
   g. Click OK.
4. Remove the title by right-clicking the title *United States (AK & HI Inset)* and then clicking Hide at the pop-up menu.
5. Move the legend down to the lower right corner as shown in figure 13.17. To do this, click once on the legend to select it, and then drag the legend to the desired location.
6. Click the Grabber tool and then move the map of the states up so more of Florida displays as shown in figure 13.17.
7. Click outside the map to deselect it.
8. Save the worksheet again with the same name (Excel Ch 13, Ex 09).
9. Print the worksheet (and map) horizontally and vertically centered on the page.
10. Close Excel Ch 13, Ex 09.

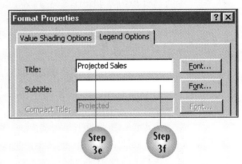

Step 3e   Step 3f

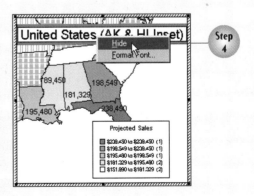

Step 4

figure
13.17

Exercise 9, Map with Title Removed and Legend Customized

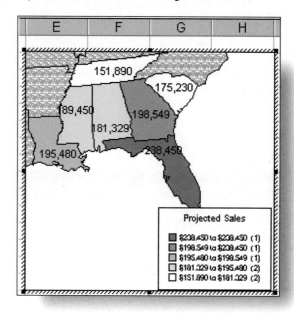

The legend in Excel Ch 13, Ex 09 identifies the shading used for the states and the value range within the shade. The legend will display five different shades. There are, however, seven states specified in the map. The same color shading is used more than once for two states, Alabama and Mississippi, and also for two other states, South Carolina and Tennessee.

Customizing a Map at the Map Control Dialog Box

The map shown in figure 13.9 used the values in the *Projected* column to create the shading for the states and the legend. Other columns of data can be used for the map with options at the Microsoft Map Control dialog box, shown in figure 13.12. For an existing map, display this dialog box by clicking the Show/Hide Microsoft Map Control button on the Map toolbar.

Show/Hide
Microsoft Map
Control

Column buttons display at the top of the Microsoft Map Control dialog box. These column buttons vary depending on the worksheet. In the Microsoft Map Control dialog box shown in figure 13.12, the column buttons display with Count of State, Projected, and Actual. The Map feature used the column headings in the worksheet for the column buttons. Notice that the Projected column button also displays below in the white box in the dialog box. The Projected button displays because this column of data was used in the map. If you want the map to display data from a different column, drag that column button down into the white box on top of the original column. When you release the mouse button, the data automatically changes in the map and the legend title changes.

Formatting buttons display along the left side of the dialog box. The name and purpose of these buttons is described in figure 13.18.

figure
13.18

Microsoft Map Control Formatting Buttons

This button	Named	Produces this effect
	Value Shading	shades map features according to numeric values
	Category Shading	colors map features according to category
	Dot Density	displays numeric data as a quantity of dots
	Graduated Symbol	displays numeric data as various sizes of symbols
	Pie Chart	displays data for specific area in a pie chart
	Column Chart	displays data for specific area in a column chart

Use the formatting buttons to customize the formatting of the map. By default, the states in the map shown in figure 13.9 display in shades from white to dark gray. Choose the Category Shading button to display the states in varying colors. To do this, you would drag the Category Shading button into the white box where the Projected button displays. When you position the arrow pointer on a formatting button, the pointer turns into a hand holding a handle. As you drag the button into the white box, the pointer turns into a hand holding a handle connected to a drawer.

Category
Shading

exercise 10

Changing Column Data and Shading in a Map

1. Open Excel Ch 13, Ex 09.
2. Save the worksheet and name it Excel Ch 13, Ex 10.
3. Change the data in the map from the *Projected* column to the *Actual* column and change the shading to Category Shading as shown in figure 13.19 by completing the following steps:
   a. Double-click the map. (This displays the Map toolbar.)
   b. Click the Map Refresh button on the Map toolbar.
   c. Click the Show/Hide Microsoft Map Control button on the Map toolbar.

d. At the Microsoft Map Control dialog box, position the arrow pointer on the Actual button that displays at the top of the dialog box, hold down the left mouse button, drag the button so it is positioned on top of the Projected button in the white area of the dialog box, and then release the mouse button.

e. Position the arrow pointer on the Category Shading button that displays at the left side of the dialog box, hold down the left mouse button, drag the button so it is positioned on top of the Value Shading button in the white area of the dialog box, and then release the mouse button.

f. Click the Close button to close the Microsoft Map Control dialog box.

4. Edit the legend by completing the following steps:
   a. Double-click the legend. (This displays the Format Properties dialog box with the Legend Options tab selected.)
   b. At the Format Properties dialog box with the Legend Options tab selected, change the title to **Actual Sales**.
   c. Click OK to close the dialog box.

5. Remove the value labels from the states. To do this, position the arrow pointer on a value, click the right mouse button, and then click the left mouse button on the <u>C</u>lear option that displays in the pop-up menu. (Do this for each value.)

6. If necessary, move the legend so it appears as shown in figure 13.19. (To do this, click the legend once to select it and then drag the outline of the legend to the desired location.)

7. Click outside the map to deselect it.

8. Save the worksheet again with the same name (Excel Ch 13, Ex 10).

9. Print the worksheet (and map) centered horizontally and vertically on the page.

10. Close Excel Ch 13, Ex 10.

figure

13.19

Exercise 10, Map Displaying Data for Actual Column

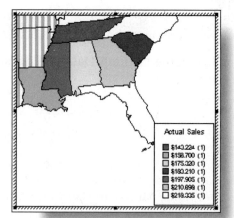

A map can display data from more than one column. For example, in exercise 11 you will create a map that displays data for the number of households owning a computer and that also displays data for the number of households that are connected to an on-line service. To display data for more than one column, drag the column button from the top of the Microsoft Map Control dialog box to just below the first row in the white box. The data in the second row will display as a series of density dots. This display can be changed to symbols of varying sizes.

Creating a Map Displaying Data from Two Columns

1. Open Excel Worksheet 19.
2. Save the worksheet with Save As and name it Excel Ch 13, Ex 11.
3. Create the map shown in figure 13.20 by completing the following steps:
   a. Select cells A4 through C7.
   b. Click the Map button on the Standard toolbar. (This causes the arrow pointer to turn into crosshairs.)
   c. Position the crosshairs in the upper left corner of cell E2, hold down the left mouse button, drag the crosshairs to the bottom right corner of cell H15, and then release the mouse button.
   d. At the Multiple Maps Available dialog box, make sure *United States (AK & HI Inset)* is selected in the list box, and then click OK.
   e. At the Microsoft Map Control dialog box, make the following changes:
      1) Position the arrow pointer (turns into a hand holding a handle) on the # On-Line button located at the top of the dialog box, drag the button to the second row in the white box where the word *Column* displays surrounded by a dashed line border, and then release the mouse button.

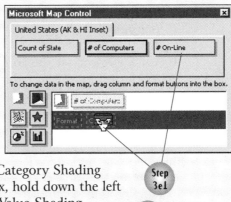

Step 3e1

Step 3e2

      2) Position the arrow pointer (turns into a hand holding a handle) on the Category Shading button at the left side of the dialog box, hold down the left mouse button, drag the button to the Value Shading button located in the first row of the white box, and then release the mouse button.
      3) Click the Close button located in the upper right corner of the Data Map Control dialog box. (If this button is not visible, drag the dialog box to the left until it is visible.)

   f. Edit the legend pertaining to dots by completing the following steps:
      1) Double-click the legend containing the title *United States (AK & HI Inset)* and the subtitle *by # On-Line* (along with information on 1 dot equalling 2,000).

2) At the Format Properties dialog box with the Legend Options tab selected, key **On-Line Users** in the Title text box. (The current title should already be selected when the dialog box is displayed.)

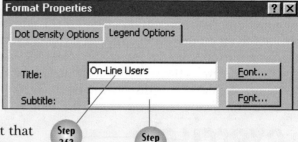

3) Select and then delete the text that displays in the Subtitle text box.
4) Click OK to close the Format Properties dialog box.
g. Edit and then move the legend that displays the number of computers by completing the following steps:
1) Double-click the legend containing the title *United States (AK & HI Inset)* and the subtitle *by # of Computers*.
2) At the Format Properties dialog box with the Legend Options tab selected, key **Homes with Computers** in the Title text box. (The current title should already be selected when the dialog box is displayed.)

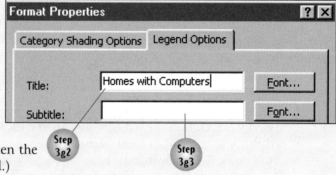

3) Select and then delete the text that displays in the Subtitle text box.
4) Click OK to close the Format Properties dialog box.
5) With the legend selected (a thick gray border surrounds the legend), drag the legend to the bottom left corner of the map as shown in figure 13.20.
h. Click the legend containing the title *On-Line Users* and then drag the legend to the bottom right corner of the map as shown in figure 13.20.
i. Hide the title in the map. (To do this, right-click the title, and then click Hide at the pop-up menu.)
j. Zoom in on the three states displaying data in the map (Washington, Oregon, and Idaho). To do this, complete the following steps:
1) Click the down-pointing triangle at the right side of the Zoom Percentage of Map button on the Map toolbar and then click *400%* at the drop-down list.
2) Click the Grabber button on the Map toolbar.
3) Position the mouse pointer (hand) in the map and then drag the map until the three states display as shown in figure 13.20.
k. Click outside the map to deselect it.
4. Save the worksheet again with the same name (Excel Ch 13, Ex 11).
5. Print the worksheet (and map) centered horizontally and vertically on the page.
6. Close Excel Ch 13, Ex 11.

figure
13.20

Exercise 11, Map Displaying Data from Two Columns

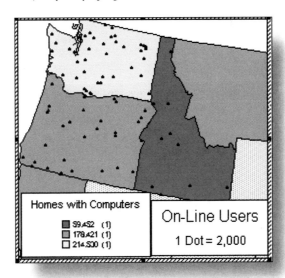

Copying a Map into a Word Document

A map created with the Map feature can be copied and then pasted in a Word document. The steps to copy and paste a map are the same as copying and pasting any other object. In exercise 12 you will be copying and pasting a map into a Word document.

exercise 12

Copying and Pasting a Map into a Word Document

1. Open Excel and Word.
2. With Word the active program, open Word Memo 01.
3. Save the memo with Save As and name it Word Ch 13, Ex 12.
4. With Word Ch 13, Ex 12 open, change to the Print Layout view and then change the Zoom to *Whole Page*.
5. Make Excel the active program and then open Excel Ch 13, Ex 11.
6. Save the worksheet with Save As and name it Excel Ch 13, Ex 12.
7. Copy and paste the map into the Word memo by completing the following steps:
   a. Click once on the map to select it.
   b. Click the Copy button on the Standard toolbar.
   c. Make Word the active program.
   d. Click the Paste button on the Standard toolbar.

8. Drag the map so it is positioned between the first and second paragraphs in the body of the memo.
9. Click outside the map to deselect it.
10. Change the Zoom back to *100%*.
11. Save the document again with the same name (Word Ch 13, Ex 12).
12. Print and then close Word Ch 13, Ex 12.
13. Exit Word.
14. Close Excel Ch 13, Ex 12 saving the changes and then exit Excel.

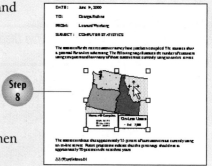

Step 8

chapter summary

► Clip art images are available from the Insert ClipArt dialog box. The steps to insert a clip art image into any of the Office applications are basically the same.

► Display the Insert ClipArt dialog box by clicking Insert, pointing to Picture, and then clicking Clip Art or clicking the Insert Clip Art button on the Drawing toolbar. Display the Microsoft Clip Gallery (which contains the same images as the Insert ClipArt dialog box) by clicking Insert and then Object. At the Object dialog box with the Create New tab selected, double-click *Microsoft Clip Gallery* in the list box.

► To insert a clip art image in a document, click the desired image in the Insert ClipArt dialog box, and then click the Insert clip button that displays at the callout side menu.

► A clip art image inserted in a document can be moved by selecting and then dragging the image.

► Size a clip art image using the sizing handles that display around the image when the image is selected.

► Use buttons on the Picture toolbar to customize a clip art image.

► The Microsoft Web site offers a clip gallery with hundreds of clip art images you can download. To display the Microsoft Clip Gallery, make sure you are connected to the Internet, and then click the Clips Online button that displays towards the top of the Insert ClipArt dialog box.

► Use the Map feature to display data that is geographic in nature.

► The Map feature will create maps for Australia, Canada, Europe, Mexico, North America, UK Standard Regions, US with AK & HI Inset, United States in North America, and World Countries.

► Use the Map feature on geographic data in an Excel worksheet. Data must be created in columns to create a map.

► To create a map, select the cells containing the data, click the Map button on the Excel Standard toolbar, and then draw a border in which the map will be inserted.

► Customize a map with buttons on the Map toolbar. With these buttons, you can move the map using the Grabber tool, add map labels, add text, display the entire map, redraw the map, refresh the map, display the Microsoft Map Control dialog box, or zoom in on or zoom out of a specific area of a map.

► Customize a title or legend in a map by right-clicking the object and then clicking the desired option.

- A map can also be customized with options at the Microsoft Map Control dialog box. With options at this dialog box, you can change the shading option, display numeric data as a quantity of dots or as various sizes of symbols, or display data in a pie chart or column chart.
- A map, like any other object, can be copied and then pasted into another Office application.

commands review

	Mouse/Keyboard
Display Insert ClipArt dialog box	Click Insert, point to Picture, then click Clip Art
Display Microsoft Clip Gallery	Click Insert, then Object, then double-click *Microsoft Clip Gallery*
Display the on-line Microsoft Clip Gallery	Click the Clips Online button in the Insert ClipArt dialog box
Create a map in Excel	Select cells, click Map button on Standard toolbar, draw frame
Display Map Labels dialog box	Click the Map Labels button on the Map toolbar
Display Format Properties dialog with Legend Options tab selected	Double-click legend; or right-click legend, then click Edit

thinking offline

Completion: In the space provided at the right, indicate the correct term, symbol, or command.

1. Click Insert, point to this, and then click Clip Art to display the Insert ClipArt dialog box. _____
2. Click this button on the Picture toolbar to display options including the Watermark option. _____
3. Click this button on the Picture toolbar to decrease the brightness of the image. _____
4. Click this button on the Picture toolbar to specify how text will wrap around the image. _____
5. This term refers to a lightened image in a document that displays behind the text. _____
6. Click this button at the Insert ClipArt dialog box to display the on-line Microsoft Clip Gallery. _____

7. A map can be created with data in this program. _____

8. Click this button on the Map toolbar to move the map within the frame. _____

9. Click this button on the Map toolbar to display a dialog box where you can add labels to map features. _____

10. Drag this button in the Map Control dialog box to the desired row in the white area to color the map features according to category. _____

11. Double-clicking a legend in a map will cause this dialog box to display. _____

12. Look at the data in the columns below. Suppose this data were established in an Excel worksheet. List below the basic steps you would complete to create a map with the data.

State	# Franchises
Alaska	14
Washington	21
Oregon	19
Idaho	10

_____

_____

_____

_____

working hands-on

Assessment 1

1. Open Word and then open Word Notice 01.
2. Save the document with Save As and name it Word Ch 13, SA 01.
3. Make the following changes to the document:
   a. Select the entire document, change the font to 14-point Arial bold and change the font color to Blue.
   b. Insert the clip art image shown in figure 13.21. (At the Insert ClipArt dialog box, click in the Search for clips text box, key **opening doors**, and then press Enter.)
   c. Decrease the width of the image to the 2½-inch mark on the horizontal ruler (displays toward top of screen).

    d. Decrease the height of the image to the 2-inch mark on the vertical ruler (displays at left side of screen).

    e. If necessary, display the Picture toolbar.

    f. Click the Text Wrapping button on the Picture toolbar and then click <u>S</u>quare at the drop-down list.

    g. Move the image so it is positioned at the left margin as shown in figure 13.21.

    h. Deselect the image.

4. Save the document again with the same name (Word Ch 13, SA 01).

5. Print and then close Word Ch 13, SA 01.

6. Exit Word.

figure
13.21

Assessment 1

McCORMACK FUNDS

Annual Stockholders' Meeting

King Auditorium

Wednesday, January 10, 2001

6:30 p.m.

Assessment 2

1. Open Excel and then open Excel Worksheet 05.

2. Save the document with Save As and name it Excel Ch 13, SA 02.

3. Make the changes to the worksheet as shown in figure 13.22 by completing the following steps:

    a. Insert two rows at the beginning of the worksheet.

    b. Turn on bold and then key **LIGHTHOUSE FINANCING** in cell A1.

    c. Center the text *LIGHTHOUSE FINANCING* across columns A, B, and C.

    d. Make cell D1 the active cell.

    e. Insert the clip art image shown in figure 13.22. (At the Insert ClipArt dialog box, key **lighthouse** in the Search for clips text box.)

    f. Change the size of the image so the bottom of the image is aligned with the bottom of row 10 and the right side of the image is aligned with the right side of column E.

    g. Deselect the image.

4. Save the worksheet again with the same name (Excel Ch 13, SA 02).

5. Print the worksheet centered horizontally and vertically on the page.

6. Close Excel Ch 13, SA 02 and then exit Excel.

figure
13.22   *Assessment 2*

	A	B	C	D	E	F
1	LIGHTHOUSE FINANCING					
2						
3		January				
4	Name	Hours	Rate			
5	Carolyn Bentley	35	$23.15			
6	Lindon Cassini	20	$19.00			
7	Michelle DeFord	40	$18.75			
8	Javier Farias	24	$16.45			
9	Deborah Gould	15	$11.50			
10	William Jarman	15	$11.50			
11						

Assessment 3

1. Open Word and then open Word Letter 01.
2. Save the document with Save As and name it Word Ch 13, SA 03.
3. Make sure you are connected to the Internet, go to the Microsoft Clip Gallery site (do this through the Insert ClipArt dialog box), and then download a clip art image related to banking. (You determine the image you want to download. Find something appropriate for the text in the letter.)
4. Insert the downloaded clip art image into Word Ch 13, SA 03 as a watermark. (You determine the size and position of the watermark as well as the brightness and contrast. Make sure the text is legible above the watermark.)
5. Save the document again with the same name (Word Ch 13, SA 03).
6. Print Word Ch 13, SA 03.
7. Delete the downloaded chip from the Insert ClipArt dialog box.
8. Close Word Ch 13, SA 03.

Assessment 4

1. Open Excel and then open Excel Worksheet 20.
2. Save the worksheet with Save As and name it Excel Ch 13, SA 04.
3. Create a map like the one shown in figure 13.23 with the data in the worksheet, using these specifications:
   a. Create a map of the United States.
   b. Zoom in on the states specified in the worksheet (as shown in figure 13.23).
   c. Edit the legend so the title displays as *# of Customers* and the subtitle is deleted.
   d. Move the legend, if necessary, so it is positioned in the same location as shown in figure 13.23.
   e. Hide the title.
4. Save the worksheet again with the same name (Excel Ch 13, SA 04).
5. Print the worksheet (and map) centered horizontally and vertically on the page.
6. Close Excel Ch 13, SA 04.

figure
13.23
Assessment 4

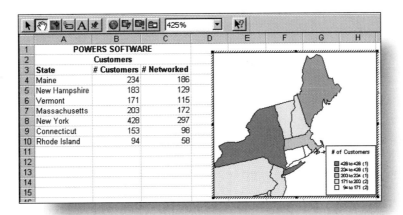

Assessment 5

1. Open Excel Ch 13, SA 04.
2. Save the worksheet with Save As and name it Excel Ch 13, SA 05.
3. Make the following changes to the map:
   a. Display the Map toolbar.
   b. Refresh the map.
   c. Display the Microsoft Map Control dialog box and then change the data column from *# Customers* to *# Networked*.
   d. At the Microsoft Map Control dialog box, change the shading button in the white area from *Value Shading* to *Category Shading*.
   e. Change the title of the legend to *# Networked*.
   f. If necessary, move the legend to the bottom right corner.
4. Save the worksheet again with the same name (Excel Ch 13, SA 05).
5. Print the worksheet (and map) horizontally and vertically centered on the page.
6. Close Excel Ch 13, SA 05.

Assessment 6

1. Borders can be added to text or objects in a document. Use Word's Help feature to learn how to insert a border. Read and then print the information you find in Help.
2. After learning how to insert borders, complete the following steps:
   a. In Word, open Word Notice 01.
   b. Set the text in the document in a larger, decorative font, and change the font color.
   c. Vertically center the text on the page.
   d. Insert a border of your choosing around the text in the document.
3. Save the document and name it Word Ch 13, SA 06.
4. Print and then close Word Ch 13, SA 06.

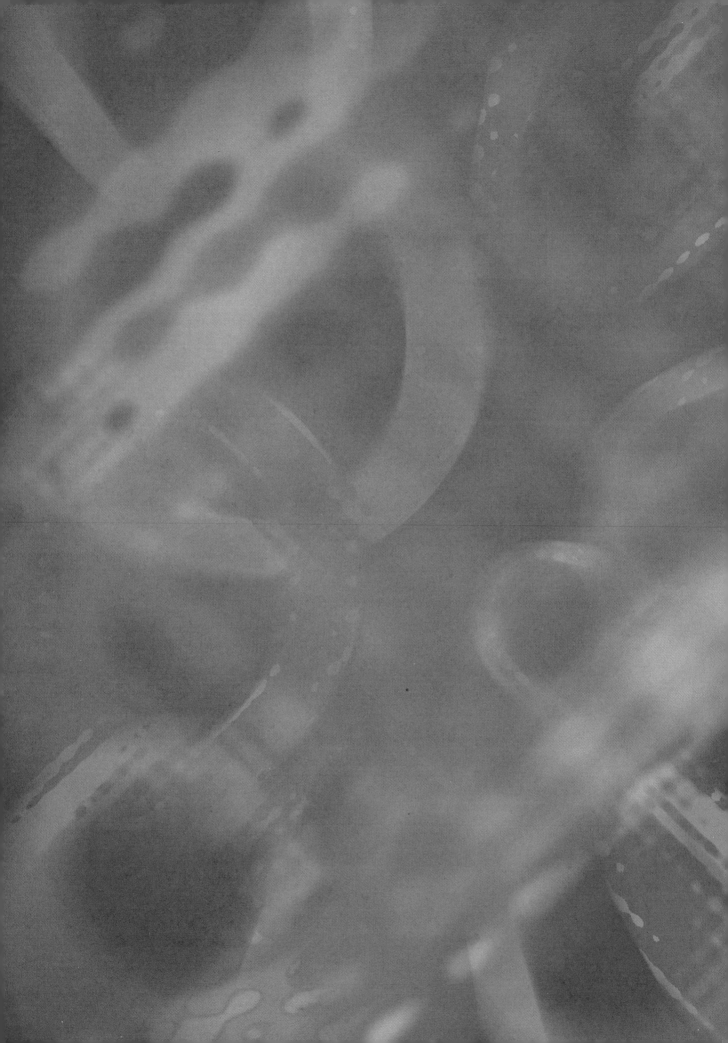

Performance

Unit 2 PA

Assessments

EXCEL

ASSESSING CORE PROFICIENCIES

In this unit, you have learned to create, save, print, edit, and format Excel worksheets. You have also learned how to work with multiple windows; move, copy, and paste data between programs; insert a clip art image in a Word document or Excel worksheet; download a clip art image from the on-line Microsoft Clip Gallery; and create a map with data in an Excel worksheet.

Assessment one

1. Create the Excel worksheet shown in figure U2.1. Format the cells as you see them in the figure. (Include a formula in cell D3 that subtracts the Quota sales from the Actual sales. Copy the formula down to D9.)
2. Save the completed worksheet and name it Excel Unit 2, PA 01.
3. Print the worksheet with gridlines and centered horizontally and vertically on the page.
4. Close Excel Unit 2, PA 01.

	A	B	C	D	E
1	SALES QUOTA REPORT				
2	Salesperson	Quota	Actual	Over/(Under)	
3	Chavis	$ 55,000	$ 63,450		
4	Hampton	$ 85,000	$ 74,000		
5	Martindale	$ 48,000	$ 51,250		
6	Enriquez	$ 93,000	$ 86,300		
7	Gorham	$ 45,000	$ 42,350		
8	Kline	$ 75,000	$ 78,560		
9	McGuinness	$ 65,000	$ 71,450		

Figure U2.1 • Assessment 1

Assessment 2

1. Open Excel Unit 2, PA 01.
2. Save the worksheet with Save As and name it Excel Unit 2, PA 02.
3. Make the following changes to the worksheet:
   a. Add a row above row 7.
   b. Key the following data in the specified cells:

A7	=	**Dillinger**
B7	=	**95,000**
C7	=	**89,650**

   c. Make cell E2 the active cell and then key **% of Quota**.
   d. Insert a formula in cell E3 that divides the actual amount by the quota. Copy this formula down to the other cells. (The result will be a decimal point. Select the decimal numbers that are a result of the formula and then click the Percent Style button on the Formatting toolbar.)
   e. Select cells A1 through E10 and then apply an autoformat of your choosing.
4. Save the worksheet again with the same name (Excel Unit 2, PA 02).
5. Print and then close Excel Unit 2, PA 02.

Assessment 3

1. Open Excel Unit 2, PA 02.
2. Save the worksheet with Save As and name it Excel Unit 2, PA 03.
3. Sort the names of the salespersons alphabetically in ascending order.
4. Save the worksheet again with the same name (Excel Unit 2, PA 03).
5. Print Excel Unit 2, PA 03, centered horizontally and vertically on the page.
6. Sort the quota amounts in column B in descending order.
7. Save the worksheet again with the same name (Excel Unit 2, PA 03).
8. Print Excel Unit 2, PA 03, centered horizontally and vertically on the page.
9. Close Excel Unit 2, PA 03.

Assessment 4

1. Open Excel Worksheet 06.
2. Save the worksheet with Save As and name it Excel Unit 2, PA 04.
3. Make the following changes to the worksheet:
   a. Delete row 2.
   b. Insert a formula to average test scores for each student.
   c. Sort the data in the worksheet by the average test scores in *ascending* order.
   d. Select all cells in the worksheet and then change the font to 11-point Tahoma (or a similar sans serif typeface).
   e. Automatically adjust the widths of columns A through N.
   f. Add shading (you determine the color) to the first row.

g. Create the header *Student Test Scores* that prints at the top center on both pages.

h. Create a footer that prints *Page x* (where *x* represents the correct page number) at the bottom center on both pages.

4. Save the worksheet again with the same name (Excel Unit 2, PA 04).

5. Print the worksheet so the column titles (names) print on both pages.

6. Close Excel Unit 2, PA 04.

Assessment 5

1. Open Excel Worksheet 17.

2. Save the worksheet with Save As and name it Excel Unit 2, PA 05.

3. Complete the following steps:

a. Select cells A1 through C11 and then copy the cells to *Sheet2*.

b. With *Sheet2* displayed, make the following changes:

1) Automatically adjust the width of columns A, B, and C.

2) Delete the contents of cell B2.

3) Change the contents of the following cells:
   A6: Change *January* to *July*
   A7: Change *February* to *August*
   A8: Change *March* to *September*
   A9: Change *April* to *October*
   A10: Change *May* to *November*
   A11: Change *June* to *December*
   B6: Change *8.30%* to *8.10%*
   B8: Change *9.30%* to *8.70%*

c. Make *Sheet1* active and then copy cell B2 and paste link it to cell B2 in *Sheet2*.

d. Make *Sheet1* active and then determine the effect on projected monthly earnings if the projected yearly income is increased by 10%.

4. Save the workbook (two worksheets) again with the same name (Excel Unit 2, PA 05).

5. Print both worksheets of the workbook so they are centered horizontally and vertically on each page.

6. Determine the effect on projected monthly earnings if the projected yearly income is increased by 20%.

7. Save the workbook again with the same name (Excel Unit 2, PA 05).

8. Print both worksheets of the workbook so they are centered horizontally and vertically on each page.

9. Close Excel Unit 2, PA 05.

Assessment 6

1. Open Excel Worksheet 36.

2. Save the worksheet with Save As and name it Excel Unit 2, PA 06.

3. Using the DATE function, enter a formula in each of the specified cells that returns the serial number for the specified date:

C5	=	February 6, 2001
C6	=	February 8, 2001
C7	=	March 2, 2001
C8	=	March 2, 2001

4. Enter a formula in cell E5 that inserts the due date (date of service plus the number of days in the Terms column).
5. Make cell A10 active and then key your name.
6. Make cell A11 active and then use the NOW function to insert the current date as a serial number.
7. Save the worksheet again with the same name (Excel Unit 2, PA 06).
8. Print and then close Excel Unit 2, PA 06.

Assessment seven

1. Plan and prepare a worksheet with the information shown in figure U2.2. Apply formatting of your choosing to the worksheet either with an autoformat or with formatting at the Format Cells dialog box.
2. Save the completed worksheet and name it Excel Unit 2, PA 07.
3. Print and then close Excel Unit 2, PA 07.

Prepare a weekly summary of orders taken that itemizes the product coming into the company and the average order size.

The products and average order size include:

Black and gold wall clock—$2,450 worth of orders, average order size of $125
Traveling alarm clock—$1,358 worth of orders, average order size of $195
Waterproof watch—$890 worth of orders, average order size of $90
Dashboard clock—$2,135 worth of orders, average order size of $230
Pyramid clock—$3,050 worth of orders, average order size of $375
Gold chain watch—$755 worth of orders, average order size of $80

In the worksheet, total the amount ordered, and also calculate the average weekly order size. Sort the data in the worksheet by the order amount in descending order.

Figure U2.2 • Assessment 7

Assessment eight

1. Open Excel and then key the following information in a worksheet:

Country	Total Sales
Denmark	$85,345
Finland	$71,450
Norway	$135,230
Sweden	$118,895

2. Using the data just entered in the worksheet, create a column chart as a separate sheet.
3. Save the workbook (worksheet plus chart sheet) and name it Excel Unit 2, PA 08.
4. Print only the sheet containing the chart.
5. Change the column chart to a line chart of your choosing.
6. Save the worksheet (and chart) again with the same name (Excel Unit 2, PA 08).
7. Print only the sheet containing the chart.
8. Close Excel Unit 2, PA 08.

Assessment 9

1. Make Word the active program and then create a letterhead with the following specifications:
   a. Include the following information in the letterhead:
      Apex Designs
      3300 Northshore Drive
      Chicago, IL 60610
      (630) 555-8822
      http://www.apexdesigns.com
   b. Insert a clip art image in the document. You determine the image as well as the size and location of the image.
2. Save the completed letterhead document and name it Word Unit 2, PA 09.
3. Print and then close Word Unit 2, PA 09.

Assessment 10

1. With Word the active program, create a notice of a telecommunications workshop with the following specifications:
   a. Include the following information in the notice (you determine how to arrange the information and what to include):
      Telecommunications Workshop
      Sponsored by Nexus Enterprises
      February 15 and 16
      9:00 a.m. to 4:00 p.m.
      Jacksonville Seminar Center
      Room 225
      Workshop fee: $250
      Contact #: (616) 555-9880
   b. Set the text in a sans serif typeface of your choosing (you determine the type size).
   c. Insert a clip art image of your choosing. (Choose a clip art image that reflects the topic of the seminar.) Size and position the image in the document.
2. Save the completed notice document and name it Word Unit 2, PA 10.
3. Print and then close Word Unit 2, PA 10.

Assessment 11

1. With Word the active program, open Word Unit 2, PA 10.
2. Save the document with Save As and name it Word Unit 2, PA 11.
3. Delete the clip art image in the document and then use the same clip art image to create a watermark. Be sure to lighten the image so the text above the image can be read.
4. Save the document again with the same name (Word Unit 2, PA 11).
5. Print and then close Word Unit 2, PA 11.
6. Exit Word.

Assessment 12

1. With Excel the active program, open Excel Worksheet 40.
2. Save the worksheet with Save As and name it Excel Unit 2, PA 12.
3. Create a map like the one shown in figure U2.3 with the data in the worksheet with these specifications:
   a. Create a Canadian map.
   b. Increase the zoom to approximately 100%.
   c. Hide the title.
   d. Move the legend as shown in figure U2.3.
4. Save the worksheet again with the same name (Excel Unit 2, PA 12).
5. Print the worksheet (and map) centered horizontally and vertically on the page.
6. Close Excel Unit 2, PA 12.

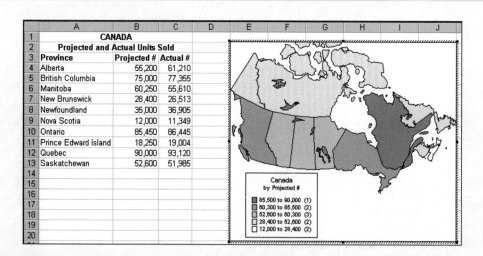

Figure U2.3 • Assessment 12

Assessment 13

1. With Excel the active program, open Excel Unit 2, PA 12.
2. Save the worksheet with Save As and name it Excel Unit 2, PA 13.
3. Make the following changes to the map:

a. Display the Microsoft Map Control dialog box and then change the data column from *Projected #* to *Actual #*.

b. At the Microsoft Map Control dialog box, change the shading button in the white area from Value Shading to Category Shading.

c. At the Format Properties dialog box with the Legend Options tab selected, change the title to *Actual Units Sold* and delete the subtitle.

4. Save the worksheet again with the same name (Excel Unit 2, PA 13).

5. Print the worksheet (and map) centered horizontally and vertically on the page.

6. Close Excel Unit 2, PA 13.

7. Exit Excel.

WRITING ACTIVITIES

The following activities give you the opportunity to practice your writing skills along with demonstrating an understanding of some of the important Word and Excel features you have mastered in this unit. (Refer to the steps in The Writing Process section of the Unit 1 Composing Activities.) Use correct grammar, appropriate word choices, and clear sentence constructions.

Activity one

Suppose that you are the accounting assistant in the financial department of McCormack Funds and you have been asked to prepare a yearly proposed department budget. The total amount for the department is $1,450,000. You are given the percentages for the proposed budget items, which are: Salaries, 45%; Benefits, 12%; Training, 14%; Administrative Costs, 10%; Equipment, 11%; and Supplies, 8%. Create a worksheet with this information that shows the projected yearly budget, the budget items in the department, the percentage of the budget, and the amount for each item. After the worksheet is completed, save it and name it Unit 2, Act 01. Print and then close Unit 2, Act 01.

Activity two

Prepare a worksheet in Excel for Carefree Travels that includes the following information:

Scandinavian Tours

Country	Tours Booked
Norway	52
Sweden	62
Finland	29
Denmark	38

Use the information in the worksheet to create a bar chart as a separate worksheet. Save the workbook (worksheet and chart) and name it Unit 2, Act 02. Print only the sheet containing the chart. Close Unit 2, Act 02.

Activity 3

Suppose you are the manager of a travel agency named Carefree Travels. Prepare a letterhead for your agency in Word that includes (but is not limited to) the following:

- Agency name: Carefree Travels
- Agency address: 1105 Sunset Drive, Phoenix, AZ 89022
- Agency telephone number: (602) 555-3344
- Include an appropriate clip art image in the letterhead

Save the letterhead and name it Unit 2, Act 03. Print and then close Unit 2, Act 03.

Activity 4

Prepare an announcement in Word for Carefree Travels that advertises a snow skiing trip. Include the following information in the announcement:

Include the following text (you can edit the text as you see fit):

Ski the Slopes of Whistler

Picture the crystal clear blue sky, the glistening snow-covered mountains, and the cool alpine air. Whistler offers some of North America's most scenic skiing, with an average annual snow pack of more than 20 feet. This is your opportunity to reserve a path down the slopes at such nationally acclaimed ski resorts such as LaJolla and Mystique. You can book your vacation today at special discount prices.

Include the following bulleted items:

- Round-trip air transportation
- Seven nights' hotel accommodations
- Four all-day ski passes.
- Compact rental car with unlimited mileage.

A bonus feature includes a two-for-one discount at many of the local ski resorts, including ski passes and ski school.

The total price of the ski package is $1,150 (double occupancy).

Include an appropriate clip art image (consider downloading an image from the on-line Microsoft Clip Gallery) in the announcement. Save the completed announcement and name it Unit 2, Act 04. Print and then close Unit 2, Act 04.

INTERNET ACTIVITY

Make sure you are connected to the Internet and then explore at least three of the sites listed below. Take notes on which part of the site was the most helpful and interesting to you. (*Note: Web sites change. If you get an error message telling you that you have reached a site that is no longer active or has changed its address, connect to the search directory site www.search-beat.com. Click* Travel Directory *in the* Themes *list box [you will need to scroll down the list to display this option] and then use resources from this site to jump to various country sites.*)

- www.africanet.com
- www.france.com
- www.okspain.org
- www.portugal.org
- www.tourindia.com

In Word, prepare a memo on the sites you visited that addresses the following:

- Compare how the sites are organized. Which site was the most helpful for actually planning a trip? Why? Though organized differently, do they offer essentially the same information or very different information?
- Which site had the most persuasive advertisements and photos? Were any so persuasive or enticing that they changed your mind about where you want to travel?
- What sites taught you the most about the geography, culture, and people of the country?

In Excel, create a travel planning worksheet for three countries you would like to visit. Include the following information in the worksheet:

- airline costs
- hotel costs (off-season and in-season rates if available)
- estimated meal costs
- entertainment costs
- car rental costs

If you cannot find specific information from all sites, leave the column(s) blank.

PowerPoint

UNIT THREE

MICROSOFT® PowerPoint 2000

CORE LEVEL MOUS SKILLS

Coding No.	SKILL	Pages
PP2000.1	Creating a presentation	
PP2000.1.1	Delete slides	623-625
PP2000.1.2	Create a specified type of slide	585-587, 593-594
PP2000.1.3	Create a presentation from a template and/or a Wizard	585-587, 593-594, 595-596
PP2000.1.4	Navigate among different views (slide, outline, sorter, tri-pane)	597
PP2000.1.5	Create a new presentation from existing slides	603
PP2000.1.6	Copy a slide from one presentation into another	624-626
PP2000.1.7	Insert headers and footers	661-665
PP2000.1.8	Create a Blank presentation	655-656
PP2000.1.9	Create a presentation using the AutoContent Wizard	595-596
PP2000.1.10	Send a presentation via e-mail	702-703
PP2000.2	Modifying a presentation	
PP2000.2.1	Change the order of slides using Slide Sorter view	627, 630
PP2000.2.2	Find and replace text	622-624
PP2000.2.3	Change the layout for one or more slides	697-698
PP2000.2.4	Change slide layout (Modify the Slide Master)	635-638
PP2000.2.5	Modify slide sequence in the outline pane	626, 630
PP2000.2.6	Apply a design template	653-654
PP2000.3	Working with text	
PP2000.3.1	Check spelling	628-629
PP2000.3.2	Change and replace text fonts (individual slide and entire presentation)	633, 635-637, 646, 648
PP2000.3.3	Enter text in tri-pane view	593-594
PP2000.3.4	Import Text from Word	696-698
PP2000.3.5	Change the text alignment	633, 637-638
PP2000.3.6	Create a text box for entering text	644-647
PP2000.3.7	Use the Wrap text in TextBox feature	644-647
PP2000.3.8	Use the Office Clipboard	698-699
PP2000.3.9	Use the Format Painter	655-656
PP2000.3.10	Promote and Demote text in slide & outline panes	609-611, 655-656
PP2000.4	Working with visual elements	
PP2000.4.1	Add a picture from the ClipArt Gallery	681-683
PP2000.4.2	Add and group shapes using WordArt or the Drawing Toolbar	647-649, 714-722
PP2000.4.3	Apply formatting	632-638
PP2000.4.4	Place text inside a shape using a text box	644-647
PP2000.4.5	Scale and size an object including ClipArt	681-683
PP2000.4.6	Create tables within PowerPoint	690-691
PP2000.4.7	Rotate and fill an object	647-649
PP2000.5	Customizing a presentation	
PP2000.5.1	Add AutoNumber bullets	659-661
PP2000.5.2	Add speaker notes	663-665
PP2000.5.3	Add graphical bullets	658-661
PP2000.5.4	Add slide transitions	601-603
PP2000.5.5	Animate text and objects	675-681
PP2000.6	Creating output	
PP2000.6.1	Preview presentation in black and white	592, 594
PP2000.6.2	Print slides in a variety of formats	587-592, 594, 596, 600
PP2000.6.3	Print audience handouts	594
PP2000.6.4	Print speaker notes in a specified format	665
PP2000.7	Delivering a presentation	
PP2000.7.1	Start a slide show on any slide	599-601
PP2000.7.2	Use on screen navigation tools	599-601
PP2000.7.3	Print a slide as an overhead transparency	655-656
PP2000.7.4	Use the pen during a presentation	599, 601
PP2000.8	Managing files	
PP2000.8.1	Save changes to a presentation	603, 606
PP2000.8.2	Save as a new presentation	585, 592
PP2000.8.3	Publish a presentation to the Web	699-702
PP2000.8.4	Use Office Assistant	596
PP2000.8.5	Insert hyperlink	691-695

Chapter 14

Preparing a PowerPoint Presentation

PERFORMANCE OBJECTIVES

Upon successful completion of chapter 14, you will be able to:

- Plan a PowerPoint presentation.
- Create a PowerPoint presentation.
- Print a PowerPoint presentation.
- Save, open, and close presentations.
- View and preview a presentation.
- Run a presentation.
- Use the pen during a presentation.
- Add transitions and sound effects to a presentation.
- Run a slide show automatically.
- Set and rehearse timings for a presentation.
- Prepare a presentation in Outline view.
- Delete a presentation.

During a presentation, the person doing the presenting may use visual aids to strengthen the impact of the message as well as help organize the presentation. Visual aids may include transparencies, slides, photographs, or an on-screen presentation. With Microsoft's PowerPoint program, you can easily create visual aids for a presentation and then print copies of the aids as well as run the presentation. PowerPoint is a presentation graphics program that you can use to organize and present information.

PowerPoint provides a variety of output capabilities for presentations. A presentation prepared in PowerPoint can be run directly on the computer. In addition, black and white overheads can be created by printing slides on transparencies, or, color transparencies can be created if you have access to a color printer. Slides can be created in PowerPoint and then sent to a film processing company to be converted to 35mm slides. Also, printouts of slides can be made for use as speaker's notes, audience handouts, or outline pages.

Planning a Presentation

With PowerPoint, you can create slides for an on-screen presentation, or for an overhead or slide projector. You can also print handouts of the presentation, print an outline, or print the entire presentation. When planning a presentation, first define the purpose of the presentation. Is the intent to inform? educate? sell? motivate? and/or entertain? Additionally, consider the audience who will be listening to and watching the presentation. Determine the content of the presentation and also the medium that will be used to convey the message. Will a computer be used to display the slides of a presentation or will overhead transparencies be created from the slides? Basic guidelines to consider when preparing the content of the presentation include:

- **Determine the main purpose of the presentation.** Do not try to cover too many topics—this may strain the audience's attention or cause confusion. Identifying the main point of the presentation will help you stay focused and convey a clear message to the audience.
- **Determine the output:** Is the presentation going to be presented in PowerPoint? will slides be used? or will black and white or color transparencies be made for an overhead? To help decide the type of output needed, consider the availability of equipment, the size of the room where the presentation will be made, and the number of people who will be attending the presentation.
- **Show one idea per slide.** Each slide in a presentation should convey only one main idea. Too many thoughts or ideas on a slide may confuse the audience and cause you to stray from the purpose of the slide. Determine the specific message you want to convey to the audience then outline the message to organize ideas.
- **Maintain a consistent layout.** A consistent layout and color scheme for slides in a presentation will create continuity and cohesiveness. Do not get carried away by using too many colors and too many pictures or other graphic elements.
- **Keep slides easy to read and uncluttered.** Keep slides simple and easy for the audience to read. Keep words and other items such as bullets to a minimum. If the presentation is done with 35mm slides, consider using a dark background color for slides. Use a light background color when creating overhead transparencies.
- **Determine the output needed:** Will you be providing audience members with handouts? If so, will these handouts consist of a printing of each slide? an outline of the presentation? or a printing of each slide with space for taking notes?

Creating a PowerPoint Presentation

PowerPoint provides several methods for creating a presentation. You can use PowerPoint's AutoContent Wizard, which asks questions and then chooses a presentation layout based on your answers. You can also create a presentation using predesigned templates. PowerPoint's templates provide a variety of formatting options for slides. If you want to apply your own formatting to slides, you can choose a blank presentation. The steps you follow to create a presentation will vary depending on the method you choose. There are, however, basic steps you will complete. These steps are:

1. Open PowerPoint.
2. Choose a slide template (or choose a blank template if you want to apply your own formatting) or use PowerPoint's AutoContent Wizard.
3. Key the text for each slide, adding additional elements as needed such as graphic images.
4. Save the presentation.
5. Print the presentation as slides, handouts, notes pages, or an outline.
6. Run the presentation.
7. Close the presentation.
8. Exit PowerPoint.

Understanding the PowerPoint Window

When PowerPoint has been opened and you have chosen the specific type of presentation you want to create, you are presented with the PowerPoint window in the Normal view. What displays in the window will vary depending on what type of presentation you are creating. However, there are consistent elements of the PowerPoint window. Figure 14.1 contains callouts specifying the various elements of the PowerPoint window. These elements are described after the figure.

figure
14.1

PowerPoint Window

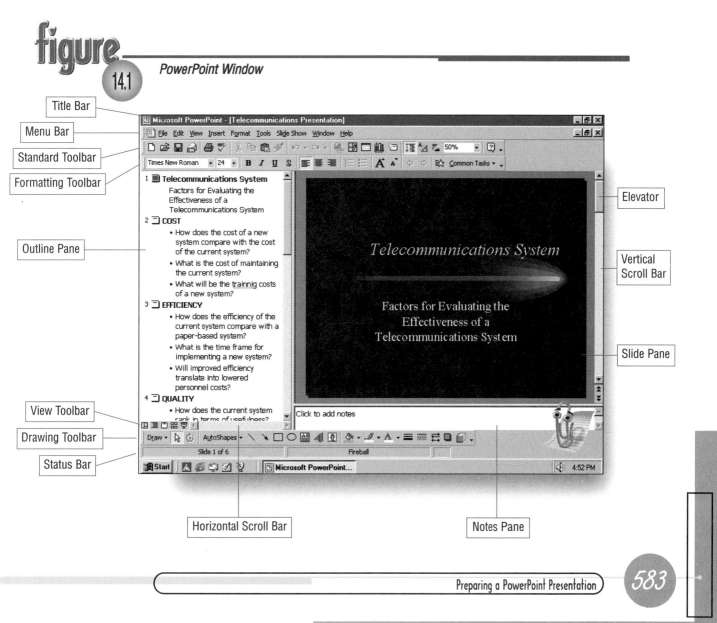

The PowerPoint window contains many elements that are similar to other Microsoft applications such as Word and Excel. For example, the PowerPoint window, like the Word window, contains a Title bar, Menu bar, Standard and Formatting toolbars, scroll bars, and a Status bar. The elements of the PowerPoint window include:

- **Title bar:** This bar displays the program name, a document title, a control menu, the Close button, and the Minimize and Restore buttons for resizing the window.
- **Menu bar:** PowerPoint commands are grouped into options that display on the Menu bar. For example, options for formatting slides can be found at the Format drop-down menu.
- **Standard toolbar:** This toolbar contains buttons for the most frequently used commands in PowerPoint such as cutting, copying, and pasting text; inserting hyperlinks, tables, and charts; and changing the zoom display.
- **Formatting toolbar:** Frequently used commands for formatting a PowerPoint presentation are grouped onto the Formatting toolbar. This toolbar contains options such as changing typeface and size, increasing and decreasing type size, adding type styles such as bold and italics, changing paragraph alignment, and adding animation effects.
- **Drawing toolbar:** With buttons on the Drawing toolbar, you can draw objects such as lines, arcs, and shapes. Buttons on this toolbar also contain options for adding attributes to objects, such as color, shading, and shadow.
- **Outline pane:** The contents of a presentation display in the Outline pane. At this pane, you can organize and develop the contents of the presentation. In a completed presentation, the Outline pane becomes the table of contents for the presentation.
- **Slide pane:** The slide pane is where slides are created and displayed. Here you can see how text looks on each slide and add elements such as clip art images, hyperlinks, and animation effects.
- **Notes pane:** Add notes to a presentation in the Notes pane.
- **Vertical scroll bar:** Use the vertical scroll bar to display specific slides in a presentation. The small box located on the vertical scroll bar is called the *elevator*. Drag the elevator on the vertical scroll bar and a yellow box displays specifying the slide number within the presentation. Use the elevator to move quickly to a specific slide.
- **Horizontal scroll bar:** The Outline pane contains a horizontal scroll bar you can use to shift text left or right in the Outline pane.
- **View toolbar:** The View toolbar, located at the left side of the horizontal scroll bar, contains buttons for changing the presentation view. For example, you can view individual slides, view several slides at once, view slide information as an outline, and also run the presentation.
- **Status bar:** Messages about PowerPoint features display in the Status bar, which is located toward the bottom of the PowerPoint window. The Status bar also displays information about the view.

PowerPoint, like other Microsoft applications, provides ScreenTips for buttons on toolbars. Position the arrow pointer on a button on any of the PowerPoint toolbars, and a ScreenTip displays (after one second) for the button.

Creating a Presentation Using a Template

To create a presentation using a PowerPoint template, you would complete the following steps:

1. Open PowerPoint by clicking the Start button on the Windows Taskbar, pointing to Programs, and then clicking *Microsoft PowerPoint*.
2. At the PowerPoint dialog box shown in figure 14.2, select Design Template, and then click OK.
3. At the New Presentation dialog box shown in figure 14.3, make sure the Design Templates tab is selected. (If not, click the Design Templates tab.)
4. At the New Presentation dialog box with the Design Templates tab selected, click the desired template (the template displays in the Preview box at the right side of the dialog box), and then click OK. You can also double-click the desired template.
5. At the New Slide dialog box shown in figure 14.4, click the desired autolayout, and then click OK.
6. Key the desired text and/or insert the desired elements in the slide.
7. To create another slide, click the New Slide button on the PowerPoint Standard toolbar, and then double-click the desired autolayout.
8. When all slides have been completed, save the presentation by clicking the Save button on the Standard toolbar. At the Save As dialog box, key a name for the presentation, and then click Save.

Design templates provided by PowerPoint were designed by professional graphic artists who understand the use of color, space, and design.

Use the Blank Presentation template if you want complete control over the presentation design.

New Slide

Save

figure

14.2

PowerPoint Dialog Box

At this dialog box, choose the AutoContent Wizard, a design template, a blank presentation, or open an existing presentation.

figure
14.3

New Presentation Dialog Box

Choose a design
template from
this list and then
preview it at the
right.

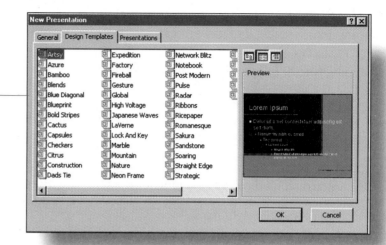

figure
14.4

New Slide Dialog Box

Click the desired
autolayout and
then click OK or
double-click the
desired autolayout.

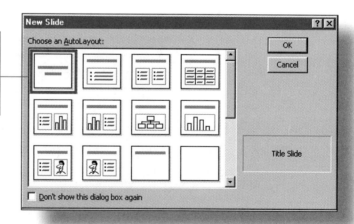

When you choose an autolayout format at the New Slide dialog box, each slide will probably contain placeholders. A placeholder is a location on the slide where information is to be entered. For example, many slides contain a title placeholder. Click in this placeholder and then key the title of the slide. When text is entered into a placeholder, the placeholder turns into a text object. An autolayout format may include some or all of the following placeholders:

- **Title:** Used to hold the title of the slide.
- **Bulleted List:** Used for a bulleted list of related points or topics.
- **Clip Art:** Holds a picture, such as a clip art image, in a slide.
- **Chart:** Holds a chart, which is a visual representation of data.
- **Organization Chart:** Used to display an organizational chart in a slide.
- **Table:** Used for a table that is inserted from Microsoft Word.

Choose a template design at the New Presentation dialog box with the Design Templates tab selected as shown in figure 14.3. Display this dialog box when you first open PowerPoint by clicking Design Template at the PowerPoint dialog box. To display this dialog box if PowerPoint is already open, click File and then New. This displays the New Presentation dialog box where you can click the Design Templates tab.

Printing a Presentation

A presentation can be printed in a variety of formats. You can print each slide on a separate piece of paper; print each slide at the top of the page, leaving the bottom of the page for notes; print up to six slides or a specific number of slides on a single piece of paper; or print the slide titles and topics in outline form. Use the Print what option at the Print dialog box to specify what you want printed.

To display the Print dialog box, shown in figure 14.5, click File and then Print. At the Print dialog box, click the down-pointing triangle at the right side of the Print what text box, and then click the desired printing format.

> Autolayouts make arranging elements in a slide easier.

> Scroll down the Choose an AutoLayout list box to view additional autolayouts.

> Printing a hard copy of your presentation helps reinforce your message.

figure
14.5 *Print Dialog Box*

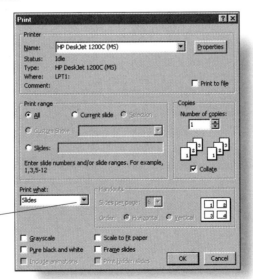

Click the down-pointing triangle to display a list of printing options.

As an example of what will print with the printing options, look at figures 14.6, 14.7, 14.8, and 14.9. Figure 14.6 shows the printing of the slides you will create in exercise 1 with the *Slides* option selected in the Print what text box at the Print dialog box. As you can see, each slide is printed on a separate piece of paper. Figure 14.7 shows the presentation as it will print when *Handouts* is selected and the Slides per page option in the Handouts is set at the default of *6*. The printing in figure 14.8 shows the slides printed in the *Notes Pages* format. At this printing, the slides are printed at the top of the page, leaving room at the bottom of the page for notes. The last printing figure, figure 14.9, shows the printing of the presentation in the *Outline View*.

figure

14.6 *Printing with Slides Selected at Print dialog box*

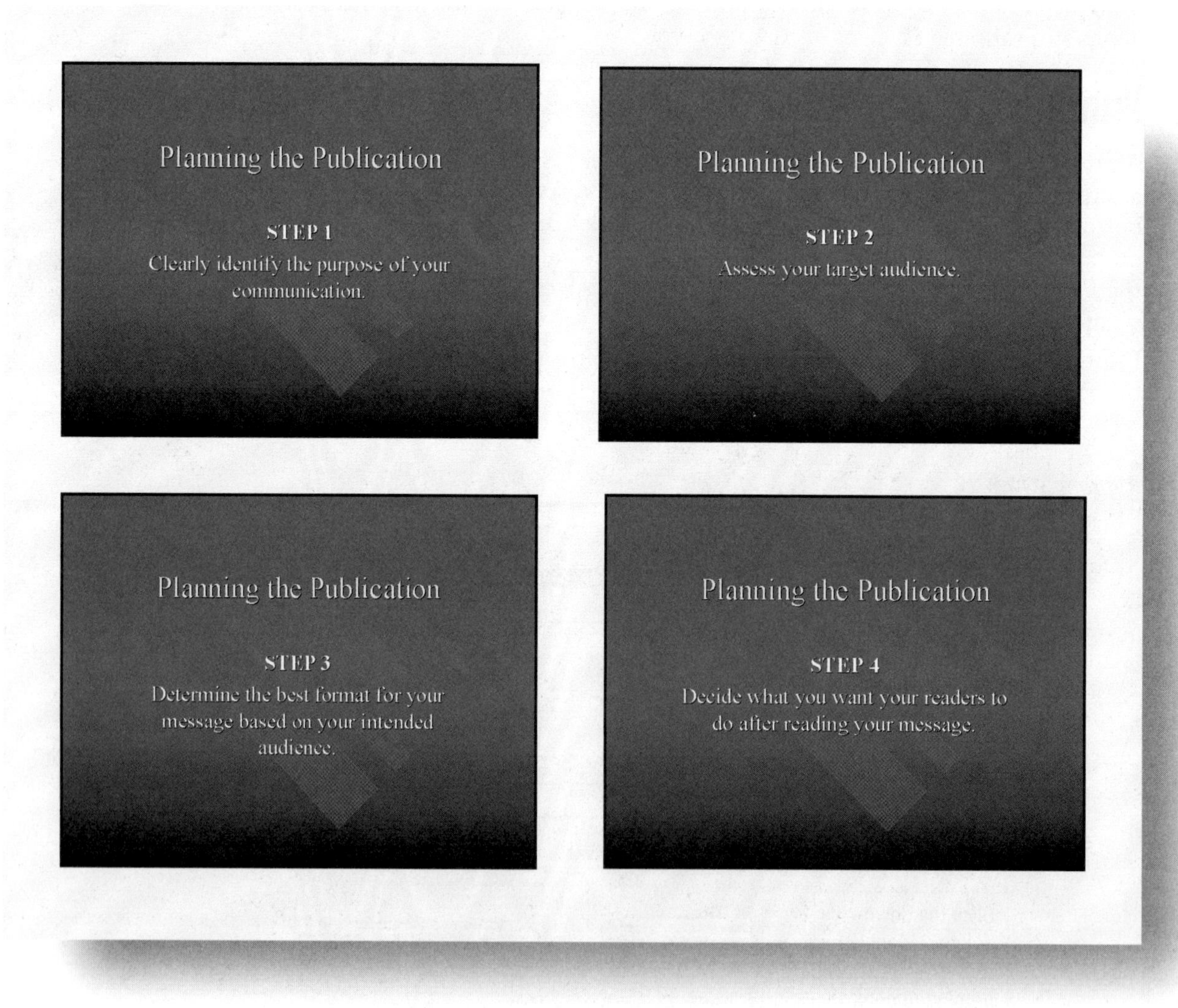

Fig. 14.6 continued

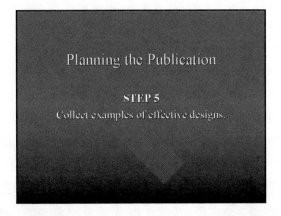

figure
14.7

Printing with Handouts Selected at Print Dialog Box

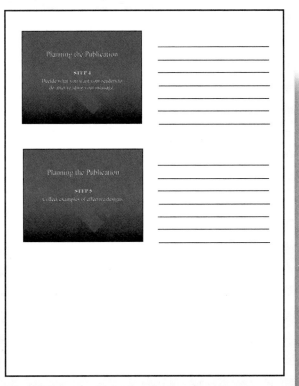

figure 14.8

Printing with Notes Pages Selected at Print Dialog Box

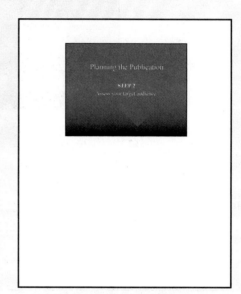

fig 14.8 continued

figure
14.9

Printing with Outline View Selected at Print Dialog Box

1. Planning the Publication
   STEP 1
   Clearly identify the purpose of your communication.
2. Planning the Publication
   STEP 2
   Assess your target audience.
3. Planning the Publication
   STEP 3
   Determine the best format for your message based on your intended audience.
4. Planning the Publication
   STEP 4
   Decide what you want your readers to do after reading your message.
5. Planning the Publication
   STEP 5
   Collect examples of effective designs.

Printing a Presentation in Grayscale and Black and White

If you do not have access to a color printer or if you are going to photocopy slides and/or notes on a black and white photocopier, consider printing slides in grayscale or black and white. To do this, display the Print dialog box and then choose either Grayscale or Pure black and white. These options display in the lower left corner of the Print dialog box.

Previewing in Grayscale and Black and White

Grayscale
Preview

Before printing in grayscale or black and white, consider previewing the slides. Preview slides in grayscale by clicking the Grayscale Preview button on the Standard toolbar. If you are in Normal or Slide view, the slide displays in grayscale and a miniature slide displays showing the color formatting. Turn off Grayscale Preview by clicking the button again. If you want to preview slides in pure black and white (with no shades of gray), hold down the Shift key and then click the Grayscale Preview button.

Saving a Presentation

After creating a presentation, save it by clicking File and then Save or by clicking the Save button on the Standard toolbar. This displays the Save As dialog box. By default, a PowerPoint presentation is saved to the *My Documents* folder. To save a presentation in the *Chapter 14* folder on your disk, you will need to change the active folder (just as you did in Word). To change to your disk that is located in drive A, click the down-pointing triangle to the right of the Save in text box, and then click *3½ Floppy (A:)*. With drive A the active folder, double-click the *Chapter 14* folder. After changing the folder, key the presentation document name in the File name text box, and then click Save or press Enter.

Closing a Presentation

After creating, viewing, and/or printing a presentation, close the presentation. To do this click, the Close button at the right side of the Menu bar or click File and then Close. If any changes were made to the presentation that were not saved, you will be asked if you want to save the changes.

Completing Computer Exercises

In previous chapters you have been copying a chapter folder from the CD that accompanies this textbook to your disk. In chapters in this unit you will copy a chapter folder to your disk and you will also be opening presentations from a folder on the CD. Presentations, particularly presentations containing images, can be quite large in size and take up considerable amount of space on your disk. For this reason, you will be instructed to open some presentations from the *Presentations* folder on the CD that accompanies this textbook.

Creating and Printing a Presentation

1. Prepare a presentation on the steps for planning a publication by completing the following steps:
   a. Open PowerPoint by clicking the Start button on the Windows Taskbar, pointing to Programs, and then clicking *Microsoft PowerPoint*.
   b. At the PowerPoint dialog box, click Design Template, and then click OK.
   c. At the New Presentation dialog box, click the Design Templates tab (if necessary).
   d. At the New Presentation dialog box with the Design Templates tab selected, double-click the *Blue Diagonal* template.
   e. At the New Slide dialog box, double-click the first autolayout in the list box. (The first autolayout is named Title Slide. The autolayout name displays in the lower right corner of the dialog box.)
   f. At the slide, click anywhere in the text *Click to add title*, and then key **Planning the Publication**.
   g. Click anywhere in the text *Click to add subtitle* and then key the following:
      1) Turn on bold, key **STEP 1**, and then turn off bold.
      2) Press Enter and then key **Clearly identify the purpose of your communication**.
   h. Click the New Slide button located on the Standard toolbar.
   i. At the New Slide dialog box, double-click the first autolayout (Title Slide) in the list box. (This inserts another slide in the Presentation window.)
   j. Complete steps similar to those in 1f and 1g to create the following text (do not key the text [(*press Enter*)]; this is an instruction):
      Title   =   **Planning the Publication**
      Subtitle   =   **STEP 2** (*press Enter*)
                          Assess your target audience.
   k. Click the New Slide button located on the Standard toolbar.
   l. At the New Slide dialog box, double-click the first autolayout (*Title Slide*) in the list box.
   m. Complete steps similar to those in 1f and 1g to create the following text:
      Title   =   **Planning the Publication**
      Subtitle   =   **STEP 3** (*press Enter*)
                          Determine the best format for your message based on your intended audience.
   n. Click the New Slide button located on the Standard toolbar.
   o. At the New Slide dialog box, double-click the first autolayout (*Title Slide*) in the list box.
   p. Complete steps similar to those in 1f and 1g to create the following text:
      Title   =   **Planning the Publication**
      Subtitle   =   **STEP 4** (*press Enter*)
                          Decide what you want your readers to do after reading your message.

The image shows a slide titled "Planning the Publication" with "STEP 1" and "Clearly identify the purpose of your communication." Labels point to Step 1f and Step 1g.

q. Click the New Slide button located on the Standard toolbar.

r. At the New Slide dialog box, double-click the first autolayout (Title Slide) in the list box.

s. Complete steps similar to those in 1f and 1g to create the following text:

Title = **Planning the Publication**
Subtitle = **STEP 5** *(press Enter)*
Collect examples of effective designs.

t. Click in the slide outside the selected area. (This should deselect the box containing the subtitle.)

2. Save the presentation by completing the following steps:

a. Click the Save button on the Standard toolbar.

b. At the Save As dialog box, click the down-pointing triangle to the right of the Save in text box, and then click *3½ Floppy (A:)*.

c. Double-click the Chapter 14 folder.

d. Select the text in the File name text, key **Planning Presentation**, and then press Enter or click <u>S</u>ave.

3. Print all five slides on the same page by completing the following steps:

a. Click <u>F</u>ile and then <u>P</u>rint.

b. At the Print dialog box, click the down-pointing triangle to the right of the Print <u>w</u>hat option, and then click *Handouts* from the drop-down list.

c. Make sure the number *6* displays in the Slides pe<u>r</u> page text box in the Handouts section of the dialog box.

d. Click OK.

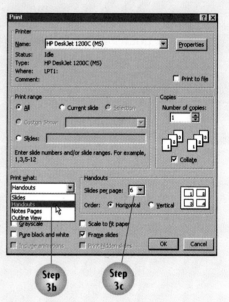

Step 3b   Step 3c

4. Preview and then print the slides in grayscale by completing the following steps:

a. Click the Grayscale Preview button on the Standard toolbar.

b. After viewing the presentation in grayscale, click the Grayscale Preview button to deactivate it.

c. Preview the presentation in pure black and white by holding down the Shift key and then clicking the Grayscale Preview button on the Standard toolbar.

d. Click the Grayscale Preview button again to deactivate it.

e. Print the five slides on one page in grayscale by completing the following steps:

1) Click <u>F</u>ile and then <u>P</u>rint.

2) At the Print dialog box, click the <u>G</u>rayscale option (located in the lower left corner of the dialog box).

3) Click the down-pointing triangle at the right of the Print <u>w</u>hat option and then click *Handouts* from the drop-down menu.

4) Make sure the number *6* displays in the Slides pe<u>r</u> page text box in the Handouts section of the dialog box.

5) Click OK.

5. Close Planning Presentation by clicking <u>F</u>ile and then <u>C</u>lose.

6. Exit PowerPoint by clicking <u>F</u>ile and then E<u>x</u>it.

Planning a Presentation with the AutoContent Wizard

PowerPoint contains an AutoContent Wizard that will help you in the planning and organizing of a presentation. You respond to certain questions from the Wizard and, based on your responses, the Wizard presents slides containing information on how to organize the presentation. For example, suppose you are an employee of an investment firm and have been asked to prepare a presentation on a variable annuity fund. You can use the AutoContent Wizard for help on how to organize this presentation. You will be doing this in exercise 2. The Wizard provides additional information on other types of presentations. Consider printing the information for these other presentations.

Getting Help from the AutoContent Wizard

1. Prepare slides for helping organize a presentation to market and sell a service by completing the following steps:
   a. Open PowerPoint by clicking the Start button on the Windows Taskbar, pointing to <u>P</u>rograms, and then clicking *Microsoft PowerPoint*.
   b. At the PowerPoint dialog box, click <u>A</u>utoContent Wizard, and then click OK. (If PowerPoint is already open, click <u>F</u>ile and then <u>N</u>ew. At the New Presentation dialog box with the General tab selected, double-click *AutoContent Wizard*.)
   c. At the AutoContent Wizard Start dialog box, click the <u>N</u>ext> button that displays toward the bottom right side of the dialog box.
   d. At the AutoContent Wizard Presentation type dialog box, click the gray button containing <u>S</u>ales/Marketing, click *Product/Services Overview* in the list box, and then click the <u>N</u>ext> button.

   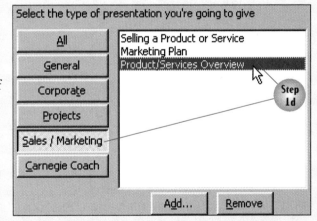

   e. At the AutoContent Wizard Presentation style dialog box, make sure the On-screen presentation option is selected, and then click the <u>N</u>ext> button.
   f. At the AutoContent Wizard Presentation options dialog box, make the following changes:

1) Click inside the Presentation title text box and then key **McCormack Annuity Funds**.
2) Press the Tab key. (This moves the insertion point to the Footer text box.)
3) Key **Variable Annuity Fund**.
4) Click the Next> button.

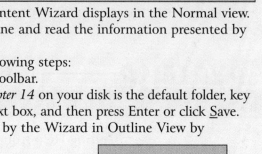

g. At the AutoContent Wizard Finish dialog box, click the Finish button.

h. The presentation created by the AutoContent Wizard displays in the Normal view. Scroll through the text in the Outline pane and read the information presented by the Wizard.

2. Save the presentation by completing the following steps:
   a. Click the Save button on the Standard toolbar.
   b. At the Save As dialog box, make sure *Chapter 14* on your disk is the default folder, key **Selling Presentation** in the File name text box, and then press Enter or click Save.

3. Print the information on the slides provided by the Wizard in Outline View by completing the following steps:
   a. Choose File and then Print.
   b. At the Print dialog box, click the down-pointing triangle to the right of the Print what option, and then click *Outline View* at the drop-down list.
   c. Click OK.

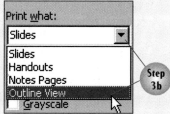

4. Close Selling Presentation. (If a dialog box displays asking if you want to save the changes, click Yes.)

5. Exit PowerPoint by clicking File and then Exit.

Using the Office Assistant

Like Word and Excel, PowerPoint contains an on-screen Help feature containing information about PowerPoint features and commands. You can use the Office Assistant to access this on-screen Help feature. To do this, click the Office Assistant or click Help and then Microsoft Excel Help. This causes a box to display above the Office Assistant. Key a question in the box about a specific PowerPoint feature and then click the Search button. The Office Assistant displays a list of topics related to the question. At this list, click the desired topic, and information will display in a Microsoft PowerPoint Help dialog box. After reading the information, click the Close button located in the upper right corner of the dialog box (contains an X). (For more information on the on-screen Help feature, refer to pages 82-87 in chapter 2.) For the last assessments in chapters 14, 15, and 16, you will be using the Office Assistant to find information on PowerPoint topics not covered in the chapters.

Opening a Presentation Document

Open

A saved presentation document can be opened at the Open dialog box. To display this dialog box, click File and then Open or click the Open button on the Standard toolbar. At the Open dialog box, double-click the desired presentation document in the list box.

Viewing a Presentation

PowerPoint provides a variety of viewing options for a presentation. The presentation view can be changed with options from the View drop-down menu or with viewing buttons that display on the View toolbar, shown in figure 14.10, located at the left side of the horizontal scroll bar. The viewing choices include:

- **Normal View:** This is the default view and displays three panes—outline, slide, and notes. With these three panes, you can work with all features in one place. This view is also referred to as tri-pane view.
- **Outline View:** The Outline view displays the organization of the presentation by headings and subheadings (see figure 14.9). Organize and develop the contents of the presentation in Outline view. Editing is probably easiest in this view since you simply click in the location you want to edit.
- **Slide View:** Use the Slide view to display individual slides. This view is useful for determining the effectiveness of elements that are positioned on the slide. Editing can also be performed in this view.
- **Slide Sorter View:** Choosing the Slide Sorter view displays all slides in the presentation in slide miniatures. In this view, you can easily add, move, rearrange, and delete slides.
- **Slide Show:** Use the Slide Show view to run a presentation. When you choose this view, the slide fills the entire screen.

A presentation displayed in Outline view makes organizing slides easy.

Key and edit text in individual slides in Slide view.

Quickly and easily reorganize slides in Slide Sorter view.

figure
14.10
View Toolbar

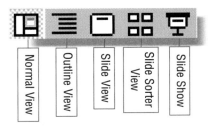

Normal View | Outline View | Slide View | Slide Sorter View | Slide Show

Change the view using either buttons on the View toolbar or options from the View drop-down menu. To use the View toolbar, click the desired button. To use the View option on the Menu bar, click View, and then click the desired view from the drop-down menu (except Outline view). The View drop-down menu contains the Notes Page option. Some presenters provide a hard copy of the information covered in the presentation. With PowerPoint, this can take the form of the slide printed at the top of the page with space available at the bottom of the page for the audience members to write notes. Choose the Notes Page view to see how the slide will display on the page along with the space for taking notes.

Previous Slide

Next Slide

In the Slide view, change slides by clicking the Previous Slide or Next Slide buttons located at the bottom of the vertical scroll bar. You can also change to a different slide by using the mouse pointer on the scroll box (called the *elevator*) on the vertical scroll bar. To do this, position the mouse pointer on the elevator, hold down the left mouse button, drag up or down until a yellow box displays with the desired slide number, and then release the mouse button. The keyboard can also be used to change to a different slide. Press the Page Down key to display the next slide in the presentation or press the Page Up key to display the previous slide in the presentation.

In addition to the Next Slide and Previous Slide buttons, you can use the Page Up and Page Down keys to move from one slide to another.

Running a Slide Show

Several methods can be used to run a slide show. Slides created in PowerPoint can be converted to 35mm slides or transparencies, or the computer screen can provide the output. An on-screen presentation saves the expense of producing slides, requires no projection equipment, and lets you use the computer's color capability.

If you are running a slide show in PowerPoint, there are several methods you can choose. You can run the slide show manually (you determine when to advance to the next slide), advance slides automatically, or set up a slide show to run continuously for demonstration purposes.

Slide Show

If you want to run a slide show manually, open the presentation, and then click the Slide Show button on the View toolbar or click <u>V</u>iew and then Slide Sho<u>w</u>. To control movement through slides in a slide show, refer to figure 14.11.

Commands for Controlling a Slide Show

To do this	Perform this action
Show next slide	Click left mouse button; or press one of the following keys: space bar, N, right arrow, down arrow, or Page Down
Show previous slide	Click right mouse button and then click desired direction at the pop-up menu; or press one of the following keys: Backspace, P, left arrow, up arrow, or Page Up
Show specific slide	Key slide number and then press Enter
Toggle mouse on or off	Key A or equal sign (=)
Switch between black screen and current slide	Key B or period (.)
Switch between white screen and current slide	Key W or comma (,)
End slide show and return to PowerPoint	Press one of the following keys: Esc, hyphen (-), or Ctrl + Break

Starting the Slide Show on any Slide

Click the Slide Show button on the View toolbar and the presentation begins with the currently active slide. To begin a slide show on any slide, make the desired slide active and then click the Slide Show button. If you want to begin the presentation with the first slide, make sure it is the active slide before clicking the Slide Show button.

Using the Pen During a Presentation

If you move the mouse when running a presentation, the *Slide Show* menu icon displays in the lower left corner of the slide. Click this icon and a pop-up menu displays as shown in figure 14.12.

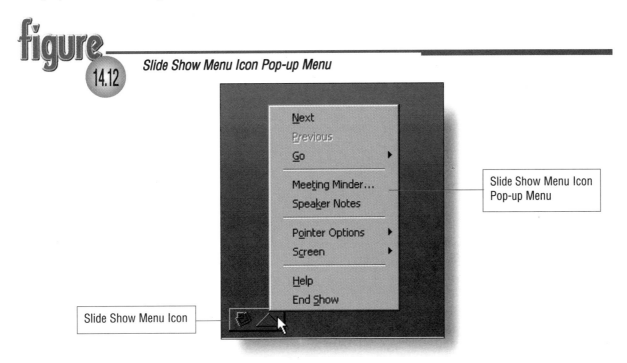

figure

14.12   *Slide Show Menu Icon Pop-up Menu*

Slide Show Menu Icon Pop-up Menu

Slide Show Menu Icon

With options at this pop-up menu, you can perform such actions as navigating within the presentation, keying speaker notes, displaying a pen, changing the screen display, getting help, and ending the presentation.

Emphasize major points or draw the attention of the audience to specific items in a slide during a presentation using the pen. To use the pen on a slide, run the presentation, and when the desired slide displays, move the mouse to display the *Slide Show* menu icon and then click the icon. At the pop-up menu that displays, point to Pointer Options, and then click Pen. This removes the pop-up menu and displays the mouse pointer as a pen. Use the pen to draw attention to specific items in the slide. If you want to draw a straight horizontal or vertical line with the pen, hold down the Shift key while drawing. Change the color of the pen by clicking the Slide Show menu icon, pointing to Pointer Options, pointing to Pen Color, and then clicking the desired color at the side menu.

If you want to erase the marks you made with the pen, click the *Slide Show* menu icon, point to Screen, and then click Erase Pen. The Erase Pen option is only available when the pen is selected. When you are finished with the pen, click the *Slide Show* menu icon, point to Pointer Options, and then click Automatic.

Viewing, Printing, and Running a Presentation

1. Open Planning Presentation by completing the following steps:
    a. Open PowerPoint.
    b. At the PowerPoint dialog box, click Cancel.
    c. With a blank Presentation window displayed, click the Open button on the Standard toolbar.
    d. At the Open dialog box, make sure *Chapter 14* on your disk is the default folder, and then double-click *Planning Presentation* in the list box.

2. With Planning Presentation open, change the views by completing the following steps:
    a. Change to the Slide view by clicking the Slide View button on the View toolbar (located at the left side of the horizontal scroll bar).
    b. Click the Next Slide button located at the bottom of the vertical scroll bar until Slide 5 is visible.
    c. Position the mouse pointer on the elevator (the scroll box) on the vertical scroll bar, hold down the left mouse button, drag the elevator to the top of the vertical scroll bar until a yellow box displays with *Slide 1* and the title of the slide, and then release the mouse button.
    d. Change to the Slide Sorter view by clicking the Slide Sorter View button on the View toolbar.

3. Print the presentation in outline view by completing the following steps:
    a. Choose <u>F</u>ile and then <u>P</u>rint.
    b. At the Print dialog box, change the Print <u>w</u>hat: option to *Outline View*.
    c. Click OK or press Enter.

4. Run the slide presentation on the screen by completing the following steps:
    a. In Slide Sorter view, click once on Slide 1. (This is to ensure that your slide show begins with the first slide.)
    b. Click the Slide Show button on the View toolbar. (This should cause *Slide 1* to display and fill the entire screen.)
    c. After viewing Slide 1, click the left mouse button. (This causes *Slide 2* to display.)
    d. Continue viewing and then clicking the left mouse button until all five slides have been viewed.
    e. At the black screen with the message *End of slide show, click to exit.*, click the left mouse button. This returns the presentation to the Slide Sorter view.

5. Run the presentation beginning with Slide 3 by completing the following steps:
    a. In Slide Sorter view, click Slide 3.
    b. Click the Slide Show button on the View toolbar.
    c. After viewing Slide 3, click the left mouse button.
    d. Continue viewing slides until the black screen displays. At this screen, click the left mouse button. (This returns the presentation to the Slide Sorter view.)

6. Run the presentation and use the pen to highlight specific words in the slides by completing the following steps:
   a. In Slide Sorter view, click Slide 1.
   b. Click the Slide Show button on the View toolbar.
   c. When Slide 1 displays, use the pen to underline a word by completing the following steps:
      1) Move the mouse to display the *Slide Show* menu icon.
      2) Click the *Slide Show* menu icon, point to Pointer Options, and then click Pen.
      3) Using the mouse, draw a circle around the text below *STEP 1*.
      4) Hold down the Shift key and then use the mouse to draw a horizontal line below the word *identify*.

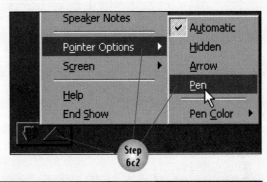

Step 6c2

      5) Erase the line by clicking the *Slide Show* menu icon, pointing to Screen, and then clicking Erase Pen.
      6) Change the color of the pen by clicking the *Slide Show* menu icon, pointing to Pointer Options, pointing to Pen Color, and then clicking Yellow.
      7) Hold down the Shift key and then use the mouse to draw a yellow line below the word *identify*.

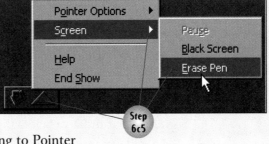

Step 6c5

      8) Turn off the pen by clicking the *Slide Show* menu icon, pointing to Pointer Options, and then clicking Automatic.
   d. Click the left mouse button until Slide 4 displays (this slide contains STEP 4) and then use the pen to underline in yellow the word *after*.
   e. Turn off the display of the pen.
   f. Click the left mouse to display Slide 5 and then use the pen to underline in yellow the word *effective*.
   g. Turn off the display of the pen.
   h. Click the left mouse button and then, at the black screen, click the left mouse button again.
7. Close Planning Presentation and then exit PowerPoint.

Adding Transition and Sound Effects

Interesting transitions and sounds can be applied to a presentation. A transition is how one slide is removed from the screen during a presentation and the next slide is displayed. Interesting transitions can be added such as blinds, boxes, checkerboards, covers, random bars, stripes, and wipes. To add transitions and sounds, open a presentation and then change to the Slide Sorter view. Select an individual slide or select all slides in the presentation, click Slide Show, and then click Slide Transition. This displays the Slide Transition dialog box shown in figure 14.13.

Make a presentation more appealing by adding effects such as sound and transitions.

figure

14.13

Slide Transition Dialog Box

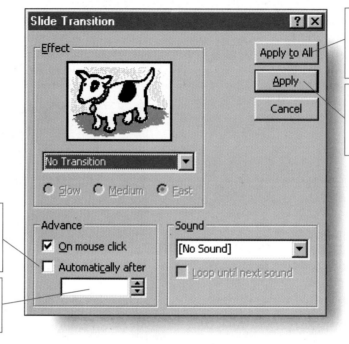

Click the Apply to All button to apply transition time to all slides.

Click the Apply button to apply transition time to selected slide only.

To advance slides automatically, insert a check mark in this check box.

Insert the desired number of seconds in this text box.

Slide
Transition

Another method for displaying the Slide Transition dialog box shown in figure 14.13 is to click the Slide Transition button on the Slide Sorter toolbar. The Slide Sorter toolbar displays below the Standard toolbar in Slide Sorter view.

To add a transition effect, click the down-pointing triangle to the right of the Effect text box (located below the picture of the dog), and then click the desired transition at the drop-down menu. When you click the desired transition, the transition effect is displayed in the picture of the dog and the picture changes to a key.

As a slide is removed from the screen and another slide is displayed, a sound can be added. To add a sound, click the down-pointing triangle to the right of the Sound text box, and then click the desired sound. You can choose from a list of sounds such as applause, breaking glass, camera, laser, and much more. When a transition is added to a slide, a transition icon displays below the slide in Slide Sorter view.

exercise 4

Adding Transitions and Sounds to a Presentation

1. Open PowerPoint.
2. At the PowerPoint dialog box, click Open an existing presentation, and then click OK.
3. At the Open dialog box, make sure *Chapter 14* on your disk is the active folder, and then double-click *Planning Presentation* in the list box.
4. Save the presentation with Save As and name it Planning Pres with Transitions by completing the following steps:
   a. Click File and then Save As.
   b. At the Save As dialog box, key **Planning Pres with Transitions** in the File name text box.
   c. Click Save or press Enter.
5. Add transition and sound effects by completing the following steps:
   a. Change to the Slide Sorter view.
   b. Click Slide Show on the Menu bar and then click Slide Transition.
   c. At the Slide Transition dialog box, add a transition effect by completing the following steps:
      1) Click the down-pointing triangle to the right of the Effect text box (containing the text *No Transition*).
      2) From the drop-down list that displays, click *Blinds Horizontal*.
   d. Add a sound effect by completing the following steps:
      1) Click the down-pointing triangle to the right of the Sound text box (containing the text *[No Sound]*).
      2) From the drop-down list that displays, click *Camera*.

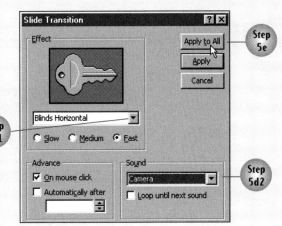

   e. Click the Apply to All button. (This closes the Slide Transition dialog box and displays a transition icon below each slide.
6. Run the presentation by clicking the Slide Show button on the View toolbar. (When the presentation is done, and the black screen displays with the message *End of slide show, click to exit.*, click the left mouse button or press the Esc key. This returns the presentation to the Slide Sorter view.)
7. Save the presentation again with the same name (Planning Pres with Transitions).
8. Close Planning Pres with Transitions.

Running a Slide Show Automatically

Slides in a slide show can be advanced automatically after a specific number of seconds with options at the Slide Transition dialog box. To automatically advance slides, click Automatically after (in the Advance section), and then key the number of seconds. If you want the transition time to affect all slides in the presentation, click the Apply to All button at the Slide Transition dialog box. If you want the transition time to affect only the selected slide, click the Apply button. The transition time is displayed below each affected slide in the presentation in Slide Sorter view.

To automatically run the presentation, make sure the first slide is selected, and then click the Slide Show button on the View toolbar. The first slide displays for the specified amount of time and then the next slide automatically displays.

In some situations, such as at a trade show or convention, you may want to prepare a self-running presentation. A self-running presentation is set up on a continuous loop and does not require someone to run the presentation. To design a self-running presentation, choose options at the Set Up Show dialog box shown in figure 14.14. To display this dialog box, open a presentation and then click Slide Show and then Set Up Show.

Set Up Show Dialog Box

Specify the type of self-running presentation with options in the Show type section.

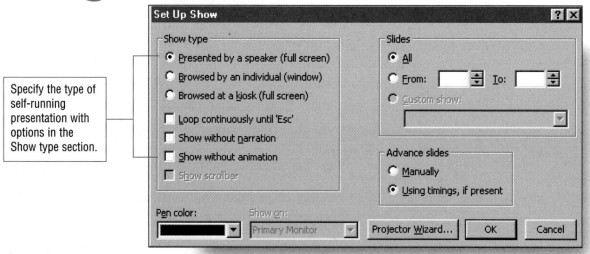

Click the Loop continuously until 'Esc' option and the presentation runs over and over again until the Esc key is pressed. With other options in the Show type section of the Set Up Show dialog, you can specify what a presentation shows when running. In the Advance slides section of the dialog box, specify whether the slides will be advanced manually or automatically. Use options in the Slides section to specify whether options are to be applied to all slides or specific slides within the presentation.

Preparing a Self-Running Presentation

1. Open History of Computers 1980s. (This presentation is located in the *Presentations* folder on the CD that accompanies this textbook.)
2. Save the presentation with Save As in the *Chapter 14* folder on your disk and name it Self-Running History.
3. Add transition and sound effects and specify a time for automatically advancing slides by completing the following steps:
   a. Change to the Slide Sorter view.
   b. Click Sli̱de Show and then Slide Transition.
   c. At the Slide Transition dialog box, click Automati̱cally after, and then key **5** in the seconds text box.
   d. Add a transition effect by completing the following steps:
      1) Click the down-pointing triangle to the right of the Effect text box (containing the text *No Transition*).
      2) From the drop-down list that displays, click *Box Out*.
   e. Add a sound effect by completing the following steps:
      1) Click the down-pointing triangle to the right of the Sound text box (containing the text *[No Sound]*).
      2) From the drop-down list that displays, click *Laser*.
   f. Click the Apply to All button. (This closes the Slide Transition dialog box and displays a transition icon below each slide as well as the transition time of 5 seconds.)
4. Set up the presentation to run continuously by completing the following steps:
   a. Click Sli̱de Show and then Set Up Show.
   b. At the Set Up Show dialog box, click the Loop continuously until 'Esc' option. (Make sure All is selected in the Slides section and Using timings, if present is selected in the Advance slides section.)
   c. Click OK to close the dialog box.

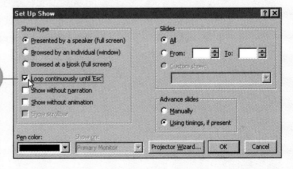

5. Make sure the first slide is selected and then run the presentation continuously by clicking the Slide Show button on the View toolbar.
6. After viewing the presentation at least twice, press the Esc key on the keyboard.
7. Save the presentation again with the same name (Self-Running History).
8. Close Self-Running History.

Setting and Rehearsing Timings for a Presentation

Setting a time at the Slide Transition dialog box sets the same time for each selected slide. In some presentations, you may want to specify a different amount of time for each slide and then rehearse the presentation to ensure that the time set is appropriate. To rehearse and set a time for each slide, you would complete these steps:

Rehearse Timings

1. Open the presentation.
2. Change to the Slide Sorter view.
3. Click the Rehearse Timings button on the Slide Sorter toolbar or click Slide Show and then Rehearse Timings.
4. The first slide in the presentation displays along with a Rehearsal dialog box shown in figure 14.15. The Rehearsal dialog box shows the time for the current slide and the total time for the presentation. The timer begins immediately. Click the Next button when the desired time displays; click the Pause button to stop the timer and leave the slide on the screen; or, click the Repeat button if you want the time for the current slide to start over.
5. When the desired time displays for the slide in the Rehearsal dialog box, click the Next button.
6. Continue in this manner until the time for all slides in the presentation has been specified.
7. After specifying the time for the last slide, a Microsoft PowerPoint dialog box displays with the total time of the presentation and asks if you want to record the new slide timings. At this dialog box, click Yes to save the new timings.

figure
14.15

Rehearsal Dialog Box

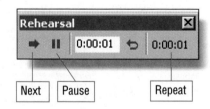

exercise 6

Rehearsing and Establishing Specific Times for Slides

1. Open Planning Presentation.
2. Save the presentation with Save As and name it Rehearsed Planning Pres.
3. Set specific times for each slide in the presentation by completing the following steps:
   a. Change to Slide Sorter view.
   b. Click the Rehearse Timings button on the Slide Sorter toolbar.
   c. With the first slide displayed, wait until the timer in the Rehearsal dialog box displays *five* seconds, and then click the Next button. (If you miss five seconds, click the Repeat button. This restarts the clock for the current slide.)
   d. With the second slide displayed, wait until the timer displays *5* seconds, and then click the Next button.
   e. Set *7* seconds for the third and fourth slides and *5* seconds for the fifth slide.
   f. After setting the time for the last slide, the Microsoft PowerPoint dialog box displays asking if you want to record the new timings. At this dialog box, click <u>Y</u>es.
4. Add a transition and sound effect to each slide by completing the following steps:
   a. Click the Slide Transition button located at the left side of the Slide Sorter toolbar.
   b. At the Slide Transition dialog box, click the down-pointing triangle at the right side of the <u>E</u>ffect text box (containing the text *No Transition*), and then click *Dissolve* at the drop-down list. (You will need to scroll down the list to display *Dissolve*.)
   c. Click the down-pointing triangle at the right side of the So<u>u</u>nd text box (containing the text *[No Sound]*) and then click *Camera* at the drop-down list.
   d. Click the Apply <u>t</u>o All button.
5. Set up the presentation to run continuously by displaying the Set Up Show dialog box, clicking the <u>L</u>oop continuously until 'Esc' option, and then closing the dialog box.
6. Make sure Slide 1 is selected and then run the presentation by clicking the Slide Show button on the View toolbar. (The slide show will run automatically. The first and second slides will stay on the screen for five seconds, the third and fourth slides for seven seconds, and the fifth slide for five seconds.)
7. After viewing the entire presentation at least twice, press the Esc key on the keyboard.
8. Save the presentation again with the same name (Rehearsed Planning Pres).
9. Close Rehearsed Planning Pres.

Preparing a Presentation in Outline View

In exercise 1, you created a slide presentation using a PowerPoint template. With this method, a slide with formatting applied was presented in the Slide pane where you entered specific text. This was a short presentation of only five slides with a small amount of text on each slide. If you are creating a longer presentation with more slides and text, consider using the Outline view to help organize the topics for the slides. Figure 14.16 displays in Outline view the Networking Presentation you will be creating in exercise 7.

figure 14.16 Presentation in Outline View

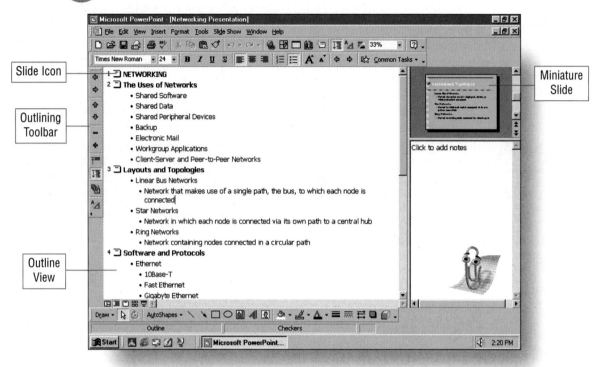

Slide Icon →

Outlining Toolbar →

Outline View →

Miniature Slide →

You can key text in the Outline pane in Normal view but consider changing to Outline view because this increases the size of the Outline pane allowing you to see more text. To prepare a presentation in the Outline view, you would complete the following steps:

1. At a blank PowerPoint screen, click File and then New.
2. At the New Presentation dialog box, click the Design Templates tab.
3. At the New Presentation dialog box with the Design Templates tab selected, double-click the desired template.
4. At the New Slide dialog box, double-click the desired autolayout format.
5. With the blank slide displayed, click the Outline View button on the View toolbar.
6. Key the title of the first slide and then press Enter. (A miniature slide displays in the Slide pane so you can view the slide with the text you key.)
7. Click the Demote button on the Formatting toolbar or press the Tab key to move to the next tab stop and then key the first heading.

Outline View

Demote

Promote

8. Continue keying the text for each slide in the presentation. Click the Demote button on the Formatting toolbar or press Tab to move the insertion point to the next tab stop (and automatically change the text formatting). Click the Promote button on the Formatting toolbar or press Shift + Tab to move the insertion point to the previous tab stop. Continue in this manner until all text is entered for the presentation.

9. When the presentation is completed, save it in the normal manner.

When keying text for a presentation in the Outline view, click the Demote button on the Formatting toolbar or press the Tab key to move the insertion point to the next tab stop. This moves the insertion point and also changes the formatting. The formatting will vary depending on the autolayout format you chose at the New Slide dialog box. For some autolayout formats, a slide title is set in a font such as 44-point Times New Roman bold. Text keyed at the first tab stop will be set in a smaller point size such as 32-point Times New Roman.

To move the insertion point to a previous tab stop, click the Promote button on the Formatting toolbar or press Shift + Tab. This moves the insertion point and also changes text formatting. Moving the insertion point back to the left margin will begin another slide. Slides are numbered at the left side of the screen and are followed by a slide icon as shown in figure 14.16.

PowerPoint contains an Outlining toolbar with buttons for editing in the Outline view (see figure 14.16). To display this toolbar, *right*-click any displayed toolbar, and then click *Outlining* at the drop-down list. You can also display the toolbar by clicking <u>V</u>iew, pointing to <u>T</u>oolbars, and then clicking *Outlining*. In the Outline view, the Outlining toolbar displays at the left side of the screen. This toolbar contains the same Promote and Demote buttons as the Formatting toolbar along with other buttons. Buttons on the Outlining toolbar are described in figure 14.17.

Outlining Toolbar Buttons

Click this button	Named	To do this
⇦	Promote	Move insertion point along with any text to the previous tab stop to the left
⇨	Demote	Move insertion point along with any text to the next tab stop to the right
⇧	Move Up	Move insertion point along with any text up to the previous line

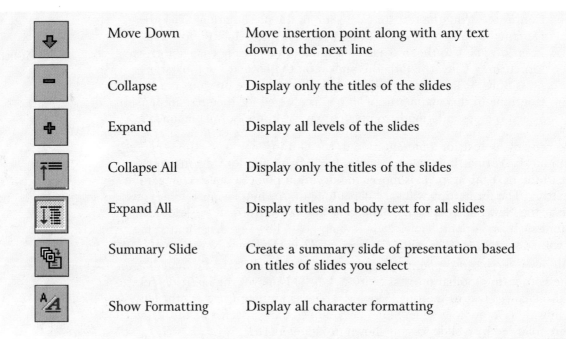

	Move Down	Move insertion point along with any text down to the next line
	Collapse	Display only the titles of the slides
	Expand	Display all levels of the slides
	Collapse All	Display only the titles of the slides
	Expand All	Display titles and body text for all slides
	Summary Slide	Create a summary slide of presentation based on titles of slides you select
	Show Formatting	Display all character formatting

Expand All

Show Formatting

Two buttons available on the Outlining toolbar are also available on the Standard toolbar. These two buttons are Expand All and Show Formatting. Clicking either of these buttons on the Outlining toolbar or the Standard toolbar accomplishes the same thing.

Preparing a Presentation in Outline View

1. Create a presentation in Outline view by completing the following steps:
    a. With PowerPoint open and a blank screen displayed, click File and then New.
    b. At the New Presentation dialog box, click the Design Templates tab.
    c. At the New Presentation dialog box with the Design Templates tab selected, double-click *Checkers*.
    d. At the New Slide dialog box, double-click the second autolayout in the list box (Bulleted List).
    e. With the empty slide displayed, click the Outline View button on the View toolbar. (Located at the left side of the horizontal scroll bar.)
    f. Turn on the display of the Outlining toolbar by clicking View, pointing to Toolbars, and then clicking Outlining.
    g. Create the outline shown in figure 14.18 by completing the following steps:
        1) Key the first slide title shown in figure 14.18 (**NETWORKING**) and then press Enter.
        2) Key the second slide title shown in figure 14.18 (**The Uses of Networks**) and then press Enter.

3) Click the Demote button on the Outlining toolbar or press Tab, key the text after the first bullet in figure 14.18 (**Shared Software**), and then press Enter.

4) Continue keying the text as it displays in figure 14.18. Click the Demote button or press Tab to move the insertion point to the next tab stop. Click the Promote button or press Shift + Tab to move the insertion back to a previous tab stop.

h. Click the Collapse All button on the Outlining toolbar. (This displays only the title of each slide.)

i. Click the Expand All button on the Outlining toolbar.

2. Save the presentation by completing the following steps:
   a. Click the Save button on the Standard toolbar.
   b. At the Save As dialog box, key **Networking Presentation**, and then press Enter or click Save.

3. View the slides by clicking the Slide Sorter View button on the View toolbar.

4. Print the four slides as notes pages by displaying the Print dialog box and then changing the Print what option to *Notes Pages*.

5. Close Networking Presentation.

figure

14.18   Exercise 7

1   NETWORKING
2   The Uses of Networks
    • Shared Software
    • Shared Data
    • Shared Peripheral Devices
    • Backup
    • Electronic Mail
    • Workgroup Applications
    • Client-Server and Peer-to-Peer Networks
3   Layouts and Topologies
    • Linear Bus Networks
      • Network that makes use of a single path, the bus, to which each node is connected
    • Star Networks
      • Network in which each node is connected via its own path to a central hub
    • Ring Networks
      • Network containing nodes connected in a circular path
4   Software and Protocols
    • Ethernet
    • 10Base-T
    • Fast Ethernet
    • Gigabyte Ethernet
    • Token Ring
    • ARCNet
    • AppleTalk

Managing Files in PowerPoint

In chapter 4, you learned how to perform file management tasks in Word, such as copying, moving, pasting, deleting, renaming, and printing documents. These same types of tasks can be performed in PowerPoint.

Delete

File management tasks in PowerPoint are performed following the same basic steps as those you learned in Word. For example, to delete a PowerPoint document, display the Open dialog box, click the PowerPoint document you want deleted, and then click the Delete button on the dialog box toolbar. At the dialog box asking if you are sure you want to delete the document, click <u>Y</u>es.

Deleting a PowerPoint Presentation

1. Delete several presentation documents by completing the following steps:
   a. With PowerPoint open, display the Open dialog box by clicking the Open button on the Standard toolbar.
   b. At the Open dialog box, click *Rehearsed Planning Pres* in the list box to select it.
   c. Click the Delete button on the dialog box toolbar.
   d. At the dialog box asking if you are sure you want to delete the presentation, click <u>Y</u>es.
   e. At the Open dialog box, delete Selling Presentation by completing steps similar to those in 1b through 1d.
   f. At the Open dialog box, delete Self-Running History by completing steps similar to those in 1b and 1d.
2. Close the Open dialog box.

chapter summary

- ► PowerPoint is a software program that lets you create slides for an on-screen presentation or for an overhead or slide projector. In PowerPoint, you can print handouts of the presentation, print an outline, or print the entire presentation.
- ► Before creating a presentation in PowerPoint, plan the presentation by defining the purpose and determining the content and medium.
- ► Follow these basic steps to create a PowerPoint presentation: 1) open PowerPoint; 2) choose a design template; 3) key the text for each slide; 4) save the presentation; 5) print the presentation as slides, an outline, or handouts; 6) run the presentation; and 7) close the presentation.
- ► The PowerPoint window contains the following elements: Title bar, Menu bar, Standard toolbar, Formatting toolbar, Drawing toolbar, Outline pane, Slide pane, Notes pane, Scroll bars, View toolbar, and Status bar.
- ► PowerPoint includes a variety of preformatted design templates you can use for creating a presentation.

- Many slides created with a PowerPoint template contain placeholders. A slide may contain all or some of the following placeholders: title, bulleted list, clip art, chart, organizational chart, and table.

- Presentations can be printed with each slide on a separate piece of paper; each slide at the top of the page, leaving room for notes; all or a specific number of slides on a single piece of paper; or slide titles and topics in outline form.

- Print a presentation in grayscale or black and white with options at the Print dialog box.

- Click the Grayscale Preview button on the Standard toolbar to preview the presentation in grayscale. Hold down the Shift key and then click the Grayscale Preview button to preview the presentation in black and white.

- Use PowerPoint's AutoContent Wizard to help in the planning and organizing of a presentation.

- Close a PowerPoint presentation document by clicking File and then Close. Open a presentation by clicking the Open button on the Standard toolbar and then double-clicking the desired presentation at the Open dialog box.

- View a presentation in one of the following five views: Normal view, which is the default and displays three panes—outline, slide, and notes; Outline view, which displays the presentation by headings and subheadings; Slide view, which displays all slides in the presentation in slide miniatures; and Slide Show view, which runs the presentation.

- A slide show can be run manually, where you determine when to advance to the next slide; automatically, where PowerPoint advances the slides; or continuously, for demonstration purposes.

- Use the pen during a presentation to emphasize major points or draw the attention of the audience to specific items in the slide. Display the pen by clicking the *Slide Show* menu icon, pointing to Pointer Options, and then clicking Pen. Draw a straight horizontal or vertical line by holding down the Shift key while drawing.

- Erase pen marks by clicking the *Slide Show* menu icon, pointing to Screen, and then clicking Erase Pen.

- A specific time can be set for how long each slide stays on the screen during a presentation.

- A presentation can be enhanced by adding transitions (how one slide is removed from the screen and replaced with the next slide) and sound.

- Consider preparing a presentation in Outline view to help organize the topics for the slides.

- File management tasks can be performed on PowerPoint presentations in the same manner as Word documents.

commands review

	Mouse
Open PowerPoint	Click Start button on Taskbar, point to *Programs*, click *Microsoft PowerPoint*
Display Print dialog box	Click File and then Print
Preview presentation in grayscale	Click Grayscale Preview button on Standard toolbar
Preview presentation in black	Hold down Shift key and then click Grayscale and white button on Standard toolbar

Save presentation	Click Save button on Standard toolbar or click File, Save
Display Save As dialog box	Click File, Save As
Close a presentation	Click File and then Close
Display Open dialog box	Click Open button on Standard toolbar or click File and then Open
Display Slide Transition dialog box	Click Slide Transition button on Slide Sorter toolbar or click Slide Show and then Slide Transition
Display Set Up Show dialog box	Click Slide Show and then Set Up Show
Display Outlining toolbar	Click View, point to Toolbars, and then click Outlining; or right-click a toolbar and then click Outlining at the drop-down list

thinking offline

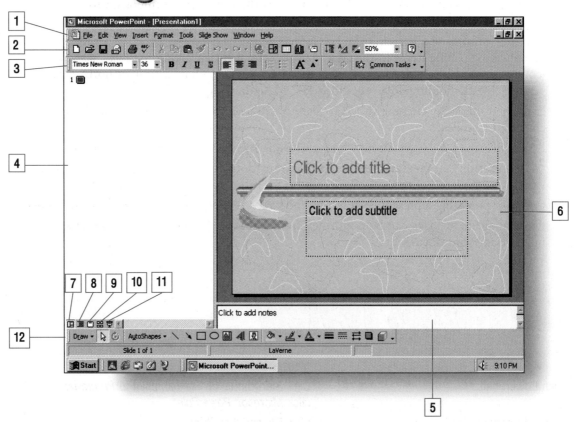

Identifying: Look at the PowerPoint screen shown on the previous page. This screen contains numbers with lines pointing to specific items. Write the name of the item after the number below that corresponds with the number in the PowerPoint screen.

1. _____   7. _____

2. _____   8. _____

3. _____   9. _____

4. _____   10. _____

5. _____   11. _____

6. _____   12. _____

Completion: In the space provided at the right, indicate the correct term or command.

1. Click this button on the View toolbar to run a presentation.

2. Click this button on the View toolbar to display all slides in the presentation in slide miniatures.

3. While running a presentation, click this button on the mouse to display the previous slide.

4. If a presentation contains six slides, click this option at the Print what drop-down menu at the Print dialog box to print all the slides on the same page.

5. Hold down the Shift key and then click this button on the Standard toolbar to display the presentation in black and white.

6. Use this during a presentation to emphasize major points or draw the attention of the audience to specific items in the slide.

7. This terms refers to how one slide is removed from the screen and replaced with the next slide.

8. To display the Slide Transition dialog box, click this option on the Menu bar, and then click Slide Transition.

9. If a time has been added to a slide, the time displays at the bottom of the slide in this view.

10. In Slide Sorter view, this toolbar displays below the Standard toolbar.

11. Click the Loop continuously until 'Esc' option at this dialog box to specify that the presentation run continuously.

12. In the Outline view, click this button on the Outlining toolbar to move the insertion point to the next tab stop. _____

13. In the Outline view, click this button on the Outlining toolbar to move the insertion point to the previous tab stop. _____

working hands-on

Assessment 1

1. Create a presentation with the text shown in figure 14.19 by completing the following steps:
   a. Open PowerPoint.
   b. At the PowerPoint dialog box, click Design Template, and then click OK.
   c. At the New Presentation dialog box, click the Design Templates tab (if necessary).
   d. At the New Presentation dialog box with the Design Templates tab selected, double-click the *Marble* template.
   e. At the New Slide dialog box, double-click the first autolayout in the list box (*Title Slide*).
   f. At the slide, click anywhere in the text *Click to add title*, and then key **DEDUCTIBLE INCOME**.
   g. Click anywhere in the text *Click to add subtitle* and then key **Exceptions to Deductible Income**.
   h. Click the New Slide button located on the Standard toolbar and then create the second slide with the text shown in figure 14.19.
   i. Continue creating the remaining slides as shown in figure 14.19.
2. Save the presentation and name it Deductible Presentation.
3. Print all the slides on one page.
4. Close Deductible Presentation.

figure

14.19 *Assessment 1*

Slide 1	Title	=	DEDUCTIBLE INCOME
	Subtitle	=	Exceptions to Deductible Income

Slide 2	Title	=	EXCEPTION 1
	Subtitle	=	Any cost of living increase if increase becomes effective while disabled.

Slide 3	Title	=	EXCEPTION 2
	Subtitle	=	Reimbursement for hospital, medical, or surgical expense.

Slide 4	Title	=	EXCEPTION 3
	Subtitle	=	Reasonable attorney's fees incurred in connection with a claim for deductible income.

Slide 5	Title	=	EXCEPTION 4
	Subtitle	=	Benefits from any individual disability insurance policy.

Slide 6	Title	=	EXCEPTION 5
	Subtitle	=	Group credit or mortgage disability insurance benefits.

Assessment 2

1. Open Deductible Presentation.
2. Save the presentation with Save As and name it Enhanced Deductible Presentation.
3. Make the following changes to the presentation:
    a. Add the transition *Split Vertical Out* to all slides in the presentation.
    b. Add the cash register sound to all slides in the presentation.
4. Save the presentation again with the same name (Enhanced Deductible Presentation).
5. Run the presentation.
6. Close Enhanced Deductible Presentation.

Assessment 3

1. Create a presentation with the text shown in figure 14.20. You determine the template and the autolayout. (*Hint: Use the first autolayout for the first slide and the second autolayout for the remaining slides.*)
2. After creating the presentation, save it and name it Newsletter Presentation.
3. Print Newsletter Presentation as an outline.
4. Print Newsletter Presentation as individual slides.
5. Close Newsletter Presentation.

figure

14.20   *Assessment 3*

SLIDE 1   TITLE   =   PREPARING A COMPANY NEWSLETTER
          Subtitle =   Planning and Designing the Layout

Slide 2   Title   =   Planning a Newsletter
          Bullets =   • If a scanner is available, use pictures of different people from
                        your organization in each issue.
                      • Distribute contributor sheets soliciting information from
                        employees.
                      • Keep the focus of the newsletter on issues of
                        interest to employees.

Slide 3   Title   =   Planning a Newsletter
          Bullets =   • Make sure the focus is on various levels of
                        employment; do not focus on top management only.
                      • Conduct regular surveys to see if your newsletter provides a
                        needed source of information.

Slide 4   Title   =   Designing a Newsletter
          Bullets =   • Maintain consistent elements from issue to issue such as:
                        - Column layout
                        - Nameplate formatting and location
                        - Formatting of headlines
                        - Use of color

Slide 5   Title   =   Designing a Newsletter
          Bullets =   • Consider the following elements when designing a
                        newsletter:
                        - Focus
                        - Balance
                        - White space
                        - Directional flow
Slide 6   Title   =   Creating a Newsletter Layout
          Bullets =   • Choose paper size
                      • Choose paper weight
                      • Determine margins
                      • Specify column layout

Assessment 4

1. Open Newsletter Presentation.
2. Save the presentation with Save As and name it Enhanced Newsletter Presentation.
3. Make the following changes to the presentation:
   a. Add a transition of your choosing to each slide.
   b. Add a sound of your choosing to each slide.
   c. Specify that all slides advance automatically after 5 seconds.
   d. Set up the presentation as continuous.
4. Save the presentation again with the same name (Enhanced Newsletter Presentation).
5. Run the presentation.
6. Close Enhanced Newsletter Presentation.

Assessment 5

1. Display the Open dialog box and then copy Planning Presentation, Newsletter Presentation, and Networking Presentation from your *Chapter 14* folder to your disk folder (the folder up one level from the Chapter 14 folder). (You will be using these persentations for exercises in chapters 15 and 16.)
2. Close the Open dialog box.

Assessment 6

1. A presentation created in PowerPoint can be sent to Word as an outline or as a handout. This might be helpful if you want to format or enhance the presentation using Word tools and features. Use PowerPoint's Help feature to learn about how to send slide images to Word. (*Hint: To get started, click the Office Assistant Title bar, key* **How do I send slide images to Word?** *and then click the* Search *button. At the list of choices that displays in the yellow box, click* Send notes, handouts, or an outline to Microsoft Word. *Continue using Help to determine the steps for sending a presentation to a Word document.*)
2. After reading the Help information, open Deductible Presentation and then send it to Word. (At the Write-Up dialog box, you choose the page layout.)
3. When the document displays in Word, print the document.
4. Close the Word document without saving it and then exit Word and PowerPoint.

Chapter 15

Editing and Formatting a PowerPoint Presentation

PERFORMANCE OBJECTIVES

Upon successful completion of chapter 15, you will be able to:

- Edit a PowerPoint presentation.
- Insert and delete slides in a presentation.
- Copy slides within and between presentations.
- Rearrange slides and rearrange objects within slides.
- Complete a spelling check.
- Format slides in a presentation.
- Format a master slide in a presentation.
- Draw objects and autoshapes with buttons on the Drawing toolbar.
- Select, move, copy, delete, and size objects.
- Draw text boxes and wrap text within an autoshape.
- Group, ungroup, flip, rotate, distribute, and align objects.
- Change slide color schemes, backgrounds, and design templates.
- Create a presentation with the Blank Presentation template.
- Format slides with Format Painter.
- Format slides with bullets and numbers.
- Insert the date and time, a header and footer, and page numbering in slides.
- Create, format, and print speaker notes.

In this chapter, you will learn to edit text and slides in a PowerPoint presentation, including inserting and deleting text and slides, rearranging slides, and formatting text and object boxes in slides. You will also learn how to change slide color schemes, apply different design templates, and insert elements in slides such as the date and time, a header and footer, and page numbering.

Editing Slides

Slides within a PowerPoint presentation can be edited. For example, text within individual slides can be inserted or deleted, slides can be deleted from the presentation, slides can be inserted into an existing presentation, and slides can be rearranged. Slides can be edited in several views—use the view that makes editing the easiest. For example, rearrange the order of slides in the Slide Sorter view; delete or insert text within slides in the Outline view or the Normal view.

Inserting and Deleting Text in Slides

To insert or delete text in an individual slide, open the presentation, change to the desired view, edit the text as needed, and then save the presentation again. If you want to delete more than an individual character, consider selecting the text first. Several methods can be used for selecting text as shown in Figure 15.1.

figure

15.1

Selecting Text

To do this	Perform this action
Select text mouse pointer passes through	Click and drag mouse
Select entire word	Double-click word
Select entire paragraph	Triple-click anywhere in paragraph
Select an entire sentence	Ctrl + click anywhere in sentence
Select all text in selected object box	Ctrl + A

Press Ctrl + F to display the Find dialog box.

Press Ctrl + H to display the Replace dialog box.

Finding and Replacing Text in Slides

Use the find and replace feature to look for specific text or formatting in slides in a presentation and replace with other text or formatting. Complete a find and replace in a PowerPoint presentation in the Normal view, Outline view, or the Slide view. Begin a find and replace by clicking Edit and then Replace. At the Replace dialog box shown in figure 15.2, key the text you want to find in the Find what text box, press the Tab key, and then key the replacement text in the Replace with text box. Click the Find Next button to find the next occurrence of the text or click the Replace All button to replace all occurrences in the presentation.

figure

15.2

Replace Dialog Box

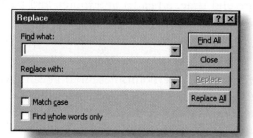

Chapter Fifteen

If you want to find specific text without replacing it with other text, click Edit and then Find. This displays the Find dialog box shown in figure 15.3. Key the text you want to find in the Find what text box and then click the Find Next button.

Find Dialog Box

Inserting and Deleting Slides

An entire slide can be deleted from a presentation at the Slide Sorter, Outline view, or Outline pane. To delete a slide from a presentation, display the presentation in Slide Sorter view, click the slide you want to delete, and then press the Delete key. A slide can also be deleted in the Outline view or the Outline pane. To do this, change to the Normal view or Outline view, position the arrow pointer on the slide icon located next to the slide you want to delete until the arrow pointer turns into a four-headed arrow, and then click the left mouse button. (This selects all text for the slide.) With the text for the slide selected, press the Delete key.

Insert and/or delete slides in Slide Sorter view or in Outline view.

A new slide can be inserted into an existing presentation at the Slide Sorter view, Outline view, or Outline pane. To add a slide to a presentation in the Slide Sorter view, you would follow these basic steps:

1. Open the presentation to which you want the slide added.
2. Change to the Slide Sorter view.
3. Click the slide that will immediately precede the new slide. (For example, if the new slide should immediately follow Slide 3, click Slide 3.)
4. Click the New Slide button located on the Standard toolbar; click the Common Tasks button on the Formatting toolbar and then click New Slide; or click Insert and then New Slide.
5. At the New Slide dialog box, double-click the desired autolayout format.
6. At the Slide Sorter view, double-click the new blank slide. (This changes the presentation to the Normal view with the new slide displayed.)
7. Add the desired text to the new slide.
8. Save the presentation again.

Copying a Slide

Slides in some presentations may contain similar text, objects, and formatting. Rather than creating a new slide, consider copying a slide. To do this, display the slides in Slide Sorter view and then select the slide you want to copy. Position the arrow pointer in the slide, hold down the Ctrl key and then the left mouse button. Drag to the location where you want the slide copied, then release the mouse button, then the Ctrl key.

Copying a Slide Between Presentations

Slides can be copied within a presentation and also between presentations. To copy a slide between presentations, open the presentation containing the slide to be copied and change to the Slide Sorter view. Click the slide you want to copy and then click the Copy button on the Standard toolbar. Open the presentation into which the slide is to be copied and then display the slides in Slide Sorter view. Click in the location where you want the slide positioned and then click the Paste button. The copied slide will take on the template design of the presentation into which it is copied.

exercise

Finding and Replacing Text and Deleting, Inserting, and Copying Slides

1. Open PowerPoint and then open Planning Presentation.
2. Save the presentation with Save As and name it Edited Planning Presentation.
3. Find all occurrences of *Planning* in the presentation and replace with *Preparing* by completing the following steps:
   a. Click Edit and then Replace.
   b. At the Replace dialog box, key **Planning** in the Find what text box.
   c. Press the Tab key.
   d. Key **Preparing** in the Replace with text box.
   e. Click the Replace All button.
   f. At the Microsoft PowerPoint message telling you that 5 replacements were made, click OK.
   g. Click the Close button to close the Replace dialog box.
4. Find all occurrences of *Publication* and replace with *Newsletter* by completing steps similar to those in step 3.
5. Delete and insert slides in the Edited Planning Presentation by completing the following steps:
   a. At the Normal view, click the Next Slide button located at the bottom of the vertical scroll bar until Slide 4 displays.
   b. Edit Slide 4 by completing the following steps:

Step 3g

Replace ? X

Find what:
Planning ▼   **Find Next**
   Close

Replace with:
Preparing ▼   Replace

□ Match case   **Replace All**
□ Find whole words only

Step 3b

Step 3d

Step 3e

1) Position the I-beam pointer on the sentence below *Step 4* and then click the left mouse button. (This inserts a frame around the text.)

2) Edit the sentence so it reads *Decide what steps you want readers to take after reading the message*. (Use deleting and inserting commands to edit this sentence.)

   c. Click the Next Slide button to display Slide 5.

   d. Edit Slide 5 in the Outline pane so it reads *Collect and assess examples of effective designs*.

6. Add a new slide by completing the following steps:

   a. Click the Slide Sorter View button on the View toolbar.

   b. Click Slide 2 to select it.

   c. Click the New Slide button on the Standard toolbar.

   d. At the New Slide dialog box, double-click the first autolayout *(Title Slide)*.

   e. At the Slide Sorter view, double-click the new slide *(Slide 3)*. (This changes to the Normal view with Slide 3 displayed.)

   f. Click anywhere in the text *Click to add title* and then key **Preparing the Newsletter**.

   g. Click anywhere in the text *Click to add subtitle* and then key the following:

     1) Turn on bold, key **STEP 3**, and then turn off bold.

     2) Press Enter and then key **Determine the available budget for the newsletter.**

7. Add another new slide by completing the following steps:

   a. Click the Slide Sorter View button on the View toolbar.

   b. Click Slide 4 to select it.

   c. Click the New Slide button on the Standard toolbar.

   d. At the New Slide dialog box, double-click the first autolayout *(Title Slide)*.

   e. At the Slide Sorter view, double-click the new blank slide *(Slide 5)*. (This changes to the Normal view with Slide 5 displayed.)

   f. Click anywhere in the text *Click to add title* and then key **Preparing the Newsletter**.

   g. Click anywhere in the text *Click to add subtitle* and then key the following:

     1) Turn on bold, key **STEP 5**, and then turn off bold.

     2) Press Enter and then key **Specify the layout of elements to be included in the newsletter.**

8. Delete Slide 2 by completing the following steps:

   a. Click the Slide Sorter View button on the View toolbar.

   b. Click Slide 2 to select it.

   c. Press the Delete key.

9. Change to the Outline view and then edit each slide so the step number matches the slide number.

10. Copy slides from a different presentation into the Edited Planning Presentation by completing the following steps:

a. Change to the Slide Sorter view.
b. Open the presentation named Company Newsletter located in the *Presentations* folder on the CD that accompanies this textbook.
c. With the Company Newsletter presentation open, change to the Slide Sorter view.
d. Click Slide 2, hold down the Shift key, and then click Slide 3. (This selects both slides.)
e. Click the Copy button on the Standard toolbar.
f. Click the button on the Taskbar representing Edited Planning Presentation.
g. Click to the right of the last slide in the presentation and then click the Paste button on the Standard toolbar.
11. Save the presentation again with the same name (Edited Planning Presentation).
12. Print the six slides on one page. (Change the Print <u>w</u>hat option at the Print dialog box to *Handouts.*)
13. Close Edited Planning Presentation.
14. Close Company Newsletter.

Rearranging Text in Slides

Text in slides can be rearranged by deleting and inserting text. Text can also be rearranged in slides using Cut, Copy, and/or Paste options. For example, to move text in a slide, you would complete the following steps:

Cut

1. Click once in the object box containing the text to be moved.
2. Select the text to be moved.
3. Click the Cut button on the Standard toolbar.
4. Position the insertion point where you want the text inserted and then click the Paste button.

Paste

Text can also be moved from one slide to another by selecting the text, clicking the Cut button, displaying the slide where you want the text inserted, and then clicking the Paste button.

To copy text in or between slides, complete similar steps. Select the text to be copied, click the Copy button on the Standard toolbar, move the insertion point to the position where the text is to be copied, and then click the Paste button.

Copy

Rearranging Text in the Outline View or Outline Pane

Text in the Outline view or in the Outline pane can be moved using the mouse. To do this, position the mouse pointer on the *slide* icon or bullet at the left side of the text, until the arrow pointer turns into a four-headed arrow. Hold down the left mouse button, drag the arrow pointer (displays with a gray box attached) to the desired location, and then release the mouse button.

If you position the arrow pointer on the *slide* icon and then hold down the left mouse button, all the text in the slide is selected. If you position the arrow pointer on the bullet and then hold down the left mouse button, all text following that bullet is selected.

Dragging selected text with the mouse moves the selected text to a new location in the presentation. You can also copy selected text. To do this, click the slide icon or click the bullet to select the desired text. Position the arrow pointer in the selected text, hold down the Ctrl key, and then the left mouse button. Drag the arrow pointer (displays with a light gray box and a plus sign attached) to the desired location, release the mouse button, and then release the Ctrl key.

Rearranging Object Boxes in a Slide

An entire selected object box can be moved easily in a slide. To do this, click once in the object box (outside any text) to select it (white sizing handles should display around the box). If white sizing handles do not display around the box, position the arrow pointer on the border of the box (small gray lines), and then click the left mouse button. Position the arrow pointer on the border around the object box until the arrow pointer displays with a four-headed arrow attached. Hold down the left mouse button, drag the outline of the box to the desired position, and then release the mouse button.

Dragging a selected box with the mouse moves the box. You can also copy a selected box. To do this, hold down the Ctrl key while dragging the box with the mouse. When the outline of the box is in the desired position, release the mouse button, and then release the Ctrl key.

Sizing an Object Box

Click an object box in a slide and sizing handles display around the box. Use these sizing handles to increase or decrease the size of the box. To increase or decrease the size, position the arrow pointer on one of the white sizing handles until the arrow pointer turns into a double-headed arrow. Hold down the left mouse button, drag the outline of the box in to decrease the size or drag the outline out to increase the size, and then release the mouse button. You can increase or decrease the size of the box at the same time by using the sizing handles that display in each corner of the selected box.

The size of a selected object box can be changed by dragging a corner or side sizing handle.

Rearranging Slides

Slides can be rearranged easily in the Slide Sorter view. To do this, change to the Slide Sorter view, position the arrow pointer on the slide to be moved, hold down the left mouse button, drag the arrow pointer (with a square attached) to the desired position, and then release the mouse button.

You can also rearrange slides in the Outline view. To do this, position the mouse pointer on the slide icon representing the slide you want to move until the pointer turns into a four-headed arrow. Hold down the left mouse button, drag to the desired position (a thin, black line displays), and then release the mouse button.

Using Buttons on the Standard Toolbar

The Standard toolbar contains the Cut, Copy, and Paste buttons along with other buttons to quickly access commonly used features in PowerPoint. The buttons on the Standard toolbar are described in figure 15.4.

PowerPoint Standard Toolbar Buttons

Click this button	Named	To do this
	New	Display the New Presentation dialog box where a blank or preformatted template can be chosen to create a presentation
	Open	Display the Open dialog box to choose a previously saved presentation file
	Save	Save the current presentation with the same name; or, save a presentation at the Save As dialog box
	E-mail	Send a slide presentation as an e-mail attachment or use the current slide text as the e-mail message
	Print	Print the presentation currently open
	Spelling	Complete a spelling check on the text in the current presentation
	Cut	Remove selected text or object to the Windows Clipboard
	Copy	Insert a copy of selected text or object in the Windows Clipboard
	Paste	Insert the contents of the Clipboard into the current slide
	Format Painter	Copy formatting from selected text or object and apply it to another object
	Undo	Undo the most recent action
	Redo	Redo (or repeat) the most recent action
	Insert Hyperlink	Insert or edit the specified hyperlink
	Tables and Borders	Display the Tables and Borders dialog box containing buttons for drawing and customizing a table
	Insert Table	Insert a blank table with number of rows and columns you specify
	Insert Chart	Embed a graph in a slide using specified data

	New Slide	Display New Slide dialog box
	Expand All	Display all levels of the slides
	Show Formatting	Display all character formatting as it will appear on the slide
	Grayscale Preview	Display a presentation in black and white (rather than color)
53%	Zoom	Increase or decrease the display of a presentation
	Microsoft PowerPoint Help	Have Office Assistant provide help topics and tips to help accomplish tasks

Completing a Spelling Check

Spelling

In chapter 3 you learned to complete a spelling check on a Word document. Perform a spelling check on a PowerPoint presentation in the same manner. Open a presentation and then click the Spelling button on the Standard toolbar. Change or ignore selected text as required.

You can press F7 to begin spell checking a presentation.

exercise 2

Creating a Presentation and then Rearranging Slides

1. Create the slides for a presentation as shown in figure 15.5 by completing the following steps:
   a. At a blank PowerPoint screen, click File and then New.
   b. At the New Presentation dialog box, click the Design Templates tab.
   c. At the New Presentation dialog box with the Design Templates tab selected, double-click the Fireball template.
   d. At the New Slide dialog box, double-click the first autolayout *(Title Slide)* in the list box.
   e. At the slide, key the text for the first slide shown in figure 15.5 by completing the following steps:
      1) Click anywhere in the text *Click to add title* and then key **Telecommunications System**.
      2) Click anywhere in the text *Click to add subtitle* and then key **Factors for Evaluating the Effectiveness of a Telecommunications System**.
   f. Click the New Slide button on the Standard toolbar.
   g. At the New Slide dialog box (with the second autolayout [Bulleted List] selected), click OK. (This inserts another slide in the Slide pane.)

h. At the slide, key the text shown in the second slide in figure 15.5 by completing the following steps:
   1) Click anywhere in the text *Click to add title* and then key **COST**.
   2) Click anywhere in the text *Click to add text* and then key the text after the first bullet in the second slide in figure 15.5 (the text that begins *How does the cost of a new system compare...*).
   3) Key the text following the remaining bullets.
i. Click the New Slide button.
j. At the New Slide dialog box (with the second autolayout [Bulleted List] selected), click OK. (This inserts another slide in the Slide pane.) Key the text in the slide as shown for the third slide in figure 15.5.
k. Continue creating the remaining slides in figure 15.5 by completing steps similar to those in 1i and 1j.

2. When all six slides have been created, make Slide 1 the active slide, and then perform a spelling check by clicking the Spelling button. Change or ignore as required during the spelling check.
3. Save the presentation and name it Telecommunications Presentation.
4. Print the six slides on one page.
5. Rearrange some of the slides in the presentation by completing the following steps:
   a. Change to the Slide Sorter view by clicking the Slide Sorter View button on the View toolbar.
   b. Move Slide 4 (QUALITY) before Slide 3 (EFFICIENCY). To do this, position the arrow pointer on Slide 4 (QUALITY), hold down the left mouse button, drag the arrow pointer (with a square attached) to the left of Slide 3, and then release the mouse button.

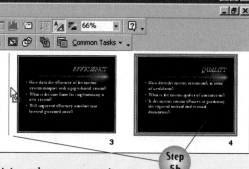

Step 5b

   c. Change to Outline view by clicking the Outline View button on the Standard toolbar.
   d. Move Slide 2 (COST) after Slide 5 (TIME) by completing the following steps:
      1) Position the mouse pointer on the slide icon representing Slide 2 until the pointer turns in four-headed arrow.
      2) Hold down the left mouse button, drag down until a thin horizontal line displays between the last bulleted item in Slide 5 and the beginning of Slide 6, and then release the mouse button.
6. Print the six slides again on one page.
7. Move and copy text within and between slides in Outline view by completing the following steps:
   a. Make sure you are in Outline view.
   b. Move the first bulleted item in Slide 6 to the end of the list by completing the following steps:

   5 ▣ TIME
      • How quickly can information be delivered?
      • What is the estimated training time for a ne
      • What is the time frame for implementing a
   6 ▢ EASE OF USE
      • Will there be a reduction in company efficie
      • Will the new system improve employee pro
      ↑ How long before users feel comfortable wit

   Step 7b3

      1) Scroll down and make sure all of the Slide 6 text displays.
      2) Position the mouse pointer on the first round bullet until it turns into a four-headed arrow.
      3) Hold down the left mouse button, drag the arrow pointer down until a thin horizontal line displays below the last bulleted item, and then release the mouse button. (Make sure that the thin black line displays before releasing the mouse button.)

    c. Copy a bulleted item from Slide 3 (EFFICIENCY) to Slide 4 (TIME) by completing the following steps:

       1) Position the mouse pointer on the last round bullet in Slide 3 until it turns into a four-headed arrow and then click the left mouse button. (This selects the text after the bullet.)

       2) With the text selected, click the Copy button on the Standard toolbar.

       3) Position the I-beam pointer immediately after the question mark in the second bulleted item in Slide 4 and then click the left mouse button.

       4) Press the Enter key. (This moves the insertion point down to the next line and inserts another bullet.)

       5) Click the Paste button on the Standard toolbar. (This pastes the item and also includes another bullet.)

       6) Press the Backspace key twice to remove the extra bullet.

  8. Add a transition and sound of your choosing to all slides.

  9. Save the document again with the same name (Telecommunications Presentation).

10. Run the presentation.

11. Print the presentation in Outline view.

12. Close Telecommunications Presentation.

figure

15.5   *Exercise 2*

| Slide 1 | Title | = | Telecommunications System |
| | Subtitle | = | Factors for Evaluating the Effectiveness of a Telecommunications System |

Slide 2	Title	=	COST
	Bullets	=	• How does the cost of a new system compare with the cost of the current system?
			• What is the cost of maintaining the current system?
			• What will be the training costs of a new system?

Slide 3	Title	=	EFFICIENCY
	Bullets	=	• How does the efficiency of the current system compare with a paper-based system?
			• What is the time frame for implementing a new system?
			• Will improved efficiency translate into lowered personnel costs?

Slide 4	Title	=	QUALITY
	Bullets	=	• How does the current system rank in terms of usefulness?
			• What is the current quality of transmission?
			• Is the current system effective in producing the required internal and external documents?

Slide 5	Title	=	TIME
	Bullets	=	• How quickly can information be delivered?
			• What is the estimated training time for a new system?
			• What is the time frame for implementing a new system?

Slide 6	Title	=	EASE OF USE
	Bullets	=	• Will there be a reduction in company efficiency during the transition?
			• Will the new system improve employee productivity?
			• How long before users feel comfortable with a new system?

Formatting a Presentation

PowerPoint provides a variety of design templates you can use to create a presentation. These templates contain formatting provided by the program. In some situations, the formatting provided by the template will be appropriate; in other situations you will want to change or enhance the formatting of a slide. Formatting can be applied to specific text in a slide or formatting can be applied to an object box.

Formatting Text in a Slide

Text formatting can include a variety of options such as changing fonts, changing font color, and changing paragraph alignment. The steps to change the formatting of a slide vary depending on the type of formatting desired. For example, to change the font of text in a slide, you would select the text first, and then change to the desired font. To change the alignment of a paragraph of text, you would position the insertion point on any character in the paragraph, and then choose the desired alignment.

The Formatting toolbar contains several buttons for applying formatting to text in a slide. The buttons, button names, and a description of what each button accomplishes are shown in figure 15.6.

figure
15.6

PowerPoint Formatting Toolbar Buttons

Click this button	Named	To do this
Times New Roman	Font	Change selected text to a different font
28	Font Size	Change selected text to a different font size
B	Bold	Add or remove bolding to or from selected text
I	Italic	Add or remove italics to or from selected text
U	Underline	Add or remove underlining to or from selected text
S	Text Shadow	Add or remove a shadow to or from selected text
≣	Align Left	Left align text
≣	Center	Center align text
≣	Align Right	Right align text
≣	Numbering	Add or remove numbering to or from selected text
≣	Bullets	Add or remove bullets to or from selected text
A	Increase Font Size	Increase font size of selected text to the next available larger size
A	Decrease Font Size	Decrease font size of selected text to the next available smaller size
←	Promote	Move selected text to the previous level (left) in an outline
→	Demote	Move selected text to the next level (right) in an outline
☆	Animation Effects	Turn on/off the display of the Animation Effects toolbar that contains buttons for adding motion and sound effects to objects in a slide
Common Tasks ▾	Common Tasks	Display a drop-down list with the options New Slide, Slide Layout, and Apply Design Template

Creating a New Line

Some of the slide autolayouts are designed to create bulleted text. You used one of these autolayouts when creating the Telecommunications Presentation. When creating bulleted text in a slide, pressing the Enter key causes the insertion point to move to the next line, inserting another bullet. There may be situations where you want to create a blank line between bulleted items to better separate them without creating another bullet. To do this, use the New Line command, Shift + Enter. When you insert a line with Shift + Enter, the new line is considered part of the previous paragraph. This lets you create a blank line without creating a bullet.

Increasing/Decreasing Spacing before/after Paragraphs

With the New Line command you can insert a blank line without creating a bullet. If you want tighter control over the amount of spacing before or after paragraphs, use options from the Line Spacing dialog box shown in figure 15.7. Display this dialog box by clicking Format and then Line Spacing. Increase or decrease spacing before a paragraph by keying the desired line spacing measurement in the Before paragraph text box. Key a line spacing measurement in the After paragraph text box to control the amount of spacing after paragraphs. By default, the measurement used is Line spacing. This can be changed to *Points* by clicking the down-pointing triangle after the list box containing the word *Lines* and then clicking *Points* at the drop-down list.

figure

15.7

Line Spacing Dialog Box

Formatting with a Master Slide

If you use a PowerPoint template, you may choose to use the formatting provided by the template, or you may want to customize the formatting. If you customize formatting in a presentation, PowerPoint's master slide can be very helpful in reducing the steps needed to format all slides in a presentation. If you know in advance that you want to change the formatting of slides, display the master slide, make the changes needed, and then create the presentation. If the presentation is already created, edit the presentation in a master slide. Any changes made to a master slide will affect all slides in the presentation.

To display the master slide, change to the Slide view, position the insertion point on the Slide View button on the View toolbar, hold down the Shift key (this causes the Slide View button to change to the Slide Master View or Title Master View button), and then click the left mouse button. You can also click <u>V</u>iew, point to <u>M</u>aster, and then click <u>S</u>lide Master. This displays a master slide similar to the one shown in figure 15.8. At this slide, make any desired changes and then click the Slide View button (do not hold down the Shift key this time).

The Slide Master contains all the elements you want to display on a slide.

Control the formatting of all slides (except a title slide) at the Slide Master. Control the formatting of a title slide at the Title Master.

figure

15.8   *Master Slide*

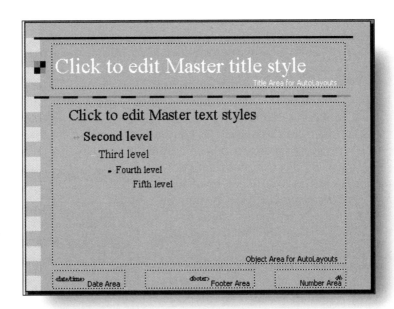

A Slide Master and/or a Title Master can be created in a presentation. If a slide was created using the first autolayout at the New Slide dialog box (Title Slide), holding down the Shift key and then clicking the Slide View button (or clicking View, pointing to Master, and then clicking Title Master) causes the Title Master slide to display. Any formatting changes made to this Title Master slide will affect only those slides in the presentation created with the Title Slide autolayout. If a slide was created using any other autolayout at the New Slide dialog box, holding down the Shift key and then clicking the Slide View button causes the Slide Master to display. Any formatting changes made to this Slide Master slide will affect all slides in the presentation that were created with any autolayout except the Title Slide autolayout.

In exercise 3, you will use a master slide to edit slides in an existing presentation. In exercise 4, you will edit a master slide and then create slides for a presentation.

exercise

Formatting Text in a Presentation Using a Master Slide

1. Open Networking Presentation.
2. Save the presentation with Save As and name it Formatted Network Pres.
3. Change the typeface and text color in slides using a master slide by completing the following steps:
   a. Change to the Slide Sorter view.
   b. Double-click Slide 1.
   c. With Slide 1 displayed in Slide view, position the arrow pointer on the Slide View button on the View toolbar, hold down the Shift key (the Slide View button turns into the Slide Master View button), and then click the left mouse button.
   d. With the master slide displayed, change the typeface and text color of the title by completing the following steps:
      1) Click in the object box containing the text *Click to edit Master title style*. (This selects the object box containing the text.)
      2) Click Format and then Font.
      3) At the Font dialog box, click *Bookman Old Style* in the Font list box. (You will need to scroll up the list of typefaces to display Bookman Old Style. If this typeface is not available, choose a similar serif typeface.)

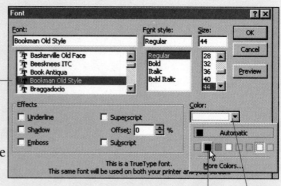

      4) Click the down-pointing triangle at the right of the Color text box.
      5) At the color pop-up menu, click the black color that displays in the Automatic section (the second color from the left).
      6) Click OK to close the dialog box.

e. Change the typeface and color of the text after bullets by completing the following steps:
    1) Click in the object box containing the bulleted text. (This selects the object box.)
    2) Position the arrow pointer on the first bullet until it displays as a four-headed arrow and then click the left mouse button. (This selects all text preceded by bullets.)
    3) With the text selected, click Format and then Font.
    4) At the Font dialog box, click *Bookman Old Style* in the Font list box. (If this typeface is not available, choose a similar serif typeface.)
    5) Click the down-pointing triangle at the right of the Color text box.
    6) Click the More Colors option that displays at the bottom of the drop-down menu.
    7) At the Colors dialog box with the Standard tab selected, click the dark blue color that displays at the right side of the top row of colors.
    8) Click OK to close the Colors dialog box.
    9) Click OK to close the Font dialog box.

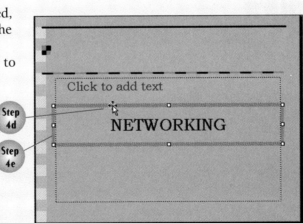

Step 3e7

f. Click the Slide View button on the View toolbar. (This displays Slide 1 with the formatting applied.)
g. Click the Slide Sorter View button on the View toolbar to see how the slides display with the new formatting.

4. Center the text in the title object box and move the object box by completing the following steps:
    a. At the Slide Sorter view, double-click Slide 1.
    b. With Slide 1 displayed in Slide view, click in the object box containing the text *NETWORKING*. (This selects the object box.)
    c. Click the Center button on the Formatting toolbar. (This centers the text horizontally in the object box.)
    d. With the object box still selected, position the arrow pointer on the object box border until a four-headed arrow displays attached to the arrow pointer.
    e. Hold down the left mouse button, drag the outline of the object box until it is centered horizontally and vertically on the slide, and then release the mouse button.

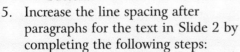

Step 4d

Step 4e

5. Increase the line spacing after paragraphs for the text in Slide 2 by completing the following steps:
    a. Click the Next Slide button until Slide 2 displays.
    b. Click in the object box containing the bulleted text.
    c. Select the bulleted paragraphs of text.
    d. Click Format and then Line Spacing.

e. At the Line Spacing dialog box, make the following changes:
    1) Click the down-pointing triangle at the right of the text box containing the word *Lines* in the <u>A</u>fter paragraph section.
    2) At the drop-down list that displays, click *Points*.
    3) Select the *0* measurement in the After paragraph measurement box and then key **6**.
    4) Click OK to close the Line Spacing dialog box.
    f. Deselect the text.
6. Add a transition and sound of your choosing to each slide.
7. Save the presentation again with the same name (Formatted Network Pres).
8. Run the presentation.
9. Print the presentation so all slides are printed on one page.
10. Close Formatted Network Pres.

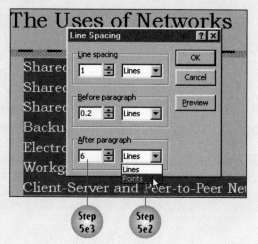

Formatting with Buttons on the Drawing Toolbar

Slides in a PowerPoint template contain placeholders where specific text or objects are inserted. Placeholders consist of an object box containing specific formatting. The formatting applied to placeholders in a template will vary depending on the template selected. These placeholders (object boxes) can be customized by changing such things as the background color or adding a border or shadow. These types of changes can be made with buttons on the Drawing toolbar. The Drawing toolbar displays toward the bottom of the screen in Normal view, Outline view, and Slide view. Figure 15.9 describes the buttons on the Drawing toolbar.

PowerPoint Drawing Toolbar Buttons

Click this button	Named	To do this
Dr<u>a</u>w ▾	Draw	Group or ungroup drawn objects and customize and edit a drawn shape or autoshape
▯	Select Objects	Select text or objects
↻	Free Rotate	Rotate selected object to any degree by dragging a corner of the object in the desired direction
A<u>u</u>toShapes ▾	AutoShapes	Display a palette of shapes that can be drawn in a slide (To draw a shape circumscribed within a perfect square, hold down the Shift key while drawing the shape.)

	Line	Draw a line in a slide
	Arrow	Insert a line with an arrowhead (To draw at 15-degree angles, hold down the Shift key.)
	Rectangle	Draw a rectangle in a slide (To draw a perfect square, hold down the Shift key while drawing the shape.)
	Oval	Draw an oval in a slide (To draw a perfect circle, hold down the Shift key while drawing the shape.)
	Text Box	Add text outside a placeholder (To add text that does not wrap, click tool, click in slide, and then key text. To add text that does wrap, click tool, drag to create a box, and then key text.)
	Insert WordArt	Insert a Microsoft Office drawing object
	Insert Clip Art	Display Insert ClipArt dialog box containing clip art images that can be inserted in a slide
	Fill Color	Fill selected object with a color, pattern, texture, or shaded fill
	Line Color	Change color of selected line
	Font Color	Format selected text with a color
	Line Style	Change thickness of selected line or change it to a compound line
	Dash Style	Change style of selected line, arc, or border to dashed
	Arrow Style	Add arrowheads to a selected line, arc or open freeform
	Shadow	Add or remove an object shadow
	3-D	Add or remove a 3-D effect

Drawing an Object

With buttons on the Drawing toolbar, you can draw a variety of shapes, such as circles, squares, rectangles, ovals. You can also draw straight lines, free form lines, and lines with arrowheads. If you drawn a shape with the Line button or the Arrow button, the shape you draw is considered a *line drawing*. If you draw a shape with the Rectangle or Oval button, the shape you draw is considered an *enclosed object*. If you want to draw the same shape more than once, double-click the shape button on the Drawing toolbar. After drawing the shapes, click the button again to deactivate it.

Use the Rectangle button on the Drawing toolbar to draw a square or rectangle in a document. If you want to draw a square, hold down the Shift key while drawing the shape. The Shift key keeps all sides of the drawn object equal. Use the Oval button to draw a circle or an oval object. To draw a circle, hold down the Shift key while drawing the object.

Creating AutoShapes

With options from the AutoShapes button, you can choose from a variety of predesigned shapes. Click the AutoShapes button and a pop-up menu displays. Point to the desired menu option and a side menu displays. This side menu will offer autoshape choices for the selected option. For example, if you point to the Basic Shapes option, a number of shapes such as a circle, square, triangle, box, stop sign, and so on, display at the right side of the pop-up menu. Click the desired shape and the mouse pointer turns into cross hairs. Position the cross hairs in the document screen, hold down the left mouse button, drag to create the shape, and then release the button.

Selecting an Object

After an object has been created in a document, you may decide to make changes or delete the object. To do this, the object must be selected. To select an enclosed object, position the mouse pointer anywhere inside the object (the mouse pointer displays with a four-headed arrow attached) and then click the left mouse button. To select a line, position the mouse pointer on the line until the pointer turns into an arrow with a four-headed arrow attached, and then click the left mouse button. When an object is selected, it displays surrounded by white sizing handles. Once an object is selected, it can be edited (for example, by changing the fill and the line), it can be moved, or it can be deleted.

If a document screen contains more than one object, you can select several objects at once using the Select Objects button on the Drawing toolbar. To do this, click the Select Objects button, position the cross hairs in the upper left corner of the area containing the objects, hold down the left mouse button, drag the outline to the lower right corner of the area containing the objects, and then release the mouse button. You can also select more than one object by holding down the Shift key as you click each object.

Each object in the selected area displays surrounded by white sizing handles. Objects in the selected area are connected. For example, if you move one of the objects in the selected area, the other objects move relatively.

Deleting an Object

An object you have drawn can be deleted from the document screen. To do this, select the object, and then press the Delete key.

Moving and Copying an Object

Select an object and then move it by positioning the mouse pointer inside the object (mouse pointer displays with a four-headed arrow attached), holding down the left mouse button, and then dragging the outline of the object to the new location. If you select more than one object, moving one of the objects will move the other objects.

Moving an object removes the object from its original position and inserts it into a new location. If you want the object to stay in its original location and an exact copy to be inserted in a new location, use the Ctrl key while dragging the object.

Sizing an Object

With the sizing handles that appear around an object when it is selected, the size of the object can be changed. To change the size of the object, select it, and then position the mouse pointer on a sizing handle until it turns into a double-headed arrow. Hold down the left mouse button, drag the outline of the shape toward or away from the center of the object until it is the desired size, and then release the mouse button.

Formatting Objects

With buttons on the Drawing toolbar you can add fill color and/or shading to an object, change the line style, and change the line color. Click the down-pointing triangle at the right side of the Fill Color or Line Color button and a palette of color choices displays. Choose a color at this palette or click an option to display more fill or line colors and fill or line patterns.

Creating a Presentation and Formatting Objects Using a Master Slide

1. Prepare the presentation on enhanced services for McCormack Financial Services shown in figure 15.10 by completing the following steps:
   a. At a blank PowerPoint screen, click File and then New.
   b. At the New Presentation dialog box, click the Design Templates tab.
   c. At the New Presentation dialog box with the Design Templates tab selected, double-click the Neon Frame template.
   d. At the New Slide dialog box, double-click the first autolayout (Title Slide).
   e. Create a Title Master slide for the presentation by completing the following steps:
      1) Position the arrow pointer on the Slide View button on the View toolbar, hold down the Shift key (this turns the button into Title Master View), and then click the left mouse button. (This displays a master slide.)
      2) With the master slide displayed, click anywhere in the text *Click to edit Master title style*.

3) Change the font to 44-point Arial bold italics.
4) With the text object box still selected (the box containing *Click to edit Master title slide*), add fill color by completing the following steps:

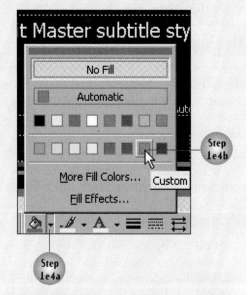

   a) Click the down-pointing triangle at the right side of the Fill Color button on the Drawing toolbar.
   b) At the pop-up menu that displays, click the second color from the right in the bottom row (a shade of green).

Step 1e4b

Step 1e4a

5) Draw diamond shapes in the lower right corner of the slide by completing the following steps:
   a) Click the AutoShapes button on the Drawing toolbar.
   b) At the pop-up menu that displays, point to Basic Shapes (this causes a side menu to display).
   c) At the side menu, click the diamond shape (last shape in the top row).
   d) Hold down the Shift key (this draws the diamond circumscribed in a square) and then position the arrow pointer (displays as a crosshair) in the bottom right corner of the slide. (You will be drawing the diamond shape over text in the master slide. Do not worry about this—the text will not display in the regular slide.)

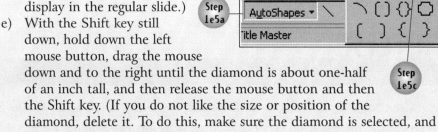

Step 1e5b

Step 1e5a

Step 1e5c

   e) With the Shift key still down, hold down the left mouse button, drag the mouse down and to the right until the diamond is about one-half of an inch tall, and then release the mouse button and then the Shift key. (If you do not like the size or position of the diamond, delete it. To do this, make sure the diamond is selected, and then press the Delete key.)
   f) If you need to move the diamond, make sure it is selected, position the arrow pointer inside the selected area, hold down the left mouse button, drag to the desired position, and then release the mouse button.
6) When the diamond is positioned in the desired location, copy it two times (you should end up with three diamond shapes in a row) by completing the following steps:
   a) With the diamond selected, position the arrow pointer inside the selected box.
   b) Hold down the Ctrl key and the left mouse button.

c) Drag the outline to the desired position and then release the mouse button and then the Ctrl key. Repeat these steps to create the third diamond shape.

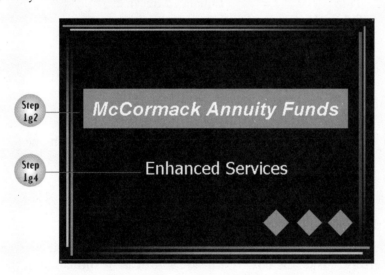

Step 1e6c

7) Click anywhere in the text *Click to edit Master subtitle style*.
8) Change the font size to 40 points.

f. Click the Slide View button on the View toolbar. (This removes the master slide and displays a slide with the formatted elements.)

g. Key the text shown in figure 15.10 by completing the following steps:
1) Click anywhere in the text *Click to add title*.
2) Key **McCormack Annuity Funds**.
3) Click anywhere in the text *Click to add subtitle*.
4) Key **Enhanced Services**.

Step 1g2

McCormack Annuity Funds

Step 1g4

Enhanced Services

h. Click the New Slide button on the Standard toolbar.
i. At the New Slide dialog box, double-click the first autolayout (Title Slide).
j. At the next slide, key the text shown in the second slide in figure 15.10.
k. Continue creating the remaining four slides shown in figure 15.10 by completing steps similar to those in 1h through 1j.

2. View all slides in the presentation by clicking the Slide Sorter View button on the View toolbar. Make any necessary adjustments to the object boxes in the slides. For example, you may want to move some object boxes to better center the text on the slide.
3. Display Slide 1 in Slide view and then increase the size of the subtitle Enhanced Services to 48 points.
4. Add a transition and sound of your choosing to all slides.
5. Save the presentation and name it Enhanced Services Presentation.
6. Run the presentation.
7. Print all six slides on the same page.
8. Close Enhanced Services Presentation.

figure

15.10   *Exercise 4*

Slide 1	Title	=	McCormack Annuity Funds
	Subtitle	=	Enhanced Services
Slide 2	Title	=	Enhanced Services
	Subtitle	=	Set up future accumulations transfers
Slide 3	Title	=	Enhanced Services
	Subtitle	=	Receive automatic statement confirmation
Slide 4	Title	=	Enhanced Services
	Subtitle	=	Faster cash withdrawals
Slide 5	Title	=	Enhanced Services
	Subtitle	=	Personal service from 8 a.m. to 11 p.m. weekdays
Slide 6	Title	=	Enhanced Services
	Subtitle	=	Multiple transfers made with one telephone call

Creating a Text Box

With the Text Box button on the Drawing toolbar, you can create a box and then insert text inside the box. Text inside a box can be formatted in the normal manner. For example, you can change the font, alignment, or indent of the text.

Wrapping Text in an Autoshape

A text box can be drawn inside an autoshape. You can also click the Text Box button on the Drawing toolbar and then click in the autoshape. This positions the insertion point inside the shape where you can key text. If you want text to wrap within the autoshape, Click Format and then AutoShape. At the Format AutoShape dialog box, click the Text Box tab. This displays the dialog box as shown in figure 15.11. At this dialog box, choose the Word wrap shape in AutoShape option. Choose the Resize AutoShape to Fit text option if you want the size of the autoshape to conform to the text. Rotate text in a text box by choosing the Rotate text within AutoShape by 90° option.

figure

15.11

Format AutoShape Dialog Box with Text Box Tab Selected

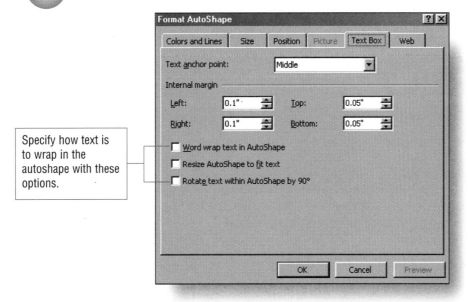

Specify how text is to wrap in the autoshape with these options.

exercise 5

Formatting at the Title Master Slide and Creating an AutoShape and Text Box

1. Open Enhanced Services Presentation.
2. Save the presentation with Save As and name it Formatted Enhanced Presentation.
3. Format objects at the Title Master slide by completing the following steps:
   a. Display the presentation in Slide Sorter view.
   b. Double-click Slide 1.
   c. With Slide 1 displayed in Slide view, hold down the Shift key, and then click the Title Master View button on the View toolbar. (Remember that the Slide View button turns into the Title Master View button when the Shift key is held down.)
   d. Change the green fill color in the top box to a shade of blue and add a border to the object box by completing the following steps:
      1) Click anywhere in the text *Click to edit the Master title style*.
      2) Click the down-pointing triangle at the right side of the Fill Color button on the Drawing toolbar.
      3) At the pop-up menu that displays, click the last color at the right in the top row (matches the blue in the diamonds).

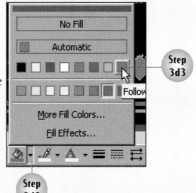

Step 3d3

Step 3d2

4) Click the Line Style button on the Drawing toolbar.
5) At the palette of line style choices that displays, click the first *4½ pt* single line choice from the top.
6) Click the down-pointing triangle at the right side of the Line Color button on the Drawing toolbar.
7) At the pop-up menu that displays, click the purple color (third color from the right in the top row).

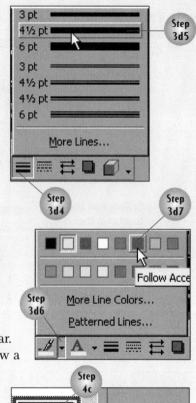

e. Click the Slide View button on the View toolbar.

4. Create the slide shown in figure 15.12 by completing the following steps:
   a. Display Slide 6. (This is the last slide in the presentation.)
   b. Click the New Slide button on the Standard toolbar.
   c. At the New Slide dialog box, double-click the last autolayout in the third row (Blank).

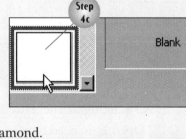

   d. At Slide 7, insert the title shown in figure 15.12 by completing the following steps:
      1) Click the Text Box button on the Drawing toolbar.
      2) Position the cross hairs in the slide and then draw a text box in the slide that will hold the title *Enhanced Services Features*.
      3) After drawing the text box, change the font to 44-point Arial bold italic.
      4) Key the title **Enhanced Services Features**.
   e. Draw the diamond at the left by completing the following steps:
      1) Click the AutoShapes button on the Drawing toolbar, point to Basic Shapes, and then click Diamond.

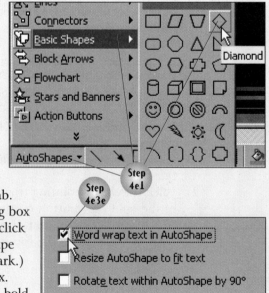

      2) Hold down the Shift key and then draw the diamond the size and position shown in figure 15.12.
      3) Insert the text and wrap the text in the autoshape by completing the following steps:
         a) Click the Text Box button on the Drawing toolbar.
         b) Click inside the diamond shape.
         c) Click Format and then AutoShape.
         d) At the Format AutoShape dialog box, click the Text Box tab.
         e) At the Format AutoShape dialog box with the Text Box tab selected, click the Word wrap text in AutoShape option. (This inserts a check mark.)
         f) Click OK to close the dialog box.
         g) Change the font to 20-point Arial bold.

h) Key the text **Personal Service**. (Make sure the word *Personal* is not split between two lines. If it is, increase the size of the diamond.)
   f. Copy the diamond to the right two times.
   g. Select the text in the middle diamond and then key **Easy to Use**.
   h. Select the text in the diamond at the right and then key **Fast and Accurate**.
5. Save the presentation again with the same name (Formatted Enhanced Presentation).
6. Print Slide 7 in grayscale.
7. Display Slide 1 and then run the presentation.
8. Close the presentation.

Exercise 5, Slide 7

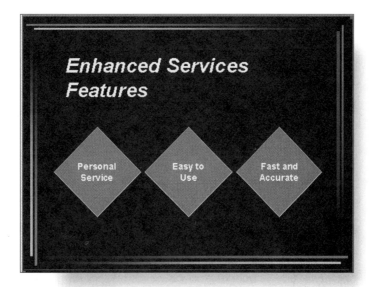

Grouping and Ungrouping Objects

You can group objects so you can work with them as if they were a single object. Grouped objects can be formatted, sized, moved, flipped, and/or rotated as a single unit. Group selected objects by clicking the Draw button on the Drawing toolbar and then clicking Group at the pop-up menu. Ungroup selected objects by clicking the Draw button and then clicking Ungroup.

Flipping and Rotating an Object

A selected object can be rotated and flipped horizontally or vertically. To rotate or flip an object, select the object, click the Draw button, point to Rotate or Flip, and then click the desired rotation or flip option at the side menu that displays. A drawn object can be rotated but a text box cannot.

Another method for rotating an object is to select the object and then click the Free Rotate button on the Drawing toolbar. This displays small green circles, called *rotation handles*, around the selected object. Use these rotation handles to rotate the object.

Distributing and Aligning Objects

Distribute and align selected objects with the D<u>r</u>aw button on the Drawing toolbar. To do this, select the objects, click the D<u>r</u>aw button on the Drawing toolbar, and then point to <u>A</u>lign or Distribute. This causes a side menu to display with options for aligning at the left, center, right, top, middle, or bottom and distributing horizontally and vertically. Depending on the objects selected, some of the options at the side menu may be inactive.

Creating, Grouping, Aligning, and Distributing AutoShapes

1. Open Formatted Enhanced Presentation.
2. Copy Slide 7 by completing the following steps:
   a. Display the slides in Slide Sorter view.
   b. Click Slide 7.
   c. Position the arrow pointer in Slide 7, hold down the Ctrl key and then the left mouse button. Drag to the right so the thin, vertical line displays at the right side of Slide 7, then release the mouse button and then the Ctrl key.
   d. Double-click the new Slide 8.
3. Create and format Slide 8 as shown in figure 15.13 by completing the following steps:
   a. Select *Features* in the title and then key **Launch Date**.
   b. Delete the triangles by completing the following steps:
      1) Click the Select Objects button on the Drawing toolbar.
      2) Draw a border around the three diamonds.
      3) Press the Delete key.
   c. Click the Text Box button on the Drawing toolbar, draw a text box the size and location of the box containing *May 1, 2001*.
   d. With the insertion point inside the text box, change the font to 48-point Arial bold, click the Center button on the Formatting toolbar, and then key **May 1, 2001**.
   e. Draw the blue arrow that displays in the upper left side of the slide by completing the following steps:
      1) Click the A<u>u</u>toShapes button on the Drawing toolbar, point to Block <u>A</u>rrows, and then click the second arrow from the left in the third row from the bottom (Notched Right Arrow).
      2) Hold down the Shift key and then draw an arrow the approximate size and location of the arrow in the upper left side of the slide. (You will rotate this arrow later in the exercise.)

f. Copy the arrow three times to the approximate positions shown in figure 15.13. (You will rotate and flip the arrows later in the next steps.)
g. Group, flip, and then ungroup the arrows at the right by completing the following steps:
    1) Click the Select Objects button on the Drawing toolbar.
    2) Draw a border around the two arrows at the right side of the slide.
    3) Click the Draw button on the Drawing toolbar and then click Group at the pop-up menu.
    4) With the two arrows selected, click the Draw button, point to Rotate or Flip, and then click Flip Horizontal.
    5) Ungroup the arrows by clicking Draw and then clicking Ungroup at the pop-up list.

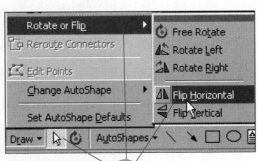

Step 3g4

h. Rotate the arrow in the upper left side of the slide by completing the following steps:
    1) Click the upper left arrow.
    2) Click the Free Rotate button on the Drawing toolbar.
    3) Position the mouse pointer on one of the green rotation handles that displays around the arrow, hold down the left mouse button, drag to rotate the arrow (as shown in figure 15.13) and then release the mouse button.
    4) Click the Free Rotate button to deactivate it.
    5) Drag the arrow to the location shown in figure 15.13.

Step 3h3

i. Complete steps similar to those in 3h to rotate the other three arrows so they display as shown in figure 15.13.
j. Align and distribute the arrows by completing the following steps:
    1) Click the Select Objects button on the Drawing toolbar.
    2) Draw a border around the top two arrows. (After the border is drawn, make sure both top arrows display surrounded by sizing handles.)
    3) Click the Draw button on the Drawing toolbar, point to Align or Distribute, and then click Align Top.

Step 3j2

    4) Draw a border around the bottom two arrows. (After the border is drawn, make sure both bottom arrows display surrounded by sizing handles.)
    5) Click the Draw button on the Drawing toolbar, point to Align or Distribute, and then click Align Bottom.
    6) Draw a border around the two arrows at the left side of the slide.
    7) Click the Draw button on the Drawing toolbar, point to Align or Distribute, and then click Align Left.
    8) Draw a border around the two arrows at the right side of the slide.
    9) Click the Draw button on the Drawing toolbar, point to Align or Distribute, and then click Align Right.
    10) Deselect the arrows.
4. Save the presentation again with the same name (Formatted Enhanced Presentation).
5. Display Slide 1 and then run the presentation.
6. Print only Slide 8 in grayscale.
7. Close Formatted Enhanced Presentation.

figure
15.13

Exercise 6, Slide 8

Formatting the Slide Color Scheme

PowerPoint design templates provide interesting and varied formatting effects and save time when preparing a presentation. Some of the formatting applied to slides by the design template can be formatted. For example, the color scheme and background of slides can be changed. To change the color scheme of a design template, open a presentation, click Format and then Slide Color Scheme. This displays the Color Scheme dialog box with the Standard tab selected as shown in figure 15.14.

figure
15.14

Color Scheme Dialog Box with Standard Tab Selected

Click the desired scheme in the Color schemes section and then click the Apply button to apply the scheme to the active slide or click the Apply to All button to apply the scheme to all slides in the presentation.

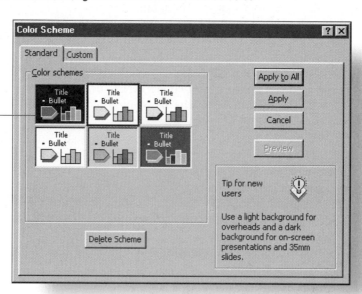

Click a color scheme in the <u>C</u>olor schemes section and then click the <u>A</u>pply button to apply the color scheme to the selected slide. If you want the color scheme applied to all slides in the presentation, click the Apply <u>t</u>o All button.

Formatting Slide Color Schemes

1. Open History of Computers 1980s. (This presentation is located in the *Presentations* folder on the CD that accompanies this textbook.)
2. Save the presentation in the Chapter 15 folder on your disk with Save As and name it Formatted History Pres.
3. Change the color scheme by completing the following steps:

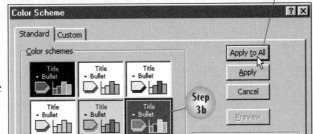

   a. Click F<u>o</u>rmat and then Slide <u>C</u>olor Scheme.
   b. At the Color Scheme dialog box with the Standard tab selected, click the last color scheme in the bottom row.
   c. Click the Apply <u>t</u>o All button.
4. Apply a transition of your choosing to each slide.
5. Save the presentation again with the same name (Formatted History Pres).
6. Run the presentation.
7. Print all six slides on one page.
8. Close Formatted History Pres.
9. Delete Formatted History Pres. (Check with your instructor before deleting this presentation.)

Customizing the Slide Color Scheme

Change the color for individual slide elements by clicking the Custom tab at the Color Scheme dialog box. This displays the dialog box as shown in figure 15.15. Click an item in the <u>S</u>cheme colors section and then click the Change C<u>o</u>lor button. At the Background Color dialog box, click the desired color and then click OK.

figure

15.15 *Color Scheme Dialog Box with Custom Tab Selected*

Click the desired element scheme in the Scheme colors section and then click the Change Color button.

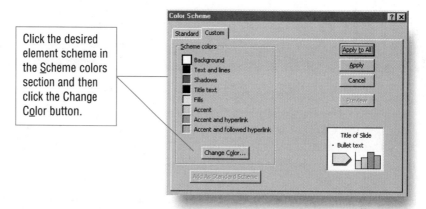

Background color can be changed with options at the Color Scheme dialog box with the Custom Tab selected or at the Background dialog box shown in figure 15.16. Display this dialog box by clicking Format and then Background. At the Background dialog box, click the down-pointing triangle at the right of the fill text box and then click the desired color at the drop-down list. Click the Apply button to apply the background color to the active slide or click Apply to All to apply the background color to all slides.

figure

15.16 *Background Dialog Box*

Click this down-pointing triangle to display a palette of color choices.

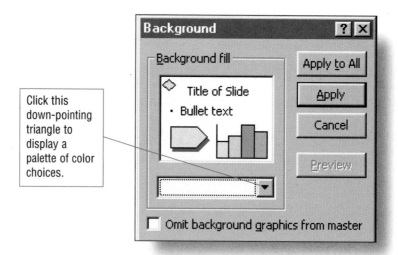

exercise 8

Customizing the Slide Color Scheme

1. Open History of Computers 1980s. (This presentation is located in the *Presentations* folder on the CD that accompanies this textbook.)
2. Save the presentation in the Chapter 15 folder on your disk with Save As and name it Customized History Pres.
3. Customize the slide color scheme by completing the following steps:
   a. Click Format and then Slide Color Scheme. **Step 3c1**
   b. At the Color Scheme dialog box, click the Custom tab.
   c. At the Color Scheme dialog box with the Custom tab selected, change the background color by completing the following steps: **Step 3c3**
      1) Click the color box preceding Background in the Scheme colors section of the dialog box.
      2) Click the Change Color button.
      3) At the Background Color dialog box, click a light blue color of your choosing.
      4) Click OK to close the Background Color dialog box.
   d. At the Color Scheme dialog box, make the following changes:
      1) Change the Shadows color to dark blue by completing steps similar to those in 3c.
      2) Change the Accent color to light green by completing steps similar to those in 3c.
   e. Click the Apply to All button.
4. Save the presentation again with the same name (Customized History Pres).
5. Run the presentation.
6. Print all six slides on one page.
7. Close Customized History Pres.
8. Delete Customized History Pres. (Check with your instructor before deleting this presentation.)

Changing the Design Template

When preparing presentations for this chapter and the previous chapter, you chose the design template first and then created each slide. A different design template can be applied to an existing presentation. To do this, click Format and then Apply Design Template; or, click the Common Tasks button on the Formatting toolbar and then click Apply Design Template at the drop-down menu. This displays the Apply Design Template dialog box shown in figure 15.17. This dialog box contains the same design templates that are available at the New Presentation dialog box with the Design Templates tab selected. Click a design template in the list box and then click the Apply button.

If you change the design template for an existing presentation, check to see how the new design formatting affects text and objects in slides. You may need to make some adjustments.

figure

15.17

Apply Design Template Dialog Box

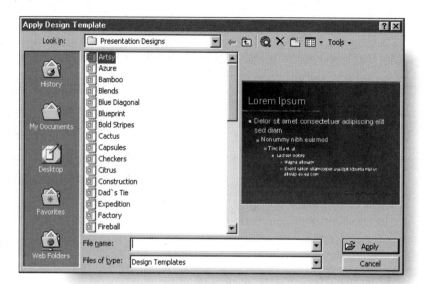

exercise 9

Changing the Design Template

1. Open History of Computers 1980s. (This presentation is located in the *Presentations* folder on the CD that accompanies this textbook.)
2. Save the presentation in the *Chapter 15* folder on your disk with Save As and name it New Design History Pres.
3. Choose a different design template by completing the following steps:
   a. Click the Common Tasks button on the Formatting toolbar and then click Apply Design Template at the drop-down menu.
   b. At the Apply Design Template dialog box, click *LaVerne* in the list box. (You will need to scroll down the list to display LaVerne.)
   c. Click the Apply button.
4. Run the presentation to see how it appears with the new design template applied.
5. Print all six slides on one page.
6. Save and then close New Design History Pres.
7. Open Telecommunications Presentation.
8. Apply a different design template of your choosing to this presentation.
9. Run the presentation to see how it appears with the new design template applied.
10. Print all six slides on one page.
11. Close Telecommunications Presentation without saving the changes.
12. Delete New Design History Pres. (Check with your instructor before deleting this presentation.)

Creating a Blank Presentation and then Applying a Design Template

Many of the presentations you have created in this and the previous chapter have been based on a design template. You can also create a blank presentation and then apply your own formatting or apply a design template. To create a blank presentation click File and then New. At the New Presentation dialog box with the General tab selected, double-click *Blank Presentation*. Create the presentation using the view you prefer and then apply formatting or apply a design template.

Preparing a Transparency

When preparing a presentation, consider using a design template with a darker background for a presentation that will be run with PowerPoint or that will be made into 35mm slides. If you are going to print slides as transparencies, consider using a lighter background. Choosing an appropriate color for a presentation or transparency is as easy as changing the design template. In exercise 10, you will apply a design template with a light background and then print one of the slides as a transparency. (Before completing this exercise, check with your instructor to see if you should print on an actual transparency or on normal paper.)

Formatting with Format Painter

If you create a blank presentation and decide to apply your own formatting, consider using the Format Painter. Use Format Painter to apply the same formatting in more than one location in a slide or slides. To use the Format Painter, apply the desired formatting to text, position the insertion point anywhere in the formatted text, and then double-click the Format Painter button on the Standard toolbar. Using the mouse, select the additional text to which you want the formatting applied. After applying the formatting in the desired locations, click the Format Painter button to deactivate it.

If you need to apply formatting in only one other location, click the Format Painter button once. The first time you select text, the formatting is applied and the Format Painter is deactivated.

Promoting and Demoting Text in the Slide Pane

In chapter 14, you created a presentation in the Outline view and used buttons on the Outlining toolbar to promote and demote bulleted text. You can also demote and promote bulleted text in the Slide pane. Press the Tab key to demote text in a slide or press Shift + Tab to promote text. If the Outlining toolbar is on, you can also promote and demote bulleted text with the Promote and Demote buttons.

exercise 10

Creating and Formatting a Blank Presentation

1. Create a blank presentation with the information shown in figure 15.18 by completing the following steps:
   a. Click File and then New.
   b. At the New Presentation dialog box, click the General tab.
   c. At the New Presentation dialog box with the General tab selected, double-click *Blank Presentation* in the list box.

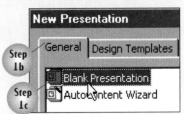

    d.   At the New Slide dialog box, double-click the first autolayout (Title Slide).

    e.   In the Slide pane, key the title and subtitle for Slide 1 as shown in figure 15.18.

    f.   Create the remaining slides shown in figure 15.19. Use the Bulleted List autolayout for Slides 2 through 5. When keying bulleted text, press the Tab key to demote text or press Shift + Tab to promote text.

2. Suppose you are going to print transparencies for the slides in this presentation. To do this, apply a design template with a light background by completing the following steps:

    a.   Change to the Slide Sorter view.

    b.   Click Format and then Apply Design Template.

    c.   At the Apply Design Template dialog box, double-click *Citrus* in the list box.

3. Change the font style and color of the terms using Format Painter by completing the following steps:

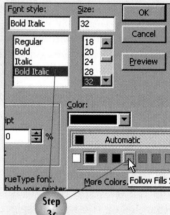

Step 3c

    a.   Double-click Slide 4.

    b.   Select the term *Balance:* (be sure to select the colon).

    c.   Display the Font dialog box, change the Font style to *Bold Italic*, change the color to the green that follows the color scheme, and then close the dialog box.

    d.   Deselect *Balance:* and then click anywhere in *Balance:*.

    e.   Double-click the Format Painter button on the Standard toolbar.

    f.   Using the mouse, select *Color Wheel:*.

    g.   Using the mouse, select each of the other terms in Slide 4 *(Contrast:, Gradient:, Hue:)*.

    h.   Display Slide 5 and then use the mouse to select each of the terms (including the colon) in the slide.

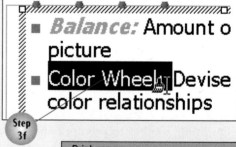

Step 3f

    i.   Click the Format Painter button to deactivate it.

    j.   Deselect the text.

4. Print only Slide 2 as a transparency by completing the following steps: *(Note: Check with your instructor to determine if you should print on an actual transparency or if you should print on paper.)*

    a.   In Slide Sorter view, click Slide 2.

    b.   Insert the transparency in your printer. (This step is optional.)

    c.   Click File and then Print.

    d.   At the Print dialog box, click the Current slide option in the Print range section.

    e.   Click OK.

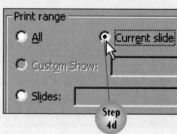

Step 4d

5. Save the presentation and name it Color Presentation.

6. Print all five slides on one page.

7. Close Color Presentation.

figure

15.18   *Exercise 10*

| Slide 1 | Title | = | COMPANY PUBLICATIONS |
| | Subtitle | = | Using Color in Publications |

Slide 2
Title = Communicating with Color
Bullets =
- Color in a publication can:
  - Elicit feelings
  - Emphasize important text
  - Attract attention
- Choose one or two colors
- Use "spot color" by using color only in specific areas

Slide 3
Title = Printing the Publication
Bullets =
- Print all copies on a color printer
- Print on a color printer and duplicate with a color photocopier
- Print on color paper
- Print on specialty paper

Slide 4
Title = Color Terminology
Bullets =
- Balance: Amount of light and dark in a picture
- Color Wheel: Devise used to illustrate color relationships
- Contrast: Amount of gray in a color
- Gradient: Gradual varying of color
- Hue: Variation of a color such as green-blue

Slide 5
Title = Color Terminology
Bullets =
- Pixel: Each dot in a picture or graphic
- Resolution: The number of dots that make up an image on a screen or printer
- Reverse: Black background on white foreground or white type against a colored background
- Saturation: Purity of a color

Formatting with Bullets and Numbers

Each design template contains a Bulleted List autolayout. The appearance and formatting of the bullets in this autolayout varies with each template. You can choose to use the bullet provided by the design template or you can insert different bullets and also can change to numbering.

Changing Bullets

Customize bullets with options at the Bullets and Numbering dialog box with the Bulleted tab selected as shown in figure 15.19. Display this dialog box by clicking in a bulleted list placeholder, and then clicking Format and Bullets and Numbering. At the dialog box, choose one the predesigned bullets from the list box, change the size of the bullets by percentage in relation to the text size, change the bullet color, and display bullet pictures and characters.

15.19 *Bullets and Numbering Dialog Box with Bulleted Tab Selected*

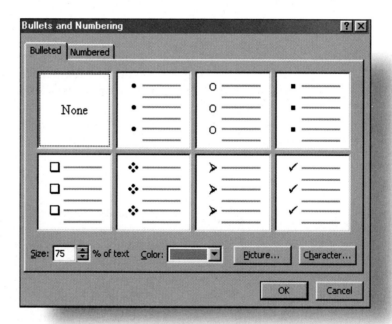

Click the Picture button located towards the bottom of the dialog box and the Picture Bullet dialog box with the Pictures tab selected displays as shown in figure 15.20. Click the desired bullet in the list box and then click the Insert clip button.

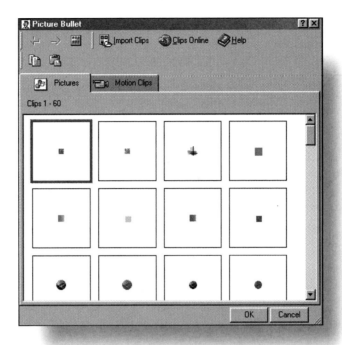

Click the Character button located towards the bottom right corner of the Bullets and Numbering dialog box and the Bullet dialog box displays. This dialog box contains the same character and symbols choices as the Insert Symbol dialog box you learned about in Word.

Inserting Numbering

A bulleted list can be easily changed to numbers. To do this, select the bulleted list and then click the Numbering button on the Formatting toolbar. You can also change to numbering by selecting the list and then displaying the Bullets and Numbering dialog box with the Numbers tab selected. Display this dialog box by clicking Format and the Bullets and Numbering. At the Bullets and Numbering dialog box, click the Numbered tab. This dialog box contains many of the same options as the Bullets and Numbering dialog box with the Bulleted tab selected.

Changing Bullets and Applying Numbering

1. Open Color Presentation.
2. Change the first-level bullets in slides 2 through 5 by completing the following steps:
   a. Display Slide 2 in Slide view.
   b. Hold down the Shift key and then click the Slide View Master button on the View toolbar.
   c. Click in the text *Click to edit Master text styles*.
   d. Click Format and then Bullets and Numbering.
   e. At the Bullets and Numbering dialog box with the Bulleted tab selected, click the up-pointing triangle at the right side of the Size option until *85* displays in the text box.
   f. Click the Picture button that displays towards the bottom of the dialog box.

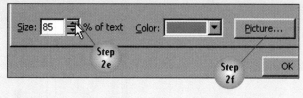

   g. At the Picture Bullets dialog box with the Pictures tab selected, click the second bullet from the left in the second row (this is a gold, square bullet).
   h. Click the Insert clip button.
   i. Click the Slide View button. (This removes the master slide.)

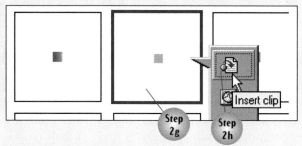

3. Print only Slide 2.
4. Change the second-level bullets in Slide 2 by completing the following steps:
   a. Make sure Slide 2 is displayed in Slide view.
   b. Hold down the Shift key and then click the Slide Master View button on the View toolbar.
   c. Click in the text *Second level*.
   d. Click Format and then Bullets and Numbering.
   e. At the Bullets and Numbering dialog box with the Bulleted tab selected, click the Character button that displays in the bottom right corner of the dialog box.
   f. At the Bullet dialog box, click the down-pointing triangle at the right side of the Color option, and then click the green color that follows the color scheme.
   g. Click the up-pointing triangle at the right side of the Size text box until *75* displays in the box.
   h. Click the pen image (first image [in the second square] from the left in the top row).
   i. Click OK to close the dialog box.
   j. Click the Slide View button. (This removes the master slide.)

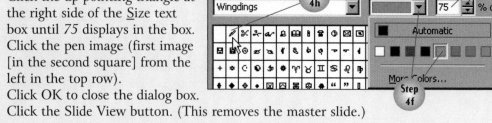

5. Print only Slide 2.
6. Save the presentation with the same name (Color Presentation).
7. Change the first-level bullets to numbers in Slides 2 through 5 by completing the following steps:
   a. Make sure Slide 2 is displayed in Slide view.
   b. Hold down the Shift key and then click the Slide Master View button on the View toolbar.
   c. Click in the text *Click to edit Master text styles*.
   d. Click the Numbering button on the Formatting toolbar.
   e. Change the color of the numbers by completing the following steps:
      1) Click Format and then Bullets and Numbering.
      2) At the Bullets and Numbering dialog box, make sure the Numbered tab is selected.
      3) Click the down-pointing triangle at the right side of the Color option and then click the orange color that follows the color scheme.
      4) Click OK to close the dialog box.
   f. Click the Slide View button. (This removes the master slide.)
8. Save the presentation again with the same name (Color Presentation).
9. Display Slide 1 and then run the presentation.
10. Print all five slides on one page.
11. Close the presentation.

Inserting Headers and Footers in a Presentation

Insert information that you want to appear at the top or bottom of each slide or on note and handout pages with options at the Header and Footer dialog box. If you want the information to appear on all slides, click View and then Header and Footer. This displays the Header and Footer dialog box with the Slide tab selected as shown in figure 15.21.

Header and Footer Dialog Box with Slide Tab Selected

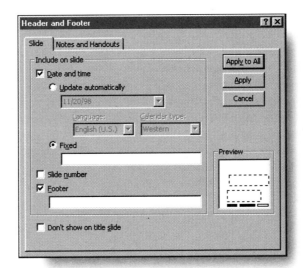

Include the date and time as fixed or automatic. To include a fixed date and time, click in the Fixed text box and then key the desired text. If you want the date and/or time inserted and then automatically updated when the presentation is opened, click the Update automatically option. Specify the format for the date and/or time by clicking the down-pointing triangle at the right side of the Update automatically text box and then click the desired format at the drop-down list. If you want the slide number inserted in a presentation, click the Slide number check box. Key any footer text desired in the Footer text box. Click the Apply button to apply the element(s) to the current slide. If you want the element(s) inserted in all slides, click the Apply to All button. Elements added to a slide or slides are previewed in the Preview section of the dialog box.

exercise 12

Inserting the Date, Time, Slide Number, and a Footer in a Presentation

1. Open Telecommunications Presentation.
2. Insert the date, time, slide number, and a footer into the presentation by completing the following steps:
   a. Click View and then Header and Footer.
   b. At the Header and Footer dialog box with the Slide tab selected, if necessary, click Date and time to insert a check mark in the check box.
   c. Click the Update automatically option.
   d. Click the down-pointing triangle at the right side of the Update automatically text box and then click the option that displays the date in numbers followed by the time (i.e., 12/01/99 12:35 PM).

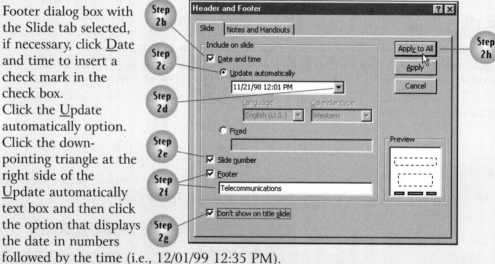

   e. Click the Slide number option to insert a check mark in the check box.
   f. Click in the Footer check box and then key **Telecommunications** in the Footer text box.
   g. Click the Don't show on title slide option to insert a check mark in the check box.
   h. Click the Apply to All button.
3. Save the document again with the same name (Telecommunications Presentation).
4. Run the presentation to see how the inserted text displays in the slides (the date, time, page number, and footer will not display on the first slide.)
5. Print all six slides on one page.
6. Close Telecommunications Presentation.

Inserting a Header and/or Footer in Notes and Handouts

Elements selected at the Header and Footer dialog box with the Slide tab selected are inserted in slides in a presentation. If you want elements inserted in notes or handouts, choose options at the Header and Footer dialog box with the Notes and Handouts tab selected as shown in figure 15.22.

15.22 Header and Footer Dialog Box with Notes and Handouts Tab Selected

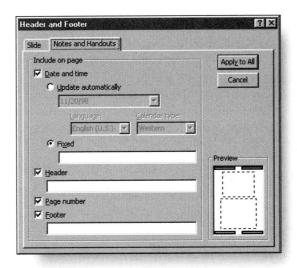

At the Header and Footer dialog box with the Notes and Handouts tab selected, choose to insert the date and/or time fixed or automatically, include a header and/or footer, and include page numbering. Choices made at this dialog box print when the presentation is printed as notes pages, handouts, or an outline.

Adding Speaker Notes

If you are going to give your presentation in front of an audience, consider creating speaker notes for some or all of the slides. Create speaker notes containing additional information about the slide that will help you during the presentation. Speaker notes do not display on a slide when the presentation is running. Speaker notes print when *Notes Pages* is selected in the Print what option of the Print dialog box.

To insert speaker notes, display slides in the Normal view, click in the Notes pane, and then key the information. Another method for inserting speaker notes is to display the presentation in Notes Page view. To do this, click View and then Notes Page. This displays the active slide with a text box below. Click inside the text box and then key the speaker note information. Format speaker notes in the normal manner. For example, you can change the font, change the text alignment, and insert bullets or numbering.

You can create and/or display speaker notes while a presentation is running. To do this, run the presentation, and then display the desired slide. Move the mouse to display the *Slide Show* menu icon. Click the *Slide Show* menu icon and then click Speaker Notes at the pop-up menu. This displays the Speaker Notes dialog box. View, key, or edit text at this dialog box and then click the Close button.

exercise 13

Inserting a Header, Footer, and the Date in Notes and Handouts

1. Open Telecommunications Presentation.
2. Insert a header and footer, the date, and page numbering in notes and handouts by completing the following steps:
   a. Click View and then Header and Footer.
   b. At the Header and Footer dialog box, click the Notes and Handouts tab.
   c. At the Header and Footer dialog box with the Notes and Handouts tab selected, click the Update automatically option. (Check to make sure the current date displays in the Update automatically text box. If not, click the down-pointing triangle at the right side of the text box, and then click the desired date style at the drop-down list.)

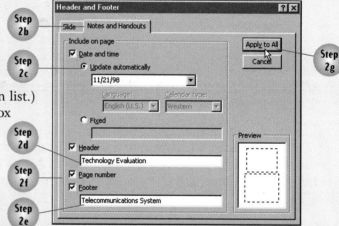

   d. Click in the Header text box and then key **Technology Evaluation**.
   e. Click in the Footer text box and then key **Telecommunications System**.
   f. Make sure there is a check mark in the Page number check box.
   g. Click the Apply to All button.
3. Add and format speaker notes by completing the following steps:
   a. Display Slide 2 in Normal view.
   b. Click in the Notes pane. (This pane displays below the slide and contains the text *Click to add notes*.)
   c. Click the Bold button on the Formatting toolbar and then click the Center button.
   d. Key **Distribute Case Study handout.**, press Enter, and then key **Discuss Case Study 1 and Case Study 4**.
   e. Display Slide 4 in Normal view.
   f. Click in the Notes pane.
   g. Click the Bold button on the Formatting toolbar and then click the Center button.
   h. Key **Elicit comments from participants regarding the current system.**, press Enter, and then key **Ask what changes individuals would like to make**.

4. Print slides 2 and 4 as notes pages by completing the following steps:
   a. Display the Print dialog box.
   b. Click the down-pointing triangle to the right of the Print what option and then click *Notes Pages* at the drop-down list.
   c. Click in the Slides text box and then key **2,4**.
   d. Click OK. (This prints each slide [slides 2 and 4] towards the top of the page on a separate piece of paper with the header, footer, date, page number, and speaker notes included.)
5. Save the presentation with the same name (Telecommunications Presentation).
6. Close Telecommunications Presentation.

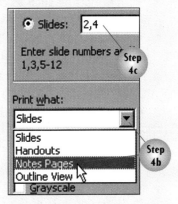

chapter summary

► Text in individual slides can be inserted or deleted, slides can be deleted from a presentation, slides can be inserted into an existing presentation, and slides can be rearranged.

► When editing a slide or text within a slide, use the view that makes editing the easiest. For example, rearrange the order of slides in the Slide Sorter view, delete or insert text within slides in the Normal view, Outline view, or Slide view.

► Use the find and replace feature to search for specific text or formatting in slides and replace with other text or formatting.

► To delete a slide from a presentation, display the presentation in Slide Sorter view, click the slide to be deleted, and then press the Delete key.

► To delete a slide in Outline view or in the Outline pane, position the arrow pointer on the slide icon located next to the slide to be deleted until the arrow pointer turns into a four-headed arrow, click the left mouse button, and then press Delete.

► Add a new slide to a presentation in the Slide Sorter view. A new slide will be inserted immediately following the selected slide.

► Copy a slide in a presentation at the Slide Sorter view by clicking the slide, holding down the Ctrl key, dragging to the location where you want the slide copied, then releasing the left mouse button and then the Ctrl key.

► Slides can be copied between presentations using the Copy and Paste buttons on the Standard toolbar.

► Move text within and between slides with the Cut and Paste buttons on the Standard toolbar. Copy text within and between slides with the Copy and Paste buttons.

► Click the Spelling button on the Standard toolbar to perform a spelling check on slides in a presentation.

► A selected object box can be moved in a slide by dragging it with the mouse.

► A selected object box can be copied in a slide by dragging it with the mouse while holding down the Ctrl key.

- Rearrange slides in Slide Sorter view by dragging the selected slide with the mouse.
- Formatting such as changing fonts, changing font color, and changing paragraph alignment can be applied to text in slides.
- To create a blank line between bulleted paragraphs without inserting a bullet, use the New Line command, Shift + Enter.
- Increase or decrease spacing before or after paragraphs with options at the Line Spacing dialog box.
- Formatting applied to a master slide will affect all slides in a presentation. Formatting can be applied to a master slide as the presentation is being created, or formatting can be applied to a master slide in an existing presentation.
- To display a master slide, change to the Slide view, hold down the Shift key, and then click the Slide View button (which changes to the Slide Master or Title Master View button).
- Use buttons on the Drawing toolbar to draw a variety of shapes and lines
- A shape drawn with the Line or Arrow buttons is considered a line drawing. A shape drawn with the Rectangle or Oval buttons is considered an enclosed object.
- A variety of predesigned shapes is available from the AutoShapes button on the Drawing toolbar.
- To select an enclosed object, position the mouse pointer anywhere inside the object and then click the left mouse button. To select a line, position the mouse pointer on the line until the pointer turns into an arrow with a four-headed arrow attached, and then click the left mouse button.
- To select several objects at once, click the Select Objects buttons, and then draw a border around the objects. You can also select more than one object by holding down the Shift key and then clicking each object.
- To delete an object, select it, and then press the Delete key.
- To move an object, select it, and then drag it to the desired location.
- To copy an object, select it, and then hold down the Ctrl key while dragging the object.
- Use the sizing handles that display around a selected object to increase or decrease the size of the object.

  Apply formatting to an object such as fill color, shading, line color, and shadows with buttons on the Drawing toolbar.
- Create a text box by clicking the Text Box button on the Drawing toolbar and then drawing the box in the document screen.
- A text box can be drawn inside an autoshape.
- Choose a text wrapping style for text inside of an autoshape with options at the Format AutoShape dialog box with the Text Box tab selected.
- Group objects you want to work with as a single unit. Grouped objects can be formatted, sized, flipped, and/or rotated as a unit. Grouped objects can be ungrouped.
- Flip or rotate a selected object by clicking the Draw button on the Drawing toolbar, pointing to Rotate or Flip, and then clicking the desired rotation or flip option.
- Distribute and align selected objects with the Draw button on the Drawing toolbar.
- Change formatting to placeholders (object boxes) such as changing background color or adding a border or shadow with buttons on the Drawing toolbar located toward the bottom of the PowerPoint window. If changes are to affect all slides in a document, make changes at the master slide.
- Choose a different slide color scheme at the Color Scheme dialog box.

- Customize individual elements of a slide with options at the Color Scheme dialog box with the Custom tab selected.
- Apply a different design template to a presentation with options at the Apply Design Template dialog box.
- Create a presentation with little formatting using the Blank Presentation template. This template is available at the New Presentation dialog box with the General tab selected.
- Use a design template with a darker background for a presentation that will run in PowerPoint or that will be made into 35mm slides. Use a template with a lighter background if the slides will be printed as transparencies.
- Use Format Painter to apply the same formatting to more than one location in a slide or slides.
- Change bullets with options at the Bullets and Numbering dialog box with the Bulleted tab selected. Click the Picture button at this dialog box to display the Picture Bullet dialog box containing bullet pictures or click the Character button to display the Bullet dialog box containing bullet symbols.
- Click the Numbering button on the Formatting toolbar to apply numbers to selected paragraphs of text, or display the Bullets and Numbering dialog box with the Numbered tab selected.
- Insert elements in a slide or slides such as the date and time, slide number, and a footer with options at the Header and Footer dialog box with the Slide tab selected.
- Insert elements in notes and handouts such as the date and time, page number, and a header and footer with options from the Header and Footer dialog box with the Notes and Handouts tab selected.

commands review

	Mouse/Keyboard
Display Replace dialog box	Click Edit and then click Replace
Display the Find dialog box	Click Edit and then Find
Start a spelling check	Click the Spelling button on the Standard toolbar
Insert a New Line command	Press Shift + Enter
Display the Line Spacing dialog box	Select object box, click Format and then click Line Spacing
Display master slide	Position arrow pointer on Slide View button, hold down Shift key, click left mouse button
Display Format AutoShape dialog box	With autoshape selected, click Format and then AutoShape
Display the Color Scheme dialog box	Click Format and then Slide Color Scheme
Display the Background dialog box	Click Format and then Background
Display the Apply Design Template dialog box	Click Format and then Apply Design Template; or click the Common Tasks button on the Formatting toolbar and then click Apply Design Template
Display New Presentation dialog box	Click File and then New
Display Bullets and Numbering dialog box	Click Format and then Bullets and Numbering
Display the Header and Footer dialog box	Click View and then Header and Footer

thinking offline

Completion: In the space provided at the right, indicate the correct term, command, or number.

1. Rearrange slides in a presentation in this view.

2. Delete or insert text within slides in the Normal view, Outline view, or this view.

3. If Slide 2 is selected in a presentation in Slide Sorter view, and the New Slide button is clicked, this is the number of the new slide.

4. To copy a selected object, hold down this key while dragging the object.

5. Press these keys to access the New Line command.

6. Increase spacing before and after paragraphs with options at this dialog box.

7. A variety of predesigned shapes is available from this button on the Drawing toolbar.

8. Click this button on the Drawing toolbar to display rotation handles around the selected object.

9. Choose a text wrapping style for text inside an autoshape with options at the Format AutoShape dialog box with this tab selected.

10. Change the color for individual elements in a slide with options at the Color Scheme dialog box with this tab selected.

11. The Blank Presentation template is available at the New Presentation dialog box with this tab selected.

12. Use this feature to apply the same formatting in more than one location in a slide or slides.

13. Click this button at the Bullets and Numbering dialog box to display the Bullet dialog box.

14. One method for displaying the Apply Design Template dialog box is to click this button on the Formatting toolbar and then click Apply Design Template at the drop-down menu.

15. If you want page numbering to print in an outline, click the Page number option at the Header and Footer dialog box with this tab selected.

working hands-on

(Note: If you are using a disk for saving presentations, consider deleting the following presentations before completing assessment 1: Color Presentation, Edited Planning Presentation, Formatted Enhanced Presentation, Formatted Network Pres, Planning Presentation, and Telecommunications Presentation.)

Assessment 1

1. Create a presentation with the text shown in figure 15.23 by completing the following steps:
   a. At a blank PowerPoint screen, click <u>F</u>ile and then <u>N</u>ew.
   b. At the New Presentation dialog box, click the Design Templates tab.
   c. At the New Presentation dialog box with the Design Templates tab selected, double-click the *Marble* template.
   d. At the New Slide dialog box, double-click the first autolayout in the list box (Title Slide).
   e. At the slide, click anywhere in the text *Click to add title*, and then key **BENEFITS PROGRAM**.
   f. Click anywhere in the text *Click to add subtitle* and then key **Changes to Plans**.
   g. Click the New Slide button located on the Standard toolbar.
   h. At the New Slide dialog box, double-click the second autolayout.
   i. Create the second slide with the text shown in figure 15.23. (Use the New Line command, Shift + Enter, and press Enter as indicated in italics.)
   j. Continue creating the remaining slides as shown in figure 15.23.
2. When all the slides are created, change the line spacing for the bulleted paragraphs in Slide 5 to 12 points. (Be sure to change to *Points* before you change the measurement.)
3. Complete a spelling check on the presentation.
4. Make the following changes to the slides:
   a. Display Slide 2 in Slide view and then make the following changes:
      1) Change to the Slide Master view.
      2) Click anywhere in the text *Click to edit Master title style*, change the font to 48-point Bookman Old Style, and change the color to white.
      3) Click anywhere in the text *Click to edit Master text styles*, change the font to 30-point Bookman Old Style, and change the color to yellow. (You will need to click the <u>M</u>ore Colors option to display the Colors dialog. At this dialog box, choose a yellow color.)
      4) Click the Slide View button to remove the Master slide.
   b. Display Slide 1 in Slide view and then make the following changes:
      1) Select the title *BENEFITS PROGRAM*, change the font to 50-point Bookman Old Style, and change the color to yellow. (Use the same yellow color you selected in step 4a3.)
      2) Select the subtitle *Changes to Plans*, change the font to 48-point Bookman Old Style, and change the color to white.
5. Add a transition and sound of your choosing to each slide.
6. Save the presentation and name it Benefits Presentation.
7. Run the presentation.
8. After running the presentation, print all the slides on one page.
9. Close Benefits Presentation.

figure

15.23   *Assessment 1*

Slide 2	Title	=	INTRODUCTION
	Bullets	=	• Changes made for 2000 *(Press Shift + Enter and then Enter.)*
			• Description of eligibility *(Press Shift + Enter and then Enter.)*
			• Instructions for enrolling new members *(Press Shift + Enter and then Enter.)*
			• Overview of medical and dental coverage

Slide 3	Title	=	INTRODUCTION
	Bullets	=	• Expanded enrollment forms *(Press Shift + Enter and then Enter.)*
			• Glossary defining terms *(Press Shift + Enter and then Enter.)*
			• Telephone directory *(Press Shift + Enter and then Enter.)*
			• Pamphlet with commonly asked questions

Slide 4	Title	=	WHAT'S NEW
	Bullets	=	• New medical plan, Plan 2002 *(Press Shift + Enter and then Enter.)*
			• Changes in monthly contributions *(Press Shift + Enter and then Enter.)*
			• Paying with pretax dollars *(Press Shift + Enter and then Enter.)*
			• Contributions toward spouse's coverage

Slide 5	Title	=	COST SHARING
	Bullets	=	• Increased deductible
			• New coinsurance amount
			• Higher coinsurance amount for retail prescription drugs
			• Co-payment for mail order drugs
			• New stop loss limit

Assessment 2

1. Create a presentation with the text shown in figure 15.24. You determine the template and the autolayout. Add a transition and sound of your choosing to each slide in the presentation.
2. After creating the presentation, complete a spelling check.
3. Save the presentation and name it Trends Presentation.
4. Run the presentation.
5. Print the slides as handouts with six slides per page.
6. Close Trends Presentation.

 figure
15.24   *Assessment 2*

Slide 1	Title	=	TRENDS IN TELECOMMUNICATIONS
	Subtitle	=	Current and Future Trends
Slide 2	Title	=	Trend 1
	Subtitle	=	Continued movement toward the deregulation of telecommunications services
Slide 3	Title	=	Trend 2
	Subtitle	=	Continued expansion and enhancement of local and wide area networks
Slide 4	Title	=	Trend 3
	Subtitle	=	Movement toward integrated services digital networks
Slide 5	Title	=	Trend 4
	Subtitle	=	Movement toward standardization of data communication protocols
Slide 6	Title	=	Trend 5
	Subtitle	=	Increased use of wireless radio-based technology
Slide 7	Title	=	Trend 6
	Subtitle	=	Continued growth of photonics (fiber optics)
Slide 8	Title	=	Trend 7
	Subtitle	=	Expansion of video teleconferencing

Slide 9	Title	=	Trend 8
	Subtitle	=	Increased power in electronic workstations
Slide 10	Title	=	Trend 9
	Subtitle	=	More sophisticated software
Slide 11	Title	=	Trend 10
	Subtitle	=	Continued growth of voice processing
Slide 12	Title	=	Trend 11
	Subtitle	=	Greater use of optical storage technologies

Assessment 3

1. Open Trends Presentation.
2. Save the presentation with Save As and name it Edited Trends Presentation.
3. Make the following edits to the presentation:
   a. Display the presentation in Slide Sorter view.
   b. Move Slide 2 between Slide 5 and Slide 6.
   c. Move Slide 10 between Slide 7 and Slide 8.
   d. Renumber the trends numbers in the titles to reflect the correct order.
   e. Display Slide 4 in Slide view, delete the subtitle text, and then key **Multimedia in integrated systems**.
   f. Display Slide 8 in Slide view, delete the subtitle text, and then key **Information as a strategic resource**.
4. Apply a different design template of your choosing.
5. Insert the current date and slide number on all slides in the presentation. (Make sure there is no check mark in the Don't show on title slide option at the Header and Footer dialog box.)
6. Save the presentation again with the same name (Edited Trends Presentation).
7. Run the presentation.
8. Print the presentation as handouts with six slides per page.
9. Close Edited Trends Presentation.

Assessment 4

1. Open Enhanced Services Presentation.
2. Save the presentation with Save As and name it Revised Enhanced Services Pres.
3. Make the following change to the presentation:
   a. Find all occurrences of *Enhanced* and replace with *Premium*.
   b. Create the header *McCormack Annuity Funds*, the footer *Premium Services* and insert the date and page number for notes and handouts. (Make sure there is no check mark in the Don't show on title slide option at the Header and Footer dialog box with the Slide tab selected.)
   c. Display Slide 2 in Normal view and then key the speaker note **Refer participants to the sample transaction**.

    d.   Display Slide 5 in Normal view and then key the speaker note **Discuss budget impact due to increased hours**.

    e.   Change the background color for all slides. (Make sure you choose a complementary color.)

4. Save the presentation again with the same name (Revised Enhanced Services Pres).

5. Run the presentation.

6. Print Slides 2 and 5 as notes pages.

7. Close Revised Enhanced Services Pres.

Assessment 5

1. Presentations can be run using PowerPoint or on a computer without PowerPoint installed. This might be useful in a situation where you travel to different locations giving a presentation and not all locations have PowerPoint available. PowerPoint contains a Pack and Go Wizard that walks you through the steps of preparing a presentation to be run on a different computer. This process is referred to as "packing" and "unpacking." Use the PowerPoint Help feature to learn how to pack and then unpack a PowerPoint presentation.

2. Prepare a memo to your instructor in Word using one of the memo templates that explains the steps to pack and unpack a presentation. Save the memo and name it Word Ch 15, SA 05. Print and then close Word Ch 15, SA 05.

3. In PowerPoint, use the Pack and Go Wizard (this feature must be installed) to pack the Edited Trends Presentation. Save the packed presentation on your data disk.

Note: Make a copy of the following presentations that you will need for chapter 16:

    Benefits Presentation (created in chapter15, assessment 1)

    Edited Trends Presentation (created in chapter 15, assessment 3)

    Enhanced Services Presentation (created in chapter 15, exercise 4)

    Networking Presentation (created in chapter 14, exercise 6)

    Newsletter Presentation (created in chapter 14, assessment 3)

 Chapter 16

Adding Animation to Presentations

PERFORMANCE OBJECTIVES

Upon successful completion of chapter 16, you will be able to:
- Add animation effects to slides.
- Add a build to slides.
- Insert clip art images in a presentation.
- Size and scale clip art images.
- Create a watermark.
- Create a table in a slide.
- Link slides in a presentation to a Web site.
- Link slides in a presentation with Word documents.
- Link slides within the same presentation.
- Import text from Word into a presentation.
- Change a slide autolayout.
- Collect and paste multiple items.
- Publish a presentation to the Web.
- Preview a Web page presentation.
- Send a presentation via e-mail.

To add visual appeal and interest to a presentation, add animation effects, such as having an element fly into a slide, drive into a slide, or display as a camera effect. You also can have body text appear one step at a time during a slide show. Add impact to a presentation by inserting clip art images representing the text in the slide. Create hyperlinks from a slide to a site on the Internet. Use action buttons to link slides in a presentation to documents in other programs or slides within the same presentation. All of these topics will be covered in this chapter along with how to copy and paste data from a Word document into a slide in a PowerPoint presentation.

Adding Animation Effects to a Presentation

With options from the Animation Effects toolbar, you can add a variety of animation effects. To display animation choices, open a presentation, select the specific object within a slide to which you want the animation added, and then click the Animation Effects button on the Formatting toolbar. This causes the Animation Effects toolbar to display. Figure 16.1 describes the buttons on this toolbar.

Animation Effects

figure

16.1   *Animation Effects Toolbar Buttons*

Click this button	Named	To do this during a slide show
	Animate Title	Drop slide title from top of slide
	Animate Slide Text	Have body text appear one step at a time
	Drive-In Effect	Make selected text or object fly in from the right along with the sound of a car
	Flying Effect	Have selected text or object fly in from the left with a whoosh sound
	Camera Effect	Have selected text or object appear as if a camera shutter was opened
	Flash Once	Make selected text or object flash once after last build
	Laser Text Effect	Make selected text or object fly in from top right accompanied by the sound of a laser (If text is selected, it appears one character at a time.)
	Typewriter Text Effect	Make selected text or object appear one character at a time accompanied by the sound of a typewriter
	Reverse Text Order Effect	Make selected text appear from bottom up
	Drop-In Text Effect	Make selected object drop in from top of slide; text drops in one word at a time
	Animation Order	Select order in which selected text or object appears
	Custom Animation	Add or change animation effects
	Animation Preview	Display a miniature slide showing a preview of the animation effect(s)

Many of the buttons on the Animation Effects toolbar are dimmed until text, an object, or an object box has been selected. To use the buttons on the Animation Effects toolbar, open a presentation, and then display a slide in the Slide pane. Select the text or object to which you want the effect applied, click the Animation Effects button on the Formatting toolbar, and then click the desired button. Continue in this manner until all animation effects have been added to selected text or objects in each slide.

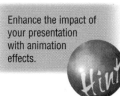
Enhance the impact of your presentation with animation effects.

Adding Animation Effects to a Presentation

1. Open PowerPoint and then open Enhanced Services Presentation. (You created this presentation in chapter 15, exercise 4.)
2. Save the presentation with Save As and name it Enhanced Pres with Animation.
3. Add animation effects to the text in each slide by completing the following steps:

   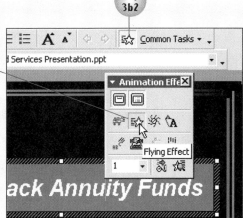

   a. Change to the Slide view. (Make sure the first slide displays in the Slide pane.)
   b. With Slide 1 displayed, add a flying effect to the title by completing the following steps:
      1) Click anywhere in the title *McCormack Annuity Funds.*
      2) Click the Animation Effects button on the Formatting toolbar.
      3) Click the Flying Effect button on the Animation Effects toolbar.
   c. With Slide 1 still displayed, add a flying effect to the subtitle *Enhanced Services* by completing steps similar to those in steps 3b.
   d. Click the Next Slide button at the bottom of the vertical scroll bar to display Slide 2.
   e. Click anywhere in the title *Enhanced Services* and then click the Animate Title button on the Animation Effects toolbar.
   f. Select the text *Set up future accumulations transfers* and then click the Laser Text Effect button on the Animation Effects toolbar.

   g. Preview the animation effects for Slide 2 by clicking the Animation Preview button on the Animation Effects toolbar.
   h. Close the Animation Preview miniature slide by clicking the Close button (contains an X) located in the upper right corner of the slide miniature.

i. Click the Next Slide button at the bottom of the vertical scroll bar to display Slide 3.
j. Format the remaining slides (there are a total of six slides in this presentation) by completing steps similar to those in 3e and 3f.
k. When all animation effects have been added to each slide, click the Close button on the Animation Effects toolbar. (This button is located in the upper right corner of the toolbar and contains an X.)
4. After formatting the last slide, change to the Slide Sorter view.
5. Click Slide 1.
6. Run the presentation by completing the following steps:
a. Click the Slide Show button on the View toolbar.
b. When the first slide displays (without the text), click the left mouse button. (This brings in the slide title.)
c. Click the left mouse button again. (This brings in the slide subtitle.)
d. Continue clicking the left mouse button to change slides and bring in text to each slide.
7. Save the presentation again with the same name (Enhanced Pres with Animation).
8. Close Enhanced Pres with Animation.

Adding a Build to Slides

With the buttons on the Animation Effects toolbar or a button on the Slide Sorter toolbar, you can display important points on a slide one point at a time. This is referred to as a *build technique*, which helps keep the audience's attention focused on the point being presented rather than reading ahead.

A build technique can be added to slides at the Slide Sorter view with the Slide Transition Effects button on the Slide Sorter toolbar. The Slide Sorter toolbar displays below the Standard toolbar. To add a build effect to a slide or slides, select the slide or slides, and then click the down-pointing triangle that displays at the right side of the Slide Transition Effects button. From the drop-down menu that displays, click the desired transition effect.

With options from the Custom Animation dialog box with the Effects tab selected as shown in figure 16.2, you can customize a build. To display this dialog box, open a presentation, display the desired slide in the Slide pane, and then click the Animation Effects button on the Formatting toolbar. At the Animation Effects toolbar, click the Custom Animation button.

No Transition ▾

Slide Transition
Effects

Custom
Animation

figure 16.2

Custom Animation Dialog Box with Effects Tab Selected

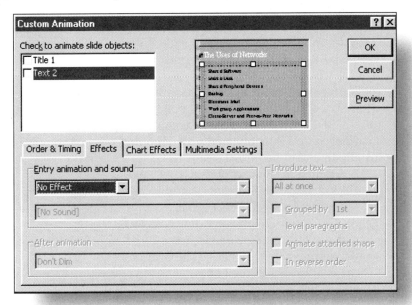

At the Custom Animation dialog box with the Order & Timing tab selected, specify the order that items display during a build with the Animation order option. With the Effects tab selected, in the Entry animation and sound section of the dialog box you can specify an animation effect such as flying, blinds, checkerboard, crawl, flash, or strip; and add sound such as a camera, laser, typewriter, or whoosh. With the After animation option, you can specify whether a previous build is dimmed when the next build is displayed. With options in the Introduce text section, you can specify that a build occurs all at once, by word, or by letter.

You were using a simple build technique in exercise 1—moving in individual objects within a slide. The build technique is very useful in slides containing more than one point. In exercise 2, you will be using the build technique on the Networking Presentation.

Add a build to bulleted items to focus the attention of the audience on a specific item.

Using the Build Technique for a Presentation

1. In PowerPoint, open Networking Presentation. (You created this presentation in chapter 14, exercise 6.)
2. Save the presentation with Save As and name it Network Pres with Build.
3. Add a build effect to each point in the slides by completing the following steps:
   a. Change to the Slide view. (Make sure the first slide is displayed in the Slide pane.)
   b. With Slide 1 displayed in the Slide pane, add an animation effect to the title by completing the following steps:

1) Click anywhere in the title *NETWORKING*.
2) Click the Animation Effects button on the Formatting toolbar.
3) Click the Animate Title button on the Animation Effects toolbar.

c. Click the Next Slide button at the bottom of the vertical scroll bar. (This displays Slide 2.)
d. With Slide 2 displayed in the Slide pane, add the Animate Title effect to the title *The Uses of Networks* by completing steps similar to those in steps 3b1 and 3b3.
e. With Slide 2 still displayed, add a build technique to the bulleted items on the slide by completing the following steps:
   1) Click once in the bulleted text. (You do not need to select all the text—the insertion point just needs to be positioned in the text object box.)
   2) Click the Custom Animation button on the Animation Effects toolbar.
   3) At the Custom Animation dialog box with the Effects tab selected, click the down-pointing triangle at the right of the first text box in the Entry animation and sound section (contains the text *No Effect*) and then click *Checkerboard* at the drop-down list.
   4) Click the down-pointing triangle at the right of the text box containing the *[No Sound]* text and then click *Camera* at the pop-up list.
   5) Click the down-pointing triangle to the right of the After animation text box containing the text *Don't Dim* and then click the first white color (Follow Title Text Scheme Color).
   6) Click OK to close the Custom Animation dialog box.
f. Click the Next Slide button at the bottom of the vertical scroll bar to display Slide 3.
g. With Slide 3 displayed, animate the title *Layouts and Topologies* by completing steps similar to those in 3b1 and 3b3.
h. With Slide 3 still displayed, add a build technique to the bulleted items on the slide by completing the following steps:
   1) Click once in the bulleted text.
   2) Click the Custom Animation button on the Animation Effects toolbar.
   3) At the Custom Animation dialog box with the Effects tab selected, click the down-pointing triangle at the right of the first text box in the Entry animation and sound section, and then click *Checkerboard* at the drop-down list.
   4) Click the down-pointing triangle at the right side of the Grouped by level paragraphs option (contains the text *1st*) and then click *2nd* at the drop-down list. (You choose *2nd* because there are two bulleted levels on this slide.)

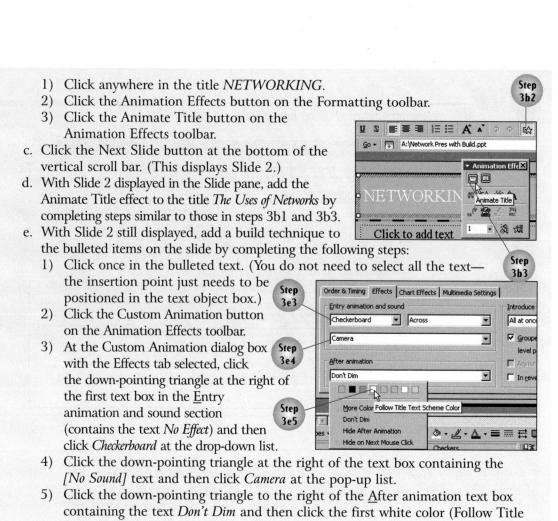

5) Click the down-pointing triangle at the right of the text box containing the *[No Sound]* text and then click *Camera* at the pop-up list.
6) Click the down-pointing triangle to the right of the <u>A</u>fter animation text box containing the text *Don't Dim* and then click the first white color (Follow Title Text Scheme Color).
7) Click OK to close the Custom Animation dialog box.
   i. Format the remaining slide with the same title animation and build technique formatting. (Be sure to change the <u>G</u>rouped by level paragraphs option to *2nd*.)
   j. Click the Close button on the Animation Effects toolbar to remove it from the screen.
4. Display the presentation in Slide Sorter view and then click Slide 1.
5. Run the presentation by clicking the Slide Show button on the View toolbar. (Click the left mouse button to display the title and each bulleted item in the slides.)
6. Save the presentation again with the same name (Network Pres with Build).
7. Close Network Pres with Build.

Inserting Clip Art in a Presentation

In chapter 13, you learned how to insert a clip art image into a Word document and an Excel worksheet. Clip art images can also be inserted in a PowerPoint presentation. Insert clip art images at the Insert ClipArt dialog box or the Microsoft Clip Gallery dialog box. (Both dialog boxes contain the same images.) Display the Insert ClipArt dialog box by clicking <u>I</u>nsert, pointing to <u>P</u>icture, and then clicking <u>C</u>lip Art. Another method is to click the Insert Clip Art button on the Drawing toolbar. Display the Microsoft Clip Gallery dialog box by clicking <u>I</u>nsert and then <u>O</u>bject and then double-clicking *Microsoft Clip Gallery*. Another method is to choose an autolayout that includes the image of a man's head and shoulders and then double-click the image.

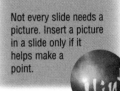

Not every slide needs a picture. Insert a picture in a slide only if it helps make a point.

Insert
ClipArt

Sizing and Scaling Images

Insert a clip art image in a slide and sizing handles display around the image. Use these sizing handles to increase or decrease the size of the image. Use the corner sizing handles to increase the height and width of the image at the same time. If you want to precisely control the size and scaling of an image, display the Format Picture dialog box with the Size tab selected. Display this dialog box by clicking the Format Picture button on the Picture toolbar. At the Format Picture dialog box, click the Size tab.

Inserting and Sizing a Clip Art Image in a PowerPoint Presentation
1. Open PowerPoint and then open Presentation 1, Ch 16. (This presentation is located in the *Presentations* folder on the CD that accompanies this textbook.)
2. Save the presentation with Save As in the *Chapter 16* folder on your disk and name it PowerPoint Ch 16, Ex 03.
3. Insert a clip art image in Slide 1 as shown in figure 16.3 by completing the following steps:
   a. Change to the Slide View and make sure Slide 1 is displayed.
   b. Click the Insert Clip Art button on the Drawing toolbar. (If the Drawing toolbar is not visible, click <u>I</u>nsert, point to <u>P</u>icture, and then click <u>C</u>lip Art.)

c. At the Insert ClipArt dialog box, click in the Search for clips text box, key **medical**, and then press Enter.

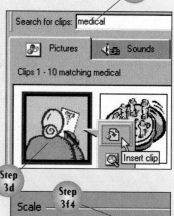

d. Click the image shown at the right and then click the Insert clip button.

e. Close the Insert ClipArt dialog box.

f. Scale the image by completing the following steps:
1) Make sure the clip art image is selected and the Picture toolbar displays. (If the Picture toolbar does not display, right-click the image and then click Show Picture Toolbar at the shortcut menu.)
2) Click the Format Picture button on the Picture toolbar.
3) At the Format Picture dialog box, click the Size tab.
4) At the Format Picture dialog box with the Size tab selected, click the up-pointing triangle at the right side of the Height text box in the Scale section until *150%* displays in the text box.

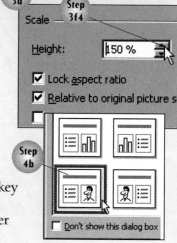

5) Click OK to close the dialog box.
g. Move the image so it is positioned in the location shown in figure 16.3.

4. Create a new Slide 2 as shown in figure 16.4 by completing the following steps:
a. Click the New Slide button on the Standard toolbar.
b. At the New Slide dialog box, double-click the first autolayout in the third row (Text & Clip Art).
c. At the slide, click in the text *Click to add title* and then key **Times to Change Medical Plans**.
d. Click the text *Click to add text* and then key the text after the first bullet as shown in figure 16.4.
e. Press Shift + Enter and then press Enter.
f. Key the text after the second bullet in figure 16.4.
g. Continue keying the bulleted text shown in figure 16.4. (Separate the bulleted text by pressing Shift + Enter and then Enter.)
h. Insert the clip art image by completing the following steps:
1) Double-click the image of a man standing.
2) At the Insert ClipArt dialog box, display the *Office* category.

3) Click the image shown at the right and then click the Insert clip button.
4) Close the Insert ClipArt dialog box.
i. Size the image by completing the following steps:
1) Make sure the clip art image is selected and the Picture toolbar displays. (If the Picture toolbar does not display, right-click the image and then click Show Picture Toolbar at the shortcut menu.)
2) Click the Format Picture button on the Picture toolbar.
3) At the Format Picture dialog box, click the Size tab.

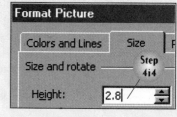

4) At the Format Picture dialog box with the Size tab selected, select the current measurement in the Height text box, and then key **2.8**.
5) Click OK to close the dialog box.

j. If necessary, move the image so it is positioned as shown in figure 16.4.
5. Animate the slide titles and add a build to the slides containing bulleted text.
6. Run the presentation.
7. Save the presentation again with the same name (PowerPoint Ch 16, Ex 03).
8. Print the presentation with two slides on a page.
9. Close PowerPoint Ch 16, Ex 03.

figure
16.3
Exercise 3, Slide 1

figure
16.4
Exercise 3, Slide 2

Inserting Images from a Disk

If you want the same clip art image on every slide, insert it on the Slide Master.

You have inserted clip art images in documents from the Insert ClipArt dialog box and you also downloaded clip art from the on-line Microsoft Clip Gallery. You can also insert images from other sources such as a disk or folder. For example, in exercise 4 you will insert images in a PowerPoint presentation from the CD that accompanies this textbook.

To insert images from a different source, click Insert, point to Picture, and then click From File. This displays the Insert Picture dialog box shown in figure 16.5. At this dialog box, change to the folder or drive containing the image. Click the desired image document name in the list box and then click the Insert button. (You can also just double-click the image document name.) Move, size, and/or format the image in the same manner as clip art from the Microsoft Clip Gallery.

figure

16.5
Insert Picture Dialog Box

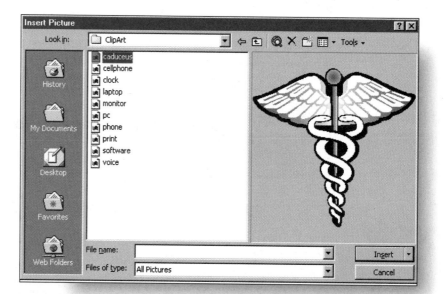

exercise 4

Inserting Images from a Disk into a PowerPoint Presentation

1. Open PowerPoint and then open Presentation 2, Ch 16. (This presentation is located in the *Presentations* folder on the CD that accompanies this textbook.)
2. Save the presentation with Save As in the *Chapter 16* folder on your disk and name it PowerPoint Ch 16, Ex 04.
3. Insert a clip art image in Slide 1 as shown in figure 16.6 by completing the following steps:
   a. Change to the Slide view with Slide 1 displayed.
   b. Display the Insert ClipArt dialog box.
   c. Display the *Communications* category.

    d. Click the telephone image shown in the slide in figure 16.6 and then click the Insert clip button.

    e. Close the Insert ClipArt dialog box.

4. Move and size the image so it displays as shown in figure 16.6.

5. Insert an image in Slide 2 as shown in figure 16.7 by completing the following steps:

    a. Click the Next Slide button to display Slide 2.

    b. Insert the CD that accompanies this textbook.

    c. Click Insert, point to Picture, and then click From File.

    d. At the Insert Picture dialog box, change to the drive where the CD is located.

    e. Double-click the *ClipArt* folder.

    f. Double-click *phone* in the list box.

6. Move and size the image so it displays as shown in figure 16.7.

7. Insert the image shown in figure 16.8 by completing the following steps:

    a. Click the Next Slide button to display Slide 3.

    b. Click Insert, point to Picture, and then click From File.

    c. At the Insert Picture dialog box, make sure the drive where the CD is located is selected, and *ClipArt* is the active folder.

    d. Double-click *cellphone* in the list box.

    e. Size and move the image so it is positioned in the slide as shown in figure 16.8.

8. Insert the image named *voice* in Slide 4 as shown in figure 16.9 by completing steps similar to those in step 7.

9. Run the presentation.

10. Save the presentation again with the same name (PowerPoint Ch 16, Ex 04).

11. Print the presentation with two slides on a page.

12. Close PowerPoint Ch 16, Ex 04.

Exercise 4, Slide 1

figure
16.7
Exercise 4, Slide 2

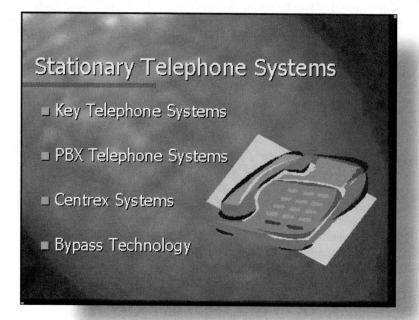

figure
16.8
Exercise 4, Slide 3

figure

16.9 *Exercise 4, Slide 4*

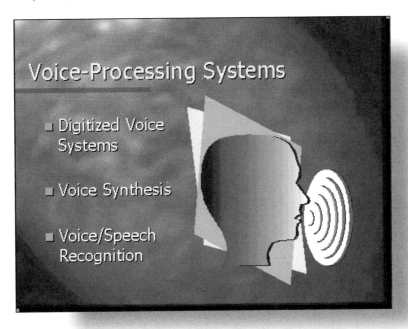

Formatting Clip Art Images in PowerPoint

The Picture toolbar that displays in PowerPoint is very similar to the Picture toolbar in Word and Excel. The only difference is that the Text Wrapping button on the Picture toolbar in Word is replaced with the Recolor Picture button on the Picture toolbar in PowerPoint. Click the Recolor Picture button and the Recolor Picture dialog box displays with options for changing the color of the various components of the clip art image.

Text Wrapping

Recolor Picture

exercise 5

Formatting a Clip Art Image in PowerPoint

1. Open PowerPoint Ch 16, Ex 04.
2. Recolor the clip art image in slide 1 by completing the following steps:
   a. Display Slide 1 in Slide view.
   b. Click the clip art image to select it.
   c. If the Picture toolbar does not display, *right-*click the image, and then click Show Picture Toolbar at the shortcut menu.
   d. Click the Recolor Picture button on the Picture toolbar.

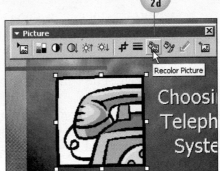

e. At the Recolor Picture dialog box, click the down-pointing triangle at the right side of the first button below the <u>N</u>ew section.

f. At the color palette that displays, click the dark blue color (third color from the left).

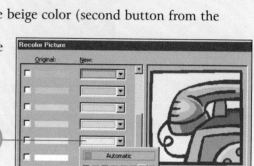

Step 2e

Step 2f

g. Scroll down to the end of the list box and then click the down-pointing triangle at the right side of the button containing the beige color (second button from the end of the list).

h. At the color palette that displays, click the light blue color (second color from the right).

i. Click OK to close the Recolor Picture dialog box.

3. Save the presentation with the same name (PowerPoint Ch 16, Ex 04).

4. Print only slide 1.

5. Close PowerPoint Ch 16, Ex 04.

6. Delete PowerPoint Ch 16, Ex 04. (Check with your instructor before deleting this presentation.)

Step 2g

Step 2h

Creating Watermarks

Image Control

Create a watermark in a PowerPoint presentation by clicking the Image Control button on the Picture toolbar and then clicking <u>W</u>atermark. Move the watermark image behind the text by clicking the D<u>r</u>aw button on the Drawing toolbar, pointing to O<u>r</u>der, and then clicking Send to Bac<u>k</u>. Use the brightness and contrast buttons on the Picture toolbar to increase or decrease the brightness and intensity of the image.

exercise 6

Creating a Watermark in a PowerPoint Slide

1. Open the presentation named History of Computers 1980s. (This presentation is located in the *Presentations* folder on the CD that accompanies this textbook.)

2. Save the presentation with Save As in the *Chapter 16* folder on your disk and name it PowerPoint Ch 16, Ex 06.

3. Create a watermark in Slide 1 as shown in figure 16.10 by completing the following steps:

a. Display slide 1 in Slide view.

b. Display the Insert ClipArt dialog box.

c. Display the *Science and Technology* category.

d. Click the clip art image shown at the right and then click the Insert clip button.

Step 3d

e. Close the Insert ClipArt dialog box.
f. Make sure the image is selected and the Picture toolbar displays. (If the Picture toolbar does not display, right-click the image and then click Show Picture Toolbar.)

g. Click the Image Control button on the Picture toolbar, and then click Watermark at the drop-down list.

Step 3g

h. Click twice on the Less Brightness button on the Picture toolbar.
i. Click the Draw button that displays at the left side of the Drawing toolbar, point to Order, and then click Send to Back.

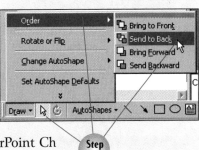

j. Move and size the watermark image so it displays as shown in figure 16.10.

4. Save the presentation again with the same name (PowerPoint Ch 16, Ex 06).

Step 3i

5. Print slide 1 only and then close PowerPoint Ch 16, Ex 06.
6. Delete PowerPoint Ch 16, Ex 06. (Check with your instructor before deleting this presentation.)

figure

16.10   *Exercise 6*

Creating a Table in a Slide

PowerPoint offers a variety of autolayouts. You have used several autolayouts including Title Slide, Bulleted List, Text & Clip Art, and Title Only. PowerPoint also includes the Table autolayout you can use to create a table in a PowerPoint presentation. To create a table in a slide, choose the Table autolayout at the New Slide dialog box, and then double-click the *Table* icon at the slide. At the Insert Table dialog box, specify the desired number of columns and rows and then click OK.

Format a table in a PowerPoint slide with buttons on the Tables and Borders toolbar. Display this toolbar by clicking the Tables and Borders button on the Standard toolbar. After formatting the table, double-click inside the first cell, and then key the text. Move the insertion point to the next cell by pressing the Tab key. (You can also click in the next cell.) Press Shift + Tab to move the insertion point to the previous cell.

Creating a Table in a Slide

1. Open PowerPoint Ch 16, Ex 03.
2. Add the new slide shown in figure 16.11 by completing the following steps:
   a. Display Slide 4 in Slide view.
   b. Click the New Slide button.
   c. At the New Slide dialog box, double-click the Table autolayout (last autolayout in the top row).
   d. At the slide, click in the text *Click to add title*, and then key **Information Resources**.
   e. Double-click the *Table* icon that displays in the middle of the slide.
   f. At the Insert Table dialog box, key **3**, press the Tab key, and then key **5**.
   g. Click OK to close the dialog box.
   h. Make sure the Tables and Borders toolbar displays. (If it does not, turn it on by clicking the Tables and Borders button the Standard toolbar.)
   i. Click the Draw Table button to deactivate the drawing tool.
   j. Select all the cells in the table and then click the Center Vertically button on the Tables and Borders toolbar.
   k. Deselect the cells.
   l. Close the Tables and Borders toolbar.
   m. Select the first row of cells, click the Bold button on the Formatting toolbar, and then click the Center button.
   n. Click in the first cell and then key the text in each cell as shown in figure 16.11. (Press the Tab key to move to the next cell or press Shift + Tab to move to the previous cell.)

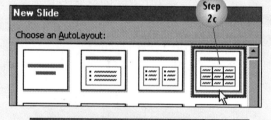

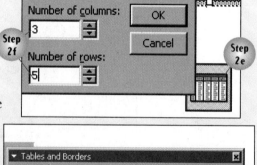

3. Save the presentation again with the same name (PowerPoint Ch 16, Ex 03).
4. Run the presentation.
5. Print all five slides on the same page.
6. Close PowerPoint Ch 16, Ex 03.

 *figure*
16.11 *Exercise 7, Slide 5*

Information Resources

Name	Region	Telephone
Jennifer Runez	Upper Peninsula	(360) 555-4300
Michael Brandt	Pierce County	(253) 555-3425
Lois Weinstein	Northwest	(206) 555-1255
Trevor Haydon	West Coast	(244) 555-0980

Creating Hyperlinks in a Presentation

In chapter 7, you learned how to jump to the Internet from within Word, display Web sites, and search for specific information. These same functions can be performed from within PowerPoint. To display the Web toolbar in PowerPoint, click <u>V</u>iew, point to <u>T</u>oolbars, and then click Web. You can also right click on any displayed toolbar and then click *Web* at the drop-down list. You may want to use the Internet to locate sites and research topics when designing and preparing a presentation. A presentation can also include hyperlinks that will connect to a specific Internet site while the presentation is running. Hyperlinks can also be created that link a slide in a presentation to another document, such as a Word document.

Creating Hyperlinks from a Slide to the Web

Creating a hyperlink from a slide in a presentation to a site on the World Wide Web is the same as you learned in chapter 7. To create a hyperlink, open the

Make a Web page out of any presentation by clicking File and then Save as Web Page. At the Save As dialog box, key a name for the Web page presentation.

Consider inserting hyperlinks in your presentation to jump to interesting sites on the Internet that pertain to the presentation.

Insert Hyperlink

presentation where you want to create a link, and then display the specific slide in the Slide pane. Select the text to which you want to apply the hyperlink and then click the Insert Hyperlink button on the Standard toolbar. At the Insert Hyperlink dialog box, key the URL in the Type the file or Web page name text box, and then click OK. When running a presentation containing a hyperlink, make sure you are connected to the Internet and then click the hyperlink.

exercise 8

Adding a Slide with Hyperlinks

1. Open Font Presentation. (This presentation is located in the *Presentations* folder on the CD that accompanies this textbook.)
2. Save the presentation with Save As in the *Chapter 16* folder on your disk and name it Linked Font Pres.
3. Add a slide to the presentation and insert hyperlinks in the slide by completing the following steps:
   a. Change to the Slide view.
   b. Click the Next Slide button until Slide 4 displays. (Slide 4 is the last slide in the presentation.)
   c. Click the New Slide button on the Standard toolbar.
   d. At the New Slide dialog box, double-click the second autolayout (Bulleted List).
   e. With the new slide displayed, click the text *Click to add title* and then key **Internet Typeface Resources**.
   f. Click the text *Click to add text* and then key **Adobe**.
   g. Press Shift + Enter, press Enter, and then key **Monotype**.
   h. Press Shift + Enter, press Enter, and then key **Publish RGB**.
   i. Press Shift + Enter, press Enter, and then key **Will Harris-House**.
   j. Add a hyperlink to Adobe by completing the following steps:
      1) Select the text *Adobe*.
      2) Click the Insert Hyperlink button on the Standard toolbar.
      3) At the Insert Hyperlink dialog box, key **http://www.adobe.com** in the Type the file or Web page name text box, and then click OK. (The word *Adobe* displays underlined and in a different color.)
   k. Add a hyperlink to Monotype by completing steps similar to those in 3j. The Web address for Monotype is **http://www.monotype.com**.
   l. Add a hyperlink to Publish RGB by completing steps similar to those in 3j. The Web address for Publish RGB is **http://www.publish.com**.
   m. Add a hyperlink to Will Harris-House by completing steps similar to those in 3j. The Web address for Will Harris-House is **http://www.will-harris.com**.
4. Save the presentation again with the same name (Linked Font Pres).
5. Make sure you are connected to the Internet and then run the presentation. When Slide 5 displays, click *Adobe* to jump to the Adobe home page. Scroll through this home page, click File and then Close to close the Internet Explorer.
6. Jump to each of the other Web sites by clicking the hyperlink.
7. After running the presentation and viewing the Web sites, close Linked Font Pres.

(Insert Hyperlink dialog box, Step 3j3:)

Insert Hyperlink
Link to:
Text to display: Adobe
Type the file or Web page name:
http://www.adobe.com
Or select from list:
Existing File or Web Page
Recent Files

Creating Hyperlinks from a Slide to a Word Document

In exercise 8, you created a hyperlink between a slide in PowerPoint and a location on the World Wide Web. A hyperlink can also be created that links a slide in PowerPoint to a document in another program such as Word. A link can be created at the Insert Hyperlink dialog box by specifying the document to which you want the slide linked or a link can be created with action buttons. To create a link between a slide and a Word document using action buttons, you would complete these steps:

1. Open the presentation to which you want a Word document linked.
2. Display the slide in Slide view that you want linked to a Word document.
3. Click the AutoShapes button on the Drawing toolbar located toward the bottom of the screen.
4. At the pop-up menu that displays, expand the pop-up menu by clicking the down-pointing arrows that display towards the bottom of the pop-up menu.
5. At the expanded pop-up menu, point to Action Buttons. (This causes a palette of button choices to display.)
6. At the palette of button choices, drag the arrow pointer to the button named *Action Button: Document* (second button from the left in the bottom row), and then click the left mouse button.
7. Position the arrow pointer inside the slide, hold down the left mouse button, drag to create the button, and then release the mouse button.
8. At the Action Settings dialog box with the Mouse Click tab selected shown in figure 16.12, click in the white circle in front of the Hyperlink to option.
9. Click the down-pointing triangle at the right side of the Hyperlink to text box (displays with the words *Next Slide*). This causes a drop-down list to display.
10. At the drop-down list, click *Other File.*
11. At the Hyperlink to Other File dialog box, change to the folder where the desired document is located, and then double-click the desired document.
12. At the Action Settings dialog box, click OK.

figure
16.12

Action Settings Dialog Box with Mouse Click Tab Selected

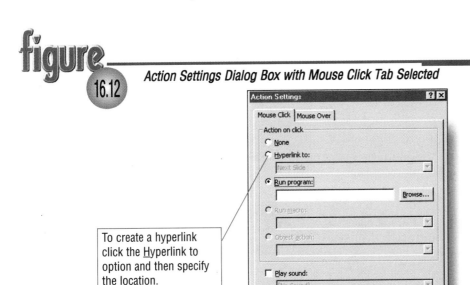

To create a hyperlink click the Hyperlink to option and then specify the location.

Once an action button has been inserted in a slide, you can click the button during the running of the presentation to display the linked document. After viewing the linked document, close the program containing the linked document and the slide redisplays. In exercise 9, you will create buttons on slides in the Font Presentation that link to Word documents.

Linking Word Documents to a PowerPoint Presentation

1. Open Font Presentation. (This presentation is located in the *Presentations* folder on the CD that accompanies this textbook.)

2. Save the presentation with Save As in the *Chapter 16* folder on your disk and name it Font Pres, Action Buttons.

3. Add a button linking Slide 2 with a Word document by completing the following steps:

   a. Display the presentation in Slide view and then display Slide 2.

   b. Click the AutoShapes button on the Drawing toolbar located toward the bottom of the screen.

   c. At the pop-up menu that displays, expand the pop-up menu by clicking the down-pointing arrows that display towards the bottom of the menu.

   d. At the expanded pop-up menu, point to Action Buttons. (This causes a palette of button choices to display.)

   e. At the palette of button choices, point to the button named *Action Button: Document* (second button from the left in the bottom row), and then click the left mouse button.

   f. Position the arrow pointer in the bottom right corner of the slide, hold down the left mouse button, drag to create the button (make the button about one-half inch in height and width), and then release the mouse button.

   g. At the Action Settings dialog box with the Mouse Click tab selected, click in the white circle in front of the Hyperlink to option.

   h. Click the down-pointing triangle at the right side of the Hyperlink to text box (displays with the words *Next Slide*).

   i. At the drop-down list that displays, click *Other File*.

   j. At the Hyperlink to Other File dialog box, change to the Chapter 16 folder on your disk and then double-click the document named *Typeface Example*.

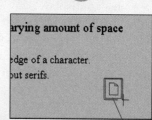

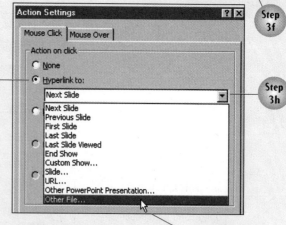

Step 3d
Step 3b
Step 3e
Step 3f
Step 3g
Step 3h
Step 3i

     k. At the Action Settings dialog box, click OK.

     l. Click outside the button to deselect it.

4. Add a button linking Slide 3 to the Word document *Type Size Example* by completing steps similar to those in 3.

5. Add a button linking Slide 4 to the Word document *Type Style Example* by completing steps similar to those in 3.

6. Save the presentation again with the same name (Font Pres, Action Buttons).

7. Run the presentation. When Slide 2 displays, click the action button that displays in the lower right corner of the slide. (This displays the *Typeface Example* document in Word.)

8. After viewing the *Typeface Example* document, click File and the Exit.

9. Continue running the presentation and clicking the action buttons in Slides 3 and 4 to display the linked Word documents. (Be sure to click File and then Exit after viewing each Word document.)

10. When the presentation is completed, close Font Pres, Action Buttons.

Linking Slides within a Presentation with Action Buttons

A slide in a PowerPoint presentation can be linked to a document in another program as you did in exercise 9. You can also link slides within the same presentation. Several methods are available for linking slides within the same presentation. One method is to insert a button that displays the "Home" slide (the first slide in the presentation) and also a button that returns to the last slide viewed. To do this, you would insert the action button named Action Button: Home in the slide you want linked to the beginning slide and insert the action button named Action Button: Return in the beginning slide.

Inserting Action Buttons to Link Slides in the Same Presentation

1. Open Newsletter Presentation. (You created this presentation in chapter 14, assessment 3.)

2. Save the presentation with Save As and name it Linked Newsletter Pres.

3. Add an action button to Slide 4 linking it to the beginning slide by completing the following steps:

     a. Display the presentation in Slide view and then display Slide 4.

     b. Click the AutoShapes button on the Drawing toolbar.

     c. Point to Action Buttons.

     d. At the palette of button choices, point to the button named *Action Button: Home* (second button from the left in the top row), and then click the left mouse button.

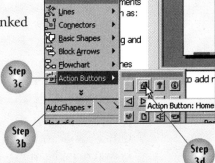

e. Position the arrow pointer in the bottom right corner of the slide, hold down the left mouse button, drag to create the button (make the button about one-half inch in height and width), and then release the mouse button.

f. At the Action Settings dialog box, make sure the Hyperlink to option is selected and that *First Slide* displays in the text box.

g. Click OK to close the Action Settings dialog box.

h. At Slide 4, click outside the button to deselect it.

4. Add an action button to Slide 1 linking it to the last slide viewed by completing the following steps:

a. Display Slide 1 in Slide view.

b. Click the AutoShapes button on the Drawing toolbar.

c. Point to Action Buttons.

d. At the palette of button choices, point to the button named *Action Button: Return* (first button from the left in the bottom row), and then click the left mouse button.

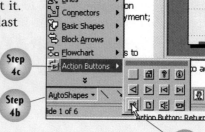

e. Position the arrow pointer in the bottom right corner of the slide, hold down the left mouse button, drag to create the button (make the button about one-half inch in height and width), and then release the mouse button.

f. At the Action Settings dialog box, make sure the Hyperlink to option is selected and that *Last Slide Viewed* displays in the text box.

g. Click OK to close the Action Settings dialog box.

h. At Slide 1, click outside the button to deselect it.

5. Save the presentation again with the same name (Linked Newsletter Pres).

6. Run the presentation. When Slide 4 displays, click the action button that displays in the lower right corner of the slide. (This displays Slide 1.)

7. After viewing Slide 1, click the action button that displays in the lower right corner of the slide. (This displays the last slide viewed—Slide 4.)

8. Continue running the presentation.

9. When the presentation is completed, close Linked Newsletter Pres.

Importing Text from Word

A variety of methods are available for sharing data between PowerPoint and other Office applications. In chapter 18 you will learn how to link and embed objects between applications. In this chapter, you will learn how to copy from one program to another by copying and pasting and by importing.

To copy and paste text between Word and PowerPoint, open the source document in Word and then open the destination presentation in PowerPoint.

Select the text in the Word document and then click the Copy button on the Standard toolbar. Make PowerPoint the active program, display the desired slide, and then click the Paste button on the Standard toolbar.

A Word document containing heading styles can be easily imported into a PowerPoint presentation. To do this, open the document, click File, point to Send To, and then click Microsoft PowerPoint. Paragraphs formatted with a Heading 1 style become the title of a new slide. Paragraphs formatted with a Heading 2 style become the first level of text, paragraphs formatted as a Heading 3 style become the second level of text, and so on. PowerPoint creates a presentation with the imported text using the Blank Presentation template. After importing the text into PowerPoint, apply the desired formatting, or apply a design template.

Changing the Autolayout

Text imported from Word into PowerPoint is inserted in a slide with a specific autolayout. In some cases, this autolayout is appropriate for the imported text. In other cases, you may need to change the autolayout. To do this, click the Common Tasks button on the Formatting toolbar and then click Slide Layout at the drop-down list. (You can also click Format and then Slide Layout.) This displays the Slide Layout dialog box that contains the same autolayout choices as the New Slide dialog box.

(Note: If you are saving presentations in the Chapter 16 *folder on your disk, consider deleting the following presentation before completing 11: Enhanced Pres with Animation; Font Pres, Action Buttons; Linked Font Pres; Linked Newsletter Pres; Network Pres with Build; and PowerPoint Ch 16, ex 03.)*

Importing Text from Word

1. Make sure PowerPoint is open and then open Word.
2. With Word the active program, open Word Outline 01.
3. Import the text (formatted with Heading 1 and Heading 2 styles) into PowerPoint by clicking File, pointing to Send To, and then clicking Microsoft PowerPoint.
4. Make PowerPoint the active program (this displays the imported text in a presentation created with the Blank Presentation template).
5. Change to the Title Slide autolayout for Slide 1 by completing the following steps:
   a. Display Slide 1 in Slide view.
   b. Click the Common Tasks button on the Formatting toolbar and then click Slide Layout at the drop-down list.
   c. At the Slide Layout dialog box, double-click the Title Slide autolayout (first autolayout from the left in the top row).
6. Apply the Factory design template to the presentation.
7. Make the following changes to the presentation:
   a. Increase the font size and line spacing of the bulleted text in Slides 2 through 4 so the bulleted lists are better spaced on the slides.
   b. Consider inserting an appropriate clip art image in one or two of the slides. (If you cannot find an appropriate clip art image in the Insert ClipArt dialog box, consider downloading a clip from the Microsoft Clip Gallery.)
   c. Add a transition and sound of your choosing to each slide.

8. Save the presentation and name it Internet Presentation.
9. Run the presentation.
10. Print the presentation with all four slides on the same page.
11. Close Internet Presentation.
12. Make Word the active program and then close Word Outline 01.

Collecting and Pasting Multiple Items

As you learned in chapter 4, Office 2000 includes a new feature called *collecting and pasting* that you can use to collect up to 12 different items and then paste them in various locations. You can display the Clipboard toolbar by right-clicking an existing toolbar and then clicking *Clipboard*. Or, the Clipboard toolbar will display when you copy two consecutive items (without pasting an item). Copied data displays as an icon on the Clipboard toolbar.

To insert an item, position the insertion point in the desired location and then click the button on the Clipboard representing the item. Position the insertion point on a button and a ScreenTip displays with information about the item. If the item is text, the first 50 characters display. When all desired items are inserted, click the Clear Clipboard button to remove any remaining items.

Usually, if you copy any two items consecutively, the Clipboard toolbar automatically displays. If you close the Clipboard toolbar three times in a row without clicking a button on the toolbar, the Clipboard toolbar will no longer appear automatically. To display the Clipboard toolbar, right-click any currently displayed toolbar, and then click Clipboard. You can also click <u>V</u>iew, point to <u>T</u>oolbars, and then click Clipboard. When you display the Clipboard toolbar and then click a button on the toolbar, the count is reset, and from that point on the Clipboard toolbar appears automatically again.

Collecting Text in Word and Pasting it in a PowerPoint Slide

1. In PowerPoint, open Internet Presentation.
2. Create a new Slide 5 by completing the following steps:
   a. Display Slide 4 and then click the New Slide button on the Standard toolbar.
   b. At the New Slide dialog box, double-click the Bulleted List autolayout.
   c. Click the text *Click to add title* and then key **Internet Terminology**.
   d. Click the text *Click to add text* and then copy terms from Word and paste them into slides by completing the following steps:
      1) Open Word and then open Word Terms.
      2) Select the first term *(Information superhighway)* and its definition by triple-clicking with the mouse.
      3) With the term and definition selected, click the Copy button on the Standard toolbar.

4) Select the second term *(TCP/IP)* and its definition and then click the Copy button. (This should display the Clipboard toolbar. If this toolbar does not display, right-click any currently displayed toolbar, and then click Clipboard.)

5) Select the third term *(ARPANet)* and its definition and then click the Copy button on the Clipboard toolbar.

6) Select the fourth term *(NSFNet)* and its definition and then click the Copy button on the Clipboard toolbar.

7) Click the button on the Taskbar representing the Internet Presentation.

8) Make sure the insertion point is positioned in the bulleted list placeholder and then click the button on the Clipboard toolbar representing the term *ARPANet*. (To find this button, use the ScreenTip.)

9) Click the button on the Clipboard representing the term *Information superhighway*.

3. Create a new Slide 6 by completing the following steps:

   a. Click the New Slide button on the Standard toolbar.

   b. At the New Slide dialog box, double-click the Bulleted List autolayout.

   c. Click the text *Click to add title* and then key **Internet Terminology**.

   d. Click the text *Click to add text* and then paste terms in the slide by completing the following steps:

      1) Make sure the insertion point is positioned in the bulleted list placeholder and then click the button on the Clipboard toolbar representing the term *NFSNet*.

      2) Click the button on the Clipboard representing the term *TCP/IP*.

4. Close the Clipboard toolbar.

5. Save the presentation again with the same name (Internet Presentation).

6. Print the six slides on one page.

7. Close Internet Presentation.

8. Make Word the active program, close Word Terms, and then exit Word.

9. Delete Internet Presentation. (Check with your instructor before deleting this presentation.)

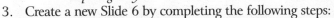

Publishing a Presentation to the Web

Save a presentation as a Web page and PowerPoint will place a copy of the presentation in HTML format on the Web. You can run a presentation published to the Web in PowerPoint or run the presentation with Internet Explorer 4.0 or later. The same presentation can be published to different locations and you can publish the entire presentation, a single slide, or a range of slides.

To make a presentation available on the Internet, you need to contact an Internet service provider that will allocate space for the Web presentation. If you want to publish a presentation to a company intranet, you must have access to a Web server.

To save a presentation as a Web page, open the presentation, click File, and then click Save as Web Page. At the Save As dialog box, key the name in the File name text box. If you want to change the Web page title, click the Change Title button. At the Set Page Title dialog box, key a new title in the Page title text box, and then click OK. Click the Publish button at the Save As dialog box and the Publish as Web Page dialog box displays as shown in figure 16.13. At this dialog box, specify whether you want to publish the entire presentation or specific slides within the presentation, and specify the browser support such as Internet Explorer or Netscape Navigator. When all changes are made to the Publish as Web Page dialog box, click the Publish button.

16.13   *Publish as Web Page Dialog Box*

When you save a presentation as a Web page, a folder is created and Web page files are inserted in the folder. A Web page generally consists of a variety of items that are inserted in individual files. For example, each bullet image and clip art image or picture in a Web page is saved in a separate image file. Inserting all of these files into a folder makes it easier for you to take this information to another location. You can copy the contents of a Web page folder to another computer or onto a disk.

Previewing a Web Page

If you want to see how the presentation displays in your Web browser, view the presentation in Web Page Preview. To do this, open the presentation you have saved as a Web page, then click File and then Web Page Preview. This displays the first slide in the Web browser as shown in figure 16.14. Figure 16.14 shows the Medical Plan Web Pres presentation in the Internet Explorer 5.0 Web browser. Your Web browser view may vary.

figure

16.14 Web Page Preview

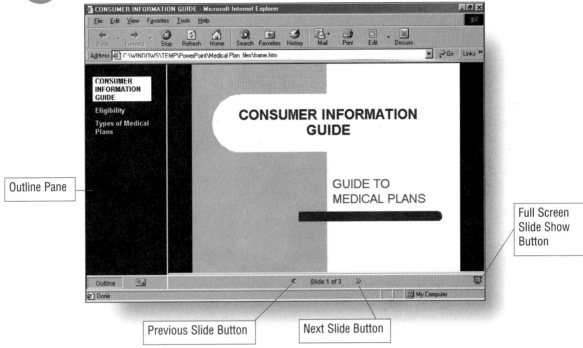

Outline Pane

Full Screen
Slide Show
Button

Previous Slide Button

Next Slide Button

When you first display the presentation in Web Page Preview, you may need to click the Maximize button located in the upper right corner of the Web browser window. Scroll through the slides in the presentation by clicking the Next Slide button located towards the bottom of the browser window (see figure 16.14). Click the Previous Slide button to view the previous slide. The Outline pane displays at the left side of the browser. Move to various slides in the presentation by clicking the title of the desired slide in the Outline pane. If you want the slide to fill the entire screen, click the Full Screen Slide Show button located in the lower right corner of the browser window. Run the presentation as you would any other presentation.

Saving a Presentation as a Web Page and Previewing the Presentation

1. Open Presentation 1, Ch 16. (This presentation is located in the *Presentations* folder on the CD that accompanies this textbook.)
2. Save the presentation in the *Chapter 16* folder on your disk with Save As and name it Medical Plan.
3. Save Medical Plan as a Web page by completing the following steps:
   a. Click File and then Save as Web Page.
   b. At the Save As dialog box, key **Medical Plan Web Pres** in the File name text box.
   c. Click the Publish button.

d. At the Publish as Web Page dialog box, notice what browser is selected in the Browser support section, and then check with your instructor to determine if this is the proper browser.

e. Click the Publish button.

4. Preview the presentation in your Web browser by completing the following steps:

a. Click File and then Web Page Preview.

b. When your presentation displays in your browser window, click the Maximize button located in the upper right corner of the browser window.

c. Click *Eligibility* in the Outline pane. (This displays Slide 2.)

d. Click *Types of Medical Plans* in the Outline pane. (This displays Slide 3.)

e. Click twice on the Previous Slide button (located below the slide). (This displays Slide 1.)

f. Run the presentation in the full screen by completing the following steps:

   1) Click the Full Screen Slide Show button located in the lower right corner of the browser window (see figure 16.13).

   2) Click the left mouse button to advance the slides.

   3) When the message *End of slide show, click to exit.* displays, click the left mouse button.

g. Click File and then Close to close your Web browser.

5. Close the presentation.

6. Look at the folder and files created by PowerPoint for the Web presentation by completing the following steps:

a. Display the Open dialog box with *Chapter 16* on your disk the active folder.

b. Double-click the *Medical Plan Web Pres_files* folder. (This was the folder created by PowerPoint.)

c. Look at the files created by PowerPoint and then click the Up One Level button. (This returns you to the *Chapter 16* folder.)

d. Delete the *Medical Plan Web Pres_files* folder.

e. Delete the Medical Plan Web Pres Web presentation document.

f. Delete the Medical Plan presentation document.

g. Close the Open dialog box.

Sending a Presentation Via E-mail

E-mail

An individual slide within a presentation or the entire presentation can be sent via e-mail. To do this, click the E-mail button on the Standard toolbar. This displays a message asking if you want to send the entire presentation as an attachment or if you want to send the current slide as the message body. If you specify that you want to send the current slide as the message body, the E-mail header displays below the Formatting toolbar as shown in figure 16.15. At the e-mail header, key the name or e-mail address of the person who is to receive the slide, identify any people who are to receive a copy, establish a priority level, and then click the Send button.

When you send a slide as the message body, the slide is sent in HTML format. The person receiving the slide can view the slide in any e-mail program that can read e-mail messages in HTML format. The recipient does not need PowerPoint installed to view the slide.

figure
16.15

E-mail Header

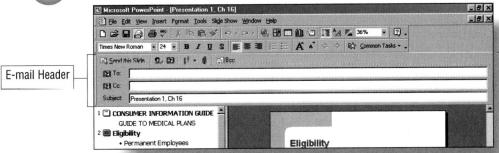

E-mail Header

If you specify that you want to send the entire presentation as an attachment, a window displays where you can enter the name or e-mail address of the person who is to receive the attached presentation and additional information such as who is to receive copies and the priority level. To view a presentation you send as an e-mail attachment, the recipient needs to use PowerPoint.

In exercise 14, you will send a slide as an e-mail to your instructor. If your system is networked and your computer is not part of an intranet system, skip the step telling you to click the Send button.

exercise 14

Sending a Slide via E-Mail

(Note: Before completing this exercise, check to see if you can send e-mail messages. If you cannot, complete all the steps in the exercise except step 3e.)

1. Open Presentation 1, Ch 16. (This presentation is located in the *Presentations* folder on the CD that accompanies this textbook.)
2. Display Slide 2 in Normal view.
3. Send the slide as an e-mail message by completing the following steps:
   a. Click the E-mail button on the Standard toolbar.
   b. At the message asking if you want to send the entire presentation as an attachment or if you want to send the current slide as the message body, click the message *Send the current slide as the message body*.
   c. At the e-mail header, key your instructor's name in the To box. (Depending on the system is configured, you may need to key your instructor's e-mail address.)
   d. Click the down-pointing triangle at the right side of the Set Priority button and then click High Priority at the drop-down list.
   e. Click the Send button. (This step is optional.)
   f. Click the E-mail button on the Standard toolbar to turn off the display of the e-mail header.
4. Close Presentation 1, Ch 16 without saving it.

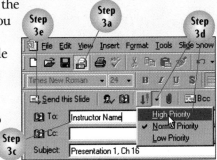

chapter summary

- Add animation effects to a slide with buttons on the Animation Effects toolbar. Display this toolbar by clicking the Animation Effects button on the Formatting toolbar. With buttons on the Animation Effects toolbar, effects can be applied to objects in slides, such as flying, camera, typewriter, laser, flash and sound effects.

- With options from the Animation Effects toolbar or a button on the Slide Sorter toolbar, important points on a slide can be presented one at a time. This is referred to as a build technique, which helps keep the audience's attention focused on the point being presented rather than reading ahead.

- Insert clip art images at the Insert ClipArt dialog box or the Microsoft Clip Gallery dialog box. A clip art image can also be inserted from another source such as a disk or folder.

- Size and scale clip art images with options at the Format Picture dialog box with the Size tab selected.

- Create a watermark in a slide using buttons on the Picture toolbar and Drawing toolbar.

- Use the Table autolayout to insert a table in a slide.

- A PowerPoint presentation can include hyperlinks that will connect to a specific Internet site while the presentation is running.

- Hyperlinks can be created that link a slide in a presentation to a document in another program. One method for linking a slide to a document in another program is to use action buttons. Action buttons are available from the AutoShapes button on the Drawing toolbar.

- Import a Word document into a PowerPoint presentation by opening the Word document, clicking File, pointing to Send To, and then clicking Microsoft PowerPoint.

- The autolayout on which a slide is based can be changed at the Slide Layout dialog box.

- Use the collecting and pasting feature to collect up to 12 different items and then paste them in various locations.

- Publish a presentation to the Web by clicking File and then Save as Web Page. At the Save As dialog box, key a name for the presentation. Click the Publish button, make any necessary changes at the Publish as Web Page dialog box, and then click the Publish button.

- When you save a presentation as a Web page, a folder is created and Web page files are inserted in the folder.

- Preview a presentation in your Web browser by clicking File and then Web Page Preview.

- An individual slide or an entire presentation can be sent via e-mail.

- Click the E-mail button on the Standard toolbar to display the e-mail header.

commands review

Mouse/Keyboard

Display Animation Effects toolbar	Click Animation Effects button on Formatting toolbar
Display Custom Animation dialog box	Click Custom Animation button on the Animation Effects toolbar
Display Insert ClipArt dialog box	Click Insert, point to Picture, then click Clip Art; or click the Insert Clip Art button on the Drawing toolbar; or double-click image in Text & Clip Art slide autolayout
Display the Format Picture dialog box	Click Format Picture button on Picture toolbar
Display Insert Picture dialog box	Click Insert, point to Picture, then click From File
Display Hyperlink dialog box	Select text and then click Insert Hyperlink button on Standard toolbar
Display Slide Layout dialog box	Click Common Tasks button on Formatting toolbar and then click Slide Layout; or click Format and then Slide Layout
Preview a Web page presentation	Click File and then Web Page Preview
Display e-mail header	Click E-mail button on Standard toolbar

thinking offline

Completion: In the space provided at the right, indicate the correct term, command, or symbol.

1. Click this button on the Animation Effects toolbar to drop a slide title from the top of the slide.

2. Click this button on the Animation Effects toolbar to have a selected text or object fly in from the left with a whoosh sound.

3. This terms refers to displaying important points on a slide one point at a time.

4. A build effect can be added to selected slides in the Slide Sorter view with this button on the Slide Sorter toolbar.

5. One method for displaying the Insert ClipArt dialog box is to click the Insert Clip Art button on this toolbar.

6. Insert an image from a different source at this dialog box.

7. Click this button on the Drawing toolbar to display a pop-up menu that contains the Action Buttons options.

8. Insert this action button in a slide to display a document in another program when the button is clicked. _____

9. Insert this action button in a slide to display the beginning slide when the button is clicked. _____

10. Import a Word document into PowerPoint by clicking File, pointing to this option, and then clicking Microsoft PowerPoint. _____

11. With the collecting and pasting feature, you can collect up to this number of items. _____

12. To save a presentation as a Web page, open the presentation, click File, and then click this option. _____

13. To see how a presentation saved as a Web page displays in your Web browser, view the presentation in this. _____

Description: In exercises in this chapter, you have used three action buttons in presentations. Several other action buttons are available from the AutoShapes button on the Drawing toolbar. List at least three other action buttons (not the ones used in the exercises) that are available from the AutoShapes button and then write an example of how the button could be used in a presentation.

1. First action button name: _____

   Example of how button can be used in a presentation: _____

   _____

   _____

2. Second action button name: _____

   Example of how button can be used in a presentation: _____

   _____

   _____

3. Third action button name: _____

   Example of how button can be used in a presentation: _____

   _____

   _____

working hands-on

Assessment 1

1. Open Edited Trends Presentation. (You created this presentation in chapter 15, assessment 3.)
2. Save the presentation with Save As and name it Animated Trends Presentation.
3. Add the following enhancements to the presentation:
   a. Display the master slide for Slide 1 and then add a fill color of your choosing to the subtitle object box.
   b. Add a flying effect to the title of Slide 1.
   c. Add a flying effect to the title and subtitle of Slides 2 through 12.
4. Save the presentation again with the same name (Animated Trends Presentation).
5. Run the presentation.
6. Close Animated Trends Presentation.

Assessment 2

1. Open Benefits Presentation. (This presentation was created in chapter 15, assessment 1.)
2. Save the presentation with Save As and name it Enhanced Benefits Presentation.
3. Make the following changes to the presentation:
   a. Add an animation effect to the title of slides 2 through 5 with the Animate Title button on the Animation Effects toolbar.
   b. Add a build technique to each bulleted paragraph in each slide. (Add a build technique that causes bulleted paragraphs to display one at a time and the previous bullet to dim. Also, consider adding a flying effect to the bulleted paragraphs.)
4. Save the presentation again with the same name (Enhanced Benefits Presentation).
5. Run the presentation.
6. Close Enhanced Benefits Presentation.

Assessment 3

1. Open Chart Presentation. (This presentation is located in the *Presentations* folder on the CD that accompanies this textbook.)
2. Save the presentation with Save As in the *Chapter 16* folder on your disk and name it Animated, Linked Chart Pres.
3. Make the following changes to the presentation:
   a. Add a build technique to the bulleted paragraphs in Slides 3, 4, and 5.
   b. Add any additional animation features that will enhance the presentation.
   c. Insert the action button named Action Button: Document in Slide 2 that, when clicked, will display the Excel document named *Excel Chart Example*.
4. Save the presentation again with the same name (Animated, Linked Chart Pres).
5. Run the presentation. (Be sure to click the *Action Button: Document* button that displays in Slide 2. This will display the Excel document named *Excel Chart Example*.)
6. Print the five slides on one page.
7. Close Animated, Linked Chart Pres.

Assessment 4

1. Open PowerPoint and then open Presentation 3, Ch 16. (This presentation is located in the *Presentations* folder on the CD that accompanies this textbook.)
2. Save the presentation with Save As in the *Chapter 16* folder on your disk and name it PowerPoint Ch 16, SA 04.
3. Insert the following clip art images:
   a. Slide 1: Insert the image shown in figure 16.16 from the CD that accompanies this textbook. The name of the image document is software. Size and move the image so it displays as shown in figure 16.16.
   b. Slide 2: Insert the clip art image and recolor the image as shown in figure 16.17. (Find this image by displaying the Insert ClipArt dialog box, keying **research** in the Search for clips text box, and then pressing Enter.)
   c. Slide 3: Insert the clip art image and recolor the image as shown in figure 16.18. (Find this image by displaying the Insert ClipArt dialog box, keying **time** in the Search for clips text box, and then pressing Enter.)
4. Create a new Slide 4 as shown in figure 16.19. (Use the Table autolayout to create this slide.) Format and enter the text as shown in the figure.
5. Save the presentation again with the same name (PowerPoint Ch 16, SA 04).
6. Print the presentation with three slides on a page. (Slides 5 and 6 will contain only a title. You will be inserting charts in these slides in assessment 5.)
7. Close PowerPoint Ch 16, SA 04.

figure

16.16   *Assessment 4, Slide 1*

figure

16.17

Assessment 4, Slide 2

figure

16.18

Assessment 4, Slide 3

figure
16.19

Assessment 4, Slide 4

PROJECT TIMELINE

Task	Begin	End
Survey of Customers	February 1	April 30
Cost Analysis	March 1	March 15
Software Design	July 1	October 31

Assessment 5

1. Open Excel and PowerPoint.
2. With PowerPoint the active program, open PowerPoint Ch 16, SA 04.
3. Copy an Excel chart into Slide 5 by completing the following steps:
   a. Display Slide 5 in Slide view.
   b. Make Excel the active program and then open Excel Chart 01.
   c. Click the chart to select it.
   d. Click the Copy button on the Standard toolbar.
   e. Make PowerPoint the active program with Slide 5 displayed in Slide view.
   f. Click the Paste button on the Standard toolbar.
   g. Increase the size and move the chart so it is positioned as shown in figure 16.20.
   h. Make Excel the active program and then close Excel Chart 01 without saving the changes.
4. Copy the chart in Excel Chart 02 to Slide 6 by completing steps similar to those in step 3.
5. Make the following changes to the presentation:
   a. Add a transition to all slides in the presentation.
   b. Add an animation effect to the title of each slide with the Animate Title button on the Animation Effects toolbar.
   c. Add a build technique to each bulleted paragraph in Slide 2 and Slide 3. (Add a build technique that causes bulleted paragraphs to display one at a time and the previous bullet to dim. Also, consider adding a flying effect to the bulleted paragraphs.)

6. Run the presentation.
7. Print the presentation so three slides print on one page (there are a total of five slides).
8. Save the presentation with the same name (PowerPoint Ch 16, SA 04).
9. Close PowerPoint Ch 16, SA 04 and then Exit PowerPoint.
10. With Excel the active program, close Excel Chart 02 without saving the changes and then exit Excel.

figure

16.20

Assessment 5, Slide 5

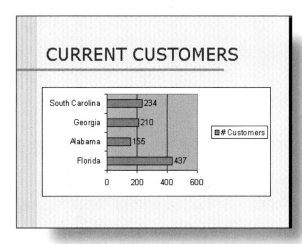

Assessment 6

1. In some presentations in this chapter, you added sound effects to slide elements. You can also record a sound or comment on an individual slide and insert a CD audio track on a slide. Use PowerPoint's Help feature to learn to add sound effects and insert a CD track on a slide. Learn about any other methods for inserting sound in a presentation. Print the information you find.
2. Using the information, open Word and then create a document describing what you have learned. You determine the formatting of the document.
3. Save the document and name it Word Ch 16, SA 06.
4. Print and then close Word Ch 16, SA 06.
5. If your computer system has a sound card and a microphone, consider adding sound to slides in a presentation.

Chapter 17

Using WordArt and Creating Organizational Charts

17

PERFORMANCE OBJECTIVES

Upon successful completion of chapter 17, you will be able to:

- Enhance the visual appeal of Word documents, Excel worksheets, and PowerPoint presentations with text created in WordArt.
- Edit, size, move, shape, and customize WordArt.
- Draw and format objects in Word and Excel using buttons on the Drawing toolbar.
- Create an organizational chart in Word and PowerPoint.
- Edit and customize an organizational chart.

Microsoft Office provides supplementary applications, including an application called WordArt that you can use to modify and conform text to a variety of shapes. With this application, create and add objects to a document, worksheet, or presentation. You can also use the WordArt application to create text in a variety of shapes and alignments and to add three-dimensional effects.

The MS Organization Chart 2.0 application is provided by Microsoft Office and is used to create an organizational chart. Customize an organizational chart with options at the Microsoft Organization Chart window. You will learn to create and customize organizational charts in Word and PowerPoint in this chapter.

Using WordArt

With the WordArt application, you can distort or modify text to conform to a variety of shapes. This is useful for creating company logos and headings. With WordArt, you can change the font, style, and alignment of text. You can also use different fill patterns and colors, customize border lines, and add shadow and three-dimensional effects.

INTEGRATED TOPIC

To enter WordArt in Word, Excel, or PowerPoint, click Insert, point to Picture, and then click WordArt. This displays the WordArt Gallery shown in figure 17.1. You can also display the WordArt Gallery by clicking the Insert WordArt button on the WordArt toolbar or the Drawing toolbar. Display the WordArt or Drawing toolbar by right-clicking a visible toolbar, and then clicking Drawing or WordArt at the drop-down list.

figure 17.1

WordArt Gallery

Insert
WordArt

Double-click the desired WordArt option.

Entering Text

Double-click a WordArt choice at the WordArt Gallery, and the Edit WordArt Text dialog box displays as shown in figure 17.2. At the Edit WordArt Text dialog box, the words *Your Text Here* are automatically selected in the Text box. Key the text in the text box and the original words are removed. Press the Enter key if you want to move the insertion point to the next line. After keying the desired text, click the OK button.

figure
17.2

Edit WordArt Text Dialog Box

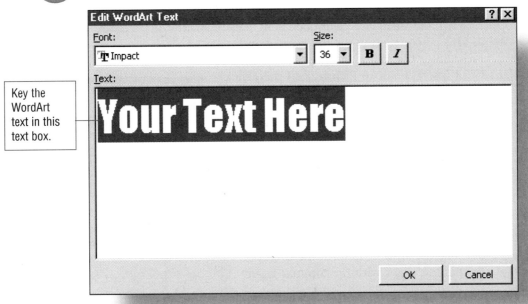

Key the WordArt text in this text box.

Sizing and Moving WordArt

WordArt text is inserted in the document with the formatting selected at the WordArt Gallery. The WordArt text is surrounded by white sizing handles and the WordArt toolbar displays near the text. Use the white sizing handles to change the height and width of the WordArt text. Use the yellow diamond located at the bottom of the WordArt text to change the slant of the WordArt text. To do this, position the arrow pointer on the yellow diamond, hold down the left mouse button, drag to the left or right, and then release the mouse button. This moves the yellow diamond along the bottom of the WordArt and changes the slant of the WordArt text.

To move WordArt text, position the arrow pointer on any letter of the WordArt text until the arrow pointer displays with a four-headed arrow attached. Hold down the left mouse button, drag the outline of the WordArt text box to the desired position, and then release the mouse button.

When all changes have been made to the WordArt text, click outside the WordArt text box. This removes from the screen the white sizing handles, the yellow diamond, and the WordArt toolbar.

Use sizing handles to change the size of a WordArt object.

exercise 1

Creating a Letterhead with WordArt

1. Open Word and then, at a clear document screen, create the letterhead shown in figure 17.3 by completing the following steps:
   a. Press Enter five times and then move the insertion point back up to the first line.
   b. Click Insert, point to Picture, and then click WordArt.
   c. At the WordArt Gallery, double-click the fourth option from the left in the third row.
   d. At the Edit WordArt Text dialog box, key **Rainbow Resort**.
   e. Click the OK button to close the Edit WordArt Text dialog box.
   f. Position the arrow pointer anywhere in the text *Rainbow Resort* until a four-headed arrow displays and then drag the outline of the WordArt box up until the top of the outline aligns with the top margin on the vertical scroll bar.
   g. Position the I-beam pointer below the WordArt text and then click the left mouse button. (This removes the white sizing handles, yellow diamond, and WordArt toolbar.)
   h. Make sure the insertion point is positioned immediately below the WordArt text and then insert the border shown in figure 17.3 by completing the following steps:
      1) Click Format and then Borders and Shading.
      2) At the Borders and Shading dialog box with the Borders tab selected, click the down-pointing triangle at the right side of the Style list box, and then click the fourth style from the end of the list.
      3) Click the down-pointing triangle at the right side of the Color list box and then click Red at the color palette.
      4) Click the None button that displays in the upper left corner of the dialog box. (This removes all the borders from the box shown in the Preview section of the dialog box.)
      5) Click on the top border of the box in the Preview section. (This inserts a border line at the top of the box.)
      6) Click OK to close the dialog box.
   i. If necessary, move the WordArt text so it is centered over the border line.
   j. Click outside the WordArt text to deselect it.
2. Save the document and name it Word Ch 17, Ex 01.
3. Print and then close Word Ch 17, Ex 01.
4. Exit Word.

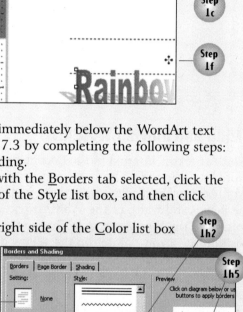

Step 1c

Step 1f

Step 1h2

Step 1h5

Step 1h4

Step 1h3

figure

17.3   *Exercise 1*

Rainbow Resort

Changing the Font and Font Size

The font for WordArt text will vary depending on the choice you make at the WordArt Gallery. You can change the font at the Edit WordArt Text dialog box with the <u>F</u>ont option. To do this, click the down-pointing triangle at the right side of the <u>F</u>ont text box. This causes a drop-down menu of font choices to display. Scroll through the list until the desired font is visible and then click the desired font.

The font size can be changed by clicking the down-pointing triangle at the right side of the <u>S</u>ize text box. This causes a drop-down menu of size options to display. Scroll through the list of sizes until the desired size is visible and then click the size.

The Edit WordArt Text dialog box contains Bold and Italic buttons. Click the Bold button to apply bold formatting to the WordArt text and click the Italic button to apply italic formatting.

Edit a WordArt object by double-clicking the object.

Delete a WordArt object by clicking the object to select it and then pressing the Delete key.

Inserting WordArt in an Excel Worksheet

1. Open Excel and then open Excel Worksheet 01.
2. Save the worksheet with Save As and name it Excel Ch 17, Ex 02.
3. Select cells A1 through D10 and then apply the Classic 3 autoformat.
4. Insert the WordArt as shown in figure 17.4 by completing the following steps:
   a. Make cell E1 the active cell.
   b. Click <u>I</u>nsert, point to <u>P</u>icture, and then click <u>W</u>ordArt.

c. At the WordArt Gallery, double-click the second option from the left in the second row.
d. At the Edit WordArt Text dialog box, key **Cambridge** in the <u>T</u>ext box and then press Enter.
e. Key **Construction**.
f. Click the down-pointing triangle at the right side of the <u>F</u>ont text box and then click *Tahoma*.
g. Click the OK button to close the Edit WordArt Text dialog box.

5. Change the location of the WordArt text by completing the following steps:
    a. Position the arrow pointer on any letter in the WordArt text until the arrow pointer displays with a four-headed arrow attached.
    b. Hold down the left mouse button, drag the outline of the WordArt text box so the upper left corner of the outline is located in cell E1, and then release the mouse button.

6. Change the size of the WordArt text by completing the following steps:
    a. Position the arrow pointer on the middle white sizing handle located at the bottom of the WordArt text until it turns into a double-headed arrow pointing up and down.
    b. Hold down the left mouse button, drag down until the outline of the WordArt box is positioned at the bottom of row 10, and then release the mouse button.

7. Click outside the WordArt text to deselect it.
8. Save the worksheet again with the same name (Excel Ch 17, Ex 02).
9. Print Excel Ch 17, Ex 02 in landscape orientation and also vertically and horizontally centered on the page. (*Hint: These options are found in the Page Setup dialog box with the Page tab selected and the Margins tab selected.*)
10. Close Excel Ch 17, Ex 02 and then exit Excel.

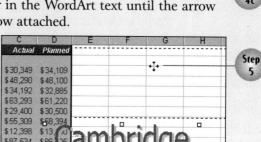

Step 4c

Step 5

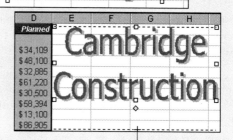

Step 6

figure
17.4

Exercise 2

	A	B	C	D	E	F	G	H	I
1	Customer	Job #	Actual	Planned					
2									
3	Sellar Corporation	2130	$30,349	$34,109					
4	Main Street Photos	1201	$48,290	$48,100					
5	Sunset Automotive	318	$34,192	$32,885					
6	Linstrom Enterprises	1009	$63,293	$61,220					
7	Morcos Media	676	$29,400	$30,500					
8	Green Valley Optics	2117	$55,309	$58,394					
9	Detailed Designs	983	$12,398	$13,100					
10	Arrowstar Company	786	$87,534	$86,905					
11									

Cambridge

Construction

Customizing WordArt

WordArt
Gallery

The WordArt toolbar, shown in figure 17.5, contains buttons for customizing the WordArt text. Click the Insert WordArt button and the WordArt Gallery shown in figure 17.1 displays. You can also display this gallery by clicking the WordArt Gallery button on the WordArt toolbar. Click the Edit Text button and the Edit WordArt Text dialog box displays.

Edit Text

WordArt Toolbar

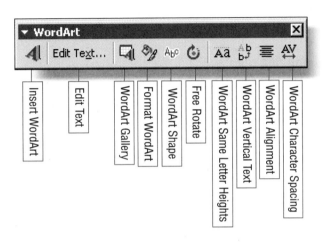

Customizing WordArt with Options at the Format WordArt Dialog Box

Customize WordArt text at the Format WordArt dialog box shown in figure 17.6. To display this dialog box, click the Format WordArt button on the WordArt toolbar.

Format
WordArt

Format WordArt Dialog Box with the Colors and Lines Tab Selected

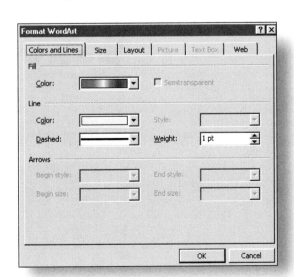

Change the color of the WordArt text and the line creating the text at the Format WordArt dialog box with the Colors and Lines tab selected. Click the Size tab and the dialog box displays options for changing the size and rotation of the WordArt text as well as the scale of the text. Choose a wrapping style and horizontal alignment with options at the dialog box with the Layout tab selected. When all changes have been made to the Format WordArt dialog box, click the OK button. This removes the dialog box and applies the formatting to the WordArt text.

The Format WordArt dialog box tabs vary depending on the active program. If you display the Format WordArt dialog box in PowerPoint, a Position tab displays instead of a Layout tab. Use options in the dialog box with the Position tab selected to specify the horizontal and vertical position on the WordArt on the slide.

Changing Shapes

WordArt
Shape

The WordArt Gallery contains a variety of predesigned WordArt options. Formatting is already applied to these gallery choices. You can, however, customize the gallery choices with buttons on the WordArt toolbar. Use options from the WordArt Shape button to customize the shape of WordArt text. Click the WordArt Shape button on the WordArt toolbar and a palette of shape choices displays as shown in figure 17.7.

figure
17.7
WordArt Shape Palette

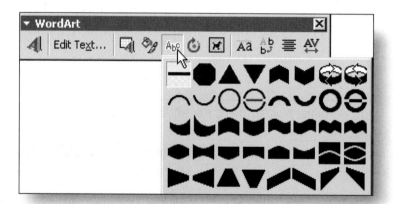

With the choices at the WordArt Shape palette, you can conform text to a variety of shapes. To select a shape, click the desired shape, and the WordArt text will conform to the selected shape. If you want to return text to the default shape, click the first shape in the first row.

exercise 3

Creating and Shaping WordArt Text in a PowerPoint Presentation

1. Open PowerPoint.
2. Create a new presentation by completing the following steps:
   a. At the blank PowerPoint screen, click File and then New.
   b. At the New Presentation dialog box, click the Design Templates tab.
   c. Double-click *Sumi Painting* in the list box.
   d. At the New Slide dialog box, double-click the last autolayout in the third row (Blank).
   e. At the blank slide, insert text in WordArt by completing the following steps:

   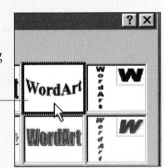

   1) Click the Insert, point to Picture, and then click WordArt.

   Step 2e2

   2) At the WordArt Gallery, double-click the second option from the *right* in the first row.
   3) At the Edit WordArt Text dialog box, key **Career Development**.
   4) Click the OK button.
   5) Change the shape of the WordArt text by completing the following steps:
      a) Click the WordArt Shape button on the WordArt toolbar.
      b) At the palette of shape choices, click the seventh shape from the left in the third row (*Double Wave 1*).

   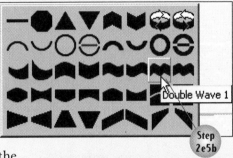

   Double Wave 1

   Step 2e5b

   6) Change the size, location, and color of the WordArt text by completing the following steps:
      a) Click the Format WordArt button on the WordArt toolbar.
      b) At the Format WordArt dialog box with the Colors and Lines tab selected, click the down-pointing triangle to the right of the Color text box in the Fill section.
      c) At the color palette that displays, click the third color from the left in the top row.
      d) Click the Size tab.
      e) At the Format WordArt dialog box with the Size tab selected, select the current measurement in the Height text box, and then key **2**.
      f) Select the current measurement in the Width text box and then key **7.5**.

   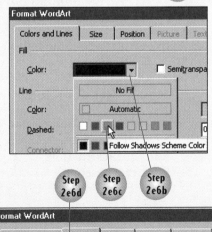

   Step 2e6d   **Step 2e6c**   **Step 2e6b**

   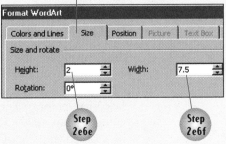

   Step 2e6e   **Step 2e6f**

g) Click the Position tab.

h) At the Format WordArt dialog box with the Position tab selected, select the current measurement in the <u>H</u>orizontal text box, and then key **1.5**.

i) Select the current measurement in the <u>V</u>ertical text box and then key **3**.

j) Click OK to close the dialog box.

7) Click outside the WordArt text (this deselects the WordArt text box).

Step 2e6g

Format WordArt

Colors and Lines	Size	Position

Position on slide

Horizontal: `1.5`   F<u>r</u>om:

<u>V</u>ertical: `3`   F<u>r</u>om:

Step 2e6h

Step 2e6i

f. Create Slide 2 by completing the following steps:

1) Click the New Slide button.

2) At the New Slide dialog box, double-click the first autolayout (Title Slide).

3) Click the text *Click to add title* and then key **Informational Interview**.

4) Click the text *Click to add sub-title* and then key **Step 1:**.

5) Press Enter and then key **Identify companies that you know employ workers in your career field.**

g. Create Slide 3 by following steps similar to those in step 2f except key the following text:

Step 2:

Prepare a script.

h. Create Slide 4 by following steps similar to those in step 2f except key the following text:

Step 3:

Telephone the contact person and explain your reason for calling.

i. Create Slide 5 by following steps similar to those in step 2f except key the following text:

Step 4:

Arrive promptly in professional dress and greet your contact person sincerely.

j. Create Slide 6 by following steps similar to those in step 2f except key the following text:

Step 5:

Get down to business as soon as possible with your questions.

k. Add a transition of your choosing to each slide.

3. Save the presentation and name it PowerPoint Ch 17, Ex 03.

4. Run the presentation.

5. Print the presentation so three slides fit on one page.

6. Close PowerPoint Ch 17, Ex 03 and then exit PowerPoint.

Customizing WordArt with Buttons on the Drawing Toolbar

The Drawing toolbar offers a variety of buttons with options for customizing WordArt. For example, you can change the letter color, line color, line style, add a shadow, and add a three-dimensional effect. To display the Drawing toolbar shown in figure 17.8, click <u>V</u>iew, point to <u>T</u>oolbars, and then click Drawing. You can also position the arrow pointer on any visible toolbar, click the *right* mouse button, and then click Drawing at the drop-down menu. Figure 17.8 identifies several buttons on the Drawing toolbar that can be used to create and then customize WordArt text.

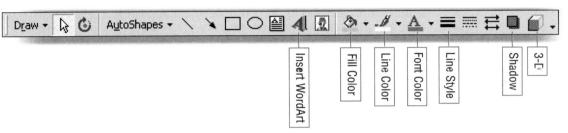

figure
17.8

Drawing Toolbar

Insert WordArt | Fill Color | Line Color | Font Color | Line Style | Shadow | 3-D

Adding Fill Shading or Color

With the Fill Color button on the Drawing toolbar, shading or color can be added
to WordArt text. Click the Fill Color button and the WordArt text will be filled
with the fill color displayed on the Fill Color button. If you want to choose a
different color, click the down-pointing triangle at the right side of the Fill Color
button. This causes a palette of color choices to display. At this palette, click the
desired fill color.

Fill Color

The Fill Color palette also includes two options—More Fill Colors and Fill
Effects. Click the More Fill Colors option and the Colors dialog box shown in
figure 17.9 displays. At this dialog box, click the desired color in the Colors
section, and then click OK.

figure
17.9

Colors Dialog Box with Standard Tab Selected

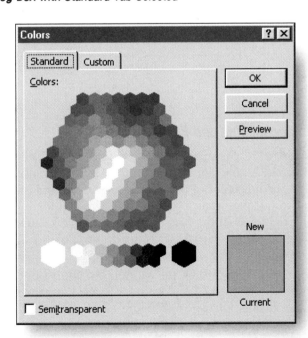

Click the other option at the Fill Color palette, Fill Effects, and the Fill Effects dialog box with the Gradient tab selected displays as shown in figure 17.10. At the dialog box with the Gradient tab selected, you can specify how many colors you want used in the gradient. You can also specify the style of gradient such as horizontal, vertical, diagonal, from the corner, or from the center The options at this dialog box will vary depending on the WordArt selected.

Click the Texture tab to choose a texture to be applied to the WordArt text. If you want to add a pattern to the WordArt text, click the Pattern tab. After making the desired choices at the dialog box, click OK.

figure
17.10

Fill Effects Dialog Box with Gradient Tab Selected

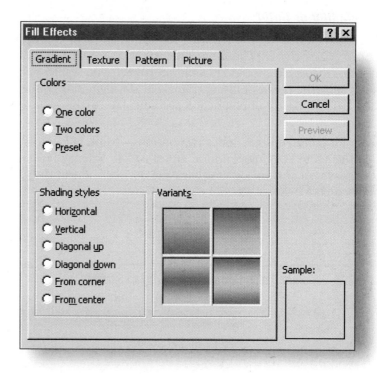

Changing Line and Font Color

Line Color

WordArt text is surrounded by a border line. The color of this line can be changed with the Line Color button on the Drawing toolbar. Click the Line Color button and the line color of the WordArt text changes to the color displayed on the button. If you want to choose a different color, click the down-pointing triangle at the right side of the Line Color button. This causes a palette of color choices to display. At this palette, click the desired color.

The Line Color palette also includes two options—More Line Colors and Patterned Lines. Click the More Line Colors option and the Colors dialog box shown in figure 17.9 displays. Click the Patterned Lines option and the Patterned Lines dialog box shown in figure 17.11 displays. Choose a pattern and a foreground and/or background color for the object at this dialog box.

figure
17.11

Patterned Lines Dialog Box

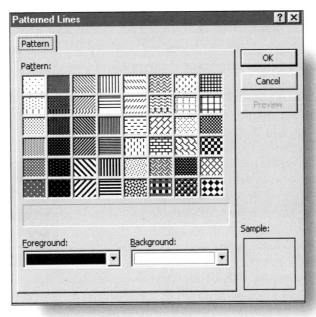

In some situations, you may want to remove the line around WordArt text. To do this, click the down-pointing triangle at the right side of the Line Color button, and then click *No Line* at the color palette.

Change the WordArt font color by clicking the Font Color button on the Drawing toolbar. At the color palette that displays, click the desired color. Click the More Colors option at the palette and the Colors dialog box displays as shown in figure 17.9.

Changing Line Style

The WordArt text line can be changed with options from the Line Style button on the Drawing toolbar. To change the line style, click the Line Style button, and then click the desired line style at the pop-up menu that displays.

Adding Shadow and 3-D Effects

Click the Shadow button on the Drawing toolbar and a palette of shadow options displays. Click the desired option or click the Shadow Settings option and a Shadow Settings toolbar displays. This toolbar contains buttons for turning shadows off or on and buttons for nudging the shadow up, down, left, or right.

If you want to add a three-dimensional look to an object, select the object, and then click the 3-D button on the Drawing toolbar. This displays a palette of three-dimensional choices as well as a 3-D Settings option. Click this option and the 3-D Settings toolbar displays. This toolbar contains buttons for turning 3-D on or off and changing the tilt, depth, direction, and light source.

Font Color

Line Style

Shadow

3-D

exercise 4

Creating and then Changing the Pattern, Color, and Shading of WordArt Text

1. Open Word.
2. Create the WordArt text shown in figure 17.12 by completing the following steps:

Step 2c

   a. At a clear document screen, make sure the Drawing toolbar is displayed (If it is not, click View, point to Toolbars, and then click Drawing.)
   b. Click the Insert WordArt button on the Drawing toolbar.
   c. At the WordArt Gallery, double-click the third option from the left in the first row.
   d. At the Edit WordArt Text dialog box, key **Surfing the Internet Workshop**, and then click the OK button.
   e. Click the WordArt Shape button on the WordArt toolbar.
   f. Click the second shape from the left in the fourth row (*Deflate*).

Step 2f

   g. Change the size and position of the WordArt by completing the following steps:

Step 2g2

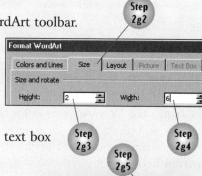

   1) Click the Format WordArt button on the WordArt toolbar.
   2) At the Format WordArt dialog box, click the Size tab.
   3) At the Format WordArt dialog box with the Size tab selected, select the current measurement in the Height text box, and then key **2**.

Step 2g3   Step 2g4

   4) Select the current measurement in the Width text box and then key **6**.

Step 2g5

   5) Click the Layout tab.
   6) At the Format WordArt dialog box with the Layout tab selected, click Center in the Horizontal alignment section.
   7) Click OK to close the Format WordArt dialog box.

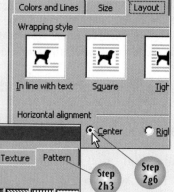

   h. Add a pattern and change colors by completing the following steps:
   1) Click the down-pointing triangle at the right side of the Fill Color button on the Drawing toolbar.
   2) At the palette of color choices that displays, click Fill Effects located at the bottom of the palette.

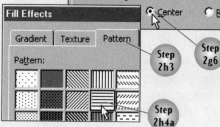

Step 2h3   Step 2g6

   3) At the Fill Effects dialog box, click the Pattern tab.
   4) At the Fill Effects dialog box with the Pattern tab selected, make the following changes:

Step 2h4a

   a) Click the fourth pattern option from the left in the second row.

b) Click the down-pointing triangle at the right side of the Foreground box.
c) At the color palette that displays, click the turquoise color (fifth color from the left in the fourth row).
d) Click the down-pointing triangle at the right side of the Background box.
e) At the color palette that displays, click the pink color (first color from the left in the fourth row).

5) Click OK to close the Fill Effects dialog box.

i. Add a shadow to the text by clicking the Shadow button on the Drawing toolbar and then clicking the second shadow option from the left in the fourth row.

j. Click outside the WordArt text to deselect the WordArt box.

3. Save the document and name it Word Ch 17, Ex 04.
4. Print and then close Word Ch 17, Ex 04.
5. Exit Word.

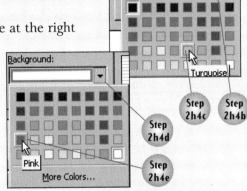
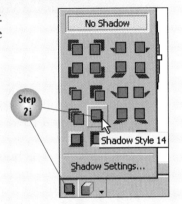

Exercise 4

Surfing the Internet Workshop

exercise 5

Changing the Font Color and Line Style of WordArt Text

1. Open PowerPoint and then open PowerPoint Ch 17, Ex 03.
2. Save the presentation with Save As and name it PowerPoint Ch 17, Ex 05.
3. Change to Slide view and make sure the Drawing toolbar is displayed. (If it is not, click View, point to Toolbars, and then click Drawing.)
4. Change the font color and line style of the WordArt text in Slide 1 by completing the following steps:
   a. Display Slide 1 in Slide View.
   b. Position the arrow pointer on any letter of the WordArt text, *Career Development*, until the arrow pointer displays with a four-headed arrow attached, and then click the left mouse button. (This selects the WordArt text and also displays the WordArt toolbar.)
   c. Customize the WordArt text by completing the following steps:
      1) Click the down-pointing triangle at the right side of the Fill Color button on the Drawing toolbar.
      2) At the palette of color choices that displays, click the light purple color (sixth color from the left in the top row).
      3) Click the Line Style button on the Drawing toolbar.
      4) At the pop-up menu that displays, click the *3 pt* line.
      5) Click the down-pointing triangle at the right side of the Line Color button.
      6) At the pop-up menu that displays, click the second color from the left in the top row.
   d. Click outside the WordArt text box to deselect it.
5. Change the color of the text in slides 2 through 6 by completing the following steps:
   a. Display Slide 2.
   b. Change to the Title Master View.
   c. Click anywhere in the text *Click to edit Master title style*.
   d. Click the down-pointing triangle at the right side of the Font Color button.
   e. At the pop-up menu that displays, click the More Font Colors button.
   f. At the Colors dialog box with the Standard tab selected, click a dark blue-gray color of your choosing.
   g. Click OK to close the dialog box.
   h. Click anywhere in the text *Click to edit Master subtitle style*.
   i. Click the down-pointing triangle at the right side of the Font Color button.

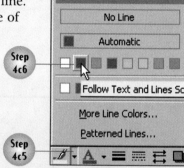

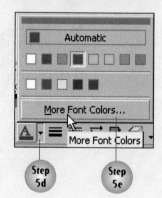

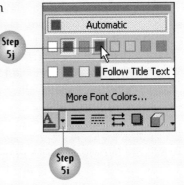

j. At the pop-up menu that displays, click the maroon color (fourth color from the left in the top row).
    Step 5j

k. Click the Slide View button to display Slide 2.

6. Save the presentation again with the same name (PowerPoint Ch 17, Ex 05).

7. Print the presentation so three slides fit on one page.

8. Close PowerPoint Ch 17, Ex 05 and then exit PowerPoint.

Step 5i

Drawing and Formatting Objects in Word and Excel

In chapter 15, you learned about the Drawing toolbar and how to draw and customize shapes, objects, and autoshapes in PowerPoint. In this chapter, you used several buttons on the Drawing toolbar to customize WordArt. Buttons on the Drawing toolbar can also be used to draw and format objects in a Word document and an Excel worksheet.

To display the Drawing toolbar in Word or Excel, right-click any currently displayed toolbar and then click Drawing at the drop-down menu. You can also display the Drawing toolbar by clicking View, pointing to Toolbars, and then clicking Drawing. For an explanation of the buttons on the Drawing toolbar, refer to figure 15.9 in chapter 15.

exercise

Drawing an Autoshape and Text Box

1. Open Word.

2. At a clear document screen, draw the star autoshape and text box shown in figure 17.13 by completing the following steps:

a. Make sure the Drawing toolbar is displayed. (If it is not, right-click any currently displayed toolbar, and then click Drawing at the drop-down menu.)

b. Click the AutoShapes button on the Drawing toolbar, point to Stars and Banners, and then click the 16-Point Star button (second button from the left in the second row from the top).

c. Position the cross hairs in the document screen, hold down the Shift key (this will keep all sides of the star equal) and the left mouse button. Drag the cross hairs to create the star and then release the mouse button and then the Shift key.

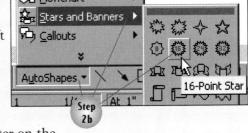

Step 2b

d. The star displays with a small yellow box inside. This box is referred to as an *adjustment handle*. Position the mouse pointer on the adjustment handle, hold down the left mouse button, and drag in so the star displays as shown in figure 17.13.

e. Fill the star with light yellow fill by clicking the down-pointing triangle at the right side of the Fill Color button on the Drawing toolbar and then clicking a light yellow color at the color palette (you choose the shade of yellow).

Step 2d

3. Create a text box inside the star by completing the following steps:

   a. Click the Text Box button on the Drawing toolbar.
   b. Draw a text box inside the star.
   c. Change the font to 14-point Arial bold.
   d. Click the Center button on the Formatting toolbar.
   e. Key **Bobbie McDaniels** inside the text box and then press Enter.
   f. Key **Employee of**, press Enter, and then key **the Month**.
   g. Click the Fill Color button on the Drawing toolbar to fill the text box with the same yellow color as the star.
   h. Remove the border around the text box by clicking the down-pointing triangle at the right side of the Line Color button and then clicking No Line at the pop-up menu.
   i. Size and/or move the text box so the text displays inside the star as shown in figure 17.13.

4. Save the document and name it Word Ch 17, Ex 06.
5. Print and then close Word Ch 17, ex 06.

figure

17.13

Exercise 6

Bobbie McDaniels
Employee of
the Month

Drawing, Customizing, and Rotating Objects

1. With Word the active program and a clear document screen displayed, create the letterhead shown in figure 17.14 by completing the following steps:
   a. Press Enter four times.
   b. Click the Center button on the Formatting toolbar.
   c. Change the font to 36-point Impact. (If Impact is not available, choose a similar typeface.)
   d. Key **In-Sync Products**.
   e. Create the red arrow at the left side of the text by completing the following steps:
      1) Click the AutoShapes button on the Drawing toolbar, point to Block Arrows, and then click *Bent Arrow* (first arrow from the left in the third row).

      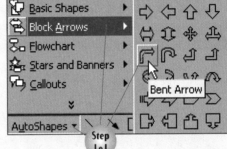

      2) Draw the arrow at the left side of the text as shown in figure 17.14. If you are not satisfied with the location of the arrow, drag it to the desired location. If you are not satisfied with the size of the arrow, use the sizing handles to increase or decrease the size.
      3) With the arrow still selected, add red fill by clicking the down-pointing triangle at the right side of the Fill Color button, and then clicking the red color at the color palette.
   f. With the red arrow still selected, copy it to the right side of the text. To do this, hold down the Ctrl key and then the left mouse button. Drag the arrow to the right side of the text, then release the mouse button and then the Ctrl key.
   g. With the arrow at the right still selected, flip the arrow by clicking the Draw button, pointing to Rotate or Flip, and then clicking Flip Horizontal.
   h. If necessary, reposition the arrow so it displays as shown in figure 17.14.
2. Save the document and name it **Word Ch 17, Ex 07**.
3. Print and then close Word Ch 17, Ex 07.

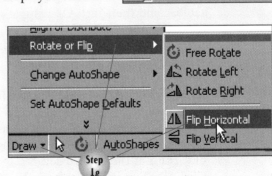

figure
17.14

Exercise 7

In-Sync Products

exercise 8

Drawing and Customizing Objects in Excel

1. Open Excel and then open Excel Worksheet 13.
2. Save the worksheet with Save As and name it Excel Ch 17, Ex 08.
3. Make the following changes to the worksheet:
   a. Delete column H.
   b. Insert a new row at the beginning of the worksheet.
   c. Select cells A1 through G1 and then click the Merge and Center button on the Formatting toolbar.
   d. Change the height of row *1* to *125*. (Do this at the Row Height dialog box.)

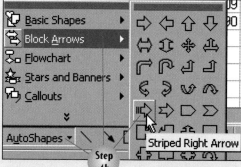

Step 4b

4. Draw the arrow and create the text inside the arrow as shown in figure 17.15 by completing the following steps:
   a. Make sure the Drawing toolbar is displayed. (If it is not, right-click any currently displayed toolbar and then click Drawing at the drop-down menu.)
   b. Click the AutoShapes button on the Drawing toolbar, point to Block Arrows, and then click *Striped Right Arrow* (first arrow from the left in the third row from the bottom).
   c. Draw the arrow the approximate size and shape shown in figure 17.15.
   d. Fill the arrow by clicking the down-pointing arrow at the right side of the Fill Color button and then clicking the blue color at the color palette.
   e. Click the Text Box button on the Drawing toolbar.
   f. Draw a text box inside the arrow large enough to figure the text shown in figure 17.15.

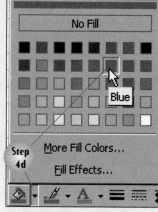

Step 4d

g. Change the font to 20-point Arial bold.
h. Click the Center button on the Formatting toolbar.
i. Key **Arrowhead Construction**.
j. Select the text box by clicking on the text box border. (When the text box is selected, the border lines change from diagonal lines to dots.)
k. With the text box selected, fill the box by clicking the Fill Color button on the Drawing toolbar. (This fills the text box with the same blue color as the arrow.)
l. With the text box still selected, click the down-pointing triangle at the right side of the Line Color button, and then click *No Line* at the color palette.
5. If you are not satisfied with the size and position of the arrow and text, click the arrow to select it, hold down the Shift key, and then click the text. (This selects both the arrow and the text box.)
6. Save the worksheet again with the same name (Excel Ch 17, Ex 08).
7. Print and then close Excel Ch 17, Ex 08.

Exercise 8

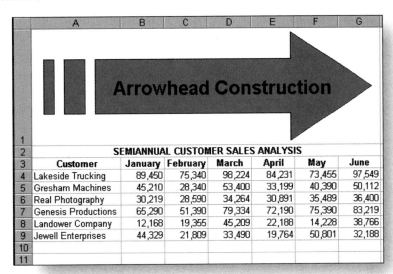

	A	B	C	D	E	F	G
1							
2		SEMIANNUAL CUSTOMER SALES ANALYSIS					
3	Customer	January	February	March	April	May	June
4	Lakeside Trucking	89,450	75,340	98,224	84,231	73,455	97,549
5	Gresham Machines	45,210	28,340	53,400	33,199	40,390	50,112
6	Real Photography	30,219	28,590	34,264	30,891	35,489	36,400
7	Genesis Productions	65,290	51,390	79,334	72,190	75,390	83,219
8	Landower Company	12,168	19,355	45,209	22,188	14,228	38,766
9	Jewell Enterprises	44,329	21,809	33,490	19,764	50,801	32,188
10							
11							

Creating an Organizational Chart

Another application provided by the Microsoft Office suite is MS Organization Chart 2.0. This application can be used in Word, Excel, or PowerPoint to create an organizational chart like the one shown in figure 17.17. You will be creating this organizational chart in exercise 9.

To create an organizational chart, make the desired program active, position the insertion point where you want the organizational chart inserted, and then click Insert and then Object. At the Object dialog box, double-click *MS*

Organization Chart 2.0 in the Object type box. This displays the Microsoft Organization Chart window shown in figure 17.16. Figure 17.16 shows the Microsoft Organization Chart window in Word. The display of this window will vary slightly in Excel and PowerPoint.

In PowerPoint, double-click *MS Organization Chart 2.0* at the Insert Object dialog box. You can also choose an autolayout containing an organizational chart icon. To display the Microsoft Organization Chart window, double-click the *organizational chart* icon.

figure

17.16

Microsoft Organizational Chart Window

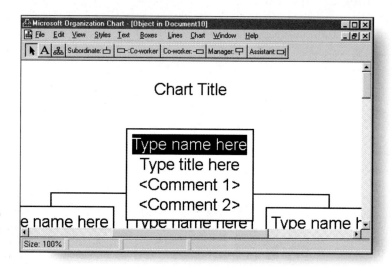

Keying Information in an Organizational Chart

At the Microsoft Organization Chart window, select *Chart Title* and then key a name for the chart. To enter information in a box, click the box, and then key the information. When you click a box, the entire box is selected. When you begin keying text, however, the text appears in the position where *Type name here* displays. Also, when you begin keying text, two additional options display at the bottom of the box: *<Comment 1>* and *<Comment 2>*. Key the text for the name and then press Enter. This selects *Type title here*. Key a title and then press Enter if you are keying more information in the box, or, click the next box. To deselect a box, click anywhere in the chart outside the box, or press the Esc key (located in the upper left corner of the keyboard).

When you click another box or close the Microsoft Organization Chart window, any options that were not chosen are removed from the box. For example, if you do not key text where *<Comment 1>* and *<Comment 2>* display in the box, they are removed from the box.

When all desired information is keyed in the chart, update the chart by clicking File and then Update *(document name)*. Close the Microsoft Organization Chart window by clicking File and then Exit and Return to *(document name)*. The chart is inserted in the document at the position of the insertion point and the chart is also selected.

Sizing and Moving an Organizational Chart

Change the size of an organizational chart using sizing handles. To display sizing handles, select the organizational chart. If you want to move an organizational chart, position the arrow pointer on the selected organizational chart, hold down the left mouse button, drag the outline of the chart to the desired position, and then release the mouse button.

Use sizing handles to change the size of an organizational chart.

Creating an Organizational Chart in Word

1. Open Word.
2. At a clear document screen, create the organizational chart shown in figure 17.17 by completing the following steps:
   a. Change to the Print Layout view.
   b. Click Insert and then Object.
   c. At the Object dialog box, make sure the Create New tab is selected, and then double-click *MS Organization Chart 2.0*. (You will need to scroll down the list to see this program.)

   Step 2c

   > **Object**
   > Create New | Create from File
   > Object type:
   > Microsoft Works 4.0 Sheet or Chart
   > MIDI Sequence
   > MS Organization Chart 2.0
   > MSCAL.Calendar
   > Music Propery Page 2.1
   > Option Propery Page 2.1
   > Package
   > Paintbrush Picture

   d. At the Microsoft Organization Chart window (shown in figure 17.16), click the Maximize button that displays at the right side of the Microsoft Organization Chart title bar.
   e. Select the words *Chart Title* and then key **Bethel Manufacturing**.
   f. Press Enter and then key **Executive Officers**.
   g. Click the top middle box. (This selects the box.)
   h. Key **Raye Lawson**.
   i. Press Enter and then key **President**.
   j. Click the box at the far left side of the next row. (This selects the box.)
   k. Key **Kenneth Erskine**.
   l. Press Enter and then key **Vice President**.
   m. Press Enter and then key **Financial Services**.
   n. Click the middle box. (This selects the box.)
   o. Key **Melissa Ingram-Hoyt**.
   p. Press Enter and then key **Vice President**.
   q. Press Enter and then key **Human Resources**.
   r. Click the box at the right side. (This selects the box.)
   s. Key **Dale Stein**.
   t. Press Enter and then key **Vice President**.
   u. Press Enter and then key **Plant Operations**.
3. Update the chart by clicking File and then Update Document1 (your document number may vary).
4. Close the Microsoft Organization Chart window by clicking File and then Exit and Return to Document1 (your document number may vary).
5. Increase the width and height of the chart and move the chart by completing the following steps:

a. Click the chart to select it. If black sizing handles display around the chart (instead of white sizing handles), complete these steps (skip these steps if white sizing handles display):
   1) With black sizing handles around the chart, right-click the chart.
   2) At the shortcut menu that displays, click Show Picture Toolbar.
   3) Click the Text Wrapping button on the Picture toolbar and then click Through at the drop-down list. (This changes the black sizing handles to white sizing handles.)
b. With the chart selected, position the arrow pointer on the middle sizing handle at the right side until it turns into a double-headed arrow pointing left and right.
c. Hold down the left mouse button, drag the outline to the right to approximately the 6-inch mark on the horizontal ruler, and then release the mouse button.
d. Position the arrow pointer on the middle sizing handle at the bottom of the chart until it turns into a double-headed arrow pointing up and down.
e. Hold down the left mouse button, drag down the outline approximately 1 inch (to about the 3-inch mark on the vertical ruler), and then release the mouse button.
f. With the chart still selected, change the Zoom to *Whole Page*, drag the chart to the middle of the page, and then change the Zoom back to *100%*.

Step 5c

6. Save the organizational chart document and name it Word Ch 17, Ex 09.
7. Print and then close Word Ch 17, Ex 09.

figure

17.17   *Exercise 9*

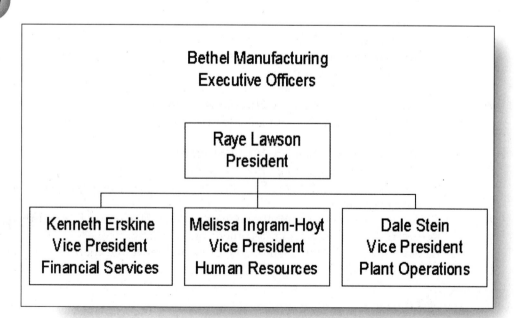

Editing an Existing Organizational Chart

Editing an existing organizational chart is similar to editing other Microsoft features. To edit an existing chart, position the arrow pointer anywhere in the chart, and then double-click the left mouse button. This displays the chart in the Microsoft Organization Chart window.

To edit an organizational chart, double-click the chart.

Adding Boxes to an Organizational Chart

The Microsoft Organization Chart window displays with a toolbar below the menu bar. Buttons on this toolbar can be used to add boxes to an organizational chart. For example, to add a box for an assistant director below a director's box, you would click the Subordinate button on the toolbar, click the director's box (this adds the new box and selects the box), and then key the information. The buttons on the toolbar contain an icon of the box that helps illustrate where the box will appear in the organizational chart. For example, if you want to add a box above another box, click the Manager button on the toolbar.

A box can be removed from a chart with the Clear option from the Edit drop-down menu. To remove a box, click the box, and then click Edit and then Clear.

Adding Boxes to an Organizational Chart

1. With Word the active program, open Word Ch 17, Ex 09.
2. Save the document with Save As and name it Word Ch 17, Ex 10.
3. Add a box above the President box by completing the following steps:
   a. Scroll down the document screen to display the organizational chart.
   b. Double-click the organizational chart. (This displays the chart in the Microsoft Organization Chart window. If necessary, maximize the organizational chart window.)
   c. Click the Manager button on the toolbar.
   d. Click the President box (contains the name *Raye Lawson*). (This inserts a box above the President box and also selects the new box.)
   e. Key **Aubrey Knowles** in the new box that displays above the President box.
   f. Press Enter and then key **Chief Executive Officer**.
4. Add a box below the box for Kenneth Erskine by completing the following steps:
   a. Click the Subordinate button on the toolbar.

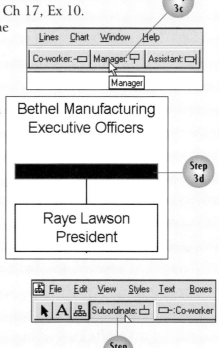

b. Click the box containing the name *Kenneth Erskine*.
c. Key **William Keeley** in the new box that displays below the box for Kenneth Erskine.
d. Press Enter and then key **Director**.
e. Press Enter and then key **Financial Services**.

5. Add a box below the box for Melissa Ingram-Hoyt by completing steps similar to those in step 4. Key the following information in the new box:

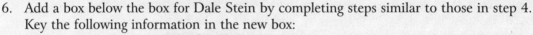

> **Dean Howell**
> **Director**
> **Human Resources**

6. Add a box below the box for Dale Stein by completing steps similar to those in step 4. Key the following information in the new box:

> **Jennifer Fleming**
> **Director**
> **Plant Operations**

7. Update the chart by clicking File and then Update Word Ch 17, Ex 10.doc.
8. Close the organizational chart by clicking File and then Exit and Return to Word Ch 17, Ex 10.doc.
9. Move the chart by completing the following steps:
   a. Change the Zoom to *Whole Page*.
   b. Use the mouse to drag the chart up until it is centered on the page.
   c. Change the Zoom back to *100%*.
10. Save the document again with the same name (Word Ch 17, Ex 10).
11. Print and then close Word Ch 17, Ex 10.

Customizing an Organizational Chart

With options on the Organizational Chart menu bar, you can customize a chart. Customizing can include adding color to a box or the chart background, changing the font of text in a box, changing the border of a box, adding a shadow to a box, and changing the alignment of text in a box.

Click the Text option on the Organizational Chart menu bar and a drop-down menu displays with the following options: Font, Color, Left, Right, and Center. Click the Font option and the Font dialog box displays where you can change the font, the font style, and the font size. Use the Color option if you want to change the text color in a box. The default alignment of text in a box is Center. This can be changed to Left or Right at the Text drop-down menu.

Click the Boxes option on the Organizational Chart menu bar and a drop-down menu displays with the following options: Color, Shadow, Border Style, Border Color, and Border Line Style. Choose the Color option to change the color of the box. Add a shadow to the box with the Shadow option. With the last three options at the Boxes drop-down menu, you can change the border style, border color, and border line style of a box.

With the options from the Lines drop-down menu, you can change the line thickness, style, and color of a line that connects boxes. To use the Lines options, you must first select the line connecting boxes that you want to change. To do this, position the arrow pointer on the desired line, and then click the left mouse button. This will change the display of the line to a dotted line.

Use the <u>C</u>hart option on the Microsoft Organization Chart menu bar to change the background color of the entire chart.

If you want to customize more than one box at a time, you can select multiple boxes. To do this, hold down the Shift key while clicking the desired boxes. If you want to select all boxes in an organizational chart, press Ctrl + A. If you select all boxes, the lines connecting the boxes are also selected.

Changing the View in an Organizational Chart

When the Microsoft Organization Chart window is open, the default display is the actual size of the chart. This can be changed with options at the <u>V</u>iew drop-down menu. The <u>V</u>iew drop-down menu contains the following options: <u>S</u>ize to Window, <u>5</u>0% of Actual, <u>A</u>ctual Size, <u>2</u>00% of Actual, and Show <u>D</u>raw Tools. With the first four options, you can specify how much of the chart you want displayed. If you click the last option, Show <u>D</u>raw Tools, four buttons display at the right side of the Microsoft Organization Chart toolbar. With these buttons, you can draw horizontal and vertical lines, diagonal lines, auxiliary lines, and rectangles.

Customizing an Organizational Chart

1. With Word the active program, open Word Ch 17, Ex 10.
2. Save the document with Save As and name it Word Ch 17, Ex 11.
3. Customize the organizational chart by completing the following steps:
   a. Double-click the organizational chart. (This displays the Microsoft Organization Chart window. If necessary, maximize the organizational chart window.)
   b. Change the view to 50% of actual size by completing the following steps:
      1) Click <u>V</u>iew on the Microsoft Organization Chart menu bar.
      2) At the drop-down menu that displays, click <u>5</u>0% of Actual.
   c. Change the color of all boxes in the organizational chart to turquoise by completing the following steps:
      1) Press Ctrl + A. (This selects all the boxes in the organizational chart.)
      2) Click <u>B</u>oxes and then C<u>o</u>lor.
      3) At the Color dialog box, click the turquoise color (fourth color from the left in the second row).

      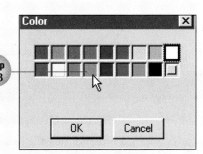

      4) Click OK to close the dialog box.
   d. Change the font for the text in boxes by completing the following steps:
      1) With the boxes still selected, click <u>T</u>ext and then <u>F</u>ont.
      2) At the Font dialog box, click Garamond (or a similar typeface) in the <u>F</u>ont list box.
      3) Click OK to close the dialog box.
   e. Change the text color to dark purple by completing the following steps:
      1) With the boxes still selected, click <u>T</u>ext and then C<u>o</u>lor.

2) At the Color dialog box, click the dark purple color (sixth color from the left in the top row).
3) Click OK to close the dialog box.

f. Change the color of the lines connecting the boxes by completing the following steps:

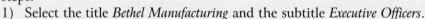

Step 3e2

1) With the boxes still selected, click Lines and then Color.
2) At the Color dialog box, click the dark purple color (sixth color from the left in the first row).
3) Click OK to close the dialog box.

g. Change the font and font color of the title of the organizational chart by completing the following steps:
1) Select the title *Bethel Manufacturing* and the subtitle *Executive Officers*.
2) Click Text and then Font.
3) At the Font dialog box, click Garamond (or a similar typeface) in the Font list box and click 18 in the Size list box.
4) Click OK to close the Font dialog box.
5) Click Text and then Color.
6) At the Color dialog box, click the dark purple color (sixth color from the left in the top row).
7) Click OK to close the Color dialog box.

h. Change the background color of the chart to light gray by completing the following steps:
1) Make sure no text or box is selected.
2) Click Chart and then Background Color.
3) At the Color dialog box, click the light gray color (seventh color from the left in the top row).
4) Click OK to close the dialog box.

4. Update the chart by clicking File and then Update Word Ch 17, Ex 11.doc.
5. Exit the Microsoft Organization Chart window by clicking File and then Exit and Return to Word Ch 17, Ex 11.doc.
6. Deselect the chart and then save the chart with the same name (Word Ch 17, Ex 11).
7. Print and then close Word Ch 17, Ex 11.
8. Exit Word.

exercise 12

Creating Organizational Charts in a PowerPoint Presentation

1. Open PowerPoint and then open Presentation 1, Ch 17. (This presentation is located in the *Presentations* folder on the CD that accompanies this text.)
2. Save the presentation with Save As in the Chapter 17 folder on your disk and name it PowerPoint Ch 17, Ex 12.
3. Create an organizational chart in Slide 5 by completing the following steps:
   a. Display Slide 5 in Slide view.
   b. Double-click the organizational chart icon.

c. At the Microsoft Organization Chart window, click the Manager button on the toolbar.

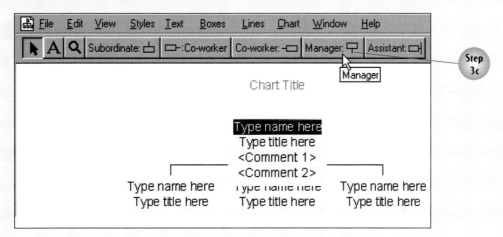

Step
3c

d. Click the first box in the chart. (This adds a new box above the original first box.)
e. Key **Michael Cruz**, press Enter, and then key **President**.
f. Click the box immediately below the Michael Cruz box. (You may need to first click outside the box to make the second box visible.)
g. Key **Cassandra Dodd**, press Enter, and then key **Vice President**.
h. Click the box at the left side of the chart.
i. Key **Harley Gleason**, press Enter, key **Director**, press Enter, and then key **Production**.
j. Click the box immediately to the right of the Harley Gleason box.
k. Key **Bonnie Cavali**, press Enter, key **Director**, press Enter, and then key **Personnel**.
l. Click the box immediately to the right of the Bonnie Cavali box.
m. Key **Teddy Arneson**, press Enter, key **Director**, press Enter, and then key **Finances**.
n. Click File and then Update PowerPoint Ch 17, Ex 12.
o. Click File and then Exit and Return to PowerPoint Ch 17, Ex 12.
4. Save the presentation again with the same name (PowerPoint Ch 17, Ex 12).
5. Print all five slides on one page.
6. Close PowerPoint Ch 17, Ex 12.

Customizing Organizational Charts in a PowerPoint Presentation

1. With PowerPoint the active program, open PowerPoint Ch 17, Ex 12.
2. Save the presentation with Save As and name it PowerPoint Ch 17, Ex 13.
3. Make the following changes to the presentation:
   a. Display Slide 3 in Slide View.
   b. Change the box color and text font of the organizational chart by completing the following steps:

       1) Double-click the chart. (This displays the Microsoft Organization Chart window.)

       2) Press Ctrl + A to select all boxes in the organizational chart.

       3) Click Boxes and then Color.

       4) At the Color dialog box, click the gold color (fifth from the left in the top row).

       5) Click OK to close the Color dialog box.

       6) With the boxes still selected, click Text and then Font.

       7) At the Font dialog box, click Times New Roman in the Font list box (you will need to scroll down the list), and click Bold in the Font style list box.

       8) Click OK to close the Font dialog box.

       9) Click File and then Update PowerPoint Ch 17, Ex 13.

      10) Click File and then Exit and Return to PowerPoint Ch 17, Ex 13.

    c. Display Slide 4 and then make the changes described in step 3b.

    d. Display Slide 5 and then make the changes described in step 3b.

    e. Add a transition of your choosing to each slide.

4. Run the presentation.

5. Save the presentation again with the same name (PowerPoint Ch 17, Ex 13).

6. Print all five slides on one page.

7. Close PowerPoint Ch 17, Ex 13 and then exit PowerPoint.

chapter summary

- With the WordArt application, you can distort or modify text to conform to a variety of shapes. With WordArt, you can change the font, size, and alignment of text. You can also add fill color, line color, change the line style, and add shadow and three-dimensional effects.

- Display the WordArt Gallery by clicking Insert, pointing to Picture, and then clicking WordArt or clicking the Insert WordArt button on the Drawing toolbar.

- Select an option at the WordArt Gallery by double-clicking the desired option.

- After an option at the WordArt Gallery is selected, the Edit WordArt Text dialog box displays.

- Use the white sizing handles around WordArt text to change the size.

- Move WordArt text by positioning the arrow pointer on any letter until it displays with a four-headed arrow, hold down the left mouse button, move the outline of the WordArt box to the desired position, and then release the mouse button.

- Specify a font and font size for WordArt at the Edit WordArt Text dialog box.

- Customize WordArt text with buttons on the WordArt toolbar.

- Create and customize WordArt with buttons on the Drawing toolbar.

- Draw and format objects in Word and Excel using buttons on the Drawing toolbar.

- Use the Microsoft Organization Chart 2.0 application to create an organizational chart in Word, Excel, or PowerPoint.
- One method for displaying the Microsoft Organization Chart window is to click Insert, Object and then double-click MS Organization Chart 2.0. In PowerPoint, you can also enter the chart window by choosing an autolayout containing an *organizational chart* icon.
- Change the size of an organizational chart by selecting the chart and then using the sizing handles that display around the chart.
- To move an organizational chart, select the chart, and then drag it with the mouse.
- To edit an existing organizational chart, double-click the chart. (This displays the chart in the Microsoft Organization Chart window.)
- Use buttons on the Organizational Chart toolbar to add boxes to an organizational chart.
- Remove a box from an organizational chart by selecting the box and then clicking Edit and then Clear.
- Customize an organizational chart with options on the Organization Chart menu bar. Customizing can include adding color to boxes or the chart background, changing the font of the text in a box, changing the box border, adding shadow, and changing the alignment of text within a box.
- To customize more than one box at a time, hold down the Shift key, and then click the desired boxes. To customize all boxes in a chart at the same time, select all boxes by pressing Ctrl + A.
- An organizational chart is displayed in actual size in the Microsoft Organization Chart window. This can be changed with options at the View drop-down menu.

commands review

	Mouse/Keyboard
WordArt Gallery	Click Insert, point to Picture, click WordArt; or click the Insert WordArt button on the Drawing toolbar
Format WordArt dialog box	Click the Format WordArt button on WordArt toolbar
WordArt shape palette	Click the WordArt Shape button on WordArt toolbar
Drawing toolbar	Click View, point to Toolbars, click Drawing; or position arrow pointer on toolbar, click *right* mouse button, then click Drawing
Colors dialog box	Click down-pointing triangle at right side of Fill Color button and then click More Fill Colors
Fill Effects dialog box	Click down-pointing triangle at right side of Fill Color button and then click Fill Effects
Patterned Lines dialog box	Click down-pointing triangle at right side of Line Color button and then click Patterned Lines
Microsoft Organization Chart 2.0	Click Insert, Object, then double-click MS Organization Chart 2.0; (or, in PowerPoint, double-click organizational chart icon)
Edit organizational chart	Double-click organizational chart

thinking offline ···

Completion: In the space provided at the right, indicate the correct term, command, or number.

1. Click Insert, point to Picture, and then click WordArt and this displays on the screen.

2. Key WordArt text at this dialog box.

3. Click this button on the WordArt toolbar to display a palette of shape options.

4. Click this button on the Drawing toolbar to change the color of WordArt text.

5. Double-click this option in the Object dialog box to display the Microsoft Organization Chart window.

6. To select more than one box in the Microsoft Organization Chart window, hold down this key while clicking the desired boxes.

7. Press these keys to select all boxes in the Microsoft Organization Chart window.

8. To delete a box from an organizational chart, select the box, click Edit, and then click this option.

9. To add a box below another box in an organizational chart, click this button on the Organizational Chart toolbar.

10. Click this button on the Organizational Chart toolbar to add a box above an existing box.

11. Use this option on the Organization Chart menu bar to change the background color of the entire chart.

12. In the space provided below, list the steps you would complete to change the text color to red and add a shadow to existing WordArt text.

_____

_____

_____

13. In the space provided below, list the steps you would complete to change the color of all boxes in an existing organizational chart to blue and change the background color to gray.

_____

_____

_____

working hands-on

Assessment 1

1. Open Word.
2. At a clear document screen, create the WordArt text and border line shown in figure 17.18 by completing the following steps:
   a. Press the Enter key eight times and then move the insertion point up to the first line.
   b. Display the WordArt Gallery.
   c. Double-click the third option from the left in the top row.
   d. At the Edit WordArt Text dialog box, key **Hightower**, press Enter, key **Financing**, and then close the dialog box.
   e. Change the shape of the text to a triangle. (*Hint: Click the WordArt Shape button on the WordArt toolbar.*)
   f. Display the Format WordArt dialog box with the Size tab selected, change the height to *1.2* and the width to *2*, and then close the dialog box.
   g. Display the Format WordArt dialog box with the Layout tab selected, click Left in the Horizontal alignment section, and then close the dialog box.
   h. Deselect the WordArt text.
   i. Insert a border below the company name as shown in figure 17.18. (*Hint: Do this at the Borders and Shading dialog box.*)
3. Save the document and name it Word Ch 17, SA 01.
4. Print and then close Word Ch 17, SA 01.
5. Exit Word.

17.18 *Assessment 1*

Assessment 2

1. Open Excel and then open Excel Worksheet 21.
2. Save the worksheet with Save As and name it Excel Ch 17, SA 02.
3. Insert WordArt into the worksheet by completing these steps:
   a. Make cell D1 the active cell.
   b. Display the WordArt Gallery.
   c. Double-click the fifth option from the left in the top row.

    d. Key the following at the Edit WordArt Text dialog box:
      1) Press the space bar, key **International**, press the space bar again, and then press Enter.
      2) Press the space bar, key **Hardware**, press the space bar again, and then press Enter.
      3) Press the space bar, key **Corporation**, and then press the space bar again.
      4) Change the font size to *28*.
      5) Close the Edit WordArt Text dialog box.
    e. Change the shape of the text to a Button (Curve). (*Hint: Click the WordArt Shape button on the WordArt toolbar and then click the fourth option from the left in the second row.*)
    f. Display the Format WordArt dialog box with the Size tab selected, change the height to *1.6* and the width to *2*, and then close the dialog box.
    g. With the WordArt text box still selected, move the WordArt so it is positioned centered horizontally between columns D through G and vertically between rows 1 through 11.
4. Save the worksheet again with the same name (Excel Ch 17, SA 02).
5. Print Excel Ch 17, SA 02 horizontally and vertically centered on the page.
6. Close Excel Ch 17, SA 02 and then exit Excel.

Assessment 3

1. Open Word.
2. At a clear document screen, create the text *International Hardware Corporation* as WordArt text. You determine the formatting of the text and include at least the following:
    a. Change the shape of the WordArt text.
    b. Add a pattern to the WordArt text.
    c. Change the foreground and background color of the WordArt text.
    d. Add a shadow or three-dimensional effect to the WordArt text.
3. Save the document and name it Word Ch 17, SA 03.
4. Print and then close Word Ch 17, SA 03.

Assessment 4

1. With Word the active program, create an organizational chart at a clear document screen with the title *Production Department*, and then key the following information in the organizational chart boxes in the order displayed: (*Hint: To remove the third box provided by Microsoft Organization Chart, select the unneeded box, and then click <u>E</u>dit and then Cl<u>e</u>ar.*)

Harley Gleason
Director

Jenna Steiner
Assistant Director

Robert Lyons   **Cheri Koesel**
Plant Manager   **Production Manager**

2. Make the following changes to the organizational chart:
   a. Add color to all boxes in the chart. (You determine the color.)
   b. Change the font of the text in the boxes. (You determine the font.)
   c. Add a background color to the chart. (You determine the color.)
3. After creating the organizational chart, select and then move the chart to the middle of the page.
4. Save the organizational chart and name it Word Ch 17, SA 04.
5. Print and then close Word Ch 17, SA 04.
6. Exit Word.

Assessment 5

1. Open PowerPoint and then open Presentation 2, Ch 17. (This presentation is located in the *Presentations* folder on the CD that accompanies this textbook.)
2. Save the presentation with Save As in the *Chapter 17* folder on your disk and name it PowerPoint Ch 17, SA 05.
3. Display Slide 1 in Slide view and then use WordArt to create the a title with the following specifications:
   a. At the WordArt Gallery, choose the fourth option from the left in the third row.
   b. At the Edit WordArt Text dialog box, key **RAINBOW ARTWORKS**.
   c. Change the shape of the WordArt text to Arch Up (Pour) (fifth option from the left in the second row).
   d. Display the Format WordArt dialog box with the Size tab selected and then change the He_ight to *8* and the Wi_dth to *8*.
   e. Display the Format WordArt dialog box with the Position tab selected and then change the _Horizontal option to *1* and the _Vertical option to *2.4*.
4. Create a new Slide 5 with the following specifications:
   a. Choose the third autolayout from the left in the second row (Organization Chart) at the New Slide dialog box.
   b. Key the title **AGENCY STRUCTURE** and then create an organizational chart with the following information:

	Monica Chun **Director**	
	Liam Randall **Assistant Director**	
Josephine Piper **Artistic Designer**	**Leska Winters** **Program Coordinator**	**Rudy Serosky** **Education Director**

   c. Center the organizational chart on the slide.
   d. Add transitions of your choosing to the slides.
5. Save PowerPoint Ch 17, SA 05.
6. Run the presentation.
7. Print the five slides on one page.
8. Close PowerPoint Ch 17, SA 05.

Assessment 6

1. With PowerPoint the active program, open PowerPoint Ch 17, SA 05.
2. Make the following changes to the organizational chart in Slide 5:
   a. Change the color of all boxes in the organizational chart to gold.
   b. Change the font of the text in the boxes to Tahoma bold.
3. Save the presentation with the same name (PowerPoint Ch 17, SA 05).
4. Print all five slides on one page.
5. Close PowerPoint Ch 17, SA 05 and then exit PowerPoint.

Assessment 7

1. Open Word and then open Word Ch 17, SA 04.
2. Save the document with Save As and name it Word Ch 17, SA 07.
3. Use the Help feature in Microsoft Organization Chart 2.0 to learn about chart styles by completing the following steps:

   a. Double-click the organizational chart. (This displays the chart in the Microsoft Organization Chart window.)
   b. Click <u>H</u>elp on the Microsoft Organization Chart menu bar.
   c. At the drop-down menu, click <u>I</u>ndex.
   d. At the Microsoft Organization Chart Help dialog box, click *Menu commands and icons*.
   e. At the next help screen, click *Styles menu*.
   f. At the next help screen, read and then print the information.
   g. Click *Rearranging boxes*.
   h. At the next help screen, read and then print the information.
   i. Exit Help.
4. Make the following changes to the organizational chart:
   a. Click one of the Co-worker buttons on the Organization Chart toolbar.
   b. Click the box containing the name *Robert Lyons*.
   c. Key **Sondra Jamison** in the new box.
   d. Press Enter and then key **Quality Control Manager**.
   e. Click the Co-worker button on the Organization Chart toolbar.
   f. Click the box containing the name *Cheri Koesel*.
   g. Key **Lloyd Harris** in the new box.
   h. Press Enter and then key **Materials Manager**.
5. Change the organizational style of the bottom four boxes by completing the following steps:
   a. Select the bottom four boxes in the organizational chart. (To do this, hold down the Shift key while clicking each of the four boxes.)
   b. Click <u>S</u>tyles.
   c. At the drop-down menu that displays, click the last group in the first row.
6. Update the organizational chart and then exit and return to the document.
7. Save the document again with the same name (Word Ch 17, SA 07).
8. Print and then close Word Ch 17, SA 07.

Chapter 18

Linking and Embedding Objects

PERFORMANCE OBJECTIVES

Upon successful completion of chapter 18, you will be able to:

- Link an Excel worksheet with a Word document.
- Edit a linked object.
- Link an object to two Word documents.
- Link an Excel chart to a presentation.
- Embed a worksheet in a Word document.
- Embed a table in a PowerPoint presentation.
- Edit an embedded object.

Microsoft Office is a suite that allows integration, which is the combining of data from two or more programs into one document. Integration can occur by copying and pasting data between programs. For example, in both Word and Excel, you have learned how to copy and paste text within and between documents. Information or objects can also be copied and pasted between programs. Copying and pasting information between programs is fairly easy but it has some drawbacks. For example, if you continually update an Excel worksheet that you had copied to a Word document, you would need to copy and paste the edited worksheet each time a change is made. This is because the changes you make to the Excel worksheet are not reflected in the worksheet in the Word document. If you are copying and pasting an object between programs, you need to remember the program in which you created the object. To edit the object, you would need to open the original program or application.

Microsoft Office offers two options for overcoming the drawbacks of copying and pasting. With the programs in Microsoft Office, you can create something in one program and then share it with another program. For example, you can create a worksheet in Excel and then share it with a Word document. This type of sharing is referred to as object linking and embedding (OLE—pronounced oh-LAY).

An object created in one program can be linked or embedded in another program. The program containing the object is called the *source* and the program

Linking provides a more direct connection between data in two programs than embedding.

the object is linked to or embedded in is called the *destination*. An object can be a table, workbook, chart, picture, text, or any other type of information you create.

There is a difference between linking and embedding. When an object is linked, the object exists in the source program but not as a separate object in the destination program. The destination program contains only a code that identifies the name and location of the source program, document, and the location in the document.

When an object is embedded, it resides in both the source and the destination programs. The difference between embedding and just copying and pasting an object from one program to another is that embedding an object makes the source application tools available for editing. Embedding causes an OLE code to be inserted in the document that points to the source application. If a change is made to an embedded document at either the source program or the destination program, the change is not reflected in the other program. For example, if you make a change to a worksheet in Excel and that worksheet is embedded in a Word document, the worksheet in the Word document is not changed. However, if you edit the worksheet that is embedded in the Word document, the Excel tools will be available for editing.

Linking does not increase the size of the document in the destination program.

The size of a document in the destination program containing a linked object does not increase. This is because the object does not reside in the document in the destination program. An embedded object in a document in the destination program will increase the document size. This is because the embedded object becomes a part of the document in the destination program.

Deciding whether to link or embed an object depends on how the information in the object is to be used. For example, if you want to insert an Excel worksheet into a Word document that contains information you do not need to update, consider embedding or simply copying the worksheet into the Word document. If the object you are copying will be continually updated and you want the updates to appear in the destination program, then link the object.

Linking Objects

Linking is one way of attaching data from one document to another.

As mentioned earlier, when an object is linked, there is only the one object, so changes made to the object will be reflected in the source as well as the destination program. By default, Microsoft Office updates a link automatically. This means that a link is updated whenever you open the destination program or you edit the linked object in the destination program. The steps to link an object between programs are basically the same regardless of the program or application. For example, to link an Excel worksheet to a Word document, you would follow these basic steps:

1. Make sure both Word and Excel are open.
2. With Excel the active program, open the workbook containing the worksheet you want to link to the Word document.
3. Select the cells in the worksheet you want to link to Word.
4. Click the Copy button on the Standard toolbar, or click Edit and then Copy.
5. Make Word the active program. (To do this, click the button on the Taskbar representing Word.)
6. Open the Word document where you want to insert the worksheet cells.

7. Move the insertion point to the location in the document where you want the worksheet cells inserted.
8. Click Edit and then Paste Special and the Paste Special dialog box displays as shown in figure 18.1.
9. At the Paste Special dialog box, choose the necessary object in the As list box, and then click Paste link.
10. Click OK to close the dialog box.

figure
18.1
Paste Special Dialog Box

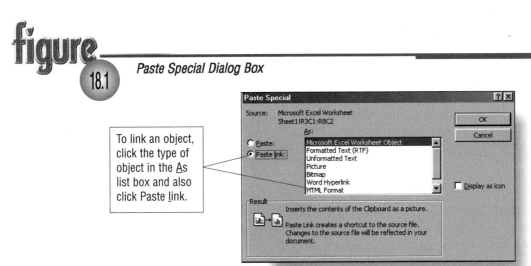

To link an object, click the type of object in the As list box and also click Paste link.

When the insertion point is positioned in the linked object in the destination program, the link is highlighted in gray. Information can be edited in the destination program but the changes made will disappear when the link is updated. A link is updated when a file is opened or printed. The gray highlighting can act as a reminder to you not to edit the linked object in the destination program.

If you want to update information in a linked object, make the changes in the object at the source program. For example, if you want to edit an Excel worksheet that is linked to a Word document, edit the worksheet in Excel. Any changes made to the Excel worksheet will be reflected in the linked worksheet in Word.

When data in a source file changes, the data in the destination file is updated. This is referred to as a *dynamic data exchange.*

exercise

Linking an Excel Worksheet with a Word Document
1. Open Excel and then open Word.
2. With Word the active program, open Word Memo 02.
3. Save the document and name it Word Ch 18, Ex 01.
4. Change to the Print Layout view and then change the Zoom to *Whole Page*.
5. Link a worksheet to the Word document by completing the following steps:
   a. Make Excel the active program.
   b. Open Excel Worksheet 05.

c. Save the worksheet with Save As and name it Excel Ch 18, Ex 01.
d. Select cells A1 through C8.
e. Click the Copy button on the Standard toolbar.
f. Make Word the active program (click the button on the Taskbar identifying Word).
g. With Word Ch 18, Ex 01 open, click Edit and then Paste Special.
h. At the Paste Special dialog box, click *Microsoft Excel Worksheet Object* in the As list box.
i. Click Paste link.
j. Click OK to close the dialog box.
k. Move the table so it is positioned between the first and second paragraphs in the body of the memo.
l. Change the Zoom back to *100%*.

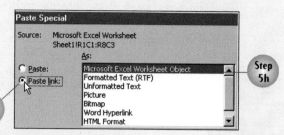

Step 5h

Step 5i

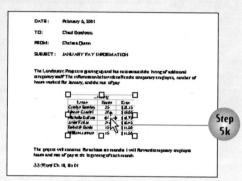

Step 5k

6. Save the Word document again with the same name (Word Ch 18, Ex 01).
7. Print and then close Word Ch 18, Ex 01.
8. Make Excel the active program and then close Excel Ch 18, Ex 01.

Editing a Document with a Linked Object

You can use Alt + Tab to cycle between two open programs.

To edit a document containing a linked object, edit the object in the source program. For example, if you want to change the number of hours worked by employees in the worksheet inserted in the Word document in exercise 1, you would make the change in Excel. Any change you make to the Excel worksheet will be reflected in the Word document. If you want the change to be saved, be sure to save the worksheet.

exercise 2

Editing a Linked Object at the Source Program

1. Make sure both Word and Excel are open.
2. Make Excel the active program and then open Excel Ch 18, Ex 01.
3. Make the following changes to the specified cells:

    B3: Change *35* to *40*
    B4: Change *20* to *25*
    B7: Change *15* to *20*
    C4: Change *$19.00* to *19.50*
    C6: Change *$16.45* to *16.90*
    C7: Change *$11.50* to *12.25*

	A	B	C
1	January		
2	Name	Hours	Rate
3	Carolyn Bentley	40	$23.15
4	Lindon Cassini	25	$19.50
5	Michelle DeFord	40	$18.75
6	Javier Farias	24	$16.90
7	Deborah Gould	20	$12.25
8	William Jarman	15	$11.50

Step 3

4. Save the worksheet with the same name (Excel Ch 18, Ex 01).
5. Print and then close Excel Ch 18, Ex 01.
6. Make Word the active program.
7. Open Word Ch 18, Ex 01.
8. Print and then close Word Ch 18, Ex 01, saving the changes. (*Note: The worksheet in Word Ch 18, Ex 01 reflects the changes made to Excel Ch 18, Ex 01 because of the linking.*)

Linking Word Documents

Linking does not have to be between two different programs—documents created in the same program also can be linked. For example, you can create an object in a Word document and then link it with another Word document (or several Word documents). If a change is made to the object in the original document, the linked object in the other document (or documents) is automatically updated. In exercise 3, you will link an object from the original Word document to two other Word documents. Changes made to the document containing the original linked object will automatically occur to the linked objects in the other two Word documents.

Linking Objects in Word Documents

1. At a clear Word document screen, open Word Memo 03.
2. Save the document and name it Word Ch 18, Linked Doc 1.
3. Change to the Print Layout view and then change the Zoom to *Whole Page*.
4. With Word Ch 18, Linked Doc 1 still open, open Word Table 03.
5. Save the document with Save As and name it Ch 18 Table 03.
6. Copy and link the table by completing the following steps:
   a. With Ch 18 Table 03 the active document, select the table.
   b. Click the Copy button on the Standard toolbar.
   c. Click the button on the Taskbar representing Word Ch 18, Linked Doc 1.
   d. With Word Ch 18, Linked Doc 1 the active document, click Edit and then Paste Special.
   e. At the Paste Special dialog box, click *Microsoft Word Document Object* in the As list box, and then click Paste link.
   f. Click OK to close the dialog box.
   g. Move the table so it is positioned below the first paragraph of the memo but above the reference initials and document name.
   h. Change the Zoom back to *100%*.
   i. Deselect the table.
7. Save the document again with the same name (Word Ch 18, Linked Doc 1).
8. Print Word Ch 18, Linked Doc 1.

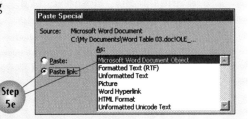

Step 5e

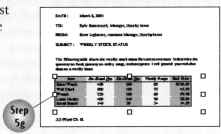

Step 5g

9. Change the name and title after TO: from *Kyle Suzenevich, Manager, Novelty Items* to *Regina Stewart, Manager, Catalog Services*.
10. Save the document with Save As and name it Word Ch 18, Linked Doc 2.
11. Print and then close Word Ch 18, Linked Doc 2.
12. Deselect the table and then print and close Ch 18 Table 03.

exercise 4

Changing Data in a Linked Object in a Word Document

1. With Word the active program, open Ch 18 Table 03.
2. Make the following changes to the table in the document:
   a. Change the following quantities in the On-Hand Qty. column:
      Change *450* to *365*
      Change *500* to *425*
      Change *230* to *170*
      Change *400* to *310*
      Change *140* to *106*
   b. Change the following quantities in the Weekly Usage column:
      Change *85* to *67*
      Change *60* to *45*
      Change *34* to *20*

Item	On-Hand Qty.	On-Order Qty.	Weekly Usage	Unit Price
Silver Watch	365	200	67	$120.00
Wall Clock	425	150	75	45.50
Wreath	170	100	45	59.98
Letter Holder	310	240	90	28.00
Bread Board	106	50	20	14.50

Step 2a   Step 2b

3. Save the edited document with the same name (Word Table 03).
4. Print and then close Ch 18 Table 03.
5. Open Word Ch 18, Linked Doc 1.
6. Change the date from *March 8, 2001*, to *March 15, 2001*.
7. Save the document with the same name (Word Ch 18, Linked Doc 1).
8. Print and then close Word Ch 18, Linked Doc 1.
9. Open Word Ch 18, Linked Doc 2.
10. Change the date from *March 8, 2001*, to *March 15, 2001*.
11. Save the document with the same name (Word Ch 18, Linked Doc 2).
12. Print and then close Word Ch 18, Linked Doc 2.
13. Exit Word.

The table in the documents Word Ch 18, Linked Doc 1 and Word Ch 18, Linked Doc 2 is automatically updated when the documents are opened. This is because the table is linked to the original table you edited in the document named Ch 18 Table 03.

Linking Objects to a PowerPoint Presentation

An object, such as a table, worksheet, or chart, can be inserted in a slide in a PowerPoint presentation. This object can be linked so that information changed at the source program will be reflected in the object in the PowerPoint presentation.

When embedding or linking objects to a presentation, consider the data and what impact you want it to have on the audience. A table or worksheet may be difficult to read when presented in a slide. For this reason, consider linking or embedding a chart into a presentation rather than a table or worksheet. A chart provides a visual display of information and has more of an impact on the audience.

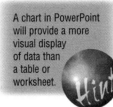
A chart in PowerPoint will provide a more visual display of data than a table or worksheet.

exercise 5

Linking Charts to a PowerPoint Presentation

1. Open Excel and then PowerPoint.
2. Open the presentation named Presentation 1, Ch 18. (This presentation is located in the *Presentations* folder on the CD that accompanies this textbook.)
3. Save the presentation with Save As in the *Chapter 18* folder on your disk and name it PowerPoint Ch 18, Ex 05.
4. Change to the Slide view and make Slide 2 the active slide.
5. Make Excel the active program and then open Excel Worksheet 23.
6. Save the Excel worksheet with Save As and name it Excel Ch 18, Slide 2.
7. Link the chart in the worksheet to Slide 2 of the presentation by completing the following steps:

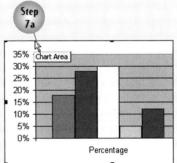
Step 7a

   a. Click once in the chart area to select it. (Click just inside the chart border. Make sure you do not select a specific chart element.)
   b. Click the Copy button on the Standard toolbar.
   c. Make PowerPoint the active program. (This should display PowerPoint Ch 18, Ex 05 with Slide 2 the active slide.)
   d. Click Edit and then Paste Special.
   e. At the Paste Special dialog box, make sure *Microsoft Excel Chart Object* displays in the As list box, and then click Paste link.
   f. Click OK to close the dialog box.
   g. Increase the size of the chart in the slide by dragging the white sizing handles that display around the chart. Increase the size of the chart so it fills a good portion of the bottom part of the slide.

Step 7e

   h. Save the presentation again with the same name (PowerPoint Ch 18, Ex 05).
8. Make Excel the active program and then close Excel Ch 18, Slide 2.
9. Open Excel Worksheet 24.
10. Save the worksheet with Save As and name it Excel Ch 18, Slide 3.
11. Link the chart in the worksheet to Slide 3 by completing steps similar to those in step 7.
12. Save the presentation again with the same name (PowerPoint Ch 18, Ex 05).
13. Print the slides as a handout with all slides on one page. (*Note: The fourth slide will be blank, except for the title. You will be inserting a chart in this slide in exercise 9.*)
14. Close the presentation and then exit PowerPoint.
15. With Excel the active program, close Excel Ch 18, Slide 3, and then exit.

As you have learned about linking, the advantage to linking over just copying and pasting is that you can change information in the object at the source program and the change will also occur in the object in the destination program. In exercise 6, you will make changes to information in the Excel charts, and this will update the charts in the PowerPoint presentation.

exercise 6

Changing Data in Linked Charts

1. Open PowerPoint and Excel.
2. With Excel the active program, open Excel Ch 18, Slide 2.
3. Make the following changes to the data in the cells in the worksheet:
   a. Change B2 from *18%* to *10%*.
   b. Change B3 from *28%* to *20%*.

	A	B
1		Percentage
2	1995	10%
3	1996	20%
4	1997	30%
5	1998	5%
6	1999	12%

Step 3

4. Save the worksheet again with the same name (Excel Ch 18, Slide 2).
5. Close Excel Ch 18, Slide 2.
6. Open Excel Ch 18, Slide 3.
7. Make the following changes to the data in the cells in the worksheet:
   a. Change B2 from *13%* to *17%*.
   b. Change B3 from *9%* to *4%*.
   c. Change B6 from *15%* to *19%*.

	A	B
1		Percentage
2	1995	17%
3	1996	4%
4	1997	18%
5	1998	4%
6	1999	19%

Step 7

8. Save the worksheet again with the same name (Excel Ch 18, Slide 3).
9. Close Excel Ch 18, Slide 3.
10. Make PowerPoint the active program.
11. Open PowerPoint Ch 18, Ex 05.
12. At the question asking if you want to update links, click OK.
13. Save the presentation with the same name (PowerPoint Ch 18, Ex 05).
14. Print the slides as a handout with all slides on one page. (*Note: The fourth slide will be blank except for the title. You will be inserting a chart in this slide in exercise 9.*)
15. Close PowerPoint Ch 18, Ex 05.
16. Exit PowerPoint and then Excel.

After printing the table and the presentation, notice that some of the bars in the charts in Slide 2 and Slide 3 reflect the changes made to the charts in Excel.

A table or chart created in Word can be linked to a PowerPoint presentation just as an Excel chart can be linked. The steps for linking a Word table or chart are basically the same as linking an Excel chart.

Embedding Objects

An object in a document in the source program can be embedded in a document in the destination program. When an object is embedded, the object resides in the document in the destination program. This is different from linking the object, which inserts only a code in the document in the destination program, not the entire object. If a change is made to the embedded object at the source program, the change is not made to the object in the destination program. Since the object is actually inserted in the document in the destination program, it is a separate object from the original object.

Since an embedded object is not automatically updated as a linked object is, the only advantage to embedding rather than simply copying and pasting is that you can edit an embedded object using the tools of the program or application in which the object was created. In exercise 7, you will embed an Excel worksheet into a Word document. In exercise 8, you will edit the worksheet while in Word.

If you take a file containing an embedded object to another computer, make sure that computer contains the necessary application before trying to edit the embedded object.

Hint

Embedding an Excel Worksheet into a Word Document

1. Open Excel and then Word.
2. With Word the active program, open Word Memo 04.
3. Save the document and name it Word Ch 18, Ex 07.
4. Change to the Print Layout view and then change the Zoom to *Whole Page*.
5. Make Excel the active program and then open Excel Worksheet 07.
6. Save the worksheet with Save As and name it Excel Ch 18, Ex 07.
7. Make the following changes to the worksheet:
   a. Add a formula to calculate depreciation by the straight-line method by completing the following steps:
      1) Make cell E3 active.
      2) Click the Paste Function button on the Standard toolbar.
      3) At the Paste Function dialog box, click *Financial* in the Function category list box.
      4) Scroll down the Function name list until the function SLN is visible and then click *SLN*.
      5) Click OK.
      6) At the second Paste Function dialog box, key **B3** in the Cost category, and then press the Tab key.
      7) Key **C3** in the Salvage category and then press the Tab key.
      8) Key **D3** in the Life category.
      9) Click OK.
   b. Copy the formula down to other cells by completing the following steps:
      1) With cell E3 active, position the mouse pointer (white plus sign) on the fill handle that displays at the lower right corner of cell E3 until it turns into a thin black cross.

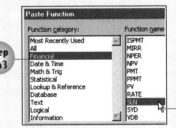

Step 7a3

Step 7a4

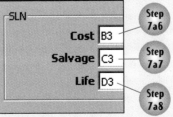

Step 7a6

Step 7a7

Step 7a8

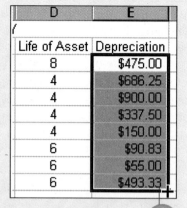

2) Hold down the left mouse button, drag down to cell E10, and then release the mouse button.

  c. Select cells A1 through E10 and then apply the Classic 3 autoformat.

  d. Select cells D3 through D10 and then click the Center button on the Formatting toolbar.

  e. Select cells E3 through E10 and then click the Currency Style button on the Formatting toolbar.

8. Embed the worksheet in the Word document by completing the following steps:

  a. Select cells A1 through E10.

  b. Click the Copy button on the Standard toolbar.

  c. Make Word the active program.

  d. With Word Ch 18, Ex 07 open, click Edit and then Paste Special.

  e. At the Paste Special dialog box, click *Microsoft Excel Worksheet Object* in the As list box.

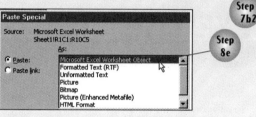

Step 7b2

Step 8e

  f. Click OK to close the dialog box.

  g. Move the worksheet so it is positioned below the paragraph of text in the memo but above the reference initials and document name.

  h. Change the Zoom back to *100%*.

9. Save the Word document again with the same name (Word Ch 18, Ex 07).

10. Print and then close Word Ch 18, Ex 07.

11. Make Excel the active program.

12. Save and then close Excel Ch 18, Ex 07.

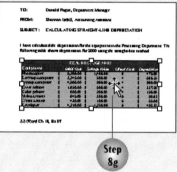

Step 8g

Editing a Document with an Embedded Object

To edit an embedded object, open the document containing the object, and then double-click the object.

An object that has been embedded can be edited in the destination program using the tools of the source program. For example, you can edit the worksheet inserted in the Word document in exercise 7 in Word. You do not need to return to the source program, Excel, to edit the worksheet.

    To edit an object in the destination program, open the destination program, open the document containing the embedded object, and then double-click the object. This causes the tools for the source program to display. For example, in exercise 8, you will double-click the worksheet located in the Word document. This will display the Excel Menu bar and Standard and Formatting toolbars at the top of the screen (rather than Word's). In exercise 8, you will be changing the formula for calculating depreciation. If the worksheet had been simply copied into the Word document, you would have had to open Excel, make changes to the worksheet, copy the worksheet again and paste it into the Word document. You also would have had to delete the original worksheet from the Word document.

exercise 8

Editing an Embedded Worksheet

1. Make Word the active program and then open Word Ch 18, Ex 07.
2. Save the document with Save As and name it Word Ch 18, Ex 08.
3. Make the following changes to the text in the memo:
   a. Change the subject from *CALCULATING STRAIGHT-LINE DEPRECIATION* to *CALCULATING DOUBLE-DECLINING DEPRECIATION*.
   b. Change the words *straight-line* that display toward the end of the sentence in the paragraph to *double-declining*.
4. Make changes to the worksheet by completing the following steps:
   a. Position the arrow pointer anywhere in the worksheet displayed in the memo and then double-click the left mouse button. (This displays Excel tools.)
   b. Add a column between columns D and E and then key the following text in the specified cells:

E2	=	**Period of Dep.**
E3	=	**1** (*Hint: Use the fill handle to copy 1 to other cells.*)
E4	=	**1**
E5	=	**1**
E6	=	**1**
E7	=	**1**
E8	=	**1**
E9	=	**1**
E10	=	**1**

   c. Insert the function to determine double-declining depreciation by completing the following steps:
      1) Make cell F3 active. (Use the horizontal scroll bar immediately below the table to display column F.)
      2) Press the Delete key to remove the formula.
      3) Click the Paste Function button on the Standard toolbar.
      4) At the Paste Function dialog box, make sure *Financial* is selected in the Function category list box.
      5) Click *DDB* in the Function name list box and then click OK.
      6) At the second Paste Function dialog box, key **B3** in the Cost category, and then press the Tab key.
      7) Key **C3** in the Salvage category and then press the Tab key.
      8) Key **D3** in the Life category and then press the Tab key.
      9) Key **E3** in the Period category.
      10) Click OK.

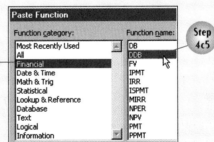

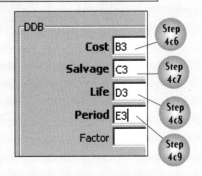

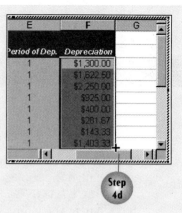

d. Copy the formula down to cells F4 through F10.
e. Use the horizontal scroll bar located immediately below the table to display column A.
f. Increase the width of the worksheet so all columns containing data display. (To do this, use the middle sizing handle at the right side of the worksheet. All columns must be visible before deselecting the worksheet.)

Step 4d

5. Click outside the worksheet to remove the Excel tools.
6. Save the document again with the same name (Word Ch 18, Ex 08).
7. Print and then close Word Ch 18, Ex 08.
8. Exit Word and then Excel.

Embedding a Worksheet in a PowerPoint Presentation

A worksheet can be embedded in a PowerPoint slide using the same steps as embedding one into a Word document. In exercise 9, you will be inserting a chart into a PowerPoint presentation and then editing the chart while still in PowerPoint but using Excel tools.

Embedding and Editing a Chart in a PowerPoint Presentation

1. Open PowerPoint and then open PowerPoint Ch 18, Ex 05. (At the message asking if you want to update the link, click OK.)
2. Save the presentation with Save As and name it PowerPoint Ch 18, Ex 09.
3. Change to Slide View and make Slide 4 the active slide.
4. Open Excel and then open Excel Worksheet 25.
5. Save the worksheet with Save As and name it Excel Ch 18, Ex 09.
6. Embed the chart in Slide 4 of the presentation by completing the following steps:

Step 6a

a. Click once in the chart area to select the chart.
b. Click the Copy button on the Standard toolbar.
c. Make PowerPoint the active program. (This should display PowerPoint Ch 18, Ex 09 with Slide 4 the active slide.)
d. Click Edit and then Paste Special.
e. At the Paste Special dialog box, make sure *Microsoft Excel Chart Object* is selected in the As list box, and then click OK.

7. Increase the size of the chart in the slide by dragging the white sizing handles that display around the worksheet.
8. Save the presentation with the same name (PowerPoint Ch 18, Ex 09).
9. Print the slides as a handout with all slides on one page.

10. Edit data in the embedded chart by completing the following steps:
    a. In PowerPoint with Slide 4 the active slide, double-click the chart. (This displays the chart with Excel editing tools available.)
    b. Click the Sheet1 tab located toward the bottom of the chart. (This displays the worksheet with the data in cells along with the chart.)
    c. Make the following changes to the data in the cells in the worksheet:
       1) Change B3 from *21%* to *12%*.
       2) Change B5 from *7%* to *15%*.
    d. Click the Chart1 tab. (This returns the display to the chart.)
    e. Click once outside the chart to remove the Excel editing tools.
11. Save the presentation again with the same name (PowerPoint Ch 18, Ex 09).
12. Print the presentation so all slides fit on one page.
13. Close the presentation and then exit PowerPoint.
14. With Excel the active program, save and then close Excel Ch 18, Ex 09.
15. Exit Excel.

Step 10b

Step 10c

	A	B
1		Percentage
2	1995	15%
3	1996	12%
4	1997	12%
5	1998	15%

chapter summary

▶ An object created in one program can be linked to another program. The program containing the object is called the source and the program the object is linked to is called the destination.

▶ A linked object exists in the source program but not as a separate object in the destination program. The destination program contains only a code that identifies the name and location of the source program, document, and the location in the document.

▶ To link an object, copy the object in the source program, and then paste it in the destination program by clicking Edit and then Paste Special. At the Paste Special dialog box, click Paste link.

▶ Edit a document containing a linked object in the source program. Any changes made will be reflected in the destination program.

▶ Documents created in the same program can be linked. Changes made to the original linked object will automatically occur to the linked object.

- An embedded object resides in the source program as well as the destination program. If a change is made to the embedded object at the source program, the change is not made to the object in the destination program.
- An embedded object can be edited using the tools of the source program. To edit an object in the destination program, double-click the object, which causes the tools for the source program to display.

commands review

	Mouse
Link object	Select object; click Copy button on Standard toolbar; make destination program active; position insertion point; click Edit, Paste Special; at Paste Special dialog box, click desired object in As list box, click Paste link, then click OK
Embed object	Select object; click Copy button on Standard toolbar; make destination program active; position insertion point; click Edit, Paste Special; at Paste Special dialog box, click desired object in As list box; click OK
Edit embedded object	In destination program, double-click object

thinking offline

Completion: In the space provided at the right, indicate the correct term, symbol, or command.

1. The program containing the original linked object is referred to as this. _____

2. The program an object is linked to is referred to as this. _____

3. To link an object, click the Paste link option at this dialog box. _____

4. If you want to update information in a linked object, make changes to the object at this program. _____

5. Use this in a presentation instead of a table or worksheet because it provides a visual display of information and has more of an impact on the audience. _____

6. When this is done to an object, only a code is inserted in the document in the destination program. _____

7. To embed an Excel worksheet in a Word document, click this option in the As list box in the Paste Special dialog box. _____

8. If this has been done to an object in a document, the object can be edited in the destination program using the tools of the source program. _____

In the space provided below each situation, indicate which of the following procedures you would choose for the described situations:

- copy and paste
- copy and link
- copy and embed

9. **Situation:** Each week you prepare a memo in Word to your supervisor that includes an Excel worksheet. The memo includes information about the number of products sold by your division, the current number of products on hand, and the number of products on order. This memo (with the worksheet) is updated each week. Which of the three procedures would you use for including the worksheet in the memo? Why?

_____

_____

10. **Situation:** Each year, you prepare an annual report for your company in Word that includes several Excel worksheets. This report and the worksheets are very different from year to year. Which of the three procedures would you use for including the worksheets in the report? Why?

_____

_____

11. **Situation:** You travel to various companies showing a PowerPoint presentation to prospective customers. The presentation includes several charts showing information such as quarterly sales figures, production figures, and projected sales. These charts are updated quarterly. Which of the three procedures would you use for including the charts in the presentation? Why?

_____

_____

working hands-on

Assessment 1

1. Open Excel and then open Word.
2. With Word the active program, open Word Letter 03.
3. Save the document with Save As and name it Word Ch 18, SA 01.
4. Link a worksheet to the Word document by completing these basic steps:
   a. Make Excel the active program and then open Excel Worksheet 03.

b. Save the worksheet with Save As and name it Excel Ch 18, SA 01.

c. Select cells A1 through D8 and then apply an autoformat of your choosing.

d. Select cells B3 through D8 and then click the Percent Style button on the Formatting toolbar.

e. Copy and then link the worksheet to the Word document, Word Ch 18, SA 01, a double space below the first paragraph in the body of the letter. (When linking, you must click *Microsoft Excel Worksheet Object* in the <u>A</u>s list box at the Paste Special dialog box.)

5. After the worksheet is linked, save the Word document again with the same name (Word Ch 18, SA 01).

6. Print Word Ch 18, SA 01.

7. Make Excel the active program (with Excel Ch 18, SA 01 open), press Esc to remove the moving border around the cells, and then make the following changes to the worksheet:

a. B3: Change *62%* to *59%*

b. B5: Change *122%* to *118%*

c. C5: Change *115%* to *110%*

8. Save the worksheet again with the same name (Excel Ch 18, SA 01).

9. Close Excel Ch 18, SA 01.

10. Make Word the active program (with Word Ch 18, SA 01 displayed).

11. Save, print, and then close Word Ch 18, SA 01.

12. Exit Word and then exit Excel.

Assessment 2

1. Open Word and then open Word Letter 04.

2. Save the document with Save As and name it Word Ch 18, SA 02 Letter.

3. Open Word Memo 05.

4. Save the document with Save As and name it Word Ch 18, SA 02 Memo.

5. Open Word Table 02.

6. Save the document with Save As and name it Ch 18 Table 02.

7. Copy and link the following:

a. Copy the table in Ch 18 Table 02 and link it to Word Ch 18, SA 02 Letter between the two paragraphs in the body of the letter.

b. Save, print, and then close Word Ch 18, SA 02 Letter.

c. Copy the table in Ch 18 Table 02 and link it to Word Ch 18, SA 02 Memo between the two paragraphs in the body of the memo.

d. Save, print, and then close Word Ch 18, SA 02 Memo.

8. Make the following changes to Ch 18 Table 02:

a. Change the title of the table to *SECOND-QUARTER INVESTED ASSETS*.

b. Change *26.5%* to *25.4%*.

c. Change *23.6%* to *22.5%*.

d. Change *38.4%* to *40.6%*.

9. Save the document with the same name (Ch 18 Table 02).

10. Print and then close Ch 18 Table 02.

11. Open Word Ch 18, SA 02 Letter.

12. Change the date from *April 9, 2001*, to *July 10, 2001*.

13. Save, print, and then close Word Ch 18, SA 02 Letter.

14. Open Word Ch 18, SA 02 Memo.

15. Change the date from *April 9, 2001*, to *July 10, 2001*.

16. Save, print, and then close Word Ch 18, SA 02 Memo.

17. Exit Word.

Assessment 3

1. Open PowerPoint and then open PowerPoint Ch 18, Ex 09. At the message asking if you want links updated, click OK. (You must have completed exercises 5 and 9 in this chapter before completing this assessment.)
2. Save the presentation with Save As and name it PowerPoint Ch 18, SA 03.
3. Add a new slide to the presentation (the new slide will be Slide 5) with the following specifications:
   a. At the New Slide dialog box, double-click the third autolayout format from the left in the third row (Title Only).
   b. Insert the title **GLOBAL EQUITIES.**
   c. Click the Center button on the Formatting toolbar to center the title in the object box.
   d. Select the title *GLOBAL EQUITIES* and then change the font size to 54 points.
4. Open Excel and then open Excel Worksheet 26.
5. Save the worksheet with Save As and name it Excel Ch 18, Slide 5.
6. Copy the chart and link it to Slide 5 in PowerPoint Ch 18, SA 03. Increase the size of the chart so it fills most of the bottom part of the slide.
7. Save the presentation again with the same name (PowerPoint Ch 18, SA 03).
8. Add another new slide to the presentation (the new slide will be Slide 6) with the following specifications:
   a. At the New Slide dialog box, double-click the third autolayout format from the left in the third row (Title Only).
   b. Insert the title **SOCIAL CHOICE.**
   c. Click the Center button on the Formatting toolbar to center the title in the object box.
   d. Select the title *SOCIAL CHOICE* and then change the font size to 54 points.
   e. Open Excel Worksheet 27.
   f. Save the worksheet with Save As and name it Excel Ch 18, Slide 6.
   g. Copy the chart and link it to Slide 6 in PowerPoint Ch 18, SA 03. Increase the size of the chart so it fills most of the bottom part of the slide.
9. Save the presentation again with the same name (PowerPoint Ch 18, SA 03).
10. Print the slides as a handout with six slides per page.
11. Close the PowerPoint Ch 18, SA 03.
12. Make Excel the active program, close Excel Ch 18, Slide 6, and then close Excel Ch 18, Slide 5.

Assessment 4

1. Make sure PowerPoint and Excel are open.
2. With Excel the active program, open Excel Ch 18, Slide 5.
3. Make the following changes to the data in the cells in the worksheet:
   a. Change B2 from *5%* to *12%*.
   b. Change B4 from *10%* to *15%*.
   c. Change B6 from *8%* to *17%*.
4. Save the worksheet again with the same name (Excel Ch 18, Slide 5).
5. Close Excel Ch 18, Slide 5.
6. Open Excel Ch 18, Slide 6.
7. Make the following changes to the data in the cells in the worksheet:
   a. Change B3 from *3%* to *11%*.
   b. Change B4 from *7%* to *15%*.

8. Save the worksheet again with the same name (Excel Ch 18, Slide 6).
9. Close Excel Ch 18, Slide 6.
10. Make PowerPoint the active program.
11. Open PowerPoint Ch 18, SA 03. (At the message asking if you want to update the links, click OK.)
12. Print the slides as a handout with six slides per page.
13. Save and then close PowerPoint Ch 18, SA 03.
14. Exit PowerPoint and then exit Excel.

Assessment 5

1. Open Excel and Word.
2. With Word the active program, open Word Letter 05.
3. Save the document with Save As and name it Word Ch 18, SA 05.
4. Make Excel the active program and then open Excel Worksheet 17.
5. Save the worksheet with Save As and name it Excel Ch 18, SA 05.
6. Make the following changes to the worksheet:
   a. Select cells A1 through C11 and then apply the Classic 3 autoformat.
   b. Select row 5 and then change the alignment to center.
   c. Select cells A6 through B11 and then change the alignment to center.
7. Embed the worksheet in Word Ch 18, SA 05 between the first and second paragraphs in the letter.
8. Save the Word document again with the same name (Word Ch 18, SA 05).
9. Print Word Ch 18, SA 05.
10. Make the following changes to the worksheet:
    a. Change B6 from *8.30%* to *9.00%*. (This will change 111,701.40 in cell C6 to 121,122.00.)
    b. Change B8 from *9.30%* to *8.60%*. (This will change 125,159.40 in cell C8 to 115,738.80.)
11. Save, print, and then close Word Ch 18, SA 05.
12. Make Excel the active program and then save and then close Excel Ch 18, SA 05.

Assessment 6

1. With Word the active program, use the Help feature to learn how to break a link. (*Hint: Use the Office Assistant and ask the question, "How do I break a link?"*) After finding, reading, and printing the information on breaking links, complete the following steps:
   a. Open Word Ch 18, SA 01 and then break the link it contains with Excel Ch 18, SA 01.
   b. Open Excel and then open Excel Ch 18, SA 01.
   c. Make the following changes to the worksheet:
      1) B5: Change *45%* to *30%*.
      2) C5: Change *39%* to *26%*.
      3) D5: Change *41%* to *28%*.
   d. Save and then print Excel Ch 18, SA 01.
   e. Make Word the active program. (Word Ch 18, SA 01 should be displayed).
   f. Save and then print Word Ch 18, SA 01. (*Note: The changes made to the Excel worksheet should not be made to the Word document since the link was broken.*)
2. Exit Word and then exit Excel.

Performance Assessments

Unit 3 PA

POWERPOINT

ASSESSING CORE PROFICIENCIES

In this unit, you have learned to create, print, save, close, open, view, run, edit, and format a PowerPoint presentation. You also learned how to add animation, build, and sound effects in a presentation and insert hyperlinks. In addition to creating and formatting PowerPoint presentations, you learned how to insert WordArt in a Word document, Excel worksheet, and a PowerPoint slide; insert organizational charts in a Word document and a PowerPoint slide; and copy and embed and copy and link objects from one program to another.

Assessment 1

1. Create a presentation with the text shown in figure U3.1. You determine the design template and the autolayout. Add the following enhancements:
   a. Transitions
   b. Builds
   c. Sound and/or fill color.
2. After creating the presentation, save it and name it Concepts Presentation.
3. Print the slides in Concepts Presentation on two pages.
4. Run and then close Concepts Presentation.

Slide 1	Title	=	TELECOMMUNICATIONS TECHNOLOGY
	Subtitle	=	Concepts of Technology
Slide 2	Title	=	ENCODING
	Bullets	=	• Common Devices
			- Microphone
			- 35 mm Camera
			- Television
			- Mouse

Slide 3	Title	=	ENCODING
	Bullets	=	• System Applications

- Broadcast Radio
- Telephone
- Still Photography
- Computer Systems
- Broadcast Television

Slide 4	Title	=	TRANSMITTING
	Bullets	=	• Common Devices

- Optical Fibers
- Amplifiers
- Transmitting Antenna
- Modems
- Lasers

Slide 5	Title	=	RECEIVING
	Bullets	=	• Common Devices

- Television Antenna
- Tuner
- Modem
- Modular Telephone Jack
- Satellite Dish

Slide 6	Title	=	STORING
	Bullets	=	• System Applications

- Television
- Computer Systems
- Telephone
- Graphic Communication Systems
- Automation Systems

Figure U3.1 • Assessment 1

Assessment 2

1. Open Concepts Presentation.
2. Create a new Slide 7 by completing the following steps:
   a. Display Slide 6 and then click the New Slide button.
   b. At the New Slide dialog box, double-click the Bulleted List autolayout.
   c. Click the text *Click to add title* and then key **APPLICATIONS**.
   d. Click the text *Click to add text* and then copy text from Word and paste it into Slide 7 by completing the following steps:
      1) Open Word and then open Word Concepts 01.
      2) Select *RECEIVING* and the paragraph below it and then click the Copy button.
      3) Select *STORING* and the paragraph below it and then click the Copy button. (Make sure the Clipboard toolbar displays.)

4) Select *TRANSMITTING* and the paragraph below it and then click the Copy button.

5) Click the button on the Taskbar representing the Concepts Presentation.

6) Make sure the insertion point is positioned in the bulleted list placeholder in Slide 7 and then click the button on the Clipboard toolbar containing the heading *TRANSMITTING*.

7) Click the button on the Clipboard containing the heading *RECEIVING*.

8) Click the Clear Clipboard button on the Clipboard toolbar and then close the toolbar.

3. Insert the footer *Concepts Presentation* and the current date and slide number so they will print on note pages.

4. Save the presentation again with the same name (Concepts Presentation).

5. Print slides 1 and 7 as notes pages.

6. Close Concepts Presentation.

7. Make Word the active program, close Word Concepts 01, and then exit Word.

Assessment 3

1. Make sure PowerPoint is open and then open Word.

2. With Word the active program, open Word Outline 03.

3. Import the text into PowerPoint.

4. Make PowerPoint the active program.

5. Make the following changes to the presentation:

   a. Change to the Title Slide autolayout for Slide 2.

   b. Change to the Title Slide autolayout for Slide 3.

   c. Apply a design template of your choosing.

   d. Insert a clip art image related to "software" in Slide 5.

   e. Check each slide and make any formatting changes to enhance the appearance of the slide.

   f. Add transitions and builds to the slides in the presentation.

   g. Create the following hyperlinks for the text in Slide 6:

Apple Computer	=	http://www.apple.com
Blizzard Entertainment	=	http://www.blizzard.com
id Software	=	http://www.idsoftware.com
Microsoft Corporation	=	http://www.microsoft.com

   h. Insert the action button named Action: Home at the bottom of Slide 3, Slide 4, and Slide 5.

   i. Insert the action button named Action Button: Return at the bottom of Slide 1.

6. Save the presentation and name it Apex Presentation.

7. Run the presentation. (When all text has displayed in Slide 3, click the Home action button. After viewing Slide 1, click the Return action button. Continue in this manner until all slides have been viewed.)

8. Print all six slides on one page.

9. Close Apex Presentation.

Assessment 4

1. Open Apex Presentation.
2. Make the following changes to the presentation:
   a. Delete the action button that displays in slides 1, 3, 4, and 5.
   b. Display Slide 1 in Slide view and then change to the Slide Master view.
   c. Change the first level bullet to a character bullet in a different color and increase the bullet size (you determine the character, the color, and the size).
   d. Make at least one other change to the Slide Master (suggestions include changing the font, font color, adding a fill color, and so on).
   e. Insert a new Slide 1 with the Blank autolayout.
   f. Insert WordArt in Slide 1 that contains the company name *Apex Cyberware*. You determine the formatting and shape of the WordArt text.
   g. Display Slide 5 in Normal view and then add the speaker note *Include specific timeline on hiring new personnel*.
   h. Display Slide 6 in Normal view and then add the speaker note *Specify the percentage of business for each category*.
   i. Insert the current date and slide number on all slides in the presentation.
3. Run the presentation.
4. Print four slides per page. (The first page will contain four slides and the second page will contain three slides.)
5. Print slides 5 and 6 as note pages.
6. Save the presentation again with the same name (Apex Presentation).
7. Close Apex Presentation.

Assessment 5

1. Open PowerPoint and then create a presentation with the following specifications:
   a. Use a design template provided by PowerPoint.
   b. Create the first slide with the following specifications:
      1) Use the last autolayout at the New Slide dialog box (Blank).
      2) Use WordArt to create the text *International Securities*. (You determine the shape and formatting of the WordArt text.)
   c. Create the second slide with the following specifications:
      1) Use the first autolayout at the New Slide dialog box (Title Slide).
      2) Key **2001 SALES MEETING** as the title.
      3) Key **European Division** as the subtitle.
   d. Create the third slide with the following specifications:
      1) Use the third autolayout from the left in the third row at the New Slide dialog box (Title Only).
      2) Key **REGIONAL SALES** as the title.
      3) Make Excel the active program. Open Excel Worksheet 28 and then save the worksheet with Save As and name it U03 Worksheet 28. Embed U03 Worksheet 28 in Slide 3.

4) Increase the size of the chart so it better fills the slide.
e. Create the fourth slide with the following specifications:
   1) Use the second autolayout in the first row at the New Slide dialog box (Bulleted List).
   2) Key **2002 GOALS** as the title.
   3) Key the following as the bulleted items:
      - **Increase product sales by 15 percent.**
      - **Open a branch office in Spain.**
      - **Hire one manager and two additional account managers.**
      - **Decrease production costs by 6 percent.**
f. Create the fifth slide with the following specifications:
   1) Use the Table autolayout (last autolayout in the top row at the New Slide dialog box).
   2) Key **HIRING TIMELINE** as the title.
   3) Key the following text in the cells in the table. (You determine the formatting of the cells.)

Task	Date
Advertise positions	03/01/01 - 04/30/01
Review resumes	05/15/01 - 06/01/01
Perform interviews	06/15/01 - 07/15/01
Hire personnel	08/01/01

g. Create the sixth slide with the following specifications:
   1) Use the third autolayout from the left in the third row at the New Slide dialog box (Title Only).
   2) Key **PRODUCTION EXPENSES** as the title.
   3) Make Excel the active program. Open Excel Worksheet 29 and then save the worksheet with Save As and name it U03 Worksheet 29. Copy and then link U03 Worksheet 29 into Slide 6.
   4) Increase the size of the pie chart so it better fills the slide. (Be sure to maintain the integrity of the chart.)
h. Create the seventh slide with the following specifications:
   1) Choose the third autolayout from the left in the second row at the New Slide dialog box (Organization Chart).
   2) Key the title **OFFICE STRUCTURE** as the title and create the following text in the organizational chart boxes:

Ricardo Miraflores
Manager

Miguel Tumbes
Assistant Manager

Audrina Chorrillos   **Hector Palencia**
Account Manager   **Account Manager**

2. Add the following enhancements to the presentation:
   a. Add a transition of your choosing to each slide.
   b. Add a build technique to the bulleted items in Slide 4.

3. Save the presentation and name it PowerPoint Unit 3, PA 05.
4. Run the presentation.
5. Print the slides as a handout with four slides per page. (The first page will contain four slides and the second page will contain three slides.)
6. Close PowerPoint Unit 3, PA 05.

Assessment 6

1. Open Excel and then open U03 Worksheet 29.
2. Make the following changes:
   a. B2: Change *38%* to *41%*
   b. B3: Change *35%* to *32%*
   c. B4: Change *18%* to *21%*
   d. B5: Change *9%* to *6%*
3. Save the worksheet again with the same name (U03 Worksheet 29).
4. Print and then close U03 Worksheet 29.
5. Make PowerPoint the active program and then open PowerPoint Unit 3, PA 05. (At the question asking if you want to update the link, click OK.)
6. Make the following changes to the embedded worksheet in Slide 3:
   a. C2: Change *2,678,450* to *2,857,300*
   b. C3: Change *1,753,405* to *1,598,970*
   c. C5: Change *2,315,600* to *2,095,170*
7. Save the presentation with the same name (PowerPoint Unit 3, PA 05).
8. Print the slides as a handout with all slides on one page.
9. Close PowerPoint Unit 3, PA 05.

Assessment 7

1. Make Word the active program and then create a letterhead with the following specifications:
   a. Insert the company name *Alpine Nursery* in WordArt (you determine the shape, font, style, etc.).
   b. Include a border line.
   c. Include the company slogan *Growing for a brighter future!* below the border line. (You determine the font, color, and alignment of the slogan.)
2. Save the letterhead and name it Word Unit 3, PA 07.
3. Print and then close Word Unit 3, PA 07.

WRITING ACTIVITIES

The following activities give you the opportunity to practice your writing skills along with demonstrating an understanding of some of the important Word, Excel, and PowerPoint features you have mastered in this and previous units. (Refer to the steps in *The Writing Process* section of Unit 1 Composing Activities.) Use correct grammar, appropriate word choices, and clear sentence structure.

Activity 1

1. Open Word and then open print, and close Key Life Health Plan. Looking at the printing of this document, create a presentation in PowerPoint that presents the main points of the plan. (Use bullets in the presentation.) Add a transition and build to the slides.
2. Save the presentation and name it Key Life Presentation.
3. Run Key Life Presentation.
4. Print the slides as handouts with six slides per page.
5. Close Key Life Presentation.

Activity 2

1. Open Word and then open, print, and then close Key Life Corporation.
2. Using the information in the Key Life Corporation document, create an organizational chart in Word with the following specifications:
   a. Include an appropriate title.
   b. Change box and text color.
   c. Add a background color.
3. Save the organizational chart and name it Word Unit 3, Act 02.
4. Print and then close Word Unit 3, Act 02.

Activity 3

1. Using PowerPoint's Help feature, find and then print information on how to save a presentation to the Web.
2. Create a memo to your instructor describing how to save a presentation to the Web and include the specific steps for doing this.
3. Save the document and name it Word Unit 3, Act 03.
4. Print and then close Word Unit 3, Act 03.

INTERNET ACTIVITY

Make sure you are connected to the Internet and then explore the Time Magazine Web site at http://www.time.com. Discover the following information for the site:

- magazine categories (for example Time Daily, Magazine, Community, and so on.)
- the type of information presented in each category
- services available
- information on how to subscribe

Using the information you discovered about the Time Magazine Web site, create a PowerPoint presentation that presents the information in a clear, concise, and logical manner. Add formatting and enhancements to the presentation to make it more interesting. Include a hyperlink in one of the slides to the Time Magazine Web site. When the presentation is completed, save it and name it Time Mag Presentation. Run, print, and then close the presentation.

Access

MICROSOFT® ACCESS 2000

CORE LEVEL MOUS SKILLS

Coding No.	SKILL	Pages
AC2000.1	Planning and designing databases	
AC2000.1.1	Determine appropriate data inputs for your database	778-781, 849-850
AC2000.1.2	Determine appropriate data outputs for your database	792-795, 871, 888, 884-886
AC2000.1.3	Create table structure	781-788
AC2000.1.4	Establish table relationships	813-815, 819-826
AC2000.2	Working with Access	
AC2000.2.1	Use the Office Assistant	805
AC2000.2.2	Select an object using the Objects Bar	853, 857, 871, 874
AC2000.2.3	Print database objects (tables, forms, reports, queries)	792-795, 850-851
AC2000.2.4	Navigate through records in a table, query, or form	850-851
AC2000.2.5	Create a database (using a Wizard or in Design View)	781-795, 899-906
AC2000.3	Building and modifying tables	
AC2000.3.1	Create tables by using the Table Wizard	832-840
AC2000.3.2	Set primary keys	815-818
AC2000.3.3	Modify field properties	797-803
AC2000.3.4	Use multiple data types	779-781, 784-785
AC2000.3.5	Modify tables using Design View	797-805
AC2000.3.6	Use the Lookup Wizard	799-803
AC2000.3.7	Use the input mask wizard	797-803
AC2000.4	Building and modifying forms	
AC2000.4.1	Create a form with the Form Wizard	853-859
AC2000.4.2	Use the Control Toolbox to add controls	866-869
AC2000.4.3	Modify Format Properties (font, style, font size, color, caption, etc.) of controls	862-869
AC2000.4.4	Use form sections (headers, footers, detail)	866-869
AC2000.4.5	Use a Calculated Control on a form	869-870
AC2000.5	Viewing and organizing information	
AC2000.5.1	Use the Office Clipboard	918-919
AC2000.5.2	Switch between object Views	788, 797, 801
AC2000.5.3	Enter records using a datasheet	789-792
AC2000.5.4	Enter records using a form	852-853
AC2000.5.5	Delete records from a table	796-797
AC2000.5.6	Find a record	796-797
AC2000.5.7	Sort records	805-806
AC2000.5.8	Apply and remove filters (filter by form and filter by selection)	948-952
AC2000.5.9	Specify criteria in a query	933-944
AC2000.5.10	Display related records in a subdatasheet	829-831
AC2000.5.11	Create a calculated field	945
AC2000.5.12	Create and modify a multi-table select query	939-941
AC2000.6	Defining relationships	
AC2000.6.1	Establish relationships	819-826
AC2000.6.2	Enforce referential integrity	821-826
AC2000.7	Producing reports	
AC2000.7.1	Create a report with the Report Wizard	871-877
AC2000.7.2	Preview and print a report	874-875
AC2000.7.3	Move and resize a control	879-883
AC2000.7.4	Modify format properties (font, style, font size, color, caption, etc.)	879-883
AC2000.7.5	Use the Control Toolbox to add controls	879-883
AC2000.7.6	Use report sections (headers, footers, detail)	879-883
AC2000.7.7	Use a Calculated Control in a report	879-883
AC2000.8	Integrating with other applications	
AC2000.8.1	Import data to a new table	915-916
AC2000.8.2	Save a table, query, form as a Web page	920-924
AC2000.8.3	Add Hyperlinks	921-924
AC2000.9	Using Access Tools	
AC2000.9.1	Print Database Relationships	822-826
AC2000.9.2	Backup and Restore a database	924-925
AC2000.9.3	Compact and Repair a database	925

Creating a Database Table

PERFORMANCE OBJECTIVES

Upon successful completion of chapter 19, you will be able to:

- Design a database table.
- Determine fields and assign data types in a database table.
- Enter data in a database table.
- Open, save, print, and close a database table.
- Add and delete records in a database table.
- Modify a database table by adding, deleting, or moving fields.
- Use the Input Mask Wizard and the Lookup Wizard.

(Note: There is no Chapter 19 *folder to copy from the CD because you will be creating your own database.)*

Managing information in a company is an integral part of operating a business. Information can come in a variety of forms, such as data on customers, including names, addresses, and telephone numbers; product data; purchasing and buying data; information on services performed for customers or clients; and much more. Most companies today manage data using a database management system software program. Microsoft Office Professional includes a database management system software program called *Access*. With Access, you can organize, store, maintain, retrieve, sort, and print all types of business data.

As an example of how Access might be used to manage data in an office, suppose a bookstore decides to send a mailer to all customers who have purchased a certain type of book in the past month (such as autobiographies). The bookstore uses Access and maintains data on customers, such as names, addresses, types of books purchased, and types of books ordered. With this data in Access, the manager of the bookstore can easily select those customers who have purchased or ordered autobiographies in the past month and send a mailer announcing a visit by an author who has just completed writing an autobiography. The bookstore could also use the information to determine what types of books have been ordered by customers in the past few months and use this information to determine what inventory to purchase.

There are a multitude of uses for information in a database. This chapter contains just a few ideas. With a properly designed and maintained database management system, a company can operate smoothly with logical, organized, and useful information. The Access program displays in the Start pop-up menu preceded by a picture of a key, and a key is displayed in the Taskbar when Access is open. The key symbolizes the importance of managing and maintaining data to a company's survival and success.

Organizing Data in a Database Table

Data is not very useful to a company if it is not organized in a logical manner. Organizing data in a manageable and logical manner allows the data to be found and used for a variety of purposes.

Organize data in tables to minimize or eliminate duplication.

Determining Fields

Microsoft Access is a database management system software program that allows you to design, create, input, maintain, manipulate, sort, and print data. Access is considered a relational database in which you organize data in related tables. In this chapter, you will be creating one table as part of a database file. In a later chapter, you will create a related table within the same database file.

A database table contains fields that describe a person, customer, client, object, place, idea, or event.

The first step in creating a table is to determine the fields. A field is one piece of information about a person, a place, or an item. For example, one field could be a customer's name, another field could be a customer's address, and another a customer number. All fields for one unit, such as a customer, are considered a record. For example, in exercise 1, a record is all the information pertaining to one employee of Premium Health Services. A collection of records becomes a database table.

When designing a database table, determine fields for information to be included based on how you plan to use the data. When organizing fields, be sure to consider not only current needs for the data but also any future needs. For example, a company may need to keep track of customer names, addresses, and telephone numbers for current mailing lists. In the future, the company may want to promote a new product to customers who purchase a specific type of product. For this situation, a field that identifies product type must be included in the database. When organizing fields, consider all potential needs for the data but also try to keep the fields logical and manageable.

After deciding what data you want included in a database table, you need to determine field names. Consider the following guidelines when naming fields in a database table:

- Each field must contain a unique name.
- Choose a name that describes the contents of the field.
- A field name can contain up to 64 characters.
- A field name can contain letters, numbers, spaces, and symbols except the period (.), comma (,), exclamation point (!), square brackets ([]), and grave accent (`).
- A field name cannot begin with a space.

In exercise 1, you will create a database table containing information on employees of a medical corporation. The fields in this table and the names you will give to each field are shown in figure 19.1.

Employee Information   **Field Name**

Employee Information	Field Name
I.D. number	*Emp #*
Last name	*Last Name*
First name	*First Name*
Middle initial	*Middle Initial*
Street address	*Street Address*
City	*City*
State	*State*
Zip Code	*Zip Code*
Date of hire	*Hire Date*
Department code	*Dept Code*

Assigning a Data Type to Fields

Part of the process of designing a database table includes specifying or assigning a data type to each field. The data type specifies the type of data you can enter in a field. Assigning a data type to fields helps maintain and manage the data and helps identify for anyone entering information into the field what type of data is expected. The data types that are available in Access along with a description of each and the field size are shown in figure 19.2.

> Assign a data type for each field that determines the values that can be entered for the field.
> *Hint*

Data Types

Assign this data type	To this type of field
Text	Assign to a field where text will be entered, such as names, addresses, and numbers that do not require calculations, such as telephone numbers, dates, Social Security numbers, and Zip Codes. A maximum number of 255 characters can be stored in a text data field; 50 characters is the default.
Memo	Assign to a field where more than 255 characters are needed. Up to 64,000 characters can be stored in a memo data field.
Number	Assign to a field where positive and/or negative numbers are to be entered for mathematical calculations, except calculations that involve money or require a high degree of accuracy. A maximum of 15 digits can be stored in a number data field.

Currency	Assign to a field where you do not want calculations rounded off during a calculation. A maximum of 15 digits can be stored in a currency data field.
Date/Time	Assign to a field where a date and/or time will be entered. Eight characters is the default.
AutoNumber	Create a field that automatically enters a number when a record is added. Three types of numbers can be generated: sequential numbers that change by one, random numbers, and replication ID numbers. A maximum of nine digits can be stored in an AutoNumber data field.
Yes/No	Assign to a field where data is to be limited to Yes or No, True or False, or On or Off.
OLE Object	Assign to an object such as an Excel spreadsheet or Word document linked to or embedded in an Access table. Up to 1 gigabyte of characters can be stored in the field.
Hyperlink	Assign to text or a combination of text and numbers stored as text and used as a hyperlink address. A hyperlink address can contain up to three parts and each part can contain up to 2048 characters.
Lookup Wizard	Click this option to start the Lookup Wizard, which creates a Lookup field. When the Wizard is completed, Access sets the data type based on the values selected during the wizard steps.

When designing a database table, determine the data type that is to be assigned to a field. The fields in exercise 1 will be assigned the data types and field sizes shown in figure 19.3.

figure

19.3 *Data Types for Exercise 1*

Field Name	Data Type
Emp #	Text (Field Size = 5)
Last Name	Text (Field Size = 30)
First Name	Text (Field Size = 30)
Middle Initial	Text (Field Size = 2)
Street Address	Text (Field Size = 30)

City	Text (Field Size = 20)
State	Text (Field Size = 2)
Zip Code	Text (Field Size = 5)
Dept Code	Text (Field Size = 2)
Hire Date	Date/Time

Data entered for some fields in exercise 1, such as *Zip Code,* will be numbers. These numbers, however, are not values and will not be used in calculations. This is why they are assigned the data type of Text (rather than Number or Currency).

During the process of creating the database table, field sizes are assigned. By default, a field is assigned the default number as described in figure 19.2. You can, however, specify a maximum field size. For example, a Text data type sets the field size at 50 characters by default. For a field in exercise 1 such as *Zip Code,* a specific maximum number can be assigned, such as 5 (if you are only using the five-number Zip Code). When assigning a field size, consider the data that will be entered in the field, and then shorten or lengthen the maximum number to accommodate any possible entries. For the *Name* field, for example, shortening the number to 30 would be appropriate, ensuring that all names would fit in the field. The two-letter state abbreviation will be used in the *State* field, so the number of characters is changed to 2.

Creating a Database Table

Once the fields, field names, and data types have been determined, you are ready to create the database table. To create a database table, you would follow these general steps:

1. Open Access. To do this, click the Start button on the Taskbar, point to Programs, and then click *Microsoft Access.*
2. At the Microsoft Access dialog box shown in figure 19.4, click Blank Access database, and then click OK.
3. At the File New Database dialog box shown in figure 19.5, change to the drive where your disk is located, key a name for the database in the File name text box, and then press Enter or click the Create button.
4. At the Database window shown in figure 19.6, double-click *Create table in Design view* in the list box.
5. At the Table dialog box shown in figure 19.7, key the first field name in the Field Name text box, and then press Tab. (This moves the insertion point to the Data Type text box and inserts the word *Text.*)
6. With the insertion point positioned in the Data Type text box and the word *Text* inserted in the box, press Tab to move the insertion point to the Description text box or change the data type and then press Tab.
7. With the insertion point positioned in the Description text box, key a description of the field, and then press Tab.
8. Continue keying field names, assigning a data type to each field, and keying a description of all fields.
9. When all fields have been keyed, click File and then Save, or click the Save button on the Table Design toolbar.

Provide full descriptions of fields in a database file if other users will be maintaining the database.

Save

10. At the Save As dialog box shown in figure 19.8, key a name for the table in the top text box, and then press Enter or click OK.
11. A message displays telling you that no primary key is defined and asking if you want to create one. At this message, click No. (You will learn more about primary keys in chapter 20.)
12. Click File and then Close to close the database table.

Microsoft Access Dialog Box

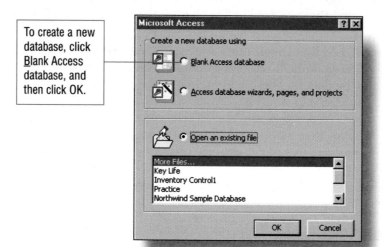

To create a new database, click Blank Access database, and then click OK.

File New Database Dialog Box

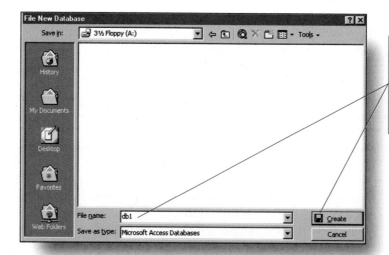

Key a name for the database in the File name text box and then press Enter or click Create.

Database Window

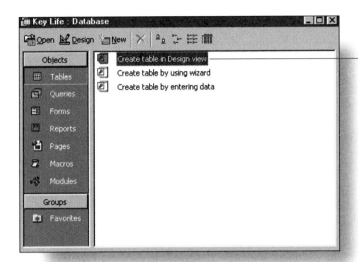

Double-click this option to create a table in Design view.

Table Dialog Box

At this dialog box, assign field names and data types; also provide a description.

figure 19.8 *Save As Dialog Box*

At the Table dialog box shown in figure 19.7, field names are entered, data types are assigned, and descriptions are keyed. When assigning a data type, Access displays information in the bottom portion of the dialog box in a section with the General tab selected. Information in this section can be changed to customize a data type for a field. For example, you can specify that only a maximum of two characters can be entered in the *Middle Initial* field.

A database file can contain more than one table. Tables containing related data are saved in the same database. In exercise 1, you will create a table named Employees that is part of the database file named Premium. In exercise 2, you will create another table as part of the Premium database that includes payroll information.

exercise 1

Creating an Employee Database Table

1. Open Access by clicking Start button on the Taskbar, pointing to *Programs*, and then clicking *Microsoft Access*.
2. At the Microsoft Access dialog box, click <u>B</u>lank Access database, and then click OK.
3. At the File New Database dialog box (see figure 19.5), change to the drive where your disk is located, key **Premium** in the File <u>n</u>ame text box, and then press Enter or click the <u>C</u>reate button.
4. At the Premium Database window, double-click *Create table in Design view* in the list box.
5. At the Table1 Table dialog box, key the fields shown in figure 19.9 by completing the following steps:
   a. Key **Emp #** in the Field Name text box and then press Tab.
   b. The word *Text* is automatically inserted in

Step 2

Step 4

the Data Type text box. Change the field size from the default of *50* to *5*. To do this, select *50* that displays after *Field Size* in the Field Properties section of the dialog box and then key **5**.

c. Position the I-beam pointer in the Description text box (for the *Emp #* field) and then click the left mouse button. (You can also press F6 to switch to the top of the dialog box and then press Tab to move the insertion point to the Description text box.) Key **Employee number** in the Description text box and then press Tab.

d. Key **Last Name** in the Field Name text box and then press Tab.

e. Change the field size to *30* and then click in the Description text box for the *Last Name* field (or press F6 and then press Tab). Key **Employee last name** and then press Tab.

f. Key **First Name** in the Field Name text box and then press Tab.

g. Change the field size to *30* and then click in the Description text box for the *First Name* field (or press F6 and then press Tab). Key **Employee first name** and then press Tab.

h. Continue keying the field names, data types, and descriptions as shown in figure 19.9. Refer to figure 19.3 for the text field sizes. To change the Data Type for the *Hire Date* field, click the down-pointing triangle after *Text* and then click *Date/Time* in the drop-down list.

6. When all the fields are entered, save the database table by completing the following steps:

a. Click the Save button on the Table Design toolbar.

b. At the Save As dialog box, key **Employees** in the text box, and then press Enter or click OK.

c. At the message telling you that no primary key is defined and asking if you want to create one, click No. (You will learn more about primary keys in chapter 20.)

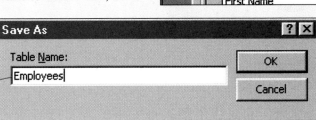

7. Close the Employees table by clicking File and then Close or clicking the Close button located in the upper right corner of the dialog box.

8. Close the Premium database file by clicking File and then Close or clicking the Close button located in the upper right corner of the dialog box.

figure

19.9

Exercise 1

⊞ Table1 : Table		
Field Name	**Data Type**	**Description**
Emp #	Text	Employee number
Last Name	Text	Employee last name
First Name	Text	Employee first name
Middle Initial	Text	Employee middle initial
Street Address	Text	Employee street address
City	Text	Employee city
State	Text	Employee state
Zip Code	Text	Employee Zip code
Dept Code	Text	Department code
▶ Hire Date	Date/Time	Date of hire

The active database is saved automatically on a periodic basis and also when the database is closed.

Hint

If you are working with a database file saved on a floppy disk, never remove the disk while the database file is open. If you do, Access will have problems when trying to automatically save the database.

Hint

In exercise 1, you saved the table containing the fields with the name Employees. Notice that the steps to save the table are the same as saving documents in Word, Excel, or PowerPoint. After saving the Employees table, you closed the Premium database file. Access automatically saves an open (or active) database on a periodic basis and also when the database is closed. If you are working with a database that is saved on a disk, never remove the disk while the database is open because Access saves the database periodically. If the disk is not in the drive when Access tries to save it, problems will be encountered and you run the risk of damaging the database.

The steps for exiting Access are the same as the other programs in the suite. You can exit (close) Access by clicking the Close button located in the upper right corner of the Access Title bar (contains an X), or you can click File and then Exit.

The Employees table contains a *Dept Code* field. This field will contain a two-letter code identifying the department within the company. In exercise 2, you will create a table named Departments containing only two fields—the department code and the department name. Establishing a department code decreases the amount of data entered in the Employees table. For example, in an employee record, you key a two-letter code identifying the employee department rather than keying the entire department name. Imagine the time this saves when entering hundreds of employee records. This is an example of the power of a relational database.

exercise 2

Creating a Department Table

1. At the blank Access screen, click the Open button on the Database toolbar. (The Database toolbar displays directly below the Menu bar and contains many buttons similar to those on a Word, PowerPoint, or Excel Standard toolbar.)

2. At the Open dialog box, make sure the drive is active where your disk is located and then double-click *Premium* in the list box.

3. At the Premium Database window, double-click *Create table in Design view* in the list box.

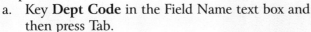

4. At the Table1 Table dialog box, key the fields shown in figure 19.10 by completing the following steps:

   a. Key **Dept Code** in the Field Name text box and then press Tab.

   b. Change the field size to *2* and then click in the Description text box for the *Dept Code* field.

   c. Key **Department code** in the Description text box and then press the Tab key.

   d. Key **Department** in the Field Name text box and then press Tab.

   e. Change the field size to *30* and then click in the Description text box for the Department field.

   f. Key **Department name** in the Description text box.

5. When all the fields are entered, save the database table by completing the following steps:

   a. Click the Save button on the Table Design toolbar.

   b. At the Save As dialog box, key **Departments** in the text box, and then press Enter or click OK.

   c. At the message telling you that no primary key is defined and asking if you want to create one, click No. (You will learn more about primary keys in chapter 20.)

6. Close the Employees table by clicking File and then Close or clicking the Close button located in the upper right corner of the dialog box.

7. Close the Premium database file by clicking File and then Close or clicking the Close button located in the upper right corner of the dialog box.

figure

19.10

Exercise 2

Table1 : Table		
Field Name	Data Type	Description
Dept Code	Text	Department code
Department	Text	Department name

Entering Data in a Table

After a database table has been designed with the necessary fields and has been created in Access, the next step is to input the data. One method for entering data into a database table is to change to the Datasheet view. A table datasheet displays the contents of a table in rows and columns in the same manner as a Word table or Excel worksheet. Each row in a datasheet represents one record. In the Employees table of the Premium database, one record will contain the information for one employee.

Opening a Database File

Before entering information into a database table, open the database file. Open a database when first opening Access or open a database starting at a blank Access screen. To open a database file as you are opening the Access program, you would complete the following steps:

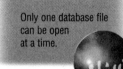

Only one database file can be open at a time.

1. Click the Start button on the Taskbar, point to Programs, and then click *Microsoft Access*.
2. At the Microsoft Access dialog box, click Open an existing file, and then double-click the desired database file name in the list box.

To open a database file at a blank Access window, you would complete the following steps:

Open

1. At the blank Microsoft Access window, click the Open button on the Database toolbar; or click File and then Open. (The Database toolbar displays directly below the Menu bar and contains many buttons similar to those on a Word, PowerPoint, or Excel Standard toolbar.)
2. At the Open dialog box, double-click the database file name displayed in the list box.

Opening a Table

Open a database file and a database window displays similar to the one shown in figure 19.11. Open a specific table in the database file by double-clicking the table name in the list box.

figure
19.11

Premium Database Window

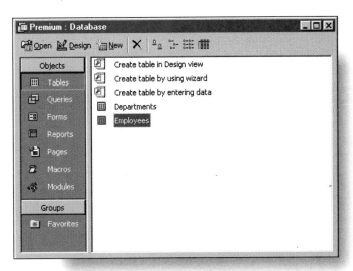

Entering Data in a Database Table

Open a database table and the table displays in the Datasheet view. This is the view needed for entering data in the table. Key data for each field in the table, pressing Tab to move the insertion point from field to field. For example, the Employees database table in the Premium database file will display as shown in figure 19.12. (Data has been entered in this database table.)

figure
19.12

Employees Table in Premium Database

Employees table in the Premium database file.

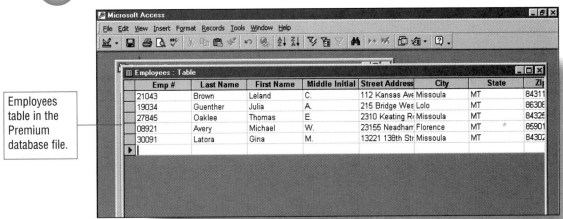

When you key data for the first field in the record, another row of cells is automatically inserted below the first row. Key the data for the first record, pressing Tab to move from field to field. The description you keyed for each field when creating the database table displays at the left side of the Access Status bar. This description can help remind you what data is expected in the field.

If the Yes/No data type was assigned to a field, a square displays in the field. This square can be left empty or a check mark can be inserted. If the field is asking a yes/no question, an empty box signifies "No" and a box with a check mark signifies "Yes." If the field is asking for a true/false answer, an empty box signifies "False" and a box with a check mark signifies "True." This field can also have an on/off response. An empty box signifies "Off" and a box with a check mark signifies "On." To insert a check mark in the box, tab to the field, and then press the space bar.

When all records have been entered in the table, save the table again by clicking the Save button on the Table Datasheet toolbar. (The Table Datasheet toolbar displays directly below the Menu bar.)

exercise 3

Entering Data in the Employees and the Departments Tables

1. At the blank Access screen, click the Open button on the Database toolbar.
2. At the Open dialog box, make sure the drive is active where your disk is located, and then double-click *Premium* in the list box.
3. At the Premium Database window, double-click *Employees* in the list box.
4. At the Employees Table dialog box, key the following data for five records in the specified fields. (Press Tab to move the insertion point to the next field or press Shift + Tab to move the insertion point to the previous field. When keying the data, not all of the data may be visible. You will adjust column widths in a later exercise.):

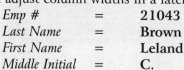

Step 3

Emp #	=	**21043**
Last Name	=	**Brown**
First Name	=	**Leland**
Middle Initial	=	**C.**
Street Address	=	**112 Kansas Avenue**
City	=	**Missoula**
State	=	**MT**

Zip Code	=	84311
Dept Code	=	PA
Hire Date	=	11/5/94
Emp #	=	19034
Last Name	=	Guenther
First Name	=	Julia
Middle Initial	=	A.
Street Address	=	215 Bridge West
City	=	Lolo
State	=	MT
Zip Code	=	86308
Dept Code	=	MS
Hire Date	=	2/15/89
Emp #	=	27845
Last Name	=	Oaklee
First Name	=	Thomas
Middle Initial	=	E.
Street Address	=	2310 Keating Road
City	=	Missoula
State	=	MT
Zip Code	=	84325
Dept Code	=	HR
Hire Date	=	6/8/95
Emp #	=	08921
Last Name	=	Avery
First Name	=	Michael
Middle Initial	=	W.
Street Address	=	23155 Neadham Avenue
City	=	Florence
State	=	MT
Zip Code	=	85901
Dept Code	=	PA
Hire Date	=	11/5/94
Emp #	=	30091
Last Name	=	Latora
First Name	=	Gina
Middle Initial	=	M.
Street Address	=	13221 138th Street
City	=	Missoula
State	=	MT
Zip Code	=	84302
Dept Code	=	HR
Hire Date	=	9/16/98

5. After keying the data, save the database table by clicking the Save button on the Table Datasheet toolbar.

6. Close the Employees table by clicking File and then Close or by clicking the Close button in the upper right corner of the window Title bar.

7. At the Premium Database window, double-click *Departments* in the list box.

8. At the Departments Table window, key the following data for four departments in the specified fields (press Tab to move the insertion point to the next field or press Shift + Tab to move the insertion point to the previous field):

Dept Code	=	**IS**
Department Name	=	**Information Services**
Dept Code	=	**HR**
Department Name	=	**Human Resources**
Dept Code	=	**MS**
Department Name	=	**Medical Services**
Dept Code	=	**PA**
Department Name	=	**Patient Accounts**

9. After keying the data, save the database table by clicking the Save button on the Table Datasheet toolbar.

10. Close the Departments table by clicking File and then Close or by clicking the Close button in the upper right corner of the dialog box Title bar.

11. Close the Premium database by clicking File and then Close or by clicking the Close button in the right upper corner of the dialog box Title bar.

Step 7

Step 8

Printing a Database Table

Print

Various methods are available for printing data in a database table. One method for printing is to open the database table and then click the Print button on the Table Datasheet toolbar. This sends the information directly to the printer without any formatting changes. In some fields created in the Employees database table, this means that you would not be able to see all printed text in a field if all the text did not fit in the field. For example, when keying the data in exercise 3, did you notice that the Street Address data was longer than the field column could accommodate? You can change the database table layout to ensure that all data is visible. You will first print the Employees and Departments tables with the default settings, learn about changing the layout, and then print the tables again.

exercise 4

Printing the Employees and Departments Tables with the Default Settings

1. At the blank Access window, open the Premium database file.
2. Open the Employees table.
3. Click the Print button on the Table Datasheet toolbar.
4. Close the Employees table.
5. Open the Departments table.
6. Click the Print button on the Table Datasheet toolbar.
7. Close the Departments table.
8. Close the Premium database file.

Look at the printing of the Employees table and notice how the order of records displays differently in the printing (and in the table) than the order in which the records were keyed. Access automatically sorted the records by the Zip Code in ascending order. Access automatically sorted the records in the Departments table alphabetically by department name. You will learn more about sorting later in this chapter.

Changing Page Setup

The Employees table printed on two pages in the Portrait orientation with default margins. The page orientation and page margins can be changed with options at the Page Setup dialog box with either the Margins or the Page tab selected. To display the Page Setup dialog box shown in figure 19.13, you would open the Employees or Departments database table, and then click File and then Page Setup.

19.13

Page Setup Dialog Box with Margins Tab Selected

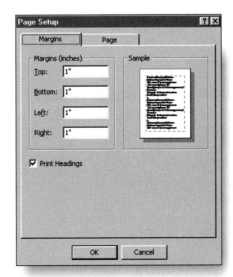

At the Page Setup dialog box with the Margins tab selected, notice that the default margins are 1 inch. Change these defaults by keying a different number in the desired margin text box. By default, the table name prints at the top center of the page. For example, when you printed the Employees table, Employees printed at the top of the page along with the current date (printed at the right side of the page). Page 1 also printed at the bottom of the page. If you do not want the name of the table and the date as well as the page number printed, remove the check mark from the Print Headings option at the Page Setup dialog box with the Margins tab selected.

Change the table orientation at the Page Setup dialog box with the Page tab selected as shown in figure 19.14. To change to landscape orientation, click Landscape. You can also change the paper size with options in the Paper section of the dialog box and specify the printer with options in the Printer for (table name) section of the dialog box.

A table can be printed in landscape orientation.

figure
19.14

Page Setup Dialog Box with Page Tab Selected

Changing Field Width

In the printing of the Employees table, not all the data is visible is the *Street Address* field. You can remedy this situation by changing the width of the fields. Notice that fields in a database table are set up in columns as in an Excel worksheet. Change the width of fields automatically to accommodate the longest entry in the field in much the same way you changed the width of columns in an Excel worksheet.

Automatically adjust column widths in an Access database table in the same manner as adjusting column widths in an Excel worksheet.

You can automatically adjust one field (column) in a database table to accommodate the longest entry in the field by positioning the arrow pointer on the column boundary at the right side of the column until it turns into a double-headed arrow pointing left and right with a double line between and then double-clicking the left mouse button. You can automatically adjust adjacent columns by selecting the columns first and then double-clicking on a column boundary.

Changing Page Setup and then Printing the Employees Table

1. Open the Premium database file and then open the Employees database table.
2. Change the page margins and orientation by completing the following steps:
   a. Click File and then Page Setup.
   b. At the Page Setup dialog box, click the Page tab.
   c. At the Page Setup dialog box with the Page tab selected, click Landscape in the Orientation section.
   d. Click the Margins tab.
   e. At the Page Setup dialog box with the Margins tab selected, select *1"* in the Top text box, and then key **2**.
   f. Click OK to close the dialog box.

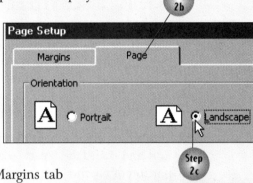

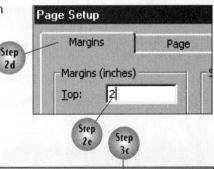

3. Automatically adjust all columns in the table to accommodate the longest entry by completing the following steps:
   a. Position the arrow pointer on the *Emp #* field name (the arrow pointer turns into a down-pointing black arrow).
   b. Hold down the left mouse button, drag the arrow pointer to the *Hire Date* field name, and then release the mouse button. (This selects all data in the table.)
   c. Position the arrow pointer on one of the column boundaries until it turns into a double-headed arrow pointing left and

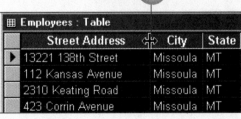

   right with a double line between, and then double-click the left mouse button. (If a column boundary is not visible, click the left scroll arrow at the left side of the horizontal scroll bar until a column boundary is visible.)
   d. Deselect the data by clicking in any field in the table.
4. Save the database table again by clicking the Save button on the Table Datasheet toolbar.
5. Send the table to the printer by clicking the Print button on the Table Datasheet toolbar.
6. Close the Employees database table and then close the Premium database file.

Maintaining a Database Table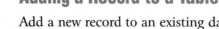

Once a database table is created, more than likely it will require maintenance. For example, newly hired employees will need to be added to the Employees table. A system may be established for deleting an employee record when an employee leaves the company. The type of maintenance required on a database table is related to the type of data stored in the table.

Adding a Record to a Table

![New Record button]

New Record

Add a new record to an existing database table by clicking the New Record button on the Table Datasheet toolbar. Key the data in the appropriate fields and then save the table again.

Deleting a Record in a Table

![Delete Record button]

Delete Record

To delete an existing record in a database table, click in any field in the row you want to delete, and then click the Delete Record button on the Table Datasheet toolbar. A message displays telling you that you will not be able to undo the delete operation and asking if you want to continue. At this message, click <u>Y</u>es.

Finding a Specific Record in a Table

To find a specific record in a table, open the table in Datasheet view, then click <u>E</u>dit and then <u>F</u>ind. At the Find and Replace dialog box, key a field entry or a portion of an entry in the <u>F</u>ind What text box, and then click <u>F</u>ind Next button. Access searches through the records and selects the first occurrence of the text you entered in the <u>F</u>ind What text box. By default, Access will search in the field in which the insertion point is positioned. If you want Access to search all fields in the table, change the <u>L</u>ook In option to the entire table. With the Matc<u>h</u> option, you can specify that you want Access to search a part of the field, the whole field, or the start of the field.

exercise 6

Adding and Deleting Records in the Employees Table

1. Open the Premium database file and then open the Employees database table.
2. Add two new records to the table by completing the following steps:
   a. Click the New Record button on the Table Datasheet toolbar.
   b. Key the following data in the specified fields:

Emp #	=	30020
Last Name	=	**Pang**
First Name	=	**Brian**
Middle Initial	=	**R.**
Street Address	=	**15512 Country Drive**
City	=	**Lolo**

State	=	MT
Zip Code	=	86308
Dept Code	=	IS
Hire Date	=	8/15/99

   c. Click the New Record button on the Table Datasheet toolbar (or, just press the Tab key).

   d. Key the following data in the specified fields:

Emp #	=	**30023**
Last Name	=	**Zajac**
First Name	=	**Elizabeth**
Middle Initial	=	**A.**
Street Address	=	**423 Corrin Avenue**
City	=	**Missoula**
State	=	**MT**
Zip Code	=	**84325**
Dept Code	=	**HR**
Hire Date	=	**8/15/99**

3. Find and delete the record for Julia Guenther by completing the following steps:
   a. Click in the first record in the Last Name column.
   b. Click Edit and then Find.
   c. At the Find and Replace dialog box, key **Guenther** in the Find What text box.
   d. Make sure the Look In option displays as *Last Name* and then click the Find Next button.
   e. When Access selects the name *Guenther,* click the Cancel button to close the Find and Replace dialog box.
   f. With Guenther selected, click the Delete button on the Table Datasheet toolbar.
   g. At the message telling you that you will not be able to undo the delete operation and asking if you want to continue, click Yes.

4. Click the Save button on the Table Datasheet toolbar to save the Employees table.

5. Print the Employees database table in landscape orientation. (You will need to change to the Landscape orientation at the Page Setup dialog box with the Page tab selected.)

6. Close the Employees table and then close the Premium database file.

Modifying a Table

Maintaining a database table involves adding and/or deleting records as needed. It can also involve adding, moving, changing, or deleting fields in the database table. These types of changes modify the structure of the database table and are done in the Design view. To display a database table in the Design view, open the database table, and then click the down-pointing triangle at the right side of the View button (first button from the left). When you click the down-pointing triangle, a drop-down menu displays with two viewing choices—Design View and Datasheet View. Click Design View to change the display of the database table. In the Design view, Field Name, Data Type, and Description display at the top of the dialog box and Field Properties displays toward the bottom of the dialog box. In the Design view, you can add fields, remove fields, and change the order of fields.

View

In addition to clicking the down-pointing triangle at the right side of the View button, you can also just click the button. If the current view is the Datasheet view, clicking the button will change to the Design view. If the Design view is the current view, clicking the button will change to the Datasheet view.

Adding a Field

Situations change within a company, and a database table must be flexible to accommodate changes that occur with new situations. Adding a field is a change that may need to be made to an existing database table. For example, more information may be required to manage the data or an additional field may be needed for accounting purposes. Whatever the reason, being able to add a new field to an existing database table is a necessity.

Insert Rows

A row for a new field can be added to an existing database table with a button on the Table Design toolbar, an option from the Insert drop-down menu, or a shortcut menu. To add a row for a new field, position the insertion point on any text in the row that will be immediately *below* the new field, and then click the Insert Rows button on the Table Design toolbar; click Insert, then Rows; or position the insertion point on any text in the row that will be immediately *below* the new field, click the *right* mouse button, and then click the left mouse button on Insert Rows. If you insert a row for a new field and then change your mind, immediately click the Undo button on the Table Design toolbar.

Undo

Deleting a Field

A field in a database table can be deleted and all data that is keyed in that field is also deleted. When a field is deleted it cannot be undone with the Undo button. Delete a field only if you are sure you really want it and the data associated with it completely removed from the database table.

Delete Rows

To delete a field, open the database table, and then change to the Design view. Position the insertion point in any text in the row containing the field you want deleted and then click the Delete Rows button on the Table Design toolbar, or click Edit, then Delete Rows. At the message asking if you want to permanently delete the field and all the data in the field, click Yes.

Using the Input Mask Wizard

For some fields, you may want to control the data entered in the field. For example, in a Zip code field, you may want the nine-digit Zip code entered (rather than the five-digit Zip Code); or you may want the three-digit area code included in a telephone number. Use the Input Mask field property to set a pattern for how data is entered in a field. An input mask ensures that data in records conforms to a standard format. Access includes an Input Mask Wizard that guides you through creating an input mask.

Use the Input Mask Wizard when assigning a data type to a field. After specifying the Field Size in the Field Properties section of the Table dialog box, click the Input Mask text box. Run the Input Mask Wizard by clicking the button containing the three black dots that appears to the right of the Input Mask text box. This displays the first Input Mask Wizard dialog box as shown in figure 19.15. In the Input Mask list box, choose which input mask you want your data to look like, and then click the Next> button. At the second Input Mask Wizard dialog box as shown in figure 19.16, specify the appearance of the input mask and the desired placeholder character, and then click the Next> button. At the third Input Mask Wizard dialog box, specify whether you want the data stored with or without the symbol in the mask, and then click the Next> button. At the fourth dialog box, click the Finish button.

figure

19.15

First Input Mask Wizard Dialog Box

Choose the desired input mask from this list box.

figure

19.16

Second Input Mask Wizard Dialog Box

Use this option to specify the placeholder character.

Using the Lookup Wizard

Like the Input Mask Wizard, you can use the Lookup Wizard to control the data entered in a field. Use the Lookup Wizard to confine the date entered into a field to a specific list of items. For example, in exercise 7 you will use the Lookup Wizard to restrict the new *Employee Category* field to one of three choices—Salaried, Hourly, and Temporary. When the user clicks in the field in the datasheet, a down-pointing triangle displays. The user clicks this triangle to display a drop-down list of available entries and then clicks the desired item.

Use the Lookup Wizard when assigning a data type to a field. Click in the Data Type text box and then click the down-pointing triangle that displays at the right side of the box. At the drop-down menu that displays, click *Lookup Wizard*. This displays the first Lookup Wizard dialog box as shown in figure 19.17. At this dialog box, indicate that you want to enter the field choices by clicking the I will type in the values that I want. option, and then click the Next> button. At the second Lookup Wizard dialog box shown in figure 19.18, click in the blank text box below *Col1* and then key the first choice. Press the Tab key and then key the second choice. Continue in this manner until all desired choices are entered and then click the Next> button. At the third Lookup Wizard dialog box, make sure the proper name displays in the What label would you like for your lookup column? text box, and then click the Finish button.

figure

19.17

First Lookup Wizard Dialog Box

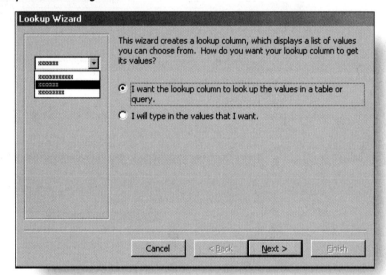

figure

19.18

Second Lookup Wizard Dialog Box

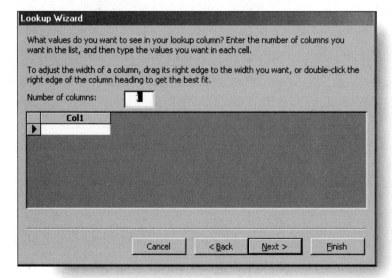

Chapter Nineteen

exercise 7

Adding a Field to and Deleting a Field from the Employees Table

1. Open the Premium database file and then open the Employees database table.
2. Add the field *Telephone* to the table and use the Input Mask Wizard by completing the following steps:

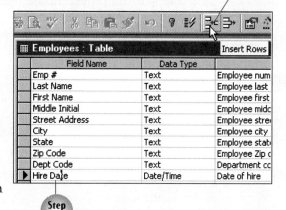

a. Click the down-pointing triangle at the right side of the View button on the Table Datasheet toolbar (first button from the left).
b. At the drop-down menu that displays, click <u>D</u>esign View.
c. Click anywhere in the text *Hire Date* that displays in the *Field Name* column. (You may need to scroll down the list to display this field.)
d. Click the Insert Rows button on the Table Design toolbar.

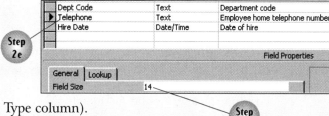

e. With the insertion point positioned in the new blank cell in the Field Name column, key **Telephone**.
f. Press Tab (this moves the insertion point to the Data Type column).
g. Select *50* that displays in the Field Size text box in the Field Properties section of the dialog box and then key **14**.

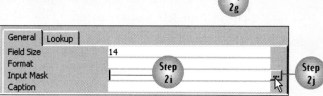

h. Click the Save button to save the table. (You must save the table before using the Input Mask Wizard.)
i. Click in the Input Mask text box in the Field Properties section of the dialog box.
j. Click the button containing the three black dots that displays to the right of the Input Mask text box.

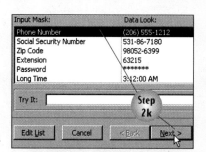

k. At the first Input Mask Wizard dialog box, make sure *Phone Number* is selected in the Input Mask list box, and then click the <u>N</u>ext> button.
l. At the second Input Mask Wizard dialog box, click the down-pointing triangle at the right side of the Placeholder character text box, and then click # at the drop-down list.

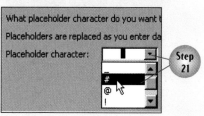

m. Click the <u>N</u>ext> button.

n. At the third Input Mask Wizard dialog box, click the With the symbols in the mask, like this option, and then click the Next> button.

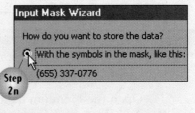

o. At the fourth Input Mask Wizard dialog box, click the Finish button.

p. Click in the *Description* column in the *Telephone* row and then key **Employee home telephone number**.

3. Delete the Hire Date row by completing the following steps:
   a. Click anywhere in the text *Hire Date* that displays in the *Field Name* column.
   b. Click the Delete Rows button on the Table Design toolbar.
   c. At the message stating that the field will be permanently deleted, click Yes.

4. Click the Save button on the Table Design toolbar to save the modified table.

5. Add telephone numbers for the records in the Employees database table by completing the following steps:
   a. Change to the Datasheet view by clicking the down-pointing triangle at the right side of the View button on the Table Design toolbar and then clicking Datasheet View.
   b. Drag the scroll box on the horizontal scroll bar to the right until the *Telephone* field is visible.
   c. Position the arrow point at the left side of the first blank cell below the new *Telephone* field until the arrow pointer turns into a thick, white plus symbol and then click the left mouse button. (This selects the entire cell.)
   d. Key **4065556841** and then press the down arrow key. (This moves the insertion point to the next blank cell in the Telephone column.)
   e. Key **4065557454** and then press the down arrow key.
   f. Key **4065553495** and then press the down arrow key.
   g. Key **4065557732** and then press the down arrow key.
   h. Key **4065550926** and then press the down arrow key.
   i. Key **4065554509** and then press the down arrow key.

6. Click the Save button again on the Table Datasheet toolbar to save the database table.

7. Add the field *Employee Category* and use the Lookup Wizard to specify field choices by completing the following steps:
   a. Change to the Design view by clicking the down-pointing triangle at the right side of the View button on the Table Design toolbar and then clicking Design View.
   b. Click anywhere in the text *Dept Code* that displays in the *Field Name* column.
   c. Click the Insert Rows button on the Table Design toolbar.

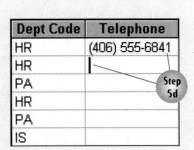

d. With the insertion point positioned in the new blank cell in the *Field Name* column, key **Employee Category**.

e. Press Tab (this moves the insertion point to the *Data Type* column).

f. Click the down-pointing triangle at the right side of the text box and then click *Lookup Wizard* at the drop-down list.

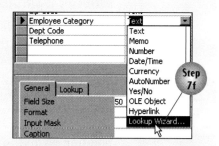

Step 7f

g. At the first Lookup Wizard dialog box, click the I will type in the values that I want option and then click the Next> button.

h. At the second Lookup Wizard dialog box, click in the blank text box below *Col1*, key **Salaried**, and then press Tab.

Step 7g

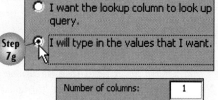

i. Key **Hourly** and then press Tab.

j. Key **Temporary**.

k. Click the Next> button.

l. At the third Lookup Wizard dialog box, click the Finish button.

Step 7h–j

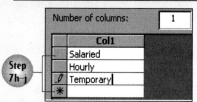

m. Click in the *Description* column in the *Employee Category* row and then key **Employee category**.

8. Click the Save button on the Table Design toolbar.

9. Insert information in the Employee Category for the records by completing the following steps:

a. Change to the Datasheet view by clicking the down-pointing triangle at the right side of the View button on the Table Design toolbar and then clicking Datasheet View.

b. Click in the first blank cell below the new *Employee Category* field.

c. Click the down-pointing triangle at the right side of the cell and then click *Hourly* at the drop-down list.

d. Click in next blank cell in the *Employee Category* field, click the down-pointing triangle, and then click *Salaried* at the drop-down list.

e. Continue entering information in the *Employee Category* field by completing similar steps. Enter the following in the specified record:

Third record	=	**Hourly**
Fourth record	=	**Hourly**
Fifth record	=	**Temporary**
Sixth record	=	**Salaried**

10. Click the Save button again on the Table Datasheet toolbar.

11. Print the table in landscape orientation with 0.5-inch left and right margins. (Change to the Landscape orientation at the Page Setup dialog box with the Page tab selected and then change to 0.5-inch left and right margins at the Page Setup dialog box with the Margins tab selected. [You must make the changes in this order.])

12. Close the Employees table and then close the Premium database file.

Moving a Record

Move records to different locations in a table in the Datasheet view. To move a record, change to the Datasheet view, and then select the row containing the record you want moved. To select a row, position the arrow pointer at the left side of the row on the gray button that begins the row until the arrow pointer turns into a black arrow pointing right, and then click the left mouse button. With the row selected, position the arrow pointer on the gray button at the left side of the selected row until the pointer turns into the normal arrow pointer (white arrow pointing up and to the left), hold down the left mouse button, drag the arrow pointer (displays with a gray square attached) to the desired position, and then release the mouse button.

Moving a Field

A field in a database table can be moved to a different location. To do this, open the database table, and then change to the Design view. Position the arrow pointer on the gray button at the left side of the field you want moved until the arrow pointer turns into a right-pointing black arrow and then click the left mouse button. This selects the entire row. Position the arrow pointer on the gray button at the left side of the selected row until it turns into the normal arrow pointer (white arrow pointing up and to the left). Hold down the left mouse button, drag the arrow pointer with the gray square attached until a thick gray line displays in the desired position, and then release the mouse button.

Moving and Deleting Fields in the Employees Table

1. Open the Premium database file and then open the Employees database table.
2. Move the *Last Name* field immediately below the *Middle Initial* field by completing the following steps:
   a. Click the down-pointing triangle at the right of the View button on the Table Datasheet toolbar and then click <u>D</u>esign View at the drop-down menu.
   b. Position the arrow pointer on the gray button (this color may vary) at the left side of the *Last Name* field until it turns into a right-pointing black arrow and then click the left mouse button. (This selects the entire row.)
   c. Position the arrow pointer on the gray button at the left side of the selected row until it turns into the normal arrow pointer (white arrow pointing up and to the left).
   d. Hold down the left mouse button, drag the arrow pointer with the gray square attached until a thick gray line displays between the *Middle Initial* field and the *Street Address* field, and then release the mouse button.

Step 2d

3. Move the *Telephone* field above the *Dept Code* field by completing the following steps:
   a. Select the row containing the *Telephone* field.
   b. Position the arrow pointer on the gray button at the left side of the selected row until it turns into the normal arrow pointer (white arrow pointing up and to the left).
   c. Hold down the left mouse button, drag the arrow pointer above the *Dept Code* field and then release the mouse button.
4. Delete the *Middle Initial* field and the data in the field by completing the following steps:
   a. Position the insertion point anywhere in the text *Middle Initial*.
   b. Click the Delete Rows button on the Table Design toolbar.
   c. At the message asking if you want to permanently delete the field and the data in the field, click <u>Y</u>es.
5. Click the Save button again on the Table Design toolbar to save the database table.
6. Click the View button on the Table Design toolbar to change to the Datasheet view.
7. Print the Employees database table in landscape orientation. (You will need to change to the <u>L</u>andscape orientation at the Page Setup dialog box with the Page tab selected.)
8. Close the Employees table and then close the Premium database file.

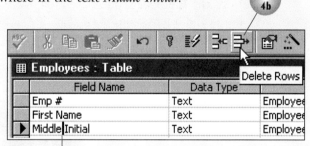

Using the Office Assistant

Like Word, Excel, and PowerPoint, Access contains an on-screen Help feature containing information about Access features and commands. You can use the Office Assistant to access this on-screen Help feature. To do this, click the Office Assistant or click <u>H</u>elp and then Microsoft Access <u>H</u>elp. This causes a box to display above the Office Assistant. Key a question in the box about a specific Access feature and then click the <u>S</u>earch button. The Office Assistant displays a list of topics related to the question. At this list, click the desired topic, and information will display in a Microsoft Access Help dialog box. After reading the information, click the Close button located in the upper right corner of the dialog box. (For more information on the on-screen Help feature, refer to pages 82-88 in chapter 2.) For the last assessments in chapters 19 through 23, you will be using the Office Assistant to find information on Access topics not covered in the chapters.

Sorting Records

The Table Datasheet toolbar contains two buttons you can use to sort data in records. Click the Sort Ascending button to sort from lowest to highest (or A-Z) on the field where the insertion point is located. Click the Sort Descending button to sort from highest to lowest (or Z-A).

Sort Ascending

Sort Descending

exercise 9

Sorting Records in the Employees Table

1. Open the Premium database file and then open the Employees database table.
2. Sort records in ascending order by city by completing the following steps:
   a. Click any city name in the database table.
   b. Click the Sort Ascending button on the Table Datasheet toolbar.
   c. Print the Employees database table in landscape orientation.
3. Sort records in descending order by employee number by completing the following steps:
   a. Click on any number in the *Emp #* field.
   b. Click the Sort Descending button on the Table Datasheet toolbar.
   c. Print the Employees database table in landscape orientation.
4. Click the Save button to save the database table.
5. Close the Employees table and then close the Premium database file.

Step 2b

Tools   Window   Help

Sort Ascending

Street Address	City
13221 138th Street	Missoula
112 Kansas Avenue	Missoula
2310 Keating Road	Missoula
423 Corrin Avenue	Missoula
23155 Neadham Avenue	Florence

Step 2a

Step 3b

Sort Descending

Step 3a

Employees : Table

Emp #	First Name	Last Name	Street Add
08921	Michael	Avery	23155 Neadham
30020	Brian	Pang	15512 Country C
30023	Elizabeth	Zajac	423 Corrin Avenu
30091	Gina	Latora	13221 138th Str
27845	Thomas	Oaklee	2310 Keating Rc
21043	Leland	Brown	112 Kansas Ave

chapter summary

- ► Microsoft Access is a database management system software program that will organize, store, maintain, retrieve, sort, and print all types of business data.
- ► Organize data in Access in related database tables in a database file.
- ► The first step in organizing data for a database table is determining fields. A field is one piece of information about a person, place, or item. All fields for one unit, such as an employee or customer, are considered a record.
- ► A field name should be unique and describe the contents of the field. It can contain up to 64 characters including letters, numbers, spaces, and some symbols.
- ► Part of the process of designing a database table is assigning a data type to each field, which helps maintain and manage data and helps identify what type of data is expected for the field. Data types include Text, Memo, Number, Currency, Date/Time, AutoNumber, and Yes/No.
- ► When assigning a data type, specific field sizes can be assigned to a field.

- Save a database table in the same manner as a Word document, an Excel worksheet, or a PowerPoint presentation. Access automatically saves a database file on a periodic basis and also when the database file is closed.
- Open a database file when starting Access or open a database file at the Open dialog box.
- Enter data in a database table in the Datasheet view. Key data in a field, pressing Tab to move to the next field or pressing Shift + Tab to move to the previous field.
- Print a database table by opening the table and then clicking the Print button on the Table Datasheet toolbar.
- Change margins in a database table at the Page Setup dialog box with the Margins tab selected.
- Change the page orientation and paper size and specify the printer with options at the Page Setup dialog box with the Page tab selected.
- Adjust field widths in a database table in the same manner as column widths in an Excel worksheet. Double-click a column boundary to automatically adjust the width to accommodate the longest entry.
- Maintaining a database table can include adding and/or deleting records.
- Modifying a database table can include adding, moving, or deleting a field.
- Use the Input Mask Wizard to set a pattern for how data is entered in a field.
- Use the Lookup Wizard to confine data entered in a field to a specific list of items.
- Sort records in a database table in ascending order with the Sort Ascending button on the Table Datasheet toolbar or in descending order with the Sort Descending button.

commands review

	Mouse/Keyboard
Open Access	Click Start, point to Programs, click *Microsoft Access*
Open dialog box	Click File, Open or click Open button on Database toolbar
Change view in table	Click View button on Table Design or Table Datasheet toolbar
Print dialog box	Open database table; click File and then Print
Send table directly to printer	Open database table; click Print button on Table Datasheet toolbar
Page Setup dialog box	Open database table, click File and then Page Setup
Add record to a table	In Datasheet view, click New Record button on Table Datasheet toolbar
Delete record in a table	In Datasheet view, click Delete Record button on Table Datasheet toolbar
Add new field to a table	In Design view, click Insert Rows button on Table Design toolbar
Delete a field in a table	In Design view, click Delete Rows button on Table Design toolbar
Move a field in a table	In Design view, drag row containing field using the mouse
Use the Input Mask Wizard	In Design view, click in the Input Mask text box in the Field Properties section and then click the button containing three black dots that displays to the right of the Input Mask text box.
Use the Lookup Wizard	In Design view, click in the desired cell in the *Data Type* column, click the down-pointing triangle that

	displays at the right side of the cell, and then click *Lookup Wizard.*
Sort records in ascending order	In Datasheet view, click Sort Ascending button on Table Datasheet toolbar
Sort records in descending order	In Datasheet view, click Sort Descending button on Table Datasheet toolbar

thinking offline

Completion: In the space provided at the right, indicate the correct term, symbol, or number.

1. All fields for one unit, such as a customer, are considered to be this.

2. A field name can contain up to this number of characters.

3. Assign this data type to a field where more than 255 characters are needed.

4. Assign this data type to a field where you do not want calculations rounded off during a calculation.

5. You would probably assign this data type to a field that will contain telephone numbers.

6. In a field assigned the Yes/No data type, a check mark in the box in the field asking a yes/no question signifies this.

7. This view is used in a database table to define field names and assign data types.

8. This is the view used in a database table to enter data in fields.

9. Display this dialog box to change the page orientation.

10. This is the default left and right margin measurements for a database table.

11. Add a new record to a database table in this view.

12. Add a new field to a database table in this view.

13. Use this wizard to set a pattern for how data is entered in a field.

14. Use this wizard to confine data entered in a field to a specific list of items.

15. Click the Sort Ascending button on this toolbar to sort records in ascending order.

16. Suppose you work for an insurance company and have been asked by your supervisor to design a database table to keep track of client claims. This database table should include the following information: client number (assigned in a separate database table), the date of the claim, type of claim, and the amount of claim. Determine the fields you would use in this database table and the data type you would assign to each and write that information in the space provided on the next page.

working hands-on

Assessment 1

1. Use Access to create a database for a store that sells vitamins and other health aids. The database table you create will keep track of what vitamins are ordered for the store. (This table assumes there are at least two other tables—one table containing information on suppliers and the other containing information on products. You will learn more about how tables are related in chapter 20.) Use the name of the store, Health Plus, as the database file name, and name the database table Orders. (There is no primary key.) Create the following fields in the Orders database table and assign the data type shown (you determine the Description):

Field Name		Data Type
Order #	=	Text (field size = 3)
Product Code	=	Text (field size = 2)
Supplier #	=	Text (field size = 2)
Date of Order	=	Date/Time
Amount of Order	=	Currency

2. Save the database table and name it Orders.
3. Change to the Datasheet view and then enter the following data:

Order #	=	214
Product Code	=	MT
Supplier #	=	10
Date of Order	=	4/5/99
Amount of Order	=	$875.50

Order #	=	223
Product Code	=	PA
Supplier #	=	27
Date of Order	=	4/6/99
Amount of Order	=	$1,005.45

Order #	=	241
Product Code	=	GS
Supplier #	=	10
Date of Order	=	4/8/99
Amount of Order	=	$441.95

Order #	=	259
Product Code	=	AV
Supplier #	=	18
Date of Order	=	4/8/99
Amount of Order	=	$772.00

4. Automatically adjust the width of fields.
5. Save the Orders database table again.
6. Print and then close the Orders table.

Assessment 2

1. With the Health Plus database file open, open the Orders table and then add the following records (remember to do this in the Datasheet view):

Order #	=	262
Product Code	=	BC
Supplier #	=	27
Date of Order	=	4/9/99
Amount of Order	=	$258.65

Order #	=	265
Product Code	=	VC
Supplier #	=	18
Date of Order	=	4/13/99
Amount of Order	=	$1,103.45

2. Delete the record for order number 241.
3. Save the Orders database table and then print the table with a top margin of 2 inches.
4. Close the Orders database table.

Assessment 3

1. With the Health Plus database file open, create a new table named Suppliers with the following fields and assign the data type shown (you determine the Description):

Field Name		**Data Type**
Supplier #	=	**Text** (field size = 2)
Supplier Name	=	**Text** (field size = 20)
Street Address	=	**Text** (field size = 30)
City	=	**Text** (field size = 20)
State	=	**Text** (field size = 2)
Zip Code	=	**Text** (field size = 10)

Use the Input Mask Wizard to specify a nine-digit Zip Code. *(Hint: At the first Input Mask Wizard dialog box, click Zip Code in the Input Mask list box.)*

2. After creating and saving the database table with the fields shown above, enter the following data in the table (remember to do this in the Datasheet view):

Supplier #	=	10
Supplier Name	=	VitaHealth, Inc.
Street Address	=	12110 South 23rd

City	=	San Diego
State	=	CA
Zip Code	=	97432-1567

Supplier #	=	18
Supplier Name	=	Mainstream Supplies
Street Address	=	312 Evergreen Building
City	=	Seattle
State	=	WA
Zip Code	=	98220-2791

Supplier #	=	21
Supplier Name	=	LaVerde Products
Street Address	=	121 Vista Road
City	=	Phoenix
State	=	AZ
Zip Code	=	86355-6014

Supplier #	=	27
Supplier Name	=	Redding Corporation
Street Address	=	554 Ninth Street
City	=	Portland
State	=	OR
Zip Code	=	97466-3359

3. Automatically adjust the width of fields.
4. Save the Suppliers database table.
5. Change the page orientation to landscape and then print the table.
6. Close the Suppliers database table.

Assessment 4

1. With the Health Plus database file open, open the Suppliers table.
2. Add the following fields and assign the data type as shown (remember to do this in the Design view):

Field		Data Type
Telephone	=	Text (field size = 14) Use the Input Mask Wizard to specify that the area code surrounded by parentheses is to be included in the telephone number.
E-mail Address	=	Text (field size = 30)
Supplier Type	=	Use the Lookup Wizard to create two categories for this field— Wholesale and Retail.

3. Save the table, change to the Datasheet view, and then add the following information in the appropriate row (key the supplier telephone number, e-mail address, and insert the supplier type in the correct row).

Supplier	=	LaVerde Products
Telephone	=	(602) 555-6775
E-mail Address	=	laverdep@gonet.com
Supplier Type	=	Wholesale

Supplier	=	**VitaHealth, Inc.**
Telephone	=	**(619) 555-2388**
E-mail Address	=	vitahealth@groupnet.com
Supplier Type	=	*Retail*
Supplier	=	**Redding Corporation**
Telephone	=	**(503) 555-6679**
E-mail Address	=	**redding@opnet.com**
Supplier Type	=	*Retail*
Supplier	=	**Mainstream Supplies**
Telephone	=	**(206) 555-9005**
E-mail Address	=	**mainsupplies@msgt.com**
Supplier Type	=	*Wholesale*

4. Automatically adjust the width of fields to accommodate the longest entry.
5. Save the Suppliers database table.
6. Change the page orientation to landscape and then print the table.
7. Close the Suppliers database table.

Assessment 5

1. With the Health Plus database file open, open the Orders table.
2. Change to the Design view and then move the fields around in the Orders database table so they are displayed in this order:
   Order #
   Date of Order
   Amount of Order
   Product Code
   Supplier #
3. Save the table, change to the Datasheet view, and then sort the records in ascending order by *Supplier #*.
4. Save, print, and then close the Orders database table.
5. Close the Health Plus database file.

Assessment 6

1. Use Access's Help feature to read and print information on assigning the AutoNumber data type to a field. (*Hint: At the Office Assistant, key the question* **"How do I add an AutoNumber field to a table?"** *and then click the* Search *button. At the list of topics that displays, click* Create a field that automatically generates numbers. *Read and then print the information that displays.*)
2. After reading information on the AutoNumber data type, open the Health Plus database file, open the Orders table, and then make the following changes:
   a. Change to the Design view and then delete the first row (the *Order #* row).
   b. Insert a row at the beginning of the table named *Order #* where the number is automatically inserted by Access.
   c. Save the Orders table.
   d. Change to the Datasheet view (notice the automatic numbers inserted by Access).
   e. Sort the records in ascending order by Order #.
   f. Print the Orders table in landscape orientation.
   g. Close the Orders table and then close the Health Plus database file.

Creating Relationships between Database Tables

PERFORMANCE OBJECTIVES

Upon successful completion of chapter 20, you will be able to:
- Create a database table with a primary key and a foreign key.
- Create a one-to-many relationship between database tables.
- Create a database table using the Table Wizard.

(Note: There is no Chapter 20 *folder to copy from the CD. You will be copying a database file from the CD to your disk.)*

Access is a relational database program that allows you to create tables that have a relation or connection to each other within the same database file. In chapter 19, you created a database table containing information on employees and another containing department information. With Access, you can connect these tables through a common field that appears in both tables.

In this chapter you will learn how to identify a primary key field in a database table that is unique to that table. In Access, data can be divided into logical groupings in database tables for easier manipulation and management. Duplicate information is generally minimized in database tables in the same database file. There should, however, be a link or relationship that connects the database tables. In this chapter, you will define primary keys and define relationships between database tables.

Creating Related Tables

There are two basic types of database management systems—a file management system (also sometimes referred to as a *flat file database*) and a relational database management system. In a file management system, data is stored without indexing and sequential processing. This type of system lacks flexibility in manipulating data and requires the same data to be stored in more than one place.

In a relational database management system, like Access, relationships are defined between sets of data allowing greater flexibility in manipulating data and eliminating data redundancy (entering the same data in more than one place). In exercises in this chapter, you will define relationships between tables in the insurance company database file. Because these tables will be related, information on a client does not need to be repeated in a table on claims filed. If you used a file management system to maintain insurance records, you would need to repeat the client information for each claim filed.

Determining Relationships

Taking time to plan a database file is extremely important. Creating a database file with related tables takes even more consideration. You need to determine how to break down the required data and what tables to create to eliminate redundancies. One idea to help you determine the necessary tables in a database file is to think of the word *about*. For example, an insurance company database will probably need a table *about* clients, another *about* the type of coverage, another *about* claims, and so on. A table should be about only one subject, such as a client, customer, department, or supplier.

Along with deciding on the necessary tables for a database file, you also need to determine the relationship between tables. The ability to relate, or *join*, tables is part of what makes Access a relational database system. Figure 20.1 illustrates the tables and fields that either are or will become part of the Southwest Insurance database file. Notice how each table is about only one subject—clients, type of insurance, claims, or coverage.

figure
20.1

Southwest Insurance Database Tables

Clients table
Client #
Name
Street Address
City
State
Zip Code

Insurance table
License #
Client #
Insurance Code
Uninsured Motorist

Claims table
Claim #
Client #
License #
Date of Claim
Amount of Claim

Coverage table
Insurance Code
Type of Insurance

Some fields such as *Client #*, *License #*, and *Insurance Code* appear in more than one table. These fields are used to create a relationship between tables. For example, in exercise 2 you will create a relationship between the Clients table and the Insurance table with the *Client #* field.

Creating relationships between tables tells Access how to bring the information in the database file back together again. With relationships defined, you can bring information together to create forms, reports, and queries. You will learn how to create forms and reports in chapter 21 and how to create queries in chapter 23.

Creating a Primary Field

Before creating a relationship between tables, you need to define the *primary key* in a table. In a database table, there must be at least one field that is unique so that one record can be distinguished from another. A field (or several fields) with a unique value is considered a primary key. When a primary key is defined, Access will not allow duplicate values in the primary field. For example, there must be a unique number in the *Client #* field in the Clients table (you would not assign the same client # to two different clients). If you define this as the primary key field, Access will not allow you to key the same client number in two different records.

In a field specified as a primary key, Access expects a value in each record in the database table. This is referred to as *entity integrity*. If a value is not entered in a field, Access actually enters a *null value*. A null value cannot be given to a primary key field. Access will not let you close a database file containing a primary field with a null value.

To define a field as a primary key, open the database table, and then change to the Design view. Position the insertion point somewhere in the row containing the field you want as the primary key and then click the Primary Key button on the Table Design toolbar. An image of a key is inserted at the beginning of the row identified as the primary key field. To define more than one field as a primary key, select the rows containing the fields you want as primary keys and then click the Primary Key button on the Table Design toolbar.

Creating a Foreign Key

A primary key field in one table may be a foreign key in another. For example, if you define the *Client #* field in the Clients table as the primary key, the *Client #* field in the Insurance table will then be considered a *foreign key*. The primary key field and the foreign key field form a relationship between the two tables. In the Clients table, each entry in the *Client #* field will be unique (it is the primary key) but the same client number may appear more than once in the *Client #* field in the Insurance table (such as a situation where a client has insurance on more than one vehicle).

Each table in figure 20.1 contains a unique field that will be defined as the primary key. Figure 20.2 identifies the primary keys and also foreign keys.

Primary Key

figure

20.2 Primary and Foreign Keys

Clients table
Client # (*primary key*)
Name
Street Address
City
State
Zip Code

Insurance table
License # (*primary key*)
Client # (*foreign key*)
Insurance Code (*foreign key*)
Uninsured Motorist

Claims table
Claim # (*primary key*)
Client # (*foreign key*)
License # (*foreign key*)
Date of Claim
Amount of Claim

Coverage table
Insurance Code (*primary key*)
Type of Insurance

In exercise 1, you will create another table for the Southwest Insurance database file, enter data, and then define primary keys for the tables. In the section following exercise 1, you will learn how to create relationships between the tables.

exercise 1

Creating a Table and Defining Primary Keys

(In step 1, you will copy the Southwest Insurance database file from the CD that accompanies this textbook to your disk. You will then remove the read-only attribute from the Southwest Insurance database file on your disk. You need to remove this attribute before you can make changes to the database file.)

1. Copy the Southwest Insurance database file on the CD that accompanies this textbook to your disk, remove the read-only attribute, and then open the database file by completing the following steps:
   a. Insert the CD that accompanies this textbook.
   b. Copy the Southwest Insurance database file from the CD to your disk.
   c. Remove the read-only attribute from the Southwest Insurance database located on your disk by completing the following steps:
      1) In Access, display the Open dialog box with the drive active containing your disk.
      2) Click once on the Southwest Insurance database file name.
      3) Click the Tools button on the Open dialog box toolbar and then click Properties at the drop-down list.
      4) At the Southwest Insurance Properties dialog box with the General tab selected, click the Read-only option in the Attributes section to remove the check mark.
      5) Click OK to close the Southwest Insurance Properties dialog box.

d. Open the Southwest Insurance database file.

2. At the Southwest Insurance Database window, create a new table by completing the following steps:

a. Double-click *Create table in Design view* in the list box.

b. At the Table1 Table dialog box, key the fields, assign the data types, and key the descriptions as shown below (for assistance, refer to chapter 19, exercise 1):

Field Name	Data Type	Description
License #	Text (Field Size = 7)	Vehicle license number
Client #	Text (Field Size = 4)	Client number
Insurance Code	Text (Field Size = 1)	Insurance code
Uninsured Motorist	Yes/No	Uninsured motorist coverage

(*Note: To create the Yes/No data type for the* Uninsured Motorist *field, click the down-pointing triangle at the right side of the* Data Type *field, and then click* Yes/No *at the drop-down list.*)

c. Specify the *License #* as the primary key by completing the following steps:

1) Click anywhere in the text *License #* (in the top row).
2) Click the Primary Key button on the Table Design toolbar.

d. Save the database table by completing the following steps:

1) Click the Save button on the Table Design toolbar.
2) At the Save As dialog box, key **Insurance** in the Table <u>N</u>ame text box, and then press Enter or click OK.

e. Close the Insurance table by clicking <u>F</u>ile and then <u>C</u>lose or by clicking the Close button located in the upper right corner of the dialog box.

3. Define primary keys for the other tables in the database file by completing the following steps:

a. At the Southwest Insurance Database window, double-click *Claims* in the list box.

b. With the Claims table open, click the View button on the Table Datasheet toolbar to switch to the Design view.

c. Click anywhere in the text *Claim #* and then click the Primary Key button on the Table Design toolbar.

d. Click the Save button on the Table Design toolbar.

e. Close the Claims table.

f. At the Southwest Insurance Database window, double-click *Clients* in the list box.

g. With the Clients table open, click the View button on the Table Datasheet toolbar to switch to the Design view.

h. Click anywhere in the text *Client #* and then click the Primary Key button on the Table Design toolbar.

i.   Click the Save button on the Table Design toolbar.
j.   Close the Clients table.
k.   At the Southwest Insurance Database window, double-click *Coverage* in the list box.
l.   With the Coverage table open, click the View button on the Table Datasheet toolbar to switch to the Design view.
m. Click anywhere in the text *Insurance Code* and then click the Primary Key button on the Table Design toolbar.
n.   Click the Save button on the Table Design toolbar.
o.   Close the Coverage table.

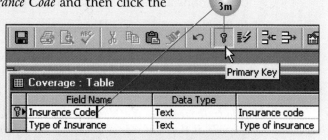

4. Open the Insurance table and then key the following data in the specified fields: (If the *Uninsured Motorist* field is Yes, insert a check mark in the field by pressing the space bar. If the field is No, leave the check box blank.)

License #	=	341 VIT
Client #	=	3120
Insurance Code	=	F
Uninsured Motorist	=	Yes

License #	=	776 ERU
Client #	=	9383
Insurance Code	=	F
Uninsured Motorist	=	No

License #	=	984 CWS
Client #	=	7335
Insurance Code	=	L
Uninsured Motorist	=	Yes

License #	=	877 BNN
Client #	=	4300
Insurance Code	=	L
Uninsured Motorist	=	Yes

License #	=	310 YTV
Client #	=	3120
Insurance Code	=	F
Uninsured Motorist	=	Yes

5. Save and then close the Insurance table.
6. Close the Southwest Insurance database file.

Establishing a Relationship Between Tables

In Access, one database table can be related to another, which is generally referred to as performing a *join*. When database tables with a common field are joined, data can be extracted from both tables as if they were one large table. Another reason for relating tables is to ensure the integrity of the data. For example, in exercise 2, you will create a relationship between the Clients database table and the Claims database table. The relationship that is established will ensure that a client cannot be entered in the Claims database table without first being entered in the Clients database table. This ensures that a claim is not processed on a person who is not a client of the insurance company. This type of relationship is called a one-to-many relationship. This means that one record in the Clients table will match zero, one, or many records in the Claims database table.

In a one-to-many relationship, the table containing the "one" is referred to as the *primary table* and the table containing the "many" is referred to as the *related table*. Access follows a set of rules known as *referential integrity*, which enforces consistency between related tables. These rules are enforced when data is updated in related database tables. The referential integrity rules ensure that a record added to a related table has a matching record in the primary table.

Creating a One-to-Many Relationship

A relationship is specified between existing tables in a database file. To create a one-to-many relationship, you would complete these basic steps:

1. Open the database file containing the tables to be related.
2. Click the Relationships button that displays at the right side of the Database toolbar; or click Tools and then Relationships. This displays the Show Table dialog box, as shown in figure 20.3.
3. At the Show Table dialog box, each table that will be related must be added to the Relationships window. To do this, click the first database table name to be included, and then click Add. Continue in this manner until all necessary database table names have been added to the Relationships window and then click the Close button.
4. At the Relationships window, such as the one shown in figure 20.4, use the mouse to drag the common field from the primary table (the "one") to the related table (the "many"). This causes the Edit Relationships dialog box as shown in figure 20.5 to display.
5. At the Edit Relationships dialog box, check to make sure the correct field name displays in the Table/Query and Related Table/Query list boxes and the relationship type at the bottom of the dialog box displays as *One-To-Many*.
6. Specify the relationship options by choosing Enforce Referential Integrity, as well as Cascade Update Related Fields and/or Cascade Delete Related Records. (These are explained in the text after these steps.)
7. Click the Create button. This causes the Edit Relationships dialog box to close and the Relationships window to display showing the relationship between the tables. In figure 20.6, the Clients box displays with a black line attached along with the number 1 (signifying the "one" side of the relationship). The black line is connected to the Claims box along with the infinity symbol ∞ (signifying the "many"

Defining a relationship between database tables is one of the most powerful features of a relational database management system.

Access provides a Table Analyzer that will analyze your database tables and restructure them to better conform to relational theory. To use the Table Analyzer Wizard, click the Analyze button on the Database toolbar.

Relationships

side of the relationship). The black line, called the *join line*, is thick at both ends if the enforce referential integrity option has been chosen. If this option is not chosen, the line is thin at both ends.

8. Click the Save button on the Relationship toolbar to save the relationship.
9. Close the Relationships window by clicking the Close button that displays at the right side of the Title bar.

Show Table Dialog Box

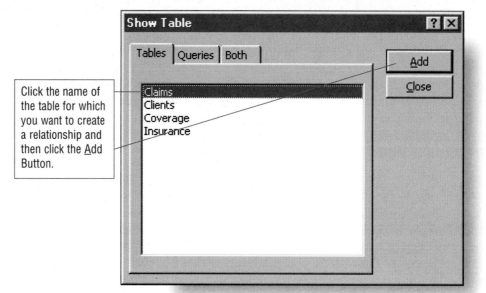

Click the name of the table for which you want to create a relationship and then click the Add Button.

Relationships Window

Insert in the Relationships window those tables for which you will create a relationship.

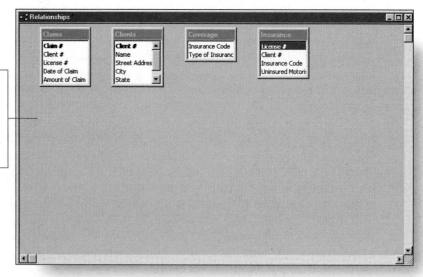

figure

20.5

Edit Relationships Dialog Box

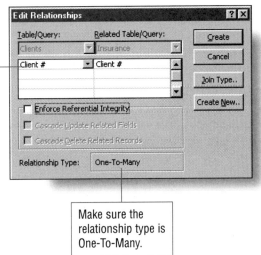

Make sure the correct field names display here.

Make sure the relationship type is One-To-Many.

figure

20.6

One-to-Many Relationship

This is an example of a one-to-many relationship where the 1 identifies the "one" side of the relationship and the infinity symbol (∞) identifies the "many" side.

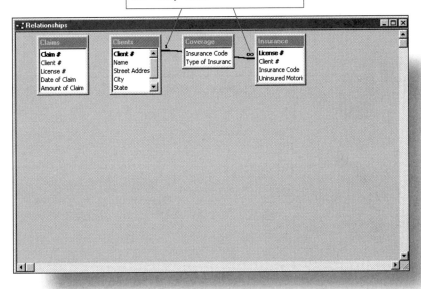

Specifying Referential Integrity

In step 6, the referential integrity of the Edit relationship was established. Choose Enforce Referential Integrity at the Edit Relationships dialog box to ensure that the relationships between records in related tables are valid. Referential integrity can be set if the field from the primary table is a primary key and the related fields have the same data type. When referential integrity is established, a value for the primary key must first be entered in the primary table before it can be entered in the related table.

If you select only <u>E</u>nforce Referential Integrity and if there is a record in the related table, you will not be able to change a primary key value or delete a primary key value in the primary table. If you choose Cascade <u>U</u>pdate Related Fields, you will be able to change a primary key value in the primary table and Access will automatically update the matching value in the related table. Choose Cascade <u>D</u>elete Related Records and you will be able to delete a record in the primary table and Access will delete any related records in the related table.

Printing Database Relationships

Access contains a Print Relationships Wizard you can use to print a report displaying the relationships between tables. To print a report of relationships between tables in a database file, you would complete these steps:

1. Open the database.
2. Display the Relationships window by clicking the Relationships button on the Database toolbar.
3. At the Relationships window, click <u>F</u>ile and then Print <u>R</u>elationships. (This displays the Relationships report in Print Preview.)
4. Click the Print button on the Print Preview toolbar to send the report to the printer.
5. Click the <u>C</u>lose button to close Print Preview.

Relating Tables in the Southwest Insurance Database File

The Southwest Insurance database file contains the four tables shown in figure 20.1. Each table contains data about something—clients, insurance, claims, and coverage. You can relate these tables so that data can be extracted from more than one table as if they were all one large table. The relationships between the tables are identified in figure 20.7.

Referential integrity makes sure that a record exists in the "one" database table before the record can be entered in the "many" database table.

figure
20.7

Relationships Between Southwest Insurance Database Tables

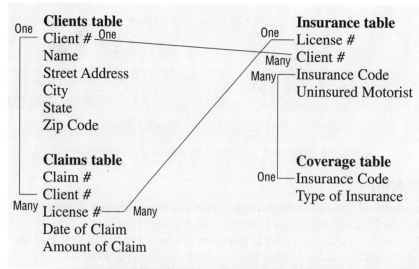

In the relationships shown in figure 20.7, notice how the primary key is identified as the "one" and the foreign key is identified as the "many." Relate these tables so you can extract information from more than one table. For example, you can design a report about claims that contains information on claims as well as information on the clients submitting the claims.

Creating a One-to-Many Relationship between Two Database Tables

1. Create a one-to-many relationship between the Clients table and the Claims table by completing the following steps:
   a. Open the Southwest Insurance database file.
   b. Click the Relationships button that displays towards the right side of the Database toolbar.

   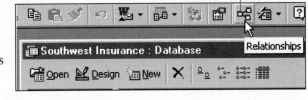

   Step 1b

   c. At the Show Table dialog box, add the Clients and Claims tables to the Relationships window by completing the following steps:
      1) Click *Clients* in the list box and then click <u>A</u>dd.
      2) Click *Claims* in the list box and then click <u>A</u>dd.
   d. Click the <u>C</u>lose button to close the Show Table dialog box.
   e. At the Relationships window, drag the *Client #* field from the Clients table to the Claims table by completing the following steps:
      1) Position the arrow pointer on the *Client #* field that displays in the Clients box.
      2) Hold down the left mouse button, drag the arrow pointer (with a *field* icon attached), to the *Client #* field in the Claims box, and then release the mouse button. (This causes the Edit Relationships dialog box to display.)

   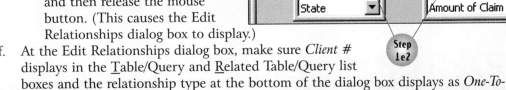

   Step 1e2

   f. At the Edit Relationships dialog box, make sure *Client #* displays in the <u>T</u>able/Query and <u>R</u>elated Table/Query list boxes and the relationship type at the bottom of the dialog box displays as *One-To-Many*.
   g. Enforce the referential integrity of the relationship by completing the following steps:
      1) Click <u>E</u>nforce Referential Integrity. (This makes the other two options available.)
      2) Click Cascade <u>U</u>pdate Related Fields.
      3) Click Cascade <u>D</u>elete Related Records.

   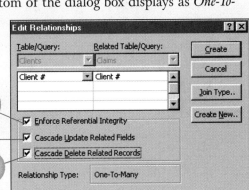

   Step 1g1

   Step 1g2

   Step 1g3

h. Click the <u>C</u>reate button. (This causes the Edit Relationships dialog box to close and the Relationships window to display showing a thick black line connecting Clients to Claims. At the Clients side, a *1* will appear and an infinity symbol ∞ will display at the Claims side of the thick black line.)

i. Click the Save button on the Relationship toolbar to save the relationship.

j. Print the relationships by completing the following steps:

1) At the Relationships window, click <u>F</u>ile and then Print <u>R</u>elationships. (This displays the Relationships report in Print Preview.)

2) Click the Print button on the Print Preview toolbar.

3) Click the <u>C</u>lose button to close Print Preview.

4) At the Report dialog box, click the Close button (contains an X) located in the upper right corner of the dialog box.

5) At the message asking if you want to save changes to the design of the report, click <u>N</u>o.

k. Close the Relationships window by clicking the Close button that displays at the right side of the Title bar.

2. Close the Southwest Insurance database file.

Once a relationship has been established between tables, clicking the Relationships button causes the Relationships window to display (rather than the Show Table dialog box). To create additional relationships, click <u>R</u>elationships on the Menu bar and then click Show <u>T</u>able. This displays the Show Table dialog box where you can specify the tables you need for creating another relationship.

exercise 3

Creating Additional One-to-Many Relationships in a Database File

1. Open the Southwest Insurance database file.

2. Create another one-to-many relationship between the Clients table and the Insurance table by completing the following steps:

a. Click the Relationships button that displays towards the right side of the Database toolbar.

b. At the Relationships window, click <u>R</u>elationships on the Menu bar and then click Show <u>T</u>able at the drop-down menu.

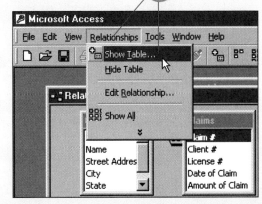

Step 2b

c. At the Show Table dialog box, click *Insurance* in the list box, and then click the <u>A</u>dd button. (You do not need to add the Clients table because it was added in exercise 2.)

d. Click the <u>C</u>lose button to close the Show Table dialog box.

e. At the Relationships window, drag the *Client #* field from the Clients table to the Insurance table by completing the following steps:

1) Position the arrow pointer on the *Client #* field that displays in the Clients box.

2) Hold down the left mouse button, drag the arrow pointer (with a *field* icon attached), to the *Client #* field in the Insurance box, and then release the mouse button. (This causes the Edit Relationships dialog box to display.)

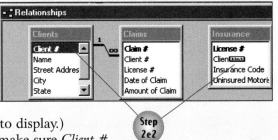

Step 2e2

f. At the Edit Relationships dialog box, make sure *Client #* displays in the <u>T</u>able/Query and <u>R</u>elated Table/Query list boxes and the relationship type at the bottom of the dialog box displays as *One-To-Many*.

g. Enforce the referential integrity of the relationship by completing the following steps:

1) Click <u>E</u>nforce Referential Integrity. (This makes the other two options available.)

2) Click Cascade <u>U</u>pdate Related Fields.

3) Click Cascade <u>D</u>elete Related Records.

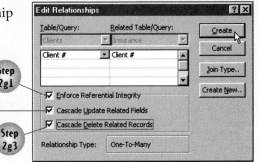

Step 2g1

Step 2g2

Step 2g3

h. Click the <u>C</u>reate button. (This causes the Edit Relationships dialog box to close and the Relationships window to display showing a thick black line connecting Clients to Insurance. At the Clients side, a *1* will appear and an infinity symbol ∞ will display at the Insurance side of the thick black line.)

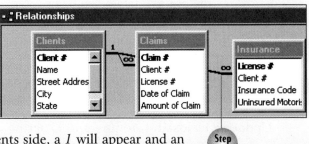

Step 2h

i. Click the Save button on the Relationship toolbar to save the relationship.

j. With the Relationships window still open, create the following one-to-many relationships by completing steps similar to those in 2b through 2i:

1) Create a relationship between *License #* in the Insurance table and the Claims table. (*License #* in the Insurance table is the "one" and *License #* in the Claims table is the "many.") At the Edit Relationships dialog box, be sure to choose Enforce Referential Integrity, Cascade Update Related Fields, and Cascade Delete Related Records.

2) Add the Coverage table to the Relationships window and then create a relationship between Insurance Code in the Insurance table and the Coverage table. (*Insurance Code* in the Coverage table is the "one" and *Insurance Code* in the Insurance table is the "many." At the Edit Relationships dialog box, be sure to choose Enforce Referential Integrity, Cascade Update Related Fields, and Cascade Delete Related Records.

k. Click the Save button on the Relationship toolbar.

l. Print the relationships by completing the following steps:

1) At the Relationships window, click File and then Print Relationships. (This displays the Relationships report in Print Preview.)

2) Click the Print button on the Print Preview toolbar.

3) Click the Close button to close Print Preview.

4) At the Report dialog box, click the Close button (contains an X) located in the upper right corner of the dialog box.

5) At the message asking if you want to save changes to the design of the report, click No.

m. Close the Relationships window by clicking the Close button that displays at the right side of the Title bar.

3. Close the Southwest Insurance database file.

In the relationship established in exercise 2, a record must first be added to the Clients table before a related record can be added to the Claims table. This is because you chose the Enforce Referential Integrity option at the Edit Relationships dialog box. Because you chose the two options Cascade Update Related Fields and Cascade Delete Related Records, records in the Clients table (the primary table) can be updated and/or deleted and related records in the Claims table (related table) will automatically be updated or deleted.

exercise 4

Updating Fields and Adding and Deleting Records in Related Database Tables

1. Open the Southwest Insurance database file.

2. Open the Clients table.

3. Change two client numbers in the Clients database (Access will automatically change it in the Claims table) by completing the following steps:

a. Make sure the Clients Table dialog box displays in the Datasheet View.

b. Click once in the *Client #* field for Paul Vuong containing the number *4300*.

c. Change the number from *4300* to *4308*.
d. Click once in the *Client #* field for Vernon Cook containing the number *7335*.
e. Change the number from *7335* to *7325*.
f. Click the Save button on the Table Datasheet toolbar.
g. Close the Clients table.
h. Open the Claims table. (Notice that the client numbers for Vernon Cook and Paul Vuong automatically changed.)
i. Close the Claims table.

4. Open the Clients table, make sure the table displays in Datasheet View, and then add the following records at the end of the table:

Client #	=	5508
Name	=	**Martina Bentley**
Street Address	=	**6503 Taylor Street**
City	=	**Scottsdale**
State	=	**AZ**
Zip Code	=	**85889**
Client #	=	2511
Name	=	**Keith Hammond**
Street Address	=	**21332 Janski Road**
City	=	**Glendale**
State	=	**AZ**
Zip Code	=	**85310**

5. With the Clients table still open, delete the record for Elaine Hueneka. At the message telling you that relationships that specify cascading deletes are about to cause records in this table and related tables to be deleted, click Yes.

6. Save, print, and then close the Clients table.

7. Open the Insurance table, make sure the table displays in Datasheet view, and then add the following records at the end of the table:

Clients : Table

	Client #	Name
+	3120	Spenser Winters
+	4308	Paul Vuong
+	7325	Vernon Cook
+	9383	Elaine Hueneka

Claims : Table

	Claim #	Client #	License #
▶	102394	9383	776 ERU
	104366	7325	984 CWS
	121039	4308	877 BNN
	153001	9383	776 ERU
*			

Clients : Table

	Client #	Name	Street Address	City	State	Zip Code
+	3120	Spenser Winters	21329 132nd Street	Glendale	AZ	85310
+	4308	Paul Vuong	3451 South Varner	Glendale	AZ	85901
+	7325	Vernon Cook	22134 Cactus Drive	Phoenix	AZ	85344
+	9383	Elaine Hueneka	9088 Graham Road	Scottsdale	AZ	85889
+	5508	Martina Bentley	6503 Taylor Street	Scottsdale	AZ	85889
+	2511	Keith Hammond	21332 Janski Road	Glendale	AZ	85310
*						

Clients : Table — Delete Record

	Client #	Name	Street Address	City	State	Zip Code
+	3120	Spenser Winters	21329 132nd Street	Glendale	AZ	85310
+	4308	Paul Vuong	3451 South Varner	Glendale	AZ	85901
+	7325	Vernon Cook	22134 Cactus Drive	Phoenix	AZ	85344
▶ +	9383	Elaine Hueneka	9088 Graham Road	Scottsdale	AZ	85889
+	5508	Martina Bentley	6503 Taylor Street	Scottsdale	AZ	85889
+	2511	Keith Hammond	21332 Janski Road	Glendale	AZ	85310

Insurance : Table

	License #	Client #	Insurance Cod	Uninsured Mot
+	310 YTV	3120	F	☑
+	341 VIT	3120	F	☑
+	877 BNN	4308	L	☑
+	984 CWS	7325	L	☑
+	422 RTW	5508	L	☑
+	130 YWR	5508	F	☐
+	795 GRT	2511	L	☑

License #	=	422 RTW
Client #	=	5508
Insurance Code	=	L
Uninsured Motorist	=	Yes

License #	=	130 YWR
Client #	=	5508
Insurance Code	=	F
Uninsured Motorist	=	No

License #	=	795 GRT
Client #	=	2511
Insurance Code	=	L
Uninsured Motorist	=	Yes

8. Save, print, and then close the Insurance table.

9. Open the Claims table, make sure the table displays in Datasheet view, and then add the following record:

Claims : Table				
Claim #	Client #	License #	Date of Claim	Amount of Claim
104366	7325	984 CWS	1/18/99	$834.95
121039	4308	877 BNN	2/3/99	$5,230.00
130057	2511	795 GRT	3/4/99	186.40

Step 9

Claim #	=	130057
Client #	=	2511
License #	=	795 GRT
Date of Claim	=	3/4/99
Amount of Claim	=	$186.40

10. Save and then print the Claims table.

11. With the Claims table still open, try to enter a record for a client who has not been entered in the Clients table by completing the following steps (Access will not allow this because of the one-to-many relationship that was established in exercise 2):

a. Add the following record to the Claims table:

Claim #	=	201221
Client #	=	5824
License #	=	640 TRS
Date of Claim	=	3/11/99
Amount of Claim	=	$895.25

b. Click the Save button on the Table Datasheet toolbar.

c. Click the Close button to close the Claims table. This causes a message to display telling you that the record cannot be added or changed because a related record is required in the Clients table. At this message, click OK.

d. A message displays warning telling you that Access cannot save the table, that closing the object will cause the changes to be made, and asking if you want to close the database object. At this warning, click Yes.

12. Close the Southwest Insurance database file.

Editing and Deleting a Relationship

The Relationships window will display any relationship that has been defined between database tables.

Hint

Changes can be made to a relationship that has been established between database tables. The relationship can also be deleted. To edit a relationship, open the database file containing the tables with the relationship, and then click the Relationships button on the Database toolbar; or click Tools and then Relationships. This displays the Relationships window with the related database tables displayed in boxes. Position the arrow pointer on the thin portion of one of the black lines that connects the related tables and then click the *right* mouse button. This causes a pop-up menu to display. At this pop-up menu, click the left mouse button on Edit <u>R</u>elationship. This displays the Edit Relationships dialog box such as the one shown in figure 20.5, where you can change the current relationship.

To delete a relationship between tables, display the related tables in the Relationships window. Position the arrow pointer on the thin portion of the black line connecting the related tables and then click the *right* mouse button. At the pop-up menu that displays, click the left mouse button on <u>D</u>elete. At the message asking if you are sure you want to permanently delete the selected relationship from your database, click <u>Y</u>es.

Displaying Related Records in a Subdatasheet

When a relationship is established between tables, you can view and edit fields in related tables with a subdatasheet. Figure 20.8 displays the Clients database table with the subdatasheet displayed for the client Spenser Winters. The subdatasheet displays the fields in the Insurance table related to Spenser Winters. Use this subdatasheet to view information and also to edit information in the Clients table as well as the Insurance table. Changes made to fields in a subdatasheet affect the table and any related table.

A plus symbol (+) displays before each record in the Clients table shown in figure 20.8. Access automatically inserts plus symbols before each record in a table that is joined to another table by a one-to-many relationship.

figure
20.8

Table with Subdatasheet Displayed

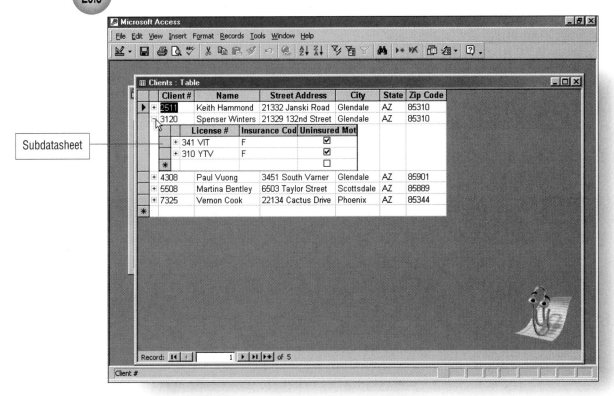

To create a subdatasheet, display the table that is the "one" in the one-to-many relationship. Click the plus symbol preceding the record for which you want to display fields in a related table. This displays the Insert Subdatasheet dialog box shown in figure 20.9. At this dialog box, click the desired table in the list box, and then click OK. The subdatasheet is inserted below the record and contains fields from the related table. To remove the subdatasheet, click the minus sign preceding the record. (The plus symbol turns into the minus symbol when a subdatasheet displays.)

Insert Subdatasheet Dialog Box

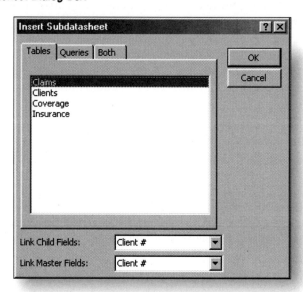

Specify a different subdatasheet in a table by clicking the Insert option on the Menu bar and then clicking Subdatasheet. This displays the Insert Subdatasheet dialog box shown in figure 20.9 where you can specify the desired table.

Viewing and Editing a Subdatasheet

1. Open the Southwest Insurance database file.
2. Open the Clients table.
3. Display a subdatasheet with fields in the Claims table by completing the following steps:
   a. Click the plus symbol that displays at the left side of the first row (the row for Keith Hammond).

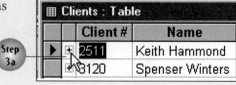

b. At the Insert Subdatasheet dialog box, click *Claims* in the list box, and then click OK.

4. Display subdatasheets for each of the remaining records by clicking the plus symbol that displays before each of the remaining four rows.

5. Remove subdatasheets for each record by clicking the minus symbol that displays before each record.

6. Suppose that the client, Vernon Cook, has moved to a new address and purchased insurance for a new car. Display the Insurance subdatasheet and make changes to fields in the Clients table and the Insurance table by completing the following steps:

a. Click Insert on the Menu bar and then click Subdatasheet at the drop-down menu.

b. At the Insert Subdatasheet dialog box, click *Insurance* in the list box, and then click OK.

c. Click the plus symbol at the beginning of the row for Vernon Cook.

d. Change his street address from *22135 Cactus Drive* to *1230 South Mesa*.

e. Change his Zip Code from *85344* to *86201*.

f. Add the following information in the second row in the Insurance subdatasheet:

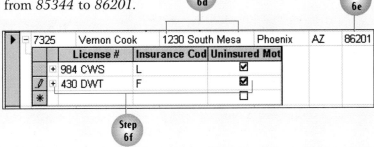

		License #	Insurance Cod	Uninsured Mot			
►	− 7325	Vernon Cook	1230 South Mesa	Phoenix	AZ	86201	
	+	984 CWS	L	☑			
✎	+	430 DWT	F	☑			
✱				☐			

License #	=	**430 DWT**
Insurance Code	=	**F**
Insurance Motorist	=	**Yes**

g. Click the Save button on the Table Datasheet toolbar.

h. Close the Clients table.

7. Open the Clients table, print it, and then close it.

8. Open the Insurance table, print it, and then close it.

9. Close the Southwest Insurance database table.

Creating a Database Table Using the Table Wizard

Access, like other programs in the Microsoft Office suite, contains a wizard that can help design an entire database as well as a database table. The database Table Wizard helps you design a table by offering possible field choices with data types already assigned. A table wizard makes the creation of a database table quick and efficient. If the Table Wizard does not offer the exact field name you require, you can edit a field name to personalize it. In exercise 6, you will use the Table Wizard to create a database table for information on products used within a medical clinic.

exercise 6

Using a Table Wizard to Create a Database File

1. Create a database table for information on products used in MedSafe Clinic by completing the following steps:
   a. Start at the blank Access window and then click the New button on the Database toolbar or click File and then New.
   b. At the New dialog box with the General tab and the *Database* icon selected, click OK.
   c. At the File New Database dialog box, make sure the proper drive is selected, key **MedSafe Clinic** in the File name text box, and then press Enter or click the Create button.
   d. At the MedSafe Clinic Database dialog box, double-click *Create table by using wizard* in the list box.
   e. At the first Table Wizard dialog box shown in figure 20.10, click *Products* in the Sample Tables list box. (This changes the fields in the Sample Fields list box.)
   f. Choose some of the sample fields in the Sample Fields list box and add them to the Fields in my new table list box by completing the following steps:

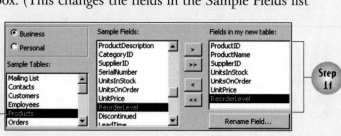

1) With *ProductID* already selected in the Sample Fields list box, click the button containing the greater than symbol (>) that displays between the Sample Fields list box and the Fields in my new table list box. (This inserts *ProductID* in the Fields in my new table list box and also selects *ProductName* in the Sample Fields list box.)

2) With *ProductName* selected in the Sample Fields list box, click the button containing the > symbol. (This adds *ProductName* to the Fields in my new table list box.)

3) Click once on *SupplierID* in the Sample Fields list box and then click the button containing the > symbol.

4) Click once on *UnitsInStock* in the Sample Fields list box and then click the button containing the > symbol.

5) With *UnitsOnOrder* already selected in the Sample Fields list box, click the button containing the > symbol.

6) With *UnitPrice* already selected in the Sample Fields list box, click the button containing the > symbol.

7) With *ReorderLevel* already selected in the Sample Fields list box, click the button containing the > symbol.

g. Click the <u>N</u>ext button located at the bottom of the dialog box.

h. At the second Table Wizard dialog box shown in figure 20.11, the wizard offers the name *Products* for the table name and also will set a primary key for the table. These choices are appropriate so click the <u>N</u>ext button at the bottom of the dialog box.

i. At the third Table Wizard dialog box shown in figure 20.12, the wizard has already selected *Enter data directly into the table*. This is appropriate for this exercise, so click the <u>F</u>inish button that displays at the bottom right corner of the dialog box.

j. At the Products Table dialog box shown in figure 20.13, notice that *AutoNumber* automatically displays in the *Product ID* field. This is because the Table Wizard assigned the data type *AutoNumber* to the field. (Access will insert a *1* in this field as soon as you move to the second field in the *Product ID* field.) Press Tab to move the insertion point to the next field *(Product Name)*.

k. Key the following in the specified fields (do not key anything in the *Product ID* field; simply press the Tab key and let Access insert the number):

Product Name	=	**Latex gloves**
Supplier ID	=	3
Units In Stock	=	243
Units On Order	=	0
Unit Price	=	0.50
Reorder Level	=	200
Product Name	=	**Syringes**
Supplier ID	=	1
Units In Stock	=	58
Units On Order	=	75
Unit Price	=	0.35
Reorder Level	=	75

	Product Name	=	1-inch gauze pads
	Supplier ID	=	4
	Units In Stock	=	144
	Units On Order	=	0
	Unit Price	=	0.05
	Reorder Level	=	125

	Product Name	=	Tongue depressors
	Supplier ID	=	1
	Units In Stock	=	85
	Units On Order	=	100
	Unit Price	=	0.03
	Reorder Level	=	100

Products : Table

	Product ID	Product Name	Supplier ID	Units In Stock	Units On Order	Unit Price	Reorder Level
	1	Latex gloves	3	243	0	$0.50	200
	2	Syringes	1	58	75	$0.35	75
	3	1-inch gauze pa	4	144	0	$0.05	125
	4	Tongue depress	1	85	100	$0.03	100
*	(AutoNumber)						

Step 1k

   l. Automatically adjust the column widths for all columns containing data.
   m. After entering the data and adjusting the column widths, click the Save button on the Table Datasheet toolbar.
  2. Change the page orientation to landscape and then print the Products table.
  3. Close the Products table.
  4. Close the MedSafe Clinic database file.

figure

20.10

First Table Wizard Dialog Box

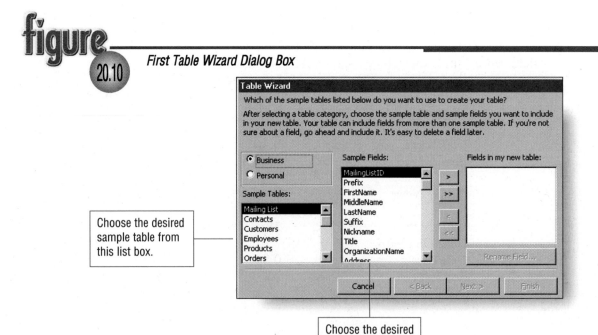

Choose the desired sample table from this list box.

Choose the desired sample fields from this list box.

figure
20.11

Second Table Wizard Dialog Box

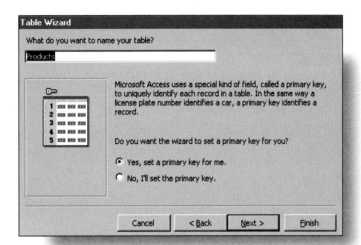

figure
20.12

Third Table Wizard Dialog Box

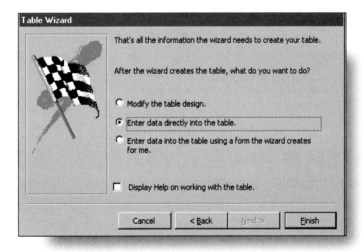

figure
20.13

Products Table Dialog Box

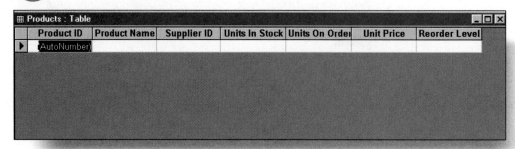

In exercise 6, step 1f, you added fields to the Fields in my new table list box by selecting the desired field in the Sample Fields list box and then clicking the button containing the greater than symbol (>). Other buttons display by the button containing the greater than symbol. Click the button containing two greater than symbols (>>) and all fields in the Sample Fields list box are inserted in the Fields in my new table list box. If you want to remove a field from the Fields in my new table list box, select the field, and then click the button containing the less than symbol (<). Click the button containing two less than symbols (<<) to remove all fields from the Fields in my new table list box.

The MedSafe Clinic database file created in exercise 6 contains only one table. Use the Table Wizard to create other tables within the same database file. In exercise 7, you will use the Table Wizard to create a table containing information about suppliers used by MedSafe Clinic.

When a second or subsequent table is created in a database file using the Table Wizard, a relationship can be created between database tables. In exercise 7, you will be creating a one-to-many relationship using the Table Wizard. The Suppliers table you create in exercise 7 will be identified as the "one" and the Products table you created in exercise 6 will be identified as the "many."

Creating Another Table and Relating Tables Using the Table Wizard

1. Create a database table for suppliers used by MedSafe Clinic by completing the following steps:
   a. At the blank Access window, click the Open button on the Database toolbar; or click File and then Open.
   b. At the Open dialog box, double-click *MedSafe Clinic* in the list box.
   c. At the MedSafe Clinic Database window, double-click *Create table by using wizard* in the list box.

d. At the first Table Wizard dialog box (see figure 20.10), click *Suppliers* in the Sample Tables list box. (You will need to scroll down the list.)

e. Add the following fields in the Sample Fields list box to the Fields in my new table list box (for help, refer to exercise 6, step 1f):

SupplierID
SupplierName
Address
City
StateOrProvince
PostalCode
(Note: This is
in a different
order than shown in the Sample Fields list box.)
PhoneNumber
E-mailAddress

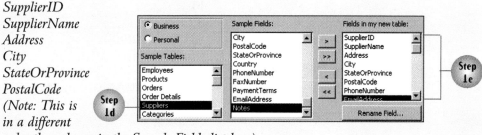

f. After inserting the fields above in the Fields in my new table list box, click the Next button located at the bottom of the dialog box.

g. At the second Table Wizard dialog box, the wizard offers the name *Suppliers* for the database table name and also will set a primary key for the table. These choices are appropriate so click the Next button at the bottom of the dialog box.

h. At the third Table Wizard dialog box shown in figure 20.14, create a one-to-many relationship between *Suppliers* (the "one") and *Products* (the "many") by completing the following steps:

1) Click the Relationships button that displays toward the bottom right side of the dialog box.

2) At the Relationships dialog box shown in figure 20.15, click the option button that displays before *One record in the 'Suppliers' table will match many records in the 'Products' table.*

3) Click OK to close the dialog box.

i. At the Table Wizard dialog box, click Next.

j. At the Table Wizard dialog box telling you that the wizard has all the information it needs to create the table, make sure *Enter data directly into the table* is selected, and then click Finish.

Relationships

How is your new 'Suppliers' table related to the 'Products' table?

○ The tables aren't related.

◉ One record in the 'Suppliers' table will match many records in the 'Products' table.

○ One record in the 'Products' table will match many records in the 'Suppliers' table.

k. At the Suppliers Table dialog box, key the following in the specified fields (the table wizard will automatically insert a number in the *Supplier ID* field):

Supplier Name	=	**Robicheaux Suppliers**
Address	=	**3200 Linden Drive**
City	=	**Baton Rouge**
State	=	**LA**
Postal Code	=	**70552**
Phone Number	=	**(318) 555-3411**
E-mail Address	=	**robi@fictional.med.com**

Supplier Name	=	**Quality Medical Supplies**
Address	=	**211 South Fourth Avenue**
City	=	**Tampa**
State	=	**FL**
Postal Code	=	**33562**
Phone Number	=	**(813) 555-8900**
E-mail Address	=	**qms@fictional.med.com**

Supplier Name	=	**Peachtree Medical Supplies**
Address	=	**764 Harmon Way**
City	=	**Atlanta**
State	=	**GA**
Postal Code	=	**73780**
Phone Number	=	**(404) 555-6474**
E-mail Address	=	**peachmed@fictional.med.com**

Supplier Name	=	**Lafferty Company**
Address	=	**12031 Ruston Way**
City	=	**Atlanta**
State	=	**GA**
Postal Code	=	**73125**
Phone Number	=	**(404) 555-8225**
E-mail Address	=	**lafferty@fictional.med.com**

Ⅲ Suppliers : Table

	Supplier Name	Address	City	State/Province	Postal Code	Phone Number	Email Address
⊞	Robicheaux Sup	3200 Linden Dri	Baton Rouge	LA	70552-	(318) 555-3411	robi@fictional.m
⊞	Quality Medical	211 South Fourt	Tampa	FL	33562-	(813) 555-8900	qms@fictional.r
⊞	Peachtree Medi	764 Harmon Wa	Atlanta	GA	73780-	(404) 555-6474	peachmed@fict
⊞	Lafferty Compar	12031 Ruston V	Atlanta	GA	73125-	(404) 555-8225	lafferty@fictiona

Step 1k

l. Automatically adjust the column widths for all columns containing data.

m. Click the Save button on the Table Datasheet toolbar to save the Suppliers table.

2. Change the top and bottom margins to *0.3* inches, change the page orientation to *landscape*, and then print the Suppliers table.

3. Close the Suppliers table.

4. Close the MedSafe Clinic database file.

figure

20.14

Third Table Wizard Dialog Box

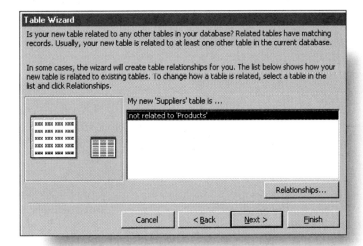

figure

20.15

Relationships Dialog Box

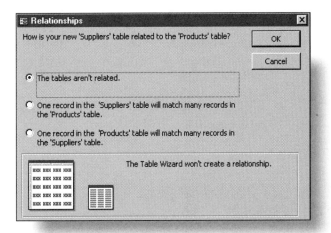

In exercise 7, a one-to-many relationship was created between the Suppliers and Products database tables. In this relationship, a record for a supplier must first be created in the Suppliers table before the supplier number can be used in a record in the Products table. In exercise 8, you will add a new supplier to the Suppliers table and then use that supplier in a record in the Products table.

exercise 8

Adding Records to the Suppliers and Products Database Tables

1. Open the MedSafe Clinic database file.
2. Open the Suppliers table.
3. With Suppliers open in Datasheet View, add the following record at the end of the table:

Supplier Name	=	**National Products**
Address	=	**2192 Second Street**
City	=	**Little Rock**
State	=	**AR**
Postal Code	=	**72203**
Phone Number	=	**(501) 555-0551**
E-mail Address	=	**natprod@fictional.med.com**

4. Save the Suppliers table.
5. Change the top and bottom margins to *0.3* inches, change the page orientation to *landscape*, and then print the Suppliers table.

Step 3

	Suppliers : Table			
	Supplier ID	Supplier Name	Address	City
+	1	Robicheaux Suppliers	3200 Linden Drive	Baton Ro
+	2	Quality Medical Supplies	211 South Fourth Avenue	Tampa
+	3	Peachtree Medical Supplies	764 Harmon Way	Atlanta
+	4	Lafferty Company	12031 Ruston Way	Atlanta
+	5	National Products	2192 Second Street	Little Roc

6. Close the Suppliers table.
7. Open the Products table and then add the following records at the end of the table:

Product Name	=	**Cotton swabs**
Supplier ID	=	**5**
Units In Stock	=	**1345**
Units On Order	=	**1000**
Unit Price	=	**0.03**
Reorder Level	=	**1500**

Product Name	=	**Thermometer covers**
Supplier ID	=	**2**
Units In Stock	=	**414**
Units On Order	=	**250**
Unit Price	=	**0.02**
Reorder Level	=	**450**

Step 8

8. Delete the record for tongue depressors.
9. Adjust the column width for Product Name.
10. Save the Products table.
11. Change the page orientation to *landscape* and then print the Products table.
12. Close the Products table.
13. Close the MedSafe Clinic database file.

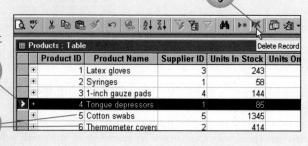

Delete Record

	Products : Table			
	Product ID	Product Name	Supplier ID	Units In Stock	Units On
+	1	Latex gloves	3	243	
+	2	Syringes	1	58	
+	3	1-inch gauze pads	4	144	
+	4	Tongue depressors	1	85	
+	5	Cotton swabs	5	1345	
+	6	Thermometer covers	2	414	

Step 8

Step 7

- ► Access is a relational database software program where database tables can be created that have a relation or connection to one another.

- ► When planning a database table, take time to determine how to break down the required data and what relationships will need to be defined to eliminate data redundancies.

- ► In a database table there must be at least one field that is unique so that one record can be distinguished from another. A field with a unique value is considered a primary key.

- ► In a field defined as a primary key, duplicate values are not allowed in the primary field and Access also expects a value in each record in the primary key field.

- ► Define a primary key field with the Primary Key button on the Table Design toolbar.

- ► A primary key field included in another database table is referred to as a foreign key. Unlike a primary key field, a foreign key field can contain duplicate data.

- ► In Access, one database table can be related to another by performing a join. When database tables that have a common field are joined, data can be extracted from both tables as if they were one large table.

- ► A one-to-many relationship can be created between database tables in a database file. In this relationship, a record must be added to the "one" database table before it can be added to the "many" database table.

- ► A relationship between tables can be edited and/or deleted.

- ► Access contains a Print Relationships Wizard you can use to print a report displaying the relationships between tables.

- ► When a relationship is established between tables, you can view and edit fields in related tables with a subdatasheet.

- ► To display a subdatasheet, display the Insert Subdatasheet dialog box (by clicking the plus symbol at the beginning of a record or by clicking Insert and then Subdatasheet), click the desired table in the list box, and then click OK.

- ► Turn off the display of a subdatasheet by clicking the minus symbol at the beginning of a record.

- ► Access contains a Table Wizard that helps create database tables. A relationship can be established between database tables during the Table Wizard steps.

commands review

	Mouse/Keyboard
Identify primary key in database table	Position insertion point in row in database table, click Primary Key button on Table Design toolbar
Display Edit Relationships dialog box	At the Relationships window, drag common field from primary table to related table
Print database relationships	At Relationships window, click File and then Print Relationships; then click Print button on Print Preview toolbar

thinking offline ....

Completion: In the space provided at the right, indicate the correct term, symbol, or number.

1. A primary key field must contain unique data while this type of key field can contain duplicate data.

2. In Access, one database can be related to another, which is generally referred to as performing this.

3. In a one-to-many relationship, the table containing the "one" is referred to as this.

4. In a one-to-many relationship, the table containing the "many" is referred to as this.

5. In a one-to-many relationship, Access follows a set of rules that enforces consistency between related tables and is referred to as this.

6. In related tables, this number displays near the black line next to the primary table.

7. In related tables, this symbol displays near the black line next to the related table.

8. The black line that connects related tables is referred to as this.

9. Click this symbol at the beginning of a record in a related table to display the Insert Subdatasheet dialog box.

10. Turn off the display of a subdatasheet by clicking this symbol that displays at the beginning of the record.

11. Click this button at the first Table Wizard dialog box to add the selected field in the Sample Fields list box to the Fields in my new table list box.

12. Click this button at the first Table Wizard dialog box to remove *all* fields in the Fields in my new table list box.

13. Suppose you have created a database table named Committees within the database file named Members. The Committees table contains a field named *Member #* that you decide should be identified as the primary key field. List the steps you would complete to identify *Member #* as the primary key field (you are beginning at a blank Access window).

14. List the steps you would complete to create a one-to-many relationship between the Member Information table and the Committees table in the Members database file. The primary key field in the Member Information table is *Member #*. (You are beginning at the Members : Database window.)

_____

_____

working hands-on

Assessment 1

1. Use Access to create a database for keeping track of books. Name the database file Books. Name the first database table you create Author Information and include the following fields in the table (you determine the data type, field size, and description):

    Field Name
    Author # (primary key)
    First Name
    Last Name ·
    Middle Initial

2. After creating the database table with the fields shown above and defining the primary key, save the table and name it Author Information. Switch to Datasheet View and then enter the following data in the table:

Author #	=	1
First Name	=	**Branson**
Last Name	=	**Walters**
Middle Initial	=	**A.**

Author #	=	2
First Name	=	**Christiana**
Last Name	=	**Copeland**
Middle Initial	=	**M.**

Author #	=	3
First Name	=	**Shirley**
Last Name	=	**Romero**
Middle Initial	=	**E.**

Author #	=	4
First Name	=	**Jeffrey**
Last Name	=	**Fiedler**
Middle Initial	=	**R.**

3. Automatically adjust the width of columns.
4. Save, print, and then close the Author Information table.
5. At the Books database file, create another table with book information with the following fields (you determine the data type, field size, and description):

Field Name
ISBN (primary key)
Author #
Title
Category Code
Price

6. After creating the database table with the fields shown above and defining the primary key, save the table and name it Book Information. Switch to Datasheet View and then enter the following data in the table:

ISBN	=	12-6543-9008-7
Author #	=	4
Title	=	**Today's Telecommunications**
Category Code	=	**B**
Price	=	**$34.95**
ISBN	=	09-5225-5466-6
Author #	=	2
Title	=	**Marketing in the Global Economy**
Category Code	=	**M**
Price	=	**$42.50**
ISBN	=	23-9822-7645-0
Author #	=	1
Title	=	**International Business Strategies**
Category Code	=	**B**
Price	=	**$45.00**
ISBN	=	08-4351-4890-3
Author #	=	3
Title	=	**Technological Advances**
Category Code	=	**B**
Price	=	**$36.95**

7. Automatically adjust the width of columns (to accommodate the longest entry).
8. Save, print, and then close the Book Information table.
9. At the Books database file, create another table with category information with the following fields (you determine the data type, field size, and description):
    Field Name
    Category Code (primary key)
    Category
10. After creating the database table with the fields shown above and defining the primary key, save the table and name it Category. Switch to Datasheet View and then enter the following data in the table:

Category Code	=	**B**
Category	=	**Business**
Category Code	=	**M**
Category	=	**Marketing**

11. Save, print, and then close the Category table.
12. Close the Books database file.

Assessment 2

1. Open the Books database file and then create the following relationships:
   a. Create a one-to-many relationship with the *Author #* field in the Author Information table (the "one") and the *Author #* field in the Book Information table (the "many"). (At the Edit Relationships dialog box, choose Enforce Referential Integrity, Cascade Update Related Fields, and Cascade Delete Related Records.)
   b. Create a one-to-many relationship with the *Category Code* field in the Category table (the "one") and the *Category Code* field in the Book Information table (the "many.") (At the Edit Relationships dialog box, choose Enforce Referential Integrity, Cascade Update Related Fields, and Cascade Delete Related Records.)
2. Print the relationships.
3. After creating, saving, and printing the relationships, add the following record to the Author Information table:

Author #	=	5
First Name	=	Glenna
Last Name	=	Zener-Young
Middle Initial	=	A.

4. Adjust the colunm width for the *Last Name* field.
5. Save, print, and then close the Author Information table.
6. Add the following records to the Book Information table:

ISBN	=	23-8931-0084-7
Author #	=	2
Title	=	**Practical Marketing Strategies**
Category	=	M
Price	=	$28.50
ISBN	=	87-4009-7134-6
Author #	=	5
Title	=	**Selling More**
Category	=	M
Price	=	$40.25

7. Save, print, and then close the Book Information table.
8. Close the Books database file.

Assessment 3

1. Use the Table Wizard to create two tables in a database file named Lafferty Company. Create the first table with the following specifications:
   a. At the first Table Wizard dialog box, click *Employees* in the Sample Tables list box.
   b. Insert the following fields located in the Sample Fields list box to the Fields in my new table list box:

      Employee ID
      First Name
      Middle Name
      Last Name
      Title
      Extension

   c. At the second Table Wizard dialog box, accept the table name of *Employees* offered by the wizard.

d. At the third Table Wizard dialog box, leave *Enter data directly into the table* selected, and then click <u>F</u>inish.

e. Key the following data in the specified fields (the *Employee ID* field will automatically be assigned a number):

First Name	=	**Samantha**
Middle Name	=	**Lee**
Last Name	=	**Murray**
Title	=	**Account Manager**
Extension	=	**412**
First Name	=	**Ralph**
Middle Name	=	**Edward**
Last Name	=	**Sorrell**
Title	=	**Director**
Extension	=	**432**
First Name	=	**Cheryl**
Middle Name	=	**Janet**
Last Name	=	**Plaschka**
Title	=	**Assistant Director**
Extension	=	**549**
First Name	=	**Brandon**
Middle Name	=	**Michael**
Last Name	=	**Perrault**
Title	=	**Administrative Assistant**
Extension	=	**653**
First Name	=	**Leland**
Middle Name	=	**John**
Last Name	=	**Nitsche**
Title	=	**Account Manager**
Extension	=	**894**

f. Adjust the column widths.

g. Save the Employees table, change the orientation to landscape, and then print the table.

h. Close the Employees table.

2. Create a second table with the following specifications:

a. At the first Table Wizard dialog box, click *Expenses* in the Sample Tables list box. (You will need to scroll down the list to display *Expenses*.)

b. Insert the following fields located in the Sample Fields list box to the Fields in my new table list box:

> *Expense ID*
> *Employee ID*
> *Expense Type*
> *Purpose of Expense*
> *Amount Spent*
> *Date Submitted*

c. At the second Table Wizard dialog box, accept the table name of *Expenses* offered by the wizard and let the wizard set the primary key.

d. At the third Table Wizard dialog box, create a one-to-many relationship where one record in the Employees table will match many records in the Expenses table. (*Hint: You must click the Relationships button at the third Table Wizard dialog box.*)

e. At the fourth Table Wizard dialog box, leave *Enter data directly into the table* selected, and then click <u>F</u>inish.

f. Key the following data in the specified fields (the *Expense ID* field will automatically be assigned a number):

Employee ID	=	1
Expense Type	=	Travel
Purpose of Expense	=	Marketing Conference
Amount Spent	=	$215.75
Date Submitted	=	2/4/99
Employee ID	=	2
Expense Type	=	Lodging
Purpose of Expense	=	Finance Conference
Amount Spent	=	$568.50
Date Submitted	=	2/10/99
Employee ID	=	3
Expense Type	=	Travel
Purpose of Expense	=	Management Workshop
Amount Spent	=	$422.70
Date Submitted	=	2/12/99
Employee ID	=	1
Expense Type	=	Business dinner
Purpose of Expense	=	Customer Relations
Amount Spent	=	$124.90
Date Submitted	=	2/16/99
Employee ID	=	4
Expense Type	=	Printing
Purpose of Expense	=	Promotional Literature
Amount Spent	=	$96.00
Date Submitted	=	2/18/99
Employee ID	=	1
Expense Type	=	Travel
Purpose of Expense	=	Customer Contact
Amount Spent	=	$184.35
Date Submitted	=	2/19/99

g. Adjust the column widths.

h. Save the Expenses table, change the orientation to landscape, and then print the table.

i. Close the Expenses table.

3. Close the Lafferty Company database file.

Assessment 4

1. Open the Employees table in the Lafferty Company database file and then add the following records:

First Name	=	**Laurie**
Middle Name	=	**Jean**
Last Name	=	**Noviello**
Title	=	**Account Manager**
Extension	=	**568**

First Name	=	**Roderick**
Middle Name	=	**Earl**
Last Name	=	**Lobdell**
Title	=	**Assistant Director**
Extension	=	**553**

2. Delete the record for Leland John Nitsche.
3. Save the Employees table and then print the table in landscape orientation.
4. Close the Employees table.
5. Open the Expenses table and then add the following records:

Employee ID	=	**4**
Expense Type	=	**Printing**
Purpose of Expense	=	**Product Brochure**
Amount Spent	=	**$510.00**
Date Submitted	=	**2/22/99**

Employee ID	=	**5**
Expense Type	=	**Travel**
Purpose of Expense	=	**Customer Contact**
Amount Spent	=	**$75.20**
Date Submitted	=	**2/23/99**

6. Save the Expenses table.
7. Print the Expenses table in landscape orientation.
8. Close the Expenses table and then close the Lafferty Company database file.

Assessment 5

1. In this chapter, you learned to create a one-to-many relationship between database tables. In Access, a many-to-many relationship can also be created between database tables. Use the Access Help feature to read and print information on creating a many-to-many relationship between database tables.
2. After reading the information, open Microsoft Word, and then create a memo to your instructor and include the following:
   a. Description of a many-to-many relationship.
   b. Steps to create a many-to-many relationship.
   c. At least one example of a situation in which a many-to-many relationship would be useful.
3. Save the Word document and name it Access Ch 20, SA 05.
4. Print and then close Access Ch 20, SA 05.

Creating Forms, Reports, Mailing Labels, and Charts

(Note: There is no Chapter 21 folder to copy from the CD. Instead, you will be copying the Outdoor Options database file from the CD to your disk.)

Access offers a variety of options for presenting data on the screen for easier data entry or for presenting data in printed form. In this chapter, you will learn to create a form from database tables, improving the data display and making data entry easier. You will also learn to prepare reports from data in a database table. A report lets you specify how data will appear when printed. In a previous chapter, you learned how to create mailing labels in Word. Mailing labels can also be created easily in Access using the Label Wizard. In previous chapters you learned to create charts from data in an Excel worksheet. A chart can also be created with data from a database table. In this chapter you will learn to create a chart with the Chart Wizard.

Creating a Form

Access offers a variety of options for presenting data in a more easily read and attractive format. When entering data in a database table at the Datasheet view, multiple records are displayed at the same time. If there are several fields within each record, you may not be able to view all fields within a record at the same time. If you create a form, generally all fields for a record are displayed and visible at one time.

Several methods are available for creating a form. In this section, you will learn how to use AutoForm to insert existing data into a form, use the Form Wizard to create a form, and use the Form Wizard to create a form with fields from related database tables.

Creating a Form Using Autoform

Use a form to easily enter, edit, and/or view data.

After creating a form, save it before working with it.

Data in a database table can be viewed, added, or edited in the Datasheet view. You can perform these functions on data inserted in a form. The advantage to a form is that the functions are generally easier to perform because the data is easier to read. Access offers the AutoForm feature, which automatically copies data in a database table and creates a form. In exercise 1, you will be using AutoForm to create a form for data contained in the Orders table, which is part of the Outdoor Options database file. When AutoForm creates the form, the first record will display as shown in figure 21.1.

Form Created from Data in Orders Table

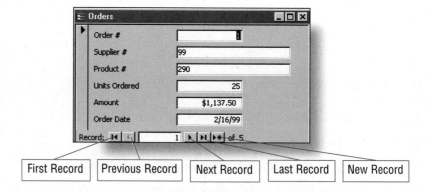

Navigation buttons display along the bottom of the first Orders record. The function each button performs is shown in figure 21.1. Using these navigation buttons, you can display the next record in the database table, the previous record, the first record, the last record, and a new record.

Printing a Form

Print a form in the same manner as a database table. If desired, changes can be made to the page margins and/or page orientation at the Page Setup dialog box. To display this dialog box, click File and then Page Setup. Print all records in the form by clicking the Print button on the Database toolbar. If you want to print a specific record, display the desired record, and then display the Print dialog box by clicking File and then Print. At the Print dialog box, click the Selected Record(s) option, and then click OK.

Creating a Form with the Products Database File

1. Copy the Outdoor Options database file on the CD that accompanies this textbook to your disk and remove the read-only attribute by completing the following steps:
   a. Insert the CD that accompanies this textbook.
   b. Copy the Outdoor Options database file from the CD to your disk.
   c. Remove the read-only attribute from the Outdoor Options database located on your disk by completing the following steps:
      1) In Access, display the Open dialog box with the drive active containing your disk.
      2) Click once on the Outdoor Options database file name.
      3) Click the Tools button on the Open dialog box toolbar and then click Properties at the drop-down list.
      4) At the Outdoor Options Properties dialog box with the General tab selected, click the Read-only option in the Attributes section to remove the check mark.
      5) Click OK to close the Outdoor Options Properties dialog box.
2. Use the AutoForm feature to create a form with the data in the Orders table by completing the following steps:
   a. Open the Outdoor Options database file.
   b. At the Outdoor Options Database window, click *Orders* in the list box.
   c. Click the down-pointing triangle at the right of the New Object button on the Database toolbar.
   d. At the drop-down menu that displays, click the AutoForm option.
   e. When the first record displays, display the next record by clicking the button toward the bottom of the Orders dialog box (see figure 21.1) that contains a right-pointing triangle.
   f. Practice displaying different records using the navigation buttons along the bottom of the Orders dialog box.
3. Save the form by completing the following steps:
   a. Click the Save button on the Form View toolbar.
   b. At the Save As dialog box, with Orders inserted in the Form Name dialog box, click OK.
4. Print all records in the form by clicking the Print button on the Form View toolbar.
5. Close the Orders form.
6. Close the Outdoor Options database file.

Adding/Deleting Records

New Record

Delete Record

Navigate through records in a form using the navigation buttons that display along the bottom of the form, as shown in figure 21.1. Add a new record to the form by clicking the New Record button that displays along the bottom of the form and contains a right–pointing triangle followed by an asterisk. You can also add a new record to a form by clicking the New Record button on the Form View toolbar that displays towards the top of the screen.

To delete a record, display the record, and then click the Delete Record button on the Form View toolbar. At the message telling you that the record will be deleted permanently, click Yes.

exercise

Adding and Deleting Records in a Form

1. Open the Outdoor Options database file.
2. At the Outdoor Options Database window, click the Forms button in the Objects bar, located at the left side of the window.
3. Double-click *Orders* in the list box.
4. With Orders open and the first record showing, add new records and delete an existing record by completing the following steps:
   a. Click the New Record button located toward the bottom of the first record.
   b. At the new blank record, key the following information in the specified fields (move to the next field by pressing Tab or Enter; move to the previous field by pressing Shift + Tab):

Order #	=	(automatically inserted)
Supplier #	=	54
Product #	=	103
Units Ordered	=	10
Amount	=	$573.25
Order Date	=	2/22/99

   c. After keying the information for the new record, press the Tab key to display the next new record (you can also click the New Record button), and then key the following information in the specified fields:

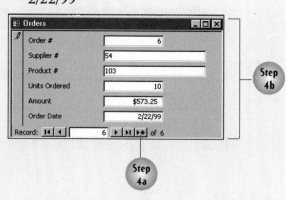

Order #	=	**(automatically inserted)**
Supplier #	=	**99**
Product #	=	**647**
Units Ordered	=	**5**
Amount	=	**$325.00**
Order Date	=	**2/22/99**

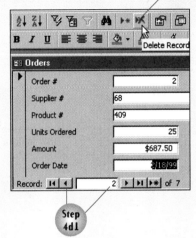

d. Delete the second record by completing the following steps:
  1) Click the button toward the bottom of the record that displays with a left-pointing triangle until Record 2 displays.
  2) With Record 2 displayed, click the Delete Record button on the Form View toolbar.
  3) At the message telling you that you will not be able to undo the delete operation, click <u>Y</u>es.
  e. Click the Save button on the Form View toolbar.
  f. Print all records in the form by clicking the Print button on the Form View toolbar.
  g. Close the Orders form.
5. Close the Outdoor Options database file.

Creating a Form Using the Form Wizard

Access offers a Form Wizard that will guide you through the creation of a form. The Form Wizard offers more formatting choices than the AutoForm feature. To create a form using the Form Wizard, open the database file containing the table for which you want to create a form. At the database window, click the Forms button in the Objects bar, and then click the <u>N</u>ew button on the window toolbar. At the New Form dialog box shown in figure 21.2, double-click *Form Wizard* in the list box and the first Form Wizard dialog box displays as shown in figure 21.3.

The Form Wizard is a general-purpose wizard that provides more flexibility than other AutoForm choices.

New Form Dialog Box

21.2

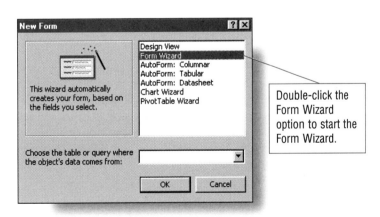

Double-click the Form Wizard option to start the Form Wizard.

At the first Form Wizard dialog box, specify the table and then the fields you want included in the form. To select the table, click the down-pointing triangle at the right side of the Tables/Queries text box, and then click the desired table. Select the desired field in the Available Fields list box, click the button containing the greater than symbol (>), and the field is inserted in the Selected Fields list box. Continue in this manner until all desired fields are inserted in the Selected Fields list box. If you want to insert all fields into the Selected Fields list box at one time, click the button containing the two greater than symbols (>>). After specifying fields, click the Next button.

figure
21.3

First Form Wizard Dialog Box

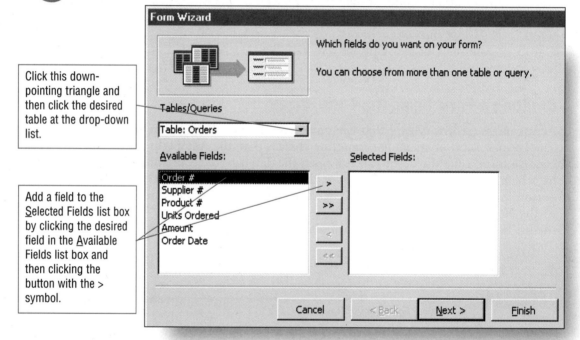

Click this down-pointing triangle and then click the desired table at the drop-down list.

Add a field to the Selected Fields list box by clicking the desired field in the Available Fields list box and then clicking the button with the > symbol.

At the second Form Wizard dialog box, shown in figure 21.4, specify the layout for the records. You can choose from Columnar, Tabular, Datasheet, and Justified (with Columnar the default). After choosing the layout, click the Next> button.

figure

21.4

Second Form Wizard Dialog Box

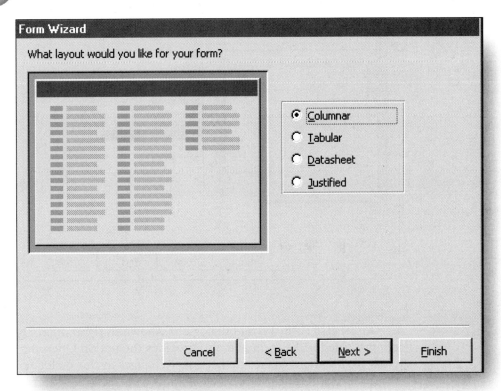

One of the advantages offered by the Form Wizard is the ability to choose from a variety of formats. At the third Form Wizard dialog box, shown in figure 21.5, you choose a format style, such as *Blends*, *Blueprint*, *Expedition*, *Industrial*, and so on. Click a format style and the results of the style are shown in the preview box. After selecting the desired format style, click the Next> button.

figure
21.5

Third Form Wizard Dialog Box

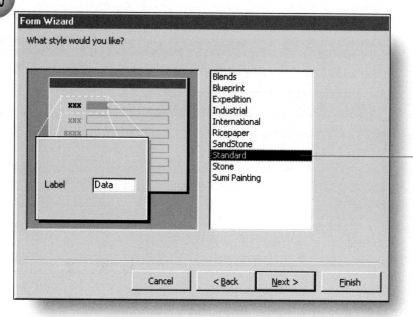

Choose the desired format with options in this list box and then preview the format in the preview box at the left side of the dialog box.

At the last Form Wizard dialog box, shown in figure 21.6, the Form Wizard offers a title for the form and also provides the option Open the form to view or enter information. Make any necessary changes in this dialog box and then click the Finish button.

figure
21.6

Fourth Form Wizard Dialog Box

Key a title for the form in this text box or accept the default name provided by the wizard.

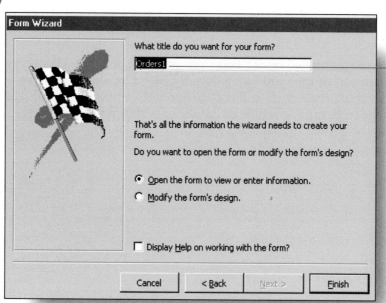

exercise 3

Creating a Form Using the Form Wizard

1. Open the Outdoor Options database file.
2. At the Outdoor Options Database window, click the Forms button in the Objects bar located at the left side of the window.
3. Delete the Orders form you created in exercise 1 by completing the following steps:
   a. Position the arrow pointer on *Orders* in the list box and then click the right mouse button.
   b. At the shortcut menu that displays, click the left mouse button on Delete.
   c. At the question asking if you want to permanently delete the form, click Yes.
4. At the Outdoor Options Database window with the Forms button selected, create a form with the Form Wizard by completing the following steps:

   a. Click the New button on the dialog box toolbar.
   b. At the New Form dialog box, double-click the *Form Wizard* option in the list box.
   c. At the first Form Wizard dialog box, click the down-pointing triangle at the right side of the Tables/Queries text box, and then click *Table: Products* at the drop-down list.

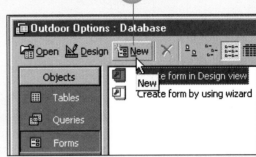

Step 4a

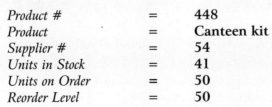

   d. Specify that you want all fields included in the form by clicking the button containing the two greater than symbols (>>), and then clicking the Next> button.
   e. At the second Form Wizard dialog box, click the Next> button. (This leaves the layout at the default of Columnar.)
   f. At the third Form Wizard dialog box, click the *International* option in the list box, and then click the Next> button.
   g. At the fourth Form Wizard dialog box, leave the options at the default, and then finish the form by clicking the Finish button.

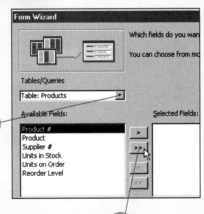

Step 4c

Step 4d

5. When the first record is shown in the form, click the New Record button, and then add the following records:

Product #	=	448
Product	=	**Canteen kit**
Supplier #	=	54
Units in Stock	=	41
Units on Order	=	50
Reorder Level	=	50

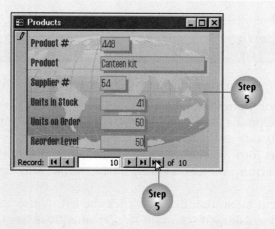

Product #	=	302
Product	=	**Pocket warmer**
Supplier #	=	31
Units in Stock	=	13
Units on Order	=	15
Reorder Level	=	15

6. Delete the record containing information on ski goggles. (At the warning message, click <u>Y</u>es.)
7. Click the Save button on the Form View toolbar.
8. Click the Print button to print all records in the form.
9. Close the form by clicking the Close button in the upper right corner of the record.
10. Close the Outdoor Options database file.

Creating a Form with Related Database Tables

The forms you have created so far in this chapter have included all the fields from one database table. Forms can also be created with fields from tables that are connected by a one-to-many relationship. You can use the Form Wizard to create a form with fields from related database tables. At the first Form Wizard dialog box (see figure 21.3), choose fields from the selected database table and then choose fields from a related database table. To change to the related database table, click the down-pointing triangle at the right of the Tables/Queries text box, and then click the name of the desired database table.

Creating a Form with Related Database Tables

1. Create a form that includes fields from the Products database table and fields from the Suppliers database table by completing the following steps:
   a. Open the Outdoor Options database file.
   b. At the Outdoor Options Database window, click the Forms button in the Objects bar.

c. Click the <u>N</u>ew button on the window toolbar.

d. At the New Form dialog box, double-click *Form Wizard* in the list box.

e. At the first Form Wizard dialog box, click the down-pointing triangle at the right of the Tables/Queries text box, and then click *Table: Products*.

f. Complete the following steps to insert fields in the <u>S</u>elected Fields list box:

1) With *Product #* selected in the <u>A</u>vailable Fields list box, click the button containing the greater than symbol (>).

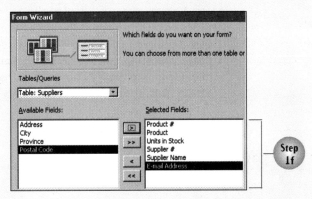

Step 1f

2) With *Product* selected in the <u>A</u>vailable Fields list box, click the button containing the greater than symbol (>).

3) Click *Units in Stock* in the <u>A</u>vailable Fields list box and then click the button containing the greater than symbol (>).

4) Click the down-pointing triangle at the right of the <u>T</u>able/Queries text box and then click *Table: Suppliers*.

5) With *Supplier #* selected in the <u>A</u>vailable Fields list box, click the button containing the greater than symbol (>).

6) With *Supplier Name* selected in the <u>A</u>vailable Fields list box, click the button containing the greater than symbol (>).

7) Click *E-mail Address* in the <u>A</u>vailable Fields list box and then click the button containing the greater than symbol (>).

8) Click the <u>N</u>ext button.

g. At the second Form Wizard dialog box, make sure *by Products* is selected in the list box that displays in the upper left corner of the dialog box, and then click the <u>N</u>ext button.

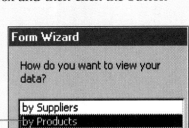

Step 1g

h. At the third Form Wizard dialog box, click the <u>N</u>ext button.

i. At the fourth Form Wizard dialog box, click *Blends* in the format style list box, and then click the <u>N</u>ext button.

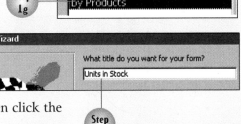

j. At the fifth Form Wizard dialog box, key the name **Units in Stock**, and then click the <u>F</u>inish button.

Step 1j

2. When the first record displays, print the record by displaying the Print dialog box, clicking Selected <u>R</u>ecord(s) in the Print Range section, and then clicking OK.

3. Close the form by clicking the Close button.

4. Close the Outdoor Options database file.

Creating a Form in Design View

A form is comprised of a series of controls. Controls are objects that display titles or descriptions, accept data, or perform actions. In the forms you created in this chapter, the AutoForm feature or the Form Wizard created the controls for the form using fields from the tables. Another method for creating a form is to use the Design view. To display the Design view, as shown in figure 21.7, click the Forms button on the Objects bar, and then double-click the *Create Form in Design view* option in the list box. In the Design view, you can use fields from a table to create controls in the Design grid and you can also add controls with buttons on the Toolbox palette. The Toolbox palette, shown in figure 21.7, appears automatically in the Design view.

Form in Design View

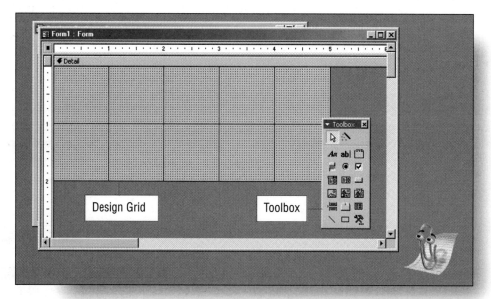

A form in Design view contains three sections—Form Header, Detail, and Form Footer. The Detail section is the only section that displays by default. (You will learn more about the Form Header and Form Footer sections later in this chapter.) The Detail section of the form in Design view is set up as a grid. Use the rulers along the top and left side of the section and the lines and dots that make up the grid to precisely position fields and controls.

Using Fields to Add Controls

Associate a table with the form to use fields to create controls. To associate a table, right-click the Form1 Form title bar and then click Properties at the shortcut menu. This displays the Form properties sheet. (You can also display the Form properties sheet by double-clicking the Form selector button that displays in the upper left corner of the Design view.) At the Form properties sheet, click the All tab, and then click in the Record Source text box. Click the down-pointing triangle that displays at the right side of the text box and then click the desired table. This displays the table fields in a field list box. (If the field list box does not display, click the Field List button on the Form Design toolbar.) Using the mouse, drag the desired field from the field list box to the Design grid.

Field List

Moving Control Objects

When a field is moved to the Design grid, a label control containing the field name and a text box control used to accept data are placed adjacent to each other on the grid. The label control containing the field name is included for descriptive purposes so that the user knows which data to key into the corresponding text box.

The label control and its corresponding text box control for a field can be moved individually or together to another location on the form. To move the two control objects together, click one of the objects. This inserts eight sizing handles around the object you clicked with a large black handle displaying in the upper left corner as shown in figure 21.8. The adjacent object displays with one large black sizing handle in the upper left corner. Position the arrow pointer on the border of the control object containing the eight sizing handles (on the border, not on a sizing handle) until the pointer turns into a hand. Hold down the left mouse button and then drag the objects to the desired position. Move multiple control objects at the same time by holding down the Shift key while clicking each object. You can also select multiple control objects by drawing a border around the desired control objects.

Selected Control Objects

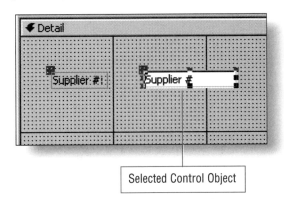

Selected Control Object

To move a control object separately from the adjacent object, position the mouse pointer on the large black handle that displays in the upper left corner of the object, hold down the left mouse button, and then drag the object to the desired position.

Resizing Control Objects

Use the sizing handles that display around a selected control to increase or decrease the size of a selected control object. Drag the middle sizing handles at the left or right edge to make the control wider or narrower; drag the middle sizing handles at the top or bottom to make the control taller or shorter; and use the corner sizing handles to resize the object both horizontally and vertically at the same time.

Formatting Control Objects

The formatting of selected control objects can be customized with options at the properties sheet. (The name of the properties sheet will vary depending on what is selected.) With the All tab selected, all formatting options are available. Click the Format tab to display only such formatting options as changing the font size, font style, font color, foreground color, background color, and caption. Click in a text box for some options and a button containing three black dots displays at the right side. Click this button to display additional formatting choices.

Aligning Control Objects

Control objects inserted in the Design grid align with horizontal and vertical lines in the grid. This is because the Snap to Grid effect is on by default. Even with the Snap to Grid effect on, you may want to control the alignment of control objects. To align control objects, select the desired objects, and then click the Format option on the Menu bar. At the drop-down menu that displays, point to the Align option, and then click the desired alignment at the side menu.

Creating and Formatting a Form in Design View

1. Open the Outdoor Options database file.
2. At the Outdoor Options window, click the Forms button in the Objects bar.
3. Create a form in Design view by completing the following steps:
   a. Double-click *Create form in Design view* in the list box.
   b. At the Design grid, right-click in the Form1 Form title bar and then click Properties at the shortcut menu.

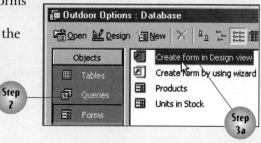

c. At the Form properties sheet, click the All tab.
d. At the Form properties sheet with the All tab selected, click in the Record Source text box, and then click the down-pointing triangle that displays at the right side of the text box.

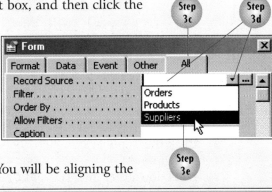

e. At the drop-down list that displays, click *Suppliers*.
f. Drag the *Supplier #* field from the field list box to the Design grid and place it at the approximate location shown at the right. (You will be aligning the control objects later in this exercise.)
g. Drag the remaining fields from the field list box to the Design grid and place them at the approximate locations shown at the right. (You will be formatting the control objects later in this exercise.)

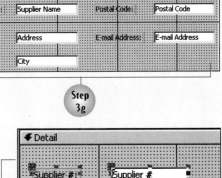

h. Align the control objects by completing the following steps:
   1) With the mouse, draw a border around all control objects located in the first column. (This selects the control objects.)
   2) With the control objects selected, click Format on the Menu bar, point to Align, and then click Right at the side menu.

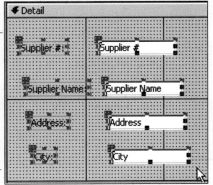

   3) With the mouse, draw a border around all control objects located in the second column.
   4) Click Format on the Menu bar, point to Align, and then click Right at the side menu.
   5) If the control objects are not positioned in the locations shown in figure 21.9, select and then drag the object to the desired position.
i. Change the *Supplier #:* caption by completing the following steps:
   1) Click the *Supplier #:* label control object (displays with a gray background).
   2) Click in the Caption text box in the Label properties sheet. (The Form properties sheet became the Label properties sheet when the label control object was selected.) (You may need to scroll up the list to display the Caption text box.)

3) Edit the text in the Caption text box so it displays as *Supplier Number:*.

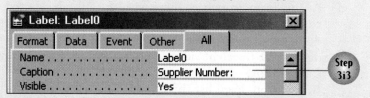

Step 3i3

4) Click anywhere in the Design grid outside a control object to deselect the object.

j. Format the label control objects by completing the following steps:

1) Click the Supplier Number label control object (displays with a gray background.)

2) Hold down the Shift key and then click each of the remaining label control objects (objects that display with a gray background).

Step 3j2

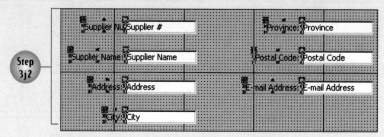

3) Click in the Fore Color text box in the Multiple selection properties sheet. (The Label properties sheet became the Multiple selection properties sheet when you selected the labels.) (You will need to scroll down the list to display the Fore Color text box.)

4) Click the button containing three black dots that displays at the right side of the text box.

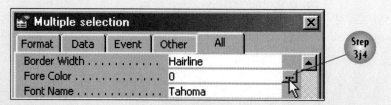

Step 3j4

5) At the color palette that displays, click the turquoise color (fifth color from the left in the top row), and then click OK to close the palette. (The color will not be visible in the Design grid until you choose another option.)

6) Click in the Back Color text box and then click the button containing three black dots.

7) At the color palette that displays, click the blue color (sixth color from the left in the fourth row from the top), and then click OK to close the palette.

8) Click in the Font Name text box and then click the down-pointing triangle that displays at the right side of the text box.

9) At the drop-down list that displays, scroll up the list to display *Arial* and then click *Arial*.

10) Click in the Font Size text box, click the down-pointing triangle that displays at the right, and then click *10*.

11) Click in the Font Weight text box, click the down-pointing triangle that displays at the right, and then click *Bold*.

k. Click in the Design grid outside a control object to deselect the objects.

l. Resize each of the label control objects so the label name displays completely. (To do this, select the label control object and then use the middle sizing handle at the left side of the object to increase the width.)

m. Format the text control objects by completing the following steps:

1) Click the *Supplier #* text control object (contains a white background).

2) Hold down the Shift key and then click each of the remaining text control objects (objects that display with a white background).

3) Click in the Fore Color text box in the Multiple selection properties sheet, click the button containing three black dots, click the blue color (sixth color from the left in the fourth row), and then click OK.

4) Click in the Back Color text box, click the button containing three black dots, click the turquoise color (fifth color from the left in the top row), and then click OK.

5) Click in the Font Name text box, click the down-pointing triangle that displays at the right, and then click *Arial* at the drop-down list. (You will need to scroll up the list to display *Arial*.)

6) Click in the Font Size text box, click the down-pointing triangle that displays at the right, and then click *10*.

7) Click in the Font Weight text box, click the down-pointing triangle that displays at the right, and then click *Bold*.

n. Click in the Design grid outside a control object to deselect the objects.

4. Close the properties sheet. (To do this, click the Close button that displays in the upper right corner of the sheet [contains an X].)

5. View the form in Form view by clicking the View button on the Form Design toolbar.

6. Save the form and name it Suppliers Form.

7. Print the currently displayed form by completing the following steps:

a. Click File and then Print.

b. At the Print dialog box, click the Selected Record(s) option in the Print Range section.

c. Click OK.

8. Close the Suppliers Form.

9. Close the Outdoor Options database file.

Exercise 5

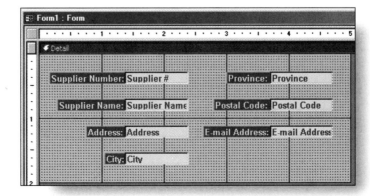

Adding Controls Using the Toolbox

The Toolbox is a palette of control object buttons that automatically appears when a form is displayed in Design view. With the buttons on this Toolbox, shown in figure 21.10, you can add and modify controls in the form. (Figure 21.10 identifies a few of the buttons on the Toolbox.) To add a control in Design view, click the desired button on the Toolbox. This causes the mouse pointer to change to a crosshair pointer with an icon attached. The icon that displays will vary depending on the control object button selected. Move the pointer to the position on the form where you want to place the object and then drag to create the object. Use the sizing handles that display around the control to increase or decrease the size.

Toolbox

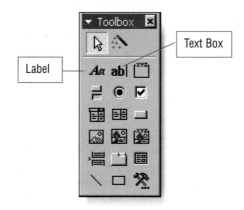

Adding a Form Header and Form Footer

A form in Design view can contain up to three sections—Detail, Form Header, and Form Footer. The Detail section is the only section that displays by default. You created a form in exercise 5 in the Detail section of the form. A Form Header displays at the top of the form in Form view and at the beginning of a printout started from the Form view screen. A Form Footer appears at the bottom of the form in Form view and at the end of a printout started from the Form view screen.

Label

Display a Form Header and Form Footer by clicking <u>V</u>iew on the Menu bar and then clicking Form <u>H</u>eader/Footer. Another method is to right-click the Form 1 Form title bar and then click Form <u>H</u>eader/Footer at the shortcut menu.

To insert text in a Form Header or Form Footer use the Label button on the Toolbox. Click the Label button and then draw the label in the Form Header or Form Footer. Key text inside the label control object and apply the desired formatting.

Apply formatting to a Form Header with options at the FormHeader properties sheet. Display this sheet by right-clicking the Form Header gray border bar and then click <u>P</u>roperties at the shortcut menu. Complete similar steps to display the FormFooter properties sheet.

Adding a Form Header and Form Footer to a Form

1. Open the Outdoor Options database file.
2. If necessary, click the Forms button in the Objects bar.
3. Double-click *Suppliers Form* in the list box.
4. Add and modify a Form Header and Form Footer in Design view by completing the following steps:
   a. Change to the Design view by clicking the View button on the Form View toolbar.
   b. Add and modify a Form Header by completing the following steps:
      1) Right-click the Suppliers Form: Form title bar and then click Form Header/Footer at the shortcut menu.
      2) Increase the height of the Form Header section by positioning the pointer at the top of the gray Detail border line until the pointer changes to a black horizontal line with an up- and down-pointing arrow, and then drag the mouse down to the approximate height shown at the right.
      3) Click the Label button on the Toolbox. (If the Toolbox is not displayed, click the Toolbox button on the Form Design toolbar.)
      4) Position the crosshair pointer with the *label* icon attached to it at the top left edge of the first black gridline in the Form Header section, drag the mouse down to the approximate height and width shown below, and then release the mouse button.
      5) A label box will appear with the insertion point automatically positioned in the top left edge of the box. Key **Outdoor Options Suppliers Form** and then click outside the box.

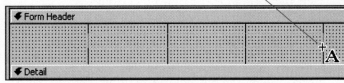

      6) Click once on the label control object to select it.
      7) Right-click the Suppliers Form: Form title bar and then click Properties at the shortcut menu.
      8) Click the Format tab at the Label properties sheet.
      9) Click in the Font Name text box (you will need to scroll down the Format list box to display this text box), click the down-pointing triangle at the right, and then click *Arial* at the drop-down menu. (You will need to scroll up the drop-down menu to display *Arial*.)
      10) Click in the Font Size text box, click the down-pointing triangle at the right, and then click *14* at the drop-down menu.
      11) Click in the Font Weight text box, click the down-pointing triangle at the right, and then click *Bold* at the drop-down menu.

12) Click outside the label control box. (Increase the height and width of the label control box so the entire title displays.)

c. Add and modify a Form Footer by completing the following steps:

1) Drag down the bottom border of the form to display the Form Footer section.

2) Click the Label button on the Toolbox.

3) Position the crosshair pointer with the *label* icon attached to it at the top left edge of the first black gridline in the Form Footer section, drag the mouse down to the approximate height and width shown below, and then release the mouse button.

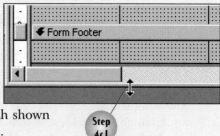

4) A label box will appear with the insertion point automatically positioned in the box. Key **Suppliers Form designed by Student Name** (key your name instead of *Student Name*) and then click outside the box.

5) Click once on the label control object to select it. (The Label properties sheet should be visible. If it is not visible, right-click the Suppliers Form: Form title bar and then click <u>P</u>roperties at the shortcut menu.)

6) If necessary, click the Format tab at the Label properties sheet.

7) Make the following changes:
   a) Change the font name to Arial.
   b) Change the font size to 10.
   c) Change the font weight to bold.

8) Click outside the label control box.

5. Close the properties sheet. (To do this, click the Close button that displays in the upper right corner of the sheet [contains an X].)

6. View the form in Form view by clicking the View button on the Form Design toolbar.

7. Click the Save button to save the form.

8. Click the New Record button that displays along the bottom of the form.

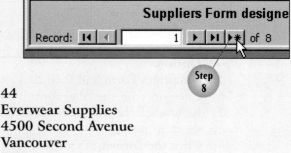

9. Add the following record:

Supplier Number	=	44
Supplier Name	=	**Everwear Supplies**
Address	=	**4500 Second Avenue**
City	=	**Vancouver**
Province	=	**BC**
Postal Code	=	**V2V 6K2**
E-mail Address	=	**everwear@recreate.fun.com**

10. Print the currently displayed form.

11. Close the Suppliers Form.

12. Close the Outdoor Options database file.

Adding a Calculated Control

A calculated control uses a mathematical equation to determine the contents that are displayed in the control object. Insert a calculated control field in Design view by creating a text box control object and then entering the mathematical equation in the text box. A calculated field is used to perform mathematical operations on existing fields but it does not exist in the table associated with the form. In exercise 7, you will create a calculated control in a form that divides the order amount by the number of units.

Key a mathematical expression in a calculated control box. Begin the expression with the equals sign (=) and insert square brackets around field names. Use mathematical operators such as +, -, *, and / to perform calculations.

Creating a Form in Design View and Adding a Calculated Control

1. Open the Outdoor Options database file.
2. At the Outdoor Options window, if necessary, click the Forms button in the Objects bar.
3. Create a form in Design view by completing the following steps:
   a. Double-click *Create form in Design view* in the list box.
   b. At the Design grid, right-click in the Form1 Form title bar and then click <u>P</u>roperties at the shortcut menu.
   c. At the Form properties sheet, click the All tab.
   d. Click in the Record Source text box, click the down-pointing triangle at the right, and then click *Orders* at the drop-down list.
   e. Drag the fields in the field list box to the Design grid and place them at the approximate locations shown in figure 21.11.
   f. Select the three label and text box control objects at the left side of the Design grid and then align them at the right.
   g. Select the two label and text box control objects at the right side of the Design grid and then align them at the right.
   h. Select the label and text box control objects located at the bottom of the design grid and align them at the right. (This moves the label control object next to the text box control object.)
   i. Add a calculated control field by completing the following steps:
      1) Click the Text Box button on the Toolbox. (If the Toolbox is not visible, click the Toolbox button on the Form Design toolbar.)
      2) Position the crosshair pointer with the *text box* icon attached below the *Amount* text box control and then drag the outline of a box approximately the same size as the text box control above it.

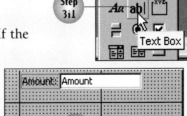

3) Click in the text box control (which currently displays *Unbound*), key **=[Amount]/[Units Ordered]**, and then click outside the control to deselect it.

4) Click the label control object adjacent to the text box control (which currently displays *Text6* [your number may vary]) to select it.

5) Click the label control object again to position the insertion point inside the label box.

6) Delete the current entry, key **Unit Price:**, and then click outside the label control to deselect it.

7) Move and/or size the calculated control and the label control to align them with the fields displayed above.

j. Click the View button on the Form Design toolbar to display the form in Form view. Notice the Unit Price amount displays aligned at the left edge of the control. Change the format properties for the calculated control by completing the following steps:

1) Click the View button on the Form View toolbar.

2) Click the text box calculated control to select it.

3) At the Text Box properties sheet, click the Format tab.

4) Click in the Format text box (you may need to scroll up to display this text box), click the down-pointing triangle at the right, and then click *Currency* at the drop-down list.

5) Click in the Text Align text box (you will need to scroll down the list to display this text box), click the down-pointing triangle at the right, and then click *Right* at the drop-down list.

```
Step        Text Box: Text6                              ×
3j3
      Format    Data    Event    Other    All

      Format . . . . . . . . . . . . . .           ▼      ▲
      Decimal Places . . . . . . . . .    Short Time    1
      Visible . . . . . . . . . . . . .   General Number 3
      Display When . . . . . . . . .      Currency      $
      Scroll Bars . . . . . . . . . . .   Euro          €
                                                    Step
                                                    3j4
```

6) Close the Text Box properties sheet.

4. View the form in Form view by clicking View button on the Form Design toolbar.

5. Save the form and name it Orders Form.

6. Display and then print the first record.

7. Close the Orders Form.

8. Close the Outdoor Options database file.

figure
21.11

Exercise 7

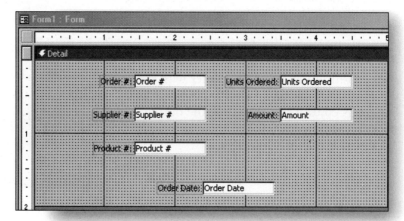

Creating Reports

The primary purpose for inserting data in a form is to improve the display of the data and to make data entry easier. Data can also be inserted in a report. The purpose for this is to control what data appears on the page when printed. Reports generally answer specific questions (queries). For example, a report could answer the question "What customers have submitted claims?" or "What products do we currently have on order?" Access includes a Report Wizard that walks you through the process of creating a report. Like the Form Wizard, you specify fields, format style, and the report name when creating a report.

> Create a report to control what data appears on the page when printed.
>
> *Hint*

To create a report using the Report Wizard, open the database file, click the Reports button in the Objects bar, and then click the New button. At the New Report dialog box, double-click *Report Wizard* in the list box. The first Report Wizard dialog box is similar to the first Form Wizard dialog box. Choose the desired table with options from the Tables/Queries text box. Specify the fields you want included in the report by inserting them in the Selected Fields list box and then clicking the Next> button.

At the second Report Wizard dialog box, shown in figure 21.12, you can increase or decrease the priority level of fields in the report. To increase the priority level, click the desired field name in the list box at the left side of the dialog box, and then click the button containing the greater than symbol (>). To decrease the priority level, click the desired field, and then click the button containing the less than symbol (<). This changes the sample information displayed at the right side of the dialog box. After specifying the field levels, click the Next> button.

figure

21.12   *Second Report Wizard Dialog Box*

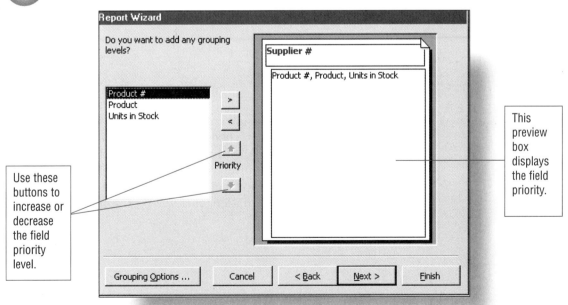

Use these buttons to increase or decrease the field priority level.

This preview box displays the field priority.

You can specify the order in which records are displayed in the report at the third Report Wizard dialog box shown in figure 21.13. To specify a sort order, click the down-pointing triangle at the right of the text box preceded by a number 1, and then click the field name. The default sort is done in ascending order. This can be changed to descending by clicking the button that displays at the right side of the text box. After identifying the sort order, click the Next> button.

Third Report Wizard Dialog Box

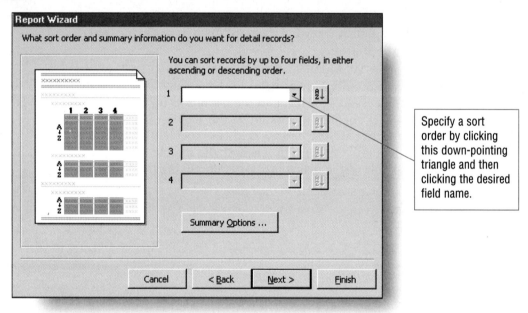

Specify a sort order by clicking this down-pointing triangle and then clicking the desired field name.

The layout of the report is determined in the fourth Report Wizard dialog box shown in figure 21.14. You can choose from a variety of layouts such as Stepped, Block, Outline 1, Outline 2, Align Left 1, and Align Left 2. Click a layout option and a sample of the layout is displayed on the sample page at the left side of the dialog box. The page orientation can also be selected at this dialog box. After choosing a layout and/or orientation, click the Next> button.

figure
21.14

Fourth Report Wizard Dialog Box

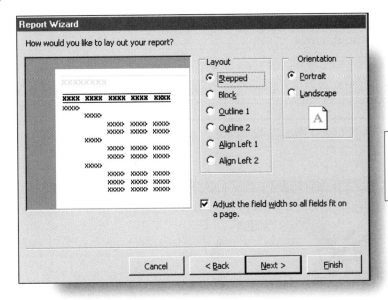

Choose a layout and orientation and then click the Next> button.

The Report Wizard offers several report styles at the fifth Report Wizard dialog box shown in figure 21.15. Click a report style and the wizard will display a sample at the left side of the dialog box. Click the Next> button to display the sixth Report Wizard dialog box.

figure
21.15

Fifth Report Wizard Dialog Box

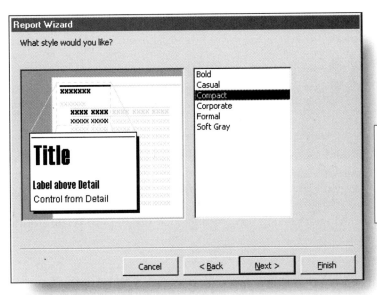

Click a style in the list box and the wizard displays a sample at the left side of the dialog box.

At the sixth Report Wizard dialog box, shown in figure 21.16, key a name for the report, and then click Finish. Creating the report may take a few moments. When the report is finished, it displays on the screen in Print Preview. In Print Preview, you can change the percentage of display of data and also send the report to the printer. To print the report, click the Print button on the Print Preview toolbar. After viewing and/or printing the report, close Print Preview by clicking the Close button.

figure
21.16
Sixth Report Wizard Dialog Box

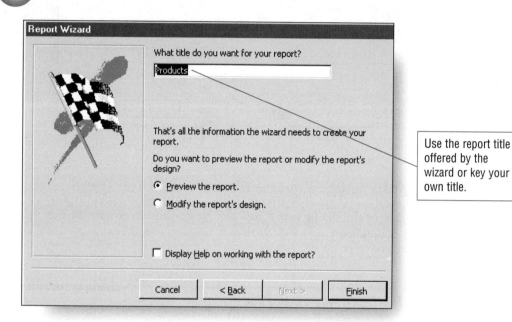

Use the report title offered by the wizard or key your own title.

exercise
8

Using the Report Wizard to Prepare a Report

1. Open the Outdoor Options database file.
2. At the Outdoor Options Database window, click the Reports button in the Objects bar.
3. Create a report with the Report Wizard by completing the following steps:
   a. Click the New button on the window toolbar.
   b. At the New Report dialog box, double-click the Report Wizard option in the list box.

c. At the first Report Wizard dialog box, click the down-pointing triangle at the right side of the Tables/Queries text box, and then click *Table: Products* at the drop-down list.

d. Insert the following fields in the Selected Fields list box:

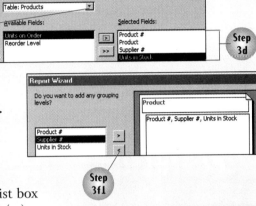

> Product #
> Product
> Supplier #
> Units in Stock

e. After inserting the fields, click the Next> button.

f. At the second Report Wizard dialog box, decrease and increase priority levels by completing the following steps:

1) Click the button to the right of the list box that displays with a less than symbol (<). (This decreases the priority level of the *Supplier #* field.)

2) Click *Product* in the list box that displays at the left side of the dialog box and then click the button to the right of the list box that displays with a greater than symbol (>). (This increases the priority level of the *Product* field.)

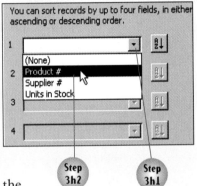

g. After specifying the priority levels, click the Next> button.

h. At the third Report Wizard dialog box, specify that the records are to be sorted by the Product # in ascending order by completing the following steps:

1) Click the down-pointing triangle at the right of the text box preceded by a 1.

2) At the drop-down menu that displays, click *Product #*.

i. Click the Next> button.

j. At the fourth Report Wizard dialog box, click Block, and then click the Next> button.

k. At the fifth Report Wizard dialog box, click *Compact* in the list box, and then click the Next> button.

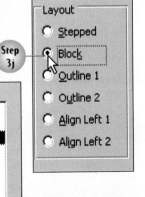

l. At the sixth Report Wizard dialog box, click the Finish button.

m. When the report displays in Print Preview, view the report, and then click the Print button that displays on the Print Preview toolbar.

n. Click the Close button at the right side of the Products title bar.

4. Close the Outdoor Options database file.

Preparing a Report Based on Two Database Tables

In the section on creating forms, you learned to create a form with fields from related database tables. Fields from related database tables can also be used to create a report. The steps to prepare a report with fields from two database tables are basically the same as those you completed in exercise 8. The only difference is that an additional Report Wizard dialog box displays during the steps asking you to specify whether the fields should be grouped by the fields from the primary table or fields from the related table. In exercise 9, you will prepare a report with fields from the Products database table and also the Suppliers table. These tables are joined by a one-to-many relationship.

Preparing a Report with Fields from Two Database Tables

1. Open the Outdoor Options database file.
2. At the Outdoor Options Database window, click the Reports button in the Objects bar.
3. Create a report with the Report Wizard by completing the following steps:
   a. Click the New button on the window toolbar.
   b. At the New Report dialog box, double-click *Report Wizard* in the list box.
   c. At the first Report Wizard dialog box, insert the following fields in the Selected Fields list box:

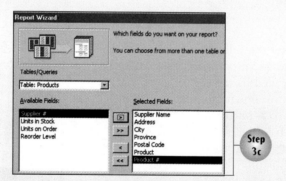

Step 3c

From the Suppliers database table:
   Supplier Name
   Address
   City
   Province
   Postal Code

From the Products database table:

      Product

      Product #

d. After inserting the fields, click the <u>N</u>ext> button.

e. At the second Report Wizard dialog box, make sure *by Suppliers* is selected in the list box in the upper left corner, and then click the <u>N</u>ext> button.

f. At the third Report Wizard dialog box, increase the priority level of the *Supplier Name* field. To do this, make sure *Supplier Name* is selected in the list box, and then click the button containing the greater than symbol (>). Click the <u>N</u>ext> button.

g. At the fourth Report Wizard dialog box, click the <u>N</u>ext> button. (Do not specify a sort order.)

h. At the fifth Report Wizard dialog box, click <u>A</u>lign Left 1, and then click the <u>N</u>ext> button.

i. At the sixth Report Wizard dialog box, click *Corporate* in the list box, and then click the <u>N</u>ext> button.

j. At the seventh Report Wizard dialog box, click the <u>F</u>inish button.

k. When the report displays in Print Preview, view the report, and then click the Print button that displays on the Print Preview toolbar.

l. Click the Close button (displays with an X) that displays at the right side of the Suppliers title bar.

4. Close the Outdoor Options database file.

Creating a Report in Design View

A report, like a form, is comprised of a series of controls, which are objects that display titles or descriptions, accept data, or perform actions. In the reports you created in this chapter, Report Wizard created the controls for the report using fields from the tables. A report, like a form, can be created in Design view. To display the report Design view, click the Reports button in the Objects bar, and then double-click *Create Report in Design view*.

A report can include up to five sections including Report Header, Page Header, Detail, Page Footer, and Report Footer. These five sections are identified in the sample report shown in figure 21.17.

figure
21.17

Sample Report

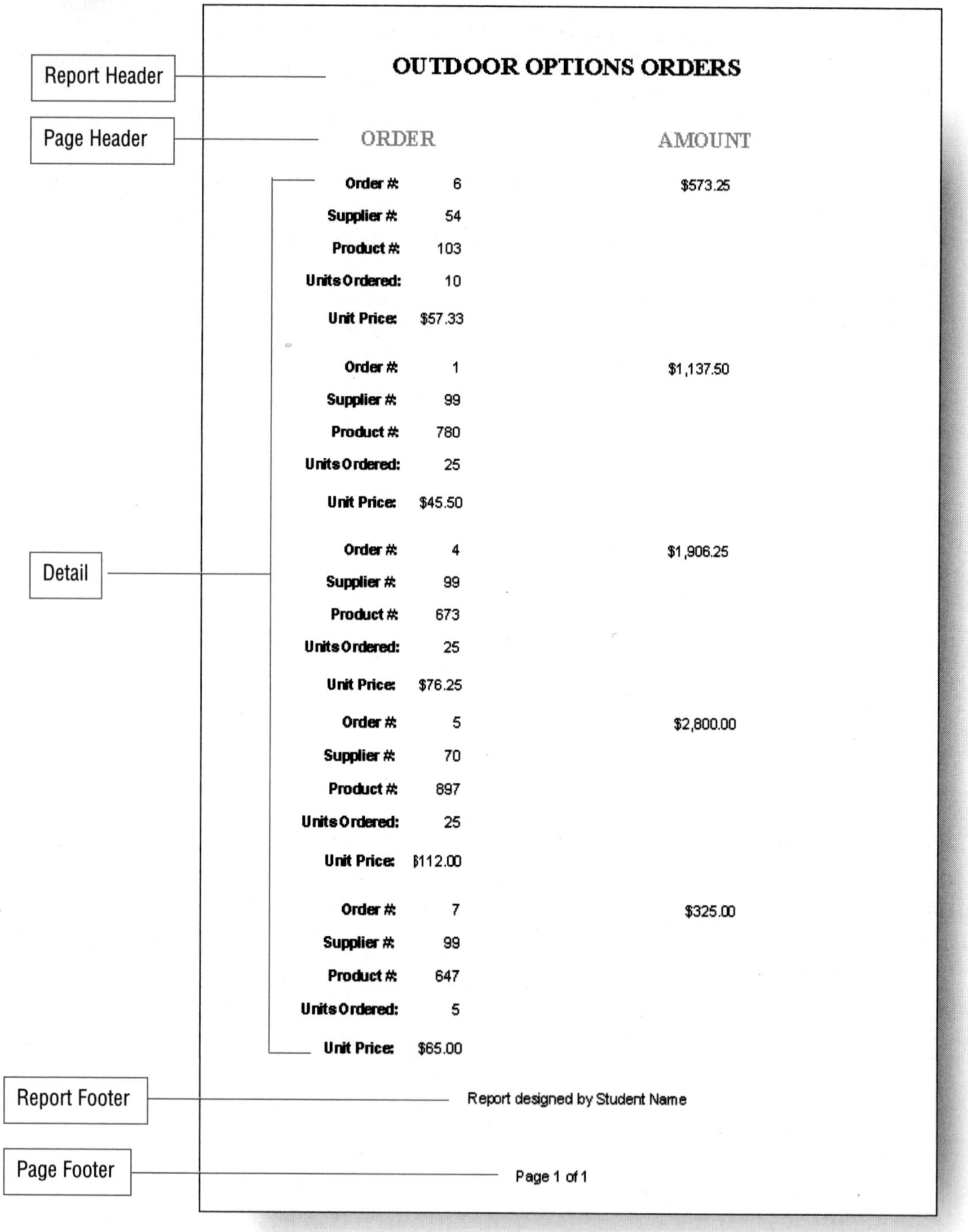

OUTDOOR OPTIONS ORDERS

Report Header

Page Header

ORDER		AMOUNT
Order #:	6	$573.25
Supplier #:	54	
Product #:	103	
Units Ordered:	10	
Unit Price:	$57.33	
Order #:	1	$1,137.50
Supplier #:	99	
Product #:	780	
Units Ordered:	25	
Unit Price:	$45.50	
Order #:	4	$1,906.25
Supplier #:	99	
Product #:	673	
Units Ordered:	25	
Unit Price:	$76.25	
Order #:	5	$2,800.00
Supplier #:	70	
Product #:	897	
Units Ordered:	25	
Unit Price:	$112.00	
Order #:	7	$325.00
Supplier #:	99	
Product #:	647	
Units Ordered:	5	
Unit Price:	$65.00	

Detail

Report Footer — Report designed by Student Name

Page Footer — Page 1 of 1

The Report Header generally includes the title of the report and/or the company logo. The Page Header appears at the top of each page and generally includes column headings identifying the data in the report. The Detail section of the report contains the data from the table. The Page Footer appears at the bottom of each page and might include information such as the page number. The Report Footer appears on the last page of the report and might include information such as the person designing the report.

Using Fields to Add Controls

To add fields to a report in Design view, associate the report with the desired table. To do this, right-click the Report1 Report title bar and then click Properties at the shortcut menu. This displays the Report properties sheet. At the Report properties sheet, click the All tab, and then click in the Record Source text box. Click the down-pointing triangle that displays at the right side of the text box and then click the desired table. This displays the table fields in a field list box. Using the mouse, drag the desired field from the field list box to the Design grid.

Moving, Resizing, and Customizing Control Objects

The steps to move, resize, and/or customize control objects in report Design view are the same as the steps to remove, resize, and/or customize control objects in form Design view. Select an object and then either move the individual object or move the label control object and the text box control object together. Customize control objects with options at the properties sheet. (The name of the properties sheet will vary depending on what is selected.)

When a field is added to the report in Design view, a label control containing the field name and a text box control used to accept data are placed adjacent to each other. The label control containing the field name is included for descriptive purposes so that the user knows which data to key into the corresponding text box. In a report, a column heading is generally included in the Page Header describing the data and, therefore, some label control objects may not be needed.

Adding Controls Using the Toolbox

Add controls to the report using buttons on the Toolbox. To add a control in Design view, click the desired button on the Toolbox. This causes the mouse pointer to change to a crosshair pointer with an icon attached. The icon that displays will vary depending on the control object button selected. Move the pointer to the position on the form where you want to place the object and then drag to create the object. Use the sizing handles that display around the control to increase or decrease the size.

Adding a Report Header and Report Footer

The Design view, by default, displays the Detail section and the Page Header and Page Footer. To add a Report Header and/or Report Footer to a report, click View on the Menu bar and then click Report Header/Footer. Another method is to right-click the Report 1 Report title bar and then click Report Header/Footer at the shortcut menu.

To insert text in a Page Header, Report Header, Page Footer, or Report Footer, use the Label button on the Toolbox. Click the Label button and then draw the label in the desired section. Key text inside the label control object and apply the desired formatting.

Creating, Customizing, and Formatting a Report in Design View

1. Open the Outdoor Options database file.
2. At the Outdoor Options window, click the Reports button in the Objects bar.
3. Create the report shown in figure 21.18 in Design view by completing the following steps:

   a. Double-click *Create report in Design view* in the list box.

   b. At the Design grid, right-click in the Report1 Report title bar and then click <u>P</u>roperties at the shortcut menu.

   c. At the Report properties sheet, click the All tab.

   d. At the Report properties sheet with the All tab selected, click in the Record Source text box, and then click the down-pointing triangle that displays at the right side of the text box.

   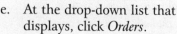

   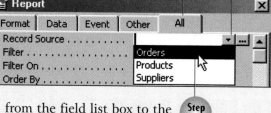

   e. At the drop-down list that displays, click *Orders*.

   f. Drag the *Order #* field from the field list box to the Design grid and place it at the approximate location shown below.

   g. Drag the other fields (*Supplier #*, *Product #*, *Units Ordered*, and *Amount*) from the field list box to the Design grid and place them at the approximate locations shown at the right.

   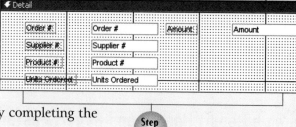

   h. Delete the label control object for *Amount*. (The label control object contains *Amount* with a transparent background [gray dots from the grid show through].)

   i. Insert a calculated control field by completing the following steps:

      1) Click the Text Box button on the Toolbox. (If the Toolbox is not visible, click the Toolbox button on the Form Design toolbar.)

      2) Position the crosshair pointer with the *text box* icon attached below the *Units Ordered* text box control and then drag the outline of a box approximately the same size as the text box control above.

3) Click in the text box control (which currently displays *Unbound*), and key **=[Amount]/[Units Ordered]**.

4) Click outside the box and then click the text box control to select it.

5) With the text box control selected, click in the Format text box in the Text Box properties sheet (you may need to scroll up the list to display the Format text box), click the down-pointing triangle at the right, and then click *Currency* at the drop-down menu.

6) Click outside the text box control to deselect it.

j. Change the caption in the new label control box by completing the following steps:

1) Click the label control box to select it (contains *Text 5* [your number may vary]).

2) Click in the Caption text box located in the Label properties sheet. (You may need to scroll up to display the Caption text box.)

3) Delete the text currently displayed in the Caption text box and then key **Unit Price:**.

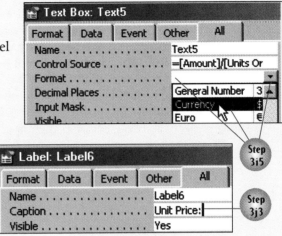

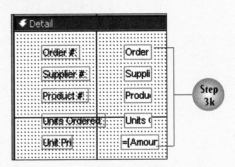

Step 3i5

Step 3j3

k. Decrease the size of the text box controls as shown at the right.

l. Select the label control objects at the left side of the Design grid (just the label control objects—not the text box control objects) and then align them at the right.

m. With the label object control boxes still selected, change the Font Weight to *Bold*.

n. With the label object control objects still selected, change the text alignment to *right*. To do this, click in the Text Align text box in the Multiple selection properties sheet (you may need to scroll down the list to display this text box), click the down-pointing triangle, and then click *Right* at the drop-down menu.

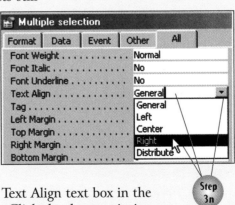

Step 3k

o. Select all the text box control objects (which contain a white background) and then click in the Text Align text box in the Multiple selection properties sheet. Click the down-pointing triangle, and then click *Right*.

Step 3n

p. Decrease the height of the Detail section by completing the following steps:

1) Position the mouse pointer on the top of the gray bar containing the text *Page Footer* until the pointer turns into an up- and down-pointing arrow with a line between.

2) Hold down the left mouse button, drag up until the border displays just below the bottom label and text box control objects, and then release the mouse button.

q. Add column headings in the Page Header by completing the following steps:

1) Click the Label button on the Toolbox.
2) Position the crosshair pointer with the *label* icon attached to it at the top left edge of the first black gridline in the Page Header section, drag the mouse down to the approximate height and width shown in figure 21.18, and then release the mouse button.
3) Key **ORDER** in the label control box and then click outside the box.
4) Use the Label button on the Toolbox to create the *AMOUNT* label shown in figure 21.18.
5) Select the two labels and then apply the following formatting:
   a) Change the Font Name to Times New Roman.
   b) Change the Font Size to 12.
   c) Change the Font Weight to Bold.
   d) Change the Fore Color to dark teal (fourth color from the left in the third row from the top).
6) Increase the size of the label control boxes so the entire text displays in each label.

r. Insert page numbering in the Page Footer by completing the following steps:

1) Click Insert and then Page Numbers.
2) At the Page Numbers dialog box, make the following changes:
   a) Click Page N of M in the Format section.
   b) Click Bottom of Page [Footer] in the Position section.
   c) Click OK to close the dialog box.

s. Add a Report Header by completing the following steps:

1) Display the Report Header and Report Footer by clicking View on the Menu bar and then clicking Report Header/Footer.
2) Increase the Report Header section by about one-half inch by dragging down the top of the gray bar (contains the words *Page Header*).
3) Click the Label button on the Toolbox.
4) Drag to create a label box inside the Report Header that is large enough to hold the title shown in figure 21.18.
5) Key the text **OUTDOOR OPTIONS ORDERS** inside the label and then click outside the box.
6) Click the label control box and then apply the following formatting:
   a) Change the Font Name to Times New Roman.
   b) Change the Font Size to 14.
   c) Change the Font Weight to Bold.
   d) Change the Fore Color to dark teal (the fourth color from the left in the third row from the top).
7) Click outside the label box to deselect it.

t. Add a Report Footer by completing the following steps:

1) Increase the height of the Report Footer section by about one-half inch. (To do this, drag down the bottom edge of the Report Footer section.)

2) Click the Label button on the Toolbox and then draw a label box inside the Report Footer large enough to hold the text shown in figure 21.18.

3) Key the text **Report designed by Student Name** (insert your name instead of Student Name).

4. Close the properties sheet. (To do this, click the Close button that displays in the upper right corner of the sheet [contains an X].)

5. View the report in Print Preview by clicking the View button on the Report Design toolbar.

6. Check the headings *ORDERS* and *AMOUNT* and make sure the headings display approximately centered over the information in columns. (If they do not, change to Design view, move the heading or headings to the desired location, and then change back to Print Preview.)

7. Print the report by clicking the Print button on the Print Preview toolbar.

8. Click the View button to return to the Design view.

9. In Design view, save the report and name it Orders Report.

10. Close the Orders Report.

11. Close the Outdoor Options database file.

Exercise 10

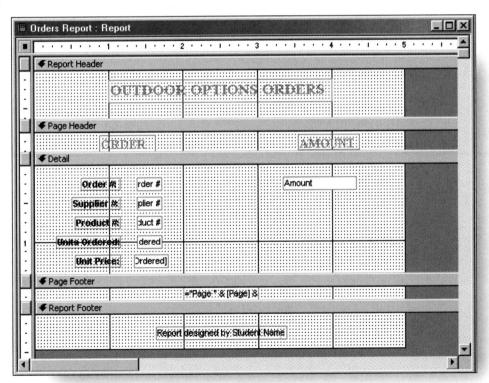

Preparing Mailing Labels

Access includes a mailing label wizard that walks you through the steps for creating mailing labels with fields in a database table. To create mailing labels, open the database file, click the Reports button in the Objects bar, and then click the <u>N</u>ew button. This displays the New Report dialog box. At this dialog box, specify the database table where the information for creating the mailing labels is located, and then double-click *Label Wizard* in the list box.

Use the Label Wizard to easily create mailing labels.

At the first Label Wizard dialog box, shown in figure 21.19, specify the label size, the number of labels across the row, the unit of measure, and the label type, and then click the <u>N</u>ext> button.

First Label Wizard Dialog Box

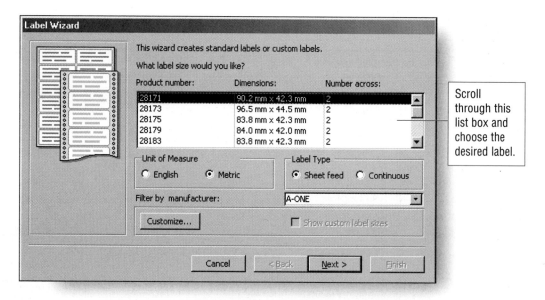

Scroll through this list box and choose the desired label.

At the second Label Wizard dialog box shown in figure 21.20, specify the font name, size, weight, and color, and then click the <u>N</u>ext> button.

figure

21.20

Second Label Wizard Dialog Box

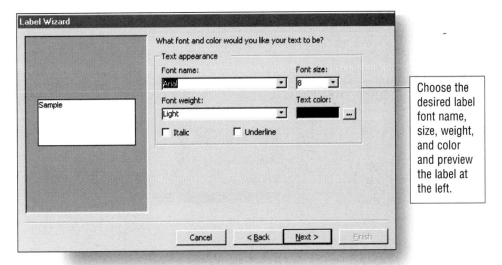

Choose the desired label font name, size, weight, and color and preview the label at the left.

Specify the fields you want included in the mailing labels at the third Label Wizard dialog box shown in figure 21.21. To do this, select the field in the Available fields list box, and then click the button containing the greater than symbol (>). This moves the field to the Prototype label. Insert the fields in the Prototype label as you want the text to display on the label. After inserting the fields in the Prototype label, click the Next> button.

figure

21.21

Third Label Wizard Dialog Box

Insert the desired fields in the Prototype label box.

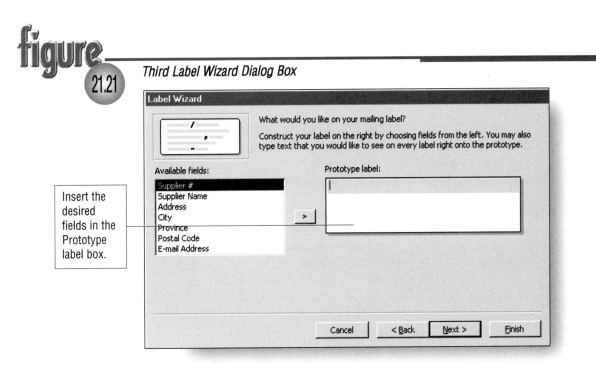

At the fourth Label Wizard dialog box, shown in figure 21.22, you can specify a field from the database file by which the labels are sorted. If you want the labels sorted (for example, by last name, postal code, etc.), insert the field by which you want the fields sorted in the Sort by list box, and then click the Next> button.

Fourth Label Wizard Dialog Box

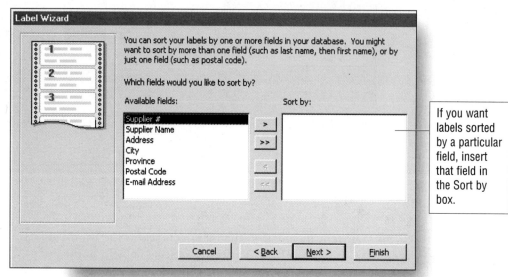

If you want labels sorted by a particular field, insert that field in the Sort by box.

At the last Label Wizard dialog box, key a name for the label file, and then click the Finish button. After a few moments, the labels display on the screen in Print Preview. Print the labels and/or close Print Preview.

Preparing Mailing Labels

(Note: The Label Wizard in early versions of Access 2000 contains a bug. If you get a message asking you to "Enter Parameter Value" when you click the Finish button in step 2f in exercise 11, click the Cancel button. (You may need to click OK at other Label Wizard dialog boxes. The labels will not display properly.)

1. Open the Outdoor Options database file.
2. At the Outdoor Options Database window, prepare mailing labels with suppliers names and addresses by completing the following steps:
   a. Click the Reports button in the Objects bar.
   b. Click the New button on the window toolbar.
   c. At the New Report dialog box, click the down-pointing triangle at the right of the *Choose the table or query where the object's data comes from* text box, and then click *Suppliers* at the drop-down menu.
   d. Double-click *Label Wizard* in the list box.

e. At the first Label Wizard dialog box, make the following changes:

1) Click English in the Unit of Measure section.

Step 2e3

2) Click the down-pointing triangle at the right side of the Filter by manufacturer option and then click *Avery* at the drop-down list.

Step 2e1

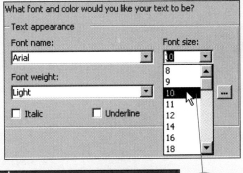

Step 2e2

3) Click *5160* in the Product number list box.

4) Click the Next> button.

f. At the second Label Wizard dialog box, change the font size to *10,* and then click the Next> button.

g. At the third Label Wizard dialog box, complete the following steps to insert the fields in the Prototype label:

1) Click *Supplier Name* in the Available fields list box and then click the button containing the greater than symbol (>).

2) Press the Enter key (this moves the insertion point down to the next line in the Prototype label).

Step 2f

3) With *Address* selected in the Available fields list box, click the button containing the greater than symbol (>).

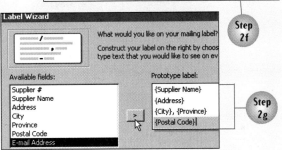

Step 2g

4) Press the Enter key.

5) With *City* selected in the Available fields list box, click the button containing the greater than symbol (>).

6) Key a comma (,) and then press the space bar.

7) With *Province* selected in the Available fields list box, click the button containing the greater than symbol (>).

8) Press the Enter key.

9) With *Postal Code* selected in the Available fields list box, click the button containing the greater than symbol (>).

10) Click the Next> button.

h. At the fourth Label Wizard dialog box, sort by postal code. To do this, click *Postal Code* in the Available fields list box and then click the button containing the greater than symbol (>).

i. Click the Next> button.

j. At the last Label Wizard dialog box, click the Finish button. (The Label Wizard automatically names the label file Labels Suppliers.) *(Note: If a message displays asking you to "Enter Parameter Value" click the Cancel button. You may need to click OK at other Label Wizard dialog boxes. The labels will not display properly.)*

3. Print the labels by clicking the Print button on the Print Preview toolbar.

4. Close the labels file. (To do this, click the Close button that displays at the right side of the Labels Suppliers Report title bar.)

5. Close the Outdoor Options database file.

Creating a Chart

In chapter 12 you learned to create charts in Excel with data in a worksheet. With the Chart Wizard, you can also create a chart with data from a database table. The Chart Wizard is available at the database file by clicking the Forms button or the Reports button in the Objects bar.

To create a chart with the Chart Wizard, open the database file, and then click either the Forms button or the Reports button in the Objects bar. Specify the database table containing the fields to be included in the chart and then double-click the Chart Wizard option in the list box. This displays the first Chart Wizard dialog box, shown in figure 21.23.

Create a chart with data from a database table to provide a visual display of data.

figure
21.23

First Chart Wizard Dialog Box

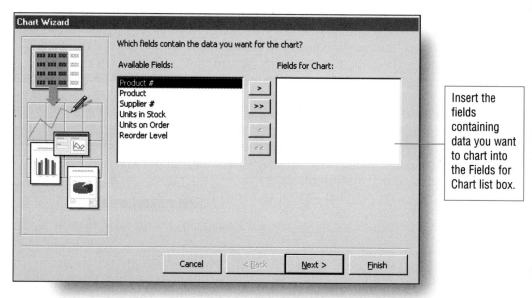

Insert the fields containing data you want to chart into the Fields for Chart list box.

At the first Chart Wizard dialog box, insert the fields you want included in the chart in the Fields for Chart list box. The first field inserted in the Fields for Chart list box will be used by the Chart Wizard as the x-axis in the chart. After inserting the fields, click the Next> button. This displays the second Chart Wizard dialog box, shown in figure 21.24.

figure
21.24

Second Chart Wizard Dialog Box

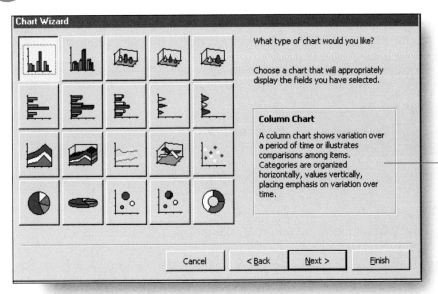

Click the desired chart, and information about the chart displays in this section.

Choose the chart type at the second Chart Wizard dialog box. To do this, click the icon representing the desired chart, and then click the Next> button. This displays the third Chart Wizard dialog box, shown in figure 21.25.

figure
21.25

Third Chart Wizard Dialog Box

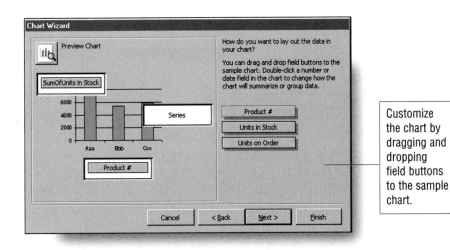

Customize the chart by dragging and dropping field buttons to the sample chart.

At the third Chart Wizard dialog box, specify how you want labels to appear in the chart. To do this, double-click a label in the preview chart. At the drop-down menu that displays, click the desired label option. At this dialog box, you can also add another field to the chart. For example, in exercise 12, you will be charting Units on Order as well as Units in Stock. To do this, you will drag the desired field from the right side of the dialog box to the appropriate location in the preview chart. When all changes have been made, click the Next> button. At the fourth, and last, Chart Wizard dialog box, key a name for the chart, and then click the Finish button.

Creating a Chart

1. Open the Outdoor Options database file.
2. Click the Tables button in the Objects bar.
3. Open the Products table by double-clicking *Products* in the list box.
4. Delete the records of those products where zero (0) displays in the *Units on Order* field (at the warning message, click Yes). After deleting the records, click the Save button on the Table Datasheet toolbar, and then close the Products database table.
5. At the Outdoor Options Database window, click the Reports button in the Objects bar.
6. Create a chart with fields from the Products database table by completing the following steps:
   a. Click the New button on the window toolbar.
   b. At the New Report dialog box, click the down-pointing triangle at the right of the Choose the table or query where the object's data comes from option, and then click Products.
   c. Double-click *Chart Wizard* in the list box.
   d. At the first Chart Wizard dialog box, complete the followings steps:
      1) With *Product #* selected in the Available Fields list box, click the button containing the greater than symbol (>).

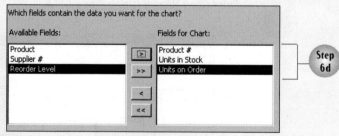

      2) Click *Units in Stock* in the Available Fields list box and then click the button containing the greater than symbol (>).
      3) With *Units on Order* selected in the Available Fields list box, click the button containing the greater than symbol (>).
      4) Click the Next> button.
   e. At the second Chart Wizard dialog box, click the Next> button.
   f. At the third Chart Wizard dialog box, complete the following steps:
      1) Position the arrow pointer on the Units on Order button at the right side of the dialog box, hold down the left mouse button, drag the outline of the button to the bottom of the *SumOfUnits in Stock* field that displays in the

preview chart, and then release
the left mouse button.

2) Double-click the *SumOfUnits in Stock* field that displays in the preview chart.

3) At the Summarize dialog box, double-click *None* in the list box. (This changes *SumOfUnits in Stock* to *Units in Stock*. By default, the Chart Wizard will sum the number of units in stock. Changing the field to *Units in Stock* tells the Chart Wizard to simply display the number of units in stock and not the sum.)

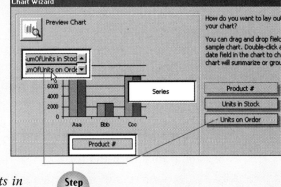

4) Double-click the *SumOfUnits on Order* field that displays in the preview chart.

5) At the Summarize dialog box, double-click *None* in the list box. (This changes *SumOfUnits on Order* to *Units on Order*.)

6) Click the <u>N</u>ext> button.

g. At the fourth Chart Wizard dialog box, key **Product Units**, and then click the <u>F</u>inish button.

7. With the chart displayed in Print Preview, print the chart by clicking the Print button on the Print Preview toolbar.

8. After the chart is printed, click the Close button that displays at the right side of the Report1 Report title bar. At the message asking if you want to save the changes to the design of the report, click <u>N</u>o.

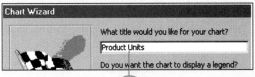

9. Close the Outdoor Options database table.

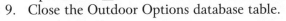

chapter summary

► A form generally improves the ease with which data is entered into a database table. A form can be created with the AutoForm feature and also with the Form Wizard.

► A record in a form displays with navigation buttons that are used to display various records in the form.

► Print a form in the same manner as a database table. Changes can be made to the page margins and/or page orientation at the Page Setup dialog box.

► Add a new record to a form by clicking the New Record button on the Form View toolbar or by clicking the button at the bottom of the record that displays with a right-pointing triangle followed by an asterisk.

► Delete a record by displaying the record and then clicking the Delete Record button on the Form View toolbar.

- The Form Wizard walks you through the steps for creating a form and lets you specify the fields you want included in the form, a layout for the records, the desired formatting, and a name for the form.

- A form can be created with fields from tables that are connected by a one-to-many relationship.

- A form is comprised of a series of controls, which are objects that display titles or descriptions, accept data, or perform actions.

- In Design view, you can use fields from a table to create controls in the Design grid and also add controls with buttons on the toolbox palette.

- Associate a table with the form to use fields to create controls.

- Move control objects in the Design grid. A label control and its corresponding text box control for a field can be moved individually or together.

- Use the sizing handles around a selected control object to change the size of the object.

- Customize control objects with options at the properties sheet.

- To align control objects in the Design grid, select the objects, click Format, point to Align, and then click the desired alignment at the side menu.

- To add a control using a button on the Toolbox, click the button, move the pointer to the position on the form where you want to place the object, and then drag to create the object.

- Turn on the display of the Form Header and the Form Footer by clicking View and then Form Header/Footer.

- A Form Header displays at the top of the form in Form view and at the beginning of a printout started from the Form view screen.

- A Form Footer displays at the bottom of the form in Form view and at the end of a printout started from the Form view screen.

- A calculated control uses a mathematical equation to determine the contents that are displayed in the control object. A calculated field is used to perform mathematical operations on existing fields but it does not exist in the table associated with the form.

- Data in a database table can be inserted in a report, which lets you control how the data appears on the page when printed.

- The Report Wizard walks you through the steps for creating a report and lets you specify the fields you want included in the report, the level of fields in the report, the order in which records display in the report, the layout of the report, the report style, and a name for the report.

- Like a form, a report can be created with fields from related database tables.

- A report, like a form, can be created in Design view. A report includes up to five sections including Report Header, Page Header, Detail, Page Footer, and Report Footer.

- To add fields to a report in Design view, associate the report with the desired table.

- Move, resize, and customize control objects in the report Design view in the same manner as control objects in the form Design view.

- Use buttons on the Toolbox to add controls to a report in Design view.

- Mailing labels can be created with data in a database table using the Label Wizard. The Label Wizard lets you specify the label type; the fields you want included in the labels; the font name, size, weight, and color; a sorting order; and a name for the mailing label file.

- A chart can be created with specific fields in a database table using the Chart Wizard. The Chart Wizard lets you specify the fields you want included in the chart, the chart type, how labels will appear in the chart, and the name for the chart file.

Mouse/Keyboard

Create a form with AutoForm	Open database table; click New Object button, then click AutoF<u>o</u>rm
Add a new record in a form	Display record, then click New Record button on Form View toolbar; or click button containing right-pointing triangle followed by asterisk
Delete a record in a form	Display record, click Delete Record button on Form View toolbar
Begin Form Wizard	Open database file, click <u>N</u>ew button, then double-click Form Wizard
Display the form Design view	Click Forms button on theObjects bar, and then double-click *Create Form in design view*
Begin Report Wizard	Open database file, click <u>N</u>ew button, then double-click Report Wizard
Display the report Design view	Click Reports button on the Objects bar, and then double-click *Create Report in design view*
Begin Label Wizard	Open database file, click <u>N</u>ew button, specify database table, then double-click Label Wizard
Begin Chart Wizard	Open database file, click <u>N</u>ew button, specify database table, then double-click Chart Wizard

thinking offline

Completion: In the space provided at the right, indicate the correct term, symbol, or command.

1. To create a form with the AutoForm feature, open the database file, click the database table in the list box and then click this button on the Database toolbar.

2. Use these buttons, which appear along the bottom of a record in a form, to display the next record in the form, the previous record, the first record, or the last record.

3. Click this button on the Form View toolbar to add a new record to the form.

4. Click this button on the Form View toolbar to delete a record from the form.

5. In the form Design view, add controls with buttons on this palette.

6. This section of the form in Design view is set up as a grid.

7. This appears at the bottom of the form in Form view and at the end of a printout started from the Form view screen.

8. This type of control uses a mathematical equation to determine the contents that are displayed in the control object.

9. Use this to guide you through the steps for creating a report.

10. When all the steps in the Report Wizard are completed, the report displays in this view.

11. This appears at the top of each page of a report and generally includes information such as column headings identifying the data in the report.

12. Use these to increase or decrease the size of a selected control object.

13. To create a chart with the Chart Wizard, open the database file, and then click either the Forms button or this button in the Objects bar.

14. When creating a chart with the Chart Wizard, the first field inserted in the Fields for Chart list box will be used as this axis in the chart.

15. Suppose you are using the Report Wizard with the Outdoor Options database file to show information on what products are currently on order, from what company, and the e-mail address of the companies. At the first Report Wizard step, what fields would you insert from the Products database table and what fields would you insert from the Suppliers database table?

16. When using the Chart Wizard, specify the fields in the Products database table (in the Outdoor Options database file) you would use to create a chart that shows the reorder level for products. Write the fields in the space provided below.

working hands-on

Assessment 1

1. Open the Outdoor Options database file.
2. Use the AutoForm feature to create a form with the data in the Suppliers database table.
3. After creating the form, add the following records to the Suppliers form:

Supplier #	=	12
Supplier Name	=	**Seaside Suppliers**
Address	=	**4120 Shoreline Drive**
City	=	**Vancouver**
Province	=	**BC**
Postal Code	=	**V2V 8K4**
E-mail Address	=	**seaside@recreate.fun.com**

Supplier #	=	34
Supplier Name	=	**Carson Company**
Address	=	**120 Plaza Center**
City	=	**Vancouver**
Province	=	**BC**
Postal Code	=	**V2V 1K6**
E-mail Address	=	**carson@recreate.fun.com**

4. Delete the record containing information on Manning, Inc.
5. Save the form with the name offered by Access (Suppliers).
6. Print and then close the Suppliers form.
7. Close the Outdoor Options database file.

Assessment 2

1. Open the Outdoor Options database file.
2. At the Outdoor Options Database window, click the Forms button in the Objects bar.
3. Delete the Suppliers form that displays in the list box. (For assistance, refer to exercise 3, step 3.)
4. Create a form for the Suppliers database table using the Form Wizard. Use all the fields in the Suppliers database table to create the form. You determine the format style. Name the form *Suppliers*.
5. When the Form Wizard is finished, add the following record:

Supplier #	=	50
Supplier Name	=	**Binder Corporation**
Address	=	**9033 East 32nd**
City	=	**Vancouver**
Province	=	**BC**
Postal Code	=	**V2V 3K2**
E-mail Address	=	**binder@recreate.fun.com**

6. Delete the record containing information on Langley Corporation.

7. Save the Suppliers form.
8. Print the Suppliers form and then close the form.
9. Close the Outdoor Options database file.

Assessment 3

1. Open the Outdoor Options database file.
2. Create a form from two related database tables using the Form Wizard with the following specifications:
   a. At the first Form Wizard dialog box, insert the following fields in the Selected Fields list box:

   From the Products database table:
   > *Product #*
   > *Product*
   > *Units on Order*

   From the Suppliers database table:
   > *Supplier #*
   > *Supplier Name*
   > *Address*
   > *City*
   > *Province*
   > *Postal Code*

   b. Do not make any changes at the second Form Wizard dialog box.
   c. Do not make any changes at the third Form Wizard dialog box.
   d. You determine the format style at the fourth Form Wizard dialog box.
   e. At the fifth Form Wizard dialog box, key the name **Units on Order**.
   f. When the first record displays, print the form.
   g. Close the record that displays.
3. Close the Outdoor Options database file.

Assessment 4

1. Open the Outdoor Options database file.
2. Open the Orders table and then make the following changes:
   a. Display the table in design view.
   b. Insert a row above Order Date.
   c. Specify the following for the new row:
   > Field Name   =   *Unit Price*
   > Data Type   =   *Currency*
   > Description   =   *Unit price*

   d. Save the table.
   e. Change to the datasheet view and then enter the following in the specified order number record:
   > Order #4   =   **72.25**
   > Order #5   =   **112.00**

   f. Save and then close the table.
3. Create a form by design with the following specifications:
   a. Create a form by design with all the fields in the Orders table. (You determine the location of the fields in the Design grid.)

b. Add a calculated control that multiplies the Unit Price by the Units Ordered. Change the format of the text box calculated control to *Currency*.

c. Apply formatting of your choosing to the label and text box control objects. (Change at least the Font Name, Fore Color, and Back Color.)

d. Add the Form Header **Outdoor Options – Orders Form**. Change the Font Name, Font Size, and Font Weight of the Form Header. (You determine the font, size, and weight.)

e. Add the Form Footer **Order Totals**. Change the Font Name, Font Size, and Font Weight of the Form Footer. (You determine the font, size, and weight.)

f. Save the form and name it Order Totals.

g. Change to the Form view.

h. Print the currently displayed record.

4. Close the Order Totals form.

5. Close the Outdoor Options database file.

Assessment 5

1. Open the Outdoor Options database file.

2. Create a report using the Report Wizard with the following specifications:

a. At the first Report Wizard dialog box, insert the following fields in the Selected Fields list box:

   From the Products database table:

   Product #

   Product

   Units on Order

   From the Suppliers database table:

   Supplier #

   Supplier Name

b. At the second Report Wizard dialog box, click *by Suppliers* in the list box.

c. Do not make any changes at the third Report Wizard dialog box.

d. At the fourth Report Wizard dialog box, identify Product # as the sort order.

e. You determine the layout style at the fifth Report Wizard dialog box.

f. You determine the style at the sixth Report Wizard dialog box.

g. At the seventh Report Wizard dialog box, key the name **Units on Order**.

h. When the report displays in Print Preview, print the report.

i. Close the report.

3. Close the Outdoor Options database file.

Assessment 6

(Note: If you got a message asking you to "Enter Parameter Value" in exercise 11, skip this assessment.)

1. Open the Outdoor Options database file.

2. Add the following records to the Suppliers database table:

Supplier #	=	59
Supplier Name	=	**DAL Manufacturing**
Address	=	**3100 Industrial Park**
City	=	**Vancouver**
Province	=	**BC**
Postal Code	=	**V2V 2K6**
E-mail Address	=	**dalmanu@recreate.fun.com**

Supplier #	=	88
Supplier Name	=	**Spinnett Corporation**
Address	=	**500 Victoria Drive**
City	=	**Port Moody**
Province	=	**BC**
Postal Code	=	**V3V 2K5**
E-mail Address	=	**spinnett@recreate.fun.com**

3. Save and then close the Suppliers database table.
4. Use the Label Wizard to create mailing labels (you determine the label type) with the suppliers' names and addresses and sorted by suppliers' names. Name the mailing label file Supplier Mailing Labels.
5. Print the mailing labels.
6. Close the mailing labels file and then close the Outdoor Options database file.

Assessment 7

1. Open the Outdoor Options database file.
2. Click the Reports button in the side bar and then click the <u>N</u>ew button.
3. At the New Report dialog box, specify that you want to choose fields from the Orders database table, and then double-click the *Chart Wizard*.
4. Create a chart with fields in the Orders database table with the following specifications:
   a. At the first Chart Wizard dialog box, insert *Order #* and *Amount* in the Fields for Chart list box.
   b. Do not make any changes at the second Chart Wizard dialog box.
   c. At the third Chart Wizard dialog box, double-click the *SumOfAmount* field, and then double-click *None* at the Summarize dialog box.
   d. At the fourth Chart Wizard dialog box, key **Order Amounts**, and then click <u>F</u>inish.
5. Print the chart and then close it without saving the changes.
6. Close the Outdoor Options database file.

Assessment 8

1. Use Access's Help feature to learn about the AutoReport feature.
2. Open the Outdoor Options database file and then create a columnar AutoReport with the Products database table. Print the report and then close it without saving it.
3. Close the Outdoor Options database file.

 Chapter 22

22

Using Database Wizards and OfficeLinks

PERFORMANCE OBJECTIVES

Upon successful completion of chapter 22, you will be able to:
- Create a database with sample data using a Database Wizard.
- Manipulate data within the database file.
- Export Access data to Excel.
- Export Access data to Word.
- Merge Access data with a Word document.
- Import data to a new table.
- Link data to new table.
- Use the Office Clipboard.
- Save a table, query, or form as a Web page.
- Apply a theme to a Web page.
- Create hyperlinks.
- Backup, restore, copy, and repair a database file.

In the previous chapter, you learned to use wizards to organize fields in a variety of formats including forms, reports, mailing labels, and charts. Access also includes a number of Database Wizards you can use to create an entire database file. In this chapter, you will create a database file using a wizard and then view the tables and forms within the database file.

Microsoft Office Professional is a suite of programs that allows easy data exchange between programs. In this chapter you will learn how to export data from Access to Excel and Word and also how to merge Access data with a Word document.

Creating a Database with a Wizard

Access provides numerous Database Wizards you can use to create database files. These wizards include all the fields, formatting, tables, and reports needed to manage data. Most of the work of creating the database file is done for you by the wizard. In exercise 1, you will be using the Contact Management Database Wizard to create a contact management database file. To see a list of available Database Wizards, click the New button on the Database toolbar (first button from the left). This displays the New dialog box. At this dialog box, click the Databases tab and the dialog box displays as shown in figure 22.1.

figure

22.1

New Dialog Box with Databases Tab Selected

Click the Databases tab to display a list of available Database Wizards.

If your dialog box displays with fewer wizards than what you see in figure 22.1, not all components of the Access program were installed. You may need to run the Microsoft Installation process again to include the Database Wizards. (For general information on adding/removing programs, refer to the Getting Started section at the beginning of this textbook.)

If Access was installed in a minimum or laptop configuration, not all wizards were installed.

At the New dialog box with the Databases tab selected, double-click the desired wizard. This displays the File New Database dialog box. At this dialog box, key a new name for the database or accept the default name provided by Access, and then press Enter or click Create.

After a few moments, the first Database Wizard dialog box displays as shown in figure 22.2. This dialog box shows information about the Contact Management database you will create in exercise 1. Depending on the database you choose, this information will vary. After reading the information in the dialog box, click the Next> button.

figure

22.2

First Database Wizard Dialog Box (for Contact Management)

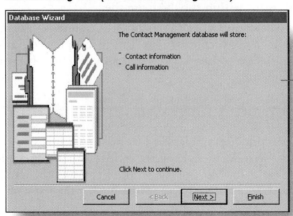

This dialog box displays information on what the database will store.

Chapter Twenty-Two

At the second Database Wizard dialog box, shown in figure 22.3, notice how the wizard provides predesigned tables displayed in the Tables in the database list box and also fields displayed in the Fields in the table list box. Most field names in the Fields in the table list box are preceded by a check mark. Some database tables may include fields in the Fields in the table list box that display in italics with no check mark in the check box. These are additional fields that are not included as part of the table. If you want one of these extra fields included in a table, click the check box to insert a check mark. When all changes are made to this dialog box, click the Next> button.

figure

22.3 *Second Database Wizard Dialog Box*

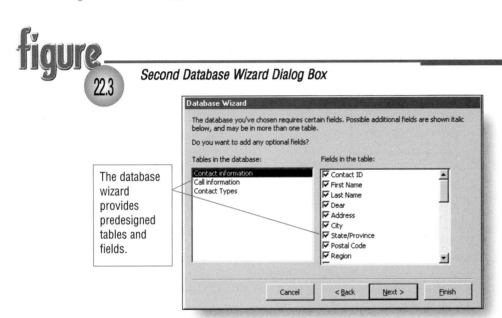

The database wizard provides predesigned tables and fields.

Choose a screen display style at the third Database Wizard dialog box, shown in figure 22.4. A sample displays at the left side of the dialog box. After choosing the screen display, click the Next> button.

figure

22.4 *Third Database Wizard Dialog Box*

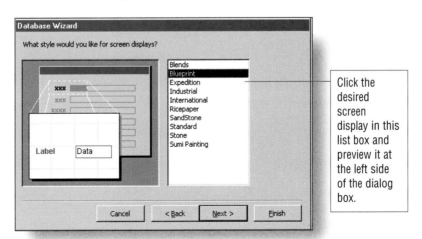

Click the desired screen display in this list box and preview it at the left side of the dialog box.

The fourth Database Wizard dialog box, shown in figure 22.5, asks you to choose a style for printed reports. As in the previous dialog box, a sample displays at the left side of the dialog box. After choosing the style, click the Next> button.

figure
22.5

Fourth Database Wizard Dialog Box

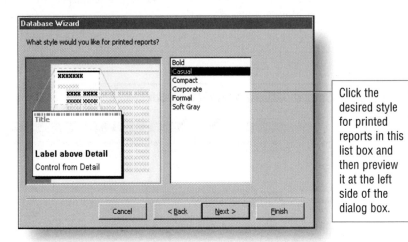

Click the desired style for printed reports in this list box and then preview it at the left side of the dialog box.

Key a name for the database or accept the default at the fifth Database Wizard dialog box shown in figure 22.6. At this dialog box, you can also choose to include a picture in all reports. After making these decisions, click the Next> button.

figure
22.6

Fifth Database Wizard Dialog Box

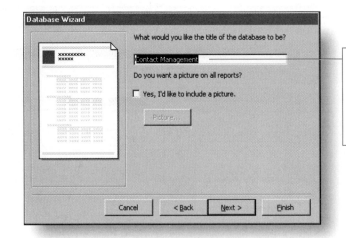

Key a name for the database in this text box or accept the default name.

The sixth (and last) Database Wizard dialog box tells you that the wizard has all the information it needs to build the database. By default, the database will start when the database is completed. Remove the check mark from this option if you do not want the database to start when completed. Click the Finish button and the wizard builds the database. This process can take several minutes.

When the database is completed, a Main Switchboard dialog box displays as shown in figure 22.7. At this dialog box, you can choose to enter or view products, enter or view other information in the database, preview reports, change the switchboard items, or exit the database.

Main Switchboard Dialog Box

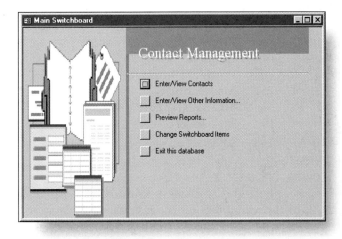

In exercise 1, you will be creating a contact management database. When the database is completed, you will enter two records and then view some of the different database tables and forms contained in the database.

Creating a Contact Management Database with a Wizard

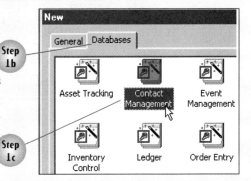

1. Create a contact management database by completing the following steps:
   a. At the blank Access screen, click the New button on the Database toolbar.
   b. At the New dialog box, click the Databases tab.
   c. Double-click *Contact Management* in the list box.

d. At the File New Database dialog box, key **Contacts**, and then press Enter or click the Create button.

e. At the first Database Wizard dialog box (see figure 22.2), read the information, and then click the Next> button.

f. At the second Database Wizard dialog box (see figure 22.3), click the Next> button. (This tells the wizard to use all default tables and fields.)

g. At the third Database Wizard dialog box (see figure 22.4), click *Blueprint* in the list box, and then click the Next> button.

h. At the fourth Database Wizard dialog box (see figure 22.5), click *Casual* in the list box, and then click the Next> button.

i. At the fifth Database Wizard dialog box (see figure 22.6), click Next>.

j. At the sixth Database Wizard dialog box, click the Finish button.

k. After a few minutes, the Main Switchboard dialog box displays.

2. At the Main Switchboard, complete the following steps:

a. Click the Enter/View Contacts button and then enter the following information in the specified fields:

First Name	=	**Robin**	*Contact ID*	=	(AutoNumber)
Last Name	=	**Osborn**	*Title*	=	**Manager**
Company	=	**Westside Storage**	*Work Phone*	=	**(612) 555-4550**
Dear	=	**Ms. Osborn**	*Work Extension*	=	245
Address	=	**403 West 22nd**	*Mobile Phone*	=	**(612) 555-1209**
City	=	**St. Cloud**	*Fax Number*	=	**(612) 555-4590**
State/Province	=	**MN**			
Postal Code	=	**55200**			
Country	=	**U.S.A.**			

b. Click the 2 button that displays towards the bottom of the record. (This displays page 2 of the record.) Enter the following information in the specified fields:

Contact Name	=	(Access automatically inserts *Robin Osborn*)
Contact Type	=	(skip this field)
Email Name	=	**rosborn@storage.com**
Referred By	=	**Samuel Eldred**
Notes	=	(skip this field)

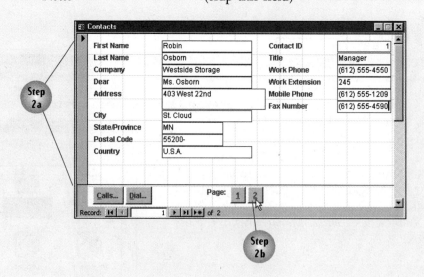

c. Click the New Record button (if necessary, click the Page 1 button located at the bottom of the form) and then key the following information in the specified fields:

First Name	=	**Carol**	Contact ID	=	(AutoNumber)
Last Name	=	**Hoyt**	Title	=	**Owner**
Company	=	**Hoyt Construction**	Work Phone	=	**(612) 555-4322**
Dear	=	**Ms. Hoyt**	Work Extension	=	**10**
Address	=	**900 North 21st**	Mobile Phone	=	**(612) 555-4100**
City	=	**St. Cloud**	Fax Number	=	**(612) 555-4201**
State/Province	=	**MN**			
Postal Code	=	**55200**			
Country	=	**U.S.A.**			

d. Click the 2 button that displays towards the bottom of the record. (This displays page 2 of the record.) Enter the following information in the specified fields:

Contact Name	=	(Access automatically inserts *Carol Hoyt*)
Contact Type	=	(skip this field)
Email Name	=	**choyt@northset.com**
Referred By	=	**Jared Snyder**
Notes	=	(skip this field)

3. Click the Save button on the toolbar to save the records.
4. Close the Contacts form.
5. Close the Main Switchboard dialog box and display the Contacts Database window by completing the following steps:
   a. With the Main Switchboard dialog box displayed, click the Close button that displays at the right side of the dialog box title bar. (This closes the Main Switchboard dialog box and displays the minimized Contacts.)
   b. Click the Restore button on the minimized Contacts title bar. (This displays the Contacts Database window with the Forms button selected.)
6. View various tables, forms, and reports in the database file by completing the following steps:
   a. Click the Tables button in the Objects bar.
   b. Double-click *Calls* in the list box, (this opens the Calls table), look at the fields in the table, and then close the table.
   c. Double-click *Contact Types* in the list box, look at the fields in the table, and then close the table.
   d. Double-click *Contacts* in the list box, look at the fields in the table, and then close the table.
   e. Click the Forms button in the Objects bar.
   f. Double-click *Contacts* in the list box, look at the layout of the form, and then close the form.
   g. Click the Reports button in the Objects bar.
   h. Double-click *Alphabetical Contact Listing* in the list box.
   i. When the report displays, print it by clicking the Print button.
   j. Close the report.
7. Investigate the relationship between tables created by the wizard by completing the following steps:
   a. With the Contacts Database window displayed, click the Relationships button on the Database toolbar.

b. At the Relationships window, notice the one-to-many relationship created by the wizard. View information about the relationship by completing the following steps:

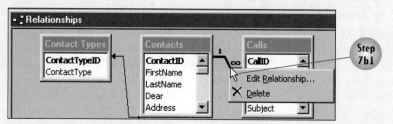

1) Position the arrow pointer on the black line connecting *ContactID* in the *Contacts* table with *ContactID* in the *Calls* table and then click the *right* mouse button.

2) At the shortcut menu that displays, click Edit Relationship. This displays the Edit Relationships dialog box, which displays information on the type of relationship created between the tables.

3) After viewing the information in the Edit Relationships dialog box, click the Cancel button.

c. Click the Close button at the right side of the Relationships window title bar.

8. Close the Contacts database file.

Viewing a database file created by the Database Wizard provides you with an example of what can be included in a database file. Consider using some of the other wizards displayed in the New dialog box with the Databases tab selected. Each database is set up differently with different tables, forms, and reports. The sample Contacts database you created in exercise 1 is fairly large—it will probably occupy over 800,000 bytes of space on your disk. For this reason, you will be deleting the Contacts database table before completing exercise 3.

Deleting a Database File

The database files created by the wizards can be quite large and take up considerable space on your disk. If you no longer need a database file, consider deleting it. To delete a database file, display the Open dialog box, click the database file to be deleted, and then click the Delete button on the dialog box toolbar. At the message asking if you are sure you want to delete the database file, click Yes.

Deleting the Contacts Database File

1. At the blank Access screen, click the Open button on the Database toolbar.
2. At the Open dialog box, click *Contacts* in the list box, and then click the Delete button on the dialog box toolbar.
3. At the message asking if you are sure you want to delete the database file, click Yes.
4. Click Cancel to close the Open dialog box.

Using OfficeLinks

One of the advantages of a suite of programs like Microsoft Office Professional is the ability to exchange data from one program to another. Access, like the other programs in the suite, offers a feature to export data from Access into Word and/or Excel. Exporting data can be easily accomplished with the OfficeLinks button on the Database toolbar.

Data can be exported from Access to Word and/or Excel.

Exporting Data to Excel

Access data saved in a table, form, or report can be exported to Excel. Use an option from the OfficeLinks drop-down menu to export data from Access to Excel. The data is saved as an Excel file in the folder where Access is installed. Excel is automatically started when the file is opened.

OfficeLinks

To export data to Excel, open the database file, and then click the name of the database table, form, or report you want saved in Excel. With the file selected, click the down-pointing triangle at the right side of the OfficeLinks button on the Database toolbar, and then click Analyze It with MS Excel at the drop-down menu. The data is converted to an Excel worksheet, Excel is opened, and the data is displayed in a worksheet. The worksheet is automatically saved with the same name as the name in the database file except the Excel extension of .xls is added to the name.

Data exported from Access to Excel is automatically saved as an Excel worksheet with the .xls extension.

exercise

Saving a Database Table as an Excel Worksheet

(Note: If you still have the Outdoor Options database you copied on your disk in chapter 21, delete that database.)

1. Copy the Outdoor Options database file from the CD that accompanies this textbook to your disk.
2. Remove the read-only attribute from Outdoor Options.
3. Open the Outdoor Options database file and then click the Tables button on the Objects bar.
4. Save the Orders database table as an Excel worksheet and format the worksheet by completing the following steps:

   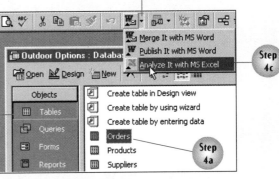

   a. Click once on *Orders* in the list box. (This selects the database table.)
   b. Click the down-pointing triangle at the right side of the OfficeLinks button on the Database toolbar.
   c. At the drop-down menu that displays, click Analyze It with MS Excel.
   d. When the data displays on the screen in Excel as a worksheet, make the following changes:

1) Select cells A1 through F6 and then apply the List 3 autoformat.

2) Select cells A2 through D6 and then change the alignment to center.

   e. Click the Save button on the Standard toolbar. *(Note: If a message displays telling you that Orders .xls is a Microsoft Excel 5.0/95 workbook and asking if you want to overwrite it, click Yes.)*

   f. Print the worksheet centered horizontally and vertically on the page.

   g. Close the worksheet saving the changes, and then exit Excel.

5. Close the Outdoor Options database file.

When you use the Analyze It with MS Excel option from the OfficeLinks drop-down menu, the table becomes an Excel worksheet. All Excel editing capabilities are available for changing or modifying the worksheet. A form can also be converted to a worksheet with the Analyze It with MS Excel option.

exercise

Saving a Form as an Excel Worksheet

1. Open the Outdoor Options database file.

2. Create a form with fields from the Orders table by completing the following steps:

   a. At the Outdoor Options Database window, click the Forms button in the Objects bar.

   b. Click the New button on the dialog box toolbar.

   c. At the New Form dialog box, double-click Form Wizard in the list box.

   d. At the first Form Wizard dialog box, insert the following fields from the Orders database tables:

   > Order #
   > Product #
   > Order Date
   > Units Ordered
   > Amount

   Step 2d

   Step 2e

   After entering the fields, click the Next> button.

   e. At the second Form Wizard dialog box, click the Next> button.

   f. At the third Form Wizard dialog box, click *Blueprint* in the format style list box, and then click the Next> button.

   g. At the fourth Form Wizard dialog box, key the name **Units on Order**, and then click the Finish button.

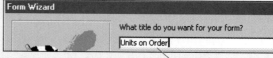

   h. When the first record displays, click the Close button.

3. Save the Units on Order form as an Excel worksheet and format the worksheet by completing the following steps:

   Step 2g

a. Click once on *Units on Order* in the list box. (This selects the form.)

b. Click the down-pointing triangle at the right side of the OfficeLinks button on the Database toolbar.

c. At the drop-down menu that displays, click Analyze It with MS Excel.

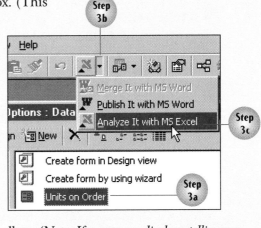

d. When the data displays on the screen in Excel as a worksheet, make the following changes:

   1) Select cells A1 through E6 and then apply the Colorful 1 autoformat.

   2) Select cells A2 through D6 and then change the alignment to center.

e. Click the Save button on the Standard toolbar. *(Note: If a message displays telling you that Units on Order.xls is a Microsoft Excel 5.0/95 workbook and asking if you want to overwrite it, click yes.)*

f. Print and then close the worksheet.

g. Exit Excel.

4. Close the Outdoor Options database file.

Exporting Data to Word

Data can be exported from Access to Word in the same manner as exporting to Excel. To export data to Word, open the database file, select the table, form, or report you want to export to Word, and then click the OfficeLinks button on the Database toolbar. At the drop-down menu that displays, click Publish It with MS Word. Word is automatically opened and the data is inserted in a Word document. The Word document is automatically saved with the same name as the database table, form, or report you selected, except the file extension rtf is added to the name. An rtf file is saved in "rich-text format," which preserves formatting such as fonts and styles. A document saved with the rtf extension can be opened with Microsoft Word and other Windows word processing or desktop publishing programs.

> **Hint**
> Data exported from Access to Word is automatically saved as an rtf (rich-text format) file.

Saving a Database Table as a Word Table

1. Open the Outdoor Options database file.

2. At the Outdoor Options Database window, click the Tables button in the Objects bar.

3. Save the Orders database table as a Word table and then add additional text to the Word document by completing the following steps:

   a. Click once on *Orders* in the list box. (This selects the table.)

   b. Click the down-pointing triangle at the right side of the OfficeLinks button on the Database toolbar.

c. At the drop-down menu that displays, click Publish It with MS Word.
d. When the data displays on the screen in Word as a table, add text to the document (not the table) by completing the following steps:
   1) Press the Enter key three times. (This will insert blank lines above the table.)
   2) Move the insertion point to the beginning of the document, turn on bold, and then key **TRANSACTIONS: 02/15/99 - 02/28/99**.
   3) Press the Enter key twice and then key the following text (the text is displayed in bold here for easier reading—do not key the text in bold):
       The following table shows the ordering transactions that occurred between February 15, 1999, and February 28, 1999.
e. Click the Save button on the Standard toolbar.
f. Print the document.
g. Close the document and then exit Word.
4. Close the Outdoor Options database file.

exercise

Saving a Report as a Word Document

1. Open the Outdoor Options database file.
2. At the Outdoor Options Database window, click the Reports button in the Objects bar.
3. Create a report with the Report Wizard by completing the following steps:
    a. Click the New button on the dialog box toolbar.
    b. At the New Report dialog box, double-click *Report Wizard* in the list box.
    c. At the first Report Wizard dialog box, insert the following fields in the Selected Fields list box:

        From the Products database table:
            Product
            Units on Order
        From the Suppliers database table:
            Supplier Name
            E-mail Address

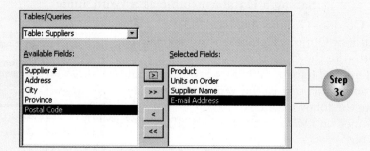

d. After inserting the fields, click the Next> button.

e. At the second Report Wizard dialog box, make sure *by Products* is selected in the list box in the upper left corner, and then click the Next> button.

f. At the third Report Wizard dialog box, increase the priority level of the *Product* field. To do this, make sure *Product* is selected in the list box, and then click the button containing the greater than symbol (>). Click the Next> button.

g. At the fourth Report Wizard dialog box, click the Next> button. (Do not specify a sort order.)

h. At the fifth Report Wizard dialog box, click Align Left 1, and then click the Next> button.

i. At the sixth Report Wizard dialog box, click *Corporate* in the list box, and then click the Next> button.

j. At the seventh Report Wizard dialog box, click the Finish button.

k. When the report displays in Print Preview, view the report, and then click the Print button that displays on the Print Preview toolbar.

l. Click the Close button (displays with an X) that displays at the right side of the Products title bar.

4. Save the Products report as a Word document by completing the following steps:

a. Click once on *Products* in the list box.

b. Click the down-pointing triangle at the right side of the OfficeLinks button on the Database toolbar.

c. At the drop-down menu that displays, click Publish It with MS Word.

d. When the data displays on the screen in Word, print the report by clicking the Print button on the Standard toolbar.

e. Click the Save button (to save the document with the default name of Products).

f. Close the document and then exit Word.

5. Close the Outdoor Options database file.

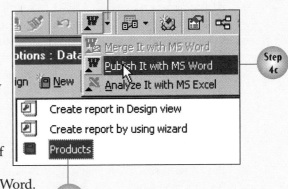

Merging Access Data with a Word Document

Data from an Access database table can be merged with a Word document. When merging data in an Access table with a Word document, the data in the Access table is considered the data source and the Word document is considered the main document. When the merge is completed, the merged documents display in Word.

When merging Access data, you can either key the text in the main document or merge Access data with an existing Word document. In exercise 7, you will merge Access data with an existing Word document and in exercise 8, you will key the main document.

Data in an Access database table can be merged with a Word main document.

exercise 7

Merging Access Data with a Word Document

1. Open the Outdoor Options database file.
2. At the Outdoor Options Database window, click the Tables button in the Objects bar.
3. Merge data in the Suppliers database table with a Word document by completing the following steps:
   a. Click once on *Suppliers* in the list box.
   b. Click the down-pointing triangle at the right side of the OfficeLinks button on the Database toolbar.
   c. At the drop-down menu that displays, click <u>M</u>erge It with MS Word.
   d. At the Microsoft Word Mail Merge Wizard dialog box, make sure <u>L</u>ink your data to an existing Microsoft Word document is selected, and then click OK.
   e. At the Select Microsoft Word Document dialog box, make the *Chapter 22* folder on your disk the active folder, and then double-click the document named Outdoor Letter.
   f. Click the button on the Taskbar representing the Outdoor Letter document, and then maximize the window by clicking the Maximize button at the right side of the Outdoor Letter title bar.
   g. Press the down arrow key six times (not the Enter key) and then key the current date.
   h. Press the down arrow key five times and then insert fields for merging from the Suppliers database table by completing the following steps:
      1) Click the Insert Merge Field button located at the left side of the Merge toolbar.
      2) At the drop-down menu that displays, click *Supplier_Name*.
      3) Press Enter, click the Insert Merge Field button, and then click *Address* at the drop-down menu.
      4) Press Enter, click the Insert Merge Field button, and then click *City* at the drop-down menu.
      5) Key a comma (,) and then press the space bar.
      6) Click the Insert Merge Field button and then click *Province*.
      7) Press Enter, click the Insert Merge Field button, and then click *Postal_Code* at the drop-down menu.

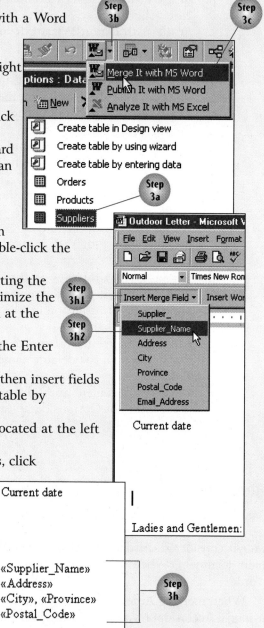

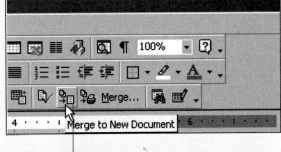

8) Replace the *XX* letters that display toward the bottom of the letter with your initials.

    i. Click the Merge to New Document button located toward the right side of the Merge toolbar.

    j. When the merge is completed, save the new document as Word Ch 22, Ex 07 in the *Chapter 22* folder on your disk.

    k. Print just the first two pages (two letters) of Word Ch 22, Ex 07.

    l. Close Word Ch 22, Ex 07 and then close Outdoor Letter, without saving the changes.

    m. Exit Word.

4. Close the Outdoor Options database file.

Merging Access Data with a New Word Document

1. Open the Outdoor Options database file.
2. At the Outdoor Options Database window, click the Tables button in the Objects bar.
3. Merge data in the Suppliers database table to a new Word document by completing the following steps:

    a. Click once on *Suppliers* in the list box.

    b. Click the down-pointing triangle at the right side of the OfficeLinks button on the Database toolbar.

    c. At the drop-down menu that displays, click Merge It with MS Word.

    d. At the Microsoft Word Mail Merge Wizard dialog box, click the Create a new document and then link the data to it option, and then click OK.

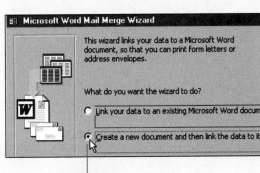

    e. Click the button on the Taskbar representing Document1, and then click the Maximize button so the blank document fills the screen.

    f. Complete the following steps to key text and insert fields in the blank Word document:

        1) Press Enter six times.

        2) Key the current date.

        3) Press Enter five times.

        4) Insert the following fields at the left margin in the order shown below (start by clicking the Insert Merge Field button at the left side of the Merge toolbar).

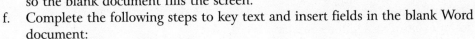

«Supplier_Name»
«Address»
«City», «Province»
«Postal_Code»

5) Press Enter twice and then key the salutation **Ladies and Gentlemen:**.

6) Press Enter twice and then key the following paragraph of text: (The paragraph is displayed here in bold for easier reading—do not key the paragraph in bold. After keying the Outdoor Options e-mail address, Word will convert it to a hyperlink. Immediately click the Undo button to remove the hyperlink and then continue keying the remainder of the paragraph.):
We just installed a new computer system in our Finance Department and are now ready to place and receive orders electronically. You can now contact us through our e-mail address at *outdoor@recreate.fun.com*. Our current records indicate that your e-mail address is «Email_Address». If this address is not correct, please let us know.

7) Press Enter twice and then key the following complimentary close (at the left margin):
Sincerely,

Mandy Generes
Director of Finances

XX:Word Ch 22, Ex 08

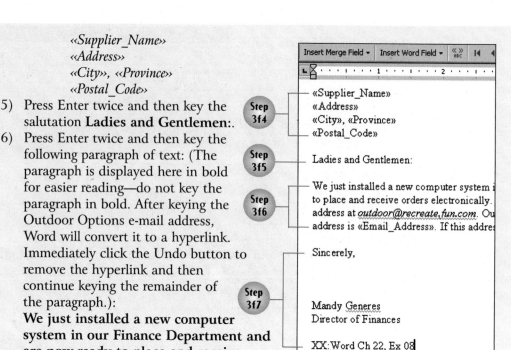

Step 3f4
Step 3f5
Step 3f6
Step 3f7

g. Click the Merge to New Document button located toward the right side of the Merge toolbar.

h. When the merge is completed, save the new document as Word Ch 22, Ex 08 in the *Chapter 22* folder on your disk.

i. Print the first two pages (two letters) of Word Ch 22, Ex 08.

j. Close Word Ch 22, Ex 08.

k. Save the main document as Word Outdoor Letter in the *Chapter 22* folder on your disk and then close Word Outdoor Letter.

l. Exit Word.

4. Close the Outdoor Options database file.

Importing and Linking Data to a New Table

In this chapter, you learned how to export Access data to Excel and Word. Data from other applications, such as Excel and Word, can also be imported into an Access table. For example, you can import data from an Excel worksheet and create a new table in a database file. Data in the original application is not connected to the data imported into an Access table. If you make changes to the data in the original application, those changes are not reflected in the Access table. If you want the imported data connected to the original application, link the data.

Importing Data to a New Table

To import data, open the database file, click File, point to Get External Data, and then click Import. At the Import dialog box that displays, double-click the desired document name. This activates the import Wizard and displays the first Wizard dialog box. The appearance of the dialog box varies depending on the document selected. Complete the steps of the import Wizard specifying information such as the range of data, whether or not the first row contains column headings, whether you want to store the data in a new table or store it in an existing table, the primary key, and the name of the table.

exercise 9

Importing an Excel Worksheet into an Access Table

*(Note: Before completing this exercise, open Excel and then open Excel Worksheet 37 [located in your Chapter 22 folder]. Save the worksheet with Save As and name it **Excel Ch 22**. Close Excel Ch 22 and then exit Excel.)*

1. Copy the Southwest Insurance database file from the CD that accompanies this textbook to your disk.
2. Remove the read-only attribute from the Southwest Insurance database located on your disk by completing the following steps:
   a. In Access, display the Open dialog box with the drive active that contains your disk.
   b. Click once on the Southwest Insurance database file name.
   c. Click the Tools button on the Open dialog box toolbar and then click Properties at the drop-down list.
   d. At the Southwest Insurance Properties dialog box with the General tab selected, click Read-only in the Attributes section to remove the check mark.
   e. Click OK to close the Southwest Insurance Properties dialog box.
3. Open the Southwest Insurance database file and click the   Tables button in the Objects bar.
4. Import an Excel worksheet into a new table in the Southwest Insurance database file by completing the following steps:
   a. Click File, point to Get External Data, and then click Import.

Step 4a

File	Edit	View	Insert	Tools	Window	Help
New...			Ctrl+N			
Open...			Ctrl+O			
Get External Data			▶	Import...		
Close				Link Tables...		

b. At the Import dialog box, make the *Chapter 22* folder on your disk the active folder.
c. Change the Files of type option to *Microsoft Excel*.
d. Double-click *Excel Ch 22* in the list box.
e. At the first Import Spreadsheet Wizard dialog box, click the <u>N</u>ext> button.

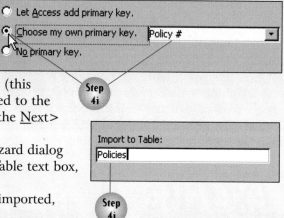

f. At the second Import Spreadsheet Wizard dialog box, make sure there is a check mark in the F<u>i</u>rst Row Contains Column Headings option, and then click the <u>N</u>ext> button.
g. At the third Import Spreadsheet Wizard dialog box, make sure the In a Ne<u>w</u> Table option is selected, and then click the <u>N</u>ext> button.
h. At the fourth Import Spreadsheet Wizard dialog box, click the <u>N</u>ext> button.
i. At the fifth Import Spreadsheet Wizard dialog box, click the <u>C</u>hoose my own primary key option (this inserts *Policy #* in the text box located to the right of the option), and then click the <u>N</u>ext> button.
j. At the sixth Import Spreadsheet Wizard dialog box, key **Policies** in the Import to Table text box, and then click the <u>F</u>inish button.
k. At the message saying the data was imported, click OK.
5. Open the new Policies table in Datasheet view.
6. Print and then close the Policies table.
7. Close the Southwest Insurance database file.

Linking Data to a New Table

Imported data is not connected to the source application. If you want the data to be connected, link the data. When the data is linked, changes made to the data in the source application are reflected in the data in the destination application and changes made in the destination application are reflected in the source application.

To link data to a new table, open the database file, click <u>F</u>ile, point to <u>G</u>et External Data, and then click <u>L</u>ink Tables. At the Link dialog box, double-click the desired document name. This activates the link Wizard and displays the first Wizard dialog box. Complete the steps of the link Wizard specifying the same basic information as the import Wizard.

Linking an Excel Worksheet with an Access Table

1. Open the Southwest Insurance database file and click the Tables button in the Objects bar.
2. Link an Excel worksheet with a new table in the Southwest Insurance database file by completing the following steps:
   a. Click File, point to Get External Data, and then click Link Tables.
   b. At the Link dialog box, make sure the *Chapter 22* folder on your disk is the active folder, and then change the Files of type option to *Microsoft Excel*.
   c. Double-click *Excel Ch 22*.
   d. At the first Link Spreadsheet Wizard dialog box, make sure Show Worksheets is selected, and that *Sheet1* is selected in the list box, and then click the Next> button.
   e. At the second Link Spreadsheet Wizard dialog box, make sure there is a check mark in the First Row Contains Column Headings option, and then click the Next> button.
   f. At the third Link Spreadsheet Wizard dialog box, key **Linked Policies** (in the Linked Table Name text box), and then click the Finish button.
   g. At the message stating the linking is finished, click OK.
3. Open the new Linked Policies table in Datasheet view.
4. Change the number *745* in the Premium column to *850*.
5. Add the following new record in the specified fields:

Policy #	=	**227-C-28**
Client #	=	**3120**
Premium	=	**685**

6. Save, print and then close the Linked Policies table.
7. Open Excel and then open Excel Worksheet 37. Notice that the information in this table contains the changes made to the Linked Policies table in Access.
8. Close Excel Ch 22 and then exit Excel.
9. In Access, close the Southwest Insurance database file.

Step 2a

File Edit View Insert Tools Window Help

New...   Ctrl+N
Open...   Ctrl+O
Get External Data   ▶   Import...
Close   Link Tables...

Linked Table Name:
Linked Policies

Step 2f

Linked Policies : Table

Policy #	Client #	Premium
110-C-39	9383	$ 1,450
122-E-30	7335	$ 850
143-D-29	3120	$ 920
192-C-29	7335	$ 1,390
201-E-91	4300	$ 1,525
215-W-32	4300	$ 734
227-C-28	3120	$ 685

Step 4

Step 5

Using the Office Clipboard

You can use the Office clipboard to collect up to 12 different items in Access or other applications and paste them in various locations. The Clipboard toolbar will display when you copy two consecutive items without pasting an item. Copied data displays as an icon the Clipboard toolbar as shown in figure 22.8. You can also display the Clipboard toolbar by right-clicking an existing toolbar and then clicking Clipboard.

figure
22.8   *Clipboard Toolbar*

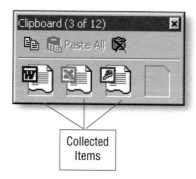

Collected
Items

To insert an item from the Clipboard to a field in an Access table, make the desired field active, and then click the button on the Clipboard toolbar representing the item. Position the mouse pointer on a button and a ScreenTip displays with information about the item. If the item is text, the first 50 characters display. When all desired items are inserted, click the Clear Clipboard button to remove any remaining items.

Usually, if you copy any two items consecutively, the Clipboard toolbar automatically displays. If you close the Clipboard toolbar three times in a row without clicking a button on the toolbar, the Clipboard toolbar will no longer appear automatically. To display the Clipboard toolbar, right-click any currently displayed toolbar, and then click Clipboard. You can also click View, point to Toolbars, and then click Clipboard. When you display the Clipboard toolbar and then click a button on the toolbar, the count is reset, and from that point on the Clipboard toolbar appears automatically again.

You can use the Office clipboard to copy data from one table to another in an Access database file or from a document in another application to an Access database file. In exercise 11, you will copy data from a Word document and paste it into a database table. Data can also be collected from documents in other applications such as PowerPoint and Excel.

Collecting Data in Word and Pasting It in an Access Database Table

1. In Access, open the Outdoor Options database file.
2. Open the Suppliers table in Datasheet view.
3. Copy data from Word and paste it into the Suppliers table by completing the following steps:
    a. Open Word, make the *Chapter 22* folder on your disk the active folder, and then open National Suppliers.
    b. Select the first company name *Ontario Center* and then click the Copy button on the Standard toolbar.
    c. Select the street address, *5402 Northridge Drive*, and then click the Copy button. (This should display the Clipboard toolbar. If this toolbar does not display, right-click any currently displayed toolbar, and then click Clipboard.)
    d. Select the city, *Toronto*, and then click the Copy button.
    e. Select the province, *ON*, and then click the Copy button.
    f. Select the postal code, *M4C 3X4*, and then click the Copy button.
    g. Select the e-mail address, *ontarioc@recreate.fun.com*, and then click the Copy button.
    h. Click the button on the Taskbar representing the Access Suppliers table. (Make sure you are in Datasheet view.)
    i. Click in the first empty cell in the *Supplier #* field and then key **42**.
    j. Click in the first empty cell in the *Supplier Name* field and then click the button on the Clipboard representing the company *Ontario Center* (To find this button, use the ScreenTip.)
    k. Click in the *Address* field and then click the button on the Clipboard toolbar representing *5402 Northridge Drive*.
    l. Click in the *City* field and then click the button on the Clipboard toolbar representing *Toronto*.
    m. Click in the *Province* field and then click the button on the Clipboard toolbar representing *ON*.
    n. Click in the *Postal Code* field and then click the button on the Clipboard toolbar representing *M4C 3X4*.
    o. Click in the *E-mail Address* field and then click the button on the Clipboard toolbar representing *ontarioc@recreate.fun.com*.
    p. Click the Clear Clipboard button on the Clipboard toolbar to remove the items.
4. Complete steps similar to those in 3b through 3p to copy the information for Explorers World and paste it into the Suppliers table. (The Supplier # is 51. You may need to scroll to the left side of the table to display the *Supplier #* field.)
5. Close the Clipboard toolbar.
6. Save and then print the Suppliers table.
7. Close the Suppliers table and then close the Outdoor Options database file.
8. Make Word the active program, close National Suppliers, and then exit Word.

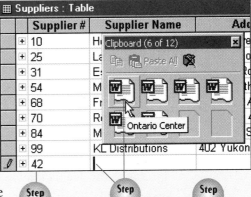

Step 3i

Step 3j

Step 3p

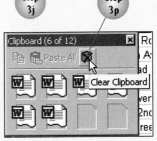

Creating a Web Page

Make Access data available for viewing on the Internet or on a company's intranet by saving the data as a data access page. A data access page is a special type of Web page designed for viewing and working with data from the Internet or intranet. Data saved as a Web page can be viewed in the default browser, formatting can be applied to the Web page, and hyperlinks can be inserted in the Web page.

Saving a Table, Query, or Form as a Web Page

Access contains a wizard that walks you through the steps for creating a data access page. To use this wizard, open the desired database file, click the Pages button in the Objects bar, and then double-click *Create data access page by using wizard* in the list box. Complete the Page Wizard steps to create the data access page.

When you create a data access page, the Page Wizard specifies a folder and subfolders for Web page files. This is because a Web page generally consists of a variety of items that are inserted in individual files. For example, each bullet image and clip art image or picture in a Web page is saved in a separate image file. Inserting all of these files into folders makes it easier for you to take this information to another location. For example, you can copy the contents of a Web page folder and all its subfolders to another computer or onto a disk.

Another way to create a data access page is to create the page in Design view. To do this, open the desired database file, click the Pages button in the Objects bar, and then double-click *Create data access page in Design view*. This displays the Design grid where you can create the form with the desired objects. Use the Toolbox to add control objects to the grid. With buttons on the Toolbox, you can also add Web page features such as hyperlinks and scrolling text.

Applying a Theme to a Web Page

Some interesting and colorful formatting can be applied to a Web page with options at the Theme dialog box shown in figure 22.9. To display this dialog box, click Format and then click Theme. Click a theme in the Choose a Theme list box and a preview displays at the right side. Click OK to close the dialog box and apply the theme to the page. (You can also double-click a theme at the Theme dialog box.)

figure

22.9

Theme Dialog Box

Choose a theme in this list box and preview it at the right.

Previewing a Web Page in Web Page Preview

When creating a Web page, you may want to preview it in your default Web browser. Depending on the browser you are using, some of the formatting may not display in the browser. To preview a Web page in your default Web browser, click File and then Web Page Preview.

Creating Hyperlinks

You can create a hyperlink in your Web page. To do this, display the Web page in Design view, and then click the Hyperlink button on the Toolbox. Using the mouse, drag in the Design view window to create a box. When you release the mouse button, the Insert Hyperlink dialog box shown in figure 22.10 displays. At this dialog box, key the text in the Text to display text box that you want to display in the Design view. Click in the Type the file or Web page name text box, key the Web site URL, and then click OK.

figure
22.10

Insert Hyperlink Dialog Box

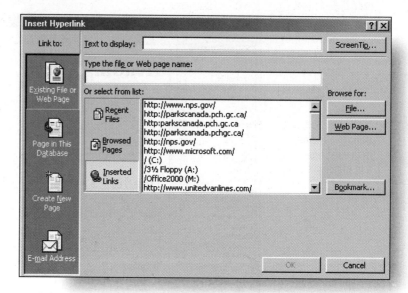

Another method for creating a hyperlink is to key the URL in a label in the Design view. When you key the complete URL, Access automatically converts the URL to a hyperlink and changes the color of the URL.

exercise 12

Saving a Table as a Web Page

1. Open the Outdoor Options database file.
2. Create a Web page by completing the following steps:
    a. At the Outdoor Options window, click the Pages button in the Objects bar.
    b. Double-click *Create data access page by using wizard* in the list box.

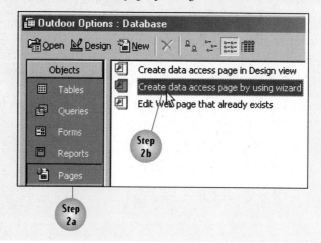

c. At the first Page Wizard dialog box, click the down-pointing triangle at the right side of the Tables/Queries text box, and then click *Table: Suppliers* in the drop-down list.

d. Click the button containing the greater than symbols (>>). This inserts all the fields in the Selected Fields list box.

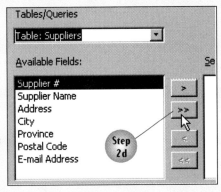

e. Click the Next> button.

f. At the second Page Wizard dialog box, click the Next> button.

g. At the third Page Wizard dialog box, click the Next> button.

h. At the fourth Page Wizard dialog box, make sure the Modify the page's design option is selected, and then click the Finish button. (The completed data access page displays on the screen in design view.)

3. Click the text *Click here and type title text* and then key **OUTDOOR OPTIONS**. (You may need to drag up the top of the data access page window to see this text.)

4. Apply a theme to the page by completing the following steps:
    a. Click Format and then Theme.
    b. At the Theme dialog box, click *Clearday* in the Choose a Theme list box, and then click OK.

5. Add two hyperlinks to the page that will allow the user to jump to the Parks Canada site and the United States National Park Service site by completing the following steps:

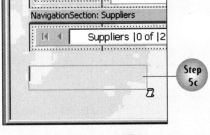

    a. Increase the size of the page window by dragging down the bottom border of the window. (This gives you space to create the hyperlinks.)
    b. Click the Hyperlink button on the Toolbox. (If the Toolbox is not displayed, click the Toolbox button on the Page Design toolbar.)
    c. Position the crosshair pointer with the *hyperlink* icon attached to it towards the bottom of the window, and then drag the mouse down to the approximate height and width shown at the right, and then release the mouse button.
    d. At the Insert Hyperlink dialog box, make the following changes:
        1) Click in the Text to display text box and then key **Parks Canada**.
        2) Click in the Type the file or Web page name text box and then key **http://parkscanada.pch.gc.ca**.
        3) Click OK.
    e. Click the Hyperlink button on the Toolbox.

    f. Position the crosshair pointer with the *hyperlink* icon attached to it to the right of the *Parks Canada* hyperlink, and then drag to create a box.

g. At the Insert Hyperlink dialog box, make the following changes:
   1) Click in the Text to display text box and then key **National Parks Service**.
   2) Click in the Type the file or Web page name text box and then key **http://www.nps.gov**.
   3) Click OK.
6. Click the View button to change to the Page view.
7. Save the access data page and name it Suppliers Web Page.
8. View the page in the default Web browser by clicking File and then Web Page Preview.
9. In Web Page Preview, use the navigation buttons along the bottom of the window to display various records.
10. Close the browser by clicking File and then Close.
11. Close the data access page and then close the Outdoor Options database file.

Managing Access Database Files

Consider performing some basic maintenance features on Access database files such as backing up, restoring, compacting, and repairing. Back up important information and then restore the information when needed. When you delete data and objects from a database file, it can become fragmented. Compact the database and repair it to more efficiently utilize the disk space.

Backing Up a Database File

Many situations may arise when you may want to backup the data in your database file. Some situations include:

- If you have multiple users who could access and change your data
- If your system is at a higher risk for viruses and/or systems failures
- If you plan to switch from one computer system to another (such as an update) and need to transfer your data

Backup any database file that contains critical data. If any unforeseen problems occur, the backup database file is available for copying. Back up a database in a similar manner to the steps you perform to copy files and folders in Windows Explorer from the CD to your disk. To backup a database, you would complete these basic steps:

1. Close the database.
2. If you are in a multi-user environment, confirm that all users have closed the database.
3. In Windows Explorer, find the drive where the database exists.
4. In the list box at the right side of the screen, click the database file you want to back up.
5. Click the Copy button on the Windows explorer toolbar.
6. Click the down-pointing triangle at the right of the Address list box and then click the drive where you want the database. (If you are using a floppy disk, make sure your disk is in the drive.)
7. Click the Paste button on the Windows Explorer toolbar.
8. You may then close Windows Explorer by clicking the Close button located in the upper right corner of Windows Explorer window.

Restoring a Database File

Restore a database from a backup copy of the database. To do this, you would complete these basic steps:

1. In Windows Explorer, click the down-pointing triangle at the right of the Address list box, and then click the drive where the database backup exists.
2. In the list box at the right side of the screen, click the database backup file you want restored.
3. Click the Copy button on the Windows Explorer toolbar.
4. Click the down-pointing triangle at the right of the Address list box and then click the drive where you want the database restored.
5. Click the Paste button on the Windows Explorer toolbar. (*Note: If the existing database file and the backup copy has the same name, restoring the backup copy may replace the existing database file. If you want to save the existing file, rename it before you copy the backup file.*)
6. Close Windows Explorer by clicking the Close button located in the upper right corner of the Windows Explorer window.

Compacting and Repairing a Database File

When data and objects are deleted from a database file, it can become fragmented and the disk space may not be used efficiently. Compacting a database rearranges how the file is stored on the disk and uses disk space more efficiently and optimizes the performance of the database. Compact a database file by clicking Tools, pointing to Database Utilities, and then clicking Compact and Repair Database.

Compacting and Repairing a Database File

1. Open the Outdoor Options database file.
2. Compact the database by clicking Tools, pointing to Database, and clicking Compact and Repair Database.
3. Close the Outdoor Options database file.

chapter summary

► Access provides numerous database wizards that will create a variety of database files including all the fields, formatting, tables, and reports needed to manage the data.

► Database wizards are displayed in the New dialog box with the Databases tab selected.

► A database file created with a wizard can be modified.

► Delete a database file by displaying the Open dialog box, clicking the desired database file, and then clicking the Delete button on the dialog box toolbar.

► A database table, form, or report can be exported to Excel with the Analyze It with MS Excel option at the OfficeLinks drop-down menu.

► When data is exported to Excel, the data becomes an Excel worksheet with all Excel editing capabilities available.

► A database table, form, or report can be exported to Word with the Publish It with MS Word option from the OfficeLinks drop-down menu.

► An Excel worksheet or a Word document created from Access data is automatically saved with the same name as the database table, form, or report selected. A different file extension, however, is added to the document name.

► Access data can be used to merge with a Word document. Access uses the data from the database table as the data source and merges the data with a Word document.

► Access data can be merged with an existing Word document or merged with a new document.

► Data from another application can be imported into an Access database table. Access contains an import Wizard that guides you through the importing data steps.

► Data from another application can be linked to an Access table. Changes made to the data in the source application are reflected in the data in the destination application and changes made in the destination application are reflected in the source application.

► Use the Office clipboard to collect up to 12 different items in Access or other applications and paste them in various locations.

► Make Access data available for viewing on the Internet or on a company's intranet by saving the data as a data access page. Data saved as a Web page can be viewed in the default browser, formatting can be applied, and hyperlinks can be inserted.

► Apply formatting to a Web page with options at the Theme dialog box.

► Preview a Web page in the default browser by clicking File and then Web Page Preview.

► One method for displaying the Insert Hyperlink dialog box is to click the Hyperlink button on the Toolbox and then drag to create a box.

► Back up an Access database file containing important information and then restore the information when needed.

► Compact and repair a database file to make it more efficiently utilize disk space.

commands review

Mouse/Keyboard

New dialog box	File, New; or click New button on Database toolbar
Open dialog box	File, Open; or click Open button on Database toolbar
OfficeLinks drop-down menu	Click OfficeLinks button on Database toolbar
Begin the Import Wizard	Open Access database file, click File, point to Get External Data, and then click Import
Begin the Link Wizard	Open Access database file, click File, point to Get External Data, and then click Link Tables
Display the Clipboard toolbar	Copy two consecutive items without pasting them; or right-click existing toolbar and then click Clipboard; or click View, point to Toolbars, and then click Clipboard
Begin Data Access Page Wizard	Open database file, click Pages button in the Objects bar, then double-click *Create data access page by using wizard*
Display the Theme dialog box	Click Format and then Theme
Preview Web page in default browser	Click File and then Web Page Preview
Display Hyperlink dialog box	Click Hyperlink button on Toolbox, drag to create a box
Compact and Repair a database	Click Tools, point to Database, and then click Compact and Repair Database

thinking offline

Completion: In the space provided at the right, indicate the correct term, symbol, or number.

1. Display a list of database wizards by displaying the New dialog box with this tab selected.

2. To display the New dialog box, click the New button on this toolbar.

3. When a database wizard is done creating a database, this dialog box displays, giving you options for entering or viewing information in the database, previewing reports, changing switchboard items, or exiting the database.

4. Delete a database file at this dialog box.

5. Click this option from the OfficeLinks drop-down menu to export the selected database table, form, or report to Excel.

6. Click this option from the OfficeLinks drop-down menu to export the selected database table, form, or report to Word.

7. Click this option from the OfficeLinks drop-down menu to merge Access data with a Word document.

8. Access data exported to Excel is saved with this file extension.

9. Access data exported to Word is saved with this file extension.

10. Use this to collect up to 12 different items in Access or other applications and then paste them in various locations.

11. Make Access data available for viewing on the Internet or on a company's intranet by saving the data as this.

12. Preview a Web page in the default browser by clicking File and then this.

13. Do this to a database file to make it more efficiently utilize disk space.

14. List the steps you would complete to create a sample database with the Music Collection Database Wizard.

_____

_____

_____

_____

working hands-on

Assessment 1

1. Use the Expenses Database Wizard to create a database with the following specifications:
   a. At the File New Database dialog box, key **Expenses** as the database file name.
   b. At the third Database Wizard dialog box, you determine the type of screen display.
   c. At the fourth Database Wizard dialog box, you determine the style for reports.

2. When the database file is completed and the Main Switchboard displays, enter information on expenses for one employee by completing the following steps:
   a. Click the Enter/View Expense Reports by Employee button that displays in the Main Switchboard.
   b. At the Expense Reports by Employee dialog box, key the following in the specified fields (you will be skipping many of the fields):

First Name	=	**Nina**
Last Name	=	**Schueller**
Title	=	**Manager**
Employee #	=	**210**

c. Click the Expense Report Form button that displays in the lower left corner of the dialog box.
d. At the Expense Reports dialog box, key the following in the specified fields (you will be skipping fields):

Exp Rpt Name	=	**Marketing Seminar**
Exp Rpt Descr	=	**Two-day Marketing Seminar**
Dept Charged	=	**Marketing Department**
Date Submitted	=	**05/14/99**

e. Create three expense categories by completing the following steps:
  1) Double-click in the first box below the Expense Category heading (located towards the bottom of the dialog box). (This displays the Expense Categories dialog box.)
  2) At the Expense Categories dialog box, enter the following three records:

Expense Category	=	**Airfare**
Expense Account#	=	**10**
Expense Category	=	**Meals**
Expense Account#	=	**20**
Expense Category	=	**Lodging**
Expense Account#	=	**30**

f. After entering the third record, click the Close button to close the Expense Categories dialog box.
g. At the Expense Reports dialog box, enter the following in the specified fields (located towards the bottom of the dialog box):

Expense Date	=	**05/10/99**
Expense Category	=	**Airfare**
Description	=	**Airline ticket**
Amount	=	**850**
Expense Date	=	**05/11/99**
Expense Category	=	**Meals**
Description	=	**Daily meals**
Amount	=	**52**
Expense Date	=	**05/12/99**
Expense Category	=	**Meals**
Description	=	**Daily meals**
Amount	=	**48**
Expense Date	=	**05/12/99**
Expense Category	=	**Lodging**
Description	=	**Hotel**
Amount	=	**220**

h. Click the Preview Report button located in the lower left corner of the dialog box.
i. When the report displays, print the report by clicking the Print button on the Print Preview toolbar.
j. Close the Expense Report.
k. Close the Expense Reports form.
l. Close the Expense Reports by Employee form.

3. View the relationships between tables by completing the following steps:
   a. Close the Main Switchboard.
   b. Click the Restore button on the minimized Expenses database file.
   c. With the Expenses Database dialog box displayed, click the Relationships button on the Database toolbar.
   d. After viewing the relationships between tables, click the Close button to close the Relationships window.
   e. Display a few tables and forms to see the how data is organized.
4. Close the Expenses database file.
5. Delete the Expenses database file.

Assessment 2

1. Copy the database file named Legal Services from the CD that accompanies this textbook to your disk. Remove the read-only attribute from the Legal Services database file.
2. Open the Legal Services database file.
3. Create a form named Billing using the Form Wizard with the following fields:

   From the Billing table:
   > *Billing #*
   > *Client ID*
   > *Date*
   > *Hours*

   From the Rates table:
   > *Rate*

4. When the form displays, close it.
5. At the Legal Services Database window, create an Excel worksheet with the Billing form.
6. Make the following changes to the Excel Billing worksheet:
   a. Automatically adjust the width of the columns.
   b. Create a column F with the heading *Total*.
   c. In cell F2, insert a formula that multiplies the Rate by the Hours.
   d. Copy the formula down to cells F3 through F12.
   e. Apply an autoformat of your choosing to the cells in the worksheet containing data.
   f. Save the Billing worksheet (at the overwrite message, click <u>Y</u>es).
   g. Print and then close the Billing worksheet.
   h. Exit Excel.
7. Close the Legal Services database file.

Assessment 3

1. Open the Legal Services database file.
2. Create a report named Client Billing using the Report Wizard with the following fields:

   From the Clients table:
   > *First Name*
   > *Last Name*

From the Billing table:
> *Date*
> *Hours*

From the Rates table:
> *Rate*

3. When the report displays, print and then close the report.
4. At the Legal Services : Database window, create a Word document with the Client Billing report form.
5. Save the Word document with Save As and name it Word Ch 22, Report.
6. Print Word Ch 22, Report, close it, and then exit Word.
7. Close the Legal Services database file.

Assessment 4

1. Open the Legal Services database file.
2. Merge data in the Clients database table to a blank Word screen. *(Hint: Use the* M̲erge It with MS Word *option from the OfficeLinks drop-down menu.)* You determine the fields to use in the inside address and an appropriate salutation. Key the following text in the body of the document:

> **The last time you visited our offices, you may have noticed how crowded we were. To alleviate the overcrowding, we are leasing new offices in the Meridian Building and will be moving in at the beginning of next month.**

> **Stop by and see our new offices at our open house planned for the second Friday of next month. Drop by any time between 2:00 and 5:00 p.m. We look forward to seeing you.**

Include an appropriate complimentary close for the letter. Use the name and title *Marjorie Shaw, Senior Partner* for the signature and add your reference initials and the document name (Word Ch 22, SA 04).

3. Merge to a new document and then save the document with the name Word Ch 22, SA 04.
4. Print only the first two letters in the document and then close Word Ch 22, SA 04.
5. Close the main document without saving it and then exit Word.
6. Close the Legal Services database table.

Assessment 5

1. Open the Legal Services database file and click the Tables button in the Objects bar.
2. Import Excel Worksheet 38 into a new table named Cases. (Use the Import Spreadsheet Wizard to do this.)
3. Open the Cases table in Datasheet view.
4. Print and then close the Cases table.
5. Close the Legal Services database file.

Assessment 6

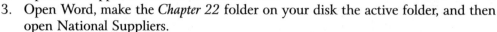

1. Open the Outdoor Options database file.
2. Open the Suppliers table in Datasheet view.
3. Open Word, make the *Chapter 22* folder on your disk the active folder, and then open National Suppliers.
4. Copy individually the company name, address, city, province, postal code, and e-mail address for Mission Suppliers and then paste the information into the appropriate fields in the Suppliers table. (Key *72* in the <u>Supplier #</u> field for Mission Suppliers.)
5. Clear the contents of the Clipboard.
6. Copy individually the company name, address, city, province, postal code, and e-mail address for Lambert-Col Outfitters and then paste the information into the appropriate field in the Suppliers table. (Key *86* in the <u>Supplier #</u> field for Lambert-Col. Outfitters.)
7. Clear the contents of the Clipboard and then close the Clipboard toolbar.
8. Save and then print the Suppliers table.
9. Close the Suppliers table and then close the Outdoor Options database file.
10. Make Word the active program, close National Suppliers, and then exit Word.

Assessment 7

1. Open the Legal Services database file.
2. Create a Web page using the Data Access Page Wizard with the fields from the Clients table. (You determine the title of the page.)
3. Apply a theme of your choosing to the page.
4. Change to the Page view.
5. Save the access data page and name it Clients Web Page.
6. View the page in the default Web browser, use navigation buttons along the bottom of the window to display various records, and then close the browser.
7. Close the data access page and then close the Legal Services database file.

Assessment 8

1. You can get help for Microsoft Office 2000 applications, such as Access, using the Help feature. Assistance is also available from resources on the Web. Use the Access Help feature to learn about the Help resources available on the Web.
2. After reading the information on Web resources, create a Word document explaining the resources available. Save the document and name it Web Resources. Print and then close Web Resources.
3. Make sure you are connected to the Internet and then visit at least one Web site that provides information on Microsoft Office 2000. Print at least one page from a site you visit.

Performing Queries and Filtering Records

23

PERFORMANCE OBJECTIVES

Upon successful completion of chapter 23, you will be able to:

- Design a query to extract specific data from a database table.
- Use the Simple Query Wizard to extract specific data from a database table.
- Create a calculated field.
- Filter data in records by selection and by form.

(Note: There is no Chapter 23 folder to copy from the CD. Instead, you will be copying individual database files from the CD as you need them in particular exercises.)

One of the primary uses of a database file is to extract specific information from the database. A company might need to know such information as: How much inventory is currently on hand? What products have been ordered? What accounts are past due? What customers live in a particular city? This type of information can be extracted from a database table by completing a query. You will learn how to perform a variety of queries on database tables in this chapter.

Access provides a Filter By Selection button and a Filter By Form button, which you can use to temporarily isolate specific records in a database table. Like a query, a filter lets you select specific field values from a database table. You will learn to use these two buttons to isolate specific data in tables.

Performing Queries

Being able to extract (pull out) specific data from a database table is one of the most important functions of a database. Extracting data in Access is referred to as performing a query. The word *query* means to ask a question. Access provides several methods for performing a query. You can design your own query, use a Simple Query Wizard, or use complex query wizards. In this chapter, you will learn to design your own query and use the Simple Query Wizard.

Designing a Query

Designing a query consists of identifying the table from which you are gathering data, the field or fields from which the data will be drawn, and the criteria for selecting the data. To design a query and perform the query, you would follow these basic steps:

1. Open the database file.
2. At the database file dialog box, click the Queries button in the Objects bar, and then click the New button.
3. At the Show Table dialog box with the Tables tab selected as shown in figure 23.1, select the table you want included in the query, and then click the Add button. Add any other tables required for the query. When all tables have been added, click the Close button.
4. At the Query1 Select Query dialog box shown in figure 23.2, use the mouse to drag the first field to be included in the query from the table box in the top of the dialog box to the first empty Field text box. If more than one field is to be included in the query, continue dragging field names from the box in the top to the Field text boxes.
5. To establish a criterion, click inside the Criteria text box in the column containing the desired Field name, and then key the criterion.
6. With the fields and criteria established, click the Run button located on the Query Design toolbar.
7. Access searches the specified table for records that match the criteria and then displays those records in the Query1 Select Query dialog box.
8. If the query will be used in the future, save the query and name it. If you do not need the query again, close the Query1 Select Query dialog box without saving it.

Run

A query can be saved.

figure

23.1

Show Table Dialog Box

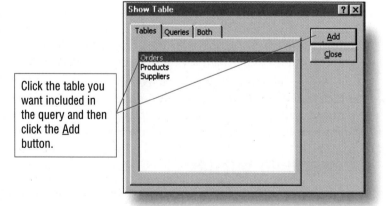

Click the table you want included in the query and then click the Add button.

figure
23.2

Query1 Select Query Dialog Box

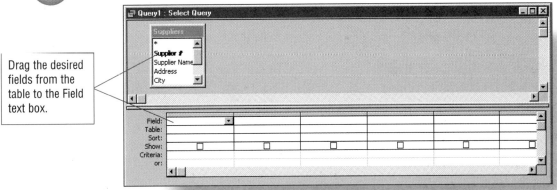

Drag the desired fields from the table to the Field text box.

In step 4 listed above, the mouse is used to drag fields from the table box in the top of the dialog box to the first empty Field text box in the lower part of the dialog box. As an example, suppose you wanted to find out how many purchase orders were issued on a specific date. To do this, you would drag the *PurchaseOrderID* field from the table to the first Field text box, and then drag the *OrderDate* field from the table to the second Field text box. In this example, both fields are needed so the purchase order ID is displayed along with the specific order date. After dragging the fields, you would then insert the criterion. The criterion for this example would be something like *#1/15/99#*. After the criterion is inserted, click the Run button on the Query Design toolbar and the results of the query are displayed on the screen.

Establishing Query Criteria

A query does not require that specific criteria are established. In the example described above, if the criterion for the date was not included, the query would *return* (*return* is the term used for the results of the query) all Purchase Order numbers with the dates. While this information may be helpful, you could easily find this information in the table. The value of performing a query is to extract specific information from a table. To do this, you must insert a criterion like the one described in the example.

Access makes writing a criterion fairly simple because it inserts the necessary symbols in the criterion. If you key a city such as *Vancouver* in the criteria text box and then press Enter, Access changes the criteria to *"Vancouver."* The quotation marks are inserted by Access and are necessary for the query to run properly. You can either let Access put the proper symbols in the criteria text box, or you can key the criterion with the symbols. Figure 23.3 shows some criteria examples including what is keyed and what is returned.

Include only those fields in a query for which you want to enter criteria or you want to display.

Hint

figure

23.3

Criteria Examples

Keying this criteria	Returns this
"Smith"	Field value matching Smith
"Smith" or "Larson"	Field value matching either Smith or Larson
Not "Smith"	Field value that is not Smith (the opposite of "Smith")
"S*"	Field value that begins with S and ends in anything
"*s"	Field value that begins with anything and ends in s
"[A-D]*"	Field value that begins with A through D and ends in anything
#01/01/99#	Field value matching the date 01/01/99
< #04/01/99#	Field value less than (before) 04/01/99
> #04/01/99#	Field value greater than (after) 04/01/99
Between #01/01/99 And #03/31/99	Any date between 01/01/99 and 03/31/99

In figure 23.3, notice that the quotation marks were used to surround field values (such as "Smith"). If you do not key the quotation marks when keying the criterion, Access will automatically insert them. The same is true for the pound symbol (#). Notice in figure 23.3 that the pound symbol (#) was used around dates. If you do not key the pound symbol around a date, Access will automatically insert the symbols. Access automatically inserts the correct symbol when you press the Enter key after keying the query criteria.

In the criteria examples, the asterisk was used as a wild card indicating any character. This is consistent with many other software applications where the asterisk is used as a wildcard character. The less than and greater than symbols were used in two of the criteria examples. These symbols can be used for fields containing numbers, values, dates, amounts, etc. In the next several exercises, you will be designing queries to extract specific information from different database tables in database files.

Performing Queries on Database Tables

(Note: If you still have the Outdoor Options database you copied on your disk in chapter 22, delete that database.)

1. Copy the Outdoor Options database file from the CD that accompanies this textbook to your disk. Remove the read-only attribute from the Outdoor Options database file.

2. Open the Outdoor Options database file.

3. Extract records of those suppliers located in Vancouver by completing the following steps:

   a. Click the Queries button in the Objects bar.

   b. Double-click *Create query in Design view* in the list box.

   c. At the Show Table dialog box with the Tables tab selected (see figure 23.1), click *Suppliers* in the list box, click the **A**dd button, and then click the **C**lose button.

   d. Drag fields from the table box to the Field: text boxes by completing the following steps:

      1) Position the arrow pointer on the *Supplier Name* field in the table list box located toward the top of the dialog box, hold down the left mouse button, drag the field icon to the first Field text box in the lower portion of the dialog box, and then release the mouse button. (When you release the mouse button, Access automatically inserts the table name Suppliers in the Table: text box and inserts a check box with a check mark in the Show: text box.)

      2) Drag the *Address* field in the table list box to the next Field text box (to the right of *Supplier Name*).

      3) Drag the *City* field in the table list box to the next Field text box (to the right of *Address*).

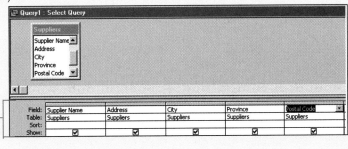

      4) Drag the *Province* field in the table list box to the next Field text box (to the right of *City*).

      5) Drag the *Postal Code* field in the table list box to the next Field: text box (to the right of *Province*).

   e. Insert the criteria text telling Access to display only those suppliers located in Vancouver by completing the following steps:

      1) Position the I-beam pointer in the Criteria text box in the *City* column and then click the left mouse button. (This positions the insertion point inside the text box.)

2) Key **Vancouver** and then press Enter. (This changes the criteria to "Vancouver.")

f. Return the results of the query by clicking the Run button on the Query Design toolbar.

g. Print the results of the query by completing the following steps:
   1) Select all columns in the table and then double-click a column boundary. (This automatically adjusts the size of each column so all data is visible.)
   2) Click the Print button on the Query Design toolbar.

h. After printing the results of the query, close the Query1 Select Query dialog box without saving the query.

4. Extract those product records with units on order greater than zero by completing the following steps:

   a. At the Outdoor Options Database window, click the <u>N</u>ew button.

   b. At the New Query dialog box, make sure *Design View* is selected, and then click OK.

   c. At the Show Table dialog box, click *Products* in the list box, click the <u>A</u>dd button, and then click the <u>C</u>lose button.

   d. At the Query1 Select Query dialog box, drag the *Product* field from the table list box to the first Field text box.

   e. Scroll down the table list box until *Units on Order* displays and then drag *Units on Order* to the second Field text box (to the right of *Product*).

   f. Insert the query criteria by completing the following steps:
      1) Position the I-beam pointer in the Criteria text box in the *Units on Order* column and then click the left mouse button. (This positions the insertion point inside the text box.)
      2) Key **>0** and then press Enter. (Make sure you key a zero and not a capital O.)

   g. Return the results of the query by clicking the Run button on the Query Design toolbar.

   h. Print the results of the query by clicking the Print button on the Query Design toolbar.

   i. After printing the results of the query, close the Query1 Select Query dialog box without saving the query.

5. Extract those orders greater than $1,500 by completing the following steps:

   a. At the Outdoor Options Database window, click the <u>N</u>ew button.

   b. At the New Query dialog box, make sure *Design View* is selected, and then click OK.

   c. At the Show Table dialog box, click *Orders* in the list box, click the <u>A</u>dd button, and then click the <u>C</u>lose button.

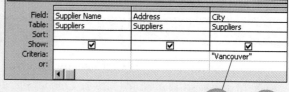

Step 3e2   Step 3f

Step 4d   Step 4e   Step 4f

d. At the Query1 Select Query dialog box, drag the *Order #* field from the table list box to the first Field text box.

e. Drag the *Product #* field to the second Field text box (to the right of *Order #*).

f. Scroll down the table list box until *Amount* is visible and then drag the *Amount* field to the third Field text box (to the right of *Product #*).

g. Insert the query criteria by completing the following steps:
   1) Position the I-beam pointer in the Criteria text box in the Amount column and then click the left mouse button. (This positions the insertion point inside the text box.)
   2) Key **>1500** and then press Enter. (Make sure you key zeros and not capital Os.)

h. Return the results of the query by clicking the Run button on the Query Design toolbar.

i. Print the results of the query by clicking the Print button on the Query Design toolbar.

j. After printing the results of the query, close the Query1 Select Query dialog box without saving the query.

6. Close the Outdoor Options database file.

In exercise 1, you performed several queries on specific database tables. A query can also be performed on fields from more than one table. In exercise 2, you will be performing queries on related database tables.

A query can be performed on two or more tables that are joined in a relationship.

Performing a Query on Related Database Tables

1. Open the Outdoor Options database file.

2. Extract information on products ordered between February 20 and February 28, 1999, and include the supplier's name by completing the following steps:
   a. Click the Queries button in the Objects bar.
   b. Click the New button on the window toolbar.
   c. At the New Query dialog box, make sure *Design View* is selected, and then click OK.
   d. At the Show Table dialog box, click *Products* in the list box and then click the Add button.
   e. Click *Suppliers* in the Show Table dialog box list box and then click the Add button.
   f. Click *Orders* in the list box, click the Add button, and then click the Close button.

g. At the Query1 Select Query dialog box, drag the *Product* field from the Products table list box to the first Field text box.

h. Drag the *Supplier Name* field from the Suppliers table list box to the second Field text box.

i. Drag the *Order Date* field from the Orders table list box to the third Field text box. (You will need to scroll down the list box to display the *Order Date* field.)

Step 2g

Step 2h

Step 2i

Field:	Product	Supplier Name	Order Date
Table:	Products	Suppliers	Orders
Sort:			
Show:	☑	☑	☑
Criteria:			)# And #02/28/99#
or:			

Step 2j

j. Insert the query criteria by completing the following steps:
   1) Position the I-beam pointer in the Criteria text box in the *Order Date* column and then click the left mouse button. (This positions the insertion point inside the text box.)
   2) Key **Between 02/20/99 And 02/28/99** and then press Enter. (Make sure you key zeros and not capital Os.)

k. Return the results of the query by clicking the Run button on the Query Design toolbar.

l. Automatically adjust the width of the columns and then print the results of the query by clicking the Print button on the Query Design toolbar.

m. After printing the results of the query, close the Query1 Select Query dialog box without saving the query.

3. Close the Outdoor Options database file.

Sorting Fields in a Query

When designing a query, the sort order of a field or fields can be specified. Notice in figure 23.2 that there is a Sort text box. Click inside one of the columns in the Sort text box and a down-pointing arrow displays at the right of the field. Click this down-pointing arrow and a drop-down menu displays with the choices *Ascending, Descending,* and *(not sorted)*. Click Ascending to sort from lowest to highest or click Descending to sort from highest to lowest.

exercise 3

Performing a Query on Related Tables and Sorting in Ascending Order

1. Open the Outdoor Options database file.
2. Extract information on orders less than $1,500 by completing the following steps:
   a. Click the Queries button in the Objects bar.
   b. Click the New button on the window toolbar.
   c. At the New Query dialog box, make sure *Design View* is selected, and then click OK.
   d. At the Show Table dialog box, click *Products* in the list box and then click the Add button.

e. Click *Orders* in the list box, click the A̲dd button, and then click the C̲lose button.
f. At the Query1 Select Query dialog box, drag the *Product #* field from the Products table list box to the first Field text box.
g. Drag the *Supplier #* field from the Products table list box to the second Field text box.

Step 2f **Step 2g** **Step 2h** **Step 2i**

Field:	Product #	Supplier #	Units Ordered	Amount
Table:	Products	Products	Orders	Orders
Sort:				Ascending
Show:	☑	☑	☑	☑
Criteria:				<1500
or:				

Step 2j **Step 2k**

h. Drag the *Units Ordered* field from the Orders table list box to the third Field text box.
i. Drag the *Amount* field from the Orders table list box to the fourth Field text box.
j. Insert the query criterion by completing the following steps:
  1) Position the I-beam pointer in the Criteria text box in the *Amount* column and then click the left mouse button.
  2) Key **<1500** and then press Enter. (Make sure you key a zero and not a capital O.)
k. Sort the *Amount* field values from lowest to highest by completing the following steps:
  1) Position the insertion point in the Sort text box in the *Amount* column and then click the left mouse button. (This will cause a down-pointing triangle to display at the right side of the text box.)
  2) Click the down-pointing triangle at the right side of the Sort text box and then click *Ascending*.
l. Return the results of the query by clicking the Run button on the Query Design toolbar.
m. Print the results of the query by clicking the Print button on the Query Design toolbar.
n. After printing the results of the query, close the Query1 Select Query dialog box without saving the query.
3. Close the Outdoor Options database file.

Performing a Query with the Simple Query Wizard

The Simple Query Wizard provided by Access guides you through the steps for preparing a query. To use this wizard, open the database file, click the Queries button in the Objects bar, and then double-click the *Create query by using wizard* option in the list box. Or, click the New button and then, at the New Query dialog box, double-click *Simple Query Wizard* in the list box. At the first Simple Query Wizard dialog box, as shown in figure 23.4, specify the database table(s) in the Tables/Queries list box. After specifying the database table, insert the fields you want included in the query in the S̲elected Fields list box, and then click the N̲ext> button.

Use the Simple Query Wizard to walk you through the steps for preparing a query.

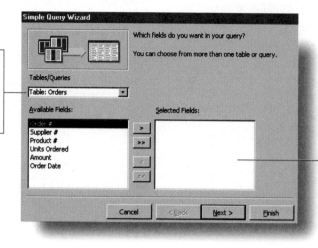

figure
23.4

First Simple Query Wizard Dialog Box

Specify the database tables in the Tables/Queries list box.

Insert the fields you want included in the query in the Selected Fields list box.

At the second Simple Query Wizard dialog box, specify whether you want a detail or summary query, and then click the Next> button. At the third (and last) Simple Query Wizard dialog box, shown in figure 23.5, key a name for the completed query or accept the name provided by the wizard. At this dialog box, you can also specify that you want to open the query to view the information or modify the query design. If you want to extract specific information, be sure to choose the Modify the query design option. After making any necessary changes, click the Finish button.

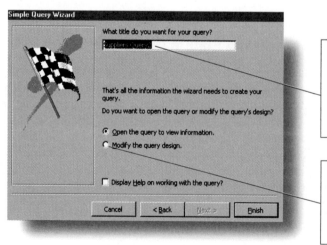

figure
23.5

Last Simple Query Wizard Dialog Box

Key a name for the query in this text box or accept the name provided by the wizard.

Click this option if you want to modify the query design.

If you do not modify the query design in the last Simple Query Wizard dialog box, the query displays all records for the fields identified in the first Simple Query Wizard dialog box. In exercise 4 you will be performing a query without modifying the design and in exercise 5 you will be modifying the query design.

Performing a Query with the Simple Query Wizard

1. Open the Outdoor Options database file.
2. Perform a query with the Simple Query Wizard by completing the following steps:
   a. Click the Queries button in the Objects bar.
   b. Double-click the *Create query by using wizard* option in the list box.
   c. At the first Simple Query Wizard dialog box, click the down-pointing triangle at the right of the Tables/Queries text box, and then click *Table: Suppliers*.
   d. With *Supplier #* selected in the Available Fields list box, click the button containing the greater than symbol. (This inserts the *Supplier #* field in the Selected Fields list box.)
   e. With *Supplier Name* selected in the Available Fields list box, click the button containing the greater than symbol.

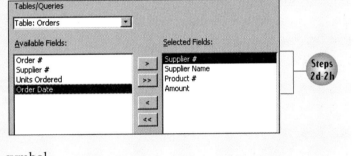

   f. Click the down-pointing triangle at the right of the Tables/Queries text box and then click *Table: Orders*.
   g. Click *Product #* in the Available Fields list box and then click the button containing the greater than symbol.
   h. Click *Amount* in the Available Fields list box and then click the button containing the greater than symbol.
   i. Click the Next> button.
   j. At the second Simple Query Wizard dialog box, click the Next> button.
   k. At the last Simple Query Wizard dialog box, click the Finish button.
3. When the results of the query display, print the results.
4. Close the Suppliers Query Select Query dialog box.
5. Close the Outdoor Options database file.

To extract specific information when using the Simple Query Wizard, tell the wizard that you want to modify the query design. This displays a dialog box where you can insert query criteria.

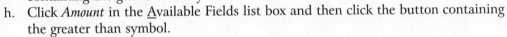

exercise 5

Performing and Modifying a Query with the Simple Query Wizard

1. Open the Outdoor Options database file.
2. Perform a query with the Simple Query Wizard and modify the query by completing the following steps:
   a. Click the Queries button in the Objects bar and then click the New button.
   b. At the New Query dialog box, double-click *Simple Query Wizard* in the list box.
   c. At the first Simple Query Wizard dialog box, click the down-pointing triangle at the right of the Tables/Queries text box, and then click *Table: Suppliers*.
   d. Insert the following fields in the Selected Fields list box:

   Supplier Name
   Address
   City
   Province
   Postal Code

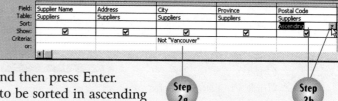

Step 2d

   e. Click the Next> button.
   f. At the second Simple Query Wizard dialog box, click the Modify the query design option, and then click the Finish button.
   g. At the Suppliers Query1 Select Query dialog box, insert the query criterion by completing the following steps:

Field:	Supplier Name	Address	City	Province	Postal Code
Table:	Suppliers	Suppliers	Suppliers	Suppliers	Suppliers
Sort:					Ascending
Show:	☑	☑	☑	☑	☑
Criteria:			Not "Vancouver"		
or:					

   Step 2g   Step 2h

   1) Click in the Criteria text box in the *City* column.
   2) Key **Not Vancouver** and then press Enter.
   h. Specify that the fields are to be sorted in ascending order by Postal Code by completing the following steps:
   1) Click in the Sort text box in the *Postal Code* column (you may need to scroll to see this column).
   2) Click the down-pointing arrow that displays at the right side of the text box and then click *Ascending*.
   i. Click the Run button on the Query Design toolbar. (Those suppliers not situated in Vancouver will display and the records will display in ascending order by Postal Code.)
   j. With the results of the query displayed, print the query.
   k. Close the query without saving the changes.
3. Close the Outdoor Options database file.

Creating a Calculated Field

In chapter 21, you learned how to create a calculated control object in the form and report Design view. A calculated control uses a mathematical equation to determine the contents that are displayed in the control object. In a query, you can insert a calculated field that performs mathematical equations.

Insert a calculated field in the Fields text box when designing a query. To insert a calculated field, click in the desired fields text box. Key the desired field name followed by a colon and then key the equation. For example, to multiply Unit Price by Units Ordered and name the field *Total Amount,* you would key **Total Amount:[Unit Price]*[Units Ordered]** in the field text box. You do not need to key the brackets around field names. When you press Enter, Access adds the appropriate symbols to the expression.

Creating a Calculated Field in a Query

1. Open the Outdoor Options database file.
2. Perform a query with the Simple Query Wizard and modify the query by completing the following steps:
   a. Click the Queries button in the Objects bar.
   b. Double-click the *Create query by using wizard* option in the list box.
   c. At the first Simple Query Wizard dialog box, click the down-pointing triangle at the right of the Tables/Queries text box, and then click *Table: Suppliers.*
   d. Insert the Supplier Name field in the Selected Fields list box.
   e. Click the down-pointing triangle at the right of the Tables/Queries text box, click *Table: Orders,* and then insert the following fields in the Selected Fields list box:
      Order #
      Units Ordered
      Amount
   f. Click the Next> button.
   g. At the second Simple Query Wizard dialog box, click the Next> button.
   h. At the last Simple Query Wizard dialog box, click the Modify the query design option, and then click the Finish button.
   i. At the Suppliers Query1 : Select Query dialog box, insert a calculated field that calculates the unit price by completing the following steps:
      1) Click in the fifth Field text box.
      2) Key **Unit Price:[Amount]/[Units Ordered]** and then press Enter.
   j. Click the Run button on the Query Design toolbar. (All records will display with the unit price calculated for each order.)
   k. With the results of the query displayed, print the query.
   l. Close the query without saving the changes.
3. Close the Outdoor Options database file.

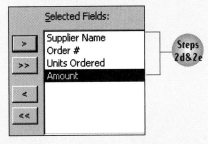

Merging Query Data with a Word Document

In chapter 22, you learned how to merge data from an Access table with a Word document. A query performed in Access can be saved, and then data from that query can be merged with a Word document. To do this, you would open the database file, complete the query, and then save the query. With the query name selected in the database file, you would click the OfficeLinks button on the Database toolbar and then click the <u>M</u>erge It with MS Word option. You would specify whether you want to merge with an existing Word document or create a new document and then insert the appropriate fields.

Performing a Query and then Merging with a Word Document

1. Open the Outdoor Options database file.
2. Perform a query with the Simple Query Wizard and modify the query by completing the following steps:
   a. Click the Queries button in the Objects bar, and then click the <u>N</u>ew button.
   b. At the New Query dialog box, double-click *Simple Query Wizard* in the list box.
   c. At the first Simple Query Wizard dialog box, click the down-pointing triangle at the right of the Tables/Queries text box, and then click *Table: Suppliers*.
   d. Insert the following fields in the <u>S</u>elected Fields list box:

   > *Supplier Name*
   > *Address*
   > *City*
   > *Province*
   > *Postal Code*

   e. Click the <u>N</u>ext> button.
   f. At the second Simple Query Wizard dialog box, click the <u>M</u>odify the query design option, and then click the <u>F</u>inish button.

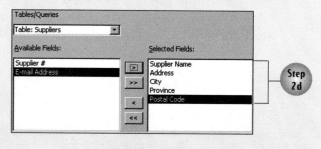

Step 2d

   g. At the Suppliers Query Select Query dialog box, insert the query criterion by completing the following steps:
      1) Click in the Criteria text box in the *City* column.
      2) Key **Vancouver** and then press Enter.

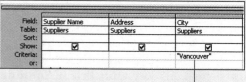

   h. Click the Run button on the Query Design toolbar. (Those suppliers situated in Vancouver will display.)
   i. Save the query as Vancouver Query by completing the following steps:
      1) Click <u>F</u>ile and then Save <u>A</u>s.

Step 2g

2) At the Save As dialog box, key **Vancouver Query**, and then press Enter or click OK.

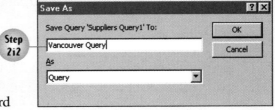

Step 2i2

j. Close the Vancouver Query by clicking the Close button at the right side of the query title bar.

3. Merge the Vancouver Query to a new Word document by completing the following steps:

a. Click *Vancouver Query* in the Outdoor Options Database window list box.

b. Click the down-pointing triangle at the right side of the OfficeLinks button on the Database toolbar.

c. At the drop-down menu that displays, click <u>M</u>erge It with MS Word.

d. At the Microsoft Word Mail Merge Wizard dialog box, click the <u>C</u>reate a new document and then link the data to it option, and then click OK.

e. Click the button on the Taskbar representing Document1, and then click the Maximize button so the blank document fills the screen.

f. Complete the following steps to key text and insert fields in the blank Word document:

1) Press Enter six times.

2) Key the current date.

3) Press Enter five times.

4) Insert the following fields at the left margin in the order shown below (start by clicking the Insert Merge Field button at the left side of the Mail Merge toolbar).

        «Supplier_Name»
        «Address»
        «City», «Province»
        «Postal_Code»

5) Press Enter twice and then key the salutation **Ladies and Gentlemen:**.

6) Press Enter twice and then key the following paragraphs of text (the paragraphs are displayed here in bold for easier reading—do not bold the paragraphs):

We have just signed with a new delivery company, Short Time Delivery, that operates within the city limits of Vancouver. This delivery company will pick up and deliver packages within a two-hour time period. The only restriction is that the pick up and delivery locations must be within the Vancouver city limits.

The next order we place with your company will be handled by Short Time Delivery. A representative from the company will pick up orders at your distribution center. If the representative needs special instructions for picking up at your company, please let us know.

7) Press Enter twice and then key the following complimentary close (at the left margin):

        Sincerely,

        Keith Watanabe
        Vice President

        XX:Word Ch 23, Ex 07

g. Click the Merge to New Document button located toward the right side of the Mail Merge toolbar.

h. When the merge is completed, save the new document to your disk as Word Ch 23, Ex 07.

i. Print and then close Word Ch 23, Ex 07.

j. Save the main document and name it Word Short Time Letter.

k. Close Word Short Time Letter and then exit Word.

4. Close the Outdoor Options database file.

Filtering Data

You can place a set of restrictions, called a *filter*, on records in a database table or form to temporarily isolate specific records. A filter, like a query, lets you select specific field values in a database table or form. Data can be filtered by selection or by form.

Using Filter By Selection

Filter By Selection

With the Filter By Selection button that displays on the Table Datasheet toolbar, you can select specific data in a field and then tell Access to display only those records containing the selected data. For example, if you want to display only those records for a specific Supplier #, select the supplier number in the appropriate database table, and then click the Filter By Selection button on the Table Datasheet toolbar. Only those records matching the selected data are displayed on the screen.

Apply Filter

The Table Datasheet toolbar contains a button named Apply Filter. When a filter is done by selection, this button changes to Remove Filter (and also displays with a light gray background). If you want to remove the filter and display the original data in the database table, click the Remove Filter button on the Table Datasheet toolbar.

exercise 8

Using Filter By Selection to Display Specific Data in a Database Table

1. Open the Outdoor Options database file.
2. At the Outdoor Options Database window, click the Tables button in the Objects bar.
3. Open the Products database table by double-clicking *Products* in the list box.
4. Use the Filter By Selection button to display only those records with no units on order by completing the following steps:
   a. Select a 0 (zero) in one of the fields in the *Units on Order* column.
   b. Click the Filter By Selection button on the Table Datasheet toolbar. (This displays only those records with no units on order.)

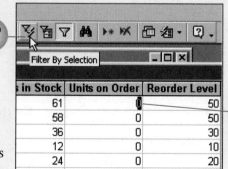

Step 4b

s in Stock	Units on Order	Reorder Level
61	0	50
58	0	50
36	0	30
12	0	10
24	0	20
0	0	0

Step 4a

c. Sort the records in ascending order by the supplier number by completing the following steps:
   1) Click in any field in the *Supplier #* column.
   2) Click the Sort Ascending button on the Table Datasheet toolbar.
d. Automatically adjust the column widths of all columns in the database table.
e. Print the database table.
f. After printing the table, click the Remove Filter button on the Table Datasheet toolbar (this redisplays all records in the database table).

5. Close the Products database table without saving the changes to the design.
6. Open the Suppliers database table by double-clicking *Suppliers* in the list box.
7. Use the Filter By Selection button to display only those records of suppliers in Burnaby by completing the following steps:
   a. Select *Burnaby* in one of the fields in the *City* column.
   b. Click the Filter By Selection button on the Table Datasheet toolbar.
   c. Print the database table in landscape orientation.
   d. After printing the table, click the Remove Filter button on the Table Datasheet toolbar (this redisplays all records in the database table).
8. Close the Suppliers database table without saving changes to the design.
9. Close the Outdoor Options database file.

Using Filter By Form

The Table Datasheet toolbar contains a Filter By Form button that, when clicked, displays the database table with a blank record. You set the values you want filtered records to contain at this blank record. Figure 23.6 shows a blank record for the Orders database table in the Outdoor Options database file. At the Orders Filter By Form dialog box displayed in figure 23.6, notice that two tabs display toward the bottom. The Look for tab is active by default and tells Access to look for whatever data you insert in a field. To display only those records for supplier # 68, you would click inside the *Supplier #* field. This causes a down-pointing triangle to display. Click this triangle and then click *68* at the drop-down menu. To filter the records, click the Filter By Form button on the Table Datasheet toolbar and only those records for supplier # 68 are displayed on the screen.

Filter By Form

figure
23.6
Orders: Filter By Form Dialog Box

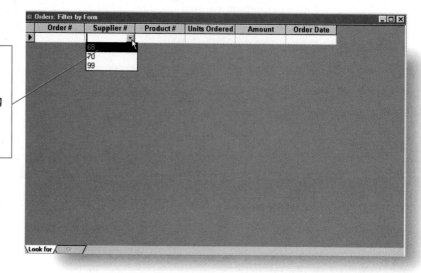

Click in the desired field, click the down-pointing triangle, and then click the desired item.

exercise
9

Using Filter By Form to Display Specific Records

1. Open the Outdoor Options database file.
2. At the Outdoor Options Database window, click the Tables button in the Objects bar, and then double-click *Orders* in the list box.
3. Use the Filter By Form button to display only those records containing supplier number 68 in the *Supplier #* field by completing the following steps:
   a. Click the Filter By Form button on the Table Datasheet toolbar.
   b. At the blank record, click in the *Supplier #* field.
   c. Click the down-pointing triangle at the right side of the *Supplier #* field and then click *68* at the drop-down menu.
   d. Click the Apply Filter button on the Table Datasheet toolbar.
   e. Print the records.
4. Close the Orders Table dialog box without saving the changes to the design.

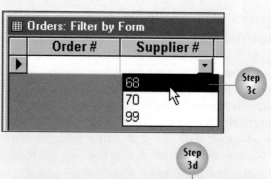

Step 3c

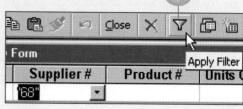

Step 3d

5. At the Outdoor Options Database window, double-click *Products* in the list box.
6. Use the Filter By Form button to display only those records containing supplier number 99 in the *Supplier #* field by completing the following steps:

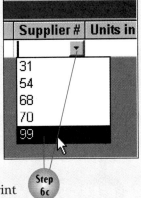

   a. Click the Filter By Form button on the Table Datasheet toolbar.
   b. At the blank record, click in the *Supplier #* field.
   c. Click the down-pointing triangle at the right side of the *Supplier #* field and then click *99* at the drop-down menu.
   d. Click the Apply Filter button on the Table Datasheet toolbar.
   e. Automatically adjust the widths of the columns and then print the records.

   Step 6c

7. Close the Products Table dialog box without saving the changes to the design.
8. Close the Outdoor Options database file.

A tab displays at the bottom of the Products Filter By Form dialog box shown in figure 23.6 with the word *Or*. Click this tab if you want to filter on two field values. When you click the Or tab, another blank record displays below the first one. As an example of when you would use the Or tab, suppose you wanted to display only those records for supplier # 68 *or* supplier # 31. You would insert *68* in the *Supplier #* field of the first blank record, click the Or button, and then insert *31* in the *Supplier #* field in the second blank record. As another example, in a database table containing suppliers' addresses, you could display only those records for suppliers located in Vancouver *or* Port Moody.

Data can be filtered on two field values.

Using Filter By Form to Filter on Two Field Values

1. Open the Outdoor Options database file.
2. At the Outdoor Options Database window, click the Tables button in the Objects bar, and then double-click *Suppliers* in the list box.
3. Use the Filter By Form button to display only those records for suppliers in Port Moody *or* Burnaby by completing the following steps:

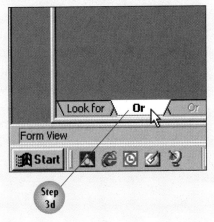

   a. Click the Filter By Form button on the Table Datasheet toolbar.
   b. At the blank record, click in the *City* field.
   c. Click the down-pointing triangle at the right side of the *City* field and then click *Port Moody* at the drop-down menu.
   d. Click the Or tab located toward the bottom of the Suppliers Filter By Form dialog box.

   Step 3d

e. At the new blank record, click the down-pointing triangle at the right side of the *City* field, and then click *Burnaby* at the drop-down menu.

f. Click the Apply Filter button on the Table Datasheet toolbar.

g. Print the records in landscape orientation.

4. Close the Suppliers Table dialog box without saving the changes to the design.

5. Close the Outdoor Options database file.

chapter summary

▶ Being able to extract specific information is one of the most important functions of a database. Data can be extracted from an Access database file by performing a query, which can be done by designing a query or using the simple query wizard.

▶ Designing a query consists of identifying the database table, the field or fields from which the data will be drawn, and the criteria for selecting the data.

▶ During the designing of a query, write the criterion (or criteria) for extracting the specific data. Access inserts any necessary symbols in the criterion when the Enter key is pressed.

▶ In a criterion, quotation marks surround field values and pound symbols (#) surround dates. The asterisk (*) can be used as a wildcard symbol.

▶ A query can be performed on fields within one database table or on fields from related database tables.

▶ When designing a query, the sort order of a field or fields can be specified.

▶ The Simple Query Wizard guides you through the steps for preparing a query. A query designed by the Simple Query Wizard can be modified.

▶ A calculated field can be inserted in a Field text box when designing a query.

▶ A query performed in Access can be saved, and then data from that query can be merged with a Word document.

▶ A set of restrictions, called a filter, can be set on records in a database table or form. A filter lets you select specific field values.

▶ Filter specific data in a field with the Filter By Selection button that displays on the Table Datasheet toolbar.

▶ Click the Filter By Form button on the Table Datasheet toolbar and a blank record is displayed. Set the values you want filtered records to contain at this blank record.

▶ When a filter is done by selection or by form, the Apply Filter button on the Table Datasheet toolbar changes to Remove Filter.

commands review

	Mouse/Keyboard
New Query dialog box	Open database file, click Queries button, click <u>N</u>ew button
Show Table dialog box	At New Query dialog box, double-click *Design View*
Simple Query Wizard	At New Query dialog box, double-click *Simple Query Wizard*
Filter specific data	Open database table, select specific data, click Filter By Selection button on Table Datasheet toolbar
Filter by form	Open database table, click Filter By Form button, at the blank record specify data, click Apply Filter button on Table Datasheet toolbar
Remove filter	Click Remove Filter button on Table Datasheet toolbar

thinking offline

Completion: In the space provided at the right, indicate the correct term, symbol, or command.

1. A query can be performed by designing your own query or using this wizard. _____

2. This is the term used for the results of the query. _____

3. This is the symbol Access will automatically insert around a field value when establishing criteria for a query. _____

4. This is the symbol Access will automatically insert around a date when establishing criteria for a query. _____

5. Use this symbol when establishing criteria to indicate a wildcard character. _____

6. This is the criterion you would key to return field values greater than $500. _____

7. This is the criterion you would key to return field values that begin with the letter L. _____

8. This is the criterion you would key to return field values that are not in Oregon. _____

9. A set of restrictions placed on records in a database table or form is referred to as this. _____

10. Click this button on the Table Datasheet toolbar to display only those records containing the selected data. _____

11. Click this tab, located at the bottom of the Filter By Form dialog box, to filter on two field values. _____

12. List the steps you would complete to display only those records with order dates between February 15, 1999, and February 20, 1999, in the Orders database table located in the Outdoor Options database file.

_____

_____

_____

_____

working hands-on

Assessment 1

(Note: If you still have the Legal Services database you copied on your disk in chapter 22, delete that database.)

1. Copy the Legal Services database file from the CD that accompanies this textbook to your disk. Remove the read-only attribute from Legal Services database file.
2. Open the Legal Services database file.
3. Design the following queries on data in the Legal Services database file:
   a. Extract records from the Billing database table with the following specifications:
      1) Include the fields *Billing #*, *Client ID*, and *Category* in the query.
      2) Extract those records with the *SE* category
      3) Print and then close the query without saving it.
   b. Extract records from the Billing database table with the following specifications:
      1) Include the fields *Billing #*, *Client ID*, and *Date*.
      2) Extract those records in the *Date* field with dates between *6/7/99* and *6/9/99*.
      3) Print and then close the query without saving it.
   c. Extract records from the Clients database table with the following specifications:
      1) Include the fields *First Name*, *Last Name*, and *City*.
      2) Extract those records with any city other than *Kent* in the *City* field.
      3) Print and then close the query without saving it.
4. Close the Legal Services database file.

Assessment 2

1. Open the Legal Services database file.
2. Extract information from two tables with the following specifications:
    a. Include the fields *Billing #*, *Client ID*, *Date*, and *Rate #* from the Billing database table.
    b. Include the field *Rate* from the Rates database table.
    c. Extract those records with a rate number greater than 2.
    d. Print the query and then close it without saving it.
3. Extract information from three tables with the following specifications:
    a. Include the field *Name* from the Attorneys database table.
    b. Include the fields *First Name* and *Last Name* from the Clients database table.
    c. Include the fields *Attorney ID, Date, and Hours* from the Billing database.
    d. Extract those records with an Attorney ID of 12.
    e. Print the query and then close it without saving it.
4. Close the Legal Services database file.

Assessment 3

1. Open the Legal Services database file.
2. Use the Simple Query Wizard to extract specific information from three tables with the following specifications:
    a. At the first Simple Query Wizard dialog box, include the following fields:
        From the Attorneys table: *Attorney ID* and *Name*
        From Categories table: *Category Name*
        From Billing table: *Hours*
    b. At the second Simply Query Wizard dialog box, click Next>.
    c. At the third Simple Query Wizard dialog box, click the Modify the query design option, and then click the Finish button.
    d. At the query dialog box, insert *14* in the Criteria text box in the *Attorney ID* column.
    e. Run the query.
    f. Print and then close the query without saving it.
3. Close the Legal Services database file.

Assessment 4

1. Open the Legal Services database file.
2. Extract records from the Clients database table of those clients located in Kent and then name the query *Kent Query*.
3. Merge the Kent Query to a new Word document using the Merge It with MS Word option from the OfficeLinks drop-down menu.
4. Click the button on the Taskbar representing Document1, click the Maximize button, and then compose a letter with the following elements:
    a. Press Enter six times, key the current date, and then press Enter five times.
    b. Insert the proper field names for the inside address.
    c. Insert a proper salutation.
    d. Compose a letter to clients that includes the following information:

> The City of Kent Municipal Court has moved from 1024 Meeker Street to a new building located at 3201 James Avenue. All court hearings after the end of this month will be held at the new address. If you need directions to the new building, please call our office.

    e.   Include a proper complimentary close for the letter. Use the name *Thomas Zeiger* and the title *Attorney* in the complimentary close.

    f.   When the letter is completed, merge it and save the new document as Word Ch 23, SA 04.

    g.   Print and then close Word Ch 23, SA 04.

    h.   Close the main document without saving it.

    i.   Exit Word.

5.   Close the Legal Services database file.

Assessment 5

1.   Open the Legal Services database file.
2.   Open the Clients database table and then use the Filter By Selection button on the Table Datasheet toolbar to display the following records:
    a.   Display only those records of clients who live in Renton. When the records of clients in Renton display, print the results, and then click the Remove Filter button.
    b.   Display only those records of clients with the Postal Code of 98033. When the records of clients with the Postal Code 98033 display, print the results, and then click the Remove Filter button.
3.   Close the Clients database table without saving the changes.
4.   Open the Billing database table and then use the Filter By Selection button on the Table Datasheet toolbar to display the following records:
    a.   Display only those records with a Category of CC. Print the CC records and then click the Remove Filter button.
    b.   Display only those records with an Attorney ID of 12. Print the records and then click the Remove Filter button.
5.   Close the Billing database table without saving the changes.
6.   Close the Legal Services database file.

Assessment 6

1.   Open the Legal Services database file.
2.   Open the Clients database table and then use the Filter By Form button on the Form View toolbar to display clients in Auburn or Renton. (Be sure to use the Or tab at the very bottom of the table.) Print the table and then click the Remove Filter button.
3.   Close the Clients database table without saving the changes.
4.   Open the Billing database table and then use the Filter By Form button on the Form View toolbar to display categories G or P. Print the table and then click the Remove Filter button.
5.   Close the Billing form without saving the changes.
6.   Close the Legal Services database file.

Assessment 7

1. Use the Access Help feature to learn how to hide fields in a query's result.
2. After reading the information on hiding fields, complete the following steps:
   a. Open the Legal Services database file.
   b. Design the following query:
      1) At the Show Table dialog box, add the Billing table, the Clients table, and the Rates table.
      2) At the Query1 Select Query dialog box, drag the following fields to Field text boxes:

      Clients table:
           First Name
           Last Name
      Billing table
           Hours
      Rates table
           Rate

      3) Insert in the fifth Field text box the calculated field *Total:Hours*Rate.* (When you press Enter, Access adds the appropriate symbols to the expression.)
      4) Hide the *Hours* and the *Rate* fields.
   c. Run the query.
   d. Print and query and then close it without saving it.
3. Close the Legal Services database file.

Using Outlook

PERFORMANCE OBJECTIVES

Upon successful completion of chapter 24, you will be able to:

- Create a Calendar, Tasks, Contacts, and Inbox personal subfolder.
- Schedule, edit, move, delete, and print appointments and events in the Calendar window.
- Set appointments using natural language phrases.
- Create and print a task list and delete items from a task list.
- Create and print a contact list and delete items from a contact list.
- Create an e-mail message.

The Microsoft Office suite includes an information management program called Outlook. Outlook is a desktop information management (DIM) application that can assist you in scheduling appointments and events, keeping track of activities, preparing a task list, and creating and maintaining a contact list. Information that you would normally keep in a calendar or daily planner can be entered into and managed by Outlook.

Outlook has a wide variety of features. In this chapter you will focus on using Outlook to manage appointments and events, create a task list and contact list, and create e-mail messages. As you become comfortable with Outlook, explore the other capabilities of the application.

Getting Started in Outlook

The first step in working with Outlook is to open it. To do this, click the Start button on the Taskbar, point to _Programs_, and then click _Microsoft Outlook_. You can also click the Launch Microsoft Outlook button located towards the left side of the Taskbar. This displays the Microsoft Outlook window with the _Inbox_ folder selected as shown in figure 24.1. (If the Office Assistant displays with a yellow box, click OK or close the Office Assistant.) The parts of the Outlook window are identified in figure 24.1. If the Outlook window does not fill the entire screen, click the Maximize button that displays at the right side of the Outlook Title bar.

Launch
Microsoft
Outlook

INTEGRATED TOPIC

figure 24.1

Microsoft Outlook Window with Inbox Folder Selected

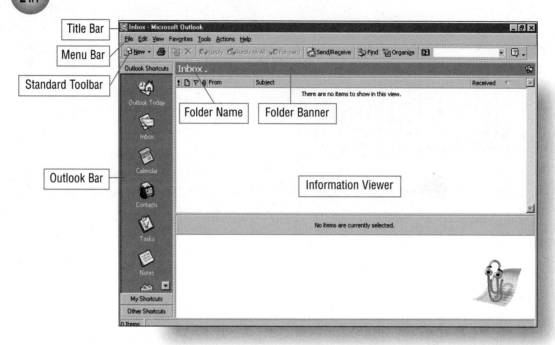

Title Bar
Menu Bar
Standard Toolbar
Folder Name
Folder Banner
Outlook Bar
Information Viewer

Another method for opening Outlook is to double-click the *Microsoft Outlook* icon on the Windows desktop.

The Outlook window contains many features that are similar to other programs in the Microsoft Office suite. For example, the Outlook window contains a Title bar, Menu bar, and Standard toolbar with elements that are similar to those features in Word, PowerPoint, or Excel.

The Title bar displays at the top of the Outlook window and displays the name of the open Outlook folder, *Inbox*. The various components of Outlook are organized in folders. For example, appointments are saved in the *Calendar* folder and contact information is saved in the *Contacts* folder. Shortcuts to these folders display as icons on the Outlook Bar located at the left side of the Outlook window. To display another folder, click the icon on the Outlook Bar representing the folder.

The Folder Banner displays below the Standard toolbar in the Outlook window. The name of the open folder displays at the left side of the Folder Banner and an icon representing the active folder displays at the right side. In figure 24.1, the Folder Banner displays the folder name *Inbox* at the left side. Clicking the name of the open folder on the Folder Banner displays the Folder List showing the various subfolders available with the folder. Right-click the folder name on the Folder Banner and a shortcut menu displays with options for working with folders and subfolders. You will be using the Folder List and the drop-down menu of folder options to create a personal subfolder.

Using the Calendar

Use Outlook's calendar to schedule appointments and events. To display the Calendar window shown in figure 24.2, click the *Calendar* icon that displays on the Outlook Bar. The items in the Calendar window are identified in figure 24.2.

figure
24.2

Microsoft Outlook Calendar Window

The Calendar Standard toolbar displays below the Menu bar. This toolbar contains buttons for managing the calendar. The buttons and a description of the buttons are presented later in this section of the chapter. The Folder Banner displays below the Standard toolbar. The name of the open folder, *Calendar*, displays at the left side. The current month, along with the next month, displays in the Date Navigator area. The current date displays highlighted in the current month in the Date Navigator. The appointment area is used to schedule appointments on specific days and at specific times. Keep track of tasks that need to be completed in the TaskPad area of the Calendar window. You will learn more about this feature later in the chapter.

Creating a Calendar Personal Subfolder

Outlook saves items of information in folders and subfolders.

Information you create at the Calendar window is saved in the *Calendar* folder. If more than one person uses the computer, consider creating a personal subfolder in which to save Calendar information. When a personal subfolder is created, individual appointment information is saved in the subfolder. In this way, many people can use Outlook on the same computer. To create a Calendar personal subfolder you would complete the following steps:

1. Position the arrow pointer on *Calendar* located at the left side of the Folder Banner and then click the *right* mouse button.
2. At the shortcut menu that displays as shown in figure 24.3, click New Folder.
3. At the Create New Folder dialog box shown in figure 24.4, key the new folder name in the Name text box, and then click OK.
4. At the message asking if you would like a shortcut to the folder added to the Outlook bar, click No.

figure

24.3

Calendar Shortcut Menu

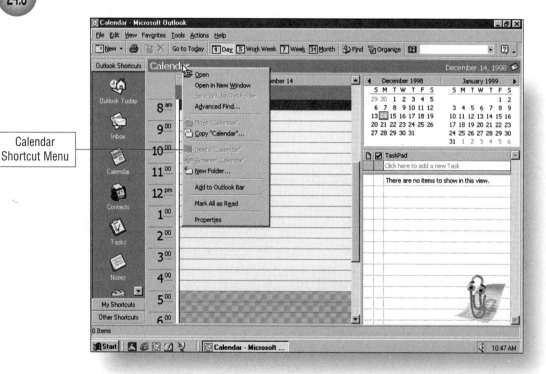

Calendar Shortcut Menu

Chapter Twenty-Four

figure

24.4

Create New Folder Dialog Box

Key a name for the new folder in the Name text box.

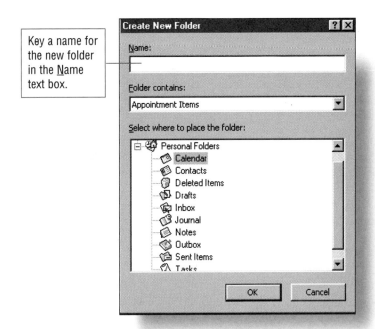

Once a Calendar personal subfolder has been created, you can select it at the Calendar drop-down menu shown in figure 24.5. To display this menu, click *Calendar* located at the left side of the Folder Banner. At the drop-down menu that displays, click the plus (+) symbol that displays before *Calendar*. A plus symbol displays before a folder containing subfolders. Select the personal subfolder by clicking the subfolder. When a personal subfolder is selected, the name of the subfolder displays at the left side of the Folder Banner (instead of *Calendar*). Also, the subfolder name displays at the left side of the Title bar (refer to figure 24.5).

Another method for displaying the Calendar drop-down menu is to click View on the Menu bar and then click Folder List.

Hint

Calendar Drop-Down Menu

24.5

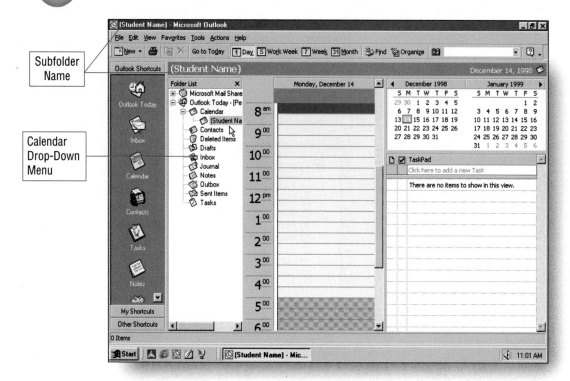

Subfolder
Name

Calendar
Drop-Down
Menu

Exiting Outlook

When you are done working in Outlook, exit the program by clicking File and
then Exit. Information keyed in Outlook is automatically saved and will be
available the next time you open the program. The next time you open Outlook,
click the *Calendar* icon on the Outlook Bar and select your personal subfolder, a
day containing appointments will display in the Date Navigator calendar in bold
print. For example, if the month displayed in the Date Navigator is January 2001
and you previously scheduled appointments for January 8, the 8 in the calendar
will display in bold print.

exercise 1

Creating a Calendar Personal Subfolder

1. Open Outlook by clicking the Start button on the Taskbar, pointing to *Programs*, and then clicking *Microsoft Outlook*. (If the Office Assistant displays a yellow box with options, click OK.)
2. Click the *Calendar* icon that displays on the Outlook Bar.
3. At the Calendar window, create a personal subfolder by completing the following steps:
    a. Position the arrow pointer on *Calendar*, located at the left side of the Folder Banner, and then click the *right* mouse button.
    b. At the shortcut menu that displays, click New Folder.
    c. At the Create New Folder dialog box, key your first and last name in the Name text box.
    d. Click OK.
    e. At the message asking if you would like a shortcut to the folder added to the Outlook bar, click No.
4. Select the new personal subfolder you just created by completing the following steps:
    a. Click *Calendar* located at the left side of the Folder Banner.
    b. At the drop-down menu that displays, click the plus (+) symbol that displays before *Calendar* (this displays Calendar subfolders).
    c. Click the subfolder containing your first and last name. (Notice that your name displays at the left side of the Folder Banner.)

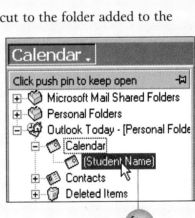

At the Calendar window (with your personal subfolder selected), the Standard toolbar displays with a variety of buttons for managing the calendar and folders. Figure 24.6 displays each button along with a description of the task the button performs.

Click this button	Named	To do this
New ▾	New Appointment	Create an appointment
	Print	Print the active file or selected items
	Move to Folder	Display a list of folders to which you can move an item
✕	Delete	Remove selected object to the *Delete Items* folder
Go to Today	Go to Today	Return to the current date
1 Day	Day	Display one day at a time
5 Work Week	Work Week	Display one work week (Monday through Friday) at a time
7 Week	Week	Display one week at a time
31 Month	Month	Display one month at a time
Find	Find	Search for items with specified criteria
Organize	Organize	Organize appointments by category
	Address Book	Display a list of e-mail addresses
	Find a Contact	Find a specific contact

Scheduling Appointments

Once a personal subfolder has been created and that subfolder has been selected, personal appointments can be scheduled. An appointment can be added in the Calendar window (with your personal subfolder selected) by clicking the desired date in the Date Navigator, selecting the desired time, and then keying the appointment information. If the appointment is longer than half an hour, drag through the times, and then key the appointment information.

If you want to include additional information for an appointment, double-click the desired appointment time, and the Untitled - Appointment window shown in figure 24.7 displays. (The title bar of the window displays *Untitled* until something is keyed in the Subject text box.) You can also display this window by clicking the New Appointment button on the Calendar Standard toolbar, or right-clicking the specific time and then clicking New Appointment at the shortcut menu.

New Appointment

Untitled - Appointment Menu

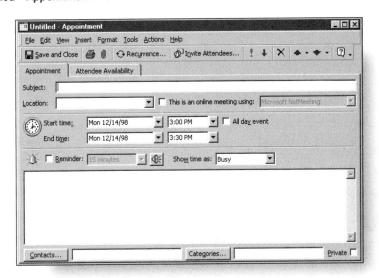

Key the subject of the meeting or appointment in the Subject text box at the Untitled - Appointment window. After keying the subject of the meeting, press the Tab key or click another option in the dialog box and the text you keyed in the Subject text box becomes the title of the Appointment window. For example, if you key **Executive Board Meeting**, the window title becomes *Executive Board Meeting - Appointment*.

Identify where the meeting will be held in the Location text box. Specify the starting time and ending time for the appointment with the Start time: and End time options. If the appointment will last all day, click the All day event check box. If you would like a reminder for an upcoming appointment, click the Reminder check box. By default, a reminder will be given fifteen minutes before the scheduled appointment. The minutes can be changed by clicking the down-pointing triangle at the right of the text box containing *15 minutes* and then clicking the desired time. You can choose from minutes, hours, or days. If a reminder is set for an appointment, a bell will sound and a Reminder dialog box will display on the screen with the appointment time and day and a description of the appointment. Key a description of the appointment or any other important information in the white text box that displays below the Reminder option.

Click the down-pointing triangle at the right of the Show time as text box and a drop-down list displays with the options *Free, Tentative, Busy*, and *Out of Office*. Click the option that describes where you will be during an appointment or if the appointment is tentative.

Outlook will warn you if you try to schedule an appointment for a time in the past or a time that conflicts with an existing appointment or meeting.

An appointment late in the day may not be visible. If there is an appointment below the bottom of the screen, a down-pointing triangle followed by an ellipsis (...) displays towards the bottom of the screen.

After all information has been entered in the Appointment window, click the Save and Close button located at the left side of the Appointment Standard toolbar. This removes the Appointment window and inserts the information you keyed in the Subject text box in the appointment area. If the subject is too long to fit on the appointment line, only a portion of the subject may display. If a reminder was included in the appointment, a *bell* icon will display at the beginning of the appointment, before the subject.

Deleting an Appointment

Delete

An appointment added to a schedule can be removed. To do this, click the appointment to select it, and then click the Delete button on the Calendar Standard toolbar. You can also delete an appointment by selecting the appointment and then clicking Edit and then Delete; or right-clicking the appointment and then clicking Delete at the shortcut menu.

Editing an Appointment

Edit an appointment by double-clicking the appointment. This opens the Appointment dialog box.

If you want to make changes to an appointment, double-click the appointment. This displays the Appointment window with the information previously entered. You can also click the appointment to select it and then click File and then Open; or, right-click the appointment and then click Open at the shortcut menu. Make any needed changes at the Appointment window and then click the Save and Close button.

Printing Appointments

Print

If you would like a printing of scheduled appointments, click the Print button on the Calendar Standard toolbar or click File and then Print. This displays the Print dialog box shown in figure 24.8. At the Print dialog box, click OK to print the current day's appointments.

figure
24.8

Print Dialog Box

Click the desired print style in this list box.

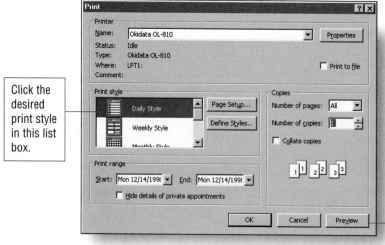

Click the Preview button to see how the calendar will appear when printed.

Adding, Editing, and Printing Appointments

1. Schedule appointments using Outlook by completing the following steps:
   a. Open Outlook by clicking the Launch Microsoft Outlook button that displays towards the left side of the Taskbar. (If your Taskbar does not contain a Launch Microsoft Outlook button, click the Start button on the Taskbar, point to Programs, and then click *Microsoft Outlook*.)
   b. At the Outlook window, click the *Calendar* icon on the Outlook Bar.
   c. Change to your personal subfolder by completing the following steps:
      1) Click *Calendar* located at the left side of the Folder Banner.
      2) At the drop-down menu that displays, click the plus (+) symbol that displays before *Calendar*. (This displays Calendar subfolders.)
      3) Click the subfolder containing your first and last name. (Notice that your name displays at the left side of the Folder Banner.)
   d. Schedule appointments for January 8, 2001, by completing the following steps:

      1) Click the right-pointing triangle that displays in the upper right corner of the Date Navigator until the months of January 2001 and February 2001 display.
      2) Click once on January 8 in the Date Navigator.
      3) Click once on 9:00 AM in the appointment area.
      4) Key **Meet with Robert Conway**.
      5) Double-click 10:00 AM (This causes the Untitled - Appointment window to display.)
      6) At the Untitled - Appointment window, make the following changes:
         a) With the insertion point positioned in the Subject text box, key **Executive Board Meeting**.
         b) Press Tab (this moves the insertion point to the Location text box) and then key **Corporate Headquarters, Conference Room**.
         c) Click the down-pointing triangle at the right side of the End time text box (the one containing *10:30 AM*), and then click 11:30 AM (1.5 hours) at the drop-down menu.

         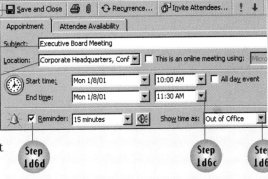

         d) Click in the Reminder check box to insert a check mark. (Leave the reminder at 15 minutes.)
         e) Click the down-pointing triangle at the right of the Show time as text box and then click *Out of Office* at the drop-down list.

f) Click the Save and Close button located at the left side of the Appointment Standard toolbar.

g) If a message displays telling you that the reminder will not appear because it is not in your Calendar or Tasks folder, click Yes. (This message displays because you are scheduling an appointment in your personal subfolder rather than the main *Calendar* folder.)

7) Double-click 2:00 PM, and then insert the following at the Appointment window:

a) Key the following in the Subject text box: **Budget Review**.

b) Key the following in the Location text box: **Meeting Room C**.

c) The ending time of the appointment is 3:00 p.m. (To change the time, click the down-pointing triangle at the right side of the End time text box [the one containing *2:30 PM*], and then click *3:00 PM* (1 hour) at the drop-down menu.)

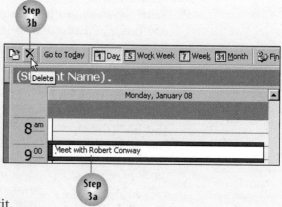

d) Add a 15-minute reminder for the meeting.

e) Change the Show time as option to *Out of Office*.

f) Click the Save and Close button located at the left side of the Appointment Standard toolbar.

g) If a message displays telling you that the reminder will not appear because it is not in your *Calendar* or *Tasks* folder, click Yes.

2. Print the daily schedule by completing the following steps:

a. Click the Print button on the Calendar Standard toolbar.

b. At the Print dialog box, make sure *Daily Style* is selected in the Print style section of the dialog box, and then click OK.

3. Delete the information on the meeting with Robert Conway by completing the following steps:

a. Click once on *Meet with Robert Conway*.

b. Click the Delete button on the Calendar Standard toolbar.

4. Print the daily schedule again following the instructions provided in step 2.

5. Exit Outlook by clicking File and then Exit.

Setting Appointments with Natural Language Phrases

Microsoft Outlook contains an AutoDate function that will convert natural language phrases to the appropriate date and time. For example, at the Untitled-Appointment window, you can enter a phrase such as "next Thursday" in the Start time: text box and the AutoDate function will convert that to the correct numeric date. You can also enter natural language time. For example, if you key **noon** in the time text box to the right of the Start time: text box, AutoDate will convert it to *12:00 PM*.

The AutoDate function uses the current date to convert natural language phrases, not the date selected in the Date Navigator. For example, in exercise 2 you displayed January 2001 in the Date Navigator and then scheduled appointments for the week of January 8, 2001. If January 8, 2001, is selected, but today's date is December 6, 1999, scheduling an appointment for "this Friday" would cause the AutoDate function to convert that language to *Fri 12/10/99*.

exercise 3

Scheduling an Appointment Using Natural Language Phrases

1. Schedule an appointment in Outlook using natural language phrases by completing the following steps:
   a. Open Outlook by clicking the Launch Microsoft Outlook located towards the left side of the Taskbar.
   b. At the Outlook window, click the *Calendar* icon on the Outlook Bar.
   c. Change to your personal subfolder by completing the following steps:
      1) Click *Calendar* located at the left side of the Folder Banner.
      2) At the drop-down menu that displays, click the plus (+) symbol that displays before *Calendar*. (This displays Calendar subfolders.)
      3) Click the subfolder containing your first and last name.
   d. Schedule an appointment for next Thursday (the date will vary depending on today's date) by completing the following steps:
      1) Click the New Appointment button on the Calendar Standard toolbar.

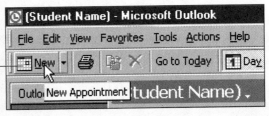
Step 1d1

      2) At the Untitled-Appointment window, make the following changes:
         a) With the insertion point positioned in the Subject text box, key **Lunch meeting with client**.
         b) Press Tab (this moves the insertion point to the Location text box) and then key **Spenser's Restaurant**.
         c) Select the current date in the Start time: text box and then key **next Thursday**.
         d) Press the Tab key. (This changes *next Thursday* to the numeric date for next Thursday and moves the insertion point to the time text box.)

e) Key **noon** in the time text box.

f) Press the Tab key twice (this changes *noon* to *12:00 PM* and moves the insertion point to the time text box after the End time text box).

g) Key **one hour** and then press the Tab key (this changes *one hour* to *1:00 PM.*

3) Click the Save and Close button located at the left side of the Appointment Standard toolbar.

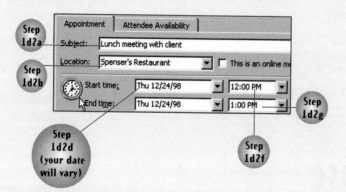

2. Display the day for the scheduled lunch meeting by clicking the specific day in the Date Navigator.

3. Print the daily schedule by completing the following steps:
   a. Click the Print button on the Calendar Standard toolbar.
   b. At the Print dialog box, make sure Daily Style displays in the Print style section of the dialog box, and then click OK.

4. Exit Outlook by clicking File and then Exit.

Changing Dates

Work Week

Month

When you click the *Calendar* icon on the Outlook Bar, the current day displays in the Calendar window (or your personal subfolder window). You can change the day on the calendar that displays in the Date Navigator section of the window by clicking the desired day. In addition to changing the day, you can change the display of the calendar. By default, the calendar displays the current day. This can be changed to work week, week, or month. Click the Work Week button on the Calendar Standard toolbar and the window display changes as shown in figure 24.9. If you click the Month button on the Calendar Standard toolbar, the window displays as shown in figure 24.10.

figure
24.9

Calendar Window with Work Week Button Selected

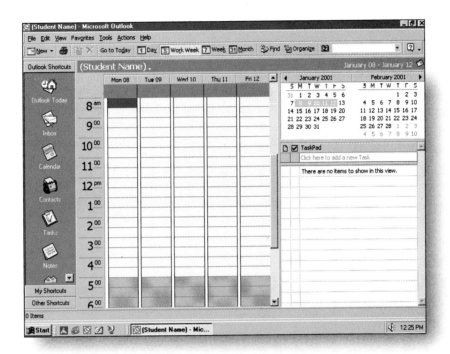

figure
24.10

Calendar Window with Month Button Selected

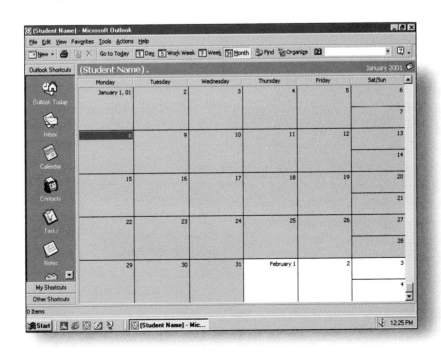

Add appointments to the weekly calendar in the same manner as the daily calendar. At the monthly calendar, click the day where you want the appointment scheduled, and then click the New Appointment button on the Calendar Standard toolbar. You can also right-click the day in the monthly calendar, and then click New Appointment at the shortcut menu.

Printing a Weekly or Monthly Calendar

In exercises 2 and 3, you printed a daily calendar. If you create a weekly schedule and want to print all the days of the week, select *Weekly Style* in the Print style section list box at the Print dialog box. If you want to print a monthly calendar, display the Print dialog box, and then click *Monthly Style* in the Print style list box. (You may need to scroll down the list box to display this choice.) If you want to see what the calendar will look like before you print it, select the desired option in the Print style list box, and then click the Preview button located in the bottom right corner of the dialog box. This displays the calendar as it will appear when printed. After viewing the calendar, click the Close button on the Print Preview toolbar.

exercise 4

Adding Appointments to a Weekly Calendar

1. Schedule and print weekly appointments using Outlook by completing the following steps:
   a. Open Outlook by clicking the Start button on the Taskbar, pointing to Programs, and then clicking *Microsoft Outlook*.
   b. At the Outlook window, click the *Calendar* icon on the Outlook Bar.
   c. Change to your personal subfolder by completing the following steps:
      1) Click *Calendar* located at the left side of the Folder Banner.
      2) At the drop-down menu that displays, click the plus (+) symbol that displays before *Calendar*. (This displays Calendar subfolders.)
      3) Click the subfolder containing your first and last name.
   d. Schedule appointments for the week of January 15, 2001, by completing the following steps:
      1) Click the right-pointing triangle that displays in the upper right corner of the Date Navigator until the months of January 2001 and February 2001 display.
      2) Click once on January 15 in the Date Navigator.
      3) Click the Work Week button on the Calendar Standard toolbar. (This will display a five-day workweek calendar beginning with Monday, January 15, 2001.)
   e. Schedule an appointment for Monday morning by completing the following steps:

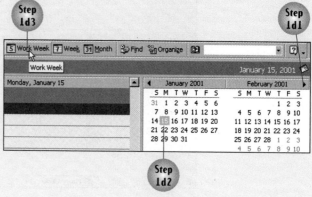

1) Double-click in the 8:30 AM time slot for Monday, January 15.
2) At the Untitled - Appointment window, add an appointment with the following specifications:

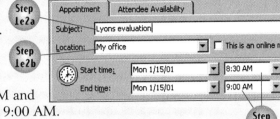

a) Key **Lyons evaluation** in the Subject text box.
b) Key **My office** in the Location text box.
c) Make sure the Start time: option is 8:30 AM and the End time option is 9:00 AM.
3) Click the Save and Close button to close the Appointment window.

f. Double-click in the 1:30 PM time slot for Monday, January 15, and then schedule an appointment at the Untitled- Appointment window with the following specifications:
1) Key **Staff meeting** in the Subject text box.
2) Key **Conference Room A** in the Location text box.
3) Make sure the starting time is 1:30 PM and change the ending time to 2:30 PM.

g. Double-click in the 8:30 AM time slot for Tuesday, January 16, and then schedule an appointment at the Untitled - Appointment window with the following specifications:
1) Key **Yang evaluation** in the Subject text box.
2) Key **My office** in the Location text box.
3) Make sure the starting time is 8:30 AM and the ending time is 9:00 AM.

h. Double-click in the 2:30 PM time slot for Tuesday, January 16, and then schedule an appointment at the Untitled - Appointment window with the following specifications:
1) Key **Meet with architects** in the Subject text box.
2) Key **Kendall Architecture office** in the Location text box.
3) Make sure the starting time is 2:30 PM and change the ending time to *4:30 PM*.
4) Key **Meet with architects to discuss preliminary plans** in the white text box below the Reminder check box.

i. Click in the 10:00 AM time slot for Wednesday, January 17, and then schedule an appointment at the Untitled - Appointment window with the following specifications:
1) Key **Client meeting** in the Subject text box.
2) Key **My office** in the Location text box.
3) Make sure the starting time is 10:00 AM and change the ending time to *11:00 AM*.

j. Click in the 3:00 PM time slot for Wednesday, January 17, and then schedule an appointment at the Untitled - Appointment window with the following specifications:
   1) Key **Review architectural plans** in the Subject text box.
   2) Key **Corporate office** in the Location text box.
   3) Make sure the starting time is 3:00 PM and change the ending time to *4:00 PM*.

k. Click in the 8:30 AM time slot for Thursday, January 18, and then schedule and appointment at the Untitled - Appointment window with the following specifications:
   1) Key **Royce evaluation** in the Subject text box.
   2) Key **My office** in the Location text box.
   3) Make sure the starting time is 8:30 AM and the ending time is *9:00 AM*.

l. Click in the 9:00 AM time slot for Friday, January 19, and then schedule an appointment at the Untitled - Appointment window with the following specifications:
   1) Key **Production meeting** in the Subject text box.
   2) Key **Room 110, Production Wing** in the Location text box.
   3) Make sure the starting time is 9:00 AM and change the ending time to *10:00 AM*.

2. Print the five-day weekly schedule by completing the following steps:
   a. Click the Print button on the Calendar Standard toolbar.
   b. At the Print dialog box, make sure *Weekly Style* is selected in the Print style list box.
   c. Click OK.

3. Exit Outlook by clicking File and then Exit.

Adding Recurring Appointments

Recurrence

Appointments that occur on a regular basis can be added to a schedule. To do this, specify the appointment at the Appointment window and then click the Recurrence button on the Appointment Standard toolbar. This displays the Appointment Recurrence dialog box shown in figure 24.11.

figure
24.11

Appointment Recurrence Dialog Box

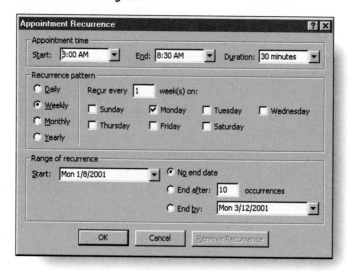

Specify the appointment beginning and ending times in the Appointment time section of the Appointment Recurrence dialog box. Identify how often the appointment will reoccur in the Recurrence pattern section of the dialog box. In this section, specify whether the appointment is to occur daily, weekly, monthly, or yearly; how often the meeting reoccurs; and on what days of the week. In the Range of recurrence section, specify the starting date and ending date of the appointment.

Adding Recurring Appointments to a Monthly Calendar

1. Schedule and print monthly appointments using Outlook by completing the following steps:
   a. Open Outlook.
   b. At the Outlook window, click the *Calendar* icon on the Outlook Bar.
   c. Change to your personal Calendar subfolder.
   d. Schedule a recurring meeting by completing the following steps:
      1) Click the right-pointing triangle that displays in the upper right corner of the Date Navigator until the months of February 2001 and March 2001 display.
      2) Click once on February 6 in the Date Navigator.
      3) Click the Week button on the Calendar Standard toolbar. (This will display a weekly calendar beginning with Monday, February 5, 2001.)

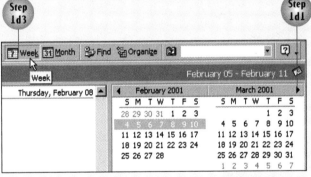

Step 1d3

Step 1d1

      4) Click the New Appointment button on the Calendar Standard toolbar.
      5) At the Untitled - Appointment window, key **Marketing meeting** in the Subject text box.
      6) Press the Tab key and then key **Conference room** in the Location text box.
      7) Click the Recurrence button on the Appointment Standard toolbar.
      8) At the Appointment Recurrence dialog box (see figure 24.11), make the following changes:

Step 1d5

Step 1d6

Step 1d7

a) Change the Start time to *9:30 AM*.
b) Change the End time to *10:30 AM*.
c) Make sure Weekly is selected at the left side in the Recurrence pattern section and that there is a check mark in the Tuesday check box at the right side.
d) Select the *1* that displays in the Recur every text box and then key **2**.
e) Click OK to close the Appointment Recurrence dialog box.

Step 1d8a   Step 1d8b   Step 1d8d

Appointment Recurrence

Appointment time
Start: 9:30 AM ▾   End: 10:30 AM ▾   Durati

Recurrence pattern
○ Daily   Recur every 2 week(s) on:
◉ Weekly   ☐ Sunday   ☐ Monday   ☑ Tuesday
○ Monthly   ☐ Thursday ☐ Friday   ☐ Saturday
○ Yearly

Step 1d8c

9) Click the Save and Close button located at the left side of the Appointment Standard toolbar.
e. Schedule a recurring Supervisor's meeting that is held in Room 10C, begins Thursday, February 8, 2001, and occurs every Thursday by completing steps similar to those in steps 1d4 through 1d9. The beginning time of the meeting is 3:00 PM and the ending time is 4:00 PM.
2. Print the monthly schedule by completing the following steps:
   a. Click the Print button on the Calendar Standard toolbar.
   b. At the Print dialog box, click *Monthly Style* in the Print style list box. (You may need to scroll down the list to display this option.)
   c. Click OK. (Printing the monthly calendar may take several minutes.)
3. Exit Outlook.

Change the ending time of an appointment by clicking and dragging the bottom border of the appointment to the new ending time.

Hint

Moving Appointments

If a scheduled appointment time has been changed, the appointment can be moved in the calendar. You can display the Appointment window for a specific appointment and then change the starting and ending times and dates, or you can use the mouse to drag and then drop an appointment in a new time or date slot.

exercise 6

Moving Appointments

1. Move appointments in Outlook by completing the following steps:
   a. Open Outlook.
   b. At the Outlook window, click the Calendar icon on the Outlook Bar.
   c. Change to your personal Calendar subfolder.
   d. Change the months in the Date Navigator to *January 2001* and *February 2001*.
   e. Click January 15 in the Date Navigator.
   f. Move the Lyons evaluation from *8:30 AM Monday* to *10:30 AM Monday* by completing the following steps:

1) Position the arrow pointer on the blue bar located immediately left of the *Lyons evaluation* appointment until it turns into a four-headed arrow.
2) Hold down the left mouse button, drag the appointment to the 10:30 AM time slot, and then release the mouse button.

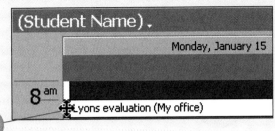

g. Move the Royce evaluation from *8:30 AM, Thursday, January 18,* to *1:30 PM on Friday* by completing the following steps:
1) Click January 18 in the Date Navigator.
2) Position the arrow pointer on the blue bar located immediately left of the *Royce evaluation* appointment until the arrow pointer turns into a four-headed arrow.
3) Hold down the left mouse button, drag the arrow pointer to January 19 in the Date Navigator, and then release the mouse button. (This displays *January 19* in the appointment area and drops the appointment into the 8:30 AM time slot.)
4) Position the arrow pointer on the blue bar located immediately left of the *Royce evaluation* appointment until the arrow pointer turns into a four-headed arrow.
5) Hold down the left mouse button, drag the appointment to the 1:30 PM time slot, and then release the mouse button.

h. Add an appointment at 1:30 PM on Wednesday, January 17. Insert the following at the Appointment dialog box:

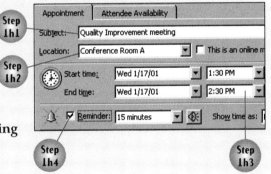

1) Key **Quality Improvement meeting** in the Subject text box.
2) Key **Conference Room A** in the Location text box.
3) Change the ending time of the appointment to *2:30 PM.*
4) Add a reminder for 15 minutes before the meeting. (If you get a message about the reminder when closing the Appointment dialog box, click <u>Y</u>es.

2. Print the weekly schedule by completing the following steps:
   a. Click the Print button on the Calendar Standard toolbar.
   b. At the Print dialog box, make sure Weekly Style is selected in the Print style list box.
   c. Click OK.
3. Exit Outlook.

Scheduling Events

Events that occur during the year that you want to remember can be included in Outlook. Events might include conferences, seminars, workshops, birthdays, anniversaries, etc. Events are different from appointments in that an event does not display in a particular time slot in the appointment area. When an event is scheduled, a description of the event displays below the date heading in the appointment area.

To schedule an event, double-click the date located at the top of the appointment area; or, click Actions on the Menu bar and then click New All Day Event at the drop-down menu. This displays the Untitled - Event window as shown in figure 24.12. At the window, specify the subject and location of the event, the beginning and ending dates, whether or not you want a reminder, and any other information needed.

An event is something that occurs during one or more days but does not necessarily occupy any of your time.

figure
24.12

Untitled - Event Window

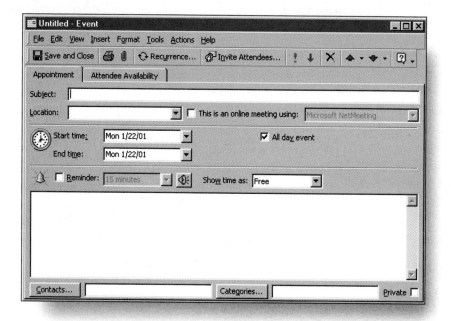

Scheduling Events

1. Schedule events in Outlook by completing the following steps:
   a. Open Outlook.
   b. At the Outlook window, click the *Calendar* icon on the Outlook Bar.
   c. Change to your personal Calendar subfolder.
   d. Schedule a sales conference for January 29 through January 31 by completing the following steps:
      1) Change the months in the Date Navigator to *January 2001* and *February 2001*.
      2) Click once on Monday, January 29.

3) Double-click *Monday, January 29* that displays at the top of the appointment area.
4) At the Untitled - Event window, key **Annual Sales Conference** in the Subject text box.
5) Click the down-pointing triangle at the right side of the End time text box.
6) At the drop-down calendar that displays, click *January 31*.
7) Click the Save and Close button located at the left side of the Event toolbar.

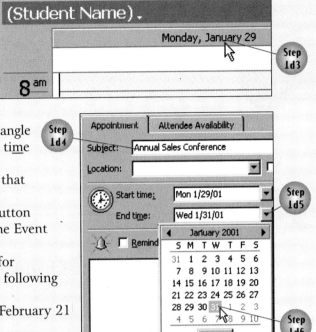

e. Schedule a marketing seminar for February 21 by completing the following steps:
   1) Click once on Wednesday, February 21 in the Date Navigator.
   2) Click Actions on the Menu bar and then click New All Day Event at the drop-down menu.
   3) At the Untitled - Event window, key **Marketing seminar for new products** in the Subject text box.
   4) Click the Save and Close button at the left side of the Event toolbar.
f. Schedule a supervisory training workshop for February 26 and 27 by completing steps similar to those in step 1d.

2. Print the February schedule by completing the following steps:
   a. Click once on February 1 in the Date Navigator.
   b. Click the Print button on the Calendar Standard toolbar.
   c. At the Print dialog box, click *Monthly Style* in the Print style list box. (You may need to scroll down the list to display this option.)
   d. Click OK. (Printing the monthly calendar may take several minutes.)

3. Print the January schedule by completing the following steps:
   a. Click once on January 1 in the Date Navigator
   b. Click the Print button on the Calendar Standard toolbar.
   c. At the Print dialog box, click *Monthly Style* in the Print style list box.
   d. Click OK. (Printing the monthly calendar may take several minutes.)

4. Exit Outlook.

Creating a Task List

The Calendar window includes a TaskPad where you can keep track of tasks that need to be completed. The TaskPad displays in the bottom right corner of the Calendar window. The TaskPad contains two sections—the new task area and the task list. The new task area is located toward the top of the TaskPad and contains the text *Click here to add a new Task*. The task list is located below the new task

area. Add a task to the TaskPad by clicking the text *Click here to add a new Task* that displays in the new task area. Key a description of the task to be completed and then press the Enter key. This inserts the task in the TaskPad.

A task can also be added to the TaskPad at the Tasks window shown in figure 24.13. To display this window, click the *Tasks* icon on the Outlook Bar. At the Tasks window, click the text *Click here to add a new Task* and then key a description of the task to be completed. Press the Tab key or click in the list box below Due Date and then key the date the task is to be completed. Press the Enter key and the task description and due date are inserted in the first list box.

Tasks Window

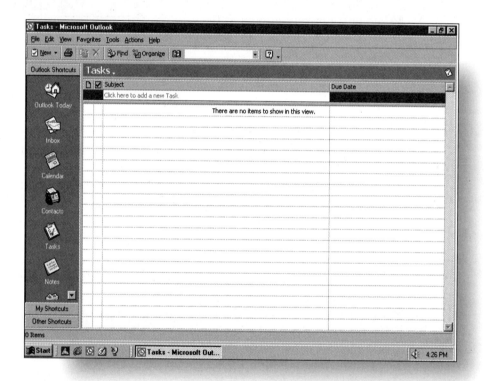

New Task

Details about a task can be added to a task at the Untitled - Task window. Details can be added, such as the status and priority of the task as well as the percentage of the task completed. To display the Untitled - Task window, click the New Task button located at the left side of the Tasks Standard toolbar.

Creating a Tasks Personal Subfolder

Information you create at the Tasks window is saved in the *Tasks* folder. If more than one person uses the computer, consider creating a personal subfolder in which to save a task list. When a personal subfolder is created, individual task lists are saved in the subfolder. A Tasks personal subfolder is created in the same manner as a Calendar personal subfolder. To create a Tasks personal subfolder, click the *Tasks* icon on the Outlook Bar. Position the arrow pointer on *Tasks*, located at the left side of the Folder Banner, and then click the *right* mouse button. At the shortcut menu that displays, click New Folder. At the Create New Folder dialog box, key the new folder name in the Name text box, and then click OK.

Once a Tasks personal subfolder has been created, you can select it by clicking *Tasks* located at the left side of the Folder Banner. At the drop-down menu that displays, click the plus (+) symbol that displays before *Tasks*. Select the personal subfolder by clicking the subfolder name. When a personal subfolder is selected, the name of the subfolder displays at the left side of the Folder Banner (instead of *Tasks*). Also, the subfolder name displays at the left side of the Title bar. You will be creating and selecting a Tasks personal subfolder in exercise 8.

Removing an Item from the TaskPad

When a task in the TaskPad is completed, it can be crossed off the list by clicking in the check box immediately preceding the task. This inserts a check mark in the check box and inserts a line through the task. To delete the task from the TaskPad, click the task to select it, and then click the Delete button on the Tasks Standard toolbar. A Delete button displays on the Calendar Standard toolbar as well as the Tasks Standard toolbar.

Printing a Task List

Items on the TaskPad will print when the Calendar daily schedule is printed. You can also print the list of tasks at the Tasks window. To do this, display the Tasks window, and then click the Print button on the Tasks Standard toolbar. At the Print dialog box, specify whether you want the task list printed in table style or memo style and then click OK.

exercise 8

Creating a Tasks Personal Subfolder and Creating a Task List

1. Open Outlook.
2. Click the *Tasks* icon that displays on the Outlook Bar.
3. At the Tasks window, create a personal subfolder by completing the following steps:
   a. Position the arrow pointer on *Tasks*, located at the left side of the Folder Banner, and then click the *right* mouse button.
   b. At the shortcut menu that displays, click New Folder.
   c. At the Create New Folder dialog box, key your first and last name in the Name text box.

d. Click OK.
e. At the message asking if you would like a shortcut to the folder added to the Outlook bar, click No.

4. Select the new personal subfolder you just created by clicking the subfolder containing your name that displays below *Tasks* in the drop-down menu.

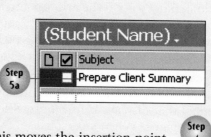

5. Create a list of tasks by completing the following steps:
   a. Click the text *Click here to add a new Task* and then key **Prepare Client Summary**.
   b. Press the Tab key. (This moves the insertion point to the text box below *Due Date* and changes the text box from blue to white [the insertion point is not visible].)
   c. Key **01/19/01**.
   d. Press the Enter key. (This adds the item to the list.)
   e. With the insertion point located in the text box immediately below *Subject*, key **Copy report**.
   f. Press the Tab key, key **01/20/01**, and then press the Enter key.
   g. With the insertion point located in the text box immediately below *Subject*, key **Proof budget**.
   h. Press the Tab key, key **01/21/01**, and then press the Enter key.

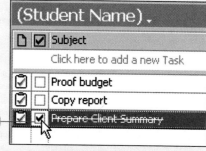

6. Print the task list by completing the following steps:
   a. Click the Print button on the Tasks Standard toolbar.
   b. At the Print dialog box, make sure *Table Style* is selected in the Print style list box, and then click OK.

7. Assume that you have prepared the Client Summary and want to remove it from the list. To do this, click the white check box immediately preceding *Prepare Client Summary*.

8. Delete the *Copy report* item from the list. To do this, click once on the text *Copy report* and then click the Delete button on the Tasks Standard toolbar.

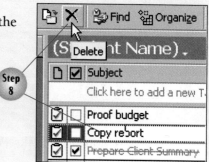

9. Print the task list again by completing step 6.
10. Exit Outlook.

Adding Contacts

With Outlook, you can keep track of contacts, (customers, clients, companies, etc.) and include information about contacts, such as a name, company name, address, telephone number, fax number, e-mail address and much more. Contact information in Outlook is stored in the *Contacts* folder or a personal subfolder within the *Contacts* folder. Information in a contact list can be printed, edited, sorted, or used as a database for mail merging in Microsoft Word. A contact is added to the contact list at the Contacts window. To display this window, click the *Contacts* icon on the Outlook Bar.

Creating a Contacts Personal Subfolder

Information on contacts that you key at the Contacts window is saved in the *Contacts* folder. If more than one person uses the computer, consider creating a personal contacts subfolder in which to save personal contact information. A Contacts personal subfolder is created in the same manner as a Calendar or Tasks personal subfolder. You will be creating and selecting a Contacts personal subfolder in exercise 9.

Creating a Contact List

After creating and selecting your Contacts personal subfolder, the Contacts window will display similar to the window shown in figure 24.14. To add a contact to the contact list, double-click the text *Double-click here to create a new Contact.* that displays toward the top of the Contacts window. This displays the Untitled - Contact window like the one shown in figure 24.15.

Contacts Window

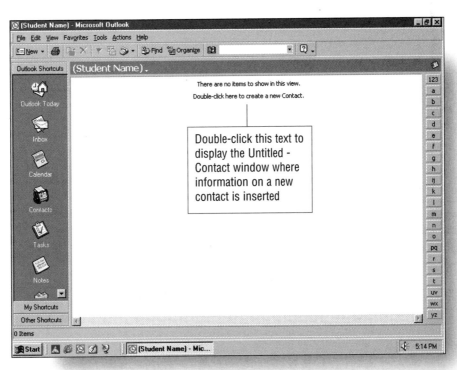

figure 24.15

Untitled - Contact Window

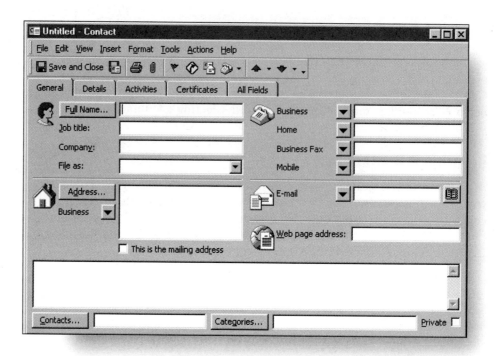

At the Contact window, add only the information you expect to need in the future. More information can always be added later. *Hint*

New Contact

At the Untitled - Contact window, key information for the first person (contact) to be added to the list. Key the specified information in the field text boxes. To move to the next field, press the Tab key. To move to the previous field, press Shift + Tab. You can also move the insertion point to another field by clicking inside the field text box. After all the information is entered, click the Save and Close button at the left side of the Contacts Standard toolbar. This displays the personal Contacts subfolder window with the contact information displayed in business card format as shown in figure 24.16. Figure 24.16 shows the contacts you will be creating in exercise 9. To create another contact, click the New Contact button located at the left side of the Contacts Standard toolbar.

figure 24.16

Contacts Window with Contacts Added

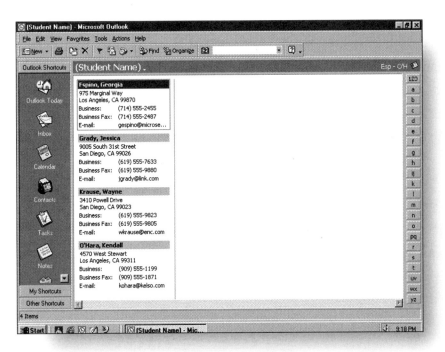

Contacts in a contact list are alphabetized by the person's last name. The range of contacts that are currently displayed in the Contacts window displays at the right side of the Folder Banner. For a contact list that contains more contacts than the window can display at one time, you can locate a specific contact by clicking the desired letter tab at the right side of the Contacts window. For example, if you want to display contact information for Georgia Espino, you would click the e letter tab. This would not only display the contact information for Georgia Espino but also any other contacts whose last name begins with E.

Deleting a Contact

A contact list should be maintained on a regular basis. Maintenance activities might include editing a contact when information has changed, such as an address, telephone number, or e-mail address; deleting outdated contacts; and adding new contacts. To delete a contact, display the Contacts window with your personal subfolder displayed. Click the name of the contact to be deleted and then click the Delete button on the Contacts Standard toolbar. If you accidentally delete a contact, immediately click the Undo button to restore the contact information.

Editing a Contact

Edit information for a contact by double-clicking the name of the contact at your personal Contacts subfolder window. This displays the contact information in the Contacts window. Change the information as needed and then click the <u>S</u>ave and Close button located at the left side of the Contacts Standard toolbar.

Printing a Contact List

Contacts can be printed in a variety of formats. Click the Print button on the Contacts Standard toolbar and the Print dialog box displays. The Print style section of the dialog box contains the following printing styles—Card Style, Small Booklet Style, Medium Booklet Style, and Phone Directory Style. You can preview how the contacts will print by clicking the desired style in the Print style section and then clicking the Pre<u>v</u>iew button located at the bottom right side of the dialog box. After previewing how the contacts will appear when printed, click the <u>C</u>lose button to close the Print Preview window.

exercise 9

Creating a Contacts Personal Subfolder and Creating a Contact List

1. Open Outlook.
2. Click the *Contacts* icon that displays on the Outlook Bar.
3. At the Contacts window, create a personal subfolder by completing the following steps:
   a. Position the arrow pointer on *Contacts*, located at the left side of the Folder Banner, and then click the *right* mouse button.
   b. At the shortcut menu that displays, click <u>N</u>ew Folder.
   c. At the Create New Folder dialog box, key your first and last name in the <u>N</u>ame text box.
   d. Click OK.
   e. At the message asking if you would like a shortcut to the folder added to the Outlook bar, click <u>N</u>o.
4. Select the new personal subfolder you just created by clicking the subfolder containing your name that displays below *Contacts* in the drop-down menu.
5. Add a contact to the list by completing the following steps:
   a. Double-click the text *Double-click here to add a new Contact.* that displays toward the top of the Contacts window.
   b. At the Untitled - Contact window, key the following text in the specified fields. (Move to the next field by pressing the Tab key; move to the previous field by pressing Shift + Tab; or move to a field by clicking inside a field text box.)

Step 4

Full Name	=	**Wayne Krause**
Job title	=	**Manager**
Company	=	**Copeland, Inc.**
Phone:		
Business	=	**(619) 555-9823**
Business Fax	=	**(619) 555-9805**
Address	=	**3410 Powell Drive**
		San Diego, CA 99023
E-mail	=	**wkrause@enc.com**

c. When all
   information for
   Wayne Krause has
   been keyed in the
   Untitled - Contact
   window, click the
   Save and Close
   button located at

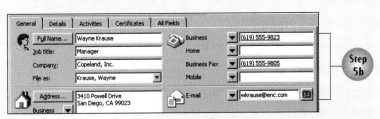

Step
5b

   the left side of the Contacts Standard
   toolbar.

6. Add another contact to the contact list by
   completing the following steps:

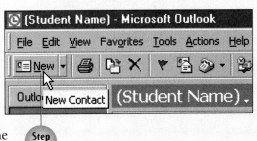

   a. Click the New Contact button located
      at the left side of the Contacts
      Standard toolbar.
   b. At the Untitled - Contact window, key the
      following information in the specified
      fields:

Step
6a

Full Name	=	**Georgia Espino**
Job title	=	**Vice President**
Company	=	**Vista Enterprises**
Phone:		
Business	=	**(714) 555-2455**
Business Fax	=	**(714) 555-2487**
Address	=	**1200 North 42nd Street**
		Los Angeles, CA 99297
E-mail	=	**gespino@microserv.com**

   c. When all information for Georgia Espino has been keyed in the Untitled -
      Contact window, click the Save and Close button located at the left side of the
      Contacts Standard toolbar.

7. Add another contact with the following information by completing steps similar to
   those in step 6.

Full Name	=	**Kendall O'Hara**
Job title	=	**Director**
Company	=	**Champion Corporation**
Phone:		
Business	=	**(909) 555-1199**
Business Fax	=	**(909) 555-1871**
Address	=	**4570 West Stewart**
		Los Angeles, CA 99311
E-mail	=	**kohara@kelso.com**

8. Add another contact with the following information by completing steps similar to those in step 6.

Full Name	=	**Jessica Grady**
Job title	=	**President**
Company	=	**Lakeland Company**
Phone:		
Business	=	**(619) 555-7633**
Business Fax	=	**(619) 555-9880**
Address	=	**9005 South 31st Street**
		San Diego, CA 99026
E-mail	=	**jgrady@link.com**

9. Print the contact list in Card Style by completing the following steps:
   a. Click the Print button on the Contacts Standard toolbar.
   b. At the Print dialog box, make sure *Card Style* is selected in the Print style list box, and then click the Pre<u>v</u>iew button located at the bottom right side of the dialog box.
   c. After viewing how the contact list will appear when printed in Card Style, click the <u>P</u>rint button located on the Print Preview toolbar.
   d. At the Print dialog box, click OK.
10. Change the address for Georgia Espino by completing the following steps:
    a. At your personal Contacts subfolder window, double-click *Espino, Georgia*.
    b. At the Georgia Espino - Contact window, click in the A<u>d</u>dress text box (or press the Tab key until the insertion point is positioned in this text box) and then change the street address from *1200 North 42nd Street* to *975 Marginal Way*. Also, change the ZIP code from *99297* to *99870*.
    c. Click the <u>S</u>ave and Close button located at the left side of the Contacts Standard toolbar.

(Student Name)

Espino, Georgia	
1200 North 42nd Street	
Los Angeles, CA 99297	
Business:	(714) 555-2455
Business Fax:	(714) 555-2487
E-mail:	gespino@microse...

Step 10a

11. Delete the contact information for Wayne Krause by completing the following steps:
    a. Click once on the name *Krause, Wayne* in the Contacts window.
    b. Click the Delete button on the Contacts Standard toolbar.
12. Print the contact list in Phone Directory Style by completing the following steps:
    a. Click the Print button on the Contacts Standard toolbar.
    b. At the Print dialog box, click *Phone Directory Style* in the Print st<u>y</u>le list box. (You will need to scroll down the list to display this option.)
    c. Click the Pre<u>v</u>iew button located at the bottom right corner of the dialog box.
    d. After viewing how the contact list will appear when printed in Phone Directory Style, click the <u>P</u>rint button located on the Print Preview toolbar.
    e. At the Print dialog box, click OK.
13. Exit Outlook.

Using the Inbox to Send Messages

When Outlook is opened, the Inbox window displays (see figure 24.1). The Inbox window can be used for a variety of functions. In this section, you will learn to use the Inbox window to create a personal subfolder and create and print e-mail messages. In a business setting, sending an e-mail message to a coworker or to a customer or client is faster and less expensive than creating, printing, and sending a traditional memo or letter. Many companies offer electronic mail (e-mail) capabilities to their employees. In this section, you will learn how to create an Inbox personal subfolder, create and print an e-mail message, and use the contact list created in exercise 9 to address an e-mail message.

Before sending and receiving mail with Outlook, you must properly configure the Internet Mail information service. Your Internet Service Provider (ISP) will need to provide most of the information for the configuration pages of the Internet Mail Information Service. In this section of the chapter, you will learn the basic steps to create an e-mail message but you will not actually send the message.

Note: If you are using Outlook on a business or home computer, you would complete these basic steps to configure the Internet E-mail information service.

1. Open Outlook.
2. Click Tools and then Services.
3. At the Services dialog box, click *Internet E-mail* in the list box, and then click the Properties button. (If *Internet E-mail* is not available, click the Add button. At the Add Service to Profile dialog box, click *Internet E-mail* in the list box, and then click OK.)
4. At the Mail Account Properties dialog box with the General tab selected, key the required information. (Some of this information you will need to get from your Internet Service Provider.)
5. Click the Connection tab and then key the required information.
6. When all information is entered, click OK.

Creating an Inbox Personal Subfolder

Messages sent and received by Outlook are displayed in the Inbox window. If more than one person uses the computer, consider creating a personal Inbox subfolder in which to save personal information. An Inbox personal subfolder is created in the same manner as a Calendar, Tasks, or Contacts personal subfolder. You will be creating and selecting an Inbox personal subfolder in exercise 10. Before sending an e-mail message, the Internet E-mail information service must be configured (see steps above). In this section of the chapter, you will create an e-mail message but not send it.

Creating an E-mail Message

To create an e-mail message, click the New Mail Message button at the left side of the Inbox Standard toolbar. This displays the Untitled - Message window shown in figure 24.17.

Outlook can be set up to send and receive e-mail messages from people in your workgroup, people with accounts on your LAN or WAN, and people who have Internet accounts.

New Mail
Message

figure

24.17

Untitled - Message Window

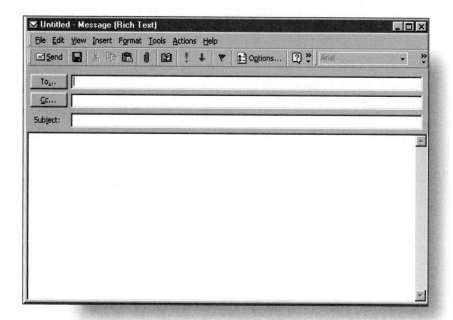

At the Untitled - Message window with the insertion point positioned in the To... text box, key the e-mail address of the person to receive the message. Key the subject of the message in the Subject text box, and then key the message in the white box below Subject. When the message is completed, send it by clicking the Send button located at the left side of the Message Standard toolbar.

If you are sending an e-mail message to someone contained in your Contacts list, you can insert his or her e-mail address in the To... text box. To do this, click the Address Book button on the Inbox Standard toolbar and the Select Names dialog box shown in figure 24.18 displays. At this dialog box, change to your personal Contacts subfolder in the Show Names from the option. This displays the name of contacts currently contained in your personal Contacts subfolder. Double-click the name of the person to receive the e-mail. This inserts the name in the Message Recipients list box. Click the OK button and the dialog box is removed from the screen and the e-mail address of the recipient is displayed in the To... text box.

When all the information for the e-mail message has been entered, send the message by clicking the Send button located at the left side of the Inbox Standard toolbar.

Address Book

figure

24.18

Select Names Dialog Box

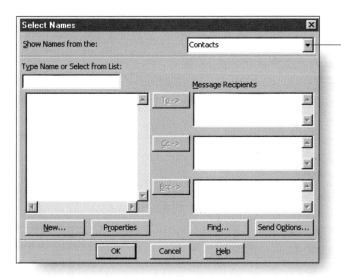

> Click this down-pointing triangle to display your personal contacts subfolder.

If your personal Contacts subfolder does not display when you click the Show Names from the option at the Select Names dialog box, you need tell Outlook to display contacts in your personal subfolder. To do this, you would complete the following steps:

1. At the Inbox window, click View and then Folder List.
2. In the list of folders, click the *Contacts* folder (this displays subfolders).
3. Right-click on your personal subfolder.
4. At the shortcut menu that displays, click Properties.
5. At the (Student Name) Properties dialog box, click the Outlook Address Book tab.
6. Click the Show this folder as an e-mail Address Book option to insert a check mark.
7. Click OK.
8. Click View and then Folder List to turn off the display of the list.

exercise

10

Creating an Inbox Personal Subfolder and Creating an E-mail Message

1. Open Outlook.
2. Complete the following steps to add your personal subfolder to the Outlook Address Book. (Check with your instructor before completing these steps—they may not be necessary.)
   a. Click View and then Folder List.
   b. In the list of folders, click the plus sign preceding the *Contacts* folder (this displays subfolders).

c. Right-click on your personal Contacts subfolder.
d. At the shortcut menu that displays, click Properties.
e. At the (Student Name) Properties dialog box, click the Outlook Address Book tab.
f. Click the Show this folder as an e-mail Address Book option to insert a check mark.
g. Click OK.
h. Click View and then Folder List to turn off the display of the list.

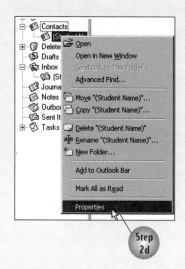

Step 2e

Step 2f

Step 2d

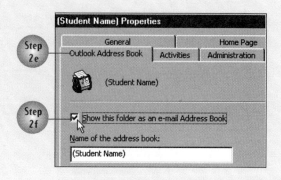

3. Click the *Inbox* icon that displays on the Outlook Bar.
4. With *Inbox* the active folder, create a personal subfolder named with your first and last name.
5. Select your new personal Inbox subfolder.
6. Compose an e-mail message to a customer in your personal Contacts folder, Jessica Grady, by completing the following steps:
   a. Click the New Mail Message button located at the left side of the Inbox Standard toolbar.
   b. At the Untitled - Message window (see figure 24.17), click the Address Book button on the Message Standard toolbar. (If this button is not visible, click the More Buttons button and then click the Address Book button.)
   c. At the Select Names dialog box (see figure 24.18), click the down-pointing triangle at the right of the Show Names from the option, and then click your name in the drop-down list. (This displays contacts in your personal Contacts subfolder.)

Step 6a

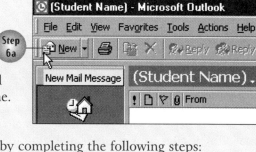

(More Buttons)

Step 6b

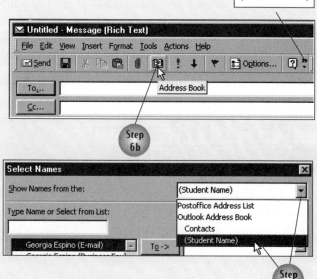

Step 6c

d. At the list of contacts that displays at the left side of the dialog box, double-click *Jessica Grady (E-mail)*. (This inserts *Jessica Grady (E-mail)* in the Message Recipients list box.)

e. Click the OK button to close the Select Names dialog box.

f. At the Untitled - Message window (with *Jessica Grady (E-mail)* displayed in the To... text box), click in the Subject box and then key **Marketing Proposal**.

g. Click in the white box below Subject and then key the following:

> **I received your marketing proposal today. I will review the proposal and then present it to the board of directors next Tuesday. I will contact you as soon as a decision is made by the board members.**

h. Print the e-mail message by clicking the Print button on the Message Standard toolbar. (If the Print button is not visible, click the More Buttons button and then click the Print button.)

i. If this was an e-mail message being sent to an actual person, you would click the Send button located at the left side of the Message Standard toolbar. You will not be sending this e-mail message since Jessica Grady, as well as her e-mail address, are fictitious. Instead, click File and then Close. At the message asking if you want to save the changes, click No.

7. Exit Outlook.

Deleting a Personal Subfolder

A personal subfolder can be deleted. To do this, change to the subfolder to be deleted. Position the arrow pointer on the subfolder name at the left side of the Folder Banner and then click the *right* mouse button. At the shortcut menu that displays, click Delete "Name" (where the name of the subfolder is displayed between the quotation marks).

exercise 11

Deleting the Tasks Personal Subfolder

1. Open Outlook.
2. Click the Tasks icon on the Outlook bar.
3. Select your personal Tasks subfolder by completing the following steps:
    a. Click *Tasks* located at the left side of the Folder Banner.
    b. At the drop-down menu that displays, click the plus (+) symbol that displays before *Tasks*.

c. Click the subfolder containing your first and last name.
4. Delete your personal Tasks subfolder by completing the following steps:
   a. Position the arrow pointer on your subfolder name at the left side of the Folder Banner and then click the *right* mouse button.
   b. At the shortcut menu that displays, click Delete "Name" (where your name displays between the quotation marks).
5. Exit Outlook.

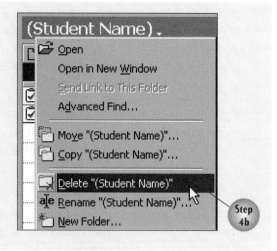

chapter summary

► Outlook is a desktop information management application that can assist you in scheduling appointments, creating a task list and contact list, and sending and receiving e-mail messages.

► Shortcuts to the folders available in Outlook display as icons on the Outlook Bar.

► The Folder Banner displays below the Standard toolbar in the Outlook window. The name of the open folder displays at the left side of the Folder Banner.

► Use the Calendar to schedule appointments and events.

► A personal subfolder can be created in which individual appointment information is saved. A personal subfolder can also be created for tasks, contact lists, and e-mail messages.

► Create a personal subfolder by right-clicking the folder name on the Folder Banner and then clicking New Folder.

► Add an appointment in the Calendar window by clicking the desired date in the Date Navigator, selecting the desired time, and then keying the appointment information.

► To include additional information for an appointment, display the Untitled - Appointment window. Display this window by double-clicking the desired appointment time or clicking the New Appointment button on the Calendar Standard toolbar.

► Delete an appointment by selecting the appointment and then clicking the Delete button on the Calendar Standard toolbar.

► Appointments can be set using natural language phrases. Outlook's AutoDate function converts the language to the appropriate date and time.

► Click the triangles in the Date Navigator to change the months displayed. Click the desired day in the month displayed in the Date Navigator.

► By default the calendar displays the selected day. This can be changed to work week, week, or month.

- A calendar can be printed in daily, weekly, or monthly style. To view how a calendar will appear when printed, click the Preview button at the Print dialog box.
- A recurring appointment can be scheduled at the Appointment Recurrence dialog box. Display this dialog box by clicking the Recurrence button on the Appointment Standard toolbar.
- Move an appointment by changing the starting and ending times or use the mouse to drag and then drop an appointment into a new date slot.
- An event can be scheduled by double-clicking the date located at the top of the appointment area or by clicking Actions and then New All Day Event.
- Keep track of tasks in the TaskPad at the Calendar window or at the Tasks window. Display the Tasks window by clicking the *Tasks* icon on the Outlook Bar. Completed items can be checked off the list or deleted.
- Use Outlook's Contacts feature to create a contact list. Information in a contact list can be printed, edited, or deleted.
- Add a contact to the contact list by clicking the New Contact button on the Contacts Standard toolbar.
- A contact list can be printed in a variety of styles including Card Style, Small Booklet Style, Medium Booklet Style, and Phone Directory Style.
- The Inbox window can be used to create and print e-mail messages. Create an e-mail message at the Untitled - Message window. Display this window by clicking the New Mail Message button located at the left side of the Inbox Standard toolbar.
- A contact name and e-mail address can be inserted in the Untitled - Message window. To do this, click the Address Book button on the Message Standard toolbar and then double-click the contact name in at the Select Names dialog box.
- Delete a personal subfolder by opening the subfolder, right-clicking the personal subfolder name at the left side of the Folder Banner, and then clicking Delete "Name" at the shortcut menu.

commands review

	Mouse
Calendar window	Click *Calendar* icon on Outlook Bar
Untitled - Appointment window	Double-click appointment time; or click New Appointment button on Calendar Standard toolbar
Appointment Recurrence dialog box	At the Appointment window, click the Recurrence button
Untitled - Event window	Double-click date at top of appointment area; or click Actions and then New All Day Event
Tasks window	Click *Tasks* icon on Outlook Bar
Untitled - Task window	Click New Task button on Task toolbar
Contacts window	Click *Contacts* icon on Outlook Bar
Untitled - Contact window	Click New Contact button on Contacts Standard toolbar
Inbox window	Click *Inbox* icon on Outlook Bar
Untitled - Message window	Click New Mail Message button on Inbox Standard toolbar

thinking offline

Completion: In the space provided at the right, indicate the correct term, command, or symbol.

1. Click the *Calendar* icon on this bar to display the Calendar window.

2. This displays below the Standard toolbar in the Outlook window and displays the name of the open folder.

3. At the Calendar window, the current month and the next month display in this area.

4. Click this button on the Calendar Standard toolbar to display the Untitled - Appointment window.

5. Click this button on the Appointment Standard toolbar to display the Appointment Recurrence dialog box.

6. After all information has been entered in the Appointment window, click this button on the Appointment Standard toolbar to remove the Appointment window and insert the appointment information in the Calendar window.

7. Click this option in the Print style section of the Print dialog box to print Monday through Sunday of the current week.

8. Click this button at the Print dialog box to see what the calendar will look like when printed.

9. This section of the Calendar window displays tasks.

10. To create an e-mail message, click this button located at the left side of the Inbox Standard toolbar.

11. In the space provided below, list the steps you would complete to schedule a staff meeting that occurs every Wednesday from 9:00 a.m. to 10:00 a.m.

working hands-on

Assessment 1

1. Open Outlook.
2. Display the Calendar window and then display your personal Calendar subfolder.
3. Display March 2001 and April 2001 in the Date Navigator and then click Monday, March 5.
4. Schedule the following appointments:
   a. Schedule a meeting with Jennifer Harris from 8:30 a.m. to 9:00 a.m.
   b. Schedule a conference call with corporate headquarters from 10:00 a.m. to 10:30 a.m. (15-minute reminder).
   c. Schedule a lunch meeting with assistant director at Spenser's Restaurant from 12:00 noon to 1:00 p.m.
   d. Schedule a finance meeting from 3:00 p.m. to 4:00 p.m. in Conference Room A.
5. Print the daily schedule.

Assessment 2

1. With Outlook open, display the Calendar window, and then display your personal Calendar subfolder.
2. Display March 2001 and April 2001 in the Date Navigator and then make the following changes:
   a. Click Monday, March 5.
   b. Move the conference call with corporate headquarters from 10:00 a.m. Monday, March 5, to 8:30 a.m. Tuesday, March 6.
   c. Move the meeting with Jennifer Harris on Monday, March 5, from 8:30 a.m. to 9:30 a.m.
   d. Change the finance meeting scheduled for 3:00 p.m. on Monday from Conference Room A to Room 14.
   e. Schedule the following appointments:
      1) Schedule a training session for Tuesday, March 6, from 1:30 p.m. to 4:30 p.m. in Room 25.
      2) Schedule a meeting with Joseph Avila for Wednesday, March 7, from 9:00 a.m. to 9:30 a.m.
      3) Schedule a product evaluation workshop for Thursday, March 8, from 9:00 a.m. to 11:00 a.m. in Conference Room A.
      4) Schedule a budget analysis meeting in the corporate office for Friday, March 9, from 10:30 a.m. to 11:30 a.m.
3. Print the weekly schedule.

Assessment 3

1. With Outlook open, display the Calendar window, and then display your personal Calendar subfolder.
2. Display March 2001 and April 2001 in the Date Navigator and then make the following changes:
   a. Move the budget analysis meeting for Friday, March 9, from the beginning time of 10:30 a.m. to the beginning time of 1:30 p.m. (on the same day).
   b. Move the product evaluation workshop from Thursday, March 8, beginning at 9:00 a.m. to Friday, March 9 beginning at 9:00 a.m.
   c. Add a recurring staff meeting for every Thursday beginning with March 8 from 9:00 a.m. to 10:00 a.m. in Conference Room A.
   d. Add a recurring meeting with the manager in the manager's office for every other Wednesday beginning with March 7 from 3:00 p.m. to 4:00 p.m.
3. Print the March monthly schedule.

Assessment 4

1. With Outlook open, display the Contacts window, and then display your personal Contacts subfolder.
2. Add the following contacts to your list:

Full Name	=	Kim Oglesbee
Job title	=	Assistant Director
Company	=	Delta Express
Phone:		
Business	=	(714) 555-6650
Business Fax	=	(714) 555-7866
Address	=	21055 Country Drive
		Los Angeles, CA 99155
E-mail	=	koglesbee@nylan.com
Full Name	=	Jeffrey Knowles
Job title	=	Manager
Company	=	Valley Enterprises
Phone:		
Business	=	(619) 555-4004
Business Fax	=	(619) 555-4333
Address	=	901 Diamond Center
		San Diego, CA 99655
E-mail	=	jknowles@valleye.com
Full Name	=	Vincent Young
Job title	=	Director
Company	=	Royer & Royer
Phone:		
Business	=	(714) 555-6688
Business Fax	=	(714) 555-0991
Address	=	1100 Third Street North
		Los Angeles, CA 99190
E-mail	=	vyoung@royer.com

3. Print the contact list in Card Style.

4. Make the following changes to the contact list:
   a. Change the address for Kim Oglesbee from *21055 Country Drive* to *4510 Magnolia Boulevard.*
   b. Change the business telephone number for Vincent Young from *(714) 555-6688* to *(714) 555-2355.*
5. Print the contact list in Phone Directory Style.

Assessment 5

1. With Outlook open, display the Inbox window, and then display your personal Inbox subfolder.
2. Create an e-mail message with the following specifications:
   a. Send the e-mail message to Kim Oglesbee.
   b. Key the following message:

   > **The catalog layout has been completed. Let's get together early next week to discuss the catalog. I have time available Tuesday morning and Wednesday afternoon. Let me know what time is good for you.**

   c. Print the e-mail message.
   d. Close the e-mail message window without sending the message.
3. Exit Outlook.

Assessment 6

1. Outlook contains more features than you learned in this chapter. Use Outlook's Help feature to learn about Notes. Learn how to create a note and print a note.

2. After learning about the Notes feature, complete the following steps:
   a. Create a personal Notes subfolder with your name.
   b. Select your personal Notes subfolder and then create the following notes:
      1) Call Kim Oglesbee regarding catalog meeting.
      2) Review Valley Enterprises contract.
      3) Contact Vincent Young asap.
   c. Print the notes.
3. Delete your personal Notes subfolder.
4. Exit Outlook.

Performance Assessments

ACCESS

ASSESSING CORE PROFICIENCIES

In this unit, you have learned to create database files in Access that include database tables, forms, and reports and create relationships between tables. You also learned how to use Access Wizards, export Access data to Word and Excel, import and link data, and perform queries and filter records in a database table. In this unit you were introduced to Microsoft Outlook and learned how to manage appointments and create a task list, a contact list, and an e-mail message.

Assessment one 1

1. Use Access to create a database for clients of a mental health clinic.
    Name the database file Lancaster Clinic. Create a database table named
    Clients that includes the following fields (you determine the field name,
    data type, field size, and description):

    Client # (primary key)
    Name
    Street Address
    City
    State
    Zip code
    Telephone number
    Date of birth
    Diagnosis ID

2. After creating the database table, save it and name it Clients. Switch to
    Datasheet view and then enter the following data in the appropriate
    fields:

    Client #: 1831
    George Charoni
    3980 Broad Street
    Philadelphia, PA 19149
    (215) 555-3482
    Date of birth: 04/12/58
    Diagnosis ID: S

    Client #: 3219
    Marian Wilke
    12032 South 39th
    Jenkintown, PA 19209
    (215) 555-9083
    Date of birth: 10/23/81
    Diagnosis ID: OCD

Performance Assessments   1003

Client #: 2874
Arthur Shroeder
3618 Fourth Avenue
Philadelphia, PA 19176
(215) 555-8311
Date of birth: 03/23/53
Diagnosis ID: OCD

Client #: 5831
Roshawn Collins
12110 52nd Court East
Cheltenham, PA 19210
(215) 555-4779
Date of birth: 11/03/63
Diagnosis ID: S

Client #: 4419
Lorena Hearron
3112 96th Street East
Philadelphia, PA 19132
(215) 555-3281
Date of birth: 07/02/84
Diagnosis ID: AD

Client #: 1103
Raymond Mandato
631 Garden Boulevard
Jenkintown, PA 19209
(215) 555-0957
Date of birth: 09/20/74
Diagnosis ID: MDD

3. Save, print, and then close the Clients database table.
4. Create a database table named Diagnoses that includes the following fields:
   Diagnosis ID (primary key)
   Diagnosis
5. After creating the database table, save it and name it Diagnoses. Switch to Datasheet view and then enter the following data in the appropriate fields:

Diagnosis ID	=	AD
Diagnosis	=	Adjustment Disorder
Diagnosis ID	=	MDD
Diagnosis	=	Manic-Depressive Disorder
Diagnosis ID	=	OCD
Diagnosis	=	Obsessive-Compulsive Disorder
Diagnosis ID	=	S
Diagnosis	=	Schizophrenia

6. Create a database table named Employees that includes the following fields (you determine the field name, data type, field size, and description):

   Provider # (primary key)
   Name
   Title
   Extension

7. After creating the database table, save it and name it Employees. Switch to Datasheet view and then enter the following data in the appropriate fields:

Provider #: 29
Name: James Schouten
Title: Psychologist
Extension: 399

Provider #: 15
Name: Lynn Yee
Title: Child Psychologist
Extension: 102

Provider #: 33   Provider #: 18
Name: Janice Grisham   Name: Craig Chilton
Title: Psychiatrist   Title: Psychologist
Extension: 11   Extension: 20

8. Save, print, and then close the Employees database table.
9. Create a database table named Billing that includes the following fields
   (you determine the field name, data type, field size, and description):
   > Billing # (primary key) (Assign the Autonumber data type to this
   >   field.)
   > Client #
   > Date of Service
   > Insurer
   > Provider #
   > Hourly Fee
10. After creating the database table, save it and name it Billing. Switch to
    Datasheet view and then enter the following data in the appropriate fields:

   Client #: 4419   Client #: 1831
   Date of Service: 03/01/99   Date of Service: 03/01/99
   Insurer: Health Plus   Insurer: Self
   Provider #: 15   Provider #: 33
   Hourly Fee: $95.00   Hourly Fee: $85.00

   Client #: 3219   Client #: 5831
   Date of Service: 03/02/99   Date of Service: 03/02/99
   Insurer: Health Plus   Insurer: Penn-State Health
   Provider #: 15   Provider #: 18
   Hourly Fee: $95.00   Hourly Fee: $90.00

   Client #: 4419   Client #: 1103
   Date of Service: 03/03/99   Date of Service: 03/04/99
   Insurer: Health Plus   Insurer: Penn-State Health
   Provider #: 15   Provider #: 18
   Hourly Fee: $75.00   Hourly Fee: $95.00

   Client #: 1831   Client #: 5831
   Date of Service: 03/04/99   Date of Service: 03/04/99
   Insurer: Self   Insurer: Penn-State Health
   Provider #: 33   Provider #: 18
   Hourly Fee: $85.00   Hourly Fee: $90.00

11. Save, print, and then close the Billing database table.
12. Close the Lancaster Clinic database file.

Assessment 2

1. Open the Lancaster Clinic database file and then create the following
   one-to-many relationships:
   a. *Client #* in the Clients table is the "one" and *Client #* in the Billing
      table is the "many."
   b. *Diagnosis ID* in the Diagnoses table is the "one" and *Diagnosis ID* in
      the Clients table is the "many."
   c. *Provider #* in the Employees table is the "one" and *Provider #* in the
      Billing table is the "many."

2. Use the AutoForm feature to create a form with the data in the Clients database table.

3. After creating the form, add the following record to the Clients form:

> **Client #: 1179**
> **Timothy Fierro**
> **1133 Tenth Southwest**
> **Philadelphia, PA 19178**
> **(215) 555-5594**
> **Date of birth: 12/07/87**
> **Diagnosis ID: AD**

4. Save the form as Clients, print the form, and then close the form.

5. Add the following records to the Billing database table:

Client #: 1179	**Client #: 1831**
Date of Service: 03/08/99	**Date of Service: 03/09/99**
Insurer: Health Plus	**Insurer: Self**
Provider #: 15	**Provider #: 33**
Hourly Fee: $95.00	**Hourly Fee: $85.00**

6. Save and then print the Billing database table.

7. Close the Billing database table and then close the Lancaster Clinic database file.

Assessment three

1. Open the Lancaster Clinic database file.
2. Create a form with fields from related database tables using the Form Wizard with the following specifications:
   a. At the first Form Wizard dialog box, insert the following fields in the Selected Fields list box:

   From the Clients database table:

   > *Client #*
   > *Date of birth*
   > *Diagnosis ID*

   From the Billing database table:
   > *Insurer*
   > *Provider #*

   b. Do not make any changes at the second Form Wizard dialog box.
   c. Do not make any changes at the third Form Wizard dialog box.
   d. You determine the format style at the fourth Form Wizard dialog box.
   e. At the fifth Form Wizard dialog box, key the name **Provider Information**.
   f. When the first record displays, print the form.
   g. Close the record that displays.
3. Close the Lancaster Clinic database file.

Assessment four

1. Open the Lancaster Clinic database file.
2. Use the Label Wizard to create mailing labels (you determine the label type) with the client names and addresses and sorted by Zip code. Name the mailing label file Client Mailing Labels.

3. Print the mailing labels.
4. Close the mailing labels file and then close the Lancaster Clinic database file.

Assessment 5

1. Open the Lancaster Clinic database file.
2. Create an Excel worksheet with the Billing database table, with the following specifications:
   a. In Excel, select the cells in the worksheet containing data and then apply an autoformat of your choosing.
   b. Save the worksheet. (Excel will automatically name it Billing.)
   c. Print the worksheet centered horizontally and vertically on the page.
3. Exit Excel.
4. Close the Lancaster Clinic database file.

Assessment 6

1. Open the Lancaster Clinic database file.
2. Merge data in the Clients database table to a blank Word screen. *(Hint: Use the Merge It with MS Word option from the OfficeLinks drop-down menu.)* You determine the fields to use in the inside address and an appropriate salutation. Key **March 10, 1999**, as the date of the letter and key the following text in the body of the document:

   The building of a new wing for the Lancaster Clinic will begin April 1, 1999. We are excited about this new addition to our clinic. With the new facilities, we will be able to offer additional community and group services along with enhanced child-play therapy treatment.

   During the construction, the main entrance will be moved to the North end of the building. Please use this entrance until the construction of the wing is completed. We apologize in advance for any inconvenience this causes you.

   Include an appropriate complimentary close for the letter. Use the name and title *Marianne Lambert, Clinic Director* for the signature and add your reference initials and the document name (Word Unit 4, PA 06).
3. Merge to a new document and then save the document with the name Word Unit 4, PA 06.
4. Print the first two letters of the document and then close Word Unit 4, PA 06.
5. Save the main document as Construction Letter and then close Construction Letter.
6. Exit Word and then close the Lancaster Clinic database file.

Assessment seven

1. Open the Lancaster Clinic database file
2. Click the Tables button in the Objects bar.
3. Import Excel Worksheet 39 into a new table named Staff Hours. (Use the Import Spreadsheet Wizard to do this.)
4. Open the Staff Hours table in Datasheet view.
5. Print and then close the Staff Hours table.
6. Use the Form Wizard to create a form with the following specifications:
   a. Use all the fields from the Staff Hours table.
   b. You determine the layout and the style of the form.
   c. Name the form Staff Wages.
   d. When the form is completed, change to Design view and add the following:
      1) Add a calculated control that multiplies the Hours by the Rate. (Name this calculated control Wages.)
      2) Format the calculated control text box so that the format is changed to *Currency* and the decimal places option is set to *2*.
      3) Insert the company name, Lancaster Clinic, in the Form Header and increase the size of the company name (you determine the size.)
      4) Make any other changes you feel are necessary to create an attractive form.
   e. Change to the Form view.
   f. Print only the first record in the form.
   g. Close the Staff Wages form.
7. Close the Lancaster Clinic database file.

Assessment eight

1. Open the Lancaster Clinic database file.
2. Design the following queries on data in the database file:
   a. Extract records from the Clients database table with the following specifications:
      1) Include the fields *Client #*, *Date of birth*, and *Diagnosis ID*. (Your field names may vary.)
      2) Extract those records with a Diagnosis ID of OCD.
      3) Print and then close the query without saving it.
   b. Extract records from the Billing database table with the following specifications:
      1) Include the fields *Client #*, *Insurer*, and *Provider #*. (Your field names may vary.)
      2) Extract those records with a Provider # of 15.
      3) Print and then close the query without saving it.

c. Extract records from the Employees database table with the following specifications:
   1) Include the fields *Provider #*, *Name*, and *Title*. (Your field names may vary.)
   2) Extract those records with a title of Child Psychologist.
   3) Print and then close the query without saving it.
3. Close the Lancaster Clinic database file.

Assessment nine 9

1. Open the Lancaster Clinic database file.
2. Open the Clients database table and then use the Filter By Selection button on the Table Datasheet toolbar to display the following records:
   a. Display only those records of clients who live in Philadelphia. When the records of clients in Philadelphia display, print the results, and then click the Remove Filter button.
   b. Display only those records of clients with the Zip code of 19209. When the records of clients with the Zip code 19209 display, print the results, and then click the Remove Filter button.
3. Close the Clients database table.
4. Open the Billing database table and then use the Filter By Selection button on the Table Datasheet toolbar to display the following records:
   a. Display only those records with a Provider # of 18. Print the records and then click the Remove Filter button.
   b. Display only those records with Health Plus as the Insurer. Print the records and then click the Remove Filter button.
5. Close the Billing database table.
6. Open the Clients form and then use the Filter By Form button on the Form View toolbar to display clients in Jenkintown or Cheltenham. Print the forms and then click the Remove Filter button.
7. Close the Clients form.
8. Close the Lancaster Clinic database file.

Assessment ten 10

1. Open Outlook.
2. Click the *Calendar* icon on the Outlook Bar and then change to your personal Calendar subfolder.
3. Display June 2001 and July 2001 in the Date Navigator and then click Monday, June 11.
4. Display the week of June 11 and then schedule the following appointments:
   a. Schedule a meeting on June 12 with the department director from 9:00 a.m. to 9:30 a.m. (no reminder).

b. Schedule a lunch meeting on June 13 with Lindsay Kerns of Southend Suppliers from 12:00 noon to 1:30 p.m. at the Sunroof Gardens Restaurant (15-minute reminder).

c. Schedule a corrective action meeting on June 13 with Louis Feldman from 4:30 to 5:30 p.m. in the conference room (no reminder).

5. Print the weekly schedule.

6. Make the following changes to the weekly schedule:
a. Move the meeting on June 12 with the department director that begins at *9:00 a.m.* so it begins at *8:00 a.m.* on the same day.
b. Delete the lunch meeting on June 13 with Lindsay Kerns.
c. Schedule a meeting with Joann Severne on June 13 from 10:00 a.m. to 11:00 a.m. in the conference room (15-minute reminder).

7. Display the monthly schedule.

8. Schedule the following appointments:
a. Schedule a planning conference for June 26 and 27.
b. Add a recurring quality control meeting for every Monday beginning with June 11 from 3:00 p.m. to 4:00 p.m. in Room 23 (no reminder).
c. Add a recurring division meeting for every other Thursday beginning with June 14 from 8:00 a.m. to 9:00 a.m. in the Human Resources conference room (no reminder).

9. Print the monthly schedule for June 2001.

10. Click the *Contacts* icon on the Outlook Bar and then change to your personal Contacts subfolder.

11. Add the following person to your Contacts list:

Full Name	=	**Jacob Richards**
Job title	=	**Director**
Company	=	**Grayson Limited**
Phone:		
Business	=	**(714) 555-3000**
Business Fax	=	**(714) 555-3210**
Address	=	**3482 South 121st Avenue**
		Los Angeles, CA 99422
E-mail	=	**jrichards@grayson.com**

12. Print your Contacts list in Phone Directory Style.

13. Click the *Inbox* icon on the Outlook Bar and then change to your personal Inbox subfolder.

14. Create and print an e-mail message to Jacob Richards with the subject *Research* that includes the following information:
Please contact Michael Langley at (714) 555-9855 before the end of this week. He needs specific information on the research completed last summer.

15. Delete your personal subfolders in the following folders: Inbox, Calendar, and Contacts.

16. Exit Outlook.

WRITING ACTIVITIES

The following activities give you the opportunity to practice your writing skills along with demonstrating an understanding of some of the important Access features you have mastered in this unit. (Refer to the steps in *The Writing Process* section of the Unit 1 Composing Activities.) Use correct grammar, appropriate word choices, and clear sentence constructions.

Activity one

The director at Lancaster Clinic has asked you to add information to the Lancaster Clinic database file on insurance companies contracted by the clinic. You need to create another database table that will contain information on insurance companies. The director wants the database table to include the insurance company name, address, city, state, and Zip code along with a telephone number and a name of a representative. You determine the field names, data types, field sizes, and description for the database table and then include the following information (in the appropriate fields):

Health Plus	**Penn-State Health**
4102 22nd Street	5933 Lehigh Avenue
Philadelphia, PA 19166	Philadelphia, PA 19148
(212) 555-0990	(212) 555-3477
Representative: Byron Tolleson	Representative: Tracey Pavone
Quality Medical	**Delaware Health**
51 Cecil B. Moore Avenue	4418 Front Street
Philadelphia, PA 19168	Philadelphia, PA 19132
(212) 555-4600	(212) 555-6772
Representative: Lee Stafford	Representative: Melanie Chon

Print the insurance company database file. Create a form with the insurance company database file and then print the form.

Open Word and then write a report to the clinic director detailing how you created the database table. Include a title for the report, steps on how the database table was created, and any other pertinent information. Save the completed report and name it Unit 4, Act 01. Print and then close Unit 4, Act 01.

Activity two

Merge data in the insurance company database file to a blank Word screen. You determine the fields to use in the inside address and an appropriate salutation. Compose a letter to the insurance companies informing them that Lancaster Clinic is providing mental health counseling services to people with health insurance through their company. You are sending an informational brochure about Lancaster Clinic and are requesting information from the insurance companies on services and service limitations. Include an appropriate complimentary close for the letter. Use the name and title *Marianne Lambert, Clinic Director* for the signature and add your reference initials. When the merge is completed, name the document containing the merged letters Unit 4, Act 02. Print the first two letters in the merged document and then close Unit 4, Act 02. Close the main document without saving it and then exit Word. Close the insurance company database table and then close the Lancaster Clinic database file.

RESEARCHING ON THE INTERNET: KEY WORDS AND EMPLOYMENT DATABASES

In this activity, you will explore employment databases on the Internet. You will record your search results by creating a database of contacts and jobs in your area of career interest.

1. Make sure you are connected to the Internet.
2. Using key search words, find at least two Web sites that advertise job listings. Key words to use might be the job title you are interested in and key phrases such as
   - Job Locator
   - Career Listings
   - Job Hunt
   - Job Openings
   - Employment Opportunities
3. If you receive too many hits, narrow your search by adding additional criteria, such as city, state, and/or more specific job titles. If your searches are not successful, try different terms. For example, if *Jobs and CD-ROM* resulted in no hits, try *Jobs and Multimedia*. If your searches continue to be unsuccessful, consider looking at these specific Web sites and use their search systems:
   - America's Job Bank (federal and state agencies) at www.ajb.dni.us/index.html
   - Career Path (ads from large newspapers) at www.careerpath.com/
   - Online Career Center at www.occ.com
   - Internet Job Locator at www.joblocator.com/jobs/
   - The World Wide Web Employment Office at www.toa-services.net/annex.html
   - What Color is Your Parachute at www.washingtonpost.com/parachute
4. Review the jobs reported. Did you find jobs in your area of interest? Which searches resulted in the most hits? the best or most helpful hits? Write down the Web sites that will help you locate jobs in the future.
5. Create a database file in Access and in that file create a database table that includes the job title, company, salary, location, and job requirements for each position you researched. Focus on companies that you may actually want to contact when you start searching for a job.
6. Enter the key words **Electronic Resume** and find out how online résumés are prepared for the Internet. For future reference, in case you decide to put your résumé on the Internet, document the guidelines you learned.

Integrated Project

Now that you have completed the chapters in this textbook, you have learned to create documents in Word; build worksheets in Excel; design presentations in PowerPoint; organize data in Access; and schedule appointments and create a contact list and an e-mail message in Outlook. To learn the various programs in the Microsoft Office 2000 suite, you have completed a variety of exercises, assessments, and activities. This integrated project is a final assignment that allows you to apply the knowledge you have gained about the programs in the Office suite to produce a variety of documents.

Situation

You are the vice president of Classique Coffees, a gourmet coffee company. Your company operates two retail stores that sell gourmet coffee and related products to the public. One retail store is located in Seattle, Washington, the other in Tacoma. The company is three years old and has seen approximately a 15 to 30 percent growth in profit each year. Your duties as the vice president of the company include researching the coffee market, studying coffee buying trends, designing and implementing new projects, and supervising the marketing, sales, and personnel managers.

Activity 1: Writing Persuasively

Using Word, compose a memo to the president of Classique Coffees, Leslie Steiner, detailing your research and recommendations:

- Research has shown a 20 percent growth in the iced coffee market.
- The target population for iced coffees is people from ages 18 to 35.
- Market analysis indicates that there are only three local retail companies that sell iced coffees in the greater Seattle-Tacoma area.
- The recommendation is that Classique Coffees develop a suite of iced coffees for market consumption by early next year. (Be as persuasive as possible.)

Save the completed memo and name it Project, Act 01. Print and then close Project, Act 01.

Activity 2: Designing a Letterhead

You are not satisfied with the current letterhead used by your company. Design a new letterhead for Classique Coffees using Word and include the following information:

- Use a clip art image in the letterhead. (Consider downloading a clip art image from the Microsoft Clip Gallery.)
- Include the company name—Classique Coffees.
- Include the company address—355 Pioneer Square, Seattle, WA 98211.

- Include the company telephone number—(206) 555-6690.
- Include the company e-mail address—ccoffees@gourmet.com.
- Create a slogan that will help your business contacts remember your company.
- Add any other information or elements (such as border lines) that you feel are appropriate.

When the letterhead is completed, save it and name it Project, Act 02. Print and then close Project, Act 02.

Activity 3: Preparing a Notice

Using Word, prepare a notice about an upcoming marketing seminar. Include the following information in the notice:

- Name of the seminar—Marketing to the Coffee Gourmet
- Location of the seminar—Conference room at the corporate office, 355 Pioneer Square, Seattle, WA 98211
- Date and time of seminar—Friday, October 19, 2001, 9:00 a.m. to 2:30 p.m.
- The topics that will be covered at the seminar:
  > identifying coffee-drinking trends
  > assessing the current gourmet coffee market
  > developing new products
  > analyzing the typical Classique Coffees customer
  > marketing a new product line
- Consider including a clip art image in the notice. (You determine an appropriate clip art image.)

When the notice is completed, save it and name it Project, Act 03. Print and then close Project, Act 03.

Activity 4: Designing a Web Page

At a recent corporate meeting, a decision was made to create a Web site home page for Classique Coffees. You have been asked to design a preliminary Web page. Create the Web page and include the following:

- Company name, address, and e-mail address
- Brief explanation of the company (see the Situation section at the beginning of this project)
- List the types of coffees sold (see Activity 7 for the list of coffees)
- Add that iced coffees will be introduced soon
- Add scrolling text that says something about the company, the products, and/or the new iced coffees
- Include some hyperlinks to interesting gourmet coffee sites (search the Web for sites, find two or three interesting sites, and then include the URL for each site as a hyperlink in your Web page)

When the Web page is completed, save it and name it CC Home Page. Print and then close CC Home Page.

Activity 5: Building a Budget Worksheet

Using Excel, prepare a worksheet with the following information:

Annual Budget: $1,450,000

Department	% of Budget	Total
Administration	10%	
Purchasing	24%	
Sales	21%	
Marketing	23%	
Personnel	12%	
Training	10%	

Insert formulas that will calculate the total amount for each budget based on the specified percentage of the annual budget. When the worksheet is completed, save it and name it Project, Act 05. Print Project, Act 05.

Determine what the impact of a 10% increase in the annual budget would be on the total amount for each department. With the amounts displayed for a 10% increase, save the worksheet again with the same name (Project, Act 05) and then print Project, Act 05.

Activity 6: Determining Depreciation Using the Straight-Line Method

Using Excel, prepare a worksheet with the following information that will determine depreciation using the straight-line method. Also, include formulas to determine the total initial costs and total salvage costs. After the depreciation amounts are inserted, insert a formula that will calculate the average depreciation amount.

CLASSIQUE COFFEES

Equipment	Initial Cost	Salvage Cost	Life of Asset	Depreciation
Espresso machine	$3,450	$500	8	
Grinding machine	$4,100	$650	10	
Telephone system	$15,350	$1,500	8	
Packaging machine	$12,800	$1,250	10	
Delivery truck	$45,000	$5,000	10	

Total Initial Costs:

Total Salvage Costs:

Average Depreciation:

Save the completed worksheet, name it Project, Act 06, and then print Project, Act 06.

Activity 7: Building a Sales Worksheet and Creating a Chart

Using Excel, prepare a worksheet with the following information:

Type of Coffee	% of Sales
Regular blend	22%
Espresso blend	12%
Regular blend decaf	17%
Espresso blend decaf	10%
Flavored blend	25%
Flavored blend decaf	14%

Save the completed worksheet, name it Project, Act 07, and then print Project, Act 07. With the worksheet still displayed, create a pie chart as a new sheet with the data in the worksheet. Title the pie chart 2001 Percentage of Sales. When the chart is completed, save the worksheet (now two sheets) with the same name (Project, Act 07). Print only the sheet containing the pie chart. Close Project, Act 07.

Activity 8: Building a Projected Sales Worksheet and Creating a Chart

Using Excel, prepare a worksheet with the following information:

Type of Coffee	% of Sales
Regular blend	21%
Espresso blend	10%
Regular blend decaf	16%
Espresso blend decaf	8%
Flavored blend	24%
Flavored blend decaf	13%
Iced	5%
Iced decaf	3%

Create a pie chart as a new sheet with the data in the worksheet. Title the pie chart Year 2002 Projected Percentage of Sales. When the chart is completed, save the worksheet (two sheets) and name it Project, Act 08. Print and then close Project, Act 08.

Analyze by comparing and contrasting the pie charts created in Project, Act 07 and Project, Act 08. What areas in the projected sales percentages have changed? What do these changes indicate? Assume that the projected annual income for Classique Coffees is $2,200,000. What amount of that income will come from iced coffees (including decaf iced coffees). Does this amount warrant marketing this new product? Prepare a memo in Word to Leslie Steiner that includes your analysis. Add any other interpretations you can make from analyzing the pie charts. Save the memo and name it Word, Project 08. Save and then print Word, Project 08.

Activity 9: Designing and Creating a Presentation

Using PowerPoint, prepare a marketing slide presentation. Include the following information in the presentation:

- Classique Coffees 2002 Marketing Plan
- Company reorganization (create an organizational chart with the following)

President

Vice President

Marketing Manager	Sales Manager	Personnel Manager
Marketing Assistants	Sales Associates	Assistant Manager

- 2001 sales percentages (insert the pie chart into the slide that is part of the Project, Act 07 worksheet).
- 2002 projected sales percentages (insert the pie chart into the slide that is part of the Project, Act 08 worksheet).
- Iced coffee marketing strategy
  - > target customer
  - > analysis of competition
  - > wholesale resources
  - > pricing
  - > volume
- Product placement
  - > stocking strategies
  - > shelf allocation
  - > stock rotation schedule
  - > seasonal display

When preparing the slide presentation, you determine the presentation design and the autolayouts. Include any clipart images that might be appropriate and add animation effects to the slides. When the presentation is completed, save it and name it Project, Act 09. Run the presentation and then print the presentation with three slides on a page.

Activity 10: Scheduling Meetings and Appointments

Use Outlook to schedule the following appointments for the week of October 15, 2001:

- Meeting in the conference room with the president, Leslie Steiner, Monday, October 15, from 10 a.m. to 11 a.m.
- Lunch with Janet Leverling of Northwind Traders, Monday, October 15, from 12:30 to 2:00 p.m. (The lunch will take place at Cervanti's Restaurant.)
- Production meeting with production department in the conference room, Tuesday, October 16, from 8:30 to 9:30 a.m. (15-minute remainder).
- Tour of Volcano Coffee with Andrew Fuller, Tuesday, October 16, from 2:30 p.m. to 4:00 p.m.
- Seminar planning meeting, Wednesday, October 17, from 8:30 a.m. to 9:30 a.m. in my office (15-minute reminder).
- Meeting with Jan Langstrom of the city zoning department in her office at the County/City Building, Room 320, Wednesday, October 17, from 2:30 p.m. to 4:00 p.m.
- Budget analysis meeting in the conference room, Thursday, October 18, from 8:30 a.m. to 9:30 a.m. (15-minute reminder).

- Meeting with Donald Wong in my office, Thursday, October 18, from 10:30 a.m. to 11:00 a.m.
- Meeting with Amanda Jenkins in my office to confirm plans for marketing seminar, Thursday, October 18, from 3 to 4 p.m.
- Marketing seminar in the conference room, Friday, October 19, from 9:00 a.m. to 2:30 p.m.

When all appointments are scheduled, print the weekly schedule.

Activity 11: Creating a Database File and Organizing Data

Use Access to create a database for Classique Coffees that contains information on suppliers and products. Include the following fields in the Suppliers table and the Products table (you determine the specific field names):

Suppliers table:
> *Supplier #*
> *Supplier Name*
> *Address*
> *City*
> *State*
> *Zip Code*
> *E-mail Address*

Products table:
> *Product #*
> *Product*
> *Supplier #*

Key the following data in the Suppliers table:

Supplier #	=	24
Supplier Name	=	**Gourmet Blends**
Address	=	**109 South Madison**
City	=	**Seattle**
State	=	**WA**
Zip Code	=	**98032**
E-mail Address	=	**gblends@coffee.com**
Supplier #	=	36
Supplier Name	=	**Jannsen Company**
Address	=	**4122 South Sprague**
City	=	**Tacoma**
State	=	**WA**
Zip Code	=	**98402**
E-mail Address	=	**jannsen@coffee.com**
Supplier #	=	62
Supplier Name	=	**Sure Shot Supplies**
Address	=	**291 Pacific Avenue**
City	=	**Tacoma**
State	=	**WA**
Zip Code	=	**98418**
E-mail Address	=	**sssupplies@coffee.com**

Supplier #	=	41
Supplier Name	=	**Bertolino's**
Address	=	**11711 Meridian East**
City	=	**Seattle**
State	=	**WA**
Zip Code	=	**98109**
E-mail Address	=	**bertolino@coffee.com**

Key the following data in the Products table:

Product #	=	**12A-0**		Product #	=	**59R-1**
Product	=	**Premium blend**		Product	=	**Vanilla syrup**
Supplier #	=	**24**		Supplier #	=	**62**

Product #	=	**12A-1**		Product #	=	**59R-2**
Product	=	**Cappuccino blend**		Product	=	**Raspberry syrup**
Supplier #	=	**24**		Supplier #	=	**62**

Product #	=	**12A-2**		Product #	=	**59R-3**
Product	=	**Hazelnut blend**		Product	=	**Chocolate syrup**
Supplier #	=	**24**		Supplier #	=	**62**

Product #	=	**21B-2**		Product #	=	**89T-3**
Product	=	**12-oz cup**		Product	=	**Napkins, 500 ct**
Supplier #	=	**36**		Supplier #	=	**41**

Product #	=	**21B-3**		Product #	=	**89T-4**
Product	=	**16-oz cup**		Product	=	**6-inch stir stick**
Supplier #	=	**36**		Supplier #	=	**41**

Print both the Suppliers table and the Products table in landscape orientation. Prepare a report with the following information: Supplier name, Supplier #, Supplier E-mail, and Product.

Merge the records of those suppliers that are located in Tacoma to a blank Word screen. You determine the fields to use in the inside address and an appropriate salutation. Compose a business letter that will be sent to the contacts in Tacoma that includes the following information:

Explain that Classique Coffees is interested in selling iced coffees in the greater Seattle/Tacoma area.

- Ask if the company offers any iced coffee products.
- If the company does not currently offer any iced coffee products, will these products be available in the future?
- Ask the company to send any materials on current products and specifically iced coffees.
- Ask someone at the company to contact you at the Classique Coffees address, by telephone at (206) 555-6690, or e-mail at ccoffees@gourmet.com.
- Include any other information you think appropriate to the topic.

Merge to a new document and then save the document with the name Project, Act 11. Print and then close Project, Act 11. Save the main document as Iced Coffee Letter and then close Iced Coffee Letter.

Activity 12: Assessing Your Work

Review the products and documents you developed and assess your own work in writing. In order to develop an objective perspective of your work, openly solicit constructive criticism from your teacher, peers, and contacts outside of school. Your self-assessment document should specify the weaknesses and strengths of each piece and your specific recommendations for revision and product improvement.

Index